Employment Practices and Business Strategy

Employment Practices
and Business Strategy

EDITED BY
PETER CAPPELLI

New York   Oxford

Oxford University Press

1999

Oxford University Press

Oxford   New York
Athens   Auckland   Bangkok   Bogotá   Buenos Aires   Calcutta
Cape Town   Chennai   Dar es Salaam   Delhi   Florence   Hong Kong
Istanbul   Karachi   Kuala Lumpur   Madrid   Melbourne
Mexico City   Mumbai   Nairobi   Paris   São Paulo   Singapore
Taipei   Tokyo   Toronto   Warsaw

And associated companies in
Berlin   Ibadan

Library of Congress Cataloging-in-Publication Data
Employment practices and business strategy /
edited by Peter Cappelli.
p.   cm.
Includes index.
ISBN 0-19-512859-1
1. Comparative management.   2. Personnel management—Case studies.
3. Organizational learning—Case studies.   4. Organizational
effectiveness—Case studies.   5. Employee selection.
6. Compensation management.   7. Employee fringe benefits.
8. Quality of work life.   9. Labor productivity.   10. Human capital.
11. Strategic planning.   I. Cappelli, Peter.
HD30.55.E47   1999
658.3—dc21   98-48334

9 8 7 6 5 4 3 2 1

Printed in the United States of America
on acid-free paper

Preface

This book is part of a study sponsored by the Committee on New American Realities (NAR), a private-sector group established in 1981 by the National Policy Association to promote a more competitive U.S. economy and to focus on both macroeconomic strategies and ways to use human resources more effectively.

Employment Practices and Business Strategy continues the long-term NAR examination of the forces that are changing the workplace and work organization. *Turbulence in the American Workplace*, published in 1991 (Oxford University Press), provided a comprehensive and compelling account of how economic turbulence is changing the U.S. labor market and workplace. *Change at Work*, published in 1997 (Oxford University Press), provided a broader look at workplace changes and their impact on employees, employers, and work organization.

Employment Practices and Business Strategy addresses the vexing question of why, in a competitive marketplace, there are good jobs and bad jobs in the economy. Even within the same occupation, some employers pay higher wages, offer training, and provide good working conditions, while other employers offer the opposite. If conventional wisdom and prevailing management thinking argue that organizations that treat their workers better will be more productive and competitive, why don't all firms in an industry strive to improve the quality of their jobs? The answer, in this book, may surprise some readers since the authors show that firms make rational choices in choosing the conditions in their workplaces—whether to offer "good" or "bad" jobs.

Through open, nonpartisan analyses and examination of U.S. economic performance, the NAR Committee defines shared interests and concerns and fosters a broad-based consensus from which effective national policies and private-sector initiatives can evolve. Although Committee members understand that consensus is not always possible, they believe that frank, informed discussion of key issues is always beneficial. The Committee's sponsored studies, such as *Employment*

Practices and Business Strategy, are meant to help private- and public-sector leaders better understand the complex economic and social issues facing the nation.

All NAR Committee members do not agree with every point raised in this important book. They do, however, believe that the authors have done a very valuable job in examining the metamorphosis that is taking place in the relationship between employers on the one hand and employees and work organizations as a whole on the other. We recommend this book to anyone seeking a serious analysis of these issues.

Alan MacDonald
Chair, New American Realities Committee

Contents

Contributors

Jeffrey B. Arthur, Fairfield University

Thomas Bailey and Carola Sandy, Columbia University

Peter Cappelli, Wharton School, University of Pennsylvania

Frits K. Pil, University of Pittsburgh

John Paul MacDuffie, University of Pennsylvania

Rosemary Batt, Cornell University

Jeffrey Keefe, Rutgers University

Larry W. Hunter, University of Pennsylvania

Geoff Mason, National Institute for Economic
   and Social Research (London)

Employment Practices and Business Strategy

Introduction

PETER CAPPELLI

Most of the headline-grabbing developments in the workplace concern trends in the economy as a whole, such as the growth in employee involvement or the increase in downsizing. Our previous study for the New American Realities Committee, *Change at Work*, examined these trends. But it is an open secret that the attention given to trends in the workplace masks the fact that the range of experience with any of these practices is huge: Despite the downsizing trend, there are a great many employers that still provide employment security, just as there are those that never did. The overall trend toward increased employee participation comprises some employers that embrace the notion fully and others that continue to reject it. Relatively little popular attention has been given to understanding the range of experience with such workplace practices as these.

Most of the important workplace issues, such as the terms and conditions of employment or the way in which work is organized, result from decisions made by individual employers or in unionized settings by management and unions through collective bargaining. So when we talk about examining the differences in practices, we really mean examining the different choices in employment practices that employers pursue. And when we look for explanations of those practices, we mean examining the factors that drive employer decisions and collective bargaining outcomes.

There are many reasons why it is important to understand both the range of practice in the workplace and why differences persist. One simple reason is to elicit a more accurate picture of the true state of the workplace than one might extract from simple statistics on average practices. Suppose, for example, that 60% of the workers in the economy are found to have employer-provided health care. Our sense about that issue is different if we find that this 60% figure results because some employers offer it to all workers and others to none of their workers than if we find that some occupations in virtually all firms are covered,

3

whereas others are not. In the former, we might lean toward believing that issues of health care coverage are rooted in firm-level decisions, but in the latter we might think otherwise.

The most important insights to be drawn from examining the variation in employment practices are in understanding the causes of these workplace facts or trends. Among the most compelling of these workplace facts is that there are good jobs and bad jobs, often in the same industry, often doing roughly the same work. Even within the same occupation, some organizations seem to offer "good" jobs with higher wages, training, and good working conditions whereas other organizations offer the opposite.

Why this is so is especially important when issues of policy arise. Given the importance of workplace outcomes such as training, job satisfaction, and wages for individuals and for societal well-being, most observers would like to see more "good" jobs in the workplace. Over the years, a wide range of policy interventions have been directed at helping expand the proportion of good jobs in the economy. It is probably fair to conclude that these efforts have had mixed success. Efforts to simply prohibit bad jobs through regulations (wage and hour legislation, occupational safety and health laws, etc.) are probably the most common attempts to change the quality of jobs. Whereas regulations certainly can eliminate bad jobs, they may do little to expand the number of good jobs.

The good jobs/bad jobs issue has received additional attention more recently with new arguments concerning the organization of work, arguments that focus on management practices and suggest how it might be in management's interest to offer more "good" jobs. Specifically, these arguments, and some empirical research backing them, assert that workplaces could be more productive if production activity were redesigned so that authority and decision making would be pushed down to the lower ranks and training and related human resource (HR) practices supported the higher skill levels that these changes demand. The phrase "high-performance work systems" is sometimes used as a general label to describe a range of work systems featuring employee involvement and teamwork and support HR practices.

The obvious question that flows from these arguments is that if high-performance work systems are truly better for employers, why are they not all adopting them? One answer to this question is to suggest that we are merely observing a temporary adjustment period and that in the long run, most companies will adopt these practices. Just as in the early 1900s, the argument might go, not all auto companies adopted assembly lines, but 30 years later, the ones that had not were no longer in business.

When we look at the contemporary scene in the United States, we see a number of arguments about the superiority of these new work systems (David Levine, *Machine That Changed the World*) and even more in the popular management field making these arguments. We also see some considerable expansion in the use of high-performance-type practices. But we still see a vast proportion of the economy where these changes have been introduced either in a very limited way or not at all, even when strong evidence suggests that they are effective.

One of the important issues to address, therefore, is Why do practices that are apparently better take so long to be adopted? This question relates to the broader issue of organizational change—the causes of resistance to change within organizations—and to the increasingly popular topic of organizational learning: how organizations learn to adapt to challenging environments.

If we relax the assumption that these practices are not necessarily better for everyone, indeed, that there may not be a "best practice" in the usual sense, then the issues become more complicated. Among academic researchers, some of the more common explanations include economic arguments, typically directed at differences in wage levels:

1. *Compensating differentials*: Workplaces differ in the terms and conditions of employment that they offer in order to respond to the different tastes that workers have. Some settings offer higher wages whereas others compensate by offering better working conditions or other benefits that are desirable to employees. So one explanation for the fact that different employers pursue different practices comes from the labor market: The different practices are designed to attract different employees.

The problem with this explanation is simply that it does not hold up that well empirically. Employers that pay more also tend to be ones that provide more training and other benefits. Jobs that are more at risk do not seem to come with a compensating wage premium.

2. *Rent sharing/efficiency wages*: Arguments like these suggest the advantages of being a better than average employer and paying above-market wages. These advantages include reduced turnover, improved morale, and generally superior employee performance. Obviously not all employers can pay above-market wages. And what causes some but not others to do it and is the crucial question that these models do not address.

3. *Dual labor markets*: These arguments suggest that the industrial structure in the economy is divided according to the nature of competition and other factors that create significant differences in the resources that are available for employees. Typically, these arguments see a "primary" sector of the economy where competition is less, prices are administered (or regulated), and opportunities for planning and long-term investments are greater, including investments in people. The "secondary" sector, in contrast, is generally one where barriers to entry are low, the firms within it are small, and cutthroat price competition is more

or less constant. Firms in the primary sector could offer better wages, internal promotion, and development and job security; those in the secondary sector, in contrast, paid low wages, made little investment in employees, and offered no security of employment.

One of the limits to this set of arguments is that they cannot explain differences within industries or sectors of the economy; for example, why firms in the same industry have different practices. These arguments have less face validity after the deregulation of the 1980s and the rise of more intense competition in every industry. It is difficult to think of any industries that meet the test of the "primary" sector these days.

But the focus on the product market was an important insight for these models, because it helped point research in a more promising direction. This new direction was to embrace the notion of strategy, that competitors try to differentiate themselves in the way they approach common product markets, and that differentiation makes possible (or indeed may require) differences in the internal makeup of the organization, including employment practices.

4. *Strategy and HR*: These arguments begin with the assumption that there are different ways to approach a product market or even different ways to produce the same product, and that it may be functional for firms to pursue different approaches. What determines why one firm pursues a given strategy and another a different one is again a vexing question that is typically pushed off onto history (i.e., it stems from actions taken decades earlier, "path dependence"), but the notion that differentiation can be functional for firms is a crucial distinction in these arguments.

Once one accepts that firms have different production or business strategies, then the next step in the argument is that different employment practices are necessary to reinforce and deliver those strategies. Why firms might pursue different employment strategies, then, begins with efforts to document how their business or production strategies differ.

Overview

Each chapter in this volume addresses the employment practices across firms within an industry and attempts to explain why they differ. The volume begins with Jeffrey Arthur's chapter on steel making in minimills, a distinct segment of the steel industry. He begins by documenting that there are distinct HR practices across employers and that they can be categorized into clear groups on criteria such as the extent of employee involvement. He also finds that the minimills are differentiated according to their business strategies, with one group focused on lowering costs and the other on creating differentiated products to address specific customer needs. Finally, he finds that business strategies seem to be driving the choices of HR practices. In those cases where the business strategies and the HR practices do not coincide, it seems to be because of prior capital investments (fixed costs) that dictate the business strategy. The minimill story may be among the best examples of business strategy driving HR practices.

Thomas Bailey and Carola Sandy examine the incidence of high-performance work systems in the apparel industry and find a more complex story. The new "quick response" production systems represent an important alternative to the traditional "progressive bundle" system (akin to Taylorism) and would seem to require HR practices associated with high-performance work. They examine what factors predict the use of more innovative HR practices and find that the number of styles produced by a company is not a good predictor of these more innovative HR practices, but that increases in the number of styles does predict them. Large firms and multifirms do more. Other issues that are thought to either advance or mitigate these practices, such as unionization, a more-educated workforce, and more immigrant workers have no effect on the relationship.

Frits Pil and John Paul MacDuffie examine the case of automobile assembly, perhaps the most powerful example of where these high-performance work practices seem to drive superior organizational performance. Given both the evidence from previous research of the superiority and the widespread attention given that research in this industry, they ask Why aren't these practices used everywhere? Further, what drives their diffusion? They reach a series of general conclusions about the factors that inhibit or advance the adoption of these practices. For example, they find that poor productivity of a plant does not lead to the adoption of these new systems. Improvements in technology may be seen as a substitute for these alternative work systems as a way to address productivity problems. Disruptions in a plant's experience, such as shutdowns, help speed these innovations. They find in general that U.S. companies have innovated the least, whereas plants in new entrant countries (joint ventures, etc.) are among the most innovative, perhaps because they have no indigenous practices and feel more free to adopt best practices from elsewhere. Finally, they examine some natural experiments that occur when the same companies operate plants in different countries in order to examine how issues of culture or union characteristics shape the diffusion process.

The above examples represent the most optimistic view of our ability to explain HR practices. Chip Hunter's chapter on retail banking takes on a much more difficult example. He finds clear differences in HR practices among banks along the criteria found in other industries (highly skilled, educated, and empowered workers in some banks, part-time work and deskilled jobs in other banks for the same occupations). But here it proves very difficult to find explanations for these differences in the basic business strategies or marketing goals of the bank. He offers some general thoughts as to why that is, including that organizations and industries that are unsure of their markets and business strategies may not give priority to aligning their practices to new strategies.

Jeffrey Keefe and Rose Batt examine the telecommunications industry and its current restructuring. Here they find that HR practices vary relatively little among companies, in part because the companies are pursuing similar business strategies in common segments of their markets. They find instead that the variation is within companies, across the different segments of their business. For example, the important differences in HR practices are in local versus long distance phone service or in business versus residential service, driven by the different strategies they pursue in each segment and the technology that impacts specific occupations.

In the final chapter, Geoff Mason raises the level of aggregation to examine how the United States differs from other countries in its HR practices in manufacturing. He focuses in particular on the diffusion of traditional practices versus employee involvement and related high-performance approaches. He finds some traditional explanations: The United States uses less "flexible" employment systems because the larger scale of U.S. production runs accommodates less-flexible manufacturing systems. But he also finds more variance in practices within the United States, and that there is greater hierarchy in manufacturing and more use of expert management, even when using the same systems as other countries. Pursuing the diffusion question examined in earlier chapters, he finds more diffusion among countries in market segments where there is more competition, and that it is easier where the skill set of workers is higher.

Implications

The evidence presented in these chapters helps us understand why employers vary in their work practices and why adoption of apparently superior practices proves so difficult. Perhaps the first lesson is that the choice of practices that an employer pursues is heavily contingent on a number of factors at the organizational level, including their own business and production strategies, support of HR policies, and cooperative labor relations. Efforts to encourage employers to develop "good" jobs or to adopt a particular set of work practices such as "high-performance" systems must confront the fact that these decisions come about as part of a complex system of prior choices. The best way to encourage firms to move toward better employment practices might be to help them adapt related, supportive practices, such as business strategies and production systems. Public policy may also play a role by supporting training and other skill development programs that reinforce better work practices. Pressures directed at the work practices themselves, such as regulations or incentives, are likely to be less successful.

It is also worth noting, however, that in competitive product markets where firms are free to choose competitive strategies, there will always be rival firms whose choices are not easily made compatible with the best work practice systems. How much effort employer groups, unions, and HR policy should direct at changing such firms, as opposed to, say, improving their business practices, is a question worth serious debate.

1

Explaining Variation in Human Resource Practices in U.S. Steel Minimills

JEFFREY B. ARTHUR

The purpose of this chapter is to describe the sources and consequences of variation in human resource (HR) practices in the minimill sector of the U.S. steel industry. The case of this industry offers a unique opportunity to study the topic of firm-level variation in HR investments. First, steel minimills are part of an industry that has experienced tremendous restructuring over the last 15–20 years.[1] In 1950, more than 45% of the world's steel was produced in the United States. The conditions under which the U.S. steel industry thrived during this period consisted of steadily increasing demand for steel products and the superiority of U.S. production technology and productivity in world markets. Historical data from the last 50 years indicate that the period from 1975 to the early 1990s represents a dramatic shift from earlier periods. The large integrated sector experienced wrenching changes in terms of declining demand for its products as well as an increase in foreign and domestic minimill competition. The impact of these changes included low operating rates, large financial losses for steelmakers, bankruptcies, massive plant closures, and manpower reductions. As a whole, the industry eliminated more than 40 million tons (25%) of capacity and reduced employment by more than 250,000 employees (60%) in the 1980s.

Facing the same economic conditions, the sector of the steel industry known as steel "mininmills" did remarkably well. Historically, the minimill sector of the steel industry has been distinguished from the rest of the industry by its technology, products, size, and market orientation. Minimills are "nonintegrated" in the sense that they use steel scrap as their main input, or "charge" which is melted down in electric furnaces. The molten steel is then continuously cast into semifinished shapes that are rolled into a number of steel products, such as wire rods, concrete reinforcing bars, and other structural shapes. Because of their technological configuration, minimills are able to achieve economies of scale at a much lower volume of output than integrated mills. Most minimills are operated as independent firms. In 1996, there were approximately 57 minimill plants spread throughout the United States operated by 33 different companies.

The success of this sector is evident by the fact that its market share has increased from less than 10% in 1970 to nearly 35% today. Minimills have almost completely taken over the market for bar shape products from both integrated producers and imports. Until recently, minimill sector growth has been limited by their inability to compete in the market for flat-rolled steel that accounts for approximately 60% of the carbon steel market. This situation has changed, however, with the commercial development of thin-slab casting technology.

Historical differences between the minimill and integrated sectors of the industry have been disappearing. In 1997, LTV Steel Co. became the first major U.S. integrated steel company to build a minimill that uses the new continuous slab-casting technology. Nucor Steel Co., the largest of the minimills, has added three new plants since 1989 that produce flat-rolled steel and is now the fourth-largest steel producer in the United States with over four million tons of annual capacity. Nucor employees and those in other new minimills are not represented by labor unions. The effect of this growing nonunion sector in the steel industry is beginning to spill over into the integrated sector and put severe strains on existing union-management relations.

Despite their similarity in technology, size, and production process, minimills have adopted very different combinations of HR practices. In this chapter, I focus on explaining this historic and ongoing variation. The chapter is organized into three sections. In the first section, I describe the characteristics of HR practices in steel minimills based on a unique survey of the industry and discuss how this variation can be understood in terms of six distinct HR systems or patterns of HR practices, ranging from "control" to "commitment" systems. The second section demonstrates how variation in these systems is related to differences in minimill business strategies. Specifically, I describe how Control-type HR systems are associated with a Low-Cost business strategy, and Commitment-type HR systems are associated with a strategy of Differentiation.

To flesh out and update these empirical results, I discuss the dynamics of business-strategy and HR-strategy fit in terms of the evolution of technology and business strategy choices as well as the impact these choices have on firm performance and industrial relations. The performance impact of the "fit" suggests that there is no one set of "best practices" in this industry. Rather, there appear to be multiple HR systems competing in this industry. In the final section I show how the continued variation in employment systems in this industry is driven by the complementarity between technology, product market, and HR system choices.

HR Practices in Minimills

Here I describe the results of a survey of HR practices in steel minimills in 1988–1989. The survey questionnaire asked the top HR/industrial relations manager at each mill to describe their mill's HR policies and practices. Completed questionnaires were obtained from 30 minimill plants (56% response rate). The average age, size, geographic location, and union status of the sample are not statistically different from the averages for the total minimill population. The data represent by far the most comprehensive information of this kind gathered with respect to steel minimills.

Description of HR Variables

Data from the survey were used to construct 10 variables that measure various aspects of the mill's workplace HR system. Specific questions were adapted from previous studies that describe the "generic" aspects of different industrial relations systems (e.g., Dyer and Holder, 1988; Walton, 1985).

The HR variables used in this study are defined in Table 1.1. The first three variables shown, decentralized decision making (DECENTRAL), employee participation programs (PARTIC), and general training (GENTRAIN) indicate the nature and intensity of employee involvement practices in the mill. Each variable consists of responses to multiple questions. Staffing and supervision practices were measured by the percentage of skilled workers (SKILL) and the number of production workers per supervisor (SUPERV). Employee-relations' socialization activity was measured by the number of employee-sponsored social activities per year (SOCIAL). The due process (DUEPROC) variable was included to measure the degree to which mills relied on formal procedures to resolve employment-related disputes.[2]

Finally, the questionnaire asked managers to indicate the total employment cost per hour (including wages, benefits, and taxes) for production employees as well as the percentage of this total employment cost accounted for by employee benefits, and bonus or incentive payments. These values are reflected in the WAGE, BENEFIT, and BONUS variables, respectively.

Table 1.1 presents the averages and ranges for each variable. These data reveal the large variation in HR practices in minimills. For example, PARTIC ranges from 0 to 100% (of employees who are involved in participation programs; average = 27.4%) and BONUS ranges from 0 to 65% (of total compensation accounted for by incentive or bonus payments; average = 21.8%). These results, which are consistent with other industry-level studies (e.g., MacDuffie, 1995), clearly indicate that within the constraints of a given product market environment and technology shared by these mills, there are still a large number of HR options available to

Table 1.1. Description of Human Resource Variables*

	Average	Range
DECENTRL (Alpha = .778): The degree to which non-supervisory employees participate in the following (1 = very little; 6 = very much): "monitoring data on quality, costs, productivity, and scrap; determining work flow or order of tasks; investing in new equipment and technology; developing new products."	2.71	1–5.25
PARTIC (Alpha = .707): Percentage of mill employees who: "receive training in group problem-solving; meet on a regular basis in small groups to discuss production or quality problems; are involved in joint (union-management or employee-management) committees."	27.3	0–100
GENTRAIN (Alpha = .770): Part of general training and development activities for production and maintenance employees accounted for by the following (1 = no part; 6 = large part): "seminars, classes, training not directly related to employee's immediate work area; general skills training not directly related to employee's current job; 'people skills' training such as communication or group problem-solving."	2.58	1–6.00
SKILL: Number of maintenance/craft workers as a percentage of all mill employees (%).	16.2	10–23.9
SUPERV: Number of production workers per supervisor.	6.62	2.75–13.94
SOCIAL: Number of times per year management organizes social gatherings for employees such as company picnics and bowling leagues.	5.45	0–40
DUEPROC: Percentage of total employee complaints or grievances that are handled through formal grievance procedures involving several steps, up to and including binding third-party arbitration.	23.2	0–90.0
WAGE: Average total employment cost per production and maintenance worker (including wage rate, benefits, bonus or incentive payments, and taxes) ($).	19.67	11.93–25.50
BENEFIT: Percentage of total average employment cost accounted for by employee benefits (%).	29.5	10–50.0
BONUS: Percentage of total average employment cost accounted for by bonus or incentive payments. (%).	21.8	0–65.0

*Source: Arthur (1992).

labor and management. In other words, investments in individual HR activities in this industry are not completely determined by technological or product market conditions.

HR Patterns in Minimills

Although it is interesting to examine variation among individual HR practices, an HR systems perspective posits that such variation is not independent. In other words, firms can be described in terms of the *pattern* or configuration of choices they make. Configuration theorists argue that there is an internal complementarity or logic to these patterns of choices.[3] For example, firms may choose to select more highly skilled workers or to invest heavily in employee training. These choices are expected to be associated with choices of HR practices in other areas, such as job design, compensation, and employee relations. Utilizing skilled workers effectively means designing jobs more broadly to allow these workers to use their skill or training in making production-related decisions. Compensation programs must be designed to attract, motivate, and retain these valuable employees. These practices can therefore be seen as complements in that their combined effects are expected to be greater than the effects of any one of the individual practices.[4]

To determine the HR patterns or systems that exist in minimills, I used a cluster analysis technique that grouped together firms with similar profiles of scores across the ten HR variables.[5] The results of this analysis are presented in Table 1.2. The "pluses" in this table indicate that the average for mills in this group is above the overall average for the sample; "minuses" indicate the opposite. The clusters are arranged in the table to reflect the range of minimill HR systems. The first three patterns in Table 1.2 have been labeled "control" HR systems. Although the scores on specific variables vary across the three groups, they have in common a focus on the control or reduction of labor cost. In contrast, the patterns of scores on HR variables in Groups 3–6 represent different ways in which firms attempt to increase employee commitment to the firm. The internal logic of the HR practices that make up these different patterns is discussed next.

Descriptions of Control HR Systems

Pure-Type Cost-Reduction System (Group 1): The pattern of scores for the eight mills in Group 1 represent a classic control HR system (Walton, 1985) or what has sometimes been referred to as the "low-road" HR strategy (Osterman, 1994). The table shows that mills in this group are below average on all ten of the HR variables and significantly below average for the GENTRAIN, SKILL, DUEPROC, WAGE, and BENEFIT variables. The primary function of this HR system is to reduce labor costs by minimizing investments in HR including wage and benefit payments to employees.

It is important to recognize the internal logic of this type of system. Jobs in these mills are designed simply to require a minimal amount of employee skill and discretion. There are a number of labor cost advantages associated with this approach to work organization. First, lower skill requirements mean that qualified employees can be obtained at relatively low wages. In addition, training costs for production workers are reduced. The combination of low skill requirements and low

Table 1.2. Description of Minimill HR Systems

	Control HR Systems						Commitment HR Systems					
	Group 1 (n = 8) Cost Reducers		Group 2 (n = 4) Conflictors		Group 3 (n = 4) Inducers		Group 4 (n = 9) Collective Bargainers		Group 5 (n = 2) Involvers		Group 6 (n = 3) Commitment Maximizers	
Variable	Average	Compared to other mills	Average	Compared to other mills	Average	Compared to other mills	Average	Compared to other mills	Average	Compared to other mills	Average	Compared to other mills
DECENTRAL	2.22	(−)	2.25	(−)*	3.00	(+)	2.38	(−)	3.62	(+)	4.58	(+)**
PARTIC	20.04	(−)	6.13	(−)**	28.08	(+)	25.48	(−)	25.00	(−)	78.88	(+)**
GENTRAIN	1.58	(−)**	1.58	(−)**	2.92	(+)	2.57	(−)	3.83	(+)	5.33	(+)**
SKILL	0.135	(−)**	.145	(−)	0.15	(−)	0.20	(+)**	0.14	(−)	0.18	(+)**
SUPERV	5.30	(−)*	7.26	(+)	10.37	(+)	6.49	(−)	4.30	(−)	6.25	(−)
SOCIAL	4.38	(−)	2.50	(−)	4.50	(−)	2.55	(−)	30.00	(+)*	6.00	(−)
DUEPROC	2.13	(−)**	73.75	(+)**	4.25	(−)**	37.83	(+)	2.50	(−)	7.00	(−)
WAGE	16.51	(−)**	17.20	(−)**	21.69	(+)	22.59	(+)**	17.20	(−)	19.73	(−)
BENEFIT	22.13	(−)**	32.75	(+)	32.25	(+)	30.79	(+)	37.00	(+)	32.33	(+)
BONUS	19.21	(−)	15.00	(−)	56.25	(+)**	14.67	(−)	7.00	(−)	15.50	(−)

*Indicates that the average for the group is significantly above (+) or below (−) the average for the rest of the mills at the 5% or 1% (**) level of confidence.

training investment reduces the costs of employee turnover. Production employees can be more easily replaced. Given these conditions, management investment in employee-commitment-enhancing HR activities, such as employee involvement, information sharing, or job security would be expected to have a very low return and could be considered counterproductive from the standpoint of labor cost minimization.

Conflictors (Group 2):   The cluster analysis revealed two other variants of the cost reduction strategy. The four mills in Group 2 are all unionized mills, whose pattern of scores appears similar to those in Group 1, except that the score on the DUEPROC variable is significantly above the average for other mills, whereas in Group 1 it is significantly below other mills. These mills reported that nearly 75% of employee complaints or grievances are handled through formal grievance procedures that include binding arbitration, whereas the average for the other unionized mills is about 30%. This pattern is consistent with what Fox (1974) calls a "low-trust/ high-conflict" labor-management relationship or what Katz and Kochan (1992:127) call a "conflict" pattern. As a group, a potential source of conflict is the relatively low level of employee compensation (WAGE).

Inducers (Group 3):   The pattern of practices in Group 3 is consistent with what Dyer and Holder (1988:22–24) call an inducement HR system. A distinguishing characteristic of this pattern is the high level of contingent or BONUS compensation that is received in these mills. As shown in Table 1.2, the total compensation accounted for by BONUS payments is 56%. These mills are also all nonunion and make very little use of formal grievance procedure to resolve disputes (DUEPROC). Unlike the pure-type cost-reduction system in Group 1, however, these mills had slightly higher-than-average levels of decentralized decision making, participation, and general training, as well as above-average wages and benefits.

Again, we can see a strong internal logic or complementarity between this set of practices, which is consistent with a goal of labor cost reduction. As Dyer and Holder (1988) note, the inducement HR system typically offers employees the *opportunity* to earn relatively high compensation. This strong monetary incentive, as well as peer pressure (in the case of the mills' group-based incentives), reduces the need for intense supervision, creating a "lean" organization that also helps to reduce costs. While incentive compensation and lean staffing provide the engine that drives down labor costs, this system also requires that employees buy into the production goals set by management and believe that their efforts to improve performance will be fairly rewarded and will not result in job loss. Thus, unlike the pure-type cost reducers, these mills must also pay attention to employee participation and employment security issues. The average annual turnover rate for this group was less than 3%, which is among the lowest for any of the groups.

Description of Commitment HR Systems

The pattern of practices for mills in Groups 4, 5, and 6 represent HR systems with a different objective than those in the first three groups. Instead of directly emphasizing labor cost reduction, the HR systems for these groups of mills focus more on increasing employee commitment to the firm. Although the objective or result is the same (i.e., employee commitment) for all three groups, the three HR patterns provide insights into the alternative means for achieving this goal.

Collective Bargainers (Group 4):   The pattern of practices in this group of nine mills is consistent with a more traditional collective-bargaining HR system. Rather than focusing on employer-sponsored employee participation or social programs, commitment in these mills is achieved through paying relatively high wages to more highly skilled workers, those with union representation. The United Steelworkers of America (USWA) represent employees at seven out of the nine mills in the group. Note that although a formal grievance procedure is used to resolve disputes in these mills, managers report that it is used only half as frequently as in the "conflictor" mills in Group 2.

This is not to say that all collective-bargaining relationships result in high employee commitment to the firm. It is clear, however, that mills in this group are unlikely to be able to compete effectively with other mills based solely on low labor costs. Instead, as I argue in the next section, this HR system is much more compatible with a competitive strategy that seeks to use the talents of a skilled work force to produce unique products or services for which higher wages could be passed on to the customer in the form of a price premium.

Involvers (Group 5):   The pattern of scores for the two mills in Group 5 provide an example of an alternate means for trying to achieve employee commitment. A distinguishing characteristic of mills in this group is the high level of informal employee-management social activities, including activities such as company picnics and bowling leagues. The theme for this group of nonunion mills is that employees and managers are part of a company "family" that can face adversity and succeed together. As in the traditional Japanese management approach, a key to the success of this type of system is a sense of reciprocal commitment between employees and employers. Managers show that they care about employees as people (through social activities and high benefits), and employees reciprocate by working hard and committing themselves to the goals of the organization.

Pure-Type Commitment-Maximization (Group 6): The pattern of scores for the mills in Group 6 provide the most obvious example of an HR system designed to maximize employee commitment to a firm. Table 1.2 shows that employees in these firms are relatively highly skilled and have a great amount of decision-making power over a variety of workplace issues. These mills also invest heavily in employee participation and general training programs. Wages and benefits are moderately high.

These HR practices appear to fit well together. The large amount of decision-making power for employees means job-specific tasks are somewhat uncertain, and that managers must trust employees to make good decisions (i.e., consistent with the interests of the firm). This type of HR system can be seen as a means of encouraging discretionary employee behaviors and decisions under conditions of high task uncertainty that are consistent with the goals of the firm. In other words, offering skilled employees high levels of involvement, general training, and wages and benefits can be seen as a way to attract, motivate, and retain qualified employees who will internalize (be committed to) the goals of the firm.

Summary: I have shown in this section that within a single sector of an industry that shares the same technology and product mix, a variety of HR practices exists. Further, I have demonstrated that we can understand this variation by examining patterns or systems of internally consistent HR practices, thus supporting the use of a configurational approach to studying variation in these practices. It is clear that multiple HR systems are consistent with minimill technology and markets. This suggests that environmental, technological, or economic factors alone will not determine which of these systems becomes dominant. Rather, we must look elsewhere for the explanation of variation in employment practices in this industry.

Explaining HR Variation in Minimills

What explains why some mills choose one type of HR system over another? One can think of a number of factors that could affect this choice. The presence of a union may have some influence (although we saw in the previous section that unionization appears to be compatible with a variety of different minimill HR systems). Perhaps it is the age of the mill and vintage of the technology that the mill uses, its size, or its location in a particular region of the country; or perhaps this choice is simply an idiosyncratic managerial decision based on individual values that cannot be predicted.

In my study, I examined all of these possibilities and found that none of them provides an adequate explanation of this choice. *Instead, I found that the single best predictor of the type of HR system used in minimills was the mills' choice of business strategy.* Specifically, I found mills that competed on the basis of being the lowest cost producer of basic steel products were likely to have one of the Control HR systems. In contrast, mills that competed on the basis of providing a unique product or service (the Differentiation strategy) were more likely to use one of the Commitment HR systems.

The Minimill Production Process

To understand more clearly why business strategy choices play such a large role in determining a mill's HR system, we need to look more closely at the production processes in these mills and how product market choices are linked to HR requirements.

The basic production process used by all the mills is essentially the same. Steel scrap is brought in to the mill by truck, rail, or barge and deposited in the scrap yard. A crane operator lifts the scrap into a high-powered electric furnace, where it is heated until the *charge* becomes a batch of molten steel with the proper metallurgical properties for the grade or quality of steel being produced. Furnace operators pour the molten steel into a smaller ladle where further metallurgical refining can be done. This ladle is then lifted by cables to the top of the continuous caster high above the shop floor. Here operators "tap" the ladle to create a stream of molten steel that moves into the *tundish* and through a set of oscillating molds, which begin to cool the outside of the steel, creating a thin film around the outside of the molten steel stream. This film thickens as the cooling steel moves down the caster to a set of rollers that bend and shape the hot metal into square billets that move parallel to the ground. These billets are then put through a series of high-power rollers where, depending on the grade and size of the billets, they are squeezed, elongated, and shaped into a variety of bar, rod, and/or structural shapes (i.e., angles, channels, I-beams). These long steel shapes are deposited onto cooling racks where material handlers bundle them up and prepare them for shipment.[6]

Although each charge of steel is in some ways a unique batch traveling through the mill, in modern mills the process becomes more or less continuous, with a new ladle of molten steel being prepared as the first one is being tapped. This is occurring at the same time that new furnace technology has reduced the tap-to-tap times significantly. Other aspects of the production process are also highly automated in modern mills. With the exception of some routine or preventative maintenance and material handling, there is very little direct interaction between steel operators and the production process. Instead, most workers spend their time in pulpits above the shop floor monitoring the flow of steel through the mill on a bank of computer terminals. The primary aim is to keep the steel moving through the mills (or "getting the tons out the door"). As long as the same type of steel is being melted and rolled into similar shapes, the work is hard and hot, but generally routine.

An exception to this occurs when the mills shift production to higher grades of steel or different types of steel shapes. Higher grades generally mean tighter tolerances, and the chemical properties of the charge must be continuously tested and closely monitored by skilled melt-shop employees. In the rolling mill, changing to different shapes requires not only changing over the rollers but also recalibrating the speed that the steel travels through the mill to avoid buckling or stretching between the rolling mill stands. Because the exact nature of these changeover activities is difficult to prescribe beforehand, mills must depend on the skill and experience of operators and maintenance workers to use their discretion in carrying out these activities in the most efficient and effective way possible. Downtime in a steel mill is very expensive.

The Link Between Business Strategy and HR Systems

As can be seen from the above description, in this industry there appears to be direct relation between the type and mix of products produced and the task characteristics and HR requirements of the people producing them. The choice of product type and mix is a core element of a mill's competitive strategy.

To examine the relationship between mills' competitive strategy and their choice of HR system, I conducted a separate survey of top minimill line managers (e.g., Plant Manager, V.P. of Manufacturing, or CEO). These managers indicated how important various product and marketing strategies were to the ability of their mill to compete with other mills. I also asked these managers to indicate the types of products produced at the mill and the number of steel sizes and grades of steel produced, as well as the percentage of production delivered to different types of customers. Out of 55 mills, 40 responded to the survey. The averages for these different variables are presented in Table 1.3.

As can be seen from this table, there was a wide range of responses for each item. Using a clustering technique similar to that used for the HR systems, I found four main types of business strategies being used by the minimills. Consistent with the typology of business strategies developed by Porter (1980), one was a classic Low-Cost or Cost Leadership strategy, and the others were variations of the Differentiation strategy in which mills were competing on some bases other than being the lowest cost producer. These different strategies are described here.

Low-Cost Producers: Fifteen of the mills in my sample were classified as Low-Cost producers. Managers at these mills emphasized the pro-

Table 1.3. Description of Minimill Business Strategy Variables*

Variable Name	Average	Range
Low cost producer: Importance of the following (1 = unimportant; 6 = very important): "Provide customers with basic steel products at prices below those of competitors"	4.05	1–6
Differentiator (Alpha = .800): Importance of the following (1 = unimportant; 6 = very important): "Provide customers with specialized sizes, shapes, or grades of steel; develop and produce new steel shapes, sizes, or grades; switch quickly between the production of different shapes, sizes, or grades to respond to fluctuations in market demand; produce shapes, sizes, and grades for the higher-priced segment of steel market; develop new techniques and methods to market products"	4.11	1–6
Focus (Alpha = .681): Importance of the following: (1 = unimportant; 6 = very important): "Serve needs of customers within a specific geographic area; create recognition of company's name and reputation in the industry"	4.63	1.5–6
Product types: Number of different product types produced	2.37	1–5
Product sizes: Number of different sizes of steel products produced	126	8–600
Product grades: Number of different grades of steel products produced	61	2–500
Contract customers: Percentage of 1987–1988 production delivered to contract customers (%)	17.69	0–100
Open market customers: Percentage of 1987–1988 production delivered to open or "spot market" customers (%)	30.7	0–100

*Source: Arthur (1992).

duction of the lowest cost basic steel products as their most important source of competitive advantage. In addition, these mills produced significantly fewer types of products in significantly fewer numbers of sizes and grades than did the other mills in the sample. They sold the majority of their products on the open or spot market.

Differentiation Strategies: The remainder of mills reported emphasizing something other than low cost as their source of competitive advantage. There were three variations of this strategy. A group of 13 mills (Versatile Differentiators) emphasized providing superior service to local market customers. Consistent with this strategy, these mills produced a significantly higher number of products and product sizes than other mills. The six Customized Differentiators emphasized their ability to fill specific customer needs. Not surprisingly, these mills tended to produce specialized steel products and shapes and sold most of their products to contract customers. Finally, six of the mills were found to be following a Specialized Differentiation strategy that emphasized specialized, high-value products at low cost. Although these mills did not produce a large variety of steel shapes, they produced a variety of steel grades to satisfy the needs of specialized, high-end steel customers (somewhat similar to specialty steel producers).

Descriptions of Business Strategy and HR-System Fit

Table 1.4 describes the relationship between business strategy and HR systems for the 29 minimills for whom data on both are available. It shows that 20 out of the 29 mills (those along the diagonal of this matrix) had the hypothesized fit between their business strategy and the HR system. This number is significantly higher than what we could expect based on chance. In addition, multivariate statistical analyses indicated that these relationships hold even after taking into account the differences in the mills' union status, age, size, and geographic location. This evidence clearly shows that in this industry, the best predictor of whether a minimill uses a Control- or Commitment-type HR system is the business strategy used by that mill.[7]

The table, however, also raises a number of important questions for both researchers and practitioners. In particular, because not all minimill firms have the prescribed fit between their business strategy and HR system, it is useful to consider: (1) What explains why some mills have fit and others do not? and (2) What impact does fit (or lack of fit) have on labor relations outcomes and plant performance? I address both of these questions next.

Does Fit Matter? The Relationship Between Fit and Performance

A central assumption of this analysis is that fit matters. In other words, performance is better for those firms that are able to achieve fit between their HR and business strategies. Is this true? Although the logic for a relationship between fit and performance is compelling, in general, research evidence to date does not support this relationship (e.g., Delery and Doty, 1996; Huselid, 1995).[8]

Table 1.4. Association Between Minimill Business Strategy and Human Resource System

HR System	Business Strategy	
	Low Cost	Differentiation
Cost Reducing	8 (89%)	8 (40%)
Commitment Maximizing	1 (11%)	12 (60%)

The minimill case indicates the complexities of studying the relationship between fit and performance. In a previous study (Arthur, 1994), I have shown that for the overall sample, the Commitment-type HR system is more effective in minimills. Specifically, scrap rates are significantly lower and productivity is significantly better for the mills with a Commitment-type HR system (after one takes into account differences in each mill's age, size, union status, and business strategy). Thus, minimills provide evidence that the elements of a Commitment-type HR system represent a set of "best practices" regardless of the business strategy that a mill is following.

The obvious question that this raises is, If all firms benefit from a Commitment-type HR system, then why don't they all adopt one? If we assume that employees would prefer a Commitment-type system, then one conclusion may be that managers are simply not knowledgeable about the benefits and require additional information and incentives. I believe, however, that this type of conclusion, and the policy initiatives it suggests, are premature. This case indicates the difficulty of determining the existence of a fit-performance relationship with this type of data.

An alternate interpretation of these results is that although having a Commitment-type HR system is beneficial to all mills, the economic benefits for an investment in this type of HR system is much smaller for mills following a Low-Cost business strategy than for mills following a Differentiation strategy. If the costs for a Commitment-type HR system exceeded the benefits from these investments in Low-Cost mills but not in the Differentiation mills, then the fit patterns that exist in these mills may be seen as rational from an economic perspective.

This alternate interpretation has a strong intuitive appeal. Differentiation can be seen as a more difficult and demanding business strategy to implement from a HR standpoint. When the success of the business depends on producing higher value, sophisticated products, or switching between the production of many different types of products, then the need for a Commitment-type HR system with more broadly trained, skilled, committed workers is critical. In contrast, pursuing a Low-Cost strategy appears to require much less-conscious effort in the HR area. The Control-type HR system is distinguishable mainly by its lack of formal job design, participation, and formal training programs. While adding investments in these areas may not hurt performance, the more routine and standardized jobs in these mills pursuing the Low-Cost strategy suggests that the payback will be relatively small.

Unfortunately, because costs associated with implementing these different systems are not available, I cannot test this possibility directly. I can, however, consider some differences in paybacks of fit for firms following different business strategies in terms of productivity, quality, and employee turnover. Table 1.5 reports differences between the Fit and No-Fit groups for the full sample (which includes Low-Cost pro-

Table 1.5. Comparison of Manufacturing Performance and Turnover in "Fit" and "No Fit" Mills

	Full Sample		Only Differentiators	
Variable	"FIT" ($n = 18$) Average	"NO FIT" ($n = 9$) Average	"FIT" ($n = 11$) Average	"NO FIT" ($n = 8$) Average
Number of labor hours per ton	2.20	2.38	1.91*	2.55
Scrap rate	.149	.194	.128*	.194
Turnover rate	.053	.063	.022*	.067

*The difference with the No Fit mills is statistically significant.

ducers) compared to the subgroup of mills following the Differentiation strategy.[9]

This table shows that the relationship between fit and performance measures is much stronger (and statistically significant) for the subsample of mills following a Differentiation business strategy. This result is consistent with the view that Fit is a more important characteristic for these mills than it is for mills following the Low-Cost strategy.

Further evidence of the differential payback to HR investments comes from comparing the relative costs of turnover in mills using a Control-type HR system with those using a Commitment-type HR system. This analysis (described in Arthur, 1994) shows that for mills following a Control strategy, there is no relationship between the level of turnover and productivity or scrap rate. In contrast, for the mills with a Commitment strategy, higher turnover is associated with significantly worse productivity and scrap rate. This suggests that the payback for HR programs that might reduce the level of turnover is much lower for firms following a Control-type HR system. The economic incentive, therefore, of mills with a Control-type HR system (and Low-Cost business strategy) to invest in HR programs that would provide for employment stability (i.e., reduce turnover levels) is considerably lower than for mills with a Commitment-type HR system (and Differentiation business strategy).

Implications for Research and Practice: The above discussion of fit and performance in the minimill industry illustrates the complexity of this relationship and the difficulty facing researchers trying to come up with any firm conclusions. The results from this study and others, which have consistently shown a relationship between business strategy and HR practices, indicate that firms are *acting* as if fitting their business strategy and HR system is important, even if researchers have not been able to provide the economic justification for this action. At one level, the economic justification may not matter. If we assume that both a Low

Cost and Differentiation strategy are viable options for competing in today's economy, and that firms will continue to make decisions about HR investments based on their choice of business strategy, then we will continue to see a variety of HR systems in these firms. In other words, economic market forces alone, at least in this industry, appear unlikely to lead to investments in Commitment-type HR systems.

Dynamics of Fit in Minimills

To answer the question of what causes fit in some mills and not in others, we need to develop a more dynamic understanding of the fit construct. To start, we can look more closely at the characteristics of mills in the Fit and No-Fit groups. This comparison reveals that the No-Fit group consists of mills that are significantly older and smaller than the mills in the Fit group. On average, the mills in the No-Fit group were built in the 1960s and have some 325 employees, whereas the Fit group mills were built in the 1970s and have over 500 employees. In addition, we find that 90% of the No-Fit mills changed ownership in the 1980s versus 45% of the Fit mills. When we combine these differences with the evolution of this industry, a clearer picture of the dynamics of fit in the industry begins to emerge.

Evolution of Minimill Industry

Even though the history of the modern steel minimill industry in the United States dates back only about 35 years, the industry has gone through a number of dramatic changes during this period. The characteristics and strategies of minimills built in earlier periods are radically different than those currently being built. Understanding the importance of minimill age (and size) requires understanding the various stages of minimill evolution. The industry evolution since 1960 can be divided into four stages: Development (1960–1970), Rapid Growth (1970–1980), Restructuring (1980–1990), and Consolidation and Expansion (1990–).

1960–1970: Development.   The 1960s was a period of rapid development for the minimill industry. In this decade, 11 new steel companies, including current market leaders such as Nucor, North Star Steel, Georgetown Steel, and the second plant of Florida Steel, joined the existing 18 companies. Annual steel capacity of minimill plants doubled from 3.5 million tons to over 7 million tons (U.S. Dept. of Commerce, 1986). Much of this early growth can be attributed to the commercial development of continuous casting technology that resulted in significant cost savings and made the small-scale production of minimill products commercially viable. Some of the early mills, such as those of

Florida Steel and Nucor Steel, which began as internal sources of steel for their fabricating operations, soon realized that they could find substantial external markets for their low-cost steel products as well.

The early success of these mills came directly at the expense of the large integrated steel producers. The advantages of the minimills over the integrated mills came not only from their lower production costs for a narrow range of steel products, but also from their ability to serve more effectively the needs of local customers (see Arthur, 1987; Barnett and Schorsch, 1983). As Barnett and Crandall (1986:23) note: "The earliest minimills catered to specific geographic regions offering a fairly broad product mix of small bar shapes, merchant bars, and reinforcing bars, and were protected from integrated mills' competition by high transport costs."

1970–1980: Growth.   The minimill sector of the steel industry expanded rapidly in the 1970s. Spurred by the success of the earlier mills, 22 new plants were built and 14 new companies entered the market. The character of the plants built during this period differed from those of the earlier period. They were generally larger, more technologically sophisticated mills that focused on higher volume production of a relatively narrow range of products. Low production costs of these products enabled mills to sell outside of local areas to larger regional or national markets. These mills, sometimes referred to as "market mills," were no longer tied to a specific geographic region but focused on a specific product niche that was sold in a wide geographic area. Examples of mills built during this period include New Jersey Steel, which produces only steel reinforcing bars (rebar); Georgetown Steel and Raritan River Steel, which are high-volume, state-of-the-art facilities producing wire rod exclusively. Three new Nucor Steel Plants in Texas, Nebraska, and Utah, which focus on high-volume, low-cost production of relatively few basic minimill products, were also built during this period.

1980–1990: "Restructuring."   The tremendous minimill growth in the 1970s, combined with an overall decline in demand for steel in the early 1980s, led to problems of overcapacity in the minimill sector. The industry experienced market saturation for traditional minimill products, inter-minimill competition, and a "shakeout" of a number of poorer performing mills. Trade journals were reporting that the minimill "honeymoon" was over: "By the mid-1980s the steel industry's bright stars have started to tarnish. The minimill industry is undergoing a restructuring almost as wrenching as the integrated steel industry" (*American Metal Market*, April 24, 1986:6). This restructuring was evidenced by the wave of bankruptcies, closures, and ownership changes among the minimills. In 1985–1986 alone, five minimill firms went bankrupt and closed down. Between 1982 and 1986, 19 of the 59 minimill plants changed ownership (Sheets, 1985). The problem for many of these mills was that, with the expansion of minimill capacity, they were no longer only competing against integrated mills for small regional markets, but against other minimills as well. As one steel analyst put it: "Initially all the minimills were protected by the integrated mills' price umbrella. Now, it's one minimill after another" (*American Metal Market*, April 24, 1986:6). The inherent production cost advantages that the early minimills enjoyed over the integrated producers disappeared when they were competing with other minimills.

1990s and Beyond: Consolidation and Market Expansion: One response to the intensified competition has been the consolidation and closure of many smaller and older minimills. This consolidation has been necessary for older mills trying to compete with the newer, more-efficient mills, whose larger volume and "market-mill" strategy allow them to undercut prices in the regional markets of the existing (older) mills. Unable to finance the large capital investments required to lower production costs, these older mills have been forced to sell assets to larger, financially stronger competitors.

Birmingham Steel Company in Birmingham, Alabama has been a prime beneficiary of this consolidation strategy. In 1980, Birmingham Bolt Co. owned two steelmaking facilities that primarily produced bolts for the mining industry. Since that time it has purchased nine older minimill plants. Five of the mills were refurbished and expanded and four were shut down. The majority of Birmingham Steel's acquisitions and investments were part of an effort to pursue a Low-Cost business strategy for basic minimill products. In 1996, rebar accounted for over 50% of Birmingham Steel's production. Rebar, used in primarily in construction, is the standard low-margin-commodity product produced by minimills.[10] With these acquisitions, Birmingham Steel has joined Nucor, Ameristeel, Northstar, and several others as the dominant producers in this segment of the U.S. steel market.

A second option for responding to increased inter-minimill competition has been to move away from lower-margin commodity products and into the production of higher grade special bar quality (SBQ) and rod products used in autos, aerospace, and other higher end applications. Minimill firms that make up this segment of the market include MacSteel, Republic Engineered Steel (former LTV plant), Chaparral Steel, American Wire and Steel, Georgetown Steel, and several of North Star Steel's plants. Although a number of these mills have also changed ownership in the 1980s and 1990s, very few have shut down. In fact, higher end quality steel production appears to be an area of growing minimill strength (Schriefer, 1995). As noted earlier, the higher quality steel grades produced by these mills generally require more sophisticated equipment and processes and relatively highly skilled employees.

Finally, the most significant development in the minimill sector in the 1990s has been the growth of new mills producing flat-rolled steel products. The commercial development in the late 1980s of casting technology that allowed minimills to produce flat-rolled products using their basic minimill (i.e., scrap-based, electric furnace) configuration drove this market expansion strategy. The first mill to use the new casting technology was Nucor's Crawfordsville, Indiana plant, which started production in 1989 with nearly 1.8 million tons of annual capacity. This was followed by the second successful Nucor start-up of a 2.0-million-ton mill in Hickman, Arkansas and a third similar-sized mill in Berkeley, South Carolina. Other firms have quickly followed suit. Gallatin Steel (Co-owned by Co-Steel and Dufasco, Canada) built a new minimill in Ghent, Kentucky in 1995 with about 1.5 million tons of annual flat-rolled capacity. Steel Dynamics, Inc. (SDI; Butler, Indiana) also built a 1.5-million-ton flat-rolled mill the same year. Since that time, three other companies have built flat-rolled mills: North Star BHP (a joint venture between North Star Steel and BHP, an Australian integrated producer with 1.5 million tons of capacity) in Delta, Ohio; Trico Steel (a joint venture between LTV Steel, British Steel, and Sumitomo Metals of 2.2 million tons) in Decatur, Alabama; and an IPSCO Steel mill in Montpelier, Iowa (Schriefer, 1996). Together, these mills represent over 11 million tons of new flat-rolled capacity (about 20% increase in this market). Added to this are existing mills that have significantly upgraded or expanded their electric furnace, slab casting capacity, such as ACME Steel, Armco, and Geneva Steel.

Implications for Labor Relations and Fit

This description of industry dynamics establishes a clearer picture of how product market competition and technological changes, along with firm-specific choices about how to respond to these changes, contribute to the diversity in HR outcomes. As noted above, the majority of the No-Fit mills in my sample were older, smaller, and mostly unionized mills that tended to follow the traditional Collective Bargaining type of commitment model. Faced with low-price competition from newer, technologically sophisticated mills, many of the older mills were forced to reduce costs significantly. In unionized mills, this generally meant attempting to shift from the Collective Bargaining HR system to one of the Control-type systems (either Cost Reducer or, in the face of strong resistance from unionized employees, a Conflictor system). This Control-type HR system was typically incompatible with a regionally focused Versatile Differentiator business strategy being pursued by these mills.

Thus these industry dynamics help to explain why eight of the nine No-Fit mills in the sample are in the upper right quadrant of Table 1.4 (i.e., mills having a Differentiation-type business strategy and Control-type HR strategy). In the late 1980s, these mills were still pursuing a Differentiation-type business strategy, but their HR strategy focused on reducing costs. Ultimately, in the absence of resources for large, new capital investments, most of the older mills have been forced to shut down or sell to larger firms. In many cases, the purchasing firm has realigned the business strategy and HR strategy fit by investing in technology that shifted the mill from a regional Versatile Differentiator to a more-efficient Low-Cost producer, while at the same time emphasizing and reinforcing a Control-type HR system.

This was certainly the case for the acquisitions by Birmingham Steel referred to earlier. Nearly all of Birmingham Steel's acquisitions have been older unionized mills. After acquiring these mills, Birmingham has been able to nullify the union contract and/or decertify the existing union. To date, the union has not been unable to reestablish itself in these plants.[11]

Birmingham's recent acquisition of Atlantic Steel's unionized plant in Catersville, Georgia is typical of this pattern. The company bought the mill in November 1996 for $43 million from Ivco, a Canadian steel company. Birmingham immediately shut the mill down, issuing a plant closure notification on November 15 and effectively eliminating the approximately 340 USWA bargaining unit jobs at the mill. The company has combined this plant with an existing plant in Mississippi and formed a joint venture, Birmingham Southwest, LLC, in which Birmingham owns 85% and Ivco owns 15%. The company is planning to reopen the plant as a nonunion mill with less than one-half the employees. Although the union is appealing this decision, it does not appear that the successorship language in the existing union contract can prevent the company from implementing its plan.

The HR strategy being pursued in Birmingham's nonunion mills is a variant of Nucor's "inducement strategy" model. About 25% of employees' pay is in the form of an incentive-based production bonus (compared with nearly 50% at Nucor). With the bonus, total compensation for production workers ranges between $35,000 and $50,000 per year, which is comparable to approximately $40,000 per year for a typical unionized minimill worker. Compared with most unionized mills, there are fewer job classifications and work rules. As in the Atlantic steel plant already discussed, these plants typically run extremely lean. This HR system appears to be successful in improving productivity by driving down labor costs. Birmingham reports labor hours per ton at 1.16, among the lowest in the industry (Ninneman, 1997).

Response to Minimill Developments by Unions and Integrated Producers

In addition to explaining the dynamics of fit in the industry, the evolution of the minimill sector presents a number of challenges for the

USWA, which represents more than half of the approximately 30,000 minimill hourly employees in North America (including 11,000 of the 23,000 minimill employees in the United States and nearly all of the 6,000 Canadian minimill workers). In addition to the loss of unionized employees within the minimill sector described previously, the new minimill capacity in flat-rolled steel has been almost entirely nonunion, creating a lost opportunity for additional union members. Finally, and perhaps most important, the growth of the nonunion minimill sector has begun to strain relationships between the union and existing integrated producers who see the new low-cost nonunion mills beginning to erode their market share.

The USWA has not been idle in the face of these threats. The union has been engaged in a number of struggles with steel companies that have been trying to move toward a cost-reduction strategy by "escaping" union representation (c.f. Walton, Cutcher-Gershenfeld, and McKersie, 1994). In fact, nearly all of the recent labor-management disputes in steel industry involve minimills or are minimill related (Becker, 1996). These include strikes at Bayou Steel, WCI, CF&I/Oregon Steel, and Northwestern Steel and Wire, as well as confrontations with LTV and IPSCO Steel over the opening of new nonunion minimill plants. In addition to work stoppages and corporate campaigns, the union has been using its bargaining leverage in existing unionized companies to get language into contracts that would force management to be "neutral" in organizing efforts in any new facilities that are built or acquired by the company (Becker, 1996). These recent labor-management confrontations are in contrast to the largely cooperative relationships that the union has been able to forge with integrated steel producers under the rubric of the "New Directions" bargaining program instituted in the 1993 round of bargaining.

In addition to strikes and contractual remedies with existing unionized steel mills, the USWA has launched a new organizing effort in steel. Labeled "SWOC II," this group, formed at the February 1997 Basic Steel Industry Conference, consists of leaders of USWA locals who have pledged money and resources to organize the growing nonunion sector within the industry. The name is significant. The original Steelworkers Organizing Committee (SWOC) was the precursor to the current USWA. Led by Phillip Murray, the first USWA president, it organized tens of thousands of U.S. steelworkers in the 1930s and early 1940s. By recalling this name, the union is not only providing a reminder of its past but also indicating the seriousness of the current threat posed by nonunion minimills to the industry.

Although USWA efforts have had some limited success at keeping existing plants organized and generating a few new members, they have not been able to organize the growing number of new minimill plants. The resistance of these new plants to unionization can be explained in part by their rural location in generally low union-density areas, the "positive" HR practices in these plants (e.g., no layoffs, relatively high wages), as well as aggressive antiunion positions taken by the mills (Kuster, 1995).

Competing HRM Systems. Using the broader strategic HRM perspective, evolving industry dynamics appear to be consolidating HR systems in the steel industry around at least two successful HR strategies. Nucor Steel represents the first strategy. The tremendous growth and success of this company has led a number of minimills and integrated steel firms to attempt to imitate both the technology and the HR system of Nucor. Throughout the industry, firms are moving toward reducing the number of organizational levels, eliminating work rules, and making a larger percentage of pay contingent on production goals and company performance. As stated in a recent press report, "Nucor has become the very model of a lean, low-cost company" (Baker, 1995:58). David H. Hoag, Chairman of LTV Corp. (an integrated steel producer), is quoted as saying, "We benchmark against Nucor" (Baker, 1995:58). To date, this model has proven to be successful only in nonunion minimills that pursue a low-cost position in the industry. It has been described by both industry and union sources as incompatible with unionization (*New Steel*, August 1996:87–91).

The alternative to Nucor's Inducement HR strategy in steel is a Commitment model, which has both a union and a nonunion variant. The union variant is known as the New Directions Program or Cooperative Partnership model, which has become the dominant model in the integrated sector of the industry. This program essentially consists of providing union workers with enhanced job security, employee involvement and information sharing, and union involvement at all levels of decision making (including a seat on the board of directors). In exchange, companies get a long-term labor agreement (six years), significant quality and flexibility-enhancing work restructuring, and a larger percentage of compensation tied to firm performance (in the form of profit sharing and gainsharing). The Cooperative Partnership agreement was first negotiated with National Steel in 1986. This type of agreement (with some minor variations) then became the pattern for the other integrated steel firms, including U.S. Steel, in the 1993–1994 round of bargaining (Arthur and Smith, 1994).

As can be seen from the above discussion, the Cooperative Partnership model has most of the characteristics of the Commitment Maximizing HR system (Cluster 6 in Table 1.2). This strategy appears to be very successful in the steel industry among both minimills and integrated steel producers. In particular, it appears to work especially well in firms pursuing a product market strategy that emphasizes high-value, high-quality, customized steel production. Most integrated producers appear to be pursuing this strategy along with, as we have seen, many minimill firms.

The growth and evolution of the nonunion minimill sector has begun to undermine a foundation of the Cooperative Partnership model— namely, the company's acceptance of the union as a legitimate and co- equal partner in the success of the firm. This is precisely what appears to be occurring at Trico steel. Trico is a nonunion minimill joint ven- ture between LTV Steel, British Steel, and Sumitomo Metals in Decatur, Alabama with a flat-rolled steel capacity of about 2.2 million tons. LTV owns a 50% stake in the company. The HR system at Trico appears to be a variant of the Nucor system. Staffing levels are very lean and there are only three levels of employees: officers, process managers, and manufacturing technicians. Like Nucor, a large percentage of employee compensation is in the form of performance-based incentives and bo- nuses. Base pay accounts for only 45% of employee earnings. The pro- duction bonus is based on prime tons shipped as well as quality and uptime. There is also a strong egalitarian culture. Everyone gets the same percentage pay supplement due to profit sharing. Unlike Nucor, employ- ees receive skill-based pay increases in addition incentive pay and are involved in cross training. The plant has been able to recruit from a large number of applicants. For the 175 hourly positions, the company re- ceived 8,500 applications and interviewed 450 candidates. Management looked for people with some college education, but who had no steel- making experience. Forty of the 175 new hires have four-year college degrees and another 135 have two-year degrees. Only two, however, had ever seen steel made before being hired. The USWA claims that this extensive screening process allows the company to "weed out" union supporters, making union organizing at the plant extremely difficult.

From the standpoint of the union, the Trico mill represents a com- plete betrayal of the cooperative partnership agreement negotiated with LTV. Because the mill produces flat-rolled products similar to integrated mills, the USWA sees this mill as a direct threat to unionized employ- ees at LTV and other unionized steel companies. It certainly appears that the company is trying to escape union representation with Trico. The announcement of the Trico project in December 1994 was made shortly after the labor agreement with LTV in June of that year. The labor agree- ment called for the company's neutrality in organizing any new plants in which the company had "a majority stake." Because LTV controls exactly 50% of the joint venture, this clause does not apply.

The USWA has fought back in many ways. Union members protested at the annual LTV stockholders' meeting and staged local rallies charg- ing that LTV got sweetheart deals from the state in the form of tax abate- ments and unusually low energy rates. Although the six-year labor contract prevents the union from taking strike action against the com- pany prior to 1999, Trico will clearly be a central issue in the next bargaining round. The confrontation over the plant has been a major blow to any hope the union had of maintaining a cooperative partnership arrangement with the company. USWA President Becker is quoted as saying, "If the [LTV Steel] contract was up, if there hadn't been this long-term agreement, we'd strike. Dead in their tracks, we'd shut them down" (Berry, 1996:33).

The union fears that other steel companies will follow LTV's lead on this issue and begin opening their own nonunion minimill joint ventures. The USWA has in fact been able to get language in its agreement with Gulf States Steel that would prevent the company from entering into joint ventures (even with a minority stake) unless they agree to card-check recognition at the new facility with the union. None of the other steelmakers, however, have been willing to talk about this so-called "Trico clause."

Barriers to Imitation

Can LTV and other integrated and minimill producers imitate Nucor's success by building their own nonunion flat-rolled minimills? Does this expansion of the minimill technology mean the end of the Cooperative Partnership model and Commitment Maximizing HR system in steel? Although the future of the Cooperative Partnership will depend on choices by steel industry management and unions, there is strong evidence to suggest that variation in HR systems will continue in the industry. In particular, I show in the following section how the competitive advantage created by the synergy between technology investments, product market, and HR strategies at Nucor create barriers to imitation. Because mills compete in different ways, we will continue to see differences in HR systems.

At one level, imitating Nucor's success appears to be very straightforward. The flat-rolled casting technology is not proprietary. Nucor has no formal R&D department. This technology is available to other competitors from the same suppliers that Nucor uses. Nucor's internal organization, its organizational structure and HR policies and practices, which F. Kenneth Iverson, Nucor's Chairman and CEO for 20 years, identifies as Nucor's "secrets of success" (Iverson, 1993), also do not appear to be difficult to imitate. The essential features of this system, very lean staffing and supervision and a high percentage of compensation as group incentive pay, are well known. Two factors, however, help to explain the barriers to the imitation of this strategy and suggest why we should expect to see a continued existence of multiple HR systems in this industry despite the success of Nucor's system (or maybe because of it).

First, although the elements of Nucor's internal organization are well known, the successful implementation of this system is much more subtle and complex than it may first appear. For example, when Nucor opens a plant, like the one in Crawfordsville, Indiana, it spends a fair amount of time and effort selecting employees, using probationary periods and interviews by psychologists to get the "right" kind of employees (and, presumably, to weed out union supporters). Although other firms can also use these selection techniques, part of this selectivity depends on their ability to offer high pay and stable jobs—Nucor has not had a layoff in 20 years. The ability to offer this kind of job security and pay level in a cyclical industry such as steel, and still keep costs down, is not something most steel firms can afford to do.

Nucor's culture and reputation, unique to the company, also play a part in the success of this system. Lean staffing and supervision as well as high-powered group incentives depend critically on employees' perceptions of fairness of and trust in management. In the absence of formal rules and contractual obligations, a key vulnerability of this type of system is managerial opportunism. In other words, a perception that additional effort would result in job loss or an arbitrary increase in production standards would seriously undermine this system. Unlike other companies in the industry, Nucor can point to its 20-year history of no layoffs. It relies on a very strong culture of egalitarianism, openness, and fairness to control other types of opportunistic behaviors. Executive privileges are minimized, and all employees and managers take pay cuts when production and sales drop (Overman, 1994). Performance standards are measured objectively and production levels are communicated continuously to employees (Berry, 1993). Management reports that all nonproprietary company information is available to employees (Iverson, 1993).

Link to Business Strategy: A second reason that not all firms are likely to be able to successfully implement Nucor's HR system is that few other steel firms are able or willing to pursue Nucor's Low-Cost business strategy. Pankaj Ghemawat of Harvard University provides some important insights into the ways in which Nucor's HR system and Low-Cost competitive strategy are interdependent and mutually reinforcing (Ghemawat, 1995). According to Ghemawat's analysis, Nucor's low-cost position has led to two "virtuous cycles." First, a Low-Cost strategy enabled Nucor to expand rapidly in the 1970s and 1980s. This rapid expansion was combined with a capital resource strategy that included self-financing of most new projects (low debt) and an insistence on a 25% return on assets in five years to create a number of investment efficiencies. Low costs and broadly defined markets were associated with high-capital utilization in the mills. This brought down costs even more and allowed the company to continue expanding by continuing to build new mills and to expand markets. Rapid expansion of its product market is one reason why Nucor has not had to lay people off and can convince employees that developing labor-saving ideas will not result in job loss.[12]

Other aspects of Nucor's HR system complement, and in many ways directly depend, on their strategy of expanding production of relatively few steel products to achieve a low-cost position in the market. Consider Nucor's use of incentive compensation:

> The effectiveness of high-powered, output-based compensation for production workers at Nucor appears to have been related to its low-cost strategy: It would have been less successful with an output based compensation formula if it had been following a differentiated strategy instead since quality tends to be harder to meter than quantity. Nucor's low costs also increased its optimal capacity utilization level relative to its competitors, narrowing the scope for divergence between output and profit maximization. (Ghemawat, 1995:695–96)

Nucor's product focus and plant designs enable the company to maintain a low-cost position by maximizing capacity utilization and throughput of good tons. Nucor's incentives fit nicely with this objective. There is an easily measured, consistent, output and a single goal that can be directly impacted by increased employee effort. Moreover, the employee goal of maximizing income by maximizing production output corresponds directly to the company goal of being a low-cost producer. This confluence of goals reduces the need for monitoring or investing in other HR policies to direct and control employee efforts, which further reduces costs. It is the tight configuration of complementary technology, product, and HR practices that makes this system so successful in achieving a low-cost position.

However, by definition only one firm can be *the* low-cost producer in a given product market. Given Nucor's lead in this area and the barrier to imitation discussed previously, it seems clear that other steel firms will continue to find other ways to compete. The choice to follow a different competitive strategy implies different choices in terms of technology, products, and HR practices. Chaparral Steel, for example, was also theoretically in a position to copy Nucor's move into the flat-rolled steel market in the late 1980s using the same technology provided by the German supplier, SMS. Chaparral's competitive strategy of differentiation by providing a variety of higher value-added steel products, however, made the pursuit of this investment less attractive (Ghemawat, 1993). Furthermore, the pursuit of Nucor's flat-rolled production strategy would not have fit well with Chaparral's Commitment-type HR system. Unlike Nucor, Chaparral invests heavily in employee and management training, both on and off the job. Instead of group production incentives based on weekly output, Chaparral offers individual employees profit sharing and an opportunity to purchase company stock. All employees are salaried and increases are based on job knowledge and supervisors' performance evaluations. Yearly performance reviews emphasize achievement of individual goals.[13]

Even among the new flat-rolled minimill producers, differences in product market strategies and HR practices are persisting. Galatin Steel, a flat-rolled minimill joint venture between Co-Steel and Dufasco, which started producing steel in 1995, has chosen to compete based on speed and customization, rather than as the lowest cost producer. This high-tech plant is able to produce short production runs efficiently and to provide precision-made, customized steel products to customers quickly, on demand. To accomplish this they utilize highly trained employees who work in self-managing teams empowered to make "on-line" production changes (Freedman, 1997). In short, both the Control-type and Commitment-type HR systems are continuing to thrive.

It should be noted that the HR systems used in the new minimill firms share many of the same general characteristics of "best practices" described in the literature (e.g., Pfeffer, 1994). HR practices at these companies, for example, emphasize selectivity in recruiting, relatively high wages, information sharing, teams, symbolic egalitarianism, measurement of practices, and an overarching philosophy.[14] The companies, however, have chosen very different means for implementing these concepts. These differences are integrally tied to the different competitive strategies being pursued in these firms. As Ghemawat (1995:714) notes:

> Competitive heterogeneity provides an additional, albeit partial, explanation of why organizational arrangements that appear to be associated with a particular firm's superior performance aren't more widely imitated by its rivals: Some rivals may be pursuing alternate strategic paths.

For minimills, these alternate strategic paths and the different HR systems associated with them appear to be a persistent feature of this industry.

Notes

1. The story of the integrated steel industry's decline and transformation in the 1980s and 1990s has been well documented. Interested readers should consult Alhbrant et al., 1996; Barnett and Crandall, 1986; and Tiffany, 1988. The industrial relations implications of these changes can be found in Arthur and Smith, 1994; and Hoerr, 1988.

2. Estimating the percentage of grievances or complaints handled through formal mechanisms for this question also required managers in most cases to estimate the number of grievances handled informally. Because it is highly unlikely that any personnel manager could know the total number of employee grievances that are resolved informally with a supervisor, it is assumed that managers are responding to this question based

on their knowledge of some subset of such grievances. In addition, it should be noted that interpretation of this variable will differ depending on whether one is analyzing a union or nonunion HR system. In nonunion mills, the use of formal due process procedures indicates that management has voluntarily agreed to give up some of its decision-making power and to abide by certain rules and procedures in dealing with employee grievances. In a unionized setting, there is no such indication, because the union has already won the right to a formal procedure and may initiate its use with or without management's consent. Among unionized mills, a high percentage of grievances handled through formal procedures may be seen as indicating a low-trust/high-conflict labor-management relationship (Fox, 1974; Katz, Kochan, and Weber, 1985).

3. For a more general discussion of these issues see Meyer, Tsui, and Hinnings, 1993; Milgrom and Roberts, 1995. As complementarities apply specifically to combinations HR practices, see Arthur, 1995; Delery and Doty, 1996.

4. For an empirical study that explicitly tests these arguments, see Ichniowski, Shaw, and Prennushi, 1994.

5. Details of this analysis are presented in Arthur (1992).

6. For the newer mills producing flat-rolled products, the up-front process is essentially the same. The only differences are that instead of casting a billet shape, they cast a steel slab, which is then flattened, elongated in the rolling mills, and wound into multiton steel coils.

7. These statistical analyses can be found in Arthur, 1992.

8. For a discussion of the conceptual and methodological issues involved in determining this relationship, see Arthur, 1996, and Becker and Gerhart, 1996.

9. Because only one of the mills following a Low-Cost business strategy was in the No-Fit category, describing meaningful differences in this subgroup is not possible.

10. With Birmingham's most recent acquisition of American Wire and Steel and Atlantic Steel, they are moving somewhat away from rebar and toward higher margin special quality bar (SBQ).

11. The sole exception to this is the Joliet, Illinois plant of the former American Steel and Wire Company that was purchased in 1994 by Birmingham whose 60 employees are represented by the USWA. There is some indication, however, that the union at this location may also be "at risk." Only 3 of the original 18 managers remain and the current Birmingham CEO Robert Garvey is quoted as saying that if the mill does not achieve production and profit goals, "we will shut the facility down" (Ninneman, 1997). This would be consistent with Birmingham's previous decisions to shut down formerly unionized mills in California, Washington, and Virginia.

12. This strategy obviously cannot work for all firms in the industry. Nucor's expansion in a stagnant or shrinking market for steel products means that other steel companies have to bear the layoff burden.

13. Information on Chaparral's HR practices and business strategies can be found in Forward et al. (1991).

14. Becker and Gerhart (1996) make the argument that "best practices" should be viewed at different levels. Many of the best practices identified by Pfeffer (1994) and others are really general principles and guidelines such as "linking pay to performance" or having an "overarching HR philosophy." The use of these general principles may provide benefits to all firms over firms that do not follow them. The question of how these principles are implemented in terms of specific policies or practices, however, may still depend on business strategy.

References

Ahlbrant, Roger S., Fruehan, Richard J., and Giarranti, Frank. 1996. *The renaissance of American steel*. New York: Oxford University Press.

American Metal Market. 1986. Minis facing turbulent era of competition. April 24, p. 6.

Arthur, J. B. 1987. Industrial relations practices in steel minimills in the United States. Master's Thesis, Cornell University.

Arthur, Jeffrey B. 1992. The link between business strategy and industrial relations strategies in American steel minimills. *Industrial and Labor Relations Review*, 45: 488–506.

Arthur, Jeffrey B. 1994. Effects of human resource systems on manufacturing performance and turnover. *Academy of Management Journal*, 37: 670–687.

Arthur, Jeffrey B. 1995. Testing the strategic human resources perspective: Contingency and configurational approaches. Paper presented at the annual meeting of the Academy of Management, Vancouver.

Arthur, Jeffrey B. 1996. Putting the pieces together: Making sense of the evidence on external fit in high performance work systems' research. Background paper prepared for Workshop on High Performance Work System, American Society for Training and Development, Washington, DC.

Arthur, Jeffrey B., and Smith, Suzanne Konzelmann. 1994. The transformation of industrial relations in the American steel industry. In Paula B. Voos (ed.), *Contemporary collective bargaining in the private sector*. Madison, WI: Industrial Relations Research Association Series.

Baker, S. 1995. Testing Nucor's mettle. *Business Week*, 5 June, 58–60.

Barnett, D. F., and Schorsch, L. 1983. *Steel: Upheaval in a basic industry*. Cambridge, MA: Ballinger Press.

Barnett, Donald F., and Candall, Robert W. 1986. *Up from the ashes: The rise of the steel minimill in the United States*. Washington: Brookings Institution.

Becker, Brian, and Gerhart, Barry. 1996. The impact of human resource management on organizational performance: Progress and prospects. *Academy of Management Journal*, 39 (4): 779–801.

Becker, George. 1996. Keynote address. 28th Constitutional Convention, United Steelworkers of America, 5 August, Pittsburgh, PA.

Berry, Bryan. 1993. Hot band at 0.66 manhours per ton; Nucor Corp.'s Hickman, Arkansas, plant. *New Steel*, 1 (October): 20–25.

Berry, Bryan. 1996. George Becker: compassion vs. the god of the bottom line. *New Steel*, 12 (May): 30–34.

Delery, John E., and Doty, D. Harold. 1996. Modes of theorizing in strategic human resource management: Tests of universalistic, contingency, and configurational performance predictions. *Academy of Management Journal*, 39 (4): 802–835.

Dyer, Lee, and Holder, Gerald W. 1988. A strategic perspective of human resource management. In Lee Dyer (ed.), *Human resources management: Evolving roles and responsibilities*. Washington: Bureau of National Affairs: 1–46.

Forward, Gordon E., Beach, Dennis E., Gray, David A., and Quick, James Campbell, 1991. Mentofacturing: A vision for American industrial excellence. *Academy of Management Executive*, 5(3): 32–43.

Fox, A. 1974. *Beyond contract: Work, power, and trust relations*. London: Faber and Faber.

Freedman, D. H. 1997. Steel edge. *Forbes*, 6 October, 46.

Ghemawat, P. 1993. Commitment to a process innovation: Nucor, USX, and thin-slab casting. *Journal of Economics and Management Strategy*, 2 (1): 135–161.

Ghemawat, P. 1995. Competitive advantage and internal organization: Nucor revisited. *Journal of Economics and Management Strategy*, 3 (4): 685–717.

Hoerr, J.P. 1988. *And the wolf finally came: The decline of the American steel industry*. Pittsburgh, PA: University of Pittsburgh Press.

Huselid, M.A. 1995. The impact of human resource management practices on turnover, productivity, and corporate financial performance. *Academy of Management Journal*, 38 (3): 635–672.

Ichniowski, C., Shaw, K., and Prennushi, G., 1994. The effects of human resource management practices on productivity. Working Paper. Columbia University, New York.

Iverson, F. Kenneth. 1993. Changing the rules of the game. *Planning Review*, September/October, 9–12.

Katz, H.C., and Kochan, T.A. 1992. *An introduction to collective bargaining and industrial relations*. New York: McGraw-Hill.

Katz, H.C., Kochan, T.A., and Weber, M. 1985. Assessing the effects of industrial relations and quality of worklife on organizational effectiveness. *Academy of Management Journal*, 28: 509–526.

Kuster, T. 1995. The USWA's battle for the minimills. *Iron Age New Steel*, May, 24–29.

MacDuffie, J.P. 1995. Human resource management bundles and manufacturing performance: Organizational logic and flexible production systems in the world auto industry. *Industrial and Labor Relations Review*, 48: 197–221.

Meyer, Alan, Tsui, Ann, and Hinnings, C.R. 1993. Guest co-editors' introduction: Configurational approaches to organizational analysis. *Academy of Management Journal*, 36: 1175–1195.

Milgrom, P., and Roberts, J. 1995. Complementarities and fit: Strategy, structure, and organizational change in manufacturing. *Journal of Accounting and Economics*, 19 (2): 179–208.

New Steel. 1996. The people and the technology: what we've got to work with. Panel Discussion. Vol. 12 (August): 87–91.

Ninneman, P. 1997. From sea to shining sea: The growth of Birmingham Steel. *Iron Age New Steel*, 13 (4), 90–96.

Osterman, P. 1994. How common is workplace transformation and how can we explain who adopts it?: Results from a national survey. *Industrial and Labor Relations Review*, 47: 173–188.

Overman, Stephenie. 1994. No-frills HR at Nucor. *HR Magazine*. July, 56–60.

Pfeffer, Jeffrey. 1994. *Competitive advantage through people*. Boston, MA: HBS Press.

Porter, M.E. 1990. *Competitive strategy*. New York: Free Press.

Schriefer, J. 1995. Growing by leaps and bounds. *Iron Age New Steel*, 11 (1): 38–42.

Sheets, K.R. 1985. U.S. minimills getting caught in steel trap. *U.S. News and World Report*, 9 December, 51.

Tiffany, Paul A. 1988. *The decline of American steel: How management, labor, and government went wrong*. New York: Oxford University Press.

United States Department of Commerce. 1986. *Growth patterns of the U.S. minimill industry*. International Trade Administration: Washington, DC.

Walton, Richard E. 1985. "From control to commitment in the workplace." *Harvard Business Review*, 63 (2): 77–84.

Walton, R.E., Cutcher-Gershenfeld, J.E., and McKersie, R.B. 1994. *Strategic negotiations: A theory of change in labor-management relations*. Boston: Harvard Business School Press.

2

The Characteristics and Determinants of Organizational Innovation in the Apparel Industry

THOMAS BAILEY
CAROLA SANDY

1. Introduction

For several years, policymakers have advocated the adoption of work and human resource (HR) reforms, which are often called "high-performance" or "high-involvement" work organization. A growing number of reports, which systematically measure the effects of these practices, show that there are positive effects on quality, cost, financial performance, and productivity (Berg et al., 1996; Dunlop & Weil, 1996; Huselid & Becker, 1996; Ichniowski et al., 1997; Kochan & Osterman, 1995; U.S. Department of Labor, 1993; Womack, Jones, & Roos, 1990). Yet despite the widespread enthusiasm, the diffusion of these apparently beneficial practices seems slow. Osterman (1994) argued that nearly one-third of firms have made significant changes, but a 1996 review of the diffusion of HR innovations suggested that although a majority of firms have made some changes, "only a small percentage of businesses . . . have adopted a full set of innovative work practices" (Ichniowski et al., 1996: 325). Furthermore, many of the firms that have made innovations often introduce reforms in a partial and truncated manner (Applebaum & Batt, 1994; Bassi, 1992), and history suggests that for many firms, reforms are short-lived (Bailey, 1993a).

This apparent puzzle has generated a growing body of research that examines the extent and causes of the spread of organizational reform, the specific nature and characteristics of those reforms, and how they relate to the economic and institutional environment in which they are introduced. This chapter contributes to that discussion by examining these issues in the context of a study of the apparel industry. We examine three broad questions related to the apparel industry:

(1) What are the characteristics of HR and organizational reform in the apparel industry, and how are the various practices combined or substituted?
(2) How widespread are high-involvement practices?
(3) What are the determinants of adoption of these practices?

The analysis combines information from extensive fieldwork with data from an establishment survey conducted in 1992 based on a random sample of apparel factories. The latter approach allows us to produce measures of the spread of various practices and perform a quantitative analysis of the characteristics of adopting firms, while the detailed information on the industry from fieldwork, provides rich contextual information for the interpretation of the quantitative results.

The apparel industry has several interesting features. Traditional apparel production is an extreme example of a classic mass production approach in which processes are divided into minute tasks, each to be carried out by one operator who specializes in that task. Therefore, apparel factories are loaded with in-process buffer inventories. Time and motion studies are still widespread in the industry, and beginners can reach standard proficiency in most tasks within a few weeks. Moreover, apparel is considered an important source of jobs for Americans with lower educational levels, a first step up the employment ladder for recent immigrants and workers living in rural areas. However, the low skill levels and moderate capital requirements also make the industry vulnerable to low-wage offshore (foreign) competition.[1] Organizational and HR innovations are advocated as a strategy for preserving and perhaps improving import-threatened apparel jobs in the United States, an issue that has become increasingly urgent because the United States lost almost 600,000 apparel jobs between 1970 and 1997 (close to one-half of total apparel employment).

The rest of this chapter is organized as follows. Section 2 briefly discusses the controversies about the nature, extent, and causes of the spread of innovative HR practices. Section 3 discusses some possible explanations for the adoption of organizational innovations. We organize the discussion around a set of seven general hypotheses about work organization practices that are later applied to the apparel industry (Section 6). Section 4 provides some background on the apparel industry and discusses the specifics of organizational innovation in apparel. This section also introduces and describes the sample. Section 5 examines various measures of the spread of innovative practices and presents an analysis of the characteristics of establishments that have introduced those practices. Section 6 presents the empirical evidence on the determinants of innovative practices. Section 7 concludes.

2. The Nature and Spread
of Organizational Innovation

What is a "high-performance work organization"? This term was apparently coined by the Commission on Skills in the American Workplace (1990). They state that the guiding principle of high-performance work "is to reduce bureaucracy by giving authority to direct workers for a wider variety of tasks" (p. 39). More recently, other authors have argued that the use of the term "high-performance" is misleading, because much of the research in this area is aimed at determining the extent to which "high-performance" practices indeed lead to higher performance. Pil and MacDuffie (1996) suggest the use of "high involvement" in this term reflects the emphasis in this literature on changing the behavior and management of workers.

One broad theme that underlies all work reform efforts, especially among advocates of high-involvement innovations, is that HR is underutilized—in effect, workers can contribute more to their organizations and that greater contribution outweighs the resources needed to elicit the improvement. This extra effort is more than simply getting people to work harder, although there was much of this in the earliest work reform programs. Rather, the objective is to get workers to apply their creativity and imagination as well as to exploit their intimate, and often unconscious, knowledge of the work process. Self-managed teams, quality circles, off-line teams, suggestion systems, and broadened responsibilities all give workers a chance to provide more significant input into their work. Training and education are important to provide the skills needed for workers to make an effective contribution, and performance-based compensation systems and group incentives give workers an incentive to participate (Bailey, 1993b).

How are these innovations operationalized? Research in the 1980s tended to look at the effects of specific practices, particularly the use of teams (Katz, Kochan, & Keefe, 1987). Although some studies still examine the use of specific techniques (Berg et al., 1996; Dunlop & Weil, 1996), most analyses now emphasize that successful adoption of these innovations requires the use of several complementary practices (Bailey, 1993b; Ichniowski et al., 1997; MacDuffie, 1995). Researchers now use two broad approaches to measuring innovative systems. One approach combines measures of many practices associated with high-involvement strategies, including training, compensation methods, teams, off-line groups of quality circles, suggestions, or changes in responsibility and authority (Huselid & Becker, 1996; Ichniowski et al., 1997). Another approach distinguishes practices that influence the role of workers—such as production teams, off-line teams, suggestion systems, more-varied work, and increasing responsibility among workers—from supporting HR practices, such as training and compensation (Osterman, 1994; Pil & MacDuffie, 1996).[2] Authors use a variety of formal and informal clustering techniques to produce indices and group firms with respect to their level of innovation.

There is also a growing body of research using both broad-based and industry-specific surveys designed to identify the diffusions of work reform and employee involvement practices. In general, surveys conducted in the 1980s found that often a majority of respondents reported adopting some work reform or employee involvement technique (Alper, Pfau, & Sirota, 1985; Eaton & Voos, 1992; Freund & Epstein, 1984; Lawler, Mohrman, & Ledford, 1992). Eighty-two percent of the respondents to a General Accounting Office survey of the 1986 Fortune "1000" reported use of some technique (Lawler, Ledford, & Mohrman, 1989). However, these studies examined the use of individual techniques rather than more significant organizational transformation. At least by the mid-1980s, relatively few organizations could be said to have made a significant organizational transformation. Results from the GAO survey suggest that "between 20 and 30 percent [of the respondents] have a substantial effort in place that uses a number of different kinds of approaches with a large percentage of employees." Osterman (1994), reporting results from a random sample of U.S. establishments with 50 or more employees, argued that 36% of all such establishments were "transformed." But this definition of "transformed" is not particularly demanding.[3] A recent review concluded that only a small percentage of firms had introduced a full package of reforms (Ichniowski et al., 1996).

3. Determinants of Organizational Innovation

Researchers have begun to look for explanations for why some firms introduce innovations, whereas others stick with traditional approaches. Explanations for why firms adopt HR innovations can be categorized into three broad groups. The first involves responses to market pressures for greater flexibility, better quality, and faster production. The second emphasizes general production efficiencies that relate to firms in all markets. The third focuses on internal firm factors that facilitate or thwart organizational innovation.

3.1. Market-Related Reasons

Much of the current wave of discussion about innovative production practices has been influenced by Piore and Sabel (1984), who argued that changing markets favored firms that used more flexible and responsive production systems. Markets now require greater variety and faster turnaround times. Mass production techniques that drove down the cost

of producing individual units of standardized goods are no longer practical in a world of niche markets, fast-changing styles and short production runs. Innovative HR practices allow firms to respond to market
changes and permit profitable production of shorter runs without exor-
bitant price increases. Thus, because, on average, mass markets are
breaking down, the average firm will tend to move toward strategies that
are more flexible. This implies that firms that must produce a greater
variety of products and a changing mix of products will want innovative work organization.

This is an historical demand-oriented argument, but it could be
applied in a cross section as well. Whatever the long-term trends, firms
in sectors in which markets are characterized by varied and changing
styles and products are more likely to adopt flexible practices. When
there is still a market for large quantities of standardized products, mass-
production techniques may still be superior.

> HYPOTHESIS 1: Firms facing markets that demand greater varieties
> of styles will be the most likely to introduce HR and organiza-
> tional innovations.

3.2. General Productivity Factors

Alternatively, innovative practices may have general productivity effects
that are important in all types of markets. These techniques improve
quality, reduce inventories, and therefore inventory carrying costs. Moreover, new forms of work organization engage workers in such a way that
they begin to contribute to the general increase in efficiency of the production process even in the production of standardized goods. Indeed,
there has been a long history of experimentation with various types
of work reform throughout the height of the mass-production era (Bailey,
1993b). Advocates of these strategies argued that these were simply
superior to more traditional approaches to production. Thus, HR innovation is in effect a widely applicable technological innovation. Recent
growth has resulted more from improvements in the techniques and strategies themselves than from market changes that favor those techniques.

> HYPOTHESIS 2: The factors that lead firms to introduce high-
> involvement innovations lie more in general efficiency benefits
> than in market factors requiring flexibility.[4]

3.3. Factors That Facilitate or Thwart Innovation

Although there are potential market and productivity benefits associated with organizational innovation, there are costs as well. Pil and
MacDuffie (1996) argued that rapid change might destroy competencies.

Thus, even if these innovations eventually lead to improved performance, firms must absorb costs in the short run. These costs, in turn, can increase or decrease as a result of several factors.

For example, some analysts argue that unions stand in the way of organizational innovation, because unions seem to defend established job definitions.[5] Alternatively, unions could promote innovation by helping to assure workers that they will share in any benefits (Kochan, Katz, & McKersie, 1986). Unions may play a particularly supportive role in import-threatened industries, such as apparel, if they see high-involvement innovations as part of a strategy to strengthen domestic employment.

HYPOTHESIS 3: In industries subject to increased competition, unionized firms will be more likely to introduce high-involvement innovations.

Plants that employ many immigrant workers may also be less likely to introduce organizational innovations. The presence of many languages in a plant may thwart the type of communication among workers and between workers and managers that is needed for successful implementation of innovative organizational practices.

HYPOTHESIS 4: Plants with a large immigrant workforce will be less likely to introduce high-involvement practices.

As many authors have emphasized, the introduction of high-involvement practices is a risky and expensive process that can be expected to lead to deteriorating performance in the short run (Pil & MacDuffie, 1996) and often requires more capital equipment per worker (Applebaum et al., 1994). This suggests that larger, more sophisticated firms may have better access to the knowledge and resources needed to make the investment and take on the risks that are required to implement these innovations. Larger organizations not only have access to the experience of other parts of the organization, but they may have personnel who could specialize in learning about new approaches. In the same vein, Osterman (1994) argues that firms operating in international markets will have better access to successful practices that are used abroad. Establishments that are part of large organizations may simply have more resources or better access to credit as well, which allows them to introduce costly practices with uncertain or far-off benefits.

HYPOTHESIS 5: Larger firms and multiplant firms will be more likely to introduce high-involvement practices.

High-involvement innovations usually require broader skills and often include increased firm-provided training. Research on training usually suggests that schooling and training are complementary. Educated workers also are believed to be more adaptable. Thus, a firm with a more highly educated workforce may have advantages in introducing organizational innovations.

> HYPOTHESIS 6: Firms that employ workers who are more educated are more likely to introduce organizational innovations.

Finally, a general environment of change can promote the chances of innovation. Pil and MacDuffie (1996) found that auto assembly plants that had introduced more new models over the previous five years were more likely to introduce high-involvement practices. They argued that model introductions offered opportunities for innovation because they "unfroze" traditional methods. In the apparel industry, many firms have traditionally produced many styles, even before the development of high-involvement innovations that have received so much attention in the last decade. Therefore, a recent increase in the number of styles produced in apparel, independent of the absolute number of styles produced, may offer "unfreezing" opportunities for innovation in the apparel industry.

> HYPOTHESIS 7: Holding constant the total number of styles or models produced, plants that have had to increase the number of styles that they produce are more likely to introduce high-involvement innovations.

3.4. Technology and Organizational Innovation

There is a complex relationship between advanced technology and organizational innovation. In general, flexible technology is often associated with organizational innovations. For example, computers can facilitate the spreading of responsibility to wider segments of the work force, by giving them easy access to information and by helping them control large and complex processes. Alternatively, firms can attempt to use flexible technology to avoid the need to introduce more difficult and uncertain flexibility-enhancing HR practices (Bailey, 1993a).

4. The Apparel Industry and Its Strategies for Competitiveness

During the last two or three decades, foreign producers have absorbed large portions of the U.S. apparel market. By the early 1990s, imports exceeded domestic production in many lines, including sweaters and most women's wear (American Apparel Manufacturers Association, 1993, Table 25). National employment in the apparel industry has fallen from a high of nearly 1.4 million in the 1970s to about 810,000 in mid-1997 (Bureau of Labor Statistics, 1997) while apparel wages have fallen from 86% of manufacturing wages in 1950 to only 60% in 1995 (AAMA, 1996).

As production opened in Asia and Latin America, many U.S. firms have moved some or all of their production offshore. Indeed, most apparel imports are garments produced abroad by contractors working for U.S.-owned companies. Firms that have attempted to maintain domestic production have followed three strategies: maintaining low wages, labor cost reduction through engineering and automation, and a strategy referred to as Quick Response—the apparel industry's version of "high-performance work organization" with an emphasis on relationships between customers and suppliers.[6]

4.1. Low Wages

Historically, apparel makers have sought to locate in low-wage regions such as the South or have recruited recent immigrants, especially in large cities like New York and Los Angeles, who are willing to work for low wages. This strategy is also reflected in falling apparel wages relative to wages in manufacturing as a whole. But given the extreme wage differentials between the United States and many countries in which apparel production is growing, such as Bangladesh, Thailand, and Guatemala, this cannot be a viable long-term strategy despite popular reports that suggest that the burgeoning sweatshop sector employing illegal immigrants in Los Angeles, and perhaps New York, is making some attempt to follow this strategy.

4.2. Labor Cost Reduction

The second strategy involves labor cost reduction through job simplification and automation—the classic U.S. mass-production approach to productivity increases and cost reduction. In apparel production, this approach is characterized by the progressive bundle system (PBS). In the bundle system, the assembly of each item is broken down into many discrete tasks, each performed by a different operator. Material is moved from operator to operator in bundles of about 30 pieces. Operators typically have one or two bundles at their workstations.

The bundle system has many advantages. It allows engineers to focus on reducing the time required to perform each task. Simplifying tasks has also facilitated automation, and by squeezing time out of each task, the total "standard allowed minutes" (SAM) can be reduced, thereby reducing the total labor required for assembly of the garment. Furthermore, the bundles contain in-process inventory, which prevents delays or problems with one operator, machine, or area from spreading quickly. In turn, the isolation of each operator facilitates the piece-rate system, which is seen as the key to motivation in the industry. Breaking assembly processes into many separate tasks also minimizes skill requirements and allows workers to specialize in one or two simple tasks, thereby reducing upward pressure on wages. Thus, the bundle system reduces labor costs through close engineering of the labor tasks, facilitating automation, and keeping skill requirements down.

However, these advantages come at a price. The bundle system generates a tremendous amount of in-process inventory. At any moment, in-process inventory equivalent to several days of output can be stored in the bundles, which complicates quality control.[7] It also slows throughput time. Many days may elapse between the time the textiles are cut and the completion of the article even if the garment may require only a few minutes of sewing time. Style changes are also more difficult since even minor changes in operations upset the balance of highly engineered balanced production lines. Despite these problems, the progressive bundle system has dominated the industry for several decades. Even through the 1980s, a strategy based on automation and low wages appears to have been at least as successful as other approaches. Those apparel sectors that had the lowest import penetration also tended to be those with the highest capital per worker and the lowest wages (Office of Technology Assessment, 1992).

But automation of apparel manufacturing is limited by technological constraints. Limp fabric makes full automation almost impossible, and even in the most advanced plants, individual operators must sit at individual sewing machines assembling garments. Furthermore, the disadvantages of the highly engineered bundle system with large amounts of in-process inventory become more problematic in operations that must produce many and faster changing styles. In any case, the system has not been able to reduce labor costs enough to stop the continued growth of offshore production. The processes are already so highly engineered that further reductions in SAMs in the bundle system could not possibly compensate for the significant wage differentials between the United States and even nearby areas like Mexico and the Caribbean.

4.3. Quick Response

The third strategy, often referred to as Quick Response, has attracted a great deal of attention since the mid-1980s. Indeed, this has received so much space in the industry press that one gets the impression of extensive diffusion of the strategy. As a competitive strategy, Quick Response emphasizes the area in which the traditional bundle system is weakest: accelerated throughput time and flexibility. If U.S. producers could significantly speed up their throughput time, their physical proximity to U.S. markets would be an even greater advantage.

To the extent that markets now demand more varied and faster changing styles, a more-flexible system with faster throughput times would seem to have many advantages. Indeed, interviews with apparel managers and retailers do suggest that retailers are putting pressure on producers to be more flexible and responsive. For retailers, these changes can reduce the high costs of holding inventory, markdowns, and stockouts (when retailers run out of popular items) (Office of Technology Assessment, 1987). Under the traditional system, more than a year may elapse between the design of an item and its delivery to the retailer. Retailers would prefer to make smaller initial orders close to the selling season and reorder hot items. Fundamentally, the advantages of Quick Response are based on shortening that overall production cycle.

From the point of view of the apparel producer, Quick Response requires changes in almost all activities, from the ordering and receipt of raw materials and other inputs, to the delivery to wholesalers or retailers. If fully implemented, Quick Response and associated changes in the way that apparel is produced and in the relationships between producers and retailers would indeed be a revolutionary change.

We divide the changes associated with Quick Response into four broad areas: high-involvement work practices, HR strategy, relations with suppliers and customers, and flexible technology.

4.3.1. High-Involvement Work Practices In the apparel industry, the modular production system corresponds most closely to the general high-involvement model. In modules, small teams of operators—often ten or fewer—work together to assemble a garment with minimal in-process inventory. Workers must be trained to do several tasks. Items that take several days to be assembled using the bundle system can be produced in a few hours in modules. The modular approach also facilitates a more integrated strategy for quality control in which all workers take on the responsibility to improve the quality of the whole product rather than being concerned only with quality problems that arise from their own tasks. Other less-ambitious, team-based strategies are also used. These are sometimes referred to as minilines or vertical teams, which maintain some of the benefits of teams, such as group problem solving and self-management but, by using larger teams, maintain some of the task-specialization characteristics of the bundle system.

There are other high-involvement practices used in apparel that do not involve teams. These include holding various types of meetings to solve problems off-line as well as practices that involve broader activities (competence at more tasks) and other types of increased input and responsibility for production workers.

4.3.2. Human-Resource Strategy   With Quick Response and related innovations, employers need more skilled and flexible employees who can work in a more varied and rapidly changing environment and who can contribute ideas and suggestions for improving products and manufacturing processes. This requires different approaches to motivating, training, and deploying workers. The piece-rate system was the foundation of motivation in the apparel industry. Operators who produced more were paid more. But in modules or other team-based strategies, output is produced collectively and piece rates must be dropped. In these cases, employers have experimented with straight hourly pay or some type of group incentive.

When workers participate in teams, two conditions must exist. First, workers must be given the opportunity to make a contribution; for example, through eliciting employee input or encouraging them to work together to find improvements or solutions. Second, workers must have appropriate training and education so that their suggestions and participation will be well informed and they can work effectively in a sophisticated fast-changing environment.

4.3.3. Relations With Suppliers and Customers   Quick Response also requires a decrease in the elapsed time between ordering and receipt of inputs. Apparel makers often argue that a large part of the total time required to produce apparel is not under their control: What difference does it make to reduce production time by a few hours or even days if textiles must be ordered months in advance?

Communications and interactions with retailers must also be improved so that producers can do a faster and more effective job in meeting the shifting retailer needs. Ever since the beginning of the widespread discussion of Quick Response, retailers and apparel and textile makers have been working to develop common nomenclature that will facilitate the use of electronic data interchange (EDI). The development of these systems of terminology has been one of the most significant achievements of the Quick Response movement, creating the impetus for many manufacturers and retailers to use bar coding to improve inventory control and communication with customers and suppliers.

4.3.4. Flexible Technology   As in other industries, the apparel employers have also sought to achieve higher throughput and flexible production through technology. The unit production system (UPS) is a flexible assembly line approach, which can speed up production, but, at least in principle, does not require significant changes in HR practices (Bailey, 1993a). The UPS eliminates bundles by moving material from operator to operator using a computerized routing system that consists of a ceiling-mounted rail. Apparel parts are attached to a hanger that can be routed to different workstations. This speeds up throughput time and reduces in-process inventory, but it does allow the maintenance of piece rates and does not require the introduction of teams (although UPS can be used with teams or modules).

5. Empirical Evidence on Organizational Innovation in the Apparel Industry

This section starts with a review of existing information about the extent to which apparel firms have adopted high-involvement innovations as well as the characteristics of the adopting firms. The analysis uses the results from a survey conducted in 1992 of 313 managers of apparel production facilities.[8] Missing data reduced the number of observations for the regression analysis to 234 observations. See the appendix for a brief description of the sample and sampling procedure.

What do we know from past research about the spread of Quick Response? The industry press gives the impression of widespread diffusion. Indeed, some employers and employer associations have taken steps to facilitate innovations. For example, groups of employers have worked out universal nomenclature and bar-coding protocols to promote more-efficient interfirm communications, and many consultants, employer organizations, and the industry's unions can provide assistance to firms seeking to implement Quick Response–related practices. Surveys by the American Apparel Manufacturing Association (AAMA) have found a small but growing number of employers trying the new approaches. For example, the AAMA (1988, 1996) reported that 7% of apparel firms used modules in 1988, and that share had grown to 15% by 1992.

Data from the apparel survey conducted for this project reveal some indication of change, but still only a small proportion of establishments have made significant and comprehensive changes. The following sections present evidence on the use of individual practices within the four components of Quick Response and high-involvement practices outlined previously.[9] We organize the discussion into the areas that we outlined earlier: (1) high-involvement practices, (2) HR policies, (3) communication with customers and clients, and (4) flexible technologies. Table 2.1 presents definitions and summary statistics for the individual practices as well as the indices that combine individual practices in a variety of ways. The composite indices are constructed to have a mean of zero and correspond to the unweighted sum of the standardized values of the individual variables. We assumed that each practice contributes roughly the same amount of information about the establishment, because we could not find any convincing theoretical argument for assigning different weights.[10] Table 2.2 displays more information about the adoption of individual practices. The first column shows the number of plants that use the practice at all, and the second column indicates their share in the entire sample. The mean displayed in the third column corresponds only to those firms that use at least some of the practice. Finally, the fifth column shows the percentage of plants that have adopted the practice for at least 50% of their workers.

5.1. High-Involvement Practices

Modular manufacturing represents the most ambitious organizational innovation currently used in the industry. *Module* (terms in italics correspond to the variable names used in the tables) measures the percentage of machine operators involved in modular production. Thirteen percent reported making at least some use of modules, but of those, only some 6% used them for more than one-half of the production work force.[11]

Innovative workplaces that require more involvement from workers are also characterized by a broadening of the scope of work among production workers; therefore, job rotation is a measure of innovation. Plants that produce a larger number of styles usually expect that their workers carry out a variety of tasks. *More Tasks* indicates if the average number of jobs performed by a sewer has increased over the last five years. Just over 40% of the plants reported that the number of tasks performed by sewing machine operators has increased since the mid-1980s. Even with this increase in operator responsibility, the number of different operations that sewers are expected to perform over the course of one month is still quite limited. Indeed, on average, managers report that about two-thirds (61%) of their sewing machine operators perform only one operation over the course of a month, whereas only about one-fifth (22%) perform four or more operations. *Four Tasks* is the percentage of sewing machine operators who perform four or more jobs over the course of one month. The survey asked if sewers are expected to diagnose the cause of machine stoppage, make a record of machine problems, perform minor repairs on the equipment, and perform equipment maintenance. *Addt'l Tasks* measures the extent to which sewing machine operators perform these additional tasks. We combine the last three variables into a *Broad Skills Index*, which will give an indication of the breadth of skills needed by workers.

High-involvement practices also include nonproduction (or off-line) practices designed to engage workers in problem solving and improvements in the products and operation of the firm. The data show that plants have made some efforts to allow a more-extensive participation by employees. For example, 6% of the plants in the sample had regularly scheduled meetings (*Meeting*) "in which hourly employees discuss problems and the solutions to those problems or other topics with other workers, supervisors, and management." Of those, about one-half have meetings at least once a week. The survey also asked if production workers and me-

Table 2.1. Quick Response Practices: Definitions and Summary Statistics

Variable	Definition	Mean	Std. Dev.	N
High Involvement Index	Standardized sum of modular production, broad skills, and off-line involvement indices	0	1.64	313
Modular production	Standardized value of module	0	1	313
Module	Percentage of machine operators involved in modular production	6.34	20.91	297
Broad skills index	Standardized sum of more tasks, four tasks, and additional tasks	0	0.67	313
More tasks	= 1 if the average number of jobs performed by a sewing machine operator has increased in the last five years; 0 = otherwise	0.45	0.5	303
Four tasks	Percentage of machine operators who perform four or more jobs during the course of one month	22.29	33.85	294
Additional tasks	= 0, 1, 2, 3, 4 if sewers are expected to carry out any of the following tasks: diagnose the cause of machine stoppage, make a record of machine problems, perform minor repairs on the equipment, and perform equipment maintenance	1.17	1.07	306
Off-line involvement	Standardized sum of meeting and labor input	0	0.8	313
Meeting	= 1, 2, 3, 4 depending upon the frequency of meetings (1 = no meetings, 2 = monthly or quarterly meetings, 3 = weekly or several times a month, and 4 = daily or several times a week	1.65	0.86	313
Labor input	= 0, 1, 2, 3, 4 if direct labor has input in any of the following decisions: organization of production tasks; selection of machinery, equipment, or production technology; in the use or adaptation of machinery; or in quality control	1.98	1.33	301

56

Human Resources Index	Standardized sum of training and group incentive indices	0	1.26	313
Training index	Standardized sum of training, training in literature or math, and other training	0	0.66	313
Training	Percentage of machine operators who received formal training provided by the plant or company	20.89	33.3	286
Training in lit. or math	= 1 if the plant offers training in literary or arithmetic skills = 0 otherwise	0.12	0.33	299
Other training	= 0, 1, 2, 3, 4 if sewing machine operators are offered zero or more of the following types of instruction: information about the firm's products or markets, information on the tasks and responsibilities of other employees, social skills, and teamwork	1.15	1.12	301
Group incentives	Standardized value of group pay	0	1	313
Group pay	Percentage of machine operators who are paid group incentives	4.03	17.12	308
EDI Index	Standardizes sum of EDI1, EDI2, and IMPCOM	0	0.65	313
EDI inc. orders	Percentage of incoming orders placed through computer links	21.63	36.57	276
EDI out. orders	Percentage of outgoing orders placed through computer links	7.82	21.37	149
Inter-plant comm.	Percentage of mechanics and supervisors who have direct interaction with individuals outside the plant	20.17	21.83	291
Flexible Technology				
UPS	Standardized value of UPS	0	1	313
UPS	Percentage of sewers working under the unit production system	8.38	24.4	297

Table 2.2. The Adoption of Quick Response

Variable	Number of Plants Using the Practice	Share in Sample (%)	Mean[a]	Std. Dev.	50% Utilization Rate[b] %
Module	40	12.8	49.98	35.82	6.4
More tasks	136	43.5	1	0	NA
Four tasks	175	55.9	37.45	36.86	34.2
Additional tasks	203	64.9	1.77	0.83	NA
Meeting	313	100	1.65	0.86	NA
Labor input	252	80.5	2.36	1.10	NA
Training	123	39.3	48.58	35.13	16.9
Training in lit. and math	181	57.8	1.91	0.81	NA
Group pay	31	9.9	39.39	39.20	2.5
EDI inc. orders	91	29.1	65.60	34.21	20.8
EDI out. orders	26	8.3	44.81	31.29	5.8
Inter-plant comm.	199	63.6	29.49	20.53	50.2
UPS	41	13.1	60.71	33.94	9.3

[a] Average for plants that use some of the practice.
[b] Percentage of plants using the practice for at least 50% of their workers.
NA = Not applicable

chanics had input into the organization of production tasks, in the selection of machinery, equipment, or production technology, in the use of adaptation of machinery or in quality assurance or control. A majority of plants does elicit input from operators and mechanics. *Labor Input* measures the extent to which direct labor participates in managerial decisions. We combined *Meeting* and *Labor Input* to form an *Off-Line Involvement Index*.

Finally, we created a *High-Involvement Index* by adding together the module, broad-skills, and off-line-involvement indices. This index should provide an indication of the overall level of worker involvement in the production process. Figure 2.1 displays the distribution of the High-Involvement Index, which is characterized by a thin tail. The majority of plants fall below the mean (58%). The most innovative plants in the sample, the 31 plants in the highest decile of the distribution, have a High-Involvement Index greater than 1.7. The average plant in the top decile has 55% of its sewers working in modules, and 42% of them perform four or more tasks; moreover, sewers in these plants have a significant influence on managerial decisions and meet monthly or quarterly. The influence of modular production is even more important among the plants that make up the highest 5% of the distribution (16 plants for which the High-Involvement Index is greater than 3.5). On average, 85% of the sewers work in modules; the use of the other High-Involvement practices does not change considerably. Finally, we also found that plants where involvement is high also make significant use of HR, an issue we will now discuss.

Figure 2.1. High-involvement index.

5.2. Human Resources

Two types of HR policies support innovative work organization. The first type of HR policy is training, which gives workers the skills necessary for them to make an effective contribution in a more-involving work setting. The second set of HR policies includes measures that create incentives for workers to participate and become more involved with their work. This usually includes group bonuses or incentives that reward workers when productivity rises or quality improves.

Training is needed because apparel firms are facing a rapidly changing environment and need workers who are adaptable and able to cope with the increased demands. Sewing machine operators must be proficient at a larger number of tasks, be able to interact with other employees, and have good understanding of work processes and business operations. We developed three measures of training. *Training* measures the percentage of machine operators who receive formal training (inside or outside the plant) paid by the plant or company. The data showed that training is not widely provided, and more than one-half of the plants provide no training to sewing machine operators.[12] Apparel establishments also offer their workers more-general training, such as instruction in literacy or arithmetic skills. This occurs because a solid general education helps individuals adjust to change, and because weak basic skills in lower-level workers are a potential problem for the adoption of high-performance practices. Furthermore, experienced lower-level employees are the primary source of mechanics and supervisors, and retraining and upgrading is the key to effectiveness of these increasingly demanding positions (Bailey, 1989). *Training in Literary or Arithmetic* measures whether the plant offers training in literary or arithmetic skills to sewing machine operators. Finally, *Other Training* indicates if sewing machine operators are offered instruction about the plant's products or markets, information on the tasks and responsibilities of other employees, social skills, teamwork, or how to work with others. We combined these training variables into a *Training Index*.

Alternative forms of compensation to the piece-rate system are particularly important in the apparel industry. Piece rates had been the foundation of motivation, as operators who produced more were paid more. When apparel plants use modular manufacturing or other forms of team production, output is produced collectively and piece rates must be dropped. Employers have experimented with straight hourly pay or some type of group incentive in these cases. The use of group incentives is an indication of an innovative approach to HR management. *Group Pay* represents the percentage of machine operators who are paid a piece or hourly rate plus group incentives. The data show that few employers have introduced innovative compensation systems. Indeed, 87% make no use of group incentives and less than 3% use group incentives—either alone or in combination with other compensation systems—for over one-half of their employees.

The *Training Index* was then combined with *Group Pay* to create the *Human Resources Index*. Figure 2.2 displays the distribution of this index and illustrates the limited extent of HR innovation in the industry.

5.3. Relations with Customers and Suppliers

Communications and interactions with retailers and textile makers must also be improved so that producers can do a faster and more-effective job in meeting the shifting retailer needs. Since the beginning of the widespread discussion of Quick Response, retailers and apparel and textile makers have been working to develop a common nomenclature that will facilitate the use of electronic data interchange (EDI). The development of these systems of terminology has been a significant achievement of the Quick Response movement, creating the impetus for many manufacturers and retailers to use bar coding to improve inventory control and to communication with customers and suppliers. One goal of many retailers is to have merchandise-ordering systems based on point-of-sale inventory control with computer links to suppliers. *EDI Incoming* measures the percentage of incoming orders placed directly

Figure 2.2. Human resources index.

with the plant through computer links. About one-third of the plants in our sample received at least 60% of their orders through direct computer links, although close to one half still make no use of computer links. Similarly, *EDI Outgoing* measures the percentage of outgoing orders sent directly to the supplier by computer means.

Another indication of interplant communication involves the interaction among employees and people outside the plant. Modern systems such as total quality management emphasize the need for employees to interact with internal and external "customers." About 40% of the plants in our survey report that none of their supervisors (and mechanics) interacts with individuals outside the plant, whereas one-quarter report that all of their supervisors (and mechanics) have this interaction. *Inter-Plant Comm.* is the percentage of mechanics and supervisors who have direct interaction with individuals not employed at the plant. These three variable are combined to create an *EDI Index* (Figure 2.3).

5.4. Flexible Technology

The UPS is a technological alternative to modules for creating a more-flexible system of apparel assembly. The variable UPS measures the per-

Figure 2.3. Relations with customers and suppliers.

centage of sewers working under the UPS. The utilization of UPS, a technological approach to flexibility, is slightly higher than the utilization of modules. About one-fifth of the plants reported making some use of UPS, but less than one-tenth use it for more than one-half of their direct labor.

5.5. Clusters of Practices and the Presence of Complementarities

Recent studies on organizational innovation stress the idea that the adoption of individual high-performance practices often has little effect on productivity (Bailey, 1993b; Ichniowski et al., 1997; Kochan & Useem, 1992). The impact from teamwork and training, for example, will be minimal if the workers lack the incentives to participate enthusiastically. Likewise, workers who have the skills to carry out several tasks and the ability to work in groups will not be fully efficient if they are confined to one activity. Only when the workplace is "transformed," i.e., a larger set of innovative practices is introduced, can we expect significant effects.

Table 2.3 presents the correlations among the individual innovative practices. The positive (and statistically significant) correlations among the practices that belong to a given category support the division of Quick Response practices in these four groups described previously—high-involvement practices, HR innovations, communications with customers and suppliers, and flexible technology. More importantly,

Table 2.3. Correlation of Quick Response Practices

	Module	More Taks	Four Tasks	Addt'l Tasks	Meeting	Labor Input	Training	Training in Lit and Math	Other Training	Group Pay	EDI Inc.	EDI Out.	Inter-plant comm.	UPS
Module	1.00													
More Tasks	0.19 ***	1.00												
Four Tasks	0.10 *	0.16 ***	1.00											
Addt'l Tasks	0.01	0.19 ***	0.15 ***	1.00										
Meeting	0.13 **	0.08	−0.16 ***	0.10 *	1.00									
Labor Input	0.16 ***	0.14 **	0.05	0.10 *	0.28 ***	1.00								
Training	0.13 **	0.16 ***	0.02	0.07	0.14 ***	0.18 ***	1.00							
Training Lit and Math	0.17 ***	−0.05	−0.11 **	0.11 **	0.30 ***	0.14 *	0.15 ***	1.00						
Other Training	0.14 ***	0.12 **	−0.02	0.15 ***	0.30 ***	0.40 ***	0.26 ***	0.24 ***	1.00					
Group Pay	0.38 ***	0.08	0.10 *	B	0.08	0.06	0.05	0.12 **	0.03	1.00				
EDI Inc.	0.04	−0.03	−0.16 ***	0.14 **	0.25 ***	0.11 ***	0.10 *	0.18 ***	0.16 ***	B	1.00			
EDI Out	−0.04	−0.01	−0.07	0.12 **	0.13 **	0.09	B	−0.05	0.05	−0.06	0.29 ***	1.00		
Inter-Plant Comm	0.04	0.08	−0.05	0.03	−0.01	0.07	−0.01	−0.02	0.04	−0.01	B	0.13 **	1.00	
UPS	−0.02	−0.02	0.03	−0.02	0.04	0.08	−0.01	−0.06	−0.06	0.05	0.01	0.03	−0.07	1.00

*** significant at the 99% level; ** significant at the 95% level; * significant at the 90% level.
B = correlation coefficient < 0.001

these correlations allow us to explore the possibility of complementarities among practices. As we expected, modular production is positively correlated with all our measures of training, employee involvement, and (naturally) the use of group incentives. Similarly, the measures of employee involvement are correlated with training and the use of EDI. The only practice that seems to be adopted independently of any other practices is the use of UPS; the correlations between UPS and the other Quick Response practices are all very low. These relationships do not change when we look at the aggregate indeces: Tables 2.4 and 2.5 present the correlations among the indices described in Table 2.1. The correlations among off-line involvement, training, and modular production are the strongest (and also statistically significant); thus, we can conjecture that these practices exhibit a significant level of similarity. The correlation between the High-Involvement Index and the HR Index is high and statistically significant which, again, suggests strong complementarities. Moreover, this is consistent with the observation that the distributions of these indices have similar shapes (Figure 1A, B).

A second method of exploring the hypothesis of complementarities among practice is by using cluster analysis, which allowed us to identify groups of plants that share characteristics concerning the introduction of innovative practices.[13] Cluster analysis using the entire set of innovative practices revealed six distinct groups. The result of this analysis supports the conjectures about complementarities that we made above based on the correlations among practices. Table 2.6 shows the characteristics of these six clusters.

- Cluster 1 is the largest and the least innovative group. These firms, on average, make very little use of any of the practices. Because this group comprises one-half of all plants in the sample, we con-

Table 2.4. Correlations of Quick Response Indices

	Broad Skills Index	EDI	Off-line Involvement	Training	Modules	Group Incentives	UPS
Broad Skills Index	1.000						
EDI	0.012	1.000					
Off-line involvement	0.095 *	0.207 ***	1.000				
Training	0.119 **	0.122 **	0.641 ***	1.000			
Modules	0.149 ***	0.023	0.183 ***	0.233 ***	1.000		
Group Incentives	0.093	−0.031	0.090	0.118 **	0.376 ***	1.000	
UPS	−0.003	−0.018	0.074	0.008	−0.022	0.046	1.000

*** significant at the 99% level; ** significant at the 95% level; * significant at the 90% level.

Table 2.5. Correlation of Aggregate Quick Response Indices

	High Involvement Index	Human Resources Index	EDI	UPS
High involvement index	1.000			
Human resources index	0.511 ***	1.000		
EDI	0.120 **	0.039	1.000	
UPS	0.022	0.041	−0.018	1.000

*** significant at the 99% level; ** significant at the 95% level; * significant at the 90% level.

firm the presumption that a significant proportion of apparel plants has not adopted any innovative practices.

- Clusters 2 and 4 account for about 35% of the sample, and they include plants that use a moderate amount of a variety of practices. There is no clear pattern for the adoption of practices among these plants: The first group provides some training to its workers and has a high degree of employee involvement, whereas the second group focuses on the adoption of modular production and requires their workers to carry out multiple tasks, with very modest levels of training.
- Cluster 3 comprises the firms that use UPS. As expected from the correlation coefficients, on average, these firms do not adopt any other innovative work practices.
- Cluster 5 includes the plants that have implemented practices that increase the speed of communication with their customers and suppliers. These plants make significant use of EDI, both for incoming as well as outgoing orders, and their mechanics and supervisors have relatively more interaction with personnel outside of the firm. As with the UPS, EDI is adopted by itself without many of any other innovative practices.
- Cluster 6 comprises most establishments where there is a significant use of modular production and where the complementarities are strong. These are also the "most innovative" of the plants in terms of any of the indices. This group, however, only includes 12 firms (4% of our sample).

There is no group that is strong on all of the indices. Even the very small Cluster 6, which has innovative HR and work organization practices, has not developed strong links to suppliers and customers. Clusters 3 and 5 are also small groups (each comprising about 5% of the sample) that have focused on one component of the overall Quick Response strategy. The plants in Cluster 3 have sought a technological solution to the need for flexibility and faster throughput. On the other measures, they look very much like Cluster 1, the least-innovative plants. The plants in Cluster 5 have developed links to suppliers and custom-

Table 2.6. Cluster Analysis

	Cluster 1 (None) N = 156	Cluster 2 N = 66	Cluster 3 (UPS) N = 17	Cluster 4 N = 47	Cluster 5 (EDI) N = 15	Cluster 6 (Modules) N = 12
Broad skills index	−0.24	−0.13	−0.09	0.91	−0.01	0.33
More tasks	−0.15	−0.04	−0.08	0.42	0.48	0.10
Four jobs	−0.44	−0.26	−0.15	1.91	−0.46	0.42
Addt'l tasks	−0.11	−0.08	−0.05	0.41	−0.07	0.47
EDI index	−0.11	0.01	−0.23	−0.14	1.95	−0.19
EDI out. orders	−0.23	−0.18	−0.24	−0.14	4.11	−0.24
Inter-plant comm.	−0.01	0.04	−0.40	−0.01	0.54	−0.23
EDI inc. orders	−0.09	0.17	−0.04	−0.27	1.19	−0.09
Off-line involvement index	−0.36	0.76	0.09	−0.15	0.35	0.49
Labor input	−0.38	0.67	0.12	0.10	0.22	0.38
Meeting	−0.33	0.84	0.07	−0.41	0.48	0.60
Training index	−0.32	0.76	−0.21	−0.05	−0.03	0.50
Other training	−0.31	0.77	−0.20	−0.07	0.09	0.21
Training in lit. and math	−0.36	0.97	−0.18	−0.29	−0.15	0.94
Training	−0.28	0.53	−0.27	0.21	−0.04	0.34
Use of modules	−0.48	0.11	−0.08	0.71	0.32	2.57
Use of group incentives	−0.17	−0.20	−0.14	−0.22	−0.23	4.64
Unit production system	−0.31	−0.15	3.57	−0.13	0.11	0.15
Overall index	−0.24	0.21	0.12	0.16	0.44	0.70

ers but have only made moderate use of modules and off-line involvement practices.

Therefore, what share of the plants in this sample could we say has been transformed? Even though hardly any plants have introduced a comprehensive package of reforms, including organizational change and sophisticated links to suppliers and customers, certainly the 12 plants in Cluster 6 could be said to have introduced a significant package of reforms, and the 15 plants in Cluster 5 are somewhat less innovative with respect to skills and modules but are much more advanced in links to other firms. Thus these two groups, which account for about 9% of the sample, could be categorized as having made significant reforms. Alternatively, looking at the high involvement index, we saw that 6% of the plants were clustered at or above two standard deviations above the mean. At the other extreme, the 170 (55%) firms in Clusters 1 and 3 have made almost no changes.

6. The Determinants of the Adoption of Innovative Practices

The discussion of Quick Response in the industry press and among consultants and employer associations reveals both market-oriented arguments emphasizing sectoral differences, the changing nature of markets, and arguments about general increases in efficiency (independent of demand factors). Improved quality, reduced inventory carrying costs, improved production techniques through employee involvement, reduced lead times and other benefits imply a more-efficient operation that would be generally useful across sectors of the industry. On the other hand, the emphasis on shortened selling seasons and the explosion of styles and colors suggest that changing markets have at least created additional advantages for the Quick Response approach. The AAMA sees Quick Response and related innovations such as modules as more appropriate for some products than others. For example, according to AAMA (1988) projections, modular manufacturing is superior to the bundle system for dresses, whereas the bundle system appears to work better for the production of basic western jeans.

For the apparel industry, individual examples can be marshaled to reveal both market and general efficiency arguments. The original Piore and Sable (1984) thesis drew heavily from the example of the production of style-sensitive Italian knitwear that appeared to support the flexibility thesis. During recent visits to apparel plants, the authors found one situation in which a firm maintained transformed plants based on modules and teamwork as well as plants that used the bundle system. The style-sensitive products and short runs were all produced in the transformed plants. Another firm maintained different approaches in the same plant and again depended on the modules to produce the short runs. On the other hand, another plant that was considered highly progressive among apparel producers employed 200 workers in teams and modules to produce one style of pants in one color.[14] And many of the companies that are known for their use of innovative approaches produce basic apparel, such as jeans and underwear, that have little style content. Moreover, Wal-Mart, hardly known for its emphasis on style, is a leader in developing Quick Response relationships with producers. Indeed, in their study of 118 apparel "business units" in 84 companies, Abernathy, Dunlop, Hammond, and Weil (1995) found no statistically significant relationship between the fashion content of the output or the use of modules and requirements by retailers that orders be "replenished" on a daily or weekly basis.[15] They did find a positive and statistically significant relationship between the total volume of the business units production and the use of modules.

In this section, we explore the empirical validity of the seven hypotheses outlined earlier by regressing proxies for these hypotheses on measures of innovation. Table 2.7 presents the summary statistics and definitions for the independent variables used in the regressions.[16] The regression results are presented in Table 2.8.[17]

We use two measures of innovation as dependent variables. The first is the high-involvement index that combines information on modules, off-line involvement, and the breadth of required skills. This approach follows the practice of considering training a supporting HR practice rather than a core part of the high-involvement strategy. The second measure of innovation combines the high-involvement index with the HR and EDI indices. This follows the practice of viewing organizational innovations as a comprehensive cluster of complementary practices. The results from these two regressions are similar. This is not surprising, because the high-involvement and HR indices are highly correlated.

Our first hypothesis suggested that firms facing markets that demand greater varieties of styles would be the most likely to introduce HR and organizational innovations. We have two approaches to this hypothesis. First we test the hypothesis that there are important differences among market sectors in the propensity to innovate. The argument that firms are driven to the introduction of HR innovations because of the need to be flexible and to respond to changing styles suggests that firms in the women's wear sector would be the most interested in those innovations. Products are more standardized in menswear, underwear, and nightwear. This hypothesis is tested by the inclusion of dummy variables for each of the sectors on the industry. We see that there are no statistically significant differences between the level of innovation in menswear and women's wear (the variable that was left out of the regression), or in menswear and underwear. Second, the variable *Styles* (the number of styles produced in the plant) tests the flexibility hypothesis directly.

Table 2.7. Explanatory Variables in Regression Analysis: Definitions and Summary Statistics

Variable	Definition	Mean	St. Dev.	Min.	Max.
Percentage change in styles	Percentage change in the number of styles produced	0.96	1.92	−0.92	14.00
Styles	Largest number of styles produced in the plant	117	433	1	4000
Total firm emp.	Total firm employment in 1991 (in thousands)	3.04	8.10	0.001	60
Age	Number of years since plant began production	24.3	20.1	0	114
Multi-plant	= 1 if the company that owns the plant, also owns other plants	0.56	0.50	0	1
Union	Percentage of the plant's labor force that belong to a union	25.40	40.41	0	100
Manufactured	= 1 if the plant is owned by a manufacturer,	0.18	0.38	0	1
Owned	= 0 if owned by a contractor				
Immigrants	Percentage of the plant's labor force who are foreign born	21.48	32.21	0	100
Education	Percentage of the plant's labor force who have a high school diploma	61.61	25.46	0	100
Knitted	Knitted apparel and accessories (SIC code 225)	0.09	0.28	0	1
Men's	Men's, youth's and boys' suits, coats, overcoats (SIC codes 231, 232)	0.34	0.47	0	1
Womens	Women's, Misses' and Juniors outerwear (SIC code 234)	0.17	0.38	0	1
Underwear and nightwear	Underwear and Nightwear (SIC code 234)	0.12	0.32	0	1
Misc. apparel	Hats, caps, millinery, miscellaneous apparel and accessories (SIC codes 235, 238)	0.04	0.20	0	1
Fabric. textiles	Fabricated Textiles (SIC codes 221, 239)	0.21	0.41	0	1
NE	ME, NH, VT, MA, RI, CT, NJ, PA	0.21	0.41	0	1
MW	OH, IN, IL, MI, WI, MN, IA, MO, ND, SD, NE, KS	0.10	0.31	0	1
SE	DE, MD, DC, VA, WV, NC, SC, GA, FL, KY, TN, AL, MS	0.47	0.50	0	1
SW	AR, LA, OK, TX, NM, AZ	0.07	0.26	0	1
W	MT, ID, WY, CO, UT, NV, WA, OR, AK, HI	0.03	0.18	0	1
NY	NY	0.05	0.22	0	1
CA	CA	0.05	0.22	0	1

Table 2.8. Regression Analysis

	Dependent Variable	
	High Involvement	High Involvement + Human Resources + EDI
Percentage change in styles	0.1236 **	0.1365 *
	(2.34)	(1.64)
Styles	0.0001	0.0001
	(0.47)	(0.38)
Total firm emp.	0.0200	0.0400 **
	(1.30)	(2.01)
Age	−0.004	−0.0030
	(−0.83)	(−0.36)
Multi–plant	0.7630 ***	1.1714 ***
	(3.30)	(3.22)
Union	−0.0027	−0.0043
	(−1.02)	(−1.02)
Manufactured (owned)	−0.1122	−0.1827
	(−0.41)	(−0.42)
Immigrants	0.0061	0.0029
	(1.30)	(0.39)
Education	0.0060	0.0010
	(1.29)	(0.13)
Knitted	−0.0567	−0.0958
	(−0.14)	(−0.15)
Men's	0.3021	0.6203
	(1.02)	(1.33)
Underwear and nightwear	0.0296	0.3666
	(0.08)	(0.63)
Misc. apparel	1.0517 **	0.7868
	(2.00)	(0.95)
Fabric. textiles	0.4435	0.5947
	(1.43)	(1.21)
NE	−1.6940 ***	−2.9238 ***
	(−3.23)	(−3.54)
MW	−0.9076	−1.4360
	(−1.49)	(−1.50)
SE	−1.4894 ***	−2.5312 ***
	(−2.68)	(−2.90)
SW	−2.2306 ***	−3.3898 ***
	(−3.62)	(−3.50)
W	0.7798	0.3539
	(1.10)	(0.32)
NY	−2.0296 ***	−3.5433 ***
	(−3.14)	(−3.49)
Constant	0.3489	1.3023
	(0.48)	(1.13)
N	229	229
Adjusted R^2	0.21	0.18

*** significant at the 99% level; ** significant at the 95% level; * significant at the 90% level.

There is no statistically significant relationship between any of the measures of innovation and the number or styles produced.

Our second hypothesis was that the factors that lead firms to introduce high-involvement innovations lie more in general efficiency benefits rather than in market factors that require flexibility. We have no individual variable that tests this hypothesis. On the other hand, an absence of a strong relationship with the market-oriented variables in our model suggests that there are benefits to these innovations that can accrue to firms in all market segments. Thus, the explanation of differences in diffusion may lie in internal factors that facilitate or thwart implementation.

According to our third hypothesis, unionized firms are more likely to adopt innovative practices. Indeed, in the last few years, the main union in the industry (UNITE) has worked hard to promote modules and other types of high-involvement practices. Union representatives agree with many industry managers that Quick Response and related practices can help preserve apparel jobs in the United States. Thus, the union has devoted considerable effort to encouraging its members to cooperate and to helping employers introduce new practices. The union and its predecessors—the International Ladies Garment Workers Union and the Amalgamated Clothing and Textile Workers Union—were instrumental in establishing the Textile Clothing Technology Center (TC²), which is an organization that has aggressively promoted the concept of modules and the training necessary to make modules and other innovations effective. Nevertheless, the analysis of our data set does not show that unionized firms (*Union*) are more likely to introduce these changes. One explanation is that the date of the survey predates much of the work that the UNITE has done in this area. Also, organizations such as TC² promote a general awareness of the practices in the industry, including among nonunion firms.

Our fourth and fifth hypotheses suggest that firms with more educated work forces are more likely to adopt work organization practices, whereas firms with large numbers of immigrants are less likely to do so. There is no support for either of these hypotheses. In this sample, the education level of the work force (*Education*) neither encourages nor discourages HR innovations.[18] Similarly, the presence of immigrants (*Immigrants*) is not related to a plant's propensity to introduce HR innovations. Indeed, in fieldwork we have found many cases in which successful teams are composed of natives of several countries, some of whom do not share a common language. It is possible that the need to collaborate in teams promotes communication among workers from different countries and cultures that would not happen in the more individualistic bundle system.

Our sixth hypothesis suggested that larger firms and multiplant firms would be more capable of introducing high-involvement practices. Indeed, there is a statistically significant positive relationship between level of innovation and firm size (*Total Firm Emp.*) in one regression and whether the plant is part of a multiplant firm (*Multi-Plant*). The coefficients for firm size are 0.00002 and 0.00004. This suggests that an increase of one standard deviation of TFE (i.e., an increase in the size of total firm employment of 8102) will increase our innovation indices by 0.16 and 0.32, respectively. The increases are modest relative to the standard deviations of the innovation indices (1.64 and 2.53). On the other hand, an increase in the probability that the plant is part of a multiplant firm increases the innovation indices by 0.38 and 0.59. The implication is that available resources and knowledge, associated with larger firms, are extremely important. Larger firms have the resources and personnel and perhaps the financial stability necessary to seek out new techniques and take the risk of implementing them.

Finally, according to our last hypothesis, holding constant the total number of styles or models produced, plants that have had to increase the number of styles that they produce are more likely to introduce high-involvement innovations. Although there is no relationship between the number of styles produced and the level of innovation, we do find a strong relationship between innovation and an increase in the number of styles produced (*Percent Change in Styles*) in the previous five years. The increase in the number of styles produced by the plants is important; on average firms have increased the number of styles produced by 96%. The coefficient on *Percent Change in Styles* suggests that when plants increase the number of styles by one standard deviation, the use of innovative practices (measured by the indices) increase by 0.23 and 0.26, respectively.

What do these results suggest about the explanations for the adoption of innovative HR practices? Surprisingly, the number of styles typically produced by a plant does not have an effect on the use of innovative practices. This certainly suggests that there are many advantages to Quick Response that are not necessarily related to the need to produce many styles. Supply-side considerations, such as savings on inventory costs, improved quality, more productive ideas from employees, and similar factors are independent of style variation. Indeed, several factors may create stronger incentives for innovation for large producers of basic apparel rather than of style-sensitive apparel.

First, retailers may have special incentives to demand fast inventory replenishment from producers of basic standardized products. Retailers have traditionally been concerned with the gross markup of an item—the difference between what they pay for it and what they charge for it. More recently, retailers have been concerned with what is referred to as gross margin return on investment (GMROI). GMROI is calculated by a combination of gross margin and inventory turnover. Fast inventory turnover depends on maintaining low levels of inventory and developing a system of rapid inventory replenishment. If standardized products are more price competitive, then gross margins will be lower, and retailers will look more to inventory turnover to raise their GMROI. This may explain why retailers would be particularly interested in Quick Response relationships with producers of basic standardized items. The Wal-Mart strategy is a good example. The discounter's success partly results from its low prices, but Wal-Mart has achieved high profitability with low prices by redefining retailing as a process of moving goods rather than selling them.[19]

Second, the introduction of workplace innovation is costly and risky. Even under the best circumstances, the payoff will come only after some time. The costs and risks favor large firms that have the resources to make these investments and that are the most likely to know about new approaches and to have the resources needed to introduce them.

Third, modules, in particular, require more capital and therefore higher fixed costs. Since workers move among different tasks, sewing machines must be available for their use. For example, the number of sewing machines in a plant with a workforce of about 325 increases from 375 to 700 after a complete switch from the bundle system to the modules. It is these high fixed costs that make innovation more difficult for firms, such as those in style-sensitive segments, facing volatile demand. Producers of underwear and blue jeans are likely to have more stable demand (Applebaum et al., 1994).

The positive effect of the increase in the number of styles is intriguing. Apparently, innovation appears to be taking place, not among plants that have traditionally produced large numbers of styles, but rather among those that have recently increased the variety of their production. Firms that have tried to increase the number of styles in the last few years have looked for new ways to achieve the needed flexibility. Thus, it is the new demands that seem to be important or possibly the opportunities that arise in a general climate of change. Firms that have not sought to increase the variety of their production are less willing to take on the uncertainties of innovation. Thus, to the extent that the market is forcing an increase in variety (and there is some evidence that, on average, this is happening), it does appear that recent market developments are encouraging HR innovation.

Firms that have traditionally produced many styles are able to accomplish that using different techniques. Interestingly, the variable for New York was the strongest regional dummy. HR innovation appears to be almost unknown in New York, yet New York has never been characterized by mass production approaches. Apparently, managers of New York firms, to the extent that they can continue to exist, appear to believe that they can meet the small-lot, fast-turnaround demands without modules, training, and other techniques.

It is interesting that it is the women's wear sector that also has the largest import penetration. This would perhaps be surprising if the proximity of production to markets were particularly important for style-sensitive items. On the other hand, the production sectors that produce many styles, such as women's wear, are also more labor intensive and less possible to automate than production in other sectors. Thus, the lower wages for offshore production may offset any possible benefits from lower inventory costs or faster response that would be possible from local production. The demand for those items that do need to be produced rapidly appear to be satisfied by production in apparel centers like New York by using traditional production practices.

7. Summary and Conclusion

We started with three broad questions, concerning the nature and characteristics of organizational innovation, the extent of the spread, and the determinants of those innovations. We will summarize the conclusions in each of these three areas.

Certainly many employers in the industry have begun to work with high-involvement practices. One of the most interesting conclusions from this research, though, is that firms tend to specialize in one cluster of techniques. In particular, the firms that are most innovative with respect to their work organization and HR policies do not particularly show progress in their interfirm relationships. And those firms that rely on flexible technology maintain traditional approaches to HR and interfirm policies. This suggests that firms may not be taking advantage of the full potential for flexible production and Quick Response. Rapid assembly on short notice will have much less effect if poor coordination with customers and suppliers requires large stocks of inventories of materials and finished goods.

One of the most striking conclusions concerns the large number of firms that are not using any of these practices. If we include those who have introduced unit production systems but have made no other changes, then about 55% of the sample falls into this traditional group. If the consensus is that somewhere between a very small percentage (Ichniowski et al., 1996) and about one-third (Osterman, 1994) have so far made a significant transformation to more-flexible and innovative production processes, this analysis falls somewhere near the lower margins of that consensus. Given the traditional image of the industry, it may not be surprising that apparel makers have not been in the forefront of HR innovation. Only some 10% have made substantial changes, and the remaining 35% fall somewhere in the middle. Overall, the jobs of typical operators have changed little, despite some increase in the number of tasks performed by each. They still perform only a very limited number of tasks—a majority perform only one task, they are likely to work in a plant that uses the progressive bundle system and pays piece rates, they have little need to read to perform their jobs, and they receive little or no formal training.

This analysis clearly shows that the determinants of change are complicated. One of the most obvious explanations, the need for flexibility and fast turnaround time, is certainly incomplete. Firms or plants producing more styles were no more likely than other plants to use Quick-Response-related practices. This conclusion is further reinforced by the result that firms do not seem to be taking full advantage of the potential for flexibility in combining organizational reform with more effective relationships with their customers and suppliers. Managers perceive that there are important benefits to Quick Response that are independent of market demand for flexibility and style variation.

The industry is clearly in a period of transition, and this transition is reflected in the pattern of adoption of Quick Response. Although plants that have traditionally produced many styles and are in style-oriented sectors are no more likely than other plants to introduce Quick-Response-related practices, plants that have increased the number of styles do tend to be more oriented toward flexible production processes.

The importance of firm size and the effect of being part of a multiplant firm are among the strongest and most robust conclusions. It may be that in the present period of transition, when the initial costs of implementing Quick Response are high and the benefits uncertain, larger firms have better access to relevant information and have the resources and specialized personnel needed to take on the costs and risks associated with these innovations. If this is true, then it suggests that in industries like apparel with many smaller firms, a policy that provides technical assistance and targeted loans or credits may be effective in promoting innovative practices.

Appendix: The Data

The data for this study come from a size-stratified random sample of 540 sites from Dunn and Bradstreet's (D&B) universe of manufacturing locations. The survey was conducted at the establishment level, thus it is possible that two or more sites are owned by the same firm. Each site was called to substantiate the information supplied by D&B and to verify that manufacturing was carried out at each site. The survey was administered in 1992 by the Center for Survey Research at the University of Massachusetts in Boston. The sample fell into four size categories (Table 2.9).

There were two initial survey mailings, yielding 150 responses (25.9%). The remaining 193 responses were obtained over the phone to yield an overall response rate of 59%. The survey asked questions about the plant's work force, training practices, work organization, and production. In most cases, the person who answered the questionnaire was the manager of the plant.

Table 2.9. Employee-Size Characteristics of Establishments in the Sample

Number of Employees	Firms Surveyed		Firms that Responded		Firms in Final Sample		Firms in Regression	
	n	%	n	%	n	%	n	%
<20	47	9	19	6	12	4	5	2
20–199	142	26	85	25	75	24	59	25
200–249	173	32	114	33	109	35	85	36
≥250	178	33	125	36	117	37	85	36
Total	540	100	343	100	313	100	234	100

The sample used in the analysis contains 313 observations. Thirty observations were dropped because the survey revealed that the plant does not do any sewing, even though it is considered an apparel establishment.

Observations for some of the variables used in the analysis were missing, although we do not believe the pattern is systematic. The non-response rate was low for all variables, but in aggregate the number of incomplete observations was substantial, and it meant that a significant number of observations would have to be dropped. Because of the loss of efficiency associated with ignoring the incomplete observations in the regression analysis, we imputed values for the variable that had the largest nonresponse rate: the percentage of sewer machine operators with a high school diploma (21% nonresponse rate). We used the imputation method suggested by Little and Rubin (1987) by which the missing observations for a variable are computed based on the regression estimates of the subsample of complete observations. In order to test for the possibility that our final sample was biased, we computed *logit* regressions in which the dependent variable was the presence in the final sample versus the exclusion for the sample. Dummy variables for the size and sector categories were used as independent variables. These tests showed that the smaller firms were underrepresented in the sample, although we do not believe that this significantly affects our results. There was no statistically significant difference between the full sample and the regression sample for all other categories.

Notes

1. The passage of the North American Free Trade Agreement and the completion of negotiations for the Uruguay round of the General Agreement on Tariffs and Trade all point to significant reduction and eventual elimination of restriction on imports of textiles and apparel.

2. In practice, the adoption of high-involvement practices and the related HR policies are highly correlated.

3. Osterman categorizes a firm as "transformed" if it uses two of the following four practices for at least 50% of its "core" workers: quality circles, self-directed work teams, total quality management, and job rotation.

4. For the apparel industry, an absence of strong market-segment-associated patterns would provide evidence for this hypothesis.

5. Lawler, Mohrman, and Ledford (1992) found that unionization seemed to discourage the use of Total Quality Management.

6. For more detailed discussions of these alternatives, see Abernathy et al. (1995), Applebaum et al. (1994), Bailey (1993a), and Berg et al. (1996).

7. As is true in any process that accumulates in-process inventory, many errors can accumulate in the bundles (in-process inventory) before they are detected.

8. The survey was based on a random sample of 540 apparel production sites provided by Dunn and Bradstreet.

9. Evidence on individual practices is reported using all the observations for which we have data; thus, the sample size changes slightly for the analysis of each practice.

10. We considered alternative specifications for the indices, where the practices receive different weights and the results did not change significantly. We should also note that when we constructed the indices we made the additional assumption that a missing observation for a given practice meant that such practice was not being used by the establishment; that is, we replaced all missing values by zeroes. This assumption implies that all our indices will be biased toward zero. We also constructed indices from complete observations that yielded similar results in the regression analysis; however, the size of the sample decreased considerably.

11. This is close to the result from the 1996 AAMA survey.

12. The survey also asked about training for other types of employees; a similar share did not provide any training to their mechanics.

13. We used Ward's Minimum Variance clustering algorithm to produce clusters of plants based on their use of Quick Response practices. Ward's algorithm is designed to minimize the variance within clusters. Initially, each observation is a cluster. The algorithm calculates the means for all variables in a cluster and then, for each cluster, it computes the squared within-cluster distance (the sum of Squared Euclidean distances from each observation in the cluster to the cluster means). Then those clusters or observations that result in the smallest increase in the sum of the squared within-cluster distances are merged.

14. This field work was conducted in 1994 as part of a "Cross Industry Employer-Employee Survey," funded by the Sloan Foundation and directed by the Economic Policy Institute.

15. The replenishment variable is a proxy for demands by retailers for fast production, and the fashion categorization is based on the number of styles and the frequency of style change.

16. In addition to the variables needed to test the hypothesis, we include regional dummies to control for labor market differences. The age of the plant (AGE) is another important control variable because newer plants might face fewer barriers to innovation. Pil and MacDuffie (1996), for ex-

ample, hypothesize that plants with less experience with traditional methods will have to overcome less opposition to innovation.

17. Standard tests could not reject the possibility that our regressions are affected by heteroskedasticity. Heteroskedasticity does not bias the coefficients but affects the estimates of their variance. We used White's method to control for heteroskedasticity, after which the statistical significance of our estimates increased. We also controlled for outliers by using robust regressions methods and down-weighting outliers; our results are not sensitive to this procedure.

18. Levi Strauss has looked to the Amalgamated Clothing and Textile Workers Union to help introduce teams, group-oriented compensation reforms, and other innovative practices. In return for helping promote the reforms, the union won the right to organize more of the company's workers with less resistance. The manager of one Levi's plant stated, "The more workers in the union, the greater their voice, and that drives the process forward" (Uchitelle 1994). But this sort of attitude is rare among apparel makers.

Other studies, for example, Bartel and Lichtenberg (1987), found that firms with more-educated work forces are more likely to adopt new technologies.

19. This paragraph is based on Quigley (1994).

References

Abernathy, F., Dunlop, J. T., Hammond, J., & Weil, D. (1995). The information-integrated channel: A study of the U.S. apparel industry in transition. *Brookings Papers on Economic Activity: Microeconomics* (Spring): 175–246.

Alper, W. S., Pfau, B., & Sirota, D. (1985, September). *1985 national survey of employee attitudes executive report.* Sponsored by *Business Week* and Sirota and Alper Associates.

American Apparel Manufacturers Association. (1988). *The coming revolution: Flexible apparel manufacturing.* Technical Advisory Committee. Washington: AAMA.

American Apparel Manufacturers Association. (1996*). Focus: An economic profile of the apparel industry.* Arlington, VA: American Apparel Manufacturers Association.

Applebaum, E., Bailey, T., Berg, T., & Kalleberg, A. (1994). *Cross industry employer/employee survey. Report of a Pilot Project.* Washington: Economic Policy Institute.

Applebaum, E., & Batt, R. (1994). *The new American workplace.* Ithaca, NY: ILR.

Bailey, T. (1989, November). Technology, skills, and education in the apparel industry. Technical paper No. 7, National Center on Education and Employment, Teachers College, Columbia University, New York.

Bailey, T. (1993a). Organizational innovation in the apparel industry. *Industrial Relations*, 32 (Winter): 30–48.

Bailey, T. (1993b). Discretionary effort and the organization of work. Report prepared for the Sloan Foundation, New York.

Bartel, A., & Lichtenberg, F. (1987). The comparative advantage of educated workers in implementing new technologies. *Review of Economics and Statistics*, 69: 1–11.

Bassi, L. (1992). *Reorganization of Work and Workplace Education: Scope and Impact.* Washington: Southport Institute.

Berg, P., Applebaum, E., Bailey, T., & Kalleberg, A. L. (1996). The performance effects of modular production in the apparel industry. *Industrial Relations*, 35 (3): 356–373.

Commission on the Skills of the American Workforce. (1990). *America's choice: High skills or low wages!* Rochester, NY: The National Center on Education and the Economy.

Dunlop, J. T., & Weil, D. (1996). Diffusion and performance of modular production in the apparel industry. *Industrial Relations*, 35 (3): 334–355.

Eaton, A. E., & Voos, P. B. (1992). Union and contemporary innovations in work organization, compensation, and employee participation. In L. Mishel and P. Voos (eds.), *Unions and economic competitiveness*. Armonk, NY: M.E. Sharpe.

Freund, W. C., & Epstein, E. (1984). *People and productivity: The New York Stock Exchange guide to financial incentives and the quality of work life.* Homewood, IL: Dow Jones Irwin.

Huselid, M. A., & Becker, B. E. (1996). Methodological issues in cross-sectional and panel estimates of the human resource-firm performance link. *Industrial Relations*, 35 (3): 400–422.

Ichniowski, C., Kochan, T. A., Levine, D., Olson, C., & Strauss, G. (1996). What works at work: Overview and assessment. *Industrial Relations*, 35 (3): 229–333.

Ichniowski, C., Shaw, K., & Prennushi, G. (1997). The effects of human resource management practices on productivity: A study of steel finishing lines. *American Economic Review*, 87(3): 291–313.

Katz, H., Kochan, T., & Keefe, M. (1987). Industrial relations and productivity in the U.S. automobile industry. *Brookings Papers on Economic Activity*, 3: 688–715.

Kochan, T., Katz, H., & McKersie, R. (1986). *The transformation of American industrial relations.* New York: Basic Books.

Kochan, T. A., & Osterman, P. (1995). *The mutual gains enterprise.* Boston, MA: Harvard Business School Press.

Kochan, T. A., & Useem, M. (eds.). (1992). *Transforming organizations.* New York: Oxford University Press.

Lawler, E. E. III, Mohrman, S., & Ledford, G. E. Jr. (1992*). Employee involvement and TQM: Practice and results in Fortune 1000 companies.* San Francisco, CA: Jossey-Bass.

Lawler, E. E. III, Ledford, G. E. Jr., & Mohrman, S. A. (1989). *Employee involvement in America: A study of contemporary practice.* Houston, TX: American Productivity and Quality Center.

Little, R. J., & Rubin, D. (1987). *Statistical analysis with missing data.* New York: Wiley.

MacDuffie, J. (1995). Human resource bundles and manufacturing performance: Organizational logic and flexible production systems in the world auto industry. *Industrial and Labor Relations Review*, 48 (2): 197–221.

Office of Technology Assessment (OTA). (1987). *The U.S. textile and apparel industry: A revolution in progress.* Washington: U.S. Government Printing Office.

Office of Technology Assessment (OTA). (1992, October). *U.S.-Mexico trade: Pulling together or pulling apart?* ITE-545. Washington: U.S. Government Printing Office, ch. 9.

Osterman, P. (1994, January). How common is workplace transformation and who adopts it? *Industrial and Labor Relations Review*, 47 (2): 173–188.

Pil, F. K., & MacDuffie, J. P. (1996). The adoption of high-involvement work practices. *Industrial Relations*, 35 (3): 423–455.

Piore, M. J., & Sabel, C. F. (1984). *The second industrial divide.* New York: Basic Books.

Quigley, J. (1994). Department store merchandising: A case study of federated department stores. Unpublished. Institute on Education and the Economy, Teachers College, Columbia University, New York.

Uchitelle, L. (1994). A new labor design for Levi Strauss. *New York Times*, October 13, 1994, D1–D6.

U.S. Department of Labor. (1993). *High performance work practices and firm performance.* Washington: U.S. Department of Labor.

Womack, J., Jones, D., & Roos, D. (1990). *The machine that changed the world.* New York: Rawson-Macmillan.

3

Organizational and Environmental Factors Influencing the Use and Diffusion of High-Involvement Work Practices

FRITS K. PIL
JOHN PAUL MACDUFFIE

High-involvement/high-performance work practices have been shown to affect performance in a variety of settings, ranging from process to batch manufacturing, and service industries. Performance improvements resulting from such work practices range from improved quality and higher productivity to lower scrap rates, lower turnover, and higher levels of customer satisfaction (Arthur 1992; Eaton and Voos, 1993; Ichniowski et al., 1994; Kochan and Osterman, 1992; MacDuffie 1995; MacDuffie & Pil, 1996). Cross-industry studies have found similar results using financial performance measures (Huselid, 1995). Indeed, a review by the Department of Labor found that of 29 studies focusing on the links between high-involvement work practices and performance, the majority found significant positive effects, and only two found negative effects (1993). A more recent review by Ichniowski and Kochan concluded that high-involvement work practices have a clear and demonstrated effect on productivity, and such effects "are large enough to be economically important to the businesses which adopt the new practices" (1995, p. 60). Despite the laudatory praise of high-involvement work, we have found tremendous variance in its implementation in the automobile industry (Pil and MacDuffie, 1996).

Even though much has been written about high-involvement work practices and their links to performance, there is very little evidence of what determines why some organizations use them and others do not (Pil and MacDuffie, 1996). The fact that there is substantive variance in practices in the automobile industry, even when there appears to be an accepted best practice model, suggests something fundamental is at work. In this chapter, we will provide a detailed analysis of the factors that explain why changing to high-involvement work is hard, successful change is rare, and variance in work practice is widespread.

We will start within the organization, focusing on the costs of implementing high-involvement work practices and the factors that enhance the benefits or reduce the costs of undertaking change. Moving to the level of the corporation, we will show that companies are constrained by their history in changing their work practices. We will look at the tools that companies use to overcome the challenges inherent to undertaking change and why not all are effective. Labor plays an important role that varies from region to region, and we'll show how unions can be facilitators or insurmountable foes in the change process. We will conclude with a discussion of how even the masters at high-involvement work, the Japanese, need to adapt their work practices to the demands of local environments.

Let us first set the stage with an overview of why the automobile industry is the ideal setting to explore change and diversity in work practices, along with a brief description of our data sources.

Why the Auto Industry?

The auto industry provides a particularly fruitful venue for exploring high-involvement work practices for four reasons: (1) the well-established relationship between work practices and performance, (2) the labor intensiveness of the industry, (3) the global nature of the industry coupled with the comparability of process and output across nations, and (4) the importance of the industry to the global economy. Let us look at each of these in turn.

The relationship between high-involvement work practices and performance is well established in the auto industry. The first clear indicators of the tie between work practices and performance came with the establishment of the GM-Toyota joint venture known as NUMMI in Fremont, California. GM had shuttered the Fremont factory in 1982 because of limited product demand and continual labor strife. The factory was reopened under a joint venture with Toyota in 1985. The joint venture kept most of the same equipment from the original Fremont factory and rehired about 85% of the original work force. One of the major changes that took place, however, was that Toyota put in place a coherent set of high-involvement work practices along with complementary human resources (HR) practices. A year after starting production, the Toyota-GM joint venture required under 20 hours to build a standard vehicle, less than half the 48 hours it had taken at the old GM Fremont plant (Krafcik, 1986). Furthermore, quality at the new plant was superior to that of any other U.S. plant.

The evidence linking high-involvement work practices to automobile-assembly-plant performance has been substantially expanded since then through survey-based research of the industry (MacDuffie, 1991, 1995; MacDuffie and Pil, 1998). This research showed that high-involvement work practices result in both superior labor productivity and better product-quality controlling for complementary HR practices and lean buffers. Much of the research relating work practices to performance in the auto industry was performed under the auspices of M.I.T.'s International Motor Vehicle Program and received significant attention through *The Machine That Changed the World* (Womack et al., 1990). The findings relating work practices and other complementary characteristics (more broadly known as "lean production systems") to performance are widely known and accepted in the industry. This is advantageous for the study of who uses and who adopts high-involvement work practices, because it rules out "ignorance" of superior practices as an explanation.

High-involvement work practices are of particular significance to the auto industry because of its high labor requirements. Indeed, the average car factory employs almost 5000 people, and the most labor-intensive area within the factories, final trim and assembly of the vehicles, is extremely hard to automate. This makes labor substitution by capital a difficult task to undertake and increases the importance of how labor is utilized and deployed. This importance is further accentuated by the sheer numbers of individuals who derive their livelihood from automobile production. The Motor Vehicle and equipment industry employed 985,000 people in 1997 (Department of Commerce, 1998). While this figure includes more than passenger vehicle and truck production, it does provide some indication of the total impact of motor vehicle production in the United States.[1] The automobile assembly factories participating in the International Assembly Plant Study (MacDuffie and Pil, 1995), which form the basis for analyses in this chapter, employ a total of almost 400,000 people. As a result, there are multiple stakeholders, not just within the plants but also in the external environment, who have a strong interest and concern in the competitiveness of the plants.

Another advantage of the auto industry is that it is truly a global industry with assembly factories in many countries and most regions of the world. Automobile assembly plants around the world produce quite similar products using comparable processes, thus making it a good industry to study location effects on the use of work practices. Despite the importance of high-involvement work practices for competitiveness and the general acceptance of the link between such practices and performance, we will see that the adoption of high-involvement work practices has been far from uniform across automobile assembly plants.

In addition to the advantages of looking at the auto industry, our data offer the additional advantage of being drawn from the establishment or plant level. Although there have been studies of work practices at levels other than the establishment level (e.g., Huselid, 1995), there is a general indication that they are best researched at the establishment level[2] (Hunter and Pil, 1995; Ichniowski, et al., 1994; MacDuffie, 1991; MacDuffie and Pil, 1995; Osterman, 1995).

Assembly Plant Study as Data Source

For this chapter we will be drawing on data collected as part of the International Assembly Plant Study. This is establishment-level data that we collected through an in-depth survey designed to capture information from a number of knowledgeable respondents within the assembly plants. In addition to using a number of cross-checks within the survey to ensure accuracy, we have also undertaken research visits to the majority of plants participating in the study.

Round 1 of the International Assembly Plant Study took place between 1988 and 1989. Seventy assembly plants from around the world were surveyed on a host of topics in an effort to understand their production systems and concomitant productivity. The data presented in chapter 4 of Womack et al. (1990) are based on this research.

In 1993–1994, Round 2 of the International Assembly Plant Study was carried out. It collected more in-depth information related to production systems as well as a host of new topics and was designed to ensure that where the question formats differed, data could be collapsed to make it directly comparable to the data collected in Round 1. A total of 89 surveys were returned from assembly plants in all parts of the world and from all major automakers. It represents the most comprehensive data collection effort of its kind ever carried out in automobile assembly plants.

Table 3.1 shows the response levels by region of the world for Round 1 and Round 2. The Round 2 sample is about 20% larger than the Round 1 sample and contains more plants in virtually every part of the world except for Europe, where we have experienced a drop in response rate. There are 43 plants that participated in both rounds of data collection.

What Do We Mean by High-Involvement Work?

Companies use a variety of different practices to increase worker involvement, knowledge sharing, and commitment. We identify five key practices affecting the structural aspects of work: "on-line" work teams, "off-line" employee involvement activities and problem-solving groups, job rotation, suggestion programs (both number of suggestions and percentage implemented), and the decentralization of quality efforts. These practices generally entail despecialization of resources, an integration of conception with execution, a decentralization of information and

Table 3.1. Sample Distribution of Assembly Plant Data

Regional Group	Round 1	Round 2	Matched 1 & 2
U.S. plants in North America	16	26	11
Japanese plants in North America	4	8	3
Japanese plants in Japan	9	12	6
European plants	24	20	13
New Entrant plants	11	11	7
Australian plants	6	4	3
South African Plants	0	6	0
Total	70	88	43
Number of companies	24	21	18
Number of countries	17	20	17

authority, and have a positive effect on both assembly plant productivity and quality (MacDuffie, 1991, 1995; MacDuffie and Pil, 1996). We find that plants vary dramatically in how they use and understand these work practices. Next are brief descriptions of each work practice we assess; keep in mind that there is variance in how these are implemented at the plants.

Work Teams: These are formally designated groups of workers that form a social unit, hold regular meetings to discuss work-related issues, and have a team leader whose job status is the same as that of team members. Team members engage in job rotation and hold regular meetings, where they take on many issues that would traditionally fall under the responsibility of functional specialists (e.g., they may do their own quality control, vacation scheduling, scrap assessment, and a host of other things). A key idea behind teamwork is to integrate "conception and execution by helping build understanding of the production system" (MacDuffie, 1991, p. 86).

Problem-Solving Groups: Because they spend so much time working as part of the production system, production workers observe problems and limitations in that system. Problem-solving groups are a very important arena where workers can explore those problems in more detail and find ways to keep them from recurring. These problems can be repeated equipment problems or infrequent quality problems that are slated to be eliminated. Problem-solving groups are a means by which those most knowledgeable about the system can search for means to improve it. As Levine and Tyson (1990) point out, they are a conduit by which information flow can be enhanced within the organization and a means to ensure better use of the information that resides on the shop floor. Unlike on-line teams that have a well-defined membership and are focused on specific tasks or set of operations, problem-solving groups are as the name suggests, problem-oriented. As such, they may consist of workers from multiple parts of the plant, and some plants disband these groups once a problem is resolved.

Job Rotation: Rotating employees on a periodic basis provides various benefits to an organization. By rotating within their work groups, as well as across work groups and departments, workers develop a broader knowledge base and a more comprehensive understanding of the production process. Even though job rotation is found in on-line teams, it may also be present in the absence of team work.

Suggestion Programs: Workers on the shop floor observe opportunities for change and improvement around them. Problem-solving activities are one means whereby these observations can come to fruition. However, sometimes employees are able to identify significant improvement potential without the need for quality circle meetings. Suggestion programs are a means by which these ideas can be brought to the forefront. Although some organizations believe that important suggestions can be implemented automatically by production workers, we find this does not appear to be true, either from a technical or an organizational control/coordination perspective. Having suggestions submitted in a formal fashion has several advantages. For one, it allows time to evaluate the merits of the suggestion and review the impact that a change in one location may have on other aspects of the production system. Furthermore, it provides a written record of changes and improvements that have been made. This is extremely useful in managing the development and evolution of the production system. For example, automobile plants introduce model changes on a periodic basis. At that time, several weeks are spent debugging and modifying the production system to reoptimize production flow and manpower and equipment utilization. Having a written record of the actions taken the previous year helps provide a codified basis from which incremental improvement can then take place.[3] Last, recording of suggestions simplifies standardization of the production process, which is critical to high quality. We measure not only the number of suggestions per employee, but also the percent that are ultimately implemented as evidence of management's responsiveness to worker suggestions.

Decentralization of Quality Tasks: Workers can be involved in quality improvement through problem-solving groups and suggestion programs, but responsibility for quality can also be integrated into workers' job tasks. This may include shifting to workers on the line the responsibility for inspection of incoming parts, inspecting work in progress and final output, and tracking statistical process control information from quality specialists (e.g., quality control inspectors and engineers).

To explore the use of high-involvement work practices in the International Assembly Plant Study, we will use a composite index, referred to as the "Work Practices" index. This index reflects the five work practices outlined above.[4] The plant with the lowest level of high-involvement work practices has a score of 0, and the plant with the highest level has a score of 100.

Inside the Plant—What Determines Change?

As can be seen from Table 3.2, there has been an overall increase in the use of high-involvement work practices by these plants from Round 1 to Round 2. The most striking increases are in the use of on-line work teams and off-line problem-solving groups (e.g., employee involvement groups, quality circles). The average plant had nearly 16% of its workforce in teams in 1989 and almost tripled that by 1993–1994 to 46.3%.[5] The average number of employees in problem-solving groups increased from 28.9% to 48.8%. There was a slight increase in job rotation, with the average plant having employees who rotate within their work groups. Plants now receive an average of almost 13 suggestions per employee, up from 9.2 in 1989, and implement over half of those.[6] Indeed, with the exception of decentralized quality control that remains at about the same level, there was a significant increase in the use of all high-involvement work practices between 1989 and 1993–1994.

Table 3.2 suggests that plants can and do increase their use of high-involvement work practices and that this is the prevailing trend worldwide. However, there remains large variance in the degree to which plants change. Although the average change in the work systems index was 12.3 (on a 0–100 scale), the standard deviation for the change was 22.2. Some plants undertook only minor change in their use of high-involvement work practices between 1989 and 1993–1994 while other plants showed dramatic increases.

What explains the change in work practice use over time? High-involvement work practices may represent "competence-destroying" change. This type of change implies unlearning existing practices or accepted ways of doing things—this is difficult to undertake and may lead to worsened performance in the short term (i.e., it may not be an economically rational choice for individual managers held accountable for short-term results). The introduction of new practices also requires up-front investments in time and energy, but the benefits take some time to show. For both of these reasons, firms may be discouraged from making changes in work practices (particularly change involving "bundles" of interdependent practices rather than individual practices) or from continuing with change efforts beyond an initial trial period. Given these impediments to change, we argue that there are three key factors at the plant or establishment level that drive the adoption of new work practices (and "bundles" of practices): (1) the level of complementary organizational practices and technologies that would increase the *benefit* from the new practices, (2) the performance levels the organization is achieving with its current practices, and (3) organizational characteristics or actions that alter the *cost* of introducing the new practices. We tested for this empirically, using both rounds of the International Assembly Plant data. (See Pil and MacDuffie [1996] for a comprehensive discussion of the theory and data presented in this section.)

Table 3.2 indicates that there was an overall increase in the use of high-involvement work practices in automobile assembly plants around the world from Round 1 to Round 2, but with high variance in the degree to which existing plants changed their use of these practices. Appendix A provides results from multivariate analyses that explored the relative importance of various intraplant drivers of changes in work practices. We first looked at the effect of enabling HR practices and technology. In terms of HR practices, we used an index that captures the amount of training provided to new and experienced workers, the use of selection mechanisms to identify workers amenable to working in high-

Table 3.2. Change in High-Involvement Work Practices at Matched Plants: Mean, (Standard Deviation)

	Plants in 1989	Same plants in 1993/94	t-test
High-Involvement Work Practices Index (0 = low; 100 = extensive use of "high-involvement" work practices)	34.6 (24.9)	46.9 (23.2)	***
Individual Practices in High-Involvement Work Practices Index			
Employees in work teams (%)	15.7 (29.1)	46.3 (39.3)	**
Employees in problem-solving groups (e.g., quality circles, employee involvement groups) (%)	28.9 (37.6)	48.8 (38.7)	***
Job rotation (1 = none, 5 = within and across work groups and departments)	3.0 (1.2)	3.2 (1.2)	*
Suggestions per employee	9.2 (28.3)	12.8 (33.2)	***
Suggestions implemented (%)	38.2 (36.6)	50.8 (32.3)	***
Responsibility for quality (1 = production workers, 4 = specialists)	1.6 (1.2)	1.7 (1.3)	—
n	43	43	

* = significant at 10% level; ** = significant at 5% level; *** = significant at 1% level.

Source: (Pil & MacDuffie, 1996)

involvement work settings, the use of pay for performance programs, and the extent of status barriers between management and line workers. We found that plants with HR practices that complement the use of high-involvement work practices were more likely to increase their use of those work practices.

For automation, we looked at the use of robotics. Even though higher levels of robotics potentially enhance a plant's ability to handle greater variety and are more amenable to worker-driven enhancements, these benefits are only realized in organizations that utilize high-involvement work practices. However, contrary to our expectations, we found that the Round 1 level of flexible automation was *not* a significant predictor of the use of high-involvement work practices in Round 2. This may be the result of different strategies for flexible automation that are reflected in the sample of Round 1 plants. Using joint estimation of high-involvement work practices and robotics, we found the Round 1 level of work practices *was* a strong predictor of the Round 2 level of flexible automation but not the converse (see Pil, 1996; Pil and MacDuffie, 1996). This suggests that either some "high-tech" plants in Round 1 did *not* increase their use of high-involvement work practices or that some "low-tech" plants in Round 1 *did* increase their use of such practices.

We believe that both are true. Round 1 plants that turned to technology investments as a means to improve their competitive position in the mid-1980s were also the plants least likely to turn to new work practices in the 1990s. In part, this is the result of some underlying preconceptions regarding the role of labor in enhancing performance. On the other hand, many plants in newly industrialized countries are choosing to invest in high-involvement work practices rather than investing heavily in any type of new technology. Indeed, even in industrialized nations we have found a trend away from the 1980s push for all-out use of automation. In particular, plants have moved away from full automation of assembly steps. Instead, there has been expanded use of what we term "automation assist." These are forms of automation that support, but do not necessarily replace, the production worker. Examples include carts moving with the line that contain parts, delivery mechanisms for parts or tools, bolt tighteners, platforms that move workers under vehicles—generally automation designed to either enhance ergonomics, reduce extraneous production-worker movement, eliminate errors related to variety, or improve quality. Automation assist is most often found in conjunction with high-involvement work practices and consists of low-cost automation developed and produced in-house by teams of technicians and production workers.

Our multivariate analyses suggest only limited evidence that change in work practices is performance driven. Although the coefficient for quality was positive and relatively large, indicating that plants whose 1989 quality was poor were more likely to implement new work practices, it was not quite statistically significant. Furthermore, productivity in 1989 had a much smaller coefficient (also positive) and was not a significant predictor of change in work practices. This is explained in part by other analyses (MacDuffie and Pil, 1998), which find that a subset of assembly plants in the Round 2 sample have been able to achieve impressive productivity results through top-down reengineering without fundamental changes in work practices; however, the quality performance of these plants has not been very strong.

Despite this finding, it is worth noting that the coefficients for the performance variables were not negative, challenging the view that poorly performing plants would be *less* likely to make changes in work practices (resulting from such factors as escalating commitment to past, ineffective policies; lack of financial resources for change; adversarial labor relations; or incompetent management) than average performers. Furthermore, as we will discuss later, *company* performance is often an important driver of plant-level change.

Beyond complementary HR practices, automation, and organizational performance, we investigated a series of factors that would alter the benefits and costs of introducing new practices. We expected that organizations that had a lot of experience with existing practices (as measured by employee tenure), as well as organizations that had undertaken measures that eradicate employee trust, would have a more difficult time introducing high-involvement work practices. This was not borne out by the data. As can be seen in Table 3.3, layoffs bore no significant relationship to the likelihood of introducing new high-involvement work practices. Furthermore, plants with a more experienced management team were more likely to introduce new work practices. In the intensely competitive environment in the worldwide auto industry over the past decade, there has been a strong external impetus for change that has overwhelmed differences between low-tenure and high-tenure workers and managers in terms of receptivity to new work practices. In this context, the benefits—particularly among members of the plant management team—of working together for longer periods of time, with respect to increased trust and cooperation, may come to the fore. We did not find support for the popular perception that older, more experienced managers and workers are more resistant to change in work practices than younger, newer employees.

With regard to layoffs, it is important to note that downsizing actions can certainly damage the "psychological contract" between employees and the firm. However, they may also provide additional impetus to efforts to change work practices. The story is further complicated by the fact that plants that have traditionally used few high-involvement work practices were also the plants that were most likely to undertake employee downsizing. (However, even when the implementation of new work practices is spurred forward in a climate of layoffs and downsizing,

Table 3.3. Understanding Change in Use of High-Involvement Work Practices (N = 39, 1989 to 1993/94). Dependent Variable = High-Involvement Work Practices in 1993/94

Variable	Equation 1		Equation 2[a]		Equation 3		Equation 4		Equation 5	
	B	SE	B	SE	B	SE	B	SE	B	SE
High-Involvement Work Pract. 1989	0.44***	0.15	0.43**	0.19	0.34**	0.15	0.37*	0.21	0.40***	0.14
Complementary HRM Index in 1989	0.41**	0.18	0.62**	0.23	0.31*	0.19	0.39*	0.23	0.32*	0.17
Flexible Automation in 1989	−0.36	0.32	−0.13	0.39	−0.05	0.33	−0.36	0.34	−0.47	0.30
Log Productivity in 1989			4.42	11.1						
Log Quality in 1989			16.92	11.4						
Production Worker Tenure					−0.13	0.63				
Managerial Tenure					1.50**	0.57				
Layoffs of Production Workers							−5.24	8.43		
Major Addition to Plant									2.1	7.45
% of Plant's Output that is New									19.17**	7.16
Constant	19.3***	6.59	−77.4	74.6	9.61	12.2	26.03**	10.97	12.84*	6.57
F-statistic	8.43***		4.8***		5.7***		4.91***		7.37***	
R Squared adj.	0.37		0.38		0.45		0.32		0.46	
Significance Levels: * = 10%, ** = 5%, *** = 1%										

[a]Regressions including productivity and quality represent a reduced n of 32 because quality data is not available for any non-U.S. plants that do not export to the United States.

Source: Pil & MacDuffie, 1996

it remains to be investigated whether its impact on economic performance is as great as if this change occurred in a climate of trust and cooperation.) We did find strong evidence that plants that undergo a major disruption in their operations—creating a window of opportunity for various organizational changes—were more likely to adopt high-involvement work practices. What is particularly important about this finding is that some types of disruptions (e.g., model changes) occur naturally and periodically in an organization's life cycle and as such provide perfect opportunities to undertake competence-destroying change in a way that minimizes the costs of the transition.

Company Trajectories and Their Influence on Work

We have discussed how various intraplant factors affect change in work practices. There are also a number of company-level factors that can facilitate or inhibit change. In this section, we explore how history and trajectory can influence plant-level use of high-involvement work practices by looking at General Motors.

In the late 1970s, General Motors, jointly with the United Auto Workers (UAW), embarked on an ambitious "Quality of Work Life" (QWL) program. This program emphasized QWL groups of line workers that addressed non-production-related issues in an attempt to boost worker satisfaction. At the same time, GM unsuccessfully tried to open some nonunion "team concept" plants in the South (the so-called "Southern strategy"). This strategy failed almost immediately, as the UAW successfully organized the new plants in Oklahoma City and Shreveport, Louisiana. The outcome of this failed strategy was that the UAW associated team work with antiunion efforts. Team initiatives in Michigan and elsewhere soon ground to a halt. Furthermore, the closing of the most advanced team plant at GM at this time, the Fiero plant in Pontiac, Michigan, did nothing to enhance the image of teams in the eyes of the UAW.

With their involvement in NUMMI, the GM-Toyota joint venture, GM and the UAW had another opportunity to learn more generally about high-involvement work practices and lean production. Unfortunately, little learning took place on the part of GM. Although thousands of managers, engineers, and workers were exposed to NUMMI, most went for short, one-day visits, visits that lacked the depth necessary to appreciate the fundamentally different logic of the production system at work in NUMMI and the role that high-involvement work practices played in that logic. By the early 1990s, a combination of market share losses, financial problems, and plant closures at GM made shifting to high-involvement work practices very difficult. Workers were distrustful of management, and cynicism toward new work practices was widespread. Whereas efforts were needed to reduce costs, these consisted primarily of GM's Synchronous Manufacturing Program—a top-down process-reengineering effort. Some headway has since been made in the implementation of team work and other high-involvement work practices, but GM and the UAW's earlier experiences continue to have a dampening effect.

GM Europe, although influenced by GM headquarters in the United States, followed a different path from GM North America. In the 1980s, the GM Europe plants decided to turn to high-involvement work practices as one avenue to enhance productivity and quality. In part, the difference between the GM plants in Europe and those in North America was a different union environment—an environment in which unions generally embrace high-involvement work as a better means to utilize high levels of worker education and skills. It also reflected a leadership more amenable to high-involvement work practices. This leadership included Jack Smith and then Lou Hughes, who had helped to set up the NUMMI joint venture and had become convinced of the value of lean-production principles. As a result, GM Europe undertook far-reaching reforms in work organization at some of its plants (Turner, 1991). Some variance does persist among individual plants as a result of country differences, but the general trend within GM Europe has been toward an extensive implementation of high-involvement work.

For example, one of the most advanced lean-production plants in Europe that is not Japanese-owned is the new GM Europe plant in Eisenach, located in the former East Germany. It is run primarily by a combination of German managers and young American and Canadian managers and advisors, who previously worked either at NUMMI or at GM's joint venture plant with Suzuki in Canada (CAMI). An even more dramatic example of GM Europe's efforts are found at GM's Antwerp plant in Belgium, where a cadre of American managers hired away from Toyota in Kentucky are working to transform a brownfield plant and thus to set an example for the rest of Europe. Eisenach and Antwerp owe much of their early success to GM Europe's strategy of trying to replicate successful principles developed elsewhere, without major efforts to reinvent or modify them, and to the extensive transfer of managers with substantive "hands-on" experience with lean production and high-involvement work practices to oversee the launch and change efforts.

The GM North America versus GM Europe example shows that even within the same company, different historical experiences with high-involvement work practices and differences in unions and management can result in divergent approaches to work practices. In reviewing the behavior of automobile companies around the world, we have found that companies that moved most rapidly to adopt new work practices from 1989 to 1993–1994 typically shared many of the following: (1) they faced a serious competitiveness crisis in the late 1980s and early 1990s; (2) their senior managers (and, in some cases, senior union officials) perceived the source of the crisis as internal rather than external—the result of problems with organizing the production system according to traditional mass-production principles. Furthermore, they often validated this perception with benchmarking data that evaluated competitors in various countries; (3) both top managers and union officials reached the conclusion that lean-production principles should be implemented; (4) they had relatively little previous experience with work reforms; (5) managers and union officials held neutral or positive views about the value of work reforms as a means of improving performance; (6) they found effective ways to cultivate organizational learning across internal functional or divisional boundaries; and (7) frequently they had, or sought access to, some "learning model," that is, establishing some kind of learning relationship, ranging from a joint venture to informal sharing of benchmarking data with another company already using these principles.[7]

Factors such as these help explain regional and company-level differences in the adoption of high-involvement work practices. These conditions were met for a number of European companies as well as some New Entrant plants (i.e., Korea, Mexico, Brazil, Taiwan, India) that proved to be the most aggressive adopters of high-involvement work practices. As mentioned earlier, there is also some indication that plants in any region producing high levels of product complexity, either as a function of manufacturing strategy or because the plant serves many export markets, are more likely to adopt both flexible automation and high-involvement work practices. In contrast, many plants in the United States and Canada retained relatively traditional work practices for the following reasons: (1) management and union ambivalence about work reform developed in response to earlier change efforts in the late 1970s and early 1980s; (2) competitive crises were not necessarily interpreted as having internal sources or as requiring a change in fundamental production principles; (3) organizational learning, with respect to innovations both inside and outside of the plant, was not always carried out effectively; and (4) the fact that most of these plants remained highly focused on building a single car or truck model at relatively high volume provided less incentive to become more flexible by changing work practices.

Learning About High-Involvement Work

Although influenced by their past, companies look to change their future through explicit learning and unlearning mechanisms and strategies to facilitate the shift to a high-involvement work environment. Some of these, such as joint ventures and alliances, operate at the company level. All Korean automobile producers, for example, have partnerships with foreign companies—Kia with Ford and Mazda, Hyundai with Mitsubishi, Daewoo with Honda, and Samsung with Nissan. These ties can provide, in part, mentoring relationships and access to role models to facilitate change. However, to date, most of what has been transferred to the Korean partners relates to technical expertise and product design rather than work organization.

Another company-level approach used to induce change involves the use of a lead plant. Here the company focuses its energy on changing one plant with the hope that what is learned at that plant will help inform change at other locations. Saturn was originally intended to be such a plant, although at this stage it does not have a strong influence on the remainder of GM in the work practices arena (Pil and Rubinstein, 1998). As mentioned earlier, GM's Eisenach and Antwerp plants have risen to prominence as exemplars for GM's European operations.

Two common problems we observe with the lead plant approach is that when assembly plants are told to use another plant as a model, they (1) fall back on the "they are different" excuse or (2) fall into the "not invented here" syndrome. On the other hand, we have seen some plants actively engaged in learning from a lead plant. Generally this occurred when the lead plant and learning plant were located in different parts of the world, and the lead plant was not viewed as a potential usurper of resources. A good example of this are the older General Motors plants in Brazil, which have an active program to learn from NUMMI's experience in the United States. The lead plant may also change over time. While Eisenach continues to be a model for new GM plants in Brazil, Argentina, Poland, and China, the new Brazil plant will provide the template for new modular assembly plants planned for the United States.

In addition to company change strategies, there are also strategies that operate or have their effect at the plant level. Some plants, for example, are assigned a "sister-plant" by their parent company—a plant that has successfully introduced high-involvement work practices and is willing to provide assistance. Other plants have brought in advisors or "champions" who have experience in workplaces that have successfully introduced high-involvement work practices. The latter is a particularly intriguing strategy.

The selection of champions may take different forms. One common approach is to send a small number of employees to a transformed plant to learn new ideas. Following their return, these employees are then expected to help introduce new work practices at their work site. In this instance, the employees serve the dual function of repositories of information they acquired during their visit, and equally important, as boundary spanners. An alternate approach is to hire employees from a plant that is using high-involvement work practices—"informed outsiders." These employees generally do not maintain active links with their former organization, but because of their greater experience actually working in a high-involvement work environment and perhaps even in implementing high-involvement work practices, they possess greater immediately accessible knowledge.

We have seen very few examples of plants that successfully used champions or informed outsiders to implement high-involvement work practices. One possible reason may be what Simon termed "bounded rationality." Implementing and utilizing high-involvement work practices is extremely complex and involves an understanding of not just the work practices but also a host of complementary practices. It could be the case that it is not possible for one, or even a few, individuals to fully understand how to implement such practices. It may also be that undertaking a fundamental change in work practices requires a concerted effort on the part of all employees in a plant, and the champions can do little to alter the status quo unless they have the support and resources from all levels within the organization. The GM plant in Antwerp mentioned earlier is particularly intriguing, because the "champions" brought into that plant initially started out as advisors, but under the guidance of Doug Friesen, the plant manager, whose background included a stint at Toyota Kentucky, a number of advisors have been moved into line positions.

Companies and plants may develop strategies for change, but so may actors in the external environment. Unions, for example, may strongly oppose or promote change toward high-involvement work practices, as in the case of the Canadian Autoworkers Union (CAW) and IG-Metall, respectively. Governments too may play a role. The Australian government, for example, has threatened Australian auto producers with reduced import tariffs if they do not undertake change. Similarly, the British government provided large incentives to Japanese transplants in the hopes that the presence of those transplants would assist change in the remainder of the British auto industry. Let us look explicitly at the role that unions can play in the change process.

The Role of Unions: The Case of the CAW

While company trajectories and choices play a role in plant use of high-involvement work practices, plants are also constrained and influenced by their labor environment. Unions, for example, can play an extremely significant role. The Canadian situation is particularly interesting because the Canadian auto workers split from the U.S. auto workers over work-practice issues. Let us look in more detail at what happened.

The Canadian Autoworkers Union

During the recession of the early 1980s, the UAW and the Big Three automakers looked for means by which to enhance the performance of the North American assembly plants. New efforts included increases in automation, profit sharing at the corporate level, increased flexibility in worker deployment, and efforts to enhance worker involvement through team-based work, quality circles, and so forth. The UAW was to be a partner in efforts to make the automobile plants more competitive. However, the Canadian Autoworkers felt the UAW was going too far in its cooperation with management (Kumar and Ryan, 1988). The most important initial sources of divergence between Canadian and U.S. auto workers was how wages are determined and the UAW's receptivity to high-involvement work (Katz and Meltz, 1991). In 1980 at Chrysler and 1982 at Ford and GM, profit sharing was introduced. In 1984, the practice of providing annual wage increases based on base-line productivity improvement was eliminated at Ford and GM in the United States in exchange for lump sum increases and the continuation of the profit-sharing plan. The Canadian auto workers, however, refused to adopt profit sharing. Furthermore, they were strongly against participative work arrangements. In 1984, the Canadian auto workers refused the U.S. agreement reached between GM and the UAW. After a two-week strike, the Canadian workers attained a contract that excluded the provisions for worker involvement, team-based activities, and gain sharing found in the U.S. contracts. It also included provisions for greater base wage rate increases than found in the U.S. contracts in the form of new annual improvement factors at GM and Ford in Canada (Chrysler followed in 1987). As a consequence, the Canadian auto workers split from the UAW and formed the CAW in 1985.

Table 3.4 portrays the extent to which lean work practices are utilized in U.S.-owned plants in the United States versus those in Canada. While only one Canadian plant has officially moved to a team structure, almost half of the U.S. plants have made that transition. Furthermore, teams are more extensively used within the U.S. plants that have adopted team arrangements. Even though some Canadian plants have moved to reduce the number of supervisors and delegate a portion of authority to production workers who are given a title akin to that of team leader, such team leaders still have little authority beyond the requirements of day-

Table 3.4. Work Practices at Big 3 Plants: United States vs. Canada

	Average US/US	Average US/CA
Workforce in Teams if Teams Present (%)	48	25
Plants in Region with Teams	9	1
Workforce in EI or QC Groups (%)	33	4
Suggestions per Employee	0.3	0.2
Suggestions Implemented (%)	42	37
Extent of Job Rotation	2.1	1.8
(1 = none; 5 = frequent, in and across work groups)		

to-day production. In contrast, teams at U.S. plants are more involved in work redesign and some problem-solving activities. Finally, teams at U.S. team plants are found in all areas of the plant, including the paint shop and the stamping plants, while teams in Canada are generally found only in the assembly area. The U.S. plants have many more teams than their Canadian counterparts, but both U.S. and Canadian plants have fairly low levels of job rotation compared with Japanese plants in North America as well as in Japan.

In the area of quality efforts, there is a marked difference between the Big Three plants in the United States and Canada. The U.S. plants make moderate use of quality circles, or organized group activities, geared toward quality improvement. This is in sharp contrast with Canada where virtually no employees participate in them. Like team work, quality circles are another formalized group structure that the CAW does not support.

Understanding Intraregional Differences in Change in Work Practices

So far we have focused within the plants, companies, and unions; Table 3.5 makes it clear that regional factors are also important drivers of change in the use of high-involvement work practices. Perhaps the most dramatic change shown in the table is the increase in Europe of the use of small-group activities. This includes an increase in on-line work teams, as well as off-line group activities such as quality circles and employee involvement groups. European plants also exhibited an increase in other work practices such as job rotation and suggestion programs.

Plants in New Entrant countries (Korea, Taiwan, Mexico, and Brazil in these data) as well as plants in Australia also exhibited significant increases in their use of high-involvement work practices. In contrast, U.S.-owned plants in North America have implemented relatively few of these practices. With the exception of job rotation, these plants make very little use of high-involvement work. This is in contrast with the Japanese-owned transplants in North America, which have continued to increase their use of high-involvement work practices and are converging on the levels found in Japan. The use of employee-involvement groups is the only work practice that has not experienced a significant increase in use at the transplants.

The Japanese plants in Japan continue to be the most significant users of high-involvement work practices. The only exception is the decentralization of quality control, where these plants have experienced a shift away from line-worker involvement back toward the use of specialists. Let us look in more detail at the role of the external environment in how plants operate by studying how Japanese-owned plants in the United States differ from their counterparts in Japan.

Table 3.5. High-Involvement Work Practices by Region

Plant Ownership/Location	US/NA	JP/JP	JP/NA	EUR	KOR	AUS	S. AFR
Work Systems Index (100 = High-involvement; 0 = Low involvement)	32	78	62	54	71	54	31
(%) of Workforce in teams if teams present	46	70	70	64	70	65	57
# Plants in region with teams	10/25	12/12	8/8	20/20	4/6	3/4	4/5
(%) of Workforce in EI or QC groups	26	81	27	47	92	51	29
Suggestions per employee	0.3	23	4	0.8	37	1.2	0.1
(%) of Suggestions implemented	41	84	70	40	44	23	15
Extent of job rotation (1 = none; 5 = frequent, in and across work groups)	2.0	3.9	4.0	3.6	3.0	4.0	3.8

US/NA = US owned plants in North America; JP/JP = Japanese plants in Japan; JP/NA = Japanese owned plants in North America; KOR = Korean plants in Korea; AUS = Australian plants; and S.AFR = South African Plants.

The Japanese Transplants: We did an in-depth comparison of work practices at Japanese transplants in North America with practices at Japanese plants in Japan, and U.S.-owned plants in North America. (See Pil and MacDuffie, 1999 for additional detail on the material covered in this section.) The goal was to explore the extent to which work practices that developed in Japan are modified and adapted to fit the U.S. context. The success of Japanese automobile producers is often attributed to their work systems, and a key question this raises is what adaptations and alterations of the work practices take place when Japanese companies establish operations overseas.

The success of the high-involvement work practices in Japan is often attributed to the "three pillars" of the Japanese employment system. These are: lifetime employment, enterprise unionism, and a seniority wage system. The Japanese transplants in the United States have opted to implement, at least in part, two of these "pillars." All of the transplants offer employment guarantees to core employees. Even though U.S. labor law does not permit enterprise unionism, the transplants have introduced many of the employee consultation mechanisms associated with such unionism. However, the transplants have not put into practice the third of the three pillars: seniority wage systems. In part this may be due to a recognition in Japan that such a wage system has negative effects on morale and does not provide commensurate benefits. In addition to transferring many of the elements of enterprise unionism as well as lifetime employment, the transplants spend considerable resources on socialization and selection programs aimed at developing a work force amenable to high-involvement work practices. The transplants are incredibly selective, hiring on average only 1 in 25 applicants.[8] Furthermore, they spend a large fraction of their new employee training time on teaching workers their production philosophy.

While the three pillars were not transferred in full, the transplants' work practices are very similar to those of their Japanese counterparts. They make extensive use of team work, their suggestion programs garner significantly more suggestions than those of their U.S.-owned counterparts, many more of those suggestions are implemented, and their employees do extensive job rotation. The only area where the transplants differ in a major way from their Japan-based counterparts is in their use of quality circles. These are not used as widely at the transplants as they are in Japan.

The transplants use most of the high-involvement work practices found at their Japanese counterparts, but that does not mean these practices have been transferred blindly. Almost all have been modified or adapted in some way, reflecting the conditions of the North American labor environment. Let us consider team work as an example. The importance of on-line teams in Japanese plants has long been recognized by scholars (Aoki, 1990; Koike, 1989). Like plants in Japan, the transplants make extensive use of such teams. They differ significantly from their American counterparts in this area. While only one-third of the Big Three plants use teams, all the Japan plants and transplants do. Furthermore, about 70% of production workers at transplants and Japan plants are in work teams, compared with about one-half at Big Three plants.

On the surface, it appears that transplants are copying the practices of their Japanese counterparts. However, teams at the transplants differ in structure and function from those found in Japan, in ways that fit the North American institutional and social environment. Table 3.6 reveals that, at the transplants, management generally appoints team leaders (although at the unionized transplants, union officials are often involved in team leader selection). In contrast, at the Big Three plants with teams, management indicates that team members have more say in team leader selection. Teams in Japan plants are reported by management to have the most influence over work allocation and methods of work and the least influence over the selection of team leaders and the amount and pace of work. The transplants also report that team members have influence on issues related to work methods and problem solving. The Big Three teams have less influence in this area. However, there are key statistically significant differences between the transplants and plants in Japan. These are found in the area of employee voice, with teams in the Japan plants reporting more influence over performance evaluations and settling grievances and complaints. Like their Big Three counterparts, the transplants have little influence in this area (see Table 3.6).

There are many other differences between the work practices found in Japanese transplants and those found in Japan. These include subtle

Table 3.6. Team Influence at Japanese Plants in Japan, Big 3 Plants, and Transplants

Team influence	Japan	Transplants	U.S.	test JP vs. T	test T vs. U.S.
Use of new technology on job	2.8	2.0	2.7		
Who should do what job	4.3	3.1	3.1	**	
The way work is done; revising methods	4.3	4.1	2.9		**
Performance evaluations	3.2	1.4	1.3	**	
Settling grievances/complaints	4.2	2.1	1.6	***	
Pace of work	2.7	2.0	2.2		
Work to be done in a day	2.4	1.6	2.0		
Selection of team leader	1.51	2.1	3.4		

U.S. category includes only plants with teams. Measured on 1–5 Likert-type scale, where 1 indicates no influence over decisions, and 5 indicates extensive influence. Mann-Whitney tests done using two-sided confidence intervals levels: * = .1, ** = .05, *** = .01.

Source: Pil & MacDuffie, 1999.

changes such as having quality circles meet during paid time and not providing bonuses at the individual level at the transplants to more substantial changes in terms of information shared with employees. In some cases, this makes the transplants resemble their American counterparts (e.g., in large pay differentials between the lowest and highest paid employees) and, in some instances, makes them different from both their Big Three and Japanese counterparts (e.g., in drastically limiting the number of job classes that exist for production workers). These changes have helped the transplants manage some of the cultural and institutional differences between North America and Japan. They are significant because they show that although it is possible to implement high-involvement work practices in very different cultural and institutional environments, some adaptation is needed.

Conclusion

Despite clear evidence that they result in superior performance, there is tremendous variance in the use and implementation of high-involvement work practices. This chapter sheds light on this seemingly anomalous observation. We started at the plant level, showing that change to high-involvement work is by no means universal and is driven by a host of factors, not all of which are intuitive. For example, management teams with longer tenure are more likely to undertake change than those that are new. The main drivers of change in work practices at the plant level are related to complementary factors that enhance the benefits of high-involvement work, the performance the plants achieve with their existing practices, and natural opportunities for change that present themselves.

However, change and use of work practices is a very complex phenomenon and is influenced by a series of factors outside the direct control of the assembly plant. For example, we showed how a company's past experiences can hinder or facilitate the implementation of new work practices. We highlighted specific tools that companies employ to drive change and the limitations inherent in such tools. Our discussion of the Canadian Autoworkers Union highlighted the importance of considering the labor context in understanding the use and diffusion of high-involvement work. Last, we highlighted the importance of regional factors in understanding the use of new work practices and the complex interrelationship between the work practices and the institutional and cultural environment.

This chapter highlights the need to transcend levels of analyses and accentuates the complexity inherent in the implementation and use of high-involvement work. Indeed, a complex interplay of plant-level, company-level, union-level, and country-level factors influence the use and diffusion of high-involvement work practices. As a result, the implementation, and even the understanding, of high-involvement work practices is far from universal, and efforts to change are not always successful.

Notes

1. Automobile manufacturing is a major economic enterprise as well as a growing one in almost all regions of the world. In 1994, for example, the total world automobile output exceeded 36 million vehicles (Automotive News, 1995), and that figure has been growing at the rate of about 500,000 vehicles per year since the early 1980s.

2. The diversity of jobs, technologies, and institutional environments faced by different establishments in many large corporations limits the usefulness of corporate-level surveys of work and HR practices. Establishments within one company can exhibit radically different work practices. For example, a corporate survey that measures work practices at GM would not distinguish between traditional automobile assembly plants, NUMMI with its Toyota influence, Saturn and its innovative union agreement, and the overseas operations of GM, let alone activities on the nonmanufacturing side in marketing, design, and finance (Hunter and Pil, 1995).

3. Kanter's analogy between innovations and flowers is a useful one. According to Kanter (1983), innovations can grow wild in an organization (almost like weeds), or they can be purposefully cultivated. Under the latter situation, it is much easier to harvest them for the long-term benefit of the organization.

4. It is calculated by pooling the data across the two time periods (1989 and 1993–1994), standardizing the data for each practice through a z-score transformation, and then additively combining the standardized scores. The Cronbach's standardized alpha score for this index was 0.69. Using principal components analysis, we found that all variables in this index loaded on one factor. In order to have an index value that is easier to interpret, we applied a linear transformation to the sum of the z-scores, such that the plant with the lowest level of these high-involvement work practices has a score of 0 and the plant with the highest level has a score of 100. The distribution of the variable is unaffected by this transformation. Because we pool the data before these transformations, a specific bundle of practices will yield the same index score in either 1989 or 1993–1994.

5. While these are average figures, there is tremendous variance in each time period, with a number of plants having no employees in teams and others having a large number in teams. A big portion of the increase of employees in teams stems from the fact that more than twice as many plants had teams in 1993–1994 as did in 1989.

6. As with teams, there is very high variation in the number of suggestions received per employee across plants. As we will see later, there is also tremendous regional variation.

7. This list reflects some of the common characteristics of firms making the most changes in their use of high-involvement work practices and

should not be interpreted as either a checklist of "must do's" or as the result of statistical analyses of the distribution of these characteristics.

8. Based on the four transplants that did extensive hiring in 1993.

References

Aoki, Masahiko. 1990. Toward an economic model of the Japanese firm. *Journal of Economic Literature*, 28(1): 1–27.

Arthur, Jeffrey B. 1992. The link between business strategy and industrial relations systems in American Steel minimills. *Industrial and Labor Relations Review*, 45(3): 488–506.

Automotive News. 1995. Market Data Book. Detroit, MI: Crain Communications.

Department of Commerce. 1998. Statistical Abstracts of the United States, Washington DC: US Bureau of the Census.

Department of Labor. 1993. "High performance work practices and firm performance." Background material for the Conference on the Future of the American Workplace.

Eaton, Adrienne, and Paula Voos. 1992. Unions and contemporary innovations in work organization, compensation, and employee participation. In Lawrence Mishel and Paula Voos (eds.), *Unions and Economic Competitiveness*. Armonk, New York: M.E. Sharpe, pp. 173–216.

Hunter, Larry W., and Frits K. Pil. 1995. How do you survey firms? In Paula Voos (ed.), *Proceedings of the forty-seventh annual meeting*. Madison, WI: Industrial Relations Research Association, pp. 152–162.

Huselid, Mark. 1995. The impact of human resource management practices on turnover, productivity, and corporate financial performance. *Academy of Management Journal*, 38(3): 635–672.

Ichniowski, Casey, and Thomas A. Kochan. 1995. What have we learned from workplace innovations? Unpublished manuscript.

Ichniowski, Casey, Kathryn Shaw, and Giovanna Prenushi. 1994. The impact of human resource management practices on productivity. Working paper no. 15, Carnegie-Mellon University, Pittsburgh, PA.

Kanter, Rosabeth, 1983. *The change masters: Innovation and entrepreneurship in the American corporation*. NY: Simon & Schuster.

Katz, Harry, and Noah Meltz. 1991. Profit sharing and auto workers' earnings: The United States vs. Canada. *Relations Industrielles*, 46(3): 515–530.

Kochan, Thomas, and Paul Osterman. 1994. *The mutual gains enterprise*. Boston, MA: Harvard Business Press.

Koike, Kazuo. 1989. *Understanding industrial relations in modern Japan*. Translated by Mary Saso. New York: St. Martin's Press.

Krafcik, John F. 1986. Learning from NUMMI, Working paper, International Motor Vehicle Program, Massachusetts Institute of Technology, Cambridge, MA.

Kumar, Pradeep, and Dennis Ryan. 1988. "Canadian union movement in the 1980's. Perspectives from union leaders." Kingston Ontario: Industrial Relations Center, Queen's University.

Levine, David, and Laura D'Andrea Tyson. 1990. Participation, productivity, and the firm's environment. In Alan Blinder (ed.), *Paying for productivity*. Washington: The Brookings Institution, pp. 183–244.

MacDuffie, John Paul. 1991. Beyond mass production: Flexible production systems and manufacturing performance in the world auto industry." Dissertation, Sloan School of Management, Massachusetts Institute of Technology, Cambridge, MA.

MacDuffie, John Paul. 1995. Human resource bundles and manufacturing performance: Organizational logic and flexible production systems in the world auto industry. *Industrial and Labor Relations Review*, 48: 197–221.

MacDuffie, John Paul, and Frits K. Pil. 1995. The international assembly plant study: Philosophical and methodological issues." In Steve Babson (ed.), *Lean work: Empowerment and exploitation in the global auto industry*. Detroit, MI: Wayne State University Press, pp. 181–198.

MacDuffie, John Paul, and Frits K. Pil. 1996. Flexible technologies, flexible workers." In Takahiro Fujimoto and Ulrich Jurgens (eds.), *Transforming auto assembly—International experiences with automation and work organization*, Frankfurt: Springer-Verlag, forthcoming.

MacDuffie, John Paul, and Frits K. Pil. 1998. 'High-involvement' work systems and manufacturing performance. Working paper, Department of Management, Wharton School, Philadelphia, PA.

Osterman, Paul. 1995. "How common is workplace transformation and who adopts it?" *Industrial and Labor Relations Review*, 47: 173–87.

Pil, Frits, K. 1996. The international and temporal diffusion of high-involvement work practices. Ph.D. diss., Wharton School.

Pil, Frits, K., and John Paul MacDuffie. 1996. The adoption of high-involvement work practices. *Industrial Relations*, 35(3): 423–455.

Pil, Frits K. and John Paul MacDuffie. (1999). "What makes transplants thrive: Managing the transfer of 'best practices' at Japanese auto plants in North America." *Journal of World Business*; reprinted in extended form as "Transferring competitive advantage across borders: A study of Japanese transplants in North America." In Jeffrey Liker, Mark Fruin, and Paul Adler, *Remade in America: Transplanting and transforming Japanese production systems*, Oxford University Press.

Pil, Frits K., and Saul Rubinstein. 1998. Saturn: A different kind of company? In M. Boyer, S. Tolliday, U. Jurgens, and E. Charron (eds.), *Between imitation and innovation*. Oxford University Press, pp. 361–373.

Turner, Lowell. 1991. Democracy at Work: Changing world markets and the Future of Labour Unions. Ithaca, NY: Cornell University Press.

Womack, James, Daniel Jones, and Daniel Roos. 1990. *The machine that changed the world*. New York: Rawson Associates.

4

Human Resource and Employment Practices in Telecommunications Services, 1980–1998

ROSEMARY BATT
JEFFREY KEEFE

1. Introduction

In the academic literature on manufacturing, much research and debate have focused on whether firms are adopting some form of "high-perfor-mance" or "high-involvement" work organization based on such prac-tices as employee participation, teams, and increased discretion, skills, and training for frontline workers (Ichniowski et al., 1996; Kochan and Osterman, 1994; MacDuffie, 1995). Whereas many firms in the telecom-munications industry flirted with these ideas in the 1980s, they did not prove to be a lasting source of inspiration for the redesign of work and employment practices. Rather, work restructuring in telecommunica-tions services has been driven by the ability of firms to leverage net-work and information technologies to reduce labor costs and create customer segmentation strategies. "Good jobs" versus "bad jobs," or higher versus lower wage jobs, do not vary according to whether firms adopt a high-involvement model. They vary along two other dimensions: (1) within firms and occupations, by the value-added of the customer segment that an employee group serves; and (2) across firms, by union and nonunion status.

We believe that this customer segmentation strategy is becoming a more general model for employment practices in large-scale service operations; telecommunications services firms may be somewhat more advanced than other service firms in adopting this strategy because of certain unique industry characteristics. The scale economies of network technology are such that once a company builds the network infrastruc-ture to a customer's specifications, the cost of additional services is essentially zero. As a result, and notwithstanding technological uncer-tainty, all of the industry's major players are attempting to take advan-tage of system economies inherent in the nature of the product market and technology to provide customized packages of multimedia products to identified market segments. They have organized into market-driven business units providing differentiated services to large businesses and institutions, small businesses, and residential customers. They have used information technologies and process reengineering to customize specific services to different segments according to customer needs and ability to pay. Variation in work and employment practices, or labor market segmentation, follows product market segmentation. As a result, much of the variation in employment practices in this industry is within firms and within occupations according to market segment rather than across firms.

In addition, despite market deregulation beginning in 1984 and opportunities for new entrants, a tightly led oligopoly structure is replacing the regulated Bell System monopoly. Former Bell System companies, the giants of the regulated period, continue to dominate market share in the post-1984 period. Older players and new entrants alike are merging and consolidating in order to have access to multimedia markets. What is striking in this industry, therefore, is the relative lack of variation in management and employment practices across firms after more than a decade of experience with deregulation. We attribute this lack of variation to three major sources. (1) Technological advances and network economics provide incentives for mergers, organizational consolidation, and, as indicated above, similar business strategies. (2) The former Bell System companies have deep institutional ties, and they continue to benchmark against and imitate each other so that ideas about restructuring have diffused quickly among them. (3) Despite overall deunionization in the industry, they continue to have high unionization rates; de facto pattern bargaining within the Bell system has remained quite strong. Therefore, similar employment practices based on inherited collective bargaining agreements continue to exist across former Bell System firms.

There is significant variation across firms, however, based on union and nonunion status. Here, despite downward cost pressures on union standards and the growth of some contingent employment practices in the unionized core, the differences between union and nonunion firms have increased, particularly with respect to compensation practices. To a lesser extent, there is also variation in labor-management relations within the unionized segment.

The remainder of the chapter is divided into five sections. The next section (Section 2) briefly describes the legacy of the Bell System, which is important for understanding the inherited characteristics of the industry that continue to shape current employment practices. Section 3 describes the changes in technology and the problem of network economics that are affecting industry structure and strategy under deregulation; it also provides a powerful explanation of why we see quite similar practices across firms. Section 4 describes current business strategies. The last two sections analyze variation in employment practices within firms (Section 5) and across firms (Section 6). Conclusions follow.

2. The Legacy of the Bell System

As deregulation began in the early 1980s, the industry was dominated by the regulated Bell System monopoly. The Bell System provided virtually all long distance service to the U.S. population, supplied 92% of local service, and accounted for over 90% of the industry's 1.1 million employees. AT&T also owned the world's largest telecommunications equipment manufacturer, Western Electric, with 175,000 employees, and the premier research laboratory, Bell Labs, with 21,000 employees. The remaining work force was based in hundreds of small independent companies in small towns and rural America. Under the court-ordered divestiture of AT&T, Judge Green promoted competition in long distance and equipment markets, but not local service markets. He allocated the long distance and equipment manufacturing businesses to AT&T; he reorganized the 22 local Bell companies into seven regional Bell operating companies (RBOC), which continued to provide local service under monopoly conditions (Temin, 1987).

The inherited telephone network was built under federal and state regulations to realize substantial economies of scale inherent in the telephone network and to achieve universal and ubiquitous telephone service. To achieve that goal, basic telephone service rates were set below cost through an elaborate system of internal cross subsidies. The communications markets that generated the cross subsidies, business equipment leasing, and long distance service, also created strong incentives for new firms to enter. Beginning in 1968, the FCC started down the slippery slope of allowing entry into those markets, which eventually threatened the entire rate structure and put an end to the telephone monopoly, for which AT&T served as national network manager.

The Bell System had also sought to minimize both transactions through vertical integration and marketing costs by offering a standardized regulated service. Under regulation, the Bell System evolved into a public service bureaucracy that defined its universal service obligation according to engineering standards, not to market revenue nor consumer needs. Profits were determined by regulatory review. Regulation provided for a reasonable rate of return on necessary investments and for legitimate costs of operating the system. Engineers and accountants determined what was necessary and legitimate. In 1982, the telephone system delivered a highly standardized and reliable product, Plain Old Telephone Service (known within the industry as POTS), to 92% of all households and all businesses. It was a highly efficient undertaking from a network engineering perspective. All Bell System companies operated under standard AT&T operating procedures with standard AT&T equipment and with collectively bargained contracts that established common human resource (HR) practices for virtually all 725,000 union-eligible employees across the system. AT&T similarly established an HR system for managerial employees that was standardized and created national internal labor markets for these employees.

In the old Bell system, employment practices were uniform within occupational groups but varied across occupations according to the nature of work and technology. There were three occupational groups that were segregated by sex: telephone operators and business office (later called customer service) jobs were female-dominated, whereas network installation, repair, construction, and maintenance were male-dominated (Hacker, 1979). AT&T successfully rationalized and automated the work of operator services early on, displacing the last workers who were directly involved in providing telephone service (Kohl, 1993). With the introduction of direct-dial long distance service in the 1950s, telephone service was completely converted to continuous process industry. Local business office jobs provided women with better jobs and offered customers a broad range of service, billing, repair, and problem-solving services. Women climbed internal job ladders from entry-level clerical and operator jobs to business office and/or management positions. The critical and high-paying jobs, however, were male-dominated plant construction and maintenance, business customer equipment installation and repair, and central office maintenance and repair. With a fourfold increase in demand for telephone service (measured by calling volume), employment in these hard-to-monitor craft jobs (skilled, semiautonomous, geographically dispersed) grew rapidly from 107,000 in 1950 to 275,000 at divestiture.

To manage a skilled labor force in geographically dispersed network and customer service jobs, AT&T developed a quantitative system of performance measurements and expanded the managerial work force to supervise these hard-to-monitor jobs. The managerial work force grew from 13.5% of the Bell system in 1950 to 29.3% in 1980, a ratio of managers to workers of 1:2.4 (Keefe and Boroff, 1994: p. 313).

The Bell work system in 1980 had many of the features of high-performance work systems currently being advocated. For its time, it offered quality service at relatively low cost through state-of-the-art technology. With the exception of operator jobs, which represented less than 11% of the work force in 1980, jobs in network installation and repair were highly skilled, semiautonomous, and problem solving in orientation. The universal customer service jobs (which required considerable skill, responsibility, and problem solving to meet individual customer needs) provided the kind of "one-stop-shopping" that current analysts advocate as the key to quality service (e.g., Schlesinger and Heskett, 1991). Employees frequently knew their customers well, either as neighbors or through repeated transactions; according to surveys, customer satisfaction was high.

Skill and training levels were high. Most entry-level jobs required a high school education; entrance examinations and selection procedures were highly selective; the average educational levels of employees included some postsecondary training; and employees received high levels of company-paid formal training and retraining. The well-developed system of internal job ladders created ongoing opportunities for advancement and lifetime security. Informal training supported continuous learning, as technologies and procedures regularly changed. The broadly defined job classifications provided management with high levels of flexibility, and when coupled with job security, new technologies and productivity improvements were rarely resisted by workers. Job security was part of the social contract, and workers reciprocated with high levels of loyalty, commitment, and obedience.

Telephone jobs were considered public service jobs, and employees took great pride in their work. Employee satisfaction was high, according to surveys of the time. To build commitment to the corporate mission, each employee was indoctrinated into the Bell System's "Spirit of Service." This doctrine rested on a basic commitment to provide every home and business with affordable and reliable telephone service. The "Spirit of Service" ethic became the integrating value among the disparate occupations and the cornerstone of the Bell System's public service ideology. Chester Barnard, the president of New Jersey Bell Telephone, writing in 1938, argued that "the endurance of organization depends upon the breadth of leadership; and that quality derives from the breadth of the morality upon which it rests" (Barnard, 1938: p. 282). The "Spirit of Service" was the moral purpose that integrated the formal and informal structures of the geographically dispersed Bell System and, according to Barnard, created the moral basis for governance by consent, serving as the ideological basis for each employee's commitment to the organization's mission. Supervisors were schooled in human relations techniques, and the company sponsored a variety of programs to integrate employees, their families, and even the union into the company community. Relations between labor and management at the corporate level were also cooperative, although they varied across states, localities, and workplaces. The highly stable demand and guaranteed profits led to a system of promotional ladders and employment security much more stable than that found in most other private sector enterprises.

3. Technology and Industry Consolidation Under Deregulation

Before examining current business strategies and employment practices, it is important to assess the implications of recent changes in technology, product markets, and industry structure for management strategies under deregulation. What is striking in the telecommunications industry is that despite almost two decades of attempts at deregulation, in 1998 the former Bell companies continue to employ over 70% of the industry's work force and comprise most of the dominant players. AT&T still accounts for over one-half of the long distance market, and the regional Bells and GTE provide 95% of wireline local service. Despite the 1996 Telecommunications Act designed to deregulate local service, the Regional Bells continue to act as regulated monopolies. AT&T, the Regional Bells, and GTE supply over 90% of wireless cellular service, although Personal Communications Services (digital wireless) will start off with many more firms in each market.

Moreover, mergers, acquisitions, and joint ventures have accelerated in the 1990s, not only among the former Bell companies, but among new entrants as well. Seven regional Bells are now five after the mergers of Pacific Bell and Southwestern Bell, and NYNEX and Bell Atlantic. SBC (Southwestern Bell) is acquiring Southern New England Telephone, a former Bell affiliate that was fully divested by AT&T in 1984. AT&T's proposed acquisition of Teleport will provide it with immediate local access to many of the largest urban business customers and transforms its position in competitive local access markets almost as dramatically as its earlier acquisition of McCaw Cellular, which overnight made AT&T the nation's largest wireless provider. Upstart WorldCom has transformed itself into a major telecommunications powerhouse through merger and acquisition. Since the AT&T divestiture in 1984, WorldCom has been the only firm to become a major player in the procompetitive telecommunications industry—all other firms (e.g., MCI and Sprint) were already in existence at that time.

WorldCom, formerly LDDS, became the fourth largest long distance carrier through a process of almost continuous merger. It now plans to acquire MCI for $37 billion in stock. Through merger and acquisition, WorldCom became the largest supplier in long distance leased data lines, acquired the second largest local competitive access carrier, MFS, and may come to dominate the Internet backbone with a 60% market share after its acquisition of MCI, the second largest long distance carrier (Keefe, 1998). GTE has grown from a handful of rural telephone companies into the largest provider of local telephone access and major competitor on the Internet with acquisitions, such as BBN, after selling its share of Sprint and its equipment businesses. On the other hand, ITT (formerly International Telephone and Telegraph) has divested or sold all of its telecommunications assets and left the industry.

Small upstarts do play an important role in the industry. They disrupt established practices within narrow market segments; their success in determining new methods, technologies, and approaches to competition is measured by their valuations at acquisition or merger. Failure to establish successful innovations, however, may also be measured in bankruptcy and liquidation. Nevertheless, the core of the industry remains, oligopolistic, and the extent of industry concentration has important implications for the extent of variation in employment practices.

One explanation for this level of industry concentration is an institutional one: The legacy of the Bell System continues to dominate the industry. This would suggest that there is a time lag due to institutional inertia, and that over time the power of institutional forces would erode; for example, as new entrants come into the market and deunionization continues. However, this does not fully explain the abundance of mergers and consolidations among new entrants such as MCI and WorldCom.

Another explanation is that the nature of the product markets and technology provide incentives for merger and consolidation. Bringing competition to the industry has been complicated by the presence of network externalities, scale economies, excess capacity, and technological uncertainty. Networks exhibit positive consumption and production externalities (Economides, 1996). Consumption externalities arise because every communication involves at least two parties, the originator and the receiver. A decision by one person to contact another can generate an uncompensated benefit (or cost) for the contacted party, creating a consumption externality. Production network externalities arise because the private benefit to any one individual of joining a network, as measured by the value he or she places on communicating with others, is less than the social benefits to all other subscribers. Again, the subscription decision creates benefits that are not compensated through the market mechanism. Prices chosen by competitive markets are not economically efficient when externalities are present (Gong and Srinagesh, 1997). Perfect competition will provide a smaller network than is socially optimal (Economides, 1996).

Firms that operate network production processes are subject to economies of scale. They invest in costly communications networks that represent a substantial sunk fixed cost embedded in long-lived facilities with excess capacity. Once the network is constructed, the marginal cost of another communication is essentially zero (Gong and Srinagesh, 1997). The competitive standard that prices be set equal to marginal costs is a recipe for bankruptcy (Baumol and Sidak, 1994). The standard competitive model cannot aid us in making an economic analysis of networks nor can it help regulators or managers in setting prices.

Furthermore, all participants in the industry face substantial technological uncertainty as they build, modernize, and maintain their networks. The inherited publicly switched network faces a substantial challenge from the packet-switched networks used in data transmission and for the Internet. The traditional telephone networks are circuit based, where switched circuits are set up for the duration of a call. This entails an end-to-end circuit being set up to complete each telephone call. By contrast, the Internet uses a connectionless adaptive routing system in which no dedicated end-to-end channel is established for each communication. Instead, traffic is split into "packets" that are routed among multiple points, making the Internet an interconnected global network of packet-switched networks that use the Internet protocol (Werback, 1997). Internet telephony can rely on a seamless connection, where packets are routed on high-speed networks that create for any user the impression of a circuit connection. This, however, provides for a much more efficient utilization of expensive network elements. Congestion on the Internet that causes packets to be lost and concerns about the Internet's reliability, however, still need to be resolved before packet-switched networks become full-fledged challengers to the publicly switched network. Even once these problems are resolved, the transition from a circuit to packet-based network will be lengthy. Internet access currently requires consumers to own a device (computer, terminal, or WebTV) that is considerably more expensive than a telephone set. The difficulty in changing consumers' equipment is reflected in the fact that many consumers still use a rotary dial telephone.

Internet telephony also threatens the public policy commitment to universal service. The Internet operates as an enhanced service and is not required to contribute to access charges nor does it make a direct contribution to the provision of universal service. Even though there is uncertainty about the future of switching technologies, local access technologies are also competing with each other. At divestiture in 1984, all relevant or potential local access technologies were analog. These technologies were provided by the newly formed cellular service companies, the traditional telephone companies supplying wireline service, and potentially by the cable TV coaxial distribution networks. In 1998, each of these access technologies is in the early stages of digital transformation. There are several advantages associated with digitalization. First, because all information is transmitted in bits, the source does not matter; it can be voice, data, facsimile, or video. Second, given the advances in digital compression technologies, substantially more information can be transmitted at higher speeds over the same medium than in the past. Third, there is often less signal distortion in a digital transmission. Finally, digitalization places all transmission media in direct competition with one another. For consumers, this offers many more options, whereas for providers, it creates many more uncertainties. Betting on the wrong media will have dire consequences. The economic advantages and disadvantages among the competing media are ever-changing, which makes forecasting a nightmare, but unavoidable when investing in long-lived network elements.

In sum, the economics of the industry as well as technological uncertainty create incentives for companies to merge, form partnerships, and diversify across competing technologies. These factors, coupled with the legacy of the Bell system, help explain why we see relatively little variation in business strategy and employment practices in this industry, the subjects to which we now turn.

4. Post-Divestiture Business Strategies

Given the continued dominance of the former Bell companies under deregulation and the fact that they enjoyed a highly skilled and committed work force, it would be plausible to think that they would embrace high-commitment HR strategies to compete on quality, service, brand name, and customer loyalty. They were unlikely to match the lower cost structures of new entrants such as MCI (formerly Microwave Communications Inc.) and Sprint in long distance and Teleport and Metro-Fiber Systems in local services. New entrants have lower unit-cost structures because they have little overhead and began with new more maintenance-free technologies. They also have lower labor costs because they start with fewer people per access line, they use nonunion labor with lower wages and benefits, and they have a younger labor force. MCI and Sprint also received support from the FCC in the long distance market by being allowed to charge lower prices and to not pay access charges during the transition period. No company, however, pursued a high-commitment strategy.

4.1. Cost-Cutting and Downsizing Strategies

The cost pressures of competing with real and anticipated new entrants led Regional Bell companies to focus heavily on cost-cutting and across-the-board downsizing, which starting in 1989 became their dominant strategy after they decided to pursue deregulation. AT&T faced competition after divestiture in 1984 and responded by benchmarking itself against its lowest cost competitor. While initially viewed as a temporary strategy, downsizing became an increasingly routine part of business operations for AT&T in the decade following deregulation. AT&T reduced its domestic nonmanagement work force by 60% between 1984 and 1995 (from 250,000 to 100,000). It cut approximately one-third of the management work force.

Over time, three trends emerged. First, increasingly higher percentages of surplused employees were managers. For example, in the first few years following divestiture, roughly one-third of displaced employees were managers. In the January 2, 1996 downsizing announcement, by contrast, 60% of the 40,000 targeted positions were in management. Second, the company began hiring new lower cost employees as it downsized incumbent employees. Third, involuntary rather than voluntary separations represented an increasing proportion of the terminations, with later rounds of downsizing offering employees smaller severance or early retirement packages. In the first two years of post-divestiture operations, for example, AT&T reduced its head count by 56,000 positions; only 25% involved layoffs. The remainder left through attrition, voluntary severance and early retirement programs, transfers within AT&T, or retreats back to the RBOCs. Between 1984 and 1992, 58% of separations in the unionized work force involved layoffs, and 42% involved voluntary separations. In 1996, the company downsizing announcement envisioned that most surpluses would occur through layoffs; however, the company backed away from this approach after considerable media scrutiny and public outcry.

The Regional Bell companies followed the lead of AT&T, but because they retained their regulated monopoly status until 1996, they were able to downsize through attrition in the 1980s. Increased and anticipated competition from local access providers led them to step up downsizing efforts in the 1990s and introduce forced separations for the first time. Overall, the RBOCs reduced the work force in their regulated businesses by 28% between 1984 and 1993. Most of these reductions occurred through attrition or voluntary retirement programs. In anticipation of the 1996 National Telecommunications Act, however, regional Bell companies announced a reduction of another 100,000 in the regulated core, or roughly 20% of the workforce, to take place largely through forced reductions. Many of these proved unnecessary, however, because competition in local services has largely failed to develop by 1999, because growth in the demand for local access lines was grossly underestimated (particularly, second lines for Internet access), because the forecasted rapid transition to a fiber optic local access network proved to be wrong, and because of the economic expansion beginning in 1991.

4.2. Network Investment Strategies

Even though Bell companies downsized their work force, they invested in their networks, as did the new entrants. At divestiture, AT&T owned the only complete long-distance network. MCI and Sprint were able to gain market share by reselling AT&T service at substantially lower prices during the transition period. They each built digital networks and actively courted large business customers, who needed high-speed data networks, whereas AT&T remained committed to its analog network with all its sunk cost. AT&T quickly lost some of its most lucrative business customers, who switched to MCI and Sprint. AT&T then aggressively depreciated its embedded network, incurring substantial restructuring charges, in order to convert to a fully digital network by 1991.

The Regional Bells have also been concerned that their embedded analog network might constitute a barrier to effectively competing in lucrative local access markets. They have aggressively depreciated their analog network based on twisted-pair copper access lines. By the mid-1990s, most companies had replaced all of their network (trunk) cable with fiber optic, and they use fiber optic to serve large business customers and on a very limited basis as residential feeder cable; however, 92% of the cable (which links switches to customer premise) remains traditional twisted-pair analog access lines. By 1996, further conversion had stalled because of technical problems, market uncertainty, and advances in digital transmission technology that would allow the companies to provide digital access on existing twisted-pair access lines.

4.3. Market Organization and Customer Segmentation

In addition to force reductions and technology investments, a central concern of top management in the Bell companies has been to turn their engineering bureaucracies into market-oriented enterprises. As with cost cutting and technology strategies, AT&T was the first to move; the RBOCs and GTE in turn adopted similar market strategies, but with some lag time. Whereas AT&T began changes in strategy and organizational structure in the mid-1980s, the Bell companies began in earnest in the late 1980s and early 1990s. AT&T embraced total quality management in the mid-1980s, the Bell companies did so three to five years later. AT&T embraced customer segmentation, separate lines of business organization, and reengineering in the late 1980s; the Bell companies and GTE followed in the early 1990s. In response to market deregulation, therefore, the business and organizational strategies of the former Bell companies have been more similar than different, varying in emphasis or timing rather than in substance.

Table 4.1 compares the system of markets, business strategy, and management organization under the pre- and postderegulation rules. Whereas in the past, companies geared their strategy and structure to state and federal regulators, they now respond to shareholders and segmented consumer markets. The RBOCs pushed legislative reforms on a state-by-state basis to shift pricing mechanisms from fixed-rate to incentive-based systems; the latter allow companies to keep a greater share of the gains from cost cutting and productivity improvements, provided they meet service standards. The availability of new digital broadband wireline and wireless technologies gives companies an increasing capability to shift from one standardized product (voice communication) over an analog system to providing a variety of products (including voice, enhanced features such as call waiting, voice messaging, data, video, and imaging) over a single network. The 1996 Telecommunications Act furthers this process by eventually collapsing industry boundaries and allowing companies to use the new technologies to provide long distance, local, cable, data, and other services to their customers. Consumer demand also favors service integration. Two-thirds of consumers in a recent poll said that they wanted their local and long dis-

Table 4.1. Telecommunications Services: Business Strategy and Structure

Components	Old System	New System
Capital market	Regulated by FCC, State PSCs: Bonds and bond-like stocks Stable rate of return 11% to 13%	Partially regulated: Growth stocks Rate of return 18% since 1984
Pricing mechanism	Regulated: Cost plus return Cross-subsidized: (long distance to local) (business to residence)	Partially regulated: "incentive-based" "cost-based" to promote competition
Product market	Standardized: analog, voice, and data	Differentiated: digital, voice, data, video, image
Technology	Cable twisted-pair copper cable, electrical analog signal, and T-Carrier digital radio transmission; electronic and electromechanical switching	Cable twisted-pair copper cable, fiber optic cable with digital multiplexed light transmission; digital circuit and packet switching, digital wireless and wireline access.
Competitive advantage	Low-cost, substantial scale economies, and labor productivity growth over 6% annually	Scale economies, declining costs, high reliability, customer service, brand name identification, and marketing promotions
Business strategy	Universal public service, "engineering driven"	Segment service markets, "market driven"
Mission	"Service is our moral purpose"	Enhance shareholder value
Employment contract	Lifetime employment, loyalty	Employability, be prepared to move
Labor relations	Union workplaces set employment standards	Nonunion workplaces set employment standards
Management structure	Vertical command and control Lifetime bell managers Stable bureaucratic–centralized	Lean bureaucracy experts and organizational professionals Market-driven–centralized

tance needs met by one provider (J.D. Power and Associates, 1996). Once a provider establishes a line to a consumer, the marginal costs of providing additional services are minimal. In sum, consumer demand, on the one hand, and the logic of network technology, on the other, call for the consolidation, centralization, and integration of service delivery systems, the opposite of what was advocated at divestiture (Temin, 1987).

With respect to customer segmentation strategies, all of the major players (former Bell companies, independents, and new entrants) are attempting to develop the most cost-effective ways to provide customized packages of information services, particularly to higher end business and residential consumers. All players seek to compete on cost, quality, and customer service by taking advantage of network system economies and becoming single-source providers of all information services to these customers. To do so, they have adopted segmented marketing strategies that differentiate customers by value-added, ranging from high value-added corporate clients to various business segments to differentiation among lower-value-added residential consumers as well. In addition, there are ongoing efforts to package particular sets of enhanced services to different commercial clients, according to the particular demand characteristics of industries, occupations, or other niches. Each is also investing billions of dollars in trying to differentiate their highly standardized network service offerings by building brand names. To support segmentation strategies, most companies have organized themselves away from state-based organizations to market-focused, line-of-business organizations. Customer-focused organizations combine sales, marketing, and service functions and incorporate streamlined support functions such as HR. Network Services, because of the "systemness" of the infrastructure, function as regional (or national in the case of AT&T and GTE) internal suppliers to the marketing organizations.

4.4. Reengineering and
Organizational Consolidation

Most major players have used advanced information systems and process reengineering to support their market segmentation strategies, at the same time reducing costs. Advanced information systems allow companies to consolidate operations into large remote service centers, each dedicated to a particular clientele; process reengineering automates many service functions, so that telephone service may be turned on remotely without the help of field technicians on the ground. Reengineered information systems also allow remote diagnosis and repair of services. Overhead and direct labor costs fall and customer response time improves. After reengineering at GTE (see appendix), for example, the percentage of residential phone orders that are automatically established doubled, from 33 to 61%. Given these anticipated improvements in service and scale economies, most major telecommunications carriers undertook multimillion dollar reengineering projects, some more successful than others. It should be noted that MCI and other new entrants also undertook reengineering projects because of the rapid changes in information technologies and associated gains from scale economies.

The most dramatic examples of consolidation occurred at AT&T and GTE—both of which faced an early challenge of creating standardized customer service and network organizations to serve national markets. By the early 1990s, for example, AT&T had consolidated hundreds of customer service bureaus into six national mega-centers. It reduced the number of network operations centers to two. AT&T currently operates one operations center to serve the eastern United States and one center to run its network west of the Mississippi. Similarly, GTE, historically composed of 22 small independent telephone companies spread across the country, initiated a massive consolidation effort in 1993–1996; it consolidated 258 local worksites into 58 regionally based service centers and has built a single network operations center in Dallas. Regional Bell companies have undertaken similar consolidation strategies, but at the regional level: they have dissolved their state-level telephone companies and reorganized them into regional corporate entities, with external facing market-based lines of business and a single network operations division. Each line of business has consolidated local business offices and network operations centers into regional mega-centers. Between 1993 and 1996, for example, US West consolidated hundreds of local customer service offices in its 14-state region into two large business centers, 12 small business centers, and 12 residential offices.

5. Variation in Employment Practices Within Firms

Powerful new information technologies, coupled with reengineering strategies, therefore, have driven organizational change within former Bell companies as well as among new entrants. HR and employment strategies in the post-divestiture period have been derivative of technology and reengineering strategies. The potential of reengineering, however, varies by product complexity and customer segment. It has been most successfully applied to simple transactions, such as orders for basic residential phone service. Business and more complex orders are less amenable to automation. This variation in product complexity and the capacity of information technologies is the source of variation in employment practices across customer segments.

5.1. Matching Customer Segments to Labor Market Segments

Unlike the past, when business office employees handled a wide variety of customers and types of inquiries, now service representatives are divided into residential, small business, and large business representatives. Job functions are further divided into sales and service, billing, collections, and repair services. Job fragmentation has been more extensive at AT&T than at the RBOCs. Comparing the 1984 and 1995 contracts between AT&T and the Communications Workers of America (CWA), for example, the number of wage grades for office workers doubled, from 11 in 1984 to 26 in 1996; the number of job titles (in grades) tripled, from a total of 53 to 149.

A major task of each company has been to transform their customer service operations into aggressive marketing organizations. The nature of the transformation depends on the market segment served by the center. A typical *residential* call center houses between 500 and 1,000 customer service representatives (CSR), each of whom handles 90–100 customers per day at a call cycle time of about 3–5 minutes. CSRs complete transactions with customers on-line and are discouraged from interacting with fellow employees. As soon as one call ends, an automatic call distribution (ACD) automatically sends another customer call to the "open" representative. Many of the interactions with customers are scripted by expert systems. Selling opportunities are prompted by the system software. CSRs need to master the art of sincere and authentic customer interactions while largely reading from a scripted text. In most companies, CSRs are supposed to have at least one-half hour per day of "closed time" away from the computer to finish up orders; but when call loads are heavy, closed time is often eliminated.

Managers and union representatives alike agree that residential CSR jobs are the most stressful ones in the industry—higher than the short-cycle, highly demanding telephone operator jobs—because of intense pressure to simultaneously sell, to provide "quality" service, and to turn over calls, all in the context of pervasive electronic monitoring. Monitoring and discipline occur through electronic monitoring, which both records the content of customer-employee interaction and the time that employees spend in each type of work activity: on-line open to receive a customer, on-line with a customer, on hold with a customer (e.g., checking information or completing an order), closed (completing paper work, going to the restroom or lunch, etc.). Company-developed algorithms provide guidelines for the amount of time allowable in each type of activity; managers at a central control panel watch for flashing lights (green, blue, red, etc.) that indicate if an employee has gone beyond the allotted time in any one area. Supervisors then use their discretion to counsel and/or discipline employees who are at variance with the targeted time allotments or schedule (known as "out of adherence"). Bell companies have universally adopted policies to enforce 90% "adherence" to schedules. If CSRs are late in taking their breaks because they are handling a customer call, they must go to their supervisor to get special approval. In some residential service centers, CSRs must raise their hands and request a supervisor's permission to take a rest room break. The electronic monitoring system times rest room breaks, and those that fall outside of adherence standards are a subject to disciplinary action. Recently, Excel, a highly competitive reseller of telecommunications services, has set even more stringent standards for performance with a lower compensation structure. The company supplements this approach with an Amway-type sales scheme, where sales representatives recruit family and friends, not only as customers, but as commissioned part-time sales agents for Excel. AT&T and other major companies now have subcontracts with Excel.

Call centers for *small business* representatives generally house 100–200 employees, and business reps handle approximately 30 customers per day. Because their orders are somewhat complex, they cannot be handled on-line with the customer on hold. Rather, the business representative takes down the information and enters some of it into a computerized database, but spends considerable time off the telephone completing the order. More-complex order entry may also be handed-off to another employee. The pace in small business centers varies; however, they still tend to be fairly reasonable, and representatives freely consult with each other to solve nonroutine problems or to get advice on how to handle a customer.

For *large business and institutional accounts*, companies hire college-educated account executives who are supposed to provide "one-stop shopping" to corporate clients. These sales people are either on purely commission pay plans or compensation plans based on salary plus commission pay, depending on the customer and market segment. There are several levels of account executives, which vary by client type and client load. But what matters is their ability to sell. They provide customized and personalized service through on-site and electronic exchanges and usually rely on additional support staff and CSRs to handle the mechanics of orders and service requests. The former internal career ladders in female-dominated jobs have been broken up somewhat: residential, small-business, and large business offices in the same company are often located in different cities; residential reps may move to small business centers, but further advancement usually depends on getting a college degree and having the demonstrated ability to sell.

In operator services, MCI has set the standards. In response to MCI's successful entry in the consumer market, in 1992, AT&T massively reengineered its Consumer Services business unit, which had just won the Malcolm Baldrige Award for quality. In order to compete with MCI's highly successful "Friends and Family" marketing program, AT&T decided that the business unit needed to cut several hundred million dollars in costs. A major target for cost reduction was operator services, which assisted customers in call completion. MCI had hired an internal facilities manager, First Data Corporation, a subsidiary of American Express, to run its operator services. MCI then laid off all its operators, who were offered jobs at $5 to $6 an hour, without benefits, to work for First Data.

AT&T estimated that it paid an average operator $12.83 an hour plus an additional $8 an hour in benefits. Although AT&T operators were 20% more productive and had a 50% lower error rate in call completion, it was unable to compensate for MCI's 70% lower labor costs. Hard bargaining ensued between the unions and the company. The result was an new part-time job title, paying $7 per hour with limited benefits, while retaining the full-time title, rate, and benefits. A new low standard was set: lower compensation, lower productivity, and lower quality, which all translated into substantially lower operating costs. Within a year, 70% of the operators were part-time. This occurred as a result of the simultaneous consolidation of operator services into mega-centers. Traditional operators were forced to geographically relocate, to follow their work into the mega-centers, or lose their jobs. Most chose to leave; less than 30% were retained. This two-tier approach had spillover effects for operator services in 1995 bargaining at the regional Bells, several of whom have followed the pattern.

5.2. Network Occupations

In contrast to the market-driven service and sales organizations, network operations have simplified their occupational structure by moving toward single top craft occupations that are organized by functional activity, such as outside plant technician or central office technician. The single-title concept, however, should not be confused with the concept of the fully cross-trained worker; virtually no technicians are fully cross trained. Although technicians carry the same title and pay, they do not perform the same work. New technologies and new organizational structures have given rise to new subspecialties. The single title gives operations management the flexibility from each company's HR bureaucracy to rapidly redeploy the work force according to changes in technology and in the demand for network services, without testing, job posting, or job bidding. Some operations management groups have also created their own training organizations to facilitate this mobility without relying on corporate HRs.

Technical work involving customer premise service and equipment, however, does follow the model where market segmentation leads to occupational segmentation. For example, Bell Atlantic bargained a new second-tier unionized subsidiary in 1995, Bell Atlantic Communications and Construction Services Incorporated (BACCSI). BACCSI technicians perform work, earning 50% of top craft compensation, work that was formerly done by Bell Atlantic Network Operations Installation and Repair Technicians, who earned 90% of top craft compensation. The BACCSI technicians compete directly with nonunion electricians for inside wire work. (Since divestiture, Bell Atlantic has lost 80% of the residential inside wire work to nonunion contractors.) Most of the former Installation and Repair Technicians have been promoted to top craft to work on cable and network modernization. During its first two years of operation, BACCSI hired and trained over 1,500 technicians. These workers are expected to home-garage their company vehicle and report directly to their first job by their starting time each morning. The workers drive their company vehicle both to and from work; however, they are not allowed to use the vehicle for personal business and are responsible for the vehicle at all times. Their day starts when they report to their first job at 8 A.M., which means their travel time to their first job and from their last job is uncompensated. In the first two years of operations, some 500 BACCSI technicians in New Jersey have received transfers to work for Bell Atlantic Network Operations as "core" technicians at the top union wage scale.

In contrast to residential customers, large business customers are serviced by "enhanced crews" of highly trained top craft cable splicers and special services technicians, who work on fiber optics, multiplexors, subscriber loop carrier systems (SLCS; pronounced "slick") and other advanced loop electronics. Market segmentation now means that a customer can receive service from technicians who are compensated at a 2:1 ratio (greater with overtime) and are trained in 3 weeks versus 3 to 5 years of combined school and on-the-job learning. At the customer's request, the market segment determines the technician and his or her level of training and compensation.

The variance in technician skill, training, and compensation has expanded through the use of two-tier agreements, which have been supplemented with the use of contractors and contract labor. Some contractors recruit former Bell employees who took early retirement and receive Bell company-provided pensions and benefits for their labor force. They gain a cost advantage by not having to pay benefits. Other contractors follow the low-cost cable TV model: Some recruit workers who cannot pass drug and alcohol screens, aptitude or ability tests, background checks, or training regimens at any of the incumbent firms. These contractors gain an advantage by paying low wages for work that hopefully requires low reliability.

Throughout the industry, but particularly in residential service markets, firms, as they compete to match or lower labor costs, are testing new lower cost compensation packages and are recruiting workers who previously were not considered employable in the telephone industry. At the other end of the market, large business customers are increasingly served by sales and technical professionals who are no longer the product of an enterprise-internal labor market, but are college-educated professionals who are directly hired into their functional specialty.

5.3. Variation in Employment Practices by Occupation, Race, and Sex

Even though variation within occupations has grown, variation across occupations has in some ways diminished. Companies have reduced management hierarchies to some extent and have replaced front line supervisors with monitoring through the use of information systems. The electronic monitoring that was initially introduced into operator services is now uniformly applied to customer services. Electronic monitoring of field technicians also occurs through the widespread use of handheld computers through which job completion reports and task assignments are made. Consequently, many workplaces have less direct supervision, but more systematic managerial control (Vallas, 1993). Managerial control, however, has changed form; it has become less personal, but more constant, and more amenable to management by numbers.

Another striking trend is that variation in employment practices by gender and race occupational segregation has declined. This issue is important in this industry because AT&T became the most significant target of federal enforcement of equal employment statutes in the 1970s (Wallace, 1976). In 1970, the Equal Employment Opportunity Commission (EEOC) and several civil rights organizations sought to intervene in an AT&T rate case brought before the Federal Communications Commission (FCC). After two years of administrative hearings and negotiations between AT&T and the federal government, represented by the EEOC, the Justice Department, and the Labor Department, an EEO Consent Decree was approved on January 18, 1973 by the United States District Court in Philadelphia. The Decree provided for a six-year program to restructure the AT&T personnel system. Women comprised the majority of the nonmanagement, union-eligible work force in the Bell System. Until 1970, occupations in the Bell System were sex segregated. Table 4.2 reports the trends in AT&T employment between 1950 and 1980. During this period, as discussed above, the expansion of telephone service resulted in a steady growth of the telephone crafts and management, a relative decline in the female nonmanagement work force, and a dramatic decrease in the number of operators.

The EEOC demonstrated that sex discrimination was the fundamental organizing principle for the Bell System's personnel system. The EEOC found that 92% of all Bell System employees worked in sex-

Table 4.2. AT&T's Employment Distribution by Occupation and Gender, 1950–1980

	1950	1960	1970	1980
AT&T Employment	602,466	735,766	1,005,380	1,044,041
Bell System	523,251	580,405	772,980	847,768
Western Electric	73,458	143,352	215,380	174,372
Bell Labs	5,757	12,009	17,020	21,901
Bell System Employment				
Bell System management	70,630	105,833	169,401	248,562
Percentage of total (%)	13	18	22	29
Bell System nonmanagement	446,129	466,795	574,534	589,939
Plant craft forces (%)	24	30	35	44
Traffic operators (%)	47	34	29	16
Office, clerical (%)	19	23	24	10
Other (%)	10	12	12	31
AT&T Female Employment				
AT&T: Women	363,363	378,070	503,728	517,439
Percentage of AT&T Total (%)	60	51	50	50
Bell System: Women	340,504	331,780	425,428	443,819
Women as percentage of total (%)	65	57	55	52
Women in management	23,266	34,084	56,749	95,739
Women in nonmanagement	310,998	290,914	341,989	339,369
Percentage of management (%)	33	32	33	39
Percentage of nonmanagement (%)	70	62	60	58
Women as a percentage of:				
Plant craft forces (%)	0	0	1	23
Traffic operators (%)	100	100	93	90
Office, clerical (%)	92	93	93	93
Other (%)	54	52	64	79
Average age (years)	30	34	33	37
Average service (years)	9	11	9	12
Annual turnover (%)	19	20	27	n.a.

Source: Bell System Statistical Manual, 1950–1980. June 1982, AT&T Comptroller's Office. (NY: AT&T)

segregated jobs (using a standard of 90% of the occupation being of one sex to determine sex segregation). To break down gender segregation, the EEO Consent Decree contained an Affirmative Action Override. If it was necessary in order to meet the Decree's goals and timetables, the Override permitted the company to bypass seniority and the well-established trainability standards for identifying the best qualified candidate and select a candidate from the pool of basically qualified applicants. By 1979, AT&T showed significant improvements and was released from the court order (Northrup, 1979). With the downsizing and displacement over 15 years, however, it is important to revisit the question of how downsizing strategies affect work force diversity. Surprisingly, industry-wide data from the EEOC show that women and minority employees have continued to gain employment in higher skilled and paid occupations, as indicated in Table 4.3. Occupational segregation by race and gender has continued to decline. Women have increased their relative representation in higher paid and traditionally white male occupations: craft, sales, professional, and managerial—but not technical—occupations. In 1995, women composed 40% of managers, 38% of professionals, 21% of technical employees, and 15% of craft workers. This pattern is particularly striking, given the 38% fall in the overall number of skilled craft jobs and the slight fall in managerial jobs. Minority representation in all occupations increased.

6. Variation in Employment Practices Across Firms

In the last section, we analyzed the dominant trends in business strategy and work organization in the industry and argued that there is relatively little variation in these practices across firms in the industry. There is more variation, however, with respect to specific employment practices. In this section, we explore differences among unionized firms and between union and nonunion firms with respect to union relations, compensation practices, training, and employment security systems.

6.1. Deunionization and Union Density

Despite only partial deregulation of the industry between 1983 and 1996, union density fell significantly from 55.5% of the total work force to 28.7% over the period. Among clerical and sales workers, union density fell from 63 to 35%, and among technical workers it fell from 68 to 52%. Deunionization occurred primarily because the traditional unionized companies cut labor costs by reducing employment levels rather than wages. At the same time, employment grew among new, nonunion firms. Deunionization was higher among clerical and sales workers, presumably because nonunion jobs expanded more quickly in these areas. (Most nonunion new entrants leased the use of the Bell network rather than build and maintain their own.) The rate of deunionization also accelerated: Over two-thirds of the decline occurred between 1990 and 1996 (see Table 4.4). Newer entrants, such as MCI and Sprint, and cable TV giants, such as TCI, have fiercely fought union drives in their facilities. For example, Sprint closed a San Francisco call center after workers began an organizing campaign; Sprint's action was found by the National Labor Relations Board to be in violation of labor laws.

Deunionization is also occurring among the Bell Companies in three ways: They have redefined traditional bargaining unit titles as managerial and exempt from labor laws; they have created unregulated "enterprise units" to handle wireless and other activities; and they have

Table 4.3. Change in Diversity, by Occupation: Telecommunications Services, 1982–1995

Occup. Group	Total # 1982	Occupation as % of 1982 Total	% Female 1982	% Min. 1982	Total # 1995	Occupation as % of 1995 Total	% Female 1995	% Min. 1995	% Change Occup.	% Change % Female	% Change % Min.
Manager	223,120	20.51	37.26	11.13	136,944	17.08	40.42	16.90	-38.62	8.48	51.86
Prof.	68,871	6.33	30.97	12.23	103,298	12.88	38.48	19.82	49.99	24.24	62.09
Technical	24,538	2.26	26.25	11.97	53,868	6.72	21.24	17.88	119.53	-19.1	49.33
Sales	26,169	2.41	55.08	16.46	66,280	8.26	59.83	29.08	153.28	8.62	76.7
Clerical	430,410	39.56	88.66	26.04	260,415	32.47	84.05	34.47	-39.5	-5.2	32.36
Craft	262,484	24.13	8.59	12.3	149,611	18.66	15.11	17.87	-43.0	75.86	45.31
Operative	40,435	3.72	52.75	26.77	25,963	3.24	51.01	33.73	-35.79	-3.3	25.99
Labor	4,700	0.43	36.09	17.23	899	0.11	16.57	25.70	-80.87	-54.08	49.13
Service	7,261	0.67	41.07	38.04	4,697	0.59	60.17	50.31	-35.31	46.5	32.25
Total	1,087,988	100.00	51.06	18.32	801,975	100.00	50.36	24.99	-26.29	-1.37	36.41

Source: EEOC data, 1982–1995.

Table 4.4. Deunionization and Union/Non-union Wage Inequality, by Occupational Group: Telecommunications Industry, 1983–1996

	1983	1996	Change (%)		
			1983–1990	1990–1996	1983–1996
Clerical & Sales Workers					
Total employment	450,755	388,655	−5.0	−8.7	−13.8
Percentage union (%)	62.6	34.5	−14.1	−30.9	−44.9
Median weekly earnings					
Union	$360	$553	32.5	21.1	53.6
Non-union	$380	$480	23.7	2.6	26.3
Real median weekly earnings*					
Union	$361	$352	1.0	−3.5	−2.5
Non-union	$382	$306	−5.7	−14.1	−19.8
Ratio: Union/nonunion median weekly earnings	0.95	1.15	7.1	14.5	21.6
Technical Workers					
Total employment	374,400	294,359	−8.9	−12.4	−21.4
Percentage union (%)	67.5	51.7	−4.4	−18.9	−23.3
Median weekly earnings					
Union	$486	$772	31.7	27.2	58.8
Non-union	$500	$694	28.0	10.8	38.8
Real median weekly earnings*					
Union	$488	$492	0.4	0.5	0.8
Non-union	$502	$442	−2.5	−9.4	−11.9
Ratio: Union/nonunion median weekly earnings	0.97	1.11	2.9	11.6	14.4

Source: CPS merged annual earnings files; * CPI-U adjusted (Batt and Strausser 1997).

acquired nonunion subsidiaries. AT&T has been the most aggressive in pursuing a deunionization strategy, transforming itself from a predominantly unionized employer (67% organized) into a nonunion employer (42% organized in the United States). For example, by 1994, over 50% of AT&T employees were classified as either managerial or supervisory (and not eligible for union membership), compared with 29% in 1984. In addition, when downsizing the unionized core, it developed two nonunion subsidiaries, American Transtech, the largest U.S. telemarketing service, and AT&T Universal Card, the second largest credit card company. It also acquired two nonunion equipment manufacturers: Paradyne (data communications equipment) and National Cash Register (NCR). NCR, the sixth largest computer company, with 1,300 locations in 130 countries, was subsequently spun off at trivestiture in 1996. The RBOCs, by contrast, continue to have over 60% of the work force unionized.

6.2. Union Relations and
Labor-Management Partnerships

Overall, union–management relations in the former Bell companies went from cooperative prior to divestiture to highly adversarial after 1984, but the degree of conflict has been greater in some companies than in others. The most aggressive corporate labor relations strategies emanated from AT&T and NYNEX in the 1980s and Bell Atlantic in the 1990s. NYNEX subsequently sued for labor peace and in 1992 negotiated neutrality and card-check recognition that apply in all nonunion NYNEX entities. Even though companies have signed a variety of neutrality agreements, it remains legally unclear how binding any of these agreements are on their nonunion subsidiaries.

The most sustained joint union–management productivity pacts emerged in companies located in right-to-work states having a mature collective-bargaining relationship and unions facing weak labor laws: BellSouth with CWA District 3 and US West with CWA District 7. CWA District 3 has a long history of a mature bargaining relationship with BellSouth. Unlike other companies, following divestiture it immediately agreed to bargain with the union on a regional, rather than local basis. It agreed without a fight to recognize the union as a newly created enterprise unit, and it agreed to joint study committees to assess the content of jobs and return inappropriately defined "managerial" jobs to the bargaining unit; 500 such jobs were returned to the union by the end of the 1980s. Based on the experience of the 1980 Quality of Worklife Programs (QWL), the union and company also agreed to jointly sponsor a Total Quality Management (TQM) program in the late 1980s and early 1990s. In the early 1990s, they formalized union participation in monthly business meetings and set up a three-tiered joint structure for union-management collaboration to improve quality. The parties also negotiated the parameters for local experimentation in a range of workplace innovations, including telecommuting, self-managed teams, and bringing work back into the bargaining unit that was historically subcontracted. The company funded pairs of union and management trainers to assist local managers and workers with workplace initiatives in order to improve quality.

The initial results were impressive. A 1994 survey of lower and middle-level managers and local union presidents found that 92% of managers and 81% of local presidents supported the union's participation in total quality as a competitive strategy for improving service quality, maintaining BellSouth's loyal customer base, and saving jobs. Seventy-seven percent of managers and 77% of union presidents believed that union participation was critical to the success of TQM. Ninety-seven percent of local union presidents were participating in monthly business meetings, and 32% were participating in weekly management staff meetings. Similarly, 90% of workers believed the union should participate in total quality, and 60% believed union participation was critical to the program's success. Twelve percent of workers in network and customer services had actually participated in total-quality problem-solving groups, and 5% of workers in core occupations were participating in self-managed teams. Quantitative evaluation comparing performance of self-managed teams and traditionally supervised work groups showed significant positive effects of teams for the company, workers, and the union: Performance of teams was significantly higher, indirect labor costs fell, workers preferred the arrangements, and nonmanagement jobs were saved at the expense of management jobs. The union also supported the company in going before state Public Utility Commissions (PUCs) to gain regulatory reforms that would shift rate regulation from fixed to incentive-based systems, a shift that allowed the company to keep some of the profits from efficiency gains (Batt, 1995, 1996).

US West and CWA District 7 devised a similar joint strategy in the late 1980s. In the 1989 contract, the company agreed to a $10 million fund to support pairs of management and union representatives to work as "change agents" with local managers and workers to improve labor relations and initiate process improvements. A two-year (1992–1993) jointly sponsored job-redesign team developed a complete redesign for the 5,000 customer service representatives in the company—from a functionally specialized position to a "universal" one with a broad set of functions and responsibilities (U.S. Congress, 1993).

In the case of AT&T, the newly created business unit structure became a vehicle for differentiated labor relations strategies within the company: one seeking collaboration and high-performance teams among highly skilled technical workers and another aggressively cutting costs and downsizing among low-skilled occupations (e.g., operator services). AT&T's much-publicized "Workplace of the Future," negotiated with the CWA and International Brotherhood of Electrical Workers (IBEW) in 1992, was an attempt to improve union-management relations after a decade of job loss. The Workplace of the Future agreement created a four-tiered structure for union participation in workplace innovations at the work unit, divisional, business unit, and corporate levels. As of 1996, however, successful implementation of Workplace of the Future had occurred only in Network Services, where the union has considerable bargaining power based on the critical role of the skilled work force in maintaining the network infrastructure. In the business units, where the union is weak or the skills of the labor force less critical, union participation in business decision making often has been ephemeral or limited to post–decision-making consultation.

NYNEX and Bell Atlantic have experienced the most adversarial labor relations in the post-divestiture period and virtually no jointly sponsored employee participation or job redesign efforts. At NYNEX, a bitter 1989 strike led the company to rethink its labor relations strategy and attempt to build a more positive bargaining relationship in the 1990s. Although it achieved considerable success in doing this, as we will describe in more detail, the better relations have not led to any labor-management partnerships with respect to work reorganization and performance improvement. Rather, until 1996, when the regional leadership changed, district leaders explicitly told local leaders not to become involved in participation or total quality programs; only a handful of renegade locals acted against regional policy. Instead, the union's strategy was a traditional one of "effects bargaining," augmented by internal membership mobilizations in combination with considerable external political and public relations pressure on the company. The result was the most far-reaching retraining, transfer, and employment security system in the industry. In the same 1994 agreement, CWA District 1 in New York surrendered its ability to fight the company on rate reform, where it repeatedly went before the state Public Service Commission (PSC) to complain of NYNEX's business practices and poor service quality. New York Telephone was ordered to hire 1,000 new employees as a condition of the PUCs support of its merger with Bell Atlantic in order to address chronic service problems formerly highlighted by the union.

In the Bell Atlantic case, top management unilaterally introduced quality programs and a culture change program, known as "The Bell Atlantic Way," both of which largely failed to accomplish stated objectives. In the 1990s the company became the most aggressive of the RBOCs in demanding wage and benefit concessions from the unions without being willing to offer much in terms of employment or union institutional security. Its aggressive 1995 contract concession strategy ultimately led to six months of union–management hostility and negative publicity. Workers reported high levels of acrimony at work and particularly resented unilaterally imposed policies of forced overtime. The state PUCs investigated service quality during this period, found repeated violations of service standards, and ordered the company to hire an additional 500 customer service representatives among other measures. The union conducted a highly effective corporate campaign targeting Bell Atlantic as Heartless (Not the "Heart of Communications") as its commercials claim. In December 1995, the CWA began to air an ad on television about Larry, the slob of a contractor who could be sent to your house as a Bell Atlantic contractor. The ad was an immediate success; customers who needed new installations or repairs emphasized that they did not want Larry. In this one instance, Bell Atlantic's need to establish its brand name gave the CWA some leverage with the public. Shortly after Larry appeared, the contract was settled.

Even though variation in union-management relations and the use of participation programs existed through the early 1990s, however, even the RBOCs with exemplary joint programs gave way to cost pressures in anticipation of local market deregulation. In 1992, US West retreated from the strong contract language of "partnership" that it had negotiated in the 1989 contract and did away with its joint "change agent" teams. By the end of 1993, it suspended its joint job redesign team in customer services, stating that it was undertaking a massive reengineering project instead (U.S. Congress, 1993). Similarly, BellSouth and CWA District 3 agreed to virtually dismantle the joint quality program in 1995 bargaining.

6.3. Compensation Strategies

Several trends in compensation strategies stand out in the post-divestiture period. First, the Bell companies and unions have negotiated wage increases that basically track the consumer price index. In fact, between 1986 and 1994, in successive rounds of bargaining, across-the-board wage increases rose as a percentage of base pay. Second, despite the fact that collective bargaining was decentralized to the enterprise level (AT&T, regional Bells, and in some cases, local telephone companies), Bell companies continued to offer wages and benefits that formed a pattern (Cappelli and Perry, 1986, 1988; Keefe and Batt, 1997). This pattern continues through the 1990s, with few exceptions. Third, and perhaps most important, the union/nonunion wage gap was fairly small until 1990 but grew significantly between 1990 and 1996. Finally, the downward pressure of the union/nonunion compensation differential has led AT&T and the RBOCs to seek reductions in health care costs and to introduce various forms of contingent pay.

Tables 4.5, 4.6, and 4.7 compare negotiated wage raises, cost-of-living adjustments, and contingent pay strategies among AT&T and the regional Bell companies. The post-divestiture trend shows a steady increase in each successive contract. Across-the-board wage increases averaged 2.78% between 1986 and 1994, but they rose on average from 2.2% in 1986 to 3.3% in 1994. Slight variation in the pattern exists among the Bell companies, with BellSouth consistently negotiating the lowest annual increases (averaging 2% annually) and AT&T negotiating the highest (3.2% on average). Previously negotiated cost-of-living-adjustments were either restricted, suspended, or eliminated in all companies over the course of the decade. In 1995 bargaining, the patterned wage bargaining continued, with base wage increases of either 10.9% or 11% in each contract.

Each company also pursued some form of contingent pay based on business performance, including profit sharing, team awards, and success sharing, which is either linked to increases in stock prices or is a stock award. The unions resisted contingent pay methods in negotiations, treating them as company add-ons outside of the basic economic package. The firmness of union resistance to contingent pay, however, var-

Table 4.5. Post-Divestiture Base Wage Increases in %

Company	1986	1987	1988	1989	1990	1991	1992	1993	1994	1995	1996	1997	Ave
AT&T	2	3	3	4	2.5	2.5	4	3.9	3.9	3.6	3.5	3.4	3.3
Ameritech	2	2	2	2	2.5	3	3.5	3.5	3.5	3.5	3.5	3.5	2.9
Bell Atlantic	2	3	3	3	2.3	2.3	4	3.7	4	3.5	4	3.5	3.2
Bell South	2	1.5	1.5	4	1	1	4	1.7	1.7	3.6	3.5	3.4	2.4
NYNEX	2.5	1	1	3	1.5	1.5	4	4	4	4	3.5	3	3.0
Pacific Telesis	2	2	2	3.1	3.7	2.6	4	3.5	3.5	3.6	3.5	3.4	3.1
Southwest Bell	3	1.5	1.5	5	3	3	$5–$22	$7–$24	$7–$26	3.7	3.5	3.4	3.1
US West				5	2.5	2.5	5	3	3	3.6	3.5	3.5	3.2
Average Change	2.2	2.0	2.0	3.6	2.4	2.3	3.9	3.3	3.3	3.7	3.5	3.4	3.0

Table 4.6. Post-Divestiture Cost of Living Adjustment (COLA)

Company	1986	1989	1992	1995
AT&T	Suspended	Eliminated	None	None
Ameritech	In base and lump sum	Eliminated or no pay out	None or no pay out	None
Bell Atlantic	Restricted and lump sum	Restricted paid in base wages	Restricted paid in base wages < 1%	None
Bell South	Restricted paid in base wages	Restricted paid in base wages	Restricted 1.4% increase paid in base wages	None
NYNEX	Capped paid in base	Capped paid in base	Restricted pays CPI over > 9%	Restricted pays CPI > 9%
Pacific Telesis	COLA eliminated	None	None	None
Southwest Bell	Capped and lump sum payment	Capped split between lump sum and base	Eliminated	None
US West	Eliminated	None	None	None

135

Table 4.7. Post-Divestiture Contingent Pay

Company	1986	1989	1992	1995
AT&T	None	Profit sharing	Stock shares: $3300	Stock shares: $2,400 $1000 signing bonus
Ameritech	None	Profit sharing	Profit sharing	Success sharing $500 signing bonus
Bell Atlantic	$300 Lump sum signing bonus	Profit sharing	Profit sharing	$1500 signing bonus
Bell South	Lump sum bonus	Team incentive bonus based on profit and quality	Team incentive bonus increased	Lump sums in cash or stock $2,200
NYNEX	None	None	None	Stock shares $1,800
Pacific Telesis	Team award	Team award	Team award	Incentive plan
Southwest Bell	Team award $600 signing bonus	None	Profit sharing	Team performance $1,400
US West		Team award $600 signing bonus	None	None $1500 signing bonus

ied. CWA at BellSouth offered less resistance than the union at NYNEX and US West, who successfully rejected contingent pay in 1992 negotiations. In 1994, however, CWA at NYNEX accepted stock and cash bonuses amounting to 3.23% between 1995 and 1997. There has been increased reliance on signing bonuses to insure ratification and a shift away from profit sharing and team awards toward stock ownership plans. The companies have particularly pushed for commission pay for customer service and sales representatives. CWA and AT&T negotiated commission pay for top union jobs in sales; CWA District 7 at US West accepted trials of commission pay on a voluntary basis in 1995. In the first year, the employee "take rate" of volunteers was 58%. GTE also negotiated commission pay in some of its local contracts in 1996.

Greater conflict erupted over post-divestiture health care bargaining in which companies pushed for some form of employee cost-sharing of benefits. By 1992, all companies except NYNEX had successfully shifted to managed-care frameworks for basic health coverage, although four companies (Bell Atlantic, NYNEX, Pacific Telesis, and US West) endured strikes over the issue in 1989. Only at NYNEX did employees, after the bitter four-month strike, hold on to traditional coverage.

6.4. The Union-Nonunion Wage Gap and Wage Inequality

Given the significant decline in unionization, one might expect that union wages would converge toward nonunion rates. Theoretically, when union density is high, one would expect nonunion firms to imitate the dominant practices of union firms in order to attract skilled employees; but as union density falls, the dominant model erodes and the nonunion model should exert downward pressure on union standards, leading to a reduction in the union-nonunion wage gap. This has not occurred in telecommunications, however. Until 1990, union density fell slightly and union wage standards prevailed in the industry, with the gap between union and nonunion wages being relatively small. Since 1990, however, the acceleration in deunionization has been accompanied by a dramatic rise in the union-nonunion wage gap. This has occurred through a decline in the real wages of nonunion workers: by 14.4% among technical workers and by 21.6% among clerical and sales workers (Table 4.8). This figure underestimates the differences in total compensation, however, by failing to take into account the higher levels of nonwage benefits for union workers and the greater use of part-time and contingent workers among nonunion employers.

Another source of rising wage inequality is the increase in dispersion within both the union and the nonunion segments. Tables 4.9 and 4.10 illustrate these trends. Among unionized sales and clerical workers, the 9:1 wage ratio increased from 2.00 in 1983 to 2.43 in 1996; for

Table 4.8. Growth of Wage Inequality Within Union and Non-union Segments, by Occupation: Telecommunications Industry, 1983–1996

			% Change (%)		
	1983	1996	1983–1990	1990–1996	1983–1996
Clerical & Sales Workers					
Union real weekly earnings*					
10th percentile	$223	$188	−3.9	−11.8	−15.6
90th percentile	$446	$456	3.0	−0.6	2.4
Non–union real weekly earnings*					
10th percentile	$221	$153	−13.4	−17.3	−30.7
90th percentile	$729	$650	−16.0	5.2	−10.8
Ratio of 90th to 10th percentile					
Union	2.00	2.43	7.1	14.2	21.4
Non-union	3.30	4.25	−3.0	31.8	28.8
Technical Workers					
Union real weekly earnings*					
10th percentile	$351	$306	−12.9	0.0	−12.9
90th percentile	$602	$690	1.6	12.9	14.5
Non-union real weekly earnings*					
10th percentile	$241	$224	1.6	−8.5	−6.9
90th percentile	$753	$701	1.6	−8.5	−6.9
Ratio of 90th to 10th percentile					
Union	1.71	2.25	16.7	14.8	31.5
Non-union	3.13	3.13	0.0	0.0	0.0

Source: CPS merged annual earnings files; * CPI-U adjusted (Batt and Stausser 1997).

the nonunion group, it grew at a higher rate, from 3.30 to 4.25 over the same period. The story of the changing wage structure among union and nonunion technical workers is quite different than for clerical and sales workers. For nonunion workers, the 9:1 ratio remained unchanged (at 3.13) for the period. In the union segment, the opposite occurred: the 9:1 ratio increased 31.5% for union workers (from 1.71 to 2.25). The increased wage dispersion is about equally attributable to a decline in the lower tenth percentile (during the 1980s) and an increase in wages in the upper 90th percentile (in the 1990s).

The increase in wage dispersion in the union segment has several sources (previously discussed). These include (1) labor segmentation strategies designed to fragment job functions and link employee groups to market segments, raising wage dispersion across wage grades; (2) contingent and commission pay strategies; (3) negotiated two-tier wage structures, as in AT&T operator services and the Bell Atlantic network agreement; and (4) union strategies to negotiate pay raises primarily at the high end of any wage grade—for workers with 5-years seniority who traditionally comprise the bulk of the work force. In the 1990s, the companies misjudged the demand for new services, particularly the Internet,

Table 4.9. Post-Divestiture Employment Security Bargaining Outcomes Showing Training and Education

Company	1986	1989	1992	1995
AT&T	Joint alliance and ETOP programs established	Alliance funding increased Broader tuition assistance	Alliance funding increased	Alliance funding continued
Ameritech	No change	Increase tuition assistance Training Opportunity program (TOP)	Educational sabbaticals TOP expanded	Career and personal development plan $3500 per year
Bell Atlantic	$5 million training and development fund	$3 million for training fund	$3 million for training fund	
Bell South	Limited training and retraining	Training and retraining open to all	Educational sabbaticals added	Improved education and training partnership
NYNEX	No change	No change	No change	Two-year college technician program and sabbaticals
Pacific Telesis	Joint training fund	Joint training fund	$3 million for training fund	Horizons retraining $16 million
Southwest Bell	No change	No change	No change	No change
US West	No change	Pathways retraining programs	Surplus priority access to training	No change

Table 4.10. Post-Divestiture Employment Security Bargaining Outcomes Showing Severance and Voluntary Incentives

Company	1986	1989	1992	1995
AT&T	Income protection program enhanced	Income protection program enhanced	Income protection program enhanced	No change
Ameritech	No change	Expanded early retirement income	Increase in income protection	No change
Bell Atlantic	No change	Income security plan	Income protection program enhanced	No change
Bell South	No change	No change	Improved early retirement income	No change
NYNEX	Income protection program	Incentives for early retirement	Incentives for early retirement	Add 5 years to service and seniority for pension eligibility
Pacific Telesis	No change	No change	New early retirement severance increased	Improved income protection and separation benefits
Southwest Bell	Incentives for voluntary separation	Early retirement income improved	Voluntary severance expanded	No change
US West	Enhancements for voluntary separation	Enhancements for voluntary separation	Enhancements for voluntary separation	No change

and downsized more than necessary. As a result, they have hired more new employees at entry-level wages, which raises dispersion within wage grades.

In the nonunion segment, the story is different. The data suggest that nonunion employers attempted to keep up with union wage practices until the late 1980s but then broke with the pattern and pursued a lower wage strategy. The dramatic fall in real wages since 1990 is striking. Moreover, it is also notable that for both occupational groups, nonunion workers at the high end (90th percentile) experienced falling real wages: 11% among clerical and sales workers and 7% among technical workers. This finding runs contrary to the idea that the market demand for high technical skills (whether in office computers or programming skills) would raise wage dispersion. That is, among nonunion workers, the higher skilled workers found their wages falling despite the common perception that technical skills are in short supply.

Another example of a two-tier wage system is a 1995 agreement at Bell Atlantic for telephone installation and repair, covering the inside protector, wire, and jacks. A new subsidiary, Bell Atlantic Communications and Construction Systems Inc. (BACCSI; previously discussed), was the result of early bargaining with the IBEW, then with the CWA. In return for a compensation structure topping at 50% of the incumbent workforce with fewer rights, the IBEW obtained a 5-year contract that provides their outside network operations work force with job protection and also upgraded all installation and repair technicians to top craft titles. The BACCSI agreement sets wages and benefits below nonunion levels in the cable TV industry. The IBEW continues to recognize the need for a lower wage technician but plans to roll BACCSI into the core agreement over the next five years. Other agreements have created lower wage job titles to perform some multimedia coaxial and fiber work, which is in direct competition with cable TV. Generally, these agreements preserve splicing work inside the core contracts at existing wage rates. Both unions seek to reduce and eliminate nonunion contractors in network construction and maintenance. Similar agreements have been negotiated at BellSouth to bring in previously subcontracted buried-service wire work and at US West and PacBell to provide union coverage to contingent customer service and telemarketing employees.

6.5. Training, Advancement, and Employment Security

Downsizing, consolidation, and reengineering have significantly altered the prior Bell system internal labor markets that provided a steady supply of skilled employees for firms in exchange for upward career mobility and lifetime employment security for employees. Because of the ongoing nature of downsizing, the break in organizational career structures and employment security is more than a temporary phenomenon. Downsizing destroyed the social contract and the sense of shared mission in the industry. For many employees, the external conditions did not warrant the reductions in force through layoffs in the period 1992–1994. When the companies undertook downsizing, they were reporting excellent profits (between 1984 and 1997, the industry outperformed the S&P 500 by earning an annual average rate of return of 18% compared with 15% for the S&P 500), and the new competitors were years away from presenting a real threat to market share or margins. People could not understand why their company so abruptly and aggressively decided to get rid of dedicated and loyal employees rather than rely on attrition and retirement incentives. As they understand it now, it was to send the message, "Your service, your loyalty, your dedication, and your experienced-based skills are not appreciated. Your career and your family's livelihood are expendable compared to the bottom line." Going forward with downsizing has made any other change programs highly suspect; from the employees' perspective, executive management is simply not to be trusted; they have no moral purpose.

Bell companies also have not developed coherent alternative strategies to replace the internal training and development systems of the past. At least in this transitional period, there is considerable evidence that internal promotional systems are stalled, whereas the employment security bargain has been replaced by an "employability" doctrine. Even though companies still have high levels of training for new entrants to jobs at all levels of the organization, many have outsourced their training departments to specialized training providers. Opportunities for company-sponsored training for career development purposes are curtailed. Instead, the companies continue to provide tuition reimbursement and encourage employees to gain skills and competencies on their own in order to improve their "employability." Training on company time for development purposes or special programs for total quality, team-building, and other behavioral skills are severely curtailed.

For the nonmanagement workforce, all Bell companies and unions have negotiated various forms of voluntary severance packages and pension enhancements to encourage early retirement (see Table 4.11). They have also negotiated retraining and transfer programs as a form of employment security—either for displaced workers who plan to leave the company or for those in populations targeted for downsizing who seek new jobs in growing areas of the business (see Tables 4.9 and 4.10). AT&T's "Alliance for Employee Growth and Development," negotiated in 1986 and renegotiated with expanded funding in 1989, 1992, and 1995, is among the most publicly well known of any joint union-management retraining program. Between 1986 and 1992, the Alliance spent $80 million providing courses in career counseling, financial counseling, and résumé writing to 59,451 union members, 60% of whom

Table 4.11. Post-Divestiture Employment Security Bargaining Outcomes Showing Transfer and Recall Rights

Company	1986	1989	1992	1995
AT&T	Job information center	Automated transfer system Displaced priority	Access to nonunion subsidiaries for transfer	No change
Ameritech	No change	Relocation allowance Increased medical benefits of laidoff employees	Priority placements for displaced workers	Hometown jobs Employment guarantees within market area
Bell Atlantic	Job information center for displaced employees	Employee career resource centers	No change	Job security for some occupations
Bell South	Career continuation program	Employment security partnership	Joint committee on subcontracting	Increase mobility rights Extend bargaining unit
NYNEX	Priority placement for displaced	No change	No change	No layoff
Pacific Telesis	No layoff agreement	No layoff agreement Transfer and relocation assistance improved	No layoff Automated transfer system	Broad transfer rights Improve work force movement
Southwest Bell	Career resource center Notice increased to 90 days	No layoff agreement	No change	Home town jobs Find jobs in market area
US West		Upgrade and transfer plan	Joint committee on skill needs	Broader recognition Transfer to mobile

were active employees. Employees generally used the program either to retrain for occupations outside of AT&T or to train to pass entrance exams for higher skilled positions inside the company; they also used other AT&T tuition reimbursement programs for post-secondary technical and/or college training (Batt and Osterman, 1993). Additionally, AT&T established a national, automated transfer system in 1989 and access to transfer to nonunion subsidiaries in 1992. Despite these efforts, AT&T faced profound employee demoralization. The 1991 AT&T Employment Security Survey, for example, found significant declines in the attitudes of the unionized work force. A 1981 Bell System survey found that 68% of nonmanagement employees felt that the company was providing job security and only 8% did not, whereas by 1991 the numbers at AT&T had more than reversed themselves, with over 73% feeling that there was little job security. In some business units, less than 4% of the nonmanagement employees felt there was any job security. Less than 20% of the employees surveyed had confidence in management's ability to lead and solve the corporation's competitive problems. Over two-thirds felt they were unable to influence events that affected their employment at AT&T. And, almost one-half of the employees surveyed had been surplused (their job abolished) at least once. The surplused employee group on average had been surplused two-and-one-half times.

When compared with attitude data collected at other traumatized organizations, the intensity of AT&T employees' pessimism goes beyond the negative attitudes found in many of those organizations. There are several reasons for these catastrophe-like responses. First, many employees chose to work at AT&T because of the Bell System's commitment to employment security, and now they face chronic insecurity. Second, downsizing has been a protracted ordeal that started in 1984 and still persists today. Third, AT&T employees use the former Bell System employment standards, which until recently have remained largely intact at the local Bell Operating Companies, to judge AT&T's new employment practices. Finally, AT&T is widely recognized as a progressive, innovative employer for its retraining, out-placement assistance, employee participation, and family leave programs. Many employees find it difficult to reconcile AT&T's positive public image with their recent personal experiences. Employees systematically underestimate (by 60%) the amount of downsizing that has occurred at AT&T (Boroff and Keefe, 1992).

Of particular significance is the fact that although retraining and transfer programs exist on paper, many employees find themselves unable to take advantage of them. When AT&T reconfigured its national organization, it consolidated offices and located them in geographically dispersed areas. Whereas in the past, employees would follow job ladders in local offices, now they often must move across the country to gain promotional opportunities. According to the 1991 survey, however, the average worker who survived successive downsizing is immobile with family commitments; he or she is White, 43 years old, married with children at home, a homeowner, a high school graduate with some college, a CWA member with 18 years of AT&T service, and annually earns $26,000 with good benefits. Some 87% of the survey respondents said they wanted to keep their current jobs until they retire, but less than 10% believed that there is any opportunity for advancement at AT&T. RBOC retraining and transfer programs have been similar to those of AT&T but have tended to have lower funding. Some, but not all, provide access to jobs in nonunion subsidiaries; some, but not all, make an explicit commitment to employment security (see Tables 4.9 and 4.10).

Despite the slower pace of downsizing, frustration with declining employment security was also high among regional Bell company employees recently surveyed (Batt, 1995), and in this case, managers were more adversely affected and critical of top management than were non-management employees. Eighty-six percent of workers and 92% of managers said job security had decreased in the previous two years; less than one-quarter were satisfied with the current level of job security. In this case as well, demoralization not only centered on job insecurity, but on the perceived lack of alternative strategies for the future. Downsizing reduced opportunities for mobility: 83% of workers and 89% of managers indicated that opportunities for promotion had declined; 72% of workers and 78% of managers said opportunities for lateral transfer had declined. Only 5% of managers at the company were promoted to higher pay grades in 1990, a fraction of what existed during the 1950s through 1970s (Howard and Bray, 1988). Moreover, where mobility existed, it often meant forced relocations to save jobs: 38% of managers in the 1994 survey said they had to relocate in the prior three years as a result of organizational restructuring. The experience of organizational instability and uncertainty is reflected in employee dissatisfaction over particular aspects of their jobs and of corporate leadership more generally. Whereas over two-thirds of workers were satisfied with their jobs, benefits, and pay, only 14% were satisfied with their opportunities for promotion and 27% were satisfied with their job security. The pattern was similar among managers: whereas 70% or more were satisfied with their jobs, pay, and benefits, less than 20% were satisfied with their employment security or opportunities for advancement. In sum, employees appeared to like the work they do and the skills they used, and they had very low absentee rates. Most scored high on commitment variables such as their willingness to work harder for the company, their pride in working for the company, and the loyalty they felt. But they were critical of top management's commitment to them: to employment security and advancement, to providing adequate resources for getting the job done, and to taking into consideration the interests of employees when making technological and organizational decisions (Batt, 1995).

In contrast to AT&T and the other regional Bell companies, NYNEX negotiated the most far-reaching employment security framework in the industry. The 1994 contract provided a special retirement incentive that adds six years to both service and age; it also included a 30% Social Security supplement until age 62 or a $500 annual bonus, whichever is greater. The incentive program was aimed at voluntarily eliminating 16,800 of 57,000 (or 30%) of the nonmanagement jobs at NYNEX and was estimated to cost over $2 billion or $77,000 per participating employee. Other components of the agreement sought to create a future for the surviving work force. NYNEX committed itself to a no-layoff clause where displacement is due to changes in organization, work process, or new technology. Layoffs are permitted only in response to volume reductions. A major innovation was the creation of a two-year Associate's Degree program in telecommunications technology, open to all bargaining unit employees. The employees work four days a week and go to school the fifth day on company time. All educational expenses are paid by the company. After graduation, employees receive a $50 per week increase. NYNEX's strategy recognizes that it is a high labor cost supplier and offsets this cost disadvantage with a highly educated, flexible, and productive work force. In the first two years of the program, roughly 1,100 employees enrolled (Clifton, 1995; personal communication, November 24, 1996). In addition, all NYNEX employees with five years of service are eligible to take a two-year educational leave. They can receive $10,000 per year for educational expenses while retaining full benefits, seniority, and a guaranteed job when they return. The contract also created a job bank and a new job sharing provision. Union workers are guaranteed access to all new NYNEX ventures in the information industry. New subsidiaries are required to start up by offering union workers the opportunity to bid into the new jobs. Wage increases were 4% in 1994 and in 1995, 3.5% in 1996, and 3% in 1997, with an additional 3.23% in stock and cash bonuses over the term. Cost-of-living protection kicks in if inflation should exceed 8%. The fully paid medical plan was maintained for the life of the agreement.

7. Conclusion

We have argued that the economies of system in the telecommunications industry coupled with the dominance of former Bell system companies has created a set of unique circumstances that shape the direction of management and employment practices in this industry. Despite market deregulation and opportunities for new entrants, technological advances have provided incentives for mergers and organizational consolidation. Despite technological uncertainty, the major players have undertaken quite similar approaches to business strategy, organizational restructuring, and the use of technology and process reengineering. All companies are attempting to take advantage of system economies inherent in the nature of the product market and technology to provide customized packages of multimedia products to identified market segments. They have reorganized into market-driven business units providing differentiated services to long distance carriers, large businesses and institutions, small businesses, and residential customers.

Companies have looked to new technologies and process reengineering to accomplish the twin goals of improving sales and reducing costs. The shift from analog to fully digital systems has improved the quality and speed of transmissions; it has shifted the demand for skill away from traditional mechanical (blue-collar craft) skills and toward digital (white-collar technical) skills. Similarly, companies have used reengineering to accomplish business unit reorganization and reduce response time through the automation of the service order process. Because reengineering has tended to be more successful in automating simple transactions, it has eliminated lower skilled clerical and customer service jobs, also resulting in an upward shift in the demand for skills.

Human resource practices are derivative of market and technology strategies. They increasingly vary within companies and within occupations by market segment. Within the unionized core, some variation in HR practices may be traced to variation in union-management relations. Those companies and unions with mature bargaining relationships and weaker unions (e.g., BellSouth, US West) have been temporarily successful in creating partnership strategies to enhance quality and customer service. In other cases, aggressive union (e.g., NYNEX) or management (e.g., Bell Atlantic) strategies have led to new employment practices that break from a de facto pattern among former Bell companies.

Far greater variation, however, exists between the union and non-union segments of the industry. The growth in the union-nonunion compensation gap has put increasing downward pressure on historically bargained union standards. We suspect that recent examples of two-tier wage structures, commission pay, and contingent employment practices found within the unionized core are likely to diffuse more rapidly in the next decade, particularly as the traditional work force retires and gives way to a younger generation.

Finally, we did not find examples of successful integration of macro-organizational restructuring and reengineering on the one hand, and the use of team-based systems on the other. Rather, there is considerable evidence that downsizing and restructuring has led to employee demoralization. As a result, we do not yet have a "best practice" model within this industry. Instead, the telecommunications industry does have something to offer the high-performance literature. In this industry, even though it is oligopolistic in structure, no single firm defines the performance standards. The telecommunications industry with high rates of productivity growth, rapid advanced technological diffusion, and decades of high and sustainable levels of performance improvement has distinguished itself as a high-performance industry. In a highly dynamic market such as telecommunications, it may be industrial performance that ultimately defines the firms—who they are, what they do, how they are organized, and what their employment practices are.

The big issue confronting the industry, and crucial for continued productivity growth, is how continuous learning and coordination among employees takes place. Historically, among professional, technical, and frontline employees, formal job ladders and long-term employment relations coupled with informal social organization provided continuous training. Informal collaboration with other skilled employees was an important source of continuous learning. Large-scale reorganization has broken up formal job ladders and informal social networks, and companies have not yet developed new organizational forms to replace the old ones.

Acknowledgment   We would like to thank the Alfred P. Sloan Foundation for generous support for this project. We would also like to thank Heidi Goldfarb and Michael Stausser for their excellent research assistance on this project.

Appendix

Reengineering the Service Order Function at GTE

The service order fulfillment process consists of three basic processes: order creation, facilities assignment and/or design, and dispatch and installation. Traditionally, service representatives would take orders from customers and create an order either manually, or increasingly in the 1980s, on-line. The service rep would give the customer a standard interval for service to be activated because she did not have access to inventory and dispatch information. Instead, she would pass the order to the Facilities Assignment Center (FAC), where an assignment clerk would check the inventory of physical plant to identify whether or not a line was available for the customer. FAC clerks would then send the assignment to dispatch clerks at the Dispatch Assignment Center (DAC), who would manually prioritize and dispatch each job to a field technician. Customers would call in to get a status update, and service reps would call the local FAC or DAC and report back to the customers. Once the field tech had completed the installation, he would call back into dispatch to report and get another assignment. When service is disconnected, the technician manually disconnected the wires.

In summary, service activation entailed numerous hand-offs to employees working in other departments, who input the appropriate customer information into distinct databases (a source of additional errors), including billing, 911 services, directory assistance, and central office switches, causing duplicate entry of information, and lost time among employees who routinely called in for updated information and waited on hold to obtain or gain information or to receive new assignments.

Over time, telephone companies have sought ways to automate this process in order to reduce response time and improve efficiency. By creating dedicated lines to each customer premise, for example, companies may turn services on and off without manually connecting and disconnecting service wires. Process reengineering is another attempt to mechanize service order fulfillment. The goal at GTE was to reduce costs per call and achieve "*OneTouch*" service for 85% of residential consumers. "*OneTouch*" means that customers interact only once with the telephone company, at the point of initial contact, and service is automatically activated.

Under the new system, the customer service associates take all of the relevant information on-line. Because the order entry and inventory data systems are now linked, service associates can see whether inventory is available and whether service may be automatically activated; therefore, while on the phone with the customer, they can set a date for service activation or book an available date for a technician to go on-site. Using interlinked databases, the service associate currently absorbs some of the assignment and scheduling work previously performed by clerks in the FAC and DAC. A centralized resource management group monitors the volume of activity and resource availability.

GTE Business orders have been similarly automated, but because these orders are more complex, a much lower percentage may be automatically assigned. In complex orders involving Centrex systems or ISDN, for example, existing inventory must be configured to provide the service before the inventory is assigned to a customer premise. At the other end of the system, an automatic work distribution system lists jobs for the day by one or more geographic areas. In theory, the redesign creates zone technicians, most of whom home-garage their vehicles and are dispatched from home each morning to their first job. Using their laptop computers to receive a list of jobs for the day, they can set their priorities for completing jobs depending on location and whether commitment time for completion is morning or afternoon. They are also to report completion of jobs through laptop computers. Ideally, they would gain a sense of ownership over their zone, transforming the outside technicians into inside independent contractors, who are accountable for the service in their zone. Implementation of the design in the field has been problematic, however, for several reasons: the outside world is nonstandard; work load varies by geography; no technician can carry all the tools, supplies, and equipment needed for every installation and repair; and not all are equally qualified to perform the work. In these cases, the zone model breaks down, and more employees report to the work center each day. To date, there are no measurable improvements in technician productivity, morale, or sense of ownership. The use of laptop computers, however, has improved reporting and efficiency in the hand-off of work (as compared with the old system, where technicians often had to wait on hold or call back to file reports and would give up or not bother). Under the reengineered model, network labor costs are lower for at least two reasons: first, the span of control of supervisors has increased from 1/10 to 1/15 or 1/20; second, a sizable portion of the technician work force has been converted to seasonal status, working in the summer months when the installation and repair workloads are heavy and getting laid off in the winter with no commitment for recall.

Overall gains resulting from reengineering are substantial: in 1993, 33% of all residential orders were One-Touch; after reengineering, the rate was 61%. Average handling time decreased from 520 seconds per call to 450 seconds per call. Reengineering also eliminated one million, or almost one third, of all dispatches to customer premises and accounted for $95 million in savings. Between 1994 and 1995, revenues per call increased from $9.20 per call to $11.41 per call. (This is a conservative estimate because it excludes new products sold and compares sales on the same set of products.) If new products are included, revenues rose to $18.00/call. Reengineering reduced costs per call and improved efficiencies through a number of changes:

- Overhead was reduced through the closure of 153 offices (19 remain)
- Incoming calls were reduced by 25% through the use of an intelligent voice response unit system (IVRU technology), which informs customers of the status of their requests
- Automatic call distribution systems route customer, by segment, to correct call center
- Automated order process and EDT lines cover 9.1 of 21 million order calls, or 43%; in residential services, an icon-driven windows environment allows service associates to more quickly enter customer information and switch between several databases at once
- The OMEGA assignment system has reduced dispatches by 20% and manual design by 10%.

References

Barnard, Chester. 1938. *The Functions of the Executive.* Cambridge: Harvard University Press.

Batt, Rosemary. 1995. Performance and welfare effects of work restructuring: Evidence from telecommunications services. Ph.D. diss., Sloan School of Management, M.I.T.

Batt, Rosemary. 1996. From bureaucracy to enterprise? The changing jobs and careers of managers in telecommunications service. In Paul Osterman (ed.), *Broken ladders*. New York: Oxford University Press, Chapter 3.

Batt, Rosemary, and Paul Osterman. 1993. Workplace training policy: Case studies of state and local experiments. Working paper no. 105, Economic Policy Institute.

Baumol, William J., and J. Gregory Sidak. 1994. *Toward Competition in Local Telephony*. Cambridge, MA: M.I.T. Press and The American Enterprise Institute.

Boroff, Karen, and Jeffrey H. Keefe. 1992. AT&T employment security survey. New Brunswick, NJ: Rutgers University, Institute of Management and Labor Relations.

Cappelli, Peter, and Charles R. Perry. 1986. Bargaining in telecommunications after divestiture. Working paper series #628, Wharton School, Philadelphia, PA.

Cappelli, Peter, and Charles R. Perry. 1988. Labor relations in telecommunications. Discussion paper #37, University of Pennsylvania, University Park, PA.

Clifton, Jean. 1995. Employee choice for training and career development in a downsizing environment: Evidence from NYNEX Corporation. Unpublished manuscript.

Economides, Nicholas. 1996. The economics of networks. *International Journal of Industrial Organization* 14(2) (March): 673–699.

Gong, Jiong, and Padmanabhan Srinagesh. 1997. The economics of layered networks. In Lee McKnight and Joseph Bailey (eds.), *Internet economics*. Cambridge, MA: M.I.T. Press.

Hacker, Sally L. 1979. Sex stratification, technology and organizational change: A longitudinal case study of AT&T. *Social Problems* 26(5) (June): 539–557.

Howard, Ann, and Douglas Bray. 1988. *Managerial lives in transition: Advancing age and changing times*. New York: Guilford Press.

Ichniowski, Casey, Thomas A. Kochan, David Levine, Craig Olson, and George Strauss. 1996. What works at work: Overview and assessment. *Industrial Relations* 35(3) (July): 299–333.

J.D. Power and Associates. 1996. *Study of residential local telephone companies*. Agoura Hills, CA.

Keefe, Jeffrey. 1998. *Monopoly.com: Will the WorldCom-MCI merger tangle the internet?* Washington: Economic Policy Institute.

Keefe, Jeffrey, and Rose Batt. 1997. United States. In Harry Katz (ed.), *Telecommunications: Restructuring work and employment relations worldwide*. Ithaca, NY: Cornell University Press.

Keefe, Jeffrey, and Karen Boroff. 1994. Telecommunications labor management relations after divestiture. In Paula Voos (ed.), *Contemporary collective bargaining in the private sector*. Madison, WI: Industrial Relations Research Association.

Kochan, Thomas, and Paul Osterman. 1994. *The mutual gains enterprise: Forging a winning partnership among labor, management, and government*. Boston, MA: Harvard Business School Press.

Kohl, George. 1993. Information technology and labor: A case study of telephone operators. *Workplace Topics* 3(1): 101–111.

MacDuffie, John Paul. 1995. Human resource bundles and manufacturing performance: Organizational logic and flexible production systems in the world auto industry. *Industrial and Labor Relations Review* 48(2) (January): 197–221.

Northrup, H. 1979. *The impact of the AT&T-EEO consent decree.* Wharton Industrial Research Center, Philadelphia, PA.

Schlesinger, Leonard, and James Heskett. 1991. Breaking the cycle of failure in services. *Sloan Management Review* 32(Spring): 17–28.

Temin, Peter. 1987. *The fall of the Bell System: A study in prices and politics.* Cambridge, England: Cambridge University Press.

U.S. Congress. 1993. *Pulling together for productivity: A union: management initiative at US West, Inc.* Office of Technology Assessment. September.

Vallas, Steven Peter. 1993. *Power in the workplace: The politics of production at AT&T.* Albany, NY: State University of New York Press.

Wallace, Phyllis. 1976. *Equal employment opportunity and the AT&T case.* Cambridge, MA: M.I.T. Press.

Werback, Kevin. 1997. Digital tornado: The Internet and telecommunications policy. Washington: Federal Communications Commission, Office of Policy and Plans Working paper Series 29.

5

Transforming Retail Banking

Inclusion and Segmentation in Service Work

LARRY W. HUNTER

Introduction

A substantial segment of the American work force may be facing a future of "lousy jobs." The essays collected in Burtless (1990), for example, suggest that workers with high levels of education and sought-after skills face excellent opportunities, but that prospects for workers with high school educations or less are bleak. Employers seem increasingly to be constructing jobs for low-skilled workers that offer low wages and benefits, minimal training, and little opportunity for advancement.

Not all lower-skilled workers, however, will find themselves employed in these situations. What will drive the differences in the employment practices faced by lower-skilled workers? Collective bargaining or government intervention might move lower-skilled workers into better jobs. The low rate of union membership in many industries, however, combined with relatively little enthusiasm for increased regulation of employment practices, suggest that what is likely to matter most will be employers' strategies and choices as they structure human resource (HR) practices in organizations.

American retail banking, a sector prototypical of the massive U.S. service economy, provides one window into these strategies and choices. Retail banking has featured many of the substantial changes in employment practices (Cappelli, 1995) typical of the 1990s. Jobs in bank branches and telephone call centers are typical of many front-line service jobs in turbulent environments. Technology, deregulation, and the proliferation of process reengineering have catalyzed changes in service sector employment practices. The forces driving these choices and changes are the subject of this chapter.

Choice in Employment Practice

Employment practices vary and evolve in part because managers institute practices in order to achieve solutions to differing and changing sets of functional problems. Osterman's "theory of choice" (1987) suggests that variance in employment practice results from a process of incremental change in practices governing groups of related jobs in organizations. Practices are the outcomes of managerial choices aimed at achieving goals for their organizations in an environment of technological, institutional, and market-based constraints.

Choice in practices is straightforward when managers see clear connections between the goals they have for their organizations and the practices they are implementing. Such connections have led to the emergence of what has been termed strategic human resource management (HRM). A number of empirical studies document links between business strategies and HR practices in organizations (Arthur, 1992; Hunter, 1998; Jackson, Schuler, and Rivero, 1989; Osterman, 1994; Schuler and Jackson, 1987; Snell, 1992).

The evidence for strategic fit, however, is not overwhelming. In fact, such fit may actually be observed only under conditions of environmental stability and strategic clarity. When markets change radically or institutions break down, organizational actors are less sure about the sorts of practices required, or about how to align those practices with broader organizational goals. During such periods, organizations have difficulty establishing not only which practices are effective but even in establishing criteria by which to evaluate any choices in practices they might make (Aldrich and Fiol, 1994). During such "eras of ferment" (Rosenkopf and Tushman, 1996), neither the value of outcomes nor the relationships between outcomes and employment practices is clear.

Effects of intraorganizational politics, and the distribution of power inside organizations, on employment practices (see, e.g., Pfeffer and Cohen, 1984; Cohen and Pfeffer, 1986) are heightened when organizations are unable to construct consensus around which practices are appropriately matched to the environment. During such periods, organizational imperatives are less clearly associated with practices. The interplay of local actors and interests is thus likely to prevail until new employment systems emerge as obviously competitively superior or at least become recognized as legitimate.

In turbulent environments, aggregate evidence of "strategic fit" may be hard to find, even as more detailed case studies establish rationales for links between strategies and practices. Retail banking provides a case study of the evolution of practice in an industry characterized by uncertain, loose connections between practices and goals. Local case studies detailed in this chapter and in other papers (e.g., Keltner, 1995; Keltner and Finegold, 1996) describe ways in which HRM practices may complement retail banking strategies. But until this evidence accumulates and consensus emerges in the industry on the relationship between strategies and practices, HRM practices for frontline retail bank employees are more likely to result from a melange of local compromises and accommodations than to reflect particular strategic initiatives in any systematic ways.

Retail Banking: Economics and Institutions

From the 1940s until the early 1980s, banks, and especially the retail functions within banks that did business with individual customers, were characterized by stability in employment. Job security was the rule, and, although salaries were not particularly high in comparison with other industries, benefits tended to be generously extended throughout organizations. Typically, retail banks were structured pyramidally; tellers, responsible for routine transactions, occupied the base of the pyramid, with "platform" employees who opened new accounts and provided other advanced services at the next level. Above these employees were layers of local and then remote branch management and specialist functions typically based around products or segments such as mortgage loans, small business accounts, and the like. The jobs were embedded in a bureaucratic, firm-based internal labor market (Althauser and Kalleberg, 1981) with narrowly defined, hierarchically located jobs. This structure featured two modifications from the ideal type with a port of entry at the bottom of a job ladder. First, moving upward, each family of jobs featured a tighter attachment between employer and employee. Entry-level tellers, for example, were typically managed in higher turnover, looser employment relationships (still featuring prospects for advancement), with turnover rates decreasing for platform and managerial employees. Second, it was possible for potential employees to enter (depending on education and previous experience) at higher levels of the pyramid. The industry provided opportunities for advancement even for those entering as tellers with only high school education and featured extremely low risk of layoffs. For the most part, retail banking jobs were good, steady jobs.

This stability fit nicely with a strongly institutionalized (DiMaggio and Powell, 1983) surrounding environment. The industry was buffered from other sectors of financial services, such as insurance and investment banking, by regulatory barriers, most prominently the Bank Act of 1933 (usually called the Glass-Steagall Act), which established commercial banking as a distinct entity by separating both the ownership and the activities of commercial banks from those of other enterprises. American commercial bankers, particularly those on the retail side, possessed a strong sense of the uniqueness of their industry, and this was reinforced through participation in industry associations and lobbying groups.

Competition in the industry was severely restricted by regulation, and commercial banking, especially its retail side, was considered neither risky, dynamic, nor lucrative. The Federal Deposit Insurance Corporation (FDIC) insured deposits up to $100,000; further, banks with FDIC charters were prohibited from offering many investment and all insurance products, and many states had strict regulations prohibiting or limiting branch and interstate banking. The stability of the industry was summed up beautifully by what bankers referred to as the "three, six, and three" rule: paying 3% on deposits; lending money at 6%; getting on the golf course by 3 o'clock.

The period hence has been anything but stable. One comprehensive review of the industry notes that the 1980s and early 1990s were "undoubtedly the most turbulent period in banking since the Great Depression" (Berger, Kashyap, and Scalise, 1995). A series of regulatory changes included expansion in the number of products that banks were allowed to offer, removal of interest rate ceilings on bank deposits, reductions in reserve requirements, the formalization of capital requirements, the expansion of bank powers through the dilution of Glass-Steagall restrictions, and relaxation of geographic banking rules. Financial innovations under the broader umbrella of regulatory reform permitted reorganization of the industry, with disaggregation and reaggregation of particular financial functions. For example, mortgage lending and personal savings were formerly both administered by banks. Today, specialist mortgage companies backed by complex financial instruments do a considerable amount of lending for homes, whereas savings are increasingly held in money market funds.

Over this same period, technological innovation accelerated. The rapid introduction of Automatic Teller Machines (ATMs), as well as new back-office technologies, dramatically decreased the costs associated with handling and processing individual transactions. First telephone banking, and then home and PC-based banking, appeared as alternative channels for delivery of retail financial services. Information technology and process redesign (popularly, "reengineering") have combined to remove from employees many basic servicing tasks. These tasks—simple inquiries, transactions, and movement of funds— are being automated or turned over to customers, as with the proliferation of telephone banking and voice-response units. Reengineering frees remaining employees to concentrate more effort on activities that have potentially higher added-value. Customized financial advice coupled with sales efforts, for example, may be a way for banks to shift their customers toward more deeper and broader relationships with them.

Information technology can also give to a bank's employees a full picture of each customer's financial position and potential; this enhances sales efforts, enabling tellers and customer service representatives to suggest a fit between customers and services and to refer the customers to employee-teammates with particular expertise in a product if that should become necessary. Information systems provide "cross-sell prompts"—

the financial equivalent of fast food's "Would you like fries with that?"—for financial products such as home equity loans for customers who are prone to large credit card balances or mutual funds for customers who keep large amounts in cash accounts. Information systems may also guide bank employees as to the relative importance of individual customers. The system for one leading bank, for example, features a small box in the corner of the customer's account screen that contains either an X, an N, or a $. Employees are instructed to treat "$" customers with the utmost courtesy; X's, on the other hand, are most unlikely to receive favorable responses to complaints or requests for fee waivers.

Deregulation and technological and financial advances have also paved the way for a vast, ongoing consolidation of the industry. The banking industry shrunk from over 12,000 banks in 1987 to some 8,000 banks by 1995 (Berger, Kashyap, and Scalise, 1995), and consolidation continues. Nearly all large banks are engaged actively in some kind of merger discussion. In 1998 alone, mergers between BancOne and First Chicago, NationsBank and Bank of America, FirstUnion and CoreStates, NationsBank and Barnett Banks, and Wells Fargo and Norwest, each eclipsed the largest previous mergers in the industry. Mergers have also begun to feature not simply commercial banks merging with one another, but the joining of organizations across sectors, the 1998 blockbuster between the commercial bank Citicorp and the insurance conglomerate Travelers Group (which itself had previously acquired the investment banking house Salomon Brothers) being the most prominent example.

The merger wave is driven in part by a belief in economies of scale in operations, for mergers bring with them immediate opportunities for cost savings through consolidation of both back office operations and front office branch networks. One typical early result of mergers is substantial job reductions. Mergers also enable diversification and the quick acquisition of broader customer bases (Akhavein, Berger, and Humphrey, 1996).[1] Mergers across traditional sector boundaries include these goals as well as the hope that efficiencies in cross-selling products might be gained.

Deregulation, consolidation, and technological change have produced what might be termed a crisis in "regulation" in the sense suggested by Piore and Sabel (1984); the institutions that formerly held the industry together no longer do so. Competition between different kinds of financial organizations has blurred the lines between banks and rivals such as mutual funds, brokerage houses, and insurance and finance companies. Government restrictions have not only been weakened, but the remaining rules have been reopened for interpretation.

Banks now face the prospect of radical transformation, with their fundamental nature open to change (Crane and Bodie, 1996). During this period, the retail market has actually grown in relative importance. Over the past two decades, banks have lost a substantial share of their business with large corporate customers; such customers have turned to alternative sources of finance, and medium-sized and even small businesses have begun to follow suit. Thus, where retail banks were once seen by executives chiefly as sources of funds that could be used in turn to underwrite lending to corporate customers, they are now emerging as distinct profit centers in their own right.

Pressures for changes in the employment practices of retail banking divisions have grown correspondingly powerful.[2] Managers believe these pressures require adaptation or transformation[3] of the ways that their banks relate to their customers. Technologies such as ATMs, telephone banking, and, most recently, home banking, mean that banks require fewer and fewer employees to deliver standardized services that customers already understand well. Rather, banking employees must be able to encourage customers to explore a much wider range of products. This range includes not only retail products that are linked to each other in more inventive ways (such as credit cards, home equity loans, and checking accounts), but increasingly, investment products such as mutual funds. At the same time, the referent set of institutions from which banks learn has expanded dramatically. Where bank executives once looked to one another for models of service delivery, they are now beginning to explore the universe of financial service providers and even other nonfinancial retailers.

Under the old model, banks and their employees took orders from their customers for a few, standardized products and then serviced those products. Reconstructed retail banks are becoming more-sophisticated sales organizations, endeavoring to match customers with an appropriate set of financial products. It is difficult to find retail banks that have not launched initiatives to become more directed toward the needs of customers. The language of change permeates the trade industry literature, professional meetings, and conferences. Correspondingly, a scramble to construct new employment arrangements has also ensued.

The Retail Banking Studies

In this chapter, I draw from a series of retail banking studies[4] to elaborate on the practices governing front-office employees in the major delivery channels of retail banks: workers in the branch networks and telephone service centers involved directly in delivering financial services to individuals. The chapter draws on over 150 interviews with top executives, line managers in retail banking, HR managers, executives responsible for the implementation of information technology, retail bank employees, and industry consultants. The interviews began in 1993 and continued through 1997. One early phase of the study, beginning in summer 1993, featured site visits to 13 U.S. retail bank headquarters and interviews of dozens of other managers and employees in branches and telephone centers. The succeeding year also featured a number of site visits and follow-ups. Because much of the data were collected under conditions of confidentiality, in this chapter I use pseudonyms for the banks from which I draw examples.

Data on the frequency of use of particular kinds of practices come from a detailed 1994–1995 survey of technology, work practices, organizational strategy, and performance in 135 U.S. retail banks. The survey population comprised the 400 largest bank holding companies (BHC) in America at the beginning of 1994. Factors such as merger activity or the lack of a retail banking organization reduced the list to 335 BHCs. Participation in the study was confidential but not anonymous, which enabled surveys to be matched with data from other sources (such as data from the Federal Deposit Insurance Corporation). Participation in the study required substantial time and effort on the part of organizations. A research team therefore sought participation by approaching the 70 largest U.S. BHCs directly, and in the second half of 1994 requested the participation of one retail banking entity from each BHC. Forty-seven BHCs agreed to participate. Of these, seven BHCs engaged the participation of two or more retail banks within the BHC, yielding a total of 64 retail banks that participated in this sample. Each organization in this sample received multiple questionnaires, including questionnaires for multiple bank branches in the retail bank.

In late 1994, the team mailed survey questionnaires to top executives of the next largest 265 BHCs and followed the mailing with a telephone call requesting the participation of one of their retail banking organizations. Sixty-four of these BHCs agreed to participate in the study, and four of these engaged the participation of two or more retail banks in the BHCs so that there was a total of 71 retail banks participating in the mailed survey. Each of the banks in the mailed survey provided data from one local branch. The two-pronged approach, while yielding a sample that was not representative of the industry (which comprises some 8,000 banks), did produce substantial coverage: Banks holding over 75% of the total assets in the industry as of year-end 1994 participated. Questionnaires targeted the "most informed respondent" (Huber and Power, 1985) with a variety of questions.

The chapter also draws on a continuing case study of one leading American bank's attempt to transform its geographically dispersed retail banking operation. "National Bank," one of the larger American commercial banks, with branches in many states, has a retail banking arm that is typical of the industry. The case study has tracked the implementation of a major redesign of the retail delivery system at National since its conception in early 1996.

Strategies and Employment Practices

A number of prominent strategic initiatives characterize the American retail banking industry of the 1990s. Product diversification, cross-selling, and increased focus on segmentation of customers and serving of niche markets all require improved sales efforts. Growth through merger activity and focus on internal efficiencies require aggressive attempts to reduce costs. Managers have found the civil-service-like character of the traditional bureaucratic internal labor market structure unsuited to accomplishing either sales-driven or cost-driven strategies.

The traditional system gave employees little incentive to seek out sales opportunities, and few developed the necessary skills to do so. The traditional system has also proved costly to maintain in comparison with streamlined delivery channels in other financial sectors. For example, the money market funds that have attracted an increasing share of retail customers' savings typically have costs that run about 10% of those of banks.

There is consensus that the old system is on its way out, and two very different trends are competing to guide the reshaping of employment practice in leading American banks (see Table 5.1). An *inclusive* strategy involves investment in the work force at all levels of the retail system. Here, tellers' jobs are enriched to include sales responsibility and cross-training to platform functions, such as account opening and the communication of product information. Similarly, telephone center representatives' jobs include sales responsibilities as well as basic account servicing. In this model, all employees are to some extent responsible for initiating and maintaining customer contact; tellers provide more basic services while platform employees engage in relationship management and active selling. For example, a site visit to Financial Bank revealed that every telephone representative was college educated and received considerable training. Although their jobs had no face-to-face customer contact and typically comprised mostly routine and mundane work, such as verifying account balances, the telephone representatives dressed in business attire—coats and ties for men, dresses and suits for women. Most of these representatives had accepted the telephone service job with the expectation that the position would serve as a first step toward advancement and a career in the bank.

An ideal-typical inclusive system couples relatively high wages with incentive pay for effective sales and sales referrals. The model also includes elements of teamwork within the branch and phone center, cross-functional cooperation between different job families, and branch or unit-based performance bonuses. Local managers in this environment are facilitators and product experts, with overall responsibility for unit performance. Under the inclusive model, all employees have access to the vast array of rapidly changing information systems in the

Table 5.1. Two Models of Employment Practice for Bank Branches

HRM Practice	Inclusive Model	Segmented Model
Selection criteria	High school, some college Trainability Customer focus	College required for platform High school for tellers
Training emphasis	Broadly cast	Focused on platform
Compensation	At or above market Incentives for team/group Returns to tenure	Above market for key platform employees Low for others Individual incentives
Job design	Broad cross-training Teamwork	Narrow, specialized Autonomy within specific tasks
Use of part-timers	For retention reasons	Use where possible, cost-control–oriented
Role of local manager	Facilitator/trainer Customer relations Generalist	Supervisor and scheduler Facilitator to platform Product specialist
Organizing logic of worksite	Team of generalists	Collection of specialists

bank and become responsible for convincing customers to hold multiple products by using the bank as a first stop for investment and lending choices.

An alternative ideal-typical strategy for organizing the retail front office, the *segmentation* approach, focuses chiefly on cost containment in the mass market, providing specialized services only for a more elite segment of customers.[5] In this model, the employment systems in the retail bank are divided, and banks attempt to match different kinds of employees to sharply distinct roles. A small number of specialized employees are responsible for managing relationships between the bank and qualified customers. These product specialists and "personal bankers" (or "investment specialists," or "financial planners"—the names for upgraded platform positions vary from bank to bank) target customers with high profit potential, such as upper-income professionals and owners of small businesses. Employees responsible for serving such customers—whether in the branch or over the telephone—are carefully screened, typically college educated, and, increasingly, licensed to sell investment products. They are well paid, and embedded in the internal labor market of the bank, with opportunities for advancement and access to training.

In the segmented model, however, the majority of branch and telephone center employees receive considerably less compensation and training. They are often employed on a part-time basis and their compensation may not include benefits. Typically they are shut off from promotion opportunities unless they acquire an external credential such as a college degree. The positions, typically, tend to be high turnover and to have relatively flat wage profiles. Further, the distinctions between the two job families are quite sharp: cross-training is scant and there are few cross-functional responsibilities. In this model, the role of the branch manager is less that of a facilitator and more that of a traditional supervisor. Here, technology simplifies the majority of the jobs, makes them easier to learn, and decreases the costs of turnover. Only the high value-added, personal banking jobs have access to the broad range of information that might be useful in generating sales leads and opportunities.

Under the *inclusive* model, jobs in retail banking will continue to be good jobs. Particularly for lower-level employees, jobs may be better compensated, feature more training, and have more opportunity for teamwork, discretionary decision making, and advancement than those under the old bureaucratic system. The *segmented* model is more consistent with recent broad trends in the distribution of income. Under this model, a smaller number of highly skilled employees will attract the bulk of banks' investments in HR. Less-educated employees will find themselves less and less likely to gain skills or to advance, and they will be increasingly vulnerable to replacement by technology.

Platform Employees

The jobs in the industry that are likely to be good jobs, with interesting work, decision-making authority, relatively high levels of compensation accompanied by benefit packages, and opportunities for skill development and advancement, are those jobs that will be done by those employees with responsibility for maintaining customer relationships, particularly with those customers considered valuable by the bank. Banking positions in which employees are responsible only for simple transactions, on the other hand, are likely to be worse jobs, subject to downward pressure on wages and simplified or replaced by technology, so that little training is required and advancement is difficult. But this begs the key questions: Which employees will these be, what jobs will they do, and what practices will govern them?

For the platform jobs in which employees have traditionally done the less-routine and more-challenging work of sales and account servicing, site visits and the survey reflect a proliferation of local experimentation rather than systematic approaches to changes in employment practice. Nevertheless, the outline of a new approach to employment practice has begun to emerge on the retail platform. Table 5.2, which reports practices in head office branches of 135 U.S. retail banks, shows that over one-half of the banks in the survey had either quality circles, total quality management programs, or self-directed work teams for their platform employees.

Table 5.2. Employment Practices for Platform Employees in Head Office Branches (WFIC Retail Banking Survey 1994–1995) in %

Work Organization

	% with Practice	% of Banks with > = 50% Participation
On-line employee involvement (wording identical to Osterman 1994)		
Do platform employees participate in:		
• Quality circles?	24.1	22.7
• Total quality management programs?	17.4	19.5
• Self-directed work teams?	38.4	40.6
• At least one of the above practices?	53.3	38.5
Off-line employee involvement		
Do platform employees participate in focus groups?	53.8	44.9
Are there two or more different job titles on the branch platform?	57.2	—

	% of Banks with 100% of Staff X-Trained	% of Banks with >50% of Staff X-Trained	% of Banks with 0% of Staff X-Trained
What share of platform employees can fulfill all the functions of a teller?	5.7	12.0	72.2
What share of platform employees can fulfill some of the functions of a teller?	24.7	62.3	16.8

(continued)

Table 5.2. (*Continued*)

Do platform employees have the authority to correct:	% with Practice
• Check posted twice?	71.5
• CD sold at incorrect rate or term?	76.9
• Incorrect ATM order information?	80.4
• Incorrect check order information?	94.7
• Loan payment not credited to account?	73.3

Can platform employees change rates or waive fees for:	Change Rates	Waive Fees
• Checking accounts?	4.4	53.3
• Home equity loans?	9.1	16.3

Selection Criteria

	% of Banks with 100% of platform employees w/ college degrees	% of Banks with >= 25% of platform employees w/ college degrees	% of Banks with 0% platform employees w/ college degrees
What share of platform employees have college degrees?	7.1	45.2	50.8

Selection Technique

Before hiring:	% with Practice
• Do platform employees have multiple interviews?	72.4
• Are platform employees tested for interpersonal skills?	21.1

Compensation—Methods

	% with Practice
Do banks pay bonuses or give raises based on:	
• Commissions?	61.4
• Group or branch performance?	38.6
• The performance of the whole organization?	32.3

Compensation—Variability

	% of Banks with > = 4% at risk for group
What share of pay for platform employees is variable (or "at risk")?	36.2

Training Programs

	% of Banks with > = 50% participating
Do platform employees:	
• Participate in off-site training?	69.1
• Receive tuition reimbursement?	24.2

Contingent Employees

	% of Banks with > = 25% in category
	Mean Share
What share of platform employees:	
• Work part-time and receive benefits?	5.6 / 14.3
• Work part-time and receive no benefits?	3.4 / 8.2

165

One should not overstate this trend; most banks have implemented only some of the reinforcing elements of a "high-performance work system" (e.g., Huselid, 1995) that might be more broadly innovative. Careful screening, more training, and pay at risk are typical elements of such a work system. Table 5.2 also shows the variety in approaches to these practices. The survey data provide modest evidence for what might be considered "bundling" of practices (MacDuffie, 1995). A principal component analysis of key practices for platform employees (Table 5.3) yields five factors with eigenvalues greater than one,[6] with the component explaining the most variance features positive loadings for all variables except the use of part-time workers. This might be considered a "high-performance workplace" factor. The data also confirm, however, that banks in the sample have implemented many combinations of practice.[7]

Can Strategic HRM Explain the Diversity in Practice?

The literature on strategic fit suggests that differences in banks' approaches to HRM practice for their frontline employees may reflect differences in strategy. The data collected in the retail banking survey allow me to test that notion. I focus here on five types of strategic differences across retail banks. Previous literature has shown that some of these strategic types are associated with differences in HRM practice; some have been established in the strategy literature as effectively differentiating banks, and they allow me to examine both self-reports and independently derived measures of strategy.

Table 5.3. Results of Principal Components Factor Analysis of HRM Practices for "Platform Workers" in Retail Banks

Variables	Factor Loadings				
	1	2	3	4	5
Percentage part–time	−0.28	0.00	0.40	0.19	−0.03
Group bonus	0.19	0.46	0.36	0.19	−0.18
Organization bonus	0.26	0.35	0.34	0.30	−0.19
Share of pay at risk	0.25	−0.37	0.40	0.16	−0.03
Percentage with college education	0.32	−0.07	0.09	−0.62	−0.04
Percentage off-site training	0.34	−0.21	−0.36	0.31	0.02
Percentage with tuition reimbursement	0.45	−0.33	0.09	0.26	0.30
Percentage on-line E.I.	0.23	0.54	−0.30	−0.09	0.04
Percentage off-line E.I.	0.45	0.09	−0.26	0.07	−0.16
Eigenvalue	1.93	1.49	1.35	1.21	1.01
Percentage of variance explained	0.18	0.14	0.12	0.11	0.09

Two of my measures are self-reported by the head of the retail bank. One useful conceptualization of strategy in predicting differences in HRM practice is suggested by those who have found that emphasis on low-cost production ought to distinguish firms from those following niche-based or quality-based strategies. The low-cost strategy ought to be associated with segmentation strategies; niche- and quality-based strategies may require more inclusive practices. I operationalize this distinction using the same measure as Osterman (1994) (see Table 5.4). Second, I measure the extent to which the retail bank follows a "niche" rather than a mass market strategy, by creating an index (alpha = 0.88) from a series of ten survey questions (see Table 5.4) adapted from Nayyar (1993). To provide independent, observed (rather than self-reported) measures of strategies, I also look at observed measures of market-based strategic differentiation. Here I draw on the recent work of Mehra (1996), who identifies a number of market-based strategic distinctions in the banking industry. I ask whether more-diverse product ranges or a more-central role for the retail bank are associated with more inclusive practices and, conversely, whether greater focus on growth through mergers (which require cost containment) is associated with a segmentation strategy.

There is no evidence of correspondence between business strategies (whether observed or self-reported) and individual HRM practices in the industry. Table 5.4 reports comparisons by strategy across nine HRM practices governing platform employees. For each practice, I divided the sample into two groups, those banks that reported using the practice and those that did not. I then compared the means for the variables capturing the different business strategies of banks across the two groups and test for significant differences in strategy. Of 45 comparisons, only one difference in means was statistically significant at the 0.05 level.[8]

Muddy Waters: What's Driving Choices in Branch Networks?

Whereas many individuals in the industry are able to articulate clear differences between alternative models for organizing work in the retail bank, few organizations have deliberately chosen to move unambiguously toward one model or the other. Here uncertainty reigns at a number of levels. Most fundamentally, there are profound disagreements within banks on the necessity, primacy, and future of their branches, where most retail employees work. Interviews with top managers in virtually every bank in our study yielded predictions of dramatic decreases in the number of branches that the bank would operate and of equally rapid growth in the number of customers that would use telephone and computer banking almost exclusively. In this view, bank branches would provide only a few routine types of activities (e.g., the

Table 5.4. Comparisons of Means for Strategy Variables by HRM Practices on Platform

HRM Practices		Low Cost[1]	Niche[2]	Diversity[3]	Growth[4]	Retail Bank Centrality[5]
				Strategies		
Part-time (%)	No	−.11	3.10	.17	.16	.42
	Yes	.88	3.03	.16	.39*	.37
Group bonus	No	−.01	3.07	.16	.18	.42
	Yes	−.10	3.13	.17	.20	.39
Organization bonus	No	−.07	3.09	.17	.21	.42
	Yes	.03	3.11	.16	.13	.38
Share of pay at risk	No	.03	3.07	.16	.21	.41
	Yes	−.08	3.15	.18	.15	.41
College ed. required	No	.08	3.09	.16	.20	.41
	Yes	−.35	3.17	.18	.14	.44
Off-site training	No	.00	3.04	.13	.15	.39
	Yes	−.04	3.11	.18	.20	.42
Tuition reimbursement	No	.20	3.14	.16	.17	.42
	Yes	−.32	3.09	.18	.22	.40
On-line employee inv.	No	.14	3.14	.17	.21	.40
	Yes	−.22	3.06	.16	.16	.43
Off-line employee inv.	No	−.17	2.99	.14	.21	.41
	Yes	.07	3.18	.17	.17	.42

*Difference is statistically significant at $p < 0.05$.

[1]Low cost emphasis score: Following Osterman (1994), respondents were asked to assign 100 points to the goal of competing on the basis of cost control and to assign points to each of the following goals relative to cost control: error-free services, giving customers a wide choice of products, and giving customers products when and where they want them (e.g., if error-free delivery of services was twice as important as cost control, it would receive 200 points). An index score used the first principal component of the three variables. (The eigenvalue for this component is 2.06 and it explains 69% of the variance.) Low scores indicate a focus on cost control; high scores, emphasis on factors other than cost control.

[2]Niche strategy scale (alpha = 0.88). This scale uses ten questions from the survey: two questions each about strategies for five banking products and services from Nayyar (1993). The respondent was asked for the degree of emphasis (on a scale from 1 to 5 from "no emphasis" to "major, constant emphasis") on first, "selling customized services," and second, "serving special market segments," for checking accounts, certificates of deposits, investment products, home equity loans, and small business loans.

[3]Diversity in the product market is measured from FDIC data by the ratio of noninterest revenue to total revenue. This shows the extent of nontraditional or fee-based banking operations.

[4]Growth orientation is the annual average asset growth rate for the bank from 1990 to 1995 from FDIC data. This chiefly captures the merger activity engaged in by the bank.

[5]Retail Bank Centrality is measured from FDIC data by the ratio of loans other than commercial and industrial loans to total loans; the higher this ratio, the more the bank is involved with the retail market and less with the wholesale market.

collection and distribution of cash and coins), gradually evolving into vestigial appendages of larger, technologically vast and impressive financial delivery systems.

Visits to the *same* banks, however, also identified equally highly placed managers who expressed the belief that the branch network was in fact one of the few strategic advantages banks held over their competitors, and that customer migration would be slow. If some managers believed that branches were dinosaurs, in need not simply of adaptation but heading toward extinction or at the least toward fundamental reform, this rival group was quick to point out that nonbank competitors, such as brokerage houses and mutual fund companies, were actually opening branches. In this view, branches have a bright future as banks adapt them into "financial stores" aimed at preserving market share against non-bank competitors. Few banks have made clear decisions about the future of their branches; hedging rules the day. A recent estimate notes that nearly 87% of banking customers still use branches (Kennickell and Kwast, 1997), and the number of bank branches in the United States has actually increased rather than decreased in the past decade (Rhoades, 1996), even as the number of banks has decreased by one-third.

A second fundamental level of uncertainty revolves around the effective segmentation of customer markets. Just as deep as the divisions over the future of the branch network are internal debates over how best to segment customers. Formulas featuring mixes of geographic, demographic, and financial profiles abound, and hordes of consultants sell segmentation advice. But profound questions remain: For example, over what time horizon should customer profitability be calculated? Today's college student or young professional with a small checking balance may be a future mortgage and investment customer, whereas today's senior citizen with a large certificate of deposit will be less and less profitable over time. Even if banks actually were able to identify unprofitable customers, more problems abound. It is difficult and awkward to offer separate services to "segmented" customer groups in and across branches. (More than one large bank has attempted to open separate offices for "qualified" personal banking customers. To date, these approaches seem only to have confused consumers.) Further, regulation continues to raise challenges: Banks are mandated to make a portion of their services available to all members of the community and therefore are constrained from embarking on strategies explicitly designed to drive unprofitable customers away. These basic debates—which customers merit the bank's attention and how the banks ought to organize to serve them—continue inside most leading American banks.

Comparison of two case sites, Regional Bank and MultiState Bank, is instructive. At Regional, the strategy appeared clear. The bank was reorienting itself to sell aggressively. The idea was the bank would focus

especially on the most profitable of its customers and use all of its platform employees to drive the sales increases. Regional's responses to the
survey questionnaire were consistent with this expressed strategy.

A central marketing department, backed by leaders of the retail division, played a leading role in the redirection of Regional's retail bank.
At Regional, all employment practices on the platform were reorganized
with the primacy of customer relationships and sales in mind. Regional
introduced sales incentive programs and invested heavily in sales
training. Platform jobs were reconfigured in teams to free up time for
selling, and employees were granted wide discretion over servicing
decisions in order to augment their ability to make customers happy
and to follow this with a sale. A new selection program carefully targeted potential employees for sales aptitude, at the same time narrow-
ing the range of applicants considered to those with college degrees.

MultiState Bank responded similarly to the survey questions on bank
strategy, and their company literature suggested a nearly identical
focus on sales as a defining strategy. At MultiState, however, the changes
in HRM practice on the retail platform were minuscule in comparison
with those at Regional. Marketing and the retail division were less central in the redesign of retail jobs. At MultiState, a branch reengineering
initiative was being driven by those with responsibility for finance and
technology. Here, a heavy dose of individual sales incentives were introduced for platform employees, but these were coupled only with the
introduction of a massive investment in technology aimed at automating basic tasks and moving them out of the branch system entirely. Almost no attention was given to job redesign, new selection criteria, or
training.

These two cases demonstrate in a different way the point made
through analysis of the survey data. There is no consensus in the industry on the best way to organize or manage platform employees, even
when it might seem that these employees are critical to the performance
of the bank. It is not clear, for example, whether the considerably larger
investment of time and resources at Regional in platform job redesign
will yield clear performance benefits. In fact, no clear template exists
for the reorganization of platform jobs in order to carry out a strategy
that requires the development of richer customer relationships.

The ongoing case study at National Bank dramatizes some of the
key dimensions of uncertainty. For example, National has not decided
whether branches ought to be organized as "teams." An early version
of the redesigned work system referred to platform employees as an
"autonomous work team," but in subsequent literature the word "autonomous" was dropped, and then the staff responsible for implementing the redesign stopped referring to the groups as "teams" entirely. The
proportion of pay based on individual sales incentives also increased
dramatically between the original plan and the introduction of the new

design. Nevertheless, the central group responsible for the phased-in introduction of the new work system continues to press to organize employees in each branch as a team. The debates pit the central staff at National, who believe that teamwork is critical to sales and customer retention, against regional management. The regional managers, who bear direct responsibility for cost containment and short-run results, advocate more pay-at-risk on an individual basis, coupled with tighter supervision of platform employees.

Although the precise practices for platform employees' jobs vary, as does the speed at which banks are adopting new practices, general trends suggest that these jobs will increasingly employ college-educated workers who will have fairly wide discretion and substantial responsibility. Even where banks are following segmentation strategies, many platform jobs are being recast as jobs aimed at serving the upper end of the bank's customer segment. (Incidentally, the case study at National Bank suggests that even though these jobs may be more lucrative, the increased sales pressures will also make them more stressful.) Still, trends suggest that these jobs will emerge as "good jobs"; perhaps, along a number of dimensions, better jobs. No such clarity exists, however, with respect to tellers, to whom I turn in the next section.

Tellers

Tellers comprise about two-thirds of the employees in retail banks' branch systems. Here, the constellation of forces driving firm choices, and the resulting muddle, have serious ramifications for differentiating good jobs from bad jobs. In a typical retail bank, the future of tellers' jobs are considered neither systematically nor regularly. When the discussions do arise, however, contradictions abound. Tellers are sometimes considered as a cost to be minimized, sometimes as key point of customer contact worthy of substantial investment, and occasionally as both. (Analysis of tellers' practices, not reported here, replicated the results for lack of fit between strategy and HRM practices for platform employees.)

First, it is critical to realize that just as bank branches are not disappearing, neither are bank tellers, at least not nearly as quickly as one might expect. Despite a dramatic increase in what might have been thought of as labor-saving technology—the number of ATMs in U.S. banks increased eightfold from 1979–1994 (Berger, Kashyap, and Scalise, 1995)—the number of tellers employed in American banks has held remarkably steady over this same period (Demsetz, 1997). There are several partial explanations for this paradoxical result. First, customers have reaped most of the gains from ATMs; they have simply been able to reduce their holding balances (Daniels and Murphy, 1994) and to go to the bank more often (Bank Administration Institute, 1994).

Perhaps more to the point here, however, banks have begun to adapt the teller job. The change is uneven. Practices vary by bank, branch by branch within banks, and even teller station by teller station within branches. Some retail bank branches now have in place some practices characteristic of the inclusive model for their tellers. There is an expressed consensus that this is a sensible direction for the industry to take. For example, a 1994 report sponsored by a consortium of 10 leading banks emphasized the necessity of moving the teller role from that of simple transaction processor to that of an outwardly engaged, customer relations specialist with some expertise and sales responsibility (Bank Administration Institute, 1994).

Table 5.5 draws on the survey of retail banks to display some of the current variance in practice at the bank level by describing practices that govern tellers in the same head office branches as the platform employees of Table 5.2. Even though teller skill requirements may be rising, we found only one bank that required its tellers to have college educations; in some others, college-educated tellers were common. Banks further varied in the extent to which they invested in time-intensive screening techniques for teller positions, including selection procedures, such as multiple or team interviews, and, less commonly, personality or skills testing of applicants. Similarly, there was considerable variation in teller training, with a range of commitment to formal in-house training programs, arrangements for tuition reimbursement, and other informal training programs not detailed here.

As with the platform employees, selection, training, and compensation naturally raise questions about "bundling" of tellers' practices. Here the survey provided no empirical evidence for systematic linkage across practices. The practices in high-performance work systems may be complements. Regional Bank, for example, shared with us memos that expressed consistent directives, with involvement from branch managers, top retail executives, and HR staff in the redesign of the system. But such "high-performance practices" were explicitly described as substitutes elsewhere. For example, branch managers across Central Bank found themselves with severe constraints on pay stemming from merger-driven cost-cutting initiatives. They worked with HR staff to devote extra attention to recruiting in order to generate better pools of candidates and to implement training programs to remedy skill deficiencies.

In many banks, relationships between selection, compensation, training, and job design policies seemed not to have been considered in relation to one another at all. This in turn yielded a rich set of accounts of internal difficulties and contradictions. For example, increased entry requirements driven by HR or marketing functions in their search for more highly skilled employees went unaccompanied by corresponding pay increases, as those with cost responsibility refused to budget for raises. This left some banks with shortages of qualified tellers; or man-

Table 5.5. Employment Practices for Tellers in Head Office Branches (WFIC Retail Banking Survey 1994–1995) (in %)

Work Organization

	% with Practice	% of Banks with > = 50% Participation
On-line employee involvement (wording identical to Osterman 1994)		
Do tellers participate in:		
• Quality circles?	21.6	10.6
• Total quality management programs?	18.9	16.2
• Self-directed work teams?	18.2	13.9
• At least one of the above practices?	43.0	25.9
Off-line employee involvement		
Do tellers participate in focus groups?	51.5	16.3
Do tellers have the authority to correct a:		
• Check posted twice?	28.5	
• CD sold at incorrect rate or term?	7.1	
• Incorrect ATM order information?	34.4	
• Incorrect check order information?	51.2	
• Loan payment not credited to account?	25.4	

	% of Banks with 100% of Staff X-Trained	% of Banks with >50% of Staff X-Trained	% of Banks with 0% of Staff X-Trained
What share of bank tellers are trained to:			
• Open a checking account?	3.8	16.9	50.8
• Replace a lost ATM card?	24.0	37.2	45.7
• Sell a Certificate of Deposit?	6.9	19.2	53.1
• Correct a payment not credited to a home equity loan?	11.9	23.3	61.9

(continued)

Table 5.5. (Continued)

	% with Practice		
What share of banks have limited function tellers?	13.3		
Selection Criteria			
	% of Banks with 100% of Tellers w/College Degrees	% of Banks with >= 25% of Tellers w/College Degrees	% of Banks with 0% of Tellers w/College Degrees
What share of tellers have college degrees?	0.8	26.6	54.7
Selection Technique			
	% with practice		
Before hiring:			
• Do tellers have multiple interviews?	61.5		
• Are tellers tested for interpersonal skills?	40.8		
Compensation—Methods			
	% with Practice		
Do banks pay bonuses or give raises based on:			
• Commissions?	50.8		
• Group or branch performance?	32.6		
• The performance of the whole organization?	35.6		

Compensation—Variability

	% of Banks with > = 4% at Risk for Group
What share of pay for tellers is variable (or "at risk")?	17.6

Training Programs

	% with Practice	% of Banks with > = 50% Participating
Do tellers:		
• Participate in off-site training?	60.6	53.4
• Receive tuition reimbursement?	25.5	16.2

Contingent Employees

	Mean Share	% of Banks with > = 25% in Category
What share of tellers:		
• Work part-time and receive benefits?	13.9	23.7
• Work part-time and receive no benefits?	19.9	38.5

175

agers found recently hired tellers unsuited to the training initiatives they hoped would improve the tellers' ability to sell.

Perhaps nowhere was the lack of systematic attention to complementary practices more evident than with respect to incentive pay. The survey data showed that the share of pay attributable to performance incentives was fairly low for tellers, but it is worth noting that the introduction of performance-based incentive programs for tellers (as opposed to penalties for losses due to error), represented a sea change from the traditional model.

The exact design of the incentive plans varied not only from bank to bank but within banks from local area to local area and from branch to branch. Different banks offered individual incentives (including performance bonuses and commissions), small-group incentives (such as those based on the performance of the teller group or the branch), organization-wide incentives (such as profit sharing), and various combinations. Sources of the incentive plans were varied, driven by the marketing or sales staff, by top retail management, local managers, or combinations of the three, but typically without consensus on the implementation of broader changes. Bank after bank introduced incentive plans with only fleeting relationships to training programs or to the organization of work. Whether successful or unsuccessful, however, the plans tended to remain on the books, occasionally in practice, and sometimes such plans even accumulated in layers on top of one another.

The Role of Local Initiatives

Local managers continue to exercise considerable discretion over the design of tellers' jobs. The ways in which managers exercise this discretion often reflect less their own banks' explicit policies and more their understanding of the broader institutional environment; that is, what they see as the proper way to run a branch. These views in turn developed through their own experiences in the industry as well as through their customers' expectations.

Even though some banks (such as National Bank) are attempting to introduce systematic, bank-wide approaches to practices for tellers, this remains the exception. Even at National, an early attempt to forge one common design for the entire bank was abandoned after the very first pilot study, in one small region. The planning team agreed that all of the bank's rural branches would be allowed to deviate from the new design and to retain more traditional approaches to teller and platform jobs.

Participation in the official introductory training for tellers at Standard Bank illustrated the extent to which local discretion can be taken. Part of the teller training—we dubbed this "Move 'em Through Day"— was devoted to ensuring that customer lines moved swiftly, and aspects of the job and technology were designed by operations specialists with exactly this in mind. Here, the simple and routine aspects of tellers' jobs were paramount. A second significant training period—"Highly Suspicious Week"—was spent ensuring that tellers carefully followed all procedures to prevent fraud, theft, and deception. The policies here were generated by managers responsible for minimizing risk. Again, focus was on the routine aspects of tellers' work (although much of the advice contradicted the approach of the earlier segment).

A third training segment, "Would You Like a Mutual Fund With That?", was designed and delivered by marketing managers in the bank and focused entirely on sales and service activities. In it, tellers were introduced to a wide array of Standard's products and services and were encouraged to take an interest and to develop their knowledge of products and customers. Here, flexibility and breadth were paramount, in almost direct opposition to the lessons of the earlier sessions.

Not surprisingly, some newly hired tellers expressed confusion at these conflicting demands. How were they supposed to behave in the branches? Should they expect their jobs to be simple and routine or broad, with sales and product responsibilities? Standard Bank's trainers told the newly hired tellers that they should expect to adapt to the policies of the local branch manager to which they would eventually be assigned. Further investigation revealed variation in tellers' job design and incentive plans from branch to branch within the bank. However, this variation was apparently unconnected to other practices: the design features of the platform jobs in the same bank, the bank's centralized criteria for hiring tellers, or the use of varying types of incentive systems.

Tellers, Cross-Training, and Employee Involvement

Central challenges to the further development of the inclusive model for tellers are those associated with increasing the breadth and discretion of tellers' work. One natural direction that banks take is to train tellers to perform some of the functions that traditionally fall to platform employees. This cross-training may exist as part of a hierarchical structure in which tellers are groomed for promotion to the platform. Cross-training may also introduce the notion of the deeper transformation required of a fully inclusive branch model, relating less to a promotion-based internal labor market structure than to the desire to break down job categories completely.

Inclusive-model branches of the future might, at the extreme, feature teams in which all employees are able to provide a comprehensive range of customer services. Under this most radical redesign, "tellers" might disappear. Signs of this can already be detected in minibranches (for example, in supermarkets) staffed by only a few employees. Marketing and sales functions tend to especially favor this design. Those with more direct responsibility for cost control, however, cannot bring themselves to support such a transformation. Keeping a sharp eye on direct labor costs leads them to believe that there is significant waste associated with having overqualified employees perform teller functions.

In practice, tellers' cross-training is evidently not associated with banks' broader strategic direction or initiatives. Rather, local effects predominate. First, the survey data suggest that branch size matters greatly. Smaller branches, less likely to seek economies of scale through specialization, are significantly more likely to have tellers cross-trained to perform a range of platform functions.[9] The effect is roughly one-to-one. Branches with twice as many tellers have, on average, half the share of cross-trained tellers. Second, there is considerable scope in this area for influence by local branch managers. The survey gathered data from multiple (up to six) branches at 64 of the 135 banks in the survey. For these banks, the within-bank variance on the cross-training index actually exceeded the variance in the index across the different banks.

Fundamental change is also stymied by the feebleness of attempts to leverage investment in HR through the devolution of decision making and the establishment of programs that encourage employee involvement (EI). EI structures are not extensive in banking. Although retail banks tend to share information on organizational goals and performance with employees, other structural programs for involving tellers are less common, as are job definitions that grant broader discretion or authority. The levels of use of structural EI programs such as Quality Circles and self-directed work teams in bank branches, for example, fell well below the means for the general populations surveyed by Osterman (1994). And managers were further reluctant to push down specific decision making regarding key choices in customer service processes.

Here the legacy of the industry, one focused on command-and-control, hierarchical structures, and risk avoidance, plays a powerful role. Managers attributed lack of employee participation to the regulatory environment, which, they claimed, provided incentives for establishing and enforcing strong routines that limited discretion. Interestingly, however, not all managers shared this view. The general weakening of the historically strong environment has created new scope for interpretation of institutional imperatives. One manager at National Bank, pushing hard for EI, for example, had only recently moved into retail banking from another industry. She believed most bankers were reluctant to push decisions down to their branch employees, not because they were constrained by regulators, but because they were either too cheap to invest in other supportive practices (such as training) or were simply scared to share power.

Movement toward the inclusive model may be further weakened by the fact that, despite relatively few job cuts to date, nearly all banks *expect* the number of tellers to decrease dramatically in the fairly near future. National Bank's early strategic plan, for example, envisioned reducing the total number of tellers in the bank by nearly two-thirds, leaving about 35% of the current number after four years. Several other banks shared similar estimates. Banks therefore continue to be reluctant to invest much in training or compensation or in the time it might take to develop effective employee involvement for employees they eventually expect to lose.

Curiously, the cuts in tellers never quite seem to come. National's strategic plan, for example, has been continually revised so that the total reductions envisioned at latest writing are only about 25%, and almost two years into the four-year plan, no cuts had actually been implemented. Still, such plans, introduced in the absence of explicit strategies to promote or retrain tellers, make it difficult to sustain other commitment-based practices, and it is further possible that deep cuts in teller levels may occur should the pressure for cost containment grow more acute. Even though consolidation (or the threat of acquisition) provides incentives for cuts, it is worth noting that the industry in the middle 1990s enjoyed generally high profits, mostly attributable to favorable macroeconomic conditions.

Contingent Workers

Overall employment levels of tellers also mask another trend: the increasing use of part-time tellers. The secular trend is clear from national labor market data (e.g., Demsetz, 1997), these data obscure considerable variance within the industry. Some banks use part-timers extensively, others, rarely (Table 5.5). Even then, alternative models for the use of part-time tellers make the overall impact of these choices difficult to interpret. Put another way, this picture is complicated by segmentation *within* the teller position. Banks vary in the extent to which tellers actually do different jobs. Even banks that tend to embrace cross-training and investment in some tellers may employ other tellers in limited-function roles. About one in every eight banks in the survey sample, for example, had established simple-transaction teller lines. Such lines are staffed by part-time tellers with lower pay and less training than regular tellers.

By far the most common justification for using part-time tellers is to control costs. First, part-timers, when they do not receive benefits, are cheaper to employ on a per-hour basis. Second, the use of part-time and especially "peak-time" tellers enables the bank to match staffing to customer patterns, as most leading banks now use sophisticated staffing models to decrease tellers' idle time. Not all banks use part-timers so extensively, however, finding the extensive use of part-time employees, who tend to have higher turnover rates, inconsistent with the maintenance of customer relationships. For example, one manager responsible for a 20-branch local area argued strongly that part-time tellers were unlikely to provide the levels of customer service and sales referrals that he expected, and that he therefore had staffed his branches almost entirely with full-time workers. A variant on this approach is for banks to use part-timers, but more for "retention" than "secondary" reasons (Tilly, 1992); part-timers in these banks might be experienced workers who receive benefits and prefer to work part-time because of family commitments. One top executive claimed that his most effective branch employees were part-time working mothers. His bank, however, paid these workers prorated benefits and found them no less expensive to employ on a hourly basis than full-timers.

Call Center Representatives

Virtually all leading retail banks are rapidly expanding telephone banking. Most are consolidating telephone customer services into large centers and investing considerably in technologies that will enable more and more banking to be conducted over the telephone. Here, again, there is considerable variance in the extent to which higher investment practices are used and for which employees.

One choice, as in branches, is to segment call center work. The majority of simple customer service tasks can be done by relatively low-paid representatives with little training. Where possible, these services are then increasingly provided purely through automation with the involvement of the customer. More specialized sales and service activities can be directed to a smaller number of more sophisticated employees who are more carefully selected, have higher levels of education, receive more training, and command higher levels of base and incentive compensation. Calls can be directed to the appropriate channel through the use of technology and different routing schemes.

Not all call centers choose to segment sales and service functions, however. Some retail banks have chosen to implement a more broadly based high-commitment system, in which most or all representatives are capable of handling many sorts of calls and are able to pursue sales opportunities. Such workplaces are typically accompanied by higher rates of training, higher levels of compensation, lower levels of employee turnover, and more structures for employee involvement. Table 5.6 suggests that in the large banks we surveyed, the segmented model is more common, though neither universally nor clearly adopted.

One merger of two very large banks that we visited, both before and after the consolidation, illustrates both of the different models and fac-

Table 5.6. Employment Practices for Telephone Call Center Employees (WFIC Retail Banking Survey 1994–1995) (in %)

Work Organization

	% with Practice	% of Banks with > 50% Participation
On-line employee involvement (wording identical to Osterman 1994)		
Do call center employees participate in:		
• Quality circles?	38.8	7.0
• Total quality management programs?	25.6	11.6
• Self-directed work teams?	14.0	2.33
• At least one of the above practices?	46.6	15.3
Off-line employee involvement		
Do call center employees participate in focus groups?	76.7	25.6

	% of Banks with 100% of Call Center Employees in Category	% of Banks with > 50% of Call Center Employees in Category
What share of call center employees:		
• Regularly do sales referrals?	42.1	62.8
• Take sales calls	33.9	37.2
• Perform telemarketing?	5.8	10.7
• Can perform all tasks?	11.6	19.0

(continued)

181

Table 5.6. (continued)

Selection Criteria

	% of Banks with 100% of Call Center Employees w/College Degrees	% of Banks with > 25% of Call Center Employees w/College Degrees	% of Banks with 0% of Call Center Employees w/College Degrees
What share of call center employees have college degrees?	1.1	35.8	26.1

Selection Technique

	% with Practice
Before hiring:	
• Do call center employees have multiple interviews?	68.2
• Are call center employees tested for interpersonal skills?	25.9

Compensation—Methods

	% with Practice
Do banks pay bonuses or given raises based on:	
• Commissions?	42.6
• Group or team performance?	20.7
• The performance of the whole organization?	20.7

Compensation—Variability

	% of Banks with > 4% at Risk for Group
What share of pay for call center employees is variable (or "at risk")?	20.4

Training Programs

	% of Banks with > 50% Participating
	15.2
	6.7

	% with Practice
Do call center employees:	
• Participate in off-site training?	16.7
• Receive tuition reimbursement?	10.2

Contingent Employees

	% of Banks with > 25% in Category
	52.3
	30.7

	Mean Share
What share of call center employees:	
• Work part-time and receive benefits?	17.4
• Work part-time and receive no benefits?	9.2

183

tors affecting the choice. Prior to the merger, Financial Bank had invested considerably in professionalizing several of its call center operations. Well-paid college graduates, dressed in business attire, spent long workdays on telephones with retail customers; over time, they learned about the customer base of the bank as well as its product offerings. They were hired into the call center as an introduction to the bank; they received considerable training and expected opportunities for advancement. The underlying idea was that each representative should be broadly skilled, able quickly to meet a large array of customer needs or to identify others in the bank who could do so. Central Bank's call centers, on the other hand, clearly segmented sales and service. The service representatives, who made up the preponderance of the work force, had high rates of turnover. They were typically high-school-educated, not well paid, received relatively little training, and had few clear routes to advancement.

Shortly after the merger, it became clear that the managers of the former Financial Bank would be making all of the major decisions for the merged entity. One of the decisions they made was to abandon their own inclusive model when the call centers of the two banks were consolidated. The "professionalized" call centers were seen as more costly to run; their benefits, while clear in principle, were diffuse and difficult to measure, and, whereas the retail-bank-level strategy clearly called for enhanced attention to customer needs, this attention was swamped by the corporate-level strategy that quickly required measurable cost savings in the context of the merger. It should be noted that, though it was abandoned, the Financial Bank call center model was not seen to have failed. Inside the new, merged bank, discussions over reviving the model continue, as managers continue to search for ways to serve customers more effectively.

Functional "Silos" and Local Decisions

Banks continue to find it difficult to predict what retail customers want and which retail customers are the most profitable to serve. Each customer represents a purchaser of multiple products that require ongoing servicing and have uncertain value, and each has different preferences for using the various channels through which the products might be serviced. The typical bank as a whole organization is therefore committed to multiple principles: cost efficiency, risk minimization, better relationships with existing customers, and increasingly active prospective sales work. Responsibility for achieving success on these dimensions typically is split across the different functions (not-so-jokingly referred to as "silos" in many banks) around which banks remain organized.

Employment practices in the retail divisions of large banks typically represent the accumulation of programs, some complementary and some contradictory. Clashes between those responsible for making the bank more cost efficient and those focused on customer initiatives play out as conflicts over choices in employment practice. For example, interviews with marketing and retail managers at New World Bank revealed that a sales-focused redesign had been thwarted by pressures to contain costs. With merger discussions looming, training programs and selection initiatives coupled with above-market pay were abandoned. However, the sales incentive programs and redesigned branch jobs remained in place.

Equally salient are conflicts between the interests of those responsible for minimizing risks and those responsible for generating revenue. Risk avoidance is expressed through tight control procedures and narrowly defined, carefully separated jobs and routines. A focus on revenue generation, in contrast, is reflected in experimentation with broader jobs, more discretion, and supporting practices characteristic of the high-commitment model.

Considering the retail delivery system—its branches and call centers—as an object of organizational-level strategic change embodied in employment practices, the strategic direction of most banks appears incoherent. Mutually supportive HR practices integrated to achieve a set of goals related to organizational strategies are rare; the norms are bundles of internal contradictions. For example, technologies may be designed to increase workers' abilities to make sensible point-of-sale decisions, but restrictive job designs prevent workers from exercising these choices. Or, vice versa, technology is restrictive but rules are broadening.[10] Incentive-driven compensation is not backed by training, or training is not backed by a reward structure. These collections of practice themselves are the expression of different interests inside the bank, as different functional actors may hold different notions of the role and the future of the retail bank and the fate of its delivery systems.

Integration across these different functional areas, and responsibility for performance on multiple dimensions, occurs at high levels, where the details manifested in employment practices receive relatively little attention. The task of balancing contradictory strategic and functional initiatives, therefore, falls much closer to the workplace. Much of it is done by local managers who are, in turn, constrained by forces above them: technological choices, cost considerations, and the extent to which others value broader consistency in policy. Where these local managers retain their discretion, their choices are guided by their own industry experiences and their sense of what kinds of practice are necessary if customers are to be served effectively.

Uncertainty and Strategic Fit

Continuing uncertainty creates a space in which functional battles may be waged over the content of employment practice. Even those organizational decision makers who see the retail bank as a sales-focused profit center may have differing views on which practices and employees are crucial to maintaining and improving customer relationships. No model has emerged as obviously superior economically. Customers are won or lost only gradually; the profitability of doing business with particular customers emerges only after even longer periods. And the relationship-based aspects of performance that the retail bank most directly affects are swamped by those shorter term considerations that attract most attention from financial markets, particularly cost savings and merger activity.

The institutional consensus over what practices are legitimate continues to erode. This lack of consensus, combined with the absence of observable obstacles to change, creates opportunities for the introduction and withdrawal of particular practices at a fairly rapid rate. Few constraining fetters prevent experimentation. The tiny share of employees organized by unions (under 2% in 1995) means that management has the latitude to introduce changes in employment practice without negotiation, and the rapid rate of consolidation of the industry has created such a sense of insecurity among employees with industry experience that adverse labor market reaction is also unlikely to discourage experimentation.

What we might expect to observe in the coming years is therefore a process akin to the development of consensus over technologically dominant designs (e.g., Utterback and Abernathy, 1975; Van de Ven and Garud, 1994). Different groups within and across organizations will attempt to build coalitions to support their vision of a best approach to the organization of the retail system and will also engage in constructing norms in the broader institutional environment. Again, however, not all actors will interpret the conditions similarly. Some see the opportunity for deep transformation of the system. Where there is questioning of the basic premise of what ought to be done in branches, both radically inclusive and sharply segmented approaches to branch work may appear better suited to the new environment than do minor adaptation of tellers' and platform employees' jobs. But this vision of transformation is not widely shared. Much more commonly, employment practices change piecemeal through coalition and compromise among competing interests.

A process of transformation might be sharpened and hastened somewhat even if no dominant best practices emerge, to the extent that best practices are discovered (or believed) to be contingent on particular business strategies. For example, some argue that workers will be in better jobs where their employers emphasize competition on the basis of quality, product adaptability, or superior service rather than on the basis of low-cost production. The premise is that niche strategies require training, income maintenance, some level of employment security, and employee involvement; cost-based strategies produce downward pressure on wages, decreased expenditure on training, downsizing, and reduced employee discretion.

In retail banking, two factors militate against any straightforward correspondence between strategies and jobs. First, it is true that the banking industry comprises firms that are growing quickly and those growing at a more moderate pace, some specializing in serving up-market customer bases, others focusing more on the mass market. But for many banks, these strategic differences are neither sharp nor clearly intentional. Rather, strategy is often emergent rather than deliberate (Mintzberg and Waters, 1985), the product of a sequence of what are, only in time, revealed to be critical decisions. Thus HR choices are less explicitly complementary to strategy.

Second, even given clarity on strategy, there are no assurances that particular strategies will evoke unique approaches to employment practice (Cappelli and Singh, 1992). Unless dominant models of best practice crystallize, even contingent on strategy, linkages between business strategy and particular HR practices may be weak at best. More specifically, either an inclusive or a segmented approach to employment systems in the branch, for example, might be well suited to a high-customization, relationship-focused approach to the retail market.

Future Prospects

Whether the inclusive model or the segmented model is more likely to prevail, therefore, depends on a set of considerations that include, but are not limited to, performance-based tests of each model. Should one or the other model be better suited to a particular strategic approach (such as continued merger activity) that emerges as dominant, this will have significant effects on practice. Should there be a variety of possible strategic routes to success in the industry, however, the prognosis is less certain. Those responsible for designing the system may find it difficult to separate effects of strategy from effects of implementation or to identify better practices, and there may be more scope for the legitimation of approaches to practice that is less dependent on performance and more on constructed consensus around appropriate models. For example, the prevailing command-and-control ideology in the industry, and the persistent vision of technology as labor-saving, may largely work against the upgrading of tellers' jobs unless alternative systems display clear, compelling performance advantages.

Assuming the industry continues to survive in the face of increasing cross-sector competition, the next decade will continue to feature the emergence of some good jobs in retail banking under a new employment paradigm. The new systems will look less and less like a bureaucratic internal labor market and more like a high-performance work environment with increased responsibility and pay incentives for at least some employees. The open question is, What share of the jobs will be good jobs? Initiatives developed from line management, marketing and sales functions, and HR staff focus on orienting employees toward customer relationships and the use of new technology. But these initiatives are being implemented in the context of broader market and technological forces that undermine the same initiatives, by driving wages and full-time work down, decreasing the availability of funds for training, and encouraging the implementation of technologies that replace rather than empower workers. Responsibility for choosing and implementing practices is spread throughout organizations, many functions have an interest, and frequent reorganizations (whether along product lines, geographies, or, most recently, customer segments) bring little clarity to the problem.

Aspects of both the inclusive and segmented models may continue to hold their appeal for some time. The segmented model offers rationalization and immediate cost savings, hedging this bet with its attention at the top end to premium or high-value customer relationships. The inclusive model, however, has its appeal too. It is especially attractive to retail bankers who believe that the future of their organizations lies in being able to serve a broad range of customers profitably, and that where employees are not contributing positively to customer relationships, they are being misused.

We might expect similar choices to play out broadly across major portions of the growing service sector of the American economy. These choices in turn may have considerable impact on the labor market experiences of American workers, particularly those with relatively low levels of education. On the one hand, the high-school-educated workers in the American service sector will find themselves drawn into jobs that feature economic security, training and growth, and the opportunity to do interesting work. On the other, they will be excluded from such opportunities.

Acknowledgment Thanks to the National Policy Association, the Sloan Foundation, the National Science Foundation, and the Wharton Financial Institutions Center for underwriting the research on which this paper is based.

Notes

1. Interestingly, the evidence for actual economies from mergers is limited at best (Berger, Hunter, and Timme, 1993).

2. Osterman (1984) suggests anecdotally that stable employment arrangements for bankers working with corporate customers were beginning to break down at least a decade earlier due to intensified competition.

3. I use these two terms in the sense suggested by Meyer, Brooks, and Goes (1990). Adaptation refers to "first-order" change, in which fundamental assumptions and organizing principles are not questioned. Transformation, or "second-order" change, allows the possibility of change in basic principles and assumptions.

4. These studies were sponsored by the Alfred P. Sloan Foundation and by the National Science Foundation, and conducted under the auspices of the Wharton Financial Institutions Center at the University of Pennsylvania.

5. In principle, one could envision a third model, one focused purely on cost containment, with minimal investment in any front office employees. In practice, our research has identified no banks pursuing this avenue.

6. Rotation produces equally murky results.

7. Coherent groupings or clusters of practices are not distinguishable. I applied several clustering methods to the sample, both within and across the employee job groups, using subsets of the employment practices summarized in Table 5.2 (as well as many others not included in the tables). Whereas the algorithms produce clusters (the nature of the methods ensures this result), the clusters were not obviously interpretable. For each method and group of variables, I applied Mojena's (1981) heuristic for "stopping rules." I was typically unable to reject the hypothesis that the data belonged to one large cluster.

8. I also employed a multivariate analysis, allowing me to estimate the effects of one type of strategy while controlling for the others and to control for size and profitability of the banks (I proxied the former by 1995 total assets, the latter by 1995 return on assets). I estimated ordinary least squares regression models using the continuous measures in Table 2 as dependent variables and logistic regression models on the binary measures reported in the table. I specified full models with all five measures of strategy plus the two control variables. In the full models, about the same number of relationships emerged as one might expect by chance. The only reasonably robust result was that larger, faster growing banks were more likely to use part-time workers and used a larger share of such workers; the model for the use of contingent workers was the only one in which the strategy variables as a group significantly ($p < 0.05$) explained variation in HRM practice.

The general failure to reject the hypothesis that there is no relationship between strategy and HRM practices appears robust to a range of definitions and constructions of independent and dependent variables. I also analyzed both scales and single-item measures of strategy and practice, including a wider set of HRM practices for platform employees, and a similar range of practices for tellers and branch managers. No patterns of results emerged, and the results scarcely differ from those one would expect by chance.

9. Cross-training was indicated with an index (Cronbach's alpha = 0.77) of the share of tellers cross-trained to perform the four platform tasks listed in Table 5.5.

10. See Hunter and Lafkas (1998).

References

Akhavein, J. D., Berger, A. N., and Humphrey, D. B. (1996). The effects of bank megamergers on efficiency and prices: Evidence from the profit function. *Review of Industrial Organization*, 12 (1): 95–139.

Aldrich, H. and Fiol, M. (1994). Fools rush in? The institutional context of industry creation. *Academy of Management Review*, 19: 645–670.

Althauser R. P. and Kalleberg, A. L. (1981). Firms, occupations, and the structure of labor markets: a conceptual analysis. In I. Berg (ed.), *Sociological perspectives on labor markets*. New York: Academic Press.

Arthur, J. B. (1992). The link between business strategy and industrial relations systems in American steel minimills. *Industrial and Labor Relations Review*, 45 (3): 488–506.

Bank Administration Institute. (1994). The RDS report on the future of retail banking delivery. Chicago, Ill.: BAI.

Berger, A. N., Hunter, W. C., and Timme, S. G. (1993). The efficiency of financial institutions: A review and preview of research past, present, and future. *Journal of Banking and Finance*, 17: 221–250.

Berger, A. N., Kashyap, A. K., and Scalise, J. M. (1995). The transformation of the U.S. banking industry: What a long, strange trip it's been. *Brookings Papers on Economic Activity*, 2: 55–218.

Burtless, G. (ed.) (1990). *A future of lousy jobs? The changing structure of U.S. wages*. Washington: The Brookings Institution.

Cappelli, P. (1995). Rethinking employment. *British Journal of Industrial Relations*, 33 (4): 563–602.

Cappelli, P. and Singh, H. (1992). Integrating strategic human resources and strategic management. In D. Lewin, O. S. Mitchell, & P. Sherer (eds.), *Research Frontiers in Industrial Relations and Human Resources*. Madison, WI: IRRA, pp. 165–192.

Cohen, Y. and Pfeffer, J. (1986). Organizational hiring standards. *Administrative Science Quarterly*, 31 (1): 1–24.

Crane, D. B. and Bodie, Z. (1996). The transformation of banking. *Harvard Business Review*, March–April: 109–117.

Daniels, K. N. and Murphy, N. B. (1994). The impact of technological change on household transactions account balances: An empirical cross-section study. *Journal of Services Research*, 8 (2): 113–119.

Demsetz, R. (1997). Human resource needs in the evolving financial sector. *Current Issues in Economics and Finance*, 3 (13).

DiMaggio, P. J. and Powell, W. W. (1983). The iron cage revisited: Institutional isomorphism and collective rationality in organizational fields. *American Sociological Review*, 48: 147–160.

Huber, G. P. and Power, D. J. (1985). Retrospective reports of strategic-level managers: Guidelines for increasing their accuracy. *Strategic Management Journal*, 6: 171–180.

Hunter, L. W. (1998). Customer differentiation, institutional fields, and the quality of entry level service jobs. Unpublished manuscript, Wharton School, Philadelphia, PA.

Hunter, L. W. and Lafkas, J. J. (1998). Information technology, work practices, and wages. Paper presented at the 50th Annual Meeting of the Industrial Relations Research Association, Chicago, IL.

Huselid, M. A. (1995). The impact of human resource management practices on turnover, productivity, and corporate financial performance. *Academy of Management Journal*, 38: 635–672.

Jackson, S. E., Schuler, R. S., and Rivero, J. C. (1989). Organizational characteristics as predictors of personnel practices. *Personnel Psychology*, 42 (4): 727–786.

Keltner, B. (1995). Relationship banking and competitive advantage: Evidence from U.S. and Germany. *California Management Review*, 37 (4): 45–72.

Keltner, B. and Finegold, D. (1996). Adding value in banking: Human resource innovations for service firms. *Sloan Management Review*, 38 (1): 57–68.

Kennickell, A. B. and Kwast, M. L. (1997). Who uses electronic banking? Results from the 1995 survey of consumer finances. Working paper, Division of Research and Statistics, Board of Governors of the Federal Reserve System, Washington, DC.

MacDuffie, J. P. (1995). Human resource bundles and manufacturing performance: Organizational logic and flexible production systems in the world auto industry. *Industrial and Labor Relations Review*, 48: 197–221.

Mehra, A. (1996). Resource and market based determinants of performance in the U.S. banking industry. *Strategic Management Journal*, 17: 307–322.

Meyer, A. D., Brooks, G. R., and Goes, J. B. (1990). Environmental jolts and industry revolutions: Organizational responses to discontinuous change. *Strategic Management Journal*, 11: 93–110.

Mintzberg, H. and Waters, J. A. (1985). Of strategies, deliberate and emergent. *Strategic Management Journal*, 6: 257–272.

Mojena, R. (1981). Hierarchical grouping methods and stopping rules—An evaluation. *Computer Journal*, 20: 359–363.

Nayyar, P. R. (1993). On the measurement of competitive strategy: Evidence from a large multiproduct U.S. firm. *Academy of Management Journal*, 36: 1652–1670.

Osterman, P. (1984). White-collar internal labor markets. In P. Osterman (ed.), *Internal labor markets*. Cambridge, MA: M.I.T. Press, pp. 163–190.

Osterman, P. (1987). Choice of employment systems in internal labor markets. *Industrial Relations*, 26: 46–67.

Osterman, P. (1994). How common is workplace transformation and how can we explain who adopts it? Results from a national survey. *Industrial and Labor Relations Review*, 47: 173–188.

Pfeffer, J. and Cohen, Y. (1984). Determinants of internal labor markets in organizations. *Administrative Science Quarterly*, 29: 550–572.

Piore, M. J. and Sabel, C. F. (1984). *The second industrial divide*. New York: Basic Books.

Rhoades, S. A. (1996). Bank mergers and industrywide structure, 1980–1994. Board of Governors of the Federal Reserve System *Staff Studies*, New York.

Rosenkopf, L. and Tushman, L. M. (1996). The coevolution of community networks and technology: Lessons from the flight simulator industry. Working paper, Wharton School, Management Department, Philadelphia, PA.

Schuler, R. S., and Jackson, S. E. (1987). Organizational strategy and organization level as determinants of human resource management practices. *Human Resource Planning*, 10 (3): 125–141.

Snell, S. A. (1992). Control theory in strategic human resource management: The Mediating effect of administrative information. *Academy of Management Journal*, 35 (2): 292–327.

Tilly, C. C. (1992). Dualism in part-time employment. *Industrial Relations*, 31: 330–347.

Utterback, J. and Abernathy, W. (1975). A dynamic model of process and product innovation. *Omega*, 3: 639–656.

Van de Ven, A. and Garud, R. (1994). The coevolution of technical and institutional events in the development of an innovation. In J. Baum and J. Singh (eds.), *Evolutionary dynamics of organizations*. London: Oxford University Press.

6

Product Strategies, Work Force Skills, and "High-Involvement" Work Practices

GEOFF MASON

1. Introduction

In recent years, much attention has been given in industrialized nations to the potential efficiency gains for manufacturing enterprises of adopting new "leaner" production practices and more systematic approaches to product "quality management." Common examples of the objectives pursued under these headings include faster turnover of stocks of components and work-in-progress; lower product reject rates; improved communications between design, engineering, and production departments; a reduction in the number of suppliers; and the imposition of higher quality standards on incoming raw materials and components.

In many cases, this search for efficiency and product quality gains has been associated with changes in work organization designed to secure higher levels of task flexibility among production workers and greater involvement of such workers in day-to-day decision making and performance improvements. Several recent studies suggest that "high-involvement" work practices, such as the use of self-directed work teams, flexible job definitions, and employee problem-solving groups can contribute to enhanced productivity and/or profitability as long as they are accompanied by appropriate changes in work systems as a whole; for example, in shop floor layout, training levels, and pay-setting procedures (see Ichniowski et al., 1996, for an assessment of recent empirical studies of the links between innovative work practices and business performance).

However, despite the wide publicity given to the potential benefits of high-involvement work practices, there is also much evidence that the diffusion of such practices is still rather slow and piecemeal (Osterman, 1994; Ichniowski and Shaw, 1995). In a recent study based on automobile assembly plants in several different countries, Pil and MacDuffie (1996) argue that the rate of adoption of high-involvement work practices is closely related to the complementarity of pre-existing human resource (HR) strategies and to a range of organizational charac-teristics affecting the perceived costs and benefits of changing work practices. Thus, for example, they find the recent extension of high-involvement work practices at plant level to be strongly associated with "disruptions" in routine, such as the introduction of new models of automobile.

Pil and MacDuffie also report that many U.S. and Canadian auto as-sembly plants had retained traditional low-involvement work practices because, among other things, they tended to be engaged in high-volume production of single models and thus had less incentive to introduce more flexible work systems than assembly plants elsewhere that had a more-diverse product mix. This point is consistent with the findings of other cross-country studies at the establishment level, which have identified correspondences between predominant product strategies, production technologies, and modes of work organization in different national in-dustries. For example, British-German comparisons of matched samples of establishments in several different branches of manufacturing suggest that British enterprises tend to specialize in more standardized and lower value-added product areas than their German counterparts. These differ-ences in product strategy are associated with markedly less flexible and less skill-intensive forms of machinery utilization and work organization in Britain than is found in Germany (Steedman and Wagner, 1987, 1989; Mason, van Ark, and Wagner, 1994).

Several of these comparisons of matched samples of production es-tablishments in Western European countries have now been extended to the United States. This chapter draws on the results of these U.S.–European studies to examine how inter-country and inter-industry dif-ferences in the rate of adoption of new work practices are closely related to differences in the predominant product strategies (and associated use of physical and human capital resources) pursued by enterprises in each country. The overall aim is to place the recent uneven diffusion of high-involvement work practices in U.S. industry—as surveyed in other chapters in this book—in some international perspective.

As shown in Tables 6.1–6.3, the different sets of cross-country com-parisons to be considered covered selected branches of food process-ing (cookies and crackers) and industrial machinery and equipment (pumps, valves, and springs; high-speed machinery and vehicle com-ponents). In each case, the samples of plants were carefully matched for principal product area. Information was gathered during visits to individual plants where detailed semi-structured interviews were held with senior managers (managing directors or factory managers, in the case of smaller plants; production and personnel managers in larger plants). Each visit also included direct observation of production pro-cesses and work organization on the shop floor, and it was therefore sometimes possible to speak with production supervisors as well as

Table 6.1. Number of Plants Visited by Employment Size Group
in Cookie and Cracker Manufacturing Industries

Employment size-group	U.S.	Britain	Netherlands	Germany	France
<200	1	2	2	3	1
200–499	2	2	2	1	3
500–999	5	2	1	2	2
≥1000	0	4	0	2	0
Total	8	10	5	8	6

Dates of fieldwork: U.S., 1993–1994; Britain, The Netherlands, Germany, and France, 1989–1991.

other employees. The visits lasted between one-half day and one day
and, if necessary, were followed up with further detailed enquiries by
telephone or letter. Although the heavy costs of this kind of field work
necessitated reliance on relatively small national samples of plants, care
was taken to ensure that the mixes of small, medium-sized, and large
plants in each sample were reasonably representative of national populations of plants.

The chapter proceeds as follows: Section 2 compares the extent of
work force flexibility and team-working in the process departments of
cookie factories in five countries: the United States, Germany, Netherlands, France, and Britain. Section 3 reports on the development of
"cellular" modes of shop floor organization in the United States, Dutch,
and British precision engineering industries. Section 4 compares the
extent and nature of shop floor team-working systems in high-speed
machinery and vehicle component plants in the United States, Britain,
and Germany, with particular emphasis on the role of production supervisors. In Section 5, the main findings of the three studies are brought

Table 6.2. Number of Plants Visited by Product Area and Employment
Size Group in Precision Engineering Industries

	U.S.	Britain	Netherlands
Product area			
Pumps	8	5	3
Valves	4	4	3
Springs	6	4	3
Total	18	13	9
Employment size-group			
<100	8	2	3
100–199	3	7	6
≥200–499	4	3	0
500	3	1	0
Total	18	13	9

Dates of fieldwork: U.S., 1994; Britain and The Netherlands, 1991.

Table 6.3. Number of Plants Visited by Product Area and
Employment Size Group in High-Speed Machinery and Vehicle
Components Industries

	U.S.	Britain[a]	Germany[b]
Product area			
High-speed machinery	5	4	3
Vehicle components	5	5	5
Total	10	9	8
Employment size-group			
<250	3	2	1
250–499	3	2	0
500–999	1	2	1
1000–1999	2	2	4
≥2000	1	1	2
Total	10	9	8

Dates of fieldwork: U.S., 1995; Britain and Germany, 1993 and 1996.
[a]Excludes one of the ten British sample establishments visited in 1993 (in the 500–999 size-group), which could not be contacted for follow-up interviews in 1996.
[b]Excludes one of the nine German sample establishments visited in 1993 (in the 1–249 size-group), which had closed down by 1996.

together for an assessment of the links between product strategies, work force skills, and employment practices.

2. Work Force Flexibility and Team-Working in Cookie Production

Modern cookie manufacturing typically employs continuous-flow methods of production with output and employment in most countries being heavily concentrated in highly mechanized—sometimes highly automated—plants. In both the United States and Western Europe, the great majority of employees in wrapping and packing departments were assigned to low-skill tasks of a highly repetitive nature. Hence, the main inter-country differences of interest in terms of shop floor work organization were identified among "process" departments covering the ingredient handling, dough-mixing, cookie-forming, and baking stages of production.

In German, Dutch, and French plants, nearly all process workers had been trained to be able to switch flexibly as required between all main areas of operation (mixing, cookie-forming, and oven control). In the German plants, initial on-the-job training for these tasks averaged only four months, reflecting the fact that 90% of trainees had previously completed apprenticeships in the craft-baking sector (Table 6.4). In the Netherlands and in France, where few newly recruited process workers had relevant previous experience, initial on-the-job training times were roughly two to three times longer than in Germany. In all three Conti-

Table 6.4. Qualifications and Training of Production Process Workers and Supervisors in National Samples of Cookie Manufacturing Plants

	U.S.	Britain	Netherlands	Germany	France
Process workers	No vocational qualifications	No vocational qualifications	40% qualified at junior vocational schools	90% craft-skilled bakers	10% craft-skilled bakers
Initial on-the-job training (average)	2 months	2 months	7 months	4 months	12 months
	Usually single task area	Usually single task area	Full range of tasks	Full range of tasks (but not always all products)	Usually full range of tasks (but not always all products)
Production supervisors	Approx. 10–15% with vocational qualifications (mainly 4-year graduates)	15% with vocational qualifications (mainly university graduates)	Two thirds with vocational qualifications	All craft-skilled bakers (almost 75% *Meister*-qualified)	40% with vocational qualifications

nental European industries, the great majority of plants had been operating for many years with three-person teams of process workers taking responsibility for the mixing and baking stages of production on at least two oven-lines at a time. However, these teams were typically not "self-directed" but rather were managed on a day-to-day basis by traditional supervisors with overall responsibility for work assignments and discipline; indeed, in German plants, three quarters of production supervisors had gained a specialist supervisory qualification (the *Meisterbrief*) (Mason, van Ark, and Wagner, 1994, 1996).

In the U.S. and British samples, average initial on-the-job-training times for process workers were much shorter (roughly two months in each case) and typically covered only a single narrowly defined task area (e.g., mixing). At later stages of their careers, American and British process workers could receive further training for other jobs (e.g., oven-operator) but—in contrast to their counterparts in Continental Europe—they were still rarely expected to take responsibility for more than one task area at a time during any given production shift. Hence, in the American and British plants visited, each individual oven-line typically had three process workers assigned to it with hardly any "functional flexibility" (between task areas on the same line) or "horizontal flexibility" between jobs on different oven-lines (Mason and Finegold, 1997).

These inter-country differences in training and deployment of process workers reflected important differences in product mix and production scale. For example, in the Continental European industries—and particularly in Germany—most plants were engaged in small- and medium-batch production of elaborate, multitextured kinds of cookies involving multiple production processes (Table 6.5). The skills and know-how required to deliver this relatively diverse product mix were also capable of supporting the greater incidence of functional and horizontal flexibility found in those plants. By contrast, product strategies in U.S. and British plants were typically focused on more simple, undecorated, low-value-added kinds of cookies—and in the United States, in particular, were geared to manufacturing these kinds of products on a much larger scale than elsewhere. Hence the more-limited training received by American and British process workers was consistent with the greater degree of repetition in the day-to-day tasks and problem-solving activities required of them.

In both the U.S. and British samples, there were a few isolated examples of current or past experimentation with functional flexibility among process workers (with associated extra investments in training). In the United States, recent union agreements with large cookie producers have led to reductions in the number of job classifications and more cross-training between different jobs carried out by process workers. However, increases in flexibility have been confined to activities within separate departments such as mixing or baking, and do not cross over between different de-

Table 6.5. Distribution of Output (Tonnage) by Quality-Grade in
National Samples of Cookie Manufacturing Plants*

Quality	U.S.	Britain	Netherlands	Germany	France
Basic-single wrapping[a]	15	35	25	15	20
Basic-multiple wrappings[b]	30	0	0	0	0
Medium[c]	50	60	60	50	70
High[d]	5	5	15	35	10
Total	100	100	100	100	100

*% shares of output, rounded to nearest 5%

[a]"dry" undecorated cookies or crackers made from relatively cheap ingredients (e.g., vegetable or animal fats), stacked in cylinder form and wrapped in a single layer of plastic film.

[b]As described for [a] but with more than one layer of packaging (very commonly found in the U.S. but rare in the European countries).

[c]Cookies requiring at least one secondary production process after baking, such as chocolate coating or sandwich-filling with cream or jam; usually sold with at least two layers of packaging. Undecorated cookies made with more expensive ingredients such as butter are also included in this category.

[d]Elaborate, multitextured cookies requiring two or more secondary (postbaking) production processes, usually stacked in successive small piles, multiwrapped and boxed; includes assortments of cookies made from expensive ingredients.

partments as in Continental Europe.[1] Similarly, in Britain some employers have recently developed a new grade of multi-skilled employees who have been trained to work in different departments, but these people stay within a fixed task area during each production shift.[2]

In part, this can be attributed to the sheer length and width of some oven-lines and sometimes the positioning of departments on different floors, which make it physically unrealistic for workers to move beyond single task areas on individual lines, especially in some American plants. But employment practices in both the United States and Britain still tend to be driven by long-established managerial policies of removing the "craft" element from cookie production and attempting to develop it as a scientifically controllable process with strictly defined limits on manual intervention by individual workers. For example, some managers in both countries were openly concerned about excessive "tampering" with the production process by shop floor employees, and U.S. plants in particular were often distinguished by their systematic efforts to develop new control systems and sampling test procedures that would "simplify" (rather than upgrade) the work of semi-skilled or low-skilled machine operators.

In the case of the U.S. industry, this low-skill mode of shop floor work organization was reinforced by decisive advantages in terms of the level of automation, the use of larger-capacity equipment (for example, longer and wider oven-lines) and, in particular, the ability to run machinery uninterrupted for much longer periods of time than in European countries. By contrast, in Britain, only a small minority of leading plants were able to specialize in the highly automated production of standardized cookies on the same scale as is widespread in the U.S. industry. And in the great majority of British plants—as in the German, French, and Dutch industries—the pattern of customer demand is such that changeovers of product recipes and machinery need to be much more frequent than in the United States.

Comparisons of average productivity levels in the five countries found crude output (tonnage) per employee-hour in U.S. sample plants to be approximately 25–40% higher than in the Dutch, French, and British samples and about 80% higher than in German plants.[3] Even when some account was taken of inter-country differences in the mix of product qualities, estimates of "quality-adjusted" productivity levels still placed the United States ahead of all four European countries, albeit with a much smaller lead over the German industry than that implied by the crude tonnage-based productivity measure.

To recapitulate, therefore, in U.S. cookie plants, the scarcity of high-involvement shop floor work practices is associated with the continued relative success of existing low-skill, low-involvement practices tailored to large-scale production of largely standardized product varieties. Given the limited role of foreign trade in the U.S. cookie market, it is likely that the main U.S. producers will continue to be able, through mass advertising and other techniques, to influence the pattern of domestic consumer demand that underpins their predominant product strategy. In Continental European industries, existing consumer tastes and preferences call for a more diversified and complex product mix, and the process skill levels required to deliver this type of output support a significant amount of flexible team-working. However, the forms of work organization found in Continental European plants predate the current wave of interest in innovative work practices, and day-to-day management of their process teams typically remains in the hands of traditional supervisors.

In general, therefore, this industry appears to be characterized by a degree of stability in product market conditions that provides little incentive for radical changes in existing product strategies (or in associated work practices). The next two sections consider an industry in which competitive pressures to move into higher value-added product areas appear to be creating more of a mismatch between product strategies and traditional low-involvement modes of work organization and skill formation.

3. "Cellular" Production in Precision Engineering

International comparisons in this industry covered three countries—the United States, Britain, and the Netherlands—and three selected branches of high-precision metal-working; namely, centrifugal pumps, hydraulic valves, and compression springs. In contrast to cookie manufacturing, there was considerable diversity among U.S. engineering plants in product strategies and in workplace organization. Large-batch production of relatively standardized products represented a much larger share of output in the U.S. sample of plants than in the two Western European countries whose engineering industries have long been exposed to severe competition from low-cost producers of standardized goods in southern Europe as well as in Asia. However, a majority of U.S. employees were engaged to varying degrees in production to-order (to detailed customer specifications) rather than bulk production for stock.

Detailed comparisons of matched production operations in sample plants found average outputs per direct person-hour in U.S. plants to be some two-thirds higher than in British plants and about 25% higher than in the Netherlands (Mason and Finegold, 1997). As in cookies, the U.S. productivity lead was closely related to advantages in production scale: For example, in the case of matched machine set-up operations, relatively slow set-up times in U.S. plants were more than offset by larger component batch sizes (fewer machine changeovers per shift), which helped reduce the average set-up labor input per unit of production in U.S. plants. Several American plants also made greater use of automated and/or dedicated production equipment than did any British or Dutch plants.

In all three countries, competitive pressures to reduce costs and the general climate of awareness in recent years about practices such as "just-in-time" manufacturing and "Quality Assurance" had prompted many plants to pursue objectives such as reductions in inventories and product reject rates. However, new production practices were typically being implemented in a cautious and pragmatic way: For example, small plants often felt obliged to carry some "excess" stock of components or finished goods to be able to compete on delivery and accommodate important large customers. In terms of high-involvement work practices, the most common and systematic efforts to improve performance in both the United States and Europe centered on two related areas of production reorganization: (1) a shift away from primary reliance on separate inspection departments toward increasing the element of self-inspection by shop floor workers in the course of production, (2) reconfiguration of shop floor layouts (e.g., to achieve a more logical sequencing of production operations and reduced movement of materials and work in progress around the shop floor).

In the earlier Anglo-Dutch comparison, one-half of the 12 British plants still reported problems, such as machine-setters having to walk long distances to find tools and work-holding equipment they needed and machines being grouped together according to their function (turning, drilling, etc.) rather than with regard to common sequences of operations. Indeed, no fewer than three British plants were in the throes of upheaval during the visits (in 1991), attempting to improve factory lay-out. By contrast, in the Netherlands, most such problems had either never arisen (in the smallest plants) or had been addressed some time ago, and only one of the nine Dutch plants visited still had significant difficulties with shop floor layout (Mason and van Ark, 1996).

In the U.S. sample in 1994, a third of the 18 plants had clearly identifiable layout problems similar to those encountered in Britain, especially at larger sites where components often have to travel long distances between different operations. However, the traditional grouping of machines by function was increasingly recognized by pump and valve manufacturers as unsuited to small- and medium-batch production of semi-customized products. Hence, four of the ten U.S. plants making pumps or valves had fully redesigned shop floor layouts in the course of formally introducing "cellular" (or "focused factory") production systems and two of the plants with layout problems had begun to implement such systems (Table 6.6).[4]

Cell production typically involves relocating machines so that teams of workers can carry out all the operations required on particular components from rough casting to finished product. This approach to shop floor layout actually derives from concepts of "group technology" first developed in the Soviet Union after World War II. (See Buchanan and Preston, 1992, for a survey of the relevant literature.) However, in the present climate of awareness about lean production objectives, it has become closely associated with the development of high-involvement work practices. In order to maximize the potential for improved productivity performance (lower machine downtime) and product quality standards (lower reject or rework rates), cellular reorganization is now often accompanied by moves toward practices such as quality self-inspection (previously described), job rotation (multiskilling), and varying degrees of team self-management in areas such as ordering of materials and day-to-day machine scheduling (sometimes linked to the elimination of traditional supervisory layers of staff).

As might be expected, the additional training needs associated with quality self-inspection and increased flexibility were particularly large in U.S. plants where an estimated two thirds of shop floor workers could be regarded as only "semi-skilled," in that they had not gained formal vocational qualifications of any kind and their previous on-the-job training had typically been confined to only a narrow range of machine operations and other tasks. By contrast, just under 80% of Dutch shop floor workers were vocationally qualified in some way and had already been trained to switch flexibly between different products and machines; in the British sample, the proportion of semi-skilled shop floor employees was not far short of that in U.S. plants, but this was partially offset by much larger numbers of apprentice-trained craft workers in Britain

Table 6.6. Shop Floor Organization in National Samples of Precision Engineering Plants

	Number of Plants			Percent of Shop Floor Work Force		
	U.S.	Britain	Netherlands	U.S.	Britain	Netherlands
Cellular production systems in operation[a]	6	3	1	46	24	16
Cellular reorganization not necessary or appropriate[b]	8	6	7	20	40	73
Shop floor in need of reorganization	4	4	1	34	36	11
Total	18	13	9	100	100	100
Total shop floor employment				2775	1264	438

[a]Includes two U.S. plants and two British plants that were in the process of addressing layout problems by implementing cellular systems at the time of the research visits (U.S., 1994; Britain, 1991; Netherlands, 1991).

[b]For example, plants where most products are manufactured on single machines or small plants without visible layout problems (see text for further discussion).

(Table 6.7). However, despite the relatively high costs of skills upgrading in the U.S. industry, six of the 18 U.S. plants had mounted comprehensive adult training programs designed not just to develop skills in quality-related areas, such as the use of Statistical Process Control (SPC) techniques, but also to tackle the identified deficiencies of individual shop floor workers in areas such as blueprint reading, shop math, and computer numerically controlled (CNC) machine operation and programming (Mason and Finegold, 1997). In three of these plants, this systematic training provision was directly related to the higher skill needs associated with cellular production (in particular, the need for machinists to be able to set and operate a wider range of machines).

By contrast, in the two European samples adult training of a comprehensive nature—targetting the bulk of direct workers—was typically confined to one- or two-day courses in the use of SPC and other aspects of quality management.[5] This partly reflects the fact that, especially in the case of the Dutch sample, there was much less of a skills gap to make up, but it may also be attributed in part to the more limited progress toward cell production and other new work practices in European plants at the time of our visits compared with the U.S. plant. Only one of the nine British plants making pumps or valves had a full cell system up

Table 6.7. Shop Floor Qualification Levels in National Samples of Precision Engineering Plants[a]

U.S.	2%	Two and four-year college graduates (mainly new Immigrants)
	3–4%	Craft apprentice-trained
	20–30%	Vocational certificates plus on-the-job training
	65–75%	No formal qualifications, on-job training only
Netherlands	12%	Technician-qualified
	8%	Craft apprentice-trained
	58%	Vocational certificates plus on-the-job training
	22%	No formal qualifications, on-job training only
Britain	41%	Craft apprentice-trained
	59%	No formal qualifications, on-job training only

Notes: Classification of vocational qualifications: Four-year graduates: U.S. Bachelor's degrees; British university First degrees; Dutch university degrees and HTS certificates. Two-year graduates (U.S.): Associate's degrees. Technician (Netherlands): MTS (intermediate technical) certificates and advanced apprenticeship awards. Craft: U.S. apprentice diplomas or foreign equivalents (includes "time-served" journeymen); British City & Guilds Part II passes or equivalent (includes "time-served" trade apprenticeships); Dutch primary apprentice awards. Vocational certificates (U.S.): Includes certificates awarded by public technical/community colleges, private training schools, and military training schools. Vocational certificates (Netherlands): Refers to certificates awarded by full-time vocational (LTS) schools that provide initial workshop training in conjunction with classroom study.
[a]Total shop floor employment): U.S. 2775; Britain, 1264; Netherlands, 438.
[b]Percentage of employees.

and running in its machine shop; two others were in the early stages of introducing such a system. Of the six Dutch plants in these two product areas only one was organized on cellular lines; in most of the smaller Dutch plants, there was little to be gained from radical redesign of the shop floor layout (Table 6.6).

In summary, therefore, the U.S. sample was notable for a wide diversity in work practices. As outlined, some American plants were conspicuously willing to incur the costs of extensive upgrading of shop floor skills needed to establish high-involvement work practices. However, several others (usually, but not always, those geared to large- or medium-batch processing of components) were still committed to distinctly *low*-involvement practices, with graduate manufacturing engineers laying out detailed instructions for semi-skilled operators to follow and making themselves readily available to deal with any problems that arose. In one case, this mode of organization was being used even in the production of small batches of highly engineered special-purpose pumps: The managers concerned attributed their ability to carry out such work with a low- and semi-skilled shop floor work force to "rigid documentation," with detailed process specifications being drawn up on a daily basis by manufacturing engineers, who were also responsible for all CNC programming and for day-to-day "trouble-shooting."

Even in plants that had sought to develop high-involvement shop floor work practices, small groups of manufacturing engineers were still readily available in emergencies and were regularly involved in incremental improvements to machinery and shop floor layout designed to enhance machine operators' performance (e.g., by reducing set-up times or product reject rates). Graduate engineers were also typically involved, not just in the design and implementation of skill-intensive new work practices, such as cell-working, but also in the provision of on-the-job training. In one case, manufacturing engineers had even been required to shift their desks into the middle of shop floor cells and to be available if necessary to "stand at the operator's shoulder" whenever a new CNC program was being run for the first time.

The next section reports on more recent evidence on the development of high-involvement work practices in United States and Western European engineering industries; in particular, the spread of team-working systems.

4. Team-Working in High-Speed Machinery and Vehicle Components Industries

Comparisons based on these two branches of engineering also involved an extension to the United States of an earlier intra-European study, in this case covering Britain and Germany (Mason and Wagner, 1994). However, for the second phase of the project, follow-up telephone interviews with managers in the British and German plants facilitated a direct comparison of work practices in the three countries and also provided a useful longitudinal perspective on shop floor organization in the two European countries (Mason, 1996).

Both the specialized high-speed machinery and vehicle components industries are characterized by highly competitive world product markets with a majority of producers under growing pressure to improve the quality and performance of their products and shorten product lead times while simultaneously having to compete on price as well. In consequence, there was widespread interest among managers in all three countries in the potential efficiencies to be gained from the introduction of new work systems, such as cell production and/or team-working. The objectives of such reorganization were typically expressed in terms of "empowering" ordinary workers, seeking to widen their responsibilities and get them involved in generating ideas for process improvements (e.g., adaptations to machinery) in ways that would be unlikely to occur with traditional hierarchical modes of supervision. For this reason, inter-country differences in the employment and deployment of production supervisors are of considerable interest in evaluating the diffusion of high-involvement work practices in each national sample of plants. In addition, the three samples predictably differed in terms of work force qualification levels, with U.S. plants falling well behind their European counterparts in terms of apprentice-trained production workers but relatively well endowed with graduate engineers (Table 6.8). Hence, the study provided a useful opportunity to observe how the implementation of high-involvement work practices was affected by the relative costs of achieving the required skill levels.

At the time of our visits, functioning cell systems were up and running in core production areas in three out of ten U.S. sample plants. One plant had recently reorganized its shop floor layout to reduce the time lost "tracking parts around the place" but had not formally adopted a cellular mode of operation. In four other U.S. plants, there had been no radical changes to shop floor layout in recent years, but (for different reasons in each case) this was not a pressing issue.[6] Only two American plants were visibly suffering from poor layout, with each shop floor littered with boxes of components waiting to be put through different operations or continue their travels around the factories.

A similar pattern of change was found with regard to team-working in U.S. plants. Six of the ten plants—including all three running production cells—had organized employees into teams with varying degrees of responsibility for self-inspection of quality standards and daily production planning (Table 6.9). However, it was notable that even though in most cases the move towards team-working had led to a small reduction in the different *layers* of supervision—for example, abolition of job categories such as "superintendent" or "general foreman" (superior to

Table 6.8. Employment Ratios and Shop Floor Qualifications
in National Samples of High-Speed Machinery and Vehicle
Components Plants

	U.S.	Britain	Germany
Shop floor employees (including supervisors) as proportion of total employment (%)	49	52	45
Average direct workers per supervisor:	18.0	22.5	32.1
1995–1996 (1993)	(17.6)	(22.9)	(28.4)
Craft-skilled and above as proportion of employees in direct production (%)	n a	20	57
Total shop floor employment	4357	4747	5435
Highest formal qualifications held by supervisors			
(rounded to nearest 5%)			
Four-year graduate or above	35	20	0
Two-year graduate	5	—	—
Meisterbrief	—	—	85
Craft (apprentice-trained)	5	55	10
Vocational certificates	15	—	—
No vocational qualifications	40	25	5
Total	100	100	100
Total no. of supervisors	229	202	164

Note: Classification of qualifications: Four-year graduates: U.S. Bachelor's degrees; British university First degrees; German *Hochschulabschluss* or *Fachhochschulabschluss*. Two-year graduates (U.S.): Associate's degrees. Craft: U.S. apprentice diplomas or equivalent (includes "time-served" journeymen); British City & Guilds Part II passes or equivalent (includes "time-served" trade apprenticeships); German *Berufsabschluss* or equivalent. Vocational certificates (U.S.): Includes certificates awarded by public technical/community colleges, private training schools, and military training schools.

foreman)—there were no reports of significant reductions in the over-all ratio of supervisors to those supervised in the plants concerned.[7] Rather, as more of the daily responsibilities of production management (machine-loadings, attendance records, monitoring of quality, etc.) had been taken over by designated "team leaders," supervisors had typically not been replaced so much as "freed" to take a more strategic view of how shop floor efficiency could be enhanced, while still retaining overall responsibility for such areas as hiring, discipline, training, materials allocations, and machinery maintenance.

Individual supervisors in plants with established team-working practices generally spoke enthusiastically about their new opportunities to participate in medium-term planning meetings involving the managers to whom they reported as well as with staff from other departments. They also reported having more time for both informal discussions with manufacturing engineers about production issues (such as the purchase of new machinery) *and* formal participation in cross-functional product development teams. Such involvement by supervisors in new product design processes has the twofold advantage of enabling them

Table 6.9. Extent of Team-Working in National Samples of High-Speed Machinery and Vehicle Components Plants

Type of work organization	Number of plants			Percent of total shop floor employment		
	U.S.	Britain	Germany	U.S.	Britain	Germany
Team-working with team members taking degree of responsibility for ensuring that daily production and delivery targets are met	6	7	6	42	72	63
Hierarchical work organization: supervisors primarily responsible for ensuring that daily production and delivery targets are met	4	2	2	58	21	37
Total	10	9	8	100	100	100
Total shop floor employment				4357	4747	5435

to contribute their knowledge of shop floor production constraints at an early stage in proceedings, at the same time learning more about customer requirements that new products need to meet.

In nearly all of the U.S. plants where team-working had helped to free supervisors from their former absorption in short-term problem solving, this had been accomplished by passing responsibility for meeting day-to-day production and delivery targets to individual team leaders, albeit with more-limited authority over hiring, discipline, and budget planning than that possessed by traditional supervisors. Ordinary team members typically had little involvement in day-to-day decisions of a managerial nature, but they were expected to be more involved in meeting output targets (e.g., through greater job flexibility) and to participate in collective problem solving.

Similar conclusions emerge from information supplied by British managers about the move to cellular production organization and team-working in their plants. In concerted efforts to improve shop floor efficiency in recent years, five of the nine British sample plants contacted in 1996 had reportedly introduced production cells combined with some degree of team-working, and another two plants had shifted to a team-based system without moving to cells. In nearly all of these plants, the traditional responsibilities of supervisors for day-to-day production management were reported to be systematically divided up between supervisors and team leaders. For example, team leaders were typically responsible for daily work allocations, progress chasing, and "first-line" responses to queries and problems that arose. Supervisors had a wider brief to think strategically about new techniques and processes and to represent production areas in inter-departmental project meetings, but their responsibilities for hiring, general discipline, budgeting, organization of on-the-job training, and so forth, had either remained the same or had even been extended. As in U.S. plants, the estimated ratio of supervisors to other shop floor employees in the British sample of plants as a whole had hardly changed between 1993–1996 (Table 6.8).[8]

In German sample plants, the need for cellular reorganization—or any full-scale relocation of machinery—has typically been less pressing than in the United States and Britain, reflecting a long heritage in Germany of incremental improvements over the years that have sought to minimize the movement of materials and components around the shop floor and to reduce downtime (e.g., ensuring that machine-setters rarely have to walk far to find tools and work-holding equipment they need). Indeed, in some of the German sample plants, the overall smoothness of production flow was judged to be "immaculate" during the earlier set of visits (Mason and Wagner, 1994). However, in recent years, German managers have developed a sudden and intense interest in the possibility that the deployment of self-directed work teams on the shop floor could improve shop floor efficiency still further by drawing more effectively on the skills and knowledge of ordinary production workers.

At the time of the initial fieldwork in German plants in 1993, the majority were visibly suffering from a slump in home market demand, which had contributed to a sharp drop in capacity utilization and reduced their ability to cover existing labor costs and overhead. In response to this sharp weakening of their international competitiveness, several plants had begun to experiment with leaner production methods (e.g., reducing stocks of raw materials and components), but there was little interest in making more fundamental changes in shop floor organization. By contrast, in the follow-up telephone interviews in 1995–1996, managers in six of the eight German plants reported recent progress toward team-based production systems.

In three of those plants, many former daily responsibilities of supervisors (*Meister*) in areas such as materials and production scheduling and product quality were said to have been handed over to team members.[9] The managers concerned commented favorably on the ability of their largely apprentice-trained machine operators and assemblers to take on wider responsibilities. The new role of *Meister* was variously described as one of "coordination and motivation" of the production teams, "keeping discussions going about (process) improvements," and a "link between team leaders and senior management" while retaining (or expanding) their involvement in areas such as recruitment, training, and the coordination of machinery maintenance and repair.

In the absence of new detailed on-site investigations in these German plants, no assessment can be made of the extent to which such teams have become truly "self-directed" without the traditional interventions of *Meister* in day-to-day decision making. In the other three German plants that reported moves toward team-working, the *Meister* had apparently been appointed as team leaders, and the only indication that some of their traditional daily responsibilities may have been at least partially dispersed to team members was the virtual disappearance of the position of *Vorarbeiter* (chargehands or assistant *Meister*) in these plants. However, in contrast to the British and U.S. samples, the average span of responsibility for supervisors in the German sample had risen in the three years since the initial visits, up from 28 to 32, reflecting sharp reductions in the number of designated shop floor supervisor positions in three of the eight German plants.[10]

These findings on the extent and nature of team-working practices in U.S., German, and British engineering plants may be briefly summarized as follows: Under intense and growing competitive pressure in international product markets, there are now widespread efforts in all three countries to involve production workers more in day-to-day decision making and problem solving and to dispense with traditional hierarchical modes of supervision. In many of the plants concerned, supervisors are now expected to take a broader responsibility for coordinating and supporting the activities of production teams and have more opportunities to participate in strategic planning affecting shop floor production. However, only in German plants is there any evidence of a recent increase in the average span of responsibility of supervisors, as might be expected to result from dispersion of day-to-day responsibilities for production management. This latter finding supports an argument that high-involvement team-working is likely to be most easily and quickly implemented in workplaces with relatively high preexisting skill levels among the shop floor work force as a whole.[11]

5. Summary and Assessment

This chapter has drawn on several recent comparisons of matched samples of manufacturing establishments in the United States and Western Europe to examine how inter-country and inter-industry differences in the rate of adoption of new work practices are related to differences in predominant product strategies and associated forms of work organization, machinery utilization, and work force skills development.

The main conclusions emerging from the different studies may be summarized as follows:

1. There are marked variations between industries and national economies in the extent to which high-involvement work practices are actually new or, if not in use, are ever likely to be appropriate.

For example, the comparisons based on a selected branch of food manufacturing (cookies and crackers) revealed pronounced inter-country differences in work organization that have existed for several decades. In Continental European countries such as Germany, the industry is mainly geared to meeting consumer tastes and preferences for a wide variety of high-quality, elaborate products, and the process skill levels required to deliver this type of output support a significant amount of flexible team-working (albeit with day-to-day management remaining in the hands of traditional supervisors). This form of work organization was well established before the current wave of interest in high-involvement work practices.

In U.S. cookie plants, by contrast, the scarcity of high-involvement shop floor work practices is associated with the continued relative success of existing low-skill, low-involvement practices tailored to large-scale production. Given the limited role of foreign trade in the U.S. cookie market, it is likely that the main U.S. producers will continue to be able, through mass advertising and other techniques, to influence the pattern of domestic consumer demand which underpins their existing product strategies and work practices.

2. New high-involvement work practices are most likely to be introduced where a mismatch develops between product market requirements and existing low-involvement modes of work organization.

In some branches of engineering—particularly those, such as specialized high-speed machinery and vehicle components, where product markets are highly internationalized—high-involvement work practices were found to be diffusing rapidly on both sides of the Atlantic. The driving factor appears to be strong competitive pressures to improve the quality and performance of products while simultaneously having to compete on price as well. In this context, high-involvement work practices, in conjunction with appropriate changes in shop floor layout and work force training, are widely viewed as an aid to meeting tighter quality objectives as well as a potential means of stimulating cost-saving initiatives by shop floor workers.

For example, a principal aim of cellular production systems is to achieve a more logical sequencing of production operations and reduced movement of materials and work in progress around the shop floor. Such reorganization is typically most successful in achieving efficiencies in large plants where wasteful layout problems have accumulated over time. Hence it was more commonly found in the U.S. engineering industry than, for example, in Germany (where there was a long heritage of incremental improvements to shop floor layout over the years) or in the Netherlands (where most plants are relatively small and already well organized).

In several U.S. plants, the introduction of cell systems was accompanied by moves toward new work practices, such as quality self-inspection, job rotation (multiskilling), and varying degrees of team self-management in areas such as ordering of materials and day-to-day machine scheduling. The combination of improved factory layout, increased training, and the development of high-involvement work practices represented a concerted response to market pressures to reduce production costs while simultaneously catering to demand for a more diversified and complex mix of products.

In Western Europe, there was some variation among national engineering industries in the pattern of response to such competitive pressures. The linking of high-involvement work practices to cellular reorganization was more often found in Britain than in Germany where, as noted, most plants had little to gain from the disruption involved in introducing cells. However, as in the United States, many plants in both the German and British samples had recently moved swiftly to deploy self-directed work teams on the shop floor in the hope of improving efficiency by involving production workers more in the search for process innovations and cost savings.

3. In industries where there are strong competitive pressures to seek efficiency gains from high-involvement work practices, the United States appears to be characterized by much wider variation in the implementation of such practices than is the case for Western Europe.

The training costs associated with new practices are inevitably higher in the United States (with historically low shop floor skill levels) than in Continental European countries with well-established vocational education and training systems. A significant proportion of American engineering companies now appear willing to devote substantial resources to comprehensive adult training to develop the skills and work practices necessary to introduce high-involvement work practices. However, these "heavy trainers" coexist with many other U.S. plants that are geared to low-involvement work practices; for example, with graduate manufacturing engineers laying out detailed instructions for semiskilled operators to follow, while supervisors maintain their traditional authority over day-to-day production issues.

This pronounced variation in employment practices within the U.S. industry partly reflects differences in product strategies, with low-involvement plants more likely to be engaged in long production runs of standardized products (less common in Continental Europe) than in small- and medium-batch production of high-value-added products. However, at enterprise level, a great many other factors besides product strategy may impinge on management decisions on work practices; for example, plant size, foreign trade exposure, union presence, or the parent company's financial resources. A much larger statistical study of U.S. plants would be necessary to identify the relative importance of these and other factors in the diffusion of high-involvement work practices.

4. Although the rate of adoption of high-involvement work practices across countries does not appear to be inversely related to the direct costs to employers of developing the required skill sets, there is some evi-

dence that such practices can be established more quickly and effectively in countries where pre-existing work force skill levels are relatively high.

For example, the widespread efforts in the American, German, and British engineering industries to dispense with traditional hierarchical modes of supervision are aimed at involving production workers more in day-to-day decision making and problem solving through teamworking. However, only in the German sample plants—with much higher proportions of fully craft-trained employees than in the other two countries—was there any evidence of a recent increase in the average span of responsibility of shop floor supervisors that might be expected to accompany genuine dispersion of day-to-day responsibilities for production management. In U.S. and British plants, the average span of responsibility of supervisors remained unchanged—and considerably lower than in Germany—suggesting that attempts to introduce high-involvement forms of team-working in the United States and Britain were constrained by relatively low levels of pre-existing skill and self-reliance among production workers.

Acknowledgments   This chapter draws on several research projects carried out in conjunction with other colleagues; in particular, Bart van Ark, David Finegold, Joe Hight, Sig Prais, and Karin Wagner. I am grateful to them for their advice and support over the years. Responsibility for any errors in this chapter is mine alone.

Notes

1. Bakery, Confectionery and Tobacco Workers Union, Kensington, MD, private communication.

2. Bakers, Food and Allied Workers Union, Hatfield, Herts., England, private communication.

3. These productivity calculations take account of estimated productivity growth in the European industries during the time interval between European and U.S. visits.

4. Note that physical reorganization along cellular lines does not promise the same advantages in spring plants where most products are manufactured on single machines.

5. The distinction here is between comprehensive adult training aimed at the bulk of the shop floor work force and other types of continuing training course targeted at specific sections of the work force. Intermittent short courses (usually no more than 1–5 days in length) were widespread in all three countries and included training courses provided by machinery vendors for selected machinists and specialist short courses for supervisors and small groups of technical support staff.

6. For example, because the plants concerned were using automated transfer-line equipment or, in some cases, were physically small and already reasonably well organized.

7. That is to say, in those few plants where the total number of production supervisors had been reduced in recent years, it had typically not declined any faster than the total number of shop floor employees.

8. In a few cases, these individuals had been retitled as "managers" of some kind but for the purposes of this assessment they were still classified as "supervisors" because they retained many traditional supervisory functions and were also reported to still be largely based on the shop floor and to have an explicit role of providing support for team leaders.

9. Some 85% of production supervisors in German sample plants had gone on beyond their apprentice training to study for *Meister* certificates, which typically involve two to three years of part-time evening and/or weekend study in areas such as logistics, cost control, business organization, instructional techniques, and relevant technical subjects.

10. Note that in 1995–1996, the average number of direct workers per supervisor in the U.S. and British samples was, respectively, 18 and 23 (Table 6.8). The historically wider span of responsibility of supervisors in German plants, even before the recent development of team-working, is consistent with expectations that the burden of supervision is inversely related to the skill levels of those being supervised (Mason, 1996).

11. At a micro level, this point is reinforced by two recent studies of single British plants in which new team-based production systems had failed to take root, in part because neither supervisors nor team members had received adequate training to cope with their ostensible new responsibilities (Buchanan and Preston, 1992; Lowe, 1993).

References

Buchanan, D. and Preston, D. (1992). Life in the cell: Supervision and teamwork in a manufacturing systems engineering environment. *Human Resource Management Journal*, 2 (4): 55–76.

Ichniowski, C., Kochan, T., Levine, D., Olson, C., and Strauss, G. (1996). What works at work: Overview and assessment. *Industrial Relations*, 35 (3): 299–333.

Ichniowski, C. and Shaw, K. (1995). Old dogs and new tricks: Determinants of the adoption of productivity-enhancing work practices, *Brookings Papers on Economic Activity: Microeconomics*. 1–69.

Lowe, J. (1993). Manufacturing reform and the changing role of the production supervisor: The case of the automobile industry. *Journal of Management Studies*, 30 (5): 730–758.

Mason, G. (1996). Shopfloor management skills in manufacturing: The formation of production supervisors in the United States, Germany, and Britain. Report to the U.S. Department of Labor. London: National Institute of Economic and Social Research.

Mason, G. and Finegold, D. (1997). Productivity, machinery and skills in the United States and Western Europe. *National Institute Economic Review*, 162 (4): 85–98.

Mason, G. and van Ark, B. (1996). Productivity, machinery and skills in engineering: An Anglo-Dutch comparison. In D. Mayes (ed.), *Sources of productivity growth*. Cambridge, UK: Cambridge University Press. (pp. 97–119).

Mason, G., van Ark, B., and Wagner, K. (1994). Productivity, product quality and workforce skills: Food processing in four European countries. *National Institute Economic Review*, 147 (1): 62–83.

Mason, G., van Ark, B., and Wagner, K. (1996). Workforce skills, product quality and economic performance. In A. Booth and D. Snower (eds.), *Acquiring skills: Market failures, their symptoms and policy responses*. Cambridge, UK: Cambridge University Press. (pp. 177–197).

Mason, G. and Wagner, K. (1994). Innovation and the skill mix: Chemicals and engineering in Britain and Germany. *National Institute Economic Review*, 148 (2): 61–72.

Osterman, P. (1994). How common is workplace transformation and who adopts it? *Industrial and Labor Relations Review*, 47 (2): 173–187.

Pil, F. and MacDuffie, J. (1996). The adoption of high-involvement work practices. *Industrial Relations*, 35 (3): 423–455.

Steedman, H. and Wagner, K. (1987). "A second look at productivity, machinery and skills in Britain and Germany." *National Institute Economic Review*, 122 (4): 84–96.

Steedman, H. and Wagner, K. (1989). Productivity, machinery and skills: Clothing manufacture in Britain and Germany. *National Institute Economic Review*, 128 (2): 40–57.

Index

SHAKESPEARE
THE PLAYWRIGHT

SHAKESPEARE THE PLAYWRIGHT

A Companion to the Complete Tragedies, Histories, Comedies, and Romances

VICTOR L. CAHN

GREENWOOD PRESS
New York • Westport, Connecticut • London

Library of Congress Cataloging-in-Publication Data

Cahn, Victor L.
    Shakespeare the playwright : a companion to the complete
tragedies, histories, comedies, and romances / Victor L. Cahn.
        p. cm.
    Includes bibliographical references.
    ISBN 0–313–27493–2 (lib. bdg. : alk. paper)
    1. Shakespeare, William, 1564–1616—Criticism and interpretation.
I. Title.
PR2976.C27   1991
822.3'3—dc20   90–34319

British Library Cataloguing in Publication Data is available.

Library of Congress Catalog Card Number: 90–34319
ISBN: 0–313–27493–2

First published in 1991

Greenwood Press, 88 Post Road West, Westport, CT 06881
An imprint of Greenwood Publishing Group, Inc.

Printed in the United States of America

The paper used in this book complies with the
Permanent Paper Standard issued by the National
Information Standards Organization (Z39.48–1984).

10 9 8 7 6 5 4 3 2 1

To Steven, my brother

After God Shakespeare has created most.

—James Joyce, *Ulysses*

(citing Alexandre Dumas, *pere)*

CONTENTS

INTRODUCTION

Since their first production four centuries ago, the plays of William Shakespeare have been the most widely produced, popularly acclaimed, and critically examined works in the world's literature. This book is intended to help readers better appreciate why.

Shakespeare was above all a man of the theater, and he was fortunate that his creative life coincided with an era when English drama flourished. His work, however, was part of a national tradition that extended back through the Middle Ages. Among the dominant forms then were miracle plays, based on the life or works of saints; mystery plays, based on biblical history; and morality plays, in which the forces of good and evil, personified by allegorical figures, battled for the soul of protagonists. The outstanding example of the morality play, and perhaps the most famous work from medieval drama, is *Everyman* (c. 1495). All these pieces were written in the vernacular, and their continual production, as well as presentations of folk plays and farces, stimulated actors and audiences across the country and over centuries. Gradually, troops of professional performers organized, but the crucial factor in this development was the steady market provided by the ever-growing city of London.

By 1558, six years before Shakespeare's birth, when Elizabeth I ascended the English throne, the spirit of the Renaissance brought a renewed interest in classical drama, specifically the Roman playwrights, including Plautus and Terence, writers of comedies, and Seneca, author of numerous tragedies. And these writers provided models for the young dramatists of the time. Furthermore, during the first two decades of Elizabeth's reign, professional acting companies were officially sanctioned in London, while theater continued to burgeon in academic institutions and private halls. Public performances were given in inn yards, where galleries were built to hold spectators.

The London companies were infused with talent from the universities of Oxford and Cambridge, whose most famous product was Christopher Marlowe, like Shakespeare, born in 1564. The author of several eminent plays, including *The Jew of Malta*, *Edward II*, and *Dr. Faustus*, Marlowe spent his life in disreputable circles, and was killed in a tavern brawl before his thirtieth birthday. But his distinctive variety of blank verse, sometimes referred to as "the mighty line," contributed enormously in establishing the poetic style that shaped drama, including Shakespeare's, for decades to come.

For all their vitality, acting companies were under constant attack. The Puritan community condemned theater, ostensibly only because such enterprises generated moral dissolution, but also because performances disrupted businesses. In addition, the Mayor of London and his council objected to productions for reasons of health and general decorum, given that most inn yard theaters adjoined unsavory areas of the city. Thus in 1574 the council decreed that no plays could be presented publicly within city limits unless the works themselves and the times and places of performance were approved by the mayor and the aldermen. In reaction to this ordinance, playhouses were built just outside the city's realm of jurisdiction, and here is where professional companies, including actors and playwrights working together, truly thrived. They did so until 1642, when the Puritans managed to close public theaters entirely.

Shakespeare joined this theatrical world in approximately 1590, when he was in his mid-twenties. His own education had been limited to grammar school in his birthplace of Stratford, but there the curriculum was heavily weighted with Latin literature, including works of Cicero, Horace, Virgil, Ovid, and the playwrights, and evidence of such study may be found throughout Shakespeare's writings. Recitation was a bulwark of classroom activity, and no doubt the emphasis on articulation and rhythmic precision gave Shakespeare an affection for both the wonders of language and the joy of performance. He also read intensively in Latin history, including Caesar's *Commentaries on the Gallic Wars*, and some of the lessons learned emerge in his Roman plays and in his sequence on English history. In 1582, Shakespeare married, and within three years was the father of three children, a girl born in 1583, and twins, a boy and a girl, born in 1585. The seven years following are the so-called lost years, for documentary evidence about Shakespeare's activities is lacking. Speculation holds that he may have been a schoolmaster or a provincial actor.

By 1592 he was established in London, for he was alluded to disparagingly by playwright Robert Greene in his book *Groats-worth of Wit*. In an attack on actors in general, Greene refers to "Shake-scene," then to an "upstart crow" with "his Tyger's hart wrapt in a Player's hyde [sic]." The last phrase parodies a line from one of Shakespeare's earliest works, *Henry VI, Part 3*: "O tiger's heart wrapp'd in a woman's hide!" (I, iv, 137). Greene may have been intimating that Shakespeare was a plagiarist, or merely that the young man was presumptuous to consider himself a playwright. Whatever the implication, the reference reveals that Shakespeare was now well enough known to be obliquely criticized.

In 1592 an outbreak of bubonic plague struck the city, and for two years theaters were closed. When they reopened in 1594, Shakespeare joined, as actor and playwright, a new company called the Lord Chamberlain's Men. Years later, after James I became monarch, the name was changed to the King's Men. During the rest of the 1590s, the company rented theaters, but by 1599 the Globe Theater had been constructed, and here is where most performances of Shakespeare's plays were presented. Thus Shakespeare enjoyed a creative environment that playwrights have always relished: the opportunity to write for a resident company of players with their own facilities at the ready. Had he lived in another period, he might nonetheless have written his 154 sonnets and several longer poems. But he would probably not have written the thirty-seven plays that remain celebrated.

Theatrical conditions helped shape the plays created during this time. In most theaters the stage, a platform without curtain, was covered and extended into the audience. Towards the rear of the stage was a higher level that could serve as a balcony or a "battlement" from which characters could look down on the rest of the action. Most of the edifices, which were open-air constructions, were round or hexagonal and of considerable size. The Globe itself could hold more than 2,000 spectators. Yet the houses encouraged an intimacy between audience and actor, and asides and soliloquies became a valued method of communicating the nature of a character. In most public theaters, two or three tiers of seats were provided for the well-to-do, who sometimes overflowed on the stage. Here they tended to behave somewhat disreputably in an effort to draw attention to themselves. Below the stage, in the pit, stood or sat the "groundlings," the less wealthy citizens, and an impatient, demanding group. Yet they were also intelligent and appreciative, and when moved by what they saw and heard on stage, responded by cheering, shouting, and even crying. Perhaps because Shakespeare's audience encompassed so wide a range of people, he created equally heterogeneous rosters of characters and placed them in a great variety of settings and moods. He also moved regularly from tragedy to comedy to history, triumphing in each genre with a virtuosity unmatched by any dramatist before or since.

Most of Shakespeare's works were written for public theaters, and their technical deficiencies influenced his writing. For instance, lighting was not available; performances took place in the daytime, and without interruption. The division of the plays into acts was the work of later editors. Therefore the audience's attention span, granting a general restlessness, must have been considerable. Nonetheless, their attention had to be held, and a premium was placed on continuous action.

Costumes were extravagant and helped elaborate character in terms of nationality and class. But scenery was minimal, and flats, curtains, and simple wooden structures had to suffice to represent houses and other edifices. Props were strictly for efficacy. Programs were not available, so the text itself had to inform the onlookers of changes in locale. Hence Shakespeare's poetic renderings of environment were not just for the sake of beauty, but to communicate the atmosphere and texture of a forest or castle that had to be suggested rather than recreated. Battles were enacted by a few performers dashing about the stage with swords. Although trapdoors and other devices were available to simulate supernatural and other spectacular effects, the unceasing movement in Shakespeare's plays, the energy we still admire, was demanding by the conditions under which he worked.

Only late in his career did Shakespeare's company perform at private theaters, which had roofs, heating, and artificial lighting. These houses, always intense rivals of the public theaters, attracted several gifted writers, including Ben Jonson, Thomas Middleton, and John Marston. But the material presented here was aimed at an elite audience and tended to be cynical, even sordid. Shakespeare's humanistic and largely sympathetic vision of the world found a more congenial home among the mass audience at the public theaters, and his popularity and acceptance by that audience is always to be kept in mind.

Theatrical conditions also imposed considerable demands on the actors. The turnover of plays was steady, and parts had to be learned after only a few rehearsals and with little direction (and while the actors were performing in other works). Thus their capacity to memorize quickly must have been astonishing. Yet we ought to remember the nature of elementary education in the England of this time. The primary activity was rote memorization, and from a very early age students were drilled into absorbing and retaining vast portions of literary material. No doubt such training proved invaluable to actors. Acting itself was carried with vigor and passion, tending towards the declamatory, and Shakespeare's distaste for what in our day would be described as "overacting" may be seen in Hamlet's instructions to the Players in Act III, scene ii. The most famous members of the Lord Chamberlain's Men were Richard Burbage, who gave the premier performance of many of Shakespeare's great tragic roles, and Will Kemp, a gifted comic star, but a renegade whose liberties on stage antagonized his colleagues and eventually led to his departure. Nonetheless, reports of the day indicate that productions were successful, and whatever his performers' deficiencies, Shakespeare was served well.

The most important limitation on the playwright was the absence of actresses. Although women were permitted on stage on the Continent, the English judged the practice immoral, and from medieval times all female roles were played by boys. One consequence of this restriction was that the parts Shakespeare wrote for males outnumber those for females by five or six to one. Moreover, the plays have a lack of extended female roles, especially for mature women, since boys could not carry off a part with the complexity of an Othello or a Lear. To be sure, Shakespeare created a few leading roles for women, including Cleopatra and Lady Macbeth, but even these lack the demands of his most challenging male roles. The Elizabethans' capacity to believe in the illusion of boys dressed as women must have been remarkable, and Shakespeare contributed to this aptitude by arranging often for his female characters to disguise themselves as men.

Although Shakespeare participated in his company's productions as an actor, his major contribution was as a playwright. For nearly twenty years he wrote an average of two plays per year, and the steadiness of the output indicates that he had little time for revision. What has been passed down to us may not be precisely first drafts, but surely the speeches and pages flowed easily from his pen.

In contrast to later playwrights, Shakespeare wrote strictly for performance, and most likely without an eye for publication. Only about half his plays were printed individually in his lifetime, and the playwright paid little attention to ensuring textual accuracy. After all, laws of his day gave him no copyright or artistic control, for prompters, actors, other collaborating playwrights, and even company bookkeepers would make script changes that satisfied their peculiar needs. Besides, once plays were published, they were no longer the special province of a particular company, which would lose a valuable commodity when a popular play was available to rival groups.

Fortunately, in 1623, seven years after Shakespeare's death, two of his former colleagues collected thirty-six of his plays into a single volume, known as the *First Folio*. Here the plays are divided into tragedies, histories, and comedies, and most are today classified under the category to which they are assigned in the original volume. This text remains generally accepted, and is the basis for virtually all editions currently in use, but innumerable questions about its authority remain. Many different editors worked on the project, so that some copies of the Folio are at variance with others. Words, stage directions, and spelling are all open to question.

No single study of Shakespeare can hope to do justice to all levels of his plays, nor can a single study encompass all perspectives from which the plays may be considered. *Shakespeare the Playwright* is based upon the conviction that the fundamental appeal of Shakespeare's works, the core of their theatrical impact, lies with his characters. So lifelike are they that though they speak either poetry or an elevated prose and though they are set in ages long past, we are inspired to probe them as we would living human beings. Part of Shakespeare's greatness is that despite the daunting complications of many of these figures, we find in them psychological consistency. We may have to struggle to resolve some of their seemingly contradictory actions and statements, but these can almost always be synthesized into what actors designate as a "through line," a consistent path of motivation. One aim of this book is to try to clarify that path for major characters in each of the plays.

Characters reveal themselves in two ways: through action and through language. We analyze them not only by what they do but also by what they say and how they say it. Thus the discussions here also focus on how specific images and words reflect the personalities, values, and intentions of the speakers. The dialogue in Shakespeare's plays ranges from the most vivid and glorious poetry, often blank verse (unrhymed iambic pentameter), to varieties of prose offered in less formal circumstances or by less exalted characters. And the richness of the language is the key to the profundity of the characters. Moreover, certain linguistic patterns occur in play after play, suggesting connections between characters. For instance, the word "honor" recurs hundreds of times in these works, and is offered by a great variety of speakers. For us, the word carries the denotation of "integrity," as it did in Shakespeare's day, but when the characters invoke it, they often mean "public acclaim for virtue," and frequently those who seek to justify themselves in the name of "honor" do so to the detriment of themselves and those around them.

Shakespeare's characters reveal aspects of humanity at large, but they themselves were created during a specific time and in a specific place. Thus the plays must be seen as reflecting aspects of the culture in which they were conceived. Elizabethan England was primarily Christian, and its view of the world followed generally from the medieval vision. This held that the universe was created by God as a perfect work, a unity in which every aspect of creation had its place. This "great chain of being" encompassed all, from the lowest inanimate objects to the angels, placing each in what were judged to be natural levels of subordination. Mankind occupied a unique place, for human beings possessed both soul and body and endured a conflict between their divine capacity, reason, and their baser appetites, or passions. Any imperfection in the world was the work of man, not God.

Within this system was a series of correspondences. As God was the highest among the angels, so the sun was the highest among the stars, fire the highest of the elements, the king the highest among men, and so on. In addition, a fundamental relationship existed between the macrocosm and the microcosm. God was ruler of the universe, the macrocosm, as a monarch was ruler of the political structure, the microcosm. And repercussions of disorder in the social microcosm extended into the universal macrocosm. Furthermore, order in the political realm corresponded to order in the human body. Just as the surrounding world, the macrocosm, was said to be composed of four elements (fire, air, water, and earth), so the human microcosm contained four parallel humors (choler, blood, phlegm, and melancholy). Any imbalance of these within an individual could lead to a disorder extending into a political plane and even into the universal plane.

This medieval vision was tempered by the influence of the Reformation and the Renaissance. The European Reformation, based primarily on religious motives, took some authority away from the Church by insisting on a personal relationship between each human being and God. In England the Reformation followed Henry VIII's rift with the Catholic Church over his divorce. Attendance in the new "Church of England" was still enforced, but now the English monarch was also the authority over all religious matters, and the psychological underpinning that the Catholic Church had provided for centuries was shattered. Movements within the Renaissance celebrated the classical heritage, further secularized aspects of human life, and emphasized personal rights and powers.

Both the Reformation and the Renaissance shook the image of the world as a static entity, and each in its own way shifted responsibility for the nature of the world more to the individual. This new perspective gave rise to new freedoms but also new uncertainties. In England the rise of the gentry reflected the alteration from a feudal system to one based on private enterprise. Furthermore, the nation was beset by a series of intellectual and moral crises springing from disputes over political rights, social rights, and the seemingly heretical results of scientific discovery. All reflected the struggle for stability between individual lives and the social order, the central subject of Elizabethan literature.

Shakespeare's plays dramatize this tension between old and new visions, between the world as a closed, structured system, and the power of individuals to find, to a certain extent, their own way. The plays celebrate individuality. At the same time they reflect a belief that the exertion of individual will creates conflict. For when that will is exercised, whether in the malevolent desire for power or wealth or a benign desire for love, the equilibrium within the individual is upset. This imbalance in Shakespeare's characters is the mainspring of the plot, the force that propels the action. In the comedies personal imbalance tends to remain localized. In the tragedies, histories, and romances, it occurs within individuals of such magnitude that their actions have ramifications that spread throughout the social and even universal structure.

Whatever the nature of the plot, all of Shakespeare's plays end with the reestablishment of personal and political equilibrium. Such restoration of order reflects the essential conservatism of both the age and the playwright. But Shakespeare's conservatism is profoundly humanitarian. Even at his most pessimistic, when cruelties and heartbreak seem overwhelming, not only these resolutions but the plays themselves communicate a faith in the benign structure of the universe as well as in humanity. That love underlies the presentation of his characters, and our embracing of them, testifies to the genius of their creator.

In the following discussions of the individual plays, I shall assume that my readers have experienced the works before. Nevertheless, we shall proceed through each as if an audience were encountering it for the first time, so as to try to capture the freshness and impact of performance. How these plays succeed as theater, how the subtleties of the characters' behavior and the nuances of their language contribute to the theatrical effect: these matters are our central concern.

The suggestions for further reading that appear throughout the book are intended to guide the interested reader in exploring the vast body of critical writing about Shakespeare.

My text is *The Riverside Shakespeare* (Houghton Mifflin), and all quotations, noted by act, scene, and line, are from that volume. Brackets around quoted words indicate that the enclosed material is open to question.

CHRONOLOGY OF PLAYS

We cannot be certain about the precise order in which the plays came, but the following list, with approximate dates of composition, is in general accord with the judgment of most scholars:

1590–92	*Henry VI, Parts 1–3*
1592–93	*Richard III*
	The Comedy of Errors
1593–94	*Titus Andronicus*
	The Taming of the Shrew
1594–95	*The Two Gentlemen of Verona*
	Love's Labor's Lost
	Romeo and Juliet
1595–96	*Richard II*
	A Midsummer Night's Dream
1596–97	*King John*
	The Merchant of Venice
1597–98	*Henry IV, Parts 1–2*
	The Merry Wives of Windsor
1598–99	*Much Ado About Nothing*
	Henry V
1599–1600	*Julius Caesar*
	As You Like It
	Twelfth Night
1600–01	*Hamlet*
1601–02	*Troilus and Cressida*
1602–03	*All's Well That Ends Well*
1604–05	*Measure for Measure*
	Othello

SHAKESPEARE
THE PLAYWRIGHT

THE TRAGEDIES

The tragic form is perhaps the noblest dramatic expression of the human predicament. Conventions of tragedy differ from age to age, but at its core is the conflict of the hero or heroine against overwhelming odds, a conflict that ends in catastrophe. Part of the struggle of these extraordinary characters is an attempt to find meaning in existence, but the answers to questions about the nature of suffering or the origin of evil remain beyond understanding, and the death of the tragic protagonist is the inevitable price of challenge and failure. Nevertheless, the battle itself so elevates these figures that their efforts dignify all of humankind.

The term *Shakespearean tragedy* covers a wide variety of plays and characters, and to establish one all-encompassing definition is impossible. Certainly the works do not conform to a set of principles such as those proposed by Aristotle as the ideal for Greek tragedy. Yet most of the plays here share several qualities we can delineate. We should note, however, that even the choice of plays that should be deemed "tragic" is controversial, and that various critics would include in their own lists works such as *Richard II*, *Richard III*, or *Troilus and Cressida*. The ten selected here are generally accepted as forming the body of Shakespearean tragedy, and in the discussion of those other plays I shall consider why I have not designated them as "tragic."

One essential part of Shakespearean tragedy is that the primary conflict of the central figure is with aspects of the social order. In this respect Shakespeare's figures differ from the tragic heroes and heroines of Greek drama, who battle against divine forces. For instance, in Sophocles' *Oedipus the King*, the title character is condemned by the gods to kill his father and marry his mother, and no actions he takes can change this destiny. He is not, however, fated to discover that he has committed these actions, and thus the tension in the drama emerges from two directions: one, Oedipus's own character, which drives him to learn that he is the man whose sins have brought a plague on Thebes; and two, his gradual realization of what he has done and his acceptance of how he will live the rest of his life under the burden of that knowledge.

This intrusion of "fate" or "destiny," the determination of human action by divine beings, is absent from Shakespearean tragedy. To be sure, several tragedies are set in a Christian society in which religious themes and images are invoked. And in all the plays the characters' view of their world is buttressed by a religious sense of some universal structuring. But so remote is this ordering force that it cannot control the individual existences of men and women. Throughout the plays characters point to the heavens to find explanation for what has occurred or to avoid responsibility for it. But never do we feel that these forces control or interfere with characters. No divine plan is at work in which human beings are pawns to be maneuvered helplessly. In Shakespeare's tragedies the cause of human suffering is human action, and thus we are always conscious that human beings are free to choose.

Is this choice in any way limited? Yes, but the limitations come from within characters, not from without. Each of the figures at the center of these plays bears responsibility for resolving extraordinary crises. The exquisite dilemma of these characters is that their qualities of greatness, those that make them worthy of the positions they hold, militate against successful resolution of the crises. In other words, the qualities that elevate the characters are the very ones that pull them to the most profound depths.

This last claim requires extensive support. Even at first glance, though, the thesis should make sense. The essence of drama is tension between an intriguing personality and a tantalizing situation that allows that personality to grapple with itself. In Shakespeare's plays we find this mixture brought together by the most gifted dramatic hand the human race has produced.

Such interaction between character and circumstance creates another quality that adds to the richness of these works. Often we are conscious of what characters do not know: how those individual drives and instincts are shaping a person's course of action. The result is dramatic irony, as we observe characters proceeding down a path that is not, strictly speaking, determined, but because of the characters' own strengths and flaws, inescapable.

Although the plays look to human character as the springboard of conflict, that focus alone does not eliminate the mystery of the tragic experience. Good and evil clash in these works, but why they should have to clash is beyond explanation. Therefore the plays are pervaded by an underlying search for the reason human beings act as they do. In experiencing these works, we ponder the nature of the human animal, a nature that allows us moments of triumph and joy, but that seems to make suffering endemic to our lives. This uncertainty is balanced by a trust in the human spirit. Such faith emerges not only because at the end of each tragedy the value of goodness is reaffirmed, but also because the plays themselves reflect how human existence, through the prism of artistic expression, may inspire our passion and wonder.

SUGGESTIONS FOR FURTHER READING

Battenhouse, Roy W. *Shakespearean Tragedy: Its Art and Christian Premises.* Bloomington: Indiana University Press, 1969.

Bowers, Fredson. *Elizabethan Revenge Tragedy*. Princeton: Princeton University Press, 1940.

Bradley, A. C. *Shakespearean Tragedy*. London: Macmillan, 1985. (Originally published in 1904).

Campbell, Lily B. *Shakespeare's Tragic Heroes: Slaves of Passion*. Cambridge: Cambridge University Press, 1930.

Champion, Larry S. *Shakespeare's Tragic Perspective*. Athens, Ga.: University of Georgia Press, 1976.

Coursen, Herbert R. *Christian Ritual and the World of Shakespeare's Tragedies*. Lewisburg, Pa.: Bucknell University Press, 1976.

Farnham, Willard. *Shakespeare's Tragic Frontier*. Berkeley and Los Angeles: University of California Press, 1950.

Goldman, Michael. *Shakespeare and the Energies of Drama*. Princeton: Princeton University Press, 1972.

Harbage, Alfred, ed. *Shakespeare: The Tragedies: A Collection of Critical Essays*. Englewood Cliffs, N.J.: Prentice-Hall, 1964.

Heilman, Robert B., ed. *Shakespeare: The Tragedies (New Perspectives)*. Englewood Cliffs, N.J.: Prentice-Hall, 1984.

Knight, G. Wilson. *The Imperial Theme: Further Interpretations of Shakespearean Tragedies including the Roman Plays*. London: Oxford University Press, 1931.

———. *The Wheel of Fire: Interpretations of Shakespearean Tragedy*. Oxford: Oxford University Press, 1930.

Leech, Clifford, ed. *Shakespeare: The Tragedies: A Collection of Critical Essays*. Chicago: University of Chicago Press, 1965.

Lerner, Laurence, ed. *Shakespeare's Tragedies: An Anthology of Modern Criticism*. Baltimore: Penguin, 1963.

McElroy, Bernard. *Shakespeare's Mature Tragedies*. Princeton: Princeton University Press, 1973.

Mehl, Dieter. *Shakespeare's Tragedies: An Introduction*. Cambridge: Cambridge University Press, 1986.

Muir, Kenneth. *Shakespeare's Tragic Sequence*. London: Hutchinson University Library, 1972.

Nevo, Ruth. *Tragic Form in Shakespeare*. Princeton: Princeton University Press, 1972.

Ribner, Irving. *Patterns in Shakespearean Tragedy*. London: Methuen, 1960.

Siegel, Paul N. *Shakespearean Tragedy and the Elizabethan Compromise*. New York: New York University Press, 1957.

Snyder, Susan. *The Comic Matrix of Shakespeare's Tragedies*. Princeton: Princeton University Press, 1979.

Stirling, Brents. *Unity in Shakespearean Tragedy: The Interplay of Theme and Character*. New York: Columbia University Press, 1956.

Whitaker, Virgil K. *The Mirror Up to Nature: The Technique of Shakespeare's Tragedies*. San Marino, Calif.: The Huntington Library, 1965.

TITUS ANDRONICUS

The first of Shakespeare's tragic plays is rarely produced in our time because it suffers from a variety of failings. Yet the work does offer a unified, if brutal, vision of humanity and society, and as such exerts a certain fascination. It belongs to the genre of the Elizabethan revenge-tragedy, of which the most famous example until Shakespeare's work was Thomas Kyd's *The Spanish Tragedy* (c. 1589). The overall form follows in the tradition of works by the Roman dramatist Seneca (4 B.C.–A.D. 65), whose plays are marked by sensationalistic violence. The plots generally focus on a single figure who pursues a path of revenge that proves not only more destructive than the initial violence that provoked it, but also brings about the revenger's downfall.

Two other elements of Senecan tragedy are found in *Titus Andronicus*. One, the language is florid, with stark, vivid imagery. Second, and most important for our purposes, the characters are drawn with little psychological subtlety, and thus to probe their language and actions for inner conflict is rarely rewarding. At moments the characters do hint at a level of complication rare in this genre, and these instances provide an inkling of what blossoms in subsequent plays of Shakespeare.

The materials of the story, set in the fourth century A.D., seem to have been taken from a variety of sources. An earlier version of Titus's career was apparently published in a small volume in 1594. The story of Lavinia was likely drawn from one of Shakespeare's favorite sources, the *Metamorphoses* of the Roman poet Ovid. Book VI of that volume describes the rape of Philomela, whose suffering is similar to that of Lavinia here. And Titus's final revenge may have been adapted from Seneca's *Thyestes*.

The opening scene reveals the primary tensions as well as some of the problems with the play. Saturninus addresses an audience of Tribunes and Senators, seeking their support in his campaign to follow his father as leader of Rome:

> Noble patricians, patrons of my right,
> Defend the justice of my cause with arms;
> And, countrymen, my loving followers,

> Plead my successive title with your swords.
> I am his first-born son, that was the last
> That ware the imperial diadem of Rome,
> Then let my father's honors live in me,
> Nor wrong mine age with this indignity.
>
>   (I, i, 1–8)

The tone is pompous, self-righteous, and hollow, as the speaker attempts to create the image of a glorified, militaristic Rome. The play soon dramatizes, however, that these words are a facade, that underneath the transcendent portrait lies fearsome savagery. As the action moves back and forth from urban Rome to the pastoral forest, brutish forces emerge from humanity in either setting. One argument that pervaded Elizabethan thought and which recurs regularly throughout Shakespeare's plays was the comparative worth of the city and the country. In this play both are the background for staggering cruelty.

Noteworthy, too, in this speech is irony characteristic of Shakespeare. Often in his plays those who proclaim their own virtues are most susceptible to corruption. And the more insistent the claims, the more painful the reality. In particular, the more a speaker relies on the word "honor," the more dangerous may be his intentions. In Act I of this play alone, "honor" appears in some form thirty-four times. Many speakers invoke it for what may appear a variety of reasons, but almost always for the same end: to legitimize a despicable act. If an atrocity is committed in the name of "honor," then it is immune from legal judgment. Such is the rationale.

After Bassianus stakes his claim to the throne, adding his own reference to "dishonor" (I, i, 13), Marcus takes over, invoking a key theme of the play: the valorous Roman heroes in contrast to "the barbarous Goths" (I, i, 28). He goes on to describe the triumphs of his brother, the great Roman leader Titus, using "honor" several times to dignify the horrors of war. He also has a suggestion for Saturninus and Bassianus:

> Let us entreat by honor of his name,
> Whom worthily you would have now succeed,
> And in the Capitol and Senate's right,
> Whom you pretend to honor and adore,
> That you withdraw you, and abate your strength,
> Dismiss your followers, and, as suitors should,
> Plead your deserts in peace and humbleness.
>
>   (I, i, 39–45)

His use of "honor" testifies to Marcus's political savvy. He knows that neither brother can maintain a claim in the face of Titus's eminence, and, indeed, both withdraw reluctantly.

Titus then enters to the Captain's words:

> Patron of virtue, Rome's best champion,
> Successful in the battles that he fights,

With honor and with fortune is return'd.

(I, i, 65–67)

Here is a great soldier whose outstanding attribute is his capacity for legal destruction carried out in the name of Rome. Here also is another irony of this play and of the tragedies as a whole. As was suggested in the introduction about all the tragic heroes, the attributes that heighten Titus eventually cause his downfall. Most of what follows results because his acclaimed talent for destruction runs uncontrolled outside the supposedly civilized arena of the battlefield. Soon distinctions between the noble Romans and "the barbarous Goths" are blurred.

First Titus stands before his family tomb to pay tribute to Rome, then to his twenty-one sons who have died in the war:

> O sacred receptacle of my joys,
> Sweet cell of virtue and nobility . . .

(I, i, 92–93)

The conflict has ended, and peace would seem at hand. Surviving son Lucius, however, has a request:

> Give us the proudest prisoner of the Goths,
> That we may hew his limbs and on a pile
> Ad [manes] fratrum sacrifice his flesh
> Before this earthly prison of their bones,
> That so the shadows be not unappeas'd,
> Nor we disturb'd with prodigies on earth.

(I, i, 96–101)

This act was a traditional Roman ritual, performed under the assumption that one final murder would end all murder. Thus Titus consents. But Tamora, Queen of the Goths, protests that her sons were likewise "valiant" (I, i, 113) in their country's cause. She, too, emphasizes "nobility" (I, i, 119). And she pleads with Titus to be merciful. He, however, is relentless, speaking of how his sons "religiously" (I, i, 124) demand a sacrifice. Then Lucius eagerly drags the body away: "Let's hew his limbs till they be clean consum'd" (I, i, 129).

Here is the first act of barbarism. And before long we realize that there is no such thing as a final murder. No matter how the winners try to adorn their act in piety, murder, on the battlefield or in a temple, brutalizes the murderer, a motif that returns again and again in Shakespeare. Here it also energizes the victims to further destruction, as Tamora and her two sons promise (I, i, 130–141). This pattern of revenge followed by further revenge dominates the rest of the play.

We see here as well a problem with the character of Titus: he is devoid of inner conflict. When the mother of his intended victim cries for mercy, Titus suffers no doubt. He reacts impassively: "Patient yourself, madam, and pardon me" (I, i, 121). Absence of inner struggle is endemic to Senecan tragedy. But for us such flatness eliminates involvement; if the character feels no anxiety, neither do we.

Another example of one-dimensionality occurs after Titus's sons return in exultation, and Lavinia, his daughter, steps forward to praise her father (I, i, 157–163). This speech is one of her few, and therefore we have little sense of her character. Thus when later Lavinia suffers horrible punishment, we do not feel outrage that such torture is inflicted on someone decent or loving. We are sickened instead that such abuse can happen to anyone. Furthermore, because we are denied personal involvement, we think instead of the overtones of her fate, and thus Lavinia becomes essentially a symbol, as we shall consider presently.

After Lavinia's tribute, Marcus officially offers Titus the position of Emperor: "And help to set a head on headless Rome" (I, i, 186). But Titus demurs:

> Give me a staff of honor for mine age,
> But not a sceptre to control the world.

(I, i, 198–199)

Marcus insists, but before Titus has a chance to respond, Saturninus bursts out in protest:

> Patricians, draw your swords, and sheathe them not
> Till Saturninus be Rome's emperor.
> Andronicus, would thou were shipp'd to hell,
> Rather than rob me of the people's hearts!

(I, i, 204–207)

Even after this threat, and Bassianus's affirmation of Titus's claim (I, i, 212–216), Titus nonetheless bestows the crown on Saturninus. In other plays of Shakespeare, parents misjudge their children and thereby invoke terrible consequences. Furthermore, when such an error takes place within a royal family, the consequences affect the entire nation. Here Titus's blunder appears incomprehensible, for Saturninus has just threatened to bring anarchy to Rome and is clearly undeserving of power. Still, the decision stands.

Saturninus tries to soothe tensions by selecting Lavinia to be his Empress (I, i, 240). Yet as he sees Tamora, his feelings change, as he reveals in an aside:

> A goodly lady, trust me, of the hue
> That I would choose were I to choose anew.

(I, i, 261–262)

Before any emotional crises arise, Bassianus seizes the passive Lavinia, and even Marcus admits that according to Roman law they have indeed been married (I, i, 280–281). Titus, however, sees this action as traitorous, and accuses his sons who help Bassianus escape.

What follows is one of the more problematic moments of the play. Mutius blocks his father's attempt to stop Bassianus and the others, but Titus does not hesitate to take action: "What, villain boy,/Barr'st me my way in Rome?" (I, i, 290–291). And Titus slays him. One way to see this apparently irrational act as part of a psychological whole is to understand Titus as a great warrior, accustomed to unquestioned obedience. When challenged, he lashes out at the immediate target, here his son.

Virtually no time is spent in remorse, though, for seconds later Saturninus returns to announce that he has taken Tamora for his wife. This action is a blatant insult to Titus: "These words are razors to my wounded heart" (I, i, 314). But even when he is not offered attendance at the wedding ("I am not bid to wait upon this bride" [I, i, 338]), he refuses to see that he has erred, and denies Marcus's request that Mutius be buried in the family tomb:

> No, foolish tribune, no; no son of mine,
> Nor thou, nor these, confederates in the deed
> That hath dishonored all our family:
> Unworthy brother, and unworthy sons!
>
> (I, i, 343–346)

Titus places loyalty to the Emperor, even a corrupt Emperor, above family, an example of one kind of divided fidelity that recurs often in Shakespeare's tragedies and histories. In his rage and bullying, Titus anticipates King Lear, who also blunders by ignoring wiser counsel and surrendering to his own pride. Then Quintus hints at Titus's subsequent loss of sanity: "He is not with himself, let us withdraw" (I, i, 368). Like Lear, Titus will eventually be mentally broken by the consequences of his own precipitous actions. Eventually Titus does relent and allows Mutius to be buried in the family tomb, but not until Marcus says: "Thou art a Roman, be not barbarous . . ." (I, i, 378). The irony is not subtle.

After the burial Marcus asks a question we have waited to hear:

> How comes it that the subtile Queen of Goths
> Is of a sudden thus advanc'd in Rome?
>
> (I, i, 392–393)

Titus's answer reflects both his naivete and his nobility:

> I know not, Marcus, but I know it is
> (Whether by device or no, the heavens can tell).
> Is she not then beholding to the man
> That brought her for this high good turn so far?
> [Yes, and will nobly him remunerate.]
>
> (I, i, 394–398)

Titus refuses to acknowledge that he is to blame for Tamora's elevation to Queen. Furthermore, he tries to convince himself that with this new rank her character will change. He does not wish to recognize that a woman such as Tamora will grow only more ruthless.

The two wedding parties return, but Saturninus has not forgiven his brother's insult:

> Traitor, if Rome have law, or we have power,
> Thou and thy faction shall repent this rape.
>
> (I, i, 403–404)

Bassianus looks to Titus for support (I, i, 411–423), but the warrior is firmly resolved against a man he judges to be a traitor. The tension is soothed by Tamora, who out loud asks forgiveness for Titus (I, i, 434–441), then privately to her husband counsels differently:

> You are but newly planted in your throne;
> Lest then the people, and patricians too,
> Upon a just survey take Titus' part . . .
>
> (I, i, 444–446)

In plays to follow, many leaders are cognizant that the force of the populace must be handled delicately. Tamora continues:

> I'll find a day to massacre them all,
> And rase their faction and their family . . .
>
> (I, i, 450–451)

Saturninus follows her advice, and agrees to public reconciliation, as all are invited to a hunting party. The irony of that activity is powerful, for the objects of the hunt are not "the panther and the hart" (I, i, 493) as Titus and the characters expect.

Act II brings a change in tone, as Aaron, who has been lurking about since the start, takes the stage. Unlike the other villains in this play, he is joyously sinister, figuratively rubbing his hands in glee as he plots to gain power:

> I will be bright, and shine in pearl and gold,
> To wait upon this new-made emperess.
>
> (II, i, 19–20)

Aaron is the first "Machiavel" in Shakespeare's plays, characters who carry out their schemes with a combination of cunning and wit. The name is borrowed from Niccolò Machiavelli (1469–1527), the Italian statesman whose book *Il Principe* (*The Prince*, 1513) contributed profoundly to the Renaissance view of political realism. Machiavelli himself became to Elizabethans a symbol of all kinds of diabolic conspiracy. Machiavels were common in the drama of Shakespeare's time, and like most of these figures, including Iago in *Othello* and Edmund in *King Lear*, Aaron is enthralling, for though his schemes horrify us, his wit and gusto ensure that we are fascinated by them. On the other hand, Aaron is not a fully developed character, because his values and reasons remain murky. We are never certain as to the purpose for his manipulations. He wants to marry Tamora and acquire status as her husband, but the explanation for his other cruelties lies perhaps in his blackness and resultant alienation.

His theatrical attractiveness is contrasted with the oafish cruelties of Tamora's sons, Chiron and Demetrius, who enter here assaulting one another over desire for Lavinia. Aaron skillfully takes them to task, claiming their squabble would shame their mother (II, i, 51–52). He warns them additionally of the threat posed by Bassianus (II, i, 63–70), then inquires casually how they propose to win her. Demetrius answers confidently:

> She is a woman, therefore my be woo'd,
> She is a woman, therefore may be won.
>
> (II, i, 82–83)

Shakespeare must have found these lines attractive, for he used versions of them lin two other plays. Suffolk muses in similar terms about Margaret, who is to be Henry VI's wife (*Henry VI, Part 1*, V, iii, 78–79). And in *Richard III*, the future King delights in the same spirit about Lady Anne (*Richard III*, I, ii, 227–228). The sentiments are least effective here, for Demetrius is so without charm that we cannot imagine his seducing anyone.

Aaron, though, does not reveal his scorn of the boys. After sneering about the thought of Saturninus's being cuckolded (II, i, 89), Aaron recalls the mythological rape of Lucrece by Tarquin, and thereby implies that such is the proper course of action. He also hints that Tamora herself would want to be involved:

> Come, come, our empress, with her sacred wit,
> To villainy and vengeance consecrate,
> Will we acquaint withal what we intend,
> And she shall file our engines with advice . . .
>
> (II, i, 120–123)

The word "sacred" suggests the cruel humor that makes Aaron both repulsive and entertaining.

In scene ii Titus and this sons enter as part of the hunting party. Titus has slept badly and takes this condition as a sign of foreboding (II, ii, 9–10). But he does not hear the threat Demetrius mutters to his brother:

> Chiron, we hunt not, we, with horse nor hound,
> But hope to pluck a dainty doe to ground.
>
> (II, ii, 25–26)

We sense that the "doe" is Lavinia.

In scene iii Aaron keeps his plot underway by burying gold. When he is joined by Tamora, she confesses her desire for him, but he clarifies his intentions:

> Madam, though Venus govern your desires,
> Saturn is dominator over mine . . .
> Vengeance is in my heart, death in my hand,
> Blood and revenge are hammering in my head.
>
> (II, iii, 30–39)

Such lines reveal the intensity of Aaron's hatred, but they do not enrich him psychologically.

Lavinia and Bassianus enter, and almost at once toss jibes at Tamora about

her affair with Aaron. First Bassianus mocks her isolation from her guard, joins
then with Lavinia and smirks about Aaron's color (II, iii, 56–80). Finally Bassianus threatens to report to Saturninus about this clandestine relationship (II,
iii, 85), an unlikely event given the brothers' mutual antagonism. Furthermore,
that these insults invite retaliation weakens events that follow, for at this point
Lavinia and Bassianus are more arrogant than sympathetic. Nonetheless, their
behavior does not warrant the horrors that unfold.

     When Chiron and Demetrius return to the stage, Tamora bursts out with a
fabrication about how Bassianus and Lavinia threatened to leave her to die of
fright in a pit of snakes. Interestingly, she also claims that they called her "foul
adultress" (II, iii, 109), suggesting that she enjoys that aspect of her treachery.
She then orders her sons to take appropriate revenge. At once both boys stab
Bassianus, who dies. Tamora is ready to do the same to Lavinia, but Demetrius
seeks another punishment:

> This minion stood upon her chastity,
> Upon her nuptial vow, her loyalty,
> And with that painted hope braves your mightiness;
> And shall she carry this unto her grave?

>   (II, iii, 124–127)

Tamora approves:

> But when ye have the honey we desire,
> Let not this wasp outlive, us both to sting.

>   (II, iii, 131–132)

The use of first-person plural intimates that Tamora wants Lavinia's rape as
much as her sons do.

     Lavinia pleads for her life:

> When did the tiger's young ones teach the dam?
> O, do not learn her wrath—she taught it thee;
> The milk thou suck'st from her did turn to marble,
> Even at thy teat thou hadst thy tyranny . . .

>   (II, iii, 142–145)

She invokes the central imagery of this play: that of animals. Shakespeare's
contemporaries envisioned humanity as caught between aspirations to be angels
and the instincts of beasts. Thus throughout his works, when human beings sink
to unspeakable levels, the playwright frequently invokes bestial images.

     Tamora, not surprisingly, recalls that her own pleas for Alarbus were ignored.
Then she adds, with malicious delight: "The worse to her, the better lov'd of
me" (II, iii, 167). Here is cruelty for its own sake, perhaps the most horrible
cruelty of all. Her sons toss Bassianus in the pit where Aaron buried gold, then
drag off Lavinia, leaving Tamora to swear revenge on all the Andronicus family
(II, iii, 188–189) and to depart to search for Aaron, "my lovely Moor" (II, iii,
190).

At this moment he enters with two of Titus's sons, Quintus and Martius, promising they will find a panther in that same pit. In an awkward sequence, Martius falls in, then calls up that he has found the body of Bassianus. The moment is almost comic, as in answer to Quintus's question about the identity of the body, Martius's inappropriately glorifies it:

> Upon his bloody finger he doth wear
> A precious ring that lightens all this hole,
> Which, like a taper in some monument,
> Doth shine upon the dead man's earthy cheeks,
> And shows the ragged entrails of this pit . . .
>
> (II, iii, 226–230)

The picturesque language is badly misplaced with respect to the victim's undignified death. Here is an example of the young Shakespeare's reaching for a dramatic coup, a poetic rendering of death that will be in his power only in his later plays.

Quintus attempts to help his brother escape, but in one more clumsily comic moment, fulfills his own prediction and falls in. When Aaron returns with Saturninus, the two trapped boys find themselves shouting up from the hole, a ludicrous position that undercuts the tension. Just as Saturninus learns the identity of the two trapped men (II, iii, 250), Tamora enters with Titus and a letter ostensibly planning the murder of Bassianus. Why Saturninus should believe the Goths, the sworn enemies of Rome, is never clear, but perhaps he is infatuated with Tamora, and accepts the accusation that Martius and Quintus conspired. He orders their torture and death, then compounds his error by believing Tamora's claim that the letter was given to her by Titus. Saturninus then orders the two boys to be executed after the torture. The outrageousness of the injustice is emphasized by Tamora, who promises Titus that she will speak for his sons (II, iii, 304–305). Even Titus recognizes the fraudulence of this claim, and stalks away with his surviving son, Lucius, who at the moment is helpless.

Scene iv continues the grotesqueries, as Demetrius and Chiron return with Lavinia, who has been raped, then left armless and tongueless so that she cannot reveal the identities of her attackers. Her condition may be taken as a symbol of Rome reduced to moral and political disorder because of Titus's errors in judgment, Saturninus's corruption, and the barbarous influence of the Goths. As Lavinia stands helplessly alone, she is discovered by Marcus, whose gradual realization of her mutilation is bizarre:

> Why dost not speak to me?
> Alas, a crimson river of warm blood,
> Like to a bubbling fountain stirr'd with wind,
> Doth rise and fall between thy rosed lips,

> Coming and going with thy honey breath.
>
> (II, iv, 21–25)

The romantic imagery is out of place. Throughout the play Marcus is the primary figure of conscience, whose awareness of right and wrong is ballast for the audience. At this moment, though, he fails to grasp the obvious, and the mood is shattered.

In Act III, scene i, Titus argues before the court of Rome for his sons' lives, invoking "honor's lofty bed" (III, i, 11), an ironically useless sentiment. He even humiliates himself by lying in the street where earlier he strode in triumph. But he speaks now to no avail, as the judges silently leave with the prisoners. Lucius tells of his own banishment, imposed after he pleaded for his brothers. Titus's response is at the core of the play:

> Why, foolish Lucius, dost thou not perceive
> That Rome is but a wilderness of tigers?
> Tigers must prey, and Rome affords no prey
> But me and mine.
>
> (III, i, 53–56)

He reaffirms the theme of animalism, and his use of "tiger" recalls Lavinia's cry to and about Tamora in Act II. Titus also clarifies that the sufferings of a royal family have implications for an entire society, a theme that returns again and again in Shakespeare's tragedies and histories. Here the brutalization of the Andronici is mirrored in the chaos that besets Rome. To the play's detriment we see little of this disorder, but the thematic import remains.

With the entrance of Lavinia and Marcus, Titus is forced to contemplate further the horrors perpetrated on his family, and he is tempted to cut off his own hands in commiseration. He then reviews the crimes committed by the nation for which he fought so bravely in war (III, i, 91–113). Lavinia's tears torment him, for they suggest to Marcus that she may know that her brothers are innocent of her husband's murder. Titus's state of imbalance is evidenced by his confused re-action. First he claims faith in human justice:

> If they did kill thy husband, then be joyful,
> Because the law hath ta'en revenge on them.
>
> (III, i, 116–117)

Then he seems to dismiss that possibility, as if overcome by human cruelty: "No, no, they would not do so foul a deed . . ." (III, i, 118). The rest of his speech is a mixture of pity for Lavinia and fury at his own inability to carry out revenge.

Aaron then enters with a perverse offer:

> Let Marcus, Lucius, or thyself, old Titus,
> Or any one of you, chop off your hand
> And send it to the King; he for the same
> Will send hither both thy sons alive,

And that shall be the ransom for their fault.

(III, i, 152–156)

That anyone should believe Aaron strains credibility, but all offer to sacrifice a limb. Titus, though, exerts his authority and volunteers (III, i, 183). While the others prepare to carry out the bloody act, Aaron enters, and Titus allows his hand to be severed just as Marcus and Lucius return. The moment is terrible, but Aaron mocks even this brutality:

> I go, Andronicus, and for thy hand
> Look by and by to have thy sons with thee.
> [*Aside.*] Their heads, I mean. O how this villainy
> Doth fat me with the very thoughts of it!

(III, i, 200–203)

From this moment we anticipate the return of the actual heads of the two boys. Stranded, Titus calls to the heavens:

> If there were reason for these miseries,
> Then into limits could I bind my woes:
> When heaven doth weep, doth not the earth o'erflow?

(III, i, 219–221)

He wonders whether a life filled with such horrors can have meaning. This question is raised far more movingly in later tragedies, as characters seek explanation for suffering they endure.

Barely has Titus finished his outcry when a messenger returns, carrying, as we suspected, the heads of Martius and Quintus. At this sight Marcus for the first time shouts his own fury (III, i, 253–263), and seems prepared to carry out revenge by himself. Titus, however, begins to go mad, in a combination of laughing and weeping. In a grotesque moment that embodies the theme of destruction, the family lifts the severed heads and hand and marches off, leaving Lucius to swear revenge.

The family's ordeal carries over to the next scene, when all are at dinner. Titus continues to review their trials until Marcus strikes at a dish. At this action Titus becomes furious:

> A deed of death done on the innocent
> Becomes not Titus' brother . . .

(III, ii, 56–57)

> How if that fly had a father and mother?

(III, ii, 60)

But when Marcus claims that the fly reminded him of Aaron, Titus attacks the fly on his own: "There's for thyself, and that's for Tamora" (III, ii, 74). Vengeance against a fly, however, borders too closely on the outlandish to be effective dramatically. The ending of the scene, the reading of a story, is also anticlimatic. Most of this act, in fact, is burdened by arbitrary violence, and the play seems stalled.

The pace picks up slightly in the next scene, as Lucius enters running from Lavinia, who is soon revealed to have information. In an extremely ungraceful sequence, Lavinia manages with her stumps to indicate to Titus and Marcus the story of Philomel in a copy of Ovid. They slowly realize that she means that she, too, was raped in the woods during the hunt (IV, i, 46–58). In response, Marcus offers a crucial line:

> O why should nature build so foul a den,
> Unless the gods delight in tragedies?
>
> (IV, i, 59–60)

Like Gloucester in *King Lear*, like a host of figures from the tragedies, Marcus seeks to deny responsibility. If the gods are in command, if nature has set up this calamity, then individuals may be absolved of guilt. However, such is not the vision in subsequent plays of Shakespeare, and such is not the vision here. We remember that Titus ordered the sacrifice of Alarbus, and Titus presented the throne to Saturninus. And the characters of Tamora, Aaron, Saturninus, Demetrius, and Chiron carried out the rest. Responsibility lies with humanity, as it does in all of Shakespeare's plays.

Marcus is then inspired to have Lavinia write on the ground, by use of her stumps and a stick, the names of her attackers. When the information is communicated in this bizarre fashion, Marcus, Titus, and young Lucius, Titus's grandson, resolve to carry out their own plot. The boy is a particularly interesting character, as he seems infected so early in life by the spirit of retribution:

> I say, my lord, that if I were a man,
> Their mother's bedchamber should not be safe
> For these base bondmen to the yoke of Rome.
>
> (IV, i, 107–109)

His courage is daunting, but violence is passing from one generation to the next. The battle goes on and on.

In Act IV, scene ii, young Lucius plays his first active part, visiting Aaron, Chiron, and Demetrius ostensibly to deliver weapons as a bribe from Titus. The boy's asides communicate his bitterness, but he carries out his task effectively. When Demetrius reads an inscription he finds on one armament, Aaron realizes that Titus knows the truth:

> The old man hath found their guilt,
> And sends them weapons wrapp'd about with lines
> That wound beyond their feeling to the quick.
>
> (IV, ii, 26–28)

That he chooses not to reveal his discovery to the brothers clarifies that Aaron's loyalty is above all to himself. This impression, however, is modified when the nurse enters with Tamora's newborn son. Because it is black and therefore obviously Aaron's, Tamora has ordered it killed (IV, ii, 66–70). But Aaron defends his offspring:

> 'Zounds, ye whore, is black so base a hue?
> Sweet blowse, you are a beauteous blossom sure.
>
> (IV, ii, 71–72)

This affection brings out another dimension of Aaron's character. Somewhere deep within him is a capacity for love that has been thwarted. The emotion is not developed, though, and thus Aaron's character is not as rich as it might be, nor as rich as that of later Machiavels.

Demetrius and Chiron are outraged: "Thou hast undone our mother" (IV, ii, 75), to which Aaron chortles: "Villain, I have done thy mother" (IV, ii, 76). He then offers a powerful tribute to the infant's color and heritage. His combination of viciousness, pride, and glee, tempered by affection for the infant, makes him the most intriguing character in the play.

So determined is Aaron that he threatens to kill Demetrius and Chiron if they harm the baby (IV, ii, 91–92). But their mother's plight still worries them, as Demetrius indicates: "By this our mother is for ever sham'd" (IV, ii, 112), and Chiron adds: "Rome will despise her for this foul escape" (IV, ii, 113). Aaron, however, has a scheme. First he ascertains that only two women besides Tamora know of the infant's existence (IV, ii, 140–142). With this knowledge secure, he kills the Nurse. Perhaps more than any other, her death reflects the world of this play. She dies for no reason but to fulfill the mad desires of a man who himself has no reason to his life. Aaron orders the baby swapped for another that will be raised as the Emperor's heir (IV, ii, 151–161), then commands that the other witness be sent to him for execution (IV, ii, 166). So ruthless is the scheme that even Chiron and Demetrius are overwhelmed (IV, ii, 169–171).

Scene iii returns us to Titus, who in his guilt now approaches madness: "Ah, Rome! well, well, I made thee miserable . . . " (IV, iii, 18). While Titus raves, Marcus orders the other men to join with the Goths against Rome and Saturninus (IV, iii, 33–35), and this shift of alliances is evidence of the disorder Titus has wrought. Titus, however, is still preoccupied, and gives his men arrows that Marcus orders directed into the Emperor's court. This desperate action reflects Titus's shattered mind and anticipates the madness of others like Lear. In this play, however, because Titus has been drawn with little subtlety, his insanity is not very moving. Furthermore, he later apparently regains control, and such inconsistency does not help.

The intensity of the story is relieved slightly with the entrance of the Clown, whom Titus assumes carries messages from heaven (IV, ii, 78–80). Although the Clown is confused by the greeting, Titus orders him to deliver a communication to the Emperor, who in scene iv is angry over Titus's behavior:

> And what and if
> His sorrows have so overwhelm'd his wits?
> Shall we be thus afflicted in his wreaks,

His fits, his frenzy, and his bitterness?

(IV, iv, 9–13)

Tamora seems to sympathize, but in an aside reveals that she is delighted with her own successes:

> But, Titus, I have touch'd thee to the quick;
> Thy life-blood out, if Aaron now be wise,
> Then is all safe, the anchor in the port.

(IV, iv, 36–38)

Her attitude, like Aaron's, is based on egoism and selfishness.

When the Clown enters, he submits Titus's letter, and Saturninus immediately commands that the messenger be hanged. The presence of comic relief anticipates Lear's Fool, the gravedigger in *Hamlet*, and other witty figures who contrast the tragic happenings around them. But this Clown is unsuccessful theatrically. Perhaps the overwhelming gore ensures the failure of any comic intrusion. In addition, the Clown is given little development. He is brought onstage, condemned to death, and quickly whisked away. We are as befuddled by his presence as he is.

Saturninus orders action against Titus, but Aemilius enters to announce that the Goths, with Lucius at their head, are preparing to attack. He refers to Coriolanus (IV, iv, 68), another Roman general who allied himself with Rome's enemies, and the subject of a later tragedy by Shakespeare. Like Titus, Coriolanus disdains a leadership position, although for different reasons. We can only speculate whether the young playwright suspected that one day he would dramatize that story. Saturninus recognizes Lucius's popularity with the people, and Tamora's invocation of the traditional images of the Roman ruler, the "sun" (IV, iv, 82) and the "eagle" (IV, iv, 83), do not assuage Saturninus's fears. But she does calm him when she guarantees that she can work on Titus to bring Lucius down (IV, iv, 89–93, 108–112).

Act V brings in Lucius, rallying the Goth army. He is interrupted first by one soldier who urges Tamora's death (V, i, 13–16), then by another who brings in Aaron with the child. The willingness of both soldiers to act against their countrymen suggests how values have been overturned. The second soldier reports having overheard Aaron comforting his "tawny slave" (V, i, 27), and the others realize that the mother was not black. Aaron then boasts that the boy is "of royal blood" (V, i, 49), but Lucius is determined to kill the child (V, i, 51). Eventually Aaron works a deal:

> For I must talk of murthers, rapes, and massacres,
> Acts of black night, abominable deeds,
> Complots of mischief, treason, villainies,
> Ruthful to hear, yet piteously perform'd.
> And this shall all be buried in my death,

Unless thou swear to me my child shall live.

(V, i, 63–68)

At last Lucius agrees, and Aaron confesses about his baby: "I begot him on the Empress" (V, i, 87). What follows is a litany of crimes joyously recounted, a summary of all the horrors we have witnessed (V, i, 98–120). The details are vivid, and Aaron's combination of malevolence and delight remains gripping:

I pried me through the crevice of a wall,
When, for his hand, he had his two sons' heads,
Beheld his tears, and laugh'd so heartily
That both mine eyes were rainy like to his . . .

(V, i, 114–117)

But none of these stories develops his character. We learn nothing new, and in that sense the material is static. Aaron proudly announces that not only is he not regretful for these actions, but sorry "that I had not done a thousand more" (V, i, 124). After Aaron offers a catalogue of nefarious deeds he might carry out, including torturing them all in hell (V, i, 147–150), Lucius orders Aaron's mouth stopped. Aemilius enters to announce a meeting with Saturninus at Titus's home, with Saturninus even promising hostages so that Lucius feels safe. Lucius brushes the request aside, asking instead that the pledges be given to Titus and Marcus. We feel that balance is slowly being restored, as Lucius is making strategically correct decisions.

This moment of transition brings back Tamora and her sons, who appear before Titus's door. She pretends to be Revenge, "sent from below / To join with him and right his heinous wrongs" (V, ii, 3–4), and Titus's reaction is bewildering. First he says he recognizes her (V, ii, 24–25). But when she denies her identity, Titus claims to believe her charade as well as her claim that her cohorts are not her sons but Rape and Murder, who will aid Titus in his revenge (V, ii, 62–63). As he feigns trust, they assume he is mad, and when Titus departs the stage temporarily, Tamora explains to her sons her scheme:

I'll make him send for Lucius his son;
And whilst I at a banket hold him sure,
I'll find some cunning practice out of hand,
To scatter and disperse the giddy Goths,
Or at the least make them his enemies.

(V, ii, 75–79)

Titus then re-enters, still claiming to be struck by the resemblance of his visitors to the Empress and her sons (V, ii, 84). He also orders them to find people just like themselves:

I pray thee do on them some violent death,
They have been violent to me and mine.

(V, ii, 108–109)

Tamora, believing Titus mad, agrees to his plan, but asks that Lucius attend a banquet where the Emperor will be vulnerable for revenge (V, ii, 111–120).

Titus agrees but insists that "Rape" and "Murder" remain with him. As Tamora
confers with her sons, Titus confides in us:

> I knew them all though they suppos'd me mad,
> And will o'erreach them in their own devices,
> A pair of cursed hell-hounds and their dame.

(V, ii, 142–144)

The pose of madness is a familiar maneuver by characters in revenge plays, but
becomes most compelling and complicated when taken on by Hamlet. Here
Titus's calculation is shrewd, but dramatically in conflict with the distraction he
manifested earlier.

As soon as Tamora leaves, Titus calls for Publius, Caius, and Valentine, and
orders them to bind and gag Chiron and Demetrius. With ferocious cold-bloodedness, Titus then approaches the boys with a knife while Lavinia enters with
a basin. Once more their crimes are recounted, and Titus then reveals his gruesome plot (V, ii, 186–195). His detailed recital takes away from the potential
twists of the final scene, for we could learn the truth when Tamora does and
thereby share her shock. But as if in compensation Shakespeare makes us feel
the revulsion twice: once by hearing how the boys will be slaughtered and served
as the repast; secondly by observing the banquet while knowing the sickening
truth.

In the final scene, which takes place in the court of Titus's house, Lucius
enters and tells Marcus that the imprisoned Aaron should be held in case the
Emperor proves treacherous (V, iii, 4–10). At this moment the royal party enters,
and Saturninus and Lucius insult one another, but Marcus temporarily alleviates
tension by inviting everyone to a banquet of reconciliation. We remember what
is about to be served, and thus our excitement remains unabated.

While the dinner is consumed amidst genial falsehood from both sides, Titus
suddenly speaks of Virginius, a Roman soldier who killed his daughter to prevent
her rape (V, iii, 36–38). When Saturninus asks the reason for this intrusive
remark, Titus suddenly turns and stabs Lavinia, then accuses Chiron and Demetrius of her rape and mutilation. Dialogue and action proceed furiously, as
Tamora demands to see her sons, and Titus exuberantly informs her that she has
consumed them. Three murders follow headlong: Titus stabs Tamora, Saturninus
kills Titus, and Lucius turns upon the Emperor. The violence proceeds so pre-
cipitously that it risks turning into burlesque, but the moment is nonetheless
terrifying.

After this succession of murders, the process of restoration begins. With the
support of Marcus and Aemilius, Lucius retells the crimes inflicted on his family
(V, iii, 96–108), then points to Aaron's child. At Aemilius's nomination, Lucius
is acclaimed the new Emperor, and his taking authority suggests that at last
balance has been restored to the Roman state, for now a proper ruler is in control.
Such reconstruction takes place at the end of each tragedy, with the implication
that whatever painful events have occurred are in some way meaningful, that a

fundamentally benign order shapes human existence. At the same time, we wonder if the tragic events that unfold are ever justifiable, and what kind of universe this is if such events can occur. This intellectual tension pervaded Shakespeare's age and dominate his plays, in particular the tragedies and histories.

Tearful farewells are offered to Titus by Lucius, Marcus, and Young Lucius, but the last moments belong appropriately to Aaron, who is ordered to be starved to death (V, iii, 180). Even facing such an end, Aaron remains full of bravado:

> If one good deed in all my life I did,
> I do repent it from my very soul.
>
> (V, iii, 189–190)

We never learn the fate of the baby. Lucius's final speech reaffirms the imagery of animals, notably "the ravenous tiger Tamora" (V, iii, 195), and the play ends with the proper note of brutality.

Titus Andronicus has an undeniable theatricality, primarily because the villains have such passion, but its flaws are myriad. Perhaps the most important is the title character, who behaves inconsistently, and who has little philosophical or intellectual depth. Furthermore, he never achieves self-knowledge, and therefore never understands his responsibility for what has occurred. Under such circumstances the wave of horror that goes on about him seems at times pointless. Still, the play does have a consolidated vision: the depths to which humanity can descend when the constraints of civilization are lifted.

SUGGESTIONS FOR FURTHER READING

Brooke, Nicholas. *Shakespeare's Early Tragedies*. London: Methuen, 1968.

Brucher, Richard T. "Tragedy, Laugh on: Comic Violence in *Titus Andronicus*." *Renaissance Drama* 10 (1979): 71–91.

Coe, Charles Norton. *Demi-Devils: The Character of Shakespeare's Villains*. New York: Brookman, 1963.

Cutts, John P. "Shadow and Substance: Structural Unity in *Titus Andronicus*." *Comparative Drama* 2 (1968): 161–172.

Sommers, Alan. " 'Wilderness of Tigers': Structure and Symbolism in *Titus Andronicus*." *Essays in Criticism* 10 (1960): 275–289.

Spencer, T.J.B. "Shakespeare and the Elizabethan Romans." *Shakespeare Survey* 10 (1957): 27–38.

Tricomi, Albert H. "The Aesthetics of Mutilation in *Titus Andronicus*." *Shakespeare Survey* 27 (1974): 17–18.

Waith, Eugene M. "The Metamorphosis of Violence in *Titus Andronicus*." *Shakespeare Survey* 10 (1957): 39–49.

ROMEO AND JULIET

Shakespeare's tragedies may be classified in two general groups: those of politics and those of love. The former category includes *Titus Andronicus*, *Julius Caesar*, *Hamlet*, *Macbeth*, *Coriolanus*, and *Timon of Athens*. The latter includes *Romeo and Juliet*, *Othello*, *Antony and Cleopatra*, and *King Lear*. To be sure, these categories overlap. For instance, in *Antony and Cleopatra* national and international ramifications surround the affair between two great rulers, and in *King Lear* civil and heavenly strife results from the fissure of the royal family. Furthermore, in all the plays a hero, and sometimes a heroine, battle against overwhelming odds, only to fall through a combination of circumstance and personal weakness. Nonetheless, the distinction between the forms is valid, for in the political tragedies the mainspring of the plot is a desire for power, while in the tragedies of love the fundamental motivation is love itself.

The basic elements of the story of *Romeo and Juliet*, that of two young lovers tragically lost, was popular in a variety of Renaissance plays and novels. Shakespeare's specific source seems to have been Arthur Brooke's poem *The Tragical History of Romeus and Juliet* (1562), but Shakespeare's alterations are many and significant. He compacted months of action into four days, thus bringing a greater urgency to the work. He developed the character of Mercutio. Thematically, he emphasized the purity of the love affair and the boldness of the disobedience against parents. His Juliet is loving and as honest as circumstances permit, and his Romeo is much more than a stereotypical lover. The most significant change is that while Brooke depicts the lovers' deaths as deserved punishment for their sins, Shakespeare glorifies their love, which soars above the world about them.

A few key questions underlie much of the critical commentary on this play. How much of what befalls the title figures is the result of their own character or the character of others? How much is the result of chance, or what may be called "fate?" If the dominant force is destiny, then the work becomes largely a portrait of situational irony, not a tragedy. Furthermore, do these title figures, who are so young, inspire the sense of tragic grandeur, or is their experience instead pathetic?

The answers to these issues begin with the Prologue:

> Two households, both alike in dignity,
> In fair Verona, where we lay our scene,
> From ancient grudge break to new mutiny,
> Where civil blood makes civil hands unclean.
> From forth the fatal loins of these two foes
> A pair of star-cross'd lovers take their life;
> Whose misadventur'd piteous overthrows
> Doth with their death bury their parents' strife.

(Prologue, 1–8)

The salient words are "fatal" and "star-cross'd." Do they imply that an inevitable providence is in control? We are told the outcome of the events to unfold. Are human choice and therefore human responsibility irrelevant? Does our awareness of the ending preclude all tension and wonder?

If fate is in charge, then this play is unique in the Shakespearean canon, the only one in which human beings are not free agents. Perhaps instead the way to view "fate" is as a combination of the weight of the past and oppression of the environment in which Romeo and Juliet exist. The "star-cross'd" element is that, given such a society, the natures of the characters, and the intensity of their love, no other outcome is possible.

Let us remember, though, that these surrounding forces are human. The Prologue clarifies that the grudge is "ancient," although we never learn the specific cause. The "strife" belongs to the parents, and "civil blood makes civil hands unclean." Thus although at moments during the play chance and coincidence seem to intrude, from the start we are directed toward human interference.

Does the inevitable ending prevent the audience's involvement? No, for the play is turned from one of suspense into one of depiction, as we watch and feel human fallibility wreak havoc with human aspiration. As the plot unwinds, we discover ourselves hoping against our knowledge for another ending. Thus we are more conscious than ever that the human personality is helpless against itself. Character is destiny, a fair estimate not only of this play, but of all of Shakespeare's plays.

The opening lines of dialogue offer a major theme: contrasting attitudes towards love. First Sampson and Gregory banter obscenely about sexual matters (I, i, 21–32). Their humor reflects the most elemental form of love: as impersonal and purely physical. And when set against these values, the emotions of the title characters become all the more enthralling. This opening tableau also suggests the comic potential of the story. Had Shakespeare been so inclined, the plot could unwind farcically and end with the lovers' victory rather than their defeat.

Before long the stage is filled with members of the two warring families, the Capulets and the Montagues, who embody another form of passion: family loyalty. Yet the rivalry seems foolish, as the servants weigh and absorb mutual insults (I, i, 41–65). The scene would be comic except that feeling runs to dangerous excess, especially when Tybalt takes over against Benvolio:

> What, drawn and talk of peace? I hate the word
> As I hate hell, all Montagues, and thee.
>
> (I, i, 70–71)

That the surrounding crowd shouts against both families suggests that both are in the wrong. Interestingly, the two fathers overhear the quarrel and struggle to participate. First, Capulet calls for his sword, but his wife mocks his militancy (I, i, 75–76). Then Montague shouts his eagerness to fight, but his wife holds him back (I, i, 79–80). The implications are that the men are the instigators of the violence, and that masculine pride keeps the feud flourishing. In many other works of Shakespeare, especially the history plays, the male ego and lust for power are dramatized as sources of destruction.

Prince Escalus, who embodies a third kind of love, that of country and civil order, elaborates on the danger of the feud:

> What ho, you men, you beasts!
> That quench the fire of your pernicious rage
> With purple fountains issuing from your veins—
> On pain of torture, from those bloody hands
> Throw your mistempered weapons to the ground,
> And hear the sentence of your moved prince.
>
> (I, i, 83–88)

He particularizes the families' crime: from an excess of fervor they have created havoc. This proclivity is dramatized several times during the play. Yet although the quality of moderation is admirable, it is not the stuff of greatness. Only when passions are untempered may they be glorious. But then they may also lead to catastrophe. Such is the path here.

The Prince also clarifies that the feud's effects have not been limited to the warring factions but have caused turmoil in the streets of Verona (I, i, 89–95). His is the only statement that suggests greater implications to the story, and otherwise events remain local. Not until subsequent tragedies are universal consequences dramatized. But the Prince's threat of punishment if further turbulence arises (I, i, 96–97) leads us to suspect that trouble is imminent.

When Montague, Lady Montague, and Benvolio are left alone, the parents inquire about their son, Romeo. Benvolio reports he is wandering about Verona in the throes of love:

> Many a morning hath he there been seen,
> With tears augmenting the fresh morning's dew,
> Adding to clouds more clouds with his deep sighs . . .
>
> (I, i, 131–133)

An Elizabethan audience would recognize these and other poses Benvolio describes as those of an ordinary courtly lover, following the tradition famous from

the sonnets of Petrarch (1304–1374). This impression is reinforced when Romeo
appears, comically sighing and suffering over his current love, Rosaline:

> Why then, O brawling love! O loving hate!
> O any thing, of nothing first [create]!
> O heavy lightness, serious vanity,
> Misshapen chaos, of well [-seeming] forms,
> Feather of lead, bright smoke, cold fire, sick health,
> Still-waking sleep, that is not what it is!
> This love feel I, that feel no love in this.

$$\text{(I, i, 176–182)}$$

The awkward rhythms and oxymorons (contrasting words in one image) comically reflect his lack of substance. These lines are those of a young man in love
with the concept of love, and Romeo reveals this shallowness when he comments:

> Tut, I have lost myself, I am not here:
> This is not Romeo, he's some other where.

$$\text{(I, i, 196–197)}$$

The theme of self-discovery through love recurs in several plays of Shakespeare,
most notably in the early comedies. When true love does strike Romeo, he finds
and understands himself, and the experience brings out the best in him poetically
as well. At the end of this opening scene, another irony intrudes, when Romeo
asks of Benvolio: "O, teach me how I should forget to think" (I, i, 226). At a
crucial moment later, he does yield to irrationality, an action that precipitates
the crisis of his life.

In scene ii, Capulet retakes the stage, speaking to Paris, a suitor for Capulet's
daughter, Juliet:

> . . . 'tis not hard, I think,
> For men so old as we to keep the peace.

$$\text{(I, ii, 2–3)}$$

The line has reverberations throughout Shakespeare's plays and throughout human history. How often, both in drama and in life, are conflicts started by old
men the cause of the deaths of young men. Here Capulet claims that his daughter
is too young for marriage. Yet Paris, a decent, if innocuous fellow, persists (I,
ii, 6). Capulet therefore invites him to a party that night, and orders a servant
to invite other guests listed on a notice.

What follows is the first of what might be termed incidents of fate in the play.
The servant comically rues his inability to read (I, ii, 38–44), and stops Romeo
and Benvolio for aid. Romeo reads the list, discovers Rosaline will be attending,
and with exaggerated claims of devotion resolves to join the affair (I, ii, 92–
93). But to claim that a meeting that serves as dramatic convention is evidence
of the thematic interference of destiny is inaccurate. Our attention therefore
remains on character, not chance.

Rosaline, a Capulet, never appears, as is theatrically suitable. This way we conceive her as we wish, and she does not gain unwarranted sympathy when Romeo's attention wanders to Juliet. Before the lovers meet, however, two more characters are introduced: the Nurse and Mercutio, both of whom savor the physical pleasures of love. Yet they have intriguingly different perspectives.

The Nurse initially endears herself to us, as she regales Juliet and Lady Capulet with bawdy recollection:

> For even the day before, she broke her brow,
> And then my husband—God be with his soul!
> 'A was a merry man—took up the child.
> "Yea," quoth he, "dost thou fall upon thy face?
> Thou wilt fall backward when thou hast more wit,
> Wilt thou not, Jule?" and by my holidam,
> The pretty wretch left crying and said "Ay."
> To see now how a jest shall come about!
>
> (I, iii, 38–45)

Her humorous delight is a warm counterpoint to the intense rivalry between the two houses. At the same time, her reaction to Paris manifests aspects of her personality that eventually prove infuriating:

> ... why, he's a man of wax ...
> Nay, he's a flower, in faith, a very flower.
>
> (I, iii, 76, 78)

She is taken with appearance, and judges according to immature standards. When later Juliet needs wisdom and understanding, the Nurse, good at heart though she is, proves garrulous and insensitive.

Juliet's reaction to her mother's suggestion of marriage hints at the girl's depth: "It is an [honor] that I dream not of" (I, iii, 66). She pretends that she believes herself unworthy, but the underlying implication is that she has not yet found the proper partner. Her mother, however, believes Paris's surface charms are all that Juliet needs:

> This precious book of love, this unbound lover,
> To beautify him, only lacks a cover.
>
> (I, iii, 87–88)

She does want the best for her daughter, but her values are weak.

The attitudes of Lady Capulet and the Nurse reinforce another aspect of this play: the absence of a villain. Romeo and Juliet are never threatened by enemies. Instead, the world in general, people who mean well but by necessity intrude into the lovers' lives, destroy them. Thus we witness not a traditional battle between good and evil, but one where good and less-good struggle. Here ardor is carried out on such an exalted plane that it must topple when forced to conform to the constricting values of the community. This theme is part of an overall irony. Most of the characters have only the best of intentions. Yet these prove

inadequate, and the lovers therefore fall victim to the weaknesses of those who
care for them most.

This tendency may be seen in Mercutio, perhaps the most charming figure in
the play, if "charm" be taken to include charisma. With his initial appearance
in Act I, scene iv, he takes over the stage: a brawling, vulgar, yet elegant man,
who guides Romeo like a younger brother. Romeo pinpoints the difference
between the two:

> You have dancing shoes
> With nimble soles, I have a soul of lead
> So stakes me to the ground I cannot move.
>
> (I, iv, 14–16)

Like almost everyone else, Romeo is captivated by Mercutio's manner. Mercutio
himself, perceptive as well as piquant, appreciates another facet of Romeo:

> You are a lover, borrow Cupid's wings,
> And soar with them above a common bound.
>
> (I, iv, 17–18)

He is laughing good-naturedly, but often in Shakespeare laughter masks truth.
Mercutio accurately perceives himself as all flash and no substance. He realizes
his inability to maintain depth of feeling, and respects in his more solemn friend
that quality absent in himself.

Mercutio's jollity builds here to the "Queen Mab" speech, a virtuoso performance. Queen Mab is a spirit, and whomsoever she visits dreams that night
of their greatest desire:

> And in this state she gallops night by night
> Through lovers' brains, and then they dream of love;
> [O'er] courtiers' knees, that dream on cur'sies straight;
> O'er lawyers' fingers, who straight dream on fees . . .
>
> (I, iv, 70–74)

But the visions eventually become violent:

> Sometimes she driveth o'er a soldier's neck,
> And then dreams he of cutting foreign throats,
> Of breaches, ambuscadoes, Spanish blades,
> Of healths five fadom deep . . .
> This is the hag, when maids lie on their backs,
> That presses them and learns them first to bear,
> Making them women of good carriage.
>
> (I, iv, 82–93)

Mercutio is likewise a dreamer, one emotionally incapable of existing in the
practical world, and with a capacity for sudden brutality. Yet whatever Mercutio's
attractions, Romeo tires of them: "Peace, peace, Mercutio, peace!/ Thou talk'st
of nothing" (I, iv, 95–96). Mercutio acknowledges this truth:

                    True, I talk of dreams,
Which are the children of an idle brain,
Begot of nothing but vain fantasy,
Which is as thin of substance as the air,
And more inconstant than the wind, who woos
Even now the frozen bosom of the north,
And, being anger'd, puffs away from thence,
Turning his side to the dew-dropping south.

                                          (I, iv, 96–103)

Mercutio recognizes that at the heart of all his laughter is an emotional vacuum. As he mocks Romeo's infatuation with Rosaline, so he will mock the subsequent relationship with Juliet. The cynicism he turns against false love he will invoke to castigate genuine love.

In Act I, scene v, the play moves to its highest manifestation of love, that between Romeo and Juliet. With his comrades Romeo invades the Capulet party, seeking Rosaline, but his eye catches someone else:

O, she doth teach the torches to burn bright!
It seems she hangs upon the cheek of night
As a rich jewel in an Ethiop's ear—
Beauty too rich for use, for earth too dear!
So shows a snowy dove trooping with crows,
As yonder lady o'er her fellows shows.

                                          (I, v, 44–49)

Contrast the simple beauty of these lines with the earlier ravings for Rosaline, in which constructions were hopelessly convoluted. Here the passion is of a fine texture, as if excessive volume would shatter it. The images of dark and light that dominate here recur throughout the play, reflecting the contrast between the glowing love of Romeo and Juliet and the seamier world around them. This world intrudes even now, as Tybalt recognizes the masked Romeo's voice and threatens to expose him (I, v, 61–63, 75–76). Only Capulet's exertion of authority, out of fear for a soiled reputation, prevents a squabble:

I would not for the wealth of all this town
Here in my house do him disparagement . . .

                                          (I, v, 69–70)

But Tybalt's parting threat assures us that however the opening moments of the romance proceed, danger is never far away:

I will withdraw, but this intrusion shall,
Now seeming sweet, convert to bitt'rest gall.

                                          (I, v, 91–92)

When Romeo approaches Juliet, the language becomes religious in the style of courtly love:

> If I profane with my unworthiest hand
> This holy shrine, the gentle sin is this,
> My lips, two blushing pilgrims, ready stand
> To smooth that rough touch with a tender kiss.

(I, v, 93–96)

What follows this invocation is a gentle parry and thrust, a secular responsive reading. Juliet opens her heart, but simultaneously tests Romeo, putting him on the defensive, subtly leading him to say the proper words to allow him to present himself as a seemly lover. At this moment she is more conscious than he of their situation and insists that he properly win her, although she is willing to help. For instance, Romeo approaches:

> O then, dear saint, let lips do what hands do,
> They pray—grant thou, lest faith turn to despair.

(I, v, 103–104)

Juliet challenges his request: "Saints do not move, though grant for prayers' sake" (I, v, 105). Therefore Romeo rewords his proposal:

> Then move not while my prayer's effect I take.
> Thus from my lips, by thine, my sin is purg'd.

(I, v, 106–107)

She accepts the proposal and returns his kiss: "Then have my lips the sin that they have took" (I, v, 108). Juliet mocks him slightly: "You kiss by th' book" (I, v, 110), implying that he is still guided by literary stereotypes, and the word "book" is associated with Romeo throughout the play. Otherwise the combination of controlled emotion, religious fervor, and simple language is winning, so much so that we are willing to believe that two people could fall in love on first sight.

But the happiness is undercut within seconds, as Romeo realizes that Juliet is a Capulet (II, i, 118–119), and a few lines later when Juliet realizes that Romeo is a Montague: "My only love sprung from my only hate" (II, i, 138). Thus the tension of the play is established economically.

At the beginning of Act II, the final couplet of the Chorus's sonnet offers an assertion that underlies the rest of the play:

> But passion lends them power, time means, to meet,
> Temp'ring extremities with extreme sweet.

(Prologue, 13–14)

Romeo and Juliet will have hardly any time together. Thus we shall ask whether their love is of such depth and quality that it transcends its brevity.

In Act II, scene i, Mercutio mocks Romeo's capacity for idealized love:

> I conjure thee by Rosaline's bright eyes,
> By her high forehead and her scarlet lip,
> By her fine foot, straight leg, and quivering thigh,

And the demesnes that there adjacent lie,
That in the likeness thou appear to us.

(II, i, 17–21)

Yet for all his scoffing at emotion, Mercutio will show himself aware of deeper feeling, particularly hate. But he does not want to distinguish between qualities of love. Rather he wants all affection reduced to the same level. What he cannot have, he pretends he does not want. Mercutio is a source of boundless energy, personal and sexual. Yet like the Nurse he proves unable to understand a love that exists beyond his sensibility. In Romeo's words: "He jests at scars that never felt a wound" (II, ii, 1).

Then Romeo turns to Juliet, offering what has become the most famous expression of idolatrous love in the world's literature:

But soft, what light through yonder window breaks?
It is the east, and Juliet is the sun.
Arise, fair sun, and kill the envious moon,
Who is already sick and pale with grief
That thou, her maid, art far more fair than she.

(II, ii, 2–6)

The imagery is familiar from Renaissance poetry, but the speech sparkles, for the language is unaffected, with few words of more than one syllable. We also note the dominant image, the conflict between night and day, reflecting a love that can flourish only in the dark.

Most important, this speech, typical of Romeo, is not tempered by reason or practicality. It is the unfettered expression of a soul, and Romeo's glory, revealed here for the first time, is that he can so give of himself. Yet in this play, as in the other tragedies, the qualities that give the hero greatness are the ones that cause his fall. And in the next act Romeo's passion leads to his descent.

The matter of Romeo's age is also intriguing. Given the maturity of his cohorts and his social maneuverability, he is probably a couple of years older than Juliet, who, as her father indicated, is not quite fourteen (I, ii, 9). Nonetheless, Juliet is more mature in this scene and throughout the story. For instance, as Romeo gambols about in the throes of romance, she blends her ardor with pertinent questions:

What man art thou that thus bescreen'd in night
So stumblest on my counsel?

(II, ii, 52–53)

How camest thou hither, tell me, and wherefore?

(II, ii, 62)

By whose direction foundst thou out this place?

(II, ii, 79)

Furthermore, she keeps in mind the omnipresent threat: "If they do see thee, they will murther thee" (II, ii, 70). As the play develops, Juliet, under the

influence of love, becomes a woman, while Romeo, despite the intensity of his
passion, remains a boy. She instinctively grasps Romeo's proper course: ''Deny
thy father and refuse thy name'' (II, ii, 34). He, however, never articulates his
dilemma: love for Juliet versus fidelity to his family. Juliet is torn between
passion and restraint:

> O gentle Romeo,
> If thou dost love, pronounce it faithfully;
> Or if thou thinkest I am too quickly won,
> I'll frown and be perverse, and say thee nay . . .

> (II, ii, 93–96)

Romeo never probes himself deeply or weighs the ethical and emotional aspects
of his crisis. Here, for instance, he impulsively swears by every convenient
symbol:

> Lady, by yonder blessed moon I vow,
> That tips with silver all these fruit-tree tops—

> (II, ii, 107–108)

Juliet sees deeper into the significance of his expression:

> O, swear not by the moon, th' inconstant moon,
> That monthly changes in her [circled] orb,
> Lest that thy love prove likewise variable.

> (II, ii, 109–111)

Like a chastened youngster, Romeo tries to amend: ''What shall I swear by?''
(II, ii, 112). Juliet maintains a more mature attitude:

> Do not swear at all;
> Or if thou wilt, swear by thy gracious self,
> Which is the god of my idolatry,
> And I'll believe thee.

> (II, ii, 112–115)

Perhaps her most telling comment is her intuition about what proves to be the
nature of their existence together:

> Although I joy in thee,
> I have no joy of this contract to-night,
> It is too rash, too unadvis'd, too sudden,
> Too like the lightning, which doth cease to be
> Ere one can say it lightens.

> (II, ii, 116–120)

Images of lightning, gunpowder, and other flashes are used regularly to characterize this love. Such language reflects both its power and the transitory nature
of an experience the world does not accept.

Juliet has one final declaration:

My bounty is as boundless as the sea,
My love as deep; the more I give to thee,
The more I have, for both are infinite.

(II, ii, 133–135)

She never falters from such commitment. Romeo, however, does waver in a moment
that impels the tragedy. Finally, after Juliet resists calls from the Nurse, the two lovers
reluctantly separate, with Juliet offering the elegant and famous farewell:

Parting is such sweet sorrow,
That I shall say good night till it be morrow.

(II, ii, 184–185)

The scene is a triumph.

In scene iii we meet Friar Lawrence, meditating on the balance of nature. His
thoughts turn to his gardening and on the qualities of various herbs:

For nought so vile that on the earth doth live
But to the earth some special good doth give;
Nor aught so good but, strain'd from that fair use,
Revolts from true birth, stumbling on abuse.
Virtue itself turns vice, being misapplied,
And vice sometime by action dignified.

(II, iii, 17–22)

Good and bad, he believes, are determined by circumstances and how materials
are used. This knowledge and attitude later have ironic implications. He also
expresses this balance in another revealing image about poison and medicine:

Two such opposed kings encamp them still
In man as well as herbs, grace and rude will;
And where the worser is predominant,
Full soon the canker death eats up that plant.

(II, iii, 27–30)

After this line, Romeo enters and we soon realize that the war between reason
and passion is to be fought within him. The Friar's prediction of death suggests
the unhappy outcome.

When Romeo reveals that he has a new object for his love, the Friar has
understandable doubt:

Holy Saint Francis, what a change is here!
Is Rosaline, that thou didst love so dear,
So soon forsaken? Young men's love then lies
Not truly in their hearts, but in their eyes.

(II, iii, 65–68)

He is unable to appreciate the depth of Romeo's affections. But his next lines
show more insight:

> If e'er thou wast thyself and these woes thine,
> Thou and these woes were all for Rosaline.
> And art thou chang'd? Pronounce this sentence then:
> Women may fall, when there's no strength in men.
>
> (II, iii, 77–80)

Juliet's destruction, in fact, occurs because of Romeo's weakness. Nonetheless, the Friar agrees to marry Romeo and Juliet, also in hope that the union will end the feud between the families (II, iii, 90–92). This desire, too, becomes ironic. Finally, the Friar gives one more piece of advice: "Wisely and slow, they stumble that run fast" (II, iii, 94). Such counsel reveals that he does not understand the nature of the love before him for Romeo's impetuosity allows him to flourish as he does. Furthermore, later the Friar's own lack of speed causes him to "stumble" and inadvertently contribute to the lovers' deaths.

In scene iv Mercutio and Benvolio enjoy themselves by mocking the absent Tybalt (II, iv, 19–26). Despite their scorn for him, they clarify that he is a dangerous man. When Romeo enters, the humor turns at his expense, as his colleagues laugh at what they imagine is one more passing infatuation. Such ribaldry, especially from Mercutio, (II, iv, 88–93), reminds us of the real world in which Romeo and Juliet must try to survive. When the Nurse enters, she, too, endures bawdy humor from Mercutio, which, she pretends, is an affront to her dignity, but her comments indicate she finds him of considerable interest (II, iv, 150–156). She and Romeo draw aside, and Romeo confides his plans about Juliet:

> Bid her devise
> Some means to come to shrift this afternoon,
> And there she shall at Friar Lawrence' cell
> Be shriv'd and married.
>
> (II, iv, 179–182)

With her customary loquaciousness, the Nurse rambles, especially about Paris, whom she still admires (II, iv, 201–206). But she agrees to tell Juliet, despite a reservation: "Doth not rosemary and Romeo begin both with a letter?" (II, iv, 206–207). The observation is yet another irony, for rosemary is the flower of remembrance used at funerals as well as weddings.

In the next scene Juliet waits anxiously for the Nurse's return:

> Had she affections and warm youthful blood,
> She would be as swift in motion as a ball . . .
>
> (II, v, 12–13)

The contrast between young and old is at the core of the play. Indeed, one reason for the play's universal appeal is that it dramatizes not just love, but young love, and that theme crosses all barriers of time and location. When the Nurse finally does arrive, she delays endlessly as she simultaneously evaluates Romeo (II, v, 38–44, 55–57) and bemoans her own aches. Eventually she reveals Romeo's directions with surprising vigor (II, v, 68–77). Perhaps we should take her dilatory response as evidence of her own ego and her desire to be at the center of the news.

In scene vi, with the plot hurtling swiftly, the Friar offers Romeo one more
warning:

> These violent delights have violent ends,
> And in their triumph die, like fire and powder,
> Which as they kiss consume. The sweetest honey
> Is loathesome in his own deliciousness,
> And in the taste confounds the appetite.
> Therefore love moderately: long love doth so;
> Too swift arrives as tardy as too slow.
>
> (II, vi, 9–15)

The words are meant benignly, but they are unrealistic. Romeo and Juliet, being
who they are, can proceed only according to the dictates of their character. This
is part of their "fate." Thus they leave this scene to be married by the Friar.

Act III, scene i brings the climactic moment of the play. In hot weather
Mercutio and Benvolio are strolling the streets, and Mercutio's attitude suggests
that what has been a long time coming is about to occur:

> Thou?
> why, thou wilt quarrel with a man that hath a hair
> more or a hair less in his beard than thou hast. Thou
> wilt quarrel with a man for cracking nuts, having no
> other reason but because thou hast hazel eyes.
>
> (III, i, 16–20)

These words, spoken to the peace-loving Benvolio, are those of a man seeking
a fight. The anger Mercutio attributes to Benvolio is his own. And the energy
Mercutio always has about him is today overflowing. At the moment his wit is
not enough of an outlet. He needs to release physically his frustration, and the
opportunity is about to present itself.

Tybalt appears and asks for "a word" (III, i, 38), but Mercutio offers to
make it "a word and a blow" (III, i, 40), then maintains a barrage of insults.
Tybalt relents: "Well, peace be with you, sir, here comes my man" (III, i, 56).
He has been waiting for Romeo. But Mercutio is eager to fight, and purposely
assumes Tybalt has used the word "man" in its alternative meaning as "servant":
"But I'll be hang'd, sir, if he wear your livery" (III, i, 57). Tybalt ignores the
implication, and approaches Romeo, who, newly married, is in a generous mood,
and welcomes Tybalt, now a relative (III, i, 62–65). At this gesture, Mercutio
is shocked: "O calm, dishonorable, vile submission!" (III, i, 73). That he uses
a form of the word "honor," almost always in Shakespeare a feeble excuse for
belligerence, suggests the hollowness of Mercutio's anger. Soon Tybalt, hardly
a pacifist, takes up the challenge. Romeo tries to separate the combatants, but
in the process Mercutio is wounded. How does he respond, and whom does he
blame? "A plague a' both your houses!" (III, i, 91). He repeats the phrase
twice more, but as much as he tries, he cannot shift guilt. He was looking for
a fight, he started the fight, and he is fatally stabbed in the fight. That he dies

punning about being "a grave man" (III, i, 98) should not blind us to his
responsibility. Mercutio remains cavalier to the end, but the energy he was
unable to give to love had to emerge somehow, and it did so violently, in both
language and action. The result is a wasted, destructive life and an early death.

Yet the full tragedy has yet to unfold. While Mercutio is borne away, Romeo
takes himself to task:

> This gentlemen, the Prince's near ally,
> My very friend, hath got this mortal hurt
> In my behalf; my reputation stain'd
> With Tybalt's slander—Tybalt, that an hour
> Hath been my cousin! O sweet Juliet,
> Thy beauty hath made me effeminate,
> And in my temper soft'ned valor's steel!
>
> (III, i, 109–115)

How misguided he is. At first glance his desire to revenge his friend's death
may seem legitimate. But in the context of the play and many other of Shakespeare's plays, Romeo is yielding to the lowest principles of his society. He
ignores that Mercutio started the fracas. More important, he equates the capacity
to kill with manhood.

Thus when Tybalt returns, Romeo has lost all perspective. The traditions of
his society demand retribution, and in this sense Romeo conforms to the values
of his environment. Spurred by a need for honor, and with all the passion he
has mustered for Juliet, he turns on Tybalt:

> Now, Tybalt, take the "villain" back again
> That late thou gavest me, for Mercutio's soul
> Is but a little way above our heads,
> Staying for thine to keep him company.
> Either thou or I, or both, must go with him.
>
> (III, i, 125–129)

The challenge may seem an expression of courage and moral fervor, but Romeo
has failed to consider the consequences. The impetuosity we admired a scene
earlier now appears to be the recklessness of a hot-headed boy.

When Tybalt falls, Benvolio shouts the immediate implications:

> Romeo, away, be gone!
> The citizens are up, and Tybalt slain.
> Stand not amazed, the Prince will doom thee death
> If thou art taken. Hence be gone, away!
>
> (III, i, 132–135)

Romeo's reaction is one of the most significant lines in the play: "O, I am
fortune's fool!" (III, i, 136). He rejects responsibility. Circumstances, he implies, have conspired against him, and his claim is echoed by characters in
several other tragedies. Other protagonists, faced with the results of a terrible

decision or action, seek to absolve themselves of the burden. And their explanations, too, are unconvincing.

Remember what Romeo has done. Throughout the play he has tried to remove
himself from the values of his society, but now he has slipped to that level. He
has thereby been a traitor to the idealized love to which he aspired. And he has
doomed any hope of a life with Juliet.

Let us also consider the overall predicament. Here is a young man, sensitive
and emotional, who ends up in a crisis where those attributes undo him. Were
he not so sensitive, he would have been less vulnerable to tradition and the
surrounding environment. Were he not so emotional, he would not have lost
control of himself. Romeo is thus the first character in these plays to face the
dilemma of the Shakespearean tragic hero. Still, because the slaying of Tybalt
is instantaneous rather than deeply considered, it lacks the resonance of more
profound reactions by later tragic heroes.

When the crowd gathers in the street, Benvolio attempts to remove blame
from Romeo by conveniently forgetting Mercutio's precipitating actions (III, i,
152–175). Nonetheless, the Prince stands by his edict of the first scene and exiles
Romeo (III, i, 187). But true culpability is established in the next scene. First
we see Juliet waiting eagerly for Romeo's return:

> Come, civil night,
> Thou sober-suited matron all in black,
> And learn me how to lose a winning match,
> Play'd for a pair of stainless maidenhoods.
> Hood my unmann'd blood, bating in my cheeks,
> With thy black mantle, till strange love grow bold,
> Think true love acted simple modesty.
>
> (III, ii, 10–16)

For Juliet, the forthcoming night will see her join with Romeo both spiritually
and physically. Yet even these hopes are undercut by her images:

> Come, gentle night, come, loving, black-brow'd night,
> Give me my Romeo, and, when I shall die,
> Take him and cut him out in little stars,
> And he will make the face of heaven so fine
> That all the world will be in love with night.
>
> (III, ii, 20–24)

Her own death is to come far sooner than she imagines. This soliloquy also
emphasizes a motif that pervades the play: the unity between love and death.
Constantly the marriage of Romeo and Juliet is explained in images that bring
together the wedding bed and the grave, with the implication that these two
young people are never to find happiness on earth, only in heaven.

When the Nurse rushes in, wailing and drowning in self-pity, she delays
telling Juliet what has happened in the streets, and Juliet's temper is frightening:
"What devil art thou that dost torment me thus?" (III, ii, 43). Love is not the

only passion she feels deeply. Eventually Juliet drags out the terrible news, and decimates any credit we may think Romeo warrants. First she manifests her simultaneous feelings of love and hate (III, ii, 75–76). Then she specifies her anger:

> O nature, what hadst thou to do in hell
> When thou didst bower the spirit of a fiend
> In mortal paradise of such sweet flesh?
> Was ever book containing such vile matter
> So fairly bound? O that deceit should dwell
> In such a gorgeous palace!
>
> (III, ii, 80–82)

To what "fiend" does she refer? Perhaps it is the spirit of her time and place, the law of revenge that possessed Romeo. Or perhaps she refers to one individual whose values infected Romeo. That would be Mercutio, who offered an attractive appearance or "book," but who proved a devil. In either case, Juliet, the most powerful ethical presence in the play, judges Romeo's actions wrong. And her decision stands.

She may seem to modify it in the lines that follow, for when the Nurse attacks Romeo, Juliet defends him passionately:

> Blister'd be thy tongue
> For such a wish! he was not born to shame . . .
>
> (III, ii, 90–91)

In other words, Juliet may criticize Romeo, but the Nurse may not. And the long speech that follows contains all the contradictory feelings that torment Juliet: despair over Tybalt's death, anger at Romeo for causing death, and desperation that Romeo committed a crime and thereby doomed them.

This issue is raised in other tragedies. Protagonists are called upon to murder, for one cause or another. Are they ever justified in doing so? The question must be answered in the context of each work.

The audience may yet excuse Romeo on the grounds that he is the victim of events, but Friar Lawrence teaches otherwise. In the scene following, Romeo rushes into the Friar's cell, berating himself and the world, as he repeats the word "banished" again and again. He even insults the Friar, whom he judges not sympathetic enough: "Thou canst not speak of that thou dost not feel" (III, iii, 64). As he defends his panic, Romeo seems like an angry boy (III, iii, 65–70). But he gets his comeuppance. First the Nurse enters to say "be a man. / For Juliet's sake" (III, iii, 88–89). The order is ironic, for Romeo's slaying of Tybalt was inspired at least partially to prove his manhood. Romeo then realizes the anguish his wife must be suffering and asks about her, but the Nurse misleads him:

> O, she says nothing, sir, but weeps and weeps,
> And now falls on her bed, and then starts up,
> And Tybalt calls, and then on Romeo cries,

And then down falls again.

(III, iii, 99–102)

Thinking that Juliet has rejected him, Romeo grabs a knife and threatens to kill himself, but the Friar reminds him of certain truths:

> Why railest thou on thy birth? the heaven and earth?
> Since birth, and heaven, and earth, all three do meet
> In thee at once, which thou at once wouldst lose.
> Fie, fie, thou shamest thy shape, thy love, thy wit,
> Which like a usurer abound'st in all,
> And usest none in that true use indeed
> Which should bedeck thy shape, thy love, thy wit.

(III, iii, 119–125)

Like all human beings, the Friar says, Romeo is the product of his world. Nonetheless, he is in control of his life, and he owes both Juliet and himself proper action. Versions of that belief resound throughout Shakespeare's plays.

Following the Friar's directive and after accepting the ring from the Nurse, Romeo leaves to join Juliet. Before they are reunited, however, we have a semicomic interlude, as Lady Capulet and her husband resolve that despite the circumstances Juliet must marry Paris:

> We'll keep no great ado—a friend or two,
> For hark you, Tybalt being slain so late,
> It may be thought we held him carelessly,
> Being our kinsman, if we reveal much . . .

(III, iv, 23–26)

Such callousness better sets off the next scene, as Romeo and Juliet awaken from the consummation of their marriage.

At first they seem to switch roles, as Juliet becomes the more romantic, denying the song of the lark, while Romeo responds that morning has come (III, v, 1–11). This moment is their last tranquil time together, and Juliet wishes to extend it. But once she faces the truth, Juliet insists that Romeo leave to save himself (III, v, 26–30). Yet she maintains the sense of doom that has always haunted her:

> O God, I have an ill-divining soul!
> Methinks I see thee now, thou art so low,
> As one dead in the bottom of a tomb.

(III, v, 54–56)

Once Romeo departs, Juliet is left alone, and her isolation quickly becomes painful. Her parents enter, full of condemnation for Romeo (III, v, 80, 84), and Juliet must pretend that her own sadness is over Tybalt's death and not Romeo's absence:

> Indeed, I never shall be satisfied
> With Romeo, till I behold him—dead—

> Is my poor heart, so for a kinsman vex'd.
> Madam, if you could find out but a man
> To bear a poison, I would temper it,
> That Romeo should, upon receipt thereof,
> Soon sleep in quiet.
>
> (III, v, 93–99)

The reference to poison is another ironic note, but more important here is Juliet's dilemma. To herself she prays that she wants to see Romeo, but to her parents she must claim she wants him dead. Thus the combination of wit and bitterness in her refusal to accept the command to marry Paris:

> I pray you tell my lord and father, madam,
> I will not marry yet, and when I do, I swear
> It shall be Romeo, whom you know I hate,
> Rather than Paris.
>
> (III, v, 120–123)

We understand that she is already married, but we also appreciate how she remains true to her own feelings while she denies her parents' order.

Juliet's pain increases when Capulet is outraged that his daughter does not accept his directive to marry Paris:

> Hang thee, young baggage! disobedient wretch!
> I tell thee what: get thee to church a' Thursday,
> Or never after look me in the face.
>
> (III, v, 160–162)

Presently he mocks her cruelly (III, v, 184–186). But Juliet cannot reveal her relationship to Romeo, and her plea to her parents is essentially directed at us:

> Is there no pity sitting in the clouds,
> That sees into the bottom of my grief?
>
> (III, v, 196–197)

Even her confidante, the Nurse, does not understand, for when the two are left alone, she counsels Juliet to forget Romeo and reverts to praising Paris: "Romeo's a dishclout to him" (III, v, 219). When the Nurse leaves, Juliet unleashes her fury: "Ancient damnation! O most wicked fiend!" (III, v, 235). After condemning the Nurse's hypocrisy, Juliet retreats to her last hope, the Friar, fully prepared to die (III, v, 242). Yet even this moment is marked by irony, as Juliet speaks of the Friar's "remedy" (III, v, 241), a foreshadowing of his failure.

Act IV brings Paris to the Friar's cell, as Paris prepares for his own marriage. The Friar's deception in seeming to approve these plans is puzzling, for Paris is a decent man, and perhaps should be told the reason Juliet's behavior is difficult to gauge. Nonetheless, when Juliet enters, Paris anticipates their marriage, and continues to do so, despite her coolish responses (IV, i, 30–31, 33–34). Only when he departs does she burst out to the Friar: "Come weep with me, past hope, past [cure], past help!'' (IV, i, 45). She is prepared to die (IV, i, 53–67), but the Friar conceives a plan by which she and Romeo may survive. First Juliet must take poison that will invest her with all the characteristics of death (IV, i, 93–106), while the Friar will send a message to Romeo explaining the plan. The scheme is characteristic of the Friar's personality: it is excessively complicated, and invites failure at several steps. Thus its going astray should be considered not fate, but miscalculation.

In scene ii, events continue to move quickly as her family's marriage plans make Juliet's plight appear more desperate and Capulet's joy ironically misplaced:

> My heart is wondrous light,
> Since this same wayward girl is so reclaim'd.
>
> (IV, ii, 46–47)

In scene iii, Juliet realizes that she cannot ask the Nurse for help (IV, iii, 19), although in retrospect such a confidence might have prevented the ultimate tragedy. Nonetheless, Juliet's strength is her independence, which, as befits a protagonist in a tragedy, contributes to her downfall. As she prepares to drink the vial of poison, her mind fills with gruesome images of death. She also wonders if the Friar himself is conspiring against her to protect himself (IV, iii, 24–27). Finally she imagines herself dying in the vault, near the body of Tybalt, and her visions have a phantasmagoric quality:

> O, if I [wake], shall I not be distraught,
> Environed with all these hideous fears,
> And madly play with my forefathers' joints,
> And pluck the mangled Tybalt from his shroud,
> And in this rage, with some great kinsman's bone,
> As with a club, dash out my desp'rate brains?
> O, look! methinks I see my cousin's ghost
> Seeking out Romeo, that did spit his body
> Upon a rapier's point. Stay, Tybalt, stay!
>
> (IV, iii, 49–57)

Desperate beyond endurance, she downs the poison.

After one more scene that depicts the marriage preparations, joyous and busy, the Nurse discovers the sleeping Juliet and cries uncontrollably. Capulet himself mourns in painfully familiar imagery:

> Death is my son-in-law, Death is my heir,
> My daughter he hath wedded.
>
> (IV, v, 38–39)

Such legitimate suffering is contrasted by the Friar's words of solace. We know he is playing a role, but again his duplicity is discomforting, especially when he proves unintentionally ironic:

> She's not well married that lives married long,
> But she's best married that dies married young.
>
> (IV, v, 77–78)

One more awkward situation occurs when Capulet orders the marriage celebration altered to fit a funeral. The gesture is too convenient, but characteristic of a man who throughout the play has acted in accordance with his own desires. In Act I, scene v, he stopped Tybalt from confronting Romeo because the disturbance would have interrupted the party. In Act III, scene v, he ordered Juliet to marry Paris to satisfy his own desires. Here he smooths over the death of his daughter, and his ease of manner leads to the comic banter of the musicians, a brief pause in the otherwise tense series of events.

In Act V, scene i, Romeo, now exiled to Mantua, has experienced his own dreams, which anticipate Juliet finding him dead, and again the image of love and death dominates (V, i, 6–11). But when Balthazar brings the news of Juliet's demise, Romeo's impulsive personality takes over: "Then I [defy] you, stars!" (V, i, 24). At last he affirms that he is responsible for his life, and without waiting for the letters from the Friar, rushes to his wife: "Well, Juliet, I will lie with thee to-night" (V, i, 34).

His first stop is the apothecary, who is reluctant to break the law and give Romeo the poison he desires. But Romeo is now willing to challenge the rules of society:

> The world is not thy friend, nor the world's law,
> The world affords no law to make thee rich;
> Then be not poor, but break it, and take this.
>
> (V, i, 72–74)

Earlier Romeo conformed to the world by obeying its values and killing Tybalt. Now, too late, he boldly goes on his own.

Scene ii reveals why the Friar's missives failed to reach Romeo. The "infectious pestilence" (V, ii, 10) may seem like fate intervening, but the Friar's plan invited such interruptions. Furthermore, too much of the tragedy has clearly been caused by human misjudgment to blame the ultimate result on "fate."

The final scene takes place in the Capulet tomb, where Paris, ever caring, has come to pay tribute to the woman he hoped would be his wife (V, iii, 12–17). When he hears an intruder, he hides, and Romeo and Balthazar step forward. Romeo speaks in images of wild animals (V, iii, 36–39), reflecting his panic, and refers to the tomb as this "womb of death" (V, iii, 45), bringing to a climax the thematic welding of love and death. Paris is outraged at this intrusion and steps forward to confront Romeo, who does not recognize Paris:

> Good gentle youth, tempt not a desp'rate man.
> Fly hence and leave me, think upon these gone,

Let them affright thee.

(V, iii, 59–61)

But Paris refuses, and once more Romeo fights and kills. Only then does he recognize Paris and mourn him as "Mercutio's kinsman" (V, iii, 75).

As Romeo stands over Juliet, he summarizes his life, and his lines reaffirm images that have dominated the play (V, iii, 85–86, 88–96). He notices that Juliet appears lifelike (V, iii, 102), and we may assume that she is recovering from the poison. The moment is an effective insertion by Shakespeare to raise our hopes against all expectation. Nevertheless, Romeo, with customary haste, does not wait long. Seconds before he drinks the poison, he invokes an intriguing metaphor:

> Come bitter conduct, come, unsavory guide!
> Thou desperate pilot, now at once run on
> The dashing rocks thy sea-sick weary bark!

(V, iii, 116–118)

In Act II, scene ii, at Juliet's balcony, Romeo used the same metaphor, but in a different tone:

> I am no pilot, yet, wert thou as far
> As that vast shore [wash'd] with the farthest sea,
> I should adventure for such merchandise.

(II, ii, 82–84)

In the earlier speech he is a young lover, uncertain how to proceed, yet boldly determined. In the later, he is a battered man who has been unequal to the tasks before him. He has, in essence, surrendered to life. Such a pattern of behavior is not unique to Romeo, but he is the first hero of a Shakespearean tragedy to voice resignation.

Friar Lawrence, appropriately, arrives too late, and Juliet soon awakens. Without explaining what has happened, the Friar tries to escape with her, to place her "Among a sisterhood of holy nuns" (V, iii, 157). That he could even contemplate such an alternative suggests how out of touch with young love he is. When Juliet delays, the Friar rushes off: "I dare no longer stay" (V, iii, 159). He fears social pressure, and we sense in him a moral cowardice, an inability to stand up for what he has done. Juliet discovers Romeo and recognizes that she has no choice. With voices closing in, she stabs herself and falls on Romeo.

When the bodies are discovered, the report spreads with great speed, suggesting the more profound implications of the story. Meanwhile the families are left to deal with their unhappiness. The Friar does gratify us with his return, and he has the strength to relate the events we have witnessed (V, iii, 231–269). The two families stand united over their dead children, but the ending is marked by a hint of disorder. First Old Capulet offers a gesture of reconciliation:

> O brother Montague, give me thy hand.
> This is my daughter's jointure, for no more
> Can I demand.

                                              (V, iii, 296–298)

Then Montague responds:

> But I can give thee more,
> For I will [raise] her statue in pure gold,
> That whiles Verona by that name is known,
> There shall no figure at such rate be set
> As that of true and faithful Juliet.

                                              (V, iii, 298–302)

We wonder if the rivalry between the two still flickers.

In considering *Romeo and Juliet*, both unto itself and as part of Shakespeare's oeuvre, we should emphasize several points. The play lacks a central figure who is the focus of the tragedy. Perhaps the lovers are too young to assume such standing, but neither has the power or authority that must be lost to create the tragic experience. Neither has sufficiently far to fall.

Individually, as well, the characters lack tragic complexity. Juliet is primarily reactive. She never takes charge of her own life, but rather waits to respond. Perhaps this role may be attributed to her age, station, or gender. Whatever the reason, despite her maturity, she remains pathetic and a victim, instead of tragic and a heroine. Only when she sees Romeo's body does she act for herself, and her suicide is carried out from resignation. And though Romeo has energy, he ultimately lacks depth. He endures no inner struggle before he murders Tybalt, and never clarifies that he is torn between Juliet and his family. His concerns are strictly romantic.

The scope of the story is also limited, for the events have no implications outside the town environs. In the first scene the Prince tries to intimate that the entire community suffers because of the feud between the Capulets and the Montagues, but that condition is never dramatized.

Yet one quality does lift this play to the realm of tragedy: our sense of irrevocable loss. Romeo and Juliet know that the love they share towers over any around them, and they resolve not to live without it. That devotion is their greatness. And the loss of that devotion makes their story tragic.

SUGGESTIONS FOR FURTHER READING

Bowling, Lawrence Edward. "The Thematic Framework of *Romeo and Juliet*." *PMLA* 64 (1949): 208–220.

Cole, Douglas, ed. *Twentieth Century Interpretations of* Romeo and Juliet. Englewood Cliffs, N.J.: Prentice-Hall, 1970.

Dickey, Franklin M. *Not Too Wisely But Too Well: Shakespeare's Love Tragedies*. San Marino, Calif.: The Huntington Library, 1957.

Evans, Bertrand. "The Brevity of Friar Laurence." *PMLA* 65 (1950): 841–865.

Evans, Robert O. *The Osier Cage: Rhetorical Devices in* Romeo and Juliet. Lexington: University of Kentucky Press, 1966.

Everett, Barbara. "*Romeo and Juliet*: The Nurse's Story." *The Critical Quarterly* 14 (1972): 129–139.

Levenson, Jill L. "The Definition of Love: Shakespeare's Phrasing in *Romeo and Juliet*." *Shakespeare Studies* 15 (1982): 21–36.

Levin, Harry. "Form and Formality in *Romeo and Juliet*." *Shakespeare Quarterly* 11 (1960): 3–11.

McArthur, Herbert. "Romeo's Loquacious Friend." *Shakespeare Quarterly* 10 (1959): 35–44.

JULIUS CAESAR

Of Shakespeare's ten tragic plays, four are set in ancient Rome: *Titus Andronicus*, *Antony and Cleopatra*, *Julius Caesar*, and *Coriolanus*. All, but in particular the last two, have a bond with Shakespeare's history plays, for in these tragedies Shakespeare explores political issues that bear closely on those raised in his two tetralogies based on the internal and external conflicts of England during the fifteenth century. Thus the "Roman tragedies" may be interpreted in part as revealing Shakespeare's view of political life.

Historically, Julius Caesar was, in 60 B.C., a member of the ruling triumvirate in Rome, along with Pompey and Crassus. Crassus died in battle in 53 B.C., and in 49 B.C., in an attempt to gain absolute authority over Rome, Caesar flouted the Roman Senate by leading his forces across the Rubicon and against the armies of Pompey. In 47 B.C. at Pharsalia, Caesar defeated Pompey, then pursued him to Egypt, where Pompey was killed, and where Caesar enjoyed a dalliance with Cleopatra. The civil war continued for two more years, and when Caesar returned to Rome, he ruled with the support of the populace until his assassination in 44 B.C.

The primary source of *Julius Caesar* is Plutarch's *Lives of the Noble Grecians and Romans*, translated into English by Thomas North in 1579, and the play borrows most from the essays on the lives of Brutus, Caesar, and Antony. The events covered actually took place over several years, which Shakespeare condenses into six days. As does Plutarch, Shakespeare dramatizes Caesar's physical weaknesses, but Shakespeare omits incidents from Plutarch that depict Caesar as far more dictatorial than the play suggests. Here Caesar is arrogant, but he is clearly a great man, a world conqueror, and respected by virtually all.

Yet who is the central character of the play? Some might claim that Caesar is at its heart, for he towers over the rest, and even in death holds a powerful influence. Other critics might say Brutus, who undergoes the crucial ethical quandary. Others might answer Cassius, the prime mover in the conspiracy, or Antony, who turns the conspiracy and Rome upside down.

But this play has a fifth major character, one too often neglected. It is the most powerful of all, one whom all the principals fear. This character is the reason the principals act, speak, and, most important, think as they do. This character is the Roman citizenry. True, Rome is not what we would call a democratic state. Yet its politicians operate with the recognition that any individual who hopes to gain power must have the support of the people.

The opening scene sets the tone. The mob is wandering aimlessly, waiting for a leader's direction, until Marullus berates them:

> You blocks, you stones, you worse than senseless things!
> O you hard hearts, you cruel men of Rome,
> Knew you not Pompey?
>
> (I, i, 35–37)

The anaphoric "you" is one element that makes this address political. How appropriate the rhythms and word patterns would sound at a convention in our day, as Marullus passionately conjures up past glories in an attempt to persuade the citizenry. After the harangue, however, and after Marullus's accusations of disloyalty to Pompey's memory, Flavius offers the other side of political oratory, the soothing benediction:

> Go, go, good countrymen, and for this fault
> Assemble all the poor men of your sort . . .
>
> (I, i, 56–57)

He makes sure the electorate does not leave disgruntled, but embraced. Like a paternal leader forgiving his momentarily forgetful charges, Flavius comforts them. Notice that the orators avoid Caesar's name. One strong implication is that the masses' enthusiasm for Caesar and against Pompey gave Caesar the power he currently wields. A second implication is that the future leader of Rome will be the man who gains that loyalty.

When the masses depart, however, cynicism surfaces, as Flavius sneers: "See whe'er their basest metal be not mov'd" (I, i, 61). He recognizes how malleable they are. Flavius then refers to those he earlier called his "good countrymen" as "the vulgar" (I, i, 70), and with Marullus sets out to destroy all symbols of Caesar. Talk will take these rebels only so far.

In their brief appearance, the two politicians demonstrate three oratorical patterns that recur throughout the play: first, arousing the listener to the matter of public need; then cajoling and flattering the listener; then, in the listener's absence, commenting ruthlessly. These styles dominate the language of the play and shape how the Roman leaders speak not only to the mob, but also to one another. Virtually every major speech in the play is a version of firebrand oratory, filled with grandiose allusion and accusation, all helping to persuade. Speakers work to catch the heart of their audience, whether it be one person or a hundred, then to sway values through demogogic tactics. Such strategy becomes self-destructive, though, for those speakers cannot avoid cultivating an intellectual duplicity. The result is that individual lives, close relationships, and finally an entire society are reduced to rubble.

In Act I, scene ii we catch a brief glimpse of Caesar. His one-word summoning of his wife (I, ii, 1) implies that he is used to being obeyed without question. Antony responds with alacrity to his own name and to Caesar's command about touching Calphurnia during the race, and thus we assume that Caesar inspires loyalty (I, ii, 9–10). We also sense a great leader who feels that his stature is deserved. Furthermore, Caesar's dismissal of the soothsayer who shouts "Beware the ides of March" (I, ii, 18) indicates Caesar's security. Such a combination of traits makes Caesar vulnerable to flattery, and that vulnerability contributes to his downfall.

Once Caesar's party leaves, we have our first glimpse of Brutus, and it ensures that he maintains our sympathy. He broods, he ponders, and he probes life with gravity. He is soon to evince an intense social conscience and concern for humanity. He is the type of man many people want to trust, because he displays no personal ambition, just deep feeling.

Yet such a man can be troublesome, especially in the political arena. Later Caesar comments about Cassius: "He thinks too much; such men are dangerous" (I, iii, 195). Brutus, who thinks differently from Cassius, is nonetheless also dangerous, albeit in a distinctive way. One reason is that Brutus holds himself in the same high esteem that the rest of the world does:

> Vexed I am
> Of late with passions of some difference,
> Conceptions only proper to myself,
> Which give some soil, perhaps, to my behaviors;
> But let not therefore my good friends be griev'd
> (Among which number, Cassius, be you one),
> Nor construe any further my neglect,
> Than that poor Brutus, with himself at war,
> Forgets the shows of love to other men.
>
> (I, ii, 39–47)

He oozes an affected profundity. Furthermore, his meaning is clear: he is too deep for anyone else to comprehend, and therefore cannot be expected to remember the trivial amenities smaller minds value.

Such vanity is susceptible to deft manipulation, as Cassius here proves. His goal is to turn Brutus towards rebellion against Caesar, Brutus's friend, but he does not use polemic against Caesar's governance. Rather he first flatters:

> I have heard
> Where many of the best respect in Rome
> (Except immortal Caesar), speaking of Brutus
> And groaning underneath this age's yoke,

>Have wish'd that noble Brutus had his eyes.

(I, ii, 58–62)

And Cassius feigns a false modesty that he knows will appeal to Brutus (I, ii, 68–78).

After a shout from the multitudes offstage, Brutus lets slip that he "fears" (I, i, 79) the people will choose Caesar for their King. (The Romans never designated a leader "King," but that term brought the play closer to the Elizabethan audience). Cassius repeats "fear" (I, i, 80) and encourages Brutus to articulate his anxiety. Its essence is that Brutus is torn between love for Caesar as a man, and worry about what Caesar as King might do to Rome. The telltale line is easily missed:

>For let the gods so speed me as I love
>The name of honor more than I fear death.

(I, ii, 88–89)

The key word is "honor." Throughout Shakespeare's plays a variety of misdeeds are legitimized in its name, and the individual who seeks honor above all is vulnerable to deception. Here Cassius improvises shrewdly: "Well, honor is the subject of my story" (I, ii, 92). And he begins a discourse on Caesar's lack of fitness for office.

The first half focuses on Caesar's physical disability, his growing feebleness that Cassius witnessed when the two were swimming (I, ii, 100–111). Cassius also dramatizes Caesar's epilepsy (I, ii, 120–128), and with calculated emotion connects the loss of masculine strength with an inability to rule:

>   Ye gods, it doth amaze me
>A man of such a feeble temper should
>So get the start of the majestic world
>And bear the palm alone.

(I, ii, 128–131)

Cassius never explains what physical deficiency has to do with effective government, and thus the railing against Caesar makes Cassius seem petty. The second part of the exhortation is the glorification of Brutus. The harangue beginning: "Why man he doth bestride the narrow world . . . " (I, ii, 135–161) is an insidious suggestion that Caesar's power could well belong to Brutus if Brutus so desired. Cassius, however, does not dwell on that power, but rather on what he claims is the sad state of Rome itself. He appeals not to greed, for he knows Brutus would scorn any blatant grab for authority, but instead to Brutus's civic pride:

>   Age, thou art sham'd!
>Rome, thou has lost the breed of noble bloods!

(I, ii, 150–151)

This declaration occurs in the midst of glowing tributes to Brutus's name and reputation. Like Marullus in scene one, Cassius attempts to rouse his audience to action. Here the audience is Cassius's best friend who, though tempted, restrains himself:

> What you have said
> I will consider; what you have to say
> I will with patience hear, and find a time
> Both meet to hear and answer such high things.

(I, ii, 167–170)

Brutus sounds as if he is trying to conceive a way to legitimize for himself actions that he knows are immoral. Cassius, meanwhile, plays the humble confidante:

> I am glad that my weak words
> Have struck but thus much show of fire from Brutus.

(I, ii, 176–177)

Throughout this scene, periodic shouts from the crowd offstage break into the conversation, like cries from a primitive horde capable of annihilation. Both men, as well as the audience, are thus subtly reminded of where real power in Rome lies.

Caesar's return with his train offers further insight into his character. He shrewdly recognizes the threat Cassius poses:

> He reads much,
> He is a great observer, and he looks
> Quite through the deeds of men.

(I, ii, 201–203)

But Caesar's pride prevents him from taking appropriate care:

> I rather tell thee what is to be fear'd
> Than what I fear; for always I am Caesar.

(I, ii, 211–212)

Caesar's deafness, mentioned in the next line, is Shakespeare's invention.

Casca's report on Caesar's public refusal of the crown is a superb example of a man's derisively commenting on the events of a world he finds despicable but amusing. He claims he scarcely noticed the proceedings (I, ii, 235–236), then recreates them with malicious accuracy. He also sneers at the mob for their cheering Caesar: "... if Caesar had stabb'd their mothers, they would have done no less" (I, ii, 274–275). But as Casca presents the details of Antony's offering the crown (I, ii, 236–242) we recognize in Caesar's turning it away the technique of a master political actor. Meanwhile Cassius uses Caesar's susceptibility to the "falling sickness" (I, ii, 256) as further evidence of his lack of fitness for office.

We should keep in mind that for Shakespeare's audience, whose nation's history was scarred with the tragic consequences of insurrection, the overthrow of a monarch was a terrifying event. And nothing Caesar has done in this play

justifies such extreme retaliation. The news that Marullus and Flavius have been
executed for treachery (I, ii, 285–286) adds another dimension to the situation,
but even this action does not reflect Plutarch's portrait of Caesar's limitless
authority, and we continue to need evidence that Cassius has legitimate grievances. More and more he seems a man jealous of power he lacks.

 Once Brutus leaves, Cassius reveals himself more fully:

> Well, Brutus, thou art noble; yet I see
> Thy honorable mettle may be wrought
> From that it is dispos'd; therefore it is meet
> That noble minds keep ever with their likes;
> For who so firm than cannot be seduc'd?

(I, ii, 308–312)

The use of "honorable" suggests that Cassius is satirizing Brutus's preoccupation
with that word. And the use of "mettle" recalls Flavius's comments about the
masses (I, i, 62). Similar patterns have been followed in both scenes: flattery,
then soothing appeal to obligation, then ridicule. Cassius also plans to pressure
Brutus by throwing through Brutus's window messages ostensibly written by
Roman citizens (I, ii, 315–320). Cassius is aware that when an individual like
Brutus judges himself the object of popular favor, vanity will take hold and he
will be drawn inexorably into the struggle for power.

 Cassius's political ambition has reduced his friend Brutus to a political tool.
In a world where machinations are inherent, where duality is the eternal companion to thought, trust and integrity must disappear. Ambition has taken hold
of Cassius, and not even his closest friendship can survive.

 Scene iii suggests some of the universal implications of the rebellion against
Caesar. In Casca's words:

> Either there is a civil strife in heaven,
> Or else the world, too saucy with the gods,
> Incenses them to send destruction.

(I, iii, 11–13)

As the storm rages, Casca fearfully reports seeing a lion, the traditional symbol
of Caesar, walking through the capital (I, iii, 20–22). And he relates a series of
other unnatural events that leave him shaken (I, iii, 22–32). When Cassius enters,
though, he coolly turns such phenomena to his advantage:

> . . . why, you shall find
> That heaven hath infus'd them with these spirits,
> To make them instruments of fear and warning
> Unto some monstrous state.

(I, iii, 68–71)

Then he moves from such portents to what he views as his own suffering under
Caesar's tyranny (I, iii, 89–100). But the political basis of his protest withers
when Cassius clarifies his feelings about his countrymen:

> What trash is Rome?
> What rubbish and what offal? when it serves
> For the base matter to illuminate
> So vile as thing as Caesar!
>
> (I, iii, 108–111)

Power over such "trash" is his only ambition. Cassius, Casca, and Cinna then resolve to meet at Brutus's house, and Cassius talks cold-bloodedly of his friend's inclinations:

> Three parts of him
> Is ours already, and the man entire
> Upon the next encounter yields him ours.
>
> (I, iii, 154–156)

Casca emphasizes why the conspiracy needs Brutus:

> O, he sits high in all the people's hearts;
> And that which would appear offense in us,
> His countenance, like richest alchymy,
> Will change to virtue and to worthiness.
>
> (I, iii, 157–160)

Brutus is a symbol of decency, and both recognize that his endorsement will lend legitimacy to an illegitimate act: the murder of a ruler. Casca's warning also confirms that no matter what the ethics of the act they plan to commit, the ultimate judges will be the masses.

   That Brutus is suffering over the dilemma of whether to take action against Caesar is clear in his soliloquy at the beginning of Act II, scene i:

> It must be by his death; and for my part,
> I know no personal cause to spurn at him,
> But for the general. He would be crown'd;
> How that might change his nature, there's the question.
>
> (II, i, 10–13)

He is caught between his concern for the good of Rome and his fear of committing an unjustified murder. Yet his thought process suggests weakness. He has no hard evidence, only supposition about what Caesar might do. Possibly we can sympathize with Brutus, who is less ambitious than the others and more devoted to the public good. We could also see him as trying to do right by everybody, and thereby failing everyone. How we take the character of Brutus goes a long way towards determining how we react towards the play as a whole.

   During the rest of the scene the nature of Brutus's crisis is further revealed. Yet he admits, too, that he has not slept since his conversation with Cassius (II, i, 61–62), and his inner disorder is paralleled by the disorder in Rome. When the conspirators enter, hidden under cloaks as befitting the thugs they are, he is annoyed that they must hide in the dark (II, ii, 77–81) and skulk through Rome.

   At last all are present, and Cassius suggests they swear an oath (II, i, 113), a suggestion Brutus decries. In a long-winded appeal, he attempts to condone the criminal act they anticipate:

> Swear priests and cowards, and man cautelous,
> Old feeble carrions, and such suffering souls
> That welcome wrongs; unto bad causes swear
> Such creatures as men doubt; but do not stain
> The even virtue of our enterprise,
> Nor th' insuppressive mettle of our spirits,
> To think that or our cause or our performance
> Did need an oath . . .

> (II, i, 129–136)

The familiar word "mettle" alerts us to his implications. Is this speech a noble attempt by Brutus to excuse an action he knows is unjustifiable? Or is it an attempt to fool himself? Again, how we answer this action will determine how we view the play.

Cassius, though, has no such doubts. After Brutus finishes moralizing, Cassius immediately gets down to business: "But what of Cicero? Shall we sound him?" (II, i, 141). In other words, enough sanctimoniousness. No one need be convinced of the validity of what is to be done. No one, that is, but Brutus, whose oral extravagances are as much for his own comfort as for the conspirators' consciences. Casca and Cinna also endorse Cicero, and Metellus notes that he will be politically valuable (II, i, 144–149), but Brutus resists:

> O, name him not; let us not break with him,
> For he will never follow anything
> That other men begin.

> (II, i, 150–152)

Perhaps Brutus does not want a rival ego involved. Whatever his reason, the others have no choice but to agree with him or lose their most important public relations figure.

Soon dispute arises as to whether Antony, too, should be murdered. Brutus's initial reaction is practical: "Our course will seem too bloody . . . " (II, i, 162). Almost immediately, however, he recoils from such cold analysis, as though he cannot admit to himself that he is cognizant of *realpolitick*, and reverts to characteristic pomposities:

> Let's be sacrificers, but not butchers, Caius.
> We all stand up against the spirit of Caesar,
> And in the spirit of men there is no blood . . .

> (II, i, 166–168)

An assassination without blood—that is what Brutus seeks:

> Let's kill him boldly, but not wrathfully;
> Let's carve him as a dish fit for the gods,
> Not hew him as a carcass fit for hounds . . .

We shall be call'd purgers, not murderers.
And for Mark Antony, think not of him;
For he can do no more than Caesar's arm
When Caesar's head is off.

(II, i, 172–182)

All of Brutus's claims in the lines above are eventually proven wrong. And despite Brutus's eloquence, Cassius knows as much, especially about Antony: "Yet I fear him . . ." (II, i, 183). Cassius realizes the fickleness of the masses and how Antony may manipulate them. Yet Brutus is a necessary spokesman for the image of the group, and none dares cross him.

After the anachronistic chiming of the clock, Cassius makes a telling point by asking how Caesar will be urged to go to the capital. Decius has a solution:

> If he be so resolv'd,
> I can o'ersway him; for he loves to hear
> That unicorns may be betray'd with trees,
> And bears with glasses, elephants with holes,
> Lions with toils, and men with flatterers;
> But when I tell him he hates flatterers
> He says he does, being then most flattered.

(II, i, 202–208)

The description applies equally to Brutus. Both he and Caesar are vulnerable to the praises of subordinates. No wonder Brutus understands and feels for Caesar and can gauge Caesar's moods. They would be Brutus's as well. When Brutus sends the conspirators off with a jolly "Good gentlemen, look fresh and merrily" (II, i, 224), he is trying to salvage dignity from this opprobrious scheme. He never succeeds.

The saddest aspect of Brutus's charade occurs when Portia asks him to open his heart to her. Some might claim that he is too ashamed to admit the truth, or that because she is a woman in this age she is not privileged to hear that truth. Neither argument is convincing, especially because Portia pierces right to the core of the problem:

> You have some sick offense within your mind,
> Which, by the right and virtue of my place,
> I ought to know of . . .

(II, i, 268–270)

Then she shames him by kneeling. He begs her to rise, while trying to dismiss her concerns (II, i, 288–290), but fails to persuade even himself:

> O ye gods!
> Render me worthy of this noble wife!

(II, i, 302–303)

No matter how we feel about Brutus, whether we see him as a noble man gone astray or a fool manipulated by allies, he loves and respects his wife, and is pained at being unable to admit the conflict ravaging him. Her feelings for him are sincere, but he is incapable of responding. The battle between his public image and his private intentions has created an inner schism, and he tries fruitlessly to fuse the two parts.

Here is an important point of comparison between Brutus and other tragic heroes of Shakespeare. By nature Brutus is a philosopher, a reflective man who tries to search out the proper course. But he finds himself in a predicament in which he is called upon to act decisively. To resolve his crisis according to a personal code, he tries to turn a murder into the reasoned action of reasonable men. Thus his strengths of character are transformed into weaknesses, a dilemma faced by many of Shakespeare's protagonists. But Brutus's predicament has a unique aspect. It is one thing to act secretly in a way one finds repulsive. It is another to have to congratulate oneself and others publicly for doing so. During what remains of his life, Brutus tries to convince everyone of what he himself does not believe, and is reduced to an ineffective rhetorician.

Act II, scene ii dramatizes once more the power of the mob. When Caesar initially hears of Calphurnia's dream and her fears about his going to the forum (II, ii, 13–26), he shrugs them aside:

> Cowards die many times before their deaths,
> The valiant never taste of death but once.

> (II, ii, 32–33)

He is simultaneously vain and heroic: "Danger knows full well/ That Caesar is more dangerous than he" (II, ii, 44–45). But eventually he consents to remain home to soothe Calphurnia. Soon, however, Decius works on him just as Cassius worked on Brutus: by appealing to ego. When Caesar, doubtless embarrassed, refuses to give Decius a reason, stating: "The cause is in my will, I will not come" (II, ii, 71), Decius reinterprets the dream (II, ii, 83–90), then slips in that the citizenry would laugh at Caesar's accepting his wife's fears as law:

> If Caesar hide himself, shall they not whisper,
> "Lo Caesar is afraid"?

> (II, ii, 100–101)

Suddenly Caesar panics. He realizes that no matter how powerful a leader seems, authority requires constant reinforcement:

> How foolish do your fears seem now, Calphurnia!
> I am ashamed I did yield to them.
> Give me my robe, for I will go.

> (II, ii, 105–107)

Indeed, he is afraid, but not of dreams, only reality.

In Act II, scene iii, Artemidorus, a scholar who, according to Plutarch, was an associate of several of the conspirators, knows what is about to happen, and his intention to reveal all adds tension. In scene iv Portia intuits that something terrible is imminent, and her conversation with the soothsayer implies that disaster is about to befall Rome. Her reflections give us respite from the talk of the main characters but also contribute suspense.

At the forum prior to the assassination, Caesar's pride grows. He dismisses the soothsayer who shouts again about the ides of March (the "ides" were the fifteenth day of a Roman month), then turns away Artemidorus (III, i, 8). For a moment our attention shifts when Popilius Lena wishes success to Cassius, who is afraid the plot is discovered (III, i, 13–22). His instantaneous assumption that he will have to kill himself comically reflects his fundamental weakness. But then we return to Caesar, who in response to Metellus Cimber's request for a pardon of his banished brother remains arrogantly untouched:

> These couchings and these lowly courtesies
> Might fire the blood of ordinary men,
> And turn preordinance and first decree
> Into the [law] of children.
>
> (III, i, 36–39)

And as the conspirators gather around him:

> But I am constant as the northern star,
> Of whose true-fix'd and resting quality
> There is no fellow in the firmament.
>
> (III, i, 60–62)

With each line he seems to demand retribution.

But consider Shakespeare's overall presentation of Caesar. He is proud, and his treatment of underlings and even his wife is cavalier. He is also ruthless, as the executions of Flavius and Marullus attest. But even though his military and political triumphs are mentioned only in passing, Caesar's stature is never questioned, not even by his enemies. Thus in the context of the play his flaws hardly justify his murder. The results of that act, soon to appear, answer firmly that the killing of a legitimate ruler invites anarchy, a theme developed in other tragedies, and at length in the sequence of history plays.

Deep down, Brutus seems to be aware of his misjudgment. After the brutal stabbing, as the bloodied body of Caesar lies before him, and the sound of "*Et tu, Brute?*" (III, i, 77) yet resounds, Brutus resumes the pose of diplomat, a role he continues to mismanage. In reply to word that chaos spreads through the city (III, i, 97–98), he moralizes:

> So are we Caesar's friends, that have abridg'd
> His time of fearing death.
>
> (III, i, 104–105)

The thought is nonsense. And the rest of his dream is equally impractical:

> Then walk we forth, even to the market-place,
> And waving our red weapons o'er our heads,

> Let's all cry, "Peace, freedom, and liberty!"
>
> (III, i, 108–110)

Reality turns out quite differently.

A servant enters to beg for Antony's safe entrance, and Brutus remains blindly idealistic:

> Tell him, so please him come unto this place,
> He shall be satisfied; and, by my honor,
> Depart untouch'd.
>
> (III, i, 140–142)

With each additional mention of "honor," the word sounds more vacuous. Cassius still fears Antony's influence (III, i, 144–146), but Brutus does not deign to answer. And when Antony arrives and mourns over Caesar, Brutus continues to rationalize absurdly:

> Though now we must appear bloody and cruel,
> As by our hands and this our present act
> You see we do, yet see you but our hands,
> And this the bleeding business they have done . . .
> Our arms in strength of malice, and our hearts
> Of brothers' temper, do receive you in
> With all kind love, good thoughts and reverence.
>
> (III, i, 165–176)

So Brutus would like to believe. But Cassius tries to recover by appealing to the politician in Antony:

> Your voice shall be as strong as any man's
> In the disposing of new dignities.
>
> (III, i, 177–178)

He knows that a man like Antony has no interest in rhetoric, only practicalities. But Brutus remains preoccupied with ensuring that his act is viewed in the best light, and resolves to placate the crowd:

> And then we will deliver you the cause
> Why I, that did love Caesar when I strook him,
> Have thus proceeded.
>
> (III, i, 181–183)

Brutus refuses to acknowledge Antony's antagonism, even as the man who was practically a son to Caesar pays tribute to the corpse:

> Here was thou bay'd, brave hart,
> Here didst thou fall, and here thy hunters stand,
> Sign'd in thy spoil, and crimson'd in thy lethe.
> O world! thou was the forest to this hart,
> And this indeed, O world, the heart of thee.
> How like a deer, strooken by many princes,

Dost thou here lie!

(III, i, 204–210)

All the imagery implies that Caesar was innocent, slain unjustly and brutally. Cassius tries to interject, but Antony puts him off, then asks for the "reasons" why Caesar was dangerous. The word soon returns with stunning irony. Brutus proudly defends himself: "Or else were this a savage spectacle" (III, i, 223). We know that it was indeed savage, but Brutus will not accept that verdict.

His worst blunder is acceding to Antony's request to speak at Caesar's funeral, a decision reached over Cassius's objections (III, i, 232–234). Brutus's plan tells more about him:

> I will myself into the pulpit first,
> And show the reason of our Caesar's death.

(III, i, 236–237)

Whether such tactics are noble or foolish is difficult to say. Brutus's faith in the power of reason is admirable, but his faith in humanity, at least according to this play, is misdirected. He compounds his ill judgment by allowing Antony to appear last, the choice position on any program. Brutus even allows Antony leeway in his address:

> You shall not in your funeral speech blame us,
> But speak all good you can devise of Caesar,
> And say you do't by our permission;
> Else shall you not have any hand at all
> About his funeral.

(III, i, 245–249)

Determined to maintain his standard of decency, Brutus lacks the cold practicality necessary for political infighting. He soon learns that where mob power is the ultimate weapon, moral niceties are a lethal luxury.

When the conspirators leave, Antony is left alone, and for the first time we learn his private thoughts. Until this moment he has been unemotional. Now he cries his pain over Caesar's murder:

> O, pardon me, thou bleeding piece of earth,
> That I am meek and gentle with these butchers!
> Thou art the ruins of the noblest man
> That ever lived in the tide of times.
> Woe to the hand that shed this costly blood!

(III, i, 254–258)

We remember that Brutus was desperate not to be thought of as one of a mob of "butchers" (II, i, 166). Antony's echo clarifies the truth. Furthermore, his earlier shaking of the hand of each conspirator (III, i, 184–189) was a fraudulent ritual, a political maneuver. Antony also reveals a more dangerous side:

> A curse shall light upon the limbs of men;
> Domestic fury and fierce civil strife

Shall cumber all the parts of Italy . . .
And Caesar's spirit, ranging for revenge,
With Ate by his side come hot from hell,
Shall in these confines with a monarch's voice
Cry "Havoc!" and let slip the dogs of war,
That this foul deed shall smell above the earth
With carrion men, groaning for burial.

                                                        (III, i, 262–275)

Antony's willingness to unleash Ate, the goddess of discord, on Rome, and to inflict such suffering in his desire for power shows a cold-heartedness that elevates Brutus's moral rectitude. Yet the outcome of the play suggests that Antony's attitude is necessary for the individual who would seek and maintain power.

Act III, scene ii is a phenomenon, an astonishing performance by Antony, whose brilliance is especially enlightening in contrast to Brutus's weak effort. Even before Brutus takes the pulpit, we suspect his speech will fall short, for he has announced his intention to explain the "reason" for Caesar's assassination. More amusing is the response from Plebeian Two, who wants to hear those "reasons" (III, ii, 9). A successful political address must be based on passion. Perhaps Brutus believes such an approach beneath him, for his speaking prose suggests an unwillingness to compromise his faith in pure ratiocination. More likely he is too self-conscious to give forth with an emotional appeal to defend a murder he knows is indefensible.

He opens by invoking "honor" (III, ii, 15), a guarantee that trouble is close. And he repeats the word throughout. Otherwise he says in essence that he killed Caesar because of Caesar's dangerous but hidden ambition (III, ii, 24–27). The rest is all fluff and filler. Brutus challenges those whom he might have offended to speak out, but adds the qualifying charge of treason to anyone who does (III, ii, 30–34). No one raises a voice, but we recognize that the speech is hollow.

The mob, however, is temporarily abated. And when Brutus assures them that each man is to receive a share in the commonwealth (III, ii, 44), their delight is particularly telling: "Let him be Caesar" (III, ii, 51) shouts one. "Caesar's better parts/ Shall be crown'd in Brutus" (III, i, 51–52) adds another. Despite Brutus's hope for them, the people do not want freedom. They want a ruler, an authority to set down laws and regulate lives. The chaos of the first scene of the play mirrors the community state of mind.

Antony's speech in response is a masterpiece, everything Brutus's is not. Antony opens in apparent accord with the mob's current feelings: "I come to bury Caesar, not to praise him" (III, ii, 74). He repeatedly echoes the word "honorable," with ironic connotations that apply to this and many other of Shakespeare's plays. With apparent humility he recreates scenes from Caesar's political life, simultaneously glorifying Caesar and diminishing the stature of the men who killed him (III, ii, 87–103). And his reference to "brutish beasts"

(III, ii, 104), with an almost subliminal pun on "Brutus," implies the lowliness and cruelty of the assassins.

Throughout his oration Antony manages to anticipate what the crowd wants to hear, then to twist that sentiment for his own purposes. One of his most ingenious moves in his shamelessly emotional appeal is the pause to reflect on Caesar's bloodied body (III, ii, 106–107). Any mutilated corpse must touch an audience, and Antony's moment of quiet gives all, onstage and off, a chance to contemplate the worth of the victim. Yet Plebeian One remarks: "Methinks there is much reason in his sayings" (III, ii, 108).

The gambit of the will drives the mob into a well-timed frenzy. As they grow more desperate to learn the contents, Antony claims that he does not mean to disclose its stipulations (III, ii, 131), then further entices his listeners: "You are not wood, you are not stones, but men . . ." (III, ii, 142). These words recall Marullus's earlier tirade: "You blocks, you stones, you worse than senseless things!" (I, i, 35). Antony's success suggests that praise moves an audience more effectively than does anger. Eventually he sends the crowd charging off in one direction, then waves the parchment and pulls them back, finally revealing that the will promises "To every several man, seventy-five drachmaes" (III, ii, 242), plus Caesar's "private arbors and new-planted orchards . . . " (III, ii, 248).

Antony's most effective stroke is bringing the mob around Caesar's body, then holding up Caesar's ripped cloak, worn, Antony claims, "That day he overcame the Nervii" (III, ii, 173). Antony graphically points to where each of the assassin's knives entered (III, ii, 174–186). He cannot, of course, know where and by whom individual blows were struck, but he conjures up a scenario of one blade after another ripping Caesar's body, and the mob feels every stab within themselves. Caesar's wounds become their own, and the conspirators become "traitors" (III, ii, 255).

Antony is brilliant, although two lines reveal his icy detachment (III, ii, 259–260). The crowd, racing off to commit destruction and murder (III, ii, 254–261), is loathsome.

The funeral oration is usually regarded as the climax of the play, but the brief scene that follows is the dramatic high point. It lasts only thirty-seven lines, but is a fearfully graphic portrait of mankind run amuck, reveling in savagery. The people realize that Cinna the poet is not the man they seek, but they kill him anyway (III, iii, 33–34). The play suggests that their brutal energy must be controlled by an authoritative government, a theme that recurs in other tragedies and histories of Shakespeare. In *Julius Caesar* this scene is the mob's final appearance, and therefore what remains with us is the montage of men running the streets like the "dogs of war" (III, i, 273) Antony invoked earlier. That they do so in revenge makes that word hard to vindicate, here and in other works where it is praised.

In acts IV and V *Julius Caesar* loses some of its vitality. Brutus, Cassius, Caesar, and Antony are primarily politicians, and politicians are interesting only as long as they are involved in politics. Once the survivors are reduced to combat, they are less intriguing. Brutus, however, remains an object of concern. Whatever his follies, we recognize him as a man finer than his world, and we wonder how much he has learned and changed.

First we see Antony in a different context: as leader and strategist. He dismisses Lepidus:

> This is a slight unmeritable man,
> Meet to be sent on errands; is it fit,
> The threefold world divided, he should stand
> One of the three to share it?

                                                                (IV, i, 12–15)

Octavius defends Lepidus: "he's a tried and valiant soldier" (IV, i, 28), but Antony is not interested in irrelevancies: "So is my horse, Octavius . . . " (IV, i, 29). As heartless as Antony is, such a realistic attitude towards the dispensation of power is here portrayed as essential to a good leader. The quality is one Brutus utterly lacks.

We see as much in scenes ii and iii, where he squabbles with Cassius. At first Brutus seems bitterly resigned to Cassius's failings (IV, ii, 18–24). Then Brutus accuses him of bribery:

> Let me tell you, Cassius, you yourself
> Are much condemn'd to have an itching palm,
> To sell and mart your offices for gold
> To undeservers.

                                                                (IV, iii, 9–12)

Cassius, shocked, denies the accusation, then endures a tirade from Brutus, who insists once more upon the nobility of all their actions (IV, iii, 18–26). His use of the word "honors" (IV, iii, 25) is also dismaying, suggesting that his ultimate goal is personal eminence. Cassius asserts that he knows the proper way to deal in war, but when Brutus retorts, the two are reduced to child-like antipathy (IV, iii, 32–34), until Brutus dismisses his erstwhile friend with a contemptuous "Away, slight man!" (IV, iii, 37). Cassius has all he can do to restrain himself for the good of the cause. When finally he threatens to take action, Brutus responds haughtily:

> There is no terror, Cassius, in your threats;
> For I am arm'd so strong in honesty
> That they pass by me as the idle wind,
> Which I respect not.

                                                                (IV, iii, 66–69)

The tone sounds like Caesar's in Act II, scene ii. A few lines later Brutus and Cassius resume their quarrel and Cassius demands that Brutus understand him better:

A friend should bear his friend's infirmities;
But Brutus makes mine greater than they are.

(IV, iii, 86–87)

Brutus's reply is revealing: "I do not, till you practice them on me" (IV, iii, 88). Earlier in the play Cassius did manipulate Brutus, but Brutus was blind.

Brutus's self-assurance finally wears Cassius down, and he essentially removes himself from the conflict (IV, iii, 93–95). Eventually he and Brutus reconcile, but we realize how slim is Brutus's understanding of the natural feelings of men. Possibly we can view him as one whose eye is ever upward, seeking only the best, and refusing to deal with men's baser desires. The play also suggests that he is unable to feel what ordinary men feel, and therefore out of touch with humanity.

When Brutus reveals Portia's death (IV, iii, 147), he does so quietly, according to the Roman Stoic ideal. Indeed, Cassius seems more moved by the news:

How scap'd I killing when I cross'd you so?
O insupportable and touching loss!

(IV, iii, 150–151)

A few lines later Brutus ends the discussion: "Speak no more of her" (IV, iii, 158). He seems to tolerate no distraction from the problem at hand. Or he may be unwilling to dwell on the misery he brought to the woman he loved and who loved him.

The information is brought out again when Messala enters. He first reports that a hundred senators have been executed by Antony, Octavius, and Lepidus, and this information suggests both the brutality of war and the ruthlessness of those who would win (IV, iii, 173–175). Brutus's confusion over the number (IV, iii, 177) may reflect his own incompetence, or the inevitable disorder of combat. Then Messala reluctantly reveals the death of Portia. Perhaps this repetition is an error on Shakespeare's part, or perhaps in hearing the report twice Brutus is proving his fortitude. The subject switches quickly to military tactics, when once more Brutus asserts his authority, and once more he makes a strategic blunder. Cassius believes, logically, that forcing the enemy to march to meet Brutus and Cassius's troops will wear the enemy out (IV, iii, 199–202). But Brutus opposes this plan, and instead advocates marching so that their own forces will end in the middle of two opposing sides. When objections are raised, Brutus offers his own speech of resignation:

There is a tide in the affairs of men,
Which taken at the flood, leads on to fortune;
Omitted, all the voyage of their life
Is bound in shallows and in miseries.
On such a full sea are we now afloat,
And we must take the current when it serves,

Or lose our ventures.

(IV, iii, 218–224)

He sees himself tossed helplessly, and his decision to act is based on a suspicion
that disaster will follow no matter how he responds. Thus whether he dies in
this battle or afterwards makes little difference to him. Cassius's answer, "Then
with your will go on . . . " (IV, iii, 224), communicates his despair at trying to
reach the intransigent Brutus.

Moments later the ghost of Caesar appears before Brutus, proclaiming itself:
"Thy evil spirit, Brutus" (IV, iii, 282). Elizabethans of all classes believed in
supernatural agencies, and ghosts in Shakespeare's plays generally fall into two
categories. Objective ghosts, such as Hamlet's father, were visible to several
people, and therefore were assumed to be actually present. Subjective ghosts,
such as Caesar here, are figments of the imagination, and in this instance we
may assume that the vision is a reflection of Brutus's conscience. The ghost's
presence recalls Caesar's claim in Act II, when Decius asked for a reason to
explain Caesar's absence from the senate: "The cause is in my will" (II, ii,
71). The ghost affirms that Brutus cannot evade responsibility by shifting blame
to fate or some other "tide." The weight of human action rests, as always in
Shakespeare, on the individual. But the ghost's threat to see Brutus at Philippi
(IV, iii, 286) indicates that Brutus has erred too often to recover.

Act V, a series of short scenes, dramatizes the madness of war. In the opening
lines, Antony and Octavius debate strategy, and Antony has no doubt that the
opponents' boldness is the product of false courage (V, i, 7–12). Octavius
disagrees, and when Antony asks if Octavius "crosses" him (V, i, 19), Octavius's reply foreshadows another play of Shakespeare's: "I do not cross you; but
I will do so" (V, i, 20). Once this battle is won, these two will be left to struggle
for power, a conflict dramatized in *Antony and Cleopatra*.

The four leaders meet in a ritual of challenges and insults more common to
medieval warfare than Roman, and Cassius taunts Antony so strongly that Antony
responds with a mixture of hatred and satisfaction: "Old Cassius still" (V, i,
63). But when left alone, Cassius grows melancholy, reflecting that today is his
birthday, and to Brutus he anticipates the worst military outcome:

If we do lose this battle, then is this
The very last time we shall speak together.

(V, i, 97–98)

Cassius, practical as always, is prepared to commit suicide. Brutus, ever the
dreamer, cannot conceive of being dragged through Rome as a prisoner: "He
bears too great a mind" (V, i, 112). But he dismisses suicide, as was committed
by Cato, Portia's father (V, i, 100–105).

In scene iii Cassius proclaims that he has slain his flagbearer, who was apparently retreating. But Titinius reports that the fault was actually that of Brutus,
who thought he saw weakness in Octavius's forces (V, ii, 4–5) and gave the
word to attack Octavius too early (V, iii, 5–8). The disorder among the troops

of Cassius and Brutus is almost comic, and again we are reminded how unsuited Brutus is for the role in which he finds himself. When Cassius is told that Titinius is not captured, he kills himself with the sword that stabbed Caesar (V, iii, 45–46). But information comes that Brutus has actually thrown back Octavius, and that Cassius acted too hastily. Messala suggests the reason: "Mistrust of good success hath done this deed" (V, iii, 66). So battered was Cassius by errors compounded by Brutus's own stubborn miscalculation that Cassius, almost eagerly, escaped the fray.

When Brutus sees the body, he has another explanation: "O Julius Caesar, thou art mighty yet!" (V, iii, 94). Caesar may be dead, but his influence carries on, and Brutus's acknowledgement emphasizes Caesar's eminence. Meanwhile Antony shows his own spirit. In scene iv, his troops capture Lucilius, who pretends to be Brutus (V, iv, 7), but when Antony discovers the mistake, he handles the captive shrewdly:

> This is not Brutus, friend, but, I assure you,
> A prize no less in worth. Keep this man safe,
> Give him all kindness; I had rather have
> Such men my friends than enemies.
>
> (V, iv, 26–29)

Here Antony demonstrates Caesar's absolute command, as well as an acute political instinct.

When Brutus senses the battle is lost, he prepares to act against his earlier dictum opposing suicide, and his final words resound with irony:

> Countrymen,
> My heart doth joy that yet in all my life
> I found no man but he was true to me.
>
> (V, v, 33–35)

How little he has learned. People have deceived him viciously, and we sense that had he opportunity to live over again, he would likely make the same mistakes.

He also tries to salvage a measure of triumph:

> I shall have glory by this losing day
> More than Octavius and Mark Antony
> By this vile conquest shall attain unto.
>
> (V, v, 36–38)

These lines, too, resound with terrible irony, for in actuality Brutus and Cassius have been judged among the most notorious traitors in history. Indeed, one measure of their reputation is that in Dante's *Inferno* they are condemned, along with Judas Iscariot, to the ninth and innermost circle of hell, where each is chewed and tortured in a mouth of Satan.

At the end Antony pays tribute to the dead Brutus:

> This was the noblest Roman of them all:
> All the conspirators, save only he,
> Did that they did in envy of great Caesar;
> He, only in a general honest thought
> And common good to all, made one of them.
> His life was gentle, and the elements
> So mix'd in him that Nature might stand up
> And say to all the world, ''This was a man!''
>
>   (V, v, 68–75)

So skillful a politician is Antony that we wonder whether these thoughts are genuine or merely a gracious gesture. Yet the final four words have one more touch of irony. In this play the great mass of men are portrayed harshly, and the few who lead them are hypocrites. Perhaps Antony is saying that Brutus was the best to which mankind can aspire.

Yet that Antony does not understand the significance of Brutus's life is evident by the last directive:

> Within my tent his bones to-night shall lie,
> Most like a soldier, ordered honorably.
>
>   (V, v, 78–79)

The telling word ''honorably'' gives Brutus what he always sought. Antony probably does not use it with the satiric connotations invoked in his funeral speech. Still, if ever a man was undeserving of a military burial, it is Brutus, who was forced into his soldierly role.

He is the first of Shakespeare's tragic heroes beset by an articulated inner conflict, torn between loyalty to a friend and duty to the state. He is beset as well by a desire to preserve his government by eliminating what he believes is a potentially evil presence. Furthermore, Brutus's struggle between power and morality carries over into Rome. The consequences of a great man's deeds must be borne by the state. The core of the tragedy is that although Brutus's motivations were benign, his own nature, in combination with that of his world, ensured that they would be ultimately destructive.

SUGGESTIONS FOR FURTHER READING

Bonjour, Adrian. *The Structure of* Julius Caesar. Liverpool: Liverpool University Press, 1958.

Charney, Maurice. *Shakespeare's Roman Plays: The Function of Imagery in the Drama.* Cambridge: Harvard University Press, 1961.

Dean, Leonard F., ed. *Twentieth Century Interpretation of* Julius Caesar. Englewood Cliffs, New Jersey: Prentice-Hall, 1968.

Foakes, R. A. ''An Approach to *Julius Caesar.*'' *Shakespeare Quarterly* 5 (1954): 259–270.

Knights, L. C. ''Shakespeare and Political Wisdom: A Note on the Personalities of *Julius Caesar* and *Coriolanus.*'' *Sewanee Review* 61 (1953): 43–55.

Simmons, J. L. *Shakespeare's Pagan World: The Roman Tragedies*. Charlottesville: University Press of Virginia, 1973.

Spencer, T.J.B. *William Shakespeare: The Roman Plays*. London: Longmans, 1963.

Traversi, Derek. *Shakespeare: The Roman Plays*. Stanford: Stanford University Press, 1963.

Velz, John W. "Orator and Impersonator in *Julius Caesar*: Style and the Process of Roman History." *Shakespeare Studies* 15 (1982): 55–75.

HAMLET

Hamlet the character is a man confronted by a series of massive problems, inside himself and outside. *Hamlet* the play is a dramatization of his attempts to solve those problems. No character has touched civilization as deeply, and no play has been analyzed as extensively.

Shakespeare's clearest source is an earlier version of the plot, now lost, but known as the "Ur-*Hamlet*," or "original Hamlet." Some critics attribute this work to Thomas Kyd, author of *The Spanish Tragedy* (c.1589), which also deals with a son's delayed revenge for a murdered father. Both plays contain a ghost, a hero who suffers madness, and a play within a play. The essentials of the story of Hamlet, however, go back several hundred years as part of Scandanavian folk tradition, and were put into literary form in the history of "Amelthus" by the Danish writer Saxo Grammaticus, who lived in the latter half of the twelfth century. Thematic influences on Shakespeare's play come from a variety of Renaissance works, including *Treatise of Melancholy* (1586) by Timothy Bright, and *Il Libro del Cortegiano* (*The Book of the Courtier*) (1528) by the Italian diplomat Baldassare Castiglione.

From the first line, "Who's there?" (I, i, 1), this play concerns identity. Hamlet's primary dilemma is that of every human being: given this time and place and these circumstances, how is he to respond? What is his role in the world? What is his responsibility? All the heroes of Shakespeare's tragedies suffer versions of this crisis. But Hamlet's dilemma is especially overwhelming. One reason is that his circumstances are never clear to him. Nor to us. They shift constantly, like colors in a kaleidoscope, and from every perspective they may be interpreted differently. At many moments Hamlet tries to establish certainty about how and where he fits. But the values by which he attempts to judge his world and find a place in it make affirmation impossible. Thus we along with Hamlet ask questions that lead to other questions that lead to still other questions. The answers grow ever more difficult to ascertain.

What further complicates Hamlet's predicament is that not only does he react to his world, but his world reacts to him. He is a royal personage, and, according to Elizabethan doctrine, the health of his state rests to a significant degree on his own physical and emotional condition. Indeed, images of disease and sickness begin immediately as Francisco confesses on watch that he is "sick at heart" (I, i, 9). The presence of the apparition itself reflects turmoil within the nation.

That ghost is also an effective theatrical device, for it creates suspense from the start. Horatio, whose opening response, "A piece of him" (I, i, 19), suggests his intellectual detachment, refuses to believe in the Ghost, as Marcellus indicates (I, i, 23–25). But in a few moments, the Ghost of the former King Hamlet does appear, dressed in armor (I, i, 60–64). Marcellus urges Horatio to speak to it, but the Ghost hurries away. Horatio, though startled, realizes the crucial point:

> In what particular thought to work I know not,
> But in the gross and scope of mine opinion,
> This bodes some strange eruption to our state.
>
> (I, i, 67–69)

We should note that Elizabethans of all social classes believed in ghosts' capacity to appear.

Marcellus then asks why the nation is arming itself so heavily, and the implication is that the Ghost's presence and such activity are related (I, i, 70–79). Horatio explains the military history: old Hamlet killed his rival Fortinbras in battle and took possession of forfeited lands (I, i, 80–95). Now young Fortinbras is preparing to fight to reclaim those lands, and Horatio describes the young man with intriguing images:

> Now, sir, young Fortinbras,
> Of unimproved mettle hot and full
> Hath in the skirts of Norway here and there
> Shark'd up a list of lawless resolutes
> For food and diet to some enterprise
> That hath a stomach in't, which is no other,
> As it doth well appear unto our state,
> But to recover of us, by strong hand
> And terms compulsatory, those foresaid lands
> So by his father lost . . .
>
> (I, i, 95–104)

Apparently Fortinbras is a bold youth determined to avenge his father's lost honor. The polarity between this son and Hamlet is one force that weighs on Hamlet's mind.

Horatio then emphasizes the unnaturalness of the Ghost's presence, referring to horrifying events that preceded the death of Julius Ceasar (I, i, 114–120). Thus when the Ghost reappears, Horatio is desperate to know its reason for coming, and poses in question the three traditional explanations:

> If there be any good thing to be done,
> That may to thee do ease, and grace to me,
> Speak to me.

If thou art privy to thy country's fate,
Which happily foreknowing may avoid,
O speak!
Or if thou hast uphoarded in thy life
Extorted treasure in the womb of the earth,
For which, they say, your spirits oft walk in death,
Speak of it, stay and speak!

                                              (I, i, 130–138)

But with the cock crowing, the spirit vanishes in silence, and Horatio wonders
if this sudden departure indicates the spirit's evil nature (I, i, 148–156). Marcellus's comment about the season of Christmas, when "no spirit dare stir
abroad" (I, i, 161), suggests that the Ghost may be in opposition to Christian
values, and this conflict, too, proves fundamental to Hamlet's crisis.

After Horatio explains that he will tell Hamlet what has transpired, the action
moves inside the court, where, in contrast, all appears serene. Claudius's opening
lines are even, his manner tranquil:

Though yet of Hamlet our dear brother's death
The memory be green, and that it us befitted
To bear our hearts in grief, and our whole kingdom
To be contracted in one brow of woe,
Yet so far hath discretion fought with nature
That we with wisest sorrow think on him
Together with remembrance of ourselves.

                                              (I, ii, 1–7)

These words do not seem those of a villain. Perhaps in retrospect they sound
oily, for the sentence structure following is almost too balanced to be natural
(I, ii, 10–16), and later we recognize the hypocrisy, but initially Claudius appears
a reasonable man. As the scene proceeds, no one in the court resists his policy
against young Fortinbras' threats, and Claudius is in control: "So much for him"
(I, ii, 25). He calmly dispatches a letter to Fortinbras's uncle, then turns to the
next matter at hand: the petition for Laertes to return to Paris. Several times
Claudius refers to Laertes by name, a political technique to ingratiate himself,
and with equal smoothness requests the permission of Laertes' father, Polonius,
who reveals his character even as he consents:

H'ath, my lord, wrung from me my slow leave
By laborsome petition, and at last
Upon his will I seal'd my hard consent.
I do beseech you give him leave to go.

                                              (I, ii, 58–61)

The tone is pompous, the construction wordy. Both qualities are part of Polonius
throughout the play.

The first hint of disorder occurs when the King addresses Hamlet as "my
son" (I, i, 64). Hamlet responds in a satiric aside: "A little more than kin, and

less than kind'' (I, i, 65). This line has various levels of meaning, for "kind" in this context also refers to "kindred," and Claudius is now not merely Hamlet's uncle, but also his father. The intricate puns tell at once about the agility of the young man's mind, his bitterness, and his preoccupation with his relationship with Claudius.

Gertrude gently chastises her son about his extended period of mourning (I, ii, 68–73), and Hamlet's response emphasizes his anger as well as one of the play's key themes: the notion of "playing" or "acting." Hamlet seizes his mother's use of the word "seems," and notes that behavior and appearance do not reveal the inner man:

> These indeed seem,
> For they are actions that a man might play,
> But I have that within which passes show,
> These but the trappings and the suits of woe.

> (I, ii, 83–86)

He is obsessed by honesty, and desperate to understand the truth about people. We feel him probing the words and actions of Gertrude, Claudius, and the others. What makes his efforts so compelling is that only much later do we see any of these other characters privately. Until then we see them precisely as Hamlet does, and thus with Hamlet's eyes. Therefore Shakespeare achieves the dramatic equivalent of first-person narrative.

The King's response to Hamlet's insinuation about false appearance is a long address intended to ameliorate Hamlet's rancor. One thought in particular stands out:

> But to persever
> In obstinate condolement is a course
> Of impious stubbornness, 'tis unmanly grief,
> It shows a will most incorrect to heaven,
> A heart unfortified, or mind impatient,
> An understanding simple and unschool'd . . .

> (I, ii, 92–97)

His undercurrent is that Hamlet is overdoing his grief and thereby neglecting duties of manhood. Throughout the play Hamlet broods over whether he is weak or cowardly. Later we understand that this first insinuation by Claudius touches something within Hamlet that pains him deeply. At this point, however, Claudius does seem to be trying to bolster Hamlet's mood:

> We pray you throw to earth
> This unprevailing woe, and think of us
> As of a father, for let the world take note
> You are the most immediate to our throne . . .

> (I, ii, 106–109)

Claudius makes this statement as if it were a revelation, a magnanimous gesture that should be a welcome surprise to Hamlet and the court. In truth, Hamlet's status has not changed at all. He remains as he was when his father was alive: next in line of succession. Thus we wonder if his being denied the throne has led to his disenchantment. After Claudius finishes, Gertrude offers her own two-line request for Hamlet to remain at the court (I, ii, 118–119), and Hamlet's reply is pointedly rude to the King: "I shall in all my best obey you, madam" (I, ii, 120).

After Claudius responds with exaggerated enthusiasm and leads away the rest of the court, Hamlet is left to offer his first soliloquy, which sets up the fundamental crisis of the play. The speech also expresses Hamlet's inner condition as clearly as he can articulate it. But it is at least partially self-deceiving. This rumination is not Hamlet's being honest, but his attempting to rationalize what bothers him. The opening lines communicate absolute despair:

> O that this too [sallied] flesh would melt,
> Thaw, and resolve itself into a dew!
> Or that the Everlasting had not fix'd
> His canon 'gainst [self-]slaughter! O God, God,
> How [weary], stale, flat, and unprofitable
> Seem to me all the uses of this world!
> Fie on't, ah fie! 'tis an unweeded garden
> That grows to seed, things rank and gross in nature
> Possess it merely.

(I, ii, 129–137)

Initially he seeks to commit suicide, but within a few lines he indicates that he resents the state of Denmark and the world, and the forces that run it. Underneath these words is frustration that Hamlet himself remains unappreciated and impotent. The anger is not only with "things rank and gross" like Claudius, but with Hamlet's powerlessness, for his own abilities remain in lesser light. We may intuit that Hamlet regards himself as a failure, and blames both the world and himself for his frustration.

Earlier Claudius urged the Prince to "think of us as of a father . . ." (I, ii, 106–107). Now Hamlet turns to that subject, and the tensions within leave him stumbling over his own thoughts:

> Why, she should hang on him
> As if increase of appetite had grown
> By what it fed on, and yet, within a month—
> Let me not think on't! Frailty, thy name is woman!—
> A little month, or ere those shoes were old
> With which she followed my poor father's body,
> Like Niobe, all tears—why, she [even she]—
> O God, a beast that wants discourse of reason
> Would have mourn'd longer—married with my uncle,
> My father's brother, but no more like my father
> Than I to Hercules. Within a month,
> Ere yet the salt of most unrighteous tears

Had left the flushing in her galled eyes,
She married—O most wicked speed: to post
With such dexterity to incestuous sheets . . .

(I, ii, 143–157)

Emotions and ideas swirl around in him. Most audiences and critics assume that
Hamlet is here truthful in his claims about how different Claudius is from old
Hamlet. But is Hamlet being truthful? We know that old Hamlet was a respected
leader, and we see that Claudius is well in command. Hamlet tells us she loved
his father, and all signs indicate that Gertrude is happy with Claudius. The two
men were brothers, and thus some resemblance would be likely. Could Hamlet
be bitter that after losing one military, political husband, his mother has taken
up with another? We should thus be sensitive to any references that suggest
Hamlet's attitude toward Claudius is close to his attitude toward his father, for
that information would complicate further a play whose involvements are already
overwhelming.

Finally Hamlet reveals his final agony:

It is not, nor it cannot come to good,
But break my heart, for I must hold my tongue.

(I, ii, 158–159)

Hamlet can tell no one of his anguish. He must bear his agony alone. We realize
that if he did have someone to trust, he would be unable to communicate his
feelings, which, as he has demonstrated, are a compendium of half-sentences,
unfinished phrases, and disjointed thoughts.

When a voice calls to him, Hamlet offers a perfunctory greeting: "I am glad
to see you well" (I, i, 160). But when he realizes that the caller is an old friend,
Hamlet's mood brightens: "Horatio—or I do forget myself" (I, ii, 161). And
before long Hamlet begins to explain some of what he said was beyond articulation:

Thrift, thrift, Horatio, the funeral bak'd-meats
Did coldly furnish forth the marriage tables.

(I, ii, 180–181)

He is not embarrassed to reveal his dissatisfactions with the marriage. When
Horatio mentions that old Hamlet was "a goodly king" (I, ii, 186), Hamlet is
oddly noncommital:

'A was a man, take him for all in all,
I shall not look upon his like again.

(I, ii, 187–188)

Is this last line ironic? Is Claudius all too much like his father? Perhaps Hamlet
does not want to dwell on his sadness at losing his father. Or perhaps Hamlet
does not want to offer false flattery to his father's memory. Furthermore, if some
antipathy to his father does lie within Hamlet, he himself may be unaware of
it.

When Horatio informs Hamlet of the Ghost's appearance, Hamlet responds in short sentences, repeating information Horatio provides and demanding affirmation. What frightens Hamlet most is that the Ghost "look'd . . . frowningly" (I, ii, 231), and was "very pale" (I, ii, 233). We may infer that when in life the figure assumed these traits, he was dangerous. Hamlet both dreads and seeks a meeting with this apparition:

> My father's spirit—in arms! All is not well,
> I doubt some foul play. Would the night were come!
> Till then sit still, my soul. [Foul] deeds will rise,
> Though all the earth o'erwhelm them, to men's eyes.

> (I, ii, 254–257)

"Doubt" in line 255 means "suspect." Hamlet thus seems to hope that the Ghost will confirm his own beliefs and provide a course of action.

Act I, scene iii is a reflection of the main action. Laertes and his sister, Ophelia, ponder Hamlet's behavior, and Laertes warns her to be careful of the Prince:

> He may not, as unvalued persons do,
> Carve for himself, for on his choice depends
> The safety and healthy of this whole state . . .

> (I, iii, 19–21)

This admonition reminds us of the burdens Hamlet bears, and which eventually prove too much for him. Ophelia agrees to follow Laertes' counsel, provided he does not behave hypocritically (I, iii, 47–51). But hypocrisy is the way of this family, as Polonius eventually demonstrates. He enters surprised that Laertes has not yet departed, then delays his son with a long-winded, if famous, list of homilies. The last has particular relevance to the play:

> This above all: to thine own self be true,
> And it must follow, as the night the day,
> Thou canst not then be false to any man.

> (I, iii, 78–80)

He himself soon proves untrustworthy, and his transgressions cost him his life. And Hamlet, too, will struggle as he tries to be true to himself. Polonius then begins to advise his daughter about Hamlet, eventually frightening himself about the danger and deceptions the Prince poses (I, iii, 115–131). Polonius concludes by commanding her not to involve herself with him (I, iii, 131–134). Ophelia consents, but we suspect her love cannot be cut off so abruptly.

In scene iv, before the Ghost appears, Hamlet comments on what he judges to be the moral degeneration of his nation:

> The King doth wake to-night and takes his rouse,
> Keeps wassail, and the swagg'ring up-spring reels;
> And as he drains his draughts of Rhenish down,
> The kettle-drum and trumpet thus bray out

The triumph of his pledge . . .

(I, iv, 8–12)

> This heavy-handed revel east and west
> Makes us traduc'd and tax'd of other nations.
> They clip us drunkards, and with swinish phrase
> Soil our addition, and indeed it takes
> From our achievements, though perform'd at height,
> The pith and marrow of our attribute.

(I, iv, 17–22)

Such revelrous behavior offends him, and he is pained that his nation has been branded. Hamlet implies that Claudius is responsible for this degeneration. But Claudius has been King only two months. Can an entire country be transformed in so brief a time, and its international reputation soiled? Or has Denmark long been this way, and is Claudius maintaining the tradition? Or is Hamlet rather a puritan, who finds any such festivity an affront? The list of questions goes on.

His next words provide further insight?

> So, oft it chances in particular men,
> That for some vicious mole of nature in them,
> As in their birth, wherein they are not guilty
> (Since nature cannot choose his origin) . . .
> Carrying, I say, the stamp of one defect,
> Being nature's livery, or fortune's star,
> His virtues else, be they as pure as grace,
> As infinite as man may undergo,
> Shall in the general censure take corruption
> From that particular fault: the dram of [ev'l]
> Doth all the noble substance of a doubt
> To his own scandal.

(I, iv, 23–38)

Hamlet articulates the quintessential predicament of the tragic hero in Shakespeare's plays: born into a set of circumstances he cannot control, possessed by qualities that under those circumstances are fatal. Hamlet is just such a man, and he knows so.

When the Ghost appears, Hamlet is horrified.

> Be thou a spirit of health, or goblin damn'd,
> Bring with thee airs from heaven, or blasts from hell,
> Be thy intents wicked, or charitable,
> Thou com'st in such a questionable shape
> That I will speak to thee.

(I, iv, 40–44)

But he has no hesitancy in following:

> I do not set my life at a pin's fee,
> And for my soul, what can it do to that,

Being a thing immortal as itself?

(I, iv, 65–67)

He is desperate for any direction. At the moment, Hamlet's life is devoid of purpose of worth, at least to him. His shout, "My fate cries out . . . " (I, iv, 82), is a plea for guidance, for he hopes the apparition will bring him out of his emotional and intellectual torpor.

The Ghost soon hints at his potential evil:

> I am thy father's spirit,
> Doom'd for a certain term to walk the night,
> And for the day confin'd to fast in fires,
> Till the foul crimes done in my days of nature
> Are burnt and purg'd away.

(I, v, 9–13)

These crimes are never specified, but what follows suggests they were terrible, for he is suffering mightily now. The Ghost then hits his key point: "Revenge his foul and most unnatural murther" (I, v, 25). Astonished, Hamlet agrees, seemingly eager:

> Haste me to know't, that I with wings as swift
> As meditation, or the thoughts of love,
> May sweep to my revenge.

(I, v, 29–31)

The lines are curiously delicate for one being called to revenge. Still, the Ghost exhorts him:

> I find thee apt,
> And duller shouldst thou be than the fat weed
> That roots itself in ease on Lethe wharf,
> Wouldst thou not stir in this.

(I, v, 31–34)

The Ghost almost bullies Hamlet, implying that nothing has ever roused him to proper action, but that perhaps this crisis, at last, will do so.

The tone sounds a bit like that of Claudius. After all, Old Hamlet was a fearsome warrior. His son, as we shall learn, is a scholar, poet, and playwright, a contemplative soul. He is a masterful swordsman, but we see him only at sport. That this father and son lived at odds is likely. Perhaps the threats the Ghost puts forth are a desperate hope that his son will become the "man" his father always wanted.

At last the Ghost states the truth for which Hamlet has waited:

> The serpent that did sting thy father's life
> Now wears his crown.

(I, v, 39–40)

Hamlet's response, "O my prophetic soul!" (I, v, 40), tells us that he has suspected as much all along. The Ghost then details the crime and reveals his

anger with Gertrude, "my most seeming virtuous queen" (I, v, 46). He explains
the details of the murder (I, v, 59–70), then adds the greatest horror of all:

> No reck'ning made, but sent to my account
> With all my imperfections on my head.
>
> (I, v, 78–79)

But he adds a qualifying thought to the order of revenge:

> Let not the royal bed of Denmark be
> A couch for luxury and damned incest,
> But howsoever thou pursues this act,
> Taint not thy mind, nor let thy soul contrive
> Against thy mother aught.
>
> (I, v, 82–86)

Whether he is angrier over the murder or the seduction of Gertrude is not clear.
Throughout the play we ask the same question of Hamlet.

Once the Ghost departs, Hamlet is left bordering on hysteria, trying to summon
the depth of feeling to impel himself to revenge:

> Yea, from the table of my memory
> I'll wipe away all trivial fond records,
> All saws of books, all forms, all pressures past
> That youth and observation copied there,
> And thy commandement all alone shall live
> Within the book and volume of my brain,
> Unmix'd with baser matter.
>
> (I, v, 98–104)

Perhaps Hamlet is trying to erase the past, to eliminate all his relationship with
his father. He seems to be seizing this order as opportunity to atone for a life
that in his father's eyes has been a failure. Here is his chance to prove himself
worthy of being Old Hamlet's son.

Yet though he claims to himself and to the Ghost that this charge inspires
him, how profoundly does he want to be such a man? As Horatio and Marcellus
approach, Hamlet continues what appears to them incoherent babbling. As Horatio says: "These are but wild and whirling words, my lord" (I, v, 133).
Meanwhile the Ghost orders Hamlet to swear them all to secrecy (I, v, 149,
155, 161), and this voice drives Hamlet to further distraction. Why is the Ghost
so insistent? Perhaps he has little faith in his son, who was off at school instead
of carrying out the business of running a court.

When the Ghost is finally gone, Hamlet is left overwhelmed:

> There are more things in heaven and earth, Horatio,
> Than are dreamt of in your philosophy.
>
> (I, v, 166–167)

The confrontation has been too much for him. Attempting to explain further, he
stumbles incoherently:

But come—
Here, as before, never, so help you mercy
How strange or odd some'er I bear myself—
As I perchance hereafter shall think meet
To put an antic disposition on—
That you, at such times seeing me, never shall,
With arms encumb'red thus, or this headshake,
Or by pronouncing of some doubtful phrase,
As "Well, well, we know," or "We could, and if we would,"
Or "If we list to speak," or "There be, and if they might,"
Or such ambiguous giving out, to note
That you know aught of me—this do swear,
So grace and mercy at your most need help you.

(I, v, 168–180)

What is his strategy? Why the need for an "antic disposition?" Why does he not carry out the assigned task?

Here is the crux of the play. In the tradition of the revenge drama, Hamlet has been ordered to take action, but unlike the cause of revenge in a comparatively crude play like *Titus Andronicus*, the role here is tangled beyond solution. What is the assigned task? Does the Ghost intend Hamlet to take revenge in the form of murder? Hamlet cannot be sure. Perhaps he is meant to kill, but he is not a murderer. His feelings about his dead father are confused, a mixture of love, fear, and possibly resentment. He hates his uncle, but he loves his mother. How will revenge, in whatever form, hurt her? The court of Elsinore is in his hands, for he must act not just to purify the royal family, but also to cleanse the state. The world is waiting. Finally, as in all revenge plays, the issue also involves the secular act of revenge versus the Christian belief of letting divine providence carry out its own punishment.

Resolving all these conflicts is impossible:

The time is out of joint—O cursed spite,
That ever I was born to set it right!

(I, v, 188–189)

And Hamlet knows that resolving them is impossible. Hence the course of the play has been set: Hamlet will try to do anything but what he has been ordered to do.

What should he do? Is revenge in the form of murder justifiable? Throughout Shakespeare's plays violence is dramatized as a convenient, simplistic solution to complex moral dilemmas. Whatever the code of the time, whatever the dictates of previous generations, the plays always come down on the side of those who oppose killing. As long as Hamlet resists the opportunity, he has our support. When he surrenders, that support wavers, but never does it fade entirely, for we see in Hamlet a man acting against himself.

In Act II, scene i, Polonius orders Reynaldo to deliver money and letters to Laertes, now in Paris. In asking Reynaldo additionally to spy, Polonius's conversation rambles, as he enjoys imagining his son's debaucheries (II, i, 25–26). The wordy instruction in the art of spying (II, i, 42–65) brings out Polonius's tendency towards deception, a contradiction of his earlier advice to be honest.

Ophelia's entrance brings us back to Hamlet's story, and her report on his appearance and behavior is startling:

> He took me by the wrist, and held me hard.
> Then goes he to the length of all his arm,
> And with his other hand thus o'er his brow,
> He falls to such perusal of my face
> As 'a would draw it. Long stay'd he so.
> At last a little shaking of mine arm,
> And thrice his head thus waving up and down,
> He rais'd a sigh so piteous and profound
> As it did seem to shatter all his bulk
> And end his being.
>
> (II, i, 84–93)

The behavior is that of a man on the edge of insanity. But as we listen to this narrative, we wonder about several points. Is Hamlet acting mad? Or has he fallen into madness? When he looks closely at Ophelia's face, is he searching for a sign of his mother? Or is he just pretending to do so? Does he believe he is acting, but is so infused with his role that he is now mad? The possibilities go round and round. Polonius, though, believes he has the solution:

> This is the very ecstasy of love,
> Whose violent property fordoes itself . . .
>
> (II, i, 99–100)

And he hurries to make his evaluation known to the King.

Claudius, in the meantime, is about to begin an investigation of his own by enlisting the aid of Hamlet's old schoolmates, Rosencrantz and Guildenstern. They accept their politely phrased instructions passively. First Rosencrantz speaks:

> Both your Majesties
> Might, by the sovereign power you have of us,
> Put your dread pleasures more into command
> Than to entreaty.
>
> (II, ii, 26–29)

Guildenstern echoes:

> But we both obey,
> And here give up ourselves, in the full bent,
> To lay our service freely at your feet,
> To be commanded.
>
> (II, ii, 29–32)

Both use the same number of syllables, and their expressions are complementary. They thus appear like halves of one personality. Indeed, the responding expressions of gratitude by the King and Queen suggest that the two are easily mistaken for each other (II, ii, 33–34).

Once they leave, Polonius enters to announce both the ambassadors from Norway and his own solution to the puzzle of Hamlet's behavior. Gertrude asserts her conclusion:

> I doubt it is no other but the main,
> His father's death and our [o'erhasty] marriage.
>
> (II, ii, 56–57)

These lines are the first indication that she is sensitive to these matters, but they do not clarify whether she was an accomplice to Old Hamlet's murder, or even whether she has knowledge or suspicions about it.

Voltemand brings news that Fortinbras has been stopped in his attack on Denmark by his uncle, the King of Norway, and his forces diverted against Poland (II, ii, 60–76). Claudius maintains the appearance of authority by preparing to grant his needed approval for troop movements across Danish territory, but is clearly preoccupied with the report on Hamlet. Polonius exercises characteristic circumlocution, but eventually reads a bad poem Hamlet has written to Ophelia, and puts this in conjunction with other behavior to propose that rejection by Ophelia, according to Polonius's orders, has left Hamlet mad (II, ii, 142–151).

After Polonius agrees to continue to spy on Hamlet, the Prince enters reading, as if distracted. The King and Queen then exit, leaving Hamlet, who indulges in obscene byplay with Polonius. Hamlet calls the old man "a fishmonger" (II, ii, 174), apparently a slang word indicating a pimp, then offers a series of vulgar remarks about Polonius's daughter. Hamlet then switches targets and makes fun of old men (II, ii, 196–203), implying that they are not to be trusted. Then he interjects seemingly suicidal thoughts (II, ii, 214–216). Polonius is utterly befuddled: "Though this be madness, yet there is method in't" (II, ii, 205–206). We recognize that at least a part of this scene is Hamlet's pretending madness, but we also recognize his genuine antagonism to Polonius (II, ii, 219). Thus we assume that in this moment, at least, he is still in control of himself. Yet that he can alternate moods so quickly, from satire to brooding melancholy, from savage wit to blithe humor, suggests a tenuous state of mind, liable to deviate at any moment.

Hamlet's exchange with Rosencrantz and Guildenstern is marked by Hamlet's clever retorts, and his wordplay is winning. Nonetheless, his animosity surfaces:

> Why then 'tis none to you; for there is
> nothing either good or bad, but thinking makes it so.
> To me it is a prison.
>
> (II, ii, 249–251)

Suddenly, however, he tires of such games, and angrily challenges them to explain their presence:

> ... be even and direct with me,
> whether you were sent for or no!
>
> (II, ii, 287–288)

When they continue to duck the issue, Hamlet releases what has been building inside him:

> I have of late—but
> wherefore I know not—lost all my mirth, forgone all
> custom of exercises; and indeed it goes so heavily with
> my disposition, that this goodly frame, the earth,
> seems to me a sterile promontory; this most excellent
> canopy, the air, look you, this brave o'erhanging
> firmament, this majestical roof fretted with golden fire,
> why, it appeareth nothing to me but a foul and pestilent
> congregation of vapors.
>
> (II, ii, 295–303)

This statement is bewildering. Even as Hamlet reveals his disillusion, he does so by praising the world that leaves him dissatisfied. He thereby confirms that he wishes he were not disillusioned, that in fact he is pretending to be disillusioned so as to excuse himself from carrying out his assignment.

Furthermore, as he claims this disillusion, he simultaneously affirms his faith:

> What [a] piece of work is a
> man, how noble in reason, how infinite in faculties, in
> form and moving, how express and admirable in
> action, how like an angel in apprehension, how like a
> god! the beauty of the world; the paragon of animals;
> and yet to me what is this quintessence of dust?
>
> (II, ii, 303–308)

The first few lines quoted reveal Hamlet the idealist. He wants to believe the best of humankind. Yet that idealism has been crushed.

With the news that the Players have come to the court (II, ii, 315–318), Hamlet blossoms. The artist in him takes over, and he peppers Rosencrantz and Guildenstern with questions about the visitors. Before the Players actually enter, Hamlet changes tone once more and confides in Rosencrantz and Guildenstern that he, too, is an actor:

> I am but mad north-north-west. When the
> wind is southerly I know a hawk from a hand-saw.
>
> (II, ii, 378–379)

Thus he yet seems in control of himself.

After an introduction by Polonius and further suggestive banter by Hamlet about a daughter, the Players enter, and Hamlet's joy is almost uncontrollable. His dialogue races, as if these visitors were his spiritual brothers:

You are welcome, masters, welcome all. I am glad to
see thee well. Welcome, good friends.

(II, ii, 421–422)

He then asks for "a taste of your quality, come, a passionate speech" (II, ii,
431–432). But Hamlet has a particular speech in mind, one about the death of
King Priam of Troy. Hamlet begins the recitation, describing the bloody state
of Pyrrhus, Achilles' son. The Player takes over, describing Pyrrhus's initial
failure to kill Priam (II, ii, 474–487), but then how Pyrrhus, inspired with a
spirit of revenge, succeeds (II, ii, 488–492). The Player concludes with a description of the anguish of Hecuba, Priam's wife (II, ii, 512–518). The similarity
to Hamlet's predicament is clear, and we note that Pyrrhus, the character, is
able to achieve what Hamlet, the man, has thus far failed to do. So taken is
Hamlet with the reading that he asks the Players to perform "The Murder of
Gonzago," with subtle alterations (II, ii, 537–543).

The drama Hamlet has ordered played will parallel events described by the
Ghost (I, v). But why is Hamlet carrying out this charade? If the Ghost has told
the truth and Hamlet has given no evidence that he doubts the narrative, why
the need for a play?

The explanation lies in the soliloquy that follows the instructions to the players:

> O, what a rogue and peasant slave am I!
> Is it not monstrous that this player here,
> But in a fiction, in a dream of passion,
> Could force his soul so to his own conceit
> That from her working all the visage wann'd
> Tears in his eyes, distraction in his aspect,
> A broken voice, an' his whole function suiting
> With forms to his conceit?

(II, ii, 550–557)

Hamlet envies the Player's capacity to lose himself in his part, to perform his
lines with conviction. As the description continues, Hamlet delineates the qualities of the Player's performance:

> He would drown the stage with tears,
> And cleave the general ear with horrid speech,
> Make mad the guilty, and appall the free,
> Confound the ignorant, and amaze indeed
> The very faculties of eyes and ears.

(II, ii, 562–566)

Hamlet can perform none of these gestures, even as he tries to rouse himself
into a fury:

> But I am pigeon-liver'd, and lack gall
> To make oppression bitter, or ere this
> I should 'a' fatted all the region kites

With this slave's offal.

(II, ii, 577–580)

He continues to curse that despite his anger and hatred, he is unable to carry out revenge.

Then he conceives a plan. And from here on he gives himself the advantage the Player enjoys: a private role. What he cannot do in life, act on behalf of his father's spirit, he hopes to do in a play. He will no longer be Hamlet the man. He will turn into Hamlet the character on the stage of Elsinore, saying lines and performing pieces of business provided by a playwright: himself. In doing so, he will enjoy several benefits. He will not have to dredge up feeling, but will perform sorrow. He will let the actions of his play inspire him as a character. He will, in a sense, remove himself one step from reality:

> I'll have these players
> Play something like the murther of my father
> Before mine uncle. I'll observe his looks,
> I'll tent him to the quick. If 'a do blench,
> I know my course. The spirit that I have seen
> May be a [dev'l], and the [dev'l] hath power
> T' assume a pleasing shape, yea, and perhaps,
> Out of my weakness and my melancholy,
> As he is very potent with such spirits,
> Abuses me to damn me. I'll have grounds
> More relative than this—the play's the thing
> Wherein I'll catch the conscience of the King.

(II, ii, 594–605)

The delight with which Hamlet makes the pun on "relative" suggests his relief at the escape from responsibility he has conceived for himself. Does he have doubts about the legitimacy of the Ghost? No. But the character Hamlet is playing has such doubts. Hamlet seeks relief from his assigned role as real-life revenger by losing himself in the self-created role of theatrical revenger. The upcoming play will be the vehicle for beginning that process.

In Act III, scene i, situational complications follow one after the other. Rosencrantz and Guildenstern claim they tried to make Hamlet reveal himself, but confess their failure to discover the core of his behavior. The only useful information they can provide is that the Players have arrived: "And there did seem in him a kind of joy/To hear of it" (III, i, 18–19). Claudius and Polonius plan to observe Hamlet secretly, and to that end Polonius gives Ophelia a book from which she is to read aloud:

> Read on this book,
> That show of such an exercise may color
> Your [loneliness]. We are oft to blame in this—
> 'Tis too much prov'd—that with devotion's visage
> And pious action do we sugar o'er

The devil himself.

(III, i, 43–48)

The irony of the moment is that these words strike Claudius. At the end of the previous scene, Hamlet hoped the play would "catch the conscience of the King." At this moment Polonius unintentionally does so:

> How smart a lash that speech doth give my conscience!
> The harlot's cheek, beautied with plast'ring art,
> Is not more ugly to the thing that helps it
> Than is my deed to my most painted word.
> O heavy burthen!

(III, i, 49–54)

Here begins one of the most fascinating twists of the play: the switching of roles between Hamlet and Claudius. Both have painful consciences, and both suffer in private. To be sure, we have not a small portion of the sympathy for Claudius that we have for Hamlet, for we know the former to be a murderer. But something in his words touches us, for he does have remorse. He is not beyond sensibility.

Hamlet then enters to offer the most famous soliloquy of the play: "To be, or not to be, that is the question" (III, i, 55). His strategies are temporarily in suspension, and he finds himself thinking to the point of inertia. He contemplates and even yearns for suicide, but fears the consequences, especially in an afterlife where he will exist oppressed by the actions he performs on earth (III, i, 69–81). Ironically, he uses the same word Claudius did above: "Thus conscience does make cowards [of us all]" (III, i, 82). Here "conscience" means not just guilt or responsibility, but the moral and psychological network within the mind that prevents human action. Nonetheless, that both characters use the same word to express their torment indicates that they have more in common than appearance would suggest.

At Ophelia's entrance, Hamlet's mood alternates once more, from the melancholy to the satiric. The two aspects of his personality are in fact different expressions of the same emotion: unhappiness with the way of the world. When Hamlet broods, he turns his unhappiness in on himself. When he mocks others, he turns his dissatisfaction against them.

This moment also raises the ever-present question as to what extent Hamlet speaks as himself, and to what extent the role he plays has superseded the man. He confronts Ophelia with rude questions, then blurts out: "I did love you once" (III, i, 114). Does he mean this statement? Is he pretending that he once loved her? Does the character he is playing mean that *he* once loved her? Has Hamlet become so imbedded in his role that reality and fiction have crossed? Suddenly Hamlet charges her: "Get thee [to] a nunnery" (III, i, 120). "Nunnery" in Elizabethan English was also slang for "brothel," and thus Hamlet's order, which he repeats several times, has at least two meanings. Then the direction of his speech changes once more:

> I am very proud
> revengeful, ambitious, with more offenses at my beck
> than I have thoughts to put them in, imagination
> to give them shape, or time to act them in.
>
> (III, i, 123–126)

He seems to be trying to play the role of frustrated revenger as powerfully as he can, perhaps to convince himself of its legitimacy as well as his capacity to carry it out. Finally he verbally assaults Ophelia as representative of all women:

> You jig and amble, and you [lisp,] you nick
> name God's creatures and make your wantonness
> [your]ignorance. Go to, I'll no more on't, it hath
> made me mad.
>
> (III, i, 144–147)

Once more we ask if Hamlet is feigning madness, falling into madness, or playing his role with such fervor that reality and acting have blurred. We cannot be certain, nor can Hamlet. But we do recognize that his anger and sexual fury are now emerging as if uncontrolled. Of more than that we cannot be sure.

When Hamlet stalks off, Ophelia's pathetic evaluation provides indication of what the young man was before we saw him:

> O, what a noble mind is here o'erthrown!
> The courtier's, soldier's, scholar's eye, tongue, sword,
> Th' expectation and rose of the fair state,
> The glass of fashion and the mould of form,
> Th' observ'd of all observers, quite, quite down!
>
> (III, i, 150–155)

Part of Hamlet's tragedy is that these noble qualities are deteriorating as a result of the task existence has left him.

The King has overheard this conversation, which leaves him confused:

> There's something in his soul
> O'er which his melancholy sits on brood,
> And I do doubt the hatch and the disclose
> Will be some danger, which for to prevent,
> I have in quick determination
> Thus set it down: he shall with speed to England
> For the demand of our neglected tribute.
>
> (III, i, 164–170)

The King, too, is acting: he claims to Polonius that Hamlet is being dispatched for the good of the court. We know that Claudius seeks to save himself from whatever threat Hamlet poses.

When the Players retake the stage, Hamlet offers extensive direction on how they are to perform. We remember that Shakespeare was an actor, part of a company, and thus intimately involved with all aspects of performance. Thus these lines are doubtless legitimate advice for his actors. But we should see Hamlet's counsel not only as directed towards actors onstage, but also reflecting his own behavior, as an actor in life:

> Suit the action to the word,
> the word to the action, with this special observance,
> that you o'erstep not the modesty of nature: for any
> thing so o'erdone is from the purpose of playing,
> whose end, both at the first and now, was and is, to
> hold as 'twere the mirror up to nature: to show virtue
> her feature, scorn her own image, and the very age and
> body of the time his form and pressure.
>
> (III, ii, 17–24)

The propriety Hamlet urges for those on the theatrical stage he will not be able to maintain by himself on the stage of his own life.

Before the royal audience arrives, Hamlet outlines for Horatio the plan at hand, and in doing so reveals much about his own conditions:

> Since my dear soul was mistress of her choice
> And could of men distinguish her election,
> Sh' hath seal'd thee for herself, for thou hast been
> As one in suff'ring all that suffers nothing.
> A man that Fortune's buffets and rewards
> Has ta'en with equal thanks; and blest are those
> Whose blood and judgment are so well co-meddled,
> That they are not a pipe for Fortune's finger
> To sound what stop she please.
>
> (III, ii, 63–71)

He lays the groundwork for the philosophy he is to adopt by play's end: his helplessness to determine the course of his life. He recognizes the extent of his quandary, that he is trapped and has no escape, and the process of rationalizing his lack of movement has begun. His entire performance to follow is therefore ostensibly aimed at discovering the truth about Claudius, but in fact is one more attempt to postpone action, decision, or both.

When the audience arrives, Hamlet speaks of being "promise-cramm'd" (III, ii, 94), confirming suspicion that the source of Hamlet's anger is unrequited ambition and jealousy for the throne. To Ophelia he makes bawdy remarks about "country matters" (III, ii, 116), confirming to the eavesdropping Polonius that Hamlet's madness emerges from frustrated love. And to Gertrude Hamlet jokes about his father's death, confirming her theory that the recent passing has left him inconsolable. All explanations are right in their own way; yet even taken together they are insufficient. For the moment, however, all provide Hamlet with temporary roles to play so as to escape the pressures of his life.

During such moments we recognize that Hamlet is a brilliant actor and writer as long as he can maintain self-discipline. This begins to crack during the performance, for Hamlet cannot resist interjecting accusatory remarks that inflame the King:

That's wormwood!

(III, ii, 181)

No, no, they do but jest, poison in jest—no
offense i'th' world.

(III, i, 234–235)

. . . this play is the image of a murther done in
Vienna; Gonzago is the duke's name, his wife,
Baptista. You shall see anon. 'Tis a knavish piece
of work, but what of that? Your majesty, and we that
have free souls, it touches us not.

(III, ii, 238–242)

'A poisons him i' th' garden for his estate.

(III, ii, 261)

[What, frighted with false fire?]

(III, ii, 266)

So taken is Hamlet with the role of master playwright dramatizing the uncertain conscience of Claudius that Hamlet the actor cannot restrain himself. He fails to let the play be "the thing," but instead interrupts and so confounds the court with his own shenanigans that an onlooker would assume that what drives the King away is not the plot of the play, but Hamlet's behavior. Furthermore, Hamlet also reveals to the King alone that further precautions must be taken against Hamlet.

Yet do any of these consequences ultimately matter? Horatio's blank comment about Claudius, "I did very well note him" (III, ii, 290), suggests that he is bewildered by what has taken place. Furthermore, what Hamlet learns does no more than confirm what the Ghost told him. No new information has been gathered. All Hamlet has done is postpone the inevitable decision and action. Yet how he has done so, by losing himself in the role of plotting avenger, soothes a pained soul that cannot bear to deal with life.

As much as he tries to retreat into his pose of madness for the court, Hamlet cannot maintain it steadily. At moments he must break out, as he perhaps did before Ophelia. Another occasion occurs now, with Rosencrantz and Guildenstern. Initially Hamlet is content to resume banter on their level, using prose, but before long he explodes:

Why, look you now, how unworthy a thing
you make of me! You would play upon me, you would
seem to know my stops, you would pluck out the
heart of my mystery, you would sound me from my
lowest note to [the top of] my compass; and there is
much music, excellent voice, in this little organ, yet

cannot you make it speak.

(III, ii, 363–369)

The central image is familiar, for earlier in this scene Hamlet spoke to Horatio about those who "are but a pipe for Fortune's finger/To sound what stop she please" (III, ii, 70–71). The need for "playing," though it provides solace, angers him. He prizes the depth of his "mystery," but he is furious that he must have such a secret. Here he momentarily wearies of his role, but no haven is available. After more wordplay with Polonius that reflects distorted perception (III, ii, 376–382), Hamlet once again needs to inspire himself to action, and therefore sets off to see his mother:

> Let me be cruel, not unnatural;
> I will speak [daggers] to her, but use none.

(III, ii, 395–396)

Given his nature, he can do nothing else.

Another turning point of the play is Act III, scene iii. Rosencrantz and Guildenstern unintentionally increase the King's anguish when they remind him how much the health of the nation is dependent upon his own state:

> The cess of majesty
> Dies not alone, but like a gulf doth draw
> What's near it with it. Or it is a massy wheel
> Fix'd on the summit of the highest mount,
> To whose [huge] spokes ten thousand lesser things
> Are mortis'd and adjoin'd, which when it falls,
> Each small annexment, petty consequence,
> Attends the boist'rous [ruin].

(III, iii, 15–22)

Rosencrantz's words of praise reaffirm the traditional belief in the divinity of the kingship, that the holder of the throne is placed there by providence, and thus action against the King is action against God. Instead of providing comfort, however, such sentiments distress Claudius, who knows that he gained the throne through regicide, murder of the King. After Polonius leaves to hide in Gertrude's room, Claudius is left alone to relive his monumental sin:

> What if this cursed hand
> Were thicker than itself with brother's blood,
> Is there not rain enough in the sweet heavens
> To wash it white as snow?

(III, iii, 43–46)

He hopes that he can find forgiveness for his appalling act. But he is also aware that at the moment he cannot pray for forgiveness:

> That cannot be, since I am still possess'd
> Of those effects for which I did the murther . . .
>
> (III, ii, 53–54)

Now we begin to grasp the extent of his lust for power and for Gertrude. He sees no escape to his suffering on earth, only in heaven:

> There is no shuffling, there the action lies
> In his true nature, and we ourselves compell'd,
> Even to the teeth and forehead of our faults,
> To give in evidence. What then? What rests?
> Try what repentance can. What can it not?
> Yet what can it, when one can not repent?
> O wretched state!
>
> (III, iii, 61–67)

Like Hamlet, he sadly contemplates his afterlife. Also like Hamlet, he is helpless on earth to do anything to secure his salvation. He wants to act, but is beyond action, and thus finds himself waiting for something or someone to direct him. The parallel to Hamlet is unmistakable.

When Hamlet sees Claudius praying, the role switching becomes more painful for us. Here is the perfect opportunity for Hamlet to carry out the appointed task, but he rationalizes that such a murder will send Claudius to heaven, an unacceptable solution (III, iii, 73–78). Instead Hamlet resolves to wait for the proper occasion:

> When he is drunk asleep, or in his rage,
> Or in th' incestious pleasure of his bed,
> At game a-swearing, or about some act
> That has no relish of salvation in't—
> Then trip him, that his heels may kick at heaven,
> And that his soul may be as damn'd and black
> As hell, whereto it goes.
>
> (III, iii, 89–95)

Throughout the play we have felt the underlying tension between Hamlet's role as earthy avenger and the Christian principle that judgment belongs to heaven. Now Hamlet attempts to exceed his bounds by making his earthly crime redeem Claudius's crime against the former King. In doing so, Hamlet assumes a new role, that of divine force, free to act without boundaries of earthly morality and justice. In overstepping these limitations, he commits a terrible transgression of his own.

Lest we doubt that he means to take such a step, consider what happens in the following scene, when Hamlet enters his mother's chamber. In response to her accusation: "Hamlet, thou hast thy father much offended" (III, iv, 9), Hamlet retorts sharply: "Mother, you have my father much offended" (III, iv, 10). And he forces her to sit so he can let loose all that he has had pent up within him. Before he can do so, however, he hears a noise from behind the curtain. Hurriedly he takes out his sword and stabs, as perhaps his anger with his mother has manifested itself in violence. He hopes the victim is the King (III, iv, 26), and in his excitement accuses Gertrude:

> A bloody deed! almost as bad, good mother,
> As kill a king, and marry with his brother.
>
> (III, iv, 28–29)

Gertrude's response (III, iv, 30) suggests that the accusation shocks her, and we have greater confidence that she had no part in the actual murder. More important at this moment, though, is Hamlet's reaction when he discovers that the hidden figure is Polonius:

> Thou wretched, rash, intruding fool, farewell!
> I took thee for thy better.
>
> (III, iv, 31–32)

He is viciously unrepentant.

Hamlet's attention turns next to his mother, against whom he releases anguish that he has until this moment kept to himself. Pointing to pictures of his father and Claudius, Hamlet rages:

> Have you eyes?
> Could you on this fair mountain leave to feed,
> And batten on this moor? ha, have you eyes?
> You cannot call it love, for at your age
> The heyday in the blood is tame, it's humble,
> And waits upon the judgment, and what judgment
> Would step from this to this?
>
> (III, iv, 65–71)

He seems repulsed by thoughts of her desires. At the end of this speech, Gertrude confesses her own pain:

> O Hamlet, speak no more!
> Thou turn'st my [eyes into my very] soul,
> And there I see such black and [grained] spots
> As will [not] leave their tinct.
>
> (III, iv, 88–91)

But her confession of guilt does not satisfy her son:

> Nay, but to live
> In the rank sweat of an enseamed bed,
> Stew'd in corruption, honeying and making love
> Over the nasty sty!
>
> (III, iv, 91–94)

His passion here suggests that what tortures Hamlet most is his mother's second marriage. He is revolted by images of sexuality, and this horror, perhaps more than loss of the crown or love for Ophelia or even the death of his father, haunts him.

Gertrude cries out her apology, but Hamlet cannot stop his tirade (III, iv, 97–101) until the Ghost reappears to Hamlet alone. Whether the Ghost is protecting Gertrude or preventing Hamlet from another murder is unclear, as is the reason the Ghost is not visible to Gertrude, who assumes Hamlet has become even madder:

> This the very coinage of your brain,
> This bodiless creation ecstasy
> Is very cunning in.
>
> (III, iv, 137–139)

After these lines, we wonder if the Ghost in this scene is a manifestation of Hamlet's conscience. Nevertheless, mother and son achieve a reconciliation. First Gertrude confesses her guilt: "O Hamlet, thou has cleft my heart in twain" (III, iv, 156). In return Hamlet has a request:

> Good night, but go not to my uncle's bed—
> Assume a virtue, if you have it not . . .
>   Refrain [to]-night,
> And that shall lend a kind of easiness
> To the next abstinence, the next more easy . . .
>
> (III, iv, 159–167)

How such behavior will help Hamlet is not clear. Still, this thought leads to another very different perspective, as Hamlet points to the body of Polonius:

> I do repent; but heaven hath pleas'd it so
> To punish me with this, and this with me,
> That I must be their scourge and minister.
> I will bestow him, and will answer well
> The death I gave him.
>
> (III, iv, 173–177)

He attempts to legitimize the murder by claiming he is under the charge of heaven. With this statement he removes himself from the realm of moral rectitude. Whatever he does subsequently, whatever violence he commits, may be excused under the title "heaven's scourge and minister."

From the initial instructions of the Ghost, Hamlet has struggled to absolve himself from the task assigned. He has feigned madness, he has arranged the play, and he has blamed his mother for her part in his predicament. Now, forced to face his crisis, Hamlet claims that he is at the mercy of other forces, an extension of heaven. Therefore he cannot be held accountable. Therefore he is without moral consequences: "I must be cruel only to be kind" (III, iv, 178). Therefore he is, in his own mind, free.

The first ramification of this new attitude emerges a few lines later, when

Hamlet schemes to be rid of the irritating presence of Rosencrantz and Guildenstern, whom he trusts, he says, as "adders fang'd" (III, iv, 203):

> For 'tis the sport to have the enginer
> Hoist with his own petar, an't shall go hard
> But I will delve one yard below their mines,
> And blow them at the moon.
>
> (III, iv, 206–209)

He displays no conscience. Their lives mean nothing to him. We deplore such heartlessness, but under the pressure of the moment Hamlet has lost much feeling, and as he drags the "guts" (III, iv, 212), he jokes about Polonius being "most grave" (III, iv, 214).

A comment about Rosencrantz and Guildenstern is appropriate. Ever since the production in 1967 of Tom Stoppard's play *Rosencrantz and Guildenstern Are Dead*, these two characters, once the quintessential nonentities of the dramatic world, have acquired a curious status. They are celebrated as twentieth-century antiheroes, lost and stumbling through a world they neither control nor understand. What is more intriguing is how much of what contemporary audiences have discovered in Stoppard's play can be found in Shakespeare's characterizations. The original Rosencrantz and Guildenstern know nothing about a murder. They hear nothing about the hasty marriage between Claudius and Gertrude. They are merely brought into court, strangers whose identities are confused by the royal couple (II, ii), and told to investigate Hamlet and report. Their scenes with him are filled with puns and witticisms at which the pair comes off a poor second, although their constant questions and forced congeniality give them a sinister quality lacking from Stoppard's version of the two.

Perhaps the moment that epitomizes their predicament occurs at the beginning of Act IV, when the King calls them onstage. Gertrude has just reported the events of the previous scene to Claudius, who utters his sorrow (IV, i, 16–23). The depth of his gloom is uncertain, and we cannot grasp his plans. Then, in the midst of this tension, as if from nowhere, Rosencrantz and Guildenstern appear and are ordered:

> Friends both, go join you with some further aid:
> Hamlet in madness hath Polonius slain,
> And from his mother's closet hath he dragg'd him.
> Go seek him out, speak fair, and bring the body
> Into the chapel. I pray you haste in this.
>
> (IV, i, 33–36)

The two then leave as silently as they entered. How easy to imagine total befuddlement on their faces. When they encounter Hamlet, several lines later, he is no help, although he does hint that they are expendable:

> But such officers
> do the King best service in the end: he keeps them,

> like [an ape] an apple, in the corner of his jaw, first
> mouth'd, to be last swallow'd. When he needs what
> you have glean'd, it is but squeezing you, and, spunge,
> you shall be dry again.
>
> (IV, ii, 16–21)

In scene iii the two bring Hamlet before Claudius, who, in a moment that borders on the comic, demands: "Now Hamlet, where's Polonius?" (IV, iii, 16). Hamlet returns with jokes about Polonius's decaying (IV, iii, 19–25), then accepts the King's decree to go to England, another comic moment. First Hamlet repeats the order: "For England" (IV, iii, 46). The King affirms: "Ay, Hamlet" (IV, iii, 46). And Hamlet playfully assents: "Good" (IV, iii, 46). Hamlet continues to toy with Claudius, confusing "mother" and "father" (IV, iii, 51–52). Meanwhile Rosencrantz and Guildenstern stand idly, until Claudius commands them to accompany Hamlet, for reasons beyond their ken. There they will die, victims of a plot which was always one step beyond them.

The depth to which Hamlet has fallen is clear in scene iv, after he meets the Norwegian Captain, who leads the troops of Fortinbras over Danish territory towards Poland. Hamlet's final soliloquy is a wretched attempt to animate a spirit so flickering that the militaristic Fortinbras has become a paragon:

> Witness this army of such mass and charge,
> Led by a delicate and tender prince,
> Whose spirit with divine ambition puff'd
> Makes mouths at the invisible event,
> Exposing what is mortal and unsure
> To all that fortune, death, and danger dare,
> Even for an egg-shell.
>
> (IV, iv, 47–53)

"A delicate and tender prince." By all accounts young Fortinbras is a killer of the first order. But Hamlet can no longer deal with the frenzy inside him, and he romanticizes the slaughter of warfare:

> Rightly to be great
> Is not to stir without great argument,
> But greatly to find quarrel in a straw
> When honor's at the stake.
>
> (IV, iv, 53–56)

The word "honor," used so often by Shakespeare's protagonists, reminds us that when no other reason for an immoral act can be found, honor is the last resort. Hamlet has managed to turn over thoughts in his mind to the point of absurdity, rallying himself to fight when no cause is to be found. Here is a man on the verge of collapse. This soliloquy is thus a death wish, the outpourings of someone who glorifies battle in the hope that he might find in it relief that he has so long sought: "O, from this time forth,/My thoughts be bloody, or be nothing worth'' (IV, iv, 65–66). Violence is its own reward. That is how far Hamlet has fallen.

Hamlet is absent from the final scenes of Act IV, but they dramatize his influence in the court. First Gertrude broods over her sins:

> To my sick soul, as sin's true nature is,
> Each toy seems prologue to some great amiss,
> So full of artless jealousy is guilt,
> It spills itself in fearing to be split.
>
> (IV, v, 17–20)

Hamlet's accusations have been ingrained within her, but her precise crimes remain uncertain. Then Ophelia enters singing bizarre lyrics, but their essence is sufficiently lewd that we realize her imbalance, in which she has taken on the role of prostitute Hamlet assigned to her. The death of her father suggests that Ophelia's madness compares to Hamlet's. But unlike Ophelia, Hamlet has managed to maintain some equilibrium. Claudius comments sadly on her deteriorated state:

> . . . poor Ophelia
> Divided from herself and her fair judgment,
> Without the which we are pictures, or mere beasts . . .
>
> (IV, v, 84–86)

This image of degeneration leads directly to the next episode, as a messenger enters to report that Laertes, in his anger over Polonius's murder, has aroused the rabble, who ''call him lord'' (IV, v, 103). Thus we see that Hamlet's actions have corrupted the state, and the order of society is threatened. Moreover, Laertes' willingness to overthrow the political structure of Denmark illuminates Hamlet's reluctance to commit a revenge that might have equally disastrous consequences. Claudius takes refuge behind divine right, but also clarifies the extent of Laertes' threat:

> There's such divinity doth hedge a king
> That treason can but peep to what it would,
> Acts little of his will.
>
> (IV, v, 124–126)

Laertes here shows no such hesitancy to commit this crime:

> To hell, allegiance! vows to the blackest devil!
> Conscience and grace, to the profoundest pit!
> I dare damnation.
>
> (IV, v, 132–133)

In seeking revenge for his father, Laertes has no conscience, no inner conflict. Instead, he brings a spirit of barbarism to the country. Perhaps most important, the actions of the populace in support of Laertes remind us of Shakespeare's fear of mob rule. As in *Julius Caesar*, *Coriolanus*, and the history plays, the threat of the mob is dangerous and subject to illicit manipulation.

The appearance of Ophelia compounds Laertes' fury with sadness (IV, v, 169–170). Claudius continues to claim his own innocence in Polonius's death, and he is willing to let Laertes' friends be the judge:

> If by direct or by collateral hand
> They find us touch'd, we will our kingdom give,
> Our crown, our life, and all that we call ours . . .
>
> (IV, v, 207–209)

Such assurance, the words of a master politician, temporarily calm Laertes, who still demands to know all the circumstances:

> His means of death, his obscure funeral—
> No trophy, sword, nor hatchment o'er his bones,
> No noble rite nor formal ostentation—
> Cry to be heard, as 'twere from heaven to earth,
> That I must call't in question.
>
> (IV, v, 214–218)

In scene vi, Horatio learns what has befallen Hamlet, whose ship was waylaid by pirates. With an energy that belies his inactivity at court, Hamlet managed to board the pirate vessel, where he was treated fairly, and he is resolved to compensate his captors (IV, vi, 22). Such an example illustrates Hamlet's potential, how he might proceed were he freed from the responsibilities imposed on him at Elsinore.

Scene vii contrasts Hamlet's actions with the plottings of Claudius and Laertes. The King reminds Laertes how profoundly Gertrude cares for her son:

> The Queen his mother
> Lives almost by his looks, and for myself—
> My virtue or my plague, be it either which—
> She is so [conjunctive] to my life and soul,
> That, as the star moves not but in his sphere,
> I could not but by her.
>
> (IV, vii, 11–16)

He claims that he is unwilling to do anything that might hurt Gertrude. Whether Claudius feels genuine devotion to his wife, or whether he does not want to be involved in another murder, particularly that of a beloved prince (IV, vii, 18–19), cannot be clarified.

Claudius continues to exert his political skills, as he persuades Laertes to follow another route to revenge. First, however, the King receives the letters mentioned earlier (IV, vi, 24), in which Hamlet flippantly addresses Claudius as "High and mighty" (IV, vii, 43), then announces that he has arrived "naked" (IV, vii, 44), or unprotected, in Denmark. Hamlet's scheme is beyond both Claudius and Laertes, but Claudius continues his own plotting, and we see fully the ruthlessness that led him to murder. He flatters Laertes shamelessly, reporting the words of a "gentleman of Normandy" (IV, vii, 82), who so praised Laertes' skill with the rapier that Hamlet became overwhelmed with envy (IV, vii, 102–105). Such jealousy on Hamlet's part is hard to imagine, but Laertes is taken in completely.

Next Claudius advises quick and resolute action:

> That we would do,
> We should do when we would; for this "would" changes,
> And hath abatements and delays as many
> As there are tongues, are hands, are accidents,
> And then this "should" is like a spendthrift's sigh,
> That hurts by easing.
>
> (IV, vii, 118–123)

Ironically, Claudius is describing Hamlet's condition through most of the play, further indication of how much they share. Laertes suggests killing Hamlet in church (IV, vii, 126), but Claudius thwarts that plan:

> No place indeed should murther sanctuarize,
> Revenge should have no bounds.
>
> (IV, vii, 127–128)

We remember Hamlet's similar reaction to the prospect of murdering the praying Claudius (III, iii). No matter how different Hamlet and Claudius are, their involvement with murder draws them together spiritually. Indeed, throughout Shakespeare's plays, acts of destruction rebound to corrupt destroyers.

Claudius explains his scheme to draw Hamlet into a sword fight with Laertes, who agrees to arrange that the tip of one of his weapons be poisoned (IV, vii, 140–148). For all his external confidence in Laertes, Claudius has another plan in reserve (IV, vii, 150–154), and conspires to have a poisoned drink in preparation. Neither plan shows foresight. A sword can easily be turned on the player, and the poisoned drink would cast suspicion on Claudius. Both men, however, are desperate to be rid of Hamlet, and thus draw plans carelessly.

Gertrude then enters to report the death of Ophelia. The detail with which the Queen fills her report is surprising, for anyone who observed the victim so long would have had opportunity to save her from drowning (IV, vii, 166–183). In any case, we recognize that Hamlet is responsible for another death, this of someone he may very well have loved.

In the first scene of Act V, the tone changes as the two gravediggers appear. Their exchange is comic relief, but as so often in Shakespeare's plays, this seemingly incidental moment bears upon the primary action. The first gravedigger, also referred to as a "clown," reflects on the nature of responsibility:

> Here lies the water; good.
> Here stands the man; good. If the man go to this water
> and drown himself, it is, will he, nill he, he goes, mark
> you that. But if the water come to him and drown him,
> he drowns not himself; argal, he that is not guilty of

his own death shortens not his own life.

(V, i, 15–20)

The gravedigger implies that one who is the target of forces greater than himself cannot be guilty. So we shall come to see Hamlet as the victim of demands that were impossible for him to resolve. The gravedigger also reflects on the equality of all men before him:

> There is no ancient
> gentlemen but gard'ners, ditchers, and grave-makers;
> they hold up Adam's profession.

(V, i, 29–31)

This theme is soon to be echoed by Hamlet.

He enters in a new mood, accompanied by Horatio, and calmer, more at ease with himself and life, than we have seen. He observes the gravedigger toss about one skull, and reflects on the identity:

> How the Knave jowls it to the ground, as if
> 'twere Cain's jaw-bone, that did the first murther.
> This might be the pate of a politician, which this ass
> now o'erreaches, one that would circumvent God,
> might it not?

(V, i, 76–80)

Both images apply well to Claudius. Then Hamlet speculates further about the same skull:

> Or of a courtier, which could say, "Good
> morrow, sweet lord! How dost thou, sweet lord?"

(V, i, 82–83)

Here he seems to refer to the hypocrisy of Polonius, or perhaps the treachery of Rosencrantz and Guildenstern. When the gravedigger tosses another skull, Hamlet assumes it to be that of a lawyer:

> Where be his quiddities now, his
> quillities, his cases, his tenures, and his tricks?

(V, i, 99–100)

Hamlet now sees all of life as futile and pointless.

So taken is Hamlet that he begins a conversation with the gravedigger, showing a lighter, more engaging side of his personality that has been recently stifled. The gravedigger explains that he is digging the grave for a woman who committed suicide, but Hamlet does not realize the woman is Ophelia. The gravedigger also clarifies Hamlet's age as thirty (V, i, 147, 162).

When the gravedigger points to one more skull, and announces it to be Yorick's, Hamlet is touched by the transcience of life:

> Alas, poor Yorick! I knew him, Horatio, a
> fellow of infinite jest, of most excellent fancy. He

hath bore me on his back a thousand times, and now
how abhorr'd in my imagination it is! my gorge rises
at it. Here hung those lips that I have kiss'd I know not
how oft. Where be your gibes now, your gambols,
your songs, your flashes of merriment, that were
wont to set the table on a roar?

(V, i, 184–191)

Then his thoughts turn to another great prince:

> Alexander
> died, Alexander was buried, Alexander returneth
> to dust, the dust is earth, of earth we make loam,
> and why of that loam whereto he was converted might
> they not stop a beer-barrel?

(V, i, 208–212)

The humor is tinged with melancholy. It suggests a man more at peace with his world, but also someone who has found justification for inaction. If all is pointless, why take on responsibility? Perhaps Hamlet has given up on his course of revenge. In the context of what follows, his ruminations on time and age are a mask that covers profound despair.

At the sight of Ophelia's funeral procession, Hamlet is shocked but when Laertes' emotions overflow and he leaps into the grave, Hamlet can no longer restrain himself. He jumps in after and, as he struggles with Laertes, shouts in desperation: "I lov'd Ophelia" (V, i, 269). The grotesque tableau of two men fighting over who loved a dead woman more is compounded by Hamlet's series of ludicrous images (V, i, 275–283), offered to convince the onlookers of his sincerity.

Or is he trying to convince himself? After all, he has murdered innocent bystanders, and he has failed to carry out his father's directives. He has, in almost every way that matters to him, failed. Now he sees another victim of his inefficacy, this one innocent. Is this overflow of passion a last attempt to give meaning to himself? As he stands at this moment, his life is, he believes, without value, and his badinage with the gravedigger, though entertaining, reflects that spirit. Perhaps, then, his claims of love for Ophelia are a final effort to tell himself that he lived for something, that a vestige of human passion remains within him.

That he is otherwise devoid of emotion is apparent in the beginning of the next and final scene. First he tells Horatio:

> There's a divinity that shapes our ends,
> Rough-hew them how we will—

(V, ii, 10–11)

The words communicate not only world-weariness, but utter disillusion, a confession of Hamlet's impotence to control his life. He seeks to be forgiven for anything that has happened and might yet occur. Providence is to blame, and he is resigned to its command.

This mood is developed further when he recounts the machinations that led to the deaths of Rosencrantz and Guildenstern. He explains about rewriting the letter that ordered his own death (V, ii, 31–47) so that they would be executed, "Not shriving time allowed" (V, ii, 47), then explains with astonishment the good fortune of his having the royal seal with him: "Why, even in that was heaven ordinant" (V, ii, 48). When Horatio questions the morality of these tactics, Hamlet answers coldly:

> There are not near my conscience. Their defeat
> Does by their own insinuation grow.
> 'Tis dangerous when the baser nature comes
> Between the pass and fell incensed points
> Of mighty opposites.
>
> (V, ii, 58–62)

To him their lives are not even worth considering. Hamlet also now views himself and Claudius as "mighty opposites." He has reached a remarkably low point. Even at this nadir, however, Hamlet retains a measure of dignity, for he vows to apologize to Laertes for any wrongs that might have been done (V, ii, 75–80).

The appearance of Osric, whom Hamlet labels "this water-fly" (V, ii, 82), suggesting effeminacy, brings a few moments of comic relief. Hamlet toys with him until Osric communicates that the King is supporting Hamlet in a challenge against Laertes (V, ii, 101–103). After the weapons and stakes are clarified, Hamlet reveals to Horatio that danger lurks: "Thou wouldst not think how ill all's here about my heart—but it is no matter" (V, ii, 212–213). He is beyond caring:

> There is special
> providence in the fall of a sparrow. If it be [now],
> 'tis not to come; if it be not to come, it will be now;
> if it be not now, yet it [will] come—the readiness is all.
> Since no man, of aught he leaves, knows what is't to
> leave betimes, let be.
>
> (V, ii, 219–223)

Life has exhausted him, and he welcomes death as deliverance. His tone is noble, but his underlying theme is the absurdity of existence. Still, when he sees Laertes, Hamlet carries out his promise of an apology:

> Was't Hamlet wrong'd Laertes? Never Hamlet!
> If Hamlet from himself be ta'en away,
> And when he's not himself does wrong Laertes,
> Then Hamlet does it not, Hamlet denies it.
> Who does it then? His madness. If't be so,
> Hamlet is of the faction that is wronged,

His madness is poor Hamlet's enemy.

(V, ii, 233–239)

The audience understands a different version of Hamlet's life: the cause of Hamlet's misdeed was Hamlet himself, but the cause of his madness was a series of other forces, including the Ghost, Claudius, and Gertrude. Hamlet tries to explain that he was never in control of his life. We know that he never had the capacity to control himself, that his abilities and the duties demanded of him clashed and left him defeated.

In the carnage of the final scene, several moments stand out. One, Claudius commands Osric to give each participant a sword, and therefore we assume that Osric is an accomplice in the King's scheme. Perhaps Claudius's dealing with such a character is evidence of how profoundly the throne of Denmark has been debased. Gertrude's giddy participation reflects her general acceptance of what has taken place over the previous months. Just as she married Claudius and added to the general decay of her court and state, so here she, in her own words "carouses" (V, ii, 289) amidst the general merriment. Whereas her actions earlier contributed to her moral disintegration, now her partaking of the tainted drink brings about her physical death.

Laertes has a moment of pause as he prepares to strike Hamlet with the poisoned sword: "And yet it is almost against my conscience" (V, ii, 296). We remember Hamlet's earlier diatribe against himself: "Thus conscience does make cowards [of us all]" (III, i, 82). And we realize how twisted the values of revenge were. But just as we hope that further fatalities might be avoided, Hamlet cannot resist taunting his opponent:

I pray you pass with your best violence;
I am sure you make a wanton of me.

(V, ii, 298–299)

His pride stung, Laertes resumes the battle. As happens in so many plays of Shakespeare, the cause of honor leads a man to death.

After Gertrude falls from the drink, Laertes tells Hamlet the truth:

In thee there is not half an hour's life.
The treacherous instrument is in [thy] hand,
Unbated and envenom'd. The foul practice
Hath turn'd itself on me. Lo here I lie,
Never to rise again. Thy mother's poison'd.
I can no more—the King, the King's to blame.

(V, ii, 315–320)

In fury Hamlet stabs Claudius. Yet so fearsome is the position of King that even after Laertes' confession, onlookers shout "Treason, treason!" (V, ii, 323). They remain loyal to the throne. The King dies, and Laertes follows, but not before he forgives Hamlet (V, ii, 329–331). Hamlet begins to expire, but has strength to solicit Horatio to resist the convenient path of suicide: "Absent thee from felicity a while . . . '' (V, ii, 347). Hamlet wants his story told, as if through narrative art it will acquire meaning.

In his last lines, Hamlet, now King after the death of Claudius, fulfills his function by bestowing authority on Fortinbras (V, iii, 355–358). The health of the state is restored, although another militaristic ruler has taken power. Some matters never change.

With corpses surrounding him, Horatio tries to salvage Hamlet's reputation. He argues that Hamlet never contributed to the deaths of Rosencrantz and Guildenstern, an outright lie. He then prepares to tell the succession of horrors:

> So shall you hear
> Of carnal, bloody, and unnatural acts,
> Of accidental judgments, casual slaughters,
> Of deaths put on by cunning and [forc'd] cause,
> And in this upshot, purposes mistook
> Fall'n on th' inventors' heads . . .
>
> (V, ii, 381–385)

He reminds us of the theatrical tradition of the revenge tragedy from which Shakespeare has moved so far.

But before Horatio can proceed, Fortinbras interrupts. In an unintentionally ironic gesture, he orders that Hamlet be carried off ''like a soldier'' (V, ii, 396). Like Brutus in *Julius Ceasar*, Hamlet is to be given a military funeral, and in this case the tribute is even more unsuitable. The final line, ''Go bid the soldiers shoot'' (V, ii, 403), is painfully fitting. It suggests that the values of this society will be maintained, that the spirit of revenge that rules this play yet lives.

The perplexities posed by Hamlet the character and *Hamlet* the play are almost beyond fathoming. What we can grasp is a hero whose disenfranchisement from the human community, in combination with his desire to belong to that community, make him the embodiment of the struggle for identity that all of us experience. Perhaps this aspect of his predicament is the reason that virtually every member of every audience that experiences this play feels at one with him. Yet despite this universality, Hamlet remains beyond us. So multitudinous are the aspects of his mind and personality that in his struggle to understand himself, he is, like existence itself, forever a puzzle, the most compelling character in world literature.

SUGGESTIONS FOR FURTHER READING

Aldus, P. J. *Mousetrap: Structure and Meaning in* Hamlet. Toronto: University of Toronto Press, 1977.

Bevington, David Martin, ed. *Twentieth Century Interpretations of* Hamlet. Englewood Cliffs, N.J.: Prentice Hall, 1968.

Bowers, Fredson. ''Hamlet as Minister and Scourge.'' *PMLA* 70 (1955): 740–749.

Charney, Maurice: *Style in* Hamlet. Princeton: Princeton University Press, 1969.

Davis, Arthur G. *Hamlet and the Eternal Problems of Man*. Jamaica, New York: St. John's University Press, 1964.

Ferguson, Francis. "*Hamlet*: The Analogy of Action." *Hudson Review* 2 (1949): 165–210.

Joseph, Bertram. *Conscience and the King: A Study of* Hamlet. London: Chatto & Windus, 1953.

Levin, Harry. *The Question of* Hamlet. New York: Oxford University Press, 1959.

Muir, Kenneth. *Shakespeare:* Hamlet. London: Edward Arnold, 1963.

Muir, Kenneth, and Stanley Wells, eds. *Aspects of* Hamlet. Cambridge and New York: Cambridge University Press, 1979.

Petronella, Vincent F. "Hamlet's 'To be or not to be' Soliloquy: Once More Into the Breach." *Studies in Philology* 71 (1974): 72–88.

Prosser, Eleanor. Hamlet *and Revenge*. Stanford Calif.: Stanford University Press, 1971.

Sterling, Brents. "Theme and Character in *Hamlet*." *Modern Language Quarterly* 13 (1952): 323–332.

Walker, Roy. *The Time is Out of Joint: A Study of* Hamlet. London: Andrew Dakers, 1948.

Weitz, Morris. Hamlet *and the Philosophy of Literary Criticism*. Chicago: University of Chicago Press, 1964.

Wilson, John Dover. *What Happens in* Hamlet. Cambridge: Cambridge University Press, 1951.

OTHELLO

For many audiences, *Othello* is the most touching and intimate of Shakespeare's tragedies. The play focuses on three characters, two of whom are happily married to each other, and a third who wishes to destroy that marriage. Such destruction is not carried out as part of some grand design, such as to win territory or power or wealth. It is carried out for its own sake, and the seeming pointlessness of this vengeance contributes to the tragedy's poignancy.

The source of *Othello* is Giraldi Cinthio's "Tale of the Moor," from a story collection known as the *Hecatommithi* (1565). Cinthio's story is a straight melodrama, and its essential features are retained in Shakespeare's play. The Moor is tormented over suspicions of his wife's infidelity, and his ensign causes these suspicions to manifest themselves in violence. Quite a few details are changed, however, and their alteration partially indicates how Shakespeare was able to take a seamy story and elevate it into poetic tragedy.

In Cinthio's tale, the unnamed Moor and his jealous ensign (Shakespeare's Iago) together kill Disdemona [sic], then try to make the murder appear to be an accident. The Moor is captured, tortured, and exiled, and eventually slain by Disdemona's family. The ensign dies during torture for another crime. Shakespeare's plot, on the other hand, concentrates on the provocation to murder, and the time period is compressed into a few days. Furthermore, the qualities of jealousy and suspicion are dramatized with singular intensity.

More important are thematic changes. Cinthio's ensign has a clear reason for his destructive actions: he is jealous of the Moor, and seeks Disdemona for his own. In *Othello*, Iago's motivation is a mystery. Another crucial adjustment is the elevation of Othello to great stature and dignity so that his manipulation by Iago has more powerful consequences that pervade the surrounding society. But although the play does have political implications, these are subordinate to the love conflict.

The problem of Iago's motivation begins right at the start of the play. Coleridge attributed Iago's behavior to "motiveless malignity," but such analysis is ultimately unsatisfactory. People act as they do for reasons, and so do well-conceived characters. Surely the play provides evidence of Iago's reasons.

In Act I, scene i, Iago and Roderigo confer, the latter complaining about the marriage of Othello and Desdemona, for Roderigo, eager to marry Desdemona himself, had paid Iago for his aid. Accused of treachery, Iago protests that he hates the Moor because Othello has given the position of lieutenant to Michael Cassio, whose refinement Iago dismisses as unmanly and unworthy:

> (A fellow almost damn'd in a fair wife),
> That never set a squadron in the field,
> Nor the division of a battle knows
> More than a spinster . . .
> And I, of whom his eyes had seen the proof
> At Rhodes, at Cyprus, and on [other] grounds
> Christen'd and heathen, must be belee'd and calm'd
> By debitor and creditor—this counter-castor,
> He (in good time!) must his lieutenant be,
> And I ([God] bless the mark!) his Moorship's ancient.
>
> (I, i, 21–33)

The references to "wife" and "spinster" suggest Iago's antagonism to women. And the contrast between Christian and heathen resounds during the play. Furthermore, Iago resents any subservience. Speaking of his general, Othello, Iago sneers:

> I follow him to serve my turn upon him.
> We cannot all be masters, nor all masters
> Cannot be truly follow'd . . .
> Were I the Moor, I would not be Iago.
> In following him, I follow but myself.
>
> (I, i, 42–58)

Iago sets himself as an enemy to service and therefore to the social order. He is devoted to self-interest, he relishes chaos and deception, and he plans to turn himself into a perverse spirit; all, he suggests, over his being denied professional advancement.

Thus here is the first possible explanation for Iago's anger. But this solution falls short. Virtually never during the rest of the play is Iago concerned with the business of the world. His preoccupation is far more immediate: obliterating the love between Othello and Desdemona. Yet his reason remains vague. Here Iago speaks of his own "peculiar end . . . " (I, i, 60), as if he himself cannot specify what he hopes to gain through his plotting.

He sets his scheme underway by convincing Roderigo to awaken Brabantio, Desdemona's father:

> Call up her father.
> Rouse him, make after him, poison his delight,
> Proclaim him in the streets; incense her kinsmen,
> And though he in a fertile climate dwell,
> Plague him with flies. Though that his joy be joy,

Yet throw such [changes] of vexation on't,
As it may lose some color.

                                                        (I, i, 67–73)

The image of poison recurs regularly, reflecting Iago's personality and method of destruction. Here we also note one of the most fascinating aspects of Iago's personality: his delight with himself and his wit. In this respect he is like his antecedent, the Vice figure from medieval morality plays, who stands for the antithesis of good. In style and attitude, Iago is also like other Machiavels in Renaissance drama, including Shakespeare's Edmund from *King Lear* and Richard III. Such smugness makes his presence theatrically irresistible, for even as we are repulsed by his cruelty we are entertained by his humor. At numerous instances we are aware of the depths of his deception, yet other characters trust him implicitly. Such irony pleases Iago inordinately, and even at some of the most painful moments of the tragedy, we feel his laughter and reluctantly join him.

When Brabantio appears, Iago, unseen in the darkness, shouts a warning that reveals another aspect of his character:

Your heart is burst, you have lost half your soul;
Even now, now, very now, an old black ram
Is tupping your white ewe.

                                                        (I, i, 87–89)

The repetition of ''now'' has an unnerving energy, as though Iago were trying to make Brabantio feel the sexual experience vicariously. But the cry should also be understood as a reflection of Iago's mind. He is outraged by the relationship between the white Desdemona and the black Othello, and he continually portrays it in brutal terminology. Interestingly, his comments about all sexuality are phrased with equal rudeness, and thus we shall consider presently if his inner wound, the cause of his anger, is dramatized as sexual in nature.

Brabantio dismisses Roderigo as an unworthy suitor (I, i, 96–101), then protests that a marriage between Desdemona and Othello is impossible: ''This is Venice/My house is not a grange'' (I, i, 105–106) He cannot believe that such illegal and uncivilized behavior can take place in his sophisticated city. Meanwhile Iago continues to taunt Brabantio with pornographic images of his daughter:

I am one, sir, that comes to tell you your
daughter and the Moor are [now] making the beast
with two backs.

                                                        (I, i, 115–117)

Roderigo offers a more courtly and dignified explanation:

Your daughter (if you have not given her leave),
I say again, hath made a gross revolt,
Tying her duty, beauty, wit, and fortunes
In an extravagant and wheeling stranger

>   Of here and everywhere.

(I, i, 133–137)

Now convinced of what has occurred, Brabantio calls for help: "Light, I say, light!" (I, i, 144). The imagery of dark and light reflects primarily two themes: one, the white Desdemona and the black Othello, and two, the goodness of Desdemona and Othello in contrast to the evil of Iago.

Once Brabantio has responded, Iago leaves quickly. Although he gives Roderigo an excuse about the importance of appearing loyal to Othello (I, i, 155–157), who is about to go to war, Iago in fact does not want to be discovered in these circumstances. After Iago scurries away, Brabantio appears on the street, and, after disjointedly shouting his anger, vows to find Othello, thus demonstrating how effective Iago's tactics can be.

In scene ii the tone of the play changes as Othello takes over. From his first lines he appears self-assured, in command of himself and his world. Speaking to Iago, who pretends concern over Brabantio's fury, Othello remains calm:

>   Let him do his spite;
> My services which I have done the signiory
> Shall out-tongue his complaints. 'Tis yet to know—
> Which, when I know that boasting is an honor,
> I shall [provulgate]—I fetch my life and being
> From men of royal siege, and my demerits
> May speak, unbonneted, to as proud a fortune
> As this that I have reach'd; for know, Iago,
> But that I love the gentle Desdemona,
> I would not my unhoused free condition
> Put into circumscription and confine
> For the sea's worth.

(I, ii, 17–28)

His fierce pride shines through. Othello has never known failure, and he cannot imagine it. The speech also reveals his singular naivete, his willingness to trust society's sense of justice. He has triumphed in war, he reasons, and he is of noble stock. Therefore the world must respect him. His view of life is simple, and it leaves him vulnerable to one such as Iago.

Other characteristics of Othello gradually appear. One, he is used to dealing in military matters, and thus solely with men. Two, he is a soldier, and lives by a soldier's code based on honor. Three, he is not experienced in a cosmopolitan social setting, and his lack of sophistication proves part of his downfall.

Cassio enters with news that Othello is needed immediately to deal with a military emergency (I, ii, 39–47). But Othello first goes back to his house, and Iago explains the reason:

>   Faith, he to-night hath boarded a land carrack,
>   If it prove lawful prize, he's made for ever.

(I, ii, 50–51)

Cassio fails to grasp this oblique, if nasty, description of marriage, and his ingenuousness anticipates his eventual downfall.

When Brabantio rushes in with sword ready for action, Iago comically deflates the moment by choosing Roderigo as his opponent (I, ii, 58). Othello's dignity temporarily disarms the protests, but Brabantio launches into his accusation. He is unable to understand the behavior of his daughter, for Desdemona has shunned "The wealthy curled [darlings] of our nation . . . " (I, ii, 68), someone like Roderigo, and instead turned "to the sooty bosom/Of such a thing as thou . . . " (I, ii, 70–71). In the face of such insult, Othello remains calm: "Whither will you that I go/To answer this your charge?" (I, ii, 84–85). Othello, however, is needed by the Duke, and thus in scene iii the action moves to a council-chamber.

Before Brabantio's party appears, however, the Duke and his counselors must deal with a threat from outside Venice: a Turkish fleet moving on Cyprus, which in 1570, the time of the play, was a colony of Venice. The first Senator warns the others:

> We must not think the Turk is so unskillful
> To leave that latest which concerns him first,
> Neglecting an attempt of ease and gain
> To wake and wage a danger profitless.

> (I, iii, 27–30)

Throughout the play the threat of the Turkish invaders, the invasion of barbarism into civilization, parallels the intrusion by Iago into the lives of Othello and Desdemona.

Brabantio rushes in amidst the chaos caused by war, and the extent of the disorder is apparent in the Duke's salutation to Othello (I, iii, 48–49) and his overlooking Brabantio, a fellow Senator. Brabantio then shouts the fate of his daughter:

> She is abus'd, stol'n from me, and corrupted
> By spells and medicines bought of mountebanks . . .

> (I, iii, 60–61)

And he accuses the Moor. Othello protests his innocence as well as his own humility (I, iii, 81–89). But Brabantio raves that his daughter could never willingly consent to such a marriage:

> It is a judgment main'd, and most imperfect,
> That will confess perfection so could err
> Against all rules of nature, and must be driven
> To find out practices of cunning hell
> Why this should be.

> (I, iii, 99–104)

The notion of Desdemona's acting against her nature returns at a startling moment.

The first Senator challenges Othello about the matter of whether he used drugs or magic to win Desdemona, and the Moor in response tells the story not only of their courtship but of his own life. After asking Iago to bring Desdemona, Othello recites a tale of extravagant adventure that emphasizes the bravery and

pride he has manifested thus far. Then he describes Desdemona's reaction to a
similar account he offered her:

> My story being done,
> She gave me for my pains a world of [sighs];
> She swore, in faith 'twas strange, 'twas passing strange;
> 'Twas pitiful, 'twas wondrous pitiful.
> She wish'd she had not heard it, yet she wish'd
> That heaven had made her such a man. She thank'd me,
> And bade me, if I had a friend that lov'd her,
> I should but teach him how to tell my story,
> And that would woo her.
>
> (I, iii, 158–166)

Here is the crux of their relationship. Desdemona fell in love not with a man,
but with an image of a man, an idealized version she drew from the stories he
told her. Even Othello understands as much: "She lov'd me for the dangers I
had pass'd" (I, iii, 167). He recognizes that she hardly knows him, but that she
finds him an object of fascination. He confesses, too, that he is taken with her
because she is taken with him: "And I lov'd her that she did pity them" (I, ii,
168). "Pity" in the Elizabethan context also has connotations of love, but,
nonetheless, he really does not know her, either. The two have married as
strangers, as if captivated with one another's portraits. Still, the intensity of their
affection is understandable, for even the Duke is impressed by Othello's narrative:
"I think this tale would win my daughter too" (I, iii, 171).

When Desdemona enters and speaks, she reveals her own strength:

> My noble father,
> I do perceive here a divided duty:
> To you I am bound for life and education;
> My life and education both do learn me
> How to respect you; you are the lord of duty;
> I am hitherto your daughter. But here's my husband;
> And so much duty as my mother show'd
> To you, preferring you before her father,
> So much I challenge that I may profess
> Due to the Moor, my lord.
>
> (I, iii, 180–189)

Her sentences are balanced, her tone resolute. She is a young woman of forceful
intelligence, and at her statement Brabantio is forced to withdraw his accusation
(I, iii, 189–198). The Duke urges reconciliation, and Brabantio offers sour
agreement:

> So let the Turk of Cyprus us beguile,
> We lose it not, so long as we can smile.
>
> (I, iii, 210–211)

Othello is then appointed to lead the war against the Turks, and asks that Desdemona be cared for properly during his campaign (I, iii, 231–239). Brabantio

turns down the suggestion that she stay at his home, but before any decision can be made, Desdemona exerts her own will:

> I saw Othello's visage in his mind,
> And to his honors and his valiant parts
> Did I my soul and fortunes consecrate.

(I, iii, 252–254)

The use of "visage" reminds us that Desdemona and Othello have fallen in love with each other's idealized image. Furthermore, the concept of "honors" will return in a most ironic context. Desdemona then requests that she be allowed to accompany her husband to Cyprus. Othello reaffirms her request, taking care to anticipate reservations others may have:

> Let her have your voice.
> Vouch with me, heaven, I therefore beg it not
> To please the palate of my appetite,
> Nor to comply with heat (the young affects
> In [me] defunct) and proper satisfaction;
> But to be free and bounteous to her mind.

(I, iii, 260–265)

He also claims that he will not be distracted from his duties (I, iii, 266–274). We cannot be certain if he wants to emphasize the spiritual qualities of their relationship or whether he downplays the physical aspect of the marriage to avoid offending anyone. In either case, we may assume that he is conscious of the racial difference between himself and Desdemona.

This awareness suggests two other aspects of Othello's personality. First, he may have a hidden doubt about Desdemona's devotion. Perhaps at this moment the doubt is miniscule, even subconscious. But if it exists, then we better understand Iago's subsequent success in making Othello insane with jealousy. Iago does not plant suspicion inside Othello. Rather the seed is there from the start, and Iago brilliantly cultivates it.

Second, as a black man alone in a white society, Othello is self-conscious. During the rest of the play his race is rarely mentioned, and many city officials speak to him respectfully, but no matter how much pride Othello manifests, the early insults from Brabantio clarify that Othello's skin color and background make him an alien in Venice. Consequently when Iago applies pressure, Othello is isolated, with no one to trust. He is therefore intensely vulnerable to hints of fallibility or weakness, and when he becomes suspicious of Desdemona, he can only turn his self-doubt inward, where it is intensified by an unspoken estrangement from the white environment.

The Duke consents to Othello's request, requesting only that Othello proceed quickly. In another moment that has ironic repercussions, Othello entrusts Desdemona's passage to Iago:

> So please your Grace, my ancient:
> A man he is of honesty and trust.

> To his conveyance I assign my wife.
>
> (I, iii, 283–285)

Often characters refer to Iago as "honest," and on each occasion, as we sense Iago smiling inside, we smile, too. Brabantio has one word of warning:

> Look to her, Moor, if thou hast eyes to see;
> She has deceiv'd her father, and may thee.
>
> (I, iii, 292–293)

The advice will be recalled by Iago at an opportune moment for him. The imagery of sight, too, will be relevant, in particular concerning the distinction between what Othello actually sees and what he imagines. At this moment, though, his trust is absolute: "My life upon her faith!" (I, iii, 294).

Then Desdemona departs, having proven herself honest and strong. She soon proves herself also moral and sublimely devoted to her husband. Nevertheless, her virtues, when combined with Othello's, invite disaster. Both are wrapped up in their own needs and feelings, and when faced with a crisis, neither is able to turn to the other for support.

Iago and Roderigo are left alone, with the latter threatening to drown himself over Desdemona. Iago scoffs at the thought:

> Ere I would say I
> would drown myself for the love of a guinea hen,
> I would change my humanity with a baboon . . .
> Virtue? a fig! 'tis in ourselves that we are
> thus or thus.
>
> (I, iii, 314–316, 319–320)

He dismisses emotion, and reduces all human activity to the law of the jungle. Only the strong-willed should survive. Iago also takes pains to clarify that he is not vulnerable to desire:

> . . . why, the power and corrigible
> authority of this lies in our wills. If the [beam] of our
> lives had not one scale of reason to poise another of
> sensuality, the blood and baseness of our natures would
> conduct us to most prepost'rous conclusions. But we
> have reason to cool our raging motions, our carnal
> stings, [our] unbitted lusts; whereof I take this that
> you call love to be a sect or scion.
>
> (I, iii, 325–332)

Throughout the play Iago delights in sneering at human affection, particularly love between a man and a woman: "It is merely a lust of the blood and a permission of the will. Come, be a man!" (I, ii, 334–335). He regularly offers this charge for masculine behavior, as if convinced that anyone who surrenders to such instincts is worthless. He then assures Roderigo that Desdemona and

Othello cannot possibly remain devoted to each other, and again his comments indicate contempt for women:

> She must change
> for youth; when she is sated with his body, she
> will find the [error] of her choice.

(I, iii, 349–351)

Thus any commitment they share is easily shattered:

> If sanctimony and a frail vow betwixt an erring
> barbarian and [a] super-subtle Venetian be not too hard
> for my wits and all the tribe of hell, thou shalt enjoy
> her; therefore make money.

(I, iii, 355–358)

Iago's scorn of sexuality and emotional bonds of any kind suggests another character from Shakespearean tragedy: Mercutio in *Romeo and Juliet*. The comparison may seem outlandish, for Mercutio is a rollicking fellow whose zest dominates a considerable portion of the play. Consider, however, Mercutio's fundamental flaw, which Romeo explains succinctly: "He jests at scars that never felt a wound" (*Romeo and Juliet*, II, ii, 1). Mercutio is unable to give himself to love, unwilling or unable to feel deep affection, and he masks this frustration with laughter. So affable is his manner, though, and so sharp his wit that his attitude is enjoyable.

Yet Mercutio's frustration takes another form: as an eagerness to fight, to release energy that has no other emotional outlet. After all, what is wit but hostility tempered by intellect? Nevertheless, at times Mercutio's mind is helpless against other forces within him, and in those moments he is dominated by an uncontrollable temper. That is the reason he fights with Tybalt.

But imagine Mercutio's frustration were greater than it is. Imagine he lacked his capacity for social interaction and conviviality. Imagine a man, therefore, of greater acrimony. He would turn into Iago.

Both characters offer sharp wordplay. Both take considerable pleasure in their own company, and both view themselves as superior. Iago, however, bears two greater burdens. One, he is trapped in a marriage which, as we shall see, is loveless. Two, his estimate of his own worth is not matched by his stature in the world nor by anyone else's opinion. Thus his virulence is compounded, as is his need to express it.

Finally, Iago's misery is aggravated by the presence of Othello. Here is a black man, an alien, who is Iago's master. Not only in battle and the social sphere, but sexually as well. Othello and Desdemona share a profound love beyond Iago's capability, and in return Iago is forced to contemplate his failure as a citizen, as a man, and as a human being. Driven by these impulses, he embarks on a mission of dissolution against everything he wants to be but cannot be; everything he sees that reminds him of his own deficiencies; everything that

unintentionally mocks his weaknesses and exacerbates the private humiliation
he bears daily.

Thus we better understand Iago's delight in disorder. He prizes anything that
tweaks the establishment and traditional values. His goal is to reduce everyone
to the emotional rubble that is his soul. He treasures playing the sycophant,
embodying in his toadyism and false amiability the fraudulence of his world and
his supremacy over it. And his malicious laughter is part of a wide-ranging desire
to subvert all institutions, social and moral.

Such a profile would explain Iago's general antagonism. It does not explain
his specific goal in the play (''my peculiar end''), and we wonder about that as
well. We must also remember, however, that Iago does not understand himself.
Even in his soliloquies, where dramatic convention holds that he tell the truth,
he offers instead what he pretends to himself is the truth about his ultimate
desires. For instance, after Roderigo leaves him here, Iago rationalizes his hatred:

> I hate the Moor,
> And it is thought abroad that 'twixt my sheets
> [H'as] done my office. I know not if 't be true,
> But I, for mere suspicion in that kind,
> Will do as if for surety.

(I, iii, 386–390)

The thought that Othello has slept with Emilia is ludicrous, and a man as keen
as Iago could not possibly believe it. Indeed, he virtually admits as much. But
the reason for his hatred remains an enigma to him, and thus he uses this concept
as reason for subsequent action. All he knows is that he wants to bring Othello
and Desdemona down to his level, to demonstrate that because of their innate
goodness, they are weaker than he:

> The Moor is of a free and open nature,
> That thinks men honest that but seem to be so,
> And will tenderly be led by th' nose,
> As asses are.

(I, iii, 399–402)

In his last two lines here, Iago puts his role in life into his own perspective:

> I have't. It is engendered. Hell and night
> Must bring this monstrous birth to the world's light.

(I, iii, 403–404)

He identifies with the devil, and the word ''monstrous'' echoes through the play
ominously.

In Act II, scene i, the action shifts to Cyprus, where Montano and two
gentlemen discuss that the ever-dangerous Turkish forces have suffered serious
losses. This area is a colony of Venice, but it is closer to raw, primitive life,
and thus symbolically Othello and Desdemona are more susceptible to attack
from subversive forces. Othello remains at sea while Cassio has come to assume

authority (II, i, 26–29). Iago has already disparaged Cassio as "bookish" (I, i, 24) and otherwise unmanly, and when Cassio does appear, he conducts himself with extreme dignity, especially when describing Desdemona to those who inquire about Othello's wife:

> . . . he hath achiev'd a maid
> That paragons description and wild fame;
> One that excels the quirks of blazoning pens,
> And in th' essential vesture of creation,
> Does tire the [ingener].
>
> (II, i, 61–65)

The flattery is excessive, and suggests that Cassio's stiff formality is a front. Such a deceptive pose in tandem with his pride in his rank helps bring about Cassio's undoing.

Iago, Desdemona, and the others enter, and Cassio continues his courtly behavior, kissing Emilia. These manners inspire Iago to toss at the women a series of barbs that the listeners take as good humored, but which we recognize as reflecting Iago's genuine feeling:

> Come on, come on; you are pictures out [a'doors],
> Bells in your parlors, wild-cats in your kitchens,
> Saints in your injuries, devils being offended,
> Players in your huswifery, and huswives in your beds.
>
> (II, i, 109–112)

When challenged about his boldness, Iago stands forth tellingly: "Nay, it is true, or else I am a Turk" (II, i, 114). Always Iago puts up a gracious style. Were his outward manner a true reflection of his inner state, he would be sullen and dislikeable. But a crucial ingredient in his success is the charm that allows him to win the confidence of others. The reference to the "Turk" keeps the parallel to Iago in our minds.

When Iago sees Cassio turn his graceful manners to Desdemona by kissing her hand, Iago is delighted:

> He takes her by the palm; ay, well
> said, whisper. With as little a web as this will I en-
> snare as great a fly as Cassio.
>
> (II, i, 167–169)

Throughout the play Iago seizes the salient weakness of those he dislikes, and exploits that weakness to his own ends.

Othello enters in triumph and greets Desdemona: "O my fair warrior!" (II, i, 182), a strange greeting from husband to wife. Moments later he adds:

> If it were now to die,
> 'Twere now to be most happy; for I fear
> My soul hath her content so absolute
> That not another comfort like to this

Succeeds in unknown fate.

(II, i, 189–193)

This statement seems to be an expression of limitless devotion, how in marrying
Desdemona Othello has done all he can. And ironically such is the case. These
two people share an idealistic love; that passion is their glory. But it exists on
so exalted a plane that it cannot survive the impending assault by reality. That
purity leads to their tragedy. Here they depart in joy after victory over the Turks,
but Iago clarifies that the real struggle has yet to start:

O, you are well tun'd now!
But I'll set down the pegs that make this music,
As honest as I am.

(II, i, 199–201)

Images of music and intonation are used throughout Shakespeare's plays to reflect
social and political order. Conversely, Iago's frequent expressions of disharmony
reflect the chaos he unleashes. The discord Othello has repelled on the military
and political front is soon to enter his life more personally, as we are aware
when he instructs Iago: "Go to the bay and disembark my coffers" (II, i, 208).
Othello does not know where the real enemy lies.

Roderigo and Iago are again left alone, and again Iago lets loose his venom.
He continues to dwell on what he imagines will be Desdemona's inevitable
distaste for Othello:

Her eye must be fed; and what delight
shall she have to look on the devil? When the
blood is made dull with the act of sport, there should
be, [again] to inflame it and to give satiety a fresh
appetite, loveliness in favor, sympathy in years,
manners, and beauties—all which the Moor is defective in.

(II, i, 225–231)

His attack slanders both Desdemona and Othello. Women, he insinuates, value
a man only for the physical pleasure he provides. And this accusation massages
the wounded ego of Iago. His apparent lack of success with women is therefore
excusable, because they are not worthy of him. They cannot appreciate him.
Hence he is right not to bother with them. Othello, on the other hand, wants to
satisfy Desdemona, but is incapable of doing so. As always, Iago's explanations
contribute to his plot, but also reflect the inner workings of his mind.

Iago eventually advises Roderigo to start a fight with Cassio, who, according
to Iago, is the main rival for Desdemona (II, i, 245–248). Once Roderigo departs,
Iago again rouses himself to action, and some critics see this speech as proof
that Iago's goal is a desire to win Desdemona for his own:

Now I do love her too,
Not out of absolute lust (though peradventure

I stand accomptant for as great a sin).
But partly led to diet my revenge.
For that I do suspect the lusty Moor
Hath leap'd into my seat; the thought whereof
Doth (like a poisonous mineral) gnaw my inwards;
And nothing can or shall content my soul
Till I am even'd with him, wife for wife;
Or failing so, yet that I put the Moor
At least into a jealousy so strong
That judgment cannot cure.

(II, i, 291–302)

What a convoluted expression. Iago claims that he desires Desdemona, but at once he throttles this emotion. Perhaps he is shocked at his own words, and to comfort himself immediately insists that he wants her for reasons other than lust, which he relentlessly disparages. He does not have real affection for her, he tells himself; he simply wants to possess her. Once more he urges himself on by asserting that Othello slept with Emilia, and he confesses that he allows the thought to pain him. Finally he admits that should his fantasy of possessing Desdemona fail, he is almost as content to see her relationship with Othello ruined. To interpret this speech as evidence of conscious love for Desdemona is a misreading. He does not consciously desire anything or anyone, but seeks instead the destruction of all around him. Yet somewhere, deep within him, lies desire of some kind.

The very brief scene ii announces a festival to celebrate the defeat of the Turkish forces, and the atmosphere of revelry provides an ideal background against which Iago may unleash his plan. For at the beginning of scene iii, Othello cautions the revelers:

Let's teach ourselves that honorable stop,
Not to outsport discretion.

(II, iii, 2–3)

Cassio's confident reply leads us to anticipate that his bounds of decorum will soon be exceeded.

When Iago enters, he starts breaking down Cassio's propriety with suggestive remarks about Desdemona, but Cassio resists (II, iii, 14–29). Iago then proposes that drinking begin in earnest, but Cassio demurs: "I have very poor and unhappy brains for drinking" (II, iii, 33–34). Such a stiff-necked attitude reminds us of other teetotalers in Shakespearean plays, characters such as Angelo in *Measure for Measure*, Prince John in *Henry IV, Part 2*, Octavius Caesar in *Antony and Cleopatra*, and Malvolio in *Twelfth Night*. All are portrayed with little sympathy. On the other hand, those who overindulge, like Falstaff, as long as they are not vicious, are generally portrayed kindly. Here Cassio's abstinence becomes a point of vulnerability, as Iago notes (II, iii, 48–51). After Cassio exits to call in the other celebrants, Iago also reveals that he managed to make three young

Cypriot guards drunk (II, iii, 55–58). The local rulers will thus be sensitive to the infiltrating behavior of the Venetians, and Othello will be under greater pressure to be rid of Cassio when the lieutenant is found intoxicated.

The others return, and the party gets underway with obscene songs and ditties. True to his prediction, the inexperienced Cassio becomes obnoxiously drunk to such an extent that he loses control. He is clearly unaccustomed to talking in casual circumstances, and thus when his defenses are lowered, he blunders by insulting Iago about the difference in their ranks: " . . . the/lieutenant is to be sav'd before the ancient" (II, iii, 109–110). When Cassio staggers off, Iago feigns sadness at his condition, which he hints to Montano is chronic:

> I fear the trust Othello puts in him,
> On some odd time of his infirmity,
> Will shake this island.

(II, iii, 126–128)

A few lines later, Montano broods on the deceptive appearance Cassio presents to Othello:

> Perhaps he sees it not, or his good nature
> Prizes the virtue that appears in Cassio,
> And looks not on his evils.

(II, iii, 133–135)

That Montano expresses this thought to Iago, whom it characterizes perfectly, is one more dramatic irony in a play filled with them.

The row between Roderigo and Cassio starts, and Iago sends Roderigo off to spread further trouble (II, iii, 157). When Othello enters to quell the disorder, his language reflects the larger predicament:

> Are we turn'd Turks, and to ourselves do that
> Which heaven hath forbid the Ottomites?

(II, iii, 170–171)

The play soon dramatizes that the primitive barbarism the Venetians think they have eradicated lurks within their own society, while Othello is to discover such dangerous instincts within himself.

The revelers are reluctant to explain what has happened, and Iago himself simulates puzzlement. He describes Cassio and Roderigo as being as close as "bride and groom" (II, iii, 180), and the reference hints at Othello's being dragged from his marriage bed to settle this squabble. No doubt Iago, with malicious wit, means for the line to upset Othello even more. Othello's fury rises, and his language again has ironic ramifications:

> My blood begins my safer guides to rule,
> And passion, having my best judgment collied,

Assays to lead the way.

(II, iii, 205–207)

Before long this description of blood and passion running wild is tragically apt. Othello ends his demand by ordering his ensign: "Tis monstrous. Iago, who began't?" (II, iii, 217). At the word "monstrous," we recall Iago's oath to himself in the last line of Act I.

Iago, with seeming reluctance, recounts his own version of the fight, and slyly puts the blame on Cassio:

> Though Cassio did some little wrong to him,
> As men in rage strike those that wish them best,
> Yet surely Cassio, I believe, receiv'd
> From him that fled some strange indignity
> Which patience could not pass.

(II, iii, 242–246)

Othello believes this recounting, and, foreshadowing a more profound betrayal, dismisses Cassio: "Cassio, I love thee,/But never more be officer of mine" (II, iii, 248–249). As if to aid in Iago's plan, Desdemona appears at this moment to see Cassio's humiliation. Othello declares a version of martial law (II, iii, 255–256), and once more we are struck by Othello's trusting Iago as an instrument of order.

Cassio is left alone with Iago, who continues his astonishing masquerade of innocence. Cassio mourns his lost reputation (II, ii, 262–265), but Iago scorns this attitude and suggests that Cassio take his case to Desdemona: "Our general's wife is now the general" (II, iii, 314–315). The remark also reflects Iago's disdain for a man who allows his life to be run by a woman. His description of Desdemona (II, iii, 319–322) is accurate. Yet Iago hopes that these attributes will be Desdemona's downfall.

Left alone, Iago again reviews Desdemona's qualities, and we recognize that he is aware of her fineness. Indeed, that she is so worthy a person is part of his pleasure:

> So will I turn her virtue into pitch,
> And out of her own goodness make the net
> That shall enmesh them all.

(II, iii, 360–362)

He is consciously perverse, as his references to "Divinity of hell!" (II, iii, 350), and "devils" (II, iii, 351) confirm. After he dismisses Roderigo with the guarantee that all plans are proceeding smoothly, Iago stands utterly self-assured.

In Act III, scene i, a brief interlude with the clown provides relief, but the character is undeveloped and in fact unnecessary. This play needs no such respite, because Iago serves as his own foil and gives us as well a comic counterpoint. Here, for instance, after he promises to aid Cassio win back Othello's favor (III, i, 36–39), Cassio muses foolishly: "I never knew a Florentine more kind and honest'' (III, i, 40). The plot continues to move energetically, as Cassio requests audience with Desdemona, and Emilia hints that her mistress is already sympathetic: "And she speaks for you stoutly" (III, i, 44). In scene ii, Othello is involved in business, and this distraction is further indication why he is susceptible to the complications to be imposed by Iago.

In scene iii Emilia shows how little understanding she has of her husband, as she comments on his attitude toward Cassio's predicament: "I warrant it grieves my husband/As if the cause were his" (III, iii, 3–4). Desdemona's reply indicates that she, too, is taken in by this "honest fellow" (III, iii, 5). After Cassio pleads his case, Desdemona reassures him, and again we feel the tragic irony:

> Therefore be merry, Cassio,
> For thy solicitor shall rather die
> Then give thy cause away.
>
> (III, iii, 26–28)

Such will be the course of events.

Iago starts his attack on Othello's mind with an improvisatory remark as Cassio departs: "Hah? I like not that" (III, iii, 34). This vague exclamation is supplemented with one more suggestion:

> Cassio, my lord? No, sure, I cannot think it,
> That he would steal away so guilty-like,
> Seeing you coming.
>
> (III, iii, 38–40)

The picture leaves Othello out of balance, just as Desdemona starts talking. She asks for Cassio's restoration to his former position, and Othello puts her off: "Not now, sweet Desdemon, some other time" (III, iii, 55). But part of her character is her boldness, and she persists, almost demanding to hear the time and place when he will listen to her (III, iii, 60–74). Eventually Othello answers more strongly:

> Prithee no more, let him come when he will;
> I will deny thee nothing.
>
> (III, iii, 75–76)

Even this response does not satisfy Desdemona, and she gently admonishes Othello for his testiness:

> Nay, when I have a suit
> Wherein I mean to touch your love indeed,
> It shall be full of poise and difficult weight,
> And fearful to be granted.
>
> (III, iii, 80–83)

She does not expect every minor request to be a test of her devotion. When she offers an opinion, it is to be regarded seriously. These assertions, though, are being presented in front of Iago, and Othello is uneasy:

> I will deny thee nothing;
> Whereon, I do beseech thee, grant me this,
> To leave me but a little to myself.
>
> (III, iii, 83–85)

The matter itself is trifling, but here again Shakespeare creates a situation where the leading characters' strengths turn into flaws. We have already considered Desdemona's independence. Othello's most distinctive characteristic is the pride that allows him to bear up under the enormous pressure from the world in which he finds himself. At this moment, as Desdemona leaves, that pride is vulnerable.

First, however, Othello seems to reaffirm his love for her:

> Excellent wretch! Perdition catch my soul
> But I do love thee! and when I love thee not,
> Chaos is come again.
>
> (III, iii, 90–92)

He is ashamed for speaking harshly to her, and dismisses ill thoughts. But the threat of "chaos" remains in our minds as well as in his.

The rest of the scene is remarkable, as Iago arouses suspicion and encourages its spreading through Othello's mind. For the audience the process creates an astonishing mixture of emotion. On one hand we are pained at Othello's vulnerability and horrified by the rage into which he ultimately falls. On the other hand we are transfixed and even reluctantly admiring of Iago's skill, insight, and wit.

When Iago hesitantly begins, Othello is disturbed by Iago's repetitions:

> [By heaven], thou echo'st me,
> As if there were some monster in thy thought
> Too hideous to be shown.
>
> (III, iii, 106–108)

Virtually every line in this scene has similarly ironic overtones, as Othello hits at the truth but remains unaware. A bit later he almost demands to be told:

> I prithee speak to me as to thy thinkings,
> As thou dost ruminate, and give thy worst of thoughts
> The worst of words.
>
> (III, iii, 131–133)

"Worst" has an unintentional dual meaning: either "the most painful" possibility or Iago's own "most vicious" image. We also realize Iago's delight:

> Though I perchance am vicious in my guess
> (As I confess it is my nature's plague
> To spy into abuses, and [oft] my jealousy

Shapes faults that are not) . . .

(III, iii, 145–148)

He downplays his capacity for understanding, but is, in these lines, being truthful.

Earlier, when Cassio mourned the loss of his reputation (II, iii, 263–265), Iago dismissed such concerns. Here Iago takes the opposite tact:

Who steals my purse steals trash . . .
But he that filches from me my good name
Robs me of that which not enriches him,
And makes me poor indeed.

(III, iii, 157–161)

He then cautions Othello against jealousy, "the green-ey'd monster" (III, iii, 166), but in the next sentence mentions the cuckold unaware of his wife's infidelity.

Yet Othello is not innately jealous and manages to regain some control:

No, Iago,
I'll see before I doubt; when I doubt, prove;
And on the proof, there is no more but this—
Away at once with love or jealousy!

(III, iii, 189–192)

At this resolution Iago seems to withdraw his implications. But suddenly he recalls Brabantio's warning (I, ii, 292): "She did deceive her father, marrying you . . . " (III, iii, 206). Then, as if attempting to hypnotize Othello, Iago asserts several times that Othello seems "moved," and the repetition does in fact depress Othello further until he offers a tormenting thought: "And yet how nature erring from itself—" (III, iii, 227).

This line, an echo of Brabantio's words (I, iii, 101), may be regarded as the climax of the play, for that Othello even considers the possibility of Desdemona's betraying him is the start of his dissolution. Within a few lines he moans:

Why did I marry? This honest creature, doubtless,
Sees and knows more, much more, than he unfolds.

(III, iii, 242–243)

The profound agony of his first four words and the ironic accuracy of the rest of the speech encapsulizes the power of this scene. Left alone, Othello lets his thoughts wander, and they leave him helpless:

Haply, for I am black,
And have not those soft parts of conversation
That chamberers have, or for I am declin'd
Into the value of years (yet that's not much),
She's gone.

(III, iii, 263–267)

Until this scene Othello seemed absolutely confident, perhaps excessively so. Here he reveals that beneath his prideful manner he feels inferiority on two

counts: his race and his age. Such vulnerability makes his collapse more understandable:

> I am abus'd, and my relief
> Must be to loathe her. O curse of marriage!
> That we can call these delicate creatures ours,
> And not their appetites!
>
> (III, iii, 267–270)

This last sentence sounds as if it came directly from Iago.

As Desdemona enters, Othello once more resists the possibility of her unfaithfulness:

> If she be false, [O then] heaven [mocks] itself!
> I'll not believe't.
>
> (III, iii, 278–279)

When Desdemona sees him suffering, she asks the cause. He indicates a pain
in his forehead, a pain we may take as psychological. She then takes out a
handkerchief, which Othello pushes away and Desdemona drops, and they leave.
She loses the handkerchief not out of neglect but out of a greater concern for
his well-being.

Emilia picks up the handkerchief, and realizes that it is one Iago has long
sought (III, iii, 290–296). We are not sure why he has wanted it, and neither is
Emilia. We are even more puzzled when moments later she allows him to take
it (III, iii, 315). Emilia's behavior in this scene and several subsequent scenes
is confusing, for she seems torn between loyalty to her husband and devotion
to her mistress. On the one hand, as will become evident, she is in some respects
worldly, especially about men. But she is still capable of being deceived by
Iago. True, everyone else in the play is also his victim, but then Emilia knows
him best, yet is still blind to his motives.

Left alone, Iago ruminates with satisfaction upon his success thus far, twice
invoking "poison," which he recognizes as his weapon (III, iii, 325, 326).
When Othello returns, he is plagued by doubt (III, iii, 336–337), and his ignorance about this portion of his life makes the rest meaningless:

> Farewell the tranquil mind! farewell content!
> Farewell the plumed troops and the big wars
> That makes ambition virtue!
>
> (III, iii, 348–350)

Once more he reverts to his faith: "Villain, be sure thou prove my love a whore
. . . " (III, iii, 359). And he takes Iago by the throat, demanding evidence.

Iago's performance here reaches new heights:

> Are you a man? Have you a soul? or sense?
> God buy you; take mine office. O wretched fool,
> That lov'st to make thine honesty a vice!
> O monstrous world! Take note, take note, O world,

> To be direct and honest is not safe.
>
> (III, iii, 374–378)

Again Iago raises the matter of manhood. He finds pleasure in other men's sufferings, as they, infatuated with women, are subject to weakness to which he, Iago, is immune. Perhaps this constant harping on that theme indicates his doubts about his own masculinity. And once more the word ''monstrous'' has ironic implications.

Othello now is torn between conflicting visions:

> I think my wife be honest, and think she is not;
> I think that thou art just, and think thou art not.
>
> (III, iii, 384–385)

Faced with the call for proof, Iago sets his imagination whirling:

> Would you, the [supervisor], grossly gape on?
> Behold her topp'd?
>
> (III, iii, 395–396)

The picture not only drives Othello further but satisfies Iago's own desires:

> It is impossible you should see this,
> Were they prime as goats, as hot as monkeys,
> As salt as wolves in pride, and fools as gross
> As ignorance made drunk.
>
> (III, iii, 402–405)

He has always enjoyed reducing human sexuality to bestial behavior. Then Iago creates his own pornographic image of himself sleeping near Cassio, who supposedly mutters lasciviously in his sleep about Desdemona and simultaneously embraces Iago and curses Othello (III, iii, 413–426). Othello, far gone, takes this fantasy as reality, and for the rest of the play is unable to distinguish truth from falsehood. He has demanded to ''see'' truth, but his own imagination takes over. Tragically, the one person who is always true to him, Desdemona, is the one person he will not trust. She is always what she says she is. But Othello never realizes her honesty. Of all the ironies in the plays, this is the most profound.

Iago mentions the missing handkerchief (which he holds), then adds one more sickening detail:

> I know not that; but such a handkerchief
> (I am sure it was your wive's) did I to-day
> See Cassio wipe his beard with.
>
> (III, iii, 437–439)

The sexual overtones drive Othello over the edge:

> Arise, black vengeance, from the hollow hell!
> Yield up, O love, thy crowned and hearted throne
> To tyrannous hate! Swell, bosom, with thy fraught,

For 'tis of aspics' tongues!

(III, iii, 447–450)

Then comes the final call: "O blood, blood, blood!" (III, iii, 451), a virtual call to the devil. Othello then kneels and swears his vengeance, and Iago, in one more moment of horror and irony, joins him, kneeling in a parody of a religious ceremony. They part together, Iago swearing his fidelity: "I am your own for ever" (III, iii, 479).

This last line has suggested to some critics that Iago's subconscious desire in destroying the marriage of Desdemona and Othello is a deep-seated homosexual love for Othello. Moreover, the text may be dramatized from such a perspective, particularly this last scene, which may be played with Iago literally hanging on Othello, embracing him in confidence. And Iago's imagining himself lying near Cassio is sometimes offered as further evidence. The description is imaginary, but that Iago even conceives this picture could hint that these desires are within him. Nonetheless, this theory seems a distortion. Iago is married, and Emilia gives no proof that he has any such leanings. Furthermore, Iago provides no evidence of homosexual desires in his soliloquies.

In scene iv Desdemona is perturbed over the loss of her handkerchief, but retains faith in her husband:

> . . . and but my noble Moor
> Is true of mind, and made of no such baseness
> As jealous creatures are, it were enough
> To put him to ill thinking.

(III, iv, 26–29)

The irony of these lines is painful, as is Emilia's reluctance to admit that she gave the handkerchief to Iago. We also note Emilia's reaction of surprise to the assertion that Othello is not jealous (III, iv, 29). Emilia knows far too much about men to believe any man immune.

Othello enters, still obsessed with what he believes is Desdemona's faithlessness, and his language is full of words that have sexual connotations, including "liberal" (III, iv, 38), "hot" (III, iv, 39), and "moist" (III, iv, 39). He then asks for the handkerchief, explaining that it was originally given to his mother by an Egyptian (III, iv, 55), and that "there's magic in the web of it" (III, iv, 69). This line contradicts the earlier scene when to Brabantio Othello denied he ever used magic in the courtship (I, iii). We cannot be certain whether Othello is lying here, or whether the handkerchief actually has magical properties. More important, his request sets Desdemona lying, as she claims it is not lost (III, iv, 83). The repetition of Othello's order for the handkerchief (III, iv, 92–96) is unnerving both to those onstage and in the audience, and Desdemona unintentionally exacerbates the tension by retorting with Cassio's name. We feel Othello ready to snap. Here he stalks off, but his temper is enough to bring out Emilia's reflections on all men:

> 'Tis not a year or two shows us a man:
> They are all but stomachs, and we all but food;
> They eat us hungerly, and when they are full

They belch us.

(III, iv, 103–106)

Emilia's words are no doubt based primarily on her marriage to Iago, and confirm
the callous attitude towards sexuality he has demonstrated. But again we wonder
why Emilia does not tell Desdemona what happened to the handkerchief. Perhaps
Emilia is afraid of being punished for her negligence. Perhaps she is angry with
Othello for his attitude and unwilling to placate him. Perhaps she is jealous of
the love Desdemona and Othello share. Whatever the reason, Emilia's motivation
remains a problem.

Iago and Cassio then enter, and Cassio once more requests that Desdemona
speak for him. She, however, resists: "My advocation is not now in tune" (III,
iv, 123). The musical image recalls Iago's threat (II, i, 199–201), and reflects
his success. Desdemona then claims that Othello is upset, and her explanation
allows Iago to divert suspicion from himself: "Is my lord angry?" (III, iv, 132).
After Iago describes the extent of Othello's temper and promises to look after
him (III, iv, 134–139), Desdemona is till inclined to forgive him (III, iv, 141–
150). Emilia, though, is less sympathetic:

> They are not ever jealous for the cause,
> But jealous for they're jealous. It is a monster
> Begot upon itself, born on itself.

(III, iv, 160–162)

She uses the familiar word "monster," echoing her husband, and we realize
that however she feels about Iago, he has influenced her thinking. Here is another
example of his "poison." Yet she fails to grasp that in Othello's case jealousy
has another cause.

Left alone, Cassio is joined by Bianca, who claims that he has stayed away
from her for a week (III, iv, 173). To assuage her annoyance, Cassio presents
her with Desdemona's handkerchief, then apologizes for his leaving on the excuse
that Othello would not want to see him with a woman (III, iv, 193–195). But
he agrees to see her later. This deception on Cassio's part, in conjunction with
his unwillingness to stand up for himself, is one more of his weaknesses. The
scene is full of minor indiscretions on the part of Emilia, Desdemona, and Cassio,
all contributing to the atmosphere of which Iago takes advantage.

In Act IV, scene i, Iago is still tormenting Othello, so much so that Othello
is reduced to incoherent phrases that reflect his disjointed mind:

> It is not words that shakes
> me thus. Pish! Noses, ears, and lips. Is't possible?
> Confess? Handkerchief? O devil!

(IV, i, 41–43)

And he falls into an epileptic fit, a collapse that provokes only greater laughter
from Iago (IV, i, 44–47), who reverts to deep concern when Cassio appears (IV,
i, 53–58). Once Cassio has gone, Iago's barrage resumes, as he invokes one of

his favorite phrases: " . . . be a man" (IV, i, 65), then dramatizes the plight of "millions now alive" (IV, i, 67) who have been deceived but are unaware of their misfortune. As always, we understand Iago's insinuations as a way not only to torment Othello, but also to relieve his own frustrations. No doubt he wants to believe that millions of men have been cuckolded so as to satisfy his own perverse values.

Iago next suggests that while he asks Cassio about Desdemona, Othello should hide to overhear the conversation (IV, i, 81–84). The sight of Othello sneaking into cover reflects how far the general has sunk. Meanwhile Iago begins to laugh with Cassio, not about Desdemona, but about Cassio and Bianca (IV, i, 132–136), and the seemingly proper young lieutenant's attempt to match Iago's sneering masculinity is mistaken by Othello for banter about Desdemona:

> Now he tells how she pluck'd him to my
> chamber. O, I see that nose of yours, but not that dog
> I shall throw it to.
>
> (IV, i, 141–143)

The reference to "dog" echoes tellingly later.

Bianca returns in a rage, having decided that Cassio has been unfaithful to her, and that the handkerchief "is some minx's token" (IV, i, 153). A few lines earlier Cassio was full of salacious humor, snickering over the prospect of marriage to Bianca. Now we realize what a pretense that bravado was, for in response to her anger he is helpless: "How now, my sweet Bianca: how now? how now?" (IV, i, 156–157). For all his dignity and courtliness, Cassio is a fraud. At times he acts the role of puritan, while on other occasions he pretends to be a young man on the prowl. At those latter moments, however, he lacks the courage of his desires. As is the case with several of Shakespeare's straight-laced characters, a virtuous front disguises weakness and corruption.

As Cassio races after Bianca to prevent her spreading more rumor (IV, i, 161), Othello bursts out to identify the handkerchief. He rails against Desdemona, but with a sense of loss:

> Hang her, I do but say what she is. So deli-
> cate with her needle! an admirable musician! O, she
> will sing the savageness out of a bear. Of so high and
> plenteous wit and invention!
>
> (IV, i, 187–190)

His anger and sadness unite in an excruciating blend:

> But yet the pity of it,
> Iago! O Iago, the pity of it, Iago!
>
> (IV, i, 195–196)

"Pity" cruelly reminds us of Act I, scene iii, when Othello informed his listeners how Desdemona pitied him.

The next few lines include some of Iago's sharpest. To Othello's shout about being cuckolded, Iago sneers: "O, 'tis foul in her" (IV, i, 201). And when Othello adds: "With mine officer!" (IV, i, 202), Iago's response is full of vicious mockery: "That's fouler" (IV, i, 203). Then Othello threatens to poison Desdemona, and Iago offers perhaps his most depraved suggestion:

> Do it not with poison; strangle her in her bed,
> even the bed she hath contaminated.

(IV, i, 207–208)

Why is he so concerned about Othello's method of murder? Because poison, figuratively if not literally, has been Iago's tool. And the throttling of Desdemona in her own bed would be symbolic rape, as close as Iago could come to sexual gratification.

After Othello enthusiastically agrees to this tableau, Desdemona enters with her cousin Lodovico, the Venetian ambassador. She innocently pleads for Cassio (IV, i, 232–233), unaware that she is driving Othello into greater fury, until perhaps the most shocking moment of the play, when Othello strikes her. He compounds the injustice by making his accusations of Desdemona public:

> Sir, she can turn, and turn; and yet go on
> And turn again; and she can weep, sir, weep;
> And she's obedient, as you say, obedient;
> Very obedient.—Proceed you in your tears.—
> Concerning this, sir—O well-painted passion!—
> I am commanded home.—Get you away;
> I'll send for you anon.—Sir, I obey the mandate,
> And will return to Venice.—Hence, avaunt!

(IV, i, 253–260)

The fragmented sentences reflected the disorder in his mind. And the final phrase before he departs the stage, "Goats and monkeys!" (IV, i, 263), is an echo of Iago's words at Act II, scene iii, 403. The line confirms that Iago's values, his "poison," have come to dominate Othello. Left with Lodovico, Iago reinforces the implications of Othello's actions:

> It is not honesty in me to speak
> What I have seen and known. You shall observe him,
> And his own courses will denote him so
> That I may save my speech.

(IV, i, 277–280)

The discord within Othello and within his marriage now turns into political chaos.

In scene ii Othello confronts Emilia, who denies Desdemona has been unfaithful (IV, ii, 12–19), although she as yet does not reveal the truth about Iago and the handkerchief. But in his state Othello remains unconvinced:

> She says enough; yet she's a simple bawd
> That cannot say as much. This is a subtile whore,

A closet lock and key of villainous secrets;
And yet she'll kneel and pray; I have seen her do't.

(IV, ii, 20–23)

Often Othello has asked to "see" proof of Desdemona's infidelity. Now he
imagines he has "seen" her in sin, and we realize how in his mind he takes the
innocent act of prayer and distorts it into something ugly. Earlier Iago vowed
to turn Desdemona's "virtue into pitch" (II, iii, 360). Now Othello does the
job.

When Desdemona enters with trepidation, Othello demands her confession:

> Come, swear it, damn thyself,
> Lest being like one of heaven, the devils themselves
> Should fear to seize thee; therefore be double damn'd:
> Swear thou art honest.

(IV, ii, 35–38)

However she responds, she is trapped. An admission will only confirm her guilt.
A denial will be taken as a lie. Othello continues to rave, his pride and innermost
being wounded:

> But there, where I have garner'd up my heart,
> Where either I must live or bear no life;
> The fountain from the which my current runs
> Or else dries up: to be discarded thence!
> Or keep it as a cestern for foul toads
> To knot and gender in!

(IV, ii, 57–62)

His language is turning animalistic, like Iago's. And as Othello's fury grows,
he climaxes by calling Desdemona a "whore" and "strumpet":

> I took you for that cunning whore of Venice
> That married with Othello.

(IV, ii, 88–89)

When Emilia enters, he tosses her money as if she were the mistress of the
brothel.

What follows is most curious. Emilia exists, then returns with Iago, who
speaks sympathetically: "What is your pleasure, madam? How is't with you?"
(IV, ii, 110). Desdemona cannot even say what Othello called her: "Am I that
name, Iago?" (IV, ii, 118). And Iago avoids answering: "What name, fair
lady?" (IV, ii, 118). A few lines later he comments: "Do not weep, do not
weep. Alas the day!" (IV, ii, 124). These words suggest an overplayed sympathy
consistent with Iago's charade. Yet as the scene continues, and Emilia storms
against whoever started this rumor that leaves Desdemona so shaken (IV, ii,
140–144), Iago's lines grow shorter. He maintains his role, but with less drive
than before, and he is silent as Desdemona, in a moment of pathetic irony, asks

for his help (IV, ii, 148–161). Thus we must ask whether something in Desdemona's plight touches him.

If we accept that Iago's character has been twisted by a frustrated capacity to love, and if we agree that he does appreciate Desdemona's quality, as lines cited earlier indicate, then we ought to assume that deep down he has affection for her. And if he can experience this twinge of remorse, then he becomes more complex. To be sure, the moment is transient, for, after a few hesitant sentences with Roderigo (IV, ii, 174–201), Iago reverts to his old self. But even so slight a variation brings one more fascinating dimension to Iago's character.

Back to himself, he proceeds to outtalk his angry dupe, who demands to know what has happened to all the jewelry he paid. Iago tells Roderigo to plan on eliminating Cassio (IV, ii, 227), but we realize that Iago intends to rid himself of both men.

In Act IV, scene iii, Othello has temporarily calmed, and leaves for a walk with an order for Desdemona:

> Get you to bed on th' instant, I will be return'd
> forthwith.

> (IV, iii, 7–8)

This moment seems to alleviate tension. But in fact it allows Othello the opportunity for premeditation, and the terror of what follows is exacerbated.

Left with Emilia, Desdemona sinks further into despair, and in a scene of unbearable sadness, her words and songs suggest she is anticipating death:

> If I do die before [thee], prithee shroud me
> In one of these same sheets.

> (IV, iii, 24–25)

She then recalls a maid of her mother's named Barbary:

> She was in love, and he she lov'd prov'd mad,
> And did forsake her.

> (IV, iii, 27–28)

The name "Barbary" recalls Iago's line about a Barbary horse (I, i, 111), and though the situation of the maid is similar to Desdemona's own plight, "Barbary" suggests that the maid was also black. Desdemona's mournful song "Willow" further emphasizes the theme of death.

Still dazed, Desdemona asks Emilia a question:

> Dost thou in conscience think—tell me, Emilia—
> That there be women do abuse their husbands
> In such gross kind?

> (IV, iii, 61–63)

Her innocence is overwhelming. When Emilia acknowledges that some such women do exist, Desdemona asks whether Emilia herself would ever be unfaithful "for all the world" (IV, iii, 68), and the response is characteristic of Emilia:

The world's a huge thing; it is a great price
For a small vice.

(IV, iii, 69)

Such cynicism contrasts with Desdemona's purity. As does Emilia's lengthy complaint on sexual equality (IV, iii, 84–103). But despite her experience, Emilia has been unable to see through the plot of her husband. Perhaps we should understand her as the victim of obsession: worldly about most matters but blindly devoted to Iago.

In Act V, scene i, we feel Iago weakening, for here is the first time he resorts to physical violence. He and Roderigo stand in the shadows, waiting for Cassio. Iago's reasoning exposes the depth of his hatred:

If Cassio do remain,
He hath a daily beauty in his life,
That makes me ugly; and besides, the Moor
May unfold me to him; there stand I in much peril.

(V, i, 18–21)

He is concerned first with Cassio's quality, then with the threat of discovery. Thus Iago is always aware of the goodness of others and consciously working against it.

Upon Cassio's entrance, Roderigo attacks, but is wounded. Then Iago stabs Cassio, whose cries are heard by the passing Othello. He believes that Iago has kept his earlier promise (IV, i, 211), and without waiting further, turns home to Desdemona:

Strumpet, I come.
[Forth] of my heart those charms, thine eyes, are blotted;
Thy bed, lust-stain'd, shall with lust's blood be spotted.

(V, i, 34–36)

What follows frustrates us enormously, for we hope that someone will have the sense to stop Othello.

As Lodovico and Gratiano bring light, Iago returns as if for the first time, and feigns confusion (V, i, 48) and sympathy (V, i, 53). Then, as if in a fit of anger, Iago kills Roderigo. Before he expires, Roderigo realizes the truth: "O damn'd Iago! O inhuman dog!" (V, i, 62). That metaphor has been used before, and will return again. When Bianca rushes in, Iago switches responsibility to her:

Gentlemen all, I do suspect this trash
To be a party in this injury—

(V, i, 85–86)

When Emilia enters, Iago characteristically condemns the events of the night as "the fruits of whoring" (V, i, 116). And even Emilia, once more taking her husband's part, condemns Bianca (V, i, 121), who protests her innocence:

> I am no strumpet, but of life as honest
> As you that thus abuse me.
>
> (V, i, 122–123)

The irony is that these words are addressed to Emilia, whose innocence is problematic. As everyone rushes off, Iago has the last words:

> This is the night
> That either makes me, or fordoes me quite.
>
> (V, i, 128–129)

This line causes us to wonder once again: what does Iago want? How could this evening possibly "make" him? Even if all worked out as he dreams, what would he have?

The power of the concluding scene comes partly from the deliberation with which Othello proceeds. His first lines indicate his state of mind:

> It is the cause, it is the cause, my soul,
> Let me not name it to you, you chaste stars,
> It is the cause.
>
> (V, ii, 1–3)

For him the need for murder is the product of reason, not of mindless passion:

> Yet I'll not shed her blood,
> Nor scar that whiter skin of hers than snow,
> As smooth as monumental alabaster.
>
> (V, ii, 3–5)

The reference to Desdemona's whiteness suggests that Othello has never lost awareness of the contrast between the colors of their skin, and that the difference has continued to haunt him: "Yet she must die, else she'll betray more men" (V, ii, 6). He tries to convince himself that in killing Desdemona he purges society of evil:

> Put out the light, and then put out the light:
> If I quench thee, thou flaming minister,
> I can again thy former light restore,
> Should I repent me; but once put out thy light,
> Thou cunning'st pattern of excelling nature,
> I know not where is that Promethean heat
> That can thy light relume. When I have pluck'd thy rose,
> I cannot give it vital growth again,
> It needs must wither. I'll smell thee on the tree.
>
> (V, ii, 7–15)

The murder must be done in darkness. Thus the candle is to be extinguished, then Desdemona's life. Othello is also struck by the finality of this act. Like the plucked rose, Desdemona can never be restored. We sense that Othello wants somehow both to kill Desdemona and to bring her back to life.

At this moment she awakens, and he bids her pray:

If you bethink yourself of any crime
Unreconcil'd as yet to heaven and grace,
Solicit for it straight.

(V, ii, 26–28)

He does not want to damn her. We think of Hamlet seeing the praying Claudius and deciding not just to kill the King but to send him to hell (III, iii). Here Othello seeks only what he believes is just punishment: "I would not kill thy soul"(V, ii, 32).

One other motif that makes this scene so moving is Desdemona's resignation. Earlier in the play her dominant quality was her bright independence. Here that assertiveness is replaced by an affection for Othello that becomes almost angelic. So devoted is she to her husband that she can only hope that he does not mean to kill her (V, ii, 42–46). Othello replays the supposed evidence of the handkerchief, and Desdemona protests her innocence, but Othello is relentless. When she learns that Cassio is dead, Desdemona cries out: "Alas, he is betray'd and I undone!" (V, ii, 76). Thinking her still disloyal, Othello loses control: "Out, strumpet! weep'st thou for him to my face?" (V, ii, 77). In fury he denies her the final prayer he solicited, and smothers her.

At Emilia's knock on the door, Othello is suddenly aware that his wife is actually dead (V, ii, 97). Emilia enters to report that "yonder's foul murthers done" (V, ii, 106), and Othello assumes she speaks of Desdemona:

It is the very error of the moon,
She comes more nearer earth than she was wont,
And makes men mad.

(V, ii, 109–111)

He cannot accept what he has done, and begins to search for reasons why he is not to blame.

Emilia instead reports that Roderigo has died, but that Cassio is only wounded, and for the first time Othello has doubts:

Not Cassio kill'd? Then murther's out of tune,
And sweet revenge grows harsh.

(V, ii, 115–116)

Here again an image of musical disharmony reflects the breakdown of order.

At Emilia's cries Desdemona struggles to say a few last words: "A guiltless death I die" (V, ii, 122). When Emilia asks who has committed the murder, Desdemona's answer reflects her ultimate loyalty to her husband:

Nobody; I myself, Farewell!
Commend me to my kind lord. O, farewell!

(V, ii, 124–125)

Othello, however, is not as strong, and initially seeks to use Desdemona's farewell as a shield: "You [heard] her say herself, it was not I" (V, ii, 127). Then he reverts to truth: "'Twas I that kill'd her!" (V, ii, 130).

When Othello accuses Desdemona of faithlessness, Emilia defends her, but not until Othello mentions Iago does Emilia begin to see the truth. Three times she echoes Othello in horror: "My husband?" (V, ii, 140, 146, 149). And her shouts of accusation at Othello (V, ii, 162–167) bring in Montano, Gratiano, and Iago.

At first Iago claims to have told only the truth and tries to prevent Emilia from speaking, but she is just as determined to do otherwise. She also invokes one of her husband's pet phrases: " . . . if thou be'st a man" (V, ii, 172). Montano sees the body of Desdemona, and with unintentional irony brands the deed: "O monstrous act!" (V, ii, 190). Meanwhile Othello desperately insists to himself and the others that the murder of Desdemona was just: "O, she was foul!" (V, ii, 200). After Gratiano reports Brabantio's death, Othello moans "'Tis pitiful," (V, ii, 210), a painful echo of his words at Act I, scene iii, line 161. At last Emilia is able to bring out the truth (V, ii, 225–229), but for her effort she is fatally wounded by Iago, who escapes momentarily. Alone with Othello, and about to die, Emilia mourns Desdemona:

> Moor, she was chaste, she lov'd thee, cruel Moor;
> So come my soul to bliss, as I speak true;
> So speaking as I think, alas, I die.
>
> (V, ii, 249–251)

We cannot help thinking that had Emilia been so honest and devoted earlier and told the truth about the handkerchief, the tragedy might have been avoided.

When Gratiano returns, Othello tries initially to avoid responsibility: "Who can control his fate?" (V, ii, 265). Like Romeo, like Brutus, like Hamlet, like other tragic heroes to follow, Othello cannot accept what he has done. Recalling the great voyages that have marked his life, he acknowledges that he has come to his end (V, ii, 267–269), and sees himself going to hell on Desdemona's gaze:

> This look of thine will hurl my soul from heaven,
> And fiends will snatch at it.
>
> (V, ii, 274–275)

Before long, he is reduced to helpless cries:

> O Desdemon! dead, Desdemon! dead!
> O, O!
>
> (V, ii, 281–282)

When Iago returns, Othello looks to Iago's feet as if to find the cloven hooves of the devil. Again Othello attempts to lay blame elsewhere. In fury, Othello stabs Iago, then tries one more way to achieve absolution, calling himself:

An honorable murderer, if you will;
For nought I did in hate, but all in honor.

(V, ii, 294–295)

Even Othello recognizes the feebleness of this excuse, as he adds the qualifying
phrase "if you will." Once again there is irony in "honor."

Iago's final words are suited to his character. When Othello orders him to
confess the reason for his plan of vengeance, Iago is blunt:

Demand me nothing; what you know, you know:
From this time forth I never will speak word.

(V, ii, 303–304)

What could he say, even if he wanted to confess? He has always rationalized
his feelings, unable to grasp what drives him. How could he articulate to anyone
else his malignancy? What lies within him is beyond his comprehension. Thus
we imagine that Lodovico's comment, "What? not to pray?" (V, ii, 305), is
greeted by Iago with a smirk.

After Iago is threatened with some unspecified torture, the details of his plot
are gradually revealed (V, ii, 308–329). Then Othello offers his final words. He
acknowledges his work for Venice, then asks that his story simply be told:

Then must you speak
Of one that lov'd not wisely but too well;
Of one not easily jealous, but being wrought,
Perplexed in the extreme . . .

(V, ii, 343–346)

For the first time he seems at peace:

And say besides, that in Aleppo once,
Where a malignant and a turban'd Turk
Beat a Venetian and traduc'd the state,
I took by th' throat the circumcised dog,
And smote him—thus.

(V, ii, 352–356)

Before he stabs himself, he recalls again the Turk as the symbol of disorder,
and symbolically makes himself responsible by calling himself the "dog." His
final act is of devotion to Desdemona: "Killing myself, to die upon a kiss" (V,
ii, 359). Montano, however, emphasizes instead the pain of the final tableau by
invocation of two dominant images: "The object poisons sight . . . " (V, ii, 364).

The ending to this play is curious, for in all the other tragedies, social or
political order is restored. Yet the denouement here is fitting, as in this play the
political story is subordinate to the love story. For the characters on stage these
events will remain forever mysterious, because what occurred between Othello
and Iago, and within each one, took place before the audience alone. Now
Othello is dead, and Iago has vowed to be silent. We, however, know that
Othello was caught between Desdemona's goodness and Iago's evil, and that in

this conflict Othello was destroyed by his own nature. What we are left to ponder is the ultimate mystery: why should innocence be made to bear such suffering?

SUGGESTIONS FOR FURTHER READING

Adamson, Jane. Othello *as Tragedy: Some Problems in Judgment and Feeling*. Cambridge and New York: Cambridge University Press, 1980.

Arthos, John. "The Fall of Othello." *Shakespeare Quarterly* 9 (1968): 93–104.

Bethell, S. L. "The Diabolic Images in *Othello*." *Shakespeare Survey* 5 (1952): 62–80.

Dean, Leonard F., ed. *A Casebook on* Othello. New York: Thomas Y. Crowell, 1961.

Elliot, G. R. *Flaming Minister: A Study of* Othello *as Tragedy of Love and Hate*. Durham, N.C.: Duke University Press, 1953.

Heilman, Robert B. *Magic in the Web: Action and Language in* Othello. Lexington: University of Kentucky Press, 1956.

Hymen, Stanley Edgar. *Iago: Some Approaches to the Illusion of His Motivation*. New York: Atheneum, 1970.

Muir, Kenneth, and Philip Edwards, eds. *Aspects of* Othello. Cambridge and New York: Cambridge University Press, 1977.

Myrick, Kenneth O. "The Theme of Damnation in Shakespeare's Tragedies." *Studies in Philology* 38 (1941): 221–245.

Rosenberg, Marvin. *The Masks of* Othello. Berkeley: University of California Press, 1961.

Spivack, Bernard. *Shakespeare and the Allegory of Evil*. New York: Columbia University Press, 1958.

KING LEAR

King Lear breaks a number of seemingly cardinal rules of dramaturgy. An outline of the story would suggest that no playwright could fashion a coherent text out of so many disparate elements. Yet of all the remarkable works considered in this book, *King Lear* may be the most remarkable.

The sources of the play are several. Lear is a character from ancient British mythology, but the first coherent story about him was written by Geoffrey of Monmouth in his *History of the Kings of Britain* (c. 1137). The more direct source is *The True Chronicle History of King Lear*, a play written in 1594 or slightly earlier. This work has a happy ending, in which Cordelia's forces triumph and Lear is restored to his throne, on which he reigns for a few years, then dies peacefully. Another important difference between the two plays is that Shakespeare's is set in pre-Christian Britain and has none of the numerous references to Christianity that pervade the older work. The Gloucester subplot is adapted from "The Tale of the Blind King of Paphlagonia" in Sir Philip Sidney's *Arcadia* (1590).

We should also note the revision of Shakespeare's text by the eighteenth-century playwright Nahum Tate, whose version was performed exclusively for over a century. Tate's most significant change was the ending, to be considered presently, but he also eliminated the Fool and France, focused more heavily on the triangle between Edmund, Regan, and Goneril, and interpolated many of his own lines.

Now to the play itself: why is it so unusual?

For one, the plot is difficult to follow. After the introductory scenes, the order of events is bewildering, even for audiences that have already experienced the play. Locale, motivation, and sequence, particularly in the military episodes, are often uncertain. The play has the quality of chaos, as if scenes were hurled together. In almost any other play such a structure would be damaging. In *King Lear* it is essential, for in part this play is about chaos.

Second, substantial background information is lacking. This work is about a father and three daughters. These daughters must have had a mother, but we are offered only an oblique reference to such a person. The detail would seem indispensable, but we do not miss it at all.

The construction of the play is unique. In most of Shakespeare's plays, the climactic scene occurs in the middle, often precisely at the center of Act III. Indeed, most plays by any author begin with scenes of exposition and development, move to a climax or series of climactic events, then resolve. In *King Lear* the exposition, development, and complication are all compressed into approximately 100 lines of the first scene. The climactic moment occurs when Lear expels Cordelia from the kingdom, then surrenders his throne and wealth to Goneril and Regan. The rest of the play, four and three-quarter acts, is all resolution, the consequences of these edicts. That so unusual a dramatic construction holds up is amazing.

This structure leads to an unusual pattern of character development. In Shakespeare's other tragic plays, certain traits of the leading figure lift him or her to greatness; later, under adverse conditions, these traits bring the figure down. But at the start of *King Lear* we never learn whether Lear the man in great. His fall comes too fast for that knowledge to be realized. Instead, his stature emerges strictly from his original position as King, and what causes his downfall and the universal calamity is his abuse of the "greatness" inherent in kingship. Afterwards he turns from a universal king into an individual man, and he achieves a different kind of greatness, one independent of social position.

The transformation does not come until late in the play, but the unrest dormant in the kingdom is apparent from the opening line, offered by Kent:

> I thought the King had more affected the
> Duke of Albany than Cornwall.

> (I, i, 1–2)

He insinuates that decisions are to be made and responsibility to be taken. Thus this play is not a portrait of a haphazard universe, although some characters do act as though the world were so ill formed. To the contrary, the play dramatizes that the individual is responsible for the path of his or her own life. These two lines also suggest a salient characteristic of Lear: his indiscretion. The nature of his world, however, demands that he wield power carefully, not impulsively, as Lear is soon to learn.

Gloucester's response reinforces these points:

> It did always seem so to us; but now in the
> division of the kingdom, it appears not which of the
> Dukes he values most, for [equalities] are so
> weigh'd, that curiosity in neither can make choice
> of either's moi'ty.

> (I, i, 3–7)

Kent's tone was of concern. Gloucester speaks with the assurance of one who believes that he has nothing to fear. He assumes himself invulnerable to suffering and does not distinguish carefully between people. As such, he is a less exalted version of the title character. Gloucester is not an evil man, but a thoughtless one. However, he lives in a society where thoughtlessness is a dangerous defect, and he, too, learns with unbearable viciousness the consequences of irresponsibility.

Next, Gloucester comments smugly about his illegitimate son, Edmund:

> His breeding, sir, hath been at my charge.
> I have so often blush'd to acknowledge him, that now
> I am braz'd to't.

> (I, i, 9–11)

Edmund, standing right by, must endure jokes about his own conception, as Gloucester snickers over past indiscretions (I, i, 13–16), then reports about his other offspring:

> But I have a son, sir, by order of law, some
> year elder than this, who yet is no dearer in my
> account.

> (I, i, 19–21)

Gloucester evinces a firm faith in this "order of law." He does not grasp that it is susceptible to ruthless forces that hold no respect or fear of it. In this play those who hold faith battle those who would subscribe to a different attitude, which holds that life is a brutal struggle in which only the fittest survive.

Gloucester is also casual about the proprieties due Edgar as both the older and the legitimate son. Gloucester jokes about the questions of primogeniture that reflect the law he lauds, and which therefore deserve deeper respect. Again, Gloucester's attitude parallels Lear's misjudgments.

With the entrance of King Lear, these themes are unified and expanded. His first words are a command, the utterance of a man accustomed to giving orders and seeing them fulfilled with alacrity. Despite Kent's earlier expression of caution, we have no reason to suspect that Lear does not have the reverence of his court. His attendants respond, and not a murmur of doubt is heard when the King explains his plan to divest himself of rule:

> Know that we have divided
> In three our kingdom; and 'tis our fast intent
> To shake all cares and business from our age,
> Conferring them on younger strengths, while we
> Unburthen'd crawl toward death.

> (I, i, 37–41)

If the court is not perturbed, the audience is, for we are aware that by relinquishing the throne Lear is abdicating a position considered in Shakespeare's society to be divinely ordained. He is creating disruption of the political and natural order, disregarding his place as the link between man and God. Furthermore, by partitioning the kingdom, he is weakening it as a whole, and inviting internal strife. This misjudgment must have tragic consequences.

The disastrous plan is compounded by further blunders, more subtle, which reveal that Lear is a failure not just as King but as father and man:

> We have this hour a constant will to publish
> Our daughters' several dowers, that future strife
> May be prevented now.
>
> (I, i, 43–45)

These lines communicate two vital thoughts. One, Lear has already decided who will receive what territories. How his daughters respond on this occasion should have no bearing on the division of the kingdom. Two, he is not blind to the personal antagonisms between his daughters nor to the potential conflicts over land and power that could ensue. He understands the situation and the people involved. Yet he proceeds along what can only be considered a second tragic path:

> Tell me, my daughters
> (Since now we will divest us both of rule,
> Interest of territory, cares of state),
> Which of you shall we say doth love us most,
> That we our largest bounty may extend
> Where nature doth with merit challenge?
>
> (I, i, 48–53)

What is he doing?

On the one hand, Lear is indulging himself, playing the proud father, and displaying for the court his love for his daughters with the expectation that they will reciprocate. In addition, he is attempting to bring some warmth to a formal event. Yet he is also doing something far more misguided. With his demand, which is an affront to his grown daughters, the King violates the relationship between parent and child. By requesting statements of love, Lear puts the royal occasion ahead of family duty. He turns the sacred bond with his children into a ceremony for the pleasure of the court and the gratification of his ego. His pride supersedes more important values.

This corruption of the royal family is another aspect of Lear's inviting the consequences that befall him. Admittedly, he does not deserve those horrors, for even now we intuit that he is a good man, and for the rest of the play he never loses the loyalty of Cordelia, Kent, and others we admire. By the end of the play we are assured of his greatness. But in the context of Elizabethan thought, when a man of such position commits errors like these and when the area of misjudgment is the welfare of his own kingdom, a tragic outcome is inevitable.

Goneril and Regan accept the humiliation stoically, and each follows Lear's wishes by offering a tribute that reeks of fraudulence, full of grandiose phrases and meaningless extravagances. Goneril's is particularly ironic, for the first quality she mentions as precious is "eyesight," (I, i, 56), dearer than "space" or liberty." "Seeing" and "eyes" become major motifs of the play, especially because of their connotations of "insight" and "understanding." Here Goneril implies that these attributes are the most valuable a person can possess, and she could be mocking her father's deficiencies. Regan's declaration, on the other hand, is phrased so that it mocks from a different direction:

> I am made of that self metal as my sister,
> And prize me at her worth. In my true heart
> I find she names my very deed of love;
> Only she comes too short, that I profess
> Myself an enemy to all other joys
> Which the most precious square of sense [possesses],
> And find I am alone felicitate
> In your dear Highness' love.

> (I, i, 69–76)

Her speech serves a dual purpose: it flatters Lear and it disparages Goneril. Such maliciousness foreshadows the future discord between the two sisters. Furthermore, that both recite so smoothly is partly a tribute to their skill at deception but also evidence that they can dismiss the inappropriateness of Lear's order. The family bond means nothing to them, nor will any other aspect of the social order.

For Cordelia, however, the situation is not as easy, and again we face a problem: why does she not simply offer flattery of her own? After all, Lear clarifies that he intends to give her the most generous share of the kingdom:

> Now, our joy,
> Although our last and least, to whose young love
> The vines of France and milk of Burgundy
> Strive to be interess'd, what can you say to draw
> A third more opulent than your sisters'? Speak.

> (I, i, 82–86)

His use of "vine" and "milk" implies that Lear sees Cordelia's marriage as more than just a political arrangement: it will establish the propagation of the royal line. He talks of growth and fruitfulness, and thus we recognize that the significance of his steps here is not lost on him. But we notice, too, that he regards France and Burgundy as having equal opportunity to bid for Cordelia's hand, and they are soon to prove themselves not in any way of like quality. In the first sentence of the play, Kent questioned Lear's judgment. Here is further evidence that Lear's "eyesight" is not what it ought to be, especially for a man of his station.

To Lear's question, Cordelia offers a reply that will echo throughout the play: "Nothing, my lord" (I, i, 87). Even after his re-asking and warning, "Nothing will come of nothing . . . " (I, i, 90), she stands by her original answer:

> Unhappy that I am, I cannot heave
> My heart into my mouth. I love your Majesty

> According to my bond, no more nor less.
>
> (I, i, 91–93)

In her own way, Cordelia presents more respect for the crown and the authority of a king than does Lear himself. She perceives that two distinct relationships are being forced into one: that of king to subject, and that of father to child. The former is a public duty, and therefore Cordelia offers her "bond," as any loyal subject should. The latter is private, and will be corrupted if displayed for political ends. Thus Cordelia is more loyal to Lear than anyone, including the King, realizes; but Lear, to use the image of the play, is too shortsighted to appreciate her fidelity. Instead he forces Cordelia to speak further, and she complies:

> Good my lord,
> You have begot me, bred me, lov'd me: I
> Return those duties back as are right fit,
> Obey you, love you, and most honor you.
> Why have my sisters husbands, if they say
> They love you all? Happily, when I shall wed,
> That lord whose hand must take my plight shall carry
> Half my love with him, half my care and duty.
> Sure I shall never marry like my sisters,
> [To love my father all].
>
> (I, i, 95–104)

Her logic is flawless. A human being may share love with several people. But Lear does not yet appreciate the nature of love, and he mistakes shared affection for divided allegiance. Over the course of the play he learns the difference.

At this moment, however, a series of agitations have coalesced. Cordelia is publicly disobeying him and seems to be flouting his authority as father and King. Furthermore, she is tarnishing what Lear believes ought to be a glorious ceremony. Finally, his favorite daughter is apparently unwilling to return his love. Ironically, from our perspective, Cordelia's pride and self-assurance prove that she is truly her father's daughter.

Thus Lear asks the foolish question: "But goes thy heart with this?" (I, i, 105). He shows his complete lack of understanding. Cordelia has managed to separate her father from her King. Lear, however, cannot reciprocate, and has gone so far as to allow his imperatives as King to supplant his love as father. The ruler has replaced the man.

Here is the core of Lear's tragedy. Much of the rest of the play dramatizes Lear's discovery of his humanity, what he shares with the rest of his subjects and with all people. He is, according to Elizabethan theology, a link between humanity and the divine, not distance from either. Kingly duties can be carried out properly only when that humanity is embraced.

Such redemption is a long way off. Thus in this scene Cordelia must try to explain herself: "So young, my lord, and true" (I, i, 107). But Lear misses the point. His ego is so wounded that he loses all judgment, and shouts the climactic lines of the play:

> Let it be so: thy truth then be thy dow'r!
> For by the sacred radiance of the sun,
> The [mysteries] of Hecat and the night;
> By all the operation of the orbs,
> From whom we do exist and cease to be;
> Here I disclaim all my paternal care,
> Propinquity and property of blood,
> And as a stranger to my heart and me
> Hold thee from this for ever.

> (I, i, 108–116)

In the name of all his authority, both divine and temporal, he unites his bequest as father with that as King. Yet though his tirade horrifies us, for even by her few words we recognize Cordelia's superiority, we remember that Lear has already broken the paternal bond by forcing Cordelia to extol him. She has tried to maintain it by answering only as his subject. He has brushed aside that response and now carries out his punishment, in doing so again blending his two roles and diminishing both. He expels her as daughter and as subject. Furthermore, he ignores that his kingdom, and the people for whom he is responsible, will now be placed in the hands of those whom Lear knows to be unworthy of such a trust. Thus in one precipitous action Lear has shattered the order of his own royal family, the order of the government, and the order of the kingdom.

Kent tries to interpose, but in fury Lear again reveals the extent of his ego:

> Peace, Kent!
> Come not between the dragon and his wrath;
> I lov'd her most, and thought to set my rest
> On her kind nursery. [*To Cordelia*] Hence, and avoid my sight!—

> (I, i, 121–124)

He admits that Cordelia is the daughter he loves best. Yet the confession is a political blunder, first because he is soon to throw himself on the good will of Regan and Goneril, second because he admits that he is leaving the country to those he respects least. How painfully ironic that when Lear invests authority in his other daughters as well as their husbands, Cornwall and Albany, he has a last request:

> Only we shall retain
> The name, and all th' addition to a king;
> The sway, revenue, execution of the rest,
> Beloved sons, be yours, which to confirm
> This coronet part between you.

> (I, i, 135–139)

He remains caught up in the protocol and trappings of office. He forgets that a human being must fill it, and that the quality of that person determines how the office will be carried out. Finally, his offer to share the coronet foreshadows the dissolution of both the kingship and national unity.

Kent sees through Lear's folly, and alone has the courage to argue boldly. Lear is fully eighty, and Kent has been with him a long time. Thus we see two old men, who hold each other in deep affection, exploding in rage. Kent holds nothing back:

> What wouldest thou do, old man?
> Think'st thou that duty shall have dread to speak
> When power to flattery bows? To plainness honor's bound,
> When majesty falls to folly. Reserve thy state,
> And in thy best consideration check
> This hideous rashness. Answer my life my judgment,
> Thy youngest daughter does not love thee least,
> Nor are those empty-hearted whose low sounds
> Reverb no hollowness.
>
> (I, i, 146–154)

He understands Regan and Goneril and their capacity for mendacity. He also warns that Lear should remember his position and not allow pride to overwhelm duty. But Lear's response is lamentable. He does not choose to explain himself. Instead he relies on grand threats, resorting to intimidation rather than reflection. After Kent and he exchange lines invoking imagery of sight (I, i, 157–159), Lear draws his sword in fury, a symbol of manhood frustrated and eager to exert itself. His expulsion of Kent is the final manifestation of his temper:

> That thou has sought to make us break our [vow]—
> Which we durst never yet—and with strain'd pride
> To come betwixt our sentence and our power,
> Which nor our nature nor our place can bear,
> Our potency made good, take thy reward.
>
> (I, i, 168–172)

Here Lear mentions another word that becomes important in this play: "nature." At this point he uses it to mean "temperament" or "personality," admitting that he has had a fit of choler and is unable to reverse himself without confessing fallibility. Other ramifications of the word are soon apparent.

Kent has no choice. Before he leaves he gives to Cordelia a blessing (I, i, 182–183) and to the other daughters offers a tentative hope that they do not prove the liars he knows them to be (I, i, 184–185). His purpose, we assume, is to remind the King on whom he may rely. But Lear has never challenged Kent's judgment. The argument is over propriety. Lear's emphasis is on the innate power of the throne, a personal version of "might makes right." No one has the authority to question one of his, the King's, actions. Throughout the tragedies and histories, Shakespeare dramatizes the need for a strong central authority in running a country. But he also dramatizes that to be effective, that authority must be responsive to the needs of the people. At this moment Lear forgets that the proper exercise of power demands responsibility. He is caught up in the rights of office and ignores his obligations as a human being.

In counterpart to Lear is France. The shallow Burgundy rejects Cordelia because she has lost her inheritance and place in court, and Lear further condemns her: "... a wretch whom Nature is asham'd/ Almost t' acknowledge hers" (I, i, 212–213). But France speaks up courageously:

> This is most strange,
> That she, whom even but now was your [best] object,
> The argument of your praise, balm of your age,
> The best, the dearest, should in this trice of time
> Commit a thing so monstrous, to dismantle
> So many folds of favor. Sure her offense
> Must be of such unnatural degree
> That monsters it, or your fore-vouch'd affection
> Fall into taint; which to believe of her
> Must be a faith that reason without miracle
> Should never plant in me.
>
> (I, i, 213–223)

He reiterates the theme of "nature," but places it in conjunction with another word that becomes a leitmotif: "monster." In his speech, "unnatural" suggests "opposing nature," or opposing the natural scheme of things. Although France questions what Cordelia has done to warrant such anger, the "unnatural" act has, in fact, been by Lear, who in tossing aside his youngest and dearest daughter, casting her from his "sight" (I, i, 124), has ripped apart his family and kingdom. "Monstrousness" can be set free only when such destruction has been perpetuated. Subsequently "unnaturalness" and "monstrousness" on a massive scale are unleashed, but all begins in this opening scene.

After a moving appeal by France (I, i, 235–241) and a slithery one by Burgundy (I, i, 241–244), Lear offers his final words on Cordelia's inheritance: "Nothing. I have sworn, I am firm." (I, i, 245). He satirically echoes Cordelia's earlier reply. But the word "nothing" comes back to haunt Lear repeatedly. Nevertheless, the lack of feeling he shows here, the inhumanity, will be transformed into a desire to place others before himself and to acknowledge his kinship with the rest of his subjects.

France accepts Cordelia's hand:

> Gods, gods! 'tis strange that from their cold'st neglect
> My love should kindle to inflam'd respect.
>
> (I, i, 254–255)

He sees the irony of the day's events. And lest we doubt Cordelia's strength, her final words to her sisters show her "insight":

> I know you what you are,
> And like a sister am most loath to call
> Your faults as they are named. Love well our father;

> To your professed bosoms I commit him,
> But yet, alas, stood I within his grace,
> I would prefer him to a better place.

(I, i, 269–274)

The sneering responses of Regan and Goneril (I, i, 276–279) hint at the evil within them. They have stood by silently while Lear has acted foolishly. Now that he has departed, they articulate their longstanding resentment with terrifying cold-bloodedness. As Goneril says:

> He always lov'd our sister most, and with what
> poor judgment he hath now cast her of appears too
> grossly.

(I, i, 290–292)

We never learn what forces have shaped these women; moreover, they do not care. All they know is that they hate their father and sister, and they are content to base their evil on that hate. They confess that their father has erred in trusting them. The know what they are, they are not dismayed by that knowledge, and they never try to explain or understand themselves. They thereby eliminate the possibility of growth or redemption.

Such anger is one-dimensional in contrast to that articulated by Edmund in the first speech of the second scene. In many respects his is the most important statement of the play, for it manifests the forces that would take advantage of errors like those Lear has committed:

> Thou, Nature, art my goddess, to thy law
> My services are bound.

(I, ii, 1–2)

"Nature" here means not the benign order to which France referred nor the individual temperament Lear described, but a brutish element in existence that can possess human beings and drive them in the struggle for survival and power. In his tone Edmund is a Machiavel like Iago in *Othello*, in that both seek to destroy through manipulation what they see as traditional good. What makes Edmund different is that he is absolutely conscious of his reasons for this course. Iago functions by instinct. The source of his hatred remains hidden, even to him. But Edmund rationally accounts for his motives:

> Wherefore should I
> Stand in the plague of custom, and permit
> The curiosity of nations to deprive me,
> For that I am some twelve or fourteen moonshines
> Lag of a brother?

(I, ii, 2–6)

He refuses to accept the values of a society that rejects his place. At the same time he reveals contempt for any ethical order based on those values. Edmund is thus the voice of humanity's outcasts, who create their own rules in the battle for supremacy.

Edmund then explains another aspect of the Nature he worships:

> Who, in the lusty stealth of nature, take
> More composition, and fierce quality,
> Than doth within a dull, stale, tired bed
> Go to th' creating a whole tribe of fops,
> Got 'tween asleep and wake?
>
> (I, ii, 11–15)

He takes the energy and passion with which he was conceived as evidence of his innate superiority. His attitude thereafter is wholly practical. The resolution to any issue is not what men ought to do, but what they can do. Action, not philosophy, is his byword. Good intentions mean nothing. In the war for power, results are all that matter.

"Now, gods, stand up for bastards!" (I, ii, 22). Here is the formidable danger that in this play confronts goodness, embodied by Kent, Cordelia, and later Edgar, the Fool, and Albany. In opposition are Goneril, Regan, Edmund, Cornwall, and soon Oswald. Monumental good battles monumental evil for the possession of the world. Good and light do triumph, or at least they emerge at the end. But survival is achieved at frightful cost, and the meaning of that survival is unclear.

At the center of the struggle are the two old men, Lear and Gloucester. The first scene showed us Lear's weaknesses and how they led him astray. Scene ii shows Gloucester's flaws beginning to undo him, a parallel emphasized by various thematic words. In reply to Gloucester's request about what he is hiding, Edmund replies "Nothing, my lord" (I, ii, 31). And Gloucester's retort reminds us of Lear's earlier smug parody:

> The quality of nothing
> hath not such need to hide itself. Let's see. Come, if it
> be nothing, I shall not need spectacles.
>
> (I, ii, 33–35)

Indeed, Gloucester is far less insightful than he realizes. He then takes from a seemingly reluctant Edmund a letter, supposedly written by Edgar, that implies that Edgar will soon be committing treason. Gloucester is outraged: "He cannot be such a monster—" (I, ii, 94), and proclaims the cause:

> These late eclipses in the sun and moon
> portend no good to us. Though the wisdom of nature
> can reason it thus and thus, yet nature finds itself
> scourg'd by the sequent effects.
>
> (I, ii, 102–106)

Like Marcus in *Titus Andronicus*, like Romeo, like a variety of figures from Shakespeare's tragedies, Gloucester tries to blame outside forces for human misjudgment:

> This villain of mine comes under
> the prediction; there's son against father: the
> King falls from bias of nature; there's father against
> child. We have seen the best of our time.
> Machinations, hollowness, treachery, and all ruinous disorders
> follow us disquietly to our graves.
>
> (I, ii, 109–114)

He recognizes that his world is threatened by anarchy, but he refuses to take responsibility on himself. Why does he not ask why Edgar, a son he knows to be loyal, turns instantly and without provocation? Why does he not wonder that Edgar would run away after giving a letter to, of all people, Edmund? Gloucester is a decent man but easily deceived, and when he attributes problems to sources other than himself, he joins that roster of tragic figures who at key moments of their lives also look to outside forces.

The response to Gloucester's musings comes at once from his own son:

> This is the excellent foppery of the world,
> that when we are sick in fortune—often the surfeits of
> our own behavior—we make guilty of our
> disasters the sun, the moon, and stars, as if we were
> villains on necessity, fools by heavenly compulsion,
> knaves, thieves, and treachers by spherical
> predominance; drunkards, liars, and adulterers by an enforc'd
> obedience of planetary influence, and all that we
> are evil in, by a divine thrusting on.
>
> (I, ii, 118–126)

Edmund's self-reliance suggests his strength and insight into human nature. Yet an Elizabethan audience would also be shocked by his divorce from any divine or supernatural agency. His reliance on his own will suggests a refusal to be bound by moral restraint, and to the Renaissance world such license was a fearsome threat.

In the latter part of scene ii Edmund convinces Edgar that Gloucester is displeased, and Edgar realizes part of the truth: "Some villain hath done me wrong" (I, ii, 165). Not for some time will he grasp that Edmund is that villain.

In scene iii the effects of Lear's abdication begin to be felt. Goneril complains to Oswald of a growing disorder:

> His knights grow riotous, and himself upbraids us
> On every trifle.
>
> (I, iii, 6–7)

We have no sympathy for Goneril, but she is doubtless accurate in her evaluation of the spreading chaos. Her resolution, though, suggests she intends to do more than soothe matters:

> . . . Idle old man,
> That still would manage those authorities

That he hath given away! Now by my life
Old fools are babes again, and must be us'd
With checks as flatteries, when they are seen abus'd.

(I, iii, 16–20)

We cannot blame Goneril's attitude on the corruptive tendencies of power, for
her temperament was this way before. Now she has an opportunity to release
hostility, and her antagonism to Lear, which she was earlier able to conceal, no
longer need be hidden.

In scene iv Kent enters, in disguise, and offers his service to Lear. The King
accepts this stranger, but is now beginning to lose self-control, as he revels
boisterously and greets Kent:

Follow me, thou shalt serve me. If I like thee
no worse after dinner, I will not part from thee yet.
Dinner, ho, dinner! Where's my knave? my Fool?
Go you and call my Fool hither.

(I, iv, 40–43)

That Lear here speaks prose rather than verse suggests his diminution.

The King asks several times for the Fool, until a loyal Knight distressed by
Lear's mistreatment (I, iv, 64–66) brings back word:

Since my young lady's going into France,
sir, the Fool hath much pin'd away.

(I, iv, 73–74)

This affection of the yet unseen Fool for Cordelia is thematically important, for
in many respects he is her surrogate. After she leaves with France at the end of
the first scene, she does not return until late in Act IV. During the interim the
Fool performs her function, for he stirs Lear's heart and is the first beneficiary
of Lear's generosity. The Fool and Cordelia never appear onstage together; often
they were performed by the same actor. One way to understand the relationship
between the two characters is to see the Fool as Lear's conscience outside the
bounds of civilization, while Cordelia fulfills that role within society.

When the Fool enters, he begins at once to exercise his right to say to Lear
with wit what others may not say at all:

Why, this fellow has banish'd two on's daughters, and
did the third a blessing against his will; if thou follow
him, thou must needs wear my coxcomb.

(I, iv, 101–103)

The Fool sings verses that imply that Lear has no idea of the damage he has
caused. When Lear dismisses the songs as "nothing" (I, iv, 128), the Fool takes
that word and replays it, as he does throughout his scenes. Finally Lear begins
to see the Fool's point: "Dost thou call me fool, boy?" (I, iv, 148). And the
Fool reveals the truth that Lear will soon learn hard:

All thy other titles thou hast given away,
that thou wast born with.

(I, iv, 149–150)

The Fool's fable of the egg has many overtones, as the Fool himself explains:

Why, after I have cut the egg i' th' middle
and eat up the meat, the two crowns of the egg.
When thou clovest thy [crown] i' th' middle and
gav'st away both parts, thou bor'st thine ass on thy
back o'er the dirt. Thou hadst little wit in thy bald
crown when thou gav'st thy golden one away.

(I, iv, 158–163)

The egg is also a symbol of life and fruitfulness, and the example intimates that Lear has not only destroyed his own royal line, but also his country's future.

When Goneril enters, she begins dismantling Lear's royal image, as she insists that his troops are out of control. What bothers Lear is not the disorder but her tone and attitude: "Are you our daughter?" (I, iv, 218). When Goneril does not apologize, Lear is forced to acknowledge that because he has abandoned the throne, he is no longer the man he was:

Does any here know me? This is not Lear.
Does Lear walk thus? speak thus? Where are his eyes?
Either his notion weakens, his discernings
Are lethargied—Ha! waking? 'Tis not so.
Who is it that can tell me who I am?

(I, iv, 226–230)

He asks these questions too late, so that now the Fool gives the only answer: "Lear's shadow" (I, iv, 231).

Goneril maintains her accusations that Lear has allowed his troops to degenerate (I, iv, 241–246). In response Lear threatens to take his forces to Regan (I, iv, 255), but his defiance is mixed with sad recognition:

O most small fault,
How ugly didst thou in Cordelia show!
Which, like an engine, wrench'd my frame of nature
From the fix'd place; drew from my heart all love,
And added to the gall.

(I, iv, 266–270)

He acknowledges that he allowed momentary pique with Cordelia to destroy his judgment, and his mention of "nature" indicates that he knows that his error is having immense consequences. He has always talked of his stature in the kingdom. Now that he has lost it, now that he has "nothing," he is aware of its importance. "Nothing" is teaching him the value of "something."

Lear's initial response to this lesson is a terrifying curse on Goneril:

Hear, Nature, hear, dear goddess, hear!
Suspend thy purpose, if thou didst intend
To make this creature fruitful.
Into her womb convey sterility,
Dry up in her the organs of increase,
And from her derogate body never spring
A babe to honor her!

(I, iv, 275–281)

His "goddess" is very different from Edmund's (I, ii, 1). Yet the ferocity of
this execration is undercut by its ineffectuality. Lear has no power of his own,
and the energy of his language is mocked by his own impotence.

The irony of the moment is increased when Lear consents to leave:

I have another daughter,
Who I am sure is kind and comfortable.
When she shall hear this of thee, with her nails
She'll flea thy wolvish visage.

(I, iv, 305–308)

He speaks of Regan, but we recognize that the daughter to whom he should turn
is Cordelia. These lines also contain the animal imagery that dominates the play,
references that reflect the descent of humanity to the bestial.

The pain of this scene is leavened slightly by the presence of Albany. As
Lear's temper rages and Goneril remains implacable, Albany's single lines evince
his growing conscience. Goneril mocks her husband's mildness (I, iv, 340–344),
and his final remark suggests his imminent break with her:

How far your eyes may pierce I cannot tell:
Striving to better, oft we mar what's well.

(I, iv, 345–346)

Scene v is a transition. After sending the loyal Kent with a letter informing
Regan that the King is soon to arrive, Lear remains alone with the Fool. He
attempts to maintain self-control, but interpolated in his comments are phrases
that indicate the anguish within him:

I will forget my nature. So kind a father!

(I, v, 32)

To take't again perforce! Monster ingratitude!

(I, v, 40)

O, let me not be mad, not mad, sweet heaven!
Keep me in temper, I would not be mad!

(I, v, 46–47)

This inner resolve against surrender, this capacity to fight madness and to endure,
becomes one aspect of Lear's greatness.

In Act II, scene i, Edmund learns from Curran that war has broken out between

Albany and Cornwall. No reason is given, but Shakespeare's audience would recognize the conflict as the inevitable emergence of greed, a sign of evil turning on itself. Yet the fact of warfare means that the entire country is now affected by the breach in the royal family, as the consequences of Lear's misjudgment spread.

Curran also tells Edmund that Cornwall and Regan are coming to Gloucester's castle. When Edgar enters, Edmund feigns concern that Edgar may be discovered and punished for words against Cornwall and for conspiring with Albany (II, i, 20–27). In a tactic reminiscent of Iago's subtler moves, Edmund starts a mock duel with Edgar, who flees. Then Edmund wounds himself for sympathy. As with Iago, we resent the effectiveness of Edmund's tactics, but we admire the skill. When Gloucester enters seconds later, Edmund easily persuades him that Edgar has escaped (II, i, 65–77), and Gloucester vows to capture his supposedly treasonous son (II, i, 80). Gloucester's blindness and mistrust once again are parallel to Lear's misjudgments.

Regan and Cornwall enter, and Regan seems to have sympathy for Gloucester's unhappiness. Speaking of Edgar, she asks:

> Was he not companion with the riotous knights
> That tended upon my father?

(II, i, 94–95)

Whether the question is serious is not clear, for the thought is ludicrous, but Gloucester is too upset to answer, so Edmund responds for him: "Yes, madam, he was of that consort" (II, i, 97). Then Cornwall congratulates Edmund on his devotion to Gloucester (II, i, 105–106), and we feel the villains instinctively banding together. As Cornwall says:

> For you, Edmund,
> Whose virtue and obedience doth this instant
> So much commend itself, you shall be ours.
> Natures of such deep trust we shall much need;
> You we first seize on.

(II, i, 112–116)

To this point Cornwall has done nothing untoward. Yet his use of "Natures" to communicate a bond with Edmund suggests a latent malevolence that soon surfaces. One theme of this play is that though evil forces may join together, they must eventually consume one another. Finally, Regan and Cornwall, having received word from Goneril that Lear is coming to their home, have departed rather than face him, and thus he is stranded.

In scene ii Kent appears in front of Gloucester's castle, and immediately assaults the effeminate Oswald verbally and physically. As Kent does throughout the play, he demonstrates boldness, but here he is also foolhardy, for he is on uncertain territory, and in a few moments pays the price. Oswald's cries bring forth Cornwall, Regan, and Gloucester, and had we any feeling for Oswald as a man set upon unjustly, that sympathy vanishes at his cowardice and his lie that he spared Kent only because of the attacker's age (II, ii, 62–63). Even in front of his royal superiors, Kent speaks forthrightly:

> I have seen better faces in my time
> Than stands on any shoulder that I see
> Before me at this instant.
>
> (II, ii, 93–95)

Cornwall reveals his nature when he orders the stocks, and despite Kent's protests, commands that the old man be bound until noon. The stocking of Kent is an insult to Lear, a complete disregard for royalty and heritage. Regan then reaffirms her malevolence by extending the period of imprisonment through the entire night. Gloucester protests (II, ii, 142–147), but remains feeble in the face of youthful energy.

When Kent is left alone, he considers a letter he has received from Cordelia, who has learned what has befallen her father. How the information could have been transmitted so quickly is not clarified, but in this play time is compressed, and her knowledge and concern are more important than a detail of plot. In addition, Kent has the strength to carry on in spite of his personal suffering: "Fortune, good night; smile once more, turn thy wheel" (II, ii, 173). The image of the wheel turning, popular in Shakespeare's day, reflects Kent's belief that justice will ultimately take hold. He has faith that the Nature Lear holds sacred, the Nature embodied by Cordelia, will triumph over more anarchic and brutal forces, embodied by Goneril, Regan, and Edmund. Whether this faith is justified, whether the world Shakespeare dramatizes is fundamentally benign, is a key issue of the play.

In scene iii Edgar appears to inform us that he has escaped and will seek anonymity in the disguise of a mad beggar:

> I will preserve myself, and am bethought
> To take the basest and most poorest shape
> That ever penury, in contempt of man,
> Brought near to beast.
>
> (II, iii, 6–9)

As does Hamlet, Edgar seeks to avoid suspicion by playing a madman. His role, however, anticipates the actual predicament to be suffered by Lear, as we are reminded when Edgar concludes: "Edgar I nothing am" (II, iii, 21).

In scene iv Lear enters to learn that his man has been put in the stocks, and tries desperately to maintain self-control:

> O how this mother swells up toward my heart!
> [Hysterica] passio, down, thou climbing sorrow,
> Thy element's below.—Where is this daughter?
>
> (II, iv, 56–58)

He moves inside to find Regan, leaving the Fool to mock Kent's boldness. Lear returns in fury at being refused:

> Deny to speak with me? They are sick? they are weary?
> They have travell'd all the night? Mere fetches,
> The images of revolt and flying off.
> Fetch me a better answer.
>
> (II, ii, 88–91)

He senses his own weakening authority, which Gloucester unintentionally mocks, referring to Cornwall:

> My dear lord,
> You know the fiery quality of the Duke,
> How unremovable and fix'd he is
> In his own course.
>
> (II, ii, 91–94)

Here is an apt description of Lear in the first scene of the play.

Lear does see the similarity, but continues to rage that he should have to request an audience with his daughter:

> Infirmity doth still neglect all office
> Whereto our health is bound; we are not ourselves
> When nature, being oppress'd, commands the mind
> To suffer with the body. I'll forbear,
> And am fallen out with my more headier will,
> To take the indispos'd and sickly fit
> For the sound man.
>
> (II, iv, 106–112)

He continues slowly to acquire self-awareness, and his vow to "forbear" anticipates much more courageous endurance to follow.

At last Regan and Cornwall appear and set Kent free. Lear bitterly acknowledges her expression of greeting:

> If thou shouldst not be glad,
> I would divorce me from thy [mother's] tomb,
> Sepulchring an adult'ress.
>
> (II, iv, 130–132)

Here is a rare mention of Lear's wife, and the context suggests that he still cannot believe that his daughter will be cruel to him. At this mention of the mother, we may speculate that because Regan and Goneril are so much alike and must have acquired their common attitude from somewhere, they may have inherited their mother's personality. Lear then explodes with complaints against Goneril, but Regan, with a mock solicitude that partially distinguishes her from Goneril, suggests that Lear himself should apologize:

> O, sir, you are old,
> Nature in you stands on the very verge
> Of his confine. You should be rul'd and led
> By some discretion that discerns your state

Better than you yourself. Therefore I pray you
That to our sister you do make return.
Say you have wrong'd her.

(II, iv, 146–152)

In desperation Lear parodies this proposal by kneeling and begging, but still
pleads to Regan that she must understand his plight:

Thy tender-hefted nature shall not give
Thee o'er to harshness. Her eyes are fierce, but thine
Do comfort, and not burn . . . Thou better know'st
The offices of nature, bond of childhood,
Effects of courtesy, dues of gratitude . . .

(II, iv, 170–179)

These sentiments reflect the bonds with Cordelia that Lear himself broke. At
this moment he suffers the kind of humiliation he inflicted on his youngest
daughter, but even though he was wrong in that action, his own debasement is
distressing to watch.

Lear continues to demand to know who put Kent in the stocks, but before
any answer is provided, Goneril enters, and the recognition that the two sisters
are allies dismays him:

O heavens!
If you do love old men, if your sweet sway
Allow obedience, if you yourselves are old,
Make it your cause; send down, and take my part.

(II, iv, 189–192)

Cornwall confesses that he imprisoned Kent, and Regan compounds this shock
by suggesting that Lear dismiss half his train and join with Goneril (II, iv, 204).
Stunned, Lear upbraids his daughter:

No, rather I abjure all roofs, and choose
To wage against the enmity o' th' air . . .

(II, iv, 208–209)

Before long that prediction comes true. When Goneril jokes in response to Lear's
shout that he would rather serve Oswald than join her (II, iv, 216–217), Lear
expels her from his presence:

We'll no more meet, no more see one another.
But yet thou art my flesh, my blood, my daughter—
Or rather a disease that's in my flesh,
Which I must needs call mine.

(II, iv, 220–223)

Even as he tries to disown her, Lear reluctantly acknowledges that he is the
origin of this evil, both the biological father and the ruler who unleashed chaos.

The daughters now cruelly toy with Lear, asking why he needs any train at

all. Lear tries to establish their debt to him: "I gave you all—" (II, iv, 250),
but Regan harshly reminds him that they were not his first choice: "And in good
time you gave it" (II, iv, 250). Under the barrage, Lear cries out:

> O, reason not the need! our basest beggars
> Are in the poorest thing superfluous.
> Allow not nature more than nature needs,
> Man's life is cheap as beast's.
>
> (II, iv, 263–266)

He attempts to explain human feeling and pride, qualities that in the first scene
of the play he ignored. He is beginning to feel his own humanity:

> You see me here, you gods, a poor old man,
> As full of grief as age, wretched in both.
>
> (II, iv, 272–273)

For the first time he regards himself as a man instead of as a king:

> If it be you that stirs these daughters' hearts
> Against their father, fool me not so much
> To bear it tamely . . .
>
> (II, iv, 274–276)

He asks a question that recurs throughout the play: What is the nature of this
world that it permits such evil to run rampant? Finally he bursts out directly at
his daughters:

> No, you unnatural hags,
> I will have such revenges on you both
> That all the world shall—I will do such things—
> What they are yet I know not, but they shall be
> The terrors of the earth! You think I'll weep:
> No, I'll not weep.
> I have full cause of weeping, but this heart
> Storm and Tempest.
> Shall break into a hundred thousand flaws
> Or ere I'll weep. O Fool, I shall go mad!
>
> (II, iv, 278–286)

The speech is a combination of anger and valor. Lear is so possessed by fury
that he cannot articulate his thoughts. But because he has abdicated his power,
he has no outlet for revenge.

The storm that begins here reflects two other storms: the disorder within the
kingdom and the disorder within Lear's mind. Yet Cornwall, Regan, and Goneril
have no sympathy for Lear. The last, in fact, blames him for his own predicament
(II, iv, 290–291). And the scene ends with their impassivity to his plight.

The storm grows in Act III, scene i, as the Gentleman reports the "eyeless
rage" (III, i, 8) to Kent, who has news of his own. Because dissension has
come between Albany and Cornwall (III, i, 21), England is on the brink of civil

war, another consequence of Lear's decision. Simultaneously, the King of
France, aware of England's vulnerability and Lear's predicament, is preparing
his own attack (III, i, 30–34). How France would have heard all this news is
another cloudy detail. In any case, such a situation places the Elizabethan audience in an odd position, on the side of Cordelia against Cornwall, Edmund,
and their forces, but also on the side of France against England. Kent has further
instructions. He urges the Gentleman to Dover where he is to report to loyal
citizens about the treatment Lear has received. He is also to take a ring of Kent's,
in case the Gentleman should meet Cordelia (III, i, 46–49).

Act III, scene ii is almost too large for any stage to encompass:

> Blow, winds, and crack your cheeks! rage, blow!
> You cataracts and hurricanoes, spout
> Till you have drench'd our steeples, [drown'd] the cocks!
>
> (III, ii, 1–3)

Lear's unwillingness to surrender is both magnificent and terrifying:

> I tax not you, you elements, with unkindness;
> I never gave you kingdom, call'd you children;
> You owe me no subscription. Then let fall
> Your horrible pleasure. Here I stand your slave,
> A poor, infirm, weak, and despis'd old man;
> But yet I call you servile ministers.
> That will with two pernicious daughters join
> Your high-engender'd battles 'gainst a head
> So old and white as this.
>
> (III, ii, 16–24)

No matter how harshly Nature treats Lear, it can never be as cruel as his
daughters. Such a moment emphasizes a man's smallness against the great ex-
panse of the universe, but brings out as well the potential dignity of man in the
face of overwhelming odds.

For the first time Lear is prepared to deal with his errors:

> Let the great gods,
> That keep this dreadful pudder o'er our heads,
> Find out their enemies now . . .
> I am a man
> More sinn'd against than sinning.
>
> (III, ii, 49–51, 59–60)

He accepts his own transgressions. This moment also shows a new humanity
from Lear, as he shelters the Fool by guiding him into a cave:

> Come on, my boy. How dost, my boy? Art cold?
> I am cold myself. Where is this straw, my fellow?
> The art of our necessities is strange

And can make vild things precious.

(III, ii, 68–71)

The absolute, unchallengable monarch has disappeared, and in his place emerges
a man of humility, grateful for life itself.

In scene iii the subplot returns. Gloucester foolishly confides in Edmund that
Lear has been mistreated, and that Gloucester himself has a letter containing
information about both the conflict between Albany and Cornwall and the imminent invasion of France. Gloucester's error in confiding to his untrustworthy
son frustrates the audience, as does his letting Cornwall take over Gloucester's
own castle. Edmund's ironic sympathy (III, iii, 7), however, is gripping, as is
his final line: "The younger rises when the old doth fall" (III, iii, 25). Here is
Edmund's pronouncement of the laws of his Nature.

In scene iv Kent urges Lear to seek refuge from the storm, but the King is
more concerned with the state of his mind:

> When the mind's free,
> The body's delicate; [this] tempest in my mind
> Doth from my senses take all feeling else,
> Save what beats there —filial ingratitude! . . .
>   In such a night
> To shut me out? Pour on, I will endure.

(III, iv, 11–18)

Such defiance gives even this battered Lear an inspiring nobility. He is also
changed in another way, as he indicates when following the Fool inside:

> Poor naked wretches, wheresoe'er you are,
> That bide the pelting of this pitiless storm,
> How shall your houseless heads and unfed sides,
> Your [loop'd] and window'd raggedness, defend you
> From seasons such as these? Oh, I have ta'en
> Too little care of this! Take physic, pomp,
> Expose thyself to feel what wretches feel,
> That thou mayst shake the superflux to them,
> And show the heavens more just.

(III, iv, 28–36)

The moment is wondrous. A king who has enjoyed absolute power and, to all
visible signs, a productive reign realizes that his life has been founded on mistaken values and the mistreatment of the people he had been entrusted to protect.
Can we doubt that were Lear restored to his throne, he would be not only a
wiser father but also a far greater king? Here is one place where the play may
be considered regenerative and hopeful.

When Edgar, disguised as poor Tom, emerges from the hovel, Lear assumes
the reason for Tom's madness:

Has his daughters brought him to this pass?
Couldst thou save nothing? Wouldst thou give 'em all?

(III, iv, 63–64)

Edgar raves about "the foul fiend" (III, iv, 46), perhaps meaning Satan, but in
reality he has been tormented by a different fiend, his brother, Edmund. Thus
we face the meeting of these three extraordinary characters: Lear, on the edge
of madness; Edgar, feigning madness; and the Fool, whose recondite wit borders
on madness. Lear interprets Tom's dilemma as a manifestation of man's puniness
in the face of the universe:

> Is
> man no more than this? Consider him well. Thou
> ow'st the worm no silk, the beast no hide, the sheep no
> wool, the cat no perfume. Ha? here's three on 's
> are sophisticated. Thou art the thing itself: unaccom-
> modated man is no more but such a poor, bare, fork'd
> animal as thou art. Off off, you lendings! Come,
> unbutton here.

(III, iv, 101–109)

He sees Edgar as man in his natural state, and Lear's request to divest himself
of clothing, after he has lost his throne, his kingdom, and his family, reflects
his desire to become the most elemental form of humanity. Such a gesture
indicates the weakening of Lear's mind. Yet, at the same time, we understand
Lear's rationale.

The Fool's next line seems to comment only on the roughness of the weather:

> Now a little fire in a wild field were
> like an old lecher's heart, a small spark, all the rest
> on's body cold.

(III, iv, 111–113)

But then Gloucester enters, and the Fool adds: "Look, here comes a walking
fire" (III, iv, 114), reminding us of Gloucester's lascivious remarks in the
opening lines of the play. Edgar, afraid Gloucester will recognize him, maintains
his pose of madness (III, iv, 129–136), and we realize that Gloucester has never
known his own son. The link between plot and subplot is emphasized in Gloucester's reflection:

> Our flesh and blood, my lord, is grown so vile
> That it doth hate what gets it.

(III, iv, 145–146)

Nonetheless, Gloucester's innate beneficence is clear at several points. He reflects
kindly upon Kent (III, iv, 163–164), then upon Edgar:

> I had a son,
> Now outlaw'd from my blood; he sought my life,
> But lately, very late. I lov'd him, friend,

No father his son dearer; true to tell thee,
The grief hath craz'd my wits.

(III, iv, 166–169)

Finally, as all seek refuge from the storm, Gloucester guides "poor Tom" inside
ahead of him. Like Lear, Gloucester has come to care for those more helpless
than he.

That this alteration is too late and too weak is apparent in scene v, as Edmund
and Cornwall confer. In line 1, Cornwall speaks of revenge, and we realize that
Edmund has revealed the plans Gloucester confided to him earlier. Cornwall's
comments also indicate that he believes the lies Edmund has told:

I now perceive, it was not altogether your
brother's evil disposition made him seek his death; but
a provoking merit, set a-work by a reprovable badness
in himself.

(III, v, 5–8)

Edmund maintains his veneer of compassion: "How malicious is my fortune,
that I must repent to be just!" (III, v, 9–10). Taking the charge of treason against
Gloucester as fact, Cornwall names Edmund Earl of Gloucester, and the two
depart together. The scene is almost blasphemous in the way these two men use
words like "loyalty" (III, v, 3), "just" (III, v, 10), "trust" (III, v, 24), and
"love" (III, v, 25) to categorize their actions, which are motivated by hatred
and lust.

In scene vi, after Gloucester leaves to find food, Lear, the Fool, and Edgar
continue their recital of outrage against the world. In his madness Lear seeks to
put his daughters on trial: "I will arraign them straight" (III, vi, 19), and with
the Fool and Edgar as judges, he conducts a mock inquisition. When questioning
an imaginary Goneril, represented by a farm stool, Lear accuses her so brutally
(III, vi, 53–56) that Edgar can barely maintain his disguise:

My tears begin to take his part so much,
They mar by counterfeiting.

(III, vi, 60–61)

In spite of his madness, Lear continues to probe for the answers to the questions
that obsess him and dominate the play:

Then let them anatomize Regan; see what
breeds about her heart. Is there any cause in nature
that make these hard hearts?

(III, vi, 76–78)

The last line is one more version of the crucial mystery of this play: How, in a
benign universe, can such evil figures as Regan and Goneril flourish?

After Kent temporarily calms Lear, the Fool offers his own farewell: "And
I'll go to bed at noon" (III, vi, 85). These words are the Fool's last in the play
and may be an anticipation of death. In any case, subsequent references to

"fool," which carries the denotations of both "clown" and "one held in affection," seem to apply both to this Fool and Cordelia.

Gloucester returns with information that a plot is underway against Lear's life,
and urges that the King be taken to Dover. He also clarifies that anyone caught
aiding Lear is in danger (III, vi, 94–95), and this warning hints at the horror of
the scene to follow. Edgar is left alone to ruminate:

> When we our betters see bearing our woes,
> We scarcely think our miseries our foes.

> (III, vi, 102–103)

He, too, wonders about the fundamental injustice of the world. How much do
his own sufferings mean in the light of the pain Lear endures?

Scene vii is almost unbearable, in some ways the most horrifying scene in
dramatic literature. The evil forces of the play are planning strategy, and Cornwall's first order is that a letter be sent to Albany communicating that French
troops have landed. Perhaps Cornwall hopes that in the face of invasion by
another country, the quarrels among the English may be laid aside. The next
order is for the retrieving of Gloucester, now judged a traitor. Regan demands
immediate punishment: "Hang him instantly" (III, vii, 4). So does Goneril:
"Pluck out his eyes" (III, v, 5). Cornwall wants to decide for himself, and
requests that Edmund leave:

> Edmund, keep
> you our sister company; the revenges we are bound to
> take upon your traitorous father are not fit for your
> beholding.

> (III, vii, 6–9)

Cornwall's scrupulousness is curious. More disturbing is Edmund's silent concession to these orders. He leaves without a word, content to let fall upon his father
whatever tortures Cornwall conceives. In retrospect we may assume that Edmund
is pleased to keep Goneril company. After Oswald reports that Gloucester has
aided Lear's escape, Cornwall's order is repeated, and Gloucester is brought in
and bound.

Cornwall clarifies the sheer lust for power that underlies the subsequent torture:

> Though well we may not pass upon his life
> Without the form of justice, yet our power
> Shall do a court'sy to our wrath, which men
> May blame, but not control.

> (III, vii, 24–27)

His revels in his freedom to inflict pain and his own version of judgment. Regan,
too, is delighted with herself, as she admits that she and Cornwall know the
answers to the questions they pose: "Be simple-answer'd, for we know the
truth" (III, vii, 43). Thus the entire episode is a sadistic charade.

The initial humiliations Gloucester suffers, such as his beard being plucked,

are, like Kent's being stocked, also insults to Lear. Gloucester does have a final
moment of courage when he boasts of his actions in protection of Lear:

> Because I would not see thy cruel nails
> Pluck out his poor old eyes, nor thy fierce sister
> In his anointed flesh [rash] boarish fangs.
>
> (III, vii, 56–58)

The irony of this expression is partly that the fate he describes is about to befall
Gloucester himself. Cornwall rips out one of Gloucester's eyes, and Regan, ever
cruel, urges her husband on: "One side will mock another; th' other too" (III,
vii, 71). Even at this gruesome moment, a trace of light emerges in the actions
of the servant who protests, then stabs Cornwall. That servant is slain immediately
by Regan, but at least some measure of good remains alive. Cornwall tears out
the other eye, and Gloucester in his agony calls for Edmund. Regan supplies
the truth:

> Out, treacherous villain!
> Thou call'st on him that hates thee. It was he
> That made the overture of thy treasons to us,
> Who is too good to pity thee.
>
> (III, vii, 87–90)

In a climax to the imagery of sight, Gloucester at last "sees" the truth when
he has lost his eyes:

> O my follies! then Edgar was abus'd.
> Kind gods, forgive me that, and prosper him!
>
> (III, vii, 91–92)

He no longer speaks of divine influences controlling existence, but realizes that
he is responsible for his own life. Regan then orders Gloucester thrown out:
" . . . and let him smell/ His way to Dover" (III, vii, 93–94). And Cornwall
commands that the rebellious servant be thrown "Upon the dunghill" (III, vii,
97). Still, as the fatally wounded Cornwall is led off by Regan, the compassion
of the servants for Gloucester reminds us that all is not evil.

In Act IV, scene i, Edgar reflects that fortune has inflicted its worst upon him
(IV, i, 1–9). But the entrance of the blinded Gloucester means that more horror
yet awaits. To the old man who aids him, Gloucester reveals his understanding
of his errors:

> I have no way, and therefore want no eyes;
> I stumbled when I saw.
>
> (IV, i, 18–19)

He also shows devotion to Edgar:

> O dear son Edgar,
> The food of thy abused father's wrath!
> Might I but live to see thee in my touch,

I'ld say I had eyes again.

(IV, i, 21–24)

As Edgar remains hidden, Gloucester thinks of poor Tom and Edgar, not realizing their common identity:

> I' th' last night's storm I such a fellow saw,
> Which made me think a man a worm. My son
> Came then into my mind, and yet my mind
> Was then scarce friends with him.

(IV, i, 32–35)

On a subconscious level, perhaps, Gloucester has always felt the presence of Edgar in Tom. Then Gloucester sinks to his point of deepest despair:

> As flies to wanton boys are we to th' gods,
> They kill us for their sport.

(IV, i, 36–37)

In scene ii of Act I, Gloucester spoke of the stars determining human action. In the scene just past, he acknowledged that he was responsible for his own errors. Now, bereft of hope, he speaks of a random, even malevolent, universe, where life is meaningless. Some audiences take this statement as Shakespeare's theme, but the remainder of the work reveals moments of hope and growth that make such utter pessimism a personal reflection of Gloucester, not the playwright.

Yet Gloucester still retains some belief in divine justice:

> That I am wretched
> Makes thee the happier; heavens, deal so still!
> Let the superfluous and lust-dieted man,
> That slaves your ordinance, that will not see
> Because he does not feel, feel your pow'r quickly . . .

(IV, i, 65–69)

Gloucester accepts his own punishment, which he believes satisfies the malevolent gods. He hopes only that others who are more deserving of retribution, and his description of such individuals fits Edmund perfectly, will also suffer.

Edgar steps forward, still in disguise, and offers to guide Gloucester, who seeks to go to Dover. Gloucester's intention on arrival is clear:

> There is a cliff, whose high and bending head
> Looks fearfully in the confined deep.
> Bring me but to the very brim of it,
> And I'll repair the misery thou dost bear
> With something rich about me.

(IV, i 73–77)

Unlike Lear, Gloucester has capitulated, and his desire for suicide contrasts Lear's never-ending struggle for sanity and life.

In scene ii Oswald reports to Goneril that her husband, Albany, is greatly altered (IV, ii, 3–11), for he is pleased that the French army has landed and angered by the treatment of Gloucester. Goneril attributes Albany's switch in allegiance to "the cowish terror of his spirit" (IV, ii, 12), and turns her attentions to Edmund, for whom her passions have increased during his absence. Goneril affirms that Oswald will work for both of them (IV, ii, 18–19). She and Edmund kiss, and Edmund pledges his loyalty: "Yours in the ranks of death" (IV, ii, 24). As always, he manages to maintain the pose of gallantry.

When Albany enters, he provides a moral upsurge. He has realized the truth about his wife and her allies, and his growth is a sign of regeneration. So are his slashing remarks to Goneril:

> Tigers, not daughters, what have you perform'd?
> A father, and a gracious aged man,
> Whose reverence even the head-lugg'd bear would lick,
> Most barbarous, most degenerate, have you madded.
> Could my good brother suffer you to do it?
> A man, a prince, by him so benefited!
> If that the heavens do not their visible spirits
> Send quickly down to tame [these] vild offenses,
> It will come,
> Humanity must perforce prey on itself,
> Like monsters of the deep.
>
> (IV, ii, 40–50)

The animal imagery crucial to the play is used to great effect to describe the degeneracy of Goneril and Regan. Albany's emphasis on justice emerging from heaven echoes Lear's earlier plea (II, iv, 189–192); both characters believe in the ultimate goodness of existence. But the source of that justice must be "visible spirits," those human beings whose lives and work will prevent humanity from destroying itself.

Goneril sneers at her husband, insulting his courage and manhood (IV, ii, 50–58, 68), but when a messenger enters with news of both Gloucester's blinding and Cornwall's subsequent death, Albany sees his fears and faith confirmed:

> This shows you are above,
> You [justicers], that these our nether crimes
> So speedily can venge! But, O poor Gloucester,
> Lost he his other eye?
>
> (IV, ii, 78–81)

Goneril, however, is concerned with more practical matters. The death of Cornwall is good news in one sense, for she and Edmund are one step closer to having all of Britain. On the other hand, Regan is now a widow, and Edmund has just gone to see her, leaving Goneril with the despised Albany. Distressed, Goneril retires to read a letter from her sister. Albany, meanwhile, now King of Britain, resolves to revenge Gloucester's blinding. We feel the balance of power shifting slowly from evil to good.

Scene iii is an interlude, building toward the momentous reunion of Lear and Cordelia. A gentleman reports to Kent that the King of France, Cordelia's husband, has been forced to return to his country, and that his Marshal has taken over (IV, iii, 1–7). This seemingly unimportant fact removes the potential dramatic awkwardness of having France invade Britain, for under these circumstances Cordelia will lead the army in support of her father. The gentleman also relates Cordelia's reaction on reading about Lear's trials:

> Ay, [sir], she took them, read them in my presence,
> And now and then an ample tear trill'd down
> Her delicate cheek. It seem'd she was a queen
> Over her passion, who, most rebel-like,
> Sought to be king o'er her.
>
> (IV, iii, 11–15)

Later, however, her emotions take hold of her:

>   You have seen
> Sunshine and rain at once; her smiles and tears
> Were like a better way: those happy smiles
> That play'd on her ripe lip [seem'd] not to know
> What guests were in her eyes, which, parted thence,
> As pearls from diamonds dropp'd.
>
> (IV, iii, 17–22)

Kent is moved to consider why Cordelia should be so different from her sisters:

>   It is the stars,
> The stars above us, govern our conditions,
> Else one self mate and make could not beget
> Such different issues.
>
> (IV, iii, 32–35)

Kent is an admirable, courageous man, but his judgment is contradicted by a recurrent theme in Shakespeare's plays, which dramatize again and again that the burden of responsibility lies not with supernatural agents but with humanity itself. The reconciliation scene between Lear and Cordelia is anticipated more intensely when Kent indicates that Lear is still ashamed to see his daughter (IV, ii, 42–47). That reunion is tied to the restoration of kingship, with news that the forces of Cornwall and Albany are moving against France.

In scene iv Cordelia returns to the stage for the first time since Act I. Here she learns that her father has escaped from camp, and now wanders:

> . . . Crown'd with rank [femiter] and furrow-weeds,
> With hardocks, hemlock, nettles, cuckoo-flow'rs,
> Darnel, and all the idle weeds that grow

In our sustaining corn.

(IV, iv, 3–6)

These adornments are mostly weeds or flowers with bitter tastes, and may reflect Lear's own state. The Doctor suggests the only possible way to help his condition:

> Our foster-nurse of nature is repose,
> The which he lacks; that to provoke in him
> Are many simples operative, whose power
> Will close the eye of anguish.

(IV, iv, 12–15)

Like Macbeth, like Henry IV, Lear can alleviate his anguish only through sleep, which so often in Shakespeare represents the natural cycle of the body and thus the order of life. When she hears that the British armies are marching, Cordelia establishes her goal:

> O dear father,
> It is thy business that I go about;
> Therefore great France
> My mourning and importun'd tears hath pitied.

(IV, iv, 23–26)

Shakespeare clarifies that France's goal is not the conquering of England but the restoration of Lear.

In scene v, tensions among Regan, Goneril, Edmund, and Albany are exacerbated. Oswald reports to Regan that Albany has begun to march against France, but "with much ado . . ." (IV, v, 2). We recognize that Albany is caught in a moral quandary between his loyalty to his country and his desire to protect Lear and Cordelia. Regan is glad that Edmund has gone with the intention of killing his father, for the longer Gloucester lives, " . . . he moves/ All hearts against us" (IV, v, 10–11). Yet she maintains the appearance of morality by implying that by killing Gloucester, Edmund would end his father's "nighted life" (IV, v, 13), as if the murder would be merciful. But the most fascinating aspect of the scene is Regan's suspicion of her own sister. As Regan says to Oswald:

> I know your lady does not love her husband,
> I am sure of that; and at her late being here
> She gave strange eliads and most speaking looks
> To noble Edmund. I know you are of her bosom.

(IV, v, 23–26)

At this invitation to embrace his confidence, Oswald acts innocent: "I, madam?" (IV, v, 27). Regan then suggests to Oswald that should Gloucester be killed: "Preferment falls on him that cuts him off" (IV, v, 38). When Oswald expresses willingness to comply with her request (IV, v, 39–40), we wonder where his loyalty, previously given to Goneril, actually lies. The entire scene reaffirms the theme of evil turning on itself.

Scene vi presents a particular theatrical challenge, as Edgar and the blind

Gloucester enter. Because of the vividness of Edgar's description, Gloucester imagines that they have arrived at the cliffs of Dover, but Edgar's words also have thematic impact:

> The murmuring surge,
> That on th' unnumb'red idle pebble chafes,
> Cannot be heard so high. I'll look no more,
> Lest my brain turn, and the deficient sight
> Topple down headlong.
>
> (IV, vi, 20–24)

The metaphor of sight returns once more. Previously the sighted Gloucester was blind to a reality that destroyed him. Here the blind Gloucester is convinced he sees a fantasy that redeems him. He kneels and prepares for suicide:

> O you mighty gods!
> This world I do renounce, and in your sights
> Shake patiently my great affliction off.
> If I could bear it longer, and not fall
> To quarrel with your great opposeless wills,
> My snuff and loathed part of nature should
> Burn itself out. If Edgar live, O bless him!
> Now, fellow, fare thee well.
>
> (IV, vi, 34–41)

In his capitulation, Gloucester acknowledges his smallness in relation to the great forces of the universe and implies his own errors and misjudgments. Despite this confession, his surrender reflects his weakness and makes Lear's inexorable struggle for life that much more moving.

On stage this moment can be awkward, for Gloucester now topples forward, as if off a high cliff. But in fact he falls only a step or so, and anticlimatic laughter from the audience must be avoided. When Gloucester awakens, Edgar pretends to be a passerby who believes Gloucester's surviving such a great fall as a miracle (IV, vi, 55). He further implies that the beggar who allowed Gloucester to jump was a "fiend" (IV, vi, 72), and thus Gloucester's preservation was an act of the gods. Gloucester accepts this explanation:

> Henceforth I'll bear
> Affliction till it do cry out itself
> "Enough, enough," and die.
>
> (IV, vi, 75–77)

He vows to hold onto life as long as he can, and in his passion he is transformed.

Such a positive moment is powerfully undercut by the entrance of Lear, now fully mad and bedecked with flowers and weeds. He proclaims "I am the King himself" (IV, vi, 84), and he dispenses commands to imaginary members of his court and country. In his ravings, which border on incoherence, he nonetheless captures the state of chaos to which his world has fallen. At the sound of

Gloucester's voice, Lear imagines "Goneril with a white beard" (IV, vi, 96), and accuses his daughters of such deceit as would destroy him (IV, vi, 96–100). He also realizes his own humanity:

> . . . they told me I was
> every thing. 'Tis a lie, I am not ague-proof.
>
> (IV, vi, 104–105)

He claims adultery is not a serious crime, for to Lear even Edmund, Gloucester's bastard son, was kinder than Lear's own daughters. He is horrified by sexuality but blames women in particular, and he views his daughters as "Centaurs" (IV, vi, 124), part human and part beast, an image that may be seen as uniting the conflicting elements of humanity seen in this play.

Gloucester at last recognizes Lear, and asks to kiss his hand, but Lear hesitates: "Let me wipe it first, it smells of mortality" (IV, vi, 133). We remember Regan's sneer after Gloucester's blinding: " . . . let him smell/ His way to Dover" (III, vii, 93–94). The word "smell" has overtones of a moral stench that pervades Lear's kingdom, as Lear suggests:

> A man may see how this
> world goes with no eyes. Look with thine ears; see
> how yond justice rails upon yond simple thief. Hark
> in thine ear: change places, and handy-dandy, which is
> the justice, which is the thief?
>
> (IV, vi, 150–154)

He then embarks on a litany of corruptions in which the powerful are as guilty as those they punish (IV, vi, 157–172). Lear thus portrays the entire universe as corrupt. In this raving, Edgar sees a searching for truth:

> O, matter and impertinency mix'd,
> Reason in madness!
>
> (IV, vi, 174–175)

Finally Lear arrives at an acceptance of his world. To Gloucester he says:

> Thou must be patient; we came crying hither.
> Thou know'st, the first time that we smell the air
> We wawl and cry.
>
> (IV, vi, 178–180)

> When we are born, we cry that we are come
> To this great stage of fools.—
>
> (IV, vi, 182–183)

Shakespeare uses the metaphor of man on stage in other works, including *As You Like It*, *Macbeth*, and *The Tempest*. Here it suggests that life itself, irrespective of individual man's actions, is absurd. Then, as if to contradict this vision, Lear changes perspectives and vows vengeance against his sons-in-law (IV, vi, 185–187). He recognizes human responsibility for the way of the world.

Yet when the Gentleman enters to bring Lear back to Cordelia, Lear refers to himself as "The natural fool of fortune" (IV, vi, 191), invoking a description similar to one used by Romeo to describe his error in killing Tybalt (*Romeo and Juliet*, III, i, 136). The line suggests that Lear has been the victim rather than the one who erred.

Throughout this scene Lear has fluctuated between two perspectives: one, that the world is corrupt and life meaningless; the other, that humanity is responsible for whatever condition in which the world exists. The Gentleman suggests that the latter view is correct when he describes Cordelia:

> Thou hast [one] daughter
> Who redeems nature from the general curse
> Which twain have brought her to.
>
> (IV, vi, 205–207)

This view implies that the world is not intrinsically evil and that humanity is not beyond redemption. Accordingly, the play, for all its misery, offers some hope. Indeed, Gloucester himself is moved to affirm life:

> You ever-gentle gods, take my breath from me,
> Let not my worser spirit tempt me again
> To die before you please!
>
> (IV, vi, 217–219)

Now he regards the forces that have spared his life as "merciful."

When Oswald enters, he prepares with delight to kill Gloucester, but Edgar, still as a peasant, defends his father and fatally wounds Oswald. The servant remains loyal to Goneril to the end, and begs that her letter to Edmund be delivered. Edgar clarifies that loyalty alone does not excuse Oswald:

> I know thee well; a serviceable villain,
> As duteous to the vices of thy mistress
> As badness would desire.
>
> (IV, vi, 252–254)

When Edgar reads the letter, he finally understands his brother's duplicity. He also understands Albany's steadfastness (IV, vi, 272). Slowly we feel the good in humanity emerging to right the terrible injustices that have been committed.

The pattern of reconciliation continues in Act IV, scene vii, which begins with Cordelia's thanks to Kent for his devotion. He is not yet prepared to make his identity public, and she accepts his request without questioning him further (IV, vii, 8–12). Such mutual trust contrasts with the constant deceptions carried out by the other sisters.

The Doctor explains to Cordelia that Lear is still sleeping, and her response reflects much of the action that has preceded:

> O you kind gods!
> Cure this great breach in his abused nature,
> Th' untun'd and jarring senses, O, wind up

> Of this child-changed father!
>
> > (IV, vii, 13–16)

Cordelia's first line indicates her faith in the fundamental goodness of the universe. Her reference to "nature" suggests belief in the bond between Lear and the universe, that as he was King, his health reflected his country and world. Her use of "untun'd" recalls the metaphor of music, which in this play, as in many others of Shakespeare, is used to dramatize the condition of the society. And the reference to "child-changed father" implies that as his two older daughters have brutalized Lear, so Cordelia's kindness will save him.

As music plays, reflecting the gradual restoration of harmony in Lear's kingdom and within Lear himself, Cordelia looks at her father and ponders all that he has endured. What moves her most, perhaps, is that he has survived:

> 'Tis wonder that thy life and wits at once
> Had not concluded all.
>
> > (IV, vii, 40–41)

As Lear awakens, he speaks of himself "Upon a wheel of fire" (IV, vii, 46), and we know that he feels his guilt as well as a desire for repentance. When Lear sees Cordelia's face, he assumes that he must be in heaven: "You are a spirit, I know; [when] did you die?" (IV, vii, 48). We recall Albany's line: "If that the heavens do not their visible spirits/ Send quickly . . . " (IV, vii, 46–47), as well as the Gentleman's comment from the last scene that Lear's last daughter "redeems nature" (IV, vi, 206). They suggest that hope for humanity does exist and that life has purpose.

As he gains consciousness, Lear's language remains humble and unaffected:

> I am a very foolish fond old man,
> Fourscore and upward, not an hour more nor less;
> And to deal plainly,
> I fear I am not in my perfect mind.
>
> > (IV, vii, 59–62)

Then he begs forgiveness of Cordelia:

> I know you do not love me, for your sisters
> Have (as I do remember) done me wrong:
> You have some cause, they have not.
>
> > (IV, vii, 72–74)

The honesty and simplicity of her next line make it perhaps the most touching of the play: "No cause, no cause" (IV, vii, 74). And when Lear asks if he is in France, Cordelia reaffirms his royal stature: "In your own kingdom, sir" (IV, vii, 75).

The scene ends with the painful realization that enemy forces have yet to be defeated. The Gentleman tells Kent, whose identity is still masked, that Edmund now leads the opposition and that Edgar and Kent himself are rumored to be in

Germany. In the scene's last lines, Kent clarifies that the final battle is about to take place, and once more we believe that good is triumphing.

In Act V, scene i, the opposition takes the stage as Edmund questions whether Albany is loyal to the cause (V, i, 1–5). Regan is more concerned with Edmund's affection for her and questions him intensely on his feelings for Goneril. Edmund teases her: "That thought abuses you" (V, i, 11), but also reassures Regan that he has never seduced Goneril. His use of the chivalric "honor" (V, i, 14) once more emphasizes his calculation and his amused delight at the prospect of two sisters squabbling over him.

Goneril then enters, brooding that she would rather lose the war than lose Edmund to her sister. Meanwhile Albany confirms his goal in leading the army:

> It touches us as France invades our land,
> Not bolds the King, with others whom, I fear,
> Most just and heavy causes make oppose.
>
> (V, i, 25–27)

He is against foreign invaders, not against those who support the King. Edmund, Regan, and Goneril all proclaim agreement with this goal, but their fraudulence is clear. Edmund and Albany head to counsel, but Edmund remains behind for a moment. As he does, Goneril and Regan, each overtly suspicious of the other, dicker over who will remain with Edmund, and eventually depart together with him. Their malicious politeness is a brief comic interlude.

Edgar, still in disguise, enters to give Albany the letter handed him by Oswald, which contains Goneril's proposal that Edmund murder Albany and marry her. Before Albany has a chance to read it, Edmund returns, warning that Cordelia's forces are drawing closer. Albany hurries to gather his army, leaving Edmund to muse pridefully on his relationship with Goneril and Regan:

> To both these sisters have I sworn my love;
> Each jealous of the other, as the stung
> Are of the adder. Which of them shall I take?
> Both? one? or neither? Neither can be enjoy'd
> If both remain alive . . .
>
> (V, i, 55–59)

He has no emotional commitment to either. Rather, he revels in his own strength and appeal. He does not plan to kill his rival Albany, who will die either in battle or at Goneril's hand afterwards (V, i, 64). But he fully intends to kill Lear and Cordelia: " . . . for my state/ Stands on me to defend, not to debate" (V, i, 68). He does not care to vie with others for the crown. As always, Edmund's loyalty is to himself.

The brief scene ii reveals the path of the war. Cordelia takes Lear under her protection while Edgar shields Gloucester: " . . . pray that the right may thrive" (V, ii, 2). The identity of the "right" is problematical, because Cordelia is fighting for the French, and Edmund leads the English along with Albany. Nevertheless, word comes quickly that the English have triumphed, and Edgar reports that Lear and Cordelia are prisoners. Gloucester is once again willing to die: "No further, sir, a man may rot even here" (V, ii, 8). But Edgar urges him onward: "Ripeness is all" (V, ii, 11). The line suggests that no matter what the external forces that play havoc with human existence, an individual's inner strength and understanding give meaning to that life. This attitude prepares us for the revelations of the final scene, when the question of life's meaning is thrust before us once more.

At the beginning of that scene, Cordelia is brought in as a prisoner, and her words reflect the theme of inner resolve:

> We are not the first
> Who with best meaning have incurr'd the worst.
> For thee, opposed king, I am cast down,
> Myself could else out-frown false Fortune's frown.
> Shall we not see these daughters and these sisters?
>
> (V, iii, 3–7)

Concerned only for her father's welfare, Cordelia promises the reuniting of the family, but Lear has no desire to see his daughters. Indeed, he is willing to dispense with all royal prerogatives, and his experience has given him the courage to endure any misfortune:

> No, no, no, no! Come let's away to prison:
> We two alone will sing like birds i' th' cage;
> When thou dost ask me blessing, I'll kneel down
> And ask of thee forgiveness. So we'll live,
> And pray, and sing, and tell old tales, and laugh
> At gilded butterflies, and hear poor rogues
> Talk of court news; and we'll talk with them too—
> Who loses and who wins; who's in, who's out—
> And take upon 's the mystery of things
> As if we were God's spies, and we'll wear out,
> In a wall'd prison, packs and sects of great ones,
> That ebb and flow by th' moon.
>
> (V, iii, 8–19)

He has lost interest in self-glorification, and emphasizes only the love he has never before shown. He sees the transience of worldly power ("who's in, who's out"), and he recognizes that political leaders ("packs and sects of great ones") come and go. What endures are kindness and the search for understanding ("the mystery of things"). At Edmund's order, the two are taken away, Lear ever bold: "We'll see 'em starv'd first" (V, iii, 25).

Edmund gives his captain a note that contains the order for the execution of Lear and Cordelia, then cautions the captain against mercy:

> Know thou this, that men
> Are as the time is: to be tender-minded

Does not become a sword.

(V, iii, 30–32)

Edmund remains ruthless, devoted to his personal code. Albany, Regan, and Goneril enter, and Albany demands that the prisoners be turned over to him for protection. Edmund attempts to put Albany off by explaining that Lear and Cordelia have been taken under guard so that they may not weaken the loyalty of the soldiers (V, iii, 45–51). Albany is outraged at what he judges as presumption by Edmund, whom he regards as a lesser officer (V, iii, 60–61). But Regan speaks up in Edmund's behalf, and Goneril is so impassioned that she takes up Edmund's side against her own husband. We are reminded of the first scene of the play, when Regan and Goneril vied hypocritically before Lear. This tableau is a grotesque parody.

As the two argue back and forth, Regan begins to feel ill, but stands by her devotion to Edmund:

> Witness the world, that I create thee here
> My lord and master.

(V, iii, 77–78)

Knowing her sister is soon to die from poison administered elsewhere, Goneril asks ironically: "Mean you to enjoy him?" (V, iii, 78). Albany interrupts by telling Goneril that she does not decide who Regan will marry, and Edmund, yet relishing his place as the object of desire of these two women, states that Albany, too, cannot make that decision (V, iii, 79). But none of the three have reckoned with Albany's new-found power, and he arrests Edmund and Goneril for treason. He apparently has read the letter given him earlier by Edgar, for Albany now tells Regan that Goneril "is subcontracted to this lord" (V, iii, 86, meaning Edmund, and that if Regan seeks to marry, she will have to marry Albany. Goneril, aware of her sister's imminent death, laughs off this bitter witticism: "An enterlude!" (V, iii, 89).

Suddenly Albany's tactics change, as he commands that a trumpet be sounded:

> If none appear to prove upon thy person
> Thy heinous, manifest, and many treasons,
> There is my pledge [*throwing down a glove*]. I'll make it
> on thy heart. . . .

(V, iii, 91–93)

We recall Edgar's instructions to Albany at Act V, scene i, line 49 and now await Edgar's reappearance. Meanwhile Regan grows more ill, to Goneril's pleasure (V, iii, 96). Edmund is eager for combat, and with braggadocio maintains the chivalric pose he has offered from the start: "I will maintain/ My truth and honor firmly" (V, iii, 100–101). After Regan is led back to her tent, the proclamation of challenge is read, and the trumpet sounds three times. Edgar appears, without revealing his identity, and declares himself as noble as Edmund. Then he reviews the catalogue of Edmund's crimes, in particular: " . . . False to thy gods, thy brother, and thy father . . . '' (V, iii, 135). We know that Edmund has been false to Edgar's god, but never to his own, the law of the jungle to which he has remained fiercely loyal.

Edmund retorts that according to the rules of knighthood, which Edmund pretends to value, this challenger might well be disdained, but Edmund consents to fight him anyway. The brothers duel, and Edmund falls, at which point Albany, who wants to ensure that Edmund stands trial, shouts ''Save him, save him!'' (V, iii, 152). Goneril tries to defend Edmund, claiming he was the victim of treachery, but Albany bullies her down and takes out the letter she wrote (V, iii, 155–158). Goneril refuses to submit and claims that she is the determinant of the law, but then strides off. Immediately Albany sends a guard after her: '' . . . she's desperate, govern her'' (V, iii, 162), for he wants her as well to stand trial. This entire sequence builds to the re-establishment of law, and such a seemingly inevitable progression makes subsequent events all the more shocking.

Recognizing that he has been mortally wounded, Edmund confesses:

> What you have charg'd me with, that have I done,
> And more, much more, the time will bring it out.
>
> (V, iii, 163–164)

Whether he means the executions of Lear and Cordelia or some other undiscovered sins is unclear. In either case, why in his repentance he does not order those executions halted sooner is difficult to say. Edmund's confession brings out the truth from Edgar:

> My name is Edgar, and thy father's son.
> The gods are just, and of our pleasant vices
> Make instruments to plague us.
>
> (V, iii, 170–172)

He reaffirms the notion that this universe is fair, and Edmund agrees:

> Th' hast spoken right, 'tis true.
> The wheel is come full circle, I am here.
>
> (V, iii, 174–175)

He concurs that his punishment is justified and that proper order is being restored. Edmund was always cognizant of his own nature and the rules by which he governed his life. He now recognizes his failure and accepts it. Albany pays tribute to Edgar's nobleness, and swears that at no time did Albany himself hold enmity for Edgar or Gloucester. Here, too, the tone of forgiveness and reconciliation suggests that all will be well.

Edgar then relates the details of his hiding out with Gloucester and the circumstances of Gloucester's death. The revelation that Tom o' Bedlam was Edgar, his son, was too much for the old man:

> But his flaw'd heart
> (Alack, too weak the conflict to support!)

'Twixt two extremes of passion, joy and grief,
Burst smilingly.

(V, iii, 197–200)

That Gloucester dies offstage reduces the impact of his death, but the nature of
his expiration anticipates Lear's final moments. Edmund is so moved by the
narrative that he urges Edgar to keep speaking. And Edgar concludes by telling
of his meeting with Kent. All strands of the story seem to be tying together
smoothly.

Edgar is interrupted, however, by a Gentleman who rushes in to report that
Goneril has stabbed herself after admitting the poisoning of Regan. Edmund sees
the grim humor:

I was contracted to them both; all three
Now marry in an instant.

(V, iii, 229–230)

Albany takes these two deaths as further evidence of the rightness of the world:

This judgment of the heavens, that makes us tremble,
Touches us not with pity.

(V, iii, 232–233)

His confidence is shaken, however, by the appearance of Kent, who reminds
Albany that Lear and Cordelia are yet to be accounted for, and Albany orders
them retrieved. When the bodies of Goneril and Regan are brought, Edmund
seems to have a revelation: "Yet Edmund was belov'd" (V, iii, 240). The two
who lusted after him may have been immoral and unnatural, but the fact of their
desire seems to touch something inside Edmund:

I pant for life. Some good I mean to do,
Despite of mine own nature. Quickly send
(Be brief in it) to th' castle, for my writ
Is on the life of Lear and on Cordelia.

(V, iii, 244–247)

He gives his sword to expedite matters, then explains that Cordelia's death would
be reported as a suicide (V, iii, 253–256). After Albany realizes that Lear and
Cordelia must be found, and once Edmund gives the order for them to be saved,
we expect this aspect of the play, like the others, to be resolved beneficently.

What follows, instead, is the most shattering moment in a play full of pain,
as Lear enters carrying the body of Cordelia. Speaking for audiences across the
centuries, Samuel Johnson found her death unendurable, and confessed himself
unable to read the play because of this ending. In Nahum Tate's adaptation,
Lear is restored to his throne while Cordelia marries Edgar. But Shakespeare
chose instead to create this devastating conclusion. Is it fitting? So much of the
last part of the play has built towards a sense of moral rectitude, of a fundamental
justice to the universe, as good triumphs over evil. And the death of Cordelia
is pointless and preventable. But that very purposelessness makes the ending

necessary, for it brings us back to the mystery of existence. Does the death of Cordelia suggest a random universe without order or structure?

Even in his weakened condition, Lear realizes that his daughter is dead. Yet he clings to hope that somehow she may be alive:

> Lend me a looking-glass,
> If that her breath will mist or stain the stone,
> Why then she lives.
>
> (V, iii, 262–264)

Kent has a different perspective: "Is this the promis'd end?" (V, iii, 264). The question suggests that after such a tragedy nothing can have meaning. Lear hopes once more that Cordelia still breathes, for her life will redeem all the sufferings he has felt. These lines in particular have suggested to some critics that Cordelia is a Christlike figure who dies for the sins of others. As Lear mourns over her, he remembers that in a last burst of energy he killed Cordelia's executioner. Then he recognizes Kent, but fails to realize that he and Caius, the loyal follower, are the same man. Finally Lear learns of the deaths of his other daughters. Yet he accepts all this information with distraction, for he is totally absorbed by Cordelia. The news that Edmund has died is tossed aside by Albany: "That's but a trifle here" (V, iii, 296).

Albany then restores Lear to his throne:

> For us, we will resign,
> During the life of this old majesty,
> To him our absolute power.
>
> (V, iii, 299–301)

But Lear does not listen. First he shouts: "And my poor fool is hang'd!" (V, iii, 306). Whether Lear refers only to Cordelia, or to both Cordelia and his own Fool, is a matter for debate. The two have had complementary roles in his life, and thus Lear's blending of their identity is appropriate. Then he asks the ultimate question:

> Why should a dog, a horse, a rat, have life,
> And thou no breath at all? Thou'lt come no more,
> Never, never, never, never, never.
>
> (V, iii, 307–308)

Why does such suffering and pain as we have witnessed exist in the world? The play provides no answer.

Suddenly Lear seems to imagine that Cordelia lives again, but the excitement of the moment is too great for him, and he expires. Whether he dies from joy or a broken heart is one more uncertainty.

Some small compensation is provided by Kent:

The wonder is he hath endur'd so long,
He but usurp'd his life.

(V, iii, 317–318)

Albany begins the process of restoring the kingdom by offering rule to Kent and Edgar, but Kent prepares to leave:

I have a journey, sir, shortly to go:
My master calls me, I must not say no.

(V, iii, 322–323)

He anticipates joining Lear in death.
Edgar then prepares to move the kingdom forward:

The weight of this sad time we must obey,
Speak what we feel, not what we ought to say:
The oldest hath borne most; we that are young
Shall never see so much, nor live so long.

(V, iii, 324–327)

Edgar seems to feel that Lear's life has taught others who will follow, and this final address unites the themes of responsibility and humanity that are the cornerstone of the tragedy.

King Lear is in many ways the most overwhelming work not only of Shakespeare but of any dramatist. At times it seems to burst beyond the bounds of the stage. Its prodigious characters encompass the full range of humanity, and the span of emotions, the heights of love and the depths of hate, are almost too much to absorb. Yet on reflection we see its thematic unity: no matter how we view the enigma of the universe, no matter how deep the suffering we endure, the capacity of the human heart to learn and forgive redeems us.

SUGGESTIONS FOR FURTHER READING

Adelman, Janet, ed. *Twentieth Century Interpretations of* King Lear. Englewood Cliffs, N.J.: Prentice-Hall, 1978.

Brooke, Nicholas. *Shakespeare:* King Lear. London: Edward Arnold, 1963.

Cavell, Stanley. *Disowning Knowledge In Six Plays of Shakespeare*. Cambridge and New York: Cambridge University Press, 1987.

Colie, Rosalie L., ed. *Some Facets of* King Lear: *Essays in Prismatic Criticism*. Toronto: University of Toronto Press, 1974.

Danby, J. F. *Shakespeare's Doctrine of Nature: A Study of* King Lear. London: Faber and Faber, 1949.

Davis, Arthur G. *The Royalty of Lear*. Jamaica, N. Y.: St. John's University Press, 1974.

Elton, William. King Lear *and the Gods*. San Marino, Calif.: Huntington Library, 1966. Reprint. Lexington: University Press of Kentucky, 1988.

Frye, Northrop. *Fools of Time: Studies in Shakespearean Tragedy*. Toronto: University of Toronto Press, 1967.

Goldberg, S. L. *An Essay on* King Lear. Cambridge: Cambridge University Press, 1974.
Heilman, Robert B. *This Great Stage: Image and Structure in* King Lear. Baton Rouge: Louisiana State University Press, 1948.
Jorgensen, Paul. *Lear's Self-Discovery*. Berkeley and Los Angeles: University of California Press, 1967.
Kernan, Alvin. "Formalism and Realism in Elizabethan Drama: The Miracles in *King Lear.*" *Renaissance Drama* 9 (1966): 59–66.
Mack, Maynard. King Lear *in Our Time*. Berkeley and Los Angeles: University of California Press, 1965.
Muir, Kenneth, and Stanley Wells, eds. *Aspects of* King Lear. Cambridge and New York: Cambridge University Press, 1982.
Rosenberg, Marvin. *The Masks of* King Lear. Berkeley and Los Angeles: University of California Press, 1972.

MACBETH

Macbeth is the shortest of Shakespeare's tragedies, and scholars have surmised that the text may have been truncated, perhaps by Shakespeare himself. Yet its brevity is a virtue, for the play's concentrated tension contributes enormously to what may be the most horrific of Shakespeare's works. Other plays are as gory. In other plays, as many or more characters are murdered. But none of the others is so preoccupied with the concept of murder, with the deliberate planning and outcome of the act. Furthermore, the motivation for this series of murders is uncomfortably clear: so eager is Macbeth to possess and maintain power that he is willing to kill in cold blood.

The creation of the play may have been influenced by the new king of England, James I, formerly James VI of Scotland, who succeeded to the throne in 1603 upon the death of Elizabeth. He had a keen interest in demonology, and even wrote a book, *Daemonologie* (1597), which Shakespeare probably used in writing the scenes involving the witches. Furthermore, James had a deep concern for Scottish history, and could trace his ancestry back to the eleventh century, the time of the story. Shakespeare's main historical reference was Holinshed's *Chronicles of England, Scotlande, and Ireland* (1577), the primary source of his history plays. In his adaptation, however, the playwright made several deviations. In Holinshed, Macbeth has a legitimate grievance against a young and incompetent Duncan. In the play, Duncan is older and decent, and Macbeth's reason for murder is not political, but personal. Banquo, Macbeth's accomplice in Holinshed, is a noble bystander in Shakespeare's play, possibly because Banquo was said to be an ancestor of James. Finally, Shakespeare dispenses with what Holinshed described as a successful ten-year reign by Macbeth and turns him into a tyrant who rules briefly and cruelly. The impact of all these alterations is an emphasis not on political ramifications, as in Holinshed, but on psychological and moral implications.

One sidelight: *Macbeth* has long been regarded as a jinxed work, because so many productions have gone awry. Thus theatrical professionals often prefer that it not be spoken of by its title, but instead referred to as "the Scottish play."

The brief opening scene sets the eerie tone and atmosphere. The storm and noise suggest chaos, but the three witches are in control, as they agree to meet again:

> When the hurly-burly's done,
> When the battle's lost and won.

(I, i, 3–4)

The emphasis on time as a symbol of order pervades the play. The battle to which the witches refer may be any one of three: the specific battle in front of them, the battle for the Scottish crown, or, most profound of all, the battle for Macbeth's soul. The structure of the phrase ''lost and won'' suggests the witches' detachment, an issue to be considered presently. The third witch adds that they will meet ''ere the set of sun'' (I, i, 5). The line refers not only to the seemingly constant darkness in the background to the action, but to the death of Duncan, for the sun was traditionally the symbol of kingship. The three witches depart with a warning in unison:

> Fair is foul, and foul is fair,
> Hover through the fog and filthy air.

(I, i, 11–12)

The couplet implies the moral ambiguity and other confusion soon to possess not only Macbeth and his wife, but all of Scotland.

After this opening tableau, some audiences may believe that the witches ordain their subsequent meetings with Macbeth and that they determine his future. According to this interpretation, the play is about fate, and in murdering Duncan, Macbeth is only playing out his destiny. Such a reading is inaccurate, as becomes apparent in scene ii. Duncan sets the tone by asking: ''What bloody man is that?'' (I, ii, 1). The sergeant then recounts the course of battle against the rebel Macdonwald, particularly Macbeth's triumph:

> For brave Macbeth (well he deserves that name),
> Disdaining Fortune, with his brandish'd steel,
> Which smok'd with bloody execution,
> (Like Valor's minion) carv'd out his passage
> Till he fac'd the slave;
> Which nev'r shook hands, nor bade farewell to him,
> Till he unseam'd him from the nave to th' chops,
> And fix'd his head upon our battlements.

(I, ii, 16–23)

This description emphasizes the brutality of war, the environment in which Macbeth flourishes. Thus his capacity for violence is easier to understand. The phrase ''Disdaining Fortune'' characterizes Macbeth's behavior, and the motif is basic to the play, for Macbeth constantly attempts to see himself as in the grip of fate. Right here, though, we learn that Macbeth is a free agent, responsible for whatever happens to him.

How, then, are we to regard the witches? Shakespeare's contemporaries generally believed in witches as in league with the devil and empowered to fly, vanish, conjure storms and images, and inflict disease. Perhaps these three figures are best viewed as invidious meddlers, toying with human action. The outcome of events matters little to them. They desire only to play upon human vulnerabilities, to tap evil within, and they have chosen as the subject Macbeth, whose frailties and vices are exploitable.

In the rest of scene ii we learn more of this man. After the Sergeant's opening description, Duncan comments: "O valiant cousin, worthy gentleman!" (I, ii, 24). The rest of the play proves this evaluation tragically ironic. The Sergeant continues to describe the invasion of the Norwegian king, whom Macbeth and Banquo have turned back. Rosse then enters to report the traitorous activities of the Thane of Cawdor, who allied himself with Norway (I, ii, 49–53). Macbeth, however, fought so boldly that the Norwegian king surrendered, now seeks an end to the fighting, and is even willing to pay indemnity. In response, Duncan orders a change of titles:

> No more that Thane of Cawdor shall deceive
> Our bosom interest. Go pronounce his present death,
> And with his former title greet Macbeth.
>
> (I, ii, 63–65)

Duncan hopes to rid his army of treachery, but here, too, irony underlies his actions, for treachery on a massive scale is soon to flourish. Furthermore, his rhyme of "death" and "Macbeth" resounds ominously. The last line of the scene, too, has ironic overtones: "What he hath lost, noble Macbeth hath won" (I, ii, 67). We remember the witch's comment in scene i (I, i, 4), and the sense of instability continues.

In scene iii the witches return. The first vows to punish a sailor whose wife cursed the witch and committed the comparatively trivial crime of refusing her chestnuts.

> But in a sieve I'll thither sail,
> And, like a rat without a tail,
> I'll do, I'll do, and I'll do.
>
> (I, iii, 8–10)

The repetition of "do" suggests that the witches' actions will be relentless, and, as such, the word becomes a motif that resounds throughout the play. The first witch then makes her scheme more specific:

> I'll drain him dry as hay:
> Sleep shall neither night or day
> Hang upon his penthouse lid;
> He shall live a man forbid . . .
>
> (I, iii, 18–21)

These lines suggest the witches' capacity for vengeance, and the punishments, sleeplessness in particular, anticipate those Macbeth will undergo. A few lines

later Macbeth enters, a protagonist distinctive among Shakespeare's tragic heroes. At this moment he is not royal. He is not a man of excessive passion. His
only outstanding feature is his skill and recklessness in the battlefield, where he
pursues his task with lusty enthusiasm. In no other way does he prove remarkable.
In fact, he is in many ways an ordinary man, and thus the battle between his
ambition and his conscience is one with which audiences may feel uncomfortably
close.

When Macbeth enters, his first line foreshadows the sequence to follow: ''So
foul and fair a day I have not seen'' (I, iii, 38). This line suggests the paradoxical
mixture of good and evil the witches offer, the promise of kingship without
explanation of the proper path. Banquo is shocked by their bizarre appearance
and questions the combination of their female identity and their beards (I, iii,
45–47). Such a clash of genders is one of the aspects of unnaturalness that
dominates the play. The witches then greet Macbeth with three titles: Thane of
Glamis, Thane of Cawdor, and King. Macbeth has no verbal reaction, but Banquo
indicates his colleague's response:

> Good sir, why do you start, and seem to fear
> Things that do sound so fair?
>
> (I, iii, 50–51)

Macbeth still does not answer, so Banquo turns to the witches:

> My noble partner
> You greet with present grace, and great prediction
> Of noble having and of royal hope,
> That he seems rapt withal; to me you speak not.
> If you can look into the seeds of time,
> And say which grain will grow, and which will not,
> Speak then to me, who neither beg nor fear
> Your favors nor your hate.
>
> (I, iii, 54–61)

Banquo's words are those of a man in possession of himself, as opposed to
Macbeth, whose behavior suggests he is already in the grip of ambition. Banquo's
reference to seeds anticipates imagery of growth and other manifestations of
nature that are essential to the play.

The witches respond with the three vaguer predictions for Banquo (I, iii, 65–
68), including a claim that he will be the father of kings. As they depart, Macbeth
desperately orders that they remain to reveal more. Banquo, however, dismisses
the trio:

> Were such things here as we do speak about?
> Or have we eaten on the insane root
> That takes the reason prisoner?
>
> (I, iii, 83–85)

But Macbeth's eager comments and questions indicate that he has indeed lost
his reason, and never does he regain possession.

Rosse and Angus enter to bring Duncan's appreciation for Macbeth's achievements in war and also to report Macbeth's new title: Thane of Cawdor. Macbeth is surprised that they dress him in the "borrowed robes" (I, iii, 109), and this imagery of clothing is another pattern that recurs. Here it suggests the misplacement of honor on Macbeth, whose behavior grows more peculiar with almost every line. He speaks an aside to himself, then a sentence aloud to Rosse and Angus, then one more aside to Banquo (I, ii, 116–119). Such fragmented speeches hint at the disorder in Macbeth's mind. As if to warn Macbeth, Banquo in his own aside muses on the witches' predictions:

> And oftentimes, to win us to our harm
> The instruments of darkness tell us truths,
> Win us with honest trifles, to betray 's
> In deepest consequence.
>
> (I, iii, 123–126)

He finds their capacity to create temptation blasphemous. Macbeth understands this perspective, as he reveals in his next aside:

> This supernatural soliciting
> Cannot be ill; cannot be good. If ill,
> Why hath it given me earnest of success,
> Commencing in a truth? I am Thane of Cawdor.
> If good, why do I yield to that suggestion
> Whose horrid image doth unfix my hair
> And make my seated heart knock at my ribs,
> Against the use of nature?
>
> (I, iii, 130–137)

He has the same doubts Banquo has. But Macbeth is less able to resist them.

> Present fears
> Are less than horrible imaginings:
> My thought, whose murther yet is but fantastical,
> Shakes so my single state of man that function
> Is smother'd in surmise, and nothing is
> But what is not.
>
> (I, iii, 137–142)

That he already conceives a "horrid image" indicates that he has previously contemplated Duncan's killing, if not consciously, then in the recesses of his unconscious. The theme of paradox here reflects Macbeth's intellect. On one side, he is obsessed with power and is capable of almost anything to achieve it. On the other, he is sufficiently respectful of the power he seeks that he is in awe of the effects of any action that might break either the legal process of achieving power or the natural order that buttresses it. Yet at the same time he is uncontrollably eager to break it. Yet he fears breaking it. Yet he is driven to break it.

In sum, he is compelled towards an action he is terrified of committing. To resolve these contradictory questions, he has a solution:

> If chance will have me king, why, chance may crown me
> Without my stir.
>
> (I, iii, 143–144)

Such concession removes Macbeth from the roster of Shakespeare's Machiavels, including Iago in *Othello*, Edmund in *King Lear*, and Richard III. They rejoice in their own power and amorality. Macbeth, however, acknowledges himself unable to resolve his crisis, and such recognition helps him maintain our sympathy. He will go in the direction of the strongest attraction:

> Come what come may,
> Time and the hour runs through the roughest day.
>
> (I, iii, 146–147)

He believes in the symbolic strength of time as a constant in his world. But even this security is shattered as Macbeth is drawn toward murder. Again, he is not going against his will, but letting himself be led. And the most powerful force leading him is to be Lady Macbeth.

Scene iv builds tension within Macbeth and within us. Duncan's first line is one among many with ironic overtones: "Is execution done on Cawdor?" (I, iv, 1). We foresee the moment when Duncan himself will be the victim. Malcolm reports that Cawdor confessed to treason but died in repentance:

> Nothing in his life
> Became him like the leaving it. He died
> As one that had been studied in his death,
> To throw away the dearest thing he ow'd,
> As 'twere a careless trifle.
>
> (I, iv, 7–11)

Such nobility will not be part of Macbeth's life or death. Duncan's response reflects his combination of decency and naivete:

> There's no art
> To find the mind's construction in the face:
> He was a gentleman on whom I built
> An absolute trust.
>
> (I, iv, 11–14)

He is soon to place trust in another deceitful man, Macbeth, whose treachery will far exceed Cawdor's.

Macbeth enters to warm greetings from Duncan, and the Thane in turn expresses his fidelity in terms so extravagant that they reek of fraudulence:

> Your Highness' part
> Is to receive our duties; and our duties
> Are to your throne and state children and servants;

Which do but what they should, by doing every thing
Safe toward your love and honor.

(I, iv, 23–27)

In retrospect, every word in this speech and, indeed, in this scene, is ironic, but we note especially the reference to children, a central theme of the play.

Duncan couches his next laudatory remarks to Banquo in images of growth (I, iv, 28–29), indicating Banquo should have honors as substantial as those given to Macbeth, and Banquo offers gratitude. Here, too, neither recipient knows how these hopes will come to fruition. Duncan then clarifies that his son Malcolm is next in line to the throne, and we wonder how Macbeth is reacting inside to this decree that seems to crush his dreams. Nonetheless, Duncan claims, all will benefit:

But signs of nobleness, like stars, shall shine
On all deservers. From hence to Enverness,
And bind us further to you.

(I, iv, 41–43)

Duncan thinks of the stars as beneficent lights. Then he announces he will visit Macbeth's castle, and Macbeth agrees to make all preparations in yet one more ironic speech (I, iv, 44–47). But in an aside he sees the occasion as opportunity, and views the stars quite differently than Duncan does:

The Prince of Cumberland! that is a step
On which I must fall down, or else o'erleap,
For in my way it lies. Stars, hide your fires,
Let not light see my black and deep desires;
The eye wink at the hand; yet let that be
Which the eye fears, when it is done, to see.

(I, iv, 48–53)

Macbeth has discovered another obstruction in his way to the kingship. Even as the possibility of murder possesses him, though, he manifests a conscience in asking the stars to hide, and thus he knows that what he plans to do is wrong. But he is compelled to go on. Duncan's final tribute, so misplaced, ends this scene of irony and expectation.

In the first lines of scene v, Lady Macbeth clarifies that she understands her husband's personality. He has written her about his honors as well as the predictions of the witches, addressing her in affectionate terms: " . . . my dearest partner of greatness" (I, v, 11). She, however, remains unemotional:

Glamis thou art, and Cawdor, and shalt be
What thou art promis'd.

(I, v, 15–16)

She assumes the kingship is already his, and wants to leave nothing to chance:

Yet do I fear thy nature,
It is too full o' th' milk of human kindness

> To catch the nearest way. Thou wouldst be great,
> Art not without ambition, but without
> The illness should attend it.

                                                                (I, v, 16–20)

The word that stands out most is "illness." Lady Macbeth knows that something malignant must lie in the soul of someone who is to fulfill what she imagines, and she is aware that her husband lacks that property:

> What thou wouldst highly,
> That wouldst thou holily; wouldst not play false,
> And yet wouldst wrongly win. Thou'ldst have, great Glamis,
> That which cries, "Thus thou must do," if thou have it;
> And that which rather thou dost fear to do
> Than wishest should be undone.

                                                                (I, v, 20–25)

In her mind he lacks the capacity for deception, the ruthlessness that must accompany successful ambition. Here again is irony, for when the act of murder is demanded, Macbeth proves bolder than his wife. We also note her repetition of various forms of "do," as if to clarify the myriad aspects of action.

At this moment, however, Lady Macbeth believes in her own capacity for aggression. Thus she urges her husband home: "That I may pour my spirits in thine ear" (I, v, 26). When she learns from the messenger that Duncan is to stay at their castle, her first reaction suggests an undiscovered guilt: "Thou'rt mad to say it!" (I, v, 31). The outburst implies that the messenger has claimed to read her thoughts. And when he leaves, the depths of her passion surface:

> Come, you spirits
> That tend on mortal thoughts, unsex me here,
> And fill me from the crown to the toe topful
> Of direst cruelty! Make thick my blood,
> Stop up th' access and passage to remorse,
> That no compunctious visitings of nature
> Shake my fell purpose, nor keep peace between
> Th' effect and [it]!

                                                                (I, v, 40–47)

She reiterates the word "blood," as though her purpose is to curse the limits femininity places on her actions. Yet like Macbeth she has a sense of foreboding. She is aware of the moral horror of what she contemplates, but feels an irresistible impulse and does not want to be inhibited by physiological constraints.

What is the origin of this impulse? The next lines indicate her particular drive:

> Come to my woman's breasts,
> And take my milk for gall, you murth'ring ministers,
> Wherever in your sightless substances

You wait on nature's mischief!

(I, v, 47–50)

The repetition of "milk" from line 15 reinforces that she is tormented by her womanliness, another instance of gender imbalance. To Lady Macbeth, her husband must be the vehicle by which she acquires the power forever denied her. Thus she calls for "nature's mischief" for two reasons. One, her own nature has already been corrupted by being trapped in the body of a woman. Two, she wants to be allowed to participate in the unnatural act of regicide. Both images, and others to follow, reflect the universal unnaturalness of the events of this play. She concludes in a triumphant shout:

> Come, thick night,
> And pall thee in the dunnest smoke of hell,
> That my keen knife see not the wound it makes,
> Nor heaven peep through the blanket of the dark
> To cry, "Hold, hold!"

(I, v, 50–54)

At this moment she seems to feel herself committing murder, and her cry that no force should stop her reinforces that she knows her vision is evil.

That Lady Macbeth's hopes will not be easy to fulfill is more apparent when Macbeth enters. Her lines of greeting are full of exclamations:

> Great Glamis! worthy Cawdor!
> Greater than both, by the all-hail hereafter!

(I, v, 54–55)

She raves on, spurring him to violence. Her husband, though, answers tentatively: "My dearest love,/ Duncan comes here tonight" (I, v, 58–59). When she asks when Duncan intends to leave, Macbeth is again meek: "To-morrow, as he purposes" (I, v, 60). When she continues to attempt to inspire him, hinting at greatness to come, he mutters indecisively: "We will speak further" (I, v, 71). She is obviously more enthralled with the plot than he, but then she has greater reason to be. As a triumphant soldier, Macbeth has garnered the plaudits of his country. What he seeks is further honor. Lady Macbeth, however, has never known personal triumph. She must live through her husband, and this set of events may be her final opportunity for glory. Thus her last words, "Leave all the rest to me" (I, v, 73), have a peculiar irony. She is looking for something to do, and she would prefer to carry out everything by herself. But she is limited to simply "wanting." "Leave all the rest to me" will end up meaning "I'll leave everything to you."

Scene vi is another ironic scene, as Duncan enters the grounds of Macbeth's home:

> This castle hath a pleasant seat, the air
> Nimbly and sweetly recommends itself

Unto our gentle senses.

(I, vi, 1–3)

Banquo echoes these thoughts with images of health and growth that clash with
the secret intentions of the hosts. "Fair" appearance masks "foul" intentions.
Lady Macbeth's appearance is greeted with enthusiasm by Duncan, and she
proves herself able to "play false," as she indicated Macbeth would not do (I,
v, 21). Duncan's tributes make her deception all the more theatrically stirring.
  Macbeth's soliloquy that opens scene vii encapsulates his dilemma:

> If it were done, when 'tis done, then 'twere well
> It were done quickly. If th' assassination
> Could trammel up the consequence, and catch
> With his surcease, success; that but this blow
> Might be the be-all and the end-all—here,
> But here, upon this bank and [shoal] of time,
> We'ld jump the life to come.

(I, vii, 1–7)

The concept of "doing" as explained here, is at the heart of the play. The murder
will not be "done" at once. Every act has consequences, and the aftermath will
linger, as Macbeth knows. Here is the core of the man: a mixture of ambition,
boldness, and fear. He is ruthless enough to plan murder and callous enough to
carry it out. But he is restrained, just barely, by dread of either legal or supernatural retribution. Macbeth's desires here are almost contradictory. He is propelled toward power he believes he deserves. But his faith constrains him. He
believes that beneficence and morality hold sway in the world, and such trust
almost prevents his achieving his life's goal:

>   But in these cases
> We still have judgment here, that we but teach
> Bloody instructions, which, being taught, return
> To plague th' inventor. This even-handed justice
> Commends th' ingredients of our poison'd chalice
> To our own lips.

(I, vii, 7–12)

Macbeth is leaning toward the "right" act: not killing. His rationale is not
admirable, but he is prepared to control himself. He continues with reasons why
the murder would be wrong, emphasizing both his relationship with Duncan and
Duncan's innocence, and the religious imagery (I, vii, 18–25) confirms that the
assassination would be blasphemous, a crime against the divine order. All these
reservations, however, cannot withstand the force of Lady Macbeth, who now
enters.
  Before she can take hold, Macbeth, as if afraid of her power, tries to assert
himself and eliminate opportunity for her to influence him:

> We will proceed no further in this business:
> He hath honor'd me of late, and I have bought

Golden opinions from all sorts of people,
Which would be worn now in their newest gloss,
Not cast aside so soon.

(I, vii, 31–35)

He does not reveal his fears, which she would have no way to answer. Instead he offers a lame excuse, inviting her to toss it aside, because he wants to be convinced. She does just that.

First she claims to doubt his love (I, vii, 35–39). Then she comments derisively about his manhood (I, vii, 39–45), and he answers brusquely that he is indeed a man (I, vii, 46–47). Her last maneuver is to dramatize her own resolve, which she does in a startling manner:

> I have given suck, and know
> How tender 'tis to love the babe that milks me;
> I would, while it was smiling in my face,
> Have pluck'd my nipple from his boneless gums,
> And dash'd the brains out, had I so sworn as you
> Have done to this.

(I, vii, 54–59)

These lines provoke the familiar question as to the existence of Lady Macbeth's children, since none is mentioned elsewhere. Possibly she had them by a first husband, since Macbeth never speaks of children of his own. The issue can be debated endlessly, but her choice of imagery is nonetheless striking. It is an attempt to concretize the depths of her desire, but the jarring details should also be seen as further indication of her frustration with womanhood. We may speculate that if her children no longer live, then her desperation for worldly power is compensation for her failure in what was in Shakespeare's day regarded as woman's essential role: motherhood.

So impressive is her energy that she wins over Macbeth. She details her plan (I, vii, 61–72), and Macbeth offers what he takes as the highest praise: "Bring forth men-children only!" (I, vii, 72). Then he expresses his resolve in essential imagery:

> I am settled, and bend up
> Each corporal agent to this terrible feat.
> Away, and mock the time with fairest show:
> False face must hide what the false heart doth know.

(I, vii, 79–82)

The concept of time traditionally stands for order and social stability. Here Macbeth shows his willingness to submit his nation to chaos, and that will be the result of this murder. His last line, which reminds us of Lady Macbeth's earlier prediction (I, v, 20–22), emphasizes the theme of appearance and reality.

In Act II, scene i, Banquo walks with his son Fleance, and the darkness they describe hints at the events to follow. In private Banquo ruminates about the predictions of the witches:

> Merciful powers,
> Restrain in me the cursed thoughts that nature
> Gives way to in repose.
>
> > (II, i, 7–9)

Banquo is not immune to ambition, but such steadfastness in the face of temptation contrasts with Macbeth's yielding. When Macbeth enters, Banquo instinctively goes for his sword, an ironically apt reaction, even as Macbeth refers to himself as "A friend" (II, i, 11). Banquo recalls the meeting with the witches, but Macbeth, clearly trying to divert suspicion, claims he gives them no thought, and casually proposes that he and Banquo should ally themselves (II, i, 21–24). We remember that the witches predicted that Banquo should be the father of kings (I, iii, 67). Perhaps Macbeth already anticipates action against Banquo, who answers noncommittally, then leaves with Fleance.

Alone, Macbeth offers another soliloquy that substantiates his ever-present doubts:

> Is this a dagger which I see before me,
> The handle toward my hand? Come, let me clutch thee:
> I have thee not, and yet I see thee still.
> Art thou not, fatal vision, sensible
> To feeling as to sight? or art thou but
> A dagger of the mind, a false creation,
> Proceeding from the heat-oppressed brain?
>
> > (II, i, 33–39)

A duality is apparent. Macbeth wishes to grasp the object he envisions, but realizes that the knife is leading him to act against his judgment. His use of the phrase "fatal vision" implies he knows what end his actions will bring. Still, he is transfixed by the blade and the energy it represents:

> I see thee yet, in form as palpable
> As this which now I draw.
> Thou marshal'st me the way that I was going,
> And such an instrument I was to use.
>
> > (II, i, 40–44)

He remains tempted by a sight that he tries to explain away as inviting him down an unwelcome road. Simultaneously he convinces himself that because the knife is leading him, that way is the one he is meant to go. Here is a mind split, but following its dominant traits: violence and ambition. Meanwhile Macbeth's imagination runs amuck with pictures of murder and blood (II, i, 45–56), images that both lure and repel him.

Macbeth even manages to make sound effects work in his favor:

> I go, and it is done; the bell invites me.
> Hear it not, Duncan, for it is a knell,

That summons thee to heaven or to hell.

(II, i, 62–64)

Sometimes a person trapped in a dilemma allows an arbitrary event to determine the outcome, to stand for a form of destiny. Here Macbeth listens to the bell and rationalizes that the tolling invites Duncan's death. We, however, view the bell as tolling for Macbeth, who will soon descend into his own hell.

In the next few lines the murder is carried out. Lady Macbeth waits anxiously, having drugged the grooms to allow her husband safe entrance into Duncan's chambers. Meanwhile she rejoices in her participation:

> That which hath made them drunk hath made me bold;
> What hath quench'd them hath given me fire.

(II, ii, 1–2)

She also reveals her fundamental weakness, for she rues her missed opportunity to kill Duncan by herself:

> Had he not resembled
> My father as he slept, I had done't.

(II, ii, 12–13)

Does Duncan resemble her father? Possibly. Does she unconsciously regard him as the father of her nation, her spiritual father? That explanation might also be valid. Far more likely than either, however, is that she lacks the courage of her convictions. She has humiliated Macbeth into murder, partially because she despises such weakness in herself. Thus not only is she angry that she is a woman and therefore denied opportunity for advancement, but her nature is, in essence, less bold than her husband's, and therefore she is perpetually disappointed with herself. For all her manipulation, for all her vivid language, Lady Macbeth is a smaller person than her husband. Not just physically, although we may assume that such is the case. Rather, she is not able to withstand the emotional battering he undergoes. As the drama proceeds, she collapses under the knowledge of what she has caused, while Macbeth allows punishment to accumulate. Thus Lady Macbeth becomes pathetic, while Macbeth, through the endurance of pain and the ability to face the ruin of his life, becomes tragic.

The difference between them appears immediately after the murder. First, the couple exchange a series of short, breathless lines that reflect the tension of the moment. Then Macbeth acknowledges that he is overwhelmed by the shock of killing. Speaking of the sleeping guards who cried out, he whispers:

> List'ning their fear, I could not say "Amen,"
> When they did say "God bless us!"

(II, ii, 26–27)

Lady Macbeth dismisses his trepidation: "Consider it not so deeply" (II, ii, 27). But he raves on, haunted by imaginary cries in which the word "sleep" tolls like that bell he heard earlier. He is afraid that hereafter he will be denied sleep, a manifestation of the natural order of a human life. Lady Macbeth attempts to remain practical, ordering her husband to wash his hands while she spreads blood over the sleeping grooms. But he is almost reduced to inaction: "I am afraid to think what I have done" (II, ii, 48). He cries that he is haunted by his deed:

> Whence is that knocking?
> How is't with me, when every noise appalls me?
> What hands are here? Hah! they pluck out mine eyes.
> Will all great Neptune's ocean wash this blood
> Clean from my hand?
>
> (II, ii, 54–58)

Her answer eventually proves ironic:

> A little water clears us of this deed;
> How easy is it then!
>
> (II, ii, 64–65)

Later the implications of her act overwhelm her, and this calculating pose shatters. When a knocking is heard at the door of the castle, Macbeth imagines the worst: "Wake Duncan with thy knocking! I would thou couldst!" (II, ii, 71). Already he regrets his crime.

   The scene with the Porter is, on one level, comic respite from the relentless tension of the previous scenes. But as is often the case in Shakespeare, this seemingly innocent interlude has thematic relevance. Here the Porter imagines that he is at the door of "Hell Gate" (II, iii, 2), and he recites a catalogue of criminals who demand entrance. All apply to Macbeth, but one is particularly close:

> Faith, here's an equivocator, that could
> swear in both the scales against either scale, who com-
> mitted treason enough for God's sake, yet could
> not equivocate to heaven.
>
> (II, iii, 8–11)

Certainly Macbeth has lied in the previous scenes, and his murder of Duncan is the greatest of treasons. Furthermore, he could not say "Amen" earlier. The other criminals, the farmer who hanged himself "on th' expectation of plenty" (II, iii, 5) and the tailor who steals also reflect Macbeth's actions. All these criminals have allowed their ambition to control them, and all end up in hell. In his responses to Macduff and Lennox, the Porter describes how drink, like lechery, may be an equivocator:

> . . . it makes him, and it mars him; it sets him
> on, and it takes him off; it persuades him, and dis-
> heartens him; makes him stand to, and not stand to; in
> conclusion, equivocates him in a sleep, and giving him

the lie, leaves him.

(II, iii, 32–36)

The addictive powers of drink and lechery as described here may be likened to the role of ambition in Macbeth's life. It has inspired him to action, but also trapped him in a perpetual hell, as becomes apparent on Macbeth's next appearance. Macduff greets him, but Macbeth responds in short, toneless lines. Lennox speaks of the extraordinary noises and actions that took place (II, iii, 54–61), but Macbeth can only answer lifelessly: " 'Twas a rough night" (II, iii, 61). He is numb with guilt.

Macduff returns in horror, and his report reveals the magnitude of Macbeth's crime:

> Most sacrilegious murther hath broke ope
> The Lord's anointed temple, and stole thence
> The life o' th' building!

(II, iii, 67–69)

The religious implications of regicide are apparent. As word spreads throughout the castle, the reactions of Lady Macbeth and Macbeth reveal their desperate states. When she is told of Duncan's murder, Lady Macbeth responds oddly: "What, in our house?" (II, iii, 88). Her preoccupation with herself takes over even as she tries to feign compassion. Macbeth tries to brood profoundly:

> Had I but died an hour before this chance,
> I had liv'd a blessed time; for from this instant
> There's nothing serious in mortality:
> All is but toys: renown and grace is dead,
> The wine of life is drawn, and the mere lees
> Is left this vault to brag of.

(II, iii, 91–96)

He is as gloomy as he says, but not because of Duncan's death. Rather, he is despondent over his own condition, soon to grow worse. Here Macbeth believes himself pretending misery. By the end of the play he speaks with even more bitterness about the meaning of human existence. Yet for all his desperation, Macbeth cannot completely hide his ambition and delight. When Donalbain, Duncan's son, rushes in and inquires, "What is amiss?" (II, iii, 97), Macbeth replies with cruel wit: "You are, and do not know't" (II, iii, 97). The joke implies that they are missing a father. Macbeth continues relentlessly:

> The spring, the head, the fountain of your blood
> Is stopp'd, the very source of it is stopp'd.

(II, iii, 98–99)

He cannot restrain his giddiness at drawing closer to the throne.

When word comes that the two grooms are dead, Macbeth admits that he has murdered them in uncontrollable anger, and Macduff, with quiet finesse, asks the reason. Perhaps he already suspects Macbeth, whose exclamation is excessively passionate:

> Here lay Duncan,
> His silver skin lac'd with his golden blood,
> And his gash'd stabs look'd like a breach in nature
> For ruin's wasteful entrance . . .

(II, iii, 111–114)

When he finishes, Lady Macbeth apparently faints. Whether the action is fake is unclarified, but we may surmise that she overheard Macbeth's narrative about the two grooms, realized that he was overplaying his part, and drew attention away from him.

Banquo urges all to stand firm together, and Macbeth adds his support:

> Let's briefly put on manly readiness,
> And meet i' th' hall together.

(II, iii, 133–134)

How ironic that after Lady Macbeth's insults in Act I, scene vii, Macbeth now calls for manhood. Malcolm and Donalbain confer, for neither can trust anyone else (II, iii, 137). Thus Donalbain suggests to Malcolm that they separate:

> There's daggers in men's smiles; the near in blood,
> The nearer bloody.

(II, iii, 140–141)

He knows that someone who has killed once will not hesitate to kill again, and that prediction proves accurate.

Scene iv dramatizes the social and political ramifications of the murder. First Rosse describes a series of unnatural phenomena that have occurred (II, iv, 5–10), as the murder of the King has repercussions through the world. When Macduff enters, he reports the general assumption that the grooms committed the murder, but his phrase "Those that Macbeth hath slain" (II, iv, 23) hints that Macbeth is in some way responsible. Macduff also reveals that because Duncan's sons have fled, Macbeth has been named King. Rather than go to Scone, however, where the coronation is to take place, Macduff sharply retorts that he plans to go home to Fife (II, iv, 36). Apparently the suspicions he manifested in the last scene have grown more serious. The Old Man's last line reveals the state of turmoil in the kingdom:

> God's benison go with you, and with those
> That would make good of bad, and friends of foes!

(II, iv, 40–41)

He offers both beneficence and warning, an appropriate mixture in this volatile environment.

In Act III, scene i, Banquo makes clear that Macduff is not the only one with doubts about Macbeth:

Thou hast it now: King, Cawdor, Glamis, all,
As the weird women promis'd, and I fear
Thou play'dst most foully for't.

(III, i, 1–3)

The rest of the speech reveals again that Banquo, like Macbeth, is ambitious, but that he is too noble to resort to illegal acts to ensure his children the crown.

When Macbeth enters, he exchanges polite conversation with Banquo, but interspersed in the dialogue and the invitation to the banquet that night are questions to determine the course of Banquo's actions for the next several hours:

Ride you this afternoon?

(III, i, 19)

Is't far you ride?

(III, i, 23)

Goes Fleance with you?

(III, i, 35)

The reason for this subtle inquisition is apparent when Macbeth is left alone:

To be thus is nothing,
But to be safely thus. Our fears in Banquo
Stick deep, and in his royalty of nature
Reigns that which would be fear'd.

(III, i, 47–50)

Here Macbeth goes beyond the bounds of rationality. The witches foretold that one day Banquo's children would possess the Scottish crown (III, i, 59–61). But Macbeth can no longer accept that prediction and resolves to claim not just the present but all eternity:

If't be so,
For Banquo's issue have I fil'd my mind,
For them the gracious Duncan have I murther'd,
Put rancors in the vessel of my peace
Only for them, and mine eternal jewel
Given to the common enemy of man,
To make them kings—the seeds of Banquo kings!

(III, i, 63–69)

Earlier we wondered if the absence of children in Lady Macbeth's life was part of what propelled her ambition. Here Macbeth seems angry that he has no offspring on whom he might bestow the crown. From that perspective he has failed to be part of the natural cycle of life, and possibly we can see his inability to procreate as one more force that drives him to prove his manhood by fighting in battle and by murdering for the throne. We also realize that here Macbeth has lost the ability to distinguish between prediction and inevitability. He has managed to persuade himself that what he knows cannot possibly happen must happen. The murder of Banquo cannot save the throne for Macbeth's nonexistent children. Yet Macbeth is now possessed by a spirit of murder, even though the rationale makes no sense.

This state of corruption is underscored by the next characters to enter, the two murderers. They are, we gather, common thugs, but now they are Macbeth's kindred souls. And the next murder he orders is fully premeditated. First he appeals to their manhood (III, i, 84–90), just as Lady Macbeth did to his. But they have little need for such urging, as they reveal. Says the second:

> I am one, my liege,
> Whom the vile blows and buffets of the world
> Hath so incens'd that I am reckless what
> I do to spite the world.

                                                        (III, i, 107–110)

An accurate description of Macbeth's current state of mind. Then the first murderer chimes in:

> And I another,
> So weary with disasters, tugg'd with fortune,
> That I would set my life on any chance,
> To mend it, or be rid on't.

                                                        (III, i, 110–113)

Such will be Macbeth's mentality before long. Macbeth then offers an explanation for his hatred. The speech also contains an obviously fraudulent excuse about Macbeth's not wanting to kill Banquo (III, i, 119–122), but the apology is wasted on these two men, who care little for moral niceties. They are killing for money, and explanations are unnecessary, as they indicate with their terse replies (III, i, 125–127). Macbeth's interruption, however, suggests his imbalance. He also informs them that he will acquaint them "with the perfect spy o' th' time . . . " (III, i, 129). Just who or what this may be is not clear. Finally, Macbeth reminds his two assassins that they are also to kill Fleance, Banquo's son, a strange point to leave until the end, since not Banquo but Banquo's children are supposed to take the throne. But Macbeth's mind is not functioning smoothly, and such disorder within him is to be expected.

By the next scene Lady Macbeth is beginning to manifest the same kind of collapse. She, too, worries about Banquo, and she, too, feels isolated, as she must ask her servant to request a few words for her with Macbeth (III, ii, 3–4). Left alone, she ponders:

> 'Tis safer to be that which we destroy
> Than by destruction dwell in doubtful joy.

                                                        (III, ii, 6–7)

Her conscience has taken hold of her. Yet when Macbeth enters, she chastizes him for allowing himself to be held by his conscience: " . . . what's done, is done" (III, ii, 12). The irony of those words is apparent even to Macbeth:

> Better be with the dead,
> Whom we, to gain our peace, have sent to peace,
> Than on the torture of the mind to lie
> In restless ecstasy. Duncan is in his grave;
> After life's fitful fever he sleeps well.
> Treason has done his worst; nor steel, nor poison,
> Malice domestic, foreign levy, nothing,
> Can touch him further.

(III, ii, 19–25)

When Duncan was alive, Macbeth envied his power. Now that Duncan is dead, Macbeth envies his serenity and freedom from responsibility. Lady Macbeth lovingly urges Macbeth to maintain a strong appearance (III, ii, 26–28), and he returns her affection but admits he is still tormented by Banquo. Still, Macbeth moves steadily ahead, although he keeps his plans private: "Be innocent of the knowledge, dearest chuck" (III, ii, 45), and he calls for the night to disguise his forthcoming actions. Then he attempts to assuage her worries:

> Good things of day begin to droop and drowse,
> Whiles night's black agents to their preys do rouse.
> Thou marvel'st at my words, but hold thee still:
> Things bad begun make strong themselves by ill.
> So prithee go with me.

(III, ii, 52–56)

The last two lines confirm the distortion of mind Macbeth experiences. He has managed to so twist his thoughts that the only cure for evil is further evil. Murder begets murder. This lesson is enforced by many of Shakespeare's tragedies and histories, but by none as graphically as in *Macbeth*.

The next scene is brief but puzzling. Macbeth's two murderers are joined by an unidentified third murderer. Is this the "perfect spy o' th' time" mentioned earlier (III, i, 129)? The first murderer demands to know who sent the intruder: "Macbeth" (III, iii, 1) is the response. This figure also has answers to all the other questions the first two pose. He hears the horses (III, iii, 8), he knows Banquo's accustomed routes (III, iii, 12–14), he recognizes Banquo (III, iii, 14), and he realizes that Fleance has escaped the assassination attempt that takes Banquo's life (III, iii, 19). Could the third murderer be Macbeth? Not likely, since he is at the castle and banquet. But can we doubt that the third murderer is some aspect of Macbeth himself? Spiritually Macbeth is with his charges. If he does not commit the actual killing, he is the author of the crime. Therefore his guilt is equal to that of the killers.

The chaos in the state is temporarily masked at the banquet, as Macbeth invites everyone to the table: "You know your own degrees, sit down" (III, iv, 1). But this false front begins to shatter with the entrance of the first murderer, as Macbeth remarks: "There's blood upon thy face" (III, iv, 13). The murderer relates Banquo's death and reluctantly admits that Fleance has escaped, but Macbeth's joy is only partially diluted:

> There the grown serpent lies; the worm that's fled
> Hath nature that in time will venom breed,
> No teeth for th' present.
>
> (III, iv, 28–30)

Lady Macbeth gently urges her husband to return to the party, for she remains conscious of amenities (III, iv, 31–36). But the social order collapses completely with the appearance of the Ghost. Shakespeare's audience believed in the power of ghosts, which are dramatized in two ways. The Ghost of Hamlet's father, which is seen by several people, is sometimes referred to as an "objective" ghost. Here the Ghost of Banquo is a "subjective" ghost, a product of an individual imagination and thus visible to only one person. Macbeth himself seems to summon the Ghost when he offers this fraudulent request:

> Here had we now our country's honor roof'd,
> Were the grac'd person of our Banquo present,
> Who may I rather challenge for unkindness
> Than pity for mischance.
>
> (III, iv, 39–42)

When Macbeth sees the Ghost and panics, his wife tries to calm him:

> This is the very painting of your fear;
> This is the air-drawn dagger which you said
> Led you to Duncan.
>
> (III, iv, 60–62)

When the Ghost leaves for a moment, Macbeth regains composure (III, iv, 83–87), but the Ghost reappears, and after Macbeth again hypocritically claims regret over Banquo's absence (III, iv, 89–91), the Ghost terrifies him once more: "Avaunt, and quit my sight! Let the earth hide thee!" (III, iv, 93). Given her husband's condition, which threatens the delicate balance of "time" (III, iv, 97) with "disorder" (III, iv, 109), Lady Macbeth has no choice but to dismiss the party with the feeble excuse that the King is now subject to illness. Alone with Lady Macbeth, he reveals his desperation:

> It will have blood, they say; blood will have blood.
> Stones have been known to move and trees to speak;
> Augures and understood relations have
> By maggot-pies and choughs and rooks brought forth
> The secret'st man of blood. What is the night?
>
> (III, iv, 121–125)

He feels the world and nature rising in opposition, and he is on the brink of collapse. Yet he summons the courage to meet the witches and learn the worst:

> I am in blood
> Stepp'd in so far that, should I wade no more,

Returning were as tedious as go o'er.

(III, iv, 135–137)

Images of blood continue to dominate his language. This combination of fear
and resolution contributes to the sympathy we feel for Macbeth, despite the
crimes he perpetrates: "We are yet but young in deed" (III, iv, 143). He knows
that more horrors await.

Scene v is regarded by most commentators as an interpolation by another
playwright. Its impact is to intensify the atmosphere of dread surrounding Macbeth. In scene vi, the forces of Scotland also begin to surround him, as Lennox
reflects how Duncan and Banquo have been close to Macbeth, then murdered.
Lennox also seems suspicious that the only evidence against Malcolm and Donalbain is the bodies of the dead grooms, killed by Macbeth in an apparent burst
of passion. Lennox offers one more thought about the current King:

> So that, I say,
> He has borne all things well, and I do think
> That had he Duncan's sons under his key
> (As, and't please heaven, he shall not), they should find
> What 'twere to kill a father; so should Fleance.

(III, vi, 16–20)

Lennox cannot be specific. But something within tells him that Macbeth is guilty.

The discussion next turns to Macduff, gathering forces to challenge Macbeth,
whom the nameless lord calls a "tyrant" (III, vi, 25). The references to the
"pious Edward" (III, vi, 27) and "Some holy angel/ Fly to the court of England"
(III, vi, 45–46) emphasize the divine nature of kingship. Furthermore, the lord
speaks of "Him above" (III, vi, 32) on Macduff's side, emphasizing the blasphemous nature of Macbeth's rule, and the Elizabethan view of religious sanction
behind an ordered state:

> . . . we may again
> Give to our tables meat, sleep to our nights;
> Free from our feasts and banquets bloody knives;
> Do faithful homage and receive free honors;
> All which we pine for now.

(III, vi, 33–37)

These sentiments should be understood as representative of the feelings of the
Scottish people under Macbeth's reign.

In Act IV, scene i, the witches are gathered about their cauldron, chanting
spells, when the second announces:

> By the pricking of my thumbs,
> Something wicked this way comes.

(iv, i, 45)

And Macbeth enters. Despite the possibility of universal destruction, which he
describes in detail (IV, i, 50–61), he no longer requests but demands to have
them order his life by outlining the future.

Three apparitions appear. The first is "an armed Head," which tells him to "beware Macduff" (IV, i, 71). It vanishes quickly. The second apparition, "a bloody Child," is more frightening, as is its warning:

> Be bloody, bold, and resolute; laugh to scorn
> The pow'r of man; for none of woman born
> Shall harm Macbeth.
>
> (IV, i, 79–81)

At this advice he assumes he need no longer fear Macduff; yet he still resolves to murder him:

> . . . thou shalt not live,
> That I may tell pale-hearted fear it lies,
> And sleep in spite of thunder.
>
> (IV, i, 84–86)

He is now planning to kill simply for the sake of convenience. Murder no longer holds terror for him. The bloody Child may also represent the children of Macduff who are to be slaughtered as well as all the children to die in the war soon to be fought because of Macbeth's reign. The image may also be a mockery of Macbeth's own childlessness.

The third apparition is "a Child crowned," which contrasts the previous image. Now the child seems to rise in opposition to Macbeth and triumph over him. Then all three apparitions speak in unison:

> Macbeth shall never vanquish'd be until
> Great Birnan wood to high Dunsinane hill
> Shall come against him.
>
> (IV, i, 92–94)

Such an obtuse message is not enough for Macbeth, who desires to "live the lease of nature" (IV, i, 99), and survive in some peace. Thus he demands to know whether Banquo's children will ever reign. And the witches reluctantly offer a show of eight Kings, with Banquo last.

In fury and frustration, Macbeth screams at the witches: "Filthy hags,/ Why do you show me this?" (IV, i, 115–116), ignoring that he asked to learn the truth. But this information does not matter to him. After Lennox enters and informs him that Macduff has fled to England, Macbeth coldly resolves to carry out the next murder:

> Time, thou anticipat'st my dread exploits;
> The flighty purpose never is o'ertook
> Unless the deed go with it. From this moment
> The very firstlings of my heart shall be
> The firstlings of my hand.
>
> (IV, i, 144–148)

He takes the coincidence of Macduff's absence as ordination of Macbeth's own right to act. In addition, he can no longer debate the merits of a particular act, for he is now afraid of his own conscience. Thus he promises to act by instinct, not rationality:

> The castle of Macduff I will surprise,
> Seize upon Fife, give to th' edge o' th' sword
> His wife, his babes, and all unfortunate souls
> That trace him in his line.
>
> (IV, i, 150–154)

Here is killing for its own sake, the inevitable outcome of Macbeth's choices. First he murdered in accordance with what he believed the witches had instructed. That murder, no matter how heinous, had an understandable goal, and in the course of carrying it out, Macbeth hesitated and weighed alternatives. Later he tried to subvert the predictions of the witches by murdering Banquo and Fleance, a plot completed with a minimum of regret. This last planned murder is completely distinct from anything the witches have ordained, for the threat to the throne is not Macduff's children, but Banquo's. And Macbeth resolves to commit this last killing with no compunction whatsoever.

Act IV, scene ii is extraordinary painful because the slaughter is pointless. At the start of the scene Lady Macduff is angry that her husband has deserted her and her children: "He loves us not/ He wants the natural touch" (IV, ii, 8–9). She means that he lacks the natural feelings of a father and husband. We suspect that Macduff wants to keep his wife safe, and thus does not make her privy to his actions. Rosse is left to explain the reasons to Lady Macduff;

> But cruel are the times when we are traitors,
> And do not know ourselves; when we hold rumor
> From what we fear, yet know not what we fear,
> But float upon a wild and violent sea
> Each way, and move.
>
> (IV, ii, 18–23)

In these days, all values are subverted by the actions of Macbeth.

The energy of Macduff's son is brief counterpoint to the gloom and lifelessness of Macbeth's world, especially when the boy's comments about traitors reflect Macbeth:

> Then the liars and swearers are fools; for
> there are liars and swearers enow to beat the honest
> men and hang up them.
>
> (IV, ii, 56–58)

Such is the condition of the world until Macbeth is overthrown. A messenger interrupts the exchange between Macduff's wife and son with a warning, but Lady Macduff is unable to leave quickly enough. Her penultimate speech embodies the horror Macbeth has unleashed:

> But I remember now
> I am in this earthly world—where to do harm

> Is often laudable, to do good sometime
> Accounted dangerous folly.
>
> (IV, ii, 74–77)

The butchery that follows clarifies the cruelty of nature under Macbeth's rule. This point is the lowest in the play, and our sympathy for Macbeth virtually disintegrates.

From here the play begins to turn upward, as Malcolm and Macduff meet in England. Macduff's comments about the pain in Scotland is ironic after the events of the previous scene:

> Each new morn
> New widows howl, new orphans cry, new sorrows
> Strike heaven on the face . . .
>
> (IV, iii, 4–6)

However, in the atmosphere of mistrust that poisons his country, Malcolm is not sure whether Macduff's sentiments can be trusted, and thus begins to test him:

> This tyrant, whose sole name blisters our tongues,
> Was once thought honest; you have lov'd him well;
> He hath not touch'd you yet.
>
> (IV, iii, 12–14)

Thus far, he claims, Macbeth has not hurt Macduff's family. Still testing, Malcolm suggests that Macduff may be seeking to win Malcolm's approval by betraying Macbeth (IV, iii, 15–17). Macduff denies he is so disloyal, and Malcolm apologizes that at this time he does not know whom to trust:

> Though all things foul would wear the brows of grace,
> Yet grace must still look so.
>
> (IV, iii, 23–24)

Here is another example of the contrast between "foul" and "fair." Still unconvinced about Macduff's fidelity, Malcolm maintains his front and asks why Macduff should have abandoned his wife and children. Disgusted, Macduff does not bother to explain, but mourns the state of his country (IV, iii, 33–34) and starts to leave. Malcolm's last test is to describe what he will be like as a ruler: " . . . black Macbeth/ Will seem as pure as snow . . . " (IV, iii, 52–53), and he continues to recite a catalogue of evil and sin that he will unleash. He speaks of his own "voluptuousness" (IV, iii, 61) and the abuse of women in which he will indulge (IV, iii, 61–66). He details his greed (IV, iii, 76–84), and he disdains the "king-becoming graces" (IV, iii, 91). The list that follows (IV, iii, 91–94) should be taken as tribute to James I. Finally, Malcolm predicts that he will reduce Scotland to rubble:

> Nay, had I pow'r, I should
> Pour the sweet milk of concord into hell,

Uproar the universal peace, confound
All unity on earth.

(IV, iii, 97–100)

The reference to "milk" recalls Lady Macbeth's comments that her husband was "too full o' th' milk of human kindness" (I, iv, 17) to be an effective murderer.

At this last boast, Macduff explodes and accuses Malcolm of destroying the kingship Duncan embodied (IV, iii, 104–111). Only now does Malcolm believe in Macduff and explains Malcolm's own innocence was the reason for the deceptions just played (IV, iii, 114–137). Macduff explains his bewilderment:

Such welcome and unwelcome things at once
'Tis hard to reconcile.

(IV, iii, 138–139)

Here is one more example of moral uncertainty.

The Doctor enters to report upon the wonderous healing powers of the English king Edward (IV, iii, 141–145). The Doctor then pays tribute to the King, and the pervasive religious imagery (IV, iii, 149–158) confirms the belief of all these characters in the alliance between the throne and divine authority. Such optimism is undercut, however, by the entrance of Rosse, evidently altered, because Malcolm does not recognize him. The cause of the change could be Rosse's knowledge of the murder of Macduff's family, or the general evil spread by Macbeth. Macduff asks about his own wife and children, perhaps out of guilt, and Rosse initially lies that they are all well (IV, iii, 176–177). But under Macduff's prodding Rosse eventually reveals the massacre of Macduff's family. Several times Macduff re-asks the question, as if the information were impossible to comprehend. His family stands as symbolic of all the murdered children of Scotland. Then his guilt surfaces:

Sinful Macduff,
They were all strook for thee! naught that I am,
Not for their own demerits, but for mine,
Fell slaughter on their souls.

(IV, iii, 224–227)

He resolves to undo Macbeth, and Malcolm asserts that together they can overthrow him:

Macbeth
Is ripe for shaking, and the pow'rs above
Put on their instruments. Receive what cheer you may,
The night is long that never finds the day.

(IV, iii, 237–240)

"Ripe" suggests that the natural order is about to be reestablished, as does the reference to day following night. After a period of darkness, light will shine.

In Act V, scene i, the depths of Lady Macbeth's fall become apparent. Her

doctor and a waiting-gentlewoman confirm that she has been sleepwalking, as
the doctor describes:

> A great perturbation in nature, to receive at
> once the benefit of sleep and do the effects of
> watching!
>
> (V, i, 9–11)

In Act II, scene ii Macbeth heard that he would sleep no more. Now a similar
curse has fallen on his wife, as she sleepwalks, reliving the murder in her
tormented conscience. When she appears, her words and actions recall moments
from previous scenes. The candle is a symbol of a feeble light piercing the dark.
She broods over Duncan's murder: "Yet who would have thought the old man
to have had so much blood in him?" (V, i, 39–40). She recalls the murder of
Macduff's wife: "The Thane of Fife had a wife; where is she now?" (V, i, 42–
43). The childish rhyme and rhythm is further evidence of her weakened condition. She struggles to rinse imaginary blood from her hands: "Out, damn'd
spot! (V, i, 35), and "All the perfumes of Arabia will not sweeten this little
hand" (V, i, 50–51), a line that recalls her earlier words of comfort to Macbeth:
"A little water clears us of this deed" (II, ii, 64). Most moving, perhaps, is
her new version of an old line. Earlier she was confident: " . . . what's done is
done" (III, ii, 12). Now she revises that opinion: "What's done cannot be
undone" (V, i, 67). The Doctor summarizes how Lady Macbeth's condition
symbolizes the state of the nation:

> Foul whisp'rings are abroad. Unnatural deeds
> Do breed unnatural troubles; infected minds
> To their deaf pillows will discharge their secrets.
>
> (V, i, 71–73)

Lady Macbeth has retreated into her private hell, and her subsequent death,
which occurs offstage, is the literal manifestation of what has occurred figuratively.

Scene ii is the first of several short scenes that dramatize the war against
Macbeth. Lennox indicates that young soldiers are preparing to fight:

> And many unrough youths that even now
> Protest their first of manhood.
>
> (V, ii, 10–11)

In Act I, scene vii, Macbeth spoke of fulfilling his manhood by killing Duncan.
Now other men fulfill theirs by looking to kill Macbeth. Angus, in dramatizing
Macbeth's untenable position on the throne, reiterates the imagery of clothing:

> Now does he feel his title
> Hang loose about him, like a giant's robe

Upon a dwarfish thief.

(V, ii, 20–22)

Cathness then speaks in terms of purging the state of illness (V, ii, 25–29), and such sickness parallels Macbeth's own health. Lennox's last word, and the last word of the scene, "Birnan" (V, ii, 31), reminds us of the witches' prediction.

By scene iii Macbeth has been reduced almost to incoherence. In his first speech he repeats thoughts and predictions, challenging other forces to attack him (V, iii, 7–10). When one of his servants attempts to bring him information about opposing troops, Macbeth curses and dismisses him. Only to Seyton does he confess his misery:

> I have liv'd long enough: my way of life
> Is fall'n into the sear, the yellow leaf,
> And that which should accompany old age,
> As honor, love, obedience, troops of friends,
> I must not look to have; but in their stead,
> Curses, not loud but deep, mouth-honor, breath,
> Which the poor heart would fain deny, and dare not.

(V, iii, 22–28)

Despite Macbeth's degradation, he offers here the self-understanding characteristic of the tragic hero. He realizes he has cut himself off from humanity and, for all his efforts, gained nothing. Therefore although Macbeth as a human being falls far short of greatness, he manages through such lines to achieve tragic stature. He is bold in putting on armor and maintaining his struggle to hold onto the throne. Yet he shows his fear in ordering Seyton to hang anyone who hints at desertion or treachery (V, iii, 36). His query to the Doctor about Lady Macbeth leads to more resignation, as he seeks the cure for Scotland's disease (V, iii, 50–51). We recognize that the only medicine is the purging of Macbeth himself.

In scene iv the isolation of Macbeth is contrasted by the growing unity of the forces in opposition to him. Malcolm orders that each of his soldiers use a branch of Birnan wood as camouflage (V, iv, 4–7), thus helping to fulfill one of the witches' prophesies. Malcolm then assures Siward that those who remain with Macbeth do so only because they are "constrained" (V, iv, 13). Gradually the order of the kingdom is being restored.

In scene v Macbeth's boldness is still evident, as he vows that his forces within the castle will be able to withstand a siege. But his confidence does not last long. He hears "the cry of women" (V, v, 8) resounding like the voices of all the mothers who mourn their dead children killed in this war he started:

> I have almost forgot the taste of fears.
> The time has been, my senses would have cool'd
> To hear a night-shriek, and my fell of hair
> Would at a dismal treatise rouse and stir
> As life were in't. I have supp'd full with horrors;
> Direness, familiar to my slaughterous thoughts,

Cannot once start me.

(V, v, 9–15)

He confesses himself emotionally deadened.

Such a sentiment prepares him for the next announcement by Seyton: "The Queen, my lord, is dead" (V, v, 16). Macbeth's initial response is passionless: "She should have died hereafter" (V, v, 17), "should" meaning "would certainly." To Macbeth, her life is meaningless, as is everything else:

> To-morrow, and to-morrow, and to-morrow,
> Creeps in this petty pace from day to day,
> To the last syllable of recorded time;
> And all our yesterdays have lighted fools
> The way to dusty death. Out, out brief candle!
> Life's but a walking shadow, a poor player,
> That struts and frets his hour upon the stage,
> And then is heard no more. It is a tale
> Told by an idiot, full of sound and fury,
> Signifying nothing.

(V, v, 19–28)

The dirge is remarkable for the measured, relentless rhythm and the simplicity of the language. Once Macbeth sought to possess time entirely; now it rolls on pointlessly, as days blend together. The ironic reference to the candle recalls the imagery of light and dark. The image of the human being as actor is familiar from *King Lear* (IV, vi, 183), *As You Like It* (II, vii, 139–166), *The Tempest* (IV, i, 148–158), and other plays. Here it epitomizes the transitory nature of man's existence. No speech in literature better expresses a vision of hopelessness.

Macbeth is brought back to awareness when a messenger reports:

> I look'd toward Birnan, and anon methought
> The wood began to move.

(V, v, 32–33)

This fulfillment of the witches' prophecy at first unnerves Macbeth:

> I pull in resolution, and begin
> To doubt th' equivocation of the fiend
> That lies like truth.

(V, v, 41–43)

The word "Equivocation" recalls the speech of the drunken Porter (II, iii, 1–21). But in desperation Macbeth falls back on the attribute that has always been his best: his courage in battle. Thus he orders his troops rallied as he himself prepares to die fighting.

In scene vi the battle is underway, and Malcolm orders his troops to drop their camouflage. Now they can face Macbeth head on. Malcolm also shows that he has taken command by referring to himself with the royal "we" (V, vi, 4). In scene vii Macbeth, in battle, is confident he will not meet one "not born of woman'' (V, vii, 3). Young Siward challenges him, shouting: ''The devil himself could not pronounce a title/ More hateful to mine ear'' (V, vii, 8–9). With his old resolution Macbeth steps into the fight and kills the boy. This action is followed by the entrance of Macduff, who swears vengeance for the murders of his wife and child. We may take him as revenging all who die in this conflict.

In scene viii, the ever-courageous Macbeth dismisses suicide and resolves to die fighting (V, viii, 1–3). At this moment Macduff enters, and Macbeth boasts that he is invulnerable to all ''of woman born'' (V, viii, 13), but Macduff shouts that he was ''from his mother's womb/ Untimely ripp'd'' (V, viii, 15–16), or born by cesarian section. At this revelation Macbeth attempts to run; however, at Macduff's shout of ''coward'' (V, viii, 23) and order to surrender in humiliation, Macbeth storms back:

> Yet I will try the last. Before my body
> I throw my warlike shield. Lay on, Macduff,
> And damn'd be him that first cries, ''Hold, enough!''
>
> (V, viii, 32–34)

He knows that whatever he tries, he is already damned. But he leaves with a traditional shout of derision to an opponent.

In the final scene, stability is at last restored to Scotland. Old Siward takes pride in his son's bravery: ''Why then, God's soldier be he!'' (V, ix, 13). Then Macduff enters, carrying Macbeth's head, an image that recalls the witches' apparition. He hails Malcolm as King, and in the play's final address Malcolm clarifies that Lady Macbeth ''by self and violent hands/ Took off her life . . .'' (V, ix, 36–37). He also invokes images of growth and order, speaking of that ''which would be planted newly with the time'' (V, ix, 31). Whatever else needs to be carried out: ''We will perform in measure, time, and place'' (V, ix, 39).

How to sum up Macbeth, this most unlikely tragic figure? Virtually every decision he makes, every action he carries out, ends up badly. Despite his devotion to his wife, his motivations are selfish and his lack of feeling eventually becomes horrifying. Yet something in him touches us. Perhaps we sense that from the start of this play he is lost: condemned to muddle amidst vague promises, the taunts of his frustrated wife, his capacity for violence, and his own stifled ambition, all wrapped in an infinite net of uncertainty from which he never manages to escape.

SUGGESTIONS FOR FURTHER READING

Bartholomeusz, Dennis. Macbeth *and the Players*. London: Cambridge University Press, 1969.

Brown, John Russell. *Shakespeare: The Tragedy of* Macbeth. London: Edward Arnold, 1963.

Hawkes, Terence, ed. *Twentieth Century Interpretations of* Macbeth. Englewood Cliffs, N.J.: Prentice-Hall, 1977.

Hobson, Alan. *Full Circle: Shakespeare and Moral Development*. London: Chatto & Windus, 1972.

Hunter, G. K. "*Macbeth* in the Twentieth Century." *Shakespeare Survey* 19 (1966): 1–11.

Jorgensen, Paul. *Naked Frailties: Sensational Art and Meaning in* Macbeth. Berkeley and Los Angeles: University of California Press, 1971.

Mack, Maynard. *Killing the King: Three Studies in Shakespeare's Tragic Structure*. New Haven: Yale University Press, 1973.

Muir, Kenneth, and Philip Edwards, eds. *Aspects of* Macbeth. Cambridge and New York: Cambridge University Press, 1977.

Paul, Henry N. *The Royal Play of* Macbeth. New York: Macmillan, 1950.

Rosenberg, Marvin. *The Masks of* Macbeth. Berkeley and Los Angeles: University of California Press, 1978.

Walker, Roy. *The Time is Free: A Study of* Macbeth. London: Dakers, 1949.

ANTONY AND CLEOPATRA

For those who approach Shakespeare's plays with the intention of seeing each character as a unified figure acting in accordance with a recognizable psychological scheme, *Antony and Cleopatra* presents a rigorous challenge. The title characters are two of the most unpredictable in dramatic literature. A considerable portion of their language and actions implies that in addition to lacking maturity and understanding, they are careless with their own emotions as well as with those of others. At many moments the behavior of Antony and Cleopatra is comically outlandish, and the mixture of love and laughter makes *Antony and Cleopatra* by far the brightest of the tragedies.

At first glance, events suggest that these two people are remarkably foolish. Antony is a man of extraordinary gifts with the world in his power, but he throws it away for the inconstant affection of Cleopatra, an enticing but selfish, clinging, and headstrong woman. Yet the language of the play seems intended to convince us that their love is ultimately worth whatever tragic ends it brings. To learn the facts alone, that Antony and later Cleopatra reconcile with each other, is not convincing. To read or hear their specific words is to experience those moments quite differently.

The primary source of the play is "The Life of Marcus Antonius" in the Thomas North translation of Plutarch's *Lives of the Noble Grecians and Romans*. The events of this play follow those dramatized in Shakespeare's *Julius Caesar*, in which Brutus, Cassius and several conspirators assassinate Caesar in 44 B.C. Historically the forces of the rebels were defeated at Philippi, and in 43 B.C. a triumvirate was formed between three leaders: Caesar's adopted son, Octavius, who took control of Italy and various northern and western territories; Lepidus, who ruled Africa; and Antony, who ruled Egypt and various territories east of the Adriatic. Antony eventually met with Cleopatra over charges that she had aided Brutus and Cassius in the war against the triumvirate, but Antony was so taken with her that he abandoned all responsibilities, both political and familial, and returned with Cleopatra to Alexandria in Egypt, where the action of this play begins in 40 B.C.

Its construction incorporates the central schism. With great speed we move from Egypt to Rome and back again: from the passion and intuitive pleasures of Cleopatra and her world to the reason and peremptory obligations of Antony's Rome; from the haven of private joy to the realm of public duty; from the florid poetry of Egypt to the austere language of Rome.

The play also fluctuates between moods of war and love. From battles for possession of the civilized world we shift to declarations of romantic love. At the axis of this turmoil is Antony, contending with his instincts, searching for the solution to an insoluble problem: how to resolve contradictory desires.

Philo's opening speech establishes the tension:

> Nay, but this dotage of our general's
> O'erflows the measure. Those his goodly eyes,
> That o'er the files and musters of the war
> Have glow'd like plated Mars, now bend, now turn
> The office and devotion of their view
> Upon a tawny front; his captain's heart,
> Which in the scuffles of great fights hath burst
> The buckles on his breast, reneges all temper,
> And is become the bellows and the fan
> To cool a gipsy's lust.
>
>   (I, i, 1–10)

Here one of Antony's followers depicts him as a great man gone hopelessly and helplessly astray. This Antony is clearly different from the cold, pragmatic leader in *Julius Caesar*, and Philo disapproves of the alteration. A question that pervades the rest of the play is to what extent this judgment, which is echoed often, is accurate.

At the start it certainly appears correct. Philo goes on to call Antony "a strumpet's fool" (I, i, 13), and the line not only disparages Antony but also clarifies how little Philo and the other Romans think of Cleopatra. Antony, furthermore, seems to conform to Philo's estimation. In his opening exchange with Cleopatra he acts as a prisoner of stereotypical conventions of romance, responding to his lady's demand to profess the extent of his passion (I, i, 14–17). At the arrival of a message from Rome, he reluctantly accepts the interruption, and Cleopatra mocks him for doing so:

> Nay, hear them, Antony.
> Fulvia perchance is angry; or who knows
> If the scarce-bearded Caesar have not sent
> His pow'rful mandate to you: "Do this, or this;
> Take in that kingdom, and enfranchise that;
> Perform't, or else we damn thee."
>
>   (I, i, 19–24)

In front of a court full of spectators, Antony is forced to acknowledge his worldly duties. Yet Cleopatra insists on humiliating him because he has a loyal wife,

Fulvia, and a youthful political rival of stature, Octavius Caesar. Antony is also conscious of his age, as his subsequent references to his "grizzled head" reveal. Thus she seizes his most vulnerable points and exposes them for all to mock.

Does she intend this banter to be amusing? Antony doesn't think so, for he hurries to his own defense:

> Here is my space,
> Kingdoms are clay; our dungy earth alike
> Feeds beast as man; the nobleness of life
> Is to do thus [*embracing*]—when such a mutual pair
> And such a twain can do't, in which I bind,
> [On] pain of punishment, the world to weet
> We stand up peerless.
>
> (I, i, 34–39)

He proclaims that he cares for nothing but her, that he is willing to toss all aside. Yet she maintains her barrage:

> Excellent falsehood!
> Why did he marry Fulvia, and not love her?
> I'll seem the fool I am not. Antony
> Will be himself.
>
> (I, i, 40–43)

She cannot resist mocking Antony's enterprises and responsibilities. Hers is not casual wit, and she does not receive casual response from Antony:

> Fie, wrangling queen!
> Whom every thing becomes—to chide, to laugh,
> To weep; [whose] every passion fully strives
> To make itself (in thee) fair and admir'd!
>
> (I, i, 48–51)

He resents her need to deflect all his business to herself, and he resents her gibes, which are aimed with full awareness of the hurt they inflict. She is joking with him, but she is not kidding. Can her approach be explained as part of an consistent attitude?

We ought to see Cleopatra as psychologically split. She is the preeminent woman of the world: Queen of Egypt, loved by great men, and now the object of devotion by the man who rules Rome. By any estimation she should be supremely self-assured. But these jokes are the product of insecurity. Why does she doubt herself? Because, as will become apparent, she suspects she does not have the capacity to win Antony completely.

At the end of scene i, her antics have kept Antony by her side, and they leave together. Philo and Demetrius are left to brood over their commander's behavior, and Demetrius hopes that Antony will regain authority over himself. At this moment, while he is betraying his marriage, his wife Fulvia is warring against Octavius Caesar in Italy, and Antony himself is failing to assist Caesar in the war against Sextus Pompey, son of the man overthrown by Julius Caesar. This younger Pompey has now claimed his right to the Roman throne, and with the aid of pirates has begun raids and skirmishes against Italy. Furthermore, Caesar lacks popular support, and the masses are threatening to ally themselves with Pompey. While all this turmoil is taking place, Antony is with Cleopatra.

In scene ii, Charmian, one of Cleopatra's attendants and also her confidante, listens with other servants to the predictions of a soothsayer. The one that strikes us is that Charmian will outlive Cleopatra (I, ii, 31), a prophecy that proves ironic. The banter continues in a sexually suggestive spirit, as the women joke lasciviously about the attributes of future husbands and lovers. Enobarbus, Antony's lieutenant and close friend, is also here, and his presence suggests the attraction of the frivolous Egyptian world to a member of the serious-minded Roman society. His line about his pleasure also hints at his cynicism:

> Mine, and most of our fortunes to-night,
> shall be—drunk to bed.

> (I, ii, 45–46)

His attitude is more complicated than mere cynicism, however, and is developed presently.

When Cleopatra enters, Enobarbus quiets the conversation, for he assumes Antony is with her, and Enobarbus does not want to be discovered making jokes about unfaithfulness, given Antony's relationship with Fulvia. But Cleopatra is alone, annoyed at Antony's change in mood:

> He was dispos'd to mirth, but on the sudden
> A Roman thought hath strook him.

> (I, ii, 82–83)

Either the gloomy Roman side of his personality has taken over, or business from home now preoccupies him. Seeing Antony coming, she childishly scurries away to avoid giving him the pleasure of finding her.

At this point all the forces in Antony's life seem to converge on uncontrollably. He learns that his wife has joined with her former enemy, Antony's brother Lucius, against Caesar in war, but that Caesar has triumphed (I, ii, 88–94). The messenger further reports that the Parthians have battled successfully against Antony's troops, and Antony assumes that his reputation in Rome is being damaged because of his time in Egypt (I, ii, 105–106). Therefore he resolves to leave (I, ii, 116–117). But before he can do so, another messenger enters to report that Fulvia has died. Antony accepts her death calmly, but with regret: "There's a great spirit gone! Thus did I desire it!" (I, ii, 122). And he resolves more firmly to resume his public duties. Almost immediately Enobarbus enters, unaware of Fulvia's death, and at Antony's order for departure makes a series of sexual jokes about how their leaving will cause the women of Egypt great suffering. He concludes with a playful reference to Cleopatra's lust: " . . . she hath such a celerity in dying" (I, ii, 144). ("Die" has a dual meaning, based on a familiar Elizabethan poetic conceit implying sexual satisfaction.) At Antony's revelation that Fulvia is dead, Enobarbus tries to lighten the moment by claiming that now his general can be with Cleopatra (I, ii, 167–170), but Antony now means to concern himself with business: "No more light answers" (I, ii, 176). He resolves to return to Rome both to defeat Pompey and to retrieve the wavering loyalty of his "slippery people" (I, ii, 185). One quality Antony here has in common with the Antony of *Julius Caesar* is a mistrust of the common people:

> Whose love is never link'd to the deserver
> Till his deserts are past . . .
>
> (I, ii, 186–187)

The speech further reflects the depths of Antony's quandary, as he is caught between two worlds and two visions of life. Antony's reference to "a serpent's poison" (I, ii, 194) is one of many references to snakes that anticipate the play's final scene.

In scene iii Cleopatra's own insecurities surface. She asks Charmian where Antony is, and gives specific instructions how he is to be treated:

> See where he is, who's with him, and what he does.
> I did not send you. If you find him sad,
> Say I am dancing; if in mirth, report
> That I am sudden sick. Quick, and return.
>
> (I, iii, 2–5)

She is desperate to keep Antony off balance, to maintain mystery about herself. But her tactics dismay Charmian:

> Madam, methinks if you did love him dearly,
> You do not hold the method to enforce
> The like from him.
>
> (I, iii, 6–8)

When the Queen asks for an alternative approach, Charmian advocates submission: "In each thing give him way, cross him in nothing" (I, iii, 9). Not surprisingly, the imperious Cleopatra rejects this advice.

Cleopatra's dilemma is that she wants conflicting qualities in one man. She wants him totally devoted to her, willing to come and go and plead and make love at her every whim. Yet she also seeks a man strong enough to make her conquest of him worthwhile. In other words, she wants a man strong enough to withstand her orders. She wants a man who controls the world. And she wants to control him.

Thus when Antony returns, Cleopatra is both pleased and distressed. She wants him to be apologetic but also strong enough to resist apology. Torn between both desires, she insults him:

> What, says the married woman you may go?
> Would she had never given you leave to come!
>
> (I, iii, 20–21)

She is furious that he has a wife, someone to love other than herself. She mocks him for betraying her, for responding to the demands of this person, because the man she desires would not kowtow to a woman's caprices. Yet a few lines later she utters one of her most eloquent declarations of love:

> Eternity was in our lips and eyes,
> Bliss in our brows' bent; none our parts so poor
> But was a race of heaven.
>
> (I, iii, 35–37)

Within a few lines she manages to cover a vast range of emotion, because she is feeling all simultaneously: love, jealousy, frustration, anger, and helplessness, each directed towards a man she longs to possess but does not really want to possess because then he will not be worth possessing.

Antony gives her the reasons he must return to Rome (I, iii, 44–54), leaving until the end the matter of Fulvia's death. Despite his overall seriousness, he, too, enjoys toying with her affections. Seeing Antony's stoic attitude, Cleopatra mocks him further:

> Now I see, I see,
> In Fulvia's death, how mine receiv'd shall be.
>
> (I, iii, 64–65)

As his anger rises, she accuses him of pretending to be angry. Antony vows by his sword, a recurring image of manhood, but Cleopatra mocks him with a disparaging reference to Hercules, from whom Antony claimed descent. When he threatens to leave, she says she has one last word, which she then pretends to have forgotten (I, iii, 90–91), just as he has forgotten her. Eventually she apologizes:

> Your honor calls you hence,
> Therefore be deaf to my unpitied folly,
> And all the gods go with you! Upon your sword
> Sit laurel victory, and smooth success
> Be strew'd before your feet!
>
> (I, iii, 97–101)

She articulates his dilemma: a desire for worldly success and acclaim, which in this case means fulfilling political responsibility, but complicated by Antony's personal desires, which must be sacrificed to the cause.

Antony, too, recognizes his trap. He cannot have both Cleopatra and Rome. He cannot dedicate himself to a woman who demands such attention while also leading the greatest empire in the history of the world:

> Our separation so abides and flies,
> That thou residing here, goes yet with me;

And I hence fleeting, here remain with thee.

> (I, iii, 102–104)

His greatness is that he is capable of being a great lover and ruler of Rome. His tragedy, too, is that he is capable of meeting either challenge, and he cannot choose between them.

In scene iv we see how Antony is viewed by his fellow triumvirs, Caesar and Lepidus, and their perspective is not flattering. Caesar speaks of Antony's revelry in disparaging tones, concluding:

> You shall find there
> A man who is th' [abstract] of all faults
> That all men follow.

> (I, iv, 8–10)

Lepidus is more sympathetic, seeing Antony as subject to his own nature (I, iv, 12–15), and this desire to speak generously of everyone reflects Lepidus's personality. But Caesar remains unimpressed, and assails what he consider's Antony's negligence (I, iv, 16–33). Throughout the play Caesar proves a strict, even harsh, man, and his stern dedication is the contrast to Antony's surrender to emotion.

The report on Pompey's success at sea further enrages Caesar against Antony, but Caesar also unknowingly agrees with Antony in an estimate of the populace, who now are joining Pompey's forces:

> This common body,
> Like to a vagabond flag upon the stream,
> Goes to and back, [lackeying] the varying tide,
> To rot itself with motion.

> (I, iv, 44–47)

Like many leaders in Shakespeare's tragedies and histories, including Antony and Cleopatra, Caesar views the mass of people as untrustworthy and in need of firm control.

Caesar is then told that Pompey is joined in his revolt by two pirates, Menecrates and Menas, and Caesar is thereafter more desperate for Antony's support. Sadly he recalls some of Antony's military ordeals, and this tribute (I, iv, 55–71) helps give Antony's inner battle tragic stature.

The leaving for the war council at the end of scene iv is contrasted by the return to Egypt in scene v, as Cleopatra indulges herself by questioning Charmian about Antony:

> Where think'st thou he is now? Stands he, or sits he?
> Or does he walk? Or is he on his horse?
> O happy horse, to bear the weight of Antony!

Do bravely, horse, for wot'st thou whom thou mov'st?

                                                        (I, v, 19–22)

The sexual connotations are amusing, but that they are coming from a royal
personage makes them also faintly ridiculous:

> He's speaking now,
> Or murmuring, "Where's my serpent of old Nile?"
> (For so he calls me). Now I feed myself
> With most delicious poison. Think on me,
> That am with Phoebus' amorous pinches black,
> And wrinkled deep in time?

                                                        (I, v, 24–29)

Cleopatra's musing on her comparatively advanced age is the action of someone
who feels that time has passed her by. Thus we better understand that her
desperation to hold onto Antony reflects her insecurity. The reference to "wrin-
kled deep in time" connotes depth of character, but communicates sadness as
well. Alexas enters with a gift from Antony, a pearl, but Cleopatra is more
concerned with Antony's mood. To avoid controversy, Alexas keeps her answers
noncommittal, and Cleopatra is pleased with the report of Antony's "well-
divided disposition" (I, v, 53). To dramatize the depth of her affection, Cleopatra
asks whether she loved even Julius Caesar this much, but Charmian misinterprets
and exclaims: "O that brave Caesar!" (I, v, 67). At this misstatement, Cleopatra
shouts in anger:

> By Isis, I will give thee bloody teeth,
> If thou with Caesar paragon again
> My man of men.

                                                        (I, v, 70–72)

In the last scene, Octavius Caesar offered disparaging words about Antony's
infatuation with Cleopatra. Here she reminds us that Julius Caesar was also one
of her lovers. The scene concludes with Cleopatra's wistful reflections on her
foolish youth:

> My salad days,
> When I was green in judgment, cold in blood,
> To say as I said then!

                                                        (I, v, 73–75)

She is proud of her better judgment now, but the lines also contain recognition
that such wisdom has come only with age.

Act II, scene i introduces Pompey, who recognizes the affection the people
have for him as well as his military advantage at sea (II, i, 9). He also shrewdly
evaluates the three triumvirs against whom he plans to take revenge:

> Mark Antony
> In Egypt sits at dinner, and will make

No wars without-doors. Caesar gets money where
He loses hearts. Lepidus flatters both,
Of both is flatter'd; but he neither loves,
Nor either cares for him.

                                                    (II, i, 11–16)

His tone is one of distaste, especially when he expresses his hope that Cleopatra
will continue to distract Antony from worldly responsibility:

Let witchcraft join with beauty, lust with both,
Tie up the libertine in a field of feasts,
Keep his brain fuming; epicurean cooks
Sharpen with cloyless sauce his appetite,
That sleep and feeding may prorogue his honor . . .

                                                    (II, i, 22–26)

With typical Roman scorn, he mocks Antony's infatuation with Cleopatra and
the luxuriousness of Egypt. Yet the lushness of Pompey's language implies that
he also envies Antony's capacity for pleasure. Pompey, however, is all business,
although so ruthless is he that in his presence the entire political atmosphere of
Rome is soiled. Varrius, however, reports that Antony has left Egypt to go to
Rome, and Pompey is unpleasantly surprised, for he respects Antony's military
skills (II, i, 34–35). Menas, however, is confident that the rift between Caesar
and Antony over Fulvia's war against Caesar will continue to keep the leaders
of the triumvirate hostile. Pompey, ever shrewd, has a different outlook:

                    . . . but how the fear of us
May cement their divisions, and bind up
The petty difference, we yet not know.

                                                    (II, i, 47–49)

   Such anticipation that the personal squabble may be put aside in the face of
a common enemy leads directly to scene ii, which begins with Lepidus's customary attempts to assuage. He pleads with Enobarbus to keep Antony conciliatory, but Enobarbus retorts sharply: "I shall entreat him/To answer like
himself" (II, ii, 3–4). Lepidus continues to play peacemaker when Caesar and
others enter:

                    When we debate
Our trivial difference loud, we do commit
Murther in healing wounds. Then, noble partners,
The rather for I earnestly beseech,
Touch you the sourest points with sweetest terms,
Nor curstness grow to th' matter.

                                                    (II, ii, 20–25)

This exhortation has little effect, as Antony and Caesar greet one another frostily.
Caesar offers criticism much milder than his outrage in Act I, scene iv, but

Antony announces at once that his time in Egypt is his business alone (II, ii, 35–36). Caesar, however, has other complaints as well:

> Your wife and brother
> Made wars upon me, and their contestation
> Was theme for you—you were the word of war.
>
> (II, ii, 42–44)

Antony denies having advocated his wife's side, and claims to have articulated his support of Caesar through letters (II, ii, 51–52). But Caesar is not convinced:

> You praise yourself
> By laying defects of judgment to me; but
> You patch'd up your excuses.
>
> (II, ii, 54–56)

Antony tries to lighten the mood by joking about his wife's uncontrollable spirit, and Enobarbus contributes:

> Would we had all such wives, that the men
> might go to wars with the women.
>
> (II, ii, 65–66)

But Caesar, always humorless, cannot be distracted from the issue, and recalls Antony's insult to Caesar's messenger as was dramatized in the first scene of the play. Antony seems to find this charge petty, but nonetheless answers politely (II, ii, 74–81), and when Caesar once more accuses him of treachery, Antony confesses the cause of Fulvia's actions against Caesar:

> Truth is, that Fulvia,
> To have me out of Egypt, made wars here;
> For which myself, the ignorant motive, do
> So far ask pardon as befits mine honor
> To stoop in such a case.
>
> (II, ii, 94–98)

Caesar is temporarily calmed, and Enobarbus adds that the two leaders should remember their enemy, Pompey, but Antony cautions Enobarbus to remember his place (II, ii, 107). Antony apparently does not want to upset further the strait-laced Caesar, who admits that he was bothered especially by Antony's "manner" (II, ii, 112), and announces that he seeks a way to strengthen their bond. Both men clearly want to alleviate their conflict.

At this point Agrippa suggests that political unity could be attained were Antony to marry Caesar's sister:

> Her love to both
> Would each to other and all loves to both
> Draw after her.
>
> (II, ii, 134–136)

The suddenness with which this deal is offered is surprising. The suddenness with which it is accepted is shocking. Antony agrees first:

> Let me have thy hand
> Further this act of grace; and from this hour
> The heart of brothers govern in our loves,
> And sway our great designs!
>
> (II, ii, 145–148)

His political conciliation is an act of convenience. He cannot take his own words seriously, for he knows where his affections lie. Nevertheless, for the good of Rome he is willing to attempt to patch up the quarrel.

Caesar, though, takes the offer as a mandate:

> There's my hand.
> A sister I bequeath you, whom no brother
> Did ever love so dearly. Let her live
> To join our kingdoms and our hearts, and never
> Fly off our loves again!
>
> (II, ii, 148–152)

This address is utterly hypocritical. Caesar claims to love his sister, and subsequent events confirm that he does. Yet he surrenders her to someone he mistrusts. A man as worldly as Caesar cannot believe that Antony, who has betrayed Fulvia, will relinquish all ties to Cleopatra. Therefore the marriage for him, too, is a political necessity. But this gesture says little for Caesar, who allows expedience to supplant personal feeling.

Even after this uniting, Antony remains reluctant to go after Pompey, who has "laid strange courtesies and great/Of late upon me" (II, ii, 154–155). No doubt Pompey, who earlier acknowledged Antony's skills, has been trying to flatter Antony out of the conflict. But after Lepidus points out the immediacy of Pompey's threat, the three resolve to work together.

They leave Agrippa, Maecenas, and Enobarbus, whose discussion turns to Cleopatra. Maecenas offers one opinion of her:

> She's a most triumphant lady, if report be
> square to her.
>
> (II, ii, 184–185)

His curiosity is piqued, and Enobarbus's response confirms the rumor. First he describes her entrance in a passage taken closely from some of the most extravagant prose in Plutarch:

> The barge she sat in, like a burnish'd throne,
> Burnt on the water. The poop was beaten gold,
> Purple the sails, and so perfumed that

> The winds were love-sick with them; the oars were silver,
> Which to the tune of flutes kept stroke, and made
> The water which they beat to follow faster,
> As amorous of their strokes.
>
> (II, ii, 191–197)

In a play full of glorious language, this homage is still astonishing. Then Enobarbus moves to Cleopatra herself:

> For her own person,
> It beggar'd all description: she did lie
> In her pavilion—cloth of gold, of tissue—
> O'er-picturing that Venus where we see
> The fancy outwork nature. On each side her
> Stood pretty dimpled boys, like smiling Cupids,
> With divers-color'd fans, whose wind did seem
> To [glow] the delicate cheeks which they did cool,
> And what they undid did.
>
> (II, ii, 197—205)

The lavish tribute continues until Maecenas reflects sadly: "Now Antony/Must leave her utterly" (II, ii, 232–233). Enobarbus knows better:

> Age cannot wither her, nor custom stale
> Her infinite variety. Other women cloy
> The appetites they feed, but she makes hungry
> Where most she satisfies; for vildest things
> Become themselves in her, that the holy priests
> Bless her when she is riggish.
>
> (II, ii, 233–239)

His praise implies not only that the union between Antony and Octavia is doomed, but that the alliance between Antony and Octavius will be short-lived.

Another curious aspect of the panegyric is the man who recites it. We might expect such a glowing description from Antony himself. Instead it comes from the mercenary and outsider. Enobarbus thus follows in the tragedies' tradition of the complicated sexual cynic. In *Romeo and Juliet*, Mercutio covers his emotional vacuum with a barrage of jokes, but is nonetheless able to appreciate Romeo's willingness to surrender himself. In *Othello*, Iago's inability to love is perverted into a murderous desire to destroy those who can. Enobarbus's tribute to Cleopatra, in combination with the bawdy wit he has demonstrated thus far, suggests that he has the capacity to fall in love, but he instead shares the emotions of others vicariously. His jokes lack the satiric edge of Mercutio's or the venom of Iago's, reflecting how Enobarbus remains emotionally detached from women. His devotion to Antony, on the other hand, indicates that Enobarbus has married himself to service, so to speak, and the extent of that loyalty is clear later.

In Act II, scene iii, Antony's first words to Octavia reveal that he means to separate himself from her regularly. And the echo of their words of parting by

Caesar (II, iii, 7–9) confirms the fragility of this marriage and the alliance it supports. The entrance of the Soothsayer, however, reminds Antony of Egypt and Cleopatra, and the Soothsayer's prediction that Caesar will outshine Antony causes Antony to dismiss him. Nonetheless, in a soliloquy, he decides to follow the Soothsayer's counsel and return to Egypt. The attraction of Cleopatra is more than Antony can resist.

After a very brief scene iv, in which comments by Lepidus remind us that political problems still flourish, we return to Egypt, where Cleopatra is indulging herself and her entourage with memories of Antony. She relates a trick she played upon him by making him drunk, then dressing him in women's clothes, while she put on his sword. She enjoys "playing" with men, and the more powerful the man, the more enjoyable the game. But when the messenger enters, Cleopatra's mood switches repeatedly. First she assumes Antony has died. Then she demands to know the essence of the report. The messenger, rightly nervous that his news will upset her, reluctantly reveals that Antony is married to Octavia, and Cleopatra bursts into anger. We recall Antony's generous attitude toward the messenger who brought him news of Fulvia's death (I, ii). Cleopatra apologizes for striking the messenger, but when he returns again, she asks him the same question, and once again she turns violent. The slapstick episode ends when Cleopatra sends Alexas to draw from the stunned messenger the details of Octavia. Meanwhile Cleopatra's own passions overflow:

> Let him for ever go—let him not, Charmian—
> Though he be painted one way like a Gorgon,
> The other way 's a Mars.
>
> (II, v, 115–117)

Earlier Enobarbus spoke of Cleopatra's "infinite variety" (II, ii, 235). Here we see her humor, her desperation, her temper, and her contradictory attitude towards Antony.

In scene vi the triumvirs and rebels at last meet after exchanging hostages. Pompey has received an offer by which he will be allowed to return to Sicily and Sardinia if he disposes of the pirates, but he is still determined to avenge his father (II, vi, 8–23). This threat is aimed at Caesar personally, but he maintains his calm: "Take your time" (II, vi, 23). Antony subtly reminds Pompey of the triumvirate's power at sea, and Pompey in return reminds Antony of his debt and longstanding conflict with Caesar:

> When Caesar and your brother were at blows,
> Your mother came to Sicily and did find
> Her welcome friendly.
>
> (II, vi, 44–46)

At this Antony and Pompey shake hands and turn the conversation to small talk about the charms of the East. Caesar, we note, stands silently. He is roused only by Pompey's reference to Julius Caesar's enjoying Egyptian cooking (II, vi, 63–65). But Octavius's terse replies do not deter Pompey, who recalls a story about Cleopatra's being taken to Julius Caesar in a mattress. He mentions these details no doubt to cause further dissension between Antony and Caesar, who, he hopes, are soon to revert to rivalry. And the tension in the conversation suggests that a rift is soon to come.

After Pompey invites all to board his ship for a party, the only two left on stage are Enobarbus and Menas, the mercenary and the pirate. The latter mutters to himself: "Thy father, Pompey, would ne'er have made this treaty" (II, vi, 83). And we wonder whether his reservations will prove accurate. Once the two men talk frankly about their careers, they seem to gain a mutual trust, and Menas confesses that he believes Pompey has made a poor deal (II, vi, 103–105). Enobarbus agrees, but admits that the marriage between Antony and Octavia is not to last long:

> He will to his Egyptian dish again. Then
> shall the sighs of Octavia blow the fire up in Caesar.
>
> (II, vi, 126–127)

Having laid the tensions of the time out honestly, the two adjourn to the party.

In scene vii the revelry is underway, and the two servants reveal that intox- ication has affected most of the celebrants, in particular Lepidus: "But it raises the greater war between him and his discretion" (II, vii, 9–10). This evaluation applies to several of the men, who under the influence of drink reveal more of themselves than they should. The first to look foolish is Lepidus, whose silliness inspires others to ply him with more. He thinks he is being clever when in fact he is the object of mock toasts and tributes. Menas, whose sobriety reflects his calculation, speaks privately to a tipsy Pompey:

> These three world-sharers, these competitors,
> Are in thy vessel. Let me cut the cable,
> And when we are put off, fall to their throats:
> All there is thine.
>
> (II, vii, 70–73)

Pompey's unthinking response shows his fundamental cowardice:

> Thou must know,
> 'Tis not my profit that does lead mine honor;
> Mine honor, it. Repent that e'er thy tongue
> Hath so betray'd thine act. Being done unknown,
> I should have found it afterwards well done,
> But must condemn it now.
>
> (II, vii, 75–80)

The use of "honor" alerts us to shady dealings. Pompey is willing to take the rewards of a despicable deed but not the responsibility. Seeing Pompey as if for the first time, Menas resolves to withdraw support.

Lepidus, meanwhile, seems to have collapsed, and is carried off to the scorn of the others. Enobarbus is his customary lusty self (II, vi, 94), as Pompey complains that the party has not yet reached the depths of an "Alexandrian feast" (II, vii, 96). In response, Antony toasts Caesar, and as the merrymaking reaches its highest din in song, Antony looks ridiculous. Here we see his capacity for self-indulgence that eventually helps bring him down. Indeed, almost all the participants behave shamefully, and in our eyes diminish the dignity of their political aspirations.

Caesar, meanwhile, refuses to partake in drink, and his sobriety manifests the strength of will that contributes to his triumph in the conflicts to follow. Yet we do not find him attractive. Like other puritanical men in Shakespeare's plays, including Angelo in *Measure for Measure*, Malvolio in *Twelfth Night*, and Prince John in *Henry IV, Part 2*, Caesar is humorless and vain. The more we see of him, Pompey, and the rest who vie for power, the more Antony and Cleopatra, whatever their fatuousness, seem increasingly likeable.

War takes over in Act III, as in scene i Antony's lieutenant, Ventidius, reflects on his conquering Antony's enemies, the Parthians. He does not choose to bask in glory for he knows such behavior could antagonize Antony:

> Better to leave undone, than by our deed
> Acquire too high a fame when him we serve's away.

(III, i, 14–15)

Ventidius also plans to let Antony take credit for the victory. Such diplomacy and foresight contrasts Ventidius with Antony himself, who in his passions dispenses with all caution.

Scene ii returns us to Antony's world. Agrippa and Enobarbus talk about Antony's imminent departure for Athens, and the conversation is full of ironic comments about all, especially Lepidus, whose attempts at universal flattery are mocked (III, ii, 7–20). When the actual parting takes place, Caesar's love for his sister is apparent:

> Most noble Antony,
> Let not the piece of virtue which is set
> Betwixt us, as the cement of our love
> To keep it builded, be the ram to batter
> The fortress of it . . .

(III, ii, 27–31)

Yet he has given her away to solve a political dilemma. Thus his affection is subordinate to his ambition. Indeed, it is Antony who speaks poetically of Octavia, as she weeps at this parting:

> The April's in her eyes, it is love's spring,
> And these the showers to bring it on.

(III, ii, 43–44)

But any compassion that we might imagine Antony feels is undercut by the cynical comments of Enobarbus, who to Agrippa dismisses even Antony's tears over the dead Julius Caesar (III, ii, 57–58).

The opposite to the passionless Caesar returns in scene iii, as Cleopatra demands from that same messenger more details about Octavia. The result is a genuinely humorous scene, as the messenger struggles to remain noncommittal and Cleopatra tries to disparage the unseen Octavia's qualities. One particularly amusing moment occurs when the Messenger tries to allay Cleopatra's worries by adding that Octavia is thirty (III, iii, 28). The Queen switches the topic back to Octavia's face, for Cleopatra is well over thirty, and does not want to hear that Antony has a younger wife.

The anticipated split between Antony and Octavia occurs in the next scene, as Antony tells her that Caesar has violated the treaty by fighting new wars against Pompey (III, iv, 1–10). Octavia bemoans her own position, trapped between two powerful men, and Antony's words do not comfort her or us:

> If I lose mine honor,
> I lose myself; better I were not yours
> Than [yours] so branchless.

(III, iv, 22–24)

Throughout the tragedies and histories, characters resort to all manners of foolish behavior to protect their "honor." Furthermore, Antony's behavior with Cleopatra has already revealed that he is willing to compromise his integrity for the pleasures of her company. That Octavia is returning to Rome to soothe the crisis is not encouraging.

Scene v, also in Antony's house in Athens, clarifies that the ruthless Caesar is consolidating his own position by turning on Lepidus:

> Caesar, having made use of him in the wars
> 'gainst Pompey, presently denied him rivality, would
> not let him partake in the glory of the action, and not
> resting here, accuses him of letters he had formerly
> wrote to Pompey; upon his own appeal, seizes him. So
> the poor third is up, till death enlarge his confine.

(III, v, 7–12)

Antony, meanwhile, is preoccupied with the death of Pompey, who was murdered by one of Antony's own officers. Thus we see the fragile alliance between Antony and Caesar falling apart, as Antony has lost control not only of Caesar but also of his own forces.

The extent of Antony's dissolution is dramatized in the next scene, in which Caesar expresses his anger. He complains that back in Alexandria Antony has committed numerous violations against Rome, ranging from Antony's allowing himself to be glorified in public with Cleopatra to his dispensing territories to his small children (III, vi, 2–5, 13–16). Caesar also feels personally affronted, for Antony has accused him of withholding spoils from the war against Pompey and imprisoning Lepidus simply to gain his wealth. Caesar has his own explanations:

I have told him Lepidus was grown too cruel,
That he his high authority abus'd,
And did deserve his change.

(III, vi, 32–34)

Caesar denies that his own ruthlessness led him to act against Lepidus. He also claims to be willing to share profits with Antony if Antony will donate portions of Armenia and other territories he has conquered on his own (III, vi, 34–37). Maecenas realizes that Antony would never agree to such terms, but Caesar refuses to admit as much. He maintains the pose that he serves strictly for the public good, and never confesses his own unscrupulousness.

When Octavia enters, Caesar's anger is exacerbated for he is shocked that she should arrive so unadorned without accompanying fanfare. Octavia tries to defend Antony, claiming that she chose to travel in this style, but Caesar is unimpressed and shocks her by reporting that Antony is back in Egypt: "He hath given his empire/ Up to a whore . . . " (III, vi, 66–67), where he also gathers troops for war against Rome. We feel Caesar coldly using his sister's unhappiness to further what he has long wanted: the downfall of Antony.

In scene vii that downfall comes closer, as Enobarbus struggles to persuade Cleopatra to refrain from taking part in the battle against Caesar. Enobarbus recklessly claims she will distract Antony (III, vii, 10–13), but she is resolved:

A charge we bear i' th' war,
And as the president of my kingdom will
Appear there for a man. Speak not against it,
I will not stay behind.

(III, vii, 16–19)

Her potential for damage is clarified immediately, when Antony enters. He is eager to fight Caesar at sea, for the foolish reason that Caesar has challenged him there (III, vii, 29). His commitment to the concept of honor continues to damage him. Enobarbus provides several logical reasons why Antony should carry the fight on land, including the experience of Caesar's troops, the maneuverability of Caesar's ships, and the skill of Antony's own forces on land (III, vii, 34–39). But Antony insists, and the cause of his obstinacy becomes clear when Cleopatra speaks: "I have sixty sails, Caesar none better" (III, vii, 49).

Antony himself knows that moving at sea is a dubious plan, for he has a backup in mind (III, vii, 52–53). Nonetheless, when he hears that Caesar has landed forces, Antony orders legions and cavalry to battle Caesar while Antony himself moves to the seas. Canidius and a fellow soldier summarize their army's plight: "So our leader's [led],/And we are women's men" (III, vii, 69). In his attempt to placate Cleopatra, Antony has lost all sense of military responsibility.

The battle of Actium, which took place in 31 B.C., is depicted in a few short episodes. In scene viii a confident Caesar orders the attack at sea, while in scene ix Antony is on the defensive. By scene x Enobarbus is distraught that Antony's troops have been defeated. The cause is Cleopatra, as Scarus implies when he

shouts " . . . we have kiss'd away/Kingdoms and provinces" (III, x, 7–8). He
then gives the details about the actions of "Yon ribaudred nag of Egypt" (III,
x, 10), who grew frightened and ordered her ship away "When vantage like a
pair o' twins appeared" (III, x, 12), or just when Antony was close to triumph.
Seeing her retreat, he followed, to his discredit:

> I never saw an action of such shame;
> Experience, manhood, honor, ne'er before
> Did violate so itself.

> (III, x, 21–23)

For so long Antony has prided himself on just those qualities. Now he is derided
because Cleopatra has robbed him of them. Canidius intends to go over to
Caesar's side, and Scarus weighs that possibility. Even Enobarbus is tempted
to desert, but his loyalty temporarily wins out.

Antony's misery in the next scene is painful to observe:

> I have fled myself, and have instructed cowards
> To run and show their shoulders.

> (III, xi, 7–8)

The words "fled myself" imply that he feels he has disregarded his obligations
and noble character. The last lines of this speech suggest that in his disgrace he
is thinking of suicide:

> . . . for indeed I have lost command,
> Therefore I pray you. I'll see you by and by.

> (III, xi, 23–24)

When Cleopatra enters, Antony can hardly look at her while he ponders his
defeat to Caesar. He remembers the battle at Philippi when Caesar held his sword
effeminately, "like a dancer" (III, xi, 36). Now Antony has lost to this man,
whom he has always judged a youthful inferior. Antony berates Cleopatra for
her actions, and she openly admits her blunder (III, xi, 55–57). Yet while he
blames her, Antony also condemns himself:

> You did know
> How much you were my conquerer, and that
> My sword, made weak by my affection, would
> Obey it on all cause.

> (III, xi, 65–68)

He recognizes his failure as well as his inability to turn away from Cleopatra.
He sees his own flaws, but when she offers, "Pardon, pardon!" (III, xi, 68),
he cannot resist her:

> Fall not a tear, I say, one of them rates
> All that is won and lost.

> (III, xi, 69–70)

Here is the crux of Antony's dilemma: worldly success versus love for Cleopatra.
What makes the quandary so compelling is that Antony cannot surrender her,

and he knows so. Thus he battles against his own mind and desires, and he cannot possibly win.

The depths of Antony's helplessness are apparent in the next scene, as his old schoolmaster, to the scorn of Dolabella, is allowed to make a petition to Caesar from Antony:

> Lord of his fortunes he salutes thee, and
> Requires to live in Egypt, which not granted,
> He lessons his requests, and to thee sues
> To let him breathe between the heavens and earth,
> A private man in Athens: this for him.
>
> (III, xii, 11–15)

He also asks that Cleopatra be allowed to keep the throne of Egypt for her heirs. These words, even through an intermediary, suggest Antony's humiliation. Caesar, however, is ungracious in triumph and turns down Antony's plea immediately (III, xii, 19–20). To Cleopatra he offers the throne, but under outlandish terms: only if she kills Antony or expels him from Egypt (III, xii, 22–23). Once the schoolteacher departs, Caesar instrucs Thidias to try to win Cleopatra over to Caesar's side. He assumes Antony's current disgrace has left Cleopatra disillusioned with him, but the command reveals Caesar's callowness. Their love cannot be destroyed so quickly. But because Caesar feels so little himself, he has no understanding of human emotion.

Contrast to such coldness is dramatized immediately, as Cleopatra asks Enobarbus how she can salvage Antony's situation. Enobarbus assures her that Antony alone is responsible for his defeat, but his words hint at resentment of her influence:

> The itch of his affection should not then
> Have nick'd his captainship, at such a point,
> When half to half the world oppos'd, he being
> The mered question.
>
> (III, xiii, 7–10)

Antony then enters, having learned of Caesar's less-than-generous offer, and explains it to Cleopatra:

> To the boy Caesar send this grizzled head,
> And he will fill thy wishes to the brim
> With principalities.
>
> (III, xiii, 17–19)

Cleopatra flirtatiously considers the proposal: "That head, my lord?" (III, xiii, 19). Even at this moment she plays the coquette. Antony ignores this jest, and returns a personal challenge to Caesar:

> I dare him therefore
> To lay his gay comparisons apart,
> And answer me declin'd, sword against sword,

Ourselves alone.

(III, xiii, 25–28)

This invitation is the last resort of a man who has exhausted all options. Fearing a dishonorable death, Antony is willing to risk personal combat, for he has nothing to lose and could escape victorious. As Antony leaves to formulate the message, Enobarbus articulates its emptiness (III, xiii, 29–37).

A messenger then enters rudely, and Cleopatra is perturbed at the lack of formality. Enobarbus overhears the embarrassment, and wonders once more if he should change sides, but for the moment maintains allegiance (III, xiii, 41–46). Thidias, Caesar's emissary, begins by flattering Cleopatra and pardoning her fidelity to Antony:

> He knows that you embrace not Antony
> As you did love, but as you fear'd him.

(III, xiii, 56–57)

When Cleopatra seems to accept this explanation, Enobarbus is taken in by what he imagines is treachery and departs to warn Antony. Meanwhile Cleopatra maintains her charade:

> Tell him, I am prompt
> To lay my crown at 's feet, and there to kneel.
> Tell him, from his all-obeying breath I hear
> The doom of Egypt.

(III, xiii, 75–78)

The extravagance of the image confirms that she is acting, but when Antony enters, he sees Thidias about to kiss her hand and explodes. He orders Thidias whipped, then rages against Cleopatra's perfidy, not allowing her to interrupt his tirade. Antony even refers to himself as a great cuckold (III, xiii, 126–128). When the whipped Thidias is brought in, Antony feels no remorse but sends a message that similar or worse punishment may be applied to Hipparchus, one of the first soldiers to desert Antony's forces (III, xiii, 147–152).

When she senses his anger is spent, Cleopatra speaks: "Not know me yet?" (III, xiii, 157). After this simple intimation of her faith, she eloquently turns away his charge:

> Ah, dear, if I be so,
> From my cold heart let heaven engender hail,
> And poison it in the source, and the first stone
> Drop in my neck; as it determines, so
> Dissolve my life!

(III, xiii, 158–162)

Once more Antony amazes us by relenting: "I am satisfied" (III, xiii, 167). And once more he prepares to resume the war.

Antony and Cleopatra depart to celebrate her birthday, leaving Enobarbus to weigh his own impasse:

> . . . and I see still
> A diminution in our captain's brain
> Restores his heart. When valor [preys on] reason,
> It eats the sword it fights with. I will seek
> Some way to leave him.
>
> (III, xiii, 196–200)

Ever the cynic, Enobarbus is astute enough to realize Antony's predicament. But he fails to understand his own. He, too, is pulled in conflicting directions, and here decides to go towards military survival, his natural path. He fails to reckon with his heart, which soon haunts him.

What may be considered Caesar's strength is apparent in Act IV, scene i, when he receives Antony's challenge. Unlike Antony, who is preoccupied with honor and therefore reacts emotionally to crises, Caesar remains detached. He laughs the offer away, reflects that many of Antony's supporters have deserted, and returns to prepare for battle (IV, i, 10–16). Yet this lack of emotion that serves Caesar so well in his role as a military leader is also his chief deficiency as a human being. Is such insensibility necessary for Caesar's eventual triumph? The play makes us wonder.

Such aloofness is contrasted to Antony's emotional foment in scene ii. Learning of Caesar's refusal to fight one-on-one, Antony nonetheless rouses himself to battle, and Enobarbus echoes the shout: "I'll strike, and cry, 'Take all!' " (IV, ii, 8). But he will soon be fighting on the other side. The next day Antony's passion in the face of death reduces his men to tears, as Enobarbus indicates (IV, ii, 34–36). The scene is bizarre in light of the military blunders Antony has committed in the name of love. Yet Antony's capacity to inspire affection is ennobling.

In scene iii, the strange music Antony's soldiers hear bodes ill for their success. And in scene iv Antony's own preparations make failure seem even more likely. He allows Cleopatra to help him with his armor, but she is not equal to the task. Nonetheless, he indulges her:

> O love,
> That thou couldst see my wars to-day, and knew'st
> The royal occupation, thou shouldst see
> A workman in't.
>
> (IV, iv, 15–18)

Cleopatra sends them off with good cheer, but her last speech implies that she suspects the worst (IV, iii, 36–38).

In scene v, Enobarbus's desertion is made known to Antony, who reacts with generosity, sending Enobarbus's money after him. The gesture suggests Antony's capacity for forgiveness, but his lines also reveal his intuition that defeat is imminent and that he is to blame: "O, my fortunes have/ Corrupted honest men!" (IV, v, 16–17).

In the opposite camp, meanwhile, Caesar foresees victory: "The time of

universal peace is near'' (IV, vi, 4), an accurate prediction. More intriguing is
the presence of Enobarbus, who receives his money from Antony in great pain:

> I am alone the villain of the earth,
> And feel I am so most. O Antony,
> Thou mine of bounty, how wouldst thou have paid
> My better service, when my turpitude
> Thou dost so crown with gold! This blows my heart.
>
>   (IV, vi, 29–33)

By the end of the scene he is ready to commit suicide. For all his cynicism,
Enobarbus is a man of feeling.

In scenes vii and viii, Antony's forces prove surprisingly successful, but his
exaltation in scene viii proves untimely, as does Cleopatra's glee (IV, viii, 16–
18). In scene ix, Enobarbus, now in the unhappy camp of Caesar, finds himself
emotionally bankrupt:

> O sovereign mistress of true melancholy,
> The poisonous damp of night dispunge upon me,
> That life, a very rebel to my will,
> May hang no longer on me . . . O Antony,
> Nobler than my revolt is infamous,
> Forgive me in thine own particular,
> But let the world rank me in register
> A master-leaver and a fugitive.
> O Antony! O Antony!
>
>   (IV, ix, 12–23)

Here he dies, apparently of a broken heart. In his own way he loved Antony,
and Enobarbus recognizes that he betrayed that love. His character is such that
he cannot live with his own version of treason.

In scene x Antony's forces continue to triumph on land, and now, still bold,
he is ready to meet Caesar at sea. But Caesar, in scene xi, remains calm, and
his order that his men stay in the ''vales'' indicates that his maneuvers by the
sea were but a ruse to draw away Antony's forces. In scene xii the strategy
works after Scarus sees the swallows, an unfortunate augury. Antony discovers
not only that the sea battle is lost but also that his troops have been defeated on
land, for the Egyptian forces have deserted:

> This foul Egyptian hath betrayed me.
> My fleet hath yielded to the foe, and yonder
> They cast their caps up and carouse together
> Like friends long lost.
>
>   (IV, xii, 10–13)

In fury he blames Cleopatra, whom he brands a ''Triple-turn'd whore'' (IX, xii,
13), recalling her past actions with Pompey and Caesar, and including what he
supposes is her treachery to him. He calls for Eros, but Cleopatra enters instead,
and Antony's anger terrifies her. He assumes she has conspired with Caesar:

Follow his chariot, like the greatest spot
Of all thy sex; most monster-like, be shown
For poor'st diminutives, for dolts, and let
Patient Octavia plough thy visage up
With her prepared nails.

(IV, xii, 35–39)

Even after she leaves in silent submission, his anger remains unabated, and he swears to kill her.

Left among her confidantes, Cleopatra plots to regain Antony's affection, and her method is characteristic of her approach to life. She orders Mardian to report to Antony that she has slain herself: "And bring me how he takes my death" (IV, xiii, 10). Play-acting rather than dealing straightforwardly, she invites disaster.

Meanwhile Antony broods over his fate:

Here I am Antony,
Yet cannot hold this visible shape, my knave.
I made these wars for Egypt, and the Queen,
Whose heart I thought I had, for she had mine—
Which whilst it was mine had annex'd unto 't
A million moe (now lost)—she, Eros, has
Pack'd cards with Caesar's, and false-play'd my glory
Unto an enemy's triumph.

(IV, xiv, 13–20)

These lines encapsulate Antony's predicament. He cannot "hold this visible shape," or withstand the pressures from both sides. He "made these wars" for both country and love, but he never understood Cleopatra's motivations, that she pretended to concede to Caesar out of self-preservation. He also recognizes how many lives have been bound up in this private squabble, and sums his fury with a familiar image: "She has robb'd me of my sword" (IX, xiv, 23). He feels his manhood lost.

Yet despite all this disaster, when Mardian enters to tell of Cleopatra's death, Antony once more forgives her. First he tells Eros: "And we must sleep" (IV, xiv, 36), a line that foretells imminent death. Then he removes his armor and makes provisions to join his dead love:

I will o'ertake thee, Cleopatra, and
Weep for my pardon. So it must be, for now
All length is torture; since the torch is out,
Lie down and stray no farther.

(IV, xiv, 44–47)

His life and happiness have been inextricably tied to her. Such recognition on Antony's part contributes to the tragic stature of his story. His affection for her was beyond his control, and thus his struggle has been futile from the start. Yet he has fought nobly to resolve irreconcilable instincts and duties.

To avoid the disgrace of capture, he orders a reluctant Eros to kill him. But
Eros chooses to kill himself instead, and Antony is forced to fall on his own
sword. In a moment that borders on the tragicomic, he only wounds himself.
Thus he must call others to finish the deed (IV, xiv, 103–104). The guards are
unwilling to complete Antony's action, but Decretas steals the sword with the
intention of using it to gain Caesar's favor. Even as Antony seeks death, harsh
reality mocks him.

The most painful moment is about to come. Diomedes enters to tell Antony
that Cleopatra is yet alive, and fearing some result as has transpired, sent
Diomedes to reveal the truth. Such coincidence and circumstances recall the
deaths of Romeo and Juliet, but the situations are different. In the earlier play
blunders and delays led to tragedy. Here Antony's life is over, whether or not
he kills himself at this moment. His military forces are in tatters, his personal
life is wrecked, and all that he has lived for has collapsed. His suicide is
inevitable. This delay, however, allows him to pardon Cleopatra and to gain
pardon from her.

The sight of the dying Antony leaves Cleopatra shattered:

> O sun,
> Burn the great sphere thou mov'st in! darkling stand
> The varying shore o' th' world! O Antony,
> Antony, Antony! Help, Charmian, help, Iras, help;
> Help, friends below, let's draw him hither.
>
> (IV, xv, 9–13)

Her cries reflect how her universe has been destroyed. Antony, however, has
reached peace with himself. He tells her that he, not Caesar, is responsible for
his wounds, then confesses:

> I am dying, Egypt, dying; only
> I here importune death awhile, until
> Of many thousand kisses the poor last
> I lay upon thy lips.
>
> (IV, xiv, 18–21)

The only passion that has ever truly moved Antony has been his love for Cleopatra. All others now seem unimportant.

His body is lifted to Cleopatra, and he offers her counsel, appropriately thinking last of her: "Of Caesar seek your honor, with your safety" (IV, xv, 46).
Second: "None about Caesar trust but Proculeius" (IV, xv, 48). And finally:

> The miserable change now at my end
> Lament nor sorrow at; but please your thoughts
> In feeding them with those my former fortunes
> Wherein I liv'd, the greatest prince o' th' world,
> The noblest; and do now not basely die,
> Not cowardly put off my helmet to
> My countryman—a Roman by a Roman

Valiantly vanquish'd. Now my spirit is going,
I can no more.

(IV, xv, 51–59)

He is dying content with what he has done and how he has lived. He acknowledges that death is his only alternative, that the dilemma of his life has long been insoluble. Now he is free.

Cleopatra's response reveals awareness that once she is without Antony, her own life is meaningless:

The crown o' th' earth doth melt. My lord!
O, wither'd is the garland of the war,
The soldier's pole is fall'n! Young boys and girls
Are level now with men; the odds is gone,
And there is nothing left remarkable
Beneath the visiting moon.

(IV, xv, 63–68)

He was the only man she loved, as well as the only man worthy of her love.

Then a surprise occurs. After uttering these words, Cleopatra faints, perhaps in an unconscious attempt to join Antony in death. She awakens almost immediately with a remarkable sentiment:

No more but [e'en] a woman, and commanded
By such poor passion as the maid that milks
And does the meanest chares.

(IV, xv, 73–75)

She relinquishes all worldly possessions, the titles and prerogatives due a queen, and thinks only as a human being. This spiritual rebirth is a sign that Antony's death has brought her knowledge of who and what she is, and the rest of her life will be devoted to proving to herself and to everyone else her commitment to Antony.

Such an intention makes the last act of the play singular. We await the culminating expression of love between two people, but one is dead. The living partner must speak for both. Cleopatra has toyed with Antony, mocked him, and wrecked his military plans. She has intruded into his relationships with subordinates and friends. She has destroyed his credibility with his countrymen. Yet throughout this final act, she will try to prove that what she and Antony shared was worth that cost.

News of Antony's passing brings temporary change in Caesar:

The breaking of so great a thing should make
A greater crack. The round world
Should have shook lions into civil streets,
And citizens to their dens.

(V, i, 14–17)

These words do not indicate a profound alteration in the speaker. Rather they suggest his private acknowledgement of the passing of a great man, a fellow triumvir, who for all his deficiencies was a titanic figure. The image of the lion, which recalls words used by Julius Caesar, Antony's mentor (*Julius Caesar*, II, ii, 46–48), denotes Antony's stature. Soon, however, Octavius Caesar shows himself the same icy patrician he has always been.

First Maecenas reminds us of the struggle Antony endured: "His taints and honors/Wag'd equal with him" (V, i, 30–31). That analysis accurately summarizes Antony's battle, as well as the predicament of the Shakespearean tragic hero. Caesar then offers an extended tribute, conscious that he is one great man paying homage to another (V, i, 40–48). Hearing from Cleopatra's messenger of her unhappiness, he resolves to treat her respectfully:

> She soon shall know of us, by some of ours,
> How honorable and how kindly we
> Determine for her; for Caesar cannot [live]
> To be ungentle.
>
> (V, i, 57–60)

The use of "honorable" hints at unsavory dealings. And almost immediately Caesar becomes the callous plotter familiar from previous scenes:

> Give her what comforts
> The quality of her passion shall require,
> Lest in her greatness, by some mortal stroke
> She do defeat us; for her life in Rome
> Would be eternal in our triumph.
>
> (V, i, 62–66)

To him Cleopatra is but another spoil of war. The sentiments are ugly and remind us that these values are the kind Antony opposed.

In the opening of scene ii, Cleopatra reflects on the vagaries of life. She describes Caesar as "Fortune's knave,/A minister of her will" (V, ii, 3–4), a phrase that recalls Romeo's calling himself "fortune's fool" (*Romeo and Juliet*, III, i, 136). Romeo suggests he was a victim of fate. Cleopatra sees Caesar as a blind tool of fate. Her brooding is interrupted by Proculeius, the one man Antony told her she could trust. But she is not interested in his offer. She says she will surrender on one condition: "If he please/To give me conquer'd Egypt for my son . . . " (V, ii, 18–19). Proculeius tries to convince her to mollify Caesar, and she seems to agree:

> I am his fortune's vassal, and I send him
> The greatness he has got.
>
> (V, ii, 29)

But the echo of "fortune" from her first speech in this scene indicates her irony. Thus when Roman soldiers burst in and take her prisoner, we are not surprised when she pulls a knife and tries to kill herself. They prevent that action now, but she is determined not to be their prize:

                    Shall they hoist me up,
And show me to the shouting varlotry
Of censuring Rome?

                                                    (V, ii, 55–57)

Dolabella enters to placate her, but she has no patience for him either, and instead offers a panegyric to Antony:

His legs bestrid the ocean, his rear'd arm
Crested the world, his voice was propertied
As all the tuned spheres, and that to friends;
But when he meant to quail and shake the orb,
He was as rattling thunder. For his bounty,
There was no winter in't; an [autumn] it was
That grew the more by reaping. His delights
Were dolphin-like, they show'd his back above
The element they liv'd in. In his livery
Walk'd crowns and crownets; realms and islands were
As plates dropp'd from his pocket.

                                                    (V, ii, 82–92)

She offers this glorious homage as much for herself as for Dolabella. Her tribute proves to her that despite all their conflicts she loved Antony, and that his sacrifice of his life for her has been and will be matched by similar devotion from her.
  She then asks Dolabella:

Think you there was or might be such a man
As this I dreamt of?

                                                    (V, ii, 93–94)

When he denies that possibility, Cleopatra turns on him:

You lie up to the hearing of the gods!
But if there be, nor ever were one such,
It's past the size of dreaming. Nature wants stuff
To vie strange forms with fancy; yet t' imagine
An Antony were nature's piece 'gainst fancy,
Condemning shadows quite.

                                                    (V, ii, 95–100)

Throughout the first four acts Cleopatra's affections seemed to vacillate. Now the intensity of her love so stirs Dolabella that under her prodding he admits that Caesar intends to use her as a prisoner.
  At this moment Caesar enters, crudely demanding: "Which is the Queen of Egypt?" (V, ii, 112). He follows with an offer of compromise (V, ii, 118–120), claiming he will hold no grudges. She responds with an apology for events of the past:

          . . . I have
Been laden with like frailties which before

Have often sham'd our sex.

(V, ii, 122–124)

Caesar proceeds in his lies, promising protection if she complies with his wishes:

> . . . but if you seek
> To lay on me a cruelty, by taking
> Antony's course, you shall bereave yourself
> Of my good purposes, and put your children
> To that destruction which I'll guard them from
> If thereon you rely.

(V, ii, 128–133)

The insinuation is nasty, for according to Caesar's proposal Cleopatra really has no choice. She, however, pretends to agree, and as an act of good faith apparently gives him an account of her wealth. Now follows a puzzling moment. Cleopatra requests affirmation of her honesty, but her treasurer, Seleucus, points out that she has omitted as much as she has listed (V, ii, 145–147). She becomes enraged, then apologizes to Caesar, saying that she kept only some "lady trifles" (V, ii, 165) and some "nobler token" (V, ii, 168) for Livia and Octavia, Caesar's wife and sister. Then she confesses:

> Be it known that we, the greatest, are misthought
> For things that others do; and when we fall,
> We answer others' merits in our name,
> Are therefore to be pitied.

(V, ii, 176–179)

The speech reflects the nature of the tragic hero, whose life affects so many others and whose stature emerges partially from the endurance of trials and pain. Caesar, with apparent grace, claims he wants none of her money and offers his solicitude. Then he leaves, and Cleopatra sneers at him:

> He words me girls, he words me, that I should not
> Be noble to myself.

(V, ii, 190–191)

This irony implies that the entire episode with Seleucus was staged, that Cleopatra feigned keeping money to see if Caesar cared about her resources. His ignoring them confirms that he does not intend her to live long, and that in any case he plans to confiscate all of her account.

After Cleopatra sends Charmian on an unspecified mission, Dolabella returns. Now allied with Cleopatra, he reaffirms Caesar's plan to bring her with her children to Rome (V, ii, 200–204). When he has departed, Cleopatra reminds Iras of the humiliations that await:

> Mechanic slaves
> With greasy aprons, rules, and hammers shall
> Uplift us to the view. In their thick breaths,

Rank of gross diet, shall we be enclouded,
And forc'd to drink their vapor.

(V, ii, 209–213)

Like other leaders from Shakespeare's tragedies and histories, figures like Cassius, Coriolanus, Antony himself, Richard II, and Richard III, Cleopatra has only scorn for the masses. She then anticipates actors performing her story:

> Saucy lictors
> Will catch at us like strumpets, and scald rhymers
> Ballad's out a' tune. The quick comedians
> Extemporally will stage us, and present
> Our Alexandrian revels: Antony
> Shall be brought drunken forth, and I shall see
> Some squeaking Cleopatra boy my greatness
> I' th' posture of a whore.

(V, ii, 214–221)

The reference to "boy" doubtless refers to the all-male theatrical companies of Shakespeare's day. Cleopatra's certainty about how simplistically she will be portrayed emphasizes that Shakespeare has in fact created a subtle, complex woman. She also comes to grips with the realization that because of who she and Antony were their follies were magnified. Grandeur was part of their joy, but endemic to their downfall.

After Charmian returns, Cleopatra asks for her robes. In a peculiar moment of comic relief, a clown enters with a basket of figs that cover snakes. Perhaps unaware of her intention, the clown warns her at length about the venom of their bites, and she jests in return not as queen, but as a woman. Eventually she dismisses him and orders herself adorned:

> Give me my robe, put on my crown, I have
> Immortal longings in me. Now no more
> The juice of Egypt's grace shall moist this lip.

(V, ii, 280–282)

As she dons the royal garb, she rejects the life of hedonism she has led:

> Methinks I hear
> Antony call; I see him rouse himself
> To praise my noble act. I hear him mock
> The luck of Caesar, which the gods give men
> To excuse their after wrath. Husband, I come!
> Now to that name my courage prove my title!

(V, ii, 283–288)

She has disposed of all jealousies and hopes to be worthy of Antony. Furthermore, Antony's life and death have taught her what she relinquishes:

> I am fire and air; my other elements
> I give to baser life.
>
> (V, ii, 289–290)

She has been purified, and only her spirit remains.

At this moment Iras falls. Like Enobarbus, she dies of a broken heart. Moments later, after applying an asp to her breast, Cleopatra tosses her dying insult to Caesar: "That I might hear thee call great Caesar ass/ Unpolicied" (V, ii, 307–308). She is delighted to have outmaneuvered him. She refers to the asp as "my baby at my breast" (V, ii, 309), as if it were a child of Antony's. Then she dies, seemingly transfigured. Fulfilling the prophecy of the soothsayer in Act I, scene ii, Charmian dies in similar fashion.

What remains is for Caesar to evaluate this sight. He enters, calm and controlled, and at first he does not understand what has happened:

> If they had swallow'd poison, 'twould appear
> By external swelling; but she looks like sleep,
> As she would catch another Antony
> In her strong toil of grace.
>
> (V, ii, 345–348)

His words recall Cleopatra's question to Dolabella:

> Think you there was or might be such a man
> As this I dreamt of?
>
> (V, ii, 93–94)

At last Dolabella notices the blood on her breast, and a guard sees the asp's trail on her skin. Even Caesar is moved, if only mildly:

> Take up her bed,
> And bear her women from the monument.
> She shall be buried by her Antony;
> No grave upon the earth shall clip in it
> A pair so famous. High events as these
> Strike those that make them; and their story is
> No less in pity than his glory which
> Brought them to be lamented.
>
> (V, ii, 356–363)

He envies their passion and eminence, and seems to repeat reluctantly Cleopatra's earlier sentiments that this story will be timeless. In its own way, then, the love between Antony and Cleopatra surmounted the worldly trappings that beset it.

Antony and Cleopatra remains difficult to evaluate from the perspective of Shakespearean tragedy. Unlike most works in the genre, it has no pervasive evil, nor are the characters' emotions tragically intense. At the end, we do not feel the world redeemed or a society purified. Instead we see a glorious, if turbulent, romance that burgeons amid circumstances that prohibit its fulfillment, and from the insoluble predicament emerges a sense of loss. Such loss, coupled with the characters' stature and the political consequences of their lives, invests the play with tragic grandeur.

Moreover, the title characters, despite their deaths, emerge triumphant. For even as Caesar wins, he senses that from another perspective he has been defeated. This play intimates that a man's first duty is to his humanity. From the beginning, Antony and Cleopatra have been trapped between desire and responsibility. Their flaws are great, but so are their passions. Though Caesar will rule Rome, his humanity is forever blunted, and a man who fails as a man cannot succeed as anything else.

SUGGESTIONS FOR FURTHER READING

Adelman, Janet. *The Common Liar: An Essay on* Antony and Cleopatra. New Haven: Yale University Press, 1973.

Brown, John Russell, ed. *Shakespeare's* Antony and Cleopatra: *A Casebook*. London: Macmillan, 1968.

Jorgensen, Paul. "Enobarbus' Broken Heart and the Estate of English Fugitives." *Philological Quarterly* 30 1951: 387–392.

Lee, Robin. *Shakespeare*: Antony and Cleopatra. London: Edward Arnold, 1971.

Markels, Julian. *The Pillar of the World*: Antony and Cleopatra *in Shakespeare's Development*. Columbus: Ohio State University Press, 1977.

Mills, Laurens Joseph. *The Tragedies of Shakespeare's* Antony and Cleopatra. Bloomington: Indiana University Press, 1964.

Riemer, A. P. *A Reading of Shakespeare's* Antony and Cleopatra. Sydney: Sydney University Press, 1968.

Rose, Mark, ed. *Twentieth Century Interpretations of* Antony and Cleopatra. Englewood Cliffs, N.J.: Prentice-Hall, 1977.

Traci, Philip J. *The Love Play of* Antony and Cleopatra: *A Critical Study of Shakespeare's Play*. The Hague: Mouton, 1970.

Traversi, Derek. *Shakespeare: The Roman Plays*. Stanford: Stanford University Press, 1963.

CORIOLANUS

This play contains many elements familiar from other tragedies and histories of Shakespeare. The subject is politics, and at its center is the mob, an uglier group than the one portrayed in *Julius Caesar* or *Henry VI, Part 2*. One prominent theme is how the struggle for political power gives rise to an inner conflict: responsibility to the state versus fidelity to one's integrity. This struggle is undergone by Brutus in *Julius Caesar*, Antony in *Antony and Cleopatra*, and several figures from the histories. The title character grows in self-awareness but is destroyed by a world in which he can no longer function. That predicament is shared by Brutus and Hamlet, among others. We are also conscious of the relationship between the welfare of a ruler and the health of the state, a theme at the heart of *Julius Caesar*, *Hamlet*, *Macbeth*, *King Lear*, and all the history plays.

But this play is unique, for it is more cynical than the other tragedies. Although the hero is young, the tone that dominates is that of angry old age. Whether Shakespeare the man was as unhappy is impossible to determine. Nonetheless, the play's bitterness is not tempered by any of the hope or regeneration that is part of other tragic plays.

The primary source is the volume that served Shakespeare for his other works about Rome: Plutarch's *Lives of the Noble Grecians and Romans*, as translated by Sir Thomas North. The fable of the belly (I, i) was apparently borrowed from William Camden's *Remains of a Greater Worke Concerning Britain* (1605). Shakespeare followed Plutarch's presentation closely, but made a few significant changes. Plutarch's Coriolanus has been raised by his mother, Volumnia, and as a result suffers primarily from a poor education. Shakespeare's Coriolanus has been totally dominated by his mother, and her indoctrination and continued influence are at the core of his personality. Shakespeare also develops minor characters more fully, in particular Menenius and Aufidius, both of whom become intriguing counterpoints to Coriolanus.

The events of the play are set in approximately 490 B.C. At the start, the mob is swarming about, grumbling in discontent. The cause of their unhappiness is the grain that the people cannot buy at what they deem a reasonable price, but this specific issue is just one example of the intense hatred that exists between the two classes of Rome, the ruling patricians and the subordinate plebeians. One man, in particular, is the target of the mob's ire: Caius Martius. The First Citizen shouts: "Let us kill him, and we'll have corn at our own price" (I, i, 10–11). As is usual in Shakespeare, the mob has a simplistic view of a complicated problem. The Second Citizen attempts to reason: "Consider you what services he has done for his country?" (I, i, 30–31), but the First Citizen remains unconvinced:

> Though soft-conscienc'd men can
> be content to say it was for his country, he did it to
> please his mother, and to be partly proud, which he is,
> even to the altitude of his virtue.

(I, i, 37–40)

The speech is striking, for here men are debating the qualities of the greatest soldier of the time, weighing his suitability as a leader, and their discussion turns on the fellow's mother. Yet the relationship between Martius and Volumnia is all-important, as the Second Citizen indicates:

> What he cannot help in his nature, you
> account a vice in him.

(I, i, 41–42)

To what extent is Martius responsible for his character? To what extent is he the victim of upbringing and environment? These are two issues before us.

Another issue is the nature of proper leadership. The Roman mob is in need of governance, and Caius Martius is, so to speak, a candidate. At this time Rome was a republic, although power was still in the hands of small class aristocrats. Plutarch devotes considerable space to debate over constitutional details, while Shakespeare keeps the essential republican structure of the society but narrows the political issue to one of class struggle. Some critics have speculated that this play was therefore a response to events in Shakespeare's day when during the early years of the reign of James I the commoners exerted a growing demand for authority over their own lives. In any case, in the world of this play, a man who wishes to hold office must adhere to certain timeless political gambits. He must flatter those he dislikes. He must smile and wangle and perform the catalogue of rituals that we recognize as part of the life of modern politicians. The play asks whether political rule is worth that price. Can an individual retain self-respect if forced to act the hypocrite? Is political power sufficient reward for what may be humiliating behavior?

We must also take into account Martius and his peculiar relationship to political life. He has more than a reasonable hate for such activities. Is his distaste legitimate? Or is he so much the product of his mother's values that he is unable to deal rationally with any social situation?

Therefore the play should be examined from at least three angles: the personality of Martius, the nature of political life, and the relationship between the two. One more aspect contributes to that extreme bitterness mentioned earlier. Virtually no character in this play is admirable or worthy of the political rule for which so many strive. Martius has his share of problems, and at his best is obstreperous and intolerant, hardly the qualities of an ideal leader. All the other politicians and rivals are slippery confidence men. In fact, everyone involved in government ends up corrupted by the tasks that world imposes.

Yet the play offers a good deal of comedy. The characters act so bizarrely at times, and what they say is so absurd, that we cannot help but laugh. Here is a political drama seemingly written by a wise if weary reporter, who has seen what personal damage a life of public service can wreak. He is haunted by the sense of loss but unable to keep from snickering at the foolishness of it all. The play should thus be viewed as a tragic satire.

Nowhere is this split attitude more apparent than in the opening scene with the entrance of Menenius. The embodiment of the clubhouse politician with a jolly demeanor and a glad hand, Menenius is skilled in defusing explosive situations like the one he encounters here:

> Why, masters, my good friends, mine honest neighbors,
> Will you undo yourselves?
>
> (I, i, 62–63)

The First Citizen clarifies the crisis. Speaking of the patricians, he says:

> They ne'er
> car'd for us yet. Suffer us to famish, and their
> store-houses cramm'd with grain; make edicts for
> usury, to support usurers; repeal daily any wholesome
> act establish'd against the rich, and provide more
> piercing statutes daily to chain up and restrain the
> poor. If the wars eat us not up, they will; and there's
> all the love they bear us.
>
> (I, i, 79–86)

The time might be any in history, for here is the universal voice of discontent and rebellion. When Menenius begins to speak, he offers in contrast the voice of the aristocracy: self-satisfied and eager to maintain the status quo. He moves quickly to the infamous tale of the belly, one of many instances in the play when the health of the body politic is put in terms of the human body:

> There was a time when all the body's members
> Rebell'd against the belly; thus accus'd it:
> That only like a gulf it did remain
> I' th' midst a' th' body, idle and unactive . . .
>
> (I, i, 96–99)

As he extends his tale to the annoyance of his listeners, he toys with them:

> I will tell you;
> If you'll bestow a small (of what you have little)
> Patience awhile, you'st hear the belly's answer.

(I, i, 124–126)

How easy to imagine Menenius himself with an expansive girth, embodying the hedonistic luxury of patrician life (I, i, 133–140).

That Menenius's analogy is completely illogical bothers no one:

> The senators of Rome are this good belly,
> And you the mutinous members . . .

(I, i, 148–149)

He assumes what he is trying to prove. The patricians, the ruling class, should be symbolized by the head of the body of the state, not its chief consumer. Nonetheless, the performance has a panache that carries the moment. When Menenius concludes by referring to the pesky First Citizen as "the great toe of this assembly" (I, i, 155), the merriment is intoxicating.

With the entrance of Martius, however, the mood darkens. He responds to Menenius's enthusiastic greeting and tribute with a terse "Thanks" (I, i, 164), then insults everyone within earshot:

> What's the matter, you dissentious rogues,
> That rubbing the poor itch of your opinion
> Make yourselves scabs?

(I, i, 164–166)

He continues by mocking their affection for certain political representatives, invoking the animal imagery that pervades the play, and that reflects Martius's view of humanity:

> He that will give good words to thee will flatter
> Beneath abhorring. What would you have, you curs,
> That like nor peace nor war? The one affrights you,
> The other makes you proud. He that trusts to you,
> Where he should find you lions, finds you hares;
> Where foxes, geese. You are no surer, no,
> Than is the coal of fire upon the ice,
> Or hailstone in the sun. Your virtue is
> To make him worthy whose offense subdues him,
> And curse that justice did it.

(I, i, 167–176)

Martius foreshadows his own end. Yet still he cannot stop:

> Who deserves greatness
> Deserves your hate; and your affections are
> A sick man's appetite, who desires most that

Which would increase his evil.

(I, i, 176–179)

Something, however, is inconsistent. Despising the masses and humanity at large is one thing. To be reticent about one's accomplishments and resist flattery is another. Martius, however, goes out of his way to be so vituperative as to invite widespread loathing. Yet the speech has a peculiar twist. He implies that only someone with the courage to condemn the populace deserves its approval. And who is the only one sufficiently courageous? Martius, of course. Thus he is in his own way soliciting support for his election as consul.

Why should he follow such a perverse route? If he desires their endorsement, why not simply smile, shake a few hands, and win easily? Because forces inside him prevent him from doing so. He cannot deal straight with himself. That Martius speaks only two soliloquies in the play is no accident, and in neither does he probe deeply. He is not given towards self-analysis. He tends instead to insist blindly that he is right, reaffirming the attitude he shows here.

He is annoyed when he reveals that the people have been allowed to elect representatives to "defend their vulgar wisdoms" (I, i, 215). And he foresees anarchy resulting. His mood improves only when news is brought of attack by the Volsces, led by Martius's great rival, Aufidius: "He is a lion/That I am proud to hunt" (I, i, 235–236). Martius is then reminded of his promise to fight against these invaders, and retorts sharply: "I am constant" (I, i, 239). In light of his subsequent behavior, that vow proves profoundly ironic.

Martius then leaves for the capital as the Citizens "*steal away*," (I, i, 251), leaving Sicinius and Brutus, the two tribunes elected to serve as representatives of the commoners. They despise Martius because of his pride, and believe that half his military honors belong to Cominius (I, i, 273). In their attitude is the pettiness Martius hates, and for the moment we sympathize with a great general forced to endure such sniping.

In scene ii we meet Aufidius, preparing for combat, and eager to encounter Martius once more:

> If we and Caius Martius chance to meet,
> 'Tis sworn between us we shall ever strike
> Till one can do no more.

(I, ii, 34–36)

Such outward aggression is almost welcome after the underhanded tactics promised by Brutus and Sicinius.

The entrance of Volumnia helps establish the reasons for Martius's curious attitude. With her first lines she establishes her personality:

> I pray you, daughter, sing, or express yourself
> in a more comfortable sort. If my son were my
> husband, I should freelier rejoice in that absence
> wherein he won honor than in the embracements of his

bed where he would show most love.

(I, iii, 1–5)

If the reference to her son as her husband is not precisely wish-fulfillment, the image is unnervingly close. The next sentence is even more telling, as she promotes the glories of worldly success under the dangerous word "honor," as superior to personal love. We have no problem envisioning how a mother with such values could have raised a son as much a misfit as Martius.

Her tirade continues:

> When yet he
> was but tender-bodied and the only son of my womb;
> when youth with comeliness pluck'd all gaze his way;
> when for a day of kings' entreaties a mother should not
> sell him an hour from her beholding; I, considering
> how honor would become such a person, that it
> was no better than picture-like to hang by th' wall, if
> renown made it not stir, was pleas'd to let him seek
> danger where he was like to find fame.

(I, iii, 5–13)

She admits to Martius's wife, Virgilia, that when he was young his spirit led him one way, but that Volumnia herself saw that he was meant for greater things:

> To a cruel war
> I sent him, from whence he return'd, his brows bound
> with oak. I tell thee, daughter, I sprang not more
> in joy at first hearing he was a man-child than now in
> first seeing he had prov'd himself a man.

(I, iii, 14–18)

An extraordinary revelation. She willingly sent him to war and risked his life in the name of honor. These lines recall the desires of Lady Macbeth, another woman frustrated with her role, who seeks to conquer the world through her husband. Volumnia saw her son as her own path to eminence and exploited his personality.

The thought of blood horrifies Virgilia, but Volumnia is ruthless in her ambition:

> Away, you fool! it more becomes a man
> Than gilt his trophy.

(I, iii, 39–40)

Her mania is clearer still when Virgilia's friend Valeria enters to report the behavior of Martius's son, who is described as chasing a butterfly, catching it, and tearing it with his teeth. Volumnia is not at all perturbed: "One on 's father's mood" (I, iii, 66). In her mind, her grandson has inherited the best of her son's traits. The image of a butterfly recurs twice more, at IV, vi, 90–95, and at V, iv, 11–14. In conjunction, all three passages suggest that Martius's early instincts led him in one direction, but that he was conditioned to act otherwise. From such a perspective the play turns into a story of what happens when a personality, an innate state of mind, is transformed by a malevolent influence. Martius has been turned by his mother into a killer. Yet sufficient vestiges of his character remain, so that when he is thrust into war, he carries on another campaign, this against himself. He hates what he has become. And his self-loathing is manifested regularly in his oral attacks on people and in his unceasing desire to kill in battle.

Such an attitude also explains why he has chosen a quiet wife like Virgilia. Here she refuses Valeria's invitation to visit a neighbor who is ill (I, iii, 109–110), for thoughts of Martius leave her too upset. Although Virgilia seems mild, she has an inner strength that allows her to resist both her mother-in-law and Valeria.

The extent to which the fighting instinct has been honed in Martius is apparent in scene iv. He boldly leads his troops against the Volsces, but the Romans are turned back, and in fury Martius lambasts his charges:

> You shames of Rome! you herd of—Biles and plagues
> Plaster you o'er, that you may be abhorr'd
> Farther than seen, and one infect another
> Against the wind a mile! You souls of geese,
> That bear the shapes of men, how have you run
> From slaves that apes would beat!
>
> (I, iv, 31–36)

When they refuse to heed his insults, Martius follows the Volsces back into their city where he is trapped alone. Somehow he emerges, after slaughtering countless enemy soldiers, and, covered with blood, leads his men to victory.

The actions are heroic, but they are also ludicrous. Common sense would dictate that when a general's entire army has dispersed, the general might do well to step back and regather them. But Martius is not fighting for Rome or against the Volsces. He is fighting to establish his manhood, to prove that he is not merely his mother's pawn, but a man unto himself. The only way he has been taught to express what he feels is through war, and he approaches this action with a boy's attitude. He never has enough. After he derogates his men, who are carrying off spoils, Martius refuses to acknowledge his wounds. Lartius tries to calm him, but Martius cannot listen:

> Sir, praise me not;
> My work hath yet not warm'd me. Fare you well.
> The blood I drop is rather physical
> Than dangerous to me. To Aufidius thus
> I will appear, and fight.
>
> (I, v, 16–20)

And off he charges, to aid Cominius.

The extent of his love for war is revealed in a telling metaphor in the next scene. Cominius is exhorting the Roman soldiers when a messenger enters to report the battle endured by Martius. Almost immediately Martius rushes in, covered with blood. Ignoring the bewildered Cominius's words of comfort, Martius shouts in desperation, lest he miss another skirmish:

> O! let me clip ye
> In arms as sound as when I woo'd, in heart
> As merry as when our nuptial day was done
> And tapers burnt to bedward!

> (I, vi, 29–32)

His uniting war and marriage suggests his incapacity to deal with matters of human feeling. He continues to disparage his soldiers:

> But for our gentlemen,
> The common file (a plague—tribunes for them!),
> The mouse ne'er shunn'd the cat as they did budge
> From rascals worse than they.

> (I, vi, 42–45)

Even when he is in battle, the possibility of the commoners having representation in government galls him (I, vi, 51–52). Yet despite his obsessions, Martius retains the capacity to inspire. He dismisses Cominius's offer of rest and treatment, then calls his forces back to action (I, vi, 76–85).

In scene vii the Roman army consolidates in preparation for the battles of Corioles that takes place in scene viii. Here Martius and Aufidius encounter each other, and even though Aufidius is joined by a number of his comrades, Martius routs them all.

Despite this triumph, his capacity to accept reward remains limited. Cominius grants great praise, but when he mentions Volumnia, Martius interrupts:

> Pray now, no more. My mother,
> Who has a charter to extol her blood,
> When she does praise me grieves me. I have done
> As you have done–that's what I can; induc'd
> As you have been—that's for my country:
> He that has but effected his good will
> Hath overta'en mine act.

> (I, ix, 13–19)

Why should he dismiss her approval? The core of his reason lies in the last word above: "act." Here is the first time he uses it, but it is the pith of his dilemma. All his life he has been forced to play the role of a killer, a role he despises. Yet it is all he knows. Therefore he goes at it with fatalistic fury, but so uncomfortably that he refuses to accept reward for his efforts. When offered money, he objects:

> I thank you, general;
> But cannot make my heart consent to take
> A bribe to pay my sword. I do refuse it,

And stand upon my common part with those
That have beheld the doing.

(I, ix, 36–40)

As he continues to downplay his achievements (I, ix, 41–53, 68–73), Martius
sounds modest and unselfish. Yet his self-absorption is made clear moments
later when he seeks to repay the kindness of a citizen of Corioles, who helped
during the fighting. Unfortunately, Martius forgets the citizen's name (I, ix, 90).
He wants to be generous, but his preoccupation with himself, the inheritance of
a mother who raised him to be so directed, makes such feeling impossible.

In the last scene of the act, Aufidius reveals his bitterness at constant defeat
by Martius: "I'll potch at him some way,/Or wrath or craft may get him" (I,
x, 16). Aufidius's willingness to resort to deceit makes Martius's integrity more
admirable. Martius's behavior may be aberrant, but he is never deceptive. Indeed,
he goes out of his way to be honest in word and emotion.

In Act II, scene i, Martius, now named Coriolanus in honor of his victory
at Corioles, is subject to unbearable political pressure, and the civilities he
managed to carry off earlier are beyond him. Moments before he enters, the
professional politicians debate their role in the city's life, and Menenius accuses the two tribunes of thinking only of their own advancement (II, i, 67–
80). But in these attacks Menenius also reveals weakness. He praises Coriolanus, and good-naturedly blames himself for his own vices (II, i, 47–54) but
dismisses the populace as "the beastly plebeians" (II, i, 95). Such a callous
attitude unmasks the smug aristocrat beneath the amiable front he put up in
the play's first scene. Then Volumnia, Virgilia, and Valeria enter and maintain the attitudes they demonstrated in Act I, scene iii. Virgilia is worried,
while Valeria is taken with the glamour surrounding Coriolanus. Most unsettling is Volumnia, who regards her son as no more than a political tool: "O,
he is wounded, I thank the gods for't" (II, i, 121). She even knows details of
his wounds, which she gleefully recites:

I' th' shoulder and i' th' left arm. There will
be large cicatrices to show the people, when he shall
stand for his place. He receiv'd in the repulse of
Tarquin seven hurts i' th' body.

(II, i, 147–150)

She regards each injury as opportunity to earn additional votes.

When Coriolanus enters, Volumnia is blatantly strategic, for as he kneels
before her, she raises him by referring to him as "Coriolanus," his title, thereby
treating him like her ruler rather than her son. She thinks only of herself until
she notices who stands next to her: "But O, thy wife!" (II, i, 175). The overlooking of Virgilia almost turns Volumnia into the traditionally comic figure of
the dominating mother-in-law. Coriolanus, though, has not forgotten his wife:

My gracious silence, hail!
Wouldst thou have laugh'd had I come coffin'd home,

> That weep'st to see me triumph? Ah, my dear,
> Such eyes the widows in Corioles wear,
> And mothers that lack sons.
>
> (II, i, 175–179)

He is happier to see her than to see anyone else, and momentarily he is gentle and good-humored. We see little of this marriage, but clearly Coriolanus has chosen a woman diametrically opposed to his mother. Virgilia's presence confirms that Coriolanus has another side, one buried by years of conditioning.

This respite is brief, as politics intrudes, first in Volumnia's hopes:

> I have lived
> To see inherited my very wishes
> And the buildings of my fancy; only
> There's one thing wanting, which I doubt not but
> Our Rome will cast upon thee.
>
> (II, i, 198–202)

Coriolanus denies his own ambitions, but Volumnia will remain insistent.

After the others depart, Brutus and Sicinius come forward again to weigh the political atmosphere. They remain a slimy pair, as Brutus scorns the affections of the people whose interests he is supposed to represent (II, i, 205–221). He also notes their fickleness (II, i, 228–231). The two again discuss Coriolanus's pride, and Brutus points out that Coriolanus has long disdained the practice of standing before the public and revealing his wounds, an essential political rite (II, i, 234–235). The two then resolve to ensure that the populace realizes Coriolanus's hatred for them:

> . . . that to 's power he would
> Have made them mules, silenc'd their pleaders, and
> Dispropertied their freedoms, holding them,
> In human action and capacity,
> Of no more soul nor fitness for the world
> Than camels in their war . . .
>
> (II, i, 246–251)

Although these two may be correct about Coriolanus's attitude, they hold exactly the same one. Furthermore, we may agree that Coriolanus is ill-suited for the position to which so many target him, but is anyone else remotely admirable or better fit? Who in this play is heroic? Not heroic on the battlefield, but in society? Where is moral courage?

The dialogue between the two officers at the beginning of scene ii reaffirms the themes dramatized thus far. The officers agree that Coriolanus's attitude toward the masses is strange, for "he seeks their hate with greater devotion than they can render it him . . . " (II, ii, 18–19). But they also concur that he deserves public acclaim and reward:

> But he hath so
> planted his honors in their eyes and his actions in their

hearts that for their tongues to be silent and not
confess so much were a kind of ingrateful injury . . .

(II, ii, 28–31)

As the scene proceeds, the public tribute begins, although Coriolanus dislikes
the performance:

I had rather have my wounds to heal again
Than hear say how I got them.

(II, ii, 69–70)

At this remark, Brutus asks ironically: "Sir, I hope/My words disbench'd you
not?" (II, ii, 70–71). He is pleased to see Coriolanus depart.

Cominius then offers a lengthy recital of Coriolanus's achievements, and
general agreement is reached that Coriolanus be nominated for consul. But when
he returns, he is reluctant to carry out the ritual expected of all who aspire to
such office:

I do beseech you,
Let me o'erleap that custom; for I cannot
Put on the gown, stand naked, and entreat them
For my wounds' sake to give their suffrage. Please you
That I may pass this doing.

(II, ii, 135–139)

He adds a subtle reminder of why the performance is distasteful to him:

It is a part
That I shall blush in acting, and might well
Be taken from the people.

(II, ii, 144–146)

The metaphor is familiar. We may think of Hamlet, like Coriolanus, obsessed
with the parts a man might play. Both are twisted by their world into acting in
accordance with principles that are anathema to them. Coriolanus's greatness is
that he is, at least in the context of the play, a figure who has no fear, whose
boyish impetuosity and courage make him an ideal soldier. These qualities have
brought him such eminence that he has been nominated to be leader of Rome,
a position calling for maturity, tact, and self-control. How can he survive?

His refusal to allow himself to be paraded before the people is interpreted by
Sicinius as a desire to deny the masses the right of approval (II, ii, 156–158).
We recognize that the tribunes care nothing for the people's right, but are
concerned only with the loss of their power that Coriolanus's election would
ensure.

In scene iii the masses gather, and their attitudes towards Coriolanus are by
now familiar. They respect Coriolanus's achievements but do not wish to support
someone who despises them. As the third citizen says:

> If he would incline to the people, there was never a
> worthier man.
>
> (II, iii, 38–39)

Coriolanus then enters in appropriate garb, muttering his resentment of the people and the process:

> Bid them wash their faces,
> And keep their teeth clean. So, here comes a brace.
>
> (II, iii, 60–61)

"Brace" is usually used for a group of birds or animals. Were his anguish not so evident, the acrimony would be funny.

One by one the citizens come before him to ask questions, and Coriolanus can barely control his anger, as he must speak politely to those he despises:

> Better it is to die, better to starve,
> Than crave the hire which first we do deserve.
> Why in this woolvish [toge] should I stand here
> To beg of Hob and Dick, that does appear,
> Their needless vouches? . . .
> Let the high office and the honor go
> To one that would do thus. I am half through:
> The one part suffered, the other will I do.
>
> (II, iii, 113–124)

This first soliloquy reveals his lack of insight. Coriolanus's question should not be why he has been asked to act in this way. The answer is obvious: politics. The real question is why he is so loath to do it, and though he hints at the cause with the word "part," he has yet to understand his maladjustment.

After Coriolanus is taken to the Senate house, Brutus and Sicinius, who have falsely given their approval to Coriolanus's candidacy, are left to speak to the mob. The pair begin a recitation of Coriolanus's insults and other transgressions, all of which amount to excessive pride. The two emphasize the single concept repeatedly, as if that one idea were all the mob can grasp. Before long the citizens have reversed their judgment and now condemn Coriolanus (II, iii, 209–212). This mob is as unintelligent as any in Shakespeare's plays, and after observing them in action we better understand Coriolanus's antagonism. Brutus and Sicinius then demonstrate further political craft by asking that the two of them be blamed for Coriolanus's nomination:

> Lay
> A fault on us, your tribunes, that we labor'd
> (No impediment between) but that you must
> Cast your election on him.
>
> (II, iii, 226–229)

Whatever the final result of the election, Brutus and Sicinius will not be accused, but instead will find allies on the winning side. The pair leaves in anticipation of Coriolanus's next public fit of temper.

At the beginning of Act III Coriolanus is disappointed to learn that the Volsces are not expected to fight soon. On the other hand, he is pleased that Aufidius has revealed hatred towards him, and Coriolanus speaks longingly of the two fighting again:

> I wish I had a cause to seek him there,
> To oppose his hatred fully.
>
> (III, i, 19–20)

His only home is the battlefield. Yet we should never think that in his impatience with politics Coriolanus is ignorant of the enterprise. When Brutus and Sicinius enter to tell him that the people have changed their opinion, Coriolanus shows that he is wise to the ways of political dirty tricks, as he condemns the tribunes:

> Are these your herd?
> Must these have voices, that can yield them now,
> And straight disclaim their tongues? What are your offices?
> You being their mouths, why rule you not their teeth?
> Have you not set them on?
>
> (III, i, 33–37)

Brutus tries to revert the charges back to Coriolanus, claiming that Coriolanus opposed an order giving the people free corn (III, i, 42–45). Despite attempts at conciliation by Cominius (III, i, 58–61), Coriolanus refuses to modify his position:

> I say again,
> In soothing them we nourish 'gainst our Senate
> The cockle of rebellion, insolence, sedition,
> Which we ourselves have plough'd for, sow'd, and scatter'd,
> By mingling them with us, the honor'd number,
> Who lack not virtue, no, nor power, but that
> Which they have given to beggars.
>
> (III, i, 68–74)

The image of the state as a garden is common in Shakespeare's plays, and most salient in *Richard II*. Coriolanus's diatribe also reflects the fear of disorder that pervaded the England of Shakespeare's day, and which is one of the dominant themes of Shakespeare's history plays.

Under the pressure of this moment and egged on by Brutus and Sicinius, Coriolanus cannot contain his rage. When Sicinius uses "shall" (III, i, 88) to describe the poisonous influence of Coriolanus's mind, Coriolanus seizes on that word of command as proof of the rudeness of his inferiors. Among other insults he refers to the masses as "the Hydra," the beast with many heads slain by Hercules, and his ravings leave Cominius comically desperate to end the scene: "Well, on to th' market-place" (III, i, 112). Nevertheless, Coriolanus continues to berate the cowardice of the masses (III, i, 120–130), and to assert the need

for strong central authority instead of bestowing power on those who are undeserving and more interested in mutiny:

> Thus we debase
> The nature of our seats and make the rabble
> Call our cares fears; which will in time
> Break ope the locks a' th' Senate, and bring in
> The crows to peck the eagles.

(III, i, 135–139)

The eagle traditionally stood for Rome, and crows are scavengers. Here is the
core of Coriolanus's vision of the anarchy that threatens his city. Yet even as
he offers political doctrine that reflects his social class, we must keep in mind
that Coriolanus's hatred of the masses is based partially on a personal misanthropy
sprung from his own upbringing.

After Coriolanus's diatribe against lessening the senators' authority (III, i,
141–161), Sicinius declares him a traitor, and despite Menenius's attempts to
calm the crisis, rouses the people into a fury: "What is the city but the people?"
(III, i, 198), a cry the masses echo. Cominius warns that such behavior will
divide Rome (III, i, 203–206), but Sicinius orders Coriolanus taken to the Tarpeian Rock, from which those who acted against the state were hurled to death.
At this threat Coriolanus draws his sword, eager to fight everyone:

> No, I'll die here.
> There's some among you have beheld me fighting;
> Come, try upon yourselves what you have seen me.

(III, i, 222–224)

After the nobles come to his aid and the crowd is beaten back, Coriolanus is
urged to escape while he can, but he remains boyishly frustrated that he was
denied combat: "I could beat forty of them" (III, i, 242) he boasts. Menenius
tries to excuse this spectacle: "His nature is too noble for the world" (III, i,
254), but that explanation is inaccurate. Coriolanus's nature, whatever that might
be, has not been allowed to survive. All that he has is the nature his mother
forced on him.

Following Coriolanus's departure is an interlude with intriguing imagery, as
Brutus and Sicinius try to arouse the plebeians to greater fury, and Menenius
tries to calm them. First he pleads:

> Do not cry havoc where you should but hunt
> With modest warrant.

(III, i, 273–274)

At these words we recall Antony's use of "Cry 'Havoc!' " in *Julius Caesar*
(III, i, 273), when before his oration he urges himself to inspire the plebeians
to run rampant. Moments later Menenius says of Coriolanus:

O, he's a limb that has but a disease:
Mortal, to cut it off; to cure it, easy.

(III, i, 294–295)

Here we remember the words of Brutus from *Julius Caesar*, when he claims that Antony is " . . . but a limb of Caesar" (II, i, 165). Finally one Senator proposes exiling Coriolanus rather than killing him: "The other course/will prove too bloody" (III, i, 325–326). In *Julius Caesar*, Brutus speaks the same way about killing Antony: "Our course will seem too bloody . . . " (II, i, 162). That these images occur in both plays is significant: both are about political life, both dramatize the plight of a misfit in that life, both dramatize distaste for the masses, and both advocate a strong central authority.

As Coriolanus's place in Roman opinion sinks, his aides, in a last desperate ploy, bring Volumnia to convince her son of the wisdom of conducting himself politically. At the beginning of the scene he insists he cannot do so and invokes a familiar image:

Why did you wish me milder? Would you have me
False to my nature? Rather say, I play
The man I am.

(III, ii, 14–16)

We understand that he plays the man Volumnia has shaped. Despite her pleas and Menenius's approval (III, ii, 31–35), Coriolanus struggles to maintain fidelity to his self-image by resisting apology:

I cannot do it to the gods,
Must I then do't to them?

(III, ii, 38–39)

One word resounds through all of Volumnia's weedling: "honor," which she invokes nearly a dozen times. But of whose honor does she speak? Here she urges him to try:

I would dissemble with my nature where
My fortunes and my friends at stake requir'd
I should do so in honor.

(III, ii, 62–64)

Her eagerness to act pierces through. But Coriolanus is not convinced. He accuses his mother of distorting his life:

You have put me now to such a part which never
I shall discharge to th' life.

(III, ii, 105–106)

Even at this moment he does not grasp the full implications of his words. Meanwhile, with unintentional irony, Cominius sustains the metaphor: "Come, come, we'll prompt you" (III, ii, 106). And Volumnia presses her argument:

> I prithee now, sweet son, as thou hast said
> My praises made thee first a soldier, so,
> To have my praise for this, perform a part
> Thou has not done before.

(III, ii, 107–110)

"Sweet son." Never have we heard her refer to him as that before. She manages to brush aside all his accusations and take them as praise. She acknowledges that she has twisted him. But as long as he has gone this far, why not achieve the ultimate goal by maintaining the lie with a new one?

Coriolanus continues to vacillate:

> Well, I must do't.
> Away, my disposition, and possess me
> Some harlot's spirit!

(III, ii, 110–112)

But then:

> I will not do't,
> Lest I surcease to honor mine own truth,
> And by my body's action teach my mind
> A most inherent baseness.

(III, ii, 120–123)

The deciding factor is Volumnia herself:

> Come all to ruin, let
> Thy mother rather feel thy pride than fear
> Thy dangerous stoutness; for I mock at death
> With as big heart as thou. Do as thou list;
> Thy valiantness was mine, thou suck'st it from me;
> But owe thy pride thyself.

(III, ii, 125–130)

The image of "sucking valor" brings to mind Lady Macbeth's envisioning herself tearing a babe from her breast (*Macbeth*, I, vii, 54–58). Volumnia confesses that what she has done to her son has been for herself. She boasts that all his best qualities are hers. If he yields to any of his own, which are his weaknesses, he lets her down, and his failure will be hers. Reluctantly Coriolanus consents to her wishes.

Before he has the chance to redeem himself, Brutus and Sicinius scheme to make his attempt futile. Sicinius tells the aedile to have the mobs respond to shouts and charges against Coriolanus:

> And when such time they have begun to cry,
> Let them not cease, but with a din confus'd
> Enforce the present execution

Of what we chance to sentence.

(III, iii, 19–22)

Brutus schemes as well to have Coriolanus lose self-control:

> Being once chaf'd, he cannot
> Be rein'd again to temperance; then he speaks
> What's in his heart, and that is there which looks
> With us to break his neck.

(III, iii, 27–30)

Both men invoke timeless strategies of mob manipulation to gain their political ends.

Their techniques work perfectly. After warning Coriolanus (III, iii, 31), Menenius starts the proceedings by once again placating the citizenry:

> Lo, citizens, he says he is content.
> The warlike service he has done, consider; think
> Upon the wounds his body bears, which show
> Like graves i' th' holy churchyard.

(III, iii, 48–51)

Initially Coriolanus offers grudging apologies. But under the prodding of Brutus and Sicinius, who once again call Coriolanus a traitor (III, iii, 66), Coriolanus falls into the trap and becomes so incensed that the masses are ready to take him to the Tarpeian Rock. At this provocation, especially because it is instigated by the two tribunes he despises, Coriolanus loses control so quickly that Menenius remarks sarcastically: "Is this the promise that you made your mother?" (III, iii, 86). But as the accusations and shouts against him grow, climaxing in cries that he be banished, Coriolanus outflanks everyone:

> You common cry of curs, whose breath I hate
> As reek a' th' rotten fens, whose loves I prize
> As the dead carcasses of unburied men
> That do corrupt my air—I banish you!

(III, ii, 120–123)

The mob's ugly breath is noted several times in this play, even by their supposed ally, Brutus (II, i, 236). The image is invoked by other characters with an aversion to the populace, including Casca in *Julius Caesar* (I, ii, 246–247), and Cleopatra when she contemplates the Roman mob's greeting her as prisoner (*Antony and Cleopatra*, V, ii, 211–213). Shakespeare's vision of mass humanity is not charitable, and the constant barrage of animal imagery does not improve it. But no one hates with the fervor of Coriolanus, who explodes in a satisfying temper tantrum, then stalks off. He has long been waiting to lash out this way, and he takes full advantage. Yet he leaves not like a man but like a boy, running away rather than meeting his foes head on, and never weighing his own responsibility.

This quality recurs in the next scene, when his impending departure is mourned by his wife and mother, standing before the young nobles of Rome. Coriolanus comments: "I shall be lov'd when I am lack'd" (IV, i, 15). What a sad reflection. He wants everyone's appreciation and affection, but simply does not have the ability to solicit it.

If at this moment Coriolanus retains some immaturity, he also evinces a new ease and grace:

> Come, my sweet wife, my dearest mother, and
> My friends of noble touch; when I am forth,
> Bid me farewell, and smile. I pray you come.
> While I remain above the ground, you shall
> Hear from me still, and never of me aught
> But what is like me formerly.
>
> (IV, i, 48–53)

For the first time we see him relaxed and realize that exile, even under these circumstances, is what he has always sought. Thus he goes away a boy, but a more reflective boy.

In scene ii the consequences of his actions begin to surface. Brutus and Sicinius are pleased with their handiwork, and scheme how to make the situation work best for themselves (IV, ii, 1–5). They try to escape the wrath of Volumnia, who curses them (IV, ii, 11–12), and even Virgilia shows her inner strength when she orders the two tribunes to remain and hear Volumnia's accusation. Virgilia is surprisingly vicious when she imagines that were her husband to meet the pair he would kill them both (IV, i, 26). This sentiment, coming from a seemingly meek wife, frightens Brutus and Sicinius, who retreat behind pious hypocrisy:

> I would he had continued to his country
> As he began, and not unknit himself
> The noble knot he made.
>
> (IV, ii, 30–32)

None of the listeners is fooled, however, and the tribunes are forced to run away.

In scene iii the ramifications of Coriolanus's departure reach the other side, as a Roman traitor and a Volsce discuss the news and conclude that Rome will now be vulnerable to attack by Aufidius (IV, iii, 31–36). This exchange is followed appropriately by Coriolanus's private reaction to his new situation. Were he truly the disillusioned man he claims to be, he would leave the territory and live in peace. Were he tired of humanity, he would be content to live alone, or at least anonymously. But he is compelled to take revenge, although precisely what he is revenging and why are not clear to him. In his second and last soliloquy he jeers at the treachery of others, then reveals that he is driven to fight, and that the cause is not important, only that he have an enemy:

> My birthplace [hate] I, and my love's upon
> This enemy town. I'll enter. If he slay me,
> He does fair justice; if he give me way,

I'll do his country service.

(IV, iv, 23–26)

Coriolanus's joining the Volsces is proof that his loyalty is, in the end, to himself. That priority is understandable, given the mother who raised him to think only of himself.

At the beginning of scene v, Coriolanus enters enemy territory, where a veneer of modesty would be appropriate strategy. Instead, he intrudes with his old arrogant self, insulting servants and pushing them aside (IV, v, 47–49). Then he identifies himself to Aufidius as "Coriolanus" (IV, v, 68), a less-than-tactful reminder of his previous conquest over these men whom he now seeks to join. The rest of his lengthy opening address is a harangue against the Roman citizenry of every level:

> The cruelty and envy of the people,
> Permitted by our dastard nobles, who
> Have all forsook me, hath devour'd the rest,
> And suffer'd me by th' voice of slaves to be
> Hoop'd out of Rome.

(IV, v, 74–78)

When Coriolanus offers his services to help Aufidius's own revenge against Rome (IV, v, 88–92), we realize that Volumnia's constant harping on honor has had an effect, for Coriolanus fights for no reason other than self-glorification. Aufidius is initially pleased to have such a potent ally, and embraces Coriolanus intimately while invoking a telling image:

> I lov'd the maid I married; never man
> Sigh'd truer breath; but that I see thee here,
> Thou noble thing, more dances my rapt heart
> Than when I first my wedded mistress saw
> Bestride my threshold.

(IV, v, 114–118)

Earlier Coriolanus referred to love and war in relation to marriage (I, vi, 29–32). Now Aufidius speaks of being married to Coriolanus, whom he subsequently calls "Mars" (IV, v, 118), the god of war. For Aufidius, Coriolanus and war are identical, and he cherishes both. Yet though the two men offer mutual pledges of support, they are bound only by love of war and hatred of Rome. Two such massive egos cannot work in tandem for long, for their splitting authority must dilute the power to which each is accustomed, as servant 3 realizes (IV, v, 191–202). This new alliance, however, pleases servant 2, who looks forward to new wars with Rome:

> Let me have war, say I, it exceeds peace
> as far as day does night; it's sprightly, [waking],
> audible, and full of vent. Peace is a very apoplexy,
> lethargy, mull'd, deaf, [sleepy], insensible, a getter

of more bastard children than war's a destroyer of
men.

(IV, v, 221–226)

Such lines remind us that foolish delight in barbarism flourishes at all levels of
society, not just among the nobles who fight for personal glory.

One inconsistency is worth noting. At Act IV, scene v, line 122, Aufidius
refers to the "Twelve several times" he was defeated by Coriolanus. Earlier,
at Act I, scene x, line 7, Aufidius mourns five such defeats. Whether such a
discrepancy is Shakespeare's error or Aufidius's is unclear.

In Act IV, scene vi, Sicinius and Brutus are pleased that the expulsion of
Coriolanus has thus far produced no negative consequences. And they revel in
praise from the citizens, mocking Coriolanus's ego (IV, vi, 29–33). But their
hypocritical self-congratulation ends when an aedile reports part of what we have
known all through this scene: that the Volsces are preparing to attack Rome.
Another messenger compounds this bad news by reporting that Coriolanus has
joined the enemy forces, as Cominius corroborates:

> He is their god; he leads them like a thing
> Made by some other deity than Nature,
> That shapes man better; and they follow him
> Against us brats with no less confidence
> Than boys pursuing summer butterflies,
> Or butchers killing flies.

(IV, vi, 90–95)

The reference to the butterfly echoes the image of Coriolanus's son eating a
butterfly, as described by Valeria in Act I, scene iii. Now Rome may suffer the
same sort of destruction at Coriolanus's hands. Menenius lashes out at the two
tribunes:

> You have made fair hands,
> You and your crafts! You have crafted fair!

(IV, vi, 117–118)

Both whine pathetically: "Say not we brought it" (IV, vi, 120), and the entrance
of the citizens confirms that Brutus and Sicinius alone have not caused this crisis.
For the citizens, too, prove hypocritical, claiming that they never wanted Coriolanus expelled (IV, vi, 139–145). Here again is the fickle, even mindless, mob
of *Julius Caesar* and the history plays.

All is not serene among the Volsces, however. By scene vii Aufidius realizes
that either he or Coriolanus will have to give way in their battle for leadership:

> He bears himself more proudlier,
> Even to my person, than I thought he would
> When first I did embrace him; yet his nature
> In that's no changeling, and I must excuse

What cannot be amended.

(IV, vii, 8–12)

We have seen Coriolanus strut for so long that we are accustomed to his behavior. Aufidius, however, is stunned, and the latter half of his statement recalls the opening scene of the play and the words of the Second Citizen:

> What he cannot help in his nature, you
> account a vice in him.

(I, i, 41–42)

Perhaps because his drive for power is close to that of Coriolanus, Aufidius understands his rival better than anyone else does:

> First he was
> A noble servant to them, but he could not
> Carry his honors even. Whether ['twas] pride,
> Which out of daily fortune ever taints
> The happy man; whether [defect] of judgment,
> To fail in the disposing of those chances
> Which he was lord of; or whether nature,
> Not to be other than one thing, not moving
> From th' casque to th' cushion, but commanding peace
> Even with the same austerity and garb
> As he controll'd the war . . .

(IV, vii, 35–45)

He enumerates three elements of Coriolanus's character that have coalesced to make Coriolanus leave Rome. Aufidius omits, however, the key element, the one that inspired the others: Volumnia. Still, despite his insights, Aufidius has little sympathy for Coriolanus:

> When, Caius, Rome is thine,
> Thou art poor'st of all; then shortly art thou mine.

(IV, vii, 56–57)

Coriolanus now faces a new treachery.

The despair in Rome continues in Act V, as Menenius and Cominius confess that they were unable to persuade Coriolanus to withdraw his plans of attack. Even Brutus and Sicinius feel helpless in the face of the upcoming invasion (V, i, 35–38). Menenius, ever the politician, hopes that Coriolanus will be more amenable after a hearty dinner (V, i, 56–58). But Cominius realizes that Rome's only hopes are Volumnia and Virgilia, who intend to meet with Coriolanus soon (V, i, 71–73).

In scene ii Menenius is stymied by the guards of the Volsces. Coincidentally, Coriolanus and Aufidius enter at this moment, but the break in their alliance is already apparent, for Coriolanus takes over completely, leaving Aufidius with but a single weak line (V, ii, 94). Meanwhile Coriolanus has become more stiffnecked than ever, and barely listens to Menenius's plea. Proud of his resoluteness, Coriolanus boasts to Aufidius:

> This man, Aufidius,
> Was my belov'd in Rome; yet thou behold'st!

(V, ii, 92–93)

We cannot be sure if Coriolanus is trying to show loyalty to the Volsces, but his delight in rejecting his old friend indicates the depth of his emotional torment. We feel him being almost perversely unresponsive, as if by doing so he will finally show himself free of his mother.

That attitude is more difficult to maintain in scene iii, when Volumnia, Virgilia, and the others come to the Volsces camp to beg for mercy to Rome. Before they arrive, Coriolanus once more demonstrates his arrogance, as he tells his "partner" Aufidius:

> You must report to th' Volscian lords, how plainly
> I have borne this business.

(V, iii, 3–4)

The use of "must" reveals who is in charge.

Soon after the supplicants arrive, Coriolanus makes his attempt at independence when he tries to deny all connection with Rome (V, iii, 33–37), but soon this stand turns to one of a fatalistic acceptance, apparent in his use of the acting metaphor:

> Like a dull actor now
> I have forgot my part, and I am out,
> Even to a full disgrace.

(V, iii, 40–42)

He gives his attention first to his wife, then bows to Volumnia, and greets Valeria. Even before the solicitations begin, Coriolanus tries to fight them off:

> Do not bid me
> Dismiss my soldiers, or capitulate
> Again with Rome's mechanics. Tell me not
> Wherein I seem unnatural; desire not
> T' allay my rages and revenges with
> Your colder reasons.

(V, iii, 81–86)

He is afraid he will be vulnerable to an emotional appeal, and tries to dismiss all argument. He wishes only to fight and end his charade, and thus orders Aufidius and the Volsces to remain and to prevent anyone from offering words in private that might change Coriolanus's opinion.

But Volumnia begins to work on him. She envisions the consequences of a war, for if his family prays for the city they love, they will be praying for the destruction of the man they love. Whatever happens, he will suffer, as either a prisoner led through the streets or as victor over his own city (V, iii, 113–118). Volumnia claims she does not want to see such humiliation, then challenges her son by warning that he will conquer Rome only by marching over his mother's body (V, iii, 124–125). To our surprise Virgilia echoes this threat, and even young Martius, Coriolanus's son, adds a similar defiance:

> 'A shall not tread on me;
> I'll run away till I am bigger, but then I'll fight.
>
> (V, iii, 127–128)

His tone sounds exactly like that of his father. When Coriolanus continues to resist, Volumnia appeals to his sense of history. Should he massacre Rome, he will be judged a turncoat, and all his achievements will be for nought (V, iii, 141–148). Then she makes her pleas more personal, that if he should deny his mother, who has given him everything, the gods would never forgive him (V,iii, 158–168). At this sentiment Coriolanus turns away, touched but still resistant. Finally she resorts to her ultimate weapon, humiliation, as she dismisses his affections:

> This fellow had a Volscian to his mother;
> His wife is in Corioles, and his child
> Like him by chance.
>
> (V, iii, 178–180)

Coriolanus's response is one of the most unusual moments in all of Shakespeare's plays, as the character is directed to hold his mother's hand and stand in silence. Suddenly he bursts out:

> O, mother, mother!
> What have you done? Behold, the heavens do ope,
> The gods look down, and this unnatural scene
> They laugh at. O my mother, mother! O!
>
> (V, iii, 182–185)

The great comedy and tragedy of his life are revealed to him. He comprehends at last what his mother has wrought, that he is trapped in his past and present, and that his future offers no escape. Thus he sees no reason to destroy Rome, and offers Aufidius instead the prospect of peace. Aufidius, of course, sees this change as contributive to his own cause (V, iii, 200–202). Coriolanus's end is now assured.

In scene iv, word has yet to come of the success of the women's mission. Thus Menenius is still gloomy and reflects to Sicinius on the danger Coriolanus poses:

> There is difference between a grub and a
> butterfly, yet your butterfly was a grub. This Martius
> is grown from man to dragon: he has wings, he's

more than a creeping thing.

                                                              (V, iv, 11–14)

The butterfly metaphor returns once more, here reflecting Coriolanus's own transformation, which we know has been the result of his mother's influence. As the two politicians weigh their helplessness, a messenger races in to tell Sicinius that the plebeians are threatening to kill him and Brutus if the women's mission fails. Once more the unreliability and latent violence of the masses are apparent. However, sudden news of the women's success ends that threat, and in scene v they are escorted back in triumph. One Senator even calls for the repeal of Coriolanus's banishment. Again we feel the uncontrollability of the masses, whose passions shift from moment to moment.

In scene vi Aufidius plans his assault on Coriolanus's loyalty. Before several members of his faction, Aufidius elaborates how he befriended Coriolanus, allowing him equal status, while in return Coriolanus has been only arrogant (V, vi, 30–39). Now that Coriolanus has failed to subdue Rome and rob the city of its spoils, because of "a few drops of women's rheum" (V, vi, 45), Aufidius condemns Coriolanus to death. His fellow conspirators approve of the plan, citing the affection of the mob for the man who only a short time before killed their children (V, vi, 51–63). Thus the Volscian aristocrats, like their Roman counterparts, view the fickle populace with scorn.

Coriolanus enters to the cheers of the commoners, proclaiming loyalty to the Volsces, and the quality of a peace that he has negotiated to bring glory to both Rome and his new countrymen. But Aufidius interrupts the presentation, branding Coriolanus a traitor:

> . . . but at his nurse's tears
> He whin'd and roar'd away your victory,
> That pages blush'd at him, and men of heart
> Look'd wond'ring each at others.

                                                              (V, vi, 96–99)

Coriolanus calls to Mars for support, but Aufidius then refers to him as "thou boy of tears" (V, vi, 100), and at the insult Coriolanus becomes furious. He storms at Aufidius, and this release of temper allows Aufidius's conspirators to call for Coriolanus's execution. The Volscean mob, its mood ever shifting, recalls the deaths caused by Coriolanus (V, vi, 121–122), and joins in the shouts of accusation. Within moments Coriolanus is murdered, not by one man, but by a crowd. How appropriate that the masses unite to kill him.

Irony accompanies his life even after its end. As Aufidius stands in ugly triumph over Coriolanus's body, the Third Lord requests that Aufidius stand aside, and the First Lord adds a touch of grace:

> Let him be regarded
> As the most noble corse that ever herald

Did follow to his urn.

(V, vi, 142–144)

Even Aufidius confesses: "My rage is gone" (V, vi, 146). As happens often at the end of these tragedies, forgiveness and reconciliation emerge. But in this play that spirit is mocked. Only one major figure dies: Coriolanus. The rest go on to live as they have. No major political changes have been instituted. The timeless conflict for power between patricians and plebeians will continue, and we feel that hardly anyone is capable of wielding that power wisely.

The play dramatizes one man's struggle to resolve irreconcilable inner conflicts, to deal with the forces that shaped him. He loses that struggle, but the course of his life does not teach any universal lesson. Aufidius claims of Coriolanus that " . . . he shall have a noble memory" (V, vi, 153). The nature of these societies, however, suggests that such a memory will not endure.

SUGGESTIONS FOR FURTHER READING

Bradley, A. C. *Coriolanus*. Oxford: Oxford University Press, 1912.

Campbell, Oscar. *Shakespeare's Satire*. New York: Oxford University Press, 1943.

Huffman, Clifford C. *Coriolanus in Context*. Lewisburg, Pa.: Bucknell University Press, 1972.

Knights, L. C. "Shakespeare and Political Wisdom: A Note on the Personalism of *Julius Caesar* and *Coriolanus*." *Sewanee Review* 61 (1953): 43–55.

Oliver, H. J. "Coriolanus as Tragic Hero." *Shakespeare Quarterly* 10 (1959): 53–60.

Palmer, John. *Political Characters of Shakespeare*. London: Macmillan, 1945.

Phillips, James Emerson, Jr., ed. *Twentieth Century Interpretations of* Coriolanus. Englewood Cliffs, N.J.: Prentice-Hall, 1970.

TIMON OF ATHENS

This play's date of composition is uncertain, as is the text itself, which may not be complete, and which may not be entirely Shakespeare's work. Yet the available script poses an intriguing variety of challenges.

The figure of Timon must have been known to Shakespeare for some time, for in *Love's Labor's Lost* Berowne mentions him as one of several great men reduced to absurdity (IV, iii, 165–168). Shakespeare probably read of Timon in a section of Plutarch's "Life of Marcus Antonius" in the North translation of *The Lives of the Noble Grecians and Romans*, the book that also provided the "Life of Alcibiades," another source of this play. Finally, Shakespeare possibly knew of an anonymous academic play, *Timon*, written in the 1580s.

The first question we must consider is whether the play is indeed a tragedy. The story is of a man who falls from great heights to profound depths, largely through his own fault. Yet what has become traditional Shakespearean character development is missing. Instead, the play is more like an extended fable or allegory in which figures personifying specific traits interact to teach about human nature. Nonetheless, the play shares several characteristics with other tragedies, notably *King Lear*, and reaffirms themes from Shakespeare's other works in this form.

The opening scene establishes important motifs, as characters designated by callings such as the Poet and the Painter debate the nature of art and reality. That these men are given no names adds to the sense of allegory. More significant is that their discussion anticipates how Timon and others are forced to evaluate human nature; what it seems and what it is, what humanity offers as image, and what the reality is behind that image. The artists have come to solicit financial support from Timon, and their reflections include extended comments on "Fortune," meaning both "money" and "chance." The crux of their argument is that man is a victim of fate, good or bad, and the Poet imagines that one day, by chance, Timon might lose his great wealth (I, i, 84–88). However, in no other play of Shakespeare's is man only a pawn of fate, and thus this section must be taken ironically. For in this work, too, the mishaps that befall humanity, specifically

Timon, are the result of not chance, but individual misjudgment and the maliciousness of others.

Another irony underlies this scene. Although the speakers put up a front for each other, implying that each has only the highest artistic intentions, their constant references to Timon and his money indicate that both are aware how they are feigning in order to gain his favors (I, i, 30–34, 42–50, 67–72). Indeed, their attitude towards him is that he is something of a dupe who gives out money without regard for the character of the recipient. Yet they are also resentful that a man should have all the money Timon has, and thus when the Poet speaks of Timon losing his resources, the Poet does so with pleasure.

With Timon's entrance the play proper begins, and immediately Timon demonstrates his limitless generosity. He pays the debt of the imprisoned Ventidius and offers to supply more money should Ventidius require it (I, i, 103). Timon then complements the dowry of an old Athenian so that the man's daughter may marry Lucilius (I, i, 144–146). After both acts of generosity, Timon receives statements of gratitude. Yet why he is so beneficent is never explained. We must instead accept that this man is devoted to helping others, even fawning sycophants like the artists. Timon hints at his rationale when he accepts one of the Painter's creations:

> Painting is welcome.
> The painting is almost the natural man;
> For since dishonor traffics with man's nature,
> He is but outside; these pencill'd figures are
> Even such as they give out. I like your work,
> And you shall find I like it.

(I, i, 156–161)

As is the case in other tragedies, the word "dishonor" suggests trouble for someone clearly preoccupied with it. Indeed, in this play, the word or variations of it are invoked dozens of times.

This tribute also suggests Timon's innocence. He does not want to hear anything unpleasant, but rather has his own vision of humanity, and accepts art as long as it supports that vision. Thus Timon is an idealist, hardly a crime, but in the context of this society a sign of foolishness. Possibly he should be seen as a distant relation of Brutus in *Julius Caesar*, with eyes on the potential grandeur of man. But Brutus at least tries to reason matters out. Timon does not think, and this deficiency makes him generally unappealing. Throughout the play, liars and mountebanks approach him, and for a long time he is unable to see through any of them. We could accept such blindness if we knew that Timon had previously met many wonderful people, or if he came from a happy family, or if we had some explanation of why he was so enthusiastic about human nature. But without that explanation, he is more of a caricature than a character. Thus as he accepts flattery from the Jeweller (I, i, 168–172), his naivete is frustrating. All these parasites see Timon as something of a fool, willing to dispense vast resources as soon as he is flattered sufficiently. Therefore, as they use Timon for their own purposes they resent him.

Alongside Timon is Apemantus, a twisted wit, whose antagonism toward the human race is as intense as Timon's love. He mocks the efforts of the Painter and the Poet, then demonstrates his own acuity:

> He that loves to be flatter'd is worthy
> o' th' flatterer.

> (I, i, 226–227)

This appraisal proves an accurate evaluation of Timon, for Apemantus sees through the false affections the others show. But why does Apemantus stay by Timon, whose views are so antithetical to his? Whatever the reason, Apemantus is an effective counterpoint to characters like the two Lords, who end scene i with tributes to Timon that are obviously hypocritical. For instance, the first Lord sums up Timon as follows: "The noblest mind he carries/That ever govern'd man" (I, i, 280–281).

In scene ii the banquet is underway, and Timon continues his beneficence by turning down the repayment by Ventidius, newly released from prison. As Timon continues to accept flattery, Apemantus grows more bitter:

> O you gods! what a number
> of men eats Timon, and he sees 'em not! It grieves
> me to see so many dip their meat in one man's blood,
> and all the madness is, he cheers them up too.
> I wonder men dare trust themselves with men.

> (I, ii, 39–43)

But attention moves away from Apemantus when Timon speaks at length, oddly enough in prose, which robs his words of dignity:

> Why, I have often wish'd myself
> poorer, that I might come nearer to you. We are born
> to do benefits; and what better or properer can we call
> our own than the riches of our friends?

> (I, ii, 100–103)

These lines reveal some of Timon's ego. He seems to delight in giving. Yet, for all his smiles, the act also keeps the recipients subordinate to him. And the more generous he is, the more superior he feels. The reason he dismisses repayment may be that such reimbursement would restore balance. As long as men do not pay Timon, even if he tells them to forget the debt, they are nonetheless in his debt. Thus Timon's generosity is not merely an expression of his link with humanity, as he claims, but also an extension of his own ego. In this respect we can also understand the antagonism of those he supports, for no matter how free Timon is with his money, his charity still makes the recipients conscious of both his wealth and their inferiority. Therefore the more they claim to love him for his kindness, the more they in fact seethe at his capacity to do kindness.

After the masque, Apemantus reflects on what he judges to be the "madness" (I, ii, 134) of the spectacle. Timon, however, is impressed, especially at the silent adoration offered to him by the Lords. To express his gratitude, he orders Flavius, his servant, to bring a jewel case. Flavius's response is the first hint of the trouble: "When all's spent, he'ld be cross'd then, and he could" (I, ii, 162). When Flavius returns with the casket, Timon continues to dispense gifts with foolish enthusiasm, and Flavius's mood grows darker:

> He commands us to provide, and give great gifts,
> And all out of an empty coffer;
> Nor will he know his purse, or yield me this,
> To show him what a beggar his heart is,
> Being of no power to make his wishes good . . .
> Happier is he that has no friend to feed
> Than such that do e'en enemies exceed.
>
> (I, ii, 192–204)

At this point we cannot be certain whether Flavius is fulfilling his servant's bond or whether his attachment to Timon is more personal. For the rest of this scene Timon continues to force gifts on various lords, even Alcibiades; and as he does, we feel his desperation to have everyone obligated to him:

> I take all and your several visitations
> So kind to heart, 'tis not enough to give;
> Methinks, I could deal kingdoms to my friends,
> And ne'er be weary.
>
> (I, ii, 218–221)

Thus the reversal that comes soon is little surprise, especially after Apemantus's steady warnings, such as:

> Friendship's full of dregs;
> Methinks false hearts should never have sound legs.
> Thus honest fools lay out their wealth on curtsies.
>
> (I, ii, 233–235)

Timon's refusal to listen to such harsh but accurate advice suggests a quick downfall.

In Act II, Timon's debts are revealed, and his creditors are determined to achieve restitution. In scene i the Senator realizes how much Timon owes him and directs Caphis to demand payment (II, i, 15–32). The ruthlessness of the order strikes us, as does the Senator's eagerness to see Timon "left a naked gull" (II, i, 31). In scene ii Flavius, too, grasps the extent of Timon's debts, but is bothered as well by Timon's ignoring reality: "What shall be done, he will not hear, till feel" (II, ii, 7).

At this point other servants enter, all seeking repayment on behalf of their masters, and all unwilling to be put off. Timon cannot believe their steadfast demands and asks Flavius:

> How goes the world, that I am thus encount'red
> With clamorous demands of debt, broken bonds,
> And the detention of long since due debts,
> Against my honor?

> (II, ii, 36–39)

Flavius does not bother to answer this naive query but tries to hold the creditors off.

Something of an answer to Timon is offered in the next part of the scene, when the waiting servants, Apemantus, a Fool whose mistress is a whore, and one of the mistress's pages indulge in obscene byplay. Their banter concerns usury, which the Fool treats as something like prostitution:

> I think no usurer but has a fool to his servant;
> my mistress is one, and I am her fool. When men
> come to borrow of your masters, they approach sadly,
> and go away merry; but they enter my master's house
> merrily, and go away sadly.

> (II, ii, 98–102)

The overall impact of the discussion is to denigrate the lending of money which Timon insists upon viewing as noble.

When Timon returns, Flavius struggles to communicate the extent of the debt Timon owes. Timon initially blames Flavius, ironically turning on the one person he can trust (II, ii, 128–132), then suggests that land be sold. When Flavius explains that all resources have been overextended, Timon still does not grasp the crisis:

> Come, sermon me no further.
> No villainous bounty yet hath pass'd my heart;
> Unwisely, not ignobly, have I given.
> Why dost thou weep? Canst thou the conscience lack
> To think I shall lack friends?

> (II, ii, 172–176)

Moments later Timon adds: "You shall perceive how you/Mistake my fortunes; I am wealthy in my friends." (II, ii, 183–184), and the ironic double meaning does not escape us. Although Timon's firm belief in mankind may seem inspiring, he sounds fatuous, especially when we have heard how his creditors are eager to get back at him. Even Flavius's report that lords Lucius and Lucullus have refused to lend him money does not shake Timon, and he orders Flavius to search out Ventidius, whose debt is, as Timon explains, profound (II, ii, 222–231). Timon's faith in humanity flourishes, but at this point he himself seems pathetic rather than noble.

The extent of the betrayal of Timon is dramatized in the opening scenes of

Act III. In Act III, scene i, Flaminius, Timon's servant, seeks funds from
Lucullus, but the latter scorns the request:

> Many a time and often I ha'
> din'd with him, and told him on't, and come again to
> supper to him of purpose to have him spend less,
> and yet he would embrace no counsel, take no warning
> by my coming. Every man has his fault, and honesty is
> his.
>
> (III, i, 23–27)

And when Flaminius tosses back money subtly offered for a bribe, Lucullus
brands him a fool like Timon (III, i, 50). In response, Flaminius's prayer that
Lucullus grow sick is feeble.

In scene ii Lucius comments to three strangers that he would be glad to give
Timon money, but his response hints at a different sentiment:

> I have receiv'd some
> small kindnesses from him, as money, plate, jewels, and
> such like trifles—nothing comparing to his—yet had
> he mistook him and sent to me, I should ne'er have
> denied his occasion so many talents.
>
> (III, ii, 20–24)

The appositive "nothing comparing to his" suggests the latent hatred in Lucius.
He dislikes being in debt to Timon, and he dislikes Timon's status and power.
Whether Timon is kind or pleasant is irrelevant. Thus when a servant enters to
request funds for Timon, Lucius finds an excuse:

> Commend me bountifully
> to his good lordship, and I hope his honor will conceive
> the fairest of me, because I have no power to be kind.
> And tell him this from me, I count it one of my
> greatest afflictions, say, that I cannot pleasure such an
> honorable gentlemen.
>
> (III, ii, 52–57)

The use of "honorable" suggests Lucius is eager to see such a trusting fool like
Timon suffer. Lucius's remark also suggests that he views life as a struggle for
survival, and that he has the need and the right to take from Timon. The three
strangers disapprove of Lucius's hypocrisy, and one is especially perturbed:

> Had his necessity made use of me,
> I would have put my wealth into donation,
> And the best half should have return'd to him,
> So much I love his heart. But I perceive
> Men must learn now with pity to dispense,

For policy sits above conscience.

(III, ii, 82–87)

But this stranger has never asked Timon for money; therefore he has no need for revenge. He can idealize about what he would do were he in a position to repay Timon, but he may be willing to offer only because he has not been asked. Furthermore, he could denote money to Timon, but chooses not to do so.

In scene iii, Sempronius, described ironically as *"another of Timon's friends,"* conceives a new excuse not to give Timon money:

I'd rather than the worth of thrice the sum
H'ad sent to me first, but for my mind's sake;
I'd such a courage to do him good. But now return,
And with their faint reply this answer join:
Who bates mine honor shall not know my coin.

(III, iii, 22–26)

Here again "honor" suggests the unscrupulousness of the speaker, and the entire address sounds deceitful.

In scene iv the servants of Timon's creditors come once more to demand money, and Flavius, who acts with the devotion of King Lear's Kent, is furious:

Why then preferr'd you not your sums and bills
When your false masters eat of my lord's meat?

(III, iv, 49–50)

But the second servant clarifies for Flavius and us the extent of the resentment others feel toward Timon:

No matter what, he's poor, and
that's revenge enough. Who can speak broader than
he that has no house to put his head in? Such may rail
against great buildings.

(III, iv, 62–65)

Flavius's anger, however, pales next to that of Timon, who learns of the rejection by his former friends and raves uncontrollably: "Tear me, take me, and the gods fall upon you!" (III, iv, 99). One of the intruding servants, Hortensius, suggests that the money he seeks will never be recovered, for Timon is now "a madman" (III, vi, 102). And after all have departed, Timon seems to support this evaluation, when he plans one last feast. Flavius claims that no money is available, but Timon has a scheme he does not articulate to Flavius. In some ways the suddenness of Timon's disillusion is parallel to Lear's upon the realization of the depth of his daughters' betrayal. Nonetheless, in this play, the transformation is less convincing, for it is sudden and has no basis in character. If we think of the play as an allegory, however, the metamorphosis is more acceptable.

In the next scene the scope of the plot widens, and we are introduced to Alcibiades, who appeared briefly in Act I as a guest at Timon's banquet. We do not learn the full background of his story, but we gather that he is defending a man accused of murder. Alcibiades' claim is that the act was self-defense:

> He is a man (setting his fate aside)
> Of comely virtues;
> Nor did he soil the fact with cowardice
> ([An] honor in him which buys out his fault),
> But with a noble fury and fair spirit,
> Seeing his reputation touch'd to death,
> He did oppose his foe;
> And with such sober and unnoted passion
> He did behoove his anger, ere 'twas spent,
> As if he had but prov'd an argument.
>
> (III, v, 14–23)

Because of his earnestness and decency, we like Alcibiades. But we also note the word "honor" in his description of his client. Could this anonymous figure be like Romeo, who in a moment of temper revenges his friend's honor? Could he be like Brutus, who always attempts to act in the name of honor? Alcibiades' client sounds too much like these men, as well as other Shakespearean figures who act according to "honor." We notice, too, Alcibiades' use of "fate." His defendant, he claims, was the victim of circumstances, and therefore not responsible for his actions.

In considering this claim in light of other tragedies, we cannot agree with Alcibiades' judgment. Instead we must reluctantly stand by the words of the First Senator, who is hard but accurate:

> You cannot make gross sins look clear;
> To revenge is no valor, but to bear.
>
> (III, v, 38–39)

That theme is reinforced in play after play. Alcibiades tries to insist on his version of "extenuating circumstances":

> To kill, I grant, is sin's extremest gust,
> But in defense, by mercy, 'tis most just.
>
> (III, v, 54–55)

But the Second Senator reminds Alcibiades that his client has not led an exemplary life:

> He's a sworn rioter; he has a sin that often
> Drowns him and takes his valor prisoner.
> If there were no foes, that were enough
> To overcome him. In that beastly fury
> He has been known to commit outrages
> And cherish factions. 'Tis inferr'd to us,

His days are foul and his drink dangerous.

(III, v, 67–73)

Apparently his client's violence was not, as Alcibiades insists, a quirk, but, as with almost all Shakespeare's characters, the product of the man's personality. This situation is thus curious, for though our sympathies tend towards Alcibiades, the lone man struggling against unfeeling authority, we agree in principle with the senators, whose harsh argument seems sensible.

But it does not make complete sense, for Alcibiades indicates that his client has killed in another context as well:

Hard fate! he might have died in war . . .
If by this crime he owes the law his life,
Why, let the war receive't in valiant gore,
For law is strict, and war is nothing more.

(III, v, 74–84)

Alcibiades implies that the same instincts condemned in society are welcome in war, where his client has served, and is willing to serve again. The First Senator cannot see the logic:

We are for law, he dies, urge it no more
On height of our displeasure. Friend, or brother,
He forfeits his own blood that spills another.

(III, v, 85–87)

Now who appears just? Alcibiades is asking for compassion on the grounds that his client has fought nobly for his country. In response the Senators are cold and unfeeling, so caught up in legalities that they are unable to temper justice with mercy. Their attitude recalls the words of Angelo in *Measure for Measure*, who, when confronted by Isabella, Claudio's sister, responds severely: "It is the law, not I, condemn your brother" (II, ii, 80). In light of the Senators' obstinancy we are comfortable feeling antagonistic to abusive power, and more so when Alcibiades protests further and is banished for his zeal in the name of freedom. As he stalks off, swearing revenge on Athens, we are sympathetic:

I'll cheer up
My discontented troops, and lay for hearts.
'Tis honor with most lands to be at odds.
Soldiers should brook as little wrongs as gods.

(III, v, 113–116)

Still, he does sound slightly preposterous acting in the name of honor, taking personal insult as reason for further destruction. Thus our attitude towards Alcibiades is mixed; he has noble intentions but misguided actions.

The relationship between Alcibiades' dilemma and Timon's is integral to the play. Both men make the same error of looking with unqualified benevolence on human behavior. At this point, neither is willing to accept that an individual may be ill-motivated. Timon refused to acknowledge selfishness and then revenge

as impulses. All he wanted to see was kindness. Alcibiades here refuses to see
a capacity for violence as leading to destruction. Both men are shocked into
reality by reactions that are, strictly speaking, legal. Timon's creditors do deserve
payment. Alcibiades' client has murdered. But in this society the law is merciless,
and thus we cannot agree totally with the system, either. Meanwhile, the two
main figures, in fits of temper, rush out to revenge themselves on the world.

Before Timon leaves, he perpetrates minor retaliation during the dinner for
his creditors. Before the actual ceremony, two lords smugly discuss Timon's
asking them for money. They pretend to be regretful that he is in need, but their
sarcasm is clear. For instance, one lord comments: "I am sick of that grief, too,
as I understand how all things go" (III, vi, 17–18). The other responds: "Every
man here's so. What would he have borrow'd of you?" (III, vi, 19–20). When
Timon enters, they revert to exaggerated pleasantries. But their dislike of him
is always evident.

After a magnanimous welcome, Timon sits the men down, then uncovers their
dishes, which contain nothing but warm water that he throws in their faces:
"Uncover, dogs, and lap!" (III, vi, 85). Then he lashes out orally:

> Live loath'd, and long,
> Most smiling, smooth, detested parasites,
> Courteous destroyers, affable wolves, meek bears,
> You fools of fortune, trencher-friends, time's flies,
> Cap-and-knee slaves, vapors, and minute-jacks!

                                                        (III, vi, 93–97)

The beast imagery reflects Timon's reversal of attitude, and but also his inability
to distinguish humanity from animals, a compounding of his earlier inability to
distinguish humanity from angels. He has never managed to come to grips with
his own kind. Thus he shouts in departure: " . . . henceforth hated be/Of Timon
man and all humanity" (III, vi, 104–105). Humanity cannot meet Timon's
idealized standard, and therefore to him humanity is worthless. This vision is
not far from Alcibiades' attitude toward the people of Athens. During the last
two acts, events force both characters to modify that viewpoint.

At the beginning of Act IV it is anything but modified, as Timon declaims
his quintessential statement of hatred, a curse against world order:

> Piety, and fear,
> Religion to the gods, peace, justice, truth,
> Domestic awe, night-rest, and neighborhood,
> Instruction, manners, mysteries, and trades,
> Degrees, observances, customs, and laws,
> Decline to your confounding contraries;
> And yet confusion live!

                                                        (IV, i, 15–21)

He seeks the destruction of the social system that humiliated him, and he is
indiscriminate in his malice. No longer is anything sacred to him:

Timon will to the woods, where he shall find
Th' unkindest beast more kinder than mankind.
The gods confound (hear me, you good gods all)
Th' Athenians both within and out that wall!
And grant, as Timon grows, his hate may grow
To the whole race of mankind, high and low!
Amen.

> (IV, i, 35–41)

As if in answer to this perverse prayer, Flavius enters and belies Timon's blanket condemnation. After parting from his servant colleagues, Flavius mourns the condition to which Timon has fallen:

Poor honest lord, brought low by his own heart,
Undone by goodness!

> (IV, ii, 37–38)

Here he places Timon in the line of Shakespeare's tragic heroes, in whom a great virtue becomes, in particular circumstances, a dangerous flaw. Yet by remaining loyal, Flavius also contradicts Timon's dismissal of all human action:

Alas, kind lord,
He's flung in rage from this ingrateful seat
Of monstrous friends; nor has he with him to
Supply his life, or that which can command it.
I'll follow and inquire him out.
I'll ever serve his mind with my best will;
Whilst I have gold, I'll be his steward still.

> (IV, ii, 44–50)

No matter what Timon says, Flavius continues to affirm faith in the potential of the human character.

In the next several scenes Timon revels in his misanthropy. In scene iii he digs for roots but comes across gold, an ironic discovery in the context of what drove him to madness. As he did earlier in the play, he throws the material away, but this time with hatred, not love:

This yellow slave
Will knit and break religions, bless th' accurs'd.
Make the hoar leprosy ador'd, place thieves,
And give them title, knee, and approbation
With senators on the bench.

> (IV, iii, 34–38)

When Alcibiades enters and reveals his own war against Athens, Timon bestows the gold with a plea for mass destruction (IV, iii, 107–124). He also complies to the greedy request for gold from the two prostitutes who accompany Alcibiades, seeing them as instruments for further ruin:

> I'll trust to your conditions, be whores still.
> And he whose pious breath seeks to convert you,
> Be strong in whore, allure him, burn him up,
> Let your close fire predominate his smoke,
> And be no turncoats; yet may your pains six months
> Be quite contrary. And thatch your poor thin roofs
> With burthens of the dead—some that were hang'd,
> No matter; wear them, betray with them.

(IV, iii, 140–147)

He rails on, peculiarly diminishing the impact of his anger. If he cannot differentiate between Alcibiades, a man of noble if misguided intent, and two women greedily soliciting gold, his outrage lacks dignity. Furthermore, Alcibiades, too, has rejected the company of Athens by taking refuge with two citizens who hardly represent the best of his society. Timon's anger, in particular, is like the one-dimensional bitterness of Apemantus, who shows up to exchange long passages of vitriol.

Apemantus also demonstrates his understanding, though, as he accuses Timon:

> Thou hast cast away thyself, being like thyself,
> A madman so long, now a fool.

(IV, iii, 220–221)

In a scene that recalls that of Lear and his Fool out on the heath, Timon and Apemantus curse humanity, and Timon asks one key question:

> Why shouldst thou hate men?
> They never flatter'd thee.

(IV, iii, 269–270)

This meeting between the cynic and the disillusioned man continues at some length. Apemantus does, however, pinpoint the key to Timon's dilemma:

> The middle of humanity thou never knew-
> est, but the extremity of both ends.

(IV, iii, 300–301)

Despite these insights, Apemantus rises little in our estimation, for he remains one-dimensional, sour that everyone is not a failure as he is. What is dramatically problematic is that Timon descends to Apemantus's level, as both join in rejection of humanity. Their diatribes reach a climax of sorts when the two hurl pure invective at one another (IV, iii, 371–374).

Nevertheless, Timon retains a special humanity that he demonstrates when he encounters the three thieves. He urges them on in their profession, in the cause of ever-more disruption:

> Love not yourselves, away,
> Rob one another. There's more gold. Cut throats,

All that you meet are thieves.

> (IV, iii, 444–446)

He still can not, or will not, distinguish between members of his species. Yet something in Timon's exhortation moves the third bandit:

H'as almost charm'd me from my profession,
by persuading me to it.

> (IV, iii, 450–451)

Vestiges of the earlier Timon touch even this hardened soul.

These feelings surface with the reappearance of Flavius, whose tearful devotion (IV, iii, 458–461) brings the madman to his senses:

What, dost thou weep? Come nearer. Then I love thee,
Because thou art a woman, and disclaim'st
Flinty mankind, whose eyes do never give
But thorough lust and laughter.

> (IV, iii, 482–485)

Forgive my general and exceptless rashness,
You perpetual-sober gods! I do proclaim
One honest man—mistake me not, but one;
No more, I pray—and he's a steward.

> (IV, iii, 495–498)

The last four words are a rueful reflection on the quality of a world that lets its sole decent man function in such a position. Timon then gives Flavius a large portion of the gold and sends him to live "rich and happy" (IV, iii, 525), a redemption, if partial and transitory, that gives the play hope.

Timon, however, is not cured of his misanthropy by one man. The Poet and the Painter return in the hope of wheedling more gold from him, but Timon overhears them. In their attempts at flattery they remind Timon and us of the general spirit of his society. Timon plays along, then treats them as they deserved earlier, by throwing gold and expelling them: "Out, rascal dogs!" (V, i, 115). The image of dogs is used throughout the play to reflect the sycophancy of those who would live off individuals such as Timon. Whether this expulsion represents Timon's recognition of the essence of these two or whether he is reverting to universal loathing is unclear.

The next episode reflects the unusual nature of Timon and his influence. Two Senators urge him to return to Athens to prevent its destruction by Alcibiades, but Timon has no stomach for them:

If Alcibiades kill my countrymen,
Let Alcibiades know this of Timon,
That Timon cares not.

> (V, i, 169–171)

Nor has he any more feeling to give:

> My long sickness
> Of health and living now begins to mend,
> And nothing brings me all things.

(V, i, 186–189)

The word "nothing" is another echo from *King Lear*. In that play it refers to the elemental condition of man without the accoutrements of society. Here the word refers to man unburdened by all that society demands. The scene ends with Timon's refusal to help Athens, and his bitter farewell (V, i, 220–223).

In scene ii Alcibiades' attack against Athens is anticipated, and the Senators announce that Timon will be of no help. In scene iii a lone soldier, wandering in the woods, comes across Timon's tomb. Both scenes emphasize the unrelenting harshness of Timon's new vision of humanity. Yet the ending of the play is in a different spirit, reflecting the side of Timon softened in the presence of Flavius. When Alcibiades returns to Athens, prepared to level it, the request of one Senator moves him:

> So did we woo
> Transformed Timon to our city's love
> By humble message and by promis'd means.
> We were not all unkind, nor all deserve
> The common stroke of war.

(V, iv, 18–22)

The Senators also plead to Alcibiades that those who have offended him are dead from shame. The Senators' message is the same as that of Timon's benediction to Flavius (IV, iii, 523–533): although evil men are part of humanity, good men do survive, and their goodness ennobles life.

Alcibiades agrees, decreeing that only enemies of himself and Timon should be punished (V, iv, 56–58). Social order is thereby restored, and, most significant, a spirit of toleration and moderation is established. After all that has happened, what Timon never achieved in life is passed on after him. Alcibiades reads the inscription of Timon's tombstone, words that urge passers-by to move on. Then Alcibiades adds:

> Dead
> Is noble Timon, of whose memory
> Hereafter more.

(V, iv, 79–81)

In other plays we are told that individual characters will be remembered, but in Timon's case we are more likely to believe so. The city of Athens owes its survival to him, and Alcibiades' last words tell us that Timon's influence will not fade:

> Bring me into your city,
> And I will use the olive with my sword:
> Make war breed peace, make peace stint war, make each

Prescribe to other as each other's leech.

(V, iv, 81–85)

For the audience, Alcibiades' regeneration is not as memorable as Timon's misanthropy, but stands as proof of the possibility of redemption through suffering.

Though not a masterpiece, *Timon of Athens* reflects key aspects of Shakespeare's tragedies. Perhaps most important is the theme of transcendence. In *Timon of Athens*, Timon's battle with his society destroys him, but his passion and his redeeming trust in Flavius reaffirm faith in humanity and ultimately in the benign order of the universe. We also think of Romeo and Juliet, Brutus, Hamlet, Othello, Desdemona, King Lear, Cordelia, Antony, Cleopatra, and others who in varying ways grapple with their world. They may die in their struggle, but the majesty of their lives gives them some triumph. And such is their stature that through their vision, strength, and endurance, they uplift us by revealing the heights to which humanity can aspire.

SUGGESTIONS FOR FURTHER READING

Bradbrook, M. C. *The Tragic Pageant of* Timon of Athens: *An Inaugural Lecture.* London: Cambridge University Press, 1966.

Butler, Francelia McWilliams. *The Strange Critical Fortunes of Shakespeare's* Timon of Athens. Ames: Iowa State University Press, 1966.

Ellis-Fermor, Una. "*Timon of Athens*: An Unfinished Play." *Review of English Studies* 18 (1942): 270–273.

Honigmann, E. A. J. "*Timon of Athens.*" *Shakespeare Quarterly* 12 (1961): 249–257.

Levin, Harry. "Shakespeare's Misanthrope." *Shakespeare Survey* 24 (1973): 89–94.

Soellner, Rolf. Timon of Athens: *Shakespeare's Pessimistic Tragedy.* Columbus: Ohio State University Press, 1979.

THE HISTORIES

In this series of plays, Shakespeare recreates some of the most stirring events from various periods of English history. He also offers a gallery of fascinating characters: some heroic, some villainous, some comic, and some a mixture of these qualities. The intricacies and effects of the confrontations between these characters, as well as their individual actions, language, and values, reflect to a great extent Shakespeare's vision of historical and political conflict.

This vision raises a variety of issues explored throughout the plays. What is the nature of kingly obligation? What values are essential in a ruler? What is the relationship between power and morality? To what extent are all who wield power susceptible to abuse of that power? What price may public figures be forced to pay in dealing with their families and other aspects of their private lives? How is the nature of the ruler reflected in the life of the populace?

As Shakespeare created these works, he was influenced by several forces. One was the explication of events provided by the leading historians of his era, Raphael Holinshed and Edward Hall. Holinshed, in his *Chronicles of England, Scotland, and Ireland*, published in a full edition in 1587, provided the playwright with details of history and genealogy. Hall's *The Union of the two noble and illustrious families York and Lancaster*, published in several editions in the 1540s and 50s, offered not only historical facts but an interpretation that underlies eight of Shakespeare's ten history plays. Hall's thesis concerned the War of the Roses, the civil strife between the Lancasters and the Yorks, two eminent houses whose rivalry created discord throughout England. Hall argued that the conflict followed directly from the deposition of Richard II in 1399 and ended only in 1485 with the marriage of the Lancastrian heir Henry VII to the Yorkist heiress Elizabeth. Shakespeare accepted this interpretation of his nation's past, and his plays may be regarded to an extent as a warning about the importance of political responsibility and the consequences of misrule.

Other forces contributed to the portrait of history that emerges from these plays. One was the political climate of Shakespeare's day. The long reign of Queen Elizabeth was obviously nearing an end, but she had not designated a successor. Thus the fear of an uncertain transfer of power and potential anarchy permeated the public consciousness. Another force was the chauvinistic tenor of Shakespeare's age, for the rulers and people of England wanted to see onstage the glory of their nation. Another was Shakespeare's own sense of the world of politics and those who participate in it. Another, in some ways the most important, was his instinct for what was theatrically viable and effective.

Finally, dominating these works is a tension between the medieval view of the state and the newly emerging Renaissance view. We must never forget the medieval belief that the king is placed on the throne by divine sanction, and that in such a position he is the linchpin of the universe, the link between the microcosm and macrocosm. Therefore the strength and security of the kingship is reflected in the stability of the world surrounding, while a throne in chaos is mirrored by a kingdom in disorder. This interpretation is partially challenged by the Renaissance sense of political reality, manifested most notoriously in the works of Machiavelli. His writings articulated an awareness of politics as a war for power waged by human beings free from divine influence. In sum, although religious feeling and theological argument pervade the plays, they are essentially secular. A universal order exists, but within it conflicts take place between independent individuals, and these conflicts are the crux of the drama.

Such overall hostility leads to a host of personal struggles that recur throughout the plays. We confront the matter of proper authority: who should rule according to divine law, but also who deserves to rule because of political and military skill, as well as because of ethical values. We see characters pulled between opposing loyalties and moralities: devotion to the good of the state versus devotion to individual desire for wealth and influence, versus alliance with competitors who seek their own wealth and influence. Although these disputes are here particularized in one era of English history, they are timeless and cast light on any age in which political antagonism flourishes, our own as much as any other.

Appendix 2 on page 827 outlines the relationships of the royal characters in the two tetralogies, and indicates the plays in which they appear.

SUGGESTIONS FOR FURTHUR READING

Armstrong, W. A., ed. *Shakespeare's Histories: An Anthology of Modern Criticism.* Harmondsworth, England: Penguin Shakespeare Library, 1972.

Blanpied, John W. *Time and the Artist in Shakespeare's English Histories.* Newark: University of Delaware Press, 1983.

Driver, Tom F. *The Sense of History in Greek and Shakespearean Drama.* New York: Columbia University Press, 1960.

Knights, L. C. *William Shakespeare: The Histories.* London: Longmans, 1962.

Leech, Clifford. *William Shakespeare: The Chronicles.* London: Longmans, 1962.

Manheim, Michael. *The Weak King Dilemma in the Shakespeare History Plays.* Syracuse, NY: Syracuse University Press, 1972.

Ornstein, Robert. *A Kingdom for a Stage; the Achievement of Shakespeare's History Plays*. Cambridge: Harvard University Press, 1972.

Palmer, John. *Political Characters of Shakespeare*. London: Macmillan, 1945.

Pierce, R. B. *Shakespeare's History Plays: The Family and the State*. Columbus: Ohio State University Press, 1971.

Prior, Moody E. *The Drama of Power: Studies in Shakespeare's History Plays*. Evanston, Ill.: Northwestern University Press, 1973.

Reese, Max M. *The Cease of Majesty: A Study of Shakespeare's History Plays*. London: Edward Arnold, 1961.

Saccio, Peter. *Shakespeare's English Kings*. New York: Oxford University Press, 1977.

Tillyard, E. M. W. *Shakespeare's History Plays*. London: Chatto & Windus, 1944.

Traversi, Derek. *Shakespeare from Richard II to Henry V*. Stanford: University Press, 1957.

Waith, Eugene M., ed. *Shakespeare, The Histories: A Collection of Critical Essays*. Englewood Cliffs, N.J.: Prentice-Hall, 1965.

THE FIRST TETRALOGY

The plays that make up the first of Shakespeare's two tetralogies based on English history are among his very earliest dramatic works, and as such they have flaws. Speakers tend to sound alike, and their language is not often memorably poetic. Few characters have depth or offer any complication; virtually all their ideas and emotions are on the surface. The result is that at too many moments we are left to watch plot develop mechanically, and amidst exposition and recitation we sometimes lose drama.

Yet these works have points of considerable interest. First, the scope of the story is massive. Perhaps only an inexperienced playwright would have had the gall to attempt to cover the panorama of sixty years in a single series of four plays, and for that reason Shakespeare's comparative innocence and youthful exuberance may have been vital to the creative process. Second, the plays themselves have an undeniable theatricality. So much territory is covered, and so many characters roam the stage that the drama seems to progress as if by the playwright's energy alone. Third, even if some scenes and acts are awkwardly composed, certain moments loom powerfully, and flashes of the Shakespeare to come emerge.

Most important, these plays are essential to an appreciation of Shakespeare's view of history and politics. Here he dramatizes a loss of national unity to be redeemed only through the rise of the Tudors, and his perspective on this era has ramifications that extend throughout his entire career.

Opinion concerning the authorship of these plays is not unanimous, for some critics believe Shakespeare collaborated with other playwrights on various sections. But the unity of style and theme suggests that the tetralogy is the product of one creative mind, and that conclusion underlies the discussion that follows.

No single figure or group of figures dominates all four plays. Henry himself is too weak and ineffectual to hold sway. Thus we shall focus on a succession of characters, including Joan of Pucelle, Talbot, Gloucester, Margaret, Suffolk, Edward, and Richard III.

Finally, let us remember that the first tetralogy is in fact the second part of the story. It dramatizes the aftermath of three historical episodes: the abdication and death of Richard II, who would thereafter be regarded by many as a martyr; the reign of Henry IV, who would always be judged by his enemies as a usurper and therefore an illegal king; and the conquests in France by Henry V, son of the usurper, yet ultimately a great ruler on his own.

These events are the subject of four plays Shakespeare will write subsequently, when he is reaching height of his powers. However, the details of the background material and the controversies and personages involved are yet fresh in the minds of the characters onstage in the first tetralogy, as well as in the collective memory of the Elizabethan audience.

HENRY VI, PART 1

This play, set against the One Hundred Years War fought by England and France from 1337 until 1453, is concerned primarily with the military and personal conflict between the French martyr, Joan of Arc, to whom Shakespeare gives the less grand title "Joan of Pucelle," and the English hero Talbot. But more subtle forces are at work. The play additionally sets up the conflict between the houses of Lancaster and York to show how strife between leaders in the English political structure not only unleashes dangerous elements within the nation, but also can damage its place in global affairs.

One more aspect is worth noting. In many cultures of the past, participation in the world of war and politics was limited to males, but in this series of plays three women are prominently involved, contributing to a fascinating theme that recurs throughout the tetralogy: the relationship between sexuality and warfare. The theme is not unique to these plays. Indeed, it is the fulcrum of Shakespeare's darkest comedy, *Troilus and Cressida*, as articulated by Thersites: "Lechery, lechery, still wars and lechery, nothing else holds fashion" (V, ii, 194–195). The words might well apply to the first tetralogy.

The play begins in 1422 with the funeral of Henry V, then, as now, a hero of English history. As his brother the Duke of Bedford, says: "England ne'er lost a King of so much worth" (I, i, 7). But the political consequences of this death are apparent at once. Exeter warns of the potential influence by England's greatest rival nation:

> What? shall we curse the planets of mishap
> That plotted thus our glory's overthrow?
> Or shall we think the subtile-witted French
> Conjurers and sorcerers, that, afraid of him,
> By magic verses have contriv'd his end?

> (I, i, 23–27)

The emphasis on the supernatural seems to anticipate the daunting presence of Joan. But a more invidious threat comes from the Bishop of Winchester, who praises Henry's achievements, then adds a note of self-congratulation for the Church's contribution:

> The battles of the Lord of hosts he fought;
> The Church's prayers made him so prosperous.

(I, i, 31–32)

This claim arouses immediate antagonism from the Duke of Gloucester, the older of Henry V's surviving brothers and Protector of the crown:

> The Church? where is it? Had not churchmen pray'd,
> His thread of life had not so soon decay'd.
> None do you like but an effeminate prince,
> Whom like a schoolboy you may overawe.

(I, i, 33–36)

Gloucester accuses the Church of working against Henry V, and of seeking a monarch who will obey church dictates. But we must recognize that Gloucester's antagonism in the name of his brother emerges not only because of policy, but also because of personality. Here, for instance, the Bishop criticizes the attitude of Gloucester's wife, and Gloucester in turn accuses the Bishop of private and professional corruption (I, i, 41–43). Moreover, although Winchester is, like Gloucester and Bedford, descended from John of Gaunt, father of Henry IV, Winchester's mother was Katherine Swynford, a lady of the court who married John of Gaunt only after her three sons by him, given the surname Beauford, were grown. Therefore they lived under the stigma of illegitimacy and outside succession to the throne. Still, the three brothers, Winchester, Somerset, and Exeter, are all prominently involved in the struggle for political influence.

This exchange of insults arouses the anger of Bedford, who shouts a central motif of the histories, fear of civil disorder:

> Henry the Fift, thy ghost I invocate:
> Prosper this realm, keep it from civil broils,
> Combat with adverse planets in the heavens!

(I, i, 52–54)

That this plea is useless is apparent moments later, as a messenger enters to announce the results of battle in France:

> Amongst the soldiers this is muttered,
> That here you maintain several factions;
> And whilst a field should be dispatch'd and fought,
> You are disputing of your generals.
> One would have ling'ring wars with little cost;
> Another would fly swift, but wanteth wings;
> A third thinks, without expense at all,
> By guileful fair words peace may be obtain'd.
> Awake, awake, English nobility!
> Let not sloth dim your honors new begot.

Cropp'd are the flower-de-luces in your arms,
Of England's coat one half is cut away.

(I, i, 70–81)

The implication is clear. Factionalism at home has caused disaster abroad. The heroic past of Henry V has been undercut by the incompetent and selfish rule of the present administration. Even when the nobles learn of elevation of the Dolphin Charles to King, their unanimous desire to fight against him is delayed by mutual antagonism (I, i, 96–102). ("Dolphin" was the Anglicized word for "Dauphin," the heir apparent to the French Crown.)

Another messenger brings word of Talbot, who in this play embodies English heroism:

More than three hours the fight continued,
Where Valiant Talbot above human thought
Enacted wonders with his sword and lance:
Hundreds he sent to hell, and none durst stand him;
Here, there and every where, enrag'd he slew.

(I, i, 120–124)

So great is his stature that even the French are in awe of him:

The French exclaim'd, the devil was in arms;
All the whole army stood agaz'd on him.

(I, i, 125–126)

Yet the cowardice of one Sir John Falstaff has brought dissension and defeat (I, i, 130–140). This character is not the famous Sir John of Shakespeare's *Henry IV*, but another soldier, actually named Sir John Fastolfe, who was acccused unfairly by the Tudors of monumental cowardice. In any case, the result is the loss of thousands of men, and the capture of Talbot. Bedford vows to rescue him by defeating the Dolphin (I, i, 148–156), and Exeter urges that all follow their oath sworn to Henry V to defeat the French.

In this play Talbot provides a dramatic balance. Will his boldness and strength of character triumph despite the dissension at court? Like the audience of Shakespeare's time, we know the ending of the story. What matters, then, is not the outcome, but the values the outcome teaches. Throughout the ten history plays two thems are linked: one, civil disorder, which occurs as the result of, two, weak rule by bickering authorities. The works repeatedly suggest that an autocracy, even one that at times goes too far in the exercise of power, is preferable to irresolution that invites overthrow and possible anarchy.

The reason for the current political disorder in England is that the surviving son of Henry V was, at the time of his father's death, only months old. Thus even though the story here is compressed, and this first scene depicts events that occurred over years, a vacuum still exists at the top of the English political hierarchy. And in the battle for control Winchester and Gloucester gradually emerge as the two chief rivals. Here the principles for which each fights are clarified. Gloucester's first loyalty is to the throne, and thus he departs from Westminster Abbey to hurry in support of the young King (I, i, 170–172). Winchester, meanwhile, ponders his own situation:

> Each hath his place and function to attend:
> I am left out; for me nothing remains.
> But long I will not be Jack out of office.
> The king from Eltam I intend to send,
> And sit at chiefest stern of public weal.
>
> (I, i, 173–177)

Such crass ambition from a supposedly pious cleric is not unusual in any of these plays. Finally, the attitude of the two men establish a central conflict of the histories: loyalty to the crown weighed against devotion to one's own career.

As the scene shifts to the French side, Shakespeare's bias shows itself. Even as the French earn victories, they do so unimpressively. Charles himself refers to "the forlorn French" (I, ii, 19), and mocks his own troops (I, ii, 22–24). Moments later Reignier warns of Salisbury (I, ii, 25), and Alanson emphasizes English courage in defeat:

> Lean raw-bon'd rascals! who would e'er suppose
> They had such courage and audacity?
>
> (I, ii, 35–36)

The weakness of the French, on the other hand, is apparent in the arrival of Joan and her subsequent place at the head of their army, an advancement that took place historically in 1429. From the beginning the French are unable to deal with her, as the Dolphin, by childishly hiding, tries to disprove her claims of supernatural power. She recognizes him at once (I, ii, 66–67) and puts forth a challenge:

> My courage try by combat, if thou dar'st,
> And thou shalt find that I exceed my sex.
> Resolve on this: thou shalt be fortunate
> If thou receive me for thy warlike mate.
>
> (I, ii, 89–92)

Although later she disdains interest in "rites of love" (I, ii, 113), Joan's final three words above foreshadow the relationship she one day shares with the Dolphin. Defiantly Charles accepts her test, but she defeats him, and leaves him in awe: "Thou art an Amazon/ And fightest with the sword of Deborah" (I, ii, 104–105). In her control of the French forces, therefore, Joan is something unnatural: a woman denying her nature while taking a man's role. Her skills and daring are overwhelming, and her inspiration will propel the French to victory, as she predicts (I, ii, 136–139). But she represents a fearsome madness that is depicted as evil.

In the first two scenes Shakespeare has set up the two opposing countries as well as the internal wars within each. In scene iii these crises develop. On

Winchester's order Gloucester is denied entrance to the Tower of London (I, iii, 18–21), but when Winchester enters, the two rivals exchange threats and lay down the reasons each thinks he is entitled to power. Gloucester, the Lord Protector and for a long time advisor to the young Henry VI, is not reserved in recalling rumors of Winchester's unsavory past:

> Stand back, thou manifest conspirator,
> Thou that contrivedst to murther our dead lord,
> Thou that giv'st whores indulgences to sin.
> I'll canvass thee in thy broad cardinal's hat,
> If thou proceed in this thy insolence.

> (I, iii, 33–37)

Winchester, oddly, does not deny any of these accusations, but bullies back with the sources of his claim: "Gloucester, thou wilt answer this before the Pope" (I, iii, 52). The squabble becomes a skirmish until the Mayor of London intercedes, and Gloucester and Winchester are left tossing accusations back and forth. This conflict between secular and religious authority is complicated by the fact that Gloucester has support of the masses while Winchester has backing by Parliament. The scene ends with a comic reflection of the Mayor:

> Good God, these nobles should such stomachs bear!
> I myself fight not once in forty year.

> (I, iii, 90–91)

Our sympathy here is probably with Gloucester, for he speaks of his dedication to the throne, while Winchester has told us that he is using the power of the Church for his own purposes. As the Mayor complains, "This cardinal's more haughty than the devil" (I, iii, 85). What is clearly lacking, though, is a strong royal voice to put an end to all this quarreling. Contrast this vacuum of power with the bravery of Talbot, who reappears in I, iv, having been ransomed for a French lord. He describes his public humiliation by the French (I, iv, 39–56), but his treatment also communicates the wonder of the French at his strength. Salisbury swears revenge, but almost instantaneously is shot. Talbot's oration over the dead Salisbury (I, iv, 72–97) reflects a concern for his men rather than his own safety and glory. Such an attitude is in contrast with that of the English nobles later on. When word comes that Joan is attacking, Talbot calls out: "Frenchmen, I'll be a Salisbury to you" (I, iv, 106), a flattering reversal of the messenger's earlier description of the French shout (I, i, 128).

In the next scene Talbot bemoans the English inability to fight (I, v, 26–32), yet somehow manages to keep the battle going. His own courage resounds, but equally important is his reaction to Joan. Historically she has always been characterized as a saint, but through Talbot and others, Shakespeare portrays her differently:

> A witch by fear, not force, like Hannibal,
> Drives back our troops and conquers as she lists:
> So bees with smoke and doves with noisome stench

Are from their hives and houses driven away.

(I, v, 21–24)

Such dark qualities in their opposition partially excuse English failure.

The dramatic impact of the battle of Orleans, therefore, is curious. Because of Joan's nature and the reliance on her by the petty French, their victory is tainted. Despite England's loss, Talbot's courage and rhetoric gives the English a peculiar grandeur. In Act I, scene vi, Charles ruefully reflects:

'Tis Joan, not we, by whom the day is won;
For which I will divide my crown with her.

(I, vi, 17–18)

The French are triumphant, yet small. The English are defeated, yet heroic.

This contrast is developed in Act II, where the conquering French are smug, "Having all day carous'd and banqueted." (II, i, 12). When Talbot, Bedford, and Burgundy attack, the French are forced to vacate half-dressed, lacking any dignity as they scurry away. Afterwards they blame one another, Charles accusing Joan (II, i, 67–71), and Joan blaming the dozing watchmen (II, i, 72–77). Such behavior ennobles the English attitude, especially that over the burial of Salisbury. The corpse is treated with deepest respect, as Talbot comments on the "treacherous manner of his mournful death . . ." (II, ii, 16). The victorious French appear more like criminals than soldiers, and for the moment the English have fulfilled their desire to avenge Salisbury's death. Burgundy scornfully describes the Dolphin and Joan escaping:

When arm in arm they both came swiftly running,
Like to a pair of loving turtle-doves
That could not live asunder day or night.

(II, ii, 29–31)

The momentary triumph is undercut by an invitation for Talbot to the Countess Auvernge. Bedford is suspicious (II, ii, 54–56), but after whispering an order to his Captain, Talbot heads off. The succeeding encounter, which is completely fictional, reinforces the French admiration of Talbot's heroism. At first the Countess is unimpressed by his comparatively diminutive stature:

I thought I should have seen some Hercules,
A second Hector, for his grim aspect
And large proportion of his strong-knit limbs.
Alas, this is a child, a silly dwarf!
It cannot be this weak and writhled shrimp
Should strike such terror to his enemies.

(II, iii, 19–24)

But when she announces that Talbot is now her prisoner, he laughs her off (II, iii, 50–56), and with a single call of his horn is able to rouse the forces in support of him. Even the Countess admits her admiration:

Victorious Talbot, pardon my abuse.
I find thou art no less than fame hath bruited,
And more than may be gathered by thy shape.

(II, iii, 67–69)

Talbot's reply is equally gracious, and thus he establishes a standard of English heroism.

Why does Shakespeare interject such a scene? Perhaps because of the episode that follows, in which he dramatizes the prelude to the War of the Roses. The actual selection of roses is from Shakespeare's imagination, but the issues are historically critical.

Plantagenet and Somerset are the two primary antagonists, and they ask Suffolk and then Warwick to adjudicate, but both decline, claiming a lack of expertise (II, iv, 5–18). Before any arguments are delineated, insults are traded, and the various nobles select either a white rose to ally themselves with Plantagenet and the House of York, or a red rose to stand by with Somerset and the House of Lancaster. The violence of the language, and the various insinuations of cowardice and treachery, suggest the incipient violence underneath the debate.

One side argues on the basis of historical precedent. Warwick claims, and accurately, that Richard Plantagenet is descended from Lionel, third son of Edward III (II, iv, 82–85). What remains unspoken here is that Henry VI is descended from Henry IV, son of John of Gaunt, a Lancaster, and the fourth son of Edward III. Thus according to rules of primogeniture, Plantagenet has the right to the throne. But Somerset opposes this assertion, pointing out that Plantagenet's father, the Earl of Cambridge, was executed as a traitor. Therefore any other considerations must be put aside (II, iv, 88–95). Plantagenet responds bitterly that his father was "Condemn'd to die for treason, but no traitor" (II, iv, 97).

The legal points raised here will be reviewed and debated again, here and in other plays. More important than this specific issue, however, is our realization that such argument reflects the fundamental tension of the play: the battle for political power. Plantagenet clarifies just how intense this battle is, when he points to the white rose as his emblem:

And, by my soul, this pale and angry rose,
As cognizance of my blood-drinking hate,
Will I for ever and my faction wear,
Until it wither with me to my grave,
Or flourish to the height of my degree.

(II, iv, 107–111)

Warwick finally takes Plantagenet's side, but warns of the destruction to come and the price he and Plantagenet are willing to pay for the crown:

And here I prophesy: this brawl to-day,
Grown to this faction in the Temple Garden,
Shall send between the Red Rose and the White

A thousand souls to death and deadly night.

(II, iv, 124–127)

Historically the resulting battles during the next few decades did not lay waste to the country at large, but did decimate the royal families of England.

These speeches establish a dichotomy crucial in appreciating what Shakespeare dramatizes here and in the other history plays. Characters continue to clash over questions of legal right to the throne, and the extended recitation by Mortimer in the next scene emphasizes the importance of these claims. At the same time we are aware that if the law does not resolve in their favor, many on both sides are eager to ignore it and to try to grab the power they seek. Thus a delicate balance exists. We are always conscious of a universal order, a system based on faith in law. And virtually all the characters believe in that order. But we are also aware that those who do not receive what they consider to be just treatment from the law are often ready to overturn it.

In fact, in scene v Richard Plantagenet tells us as much. First the dying and imprisoned Edmund Mortimer summarizes the historical justification for Plantagenet assumption of the throne. The key issue is that Henry IV forcibly removed Richard II from the throne, thereby disrupting the royal order (II, v, 62–66). The influential Percy family, seeing Richard without children, therefore proposed Edmund Mortimer for the throne, given that Mortimer by his mother (actually grandmother) was descended from Lionel, Duke of Clarence, the third son of Edward III. But when Henry V assumed the throne, Mortimer was imprisoned.

(At the risk of muddying the facts, we should note that Shakespeare follows his historical sources by confusing two characters. The one imprisoned was actually John Mortimer, who supported his cousin Edmund's claim to the throne).

After naming his nephew Richard Plantagenet as his heir, Mortimer issues a final warning:

Strong fixed is the house of Lancaster,
And like a mountain, not to be remov'd.

(II, v, 102–103)

But when left alone after Mortimer's death, Plantagenet offers his own interpretation of the situation:

And for those wrongs, those bitter injuries,
Which Somerset hath offer'd to my house,
I doubt not but with honor to redress.
And therefore haste I to the parliament,
Either to be restored to my blood,
Or make my will th' advantage of my good.

(II, v, 124–129)

If he is not granted what he deems proper compensation and authority, he will revert to methods outside the law. He invokes the word "honor," so often in Shakespeare a poor excuse for an inexcusable act. And he will let his "will" take hold. We should have no doubt that what Plantagenet threatens is anarchy. The price for abandoning law is chaos, and for Shakespeare and his contemporaries the fear of such disorder was profound.

In Act III the struggle for power within England becomes openly ruthless, as even Gloucester, who for much of the play seems to be a man of dignity, sinks to a barrage of insults. The object of concern at the beginning of scene i is a bill Gloucester supports but which Winchester opposes, and the two engage in bitter confrontation. First Gloucester calls Winchester, "Thou bastard of my grandfather" (III, i, 42), to which Winchester retorts:

> Ay, lordly sir; for what are you, I pray,
> But one imperious in another's throne?

> (III, i, 43–44)

Meanwhile Plantagenet politically maintains a pose of neutrality (III, i, 61–64), but clarifies his hatred of Winchester.

What makes the overall exchange more dramatic is that while these insults go back and forth, the King himself is standing right there listening. Historically Henry was a child at the time, but for the purpose of drama Shakespeare has made him of an age where his inability to control the nobles is more visibly a sign of weakness. Henry does attempt to interject a note of sanity:

> O, what a scandal is it to our crown
> That two such noble peers as ye should jar!
> Believe me, lords, my tender years can tell,
> Civil dissension is a viperous worm
> That gnaws the bowels of the commonwealth.

> (III, i, 69–73)

The words reflect the spirit of Shakespeare and his age. But the King's incompetence is apparent, for he cannot stop the fighting. Meanwhile a battle has broken out between the followers of the two opposing sides, and the Mayor enters to beg for it to be quelled (III, i, 76–85). Briefly the fighting is brought onstage, then quieted at Gloucester's words (III, i, 103–105). The King thereafter confesses his pain: "O, how this discord doth afflict my soul!" (III, i, 106), and such a pathetic plea soothes tempers momentarily. But even as Gloucester and Winchester shake hands, they mutter asides that tell us that hostilities have hardly been abated (III, i, 136–141). The King, however, naively believes progress has been achieved:

> O loving uncle, kind Duke of Gloucester,
> How joyful am I made by this contract!
> Away, my masters, trouble us no more,
> But join in friendship, as your lords have done.

> (III, i, 142–145)

Such enthusiasm for obviously fraudulent promises, as well as Henry's behavior throughout this scene and those to come, raises a key question about the nature of kingship. Henry is a man of feeling, neither immoral nor unintelligent. He recognizes hostility between his advisors, and he is cognizant of the potential disaster that such rivalry might cause. Is he therefore a fit King? No, because he is unable to exert authority, to make decisions, and to dispel controversy. Thus which quality in a leader is preferable: strength or morality? Obviously a combination of both would be ideal, but here and elsewhere Shakespeare suggests that if the choice is one or the other, strength is more important. In subsequent plays power goes astray. At what point does authority warrant overthrow? Here we begin to see the consequences of weakness. Consequences of a different kind of abuse will be observed later.

The feebleness of Henry's position is further exemplified by his naming Richard Plantagenet the Duke of York, as compensation due the family from past events. Warwick, who all along schemes for Plantagenet's eventual ascension to the throne, is the instigator of this gesture:

> Let Richard be restored to his blood,
> So shall his father's wrongs be recompens'd.

(III, i, 159–160)

Henry himself is so desperate to be liked and to maintain harmony that he does not consider the implications of his action:

> If Richard will be true, not that alone
> But all the whole inheritance I give
> That doth belong unto the house of York,
> From whence you spring by lineal descent.

(III, i, 162–165)

Thus the irony of Plantagenet's expression of gratitude:

> Thy humble servant vows obedience
> And humble service till the point of death.

(III, i, 166–167)

Just whose death is not clear.

Gloucester, looking on, can do nothing about Henry's extravagant gift, but tries to cut losses by urging the King to go to France and take the crown of that country. Thus even if Henry does not choose to exert authority, it will nonetheless be clearly his. Henry's mild acquiescence is not encouraging (III, i, 183–184), especially to Exeter, who expresses a pervasive motif of these plays:

> Ay, we may march in England, or in France,
> Not seeing what is likely to ensue.
> This late dissension grown betwixt the peers
> Burns under feigned ashes of forg'd love,
> And will at last break out into a flame:
> As fest'red members rot but by degree,
> Till bones and flesh and sinews fall away.
> So will this base and envious discord breed.

And now I fear that fatal prophecy
Which in the time of Henry nam'd the Fift
Was in the mouth of every sucking babe,
That Henry born at Monmouth should win all,
And Henry born at Windsor lose all:
Which is so plain that Exeter doth wish
His days may finish ere that hapless time.

(III, i, 186–200)

The accuracy of Exeter's prediction is revealed soon enough, when Joan attacks Rouen. This battle has no basis in history, for Joan died in 1431, twenty-four years before Talbot did, and Rouen remained in English control until 1449, eighteen years after Joan's death. But theatricality is all-important here. First Talbot brands Joan "that damned sorceress" (III, ii, 38), emphasizing that the only way France can defeat England is by supernatural intervention.

Talbot challenges the French to resume the battle on the field (III, ii, 64–66), but the French decline, and even Pucelle is frightened of Talbot's visage (III, ii, 72–74). Talbot manages to reorganize his forces, and they reclaim Rouen. Subsequently Talbot shouts "Now will we take some order in the town" (III, ii, 126). To his mind such a goal is the only cause that warrants warfare. He also speaks eloquently over the body of Bedford, who was killed in the battle:

A braver soldier never couched lance,
A gentler heart did never sway in court;
But kings and mightiest potentates must die,
For that's the end of human misery.

(III, ii, 134–137)

Unlike other military leaders in the histories, Talbot never romanticizes death in war. He is always conscious of the cost of human life, an awareness that is lost on far too many leaders in these works. Indeed, throughout the history plays we feel swept along by a wave of brutality, deceit, and corruption. Nonetheless, certain individuals stand out because of their humanity in the face of such force. Talbot is the first.

His nobility is contrasted with the cowardice of Fastolfe, who runs away again (III, ii, 108), as well as the treachery of Burgundy, who in this scene joins Talbot, claiming "My vows are equal partners with thy vows" (III, ii, 85). His loyalty will not last.

In the next scene Pucelle suggests that the French should not worry about Talbot, that their own army need be regathered (II, iii, 1–8). She further advises persuading Burgundy to switch allegiances, and although historically she was dead when Burgundy committed this treason, Shakespeare has her help in the persuasion:

Behold the wounds, the most unnatural wounds,
Which thou thyself hast given her woeful breast.
O, turn the edged sword another way,

Strike those that hurt, and hurt not those that help.

(III, iii, 50–53)

Burgundy calls himself "bewitch'd" (III, iii, 58), and soon is hers. The implication is that Joan's demon sexuality can divert a Frenchman's allegiance. Yet
when Burgundy does relent (III, 78–84), even Joan is disgusted: "Done like a
Frenchman—turn and turn again" (III, iii, 85).

In contrast, in the next scene Talbot, soon to lose the war, nonetheless speaks
as a paragon of English manhood:

I have a while given truce unto my wars,
To do my duty to my sovereign;
In sign whereof, this arm, that hath reclaim'd
To your obedience fifty fortresses,
Twelve cities, and seven walled towns of strength,
Beside five hundred prisoners of esteem,
Lets fall his sword before your Highness' feet,
And with submissive loyalty of heart
Ascribes the glory of his conquest got
First to my God and next unto your Grace.

(III, iv, 3–12)

Even the young, incompetent Henry realizes the stature of the man before him,
and grants Talbot the title of Earl of Shrewsbury. Such tranquility is short-lived.
Immediately upon the King's departure, Vernon and Basset begin to quarrel,
carrying on the rivalry between York and Lancaster. The point is clear. The
King's appreciation of good men like Talbot is admirable, but his blindness to
political reality is nonetheless disastrous.

In Act IV, scene i, Henry's incompetence is dramatized more graphically,
with almost comic impact. As Henry is being crowned, Fastolfe enters with a
letter from Burgundy. Talbot can barely stomach either Fastolfe's presence or
mention of Burgundy the and insults the messenger at length (IV, i, 13–29).
Eventually the King picks up Talbot's theme by expelling the knight. Then the
letter itself becomes the object of interest, for in it Burgundy declares that he
has joined with "Charles, the rightful King of France" (IV, i, 60). Yet at the
end of the letter, Henry asks plaintively, "What? doth my uncle Burgundy
revolt?" (IV, i, 64). As if to a child Gloucester explains what has happened.
The King, however, can offer only the pettiest of retaliations:

Why then Lord Talbot there shall talk with him,
And give him chastisement for this abuse.

(IV, i, 68–69)

Henry lacks the resolve and energy to maintain the stature of the crown, and
his deficiency helps bring the kingship down with him.

Yet Henry is not completely blind to reality. When Vernon and Basset enter
continuing their argument from the previous scene, Somerset and Plantagenet,
now known as York, take sides, while Gloucester and Exeter try to soothe

tensions. Henry, meanwhile, can only offer caution that France will take advantage of quarreling among his nobles:

> If they perceive dissension in our looks,
> And that within ourselves we disagree,
> How will their grudging stomachs be provok'd
> To willful disobedience, and rebel!

(IV, i, 139–142)

He has correctly identified the problem. But instead of exerting his authority as King and putting an end to all discussion, he, out of fear and weakness, tries to soothe everyone's feelings by reconciliation (IV, i, 153–155). First he puts on the Red Rose to announce his alliance with both factions; then he timidly requests that Somerset and York, "go cheerfully together" (IV, i, 167) to support Talbot in his next sally against France. The futility of either strategy is emphasized by Exeter, once again the voice of warning:

> But howsoe'er, no simple man that sees
> This jarring discord of nobility,
> This shouldering of each other in the court,
> This factious bandying of their favorites,
> But that it doth presage some ill event.
> 'Tis much, when sceptres are in children's hands;
> But more, when envy breeds unkind division:
> There comes the ruin, there begins confusion.

(IV, i, 187–194)

The didactic quality makes the address theatrically awkward, but thematically it is vital.

The tragic consequences Exeter anticipates occur first in Act IV, scene ii, when at Bourdeaux Talbot orders the French to surrender (IV, ii, 1–14). But a French general challenges back, and in scene iii the antagonism between York and Somerset prevents them from carrying out the King's order to provide support. First York blames Somerset for failing to send horsemen (IV, iii, 9–16). Then Somerset blames York's planning (IV, iv, 1–5). Talbot is thus stranded, and in between the excuses and complaints William Lucy utters another warning:

> Thus while the vulture of sedition
> Feeds in the bosom of such great commanders,
> Sleeping neglection doth betray to loss
> The conquest of our scarce-cold conqueror,
> That ever-living man of memory,
> Henry the Fift. Whiles they each other cross,
> Lives, honors, lands, and all, hurry to loss.

(IV, iii, 47–53)

Later he adds:

> The fraud of England, not the force of France,
> Hath now entrapp'd the noble-minded Talbot:

> Never to England shall he bear his life,
> But dies, betray'd to fortune by your strife.

(IV, iv, 36–39)

The repetition of this message may be unwieldy, but what is tragically ironic is that while the rivalries portrayed onstage are the province of only a few power-hungry nobles, the consequences of their disputes extend throughout the nation. "Great" figures may carry out private machinations, but many others not so grand die in war, helpless victims of those plotters.

Among the first to do so are Talbot and his son in scenes that may be regarded as the climax of the play. Talbot has been the center of the action, the model of English heroism. Now he becomes the symbol of all victims of war.

The encounters between Talbot and his son have several implications. First, the overall tragedy is personalized in the destruction of one family. Initially the price is only dissension, as in scene v when Talbot orders his son to leave the battlefield (IV v, 8–10), but the boy defies orders, and stays to fight with his father. After their reconciliation, Talbot's parting words become an elegy over every son who risks his life in battle:

> In thee thy mother dies, our household's name,
> My death's revenge, thy youth, and England's fame:
> All these, and more, we hazard by thy stay;
> All these are sav'd if thou wilt fly away.

(IV, vi, 38–41)

Second, Talbot's moving soliloquy that begins scene vii is a powerful reminder that no matter how heroic the pageant of war may seem to the historical observer, the truth is the awful cost of human life. Throughout the history plays, Shakespeare glorifies certain military leaders, individual soldiers, and courage and brilliance in strategy. But he never glorifies the actuality of battle. To the contrary, even when at his most patriotic, the playwright presents the horror of combat, the murder of one man by another, in all its barbarity.

Talbot meets his son's death and his own fatal wounds with characteristic dignity:

> Come, come, and lay him in his father's arms,
> My spirit can no longer bear these harms.
> Soldiers, adieu! I have what I would have,
> Now my old arms are young John Talbot's grave.

(IV, vii, 29–32)

As Lucy enters to search for Talbot's body, the lengthy list of titles seems odd (IV, vii, 60–72), but even this recitation is scorned by Joan (IV, vii, 72–76), reflecting a graceless French disregard for English nobility. Moments later she mocks the corpses of the two Talbots:

> I think this upstart is old Talbot's ghost,
> He speaks with such a proud commanding spirit.

For God's sake let him have ['em]; to keep them here,
They would but stink, and putrefy the air.

(IV, vii, 87–90)

As always, the French and Joan are insulting and ungracious, in victory or defeat. Shakespeare's chauvinism is unflagging.

With the death of Talbot the play loses its only gallant figure, and in Act V we move to a new, in some ways more unpleasant, dramatic plane. In hope of unifying England and France and thereby avoiding further bloodshed, Gloucester has arranged a marriage with the daughter of the Earl of Arminack, a noble close to the King of France. Henry is shyly reluctant (V, i, 21–23), but agrees. Then he unwittingly sabotages the plan by seeking the advice of other counselors.

When Gloucester proffers the marriage plan, he speaks of it on the basis of peace terms, a goal we have come to associate with him:

To stop effusion of our Christian blood,
And stablish quietness on every side.

(V, i, 9–10)

When Winchester enters here, however, he wears his Cardinal's habit, and Exeter warns that such presumption fulfills a dangerous prophecy of Henry V:

"If once he come to be a cardinal,
He'll make his cap co-equal with the crown."

(V, i 32–33)

Left alone after the announcement of Henry's betrothal, Winchester offers private analysis that confirms the danger he poses:

Humphrey of Gloucester, thou shalt well perceive
That neither in birth, or for authority,
The Bishop will be overborne by thee.
I'll either make thee stoop and bend thy knee,
Or sack this country with a mutiny.

(V, i, 58–62)

Time and time again individuals whom we should recognize as dangerous make evident their malevolence by rationalizing chaos as an acceptable alternative to defeat by legal means.

With such a threat in the air, the action switches to France, where in scene ii the French learn that the English army is unified and attacking (V, ii, 11–13). In scene iii, however, the French army has refused to follow Joan. To rally her soldiers, Joan calls on "ye charming spells and periapts" (V, iii, 2), and fiends do appear, but they depart silently, leaving Joan helpless and frustrated:

See, they forsake me! Now the time is come
That France must vail her lofty-plumed crest

And let her head fall into England's lap.

(V, iii, 24–26)

She is stranded at the mercy of York, who orders her removed: "A goodly prize, fit for the devil's grace" (V, iii, 33). But as one woman is robbed of power, another enters immediately to assume it. The juxtaposition is effective. Just when Joan is taken away, Margaret moves in. And from the lines to follow we are aware that the sexuality of both is at the root of their power.

At the start of their exchange Suffolk reminds Margaret that she is his prisoner, but that relationship does not last. Margaret announces that she is the daughter of the King of Naples (Reignier, who appeared earlier); and Suffolk, though taken with her, shows his respect by offering her freedom (V, iii, 59). But so attracted is he that immediately he recalls her. Thereafter the pair speak both to themselves and to each other, and their sheer ruthlessness is almost funny. Margaret, feigning modesty, claims she has no dowry, while Suffolk, ever charming, considers ways to control her, and through her the King. As the two alternately chat, then mutter asides, we are both amused and put off by their lack of sensibility. For instance, Suffolk, anticipating more famous words of Richard III (*Richard III*, I, ii, 227–228), says of Margaret:

> She's beautiful; and therefore to be wooed:
> She is a woman; therefore to be won.

(V, iii, 78–79)

Meanwhile Margaret coolly ponders her position:

> Perhaps I shall be rescu'd by the French,
> And then I need not crave his courtesy.

(V, iii, 104–105)

But eventually Suffolk makes his purpose clear:

> I'll undertake to make thee Henry's queen,
> To put a golden sceptre in thy hand,
> And set a precious crown upon thy head,
> If thou wilt condescend to be my—

(V, iii, 117–120)

At this last suggestion Margaret retorts sharply: "What?" (V, iii, 120). But Suffolk gracefully sidesteps: "His love" (V, iii, 121). No doubt both understand and accept his implication. With but a little more persuasion Margaret is won over, and her father is soon equally pleased (V, iii, 151–156). After Suffolk is left alone to remind us of his own ambition (V, iii, 187–195), the thought of Henry VI going against two individuals as deviously aggressive as Margaret and Suffolk is not comforting.

Other serious implications about marriage are apparent during Joan's trial. She disavows any relationship with the shepherd who is her father:

> First let me tell you whom you have condemn'd:
> Not me begotten of a shepherd swain,

But issued from the progeny of kings;
Virtuous and holy, chosen from above,
By inspiration of celestial grace
To work exceeding miracles on earth.

(V, iv, 36–41)

When this claim is ignored, Joan attempts to defend herself by claiming that she is carrying a child (V, iv, 60–64). York insinuates that she and the Dolphin have been "juggling" (V, iv, 68), but Joan insists that the King of Naples is the father. That the man is already married further shocks the English, and provides further reason to condemn Joan (V, iv, 78–85). She leaves with a curse on the "glorious sun" (V, iv, 87), traditionally a symbol of the king, and no doubt the Elizabethan audience would have taken her words as an attack on the manhood of Henry himself.

Meanwhile disorder spreads. Winchester, seeking to consolidate his own position, announces a treaty with France. He ignores the objections of York, who fears the loss of territory recently won (V, iv, 102–112), but Warwick soothes him. Meanwhile the Cardinal continues to impose his order on the French King, insisting on subordination to Henry:

And, Charles, upon condition thou wilt swear
To pay him tribute and submit thyself,
Thou shalt be plac'd as viceroy under him,
And still enjoy thy regal dignity.

(V, iv, 129–132)

Alanson is outraged, as is Charles, while York tries to force the treaty. But a few quiet words from Reignier and Alanson reveal that the French will break any treaty at their own convenience (V, iv, 155–164). Lying and cheating run wild, as scarcely a single character onstage says a word that can be taken at face value.

The ultimate chicanery, however, is carried off by Suffolk. In the last scene of the play the King is immediately smitten with Margaret (V, v, 1–9), and not even Gloucester, who has already arranged a politically powerful marriage, can change his mind:

You know, my lord, your Highness is betroth'd
Unto another lady of esteem.
How shall we then dispense with that contract,
And not deface your honor with reproach?

(V, v, 26–29)

Suffolk dwells on what is in actuality the minor title of Margaret's father, as well as Henry's own stature: "Henry is able to enrich his queen . . ." (V, v, 51). Suffolk's other arguments to the King thematically reflect the play:

For what is wedlock forced, but a hell,
An age of discord and continual strife?
Whereas the contrary bringeth bliss,
And is a pattern of celestial peace.

(V, v, 62–65)

Suffolk seizes on the universal fear of disorder and builds his case about it. He also predicts the powerful children Henry and Margaret shall bear (V, v, 70–76), and we can imagine that so weak a king is taken with such visions. Therefore Henry agrees, although his language indicates that he does so only to stop his own misery (V, v, 81–86). Characteristically he ends by leaving to be alone and "ruminate my grief" (V, v, 101). Suffolk has thus managed not only to have Henry turn his back on the marriage arranged by Gloucester, and thereby out away Gloucester's influence; not only to have the King marry Margaret, who brings no wealth or stature to the throne, and who will provide Suffolk with as much power as anyone; but also, as is revealed in the first scene of Part 2, to have the King give away major territories won by Henry V.

For Suffolk, as for so many of the other nobles near the throne, the personal antagonisms and general disarray within the kingdom represent not danger but opportunity for advancement. And like the others Suffolk is willing to use Henry's weaknesses to further private ends. Gloucester sees what is happening, but is helpless to remedy the crisis: "Ay, grief, I fear me, both at first and last" (V, v, 102).

The play ends with an appropriate couplet from Suffolk:

Margaret shall now be Queen, and rule the King;
But I will rule both her, the King, and realm.

(V, v, 107–108)

This travesty of a marriage thus reflects the entire world of *Henry VI, Part 1*. The play dramatizes social disintegration mirrored in the breakdown of institutions. Winchester embodies the corruption of the Church, the struggle for secular power by religious elements. The defeat of Talbot, caused by the failures of York and Somerset, manifests the loss of chivalry at the hands of aristocratic self-interest that gnaws at the soul of the country. The triumphs of Joan, her supernatural origins and sexual dalliances with the French King and others, represent a general unnaturalness, in particular the distortion of womanhood. And the deaths of Talbot and his son as well as the marriage of Henry are personal tragedies that are the result of greater evil. The evisceration of the monarchy has left the country at war with itself.

SUGGESTIONS FOR FURTHER READING

Bevington, D. M. "The Domineering Female in *Henry VI.*" *Shakespeare Studies* 2 (1966): 51–58.
Billings, Wayne L. "Ironic Lapses: Plotting in *Henry VI.*" *Studies in the Literary Imagination* 5 (1972): 27–49.

Candido, Joseph. ''Getting Loose in the *Henry VI* Plays.'' *Shakespeare Quarterly* 35 4 (1984): 392–406.

Kay, Carol McGinnis Kay. ''Traps, Slaughter, and Chaos: A Study of Shakespeare's *Henry VI* Plays.'' *Studies in the Literary Imagination* 5 (1972): 1–26.

Ricks, Don M. *Shakespeare's Emergent Form: A Study of the Henry VI Plays*. Logan: Utah State Unversity Press, 1968.

Riggs, David. *Shakespeare's Heroical Histories:* Henry VI *and Its Literary Tradition*. Cambridge: Harvard University Press, 1971.

Henry VI, Part 2

This play dramatizes the War of the Roses and its consequences within English society. In *Henry VI, Part 1*, the conflict is seen primarily through its effects on foreign entanglements. Here in Part 2 Shakespeare turns the story inward, as dissension among the nobles spreads to society at large. Historically the battles never evolved into national civil war as the playwright intimates. Nonetheless, the results were widespread and painful.

Part 2 also has a different tone. Whereas Part 1 is episodic, moving from locale to locale and subplot to subplot, the emphasis here is more on character development, as certain figures sketched out in Part 1 are explored more fully. We are also given further insight into the nuances of political intrigue, the strategies and subterfuges used to gain power on an ever-shifting political plane.

Finally, much of the turmoil that arises is a direct result of the fatal marriage between Henry VI and Margaret of Anjou. Their union represents the corruption of ritual and law that symbolizes the corruption of legal institutions throughout the state. The marriage also reflects a vitiation of the royal family that infects the family of the state. Even the relationship itself, between a woman who proves so strong and a man so weak, becomes a symbol of unnaturalness.

All three elements are observed in Act I, scene i, set in 1445, when Margaret of Anjou arrives in England to marry Henry. Suffolk begins the discussion as if he had never stopped talking since the end of the previous play. His central point is that along with the marriage he has negotiated a treaty which he hands to Gloucester, whose reaction is both comic and moving. Not only does the treaty exclude any marriage dowry, but according to its terms Henry agrees to surrender key territories won in battle by his father. In one of Shakespeare's rare stage directions (I, i, 53), Gloucester simply lets the document drop. Winchester gleefully picks it up, thereby aligning himself with Suffolk.

The King, too, is delighted with the arrangement, and even rewards Suffolk with a title. But Gloucester's sorrow is eloquent commentary on Henry's blindness to the public trust he has ignored. First Gloucester seizes on the historical defilement:

> What? did my brother Henry spend his youth,
> His valor, coin, and people, in the wars?
> Did he so often lodge in open field,
> In winter's cold and summer's parching heat,
> To conquer France, his true inheritance?

(I, i, 78–82)

He also foresees national disgrace:

> O peers of England, shameful is this league,
> Fatal this marriage, cancelling your fame,
> Blotting your names from books of memory,
> Rasing the characters of your renown,
> Defacing monuments of conquer'd France,
> Undoing all, as all had never been!

(I, i, 98–103)

Here Gloucester clarifies his primary motivation: loyalty to the throne of England. Not necessarily to the King, but to the throne itself. Therefore if this play has a hero, it is Gloucester. Not that he has no desire for power; one reason he so resents Suffolk and Winchester is that Gloucester does not care to see anyone between himself and the King. But ultimately he places the good of the country before his own ambition. And given the ruthlessness of all the others involved, that attribute alone makes him outstanding.

Warwick, too, regrets the loss of hard-won territory (I, i, 116–123), but Gloucester's political isolation becomes apparent when he leaves. At first Winchester (now Cardinal Beauford), Buckingham, Somerset, York, Warwick, and Salisbury seem to unite, for, indeed, no one but Suffolk and the Cardinal supports the upcoming marriage. As Buckingham says:

> Cousin of Somerset, join you with me,
> And all together, with the Duke of Suffolk,
> We'll quickly hoise Duke Humphrey from his seat.

(I, i, 167–169)

Yet as soon as the Cardinal leaves, Buckingham and Somerset join the others in a conspiracy against both Gloucester and the Cardinal (I, i, 172–176). Then Buckingham and Somerset leave, and Salisbury, Warwick, and York form their own team, ostensibly in support of Gloucester (I, i, 183–189), but we recognize that their own priorities are foremost in their minds. This pattern of alliances, all in opposition and all shifting back and forth, dominates the play. No one trusts anyone. The supreme moral principle in this court is self-promotion, and no one exemplifies that attitude better than the Duke of York.

His soliloquy that ends scene i is emotionally and thematically at the core of the play. He takes personally the loss of territory demanded by the royal marriage:

> The peers agreed, and Henry was well pleas'd
> To change two dukedoms for a duke's fair daughter.

I cannot blame them all, what is't to them?
'Tis thine they give away, and not their own.

(I, i, 218–221)

He also has plans to take the throne for himself:

> Cold news for me; for I had hope of France,
> Even as I have of fertile England's soil.
> A day will come when York shall claim his own,
> And therefore I will take the Nevils' parts,
> And make a show of love to proud Duke Humphrey,
> And, when I spy advantage, claim the crown,
> For that's the golden mark I seek to hit.

(I, i, 237–243)

Like the others, York responds selfishly to the situation, but unlike the others, he believes he has a historical right to the throne. The sources of his convictions were estabished in Part 1, and they are restated here, but they remind us that the War of the Roses is not merely a struggle for power. It also involves the question of legitimacy: what family should properly rule England? The issue has political, social, and even theological implications, and is compounded by the intrusion of individual aspiration and family loyalty along with historical and moral judgment. Who should be King according to law? But who deserves to be King because he possesses the qualities that best embody kingship? The answers may not be the same. And who is willing to forego personal aggrandizement to support a more deserving claim to the throne? All these factors whirl around, demanding resolution.

The next two scenes introduce the women who make this battle for power still more complex. Because of their gender and rank, office is beyond them, but they gain power through manipulation of the men who do wield legal authority. First Gloucester's wife, Eleanor, states the extent of her drive:

> King Henry's diadem,
> Enchas'd with all the honors of the world?
> If so, gaze on, and grovel on thy face,
> Until thy head be circled with the same.
> Put forth thy hand, reach at the glorious gold.
> What, is't too short? I'll lengthen it with mine,
> And having both together heav'd it up,
> We'll both together lift our heads to heaven,
> And never more abase our sight so low
> As to vouchsafe one glance unto the ground.

(I, ii, 7–16)

Her ambition alone is daunting, but it is joined with an element of perversity when Eleanor turns to dreams in support of her goals. Gloucester reveals his own dream, in which he prevents others from gaining the throne, and even executes Suffolk and Somerset (I, ii, 25–31). But Eleanor has her own ambition. She has fantasized that Henry and Margaret knelt before her: "And on my head did set the diadem'' (I, ii, 40). Gloucester urges his wife to be satisfied with her social standing (I, ii, 41–50), but moments later we see her consorting with Hume, a priest of dubious sanctity, who fills her with pretentious images. Here ambition runs wild. Yet even this alliance is tainted, for upon Eleanor's exit Hume confesses that he has been hired by Suffolk and Cardinal Beauford to undermine her, and that she is but a tool in his own plot:

> Well, so it stands; and thus, I fear, at last
> Hume's knavery will be the Duchess' wrack,
> And her attainture will be Humphrey's fall.
> Sort how it will, I shall have gold for all.

> (I, ii, 104–107)

As we move from one scheme to another, one treachery to another, the play acquires a grotesque fascination. As yet no one has accomplished anything, but the tableau has a blackly comic sense, and offers an undignified but absorbing spectacle.

In the next scene we move to yet another conspiracy, involving one more individual close to power, and eager for more. In the last play Margaret was tactfully demure, but here in response to petitioners who mistake Suffolk for Gloucester, and who in fact are opposed to Suffolk (I, iii, 20–22), she does not hesitate to speak out:

> What, shall King Henry be a pupil still
> Under the surly Gloucester's governance?
> Am I a queen in title and in style
> And must be made a subject to a duke?

> (I, iii, 46–49)

That Margaret is a Frenchwoman, and thus to many an interloper who has gained the throne of England, makes this whining more outrageous. But Gloucester alone does not annoy her. She resents anyone who has power:

> Beside the haughty Protector, have we Beauford
> The imperious Churchman, Somerset, Buckingham,
> And grumbling York; and not the least of these
> But can do more in England than the King.

> (I, iii, 68–71)

She is angriest with the arrogant Duchess of Gloucester: ''Shall I not live to be aveng'd on her?'' (I, iii, 82). Historically Eleanor was dead four years before Margaret arrived in England. But how dramatically effective to see the two women in counterpoint, and how telling the contrast in their ages but the similarity of their attitudes. Eleanor has been near power all her life, but she remains unsatisfied. Margaret, though the daughter of a king, has only recently come close to the potential exercise of authority on her own, and she, too, is already frustrated. The two women remind us that no matter who is involved, no power is enough power. And Margaret's tantrums, in combination with Suffolk's attempts at pacification, are almost comic, especially at Act I, scene iii, lines 88–100.

When Suffolk and Margaret are joined by Gloucester and other rivals for the post of Regent over France, insults fly fast. Everyone is conscious of the struggle taking place. Everyone, that is, except the King, who announces:

> For my part, noble lords, I care not which,
> Or Somerset or York, all's one to me.
>
> (I, iii, 101–102)

Margaret tries to exert her voice through her husband, but Gloucester dismisses her: "These are no women's matters" (I, iii, 117). She responds with an answer that pierces right to the heart of Gloucester's cause:

> If he be old enough, what needs your Grace
> To be Protector of his Excellence?
>
> (I, iii, 118–119)

This line inspires a series of vebal parries against Gloucester, who manages to hold his own. Then the action degenerates into violence, as the Queen uses her fan to swat Eleanor on the ear. The King, meanwhile, stands by helplessly.

The impact of the scene is powerful. Except for that one instant of physicality, all remains vaguely civil. Yet we know how intense hostilities are. The encounter captures one of the key points of the politics as Shakespeare dramatizes it: the drive for power must be disguised. Successful politicians cannot be openly greedy; they must hide their desires under the cloak of concern for the good of the nation. In this play and throughout the first tetralogy, characters generally maintain the veneer of politeness, although their soliloquies and private conversations reveal their naked aggression. In the second tetralogy, however, these instincts are expressed in more subtle ideas and images, and the characters themselves are not always aware of all they feel. The drama therefore is more sophisticated.

The bizarre nature of the struggle here is apparent in two more moments from Act I. Gloucester is unaware of York's private ambitions, and, ever devoted to the throne, urges that York, ostensibly Gloucester's ally, be appointed Regent (I, iii, 160–161). But York is soon confronted by Suffolk's charge of treachery (I, iii, 181–185). The charges convince Gloucester, who, despite York's denials, switches allegiances and convinces the King to give the regency to Somerset. Here York does not respond, but his antagonism to Gloucester carries into the next scene when a witch joins with Hume, another priest, and a conjurer to counsel Eleanor. Spirits come and go to answer the Duchesses's prayers, but the spectacle is so grotesque as to turn the play temporarily into a horror show. The episode is cut off when Buckingham and York, clarifying their revenge for Gloucester's betrayal (I, iv, 45–46) arrest the Duchess and her cohorts as traitors.

The conspiracy against Gloucester himself remains relentless in Act II, scene i, as opposing forces gather around him physically as well as legally. The queen,

with a hawk on her fist, Beauford, and Suffolk threaten Gloucester, but what is
most entertaining is how antagonisms are muttered surreptitiously. Because the
King is present, Gloucester and Beauford say one thing out loud, then communicate the real meaning out of the sides of their mouths (II, i, 35–53). Eventually the King senses rising tensions:

> How irksome is this music to my heart!
> When such strings jar, what hope of harmony?
> I pray, my lords, let me compound this strife.
>
> (II, i, 54–56)

"Compound" here means "settle." But the King is not strong enough to take
action and is, as we might expect, reduced to weak, if fervent, prayer:

> Now God be prais'd, that to believing souls
> Gives light in darkness, comfort in despair!
>
> (II, i, 64–65)

Here is evidence of Henry's ultimate reliance on divine intervention. Other
characters echo this sentiment, that a benign deity will evetually restore justice.
Such was the medieval view. But also present here, and what Henry refuses to
acknowledge, is the human responsibility for solving political problems. The
King's burden is especially heavy since his actions influence everyone else's.
Yet Henry does nothing.

The conspiracy against Gloucester also raises another issue that reaches beyond
the immediate world of the history plays. Gloucester is trying to conduct himself
morally in a society where immorality is rampant. Can he remain virtuous and survive, or is Gloucester's only recourse to sink to the level of his opposition? The implications of this question are profound. Which course is preferable? Should
Gloucester remain on what we might call the high road? He does, and as a result
suffers the banishment and death of his wife. Then he, too, is killed. Does the play
suggest that he change his ethical outlook and become as corrupt as the opposition?
Which is more important: maintaining moral standards or gaining power? The issue is complicated more by the reality that Gloucester is not acting only for himself. The country must live with the outcome of his actions.

The extent of the King's naivete is apparent when he is fooled by the claims
of Simpson, who asserts that his blindness has been miraculously cured at a
nearby shrine (II, 1, 81). Gloucester's shrewdness exposes the mountebank (II,
i, 144–155), but the Protector's confidence is shattered when Buckingham brings
news that the Duchess has been imprisoned (II, 1, 163–173). In response Gloucester proclaims his innocence and disowns his wife (II, i, 193–195). For him
loyalty to the throne supersedes even devotion to his wife.

The power of the forces opposing Gloucester is stated at length in Act II,
scene ii, when York, Salisbury, and Warwick explore the historical basis for
York's claim to the throne. They retell the story of Richard II's placement on
the throne, Bullingbrook's usurpation, and Richard's assassination (II, ii, 19–

27), then detail the intricate questions of inheritance and primogeniture developed in Act II, scene v, of *Henry VI, Part 1*.

As he does in the previous play, York stakes his claim to the throne on the basis of his mother's marriage to Richard Earl of Cambridge, son of Edmund Langley, Edward III's fifth son. York's mother, Anne Mortimer, was descended from Clarence, Edward III's third son (II, i, 43–50). Furthermore, she was the sister of Edmund Mortimer, who was recognized as heir presumptive by the childless Richard II. York's salient point is that as the offspring of this union, he has precedence over Henry VI, who is descended from John of Gaunt, Edward III's fourth son:

> So, if the issue of the elder son
> Succeed before the younger, I am king.
>
> (II, ii, 51–52)

Here he clarifies his right of inheritance by the older son, the tradition known as "primogeniture," which was central to the English social and political structure of the time.

Indeed, this scene reveals some of the complications caused by the law. When Edward III died in 1377, his son Eward the Black Prince was already dead. But the kingship did not then pass to the oldest surviving son of Edward III, John of Gaunt. Instead by law it was given to the oldest son of the Prince, the child who became Richard II. Years later Gaunt's son Bullingbrook expelled Richard, and seized the crown for himself as Henry IV. It has since passed through the heroic Henry V, and now is worn by Henry VI.

But the question of legitimacy remains. And York has his followers. Yet what he does not mention is that inheritance through a woman, here York's mother, is always open to question. In addition, Richard Earl of Cambridge was executed as a traitor, a controversy explored in Part 1 (II, iv). Nonetheless, York's claim wins Warwick's support (II, ii, 51–52), as it does in the earlier play. Whatever the unresolvable complications of inheritance, the matter is reduced to simple politics by York, who has no scruples:

> Do you as I do in these dangerous days:
> Wink at the Duke of Suffolk's insolence,
> At Beauford's pride, at Somerset's ambition,
> At Buckingham, and all the crew of them,
> Till they have shar'd the Shepherd of the flock,
> That virtuous prince, the good Duke Humphrey.
>
> (II, ii, 69–74)

No doubt such compliments are offered with an ironic grin:

> 'Tis that they seek, and they in seeking that
> Shall find their deaths, if York can prophesy.
>
> (II,ii,75-76)

He is also content to let Gloucester die to further York's own path to the kingship.

York's crassness brings to the fore a dilemma any public servant must face.

To what extent should conscience be pushed aside in the name of a cause? Are immoral means ever justified by moral ends? Gloucester offers a form of an answer in the next scene when his wife is banished: ''I cannot justify whom the law condemns'' (II, iii, 16). He knows his wife has conspired with witches and conjurers. Yet he also knows that the entire procedure is a farce to disgrace him and wrest away his influence with the King. Still, Gloucester is not willing to subvert the law. Henry vows to be his own Protector, and the Queen, knowing how she can control her husband, also urges Gloucester's resignation (II, iii, 22–31). Rather than disobey Henry, Gloucester agrees (II, iii, 32–38).

The legal fraud taking place in Act II, scene iii is mocked by the intrusion of the commoners, whose own quarrel suggests the disorder permeating the kingdom. Henry tries to make the intrusion seem like a lesson:

> And God in justice hath reveal'd to us
> The truth and innocence of this poor fellow,
> Which he had thought to have murther'd wrongfully.
>
> (II, iii, 102–104)

We feel his attempt to make order out of chaos.

Nonetheless, the trial of Gloucester's wife is carried out, and she is paraded barefoot through the street. Even now Gloucester's perspective does not change. As his wife walks, she harangues him for his inaction, but Gloucester is adamant:

> And had I twenty times so many foes,
> And each of them had twenty times their power,
> All these could not procure me any scathe
> So long as I am loyal, true, and crimeless.
> Wouldst have me rescue thee from this reproach?
> Why, yet thy scandal were not wip'd away,
> But I in danger for the breach of law.
>
> (II, iv, 60–66)

His faith in ultimate justice is greater than his belief that the actions of any individual will hold sway. On the one hand Gloucester is, in the context of this play, naive. Yet his trust in a greater justice is to a degree ennobling and, as will be seen, to a degree accurate.

Few other characters are beset by Gloucester's doubts. Indeed, most are guided by a single principle: obtain power at any cost. For instance, in the opening scene of Act III at Parliament, Margaret accuses Henry of foolishly listening to Gloucester, who, she claims, is looking out for himself:

> Me seemeth then it is no policy,
> Respecting what a rancorous mind he bears
> And his advantage following your decease,
> That he should come about your royal person,

Or be admitted to your Highness' Council.

(III, i, 23–27)

She also makes clear her belief that power is not to be had only in the halls of
the palace:

> By flattery hath he won the commons' hearts;
> And when he please to make commotion,
> 'Tis to be fear'd they all will follow him.

(III, i, 28–30)

She establishes a theme that develops in this play and throughout the Shakespearean canon: fear of and distaste for the masses. The nobles who here dicker
for control do so under the unspoken assumption that to gain power in the upper
echelons of society guarantees authority over the populace at large. They also
believe that if order breaks down at the top, disorder will spread through society,
creating an anarchy that will leave everyone of every rank vulnerable. But the
reverse is also considered: that the man who has the loyalty of the masses is
well on the way to gaining power at the top. And if disorder starts in the lower
ranks, that chaos can move upward. Such a pattern unfolds in the next act of
this play.

After York and Suffolk both rail against Gloucester in Act III, scene i, they
learn that all of Henry's territories in France have been lost. The King's reaction
is, typically, one of helplessness: "Cold news, Lord Somerset; but God's will
be done!" (III, i, 86). York's aside is equally telling and echoes his words at
(I, i, 237–238):

> Cold news for me; for I had hope of France
> As firmly as I hope for fertile England.
> Thus are my blossoms blasted in the bud,
> And caterpillars eat my leaves away;
> But I will remedy this gear ere long,
> Or sell my title for a glorious grave.

(III, i, 87–92)

Had we any uncertainty about York's priorities, they are at this moment clarified.
Unlike Gloucester in this play or Talbot in the last, York places private reward
ahead of the public good. And no delineation of genealogy can justify his
fundamental selfishness.

During Gloucester's trial, the defendant plays his role too loyally. He is
attacked outrageously as having taken bribes (III, i, 104–106), tortured prisoners
(III, i, 122–123), and committed all manner of immoral and treasonous acts.
Even the King recognizes the fundamental injustice of the scene: "My conscience
tells me you are innocent" (III, i, 141), but takes no steps to exert his prerogatives. Yet Gloucester never loses dignity or faith:

> Virtue is chok'd with foul ambition,
> And charity chas'd hence by rancor's hand;

Foul subornation is predominant,
And equity exil'd your Highness' land.

(III, i, 143–146)

Then he goes down the roster of his accusers.

The effect, though, is curious. On the one hand Gloucester's nobility is admirable, as is his fidelity to his country. But we are frustrated at his impotence. He will not retaliate by bringing in support of his own, by letting his accusers know that he can unleash massive popular support. And Gloucester's steadfastness to principle is undercut by the King's feebleness. After Gloucester is taken away, the King mourns:

His fortunes I will weep, and 'twixt each groan
Say, "Who's a traitor, Gloucester he is none."

(III, i, 221–222)

The King will take action only when the commoners arise, but by then the cause will be lost.

We should note that Shakespeare always dramatizes the King's weakness as just that: weakness. Never does the playwright paint the picture of mental collapse that historically became the case in 1453, when Henry went mad, a condition possibly inherited from his French grandfather Charles VI. We can understand such an omission. After all, a long line of English rulers, including those of Shakespeare's day, were descended from Henry VI, and to have their forefather portrayed as possessed by a mental condition that could be passed on would not do. Moreover, for dramatic purposes the portrait of madness would be ill-advised. How much more effective to see telling political blunders rather than a lunacy that could be interpreted as a political anomaly.

When Gloucester leaves the stage in Act III, scene i, and the King expresses the desire that Gloucester will be exonerated, York, Suffolk, Beauford, and the Queen remain to weigh strategy. All agree on the need for Gloucester's death (III, i, 257, 273, 278–80), and when the report is brought in that revolt is brewing in Ireland, York is pleased to be given authority to suppress it (III, i, 309–314). Historically York was at this time not so deeply involved in the political ring, but Shakespeare takes the intriguing step of leaving York alone to reveal his ulterior motives. Speaking as if to the nobles now offstage, York summons up a brutal picture:

'Twas men I lack'd, and you will give them me;
I take it kindly. Yet be well assur'd
You put sharp weapons in a madman's hands.
Whiles I in Ireland nourish a mighty band,
I will stir up in England some black storm
Shall blow ten thousand souls to heaven or hell;
And this fell tempest shall not cease to rage
Until the golden circuit on my head,
Like to the glorious sun's transparent beams,

Do calm the fury of this mad-bred flaw.

(III, i, 345–354)

Jack Cade (III, i, 356–375) will become the instrument of York's ruthlessness.

An interesting moment occurs in the next scene, when two murderers tell Suffolk of Gloucester's death, which historically took place in 1447. Tudor history blamed Suffolk for this act, and the playwright does not deviate from the accepted interpretation. This occasion is also the first where Shakespeare dramatizes the degradation of a leading character by having him conspire with murderers. The next time is when Richard III carries out one of his plots. And Macbeth's fall is maifested in his instructions to the murderers assigned to kill Banquo and Fleance.

The King and Queen meet the news of Gloucester's death in unsurprising fashion. Henry simply faints, then awakens to accuse Suffolk ineffectively (III, ii, 39–55). The King must then endure a long and hypocritical speech by the Queen, who is outraged that Suffolk should be so branded. More important is the news Warwick brings: that the commoners have learned of the death of their hero Gloucester, and are beginning to rise in "spleenful mutiny" (III, ii, 128). Henry's initial response is familiar:

O Thou that judgest all things, stay my thoughts,
My thoughts that labor to persuade my soul
Some violent hands were laid on Humphrey's life!

(III, ii, 136–138)

He can rely only on God.

Warwick, though, appears with Gloucester's body, and explains that the victim was murdered, providing graphic details of substantiation:

But see, his face is black and full of blood,
His eyeballs further out than when he lived,
Staring full ghastly, like a strangled man;
His hair uprear'd, his nostrils stretch'd with struggling;
His hands abroad display'd, as one that grasp'd
And tugg'd for life, and was by strength subdu'd.
Look, on the sheets his hair, you see, is sticking,
His well-proportion'd beard made rough and rugged.
Like to the summer's corn by tempest lodged.
It cannot be but he was murd'red here,
The least of all these signs were probable.

(III, ii, 168–178)

The detail of this forensic description reminds us of the power latent in Shakespeare's poetry. So strong is the passage that Henry himself is moved to his boldest statement of the play. After Suffolk denies Warwick's accusations (III, ii, 179–181), and Salisbury brings word that rioters outside demand Suffolk's execution (III, ii, 243–247), Suffolk reacts with characteristic contempt, but

Henry agrees with the mob, and condemns Suffolk to banishment (III, ii, 287–288). When Margaret protests, Henry intensifies his threat:

> If after three days' space thou here be'st found
> On any ground that I am ruler of,
> The world shall not be ransom for thy life.
>
> (III, ii, 295–297)

Never again is Henry as commanding as at this moment.

One other speech of the King's deserves comment. After he hears Suffolk's initial defense, Henry reflects on the nature of courage and truth:

> What stronger breastplate than a heart untainted!
> Thrice is he arm'd that hath his quarrel just;
> And he but naked, though lock'd up in steel,
> Whose conscience with injustice is corrupted.
>
> (III, ii, 232–235)

The speaker of these words is a man who believes in justice, who has faith in the fundamental order of the world. He is convinced that in the end right will triumph. Henry himself is not strong enough to fight for his ideals, but that he has such faith makes him more than just a weakling. Rather, he turns into an idealist in an all-too-harsh and realistic world.

After sentence is pronounced and Suffolk and Margaret are left alone, their moments together are among the more puzzling of this play. Initially Suffolk simply curses the masses that have caused his plight, but Margaret turns political rage into a frustrated love:

> O, let me entreat thee cease. Give me thy hand,
> That I may dew it with my mournful tears;
> Nor let the rain of heaven wet this place
> To wash away my woeful monuments.
>
> (III, ii, 339–342)

Never has she been so amorous, and she goes on at length in this vein. Suffolk's response is equally unusual for him:

> 'Tis not the land I care for, wert thou thence;
> A wilderness is populous enough,
> So Suffolk had thy heavenly company:
> For where thou art, there is the world itself,
> With every several pleasure in the world;
> And where thou art not, desolation.
> I can no more: live thou to joy thy life;
> Myself no joy in nought but that thou liv'st.
>
> (III, ii, 359–366)

Such passion is surprising. Yet it continues, as they part with moving expressions of affection (III, ii, 402–412). Earlier the two expressed tentative feelings for each other, but we were always conscious that each was at the same time plotting politically, and emotion seemed subordinate to ambition. Here, though, their love seems genuine. Perhaps Shakespeare was trying to give this relationship more profundity, but the attempt is too abrupt and therefore forced. In the second tetralogy characters are more fully drawn, and such roundness is more convincing.

During his wife"s trial Gloucester emphasized faith that the law would eventually right itself. The expulsion of Suffolk is one piece of evidence that Gloucester was right. Another is the sudden illness and death of Beauford, who by the next scene is mysteriously struck down. He dies unrepentant, and Warwick sums up the Cardinal's life succinctly: ''So bad a death argues a monstrous life'' (III, iii, 30). Not long after, historically in 1450, Suffolk is murdered at sea. He dies with a return to the truculence that has marked his life. First he dismisses his need for concealment: ''Jove sometime went disguis'd, and why not I?'' (IV, i, 48). Then he scorns the Lieutenant preparing to kill him:

> How often hast thou waited at my cup,
> Fed from my trencher, kneel'd down at the board,
> When I have feasted with Queen Margaret?
> Remember it, and let it make thee crestfall'n . . .
>
> (IV, i, 56–59)

In death he even salvages a measure of dignity:

>   No, rather let my head
> Stoop to the block than these knees bow to any
> Save to the God of heaven and to my king;
> And sooner dance upon a bloody pole
> Than stand uncover'd to the vulgar groom.
> True nobility is exempt from fear:
> More can I bear than you dare execute.
>
> (IV, i, 124–130)

Whether such devotion to God and country is genuine is a matter for conjecture.

Also important in the same scene is the Lieutenant who decides Suffolk's fate. This nameless man, in condemning Suffolk, manifests a loyalty to England that is vital in reassuring the audience that such fidelity does indeed exist:

> By devilish policy art thou grown great,
> And like ambitious Sylla, overgorg'd
> With gobbets of thy [mother's] bleeding heart.
>
> (IV, i, 83–85)

And he continues with a litany of Suffolk's crimes and their consequences. The Lieutenant is also an example of a curious schism in Shakespeare's attitude about the common people. Throughout his plays individual commoners become hallmarks of decency in an indecent world. Simple though they may be, they are capable of exalted human qualities. The Gardener in *Richard II* and Feeble in *Henry IV, Part 2* are two examples. Yet Shakespeare often emphasizes the stupidity and destruction that the masses can cause when they band together in disorder. We think of the mobs in *Julius Caesar* and *Coriolanus*. The most powerful and frightening mob of all shows up in this play, led by Jack Cade, a mysterious figure from Kent, who with his cohorts appeared in London in 1450 and led riots supposedly intended at political reform.

From virtually his first words, Cade is a figure of mockery. At Act IV, scene ii, line 39, he starts to recite his family history, and the references to Mortimer and Plantagenet put the claims by York and his family in unflattering light. Yet Cade, Dick, and the Yorkist hordes also deride the concept of lineage, and that attitude is unacceptable. Here is another dichotomy Shakespeare presents. On the one hand, we know that the Yorks and Lancasters, to justify all sorts of scurrilous actions, turn to lists of distinguished family members. Yet these details of ancestry are crucial to a vision of order. They are not to be dismissed rudely. Cade does so, and when he shouts "All the realm shall be in common" (IV, ii, 68), he is inviting the breakdown of the social structure. So does Dick when he urges the oft-quoted "The first thing we do, let's kill all the lawyers" (IV, ii, 76). During this play a variety of despicable acts are committed in the name of legal propriety, and more follow in others plays. But Shakespeare implies that no matter how unjust these actions are, they are at least based on a semblance of law and can be dealt with by civilized means. Cade and his followers act beyond such bounds, and the mindless savagery they unleash almost makes us long for the machinations of Suffolk and York.

First Cade's cohorts kill the clerk, ostensibly because he can read and write (IV, iii, 105–110). His death reminds us of the fate of Cinna the Poet in *Julius Caesar*, who is torn for his "bad verses" (III, iii, 30). Sir Humphrey Stafford and his brother are then brought in, and while Cade weighs their fate, he reveals his political acuity and ambition:

> Go to, sirrah, tell the King from me, that, for his
> father's sake, Henry the Fifth (in whose time boys went
> to span-counter for French crowns), I am content he
> shall reign, but I'll be Protector over him.

(IV, ii, 156–159)

This speech is one of many indications that despite his cries for the common good, Cade is, at his core, devoted only to himself. After he gives the command for the execution of the Staffords, he reminds the audience both onstage and off where his values lie:

> But then are we in order when we are most
> out of order.

(IV, ii, 189–190)

No words could be more distressing to the Elizabethans.

In scenes iii and iv, civil madness spreads, but the King stumbles ineffectually:

> I'll send some holy bishop to entreat;
> For God forbid so many simple souls

> Should perish by the sword! And I myself,
> Rather than bloody war shall cut them short,
> Will parley with Jack Cade their general.
> But stay, I'll read it over once again.
>
> (IV, iv, 9–14)

From what we have observed, we are sure that Cade has no interest in conferences. The Queen, however, is still preoccupied with Suffolk (IV, iv, 15–18). All the while Cade draws nearer, and a messenger reports that he has changed tactics:

> Jack Cade proclaims himself Lord Mortimer,
> Descended from the Duke of Clarence' house,
> And calls your Grace usurper, openly . . .
>
> (IV, iv, 28–30)

Whatever Cade's propaganda, he, too, is infected by the same desire for power that afflicts almost everyone in this world. Henry and Margaret must flee, and the King's trust in God (IV, iv, 55) is paralled by that of Lord Say, who prepares to defend the city against all odds:

> The trust I have is in mine innocence,
> And therefore am I bold and resolute.
>
> (IV, iv, 59–60)

Such faith is admirable, yet useless in the face of what is coming.

The dramatic structure of these scenes reflects the chaos of the action. They are short and choppy, as characters dash onstage and off, and brutality runs amuck. The sense in the theater ought to be the dramatic equivalent of the chaos of Picasso's 1937 masterpiece *Guernica*, that vast canvas of contorted bodies and screaming faces that depicts the horrors of war. Meanwhile the mind behind the butchery still flourishes, as Cade orders the death of a soldier who simply calls him by his own name (IV, vi, 8). Thereafter Cade proclaims his jurisdiction:

> And now henceforward it shall be treason for any that
> calls me other than Lord Mortimer.
>
> (IV, vi, 5–6)

> I have thought upon it, it shall be so. Away,
> burn all the records of the realm, my mouth shall be
> the parliament of England.
>
> (IV, vii, 13–15)

> And henceforward all things shall be in common.
>
> (IV, vii, 18–19)

In certain lines Cade sounds like the voice of anarchy, intent on putting humanity on one equal level. Other lines, though, suggest his own desire for authority. Yet his character is even more complicated. Cade lambasts the power exerted by Lord Say, accusing him of punishing men who were simply too poor to obtain justice (IV, vii, 37–47). But after the faithful Lord Say begs for his life, patiently answering each of Cade's insults, Cade murmurs an aside that hints at a grain of humanity:

> I feel remorse in myself with his
> words; but I'll bridle it. He shall die, and it be but for pleading so well
>   for his life.
>
> (IV, vii, 105–107)

The intelligence with which Lord Say speaks moves Cade, who thus shows himself more than a monster. At the same time such intelligence frightens him, for he does not want intellect nearby. The reason why is clear a few lines later:

> The proudest peer in
> the realm shall not wear a head on his shoulders,
> unless he pay me tribute.
>
> (IV, vii, 119–121)

Here is Cade's heart. His claims for universal freedom mask the familiar drive for power seen in so many more "civilized" figures. Cade's actions may be less sophisticated than those of the royalty, but the underlying motive is the same for all.

For all his primitive energy, Cade is hardly a fool. After Buckingham expresses Henry's willingness to pardon the rebels (IV, viii, 7–10), and the rebels cheer the King, Cade berates his unreliable followers:

> But you are all recreants and dastards,
> and delight to live in slavery to the nobility.
>
> (IV, viii, 27–28)

Momentarily the mob transfers allegiance back to Cade, but Clifford manages to rouse again support for the King (IV, viii, 34–52), and Cade recognizes the fickleness which Shakespeare often ascribes to the masses:

> Was ever feather so lightly blown
> to and fro as this multitude?
>
> (IV, viii, 55–56)

He may even earn a touch of our sympathy as he is forced to abandon his grand schemes:

> And
> heavens and honor be witness that no want of resolu-
> tion in me, but only my followers' base and ignomini-
> ous treasons, makes me betake me to my heels.
>
> (IV, viii, 61–64)

Cade has wit, charm, and limitless ambition. In all these qualities he is like many of the nobles who battle for the throne and the authority attached. The only major differences between Cade and the others are his unmasked aggression and the position the royals were granted at birth. With such breeding the nobles bring a touch of decorum to their war. Otherwise Cade's presence confirms that the struggle to rule is universal.

In scene ix the King expresses for the first time his wish to be other than a monarch:

> Was never subject long'd to be a king
> As I do long and wish to be a subject.
>
> (IV, ix, 5–6)

The sentiment is one he will repeat with greater desperation. But for the moment he manages to carry on. When he learns that York intends to rid the court of Somerset (IV, ix, 29–30), the King attempts to defuse the attack by having Buckingham report that Somerset is in the Tower (IV, ix, 36–40). Somerset's willingness to imprison himself for the cause (IV, ix, 41–43) is evidence of the loyalty to the throne that flourishes despite Henry's weakness.

The manner of Cade's death is appropriate; he is killed by Iden, a man whose life is the antithesis of the unbridled ambition that characterizes so many in the play:

> Lord, who would live turmoiled in the court
> And may enjoy such quiet walks as these?
> This small inheritance my father left me
> Contenteth me, and worth a monarchy.
> I seek not to wax great by others' [waning],
> Or gather wealth, I care not with what envy.
>
> (IV, x, 16–21)

Here is another simple man who stands in contrast to the greedy aristocracy. When he turns to fight Cade, he does so not to gain territory, but to defend his own home from an invader. Cade dies with appropriate swagger:

> Iden, farewell, and be proud of thy victory.
> Tell Kent from me, she hath lost her best man, and
> exhort all the world to be cowards, for I, that never
> fear'd any, am vanquish'd by famine, not by valor.
>
> (IV, x, 72–75)

Despite all his excesses, Cade is a character we are sorry to lose. In a play where so many operate in shadow, his overt lust is refreshing.

In Act V the War of the Roses at last comes to center stage. Speaking of Henry, York begins the act by proclaiming one of his fundamental principles of political theory: "Let them obey that knows not how to rule . . . " (V, i, 6). His capacity to rule is self-justifying, as he indulges in a version of "might makes right." If he can take the crown, that conquest will prove his legitimacy. Such an attitude is dangerous indeed, and across human history has been the beacon to inspire one totalitarian figure after the next. No law can withstand such an absolute view of power.

York searches out Somerset, a son of John of Gaunt, and thus York's only remaining rival for the throne, but Buckingham tells him that his quarry is already taken. Their exchange is amusingly ironic. First York asks, "Upon thine honor, is he prisoner?'' (V, i, 42). And Buckingham answers, ''Upon mine honor, he is prisoner'' (V, i, 43). Two chronic liars invoke ''honor'' at this key moment. So often in Shakespeare those who use the word do so when they are least ''honorable.'' Before York gets his comeuppance, though, we note the King's reaction to seeing the head of Cade: ''Great God, how just art thou!'' (V, i, 68). His faith is relentless. Yet Cade is dead. Perhaps Henry's trust in a benign order is not entirely out of place.

York once more publicly proclaims loyalty to the King, and even decries the actions of Cade, his own man (V, i, 58–59, 61–63). Thus when Somerset enters, we are gratified that York is forced to confess his plots. Especially satisfying is his outrage at being deceived. Here is someone who has lied and cheated his way through the play, albeit with some historical justification. In any case he has been entirely selfish. Now he finds himself the victim, and his sense of effrontery is outlandish:

> False king, why hast thou broken faith with me,
> Knowing how hardly I can brook abuse?
> King did I call thee? No; thou art not king;
> Not fit to govern and rule multitudes,
> Which dar'st not, no, nor canst not rule a traitor.
> That head of thine doth not become a crown:
> Thy hand is made to grasp a palmer's staff
> And not to grace an awful princely sceptre.

> (V, i, 91–98)

Despite York's general unattractiveness, his charges against Henry have grounds, and they reaffirm a central issue of all the history plays. Henry is an inadequate king, whose blunders have damaged his country. Does he deserve to remain on the throne? At what point does his incompetence demand that he be removed? Shakespeare gives no answer. But the qualities he invests in those who oppose Henry VI, and in characters who appear later in this tetralogy and the next, suggest that Shakespeare was firmly on the side of authority.

The accusations against York bring to the stage his two sons, Edward and Richard. Their entrance is followed by that of Young Clifford, son of Hotspur's daughter Elizabeth. Thus the rivalry between the Percies and the Nevilles continues, and economically Shakespeare moves the War of the Roses to the next generation. Richard, one day to become king himself, was historically at this point only two or three years old, but for the sake of drama he is presented as a young warrior. We can also hear in his early words the unique tones of the character who becomes Shakespeare's first larger-than-life figure:

> Oft have I seen a hot o'erweening cur
> Run back and bite, because he was withheld,
> Who, being suffer'd, with the bear's fell paw
> Hath clapp'd his tail between his legs and cried;
> And such a piece of service will you do,

if you oppose yourselves to match Lord Warwick.

> (V, i, 151–156)

The vivid imagery, the subtle threat, the veiled wit, the boldness: the core of the enthralling character to come is already here. So are the insults about his appearance, offered by Clifford, as he turns back Richard's challenge:

> Hence, heap of wrath, foul indigested lump,
> As crooked in thy manners as thy shape.

> (V, i, 157–158)

Richard absorbs many similar taunts before he has opportunity for revenge.
   That does not occur for some time. Here York offers a farewell threat to Clifford:

> I am thy king, and thou a false-heart traitor.
> Call hither to the stake my two brave bears,
> That with the very shaking of their chains
> They may astonish these fell-lurking curs.

> (V, i, 143–146)

Such hatred guarantees a long and bloody war, as does Henry's inability to stand between these opposing forces:

> O, where is faith? O, where is loyalty?
> If it be banish'd from the frosty head,
> Where shall it find a harbor in the earth?
> Wilt thou go dig a grave to find out war,
> And shame thine honorable age with blood?

> (V, i, 166–170)

The answer to the King's question is the battle of St. Albans, fought in 1455, and accepted historically as the opening of the War of the Roses. But before the actual fighting we are shown how deep feelings lie, when Salisbury and Warwick, the Nevilles, announce their allegiance to the Yorks. Salisbury's explanation suggests that he is not inspired by mere greed but by a sense of historical right:

> My lord, I have considered with myself
> The title of this most renowned duke,
> And in my conscience do repute his Grace
> The rightful heir to England's royal seat.

> (V, i, 175–178)

He thereby breaks his oath of loyalty to the King. Henry challenges the betrayal of heaven's ordained ruler (V, i, 181), a line the Elizabethan audience would no doubt have viewed ironically, as Henry is himself the grandson of a usurper. But Salisbury is firm:

> It is great sin to swear unto a sin,
> But greater sin to keep a sinful oath.
>
> (V, i, 182–183)

In such times no bond is sacred.

As the battle begins, Clifford is killed by York (V, ii, 27), and Young Clifford swears revenge with an energy that marks the best of Shakespeare's early histories:

> York not our old men spares;
> No more will I their babes. Tears virginal
> Shall be to me even as the dew to fire,
> And beauty, that the tyrant oft reclaims,
> Shall to my flaming wrath be oil and flax.
> Henceforth I will not have to do with pity.
> Meet I an infant of the house of York,
> Into as many gobbets will I cut it
> As wild Medea young Absyrtus did;
> In cruelty will I seek out my fame.
>
> (V, ii, 51–60)

The vigor of Young Clifford's prose, as well as his passion, is matched only by those of Richard Plantagenet, who lines later dispatches Somerset: "Priests pray for enemies, but princes kill" (V, ii, 71).

His statement reflects the confusion of Henry, who in the chaos of war remains his unfortuate lost self: "Can we outrun the heavens? Good Margaret, stay" (V, ii, 73). This inaction is contrasted with Margaret's unwillingness to surrender power:

> If you be ta'en, we then should see the bottom
> Of all our fortunes; but if we haply scape
> (As well we may, if not through your neglect),
> We shall to London get, where you are lov'd,
> And where this breach now in our fortunes made
> May readily be stopp'd.
>
> (V, ii, 78–83)

Her lack of feeling for Henry the man is sad. But her desire to hold the throne sets up the conflict that dominates the next play: Margaret versus York, with England the prize. The problem dramatically is that the audience does not care for either character because both are so coldly ambitious.

This lack of sympathy, however, does not detract from the power of Part 2, a fearfully graphic portrait of the consequences of weakness in government. Indeed, the play ends with York's order to prevent Henry's calling Parliament (V, iii, 23–27) and that tactic reaffirms the terrors that may unfold when lawlessness runs wild. True, the language is not always subtle, and too many characters declaim too long and too often. But the passions and tensions propel the story with ferocious energy.

SUGGESTIONS FOR FURTHER READING

Alexander, Peter. *Shakespeare's* Henry VI *and* Richard III. Cambridge: Cambridge University Press, 1929.

Blanpied, John W. "History as Play in *Henry VI, Part II.*" *Susquehanna University Studies* 9 (1971): 83–97.

Burckhardt, Sigurd. "I am But Shadow of Myself: Ceremony and Design in *Henry VI.*" *Modern Language Quarterly* 28 (1966): 139–158.

Calderwood, James L. "Shakespeare's Evolving Imagery: *2 Henry VI.*"*English Studies* 48 (1967): 481–493).

Carr, Virginia. "Animal Imagery in *2 Henry VI.*" *English Studies*, 53 (1971): 408–412.

Talbert, Ernest William. *Elizabethan Drama and Shakespeare's Early Plays*. Chapel Hill: University of North Carolina Press, 1963.

Henry VI, Part 3

The chaos that marks the last two acts of *Henry VI, Part 2* is carried over to Part 3, a veritable nightmare, filled with repeated acts and images of violence. As in perhaps no other work of Shakespeare's, turmoil surrounding the throne pervades the realm to destroy not only political and military alliances, but the social fabric of English society. The vision is terrifying and culminates in dominance by the figure who one day personifies the punishment inflicted on England, Richard Plantagenet, here the Duke of Gloucester, and eventually Richard III.

The action of the play begins in 1455 after the battle of St. Albans that ended the previous work. From the beginning Henry VI is weaker then we have ever seen, as York reports:

> While we pursu'd the horsemen of the north,
> He slyly stole away and left his men;
> Whereat the great Lord of Northumberland,
> Whose warlike ears could never brook retreat,
> Cheer'd up the drooping army, and himself,
> Lord Clifford, and Lord Stafford, all abreast,
> Charg'd our main battle's front; and breaking in,
> Were by the swords of common soldiers slain.
>
> (I, i, 2–9)

His tone suggests that combat inspires a glorious thrill. But lest we be taken in by such bombast, a few lines later Richard holds up the head of Somerset, whom he killed in battle at the end of Part 2: "Speak thou for me and tell them what I did" (I, i, 16). We are in only the first few lines of the first scene. Yet already we face the depravity to which men in war may sink. The level drops even further as the conflict continues.

All this barbarism is not without reason, as Warwick clarifies:

> This is the palace of the fearful king,
> And this the regal seat. Possess it, York,
> For this is thine and not King Henry's heirs'.
>
> (I, i, 25–27)

We are never allowed to forget that the Yorks as yet look on the Lancasters as usurpers, and that behind this conflict is the issue of legitimacy. So intense are feelings here that Warwick threatens violence unless Henry is deposed and York is established as King (I, i, 39–41). Warwick even escorts York to the throne. Entering to the sight of their enemy so placed, King Henry, Northumberland, Clifford, and Westmerland express varying degrees of action and vengeance, but Henry, ever cautious, warns that the Yorkists have popular favor on their side (I, i, 67–68). Even the naive Henry recognizes the daunting power of the mob. The question of legitimacy and right to the throne is batted back and forth, as Exeter accuses York of treachery, and York retorts that by following a usurping king Exeter is himself a traitor (I, i, 79–81). Henry turns to history to support his claim (I, i, 105–109), and he seems to be withstanding York's charges and threats, but the weakness of Henry's position, and by implication the clue to Shakespeare's attitude on the entire matter, is clear from a few lines muttered aside. First Henry speaks to himself: "I know not what to say, my title's weak" (I, i, 134). Then Exeter, heretofore a valiant supporter of the King, expresses his own doubt, as he thinks of York: "My conscience tells me he is lawful king" (I, i, 150). Immediately Henry is more fearful: "All will revolt from me and turn to him" (I, i, 151). Such confessions clarify the truth that pervades both tetralogies: that the removal of Richard II was a crime against the King and the universal order, and that England suffers because of the transgression.

Clifford, whose constant proximity to Margaret suggests that he has replaced the dead Suffolk in her favors, continues to offer his loyalty to the King:

> King Henry, be thy title right or wrong,
> Lord Clifford vows to fight in thy defense.
> May that ground gape, and swallow me alive,
> Where I shall kneel to him that slew my father!
>
> (I, i, 159–162)

The last couplet intimates that Clifford is less concerned with loyalty to Henry and more with actions against the men against whom he has sworn revenge. Meanwhile opposition to Henry becomes more virulent, and in desperation the King yields to York's demands for future reign:

> I am content: Richard Plantagenet,
> Enjoy the kingdom after my decease.
>
> (I, i, 174–175)

In response to this shocking breach of precedent, Westmorland, Northumberland, and Clifford express their outrage, then depart with almost comic synchronization (I, i, 183–188), but Henry remains firm:

> I here entail
> The crown to thee and to thine heirs for ever,
> Conditionally that here thou take an oath
> To cease this civil war, and whilst I live

To honor me as thy king and sovereign,
And neither by treason nor hostility
To seek to put me down and reign thyself.

                                                    (I, i, 194–200)

The strategy may seem a way to reconcile warring factions, as York claims: "Now York and Lancaster are reconcil'd" (I, i, 204). But the maneuver is in fact a gross corruption of law, for the English guarded few rights more zealously than that of primogeniture, inheritance by the first son, as Margaret angrily exclaims:

                    Ah, timorous wretch,
        Thou hast undone thyself, thy son, and me,
        And giv'n unto the house of York such head
        As thou shalt reign but by their sufferance.

                                                    (I, i, 231–234)

She speaks from her own selfish perspective, but Henry has nonetheless shredded his most profound ties to God. In an attempt to avoid further bloodshed the King has only exacerbated the crisis. Acting out of fear rather than with decisiveness, he has weakened himself and the throne.

     At the risk of interrupting the sense of drama, we ought to note one delightful touch that itself may break the flow of the play. As Margaret is about to enter this scene, Exeter takes one look and scurries off: "I'll steal away" (I, i, 212). Henry then turns, sees her, and mumbles, "Exeter, so will I" (I, i, 213). The response is completely unroyal, more befitting the henpecked husband in a farce. Yet Henry is about to endure another of his wife's tirades, and because he is never truly evil but rather ill-fitted for his position, he retains our sympathy. Later, when he is more helpless and under greater pressure, we grant him additional compassion.

     At the end of this scene, however, Henry is not quite so innocent. Margaret stalks off, having expelled Henry from his own bed and home, and also having sworn to retaliate against the house of York (I, i, 247–255). The King is almost grateful:

        Reveng'd may she be on that hateful duke,
        Whose haughty spirit, winged with desire,
        Will cost my crown, and like an empty eagle
        Tire on the flesh of me and of my son!

                                                    (I, i, 266–269)

Henry's use of the word "eagle," traditionally the bird that symbolized the King, reflects his own vision of York as already a figure of authority. In addition, his own desire to see York brought down makes him appear less the innocent victim and more the incompetent ruler. As such, he is in direct contrast with York in the next scene, who, in planning strategy with his sons, is determined to win the crown: "I will be king, or die" (I, ii, 35). Such energy befits a king, although our admiration for York's passion is modified by his immorality and willingness to kill others in his way along with any guiltless bystanders. In this scene we also note how closely united in ambition and ruthlessness are York and his son Richard, a bond clarified by Richard's vigorous diatribe on why any oath to Henry may be properly broken (I, ii, 22–34). The final threat in these lines also reflects Richard's personal capacity for violence that will continue to emerge.

York's plans for takeover are interrupted by the news of the advancement of Margaret's 20,000 troops. Despite his meager army of 5,000, York is unintimidated: "A woman's general: what should we fear?" (I, ii, 68). But such boldness proves misguided, for his forces are soon crushed. Before that loss, however, both the brutality of war and the link between the generations are intensified, when York's son Rutland is killed by Young Clifford: "Thy father slew my father; therefore die" (I, iii, 47). This revenge ethic will continue to prevail, and young Rutland is but one of many innocents who pay with their lives for the vengeance of York and Lancaster. That recurring theme, particularized in the slaughter of families, may be the most tragic element of the tetralogy. We understand Clifford's motivation against the man who killed his father, but the murder of the helpless Rutland remains abhorrent.

Clifford's action, however, is only a prelude to the viciousness of Margaret toward the captured York. Before his defeat, York broods miserably on the death of his uncles, although he is proud of his sons' military aggression (I, iii, 9–16). When York is taken, the language of both captor and prisoner abounds with animal imagery, as the most degenerate aspects of the human creature are pre-eminent. York is unrelenting, as he vows that his imminent death will be revenged:

> My ashes, as the phoenix, may bring forth
> A bird that will revenge upon you all . . .
>
> (I, iv, 35–36)

Clifford and Northumberland thereupon trade insults with York, but Margaret is the most vicious. First she attacks his claim to the title: "What, was it you that would be England's king?" (I, iv, 70). Then she savages his children, especially Richard:

> And where's that valiant crook-back prodigy,
> Dicky, your boy, that with his grumbling voice
> Was wont to cheer his dad in mutinies?
>
> (I, iv, 75–77)

She tortures her prisoner further by dangling before his eyes the napkin stained with Rutland's blood.

She saves her greatest insult for York himself by placing the paper crown on his head, simultaneously screaming her mockery of his ambition: "Ay, marry, sir, now looks he like a king" (I, iv, 96). For a moment our sympathy may shift to York, for Margaret's behavior borders on madness, and York does have historical justification for his actions. But Shakespeare undercuts us again, for York answers with venom equal to Margaret's:

> She-wolf of France, but worse than wolves of France,
> Whose tongue more poisons than the adder's tooth!
> How ill-beseeming is it in thy sex
> To triumph like an Amazonian trull
> Upon their woes whom fortune captivates!
>
> (I, iv, 111–115)

His images emphasize the unnaturalness not only of this spectacle, but also of Margaret's leading Henry's army and of her bestiality: "O tiger's heart wrapp'd in a woman's hide!" (I, iv, 137). For the Elizabethans, who envisioned humanity placed between angels and animals, such language suggests a descent to unspeakable depths.

Historically York died in 1460. Here his stabbing is almost a relief from the hatred spewed onstage. We continue to recognize, however, that these brutalities are the result of political disorder, royal weakness, and, previous to that, crimes against King and God committed decades before. At this moment York's plight moves Northumberland (I, iv, 169–171), and Margaret sneers at Northumberland's softness, but York's energy in the face of death may touch us:

> There, take the crown, and with the crown, my curse,
> And in thy need such comfort come to thee
> As now I reap at thy too cruel hand!
> Hard-hearted Clifford, take me from the world,
> My soul to heaven, my blood upon your heads!
>
> (I, iv, 164–168)

This horror seems pointless. We have no sense of justice triumphing or morality exerting itself. Instead, one woman, possessed by terrifying ambition, humiliates and murders a man himself responsible for widespread suffering. Such is Shakespeare's vision here.

Act II begins with the appearance of the three suns before Edward and Richard, one of the few images Shakespeare develops in the first tetralogy. The suns also provide the competing brothers an opportunity to reveal themselves. Richard seizes the phenomenon as a sign that the three surviving children of York (including George, not seen here) should blend into one, as if a single man will emerge and assume leadership (II, i, 26–32). Edward takes the suns as inspiration for battle, and assumes the three individuals will work together (II, i, 33–40). Richard comments ironically about his brother's interpretation:

> Nay, bear three daughters; by your leave I speak it,
> You love the breeder better than the male.
>
> (II, i, 41–42)

Historically Edward was known as a shameless philanderer, and Richard shows that he has little tolerance for such conduct. The line also reveals that inherent

in Richard's attitude toward his brother is mistrust, since Edward has other
concerns besides the single-minded pursuit of power. Richard has none, and
therefore he will rely not on his distracted brothers but on himself.

The news of the deaths of their father and Rutland also provokes telling
reactions. Edward mourns, reduced to weeping and inaction (II, i, 68–78).
Richard icilily vows retaliation:

> Tears then for babes; blows and revenge for me.
> Richard, I bear thy name, I'll venge thy death,
> Or die renowned by attempting it.
>
> (II, i, 86–88)

When Edward contemplates his new title (as oldest surviving son he becomes
Duke of York), Richard warns him not to settle for anything less than the crown:

> Nay, if thou be that princely eagle's bird,
> Show thy descent by gazing 'gainst the sun;
> For chair and dukedom, throne and kingdom say,
> Either that is thine, or else thou wert not his.
>
> (II, i, 91–94)

Richard's career is just starting, but already his severity and monomania emerge.
Those qualities help make him both abhorrent and energetic, an unbeatable
theatrical combination.

Even when Warwick informs Richard that their troops are fighting ineffectively (I,
i, 121–129), Richard reacts with his customary mixture of contempt and courage:

> But in this troublous time what's to be done?
> Shall we go throw away our coats of steel,
> And wrap our bodies in black mourning gowns,
> Numb'ring our Ave-Maries with our beads?
> Or shall we on the helmets of our foes
> Tell our devotion with revengeful arms?
>
> (II, i, 159–164)

Warwick offers additional warning that Margaret and the other royal supporters
are determined to defy Henry's earlier oath to give the crown to York's descendants, but the caution only inflames Richard further:

> Ay, now methinks I hear great Warwick speak.
> Ne'er may he live to see a sunshine day
> That cries "Retire!" if Warwick bid him stay.
>
> (II, i, 186–188)

Warwick, in turn, is inspired to head back to battle with renewed energy:

> King Edward, valiant Richard, Montague,
> Stay we no longer, dreaming of renown,

But sound the trumpets, and about our task.

(II, i, 198–200)

At this point Richard's behavior may seem vaguely heroic. Soon it seems psychotic. Never is it dull. The turning of Warwick here should be taken as initial evidence of Richard's power to persuade and command. So strong, in fact, is Richard's influence that Warwick urges Edward to become King by means of a victory tour through the countryside, with severe punishment for those who refuse to celebrate:

> For King of England shalt thou be proclaim'd
> In every borough as we pass along,
> And he that throws not up his cap for joy
> Shall for the fault make forfeit of his head.

(II, i, 194–197)

Warwick, too, has been infected with belief in his own absolute authority. If justice alone is not sufficient, compulsion will serve.

Before the battle of Towton, fought in 1461, Margaret, Henry, and their supporters meet at the castle of York where Margaret displays York's impaled head. Henry is horrified:

> Withhold revenge, dear God! 'tis not my fault,
> Nor wittingly have I infring'd my vow.

(II, ii, 7–8)

Clifford attempts to make Henry realize that such a sight is part of war. After all, "Ambitious York did level at thy crown . . . " (II, ii, 19). But Henry is unable to rouse himself to anger or action:

> But, Clifford, tell me, didst thou never hear
> That things ill got had ever bad success?

(II, ii, 45–46)

This attempt at moralizing is mocked by Margaret, who sneers at her husband's "soft courage" (II, ii, 57). When Edward, Richard, and their supporters enter to demand Henry's release of the throne, a barrage of insults is exchanged, while the King tries to assert himself: "I am a king, and privileg'd to speak" (II, ii, 120). But he is utterly ineffectual, as the others, especially Richard and Margaret, maintain their verbal assaults (II, ii, 135–143).

All the dickering and threatening lead inevitably to battle. In scene iii Edward realizes his forces are weakening (II, iii, 7), and the losses are compounded by news of the death of Warwick's brother at the hands of Clifford (II, iii, 14–16). This action inspires yet another oath of revenge, this from Warwick (II, iii, 29–32), and we feel the cycle of blood extending seemingly forever. It is manifested in scene iv, as Richard and Clifford, each shouting his own personal cause, fight one-on-one, until Clifford escapes.

This clash sets up what may be the most important moments of the first three

plays. Scene v opens with a long soliloquy by Henry, who summarizes the battle
with sad reflection:

> Now sways it that way, like the self-same sea
> Forc'd to retire by fury of the wind.
> Sometime the flood prevails, and then the wind;
> Now one the better, then another best;
> Both tugging to be victors, breast to breast,
> Yet neither conqueror nor conquered;
> So is the equal poise of this fell war.
>
> (II, v, 7–13)

The surrounding conflict is more than he can bear, and in the inevitable destruction he sees no purpose: no winner, no loser, just survivors. For himself he
seeks a pastoral life:

> O God! methinks it were a happy life
> To be no better than a homely swain,
> To sit upon a hill, as I do now,
> To carve out dials quaintly, point by point,
> Thereby to see the minutes how they run . . .
>
> (II, v, 21–25)

He then moves to plan each hour of the day, and his desire for order is in pathetic
contrast to the chaos around him. Henry is the first of Shakespeare's kings to
stand aside and wish for a life simpler than his own. For the moment, then, he
should be viewed as a gentle man placed in an unforgiving position in the world.
Were Henry a greater, more active, figure, he might approach tragic stature.
But he is too much a victim, helpless before forces greater than his own.

What follows immediately is not what we might expect. Instead of the savage
energy of war, Shakespeare moves directly to its tragic outcome. A nameless
boy drags in one of his victims, who turns out to be the boy's own father. The
symbolism is heavy-handed, but here the scene underscores the anti-war spirit
of the history plays, for here the battle is personalized, and we see the destruction
of this family and by extension the family of the nation. Henry's own statement
of mourning is one of his best moments:

> O piteous spectacle! O bloody times!
> Whiles lions war and battle for their dens,
> Poor harmless lambs abide their enmity.
>
> (II, v, 73–75)

The words apply universally, across eras and continents. And if throughout this
play we judge Henry harshly for his inability to govern, here Shakespeare presents
him in a kinder light.

At another part of the stage a father then drags in a body that he discovers to
be his own son, and again the cruel irony of battle is thrust before us. This father
is more accurate in mourning the causes of the tragedy that has befallen him:

O, pity, God, this miserable age!
What stratagems! how fell! how butcherly!
Erroneous, mutinous, and unnatural,
This deadly quarrel daily doth beget!

(II, v, 88–91)

The word "quarrel" suggests the private origins of this war that has extended
throughout the country. In addition, the tableaus with two fathers and two sons
emphasize further that Henry is the father of his country, who has failed in his
responsibility to his children. If any passage could be said to capture the theme
and tone of this play, the four lines above might come closest.

These moments are some of the few tranquil ones in the play. The entrance
of Margaret and her cohorts shatters the mood, and her personality, expressed
once again in images of animals, clashes sharply with Henry's pastoral vision:

Edward and Richard, like a brace of greyhounds
Having the fearful flying hare in sight,
With fiery eyes sparkling for very wrath,
And bloody steel grasp'd in their ireful hands,
Are at our backs, and therefore hence amain.

(II, v, 129–133)

The next scene returns us to the world of butchery, as Clifford staggers onstage,
an arrow through his neck. At some length he anticipates his death, essentially
justifying all the violence he has committed in the name of his cause. But this
speech is followed by an example of the awkwardness that at points mars these
early plays. When Edward, Richard, and their allies come upon Clifford's body,
they assume he is dead. Then, as if on cue, Shakespeare includes a stage direction
that reads "*Clifford groans [and then dies]*." The effect might well be comic,
unless played subtly. Even Richard's covering line does not disguise the transition.

Before the coronation of King Edward we see a series of actions intended to
create consolidation of his kingship. First Warwick orders York's head to be
taken down from the gates at York, and Clifford's put in its place (II, vi, 52–
55). At this command the three brothers all taunt Clifford's head, in lines that
are nothing short of bizarre. Warwick finally stops the threats, adding that he
will head to France to ask for the hand of Lady Bona for Edward, a marriage
that should garner French support (II, vi, 89–98). Finally new titles are awarded.
George is named Duke of Clarence, and Richard Duke of Gloucester. Richard
protests that his title is burdened by an unhappy history, but Edward is insistent.
In light of subsequent events, Richard's use of "ominous" (II, vi, 107) has
powerful irony.

At the beginning of Act III Shakespeare again invokes the contrast between
Henry and the world in which he is forced to exist. Amidst the two keepers the
King finds himself more comfortable than at court. But his words before he
encounters anyone else reassert the central theme of the history plays:

> No, Harry, Harry, 'tis no land of thine;
> Thy place is fill'd, thy sceptre wrung from thee,
> Thy balm wash'd off wherewith thou was anointed.
>
> (III, i, 15–17)

Were we to be generous to his character, we might say that the reason Henry chooses to avoid the frenzy of war is that deep down he knows that his position as King is untenable, that he has no legal right to the crown. Such an interpretation, however, is too strongly in Henry's favor. His nature, as Shakespeare dramatizes it, is simply feeble, and his doubts about his legitimacy reinforce his timidity and lack of desire to battle for a crown that holds no luster for him.

Yet Henry does have a capacity for self-awareness that distinguishes him from most of the other characters. When asked by the two gameskeepers to explain himself, the King replies with insight:

> More than I seem, and less than I was born to;
> A man at least, for less I should not be;
> And men may talk of kings, and why not I?
>
> (III, i, 56–58)

At this moment he sounds like Richard II, who at his depths philosophizes about his own predicament in similarly bittersweet words. Henry, though, lacks Richard's poetry, and he is even more passive, as when he follows the two keepers who, from loyalty to the throne (III, i, 66–71) lead him away. Henry is unable to resist:

> In God's name lead; your king's name be obey'd,
> And what God will, that let your king perform;
> And what he will, I humbly yield unto.
>
> (III, i, 99–101)

Earlier we noted that in his depiction of Henry, Shakespeare avoided the issue of congenital madness. Instead the playwright dramatizes an intense melancholia, here almost akin to a death wish, so that Henry's weakness, although not inherent in his nature, is something more than mere incompetence.

At the beginning of scene ii, Lady Grey enters, seeking to regain her slain husband's lands, but the request soon turns into Edward's attempt at courtship. While Gloucester and Clarence snicker from aside, Edward invites her affection: "An easy task, 'tis but to love a king" (III, ii, 53), while Lady Grey remains tactically distant: "That's soon perform'd, because I am a subject" (III, ii, 54). When Edward grows bolder: "To tell thee plain, I aim to lie with thee" (III, ii, 69), Lady Grey resists more bluntly: "To tell you plain, I had rather lie in prison" (III, ii, 70). But Edward is so aroused by her refusal that in desperation he changes his offer and proposes to make her his queen, much to the surprise of his two brothers (III, ii, 111–117).

After word comes that Henry has been taken prisoner, however, Richard, (now known as Gloucester), offers a key soliloquy, the first major address by the character soon to emerge as one of the playwright's most enthralling stage presences. From the beginning of this passage, Gloucester speaks with a tone and sense of self unique in this work. True, Henry has some understanding of his situation, but he uses that knowledge as an excuse to avoid anything else. Then, too, Henry deals mostly with surface matters. Gloucester is the first character to probe himself, to let the inner workings of his mind be revealed in all their complexity.

His first lines suggest his lust, which is directed only at power:

> Ay, Edward will use women honorably.
> Would he were wasted, marrow, bones, and all,
> That from his loins no hopeful branch may spring,
> To cross me from the golden time I look for!

> (III, ii, 124–127)

Such resentment towards Edward's children will one day turn into deadly violence. Richard then scrutinizes himself with singular discernment:

> Why then I do but dream on sovereignty,
> Like one that stands upon a promontory
> And spies a far-off shore where he would tread . . .

> (III, ii, 134–136)

Why should he be so self-absorbed? He provides his own explanation:

> Why, love forswore me in my mother's womb;
> And for I should not deal in her soft laws,
> She did corrupt frail nature with some bribe,
> To shrink mine arm up like a wither'd shrub,
> To make an envious mountain on my back,
> Where sits deformity to mock my body;
> To shape my legs of an unequal size,
> To disproportion me in every part,
> Like to a chaos, or an unlick'd bear-whelp
> That carries no impression like the dam.

> (III, ii, 153–162)

Shakespeare accepts the Tudor convention of Gloucester's deformity. The future King looks at the distorted body he inhabits, takes that as evidence of his misshapen values and ideals, and rationalizes his need to destroy. We feel him talking himself into his actions, urging himself on, twisting his personality and desires. The tortuous paths of his thought are fascinating.

His next step is to articulate his plans. He admits to us and himself that he is unsure of what steps he should follow, and here is where his mind takes its most intriguing convolution:

> Why, I can smile, and murther whiles I smile,
> And cry "Content" to that which grieves my heart,
> And wet my cheeks with artificial tears,

>   And frame my face to all occasions.
>
>   (III, ii, 182–185)

He relishes his own capacity for deception. Other characters in the tetralogy
have outlined schemes, but they all spoke as if they were acting from a moral
imperative, as if they were right and their opponents wrong. Gloucester takes
pride in his illegality, and revels in his alienation. He accepts his misshapen
form as a sign of his misshapen soul, as inspiration for perverse behavior.

When Gloucester departs the stage, the play sags, for no one is as intriguing
as he. Still, Margaret's schemes deserve attention. She visits Lewis, King of
France, in an effort to win that nation's support. She offers a deception of her
own, playing the wounded wife desperately in love with a man unable to do
enough for her:

>   Now therefore be it known to noble Lewis,
>   That Henry, sole possessor of my love,
>   Is, of a king, become a banish'd man,
>   And forc'd to live in Scotland a forlorn . . .
>
>   (II, iii, 23–26)

She even tries to make her personal crusade one for the good of the nation:

>   Our people and our peers are both misled,
>   Our treasure seiz'd, our soldiers put to flight,
>   And as thou seest, ourselves in heavy plight.
>
>   (III, iii, 35–37)

The performance is convincing, but not as compelling as Gloucester's, for Margaret lacks Gloucester's smug delight. Her efforts are interrupted by Warwick,
who has come to arrange the marriage between Lady Bona and Edward. Margaret
recognizes the potential for disaster: "If that go forward, Henry's hope is done"
(III, iii, 58). As Warwick and Oxford debate historical right (III, iii, 81–108),
Lewis remains pragmatic. When asked to choose between two kings, one weak
and one strong, he thinks in terms not of who will love his sister, but of who
will do best by him. As he says in agreeing with Warwick's offer:

>   But if your title to the crown be weak,
>   As may appear by Edward's good success,
>   Then 'tis but reason that I be releas'd
>   From giving aid which late I promised.
>
>   (III, iii, 145–148)

Margaret's fury with Warwick (III, iii, 156–161) does no good, for Lewis
demonstrates the cold-blooded practicality Henry lacks. Warwick's scheme,
however, is undercut by the revelation that Edward has already married Lady
Grey, in a ceremony that historically took place in May of 1464 (III, iii, 174–
178). We cannot help but think back to Part I, when Henry, at Suffolk's urging,
married Margaret, and thereby sabotaged the former Duke of Gloucester's plans.

Warwick's frustration is understandable, as is Margaret's delight (III, iii, 179–

180). But the next two turns of plot are surprising. First Warwick renounces the House of York:

> And to repair my honor lost for him,
> I here renounce him and return to Henry.
> My noble queen, let former grudges pass,
> And henceforth I am thy true servitor.

(III, iii, 193–196)

The word "honor" alerts us to the distinct possibility that this change of heart is less from deep commitment than from a desire to emerge on the winning side. Warwick virtually humiliates himself before a woman he has previously held in contempt. Now he needs her to maintain his own place. Even more surprising is Margaret's reaction:

> Warwick, these words have turn'd my hate to love,
> And I forgive and quite forget old faults,
> And joy that thou becom'st King Henry's friend.

(III, iii, 199–201)

How profoundly are these words to be taken? Not very. Shakespeare here dramatizes a timeless truth about political life: that the bitterest rivals can form an alliance if both stand to profit. At this juncture Lewis agrees to give military support (III, iii, 219–220), and Margaret and Warwick become such fast friends that Warwick agrees to an astonishing marriage:

> This shall assure my constant loyalty,
> That if our queen and this young prince agree,
> I'll join mine eldest daughter, and my joy,
> To him forthwith in holy wedlock bands.

(III, iii, 240–243)

Lest we be deceived by these shifts of emotion, Warwick at the end of the scene reminds us that the only genuine motivation for anyone in this court is power. Speaking of Edward, Warwick states:

> I was the chief that rais'd him to the crown,
> And I'll be chief to bring him down again;
> Not that I pity Henry's misery,
> But seek revenge on Edward's mockery.

(III, iii, 262–265)

Because of his wealth and influence, Warwick historically was known as "the kingmaker." Here we see the explanation for his actions. Not generosity of spirit or devotion to the country, but revenge. That and power are the bulwarks of his ambition.

How interesting, then, that Shakespeare moves next to dissension amidst the Yorks, as if to imply that they, too, are unable to handle possession of power. Edward, now King, is compelled to assert himself:

> They are but Lewis and Warwick, I am Edward,
> Your king and Warwick's, and must have my will.
>
> (IV, i, 15–16)

His ego stands front and center. Meanwhile Gloucester's attitude towards his newly crowned brother is evident in his ironic remarks about the marriage to Lady Grey:

> . . . God forbid that I should wish them sever'd
> Whom God hath join'd together; ay, and 'twere pity
> To sunder them that yoke so well together.
>
> (IV, i, 21–23)

The word "yoke" humorously connotes oxen pulling a cart, a characteristic gibe of Gloucester. Meanwhile, Edward is so taken with his newly enfranchised authority that he imagines how if he simply dispenses honors, all will automatically follow him:

> It was my will and grant,
> And for this once my will shall stand for law.
>
> (IV, i, 49–50)

Gloucester is annoyed with Edward's desire to give a wealthy young heir to Lady Grey's brother, and Clarence chimes in with his own doubts, but Edward answers condescendingly:

> Alas, poor Clarence! is it for a wife
> That thou art malecontent? I will provide thee.
>
> (IV, i, 59–60)

The belittling gesture does not persuade Clarence. Yet Edward refuses to acknowledge threats from anyone who criticizes his wife or his policies (IV, i, 75–82). Even news of the alliance between Warwick, Margaret, and Lewis does not dismay the new King: "They shall have wars, and pay for their presumption" (IV, i, 114). Clarence, however, is disgusted, and announces his plan to leave Edward's camp and marry Warwick's other daughter (IV, i, 118–120). Gloucester alone stays with Edward:

> My thoughts aim at a further matter: I
> Stay not for the love of Edward, but the crown.
>
> (IV, i, 125–126)

Gloucester is true to one cause: himself. Meanwhile Edward remains so cocky that he tells his supporters that he hardly needs them (IV, i, 137–142). The entire scene reinforces our awareness of how lust for power, which has infiltrated so many relationships, quickly takes hold here.

The royalist side, though, seems in equally poor shape. Warwick welcomes Clarence, speaks of the arranged marriage (IV, ii, 12), then plots to surprise Edward's troops (IV, ii, 25). Yet when all these allies gather together and shout "Henry" (IV, ii, 27), the enterprise seems puny. And Clarence's silence implies that he has little enthusiasm for warring against his brother. Certainly Henry the man arouses no fervor. We remember him as one who would prefer to be a shepherd, and the unity of those in his support is ludicrous.

Whatever the quality of their goals, Clarence and Warwick succeed in surprising Edward's forces. We note, however, that Edward's troops are aware of his inability to sleep. The supposed reason is Edward's vow never to rest until Warwick's forces are suppressed (IV, iii, 3–6), but Edward is here the first of several kings in the history plays whose problems in office are reflected in perpetual wakefulness.

The attack comes almost at once, and Warwick, before retaking the crown, denounces the humiliated Edward, who is still in his bedclothes (IV, iii, 35–40). Edward's reaction is intriguing:

> Though Fortune's malice overthrow my state,
> My mind exceeds the compass of her wheel.

> (IV, iii, 46–47)

For the first time he has a sense of the larger scheme of things, that his fate is not the only issue. The image of the wheel, coming around, suggests the reestablishment of proper order. Shakespeare's audience knows how this conflict ends, and faith that the wheel will eventually turn, that order will be restored, reflects a faith in the benign structure of the universe. Henry VI has uttered such expressions throughout this play, but he does so with a voice of resignation, as if he himself has no part in the restoration. The history plays affirm that the England of this play is suffering because of crimes against the King, but that the punishment itself and the eventual restoration of order is ultimately part of a beneficent universal structure.

In scene iv we see another side to the political crisis when Lady Grey, now Queen Elizabeth, reveals to Rivers that she is pregnant. To save Edward's child the two escape. In scene v, Gloucester is hardly prepared to give up his personal quest, as he plots to free his brother, now prisoner of the Archbishop of York (IV, v, 9–13). When Edward appears with his huntsmen, the former King is sent to Flanders for protection.

With the deposition of Edward in 1470, Henry is once more made king. Historically he remained away from the throne for only six months. But Shakespeare's portrait is of a man who simply does not want the job. First he transfers his power to Warwick (IV, vi, 24–25). And by making Clarence Protector, Henry abandons the throne before he possesses it:

> I make you both Protectors of this land,
> While I myself will lead a private life,
> And in devotion spend my latter days,
> To sin's rebuke and my Creator's praise.

> (IV, vi, 41–44)

Whether this retreat is a search for spiritual fulfillment or an expression of moral cowardice is a matter of interpretation.

As Warwick declares Edward a traitor whose lands should be confiscated (IV, vi, 54–55), Henry is preoccupied, and faces to the side. There he notices a youth standing nearby, and Somerset reveals that the figure is Henry, Earl of Richmond. The King intuits a truth the audience already knows:

> If secret powers
> Suggest but truth to my divining thoughts,
> This pretty lad will prove our country's bliss.
> His looks are full of peaceful majesty,
> His head by nature fram'd to wear a crown,
> His hand to wield a sceptre, and himself
> Likely in time to bless a regal throne.
>
> (IV, vi, 68–74)

At the King's lowest point, Shakespeare provides him with an almost divine ability for prophecy. Thus Henry seems more dignified, and we are more likely to accept that he does have spiritual qualities. In addition, the moment reminds us that the war between Lancaster and York will eventually end, and that the crown will be restored in the person of Richmond, who becomes Henry VII. Thus even though the report of Edward's escape and the renewed threat to the crown end the scene, the sense of universal order is never far away.

In the meantime the deposed Edward and Gloucester take action. They appear at York, where the town gates are locked, but deceive the Mayor into letting them in (IV, vii, 27–28). Then the brothers rally each other with characteristic attitudes. Edward, who has been King, albeit briefly, seeks to retrieve that authority by legal means, as he explains to Montgomery:

> Nay, stay, Sir John, a while, and we'll debate
> By what safe means the crown may be recover'd.
>
> (IV, vii, 51–52)

He wants power permanently, not by maneuvers that will be questioned and leave him vulnerable. Gloucester, on the other hand, cares nothing for rules: "Why, brother, wherefore stand you on nice points?" (IV, vii, 58). Richard's dynamism naturally carries the moment, as Edward agrees to reclaim the throne. And Montgomery supports that threat by throwing down his gauntlet before potential challengers.

Thus the move against Henry begins, although the campaign is really against two more dangerous opponents, as Edward indicates:

> We'll forward towards Warwick and his mates;
> For well I wot that Henry is no soldier.
> Ah, froward Clarence, how evil it beseems thee
> To flatter Henry and forsake thy brother!
>
> (IV, vii, 82–85)

Fraternal loyalties have long been tossed aside in the world of this play.

In contrast to Gloucester and Edward's ambition is the rambling of Henry, whose reflection raises a question that resounds through the histories. Speaking of his people, we weighs his disapprobation:

> I have not stopp'd mine ears to their demands,
> Nor posted off their suits with slow delays;
> My pity hath been balm to heal their wounds,
> My mildness hath allay'd their swelling griefs,
> My mercy dried their water-flowing tears;
> I have not been desirous of their wealth,
> Nor much oppress'd them with great subsidies,
> Nor forward of revenge, though they much err'd.
> Then why should they love Edward more than me?
>
> (IV, viii, 39–47)

He cannot grasp the personality of the masses. Their loyalties are inconstant, as are their values. What they respect most, and what Edward here embodies, is force. In play after play Shakespeare dramatizes that the populace seeks government that deals with a firm hand, a vision no doubt based on Shakespeare's own belief in the need for a powerful central authority. Whatever the reason, throughout the history plays, as well as in tragedies like *Julius Caesar* and *Coriolanus*, the masses want to follow, not lead. And what they choose to follow is not necessarily right, but only strong.

That strength takes over immediately, as Edward and Gloucester capture Henry. The helpless King has no comment, but perhaps his silence should be taken as relief that he is unburdened of rule. Shakespeare seems to suggest that just as the masses require authority, those who rule best must want to rule. Power cannot be exercised wisely by those who do not enjoy it.

The taking of Henry, however, is not the end of the war, as Edward and Gloucester advance on Warwick. The "kingmaker" refuses to acknowledge the authority of Edward, who ruthlessly dismisses his former ally (V, i, 53–57). The most interesting moment of the conquest is the revelation by Clarence, who throws down his red Lancaster rose and proclaims his loyalty to his brother (V, i, 81–102). This action, supported by a long speech, earns perfunctory acknowledgements by Edward and Gloucester (V, i, 103–106), but despite Clarence's audaciousness we do not believe he will ever be trusted by either of his brothers. The world of politics is too cruel for so vacillating a figure, and Clarence is not to survive long.

In scene ii, after battle with Edward, the dying Warwick ruminates on power, sounding very much like Henry:

> Why, what is pomp, rule, reign, but earth and dust?
> And live we how we can, yet die we must.
>
> (V, ii, 27–28)

Such perspective comes awfully late. After Warwick dies, however, Edward and Gloucester recognize that the ultimate enemy was not Warwick but Margaret:

> The Queen is valued thirty thousand strong,
> And Somerset, with Oxford, fled to her;
> If she have time to breathe, be well assur'd
> Her faction will be full as strong as ours.
>
> (V, iii, 14–17)

Meanwhile Margaret remains eager to fight, and orders Oxford and Somerset to replace Warwick and Montague. In her own way she is as ruthless as the Yorks, using people strictly for her own ends. She is joined in her efforts by her spirited son, Prince Edward, whom Oxford optimistically proclaims is the image of his grandfather, Henry V (V, iv, 53–54). That resemblance turns out to be of no value, for Margaret and Edward's troops fall in the battle of Tewkesbury, which occurred historically in May 1471. And what happens to them is a sadly fitting ending to this play.

Faced with his conquerors, the young Prince is not spiritually subdued, even before the newly restored King Edward:

> Speak like a subject, proud ambitious York!
> Suppose that I am now my father's mouth:
> Resign thy chair, and where I stand kneel thou,
> Whilst I propose the self-same words to thee,
> Which, traitor, thou wouldst have me answer to.
>
> (V, v, 17–21)

At these words Margaret bursts out with a longing we have always known she harbors: "Ah, that thy father had been so resolv'd!" (V, v, 22). But if we ever suspected that genuine honor resides in the Yorks, or that their nature was in any way noble, or that they have somehow been ennobled by their struggle for what they believe is right, their next action reveals everything. All three brothers stab the Prince, and this particular piece of brutality, even after all that has proceeded, is shocking. Gloucester is even ready to kill Margaret on the spot, but Edward manages to restrain him. Rarely do we sympathize with Margaret, but here her outcry is appropriate: "Butchers and villains! bloody cannibals! (V, v, 61). She invokes the imagery that has dominated the play. In addition, her lines below remind us of a motif vital to the tetralogy:

> You have no children, butchers; if you had,
> The thought of them would have stirr'd up remorse,
> But if you ever chance to have a child,
> Look in his youth to have him so cut off
> As, deathsmen, you have rid this sweet young prince!
>
> (V, v, 63–67)

The War of the Roses involves considerable loss of life, but the most moving deaths are those of innocent children. In addition, Margaret's curse (V, v, 82) contains a tragic irony, for the offspring of brothers Edward and Clarence will die at the hands of their brother, Richard of Gloucester.

Those deaths occur in the next play. First comes the most repulsive moment in this work, perpetrated, not surprisingly, by Gloucester, who during scene v steals away to the Tower. He is aware that Henry VI is the last of Gaunt's descendants, the final Lancaster to have a claim to the crown. Thus the penultimate scene of this play contains the event we have anticipated since early in Part I.

That Henry also anticipates it is apparent when he greets Gloucester: "What scene of death hath Roscius now to act"? (V, vi, 10). His mention of the Roman actor distinguished for his tragic roles suggests how Henry thinks of himself: as an actor ill-suited for his part. The tone of his line also implies that his imprisonment has fostered a boldness within him. Gloucester's answer has its own ironic implications:

> Suspicion always haunts the guilty mind;
> The thief doth fear each bush an officer.
>
> (V, vi, 11–12)

At the moment his own conscience is clear. It will not always be so.

When Gloucester boasts to Henry that the Prince, Young Edward, has been murdered, and by Gloucester himself (who takes full credit)(V, vi, 34), Henry's warning is even stronger than Margaret's:

> And thus I prophesy, that many a thousand
> Which now mistrust no parcel of my fear,
> And many an old man's sigh and many a widow's,
> And many an orphan's water-standing eye—
> Men for their sons, wives for their husbands,
> Orphans for their parents' timeless death—
> Shall rue the hour that ever thou wast born.
>
> (V, vi, 37–43)

And with a vigor unprecedented for him, Henry goes on to describe the circumstances of Gloucester's birth that created "an indigested and deformed lump . . . " (V, vi, 51). In his last moments Henry is at his best. Then Gloucester has his turn, and the cold-blooded stabbing of Henry is this play's culminating act of disorder. This murder has never been substantiated historically, but the Tudor view of events had Henry murdered by Gloucester, and Shakespeare follows that tradition.

Henry's last line suggests his nobler side: "O God forgive my sins, and pardon thee!" (V, vi, 60). Again we might ask if he approaches the stature of a tragic hero. But the answer remains no. Perhaps the best we can say of him is that like the truly tragic figures, Hamlet, Othello, Brutus, and others, Henry was placed in a situation where his nature worked against the successful resolution of his problems. But his inability to grapple with the events of the world and his willingness to surrender to them leave him pathetic, not tragic.

Thus in these last moments our attention is focused on Richard of Gloucester, soon to be Richard III. His curse as he stabs the dead body of Henry (V, vi, 61–67) is a sign that viciousness is now paramount inside him, unchallenged by

remnants of other emotions. He soon stands as the ultimate predator, the final
punishment visited upon England for the sins committed decades before. Yet
even in this moment of ferocity, Gloucester remains psychologically compelling:

> I, that have neither pity, love, nor fear.
> Indeed 'tis true that Henry told me of;
> For I have often heard my mother say
> I came into the world with my legs forward.
> Had I not reason, think ye, to make haste,
> And seek their ruin that usurp'd our right?
>
> (V, vi, 68–73)

His final step is complete withdrawal from mankind:

> Then since the heavens have shap'd my body so,
> Let hell make crook'd my mind to answer it.
> I have no brother, I am like no brother;
> And this word "love," which greybeards call divine,
> Be resident in men like one another,
> And not in me: I am myself alone.
>
> (V, vi, 78–83)

His pleasure in his own spiritual perversity makes him irresistibly entertaining.

It remains for Edward, temporarily secure on the throne where he will rule
until 1483, to recite a partial list of murders and deaths carried out during the
past three plays (V, vii, 5–10). But after he finishes, we sense the playwright's
eagerness for the final part of the tetralogy, the play devoted to the future Richard
III, who here kisses his young nephew, Edward, with outward words of affection:

> And that I love the tree from whence thou sprang'st,
> Witness the loving kiss I give the fruit.
>
> (V, vii, 31–32)

But aside he mutters:

> To say the truth, so Judas kiss'd his master,
> And cried "All hail!" when as he meant all harm.
>
> (V, vi, 33–34)

With such language Richard brands himself a violator of moral and religious
precepts. Yet he does so with a combination of wit and malevolence that dominates the next play, in which the values and conflicts of the first three plays
clash in bloody yet triumphant resolution.

SUGGESTIONS FOR FURTHER READING

Gerould, Daniel C. "Principles of Dramatic Structure in *Henry VI*." *Educational Theatre
    Journal* 20 (1967): 376–388.
French, A. L. "The Mills of God and Shakespeare's Early History Plays." *English
    Studies* 55 (1974): 313–324.

Jorgensen, Paul A. "A Formative Shakespearean Legacy: Elizabethan Views of God, Fortune, and War." *PMLA* 90 (1975): 222–233.

Kelly, Faye L. "Oaths in Shakespeare's Henry VI Plays." *Shakespeare Quarterly* 24 (1972): 357–371.

Utterback, Raymond V. "Public Men, Private Wills, and Kingship in *Henry VI, Part III*." *Renaissance Papers* (1978): 47–54.

Womersley, D. J. "*3 Henry VI*: Shakespeare, Tacitus, and Parricide." *Notes and Queries* 32 (1985): 468–473.

RICHARD III

The final play of the first tetralogy is by far the most theatrically successful. It is dominated by a title figure whose presence on stage, no matter how repugnant his deeds, is riveting. In addition, the drama is enlivened because Richard in his machinations is matched by two opponents sufficiently powerful to bring him down. One is Nemesis, the classical spirit of revenge, embodied here by Margaret. The other is a Christian force, that of Providence, embodied here by Richmond, soon to be Henry VII. He himself is not a fully drawn character, but represents divine order reasserting itself after the decades of chaos that have beset England.

Throughout this play Richard is depicted as the ultimate wrath of God, the culmination of civil war. He is the epitome of greed, egomania, and savagery, his downfall the inevitable self-destruction of uncontrolled ambition. Thus his end is a cleansing of the state and a purification for all who have suffered because of its disorder.

In portraying Richard as an arch-criminal, Shakespeare followed Tudor propaganda, as begun by Polydore Vergil, the Italian humanist appointed by Henry VII to write a history of England. This work, which established the basic position of Richard in the overall scheme of the War of the Roses, was followed by Sir Thomas More's account of Richard's rise and reign, an interpretation passed on to Shakespeare through Hall and Holinshed.

The historical Richard, who ruled just two years, from 1483–1485, was in fact an able administrator and effective soldier, loyal to his brother Edward IV, who led the nation through more than a decade of comparative tranquility. Clarence, the third brother, was the more fractious sibling, and after causing all sorts of difficulties he was ordered executed by Edward in 1478, then drowned, according to legend, in malmsey, a type of wine. Furthermore, Richard does not seem to have had a part in the actual killing, as Shakespeare dramatizes. In the play Richard is portrayed as having dominated Buckingham, but historically the reverse is likely the case, and the King never did succeed in making allies with other influential nobles. The great crime associated with Richard is the murder of his two nephews, the children of Edward IV, but even this act is not absolutely certain, although the body of evidence points strongly to Richard's guilt.

Whatever the truth about historical events that will likely remain murky, our concern is Shakespeare's dramatization. He takes fourteen years of history, condenses them into three months, and creates the play that stands as his first masterpiece. The intensity and unity of the work also justifies its being designated formally as "The Tragedy of Richard III." But primarily because the title figure does not experience the kind of inner struggle that characterizes the true tragic hero, the work is most often classified as a history.

From the outset Richard enthralls us as he takes us into his confidence. When he speaks directly to us, we can believe him. Unlike Iago in *Othello*, Richard is honest with himself. Iago makes us privy to his thoughts, but presents them with such convolutions that even he does not understand his own motivations. Richard never has that problem. Thus he is psychologically less complex than Iago, but more accessible.

At the opening of the play, Richard, still Duke of Gloucester, (although I shall refer to him as Richard throughout this chapter) makes his ambitions clear:

> Now is the winter of our discontent
> Made glorious summer by this son of York;
> And all the clouds that low'r'd upon our house
> In the deep bosom of the ocean buried.

                                                              (I, i, 1–4)

The pun on "sun," referring to both his family status and his plans to hold the kingship, reflect the agility of his wit, and his security and delight in himself. He also maintains one of his preoccupations in *Henry VI, Part 3*, reflecting on his own physical deformity:

> And therefore, since I cannot prove a lover
> To entertain these fair well-spoken days,
> I am determined to prove a villain
> And hate the idle pleasures of these days.
> Plots have I laid, inductions dangerous,
> By drunken prophecies, libels, and dreams,
> To set my brother Clarence and the King
> In deadly hate the one against the other . . .

                                                              (I, i, 28–35)

How different Richard is from another character who attempts such schemes, Macbeth. Both kill for power, and one symbol of their degeneration is the murder of children. Macbeth orders the slaughter of Macduff's children, Richard that of the sons of Edward IV. The Scottish thane, however, is presented as a man victimized by circumstance, and pressured by his wife into committing a heinous act that leads him to other such acts. Even as he plots and kills, he is frightened by possible moral consequences. Richard, on the other hand, is immune to such fears. He willingly sets out to destroy, with complete disregard for the forces of retribution. Again, this attitude prevents great subtlety of character, and Richard poses few questions to the audience. But the directness of his goals and the clarity of his statements propel this play forward with scarcely any retardation.

His first scheme is to set his two brothers at odds with each other, as he has done by fabricating a prophesy that someone whose name begins with G should murder King Edward's heirs (I, i, 39–40). Because Clarence's first name is George, he has automatically come under suspicion, and therefore been imprisoned. Perhaps we in the audience reflect that the prediction will eventually prove accurate, since *Gloucester* is to be that assassin.

Here Richard's skill at manipulation can be seen at once, as he maneuvers his brother George, Duke of Clarence, to the Tower. Clarence, who in the last play was traitorous to his brothers, speaks of the prophesy with naive irony (I, i, 53–61), unaware that Richard is the instigator. But Richard maintains his charade. First he blames Elizabeth, Edward's queen, for Clarence's imprisonment: "Why, thus it is, when men are rul'd by women . . ." (I, i, 62). We should also take the line as reflecting Richard's general antagonism to women, further clarified when Richard mentions the King's friendship with Jane Shore (I, i, 71–75).

Brakenbury, Clarence's guard, steps in to prevent the brothers from conspiring, but Richard quickly assures him: "We speak no treason, man" (I, i, 90). Then, with apparent confidence in Brakenbury, Richard takes him aside and whispers words of praise for both the Queen and Shore. Richard appears to show complete faith in the jailor: "Wouldst thou betray me?" (I, i, 102). Throughout the play Richard has the invaluable capacity to speak intimately to a series of individuals, and gain each one's trust. He concludes this episode by inveigling himself into Clarence's confidence:

> Well, your imprisonment shall not be long,
> I will deliver you, or else lie for you.
>
> (I, i, 114–115)

Indeed, Richard will cut short Clarence's stay in jail, and will "lie" to achieve that end.

His solicitous manner is maintained on the entrance of Hastings, who enters to complain of his own imprisonment, which, he hints obliquely, was Richard's doing:

> But I shall live, my lord, to give them thanks
> That were the cause of my imprisonment.
>
> (I, i, 127–128)

Richard innocently expresses sympathy (I, i, 129–131), then feigns amazement to learn that King Edward is ill: "Now by Saint John, that news is bad indeed!" (I, i, 138). On many occasions Richard relies on religious oaths to give himself the veneer of respectability. For us, such false piety is one more aspect of his witty malevolence. Richard also shifts the blame to Edward himself for leading such a dissolute life (I, i, 139–140). Scarcely a single line of Richard's does not have an ulterior motive.

In his next soliloquy, Richard clarifies his deadly schemes. He must make sure that Clarence dies before the King, for if Edward should die first, Clarence could become King and his children could also be in Richard's way to the crown. Richard also schemes to marry Lady Anne, widow of Edward, the son of Henry VI. That marrige was the one arranged by Margaret and Warwick in III, iii of *Henry VI, Part 3*. Later in the play Richard helped murder the son, and killed the father single-handedly. Now, with outrageous boldness, he moves against Anne:

> The readiest way to make the wench amends
> Is to become her husband and her father:
> The which will I, not all so much for love
> As for another secret close intent
> By marrying her which I must reach unto.

(I, i, 155–159)

Like the Vice figures from medieval drama, Richard gives vent to our worst instincts. Thus even as we are repulsed by him, we are attracted to him.

Scene ii begins with Lady Anne's curses on the man about to attempt to seduce her. One important aspect of her dirge over the body of the dead king is that she focuses on the animal imagery that dominates the tetralogy and reaches its culmination in this work:

> O, cursed be the hand that made these holes!
> Cursed the heart that had the heart to do it!
> Cursed the blood that let this blood from hence!
> More direful hap betide that hated wretch
> That makes us wretched by the death of thee
> Than I can wish to wolves—to spiders, toads,
> Or any creeping venom'd thing that lives!
> If ever he have child, abortive be it,
> Prodigious, and untimely brought to light,
> Whose ugly and unnatural aspect
> May fright the hopeful mother at the view,
> And that be heir to his unhappiness!

(I, ii, 14–25)

Her words also emphasize the theme of family destruction, in particular the pain of children, that throughout the tetralogy has reflected the destruction of the nation as a whole.

First Richard countermands Anne's order to remove the corpse:

> Unmanner'd dog, [stand] thou when I command.
> Advance thy halberd higher than my breast,
> Or by Saint Paul I'll strike thee to my foot,

And spurn upon thee, beggar, for thy boldness.

(I, ii, 39–42)

But this abusive manner disappears when Richard starts the courtship. No matter how she insults him, he never grows angry. To the surrounding mourners Anne points out how, as according to tradition, the victim's blood spouts in the presence of the murderer:

> Blush, blush, thou lump of foul deformity;
> For 'tis thy presence that exhales this blood
> From cold and empty veins where no blood dwells.

(I, ii, 57–59)

The subject quickly changes to Edward, who historically was only betrothed to Anne, but whom Shakespeare assumed was married to her. At first Richard denies the murder (I, ii, 91) but ten lines later has the audacity to confess it (I, ii, 101). Then Richard surprises us once more, revealing the poet within him:

> Your beauty was the cause of that effect—
> Your beauty, that did haunt me in my sleep
> To undertake the death of all the world,
> So I might live one hour in your sweet bosom.

(I, ii, 121–124)

Even though he has repeatedly denied the existence of such feelings, that he can pretend so successfully suggests frustrated love.

His next tactic is the story of his own father's suffering and death (I, ii, 155–164) and his own impassivity over the events. Only Anne, he claims, can stir him:

> And what these sorrows could not thence exhale,
> Thy beauty hath, and made them blind with weeping.

(I, ii, 165–166)

But Richard's most daring move is opening his shirt and laying himself vulnerable to the sword he hands her. The gesture moves even Anne, who refrains from stabbing him:

> Though I wish thy death,
> I will not be thy executioner.

(I, ii, 184–185)

And as he adds one passionate statement on top of another, she is finally overcome:

> With all my heart, and much it joys me too,
> To see you are become so penitent.

(I, i, 219–220)

For all his evil, Richard must be played with charm to bring off this extraordinary sequence.

The courtship of Lady Anne historically was conducted over two years. Shakespeare condenses it to 200 lines, and so convincing is the scene that an audience, too, might be swept along. But Richard's lines upon Anne's exit, a subtler expression of sentiments uttered by Suffolk in *Henry VI, Part 1* (V, iii, 78–79), reveal the real man:

> Was ever woman in this humor woo'd?
> Was ever woman in this humor won?
> I'll have her, but I will not keep her long.
>
>   (I, ii, 227–229)

These words gain power not from the meaning alone, but because of the complete alteration in tone and manner, as Richard moves from seduction to calculation with nary a moment's hesitation. Even he is amazed at his own adeptness (I, ii, 246–250). Perhaps his skill is evidence that political action is itself a form of seduction, that winning public confidence is not so different from winning private affection.

In scene iii, the discontent in the royal house is apparent, as the Queen and her advisors brood over the King's illness. Grey speaks glowingly of her son Edward, but Elizabeth is worried that the boy is under the protection of Richard (I, iii, 11–13). With the appearance of Stanley and Buckingham, however, the conversations stop. Elizabeth immediately accuses Stanley's wife of disloyalty, but he blames "envious slanders" (I, iii, 26). Stanley, father of the Richmond who is eventually to become King Henry VII, always remains calm in the face of accusation, a tactic to be examined more closely. The more important report is brought by Buckingham, Richard's confidante, who claims first that the King's health is improved, then that Richard is on his way to soothe royal tensions (I, iii, 34, 36–39).

Immediately Richard enters, in what we recognize as a false rage against anyone who mistrusts him:

> When have I injur'd thee? When done thee wrong?
> Or thee? or thee? or any of your faction?
> A plague upon you all! His royal Grace
> (Whom God preserve better than you would wish!)
> Cannot be quiet scarce a breathing while
> But you must trouble him with lewd complaints.
>
>   (I, iii, 56–61)

The performance is fascinating, but Elizabeth is not fooled, commenting on Richard's "interior hatred/ That in your outward action shows itself . . . " (I, iii, 65–66). But Richard defends himself by attacking Elizabeth, blaming her for the imprisonments of Clarence and Hastings (I, iii, 77, 90), and taunting her for having married the King, a younger man (I, iii, 100).

With the appearance of Margaret, hidden behind a curtain, the play takes on yet another tone, for in some ways she is the only character whose stature approaches Richard's. Historically she was not in England during this time, having returned in 1475 to France, where she died in 1482. But dramatically she is essential. She is the only character who spans all four plays, and her words carry a sense of historical inevitability. She is the voice of the past, of painful experience. Thus when she speaks from behind and accuses Richard of his crimes, especially the murder of her husband Henry VI and son Edward (I, iii, 118–119), she bears the weight of two decades of death and suffering that England has borne. Like the chorus in Greek tragedy, Margaret is the memory and conscience of the play.

When Elizabeth confesses her own unhappiness on the throne, Margaret is glad, for as a Lancastrian she regards the wife of a Yorkist King as a usurper (I, iii, 110–111). For a few moments she speaks only asides, as Richard continues his assault on Elizabeth. Rivers and Elizabeth accuse Richard of desiring the throne for himself (I, iii, 144–147, 150–153), but with comic shock he denies the accusation: ''I had rather be a pedlar'' (I, iii, 148). But when Margaret steps out and points to Richard, she becomes an agent of revenge, no longer passive in her pain. Richard does not accept her intrusion weakly, and the resultant assaults of the two upon each other are appalling. In a series of vicious exchanges, they review their families' histories as dramatized in the previous two plays: Margaret curses once more the deaths of her husband and son (I, iii, 167–172), while Richard recalls again the humiliation and execution of his father (I, iii, 173–180). We cannot help remembering that Henry VI was himself grandson of a usurper, Henry IV, who removed Richard II from the throne. As throughout the history plays, the theme of children suffering for the sins of earlier generations resounds.

In the end Margaret has the sharper lines, as her litany (I, iii, 187–213) overwhelms the others, and she curses Richard and his offspring, then his fate:

> Long mayst thou live to wail thy children's death,
> And see another, as I see thee now,
> Deck'd in thy rights as thou are stall'd in mine!
>
> (I, iii, 203–205)

> The worm of conscience still begnaw thy soul!
> Thy friends suspect for traitors while thou liv'st,
> And take deep traitors for thy dearest friends!
> No sleep close up that deadly eye of thine,
> Unless it be while some tormenting dream
> Affrights thee with a hell of ugly devils!
>
> (I, iii, 221–226)

That these final predictions actually occur make Margaret's voice even more daunting. Richard, however, remains calm, answering her denunciation with a simple ''Margaret'' (I, iii, 233). Turning to Elizabeth, Margaret then berates her: ''Fool, fool, thou whet'st a knife to kill thyself'' (I, iii, 243). Here she becomes an avenging fury that seeks to punish Richard as he has punished others. Buckingham tries to soothe her anger: ''Peace, peace, for shame! if not, for charity'' (I, iii, 272), but she turns aside his request and his threats, reminding those both onstage and off what will happen because of Richard:

> O Buckingham, take heed of yonder dog!
> Look when he fawns he bites; and when he bites,
> His venom tooth will rankle to the death.
> Have not to do with him, beware of him;
> Sin, death, and hell have set their marks on him,
> And all their ministers attend on him.

(I, iii, 288–293)

The end-stopped lines and the vigorous language give Margaret's passage, indeed, almost all the lines of this play, an unnerving energy. Furthermore, Margaret's reliance on ultimate judgment suggests a profound faith in the rightness of the world. She expresses such faith in hellish terms, but the theme of order restored underlies her perspective, as does the accuracy of her words, especially to Buckingham, who will pay with his life for his alliance with Richard.

Dorset and Buckingham are stunned by Margaret's venom, but Richard remains unflappable. In front of the others he expresses sympathy for Margaret's sufferings (I, iii, 305–307), then chastizes Elizabeth for her wrongdoing, and with blasphemous fraudulence asks God to pardon those responsible for Clarence's suffering. Rivers dismisses the false piety (I, iii, 315–316), while Gloucester feigns blindness to the sarcasm (I, iii, 317). But as soon as he is left alone onstage, he begins plotting the downfall of everyone, including Buckingham, his apparently loyal follower (I, iii, 328). Here, too, Richard takes inordinate pleasure in his masquerade:

> And thus I clothe my naked villainy
> With odd old ends stol'n forth of holy writ,
> And seem a saint, when most I play the devil.

(I, iii, 335–337)

His religious front is thus not a coincidence, but a calculated aspect of his entire strategy. Maintaining a saintly pose allows him to remain immune from the taunts and insults of others.

With the assistance of the two murderers who suddenly appear, Richard outlines his first step: the murder of Clarence. We recall the scheme of Suffolk and his two hired thugs from *Henry VI, Part 2*, but here the murderers are more sharply developed as characters, and their killing of Clarence turns into a far more moving event than the earlier execution of Gloucester, which occurs offstage and is only reported. In this brief episode Richard gives the murderers the warrant for Clarence's death, but not, as we later learn, Edward's reprieve.

Clarence begins his final scene by confessing regrets over previous actions. He is haunted by dreams, and anticipates the actual manner of his death: ''O Lord, methought what pain it was to drown'' (I, iv, 21). His anguish becomes dreadful:

With that ([methoughts]) a legion of foul fiends
Environ'd me, and howled in mine ears
Such hideous cries that with the very noise
I, trembling, wak'd, and for a season after
Could not believe but that I was in hell,
Such terrible impression made my dream.

                                        (I, iv, 58–63)

To his jailor Clarence admits his guilt, but insists that he only followed Edward's orders:

Ah, Keeper, Keeper, I have done these things
(That now give evidence against my soul)
For Edward's sake, and see how he requites me!

                                        (I, iv, 66–68)

Clarence further engenders our sympathy by pleading for the lives of his children and wife. She, however, was in actuality dead by this time.

When the two murderers enter, Brakenbury reluctantly leaves to allow them to fulfill Richard's command. Like others in a world where order has broken down, Brakenbury tries to excuse himself from responsibility:

I will not reason what is meant hereby,
Because I will be guiltless from the meaning.

                                        (I, iv, 93–94)

Nevertheless, Brakenbury must bear blame for what follows.

One sign of Shakespeare's evolving skill is that he individualizes the murderers. Murderer One is a brutal killer, with no touch of remorse or conscience, while Murderer Two is pained by the ethics of his task. When Murderer One inquires about his partner's condition, the response is: "[Faith,] some certain dregs of conscience are yet within me" (I, iv, 121–122). But in this play wit and horror are companions, and here Shakespeare adds a comic moment. When the first Murderer reminds his confederate: "Remember our reward when the deed's done" (I, iv, 123–124), Murderer Two jumps right back on track: "['Zounds], he dies!" (I, iv, 125). Still, his conscience returns to weigh on him:

A man cannot steal, but it accuseth him;
A man cannot swear, but it checks him; a man cannot
lie with his neighbor's wife, but it detects him. 'Tis
a blushing shame-fac'd spirit that mutinies in a man's
bosom.

                                        (I, iv, 135–139)

When Clarence awakens, realizes their mission, and demands justification, each murderer reveals himself in his reactions to the killing. Clarence insists that private murder is an act against God (I, iv, 195–200), but Murderer One is undeterred and speaks only in terms of vengeance:

> And like a traitor to the name of God
> Didst break that vow, and with thy treacherous blade
> Unrip'st the bowels of thy sov'reign's son.
>
> (I, iv, 205–207)

He conveniently overlooks that Clarence's partners in the murder of Henry's son were Edward and Richard. When Clarence claims that he has Richard's protection (I, iv, 229–230), the second Murderer tries to mollify his intended victim: "You are deceiv'd, your brother Gloucester hates you" (I, iv, 232). Even Clarence recognizes differences between the two. He judges the first's refusal to relent to be "beastly, savage, devilish" (I, iv, 262). To the second he comments, "My friend, I spy some pity in thy looks" (I, iv, 263). And when the first Murderer carries out the actual stabbing (from behind Clarence), it is the second whose conscience is sparked:

> A bloody deed, and desperately dispatch'd!
> How fain, like Pilate, would I wash my hands
> Of this most grievous murther!
>
> (I, iv, 271–273)

Murderer One; however, proceeds relentlessly, carrying the body off for drowning in the "malmsey-butt" (I, iv, 270).

Why did Shakespeare take such pains to differentiate the two killers? Perhaps because they represent the instincts warring in England during this play. Murderer One embodies the savagery let loose during civil war. Murderer Two embodies the instincts for decency thus far covered by Richard's actions, but which will gradually rise. We are touched by Clarence's death, even though we know of his treachery and the murder he committed. But by the end of his life we see him as more victim than perpetrator. And Murderer Two's attitude is evidence that the pity we feel is not absent from England itself. Thus Richard's time in power is limited.

With the beginning of Act II a contrast is established between Richard and his brother Edward, now dying. Richard has yet to grasp his mortality and inevitable fall. Edward, however, once as greedy for pleasure as his brother is for power, is conscious of his imminent death, and tries to reconcile himself with that end so that "my soul shall part to heaven . . . " (II, i, 5). All his listeners, including Hastings, Rivers, Dorset, and Elizabeth, embrace mutual loyalty. Buckingham, too, proclaims fidelity, but comments to the Queen with unintentional irony about what would happen should he, Buckingham, ever prove false:

> When I have most need to employ a friend,
> And most assured that he is a friend,
> Deep, hollow, treacherous, and full of guile

Be he unto me!

(II, i, 36–39)

Buckingham shortly allies himself with Richard, becoming what in contemporary parlance might be called a "front," one who carries out plans Richard cannot execute personally. But Buckingham's deceit comes at a cruel price, and illustrates a phenomenon demonstrated throughout the history plays: a character who works for someone deceitful inevitably becomes a victim of deceit. "Honor among thieves" does not apply to this world. Buckingham knows what Richard is, but never imagines that Richard will turn on him. And when Richard does turn, the reversal leaves Buckingham stunned.

At this moment, however, Buckingham is comfortable in his association with Richard, who traipses in with such insouciance as to ridicule the gathering and his brother's condition:

Good morrow to my sovereign king and queen,
And, princely peers, a happy time of day.

(II, i, 47–48)

Especially outlandish is his reflection on his own character:

I do not know that Englishman alive
With whom my soul is any jot at odds
More than the infant that is born to-night.
I thank my God for my humility.

(II, i, 70–73)

The word "humility" is offered with such brazen delight that we find ourselves enjoying this character's behavior far more than we feel we should.

When Richard casually reveals Clarence's death (II, i, 80), he shares the general shock by expressing grief that the order for execution was not rescinded on time, as Edward had commanded, adding:

God grant that some, less noble and less loyal,
Nearer in bloody thoughts, [but] not in blood,
Deserve not worse than wretched Clarence did,
And yet go current from suspicion.

(II, i, 92–95)

Richard seems to require the tension of living dangerously, uttering comments that mock uninformed listeners, but which if overheard by the wrong people could do him in.

How appropriate, then, that such risky words are followed by the entrance of Lord Stanley, an intriguing figure on the political landscape. Unlike Buckingham, who throws his lot totally with Richard, Stanley presents the appearance of neutrality. He never outwardly commits himself either to Richard or to anyone opposing Richard. Rather he stays loyal to the crown, England, and the good of the populace. He is the professional politician, the perpetual party insider, who never enjoys the intoxicating joys of absolute power, but always

enjoys the moderate pleasures of close association with power. He never takes
risks that might push him to the top, but he avoids risks that might leave him
vulnerable from below. When we reflect that Stanley's son Richmond eventually brings down Richard, Stanley's neutrality becomes a lesson in political
survival.

He enters with the request that a servant's life be spared. The petition, innocent enough, nevertheless reveals to Edward his helplessness: he can spare
this life but not save his own brother's (II, i, 103–106). This realization inspires the sense of inevitable punishment that awaits anyone who strives too
greedily for power:

> O God! I fear thy justice will take hold
> On me and you, and mine and yours, for this.
>
> (II, i, 132–133)

Edward's sin is like the Greek concept of *hubris*, or excessive pride, and the
sense of retribution is similar to the Greek belief in punishment for one who
challenges the gods and attempts to exceed his own place in the human community. This occasion is not the last when characters speak of such judgment
awaiting themselves and others.

Even after this extraordinary moment, Richard mocks everyone around him:

> This is the fruits of rashness! Mark'd you not
> How that the guilty kindred of the Queen
> Look'd pale when they did hear of Clarence' death?
> O, they did urge it still unto the King!
> God will revenge it.
>
> (II, i, 135–139)

Indeed, God will revenge, but not as Richard anticipates.

In the next scene we see still further evidence of the disintegration of family,
and, by implication, of the nation, that Richard has wrought. Clarence's children
blame the Duchess of York for their father's death, and they believe the lies
Richard has unleashed (II, ii, 2–26). Thus his poison spreads. News of Edward's
death brings mourning from all, as the Duchess of York and the Queen dwell
especially heavily on the cycle of historical punishment (II, ii, 39–61). But
Rivers remains practical and warns Elizabeth:

> Madam, bethink you like a careful mother
> Of the young Prince your son. Send straight for him,
> Let him be crown'd, in him your comfort lives.
>
> (II, ii, 96–98)

Rivers never speaks directly of Richard, but the implication of his threat is
palpable.

Appropriately, Richard enters at this moment, full of sanctimony, as he offers
outrageous sympathy to Elizabeth:

Sister, have comfort. All of us have cause
To wail the dimming of our shining star.

(II, ii, 100–101)

Then he asks his mother: "Humbly on my knee/ I crave your blessing" (II, ii, 105–106). Her gracious response earns only a satiric aside:

That is the butt-end of a mother's blessing.
I marvel that her Grace did leave it out.

(II, ii, 110–111)

Business takes precedence almost immediately, though, as Buckingham proposes that the young Prince head to London with "some little train" (II, ii, 123), then dismisses Rivers' reservation by implying that for safety's sake the transfer should not arouse public notice (II, ii, 124–131). Then Buckingham adds that Richard and he should go retrieve the Prince from Ludlow, and Richard agrees with enthusiasm: "My oracle, my prophet, my dear cousin . . . " (II, ii, 152). Richard's apparent acquiescence and flattery should not surprise us. By playing the sycophant, he brings Buckingham closer, ensures Buckingham's loyalty, and removes any suspicion from himself. Furthermore, the more responsibility Buckingham assumes, the greater his dependence on Richard, the greater his vulnerability when away from Richard, and the greater his need for Richard's good will.

Scene iii demonstrates a typical Shakespearean strategy: moving away from the central action to offer commentary by minor figures who reflect the greater themes. Here three citizens weigh the state of their nation, and their conversation reinforces that what the masses desire is order. To that end the first Citizen hopes that Edward's child will rule successfully (II, iii, 10). The third Citizen, however, remembering the reign of Henry VI, and perhaps of the young Richard II, knows the risks of inexperienced rule: "Woe to that land that's govern'd by a child!" (II, iii, 11). Citizen Three also articulates fears of Richard (II, iii, 27–30). But then this same citizen offers a hope that underlies these plays:

Before the days of change, still is it so.
By a divine instinct men's minds mistrust
Ensuing danger; as by proof we see
The water swell before a boist'rous storm.
But leave it all to God.

(II, III, 41–45)

Chaos, abusive management, salvation: such is the story of the England of the history plays.

In the next scene youthful Duke of York, son of the late King, and younger brother to the Prince, demonstrates his vigor by commenting derisively on his uncle, Richard (II, iv, 27–30). Such boldness wins our admiration, but also leads us to suspect that this outspoken child will not last long in Richard's world. The dangers of that society become apparent when we learn that Lord Rivers and Lord Grey, as well as Sir Thomas Vaughan, have been taken prisoner to Pomfret Castle, where many others, including Richard II, have died. The events echo the fears of the Third Citizen in the previous scene. Queen Elizabeth states deeper significance:

> Ay me! I see the ruin of my house:
> The tiger now hath seiz'd the gentle hind;
> Insulting tyranny begins to jut
> Upon the innocent and aweless throne.
> Welcome, destruction, blood and massacre!
> I see (as in a map) the end of all.
>
> (II, iv, 49–54)

Her desperation, couched in familiar animal imagery and in the context of the destruction of the family, strikes resounding themes. The nation is turning on itself, as the Duchess clarifies:

> And being seated, and domestic broils
> Clean overblown, themselves, the conquerors,
> Make war upon themselves, brother to brother,
> Blood to blood, self against self.
>
> (II, iv, 60–63)

The agent of this destruction is Richard, yet to reach the apex of his power.

In Act III he resumes his drive upward. In scene i he welcomes the young Prince, who is immediately suspicious: "I want more uncles here to welcome me" (III, i, 6). Richard claims unctuously that the privacy of the meeting is for the Prince's own protection from dangerous foes: "God keep you from them, and from such false friends" (III, i, 15). But the Prince remains unconvinced, and inquires about his mother and younger brother (III, i, 20–23). When the Mayor enters to report that they have taken sanctuary, Buckingham innocently asks for the young Duke of York to be sent here, and urges Hastings to ensure that move. The strategy is obviously intended to separate the children from their surviving parent. The Cardinal protests, but Buckingham convinces, or rather bullies, him into believing no sanctuary is necessary for one so young (III, i, 44–56). Meanwhile Richard continues maneuvering, and casually urges the Prince to retreat to the Tower of London. Edward is resistant, but eventually Richard connives so that both the Prince and young York are to head off to the Tower. The most telling line of this part of the scene is Richard's offhand statement about his own nature:

> Thus, like the formal Vice, Iniquity,
> I moralize two meanings in one word.
>
> (III, i, 82–83)

This self-awareness places him both psychologically and theatrically in the tradition of that character.

The Prince is reluctant to proceed to a place built by Julius Caesar (III, i, 68–69), but his protests are to little good. Nonetheless, we admire this bravery:

And if I live until I be a man,
I'll win our ancient right in France again,
Or die a soldier as I liv'd a king

(III, i, 91–93)

In response Richard offers a characteristic aside: "Short summers lightly have a forward spring" (III, i, 94). His joy in the knowledge that the Prince's life is soon to be cut off reflects Richard at his most sinister. When the Young Duke of York is brought in, he, too, is dubious, and his repartee with Richard is full of double meaning. For instance, the boy asks, "I pray you, uncle, give me this dagger" (III, i, 110), and Richard responds, "My dagger, little cousin? with all my heart" (III, i, 111). Even as we are revolted by Richard's eagerness to destroy these boys, the irony of his lines is compelling. The young York has his own reasons for avoiding the Tower, since he has been told that his uncle Clarence was murdered there (III, i, 144–145), but nonetheless both the Prince and the Duke head to that fatal place.

In the latter half of the scene Richard, Buckingham, and Catesby are left together, and Buckingham orders Catesby to probe Hastings' feelings (III, 1, 169–180). Richard seconds the plan, and Catesby leaves with absolute obedience. Buckingham, however, is not so compliant, and here he miscalculates. He expects favors, and does not hide his own ambition. He even goes so far as to extract a promise from Richard:

And look when I am king, claim thou of me
The earldom of Herford, and all the moveables
Whereof the King my brother was possess'd.

(III, i, 194–196)

Richard's tone drips resentment, for a man such as he cannot be pleased to be in debt to anyone. Buckingham makes an elementary political misjudgment, one Catesby avoids. Catesby does not ask favors. He restricts himself to following orders, never becoming personal, never insinuating that his service warrants reward. He wordlessly implies that the privilege to serve is enough. Buckingham, on the other hand, expects a bonus, and when he says "I'll claim that promise at your Grace's hand," (III, i, 197), he exerts too much independence, pushing his own priorities to the forefront, insinuating that he and Richard are equals in their enterprises, and trusting a man he knows to be untrustworthy.

In scene ii Hastings learns from a messenger that Stanley has had an ominous dream about a boar, the animal traditionally associated with Richard. Hastings, however, ignores the advice to flee, and his lack of circumspection is soon to cost him his life. First he foolishly trusts Catesby, one of his serving-men, who sounds Hastings out. Catesby insinuates that Richard alone can right the state (III, ii, 39–40), and Hastings carelessly speaks forth:

I'll have this crown of mine cut from my shoulders
Before I'll see the crown so foul misplac'd.

But canst thou guess that he doth aim at it?

(III, ii, 43–45)

Even when told of the deaths of members of the Queen's family (III, ii, 50), Hastings does not retract his words, and Catesby's quiet remark (III, ii, 69–70) seals Hastings' fate.

Consider Hastings' quick words in contrast to the measured responses of Stanley, who enters here as stealthily as he moves throughout the play. Hastings is the headstrong man who pays the price for his outspokenness. Stanley, on the other hand, says nothing that could be taken as opposition to Richard. For instance, he comments on the attitude of the three men taken to Pomfret:

They, for their truth, might better wear their heads
Than some that have accus'd them wear their hats.

(III, ii, 92–93)

The eventual prevailing of Stanley suggests that in politics well-tempered deception rather than honesty is the path to progress. The scene ends with Buckingham heading off for the Tower, accompanied by a naive Hastings.

Scene iii is an interlude that reinforces for the audience the historical inevitability of events taking place. The executions at Pomfret remind the condemned Rivers of the death of Richard II, and Grey recalls Margaret's curse. Once again we remember that the disposition of a lawful King led to all this bloodshed.

In scene iv Hastings pays severely for his indiscretion. Before the scheduled meeting, he boasts of his friendship with Richard, and offers to speak on his behalf (III, iv, 14–20). When Richard then enters, Buckingham communicates Hastings' assurance (III, iv, 27–28). For no apparent reason, Richard requests that some strawberries be brought in, allowing himself a chance to confer with Buckingham, confirm Catesby's report, and step aside to follow through on appropriate action against Hastings. All is conducted with such smoothness that we are hardly aware of what is taking place. Stanley, however, ever cautious, voices general suspicions (III, iv, 42–45), but these are feeble in light of what follows.

When Richard returns, his cheerful demeanor suddenly darkens. He holds up his withered left arm, blames his deformity on witchcraft, and accuses Hastings of conspiring with the notorious witch Jane Shore. Why is Richard's claim so quickly accepted? Because Richard has created an atmosphere of mistrust in which everyone is suspect. Thus when a man like Hastings is accused, the safest course for those who hear the accusation is to join it. To stand aside is to turn the apprehension on one's self. And in such a perilous environment, casting any doubt is regarded as treason. Hastings recalls the various signs of disaster that he ignored (III, iv, 80–93), then leaves for execution with a warning for all those too weak to stand up beside him:

O bloody Richard! Miserable England!
I prophesy the fearfull'st time to thee
That ever wretched age hath look'd upon.
Come, lead me to the block; bear him my head.

They smile at me who shortly shall be dead.

> (III, iv, 103–107)

Hastings is hardly innocent, for he, too, stood by while Margaret's son, young Edward, was slain. But Richard's ruthlessness remains startling.

In scene v, after Hastings' death, Richard and Buckingham perform a bizarre charade, as they stage a battle against imaginary enemies loyal to Hastings. They carry on so for the benefit of the Mayor, and Richard takes pains to justify the execution of Hastings:

> But that the extreme peril of the case,
> The peace of England, and our persons' safety,
> Enforc'd us to this execution?

> (III, v, 44–46)

Buckingham then urges that Richard's cause be taken to the people, and the Mayor blindly agrees:

> And do not doubt, right noble princes both,
> But I'll acquaint our duteous citizens
> With all your just proceedings in this [cause].

> (III, v, 64–66)

Richard still needs mass support. He knows that the power of the people should not be ignored by someone who seeks to exercise power of his own. The commoners may at times warrant contempt, but never should they be overlooked.

With Hastings eliminated, Richard moves to rid himself of Edward's children. His first tactic is comparatively indirect: he orders Buckingham to spread rumors about Edward's profligacy and thereby cast doubt on the legitimacy of the offspring (III, v, 74–75). Richard's warped nature is revealed in his language as he delineates the scheme to Buckingham:

> Moreover, urge his hateful luxury
> And bestial appetite in change of lust,
> Which stretch'd unto their servants, daughters, wives,
> Even where his raging eye or savage heart,
> Without control, lusted to make a prey.

> (III, v, 80–84)

The almost pornographic description reminds us again of Iago, who on many occasions speaks of sexuality in such ugly terms. Both men take out their emotional frustrations by demeaning the actions and emotions of others. Richard's strategy of rumor, however, is only a prelude.

In the brief scene vi, the scrivener finishes writing the indictment of Hastings, who was already executed. The episode further underlies the complete illegality of Richard's actions. However, the scrivener also warns that anyone aware of the corruption will probably be shrewd enough to remain silent, a testament to the power of the fear Richard exploits.

In scene vii Richard learns that Buckingham, despite slander of Edward and praise of Richard, was unsuccessful in rousing sufficient crowd approval for Richard's ascension to the throne (III, vii, 25–27). In response to Buckingham's suggestion, Richard plans his most outlandish public gesture: appearing before the masses positioned between two ministers, while Buckingham, on cue, will beg him to accept the crown (III, vii, 48–51).

The mayor enters, followed closely by Catesby, who describes Richard's supposed preoccupation:

> He is within, with two right reverend fathers,
> Divinely bent to meditation,
> And in no worldly suits would he be mov'd,
> To draw him from his holy exercise.
>
> (III, vii, 61–64)

Buckingham continues the charade by urging Catesby to bring Richard before them, so eager is everyone to see him, and while Catesby hurries away, Buckingham continues to praise Richard in the most extravagant religious terms (III, vii, 92–94).

Richard's subsequent appearance is astonishing for several reasons. The sheer theatricality is brilliant, as Richard seizes what seems to be a universal political phenomenon, the bond between religion and politics. Whatever the society, the presence of a secular ruler under the sanction of religious authority comforts the populace. Admittedly, in the age of this play the position of king was divinely ordained, but even so we can observe in cultures across history that citizens are reassured when they believe that their political leaders are guided by religious values.

Second, Buckingham's appeal is completely fraudulent. Yet it is phrased with such reverence as to remind all listeners of the holiness of the kingship in the thought of Shakespeare's age:

> The supreme seat, the throne majestical,
> The sceptred office of your ancestors . . .
>
> (III, vii, 118–119)

The speech ends with Buckingham's ostensibly speaking for everyone and urging Richard to take the crown.

Third, as Richard proclaims his unworthiness, he is gloriously ironic. Yet at the same time his words are accurate:

> Yet so much is my poverty of spirit,
> So mighty and so many my defects,
> That I would rather hide me from my greatness—
> Being a bark to brook no mighty sea—
> Than in my greatness covet to be hid
> And in the vapor of my glory smother'd.
>
> (III, vii, 159–164)

His mocking of traditional vows of humility is another of his blasphemies. Buckingham then appeals to Richard on the basis of Edward's sins, and the supposed illegitimacy with which he has corrupted the throne:

Yet to draw forth your noble ancestry
From the corruption of abusing times
Unto a lineal true-derived course.

(III, vii, 198–200)

Even the Mayor takes part in this solicitation, joined by Catesby and Buckingham. Yet clever though Richard and Buckingham's tactics are, they do not incite the enthusiasm of the mob before him. Thus in the funniest moment of the play, Richard interrupts his own oratory and whispers "Call them again" (III, vii, 224) to Catesby, who manages to keep the crowd listening. With feigned reluctance, Richard then accepts the offer to be King, and the mayor heartily approves. Richard's final line of the scene, "Come, let us to our holy work again" (III, vii, 246) encapsulates the gall of his performance. Most significant, however, is Richard's understanding of the art of politics, and the demagoguery he practices has implications for any age.

That Richard is fooling no one who truly knows him is apparent in the next scene. Brakenbury prevents Queen Elizabeth from seeing the young Prince and Duke of York, and in doing so refers to orders of "The King" (IV, i, 17). Elizabeth is shocked, and Brakenbury retracts his statement, but Stanley then enters to escort Lady Anne to her coronation as Queen. Helpless, Elizabeth can only hope for justice to exert itself, as she voices her frustration to Dorset:

Death and destruction dogs thee at thy heels;
Thy mother's name is ominous to children.
If thou wilt outstrip death, go cross the seas,
And live with Richmond, from the reach of hell.
Go hie thee, hie thee from this slaughter-house,
Lest thou increase the number of the dead,
And make me die the thrall of Margaret's curse,
Nor mother, wife, nor England's counted queen.

(IV, i, 39–46)

Here is the first mention of the potential of Richmond, who eventually brings down Richard. Stanley, meanwhile, always playing safe, counsels Anne to proceed with the marriage (IV, i, 47–51). She prefers torture and even death:

Anointed let me be with deadly venom,
And die ere men can say, "God save the Queen!"

(IV, i, 61–62)

Then she tearfully recounts her own suffering and predicts her end:

Besides, he hates me for my father Warwick,
And will, no doubt, shortly be rid of me.

(IV, i, 85–86)

But for someone as cold-blooded as Richard, such opposition is mild. In the next scene he is crowned, and ascends the throne. In one of the play's most chilling moments, Richard summons Buckingham and nonchalantly comments that young Edward still lives. Buckingham does not grasp Richard's innuendo, so the King clarifies his point: "I wish the bastards dead" (IV, ii, 18). For the first time Buckingham hesitates:

> Give me some little breath, some pause, dear lord,
> Before I positively speak in this.
> I will resolve you herein presently.
>
> (IV, ii, 24–26)

Buckingham acts as though Richard has made a request, not given an order. Thus Catesby's comment that the King "gnaws his lip" (IV, ii, 27) tells us that Buckingham has suddenly fallen out of Richard's favor. And anyone out of Richard's favor is doomed.

At Buckingham's momentary weakness, Richard turns to a more professional murderer, Tyrrel, then to himself puts the "witty" Buckingham out of his trust (IV, ii, 42–45). Even as the King plans his next step, Stanley enters to remind him that the Marquess Dorset has joined Richmond's forces. The opposition is gathering. For the moment Richard does not reply. Instead he orders Catesby to spread the report of Lady Anne's illness (IV, ii, 50–56). Already Richard plans her murder and his subsequent marriage to his brother's daughter. The schemes themselves are frightening, but more revealing is Richard's own reaction to them:

> But I am in
> So far in blood that sin will pluck on sin.
> Tear-falling pity dwells not in this eye.
>
> (IV, ii, 63–65)

Here he sounds uncannily like Macbeth, who also finds himself numbed by his own villainy:

> I am in blood
> Stepp'd in so far that, should I wade no more,
> Returning were as tedious as go o'er.
>
> (*Macbeth*, III, iv, 135–137)

Both reach a point of no return. Once they have murdered, they are driven to do so again and again.

Richard's command to Tyrrel is blunt: "I mean those bastards in the Tower" (IV, ii, 75). But while giving this order Richard emphasizes another point that links him with Macbeth as well as with Edward IV: the inability to sleep (IV, ii, 73). The antithesis to Richard's nervousness is Stanley's calmness. Richard warns him about Dorset's joining Richmond: "Stanley, he is your wive's son: well, look unto it" (IV, ii, 87). As usual, Stanley does not reply but quietly keeps his distance.

Such shrewdness is not the approach of Buckingham, who here makes his last error when he seizes this moment to press Richard for the earldom previously promised. With comic distaste Richard refuses to acknowledge his erstwhile crony's interruptions (IV, ii, 88–91, 94, 99, 101, 108), then dismisses him contemptuously: "I am not in the giving vein today" (IV, ii, 116) Buckingham is barely able to control his fury:

> And is it thus? repays he my deep service
> With such contempt? Made I him king for this?

> (IV, ii, 119–120)

His experience reinforces a lesson these plays emphasize strongly: those who support corruption are eventually undone by corruption.

In scene iii, Tyrrel returns, having murdered Edward's two sons. We might expect him to feel minimal remorse, given that he is a professional assassin. Instead, he is haunted by the faces of the two boys and angry that he must report to the "bloody King" (IV, iii, 22). Richard, however, has no regrets. Indeed, he seeks to revel in the details (IV, iii, 31–35). Thus the contrast between him and Tyrrel confirms that Richard has now moved beyond all human feeling.

No historical evidence exists to establish beyond question that Richard was responsible for these two murders. But Tudor tradition held that he was the perpetrator. His motivation is no mystery, for the boys, sons of his older brother, would always be a threat to his place on the throne. In any case, in 1674 two small skeletons were found in the Tower of London, and these were assumed to have been the remains of the young men.

At this point in the play, with Richard at his moral nadir, the forces in opposition gain momentum. First Ratcliffe reports:

> Bad news, my lord. Morton is fled to Richmond,
> and Buckingham, back'd with the hardy Welshmen,
> Is in the field, and still his power increaseth.

> (IV, iii, 46–48)

Richard grows concerned, although not with Buckingham (IV, iii, 49–50). But Margaret's reaction in the beginning of the next scene tells us that retribution is at last on its way:

> So now prosperity begins to mellow
> And drop into the rotten mouth of death.
> Here in these confines slily have I lurk'd,
> To watch the waning of mine enemies.

> (IV, iv, 1-4)

Her hopes open an astounding scene of mourning, as the women recite a dirge of death and pain borne by themselves and by the nation. Two points are of particular interest. One, Margaret expresses her own hopes about Richard:

> Cancel his bond of life, dear God, I pray,
> That I may live and say "The dog is dead."

> (IV, iv, 77–78)

But when Elizabeth tries to share her grief, Margaret turns on her:

I call'd thee then vain flourish of my fortune;
I call'd thee then poor shadow, painted queen,
The presentation of but what I was . . .

(IV, iv, 82–84)

Thou didst usurp my place, and dost thou not
Usurp the just proportion of my sorrow?

(IV, iv, 109–110)

Even in the throes of deepest misery, Margaret does not forgive the woman whom she judges an illicit queen. Political rivalries among women die as hard as those among men.

When Richard enters, he encounters the most profound personal rejection he will meet: that by his own mother. She curses his very existence:

No, by the holy rood, thou know'st it well,
Thou cam'st on earth to make the earth my hell.
A grievous burthen was thy birth to me,
Tetchy and wayward was thy infancy . . .

(IV, iv, 166–169)

Then she disavows him and his life:

Hear me a word;
For I shall never speak to thee again.

(IV, iv, 181–182)

Richard has a one-word answer: "So" (IV, iv, 183). It is perfectly reflective of a character who has denied himself all feeling. Nothing touches him now. Even after his mother curses him again, Richard moves blithely to his next step: acquiring the hand of Elizabeth's daughter, also named Elizabeth.

The Queen initially says "amen" to Margaret's curses (IV, iv, 198), then disdains Richard's request. He nonchalantly denies killing his cousins, then brilliantly touches Elizabeth by answering her question about what good he could do for her: "Th' advancement of your children, gentle lady" (IV, iv, 242). He recognizes her unquenchable desire for power. And in later lines he reiterates this telling point:

I mean that with my soul I love thy daughter,
And do intend to make her Queen of England.

(IV, iv, 263–264)

Elizabeth retorts with a roster of murders committed, she believes, by Richard. But he remains serene:

You mock me, madam, this [is] not the way
To win your daughter.

(IV, iv, 284–285)

Then he adds: "Look what is done cannot be now amended" (IV, iv, 291). Here, too, Richard's admission of an evil past anticipates *Macbeth*, in which

Lady Macbeth phrases the same thought more felicitously: "What's done cannot be undone" (V, ii, 68). And just as Macbeth seeks to possess the throne and all time (III, i, 63–71), so Richard promises Elizabeth:

> Again shall you be mother to a king;
> And all the ruins of distressful times
> Repair'd with double riches of content.

> (IV, iv, 317–319)

As the arguments go back and forth, and with Elizabeth insulting him at virtually every line, Richard stands by a last argument, national security:

> Without her, follows to myself and thee,
> Herself, the land, and many a Christian soul,
> Death, desolation, ruin, and decay.

> (IV, iv, 407–409)

With this barrage he finally persuades her. Is he impressed by his achievement at winning? Hardly: "Relenting fool, and shallow, changing woman" (IV, iv, 431). His mockery is unwavering.

His sense of command is not. For at this point Richard manifests another characteristic of both Macbeth and Lady Macbeth: his mind begins to weaken. He presses Catesby to deliver a message to the Duke of Norfolk, but neglects to give the message itself (IV, iv, 442). Then when asked once more by Catesby, Richard claims to have changed his mind (IV, iv, 456). Only a few lines before, Richard laughed at Elizabeth's changing her mind. This hint of breakdown is followed by the entrance of Stanley, who innocently announces that his son, Richmond, is on the way. Richard challenges Stanley's loyalty (IV, iv, 490–491), but Stanley is too shrewd to take the bait:

> Most mighty sovereign,
> You have no cause to hold my friendship doubtful.
> I never was nor never will be false.

> (IV, iv, 491–493)

Just as Richard begins to collapse inwardly, opposing forces close in from the outside.

The next blow to Richard is the news that Buckingham is leading troops against him. Richard offers a reward for anyone who can bring in that "traitor" (IV, iv, 516), and almost at once, too quickly to be believable, a report comes that Richard's former confederate has been taken. The floods that scattered his army may be taken as one more evidence of divine punishment (IV, iv, 510–513) this time for Buckingham, who transgressed by aiding Richard in all his nefarious schemes. The Act ends with a brief scene in which the forces opposing Richard are uniting. Stanley, however, still proceeds carefully, for if he changes sides too quickly, his son George will be killed by Richard, "the most deadly boar" (IV, v, 2).

The play races along now, so much does Shakespeare have to include, and we are taken directly to Buckingham's execution. The prisoner acknowledges all the lives that have been lost because of his own and Richard's "corrupted foul injustice . . . '' (V, i, 6), then adds ironically that he is about to join the list of victims. He also reflects bitterly that this is All-Souls day, the moment when he at one time anticipated that he would possess the throne, or at least some of its power. Then he remembers Margaret's curse (V, i, 25). Yet Buckingham never expresses true remorse. He regrets his sins, and that matters have worked out so badly, but we do not feel that he wishes he had led his life differently, or that had he the opportunity he would have chosen another path. What seems to bother him is not his succession of errors but the unfortunate twists of events that have gone against him. Thus in his view he goes to the "block of shame" (V, i, 28) not because he was immoral or destructive but because his plans did not turn out as he had intended. Like Beaufort before him, Buckingham offers no last-minute conversion or change of heart.

Scene ii of Act V marks the initial appearance of Richmond, and his words bring a new voice. Twice he speaks "in God's name" (V, ii, 14, 22), and his concerns are for the country, not himself. Richmond, however, stays a figure-head. His function is as a contrast to Richard, and as such he is thematically vital but dramatically flat.

Richard, though, remains of interest, and in scene iii he rallies his disheartened troops. The time is August of 1485, the place Bosworth Field. Richard points to the overwhelming size of his forces (V, iii, 11), and the very fact of the kingship as further support. But on the other side Richmond notes a new day:

> The weary sun hath made a golden set,
> And by the bright tract of his fiery car
> Gives token of a goodly day to-morrow.
>
> (V, iii, 19–21)

His image suggests that Richard's reign is soon to end. And with warm embraces he takes his men inside to prepare for the next day's battle.

Richard, however, still plots. He sends Catesby to warn Stanley that unless his forces join with Richard's, Stanley's son will be executed (V, iii, 60–62). Yet even though his generals Northumberland and Surrey are attempting to inspire their troops, Richard himself is growing dejected:

> I have not that alacrity of spirit
> Nor cheer of mind that I was wont to have.
>
> (V, iii, 73–74)

We feel the consequences of all his actions weighing him down. Meanwhile Stanley visits Richmond's tent, bringing blessing from Richmond's mother, and apologies from Stanley himself that because of the predicament of his other son George, Stanley cannot join the forces in opposition to the King (V, iii, 94–96). The holy nature of Richmond's quest is apparent in his soliloquy (V, iii, 108–117), as his battle hopes are phrased in religious terms.

In depicting Richard's end, Shakespeare again anticipates the plight of Macbeth, as Richard and Richmond are both visited by the Ghosts of Richard's victims. But whereas Macbeth is haunted by Banquo alone, Richard is set upon by so many figures that the effect is to an extent negated. Still, after the series of curses on Richard and blessings on Richmond, one more remarkable moment awaits: Richard's coming to grips with his life.

His soliloquy is not easy to follow, for he is not in control of what he says. Nevertheless, certain lines are telling:

> What do I fear? Myself? There's none else by.
> Richard loves Richard, that is, I [am] I.

> (V, iii, 182–183)

In *Henry VI, Part III*, Richard's self-reliance was a source of pride. Now it is cause for fear because he feels his smallness and helplessness.

> Is there a murtherer here? No. Yes, I am.
> Then fly. What, from myself? Great reason why—
> Lest I revenge. What, myself upon myself?
> Alack, I love myself. Wherefore? For any good
> That I myself have done unto myself?

> (V, iii, 184–188)

He realizes that he has created his own hell. He also speaks for the first time of a conscience. Previously he relished his amorality. Now he is haunted by guilt:

> My conscience hath a thousand several tongues,
> And every tongue brings in a several tale,
> And every tale condemns me for a villain.

> (V, iii, 193–195)

Here is another place where Richard differs from the other Shakespearean character he resembles most, Iago. Othello's tormentor never articulates such pangs, for he is never able to deal honestly with his own self. Richard, on the other hand, has insight into part of his makeup.

He also understands something else:

> I shall despair; there is no creature loves me,
> And if I die no soul will pity me.
> And wherefore should they, since that I myself
> Find in myself no pity to myself?

> (V, iii, 200–203)

He grasps the loneliness and lack of love that has marked his life. In speaking this way he does not minimize his villainy, nor does he weaken his resolve to fight to the death. Yet this one speech does to a degree humanize Richard, and we might even feel sympathy for him. He is, after all, a brilliant presence, and we are sorry to lose that.

After this speech, Richard confesses his fears to Ratcliffe (V, iii, 216–

222), and his terrors anticipate his inevitable downfall. Richmond, in contrast, feels his confidence increasing after the succession of ghostly visits, and offers a rallying address to his troops. It is full of patriotic fervor, but also a statement of orthodox belief about the nature of kingship. The emphasis is on the relationship between King and God, and Richard is characterized as "God's enemy" (V, iii, 252). Richmond also brings out strongly the theme of home and family (V, iii, 259–262). What he lacks is the poetic flair that sparks the speeches of similar intent and theme that are the hallmark of Henry V.

Richard's call to his forces is far less noble. He accuses the men of weakness, and his vision of both his country and his people is extraordinarily hostile. We note that Richard, too, mentions wives and children, but from a different perspective:

> Shall these enjoy our lands? lie with our wives?
> Ravish our daughters?
>
> (V, iii, 336–337)

Even at such a moment his mind follows its own twisted course. Yet his speech is stirring in its fury, and we can imagine troops being aroused to unparalleled violence. The scene ends with the news that Stanley has refused to bring his forces with Richard's, but the King is convinced to wait until after the fighting for the execution of George, Stanley's son.

When Richard dives into battle, he does so with the ironic bravura characteristic of his life: "A horse, a horse! my kingdom for a horse!" (V, iv, 13). He has always been a fighter, and he never surrenders, not even at this moment before forces greater than his own.

Richmond's triumph is notable for several reasons. One, his second line in scene v, "the bloody dog is dead" (V, v, 2), recalls Margaret's curse (IV, iii, 78), and helps provide the play and the tetralogy with a sense of unity. More contributive to that unity is Richmond's final address, which emphasizes the fusion of the houses of York and Lancaster, a union he phrases in terms of family. First he reminds us of the price England has paid:

> England hath long been mad and scarr'd herself:
> The brother blindly shed the brother's blood,
> The father rashly slaughter'd his own son,
> The son, compell'd, been butcher to the sire.
>
> (V, v, 23–26)

As we remember the four plays, we come across numerous specific instances that amplify these general truths. Then Richmond looks to the glorious future:

> And let their heirs (God, if thy will be so)
> Enrich the time to come with smooth-fac'd peace,

With smiling plenty, and fair prosperous days!

(V, v, 32–34)

He concludes by speaking of the country in terms of religious idealism, ending the play with divine blessing.

The power of this work, aside from theme, is in the title character. That historically Richard struggled to give restitution to landowners, tried to correct imbalances in the courts, and served as a patron of the arts were qualities ignored by the Tudor historians and absent from Shakespeare's portrayal, which has an expressly political purpose. *Richard III*, as well as the other parts of the tetralogy, warns England about the dangers of misrule and the frightful consequences of political disorder. Throughout the four plays, all potential rulers, including Richard, are conscious of the power of the masses. Richard himself rules with the approval of the public. Thus we see acknowledgement that the influence of the populace grows, but not its judgment.

We are also aware of the nature of the struggle for political power, and how proximity to power brings out drives and instincts that lie within virtually everyone. Some temper their ambition and subordinate it to the good of the country. But the few who do, such as Talbot and Gloucester, may well pay with their lives. Still, such sacrifices serve the greater cause, for by the end of these plays order is restored. The divine help to which Henry VI prays and that Richmond invokes does not fade away. The faith in law articulated by the Duke of Gloucester is not to be scorned. What society ought to seek is a central authority, ideally benign, but necessarily strong. That is what the nation wants, and that is what it needs.

SUGGESTIONS FOR FURTHER READING

Arnold, Aerol. "The Recapitulation Dream in *Richard III* and *Macbeth*." *Shakespeare Quarterly* VI (1955): 51–62.

Clemen, Wolfgang. *A Commentary on Shakespeare's* Richard III.

Haeffner, Paul. *A Critical Commentary on Shakespeare's* Richard III. London: Macmillan, 1966.

Hamilton, A. C. *The Early Shakespeare*. San Marino, California: The Huntington Library, 1967.

Law, Robert Adger. "Richard III: A Study in Shakespeare's Composition." *PMLA* LX (1945): 689–696.

Spivack, Bernard. *Shakespeare and the Allegory of Evil*. New York: Columbia University Press, 1958.

Toole, William B. "The Motif of Psychic Division in *Richard III*." *Shakespeare Survey* XXVII (1974): 21–32.

KING JOHN

King John is concerned with many of the same issues dramatized in Shakespeare's other history plays: the problem of an inadequate ruler, legal succession versus right by might, and fear of social chaos. Yet *King John* is for several reasons singular among these works. Its date of composition is uncertain, but the play is likely the middle piece between the two tetralogies. It is the only history that is set not against the background of the York-Lancaster rivalry and the generations succeeding, but against events that occurred roughly 100 years before. Finally, this history is the only one based on another play, *The Troublesome Reign of John, King of England*, an anonymous work published in 1591. Shakespeare was strongly influenced by the earlier piece, and perhaps that is why this play is burdened by difficulties. In fact, its lack of organization and energy has been taken as indication that Shakespeare wrote it under some obligation.

Whatever the reason, the play suffers from at least two defects. One, no single character grips audience attention. The title figure is a usurper, at times greedy and determined, but not of sufficient stature to hold center stage for long. Furthermore, his tentative acts at times clash with the boldness of his statements, and his motivations are difficult to ascertain. John should not be judged a profound character; rather he is a confusing one. In addition, the play has far too much talk about politics and too little action in politics. Many characters lack vigor, and their speeches tend to be wordy and flat. The result is a work thematically reflective of Shakespeare's view of history and kingship, but theatrically not always gripping.

In terms of historical accuracy, Shakespeare's John, although unsympathetic, does not match the incompetence and cruelty of the real King, often judged the worst monarch ever to sit on the English throne. He lost great expanses of territory won by Henry II, ruled in perpetual conflict with the English church over his own divorce and other issues, and outraged his nobles with taxation and additional demands. Eventually these abuses caused the aristocracy to unite against him, an uprising that led to the creation of the Magna Charta in 1215. Even that document, however, did not stop John, and in reneging on it he further plundered the lands of his nobles. In desperation they offered the crown of England to King Louis of France, who attempted to take it from John. In 1216 John died during that struggle. Had he survived six months longer, England likely would have lost all its territory in France.

Shakespeare's version of this monarch is not so harsh, although from the first lines of the play, which begins in 1199, his point of vulnerability is clear, as Chatillion the French ambassador refers to John as "borrowed majesty" (I, i, 4). Here is the critical argument of the play, for by order of primogeniture the English throne belongs to Arthur, Duke of Britain, son of Richard the Lion-hearted's next-oldest brother and nephew to John. But John, second-oldest brother of Richard, has seized the crown. Indeed, so militant is his claim that he announces himself willing to go to war to retain it (I, i, 19–20). Even his mother, Elinor, recognizes that by legal rights the throne belongs to Arthur (I, i, 40–41). But John's resolve may be seen in two lines in which he communicates the extent to which he is prepared to fight:

> Our abbeys and our priories shall pay
> This [expedition's] charge.

> (I, i, 48–49)

Here is John's combination of ruthlessness and determination. He has the courage to steal from churches, and he breaks laws to secure his position. Arthur, on the other hand, reveals himself weak on several counts, and this dilemma gives rise to the central question. Who is preferable on the throne: the aggressive if illegitimate John, or the legitimate but passive Arthur? Neither proves satisfactory.

A new voice appears in the next few lines, with the entrance of Philip the Bastard. His legitimacy, too, is in doubt: Is he the illegitimate son of Robert Faulconbridge and entitled to part of that family fortune? After John weighs the evidence, he surmises correctly that Philip is in fact the bastard son of Richard the Lionhearted (I, i, 128–129). Philip immediately renounces the inferior Faulconbridge inheritance and aligns himself with the royal family. He is accepted as a Plantagenet and renamed Sir Richard. Nonetheless, throughout the play he is referred to as "the Bastard," and will be so designated here.

What is curious about the Bastard's character is that he was virtually created by Shakespeare, a rare strategy in a historical play. Furthermore, the bastard traditionally was an evil figure, an outsider whose existence affirmed the positive virtues of the other characters. In this play, however, the Bastard is the hero. First, he is loyal to the throne. Not loyal to the individual who occupies the throne, but to the throne itself. This fidelity emerges from his devotion to his real father, as he explains at the end of the opening scene to his mother:

> Now by this light, were I to get again,
> Madam, I would not wish a better father.

> (I, i, 259–260)

Whatever steps the Bastard takes, he thinks in terms of what is good for the country, and this attitude sets him apart from John. Second, during the play the

Bastard is outside the primary action, and through his ironic perspective he becomes the moral ballast for a work that otherwise lacks an ethical center. Finally, the Bastard stands for a sense of political reality. He bears resemblance to the traditionally malevolent schemer, but his instincts and values are fundamentally benign. Thus he is the political realist whose aggression is modified by morality. As he himself explains:

> But this is worshipful society,
> And fits the mounting spirit like myself;
> For he is but a bastard to the time
> That doth not [smack] of observation—
> And so am I, whether I smack or no;
> And not alone in habit and device,
> Exterior form, outward accoutrement,
> But from the inward motion to deliver
> Sweet, sweet, sweet poison for the age's tooth,
> Which though I will not practice to deceive,
> Yet to avoid deceit, I mean to learn;
> For it shall strew the footsteps of my rising.
>
> (I, i, 205–216)

This sentiment is vital, for when the Bastard eventually does take charge, his behavior is legitimate even if his birth is not.

From the beginning of Act II the play becomes talky, as characters move from threat to debate and back again to threat. At the opening, Philip, King of France, restates his support for Arthur's claim to the English throne, and this assertion is backed by the Duke of Austria (II, i, 19–31), whose slaying of Richard the Lionhearted led to John's takeover. Austria advocates his cause with a spirited cry, the sort that in Shakespeare's later plays becomes the object of satire:

> The peace of heaven is theirs that lift their swords
> In such a just and charitable war.
>
> (II, i, 35–36)

The more we see, the more such enthusiasm for killing seems foolish. That attitude is maintained when Chatillion enters, for although he warns that the English are arming heavily, his tone suggests that he views war as having a certain grandeur:

> In brief, a braver choice of dauntless spirits
> Than now the English bottoms have waft o'er
> Did never float upon the swelling tide
> To do offense and scathe in Christendom.
>
> (II, i, 72–75)

The only reluctant note is sounded by Constance, Arthur's mother, who at this moment eschews unnecessary bloodshed:

> My Lord Chatillion may from England bring
> That right in peace which here we urge in war,

And then we shall repent each drop of blood
That hot rash haste so indirectly shed.

(II, i, 46–49)

But when Arthur's petition is denied, her pacific tone changes and complements the violent words of John's mother, Elinor of Aquitaine. Both women resound throughout this play with a note of wailing similar to that of the women of *Richard III*. Here, though, the effect is different. In *Richard III* the women were opposed to a demonic force, Richard, and their recitations of death and doom had a tragic quality. In *King John* the two women bemoan the fates of their sons alone, neither of whom seems worthy of such passion, let alone the office for which they compete. Thus the mothers sound shrill rather than noble. Indeed, Chatillion clarifies that Elinor is the motivating spirit behind John:

With him along is come the mother-queen,
An [Ate], stirring him to blood and strife . . .

(II, i, 62–63)

Ate was the Greek goddess of discord.

With John's entrance in Act II, scene i, the issue of legitimacy is dramatized by Philip in terms familiar from other history plays. First he mentions family and children:

But thou from loving England art so far
That thou has under-wrought his lawful king,
Cut off the sequence of posterity,
Outfaced infant state, and done a rape
Upon the maiden virtue of the crown.

(II, i, 94–98)

Here, as in the first tetralogy, destruction of the state is likened to destruction of the family. Then Philip reaffirms the place of God in the issue of royal succession. He points towards the city of Angiers ("this" [II, i, 106]), and speaks of it as coming to Arthur from God. The implication is that John, by claiming possession, is going against divine will. John's retort would stir Shakespeare's audience: that Philip is using support from the Church to interfere in English political life (II, i, 118). Thus one problem this play poses is Shakespeare's attitude toward John: he has taken the crown by usurpation, but he is an Englishman heroically opposing the Church of Rome.

Immediately Elinor and Constance clash, both accusing each other and the other's son of moral delinquency. This domination by the two mothers emphasizes the strength of the Bastard, whose healthier relationship with his mother was dramatized in Act I. Furthermore, the women's tirades are undercut by the ironic comments of the Bastard to the intruding Duke of Austria:

I'll smoke your skin-coat and I catch you right.
Sirrah, look to't, i'faith I will, i' faith.

(II, i, 139–140)

It remains for Philip to silence everyone and restate the key issue, which, to the play's detriment, tends to be lost amid diatribes the characters toss at one another:

Women and fools, break off your conference.
King John, this is the very sum of all:
England and Ireland, [Anjou], Touraine, Maine,
In right of Arthur do I claim of thee.
Wilt thou resign them and lay down thy arms?

(II, i, 150–154)

John accepts the challenge, but in a peculiar way, apparently seeking to avoid battle by offering Arthur friendship:

Arthur of Britain, yield thee to my hand,
And out of my dear love I'll give thee more
Than e'er the coward hand of France can win.

(II, i, 156–158)

Here John's character becomes more confusing. Does he make this offer out of fear of warfare? Is he more bluster than courage? Or is he using tactics to win over someone he knows is weak, namely Arthur? As the play progresses, the problem grows knottier.

Arthur gives us no such difficulties, for he is obviously feeble. As arguments rage about him, he seeks refuge:

Good my mother, peace.
I would that I were low laid in my grave,
I am not worth this coil that's made for me.

(II, i, 163–165)

Such vulnerability only arouses more antagonism between the two women, while John's inability to intercede emphasizes his ineffectiveness.

The tone of the scene alters with the appearance of Hubert and the other citizens of Angiers, for now the conflict leaves the immediate circle of royals and moves into the realm of the populace. John once again stakes his claim, insisting that he is "lawful King" (II, i, 222) and promising protection if the town stands by him. Philip counters that Arthur is the rightful king and offers protection of his own, but adds that if the citizens do not go to his side, the French will attack (II, i, 265–266). Here Shakespeare draws a subtle but important distinction so that his English audience may reflect that at least John does not threaten bloodshed.

Still, the only one to emerge from this scene with dignity is Hubert, sometimes called "the Citizen." This confusion arises over the behavior of Hubert de Burgh later on. Are these characters meant to be the same man? The problem is textual and will be considered presently, but our immediate concern is that the speaker's eloquent strategy stands in contrast to the posturing of the two kings. Hubert's initial reply clarifies the position of his people:

In brief, we are the King of England's subjects:
For him, and in his right, we hold this town.

(II, i, 267–268)

When pressed further he sidesteps both rulers:

> . . . but he that proves the King,
> To him will we prove loyal. Till that time
> Have we ramm'd up our gates against the world.

(II, i, 270–272)

The situation then degenerates into pitched battle but ends quickly and inconclusively. The vital line of this portion is uttered by Hubert: "Blood hath bought blood, and blows have answer'd blows . . . " (II, i, 329). So often in Shakespeare, in the tragedies as well as the histories, one act of destruction inevitably leads to another. Here Hubert alone grasps that fact. The two kings instead begin taunting each other (II, i, 334–349), and their images of violence are in humorous opposition to their impotence.

It remains for the Bastard to conceive the slightly ridiculous plan that both sides join forces against Angiers. The Bastard has an ulterior motive, for if Austria attacks from the North and France from the South, England's two enemies will end up firing on themselves (II, ii, 413–414). Nonetheless, the Bastard has the knack of inspiring the two kings:

> Then, in a moment, Fortune shall cull forth
> Out of one side her happy minion,
> To whom in favor she shall give the day,
> And kiss him with a glorious victory.

(II, i, 391–394)

Such palaver might succeed in energizing John and Philip were it not for Hubert, again the voice of reason, and another of Shakespeare's simple men, honest and decent. Hubert suggests a marriage between Lady Blanch of Spain, a relative of Richard the Lionhearted, and Lewis, son of Philip. Hubert advocates the marriage in language that suggests his understanding of the egos on both sides:

> O, two such silver currents when they join
> Do glorify the banks that bound them in;
> And two such shores to two such streams made one,
> Two such controlling bounds shall you be, kings,
> To these two princes, if you marry them.

(II, i, 441–445)

Eventually the marriage contract is sealed, but the terms and counterterms are almost comically deflationary, in particular by John, who surrenders vast territory to preserve his own hold on the English crown (II, i, 527–532). The Bastard notes the hypocrisy:

> Mad world, mad kings, mad composition!
> John, to stop Arthur's title in the whole,
> Hath willingly departed with a part,
> And France, whose armor conscience buckled on,
> Whom zeal and charity brought to the field
> As God's own soldier, rounded in the ear
> With that same purpose-changer, that sly devil,

That broker that still breaks the pate of faith,
That daily break-vow, he that wins of all,
Of kings, of beggars, old men, young men, maids,
Who having no external thing to lose
But the word "maid," cheats the poor maid of that,
That smooth-fac'd gentleman, tickling commodity . . .

(II, i, 561–573)

Each king has compromised his own nation in the pursuit of private gain. And
the reason, the Bastard articulates, is a word that has ramifications throughout
the history plays: "commodity," i.e., acting according to personal convenience
or advantage:

Commodity, the bias of the world—
The world, who of itself is peized well,
Made to run even upon even ground,
Till this advantage, this vile-drawing bias,
This sway of motion, this commodity,
Makes it take head from all indifferency,
From all direction, purpose, course, intent—
And this same bias, this commodity,
This bawd, this broker, this all-changing word,
Clapp'd on the outward eye of fickle France,
Hath drawn him from his own determin'd aid,
From a resolv'd and honorable war
To a most base and vile-concluded peace.

(II, i, 574–586)

He states here, with his own sense of discovery, what is dramatized over and
over in the first and second tetralogies. Throughout these works politicians and
those aspiring to power deal from commodity. Here the Bastard speaks for all
characters who modulate idealism with political reality as well as for all who
curb private ambition because of potential public reaction.

We also note recognition of his own drives:

Well, whiles I am a beggar, I will rail,
And say there is no sin but to be rich;
And being rich, my virtue then shall be
To say there is no vice but beggary.
Since kings break faith upon commodity,
Gain, be my lord, for I will worship thee.

(II, i, 593–598)

He sees a timeless verity of human nature: that those who do not have power
resent those who do, while those who have power automatically resent those
who seek to take it away. That the Bastard acknowledges such instincts in himself
demonstrates an honesty rare in these plays.

In contrast to the Bastard's perception is Constance's wailing, which dominates
the first scene of Act III. In particular she bemoans the ill fate of her son, Arthur:

But thou art fair, and at thy birth, dear boy,
Nature and Fortune join'd to make thee great.
Of Nature's gifts thou mayest with lilies boast,
And with the half-blown rose. But Fortune, O,
She is corrupted, chang'd, and won from thee;
Sh' adulterates hourly with thine uncle John,
And with her golden hand hath pluck'd on France
To tread down fair respect of sovereignty,
And made his majesty the bawd to theirs.

(III, i, 51–59)

In light of Arthur's inability to take any action, Constance's extravagant praise of his virtues seems misguided. Throughout this scene her words have energy, but she rambles on at such length and high pitch that she exhausts us. Even when the wedding party enters, Constance continues her tirade:

Arm, arm, you heavens, against these perjur'd kings!
A widow cries; be husband to me, heavens!
Let not the hours of this ungodly day
Wear out the [day] in peace; but ere sunset,
Set armed discord 'twixt these perjur'd kings!
Hear me, O, hear me!

(III, i, 107–112)

As Constance mocks him, John curiously allows her to go on without interruption. He seems powerless to act.

He is forced to do so at the entrance of Pandulph, who starts an important scene of the play. He is a representative of the Pope, and his argument with John concerns the King's refusal to accept Stephen Langton, the Pope's choice for Archbishop of Canterbury. We must keep in mind that historically, after Henry VIII's break with the Pope in 1533 over the issue of divorce, the English were enemies of the Church in Rome, and thus Pandulph's appearance aroused immediate antagonism from Shakespeare's audience. As if in accordance with such sentiments, John's answer to Pandulph becomes the King's high moment:

What earthy name to interrogatories
Can taste the free breath of a sacred king?
Thou canst not, Cardinal, devise a name
So slight, unworthy, and ridiculous,
To charge me to an answer, as the Pope.
Tell him this tale, and from the mouth of England
Add thus much more, that no Italian priest
Shall tithe or toll in our dominions;
But as we, under [God], are supreme head,
So under Him that great supremacy,
Where we do reign, we will alone uphold
Without th' assistance of a mortal hand.
So tell the Pope, all reverence set apart

To him and his usurp'd authority.

(III, i, 147–160)

Here John is speaking for a nation. At the same time the gesture is politically destructive, since by insulting the Pope and turning his back on Rome, John ruins any chance for political alliance with France, and thereafter any opportunity for reuniting the two countries with himself in charge.

His predicament is exacerbated by Pandulph, a no-nonsense politician whose severity is apparent when he replies to John's declaration:

Thou shalt stand curs'd and excommunicate,
And blessed shall he be that doth revolt
From his allegiance to an heretic,
And meritorious shall that hand be call'd,
Canonized and worshipp'd as a saint,
That takes away by any secret course
Thy hateful life.

(III, i, 173–179)

Pandulph puts a price on John's head, leaving Philip in a political vise. He wants to be loyal to the Church and therefore must obey Pandulph. But he also has agreed to a political marriage that will save his country from war. His solution reflects his weakness, as he turns for an answer to Pandulph:

Good reverend father, make my person yours,
And tell me how you would bestow yourself.
This royal hand and mine are newly knit,
And the conjunction of our inward souls
Married in league, coupled, and link'd together
With all religious strength of sacred vows.

(III, i, 224–229)

He seeks a compromise. But this world is one of absolutes, and Pandulph reminds the French ruler that Philips's first loyalty is to the Church:

O, let thy vow
First made to heaven, first be to heaven perform'd,
That is, to be the champion of our Church!

(III, i, 265–267)

Lewis, too, is ready to fight (III, i, 300), and under his pressure as well as Pandulph's, Philip, in the turning point of the play, succumbs: "England, I will fall from thee" (III, i, 320). Seconds before Philip capitulates, Constance challenges Blanch and supports Lewis's resolve:

That which upholdeth him that thee upholds,
His honor. O, thine honor, Lewis, thine honor!

(III, i, 314–315)

That word, "honor," intended to dignify men, so often proves the reason for their downfall. We ought to see Philip as hearing those words, then making the decision that brings him temporary glory but ultimate disaster. Furthermore, the entire episode is mocked by the exchange of insults from the two mothers (III, i, 321–322).

In Act III, scene i, John is at his height: bold, aggressive, willing to risk confrontation for the sake of his country's security and independence. But he never approaches such strength again. Indeed, from this point on he virtually disintegrates. In scene ii the Bastard begins to assume authority, entering with the head of the Duke of Austria, who was killed in the war. John then commands that his mother be removed from danger, but the Bastard has already seen to her security (III, ii, 7–8). In scene iii the King assures both Elinor and Arthur that they will be safe (III, iii, 1–4) but immediately after shepherding Arthur aside, John turns to Hubert de Burgh and hints about killing Arthur. The episode reminds us of Richard III's instructions to Buckingham about the death of Edward's children (IV, ii). But whereas Richard is sufficiently malevolent so as to communicate his orders in a few lines, John is neither so willful a character nor so effective a speaker, and he blunders to his point. Finally Hubert grasps the truth: "He shall not live" (III, iii, 66). John's weakness is also clear in his incoherent expression of relief:

> Enough.
> I could be merry now. Hubert, I love thee.
> Well, I'll not say what I intend for thee.
> Remember. Madam, fare you well,
> I'll send those powers o'er to your Majesty.

(III, iii, 66–70)

Whatever courage we might have attributed to John before, he now sinks permanently in our estimation.

We also wonder about Hubert. Is this man the same one who stood at Angiers and spoke for the city? He and John were strangers then. Now John takes him into his most intimate confidence, and Hubert follows a terrifying directive without questioning. Earlier Hubert had said he would be "loyal" to the victorious king. Is this scene the result? As indicated before, such confusions arise from conflicting texts.

To return to the central action. Matters do not proceed any better for Philip than they do for John, for the French King's indecision has caused revolt in his country. The misery is articulated by Constance, whose laments parallel the pain of war and its toll on France:

> No, I defy all counsel, all redress,
> But that which ends all counsel, true redress:
> Death, death. O amiable lovely death!
> Thou odoriferous stench! sound rottenness!

(III, iv, 23–26)

Her strongest opponent is Pandulph, who accuses her of madness, but she insists, with accuracy, "Thou art [not] holy to belie me so . . . (III, iv, 44). Indeed, in this scene she becomes a voice of truth, like Margaret in *Richard III*. Constance here is a symbol of the destruction of the family because of war and political struggle:

> I am not mad; too well, too well I feel
> The different plague of each calamity.
>
> (III, iv, 59–60)

Despite her claims, her ranting and tearing of her hair (III, iv, 102) suggest borderline insanity.

Pandulph's ruthlessness is apparent in his counsel to young Lewis. First the Cardinal, unashamedly corrupt, intuits that John will have Arthur killed (III, iv, 131–140). Far from being shocked by that possibility, Pandulph sees potential benefits for Lewis:

> You, in the right of Lady Blanch your wife,
> May then make all the claim that Arthur did.
>
> (III, iv, 142–143)

Lewis expresses skepticism, but Pandulph's answer reflects the cynicism of a seasoned political operator: "How green you are and fresh in this old world!" (III, iv, 145). Pandulph is the embodiment of the chicanery that is part of the politics of any institution at any time. He is also aware of the common people, for he warns Lewis that when Arthur is dead the people will revolt against John (III, iv, 165). Such acuity makes Pandulph a compelling figure. To be sure, he is one-dimensional, but he is a skillful manipulator and the most unified character in his sense of himself and his purposes. Other characters vacillate, pressured by fear and weakness. Pandulph, however, thinks in terms only of power for himself through power for the Church, and his single-mindedness gives him a vitality uncommon in this work. Here he leaves delighted with the intention of convincing Philip to invade England, a move the French people will support when they learn of the Bastard's ransacking churches (III, iv, 171–181).

From the world of political scheming the play moves next to the area of human tragedy: the plight of Arthur. Hubert has been assigned to murder the boy, but the fundamental decency of the two characters prevents the deed. Arthur accepts his fate nobly, (IV, i, 75–83), then pleads pathetically (IV, i, 97–104), and Hubert is sufficiently touched to risk his own life by letting Arthur escape. The scene extends too long, and the excessive sentiment is enervating, but the contrast between these two characters and virtually everyone else moves us.

It is especially moving in contrast to the emotional state of John, who in the next scene orders a second coronation for himself (IV, ii, 1–2). Why should he take such an action? Perhaps because he is conscious of his position as a usurper, and for all his bluster, the second coronation is a desperate attempt to better secure his place. He has enough fear and respect for the kingship and the divine order of which it is a part to try to give himself not only practical authority but also legal sanction. Pembroke realizes the King's vulnerability:

> When workmen strive to do better than well,
> They do confound their skill in covetousness,
> And oftentimes excusing of a fault
> Doth make the fault worse by th' excuse . . .
>
> (IV, ii, 28–31)

Salisbury, too, urges the King not to draw attention to his uncertainty, but like a true political sycophant compromises his integrity by backing off from his advice:

> To this effect, before you were new crown'd,
> We breath'd our counsel; but it pleas'd your Highness
> To overbear it, and we are all well pleas'd,
> Since all and every part of what we would
> Doth make a stand at what your Highness will.
>
> (IV, ii. 35–39)

Men like John attract such oily followers, for someone who deals duplicitously with others invites the same treatment in return.

The shift of influence from John to the Bastard is a central movement in this play. In Act IV it is manifested in the gradual replacement of John by the Bastard as head of the English army. John's weakness, though, takes several steps. First he retracts his plan to murder Arthur (IV, ii, 67–68). Although this judgment is morally correct, the King makes it not out of ethical considerations, but only after Pembroke's warning that Arthur's death might endanger John's own safety (IV, ii, 47–66). When news of Arthur's supposed death comes through, others mourn, but John is worried more about himself:

> Why do you bend such solemn brows on me?
> Think you I bear the shears of destiny?
> Have I commandement on the pulse of life?
>
> (IV, ii, 90–92)

He is attempting to avoid responsibility, but even Salisbury recognizes the King's role:

> It is apparent foul play, and 'tis shame
> That greatness should so grossly offer it.
> So thrive it in your game! and so farewell.
>
> (IV, ii, 93–95)

When left alone, John seems to have a turnabout: "They burn in indignation. I repent" (IV, ii, 103). That he is regretful of Arthur's fate is to his credit. But the transformation is instantaneous and not consistent with John's character.

Immediately after this line, however, action takes place as furiously as in any section of the play. First John learns of the death of his mother as well as that of Constance three days before (IV, ii, 119–124). The prophet Peter of Pomfret is brought in to predict John's fall from the throne (IV, ii, 146–151). And on top of that the King learns that French troops are gathering to revenge Arthur's supposed death (IV, ii, 161–166). John's reaction to this tumult is to try to maintain control. He orders Peter imprisoned and the Bastard to regather the King's former allies because "I have a way to win their loves again" (IV, ii, 168). Yet when alone once more, John sighs helplessly: "My mother's dead!" (IV, ii, 181).

As John is beset by events, we pity him. But that attitude fades when John accuses Hubert of Arthur's murder (IV, ii, 204–206), then claims that Hubert's face forced the hint of an order:

> But taking note of thy abhorr'd aspect,
> Finding thee fit for bloody villainy,
> Apt, liable to be employ'd in danger,
> I faintly broke with thee of Arthur's death . . .

> (IV, ii, 224–227)

The repetitive tone of this speech, which suggests hysteria, does not disguise the ineffectiveness of the excuse nor John's responsibility. But that John has awareness beyond his own situation is clear:

> Nay, in the body of this fleshly land,
> This kingdom, this confine of blood and breath,
> Hostility and civil tumult reigns
> Between my conscience and my cousin's death.

> (IV, ii, 245–248)

This theme is familiar from the first tetralogy. Nothing more frightened Shakespeare's audience than the anticipation of such anarchy. But whether John fears for his nation or for himself is not certain.

Nonetheless, the discovery of Arthur's body after the boy jumps to his death suggests that the King's fear of civil disorder is reasonable. First Salisbury dramatizes the depths of the crime:

> This is the bloodiest shame,
> The wildest savagery, the vildest stroke,
> That ever wall-ey'd wrath or staring rage
> Presented to the tears of soft remorse.

> (IV, iii, 47–50)

He then moves to blame Hubert, but when the latter shifts the culpability to John (IV, iii, 135–139), the Bastard is left to evaluate the crisis. Does he oppose the King who ordered the murder? To do so would be to place the entire kingdom in jeopardy:

> I am amaz'd, methinks, and lose my way
> Among the thorns and dangers of this world.
> How easy dost thou take all England up
> From forth this morsel of dead royalty!
> The life, the right, and truth of all this realm
> Is fled to heaven; and England now is left
> To tug and scamble, and to part by th' teeth

> The unowed interest of proud swelling state.
> Now for the bare-pick'd bone of majesty
> Doth dogged war bristle his angry crest,
> And snarleth in the gentle eyes of peace;
> Now powers from home and discontents at home
> Meet in one line; and vast confusion waits,
> As doth a raven on a sick-fall'n beast,
> The imminent decay of wrested pomp.

> (IV, iii, 140–154)

Fearful of chaos, the Bastard supports the King because the state of the kingship is more important than the individual man who temporarily occupies the throne. This spirit of nationalism makes the Bastard the hero of this play as well as its unifying character.

The Bastard's fears about disorder are justified when in the beginning of Act V, John, afraid for his own place, reverses his earlier action and allies himself with Pandulph (V, i, 1–2). The Bastard then returns, unaware of the pact but with news of military loss and desertion by nobles. Rather than give in, he attempts to rally the King:

> Be stirring as the time, be fire with fire,
> Threaten the threat'ner, and outface the brow
> Of bragging horror; so shall inferior eyes,
> That borrow their behaviors from the great,
> Grow great by your example and put on
> The dauntless spirit of resolution.

> (V, i, 48–53)

Such vigorous if simplistic language is characteristic of the man now the leader of the English forces. But when John reveals that a deal has been worked out with the Pope, the Bastard is outraged, and his cries may be taken to echo what Shakespeare's audience must have felt:

> O inglorious league!
> Shall we, upon the footing of our land,
> Send fair-play orders and make comprise,
> Insinuation, parley, and base truce
> To arms invasive?

> (V, i, 65–69)

The Bastard's heroism appears even brighter in the light of Lewis's response to news of the treaty. At first Lewis sympathizes with Salisbury, who mourns that his own country is split over the war:

> But such is the infection of the time,
> That for the health and physic of our right,
> We cannot deal but with the very hand

Of stern injustice and confused wrong.

(V, ii, 20–23)

He is in anguish that he is forced to fight his countrymen, and in his surprising
depth of feeling here Salisbury has changed from the unquestioning follower of
the King. Lewis offers understanding, then shifts tactics:

> Come, come; for thou shalt thrust thy hand as deep
> Into the purse of rich prosperity
> As Lewis himself . . .

(V, ii, 60–62)

Once more, "commodity" asserts itself, as Lewis assumes that any man will
be cheered by prospects of profit. But when Pandulph arrives, the blessing Lewis
anticipates for the war is not forthcoming. Instead Pandulph announces a treaty
with John (V, ii, 69–71), and Lewis is furious:

> What is that peace to me?
> I, by the honor of my marriage-bed,
> After young Arthur, claim this land for mine,
> And now it is half conquer'd, must I back
> Because that John hath made his peace with Rome?

(V, ii, 92–96)

How ironic that he uses "honor" to justify further military action. Lewis's
glorification of war is answered by the Bastard, who arrives to speak not of
military glory but of English glory:

> Know the gallant monarch is in arms,
> And like an eagle o'er his aery tow'rs,
> To souse annoyance that comes near his nest;
> And you degenerate, you ingrate revolts,
> You bloody Neroes, ripping up the womb
> Of your dear mother England, blush for shame . . .

(V, ii, 148–153)

Ostensibly the Bastard is speaking for John, but clearly he has supplanted the
King, whose physical illness becomes the reflection of what we have already
recognized as moral weakness.

The ending of the play is unimpressive, for events occur arbitrarily, not as
the logical outcome of character. In scene iii, John grows more ill, his physical
state mirroring his mental and emotional condition. Then, in scene iv, the English
traitors are told by Melune that their alliance with Lewis is baseless, for the
King intends to behead all the English (V, iv, 15). In reaction to this news,
Salisbury, never steadfast in allegiance, switches sides once more:

> We will untread the steps of damned flight,
> And like a bated and retired flood,
> Leaving our rankness and irregular course,
> Stoop low within those bounds we have o'erlook'd,

> And calmly run on in obedience
> Even to our ocean, to our great King John.
>
> (V, iv, 52–57)

We learn that King John has been poisoned by a monk (V, vi, 23), and therefore to maintain its power the monarchy must be reestablished in the character of Prince Henry. Hubert reports that at Henry's request John has pardoned the returning nobles, and we feel the English people uniting (V, vi, 33–36).

But none of these events is theatrically effective. Henry never becomes more than a symbol, as he relates his father's torments:

> Death, having prey'd upon the outward parts,
> Leaves them invisible, and his siege is now
> Against the [mind], the which he pricks and wounds
> With many legions of strange fantasies,
> Which in their throng and press to that last hold,
> Confound themselves.
>
> (V, vii, 15–20)

Even John's suffering near death is uncomfortable rather than touching, for his illness was caused by artificial means, and his inconsistencies of action and thought have kept us at a distance.

Shakespeare also leaves a couple of plot lines vague. At line 80 of the final scene, the Dolphin is said to be at the heels of the English army. But then we learn that Pandulph was able to talk the Dolphin out of further fighting. How this result was achieved or what has happened to Pandulph is never clarified. All we have are facts that resolve one side of the story.

The only character who leaves with stature is the Bastard. That he has the last speech suggests that even when Henry becomes King, the Bastard will embody the spirit of kingship:

> This England never did, nor never shall,
> Lie at the proud foot of a conqueror,
> But when it first did help to wound itself.
> Now these her princes are come home again,
> Come the three corners of the world in arms,
> And we shall shock them. Nought shall make us rue,
> If England to itself do rest but true.
>
> (V, vii, 112–118)

His speech brings out the thematic core of the play. England is united, but because of King John's desperation to retain his throne, a selfishness that spread through the royal world and by extension into the kingdom at large, the country was for a time fragmented. Still, the spirit of patriotism, as personified by the Bastard, brings the nation together.

King John thus reaffirms several motifs prevalent in the first tetralogy. Yet because character and plot development are weak and because the central crisis is royal legitimacy, an issue removed from us, the play does not excite a modern audience as it would have Shakespeare's. They would have been taken with the defeat of the French and the action against the Church of Rome. As a thematic link between the two tetralogies, however, this work amplifies the playwright's view of political strategy and the responsibilities of kingship.

SUGGESTIONS FOR FURTHER READING

Berman, Ronald. "Anarchy and Order in *Richard III* and *King John*." *Shakespeare Survey* 20 (1967): 51–59.

Burckhardt, Sigurd. "*King John*: The Ordering of This Present Time." *ELH* 33 (1966): 133–153.

Calderwood, James C. "Commodity and Honour in *King John*." *University of Toronto Quarterly* 29 (1960): 341–356.

Price, J. R. "*King John* and the Problematic Art." *Shakespeare Quarterly* 21 (1970): 25–28.

Simmons, J. L. "Shakespeare's *King John* and Its Source: Coherence, Pattern, and Vision." *Tulane Studies in English* 17 (1968): 53–72.

Stroud, Ronald. "The Bastard to the Time in *King John*." *Comparative Drama* 6 (1972): 154–166.

Van de Water, Julia C. "The Bastard in *King John*." *Shakespeare Quarterly* 33 (1966): 137–146.

THE SECOND TETRALOGY

In this series of plays Shakespeare reaches his apogee in the historical drama form. They are superior to his earlier efforts primarily for two reasons. The language is richer and more unified, progress that results from the second and more important cause: the subtlety and complexity of many of the characters. Here they are more than just political schemers or irresolute victims. Their moments of triumph and defeat intermingle, and what we may judge to be their personal strengths and weaknesses overlap. In sum, these characters are more fully developed and more human than the comparatively one-dimensional figures of the first tetralogy.

The issues of the plays, however, are familiar, because here is the story that precedes that of Henry VI and Richard III. Once again we are concerned with the responsibilities of kingship and the destruction wrought when a king is overthrown. But since the characters are more compelling, we are more involved in the resolution of the crises. In addition, Shakespeare offers a gallery of non-royals who provide brilliant counterpoint to the intense political struggle. Thus this tetralogy offers a greater sense of society as a whole than does the first.

These works are polished, the products of a mature dramatist in command of his skills. And even though Shakespeare is again encapsulating years into weeks, even though he is creating enormous pageantry that tests the limits of any stage, the playwright's mastery is such that we never feel that he is out of control. He offers brilliant comedy, great battlefield action, sharply drawn political intrigue, and human conflict that approaches the realm of the tragic. These works are superbly crafted. From structure to character to language to theme they represent the myriad aspects of Shakespeare the dramatist.

RICHARD II

From his opening words, the first of the play, the title character establishes his personality:

> Old John of Gaunt, time-honored Lancaster,
> Hast thou, according to thy oath and band,
> Brought hither Henry Herford thy bold son,
> Here to make good the boist'rous late appeal,
> Which then our leisure would not let us hear,
> Against the Duke of Norfolk, Thomas Mowbray?
>
> (I, i, 1–6)

The flagrant use of "old" reminds John of Gaunt that he is no longer vigorous, that his days of influence are waning. The phrase "oath and band" reaffirms for Gaunt and everyone within earshot precisely who is in charge and who demands obeisance. The word "leisure," which here indicates a lack of leisure, communicates to all the limitless bounds of kingly duty. What we have, then, is a man infatuated with the glories of his position and the range of his power. We also have a man totally unsuited to wield such power, and whose nature ensures that he will both abuse and waste that power.

We also sense a man in love with the language of kingship. Therefore it is completely appropriate that the play that bears his name should be entirely in verse. Richard's personality dominates his world, and the voices around him reflect his own.

The historical Richard became king at the age of ten, taking over for his father, Edward the Black Prince, Edward III's oldest son, who predeceased his father. This elevation gave the boy authority over all nobles, including his uncle, the eminent John of Gaunt, fourth son of Edward III. Although the ascension was appropriate according to the laws of succession and primogeniture (inheritance by the first son), the new king was the target of widespread resentment that never completely abated. Nor did his own behavior help alleviate the antagonism. The young ruler enjoyed a few glorious moments, notably in 1381 when he suppressed the Peasant Revolt by meeting face to face with the rebels. But his own desire for luxury as well as his propensity for trusting sycophants proved disastrous. The "Merciless" Parliament of 1388 contested Richard's authority, specifically his reliance on unpopular cohorts and his manipulation of the judiciary. Such disputes were never really resolved, but instead fueled anger on both sides. In 1396 Richard visited Paris, where he was apparently so taken with the grandeur of the French monarchy that he became determined to live in equal splendor. From that point on his abuse of subordinates as well as his waste of public funds for personal gain and pleasure became notorious. The nobles accused him of incompetence, and in response Richard had several arrested, including Thomas of Woodstock, the Earl of Gloucester. Woodstock was eventually murdered at Calais, possibly at Richard's command, by Thomas Mowbray, Duke of Norfolk, who as this play opens stands accused of treason by Henry Bullingbrook, Duke of Herford. Some time before, Mowbray had warned Bullingbrook that Richard intended to execute both him, Bullingbrook, and his father, John of Gaunt. Or so Bullingbrook says. This trial, which took place in 1398, has been called to resolve the controversy.

Historically Richard's complicity in the murder of Gloucester is uncertain. And Shakespeare does not offer an answer. Instead he lets the tangle carry the dramatic situation. Richard knows that Mowbray, his aide, is aware of the King's general involvement. Richard also knows that Bullingbrook, his cousin, and Gaunt, his uncle, resent him. Yet Richard is bound to maintain the disinterest due a king in legal matters, while his own nature forces him to maintain his kingly manner.

For instance, inviting the two antagonists to address him, he says:

> Then call them to our presence; face to face,
> And frowning brow to brow, ourselves will hear
> The accuser and the accused freely speak.
> High-stomach'd are they both and full of ire,
> In rage, deaf as the sea, hasty as fire.
>
> (I, i, 15–19)

He delights in metaphor as well as in dramatizing the passion of the moment and his unique place in it. He basks in his own majesty. Yet we sense, and evidence soon confirms, that he is unfit for the position. Like King Lear, Richard suffers the loss of kingship before he admits his folly. To be sure, Richard never reaches the tragic stature of Lear, who suffers as perhaps no king ever suffered, and whether Richard is even tragic is open to question. But like other tragic heroes in Shakespeare, Richard suffers because of personal flaws magnified in the circumstances in which he is trapped.

Before the trial begins, Bullingbrook greets the King:

> Many years of happy days befall
> My gracious sovereign, my most loving liege!
>
> (I, i, 20–21)

The tone is respectful, but underneath we sense ironic resentment. Then Mowbray attempts to outdo his opponent:

Each day still better other's happiness,
Until the heavens envying earth's good hap,
Add an immortal title to your crown!

(I, i, 22–24)

These sentiments are so exaggerated that Mowbray is obviously trying to curry favor. Richard's reply suggests that he knows what is happening:

We thank you both, yet one but flatters us,
As well appeareth by the cause you come:
Namely, to appeal each other of high treason.

(I, i, 25–27)

He realizes that they purposefully flatter him, but he nonetheless enjoys the flattery.

When the speeches of accusation and defense begin, the case remains murky. First Bullingbrook states his general accusation against Mowbray: "Thou art a traitor and a miscreant . . ." (I, i, 39). In response, Mowbray points out that his accuser is a relative of the King's (I, i, 58), but even so Mowbray cannot let such lies pass:

I do defy him, and I spit at him,
Call him a slanderous coward and a villain . . .

(I, i, 60–61)

By throwing down his glove (I, i, 67) Mowbray offers to fight Bullingbrook, who answers in kind (I, i, 69–72), indicating a willingness to do battle, irrespective of his royal station. Then Bullingbrook establishes what he insists is Mowbray's place in the corruption carried on by the present administration:

. . . That all the treasons for these eighteen years,
Complotted and contrived in this land,
Fetch from false Mowbray their first head and spring.

(I, i, 95–97)

He goes on to claim that Mowbray was responsible for Gloucester's death (I, i, 100), but tactfully does not add that the order probably came from the King.

Richard's reaction to these accusations, which hit him personally since his reign has been precisely eighteen years, is characteristic: "How high a pitch his resolution soars" (I, i, 109). He is intrigued more by theatrics than facts. Such an attitude is further revealed when he assures Mowbray of royal impartiality:

Now by [my] sceptre's awe I make a vow,
Such neighbor nearness to our sacred blood
Should nothing privilege him nor partialize
The unstooping firmness of my upright soul.

(I, i, 118–121)

The King is entranced by the symbols of his power. He believes at this moment and virtually until the end of his life that the divine nature of kingship shelters him from challenge. What Richard does not grasp, and what this play and

tetralogy dramatize, is that the nature of kingship is changing. Events reflect the
end of the feudal era, when the political structure of England is no longer
monolithic but in flux, moving with the ebbs and tides of shifting power. Richard
is the last of his kind. Psychologically he is removed from the common people,
but they are a central element in the contention for authority, and subsequent
rulers will have to respond to them.

To return to the first scene. Mowbray attempts to defend his actions, offering
explanation for one mission in question:

> Three parts of that receipt I had for Callice
> Disburs'd I duly to his Highness' soldiers . . .

(I, i, 126–127)

Then he moves to the more sensitive issue:

> For Gloucester's death,
> I slew him not, but to my own disgrace
> Neglected my sworn duty in that case.

(I, i, 132–134)

He is careful, however, not to accuse anyone else of the murder, and instead
moves his attack back against Bullingbrook. Before Bullingbrook has a chance
to respond, however, the King, perhaps fearing exposure of his own involvement,
tries to intervene:

> Deep malice makes too deep incision.
> Forget, forgive, conclude and be agreed,
> Our doctors say this is no month to bleed.

(I, i, 155–157)

But neither complainant listens to him. Instead they challenge one another, while
Richard remains ineffectual:

> Rage must be withstood,
> Give me his gage. Lions make leopards tame.

(I, i, 173–174)

But Mowbray is not assured:

> Mine honor is my life, both grow in one,
> Take honor from me, and my life is done.

(I, i, 182–183)

He seems to imply that he has done everything for Richard, but that now the
reward for such loyalty is that Mowbray must accept the destruction of his
reputation. He wants to fight back, but Richard will not permit him to do so.
Meanwhile the King tries to keep himself above the fray:

> We were not born to sue, but to command,
> Which since we cannot do to make you friends,
> Be ready, as your lives shall answer it,

At Coventry upon Saint Lambert's day.
There shall your swords and lances arbitrate
The swelling difference of your settled hate.
Since we cannot atone you, we shall see
Justice design the victor's chivalry.

                                                                    (I, i, 196–203)

We realize that Richard is an external king. He bears the formality of office but
not the command.

We ought to realize something else. Earlier Bullingbrook spoke of eighteen
years of treason, a remark Richard has allowed to go unchallenged. He has made
no attempt to pursue the charge further nor to deny the accusation. In other
words, he is not only weak, but possibly corrupt.

In scene ii, complaints against Richard grow. Gaunt, who historically was a
military and social bumbler, is turned by Shakespeare into a spokesman for
tradition and orthodox political belief. The Duchess of Gloucester urges Gaunt
to take revenge against the murderer of her husband, Gaunt's brother (I, ii, 30–
36) but Gaunt refuses to do so for reasons vital to the play:

God's is the quarrel, for God's substitute,
His deputy anointed in His sight,
Hath caus'd his death, the which if wrongfully,
Let heaven revenge, for I may never lift
An angry arm against His minister.

                                                                    (I, ii, 37–41)

Both suspect that Richard is responsible for Gloucester's death, but Gaunt does
not believe it is within man's rights to interfere with the ways of God. The King
is on the throne by divine order; therefore to act against the King is to act against
God. Gaunt is thus bound by political and religious values. The Duchess, however, is concerned more with familial and emotional values, and as she dismisses
Gaunt, she uses the pejorative "old" twice (I, ii, 44, 54), echoing Richard's
ironic opening words. The question, then, is whether Richard should be removed
from office. At what point does his behavior warrant expulsion? And what price
will the nation pay for such action?

In scene iii, which historically took place two years later, the controversy
between Bullingbrook and Mowbray intensifies, as the two prepare for combat.
Richard revels in the ceremonial aspects of the occasion, as he grandly orders
the Marshal to bring forth Mowbray, who formally states his cause (I, iii, 16–
25), and then Bullingbrook, who proclaims his own (I, iii, 35–41). After both
make lavish appeals to the King, Richard moves to Bullingbrook:

We will descend and fold him in our arms.
Cousin of Herford, as thy cause is right,
So be thy fortune in this royal fight!
Farewell, my blood, which if to-day thou shed,

> Lament we may, but not revenge [thee] dead.
>
> (I, iii, 54–58)

The words indicate that the King has taken sides, and that Mowbray's cause is already lost. We understand Richard's tactics, since Mowbray knows too many secrets, and Richard would no doubt be happy to see him depart. Still, we disapprove of such cold treatment of a loyal follower.

As the moment of battle approaches, Bullingbrook offers tribute to the King, then to Bullingbrook's cousin Aumerle (I, iii, 63–66). Then he asks strength from his father, John of Gaunt (I, iii, 69–77), who offers his own spirited words of encouragement. Finally Mowbray has a chance to offer everlasting devotion to Richard:

> However God or fortune cast my lot,
> There lives or dies, true to King Richard's throne,
> A loyal, just, and upright gentleman.
>
> (I, iii, 85–87)

The rest of the speech seems to be a desperate plea for the King's support, but Richard offers only a perfunctory two-line response (I, iii, 97–98), and orders the fight to begin. Clearly he wants nothing to do with Mowbray. Richard permits two heralds to shout instructions, so that events move right to the brink of physical contact. But suddenly the King interrupts by throwing down his warder (his umpire's baton), then attempts to justify this surprising decision with an explanation (I, iii, 123–143) that is staggering in its convolution. For instance, the word "peace," first in line 132 and then in line 137, is both the subject and object of the word "fright" (line 137). Such twisting of words and ideas suggests that Richard stops this battle not out of a desire for civil order as he claims, but out of fear for his own security.

Richard ends this oration with pronouncement of punishment on Bullingbrook: ten years of exile. The reaction by Bullingbrook is almost too acquiescent, as if he knows the full term will not be served:

> Your will be done. This must my comfort be,
> That sun that warms you here shall shine on me,
> And those his golden beams to you here lent
> Shall point on me and gild my banishment.
>
> (I, iii, 144–147)

We note his use of the word "sun," traditionally the symbol of the king, and we note line 145, which contains the veiled threat that one day Bullingbrook will take that sun and, by implication, the crown away from Richard.

As if to avoid response, Richard turns to Mowbray and imposes lifetime banishment (I, iii, 150–153). The heartlessness of this gesture is revealed in Mowbray's answer, one of the key speeches of the play. What pains him most is the loss of his linguistic heritage:

The language I have learnt these forty years,
My native English, now I must forgo,
And now my tongue's use is to me no more
Than an unstringed viol or a harp,
Or like a cunning instrument cas'd up,
Or being open, put into his hands
That knows no touch to tune the harmony.

(I, ii, 159–165)

In a play so much about language, Mowbray emphasizes that words are the embodiment of a culture, and their distortion or loss represents the destruction of that culture. Furthermore, to lose the sound and meaning is to lose part of one's self.

After this plea, Richard's retort seems even crueler, especially as it is made to one who has dedicated his life to the King:

It boots thee not to be compassionate,
After our sentence plaining comes too late.

(I, iii, 174–175)

He restates the impact of both sentences in all their harshness:

You never shall, so help you truth and God,
Embrace each other's love in banishment,
Nor never look upon each other's face,
Nor never write, regreet, nor reconcile
This low'ring tempest of your home-bred hate,
Nor never by advised purpose meet
To plot, contrive, or complot any ill
'Gainst us, our state, our subjects, or our land.

(I, iii, 183–190)

Richard clearly wants both men out of his way and apart from each other. The two swear obedience, but even at this moment Bullingbrook shows his shrewdness and presence of mind as he attempts to catch the emotionally vulnerable Mowbray off-guard:

Confess thy treasons ere thou fly the realm;
Since thou hast far to go, bear not along
The clogging burthen of a guilty soul.

(I, iii, 198–200)

We can imagine these words said with false sympathy, and we can also imagine Richard freezing inside, fearful that Mowbray will make such a confession. But Mowbray does not take the bait. Instead he speaks quietly about Bullingbrook himself:

> But what thou art, God, thou, and I do know,
> And all too soon, I fear, the King shall rue.
>
> (I, iii, 204–205)

Then he leaves, sparing Richard the need for action.

But Richard does act, albeit in his own way, for he reduces Bullingbrook's sentence to six years' banishment. Why does the King follow this course? Is the reason, as he claims, the look of sadness in Gaunt's eyes (I, iii, 207–208)? Or is he frightened by Mowbray's words and seeking to avoid out-and-out conflict with Gaunt, the man who in this play is the most respected in England? Whatever the reason, Gaunt expresses shock that he trusted Richard to be fair:

> You urg'd me as a judge, but I had rather
> You would have bid me argue like a father.
> O, had't been a stranger, not my child,
> To smooth his fault I should have been more mild.
>
> (I, iii, 237–240)

Now, however, Richard is firm.

Bullingbrook's private reaction to this punishment is telling. As his father tries to soften the blow (I, iii, 286–293), Bullingbrook insists on appraising his fate realistically:

> O no, the apprehension of the good
> Gives but the greater feeling to the worse.
>
> (I, iii, 300–301)

This attitude becomes his chief political attribute. He is unwilling to settle for appearance or surface value. Unlike Richard, Bullingbrook is interested in reality, not pretense.

In the next scene we see Richard alone with his confederates, off the public stage, as it were, and we realize how contemptuous he is of the common people. To this point he has been vain, impractical, and cruel. Now he sinks lower. First he dismisses Bullingbrook's affection from the masses:

> . . . How he did seem to dive into their hearts
> With humble and familiar courtesy,
> What reverence he did throw away on slaves,
> Wooing poor craftsmen with the craft of smiles
> And patient underbearing of his fortune,
> As 'twere to banish their affects with him.
>
> (I, iv, 25–30)

He sneers at Bullingbrook's behavior, but he also envies Bullingbrook's capacity to insinuate himself into public trust. Richard feels above such politicking, but he also wishes he had the skill to bring it off. He mocks the masses as if their voices do not count, but he soon learns his error. Here a hint of awareness surfaces in his detailed description of Bullingbrook.

Richard's next misjudgment has more immediate implications. He plans to go to war in Ireland, not out of moral or political commitment but to ravage the country and fill his treasury (I, iv, 45–47). For the first time, unbridled corruption can be added to the King's crimes.

Yet the question remains: does such behavior warrant Richard's being removed from the throne by force? Does such an attitude entitle his opponents to go against divine order?

At the end of this scene the crueler side of Richard shows up again, as he comments upon the imminent death of Gaunt:

> Now put it, God, in the physician's mind
> To help him to his grave immediately!
> The lining of his coffers shall make coats
> To deck out soldiers for these Irish wars.
> Come, gentlemen, let's all go visit him.
> Pray God we may make haste and come too late.
>
> (I, iv, 59–64)

We see here the derisive wit that characterizes any person too full of himself and his power. With almost every sentence Richard grows more infuriating.

The next scene is the peak of his odiousness. Before Richard enters, the dying Gaunt offers what has stood throughout the history of literature as the most stirring tribute to English glory, an extraordinary combination of religious and political doctrine (II, i, 31–68). The tone of the occasion shatters, however, when Richard struts in with a contemptuous: "What comfort, man? how is't with aged Gaunt?" (II, i, 72). Such flippancy is so outlandish as to be comic. Gaunt tries to fight back: "O no, thou diest, though I the sicker be" (II, i, 91). But Richard is flying too high to acknowledge even the possibility of his own weakness: "I am in health, I breathe, and see thee ill" (II, i, 92). He seems to find pleasure in tormenting Gaunt.

But the dying man is able to articulate his fears for Richard's kingship:

> Thy death-bed is no lesser than thy land,
> Wherein thou liest in reputation sick,
> And thou, too careless patient as thou art,
> Commit'st thy anointed body to the cure
> Of those physicians that first wounded thee.
> A thousand flatterers sit within thy crown,
> Whose compass is no bigger than thy head,
> And yet, [incaged] in so small a verge
> The waste is no whit lesser than thy land.
> O had thy grandsire with a prophet's eye
> Seen how his son's son should destroy his sons,
> From forth thy reach he would have laid thy shame,
> Deposing thee before thou wert possess'd,
> Which art possess'd now to depose thyself.
>
> (II, i, 95–108)

Gaunt clarifies that the King is not separate from his country, but a part of its life. And moral disease on the throne turns into a plague that damages the land.

To this accusation Richard responds not with apology or explanation, but with rage and threat:

> A lunatic lean-witted fool,
> Presuming on an ague's privilege,
> Darest with thy frozen admonition
> Make pale our cheek, chasing the royal blood
> With fury from his native residence.
> Now by my seat's right royal majesty,
> Wert thou not brother to great Edward's son,
> This tongue that runs so roundly in thy head
> Should run thy head from thy unreverent shoulders.
>
> (II, i, 115–123)

These words are those of a man taken with his own status and unwilling to learn from experience. Gaunt is left with little to do but to invite Richard to join him in death. Before Gaunt is carried off, he uses the image of a withered flower to characterize Richard (II, i, 134), anticipating the garden imagery that will soon be prevalent. The word "withered" suggests the current state of Richard himself.

Northumberland soon brings word of Gaunt's death:

> His tongue is now a stringless instrument,
> Words, life, and all, old Lancaster hath spent.
>
> (II, i, 149–150)

The couplet recalls Mowbray's farewell address (I, iii, 161–162), for both speakers unite images of language and music. At the grim news, however, Richard remains impassive:

> The ripest fruit falls first, and so doth he;
> His time is spent, our pilgrimage must be.
> So much for that.
>
> (II, i, 153–155)

His callousness at the passing of a great man is shocking. But with his next lines he moves from the insensitive to the illegal:

> Now for our Irish wars:
> We must supplant those rough rug-headed kerns,
> Which live like venom where no venom else
> But only they have privilege to live.
> And, for these great affairs do ask some charge,
> Towards our assistance we do seize to us
> The plate, coin, revenues, and moveables
> Whereof our uncle Gaunt did stand possess'd.
>
> (II, i, 155–162)

Here Richard unequivocally breaks the law, usurping Bullingbrook's inheritance and scorning legal precedent. He obviously believes that with the death of Gaunt his most serious threat has disappeared. But Richard has miscalculated. As York, the last surviving son of Edward III, bemoans the state of the nation, he suggests more strongly that Richard has corrupted the crown. Speaking of Richard's father, York states:

> His hands were guilty of no kinred blood,
> But bloody with the enemies of his kin.
> O Richard! York is too far gone with grief,
> Or else he never would compare between.
>
> (II, i, 182–185)

York's statement is the strongest insinuation so far of Richard's involvement in Gloucester's death. Still, the King remains oblivious: "Why, uncle, what's the matter?" (II, i, 186). Whether such a line is the result of conceit or stupidity is not certain.

Nevertheless, it inspires York to a catalogue of Richard's crimes, establishing reasons why the King might be vulnerable to overthrow (II, i, 189–194). York also clarifies the magnitude of Richard's transgressions:

> Take Herford's rights away, and take from Time
> His charters and his customary rights;
> Let not to-morrow then ensue to-day;
> Be not thyself; for how art thou a king
> But by fair sequence and succession?
>
> (II, i, 195–200)

The images of "time" permeate this work, often in conjunction with images of music. Both represent a sense of order, the proper place of men and things in a universal system that during periods of disorder is shattered. The breakdown of time, then, for York and for others, suggests a breakdown of nature. The implication is that Richard has violated not only human rights but divine right. Does York's explanation imply that Richard's opponents are entitled to further corrupt nature by removing Richard from the throne? That question remains paramount.

Richard's capacity to ignore such warning is startling:

> Think what you will, we seize into our hands
> His plate, his goods, his money, and his lands.
>
> (II, i, 209–210)

There is nothing elaborate or extravagant in Richard's language here: just cold statement of policy. Then he reminds all of his plan to go to Ireland to quash a rebellion (II, i, 218). What Richard fails to grasp is that the real rebellion will occur in his own kingdom. And he has brought this uprising on himself. Furthermore, he compounds his errors by leaving York in charge. York has just lambasted Richard, accusing him of crimes against the family, the state, and God. Yet Richard leaves with the pronouncement that York "always loved us well" (II, i, 221). Once more we ask, is Richard too proud to be realistic, or too foolish?

At this point, when Richard is at his worst, something else about him deserves mention: he still manages to retain a measure of attractiveness for the audience. We recognize his malfeasances and weaknesses. Yet we also find him a figure of fascination. He is theatrically eloquent, and he moves about the stage with a sense of his own loftiness. Something about him is irresistible. Yet we also wonder why he does what he does. Because we gradually see him as one totally unsuited for the position life has thrust upon him, no matter how he proceeds we are still sympathetic. Thus the play's tragic potential.

We also tend to be sympathetic to someone who is the object of so much resentment, and the remainder of this scene reveals the extent of the antagonism Richard has aroused. When left alone, Northumberland, Willoughby, and Ross reflect on Gaunt's death, at first speaking tentatively, for so absolute is the authority of the King that none is willing to admit antipathy to Richard. Then Northumberland opens up a bit:

> Nay, speak thy mind, and let him ne'er speak more
> That speaks thy words again to do thee harm!

> (II, i, 230–231)

As a member of the Percy family of northern England, Northumberland is as influential as any nobleman in the country, and his backing is enough to give others the courage to proceed. Then Willoughby raises the possibility of alliance with Bullingbrook (II, i, 232). Still uncertain, Northumberland points out that Richard did not himself conceive the plan for the Irish Wars, but has been "basely led" (II, i, 241). Ross, bolder now, insists on blaming Richard for almost everything:

> The commons hath he pill'd with grievous taxes,
> And quite lost their hearts; the nobles he hath fin'd
> For ancient quarrels, and quite lost their hearts.

> (II, i, 246–248)

At these lines the three realize that they are alike in their judgment of Richard, and freely articulate their resentment, reviewing crimes and attitudes familiar to us. Some mutual suspicion remains, however, and no one wants to be the first to advocate outright rebellion. For a few moments each talks about the dangers all face (II, i, 259–272). At last Ross takes a stand:

> Be confident to speak, Northumberland:
> We three are but thyself, and, speaking so,
> Thy words are but as thoughts, therefore be bold.

> (II, i, 274–276)

Now Northumberland reveals that Bullingbrook and several other nobles are sailing to England, eager to take action against the King. This report is all Ross and Willoughby need, and they race off to rally additional support. Opposition to Richard is gathering with irresistible momentum, and as his destruction runs its course we slowly turn to him. He is callous, pompous, manipulative, and corrupt. Yet we still find him deserving of compassion. That we do is part of Shakespeare's achievement.

When we meet Richard's wife, the play takes an intriguing turn. Historically she was a child, but Shakespeare usefully makes her older to give the drama another dimension. She becomes the voice of conscience Richard lacks:

> Yet again methinks
> Some unborn sorrow, ripe in fortune's womb,
> Is coming towards me, and my inward soul
> With nothing trembles; at some thing it grieves,
> More than with parting from my lord the King.
>
> (II, ii, 9–13)

She anticipates the political and personal disaster headed Richard's way. Bushy attempts to comfort the Queen by suggesting that her unhappiness is caused only by her "lord's departure" (II, ii, 21), but the Queen is inconsolable: "Howe'er it be,/ I cannot be but sad . . . " (II, ii, 29–30). The disaster she foresees is also foreshadowed by Green, who brings news that Bullingbrook has arrived at Ravensburgh (II, ii, 50–51). All three counsellors are frustrated at the King's departure for Ireland, for Northumberland and his supporters are mounting opposition forces (II, ii, 53–61). At this point York enters bemoaning his inability to deal with such strife:

> Here am I left to underprop his land,
> Who, weak with age, cannot support myself.
> Now comes the sick hour that his surfeit made,
> Now shall he try his friends that flatter'd him.
>
> (II, ii, 82–85)

How appropriate that York uses the imagery of illness Gaunt invoked. York also seems to find pleasure in that the King shall have to rely on the trio before us, as if Richard might then learn a lesson. But whatever small pleasure he may have is undercut first by the death of the Duchess of Gloucester (II, ii, 97), then by his realization that the impending battle for the throne means that he will be trapped between opposing family loyalties (II, ii, 111–115). The imminence of the crisis is made clearer by the nervousness of the three sycophants. As Green says:

> Besides, our nearness to the King in love
> Is near the hate of those love not the King.
>
> (II, ii, 126–127)

In fact, the only person who seems unaware of what is coming is Richard himself.

At this point we ought to note the fullness that these supporting characters give to *Richard II*. Such interesting figures were absent from the first tetralogy, where all we saw were comparatively one-dimensional schemers angling for control. The result is that this play is a much deeper work, with more shades of personality and levels of meaning.

Events began to turn in Act II, scene iii, when Bullingbrook and Northumberland lead forces toward Berkeley, where York was headed at the end of the
last scene (II, ii, 119). Northumberland's son, Harry Percy, enters to tell his
father that Worcester, Northumberland's brother, has joined their rebel troops,
and Northumberland takes this occasion to introduce his son to Bullingbrook.
Young Percy swears fidelity (II, iii, 41–44), a moment that ironically anticipates
the action of *Henry IV, Part 1*, when Percy, then nicknamed Hotspur, will
bitterly oppose the man whom he helps make king.

Percy reveals that Berkeley Castle is nearby, and before long York appears.
He disdains Bullingbrook's greeting of "uncle," and in one of his most passionate outbursts, reveals his frustration at his age and inability to take action:

> Were I but now lord of such hot youth
> As when brave Gaunt, thy father, and myself
> Rescued the Black Prince, that young Mars of men,
> From forth the ranks of many thousand French,
> O then how quickly should this arm of mine,
> Now prisoner to the palsy, chastise thee,
> And minister correction to thy fault!
>
> (II, iii, 98–105)

Bullingbrook attempts to explain how he has been wronged, but even at Bullingbrook's mere appearance York is outraged, for Bullingbrook has broken
Richard's order of banishment:

> Even in condition of the worst degree,
> In gross rebellion and detested treason.
> Thou art a banish'd man, and here art come,
> Before the expiration of thy time,
> In braving arms against thy sovereign.
>
> (II, iii, 108–112)

Bullingbrook answers with a speech central to this play, one with enormous
political and legal ramifications. The speech also reveals the essence of Bullingbrook's character.

First he notes that Richard has broken the law by violating Gaunt's lands:

> O, then, my father,
> Will you permit that I shall stand condemn'd
> A wandering vagabond, my rights and royalties
> Pluck'd from my arms perforce—and given away
> To upstart unthrifts?
>
> (II, iii, 118–122)

Bullingbrook also asks what York would do were his lands and inheritance stolen
(II, iii, 125–133). Then he poses the climactic issue:

> I am a subject,
> And I challenge law. Attorneys are denied me,

And therefore personally I lay my claim
To my inheritance of free descent.

(II, iii, 133–136)

Bullingbrook believes that no legal recourse is open to him. Therefore we must
ask whether Richard, in breaking so many laws, has gone beyond behavior
acceptable in a king. If so, is Bullingbrook the one to take over? Given the
political and social turmoil that England endures in the decades to come, the
answer to the first question seems to be "no." The price for overthrowing a
king is too great. But that answer is not complete.

The answer to the second question is also unclear. What kind of king does a
country warrant? Is the ideal ruler one like Bullingbrook? Aggressive, shrewd,
ruthless when need be? Or is such a man the only type who gains power, given
the nature of political struggle?

Bullingbrook's barrage leaves York helpless. Yet whatever injustice Bullingbrook has suffered, York remains on the side of the King:

But if I could, by Him that gave me life,
I would attach you all, and make you stoop
Unto the sovereign mercy of the King;
But since I cannot, be it known unto you
I do remain as neuter.

(II, iii, 155–159)

This loyalty to the throne will remain the hallmark of York's character. Here
he leaves a broken man: "Things past redress are now with me past care" (II,
iii, 171).

Scene iv relates first the disorder in Richard's Welsh forces. The Captain
reports " 'Tis thought the King is dead" (II, iv, 7), and certain omens in the
heavens (II, iv, 8–11) foretell "the death or fall of kings" (II, iv, 15). Salisbury's
soliloquy further hints at Richard's inevitable collapse: "Thy sun sets weeping
in the lowly west . . . " (II, iv, 21).

Bullingbrook's ruthlessness is apparent in the treatment of Bushy and Green
at the beginning of Act III. Bullingbrook accuses them not only of misleading
the King but of coming between the King and his wife (III, i, 12). He further
indicates that his disapproval of them is personal as well as political:

. . . Whilst you have fed upon my signories,
Dispark'd my parks and fell'd my forest woods,
From my own windows torn my household coat,
Ras'd out my imprese, leaving me no sign,
Save men's opinions and my living blood,
To show the world I am a gentleman.

(II, i, 22–27)

After this list of accusations, he does not ask for a defense. He does not hold a
trial. He simply announces their execution. We could say that Bullingbrook has
no choice here, that his strategy is an example of the pragmatism Richard lacks.

We could also say that Bullingbrook is not concerned with justice or mercy, only power. We do note, however, that he instructs his supporters to be kind to the Queen (III, i, 37). Thus the future Henry IV has gentler instincts as well.

The contrast with Richard is clearer in the next scene, as the King attempts to conduct his military campaign. First he dramatizes his love of England, but the emphasis is less on the glory of the country and more on his own qualities:

> As a long-parted mother with her child
> Plays fondly with her tears and smiles in meeting,
> So weeping, smiling, greet I thee, my earth,
> And do thee favors with my royal hands,
>
> (III, ii, 8–11)

Carlisle, often the voice of religious authority, attempts to assuage Richard's fears of Bullingbrook's treachery:

> Fear not, my lord, that Power that made you king
> Hath power to keep you king in spite of all.
> The means that heavens yield must be embrac'd,
> And not neglected; else heaven would,
> And we will not.
>
> (III, ii, 27–31)

At this moment Richard is aware of the potential uprising, but still confident that the nature of kingship will protect him:

> Not all the water in the rough rude sea
> Can wash the balm off from an anointed king;
> The breath of worldly men cannot depose
> The deputy elected by the Lord;
> For every man that Bullingbrook hath press'd
> To lift shrewd steel against our golden crown,
> God for his Richard hath in heavenly pay
> A glorious angel; then if angels fight,
> Weak men must fall, for heaven still guards the right.
>
> (III, ii, 54–62)

Many qualities of this excerpt reflect the character of Richard. First, the image of water versus fire permeates the play. Richard sees himself as the glorious fire, the highest of the four elements (the others are water, earth, and air). The fire is also parallel to the traditional image of the King as the sun. At the same time Henry is constantly compared to water, intending to extinguish Richard's brilliance. We also note the rest of the grandiose imagery, the sense of majesty Richard exudes. Here is a king for whom the symbols of office supersede the actuality. Here is a king performing his role rather than living it.

This sense of performance gradually takes over. Several lines later, for instance, Richard learns that his Welsh followers have joined Bullingbrook's forces. When Aumerle comments upon the King's pale face, Richard replies, "Have I not reason to look pale and dead?" (III, ii, 79). He is always conscious of his appearance, as if what intrigues him most about himself is the precision of his enactment. When he next remarks "I had forgot myself, am I not king?" (III, ii, 83), he both evaluates the place of kingship, and his own performance as king:

> Strives Bullingbrook to be as great as we?
> Greater he shall not be; if he serve God,
> We'll serve him too, and be his fellow so.
> Revolt our subjects? That we cannot mend,
> They break their faith to God as well as to us.
> Cry woe, destruction, ruin, and decay;
> The worst is death, and death will have his day.
>
> (III, ii, 97–103)

He is the writer, director, star, and critic of his own extravaganza, and the nature of this endeavor contributes to his capacity to elicit our sympathy.

As bad news pours in, Richard grows more theatrical about his status. When the thought is proposed that Bushy, Bagot, and Green may have made peace with Bullingbrook, the King comments, "Three Judases, each one thrice worse than Judas!" (III, ii, 132). This occasion is not the only one when he compares himself to Christ to dramatize the divinity of his royal place.

One high point of Richard's show is his series of ruminations after he is told that his cohorts have been executed. Suddenly he changes himself from general to philosopher, and the transformation works brilliantly:

> Let's talk of graves, of worms, and epitaphs,
> Make dust our paper, and with rainy eyes
> Write sorrow on the bosom of the earth.
> Let's choose executors and talk of wills;
> And yet not so, for what can we bequeath
> Save our deposed bodies to the ground?
>
> (III, ii, 145–150)

The vividness of the pictures he creates make his reflections come alive. He is the chronicler of his own life: outlandish, yet full of self-pity. And the beauty of the poetry suggests an artist's soul:

> For God's sake let us sit upon the ground
> And tell sad stories of the death of kings:
> How some have been depos'd, some slain in war,
> Some haunted by the ghosts they have deposed,
> Some poisoned by their wives, some sleeping kill'd,
> All murthered—for within the hollow crown
> That rounds the mortal temples of a king
> Keep Death his court, and there the antic sits,
> Scoffing his state and grinning at his pomp,
> Allowing him a breath, a little scene,
> To monarchize, be fear'd, and kill with looks,
> Infusing him with self and vain conceit,

As if this flesh which walls about our life
Were brass impregnable; and humor'd thus,
Comes at the last and with a little pin
Bores thorough his castle wall, and farewell king!

(III, ii, 155–170)

Richard insists upon seeing himself as part of a long line of kings, all of whom have been cut off in mid-role, so to speak. He is painfully aware of the artificiality of his place, and the reference to "scene" is one more hint of what this passage emphasizes: that Richard is an actor trying to perform a role for which he is unsuited.

The end of this speech brings out an even more important quality that suggests the start of Richard's redemption:

Cover your heads, and mock not flesh and blood
With solemn reverence, throw away respect,
Tradition, form, and ceremonious duty,
For you have but mistook me all this while.
I live with bread like you, feel want,
Taste grief, need friends; subjected thus,
How can you say to me I am a king?

(III, ii, 171–177)

Here is recognition that before a king is a ruler or instrument of God, he is first a man. We think of King Lear, who experiences the same understanding of his place among humanity.

Richard here earns pity and achieves dignity, and later he finds both again, but he never loses his tendency for posturing, which at moments becomes absurd. For instance, in response to requests for military action, he says to Aumerle:

Beshrew thee, cousin, which didst lead me forth
Of that sweet way I was in to despair!

(III, ii, 204–205)

A few lines later he adds:

Go to Flint castle, there I'll pine away—
A king, woe's slave, shall kingly woe obey.

(III, ii, 209–210)

He never loses pleasure in romanticizing his plight. And he enjoys his performance more than anyone else.

Meanwhile, however, a trace of political acumen seeps into his conversation when he says:

He does me double wrong
That wounds me with the flatteries of his tongue.

(III, ii, 215–216)

Until this moment he never admitted the possibility that he might have been deceived. Now, too late, he begins to come to grips with the nature of political corruption.

Richard's inevitable fall comes closer in the next scene, when he is confronted
by Northumberland, fronting for Bullingbrook and demanding Richard's crown.
We appreciate Bullingbrook's strategy, letting Northumberland play the knave
who demands that Richard resign from the throne. We note, too, the language
Bullingbrook chooses in preparing to challenge Richard:

> If not, I'll use the advantage of my power,
> And lay the summer's dust with show'rs of blood
> Rain'd from the wounds of slaughtered Englishmen,
> The which, how far off from the mind of Bullingbrook
> It is, such crimson tempest should bedrench
> The fresh green lap of fair King Richard's land,
> My stooping duty tenderly shall show.

(III, iii, 42–48)

Bullingbrook's willingness to resort to violence suggests his determination, a
trait essential to political success. The image of the "crimson tempest," uniting
both blood and water, emphasizes Richard's relationship to the rest of the country,
that as he is king, the populace lives through him. A few lines later Bullingbrook
reaffirms what Richard stated earlier: that Bullingbrook will extinguish Richard's
glory: "Be he the fire, I'll be the yielding water . . . " (III, iii, 58).

When Richard does make his entrance, even Bullingbrook is impressed, invoking Richard's own imagery:

> See, see, King Richard doth himself appear,
> As doth the blushing discontented sun
> From out the fiery portal of the east . . .

(III, iii, 62–64)

But York uses the appropriate phraseology:

> Yet looks he like a king! Behold, his eye,
> As bright as is the eagle's, lightens forth
> Controlling majesty. Alack, alack for woe,
> That any harm should stain so fair a show!

(III, iii, 68–71)

The quality of "show" is the core of Richard. We should also note the use of
"eagle," the bird traditionally the symbol of the king.

Richard initially challenges Northumberland's effrontery, playing his role to
the hilt:

> We are amaz'd, and thus long have we stood
> To watch the fearful bending of thy knee,
> Because we thought ourself thy lawful king;
> And if we be, how dare thy joints forget

To pay their aweful duty to our presence?

(III, iii, 72–76)

The extravagant language, extending his ideas over lines, reflects Richard's delight in his role. But when Northumberland politely but firmly lays the accusations and threats before him (III, iii, 104–120), Richard reverts to his true self:

> What must the King do now? Must he submit?
> The King shall do it. Must he be depos'd?
> The King shall be contented. Must he lose
> The name of King? a' God's name let it go.

(III, iii, 143–146)

Moments earlier he used the royal "we." Now he switches to third-person, as if questioning how the character he is playing and directing and whose words he is writing ought to proceed. Then he moves to strategies of stagecraft. First he considers exchanging props (III, iii, 147–153). Then he plans his departure from the stage (III, iii, 154–159) and outlines the emotional range of his performance (III, iii, 160–170). He concludes with a challenge:

> Well, well I see
> I talk but idlely, and you laugh at me.
> Most mighty prince, my Lord Northumberland,
> What says King Bullingbrook? Will his Majesty
> Give Richard leave to live till Richard die?
> You make a leg, and Bullingbrook says ay.

(III, iii, 170–175)

He is playing several games at once. He intimates he has the virtuosity to play his part in a variety of ways, but that Bullingbrook, who in this scene grabs at what Richard deems the supporting role, is too much the philistine to appreciate Richard's talent. Somehow Richard has managed to make the triumphant Bullingbrook, whom he now disparagingly refers to as "King" (III, iii, 173), look like a vulgar loser. And Northumberland is even more the fool for bowing to so crude a figure.

What we have here is not grief, but stylized grief, brilliant and affecting:

> Down, down I come, like glist'ring Phaëton,
> Wanting the manage of unruly jades.
> In the base court? Base court, where kings grow base,
> To come at traitors' calls and do them grace.

(III, iii, 178–181)

He leaves his place of honor with such sweep that he trivializes those who remove him. In the next act he utilizes this technique even more effectively.

We also seen another side of Richard. As he is addressed by Bullingbrook, who diplomatically, if hypocritically, kneels, the King does not permit the mockery:

Fair cousin, you debase your princely knee
To make the base earth proud with kissing it.
Me rather had my heart might feel your love
Than my unpleased eye see your courtesy.

(III, iii, 190–193)

He is aware of the hollowness of ceremony. Whereas once he relished every ritual of kingship, the seriousness of his plight has now overtaken him. Sadly, his understanding comes too late for him to salvage anything but his dignity.

Scene iv of Act III is an interlude in the primary action. Yet as is so often the case in Shakespeare's plays, this respite is crucial to the central theme. The leading speaker is the Gardener, whose comments on his own work refer to Richard's predicament as a whole. One of the Gardener's men reflects on their lives:

Why should we in the compass of a pale
Keep law and form and due proportion,
Showing as in a model our firm estate,
When our sea-walled garden, the whole land
Is full of weeds, her fairest flowers chok'd up,
Her fruit-trees all unprun'd, her hedges ruin'd,
Her knots disordered, and her wholesome herbs
Swarming with caterpillars?

(III, iv, 40–47)

We link the disorder in the garden with the chaos plaguing England, and we know that Richard is the cause of that disorder. Thus this speaker reminds us that the kingdom is a natural organism, which lives and breathes as an extension of the King himself. The Gardener's reply emphasizes that Richard, too, suffers:

He that hath suffered this disordered spring
Hath now himself met with the fall of leaf.

(III, iv, 48–49)

The King and the kingdom are one. The Gardener comments further about the nation:

Superfluous branches
We lop away, that bearing boughs may live;
Had he done so, himself had borne the crown,
Which waste of idle hours hath quite thrown down.

(III, iv, 63–66)

We may take the superfluous branches to mean friends like Bushy, Bagot, and Green, who ate away at Richard's reign from inside. We should also note the mention of time with its overtones of order.

When the Queen overhears the Gardener's words and learns that Richard has been deposed, she steps forward to hear the worst. What touches us is her predicament as well as the Gardener's compassion in dealing with her. Here is another of Shakespeare's simple men, who seem to embody the best in humanity. When the Queen leaves, angered and humiliated, the Gardener comments:

> Poor queen, so that thy state might be no worse,
> I would my skill were subject to thy curse.
> Here did she fall a tear, here in this place
> I'll set a bank of rue, sour herb of grace.
> Rue, even for ruth, here shortly shall be seen,
> In the remembrance of a weeping queen.
>
> (III, iv, 102–107)

Such generosity partially redeems humanity at large, providing a measure of hope for the country. And the image of a garden, healthy, growing, and tended by a wise and compassionate ruler, serves as an idealized vision throughout the tetralogy.

Reality, however, retakes center stage in the first scene of Act IV. Bullingbrook arranges a trial scene so as to justify further his taking the throne from Richard. He asks Bagot, who was spared from earlier execution, for further evidence of Richard's role in Gloucester's death, and Richard's former cohort, desperately in need of Bullingbrook's good graces, accuses Aumerle (IV, i, 10–11), who denies the assertion and throws down his gage to back himself in combat (IV, i, 25–29). Other onlookers take up the accusation, particularly Fitzwater and Surrey. The former claims that Mowbray, "the banished Norfolk" (IV, i, 80), blamed Aumerle, and once again Aumerle throws down his gage in challenge. Bullingbrook exerts his new authority by postponing any final judgment until Norfolk has returned (IV, i, 86–90), then assuages his squabbling subordinates:

> Lords appellants,
> Your differences shall all rest under gage,
> Till we assign you to your days of trial.
>
> (IV, i, 104–106)

He demonstrates his political adroitness by allowing those who could band together against him to fight amongst themselves. York then enters to announce Richard's abdication, and simultaneously confirms his loyalty to the throne, no matter who occupies it: "And long live Henry, fourth of that name" (IV, i, 112). Bullingbrook responds with calculated sanctity: "In God's name I'll ascend the throne" (IV, i, 113).

Carlisle's tirade in response to this self-anointing is an accurate prediction of the result of Bullingbrook's action, but we note the religious language the Bishop uses to express his outrage. First he restates the essential conflict:

> What subject can give sentence on his king?
> And who sits here that is not Richard's subject?
> Thieves are not judg'd but they are by to hear,
> Although apparent guilt be seen in them,
> And shall the figure of God's majesty,
> His captain, steward, deputy, elect,

Anointed, crowned, planted many years,
Be judg'd by subject and inferior breath,
And himself not present? O, forfend it, God,
That in a Christian climate souls refin'd
Should show so heinous, black, obscene a deed!

(IV, i, 121–131)

Then he dramatizes the consequences of Bullingbrook's treachery:

And if you crown him, let me prophesy,
The blood of English shall manure the ground,
And future ages groan for this foul act . . .
Disorder, horror, fear, and mutiny
Shall here inhabit, and this land be call'd
The field of Golgotha and dead men's skulls.
O, if you raise this house against this house,
It will the woefullest division prove
That ever fell upon this cursed earth.
Prevent it, resist it, let it not be so,
Lest child, child's children, cry against you "woe!"

(IV, i, 136–151)

Like Shakespeare's audience, we know the rampant destruction to be unleashed.
And the references to chaos and the suffering of children remind us of the action
of the first tetralogy. Therefore this address is further evidence of the belief that
the overthrow of a king, even one who has committed grievous abuses, is
invitation to disaster. But such an interpretation is not a full reading of this play.

However, before the other side of the story surfaces, Richard puts on one final
performance. His bestowing the crown on Bullingbrook is an act of resignation.
Yet so overwhelming is Richard's flair for theatrics that he turns this moment
of humiliating defeat into one of triumph. He reminds all of his closeness to
another victim of treachery:

Yet I well remember
The favors of these men. Were they not mine?
Did they not [sometimes] cry "All hail!" to me?
So Judas did to Christ; but He, in twelve,
Found truth in all but one; I, in twelve thousand, none.
God save the King! Will no man say amen?
Am I both priest and clerk? Well then, amen.
God save the King!

(IV, i, 167–174)

Then he takes the crown and thrusts it on Bullingbrook, dangling it before his
rival as if it were a prize and Bullingbrook a child reaching greedily for it.
Richard also speaks in terms of the two buckets, his image suggesting awareness
of the circle of life, the ever-changing patterns of failure and success:

Now is this golden crown like a deep well
That owes two buckets, filling one another,

> The emptier ever dancing in the air,
> The other down, unseen, and full of water:
> That bucket down and full of tears am I,
> Drinking my griefs, whilst you mount up on high.

(IV, i, 184–189)

Richard knows that Bullingbrook will one day suffer similar pain.

Richard's words help clarify the other side of this play: the value, indeed, the necessity of Richard's fall and Bullingbrook's rise. Richard here evinces a faith similar to that shown by Henry VI and Gloucester in the first tetralogy. All believe that justice will eventually exert itself, that a benign order does shape the world. Such a belief helps us better grasp Shakespeare's perspective on Richard's fall. The King's behavior has been disgraceful, but punishment by his subjects will arouse disaster as is dramatized in the first tetralogy. Yet we should keep in mind that these events have a purpose, and the takeover by Bullingbrook has its own importance. As Henry IV he will bring to the English crown a political sophistication that will help England leave the outmoded feudal era and enter the modern world. The downfall of Richard is therefore tragic but beneficial, leading to decades of pain but ultimately to glory. Thus there is no simple answer to the question of who is right and who is wrong in this play. Right and wrong exist on both sides, and Shakespeare, in this work and the next three, brings out such complication.

When Bullingbrook expresses impatience with Richard's delayed resignation, the King dispatches him with singular style:

> My crown I am, but still my griefs are mine.
> You may my glories and my state depose,
> But not my griefs; still am I king of those.

(IV, i, 191–193)

Here Richard refuses to release the performance aspect of his life. And in his series of puns on "care" (IV, i, 194–199), he wittily derogates Bullingbrook's comparatively crass ambition.

When Richard actually removes the crown, he does so with a poetic flair that intimates that he, a divinely ordained king, will always possess a majesty that Bullingbrook, forever a usurper, can only dream of:

> With mine own tears I wash away my balm,
> With mine own hands I give away my crown,
> With mine own tongue deny my sacred state,
> With mine own breath release all duteous oaths;
> All pomp and majesty I do foreswear;
> My manors, rents, revenues I forgo;
> My acts, decrees, and statutes I deny . . .

(IV, i, 207–213)

The implication is that only a lawful king can follow this ritual, and Bullingbrook will never have such status. Thus he will forever be smaller than Richard, who concludes his performance with a line of forgiveness:

God pardon all oaths that are broke to me!
God keep all vows unbroke are made to thee!
Make me, that nothing have, with nothing griev'd,
And thou with all pleas'd, that hast all achiev'd.

                                        (IV, i, 214–217)

These generous blessings mask an ironic wit, for Richard again implies that only
he can be recipient of such oaths, and therefore only he may be betrayed, yet
willing to pardon his betrayers. He ends with an expression of apparent generosity, but one that reveals utter contempt:

God save King Henry, unking'd Richard says,
And send him many years of sunshine days!
What more remains?

                                        (IV, i, 220–222)

The implication is not only that Henry is being crowned with Richard's approval,
but also that Henry actually needs that approval. The last three words suggest
that once Richard's performance is finished, nothing of interest remains, and
that the subsequent reign of Henry IV will be irrelevant. Richard's style is, to
say the least, impressive.

Northumberland resorts to comic coarseness as he attempts to force Richard
to recite a list of grievances against him. After invoking more religious imagery
(IV, i, 239–242), the deposed King manages to turn aside this order as well:

Mine eyes are full of tears, I cannot see;
And yet salt water blinds them not so much
But they can see a sort of traitors here.

                                        (IV, i, 244–246)

Again he deflects the moment, raising himself as he belittles his conquerors. In
his next speech he does so with more intensity:

O that I were a mockery king of snow,
Standing before the sun of Bullingbrook,
To melt myself away in water-drops!

                                        (IV, i, 260–262)

The use of the water image to characterize himself, not Bullingbrook, is another
step to garner sympathy. Shifting the image of the sun to Bullingbrook makes
the abdication more like a gesture of beneficence than one of resignation.

The climactic moment of this scene, perhaps of Richard's life, is his staring
into the mirror. This act has several levels of meaning. First, Richard the actor
is admiring himself. At the same time he is performing for the admiration of
the onlookers. Simultaneously we must imagine him genuinely looking to try to
understand who he is. And as he recalls the lines about Helen of Troy from
Marlowe's *Dr. Faustus*, he is doing one more thing:

Was this face the face
That every day under his household roof

> Did keep ten thousand men? Was this the face
> That like the sun, did make beholders wink?
> Is this the face which fac'd so many follies,
> That was at last out-fac'd by Bullingbrook?
>
>   (IV, i, 281–286)

He reflects on the transience of his place as king, and on his own fear of mortality.

Bullingbrook's last attempt to retrieve the occasion is to brand Richard with the word "shadow," to imply that Richard was no more than an imitation of a king (IV, i, 292–293). But Richard already knows that. Besides, he is more interested in the words than the idea:

> Say that again.
> The shadow of my sorrow! Hah, let's see.
>
>   (IV, i, 293–294)

And he takes off on another flight of fancy, graciously and ironically thanking Bullingbrook for the inspiration. Moments later he exits, casually victorious in his greatest defeat. Only Carlisle sees the greater truth:

> The woe's to come; the children yet unborn
> Shall feel this day as sharp to them as thorn.
>
>   (IV, i, 322–323)

The Richard we meet in Act V is a different man. Instead of demonstrative, he tends to be reflective. For instance, when the Queen articulates her bitterness, Richard reacts with more calm and understanding than he has ever shown:

> I am sworn brother, sweet,
> To grim Necessity, and he and I
> Will keep a league till death. Hie thee to France,
> And cloister thee in some religious house.
> Our holy lives must win a new world's crown,
> Which our profane hours here have thrown down.
>
>   (V, i, 20–25)

He exudes relief, a desire to seek spiritual comfort rather than find solace in the material world. Richard also seems to realize that he was never suited to be King:

> And ere thou bid good night, to quite their griefs,
> Tell thou the lamentable tale of me,
> And send the hearers weeping to their beds.
> For why, the senseless brands will sympathize
> The heavy accent of thy moving tongue,
> And in compassion weep the fire out,
> And some will mourn in ashes, some coal-black,

For the deposing of a rightful king.

(V, i, 43–50)

Outside his office he has acquired maturity, although we still see a man concerned about how his life will be replayed and how the audience will react. Certain parts of him never change.

Richard also shows a new political sophistication. When Northumberland comes to remove him to prison at Pomfret, away from vestiges of political support, Richard is surprisingly alert to the meaning of his removal. Speaking of the man he still calls Bullingbrook, Richard comments:

> He shall think that thou, which knowest the way
> To plant unrightful kings, wilt know again,
> Being ne'er so little urg'd, another way
> To pluck him headlong from the usurped throne.
> The love of wicked men converts to fear.
> That fear to hate, and hate turns one or both
> To worthy danger and deserved death.

(V, i, 62–68)

He accurately predicts the internal conflict that soon haunts the future Henry IV, and his insight into the nature of the human political animal is admirable. But his awareness of the innate greed that possesses ambitious men comes too late to save his kingship.

Northumberland ignores Richard's warning, and orders that the King and Queen must be separated. Initially Richard reacts characteristically, dramatizing the moment:

> Bad men, you violate
> A twofold marriage—'twixt my crown and me,
> And then betwixt me and my married wife.

(V, i, 71–73)

But to his wife he shows a depth of feeling unusual for someone who has been so long preoccupied with style, not emotion:

> Come, come, in wooing sorrow let's be brief,
> Since wedding it, there is such length in grief.
> One kiss shall stop our mouths, and dumbly part;
> Thus give I mine, and thus take I thy heart.

(V, i, 93–96)

Here, too, we see his growth as a man.

The next scene is thematically crucial. Throughout most of the play the Duke of York is a minor character, involved in the plot, yet helpless to alter its course. Nevertheless, his attitudes reflect those of the populace. Here he compares Richard to "a well-graced actor" (V, ii, 24), and Richard has his condolences. But York's allegiance has changed:

> But heaven hath a hand in these events,
> To whose high will we bound our calm contents.
> To Bullingbrook are we sworn subjects now,
> Whose state and honor I for aye allow.
>
> (V, i, 37–40)

All his life York has been loyal to the crown. Now, his faith tested, he places his loyalty in a man he knows to be a usurper. That loyalty is tested at once when he discovers his son Aumerle holding a letter that reveals him taking part in a conspiracy against the King. York cannot abide such disloyalty: "Treason, foul treason! Villain, traitor, slave!" (V, ii, 72). Here again disorder in the political life of the kingdom extends into family life. York must decide where his fidelity belongs: to his son or his king. Despite his wife's protests (V, ii, 88–94), he has no alternative, for his life has been based on obeisance to the throne. We might conclude that in turning on his son, York is consumed by self-interest, but such an estimate would be unfair. His choice follows from the fundamental commitment of his existence.

King Henry also worries about his "unthrifty son" (V, iii, 1), in a moment that must have pleased Elizabethan audiences. The future Henry V has been found frequenting taverns, "with unrestrained loose companions" (V, iii, 7), and the present King is disappointed but not disheartened:

> As dissolute as desperate, yet through both
> I see some sparks of better hope, which elder years
> May happily bring forth.
>
> (V, iii, 20–22)

That transformation is the story of the next two plays, and the protagonist emerges as one of the great heroes of English history. This incident tells us that Shakespeare knew where he was headed in this writing.

A more pressing need for Henry is a parallel crisis between father and son, as York accuses Aumerle:

> Mine honor lives when his dishonor dies,
> Or my shamed life in his dishonor lies:
> Thou kill'st me in his life; giving him breath,
> The traitor lives, the true man's put to death.
>
> (V, iii, 70–73)

Despite the intrusion of the word "honor," we appreciate the depth of York's feeling. At this moment, though, the Duchess rushes in to beg for her son's life (V, iii, 100–110), and Henry is faced with the first crisis of his reign, one that goes to the heart of his kingship. He is challenged by a crime against himself, the King, and he resolves to be merciful: "I pardon him as God shall pardon me" (V, ii, 131). This line is a statement of hope as well as policy, especially when Henry repeats himself (V, iii, 135–136). Earlier, when he dealt with Bagot, Aumerle, and the nobles, we saw Henry the practical politician. Now we see him as a human being and father to his people, and even though he has committed an offense against God, his nobility emerges.

The brief scene with Exton has an important implication. He takes the words and glances of the King to mean one thing: that he, Exton, should murder Richard. Does Henry mean that? We cannot be sure, although political expediency would warrant such instructions. With Richard out of the way, Henry's throne is more secure. But the focus here is on Exton, who wants the King's instructions to be for him alone: "I am the King's friend, and will rid his foe" (V, iv, 11). Thus he represents the forces that do not disappear with the new king but which remain unscrupulous in securing a place of power.

The objection of Exton's attention is a changed man, but still loyal to his nature. When we find Richard alone, in prison, he is still the performer, and his audience is himself:

> I have been studying how I may compare
> This prison where I live unto the world;
> And for because the world is populous,
> And here is not a creature but myself,
> I cannot do it; yet I'll hammer it out.
>
> (V, v, 1–5)

As usual, he is more interested in the poetry than the predicament. He is also conscious of what he is and how he has lived his life:

> Thus play I in one person many people,
> And none contented. Sometimes am I king;
> Then treasons make me wish myself a beggar,
> And so I am. Then crushing penury
> Persuades me I was better when a king;
> Then am I king'd again, and by and by
> Think that I am unking'd by Bullingbrook,
> And straight am nothing.
>
> (V, v, 31–38)

What we see now and what we never saw before is his awareness of the games he played and the follies he pursued. Such insight brings Richard a genuine dignity as opposed to the staged dignity he presented on earlier occasions.

As always, he is sensitive to music and image. Thus as he hears notes he places them symbolically in terms of time and intonation:

> How sour sweet music is
> When time is broke, and no proportion kept!
> So is it in the music of men's lives.
> And here have I the daintiness of ear
> To check time broke in a disordered string;
> But for the concord of my state and time

Had not an ear to hear my true time broke.

                                                           (V, v, 42–48)

He sees the disorder in the music reflecting not only the disorder in his kingdom
but that of the universe as well. And he is realistic enough to lay the blame
squarely on himself: "I wasted time, and now doth time waste me . . . " (V, v,
49). The entire passage, and this last line in particular, reminds us of the Gardener's sentiments in III, iv, especially when he spoke of the "waste of idle
hours" (III, iv, 66). The extent of Richard's change is even more apparent when
he meets a groom of the stable with "Thanks, noble peer!" (V, v, 67). He
knows he is no more than a man.

To the groom Richard inquires how Bullingbrook handled Barbary, the horse
Richard used to ride. When the groom answers that the animal strode proudly,
Richard is hurt, and wishes Barbary had not been so disloyal (V, iv, 87–89).
But soon Richard pardons the horse (V, iv, 90). After all, he wistfully reflects,
he himself has been effectively handled by Bullingbrook:

              I was not made a horse,
        And yet I bear a burthen like an ass,
        Spurr'd, gall'd, and tir'd by jauncing Bullingbrook.

                                                           (V, iv, 92–94)

The exact manner of Richard's death is historically uncertain, although he
may have died from starvation. Shakespeare dramatizes a more graphic death,
before which Richard fights back against Exton and the servants. We might view
this struggle as evidence that Richard dies more bravely than he lived, but
Richard's glory is not a spasm of violence. Rather it is the nobility and insight
he achieves. Indeed, he dies thinking of his kingdom:

                 Exton, thy fierce hand
        Hath with the King's blood stain'd the King's own land.

                                                           (V, v, 109–110)

Even Exton is moved by those words: "As full of value as of royal blood" (V,
vi, 113).

Henry, meanwhile, is preoccupied. To Northumberland, who has executed
Salisbury and others loyal to Richard, he promises future favors:

        We thank thee, gentle Percy, for thy pains,
        And to thy worth will add right worthy gains.

                                                           (V, vi, 11–12)

Ironically Northumberland will soon judge those gains to be inadequate. By the
beginning of the next play, he and his family and followers will resent what
they deem to be the ingratitude of a king who gained the throne with their aid.
Henry offers similar thanks to Fitzwater, then tries to soothe Carlisle:

        Choose out some secret place, some reverent room,
        More than thou hast, and with it joy thy life.

So as thou liv'st in peace, die free from strife,
For though mine enemy thou hast ever been,
High sparks of honor in thee have I seen.

(V, vi, 25–29)

This pardon may seem merciful, but it is also tactical, as Henry defuses antagonisms to his rule, which he knows will always be judged illegal. By his maneuverings with Northumberland, Fitzwater, and Carlisle, the King is mending political fences, a skill forever beyond Richard but necessary in the new climate that Henry has created.

Exton then returns Richard's body to Henry, expecting praise, but the King is not comforted:

Though I did wish him dead,
I hate the murtherer, love him murthered.
The guilt of conscience take thou for thy labor,
But neither my good word nor princely favor.
With Cain no wander through shades of night,
And never show thy head by day nor light.

(V, vi, 39–44)

Henry rebukes the assassin, but will never escape from under the burden of the crime.

We have seen Henry's political skill. We have seen his humanity. Now we see one more comforting side of him as he does not shirk his sin:

Lords, I protest my soul is full of woe
That blood should sprinkle me to make me grow.

(V, vi, 45–46)

Here is a rounding off of the dominant issue of the play. The overthrow of Richard will have terrible consequences for England. At the same time the action is historically necessary. For the new King himself, the fruits of triumph will be few. He says he intends to go to the Holy Land to rid himself of the blood on his hands but he never reaches his goal, and he endures intense physical and psychological ordeals. In his final address he maintains the images of growth and fruitfulness that have developed through the play. Thus he seems to anticipate the suffering that will be the price of his ascension, but hopes that ultimately God will judge him beneficently.

Of Richard we have a different impression. We recognize his predicament, a man placed in a situation in which his own character makes survival impossible. But Richard never reaches tragic stature. At times he is excessively foolish and misguided, and never do we feel his struggle against his fate. Instead he submits to his own nature. Ultimately, we know, England is better off without his influence. Yet we do feel a sense of loss at his death, for the passing of his peculiarly romantic personality marks the beginning of the end of the feudal era.

SUGGESTIONS FOR FURTHER READING

Altick, R. D. "Symphonic Imagery in *Richard II*." *PMLA* 62 (1947): 339–365.

Cubeta, Paul M., ed. *Twentieth Century Interpretations of* Richard II. Englewood Cliffs, N.J.: Prentice-Hall, 1971.

Dean, Leonard. "*Richard II*: The State and Image of the Theater." *PMLA* 67 (1952): 211–218.

Humphreys, Arthur Raleigh. *Shakespeare:* Richard II. London: Edward Arnold, 1967.

Jorgensen, Paul. "Vertical Patterns in *Richard II*." *Shakespeare Association Bulletin* 33 (1948): 119–134.

Mahood, Molly Maureen. *Shakespeare's Word Play*. London: Methuen, 1957.

Morris, Helen. *King Richard II*. London: Blackwell, 1966.

Potter, Lois. "The Antic Disposition of Richard II." *Shakespeare Survey* 27 (1974): 33–41.

Thompson, Karl F. "Richard II, Martyr." *Shakespeare Quarterly* 8 (1957): 159–166.

Winny, James. *The Player King: A Theme of Shakespeare's Histories*. London: Chatto & Windus, 1968.

HENRY IV, PART 1

In *Richard II*, the usurpation by Bullingbrook, now Henry IV, alters the kingship into a position subject to the mutabilities of political fortune. To an extent, the new king enjoys his power, but he also suffers its grievous consequences. In the first of two plays devoted to his rule, Henry seeks to promote an era of political stability but is plagued by forces of disorder that he himself has unleashed. As a result, all except the last five years of his reign, which lasted until his death in 1413, are marked by discord. The King himself is comforted partially by the maturation and ascension of his son as Henry V; yet his own physical and emotional afflictions make his years on the throne an ordeal.

The Prince's character provides the most important movement of the two plays. At the beginning of Part I, Hal is a wastrel, or at least offers the appearance of one. Historical evidence is slim on the matter, but Elizabethan legend had Hal as the embodiment of the Prodigal Son, who led a life of profligacy then reformed to lead the nation to a series of memorable triumphs. Shakespeare accepts this tradition and presents Hal as a wayward youth who indulges in all the whims common to a young man of sixteen or so as well as some not as traditional, such as highway robbery. Shakespeare's portrait of Hal also insinuates that this flippant attitude conceals an instinct for politics and an awareness of his place in the kingdom and in history. The shape of both parts of *Henry IV* thus reflects Hal's growth into a ruler of magnitude, as well as his recognition of the influences he must absorb and those he must abandon.

The primary influence, both beneficial and potentially damaging, is the fictional Sir John Falstaff, lord of the world of the tavern, as Henry IV is lord of the rest of the country. The character has two vague historical precedents. One is Sir John Oldcastle, an associate of Hal's and a successful soldier, later an adherent of John Wyclif, and thereafter executed for treason and heresy. The name *Falstaff* was borrowed from Sir John Fastolfe, who fought under Henry V, then against Joan of Pucelle. He appears briefly in *Henry IV, Part I*, in which he is dramatized unfairly as a coward. Despite these two antecedents, we should properly think of Falstaff as the product of Shakespeare's imagination. He is a remarkable creation: physically grotesque and a composite of, among other qualities, wit, lust, supreme self-indulgence, and an instinct for self-preservation. He may be seen as the embodiment of the best and worst of humanity, a second father to Hal, who must learn Falstaff's lessons, then leave behind Falstaff's principles.

The action of the play, which covers only about a year, begins in 1402, two years after the death of Richard II, and from Henry IV's opening lines the change in the political environment is apparent:

> So shaken as we are, so wan with care,
> Find we a time for frighted peace to pant
> And breathe short-winded accents of new broils
> To be commenc'd in stronds afar remote.
> No more the thirsty entrance of this soil
> Shall daub her lips with her own children's blood,
> No more shall trenching war channel her fields,
> Nor bruise her flow'rets with the armed hoofs
> Of hostile paces.

(I, i, 1–9)

He is under pressure from national unrest, but he accepts responsibility for this unrest. His subsequent lines evince a social conscience, an awareness that any suffering his country endures touches him. *Richard II* ends with Henry IV's intention of going to the Holy Land for expiation of his sins, and he still plans such a journey (I, i, 18–29). But the turmoil that he created occupies him and prevents this step. The rest of the speech also reveals that Henry feels the bond between man's actions and the cosmos, but the state of "civil butchery" (I, i, 13) he has created makes reliance on divine intervention useless.

In addition, the language of this initial speech echoes intriguingly a passage from *Richard II*. In Act 1, scene iii of that play, Bullingbrook and Mowbray, who have accused each other of treason, are about to fight a duel, when at the last moment King Richard intercedes. Included in the rambling explanation of his gesture are these lines:

> And grating shock of wrathful iron arms,
> Might from our quiet confines fright fair peace,
> And make us wade in even in our kinred's blood . . .

(*Richard II*, I, iii, 136–138)

Like Henry, Richard uses a form of "fright" with "peace," and both speak of the blood of their families. Richard invokes the imagery to disguise his own schemes. He does not anticipate that his own policies and actions will cause such suffering to come to pass. Henry's speech reveals that it has.

Then Henry turns to the immediate crisis, one between himself and the men who helped him gain the throne. Historically this argument also involved matters of finance, for the King spent his entire reign struggling to meet expenditures, and as a result imposed heavy taxes, including some on the Percies, formerly among his strongest advocates. Shakespeare, however, focuses on the plight of Mortimer, who, when fighting in the name of the King, had been taken prisoner by the fanatical Welshman Glendower (I, i, 36–41). Now Westmerland requests that Mortimer be freed. Henry's initial response is an offhand remark that the excursion to the Holy Land must once more be postponed. But beneath that seemingly innocent comment lies political savvy. Henry knows that Mortimer had been named heir to the throne by the childless Richard. (Shakespeare here follows Holinshed and confuses two cousins named Mortimer, but that error does not change the issue.) Thus the King is not eager to bring nearby a rival for the throne. At the same time he is conscious that by not immediately rescuing Mortimer he is antagonizing the men who in essence bestowed upon the King the power he exerts. But Henry does not care to surrender his political influence. The same instinct that drove him to take the authority of the kingship now drives him to consolidate it. Yet he is aware that, in all fairness, he does owe these men. Satisfying them but not yielding to them: such is the awkward political equilibrium Henry seeks to achieve.

One other offstage character intrudes here: Hotspur, Northumberland's son, Mortimer's brother-in-law, and a valiant soldier whose exploits, here described by Westmerland (I, i, 52–61), bother the King for two reasons. One, Hotspur's own achievements emphasize the failure of Henry's own son:

> Yea, there thou mak'st me sad, and mak'st me sin
> In envy that my Lord Northumberland
> Should be the father to so blest a son—
> A son who is the theme of honor's tongue,
> Amongst a grove the very straightest plant,
> Who is sweet Fortune's minion and her pride,
> Whilst I, by looking on the praise of him,
> See riot and dishonor stain the brow
> Of my young Harry.
>
> (I, i, 78–86)

The Elizabethan audience knows how young Hal will turn out. Thus the King's disillusionment is part of the irony underlying this play. But more subtle ironies exist. The use of the word "honor" alerts us to possible weakness in Hotspur. Indeed, that word is a leitmotif throughout, and no character better embodies its more dangerous implications. Here we learn of Henry's dissatisfaction with Hotspur's refusal to turn over prisoners to the King (I, i, 91–95). Westmerland tries to lay the blame for this choice on Worcester, and Henry's willingness to await further evidence reinforces the fundamental tension of his dominion: political debt versus the desire to rule effectively, and for Henry such rule means with unchallenged authority.

In scene ii the action shifts to the Prince's apartment in London, a transition that establishes the central pattern of the play: from the nobles to the tavern society and back again. These two worlds reflect one another, and they are also the two worlds Hal inhabits and which he must synthesize in himself. The relationship between Hal and Falstaff is perceptible at once, as Hal begins his good-natured yet pointed commentary:

> What a devil has thou to do with the time of the day?
> unless hours were cups of sack, and minutes capons,
> and clocks the tongues of bawds, and dials the signs of
> leaping-houses, and the blessed sun himself a fair hot
> wench in flame-color'd taffata; I see no reason why
> thou shouldst be so superfluous to demand the time
> of the day.

(I, ii, 6–12)

The focus on time and order pierces to the heart of the fat knight's character. He is a figure of anarchy and disorder, and as such must ultimately be turned away. Yet he has much to offer Hal, and the Prince's image of the "blessed sun," a pun on Hal's dual role as offspring and future monarch, emphasizes his bond with Falstaff.

The quality of Falstaff's language is apparent from the start:

> Let us be Diana's
> foresters, gentlemen of the shade, minions of the moon,
> and let men say we be men of good government, being
> govern'd, as the sea is, by our noble and chaste mistress
> the moon, under whose countenance we steal.

(I, ii, 25–29)

Yet the grace of his words does not disguise their irreverence. The image of "good government" ironically reflects the supposedly legitimate figures who will dominate the play, for as they rationalize their plot to "steal" the crown, so Falstaff conducts his life, one of thievery and lechery, according to his values. Furthermore, if the royal figures are symbolized by the sun, so Falstaff's anti-royal society is appropriately embodied by the moon. As Falstaff notes moment's later, " . . . 'tis no sin for a man to labor in his vocation" (I, ii, 104–105).

The delicate nature of the relationship between Hal and Falstaff is always apparent:

> Yea, and so us'd to that, were it not here
> apparent that thou art heir apparent—But I prithee,
> sweet wag, shall there be gallows standing in England
> when thou art king? and resolution thus fubb'd as
> it is with the rusty curb of old father antic the law?
> Do not thou, when thou art king, hang a thief.

(I, ii, 57–62)

Falstaff clarifies Hal's role, now and in the future. Falstaff also hints that no matter how boisterous their relationship, he himself is a subordinate and must be tactful. He dares not overstep certain unspoken bounds. Thus even as he jokes we sense a measure of seriousness:

By the Lord, and I do not, I am a villain,
I'll be damn'd for never a King's son in Christendom.

(I, ii, 96–97)

Here he slyly asks to be spared, for he hopes to maintain a place in the future
king's company but fears that his place will not always be available. That
suspicion proves cruelly accurate.

Throughout most of the scene the Prince acknowledges none of these hints
but only revels in his banter. And he is particularly pleased to conspire with
Poins in a robbery of Falstaff. As Poins explains:

> The virtue of this jest will be the
> incomprehensible lies that this same fat rogue will tell
> us when we meet at supper . . .

(I, ii, 186–188)

When left alone, however, Hal offers one of the key soliloquies of the tetralogy:

> I know you all, and will a while uphold
> The unyok'd humor of your idleness,
> Yet herein will I imitate the sun,
> Who doth permit the base contagious clouds
> To smother up his beauty from the world,
> That when he please again to be himself,
> Being wanted, he may be more wond'red at
> By breaking through the foul and ugly mists
> Of vapors that did seem to strangle him.

(I, ii, 195–203)

He is conscious of the role he has assumed, of the shady morality of his companions, and of the inevitability of his departure:

> So when this loose behavior I throw off
> And pay the debt I never promised,
> By how much better than my word I am,
> By so much shall I falsify men's hopes,
> And like bright metal on a sullen ground,
> My reformation, glitt'ring o'er my fault,
> Shall show more goodly and attract more eyes
> Than that which hath no foil to set it off.
> I'll so offend, to make offense a skill,
> Redeeming time when men think least I will.

(I, ii, 208–217)

Even at this stage Hall is sophisticated enough to realize that the degree to which
he alters his image will contribute to his success. And his last line about "redeeming time" shows that he is calculating every move. This thought we may
take in either of two ways: as indication that Hal is fundamentally deceptive or
that he is already politically acute. Perhaps he is a little of both. Moreover, the
entire speech, in conjunction with Falstaff's earlier words, reveals that neither

of these characters is completely honest with the other. For all their joviality, neither forgets his respective place, nor does either dwell on the dichotomy between their lives. Thus despite their mutual affection, their eventual parting is apparent from the start.

In scene iii the reality of the political world reasserts itself. Simultaneously the King feels the need to reassert himself. Not surprisingly, he expresses some of the same sentiments as his son:

> My blood hath been too cold and temperate,
> Unapt to stir at these indignities,
> And you have found me, for accordingly
> You tread upon my patience; but be sure
> I will from henceforth rather be myself . . .

                                                            (I, iii, 1–5)

In response to this quiet threat, Worcester attempts to claim his prerogatives:

> Our house, my sovereign liege, little deserves
> The scourge of greatness to be us'd on it,
> And that same greatness too which our own hands
> Have holp to make so portly.

                                                            (I, iii, 10–13)

In Worcester's eyes Henry is hardly part of any divine order, but rather another politician who must answer to his supporters. Furthermore, Worcester, Northumberland, and Hotspur, leaders of the eminent Percy clan, helped elevate Henry to the throne. How can he now ignore their demands? Such effrontery challenges the King's authority, but this attitude is a direct result of the former Bullingbrook's own overthrow of Richard. Henry changed the nature of the kingship. Now he must live with those changes, and he does so at this juncture by ruthlessly cutting Worcester off, then turning to Worcester's brother Northumberland: "You were about to speak" (I, iii, 22). Here the arrogance of power comes to the fore. Yet Henry must be so resolute if he is to maintain control.

When Northumberland's son Hotspur raises his voice, a new tone is added to the crisis. Virtually all the other characters in court speak in measured lines, weighing each syllable. But Hotspur, as his name implies, overflows with passion. His narrative about a seemingly effeminate soldier intruding on him in battle reflects both Hotspur's courage and his intolerance for anyone who does not conform to his ideals:

> I then, all smarting with my wounds being cold,
> To be pest'red with a popingay,
> Out of my grief and my impatience
> Answer'd neglectingly, I know not what—
> He should, or he should not—for he made me mad
> To see him shine so brisk and smell so sweet,
> And talk so like a waiting-gentlewoman

Of guns, and drums, and wounds, God save the mark!

(I, iii, 49–56)

The King, however, is not swayed in his judgment of Hotspur's conduct:

> Why, yet he doth deny his prisoners,
> But with proviso and exception,
> That we at our own charge shall ransom straight
> His brother-in-law, the foolish Mortimer . . .
> Shall we buy treason? and indent with fears,
> When they have lost and forfeited themselves?
> No, on the barren mountains let him starve;
> For I shall never hold that man my friend
> Whose tongue shall ask me for one penny cost
> To ransom home revolted Mortimer.

(I, iii, 77–92)

At this denial Hotspur cannot restrain himself:

> Revolted Mortimer!
> He never did fall off, my sovereign liege,
> But by the chance of war; to prove that true
> Needs no more but one tongue for all those wounds,
> Those mouthed wounds, which valiantly he took,
> When on the gentle Severn's sedgy bank,
> In single opposition hand to hand,
> He did confound the best part of an hour
> In changing hardiment with great Glendower.

(I, iii, 93–101)

Hotspur, too, regards the King as the first among equals. Furthermore, in retelling this narrative, Hotspur seems to refight the battle. Something in him is furiously romantic yet at the same time audaciously foolish. Historically, Hotspur was only a couple of years younger than the king. Shakespeare, however, makes Hotspur Hal's age so as to set off the contrast between the two as men and as soldiers and to set apart Hotspur's braggadocio from Hal's present semblance of dissipation and subsequent political acumen.

   After Hotspur urges his cause as strongly as possible, the King still stands his ground:

> Thou dost belie him, Percy, thou dost belie him;
> He never did encounter with Glendower.
> I tell thee,
> He durst as well have met the devil alone
> As Owen Glendower for an enemy.
> Art thou not asham'd?

(I, iii, 112–118)

The King challenges Hotspur's facts, and Shakespeare does not clarify whose interpretation is accurate. But we can tell Henry's attitude: he will not be pushed.

And we sense that even if he believed every word Hotspur spoke, the King
would still not consent to rescuing Mortimer. He must establish his authority,
as he does in the remainder of his speech:

> But, sirrah, henceforth
> Let me not hear you speak of Mortimer.
> Send me your prisoners with the speediest means,
> Or you shall hear in such a kind from me
> As will displease you. My Lord Northumberland:
> We license your departure with your son.
> Send us your prisoners, or you will hear of it.

(I, iii, 118–124)

Henry is reminding everyone that he is King and not a man with whom to trifle.
Still, that a discussion such as this can take place, with the King dickering as
his opponents speak right back to him, testifies to the new political environment
Henry's overthrow of Richard has created.

When the King departs, the remaining men weigh the reasons for his refusal
to ransom Mortimer, and after Worcester's reminder Hotspur repeats one possible
explanation:

> But soft, I pray you, did King Richard then
> Proclaim my brother Edmund Mortimer
> Heir to the crown?

(I, iii, 155–157)

The designation itself is not the key issue, but it does hit the question of succession. Mortimer, also known as Edmund, Earl of March, was descended from
Lionel of Clarence, the third son of Edward III. Henry IV, however, is a son
of John of Gaunt, fourth son of Edward. Shakespeare here follows Holinshed
in confusing this Edmund with his uncle, also named Edmund, but in the context
of the play, the Mortimer here noted, and who married Owen Glendower's
daughter, has a direct link to the throne. Thus Henry's reluctance to rescue him
is understandable.

Even more interesting are Hotspur's reflections on events that have left them
in this state of affairs:

> Shall it for shame be spoken in these days,
> Or fill up chronicles in time to come,
> That men of your nobility and power
> Did gage them both in an unjust behalf
> (As both of you—God pardon it!—have done)
> To put down Richard, that sweet lovely rose,
> And plant this thorn, this canker, Bullingbrook?

(I, iii, 170–176)

He cannot even call the new king by his royal name. How revealing that these
men, jealous of the usurper they have put in office, wax nostalgic for Richard,
whom they expelled. The circle goes round and round.

Northumberland understands his son:

Imagination of some great exploit
Drives him beyond the bounds of patience.

(I, iii, 199–200)

But the quintessence of Hotspur the man is his own tribute to honor:

By heaven, methinks it were an easy leap,
To pluck bright honor from the pale-fac'd moon,
Or dive into the bottom of the deep,
Where fadom-line could never touch the ground,
And pluck up drowned honor by the locks,
So he that doth redeem her thence might wear
Without corrival all her dignities;
But out upon this half-fac'd fellowship!

(I, iii, 201–208)

Hotspur ends up symbolic of a chivalric spirit as outdated as the feudal world it complements. His vision offers renown, but its limits will be defined by Falstaff and, more significantly, by Hal, who eventually blends similar youthful passion with worldly calculation.

As Hotspur continues to rave, Worcester attempts to break in with a concrete proposal. But Hotspur seems out of control. First he imagines maliciously whispering ''Mortimer'' into a sleeping Henry's ear (I, iii, 221–226). Then, as if frustrated by his inability to perpetrate that prank, he rails on purposelessly:

All studies hear I solemnly defy,
Save how to gall and pinch this Bullingbrook,
And that same sword-and-buckler Prince of Wales,
But that I think his father loves him not
And would be glad he met with some mischance,
I would have him poisoned with a pot of ale.

(I, iii, 228–233)

Calling the King by his former name indicates Hotspur's complete lack of respect. And the reference to Hal and the pot of ale reveals the scorn in which the Prince is generally held. Hotspur maintains this barrage of emotion until Worcester inquires with comic exhaustion:

Nay, if you have not, to it again,
We will stay your leisure.

(I, iii, 257–258)

Now Hotspur is finished.

Thus Worcester can finally offer his plan: first, Hotspur should release all his Scottish prisoners except Douglas, thereby ensuring the cooperation of the Scots against Henry; second, Northumberland should cultivate the friendship of the Archbishop Scroop, whose brother was executed by Henry, and who still bears a grudge against the King (I, iii, 260–271). The conspiracy immediately reminds us of the plot against Falstaff formulated in the previous scene, and Hotspur's boyish enthusiasm does not increase the stature of the royal machinations:

> Why, it cannot choose but be a noble plot.
> And then the power of Scotland, and of York,
> To join with Mortimer, ha?
>
> (I, iii, 279–281)

Moments later he adds: " . . . we'll be reveng'd on him" (I, iii, 291). Earlier the two conspiracies were linked by Hotspur's reference to "The cords, the ladder, or the hangman rather?" (I, iii, 166). We note, too, the pettiness of both conspiracies. But the conspiracy in the tavern is strictly local in effect. The stealing of a few pounds from Falstaff fades in comparison with the bloody destruction that these men consent to unleash. Accordingly, Hotspur sounds misguided, and even his closing rally rings hollow:

> Uncle, adieu! O, let the hours be short,
> Till fields, and blows, and groans applaud our sport!
>
> (I, iii, 301–302)

No matter how justified these men believe their actions and no matter how politically motivated are Henry's denials of their petitions, these individuals who would now overthrow the King seem small-minded and vengeful.

Act II, scene i centers on the concept of disorder. Two carriers are dismayed over the condition of the inn where they seek shelter, and as they use the word "house," it has overtones of the royal house of England. Gadshill, a robber mentioned by Poins earlier (I, ii, 106), and named after a road infamous for robberies, requests a lantern from the carriers, but they refuse. Chamberlain then tells Gadshill of a franklin (a landowner), who will be leaving the tavern carrying a large amount of money (II, i, 54–56). The professional highwayman has no hesitation about joining an activity carried out by more exalted comrades:

> . . . for they pray
> continually to their saint, the commonwealth, or
> rather, not pray to her, but prey on her, for they ride
> up and down on her, and make her their boots.
>
> (II, i, 79–82)

The parallel to the plot by Northumberland and Hotspur against the King is clear.

This comic inversion of the plot against King Henry takes place in Act II, scene ii, when Falstaff is beset on the road. As he rumbles along muttering to himself, he initially has no dignity. But as he proclaims at length his stature through complaints against his mistreatment, he gains that standing, and in doing so becomes the embodiment of man's capacity to create his own image. We think of Hal's earlier expression of his conception of himself (I, ii, 195–217).

However, Falstaff's words have further repercussions: "A plague upon it when thieves cannot be true to one another!" (II, ii, 27–28). He reminds us how the enemies of Richard have become enemies of one another, another instance where the shenanigans of the tavern are set against life at the court, which thereby seems far less noble.

When attacked by the disguised Prince and his gang, Falstaff offers two lines that, as much as any others, point to the heart of his character: " . . . they hate us youth" (II, ii, 85) and "What, ye knaves, young men must live!" (II, ii, 90–91). Falstaff is a thief, a parasite, a cheat, and a lecher, among other things. But he also embodies the license of youth, the laughter and freedom of expression that society grants to young people. At the same time, though, youth must one day be outgrown, and that realization is ever on our minds as well as on Hal's.

In contrast to the adolescence that Hal forsakes is the impetuosity from which Hotspur never escapes. It is again manifested in Act II, scene iii, first as he scorns a letter from a lord reluctant to conspire against the King, then in his interlude with his wife. She complains that even in sleep he seems preoccupied with battle (II, iii, 47–55), and although he displays affection for her, his immaturity shines through:

> And when I am a' horseback, I will swear
> I love thee infinitely. But hark you, Kate,
> I must not have you henceforth question me
> Whither I go, nor reason whereabout.
>
> (II, iii, 101–104)

A need for such secrecy usually betokens a man embarrassed by his task, and Hotspur looks more and more like a boy about to indulge in nasty pranks, deceptive about what he knows to be wrong.

Act II, scene iv, one of the great scenes in all of Shakespeare, signals the beginning of Hal's visible transformation. In his first speech he tells Poins and us that he is conscious of his current state of disrepute (II, iv, 9–14). He is also aware of the eminence of his great rival:

> I am not yet of Percy's
> mind, the Hotspur of the north, he that kills me some
> six or seven dozen of Scots at a breakfast,
> washes his hands, and says to his wife, "Fie upon this
> quiet life! I want work!"
>
> (III, iv, 101–105)

His tone is sarcastic. Yet he knows that he will one day assume the responsibilities of office, and those will include battle with Hotspur. Still, he takes time to indulge his taste for jokes by tormenting Francis, allying himself with Poins to call the servant back and forth, and leave him frazzled. Hal explains his reasons:

> I am now of all humors that have show'd
> themselves humors since the old days of goodman
> Adam to the pupil age of this present twelve a' clock

at midnight.

(II, iv, 92–95)

We feel him fighting off the inevitable break with this boisterous life.

When Falstaff enters, he curses the general state of cowardice, while simultaneously exalting his own bravery:

> There lives not three good men
> unhang'd in England, and one of them is fat
> and grows old.

(II, iv, 130–132)

After some typical banter with Hal, Falstaff recounts his ordeal on the road, changing the facts to suit the moment. Eventually the Prince challenges the narrative:

> These lies are like their father that begets
> them, gross as a mountain, open, palpable. Why, thou
> clay-brain'd guts, thou knotty-pated fool, thou
> whoreson, obscene, greasy tallow-catch—

(II, iv, 225–228)

But Falstaff stands by his claims. Only when the prince forces him to face the truth (II, iv, 253–264) does Falstaff relent:

> By the Lord, I knew ye as well as he that
> made ye. Why, hear you, my masters, was it
> for me to kill the heir-apparent? Should I turn upon
> the true prince? Why, thou knowest I am as valiant
> as Hercules; but beware instinct—the lion will not
> touch the true prince. Instinct is a great matter; I was
> now a coward on instinct.

(II, iv, 267–273)

The first sentence suggests that Falstaff understands the Prince as well as does the father who made Hal. Thus Falstaff is saying he is like a second father. The next sentence emphasizes that Falstaff never forgets Hal's identity, and the word "kill" surely does not refer to this one incident. Rather Falstaff knows that he must respect the man who will one day be his king, and that this future king must never be treated so coarsely that anyone forgets his place. The reference to the "lion," the traditional emblem of the king, intimates that Falstaff will try not to let Hal be hurt by his real father, another expression of solicitude.

Thus this passage hints at the deeper qualities of the relationship between the Prince and the knight. But that relationship is explored much further in the next part of the scene, where Hal plays himself, then his own father, with Falstaff playing complementary roles. After relaying a message that Hal is called to court, perhaps to fight the Percies, Falstaff inquires whether Hal is afraid of Hotspur (II, iv, 365–370). Underlying the query is Falstaff's own concern for Hal's safety, but Hal denies any apprehension, claiming he lacks the "instinct"

Falstaff claimed earlier (II, iv, 372). But the issue taps something inside Hal, who virtually orders Falstaff to pretend to be the King and to question Hal on his goals and values. Falstaff plays the role with zest:

> If then
> thou be son to me, here lies the point: why being son
> to me, art thou so pointed at? Shall the blessed sun of
> heaven prove a micher and eat blackberries? a question
> not to be ask'd.
>
> (II, iv, 405–409)

Multiple levels of truth are evident here. Earlier Falstaff had claimed about his own narrative:

> What, art thou mad? art thou mad? is not the
> truth the truth?
>
> (II, iv, 229–230)

Here he proves the contrary. First Falstaff is asking Hal how long will he, as Prince, indulge in foolery (II, iv, 407–410). Falstaff knows this question genuinely torments the King, and Falstaff knows, too, that Hal is aware of Henry's anger.

Next Falstaff turns to his own defense. Speaking of a "virtuous man" (II, iv, 417) known to be in Hal's company, he offers a flattering account of himself:

> If that man should be
> lewdly given, he deceiveth me; for, Harry, I see
> virtue in his looks. If then the tree may be known by
> the fruit, as the fruit by the tree, then peremptorily I
> speak it, there is virtue in that Falstaff; him keep
> with, the rest banish.
>
> (II, iv, 426–431)

In some respects Hal is the "fruit," the offspring of Falstaff, and the strength of Hal's character is the proof of Falstaff's virtue. Thus Falstaff is playing, but he is also pleading not to be forgotten.

This request, however, will eventually be denied, as Hal reveals. And he does so in a mask of his own as he orders Falstaff to stand down while "I'll play my father" (II, iv, 434). Falstaff's response, "Depose me?" (II, iv, 435) is one moment of recognition of Hal's inevitable transformation. From this point on, the future king in Hal emerges, and his language as he assaults himself, as it were, grows passionate, even violent:

> Swearest thou, ungracious boy? henceforth
> ne'er look on me. Thou art violently carried away from
> grace, there is a devil haunts thee in the likeness of

an old fat man, a tun of man is thy companion.

(II, iv, 445–448)

The words are offered in the familiar spirit of humor, but we should imagine
Falstaff squirming as he hears taunts about his physical deficiencies, then a
catalogue of his vices:

> Wherein is he good, but to taste sack and drink
> it? wherein neat and cleanly, but to carve a capon and
> eat it? wherein cunning, but in craft? wherein crafty,
> but in villainy? wherein villainous, but in all things?
> wherein worthy, but in nothing?

(II, iv, 455–459)

Serious implications lurk here, and the laughter of the onlookers must be strained.
Hal may smile as he says these lines, but they should be uttered with controlled
intensity.

Falstaff, as Hal, offers a more desperate defense. He recognizes his age and
mortality:

> That he is old,
> the more the pity, his white hairs do witness it, but that
> he is, saving your reverence, a whoremaster, that I
> utterly deny.

(II, iv, 467–470)

He recognizes his own weakness of spirit:

> If sack and sugar be a fault, God
> help the wicked! If to be old and merry be a sin, then
> many an old host that I know is damn'd.

(II, iv, 470–472)

Most important, he recognizes his value to Hal:

> No, my good lord, banish Peto, banish Bardolph,
> banish Poins, but for sweet Jack Falstaff, kind
> Jack Falstaff, true Jack Falstaff, valiant Jack Falstaff,
> and therefore more valiant, being as he is old Jack
> Falstaff, banish not him thy Harry's company, banish
> not him thy Harry's company—banish plump Jack,
> and banish all the world.

(II, iv, 474–480)

Falstaff warns that Hal must never lose his touch of humanity, his bond with
common people. Hal's poignant answer indicates that he knows precisely what
must be done: "I do, I will" (II, iv, 481). We should imagine that at this moment
Falstaff's face communicates laughter at Hal's wit, tainted by the pain of recognition at Hal's cold insight. The fissure has opened.

But Hal spiritually does not desert the tavern crowd. Earlier in the scene he ignored Falstaff's message to hurry to court after the message from Sir John Bracy. Now before leaving the tavern, he lies to the Sheriff who is chasing Falstaff (II, iv, 512–518). Hal is thus no paragon of virtue. On the other hand, he is not immoral or unduly cruel. He enjoys defiance of his father, but later he demonstrates loyalty and courage in battle. He is, in fact, an engrossing puzzlement. We have no indication that he is pained by the competing roles he plays. He is not tormented by conscience or duty. We never feel he is out of control. Indeed, if anything, he maintains an emotional detachment from everyone, including the King and Falstaff. After the soliloquy in Act I, scene ii, he never opens up, even to the audience. Perhaps this demeanor is one subtle theme of this play: that the successful politician must keep tight rein on himself so as to be invulnerable to any emotion that might weaken his place.

This notion is supported by scene i of Act III, which further clarifies the personalities of those who conspire against Henry. Here Hotspur, Worcester, Mortimer, and Glendower plan the division of the kingdom after they retake it, but egos are always on parade, as when Glendower boasts of his powers that supposedly verge on the supernatural. First he asserts: "I say the earth did shake when I was born" (III, i, 20). Then he boasts: "I can call spirits from the vasty deep" (III, i, 52). Hotspur does not hesitate to quash such pretension:

> Why, so can I, or so can any man,
> But will they come when you do call for them?
>
> (III, i, 53–54)

Eventually exhausted by Hotspur's challenging, Glendower then turns the others to business, and Mortimer outlines a proposed division of the kingdom:

> England, from Trent and Severn hitherto,
> By south and east is to my part assign'd;
> All westward, Wales beyond the Severn shore,
> And all the fertile land within that bound,
> To Owen Glendower; and, dear coz, to you
> The remnant northward lying off from Trent.
>
> (III, i, 73–78)

This partitioning confirms what we have suspected: the primary motivation of the rebels is not the good of the country, but the assertion of their own strength and will. The Elizabethan audience would surely have regarded any scheme to fragment the country as destructive, and thus the King and Hal, who defend the nation as a whole, emerge as heroes.

An argument ensues over territory, but eventually it is resolved, although Hotspur's temper is always at the forefront, especially when he must listen to Glendower:

> I had rather be a kitten and cry mew
> Than one of these same metre ballet-mongers;
> I had rather hear a brazen canstick turn'd,

Or a dry wheel grate on the axle-tree,
And that would set my teeth nothing an edge,
Nothing so much as mincing poetry.

(III, i, 127–132)

When Glendower momentarily leaves, Mortimer gently chastises Hotspur for
his temper, but Worcester puts the matter to his nephew more strongly:

You must needs learn, lord, to amend this fault;
Though sometimes it show greatness, courage, blood—
And that's the dearest grace it renders you—
Yet oftentimes it doth present harsh rage,
Defect of manners, want of government,
Pride, haughtiness, opinion, and disdain . . .

(III, i, 178–183)

This lesson is one Hotspur never learns. We enjoy his unrestrained passion, but
we respect Hal more, for he clearly has the mastery of his own feelings that a
leader must maintain.

The rest of the scene is a semi-romantic interlude, as Mortimer, who is married
to Glendower's daughter, must comfort his wife at his own departure. That he
speaks no Welsh and his wife no English gives the episode a comic tone, but
the Welsh music brings out a measure of sentiment in Hotspur (III, i, 245–257).
The mood lasts only briefly, however, for his mind reverts to the treaty the men
are to sign, and the episode ends with everyone headed to battle.

The growing conspiracy sets up the climatic scene of the play, the only one
in which the King and Hal are alone. Act III, scene ii has little action or distracting
adornment; it is instead an occasion for the declaration of principle, first by
Henry, then by Hal, and together they establish the responsibilities of kingship
and of the man who will be king. Historically the encounter has no basis, but
theatrically it is dynamic.

The depths of Henry's conscience are apparent in his opening words:

I know not whether God will have it so
For some displeasing service I have done,
That in his secret doom, out of my blood
He'll breed revengement and a scourge for me . . .

(III, ii, 4–7)

Surely he can answer his question. Henry has indeed offended God by overthrowing a king, and punishment is inevitable, although the specific form is
uncertain.

Hal denies his father's accusations, but Henry persists:

The hope and expectation of thy time
Is ruin'd, and the soul of every man

Prophetically do forethink thy fall.

(III, ii, 36–38)

We wonder whether Henry fears most for the kingdom or for himself. After all, he goes on at length at how he gained the crown:

And then I stole all courtesy from heaven,
And dress'd myself in such humility
That I did pluck allegiance from men's hearts,
Loud shouts and salutations from their mouths,
Even in the presence of the crowned King.

(III, ii, 50–54)

He seems to be attempting both to glorify and justify his own ambition:

The skipping King, he ambled up and down,
With shallow jesters, and rash bavin wits,
Soon kindled and soon burnt, carded his state,
Mingled his royalty with cap'ring fools,
Had his great name profaned with their scorns,
And gave his countenance, against his name,
To laugh at gibing boys, and stand the push
Of every beardless vain comparative . . .

(III, ii, 60–67)

This last passage serves two purposes. It warns Hal of the dangers of a weak reputation, and it further excuses Henry's original overthrow. Indeed, this entire lengthy recitation may be said to have a double goal. The King cautions Hal about neglecting responsibilities and simultaneously tries to vindicate himself. Why does he go on so? Upon reflection we recognize that the King has never spoken this way before, that he has never been able to trust anyone with his most profound feelings. Such is the loneliness of power. Now he is confiding in Hal, who will one day assume that power. The King seems to be seeking a pardon from his son, an expression of reassurance that as a father and monarch he has succeeded. But that expression does not come here.

Hal's one-sentence answer is the turning point of the play:

I shall hereafter, my thrice-gracious lord,
Be more myself.

(III, ii, 92–93)

He echoes the opening speech of Act I, scene iii, when Henry indicated he would "rather be myself" (I, iii, 5). The parallel image seals the bond between father and son. This line from Hal is also characteristically unemotional.

But Henry is not yet finished. Instead he persists in lecturing, next about Hotspur: "And even as I was then is Percy now" (III, ii, 96). Is the King trying to inspire Hal? Or is this meeting likely to be Henry's only chance to release all his anxiety, to express the pressure he feels from the opposition? Hotspur is his most vociferous rival: young, energetic, and antagonistic. But Henry lists

the others as well (III, ii, 118–120). By the end of Part 2 the King will die
from a combination of spiritual exhaustion, emotional collapse, and a crippling
disease like leprosy. Here he confesses his apprehension that those forces surrounding him will one day bring him down.

Hal's response to his father's desperation is powerful. He, too, personalizes
matters, promising not to rule wisely or shrewdly, but simply to defeat Hotspur:
"I will redeem all this on Percy's head . . ." (III, ii, 132). The repetition of
"honor" at lines 138 and 142 is meant to resound ironically at young Percy,
who bases his life on the connotations of that word. In sum, Hal is ready to
fight for his father's cause. Yet again he offers no deep affection for his father,
but instead speaks from political obligation (III, ii, 153–156). Henry's brief
response is in a similar vein; not an expression of gratitude, but more evidence
of the pressure he feels:

> A hundred thousand rebels die in this.
> Thou shalt have charge and sovereign trust herein.
>
> (III, ii, 160–161)

His words communicate no joy, only resignation.

As if on cue, Sir Walter Blunt reports on the progress of battle. Opposition
forces are mounting, and again they are listed individually, this time by Blunt.
Henry's war is unrelenting.

In contrast to the solemnity of the court, life at The Boar's Head Tavern
remains rollicking. Indeed, the more the Prince grows, the more Falstaff seems
an alien being. Thus when we leave Hal and the seriousness of his purpose,
Falstaff's reflections, too, seem striking:

> I was as virtuously given as a
> gentlemen need to be, virtuous enough: swore
> little, diced not above seven times—a week, went to a
> bawdy-house not above once in a quarter—of an hour,
> paid money that I borrow'd—three or four times,
> liv'd well and in good compass, and now I live out of
> all order, out of all compass.
>
> (III, iii, 14–20)

The humor is ever present, but so is a tone of self-defense. Falstaff seems to
know that he is now more than just a riotous companion; he is the antithesis of
all that the Prince must become. The phrase "out of compass" implies not only
Falstaff's girth and appetite, but the excess of his life.

Bardolph picks up on the phrase "out of compass" and inspires from Falstaff
an extended disquisition on Bardolph's nose and face: "I never see thy face but
I think upon hell-fire and Dives that liv'd in purple . . ." (III, iii, 31–32). This
virtuoso speech is interrupted by the Hostess, whom Falstaff verbally assaults,
demanding to know who picked his pocket (III, iii, 52–53). The two go back
and forth with hilarious, if vicious, insults, and when she is unable to help,

Falstaff refuses to pay his considerable bill. At this point Hal enters, and Falstaff pleads his case further. But once more he is caught by Hal:

> Why, thou whoreson,
> impudent, emboss'd rascal, if there were any thing
> in thy pocket but tavern-reckonings, memorandums
> of bawdy-houses, and one poor pennyworth of
> sugar-candy to make thee long-winded—if thy pocket
> were enrich'd with any other injuries but these, I am a
> villain. And yet you will stand to it, you will not
> pocket up wrong. Art thou not asham'd?

                                                             (III, iii, 156–163)

Now Falstaff realizes who perpetrated the crime:

> Dost thou hear, Hal? Thou knowest in the
> state of innocency Adam fell, and what should poor
> Jack Falstaff do in the days of villainy? Thou seest I
> have more flesh than another man, and therefore more
> frailty. You confess then you pick'd my pocket?

                                                             (III, iii, 164–168)

Falstaff then pardons the Hostess, and Hal comforts him that the robbery money is paid off. As always, Hal forgives Falstaff anything, as does almost everyone else. But the news that Hal and his father have reconciled brings a new order for Falstaff: "I have procur'd thee, Jack, a charge of foot" (III, iii, 186). And with war at hand, Hal has serious orders first for Bardolph, then for Peto, then for Falstaff himself:

> Jack, meet me to-morrow in the Temple Hall
> At two [a']clock in the afternoon;
> There shalt thou know thy charge, and there receive
> Money and order for their furniture.
> The land is burning, Percy stands on high,
> And either we or they must lower lie.

                                                             (III, iii, 199–204)

Were we to hear only the last two lines, we might think the speaker Hotspur. Here is more evidence of the Prince's shifting priorities. And Falstaff's casual response is one more remark that reflects the widening chasm between them.

   At the beginning of Act IV the action turns again to the opposition, and certain words and images recur. Douglas, now an ally, refers to Hotspur as "the king of honor" (IV, i, 10), and although the phrase may be meant as a compliment, the playwright's irony pierces through. Hotspur receives further messages from his father, Northumberland, stressing the theme of fathers and sons. The weight given that relationship ensures that the play can never be viewed as an abstract political drama. To the contrary, the emphasis on family reminds the audience of the personal toll that political and social conflicts take, both on the participants and on those who must live with the consequences.

This scene also brings out the theme of "sickness." Northumberland's letters indicate that he is unwell, and we remember Henry's opening lines of the play in which he indicated his physical debilitation. Hotspur, though, remains unimpressed by the imposition of disease. He acknowledges that:

> This sickness doth infect
> The very life-blood of our enterprise . . .
>
> (IV, i, 28–29)

But he is determined to carry on. Speaking of his father, he says:

> Yet doth he give us bold advertisement
> That with our small conjunction we should on.
> To see how fortune is dispos'd to us,
> For, as he writes, there is no quailing now,
> Because the King is certainly possess'd
> Of all our purposes.
>
> (IV, i, 36–41)

Why is he so eager to maintain this struggle? The answer comes in a few moments. In the meantime we may take the images of sickness as reflecting the state of the kingdom itself.

The scene is also important because of the dissension that surfaces amidst the opposition ranks. Hotspur blusters that his father is not necessary to their enterprise, but Worcester remains unconvinced:

> This absence of your father's draws a curtain
> That shows the ignorant a kind of fear
> Before not dreamt of.
>
> (IV, i, 73–76)

Hotspur has a retort:

> If we without his help can make a head
> To push against a kingdom, with his help
> We shall o'erturn it topsy-turvy down.
> Yet all goes well, yet all our joints are whole.
>
> (IV, i, 80–83)

Hotspur is dedicated to his own reputation, while Worcester, though a conniving plotter, is nonetheless concerned with the success of the cause. The conspirators have always been united in their opposition to the King. Now something else is happening. The implication of this scene and others that follow is that internal dissent is in the nature of rebellion. If these men can overthrow one king, as they have already done, and they are prepared to overthrow another, then they become primed to challenge any authoritarian structure, even one they have established among themselves. The craving for power cannot be turned on and off.

Sir Richard Vernon then enters with a report on the royal army, and his description of Hal is memorable:

I saw young Harry with his beaver on,
His cushes on his thighs, gallantly arm'd,
Rise from the ground like feathered Mercury,
And vaulted with such ease into his seat
As if an angel [dropp'd] down from the clouds
To turn and wind a fiery Pegasus,
And witch the world with noble horsemanship.

(IV, i, 104–110)

Hotspur interrupts, for he cannot hear such words about his rival. Yet at the same time he is so inspired that he can barely restrain himself from racing off. Even news that Glendower needs time to rally his troops does not discourage Percy:

Come let us take a muster speedily.
Doomsday is near, die all, die merrily.

(IV, i, 133–134)

He is a fascinating figure. But this sentiment is fundamentally mindless. And as if to emphasize just how mindless it is, Shakespeare moves us directly to the other side of war. We do not see the conferences where leaders plan sophisticated strategy. Instead, we come upon common foot soldiers, who have little sense of the cause for which they have been called to arms, and even less sense of the glory Hotspur envisions.

Falstaff derides the troops he has managed to scrape up. He acknowledges that he has abused the King's fund, hauling in not the best, who were able to bribe their way out of service, but the worst (IV, ii, 20–31). We note his phrase "ten times more dishonorable" (IV, ii, 30–31), and after Hotspur's harangues, the word has bitter connotations. Nothing is honorable in this crew or in the service of which Falstaff is a part.

When Hal enters and surveys this unimpressive lot, Falstaff offers a weak, even annoying, excuse:

Tut, tut, good enough to toss, food for
powder, food for powder; they'll fill a pit as well as
better. Tush, man, mortal men, mortal men.

(IV, ii, 65–67)

Here is the dark side of battle. Poor, uninfluential men fight to satisfy the whims of rich, powerful men. Here, too, is where Falstaff loses some of his charm. We now realize that part of his way of life demands corruption, that his cowardice involves not simply his own boisterous times, but death for others who depend on him. Suddenly he is less cheerful a figure.

The next scene returns us to the formal aspects of war, as dissension on the opposition side spreads. Vernon is nervous about the upcoming battle (IV, iii, 16–24) but the others mock his fears. Yet in the light of the previous scene, his trepidations do not seem foolish or impractical, but all too fair. Here, too, the rebels are more angry with one another than with the King.

With the entrance of Sir Walter Blunt, the official conflict begins. This episode is essential for it clarifies reasons of the opposition to Henry IV. Blunt's invitation, however, suggests the illegality of what is to take place:

> So long as out of limit and true rule
> You stand against anointed majesty.
>
> (IV, iii, 39–40)

The lines are reminiscent of Falstaff's comments about himself and his place, and the anti-order qualities of the rebels assure that our sympathies lie with the King.

Hotspur begins his explanation:

> My father gave him welcome to the shore;
> And when he heard him swear and vow to God
> He came but to be Duke of Lancaster,
> To sue his livery and beg his peace,
> With tears of innocency and terms of zeal,
> My father, in kind heart and pity mov'd,
> Swore him assistance, and perform'd it too.
>
> (IV, iii, 59–65)

The argument seems to be no more than that the rebels who helped Bullingbrook become Henry IV have not garnered their expected spoils. When Blunt dismisses this catalogue of frustrations, Hotspur retorts with more persuasive proof. First he harkens back to Richard:

> In short time after, he depos'd the King,
> Soon after that, depriv'd him of his life,
> And in the neck of that, task'd the whole state;
>
> (IV, iii, 90–92)

How ironic that Richard, once the object of derision, is now mourned. Then Hotspur's list grows, but all the crimes he reviews are against himself, his father, and their associates. Only at the end are additional malfeasances noted, but they are never explained fully. The tally is therefore unconvincing, and we feel more than ever that this rebellion is the work of disappointed power brokers fretting about their own status and not the good of the country.

A more objective version of the conflict is offered in scene iv, when the Archbishop of York orders Sir Michael to deliver messages to the allied rebel troops. These two are impressed with the power of the King, especially when he is joined by Hal, and we learn here that the army of the rebels is ready to collapse (IV, iv, 16–20). As a result of this conversation, the two previous scenes become more painful. One, the soldiers Falstaff has recruited are soon to die, and their fate appears pointless. Two, Hotspur's campaign appears more foolish, and his hope to "die merrily" more dubious.

Act V takes us to the actual arena of war, the battle of Shrewsbury fought in July 1403. From the King's opening lines the tone is gloomy:

How bloodily the sun begins to peer
Above yon bulky hill! the day looks pale
At his distemp'rature.

(V, i, 1–3)

Hereafter none of Hotspur's poetry or militaristic fervor seems appropriate. Soon, however, a curious incident occurs, when Worcester enters with a plea to stop the bloodshed. Henry consents to listen, but first insists on laying the blame for the entire conflict on the intruder:

You have deceiv'd our trust,
And made us doff our easy robes of peace,
To crush our old limbs in ungentle steel.

(V, i, 11–13)

Henry seems regretful that the war has gone this far. Worcester then offers a defense, claiming that Henry had once allied himself with the men now fighting him:

It was myself, my brother, and his son,
That brought you home, and boldly did outdate
The dangers of the time . . .

(V, i, 39–41)

. . . We were enforc'd for safety sake to fly
Out of your sight and raise this present head,
Whereby we stand oppos'd by such means
As you yourself have forg'd against yourself
By unkind usage, dangerous countenance,
And violation of all faith and troth
Sworn to us in your younger enterprise.

(V, i, 65–71)

To these charges Henry offers a contemptuous dismissal:

And never yet did insurrection want
Such water-colors to impaint his cause,
Nor moody beggars, starving for a time
Of pell-mell havoc and confusion.

(V, i, 79–83)

Instead of seeking a path away from bloodshed, Henry now seems eager to fight. Thus at the beginning of the scene the King is frustrated and saddened by the potential cost of war. But once his opponents make their case, his spirits are aroused and battle once more has its lure. Pride supersedes rationality.

Hal intervenes, warning both parties about the many deaths to come (V, i, 83–85). Then he offers a way out of the slaughter: his own single combat with Hotspur (V, i, 100). This gesture is Shakespeare's invention, with no historical substance. Henry, however, does not accept these terms, and warns that unless the rebels resign immediately:

Rebuke and dread correction wait on us,
And they shall do their office.

                                                    (V, i, 110–111)

Hal realizes that Hotspur and Douglas will never accept the King's offer for they
fully expect to win. But Henry does not back down: "And God befriend us as
our cause is just" (V, i, 120). How ironic that the character who in the previous
play challenged the grace of God by overthrowing a king now banks on that
grace to support himself. Henry's attitude suggests that whoever is king is right,
quite a change from the man who took the throne against civil law.

   Why would Shakespeare include this scene? The reason may be the next few
lines, Falstaff's musings on honor:

                        What
   is honor? A word. What is in that word honor?
   What is that honor? Air. A trim reckoning!
   Who hath it? He that died a' Wednesday. Doth he
   feel it? No. Doth he hear it? No. 'Tis insensible
   then? Yea, to the dead. But will['t] not live with the
   living? No. Why? Detraction will not suffer it.
   Therefore I'll none of it, honor is a mere scutcheon.
   And so ends my catechism.

                                                    (V, i, 133–141)

The speech is vital to this play on several levels. First, it is the clearest response
to Hotspur's orations. Second, its placement right after Henry renews his commitment to fighting suggests that the King himself is vulnerable to the same
flights of ego that motivate Hotspur. Third, it reflects the myriad aspects of
Falstaff's character: his wit, his insight, his cowardice. Fourth, and perhaps
most significant, this speech, which follows Hal's plan to avoid wholesale slaughter, shows that the Prince has learned from Falstaff, that Hal might one day
bring to his kingship a different set of values. Henry V does become one of the
great leaders of English history, and part of his greatness that Shakespeare
dramatizes is the sense of humanity he learns from Falstaff.

   The speech raises another issue, this one central to all the history plays. In
the discussion of the first tetralogy, we considered how Shakespeare presents
the ugliness of battle, that he never hides that reality behind chauvinistic or
patriotic flourishes. In the earlier plays the fighting was repulsive, but then so
many of the characters were dislikeable. Here, some of the characters are more
attractive personally, and their cause may appear to have more substance. Nonetheless, the act of war remains as horrifying as ever, and Falstaff's "catechism"
on the meaninglessness of honor thus has a place in Shakespeare's antiwar vision.
Participants may escape with their lives, and they may even earn national reward.
But we are never allowed to feel pride at someone's death. Instead we feel that
all would be better off if the entire terrible enterprise could be avoided.

   In the next scene loyalty degenerates further, as Worcester is not eager to tell

Hotspur of the King's inclination to call off the war (V, ii, 21–25). Worcester even adds an insult in the King's name:

> He calls us rebels, traitors, and will scourge
> With haughty arms this hateful name in us.
>
> (V, ii, 39–40)

Here we think back to the lies and deceits of the tavern world. Worcester's deception, the act of a nobleman supposedly fighting for his country, is far more reprehensible and leads to much greater suffering. Worcester and Vernon report only Hal's invitation, and Hotspur seems eager to hear that the challenge was insulting: "How show'd his tasking? seem'd it in contempt?" (V, ii, 50). Vernon tries to downplay further hostility, and in fact praises Hal's qualities:

> If he outlive the envy of this day,
> England did never owe so sweet a hope,
> So much misconstrued in his wantonness.
>
> (V, ii, 66–68)

But Hotspur has such antagonism for the King that he ignores common sense:

> O gentlemen, the time of life is short!
> To spend that shortness basely were too long
> If life did ride upon a dial's point,
> Still ending at the arrival of an hour.
> And if we live, we live to tread on kings,
> If die, brave death, when princes die with us!
>
> (V, ii, 81–86)

Here he is so enthusiastic about the prospect of romantic death that he cannot be regarded seriously. Yet his call does have a touch of magic. Such is the nature of war. Its savagery has a fascination, and Shakespeare acknowledges both sides through Hotspur:

> Sound all the lofty instruments of war,
> And by that music let us all embrace,
> For heaven to earth, some of us never shall
> A second time do such a courtesy.
>
> (V, ii, 97–100)

He is deluded but alluring.

The battle scenes are both graphic and intriguing. First Douglas kills Blunt, who is disguised as the King, and at that moment Blunt seems to have died an "honorable" death. Yet as Falstaff waddles on, we cannot respect any of the battle, for his very presence lampoons the event: "There's honor for you!" (V, iii, 32–33). As Falstaff pulls out a flask instead of a sword, Hal is angered: "What, is it a time to jest and dally now?" (V, iii, 56). We note the word "time," for Hal is now subject to its implications of order and stability. Falstaff responds to Hal's accusation:

> Give me life,
> which if I can save, so; if not, honor comes unlook'd
> for, and there's an end.
>
> (V, iii, 59–61)

We are sympathetic to his attitude. Yet we also realize that his irony, amusing as it is, cannot sustain someone with responsibility, which has its price.

In the beginning of scene iv, the King suggests that his two sons, a wounded Hal and John of Lancaster, temporarily rest from battle. But John is unwilling to retreat even momentarily, and after he charges off, Hal has great praise for his younger brother:

> I did not think thee lord of such a spirit.
> Before, I lov'd thee as a brother, John,
> But now I do respect thee as my soul.
>
> (V, iv, 18–20)

Earlier in the play Hal allied himself with Falstaff's values. Now, as he takes on authority and responsibility, Hal's perspective has changed.

The next curious moment occurs when the King is in danger of being killed by Douglas. Hal enters, and under the pressure of his attack Douglas flees. The King expresses his gratitude:

> Thou hast redeem'd thy lost opinion,
> And show'd thou mak'st some tender of my life
> In this fair rescue thou hast brought to me.
>
> (V, iv, 48–50)

Henry seems to be saying that skill in warfare is the true measure of a man. Hal's answer is surprising:

> O God, they did me too much injury
> That ever said I heark'ned for your death.
> If it were so, I might have let alone
> The insulting hand of Douglas over you,
> Which would have been as speedy in your end
> As the poisonous potions in the world,
> And sav'd the treacherous labor of your son.
>
> (V, iv, 51–57)

No one was more pessimistic about Hal than his own father, and thus Hal is hitting back at the King with force. He also speaks with his familiar aloofness, expressing neither loyalty nor love. Instead, the implication is that he fought Douglas out of obligation, and that the King was very lucky that Hal did so. The Prince's toughness is taking hold.

The duel between Hal and Hotspur is the culmination of the play. It is almost certainly fictional, and the manner of Hotspur's death is historically unknown. But theatrically the fight works wonderfully. Hotspur sets off the struggle with "I can no longer brook thy vanities" (V, iv, 74), and we appreciate the irony of Hotspur's being bothered by anyone else's pride. The fight goes on at length, a ferocious duel to the death and a proper reflection of the actual battle of Shrewsbury, which was protracted and gory. When Hotspur falls, he reflects with poignancy:

> O Harry, thou hast robb'd me of my youth!
> I better brook the loss of brittle life
> Than those proud titles thou hast won of me.
>
> (V, iv, 77–79)

He seems to recognize what he is: a perennial boy who has died as he has always wished he would. He even expires in mid-sentence, still tossing insults.

Hal, however, reacts with maturity. First he finishes Hotspur's sentence. Then he refers to Hotspur as "great heart" (V, iv, 87), and intimates that no longer did he have a place in this world. Hal knows what we know: that Hotspur was, in his own way, like Richard II: a relic.

When Hal spies Falstaff on the ground nearby, he is touched, and we note the juxtaposition of the two bodies, representing the extremes of Hal's life. But the symmetry of the play is unbalanced. Hotspur lies dead, his values shattered. Falstaff, however, arises unrepentent, ruminating on the word "counterfeit" (V, iv, 115–120) and adding, "The better part of valor is discretion. . . . " This play has been partially about reality versus illusion, the discovery of the real Hal and the nature of a proper king. That theme of truth is reflected in the next episode, when Hal enters to see Falstaff carrying Hotspur, whom he claims to have killed (V, iv, 141). Hal challenges Falstaff: "Why, Percy, I kill'd myself, and saw thee dead" (V, iv, 144). But Falstaff, as we might expect, plays the role of the battle-hardened soldier with glorious outrage:

> Lord, Lord, how this world is
> given to lying! . . . I'll take it
> upon my death, I gave him this wound in the thigh.
> If the man were alive and would deny it, 'zounds,
> I would make him eat a piece of my sword.
>
> (V, iv, 145–153)

Lancaster, unacquainted with Falstaff, can only remark: "This is the strangest tale that ever I heard" (V, iv, 154). Hal, however, is not surprised: "This is the strangest fellow, brother John" (V, iv, 155). And he surrenders to the grandeur of Falstaff's charade.

But in light of Hal's public revelation of his own character, Falstaff's loyalty to himself is telling. He never changes, and thus we understand him as he casually takes up Hotspur's body in the hope of receiving credit for the kill. The action is entertaining but fundamentally fraudulent. Falstaff, to both his credit and his shame, is unable to appreciate the gravity of the situation. Therefore Hal must leave him behind, as Falstaff himself intimates:

> I'll follow, as they say, for reward. He that
> rewards me, God reward him! If I do grow great, I'll

> grow less, for I'll purge and leave sack, and live
> cleanly as a nobleman should do.
>
> (V, iv, 162–165)

In the final scene Henry IV tries to restore balance to the political situation. He orders the executions of Vernon and Worcester, but adds: "Other offenders we will pause upon" (V, v, 15). Then he allows his son the right to release Douglas, and Hal does so, without ransom. We remember Henry's actions at the end of *Richard II*, when he condemns Exton and pardons Carlisle. Exton is a killer, Worcester a deceptive conspirator. Both are executed. Carlisle and Douglas, both courageous in their own way, are pardoned. Hal's similar generosity of spirit reflects the quality of the future King as he bestows the task of telling Douglas on the King's other son, John of Lancaster. Then Henry carries out this pattern of dividing responsibility. Each member of the family will lead part of the remaining battle, and the intention is that as the rebellion is quashed, familial and national order will be restored.

But the full story is not yet told. In the second part of *Henry IV* the King pays a greater price for deposing Richard and the nation bears more pain for the King's guilt. Historically Henry did leave behind a consolidated government, a remarkable achievement for a usurper, but Shakespeare focuses more on the price paid by the man rather than on legislative accomplishments. Hal, too, undergoes further transformation, as he draws closer to the crown. The mutual triumph of Part I does not last, as the relationship between father and son undergoes its severest test.

SUGGESTIONS FOR FURTHER READING

Beck, Richard J. *Shakespeare:* Henry IV. London: Edward Arnold, 1965.

Hunt, Maurice. "Time and Timelessness in *1 Henry IV*." *Exploration in Renaissance Culture* 10 (1984): 56–66.

Hunter, G. K. "*Henry IV* and the Elizabethan Two-Part Play." *Review of English Studies* 5 (1954): 236–248.

Marsh, D. R. C. *A Critical Commentary on Shakespeare's* Henry IV, Part One. London: Macmillan, 1967.

McGuire, Richard L. "The Play-within-the Play in *1 Henry IV*." *Shakespeare Quarterly* 18 (1967): 47–52.

Sanderson, James, ed. *Twentieth Century Interpretations of* Henry IV, Part One. Englewood Cliffs, N.J.: Prentice-Hall, 1969.

Toliver, Harold E. "Falstaff, the Prince, and the History Play." *Shakespeare Quarterly* 16 (1965): 63–80.

Wilson, John Dover. *The Fortunes of Falstaff*. Cambridge: Cambridge University Press, 1944.

HENRY IV, PART 2

Henry IV, Part 1 concentrates on growth and triumph. *Henry IV, Part 2* concentrates on decay and death.

The opening address by Rumor sets the tone:

> My office is
> To noise abroad that Harry Monmouth fell
> Under the wrath of noble Hotspur's sword,
> And that the King before the Douglas' rage
> Stoop'd his anointed head as low as death.
> This have I rumor'd through the peasant towns
> Between that royal field of Shrewsbury
> And this worm-eaten [hold] of ragged stone,
> [Where] Hotspur's father, old Northumberland,
> Lies crafty-sick.
>
> (Induction, 28–37)

The victories of *Part I* are undercut by lies, and the implication is that no matter how powerful the exaltation, the bitterness of the aftermath will take hold. In this work the political and military conflicts are uglier and without the romance that lent a glow to the earlier play. Here the laughter is coarser and crueler. Hal grows into the capable and confident Henry V, but simultaneously the two men who have shaped him, Henry IV and Falstaff, endure intense physical and spiritual suffering.

The long opening scene between members of one of the conspiracies emphasizes the play's anti-romantic vision. Lord Bardolph brings a series of rumors, including those of the wounding of Henry IV, the death of Hal, and the imprisonment of Falstaff, but Northumberland's suspicions reveal that Bardolph heard the news entirely second-hand (I, i, 25–27). Travers then enters with a lengthy account that has at least one accurate detail: the death of Hotspur. Despite Bardolph's comic refusal to believe any report but his own, Northumberland is shaken by word of his son's death (I, i, 48–51). It remains for Morton to bring the truth, although he must struggle to communicate through Northumberland's

rage. Morton reveals that Douglas and Worcester still live, but even mention of
Hotspur causes Northumberland to realize the worst (I, i, 83–84). He continues
to struggle with the facts, as if unable to accept the reality of his son's passing.

At last Morton is allowed to give a full account of the battle of Shrewsbury.
He tells a stirring narrative of Hotspur's loss, dramatizing how even in death
Percy was an inspiration to his troops (I, i, 110–125). Nevertheless, the result
was defeat:

>   The sum of all
>   Is that the King hath won, and hath sent out
>   A speedy power to encounter you, my lord,
>   Under the conduct of young Lancaster
>   And Westmerland.
>
>   (I, i, 131–135)

At this summation Northumberland becomes enraged:

>   Let heaven kiss earth! now let not Nature's hand
>   Keep the wild flood confin'd! let order die!
>   And let this world no longer be a stage
>   To feed contention in a ling'ring act;
>   But let one spirit of the first-born Cain
>   Reign in all bosoms, that each heart being set
>   On bloody courses, the rude scene may end,
>   And darkness be the burier of the dead!
>
>   (I, i, 153–160)

His is the first of several speeches that urges disorder, and the tirade sounds like
any of several from the first tetralogy. Here, too, Northumberland plays a dangerous game. His own rebellion, which he once deemed legitimate, is in tatters.
But rather than accept his losses and maintain equanimity for the good of the
kingdom, he chooses to advocate chaos, for to his mind anarchy is preferable
to a ruler he dislikes. The Elizabethan audience would recognize the danger of
his attitude.

Morton tries to soothe Northumberland's anger:

>   It was your presurmise
>   That in the dole of blows your son might drop.
>
>   (I, i, 169–170)

This invocation of his own responsibility temporarily calms the angry father. So
does the news that a new rebellion is beginning under the religious sanction of
the Archbishop of York:

>   [. . . But now the Bishop
>   Turns insurrection to religion.
>   Suppos'd sincere and holy in his thoughts,
>   He's followed both with body and with mind;
>   And doth enlarge his rising with the blood

Of fair King Richard, scrap'd from Pomfret stones;
Derives from heaven his quarrel and his cause;
Tells them he doth bestride a bleeding land,
Gasping for life under great Bullingbrook,
And more and less do flock to follow him].

                                                        (I, i, 200–209)

Theatrically this scene seems to follow hard upon the battle of Shrewsbury. In
fact, the end of the first conspiracy and the rise of this second did not occur
until two years later, in 1405. In any case, Northumberland now has renewed
hope:

Go in with with me, and counsel every man
The aptest way for safety and revenge.

                                                        (I, i, 212–213)

Thus disorder spreads once more.

    The next scene takes us to a parallel but at the same time contrasting atmosphere
of disappointment and frustration. In his first line Falstaff dwells on illness:
"Sirrah, you giant, what says the doctor to my water?" (I, ii, 1). We cannot
be certain whether he suffers from gout or syphilis, but never before has he
expressed worry about his physical condition. He has also grown more philosophical about his nature:

                          I am not only witty
in myself, but the cause that wit is in other men.

                                                        (I, ii, 9–10)

Yet this self-reflection is tinged with melancholy, especially about Hal:

I do here walk before thee like a sow that hath overwhelm'd all her litter but one. If the Prince put thee
into my service for any other reason than to set me off,
why then I have no judgment.

                                                        (I, ii, 11–14)

Falstaff can still enjoy the spectacle of a diminutive servant in contrast with his
own enormity. But a man telling jokes to an unappreciative audience suggests
loneliness. Falstaff is peeved that Hal has no immediate use for him, and although
he continues to toss off barbs, throughout this scene and the rest of the play his
jokes become darker. His preoccupation with his own health, his isolation from
Hal, and other reminders of his age haunt him, and despite his jests, which are
at times as rich as ever, other forces take control of his wit and heart.

    The extent of Falstaff's degeneration is apparent in the episode following with
the Chief Justice. Until this point, Falstaff's escapades, those outside military
affairs, that is, have had virtually no wider impact. Here, however, we are
conscious of Falstaff as an enemy of the social order. The Justice arrives to
question Falstaff about a robbery, but the fat knight keeps turning the conversation
elsewhere, focusing first on the Justice's health (I, ii, 94–100), then the King's

(I, ii, 104–118). At last the Justice is able to state his accusation: "Well, the truth is, Sir John, you live in great infamy" (I, ii, 136–137). The issue in question is the robbery at Gadshill. But the Justice excuses Falstaff on account of the knight's bravery at Shrewsbury (I, ii, 148–149), although we who have seen that performance in *Henry IV, Part 1* find such pardon ironic. The Justice does warn Falstaff, however, about Falstaff's advanced age, but Sir John wishes to hear none of it:

> You that are old
> consider not the capacities of us that are young, you do
> measure the heat of our livers with the bitterness
> of your galls; and we that are in the vaward of our
> youth, I must confess, are wags too.
>
> (I, ii, 173–176)

The Chief Justice picks up this very point:

> Do you set down your name in the scroll
> of youth, that are written down old with all the
> characters of age? Have you not a moist eye, a
> dry hand, a yellow cheek, a white beard, a decreasing
> leg, an increasing belly?
>
> (I, ii, 178–182)

This relentless recitation of his failings does not faze Falstaff. But he is cognizant of the Justice's implication: that Falstaff has lost some of his youth, and with that some of his aura of invincibility. The Justice also makes clear that the bond between Falstaff and Hal will inevitably break: "Well, God send the Prince a better companion" (I, ii, 200). Falstaff laughs off this possibility, and with comic gall asks the departing magistrate for a loan for one thousand pounds (I, ii, 223). But we are aware that more serious matters, particularly his own health, weigh heavily on him:

> A good wit will make use
> of anything. I will turn diseases to commodity.
>
> (I, ii, 247–248)

He resists surrendering to age, but the awareness is there all the same, and the erosion of his spirit intensifies throughout the play.

In scene iii the unrest in the kingdom is apparent, as a new conspiracy forms against the King. Hastings warns that only with Northumberland's troops can this uprising succeed (I, iii, 10–14), and the others confirm that judgment. Throughout the two parts of *Henry IV*, Northumberland, the head of the Percy family, is the most powerful lord, but he never fully commits himself to any cause. In Part 1 he retreated before battle, and in this play, too, he falls short. But more important than the general tactics of the three are their unspecified motivations. Mowbray is the son of Thomas Mowbray, formerly the confidante of Richard II. In the play of that name, the father was accused of treason by

Bullingbrook, and thereafter banished for life by the King. Thus Mowbray has his private reasons to seek the overthrow of Henry. Archbishop Scroop's brother was executed at the order of Henry IV. And Hastings is a relative of Edmund Mortimer, who was designated by Richard II as his heir, and who was captured by Owen Glendower. It was Henry IV's refusal to rescue or ransom Mortimer that led to the original deposing of the King as dramatized in *Henry IV, Part 1*.

These personal grievances are the mainspring of the conspiracy, and no matter how the three plan their maneuvers, we know that the general good is not their primary goal. Instead we are conscious of jealousy and anger, as in the Archbishop's words:

> The commonwealth is sick of their own choice,
> Their over-greedy love hath surfeited.
> An habitation giddy and unsure
> hath he that buildeth on the vulgar heart . . .
> So, so, thou common dog, didst thou disgorge
> Thy glutton bosom of the royal Richard,
> And now thou wouldst eat thy dead vomit up,
> And howl'st to find it. What trust is in these times?
> They that, when Richard liv'd, would have him die,
> Are now become enamor'd on his grave.

(I, iii, 87–102)

Certainly the speaker despises Henry. But he hates with equal force the masses. The image of vomit and the general disillusionment with his country turns this rebellion into a confluence of irritation, exasperation, and frustration with English society from top to bottom.

A word about the structure of this play. The sudden shifts of location that characterize the opening act keep us off balance. In addition, neither the title character nor Hal appears until well into Act II. Instead we are taken into the society surrounding the court, and that strategy creates a peculiar effect. We see the influence of the usurpation, and we see the society itself in ragged shape. We are not told that this condition is the direct result of the takeover by Henry IV, but the suggestion is everywhere. Thus the discomfort of the opening of Act II, when the Hostess accuses Falstaff of owing her money. The quality of the environment is apparent in speeches like this from the Hostess.

> He stabb'd
> me in mine own house, most beastly, in good faith. 'A
> cares not what mischief he does, if his weapon be
> out. He will foin like any devil, he will spare neither
> man, woman, nor child.

(II, i, 13–17)

Sexual connotations pervade the scene. Nonetheless grimness looms over everything. Perhaps the presence of the Chief Justice casts the pall, as here he questions Falstaff:

> Doth this become your place, your time, and business?
> You should have been well on your way to York.

(II, i, 66–67)

The Justice is, strictly speaking, a fair man, but he is so lacking in humor that his earnestness becomes depressing. Then, too, the law never intruded when the Prince was in the tavern to share the good times. Now reality pierces the laughter.

The Hostess adds to the doleful atmosphere when she speaks to Falstaff without her customary beneficence:

> . . . when the Prince broke thy head for
> liking his father to a singing-man of Windsor,
> thou didst swear to me then, as I was washing thy
> wound, to marry me and make me my lady thy wife.

(II, i, 89–92)

Even the thought of the Prince's striking Falstaff is disturbing, despite the fact that the blow comes in defense of Henry. We are grateful not to have viewed the moment. Falstaff tries to change the issue, but the Chief Justice holds him in check and insists that Falstaff pay (II, i, 118–121). Sir John, however, claims that he is in the King's employ and therefore immune from such charges, but the Justice refuses to indulge him:

> You speak as having power to do wrong,
> but answer in th' effect of your reputation, and satisfy
> the poor woman.

(II, i, 129–131)

Falstaff still tries to treat his antics as no more than that. He does not want to be bogged down by feeling. But without the Prince's company, the tavern is a real place, and Falstaff is held to the standards to which ordinary people must conform. Such restrictions choke him, and he resists the pressure. But given the seriousness of all around him, he is no longer a figure of joyous fantasy and games but an ornery thief who takes advantage of the vulnerabilities of those weaker than himself. And his getaway from this predicament is not as exhilarating as we might hope. Still, that the Hostess is willing to pawn her silverware to pay Falstaff's debt (II, i, 140–142) suggests that her affection for him will never diminish, no matter what he does. Our sentiments are likely to remain as warm.

The Prince's initial appearance is in Act II, scene ii, and his first line informs us that he has changed: "Before God, I am exceeding weary" (II, ii, 1). Already his office oppresses him, and he lacks the vivacity we saw in the last play. The source of his unhappiness is ostensibly his father's illness, but what may bother Hal more is his own attitude towards that illness:

> Marry, I tell thee it is not meet that I
> should be sad, now my father is sick, albeit I could
> tell to thee—as to one it pleases me, for fault of a
> better, to call my friend—I could be sad, and sad

indeed too.

(II, ii, 39–43)

He finds himself conscious of his behavior, aware that all his actions and statements will be judged from a political perspective: "What wouldst thou think of
me if I should weep?" (II, ii, 52). In the discussion of *Henry IV, Part 1*, we
noted that Hal maintains an emotional distance from everyone. Here is he emotionally distant even from himself, so preoccupied with politics that he appears
almost incapable of maintaining honest feeling. He needs to talk to someone,
and here he chooses Poins, a mild jokester, but, unlike Falstaff, more of a
sounding board than a respondent. Curiously, the more public the Prince's life
becomes and the more he is forced to involve himself with people, the more
inward he turns.

When the letter arrives from Falstaff, warning the Prince about confiding in
Poins, Hal realizes that Falstaff, too, is capable of envy and loneliness. Hal and
Poins resolve to visit Falstaff to indulge in another practical joke, but their
enthusiasm is muted:

> From a God to a bull? a heavy descension!
> it was Jove's case. From a prince to a prentice? a low
> transformation! that shall be mine, for in every thing
> the purpose must weigh with the folly. Follow me,
> Ned.

(II, ii, 173–177)

The Prince heads off reluctantly, as if out of obligation. He is isolated here, as
are many of the characters in several different situations. In *Henry IV, Part 1*
the camaraderie at the taverns and among some of the rebels was uplifting. Here
no one trusts anyone else, and no one embraces anyone else. Everyone seems
insulated from affection. Whatever their business, characters go about it with
bleak determination, and a malaise hangs over all.

That the rebellion against Henry IV suffers from this kind of dispirit is clear
in the next scene. In Act I, scene i, Northumberland was furious with the King
and prepared to unleash chaos. Here he is ready to continue the war, but his
rationale arouses our suspicions: "Alas, sweet wife, my honor is at pawn . . . "
(II, iii, 7). His daughter-in-law, Hotspur's widow, pleads that he be more ju-
dicious, and as she does she pays tribute to her late husband, a eulogy that serves
three purposes. One, she takes up Northumberland's use of "honor" to reflect
on how it drove Hotspur to his fate: "There were two honors lost, yours and
your son's . . . " (II, iii, 16). Second, she reminds her father-in-law that his grief
is overdone, considering that he stayed at home during the battle of Shrewsbury
(II, iii, 33–38). Therefore Northumberland's honor is already lost. Third, her
glorification of Hotspur (II, iii, 18–41) places him in greater contrast to Hal,
who in the last scene was subdued by the weight of office. Eventually Northumberland accedes to his wife and daughter's wishes by retreating to Scotland,

but once more, as he did when he was ill, he deserts his allies. Northumberland thus becomes another figure cut off by the events and spirit of his time.

Historically Northumberland maintained direct and indirect assaults upon the throne until his death in 1408. Thereafter Henry enjoyed relative peace from internal conspiracy, although his physical suffering was unabated.

The anti-romantic tone of the play is exacerbated during Act II, scene iv, where the world Hal has left becomes more repellent. First, the conversation between Falstaff and Mistress Doll reflects the nastier aspects of the knight's personality. He and Doll Tearsheet accuse one another of spreading sexual disease (II, iv, 35–54), and the tone is uglier than any we remember from Part 1. As the Hostess says:

> By my troth, this is the old fashion, you two
> never meet but you fall to some discord. You are both,
> i' good truth, as rheumatic as two dry toasts, you can
> not bear with another's confirmities.

(II, iv, 55–58)

The revelry is joined by Pistol, described by Doll as "the foul-mouth'd'st rogue in England" (II, iv, 72), and with his entrance vulgarities spread thickly across the stage. Pistol, the Elizabethan version of the *miles gloriosus*, the braggart soldier from Roman comedy, offers a grossly witty swagger, but he grows meaner and more grotesque almost by the minute. In this play he appears only intermittently, and his full impact is not felt until *Henry V*. Nevertheless, he contributes to the general tone of disrepute that pervades this play. When Doll berates him, he is ready to retaliate (II, iv, 160), and although we know he is a coward at heart, that he actually draws his sword and forces Falstaff to do the same eliminates some of whatever joy remains in this tavern world.

Even at this moment, though, the underlying affection that binds Falstaff to the others emerges. Doll, forever at him, phrases her feelings gently to reaffirm what Falstaff himself knows:

> Thou whoreson little tidy Bartholomew boar-pig, when
> wilt thou leave fighting a' days and foining a' nights,
> and begin to patch up thine old body for heaven?

(II, iv, 231–233)

Such sentiments do not appeal to Falstaff:

> Peace, good Doll, do not speak like a death's-
> head, do not bid me remember mine end.

(II, iv, 234–235)

She, too, recognizes his mortality, and her concern reaches to the core of his appeal. We recognize his weaknesses and foibles. Yet none of these overwhelms his loveableness because he is never hypocritical. When accused of a crime he feigns offense, but all listening to him, onstage and off, recognize that he is playing. And in doing so he welcomes everyone else into his game. They must trap him, but only by the rules of imagination. He is especially worth cherishing because he stands in contrast to the politics around him. The nobles and politicians exist in a constant state of of duplicity: undercutting, plotting, cheating, all the while posing under the guise of legitimacy. Falstaff's existence mocks that attitude, and while he stands for disorder, he is, in an intriguing way, the most truthful man in his world. That he is this anomaly also means that he will be abandoned by someone like Hal, who must join that other world, and thus Falstaff's masquerade has a unique poignancy.

His personal bitterness breaks out when the Prince enters disguised with Poins. Falstaff unknowingly insults both of them (II, iv, 244–253), implying that the Prince simply is not up to Falstaff's standard. Poins is eager to beat Falstaff "before his whore" (II, iv, 257), but the Prince is struck more by Falstaff's energy:

> Is it not strange that desire should so many
> years outlive performance?
>
> (II, iv, 260–261)

Yet even as Falstaff accepts Doll's flattery, he is, as ever, conscious of his age: "I am old, I am old" (II, iv, 271). At last the Prince and Poins reveal themselves, and Falstaff struggles to fabricate a reason for his earlier derogation of Hal:

> I disprais'd him before the wicked, that
> the wicked [*turns to the Prince*] might not fall in love
> with thee; in which doing, I have done the part of a
> careful friend and a true subject, and thy father is to
> give me thanks for it. No abuse, Hal; none, Ned,
> none; no, faith, boys, none.
>
> (II, iv, 319–324)

The wit is here, but also a desperation, a sad recognition that Falstaff is gradually losing his place in the Prince's life. The succession of insults against Bardolph and the women also demonstrates clever wordplay, but again, we sense that Falstaff feels a certain desolation among even these, his friends.

Moments later Peto enters with word that the King is at Westminster, where Hal's presence is required. Falstaff, too, has been called, but the Prince ignores that fact, for he is now preoccupied with guilt over his wasteful activities:

> By heaven, Poins, I feel me much to blame
> So idly to profane the precious time.
>
> (II, iv, 361–362)

Hal's recognition of his responsibilities is unshakable. Seconds later Bardolph enters repeating Peto's news that Falstaff is besieged by "a dozen captains" (II, iv, 372), and the fat knight, too, dashes off: "You see, my good wenches, how men of merit are sought after" (II, iv, 374–375). Worldly concerns are breaking up the old gang.

In the first scene of Act III, Henry IV finally appears. His presence augments the gloom, for he suffers from loss of sleep:

> How many thousand of my poorest subjects
> Are at this hour asleep! O sleep! O gentle sleep!
> Nature's soft nurse, how have I frighted thee,
> That thou no more wilt weigh my eyelids down,
> And steep my senses in forgetfulness?

(III, i, 4–8)

The pragmatic, energetic politician has turned into a weary figure who, although hardly helpless, nonetheless feels his strength waning: "Uneasy lies the head that wears a crown" (III, i, 31). The pressures of responsibility are different from those of ambition, and gaining the crown may be easier than maintaining it.

Warwick's entrance does not relieve the King's pain, and Henry is compelled to voice his unhappiness:

> Then you perceive the body of our kingdom
> How foul it is, what rank diseases grow,
> And with what danger, near the heart of it.

(III, i, 38–40)

He is not suicidal, as Henry VI so often is, but his misery is moving, especially because he feels that he himself is the agent of his own affliction. He regrets so much of his life after the challenge to Richard II:

>   O, if this were seen,
> The happiest youth, viewing his progress through,
> What perils past, what crosses to ensue,
> Would shut the book, and sit him down and die.

(III, i, 53–56)

He mourns the loss of friendships (III, i, 57–65), and he even mourns Richard, whose warning remains fresh in his mind:

> "The time will come, that foul sin, gathering head,
> Shall break into corruption": so went on,
> Foretelling this same time's condition
> And the division of our amity.

(III, i, 76–79)

Here Henry is not really talking to Warwick. He is talking to himself, and Warwick happens to be in the room. The import of the confession is that no matter how politically necessary Henry's overthrow was, the price he pays and the price his country pays now and later are extraordinarily high.

Warwick tries to comfort the King, telling him that Richard only guessed at the future, that no supernatural agency could control destiny (III, i, 82–92). At this advice Henry is temporarily soothed. But even after he gives military instructions, his state of mind and the state of the kingdom still oppress him:

I will take your counsel,
And were these inward wars once out of hand,
We would, dear lords, unto the Holy Land.

(III, i, 106–108)

Once again he speaks of the pilgrimage that he sought to make at the end of
Richard II and the beginning of *Henry IV, Part 1*.

At this point we might wonder whether Henry, bearing up under enormous
strain, ever reaches the stature of a tragic hero. He does not. After all, we have
seen him from only a limited vantage point. In *Part 1* he is an ambitious and
successful politician; in *Part 2* he is less ambitious, although still successful.
But our feelings about him are restrained because we have known him only as
a public man, never as a human being. In this way he is like his son, for both
have kept us set apart from them. And such distance prevents the development
of the tragic sense.

Furthermore, throughout *Part 1* and thus far in *Part 2* we have never seen
Henry battling against himself. We have never felt that he has been torn between
opposing emotions or that his character has been in conflict with circumstance.
We have never felt that his nature compelled him to act so that disaster was
brought down upon him. Any of these dramatic matrices would have helped
create a sense of tragic loss. But the play presents Henry only as a political
operative, who achieves his ambitions but then suffers predicted consequences.
That situation is not tragic.

Scene ii returns us to the world of Falstaff, but we do not escape the issue of
debilitation. Justices Silence and Shallow are wizened men, whose physical
condition mirrors the quality of the law they practice. Looming larger than their
petty corruptions, however, is their outlook on mortality:

Jesu, Jesu, the mad days that I have spent!
And to see how many of my old acquaintance are dead!

(III, ii, 33–34)

So says Shallow. And Silence follows with "We shall all follow, cousin" (III,
ii, 35). Such expressions of life's impermanence dominate their dialogue.

The placement of this episode immediately after the King's confession emphasizes that no matter what a person's place on the human ladder, all are subject
to the same patterns of life and death. And the subsequent entrance of Falstaff,
an old comrade of the justices, reinforces that theme.

Falstaff is recruiting soldiers, and once more he has gathered a ragtag bunch.
One of the men, Thomas Wart, is so pathetically thin that Falstaff lets him go.
Another member, however, stands out. His name is Feeble; he is, ironically, a
woman's tailor, and in contrast to his name, he speaks in a clear and true voice.
He is another of those simple characters who embody decency amidst corruption
and egocentricity. Feeble's line in response to Falstaff's insult sets his character:
"I will do my good will, sir, you can have no more." (III, ii, 156). And a bit

later, after Bullcalf and Mouldy bribe Bardolph to escape service, Feeble speaks
more poetically but with the same dignity:

> By my troth I care not; a man can die but
> once, we owe God a death. I'll ne'er bear a base mind.
> And't be my dest'ny, so; and't be not, so. No man's too
> good to serve 's prince, and let it go which way it will,
> he that dies this year is quit for the next.
>
> (III, ii, 234–238)

Such sentiments, however fine, seem out of place in the gross world of Falstaff,
Shallow, and Silence, who turn from stories of depravity to recalling friends
either ancient or dead (III, ii, 191–210). Falstaff speaks of his age with one of
his most memorable phrases: "We have heard the chimes at midnight, Master
Shallow" (III, ii, 214). In such a line is a mixture of humor and melancholy
that is characteristically Falstaffian. But the wistfulness of the moment is undercut
by the corruption around him. Bardolph accepts the bribes from Mouldy and
Bullcalf, but then gives Falstaff one pound less than the total (II, iv, 244),
suggesting that even those united in corruption cannot trust one another. The
scene ends with a soliloquy in which Falstaff continues to cogitate on the morality
and mortality of his colleagues:

> Lord, Lord, how subject we old men are to this
> vice of lying! This same starv'd justice hath done
> nothing but prate to me of the wildness of his youth,
> and the feats he hath done about Turnbull Street, and
> every third word a lie, duer paid to the hearer than the
> Turk's tribute.
>
> (III, ii, 303–308)

And a bit further:

> And now is this Vice's dagger become a
> squire, and talks as familiarly of John a' Gaunt as if he
> had been sworn brother to him.
>
> (III, ii, 319–320)

Falstaff, too, may be thought of in the theatrical tradition of the Vice of the
morality play. But unlike the voice of that figure, his also contains laughter and
regret, derision and whimsy, here focused on the inevitability of death.

We might ask why in this play Shakespeare places so heavy an emphasis on
mortality. In fact, during most of the first half, the incipient rebellions and the
ongoing political subterfuges are mentioned only in passing. Instead we ponder
the brittle lives of characters whose existence is a cartoon of those great sweeping
issues. Perhaps that last sentence contains the answer. By the time politics retakes
center stage, the audience has been saturated with commentary on life and death.
We have heard so many bawdy jokes that the complications of the state seem
less than momentous, and we are now ready to regard them with a cynical eye.

Thus as Act IV begins and the forces of the second conspiracy gather around Henry, the pettiness of human ambition stands diminished against the overwhelming forces of nature. Whatever these men accomplish or fail to accomplish, all will one day die.

At the beginning of Act IV the action moves to the new conspiracy, and the setting is the forest of Gaultree. The Archbishop and Mowbray clarify that without Northumberland's support their cause is much weakened (IV, i, 6–18), and we are reminded of an irony that seems never to leave the world of the history plays: no sooner does a conspiracy start than it is beset by internal problems. When Westmerland enters, representing the King, his accusations against the Archbishop have another ironic ring:

> Wherefore do you so ill translate yourself
> Out of the speech of peace that bears such grace,
> Into the harsh and boist'rous tongue of war?
> Turning your books to graves, your ink to blood,
> Your pens to lances, and your tongue divine
> To a loud trumpet and a point of war?
>
> (IV, i, 47–52)

He claims to be bothered that a clergyman would involve himself in the business of rebellion. But how convenient that a supporter of Henry IV forgets that the King himself came to power in an act of civil disobedience. Here again we see that when those who covet power finally gain authority, they become the establishment, and possessive of their power. In their eyes all subsequent rebellions are immoral rebellions, and all rebels illegal rebels.

The Archbishop responds with his own grievances, prefacing his remarks with a statement of one central theme: " . . . we are all diseas'd" (IV, i, 54). In the previous two plays, the insurrections were the work of men full of righteousness and patriotism. Here even the rebels feel corrupted. The Archbishop then attacks the King, but his charges remain ineffectually general, as Westmerland notes:

> Wherein have you been galled by the King?
> What peer hath been suborn'd to grate on you?
> That you should seal this lawless bloody book
> Of forg'd rebellion with a seal divine.
>
> (IV, i, 89–92)

Again we think back to Henry's own actions against Richard.

Mowbray interrupts, claiming he can provide more substantial reasons, but Westmerland attempts to disarm him by pointing out that the lands of Norfolk, Mowbray's father, who was exiled by Richard II, have been restored (IV, i, 108–110). What objections could Mowbray possibly hold?

The answer does not surprise us:

What thing, in honor, had my father lost,
That need to be reviv'd and breath'd in me?

(IV, i, 111–112)

Here is the crux of Mowbray's cause: honor. And he goes on to attack not the present ruler, but Richard for humiliating and ultimately destroying the Duke of Norfolk. The pointlessness of Mowbray's goals undercuts his cause. He even complains that although Henry has righted some wrongs, he has done so "from policy, not love" (IV, i, 146). The question is not justice or fairness to the people or the nobles. The question is the need for power, for emotional and intellectual redress, which Westmerland, still speaking for Henry, has no intention of bestowing. His confidence in the royal troops is clear:

Our battle is more full of names than yours,
Our men more perfect in the use of arms,
Our armor all as strong, our cause the best;
Then reason will our hearts should be as good.
Say you not then our offer is compell'd.

(IV, i, 152–156)

Westmerland seeks to avoid actual conflict. Nonetheless, he is forced to accept articles of grievance from the Archbishop (IV, i, 166–175) and claims he will show them to the King. Mowbray remains suspicious (IV, i, 181–182), but Hastings hopes the King will compromise, while the Archbishop is convinced the King is exhausted by the relentless conflict that leaves him with more enemies than ever:

His foes are so enrooted with his friends
That, plucking to unfix an enemy,
He doth unfasten so and shake a friend . . .

(IV, i, 205–207)

On such a note Westmerland returns, this time with Prince John, and the episode that follows is the logical outcome of the previous scene. In this play we have observed constant duplicity and egoism. The conspirators do not have faith in one another, nor do they trust the King. Oaths are sworn left and right, but dishonesty is rampant. How else should the rebellion be put down but by another such act?

John starts his campaign as Westmerland did: by expressing surprise that the Archbishop, a clergyman, should be involved in such an opprobrious enterprise (IV, ii, 22–30). Interestingly, John emphasizes that the King is God's substitute, and once again we remember how Henry gained the throne by ignoring such a mandate.

The Archbishop retorts with arguments that chaos has taken over, and that the rebels fear for their lives:

But as I told my Lord of Westmerland,
The time misord'red doth, in common sense,

Crowd us and crush us to this monstrous form
To hold our safety up.

(IV, ii, 32–35)

Hastings persists that even if this rebellion should fail, generation after generation
will suffer for the sins carried out now (IV, ii, 46–49).

In one sense Hastings is right, as we know, but John ignores these charges,
then offers peace:

If this may please you,
Discharge your powers unto their several counties,
As we will ours, and here between the armies
Let's drink together friendly and embrace,
That all their eyes may bear those tokens home
Of restored love and amity.

(IV, ii, 60–65)

The proposal is inviting, but we are already suspicious of John, for he prefaces
his words by swearing "by the honor of my blood" (IV, ii, 55). What is
nonetheless amusing is how the officers exchange proverbs that communicate a
variety of overtones. Mowbray responds with doubt to one toast:

You wish me health in very happy season,
For I am on the sudden something ill.

(IV, ii, 79–80)

The Archbishop tries to defuse his colleague's fears, but ironically anticipates
the outcome:

Against ill chances men are ever merry,
But heaviness foreruns the good event.

(IV, ii, 81–82)

Tensions rise subtly here, as Westmerland chimes in with his own message of
comfort:

Therefore be merry, coz, since sudden sorrow
Serves to say thus, some good thing comes to-morrow.

(IV, ii, 83–84)

The hypocrisy is overwhelming.

At last a shout of peace is heard, and the battle ends with no bloodshed.
Westmerland is then dismissed by the Prince, ostensibly to release the royal
forces, while Hastings does the same for the rebel troops. John reacts calmly:
"I trust, lords, we shall lie to-night together" (IV, ii, 97). We note the double
meaning of the word "lie." Westmerland then returns to explain that the royal
troops will not disband without a specific order from John, and he seems agree-
able: "They know their duties" (IV, ii, 101). He always claims to value order.

When Hastings announces that his soldiers have dispersed, Westmerland
shocks them:

> Good tidings, my Lord Hastings! for the which
> I do arrest thee, traitor, of high treason,
> And you, Lord Archbishop, and you, Lord Mowbray,
> Of capital treason I attach you both.

(IV, ii, 106–109)

Even more astonishing are John's additional charges:

> I promis'd you redress of these same grievances
> Whereof you did complain, which, by mine honor,
> I will perform with a most Christian care.

(IV, ii, 113–115)

We can scarcely believe that "honor" shows up once more. But the invocation of "Christian care" seems almost profane, as does John's final sentiment: "God, and not we, hath safely fought to-day" (IV, ii, 121). He tries to ennoble his hypocrisy and treachery under the banner of religious sanction.

Historically the promise of personal safety was offered by Westmerland, not John, but Shakespeare's choice better contrasts John with Hal. Without doubt John is dislikeable and his tactics reprehensible. Even more so are his pious excuses. Yet the rebellion is quashed with no loss of life. And this tactic has been set up by the previous double dealings of so many characters. The world of politics, as Shakespeare dramatizes it, is not distinguished by decency or morality. The only basis of judgment is victory, a fact that is treated as neither noble nor disagreeable. Whatever we think of John's strategy, it works. We surely do not want John for King, for his ruthlessness is alarming. Yet at the end of this scene no blame is laid on him, nor will any be placed later on. Here he takes politically expedient steps, and we have seen before that expediency, what in *King John* is called "commodity," is the essence of politics.

Act IV, scene iii moves us back to the world of Falstaff, and an action that proves a mockery of the previous treachery. Here Sir John manages to outtalk Colevile and avoid fighting, and we think back to similar tactics used by the other John, the Prince. When he enters with a group of other nobles, he warns Falstaff about the consequences of his behavior (IV, iii, 28–29). But Falstaff is undaunted, and points to the submission of Colevile as evidence of his skill (IV, iii, 37–39). He even threatens to write a ballad about the triumph that will put Prince John in a poor light (IV, iii, 47–53). Under such circumstances Hal might enjoy the joke, but John is unamused. For his own benefit he refers to Colevile as a famous "rebel" (IV, iii, 63), ignores Falstaff's insertion that "a famous true subject took him" (IV, iii, 64), and sends the prisoner off for execution. Such cold behavior and the Prince's unreliable promise to speak better of Falstaff than he deserves (IV, iii, 84–85) inspires Falstaff's evaluation of Hal's brother:

> Good faith, this same young soberblooded
> boy doth not love me, nor a man cannot make

him laugh, but that's no marvel, he drinks no wine.

(IV, iii, 87–89)

Falstaff finds John passionless, someone who feels no pleasure in the company of others. In this respect he is similar to other power-seeking men in Shakespeare's plays, including Octavius Caesar in *Antony and Cleopatra* and Angelo in *Measure for Measure*, both of whom are humorless puritans. True, Falstaff's tests of a man's quality are framed according to his own standard by which a capacity for alcohol reveals the tendencies of the body's humours, but even this singular system allows clear evaluation. Whatever else we say of Falstaff, he does understand people. Prince John is without sentiment, without warmth, without the humanity that Falstaff and we believe necessary to a ruler.

Falstaff compares this figure with Hal:

> Hereof comes it that Prince Harry is valiant, for the
> cold blood he did naturally inherit of his father, he
> hath, like lean, sterile, and bare land, manur'd, hus-
> banded, and till'd with excellent endeavor of
> drinking good and good store of fertile sherris, that he
> is become very hot and valiant. If I had a thousand
> sons, the first humane principle I would teach them
> should be, to forswear thin potations and to addict
> themselves to sack.

(IV, iii, 117–125)

Falstaff recognizes what we have seen: that Hal has inherited some of Henry IV's personality. But Falstaff also takes credit for something else: what Hal has gained from Falstaff will make him a greater King.

The price of kingship is visible when Henry IV is carried in, debilitated by worry and disease. Warwick bravely claims that Henry will soon enjoy triumph over the remaining rebels (IV, iv, 11–12), but the King is more concerned with the whereabouts and activities of Hal. As he explains to his other sons, Thomas of Clarence and Humphrey of Gloucester, his worries are first political:

> His temper therefore must be well observ'd.
> Chide him for faults, and do it reverently,
> When you perceive his blood inclin'd to mirth;
> But, being moody, give him time and scope,
> Till that his passions, like a whale on ground,
> Confound themselves with working.

(IV, iv, 36–41)

He fears that Hal's nature, still something of a mystery to him as to us, will lay waste all his own efforts.

He also fears for the good of the kingdom:

> The blood weeps from my heart when I do shape,
> In forms imaginary, th' unguided days
> And rotten times that you shall look upon,

When I am sleeping with my ancestors.

(IV, iv, 58–61)

Warwick has the proper response:

> So, like gross terms,
> The Prince will in the perfectness of time
> Cast off his followers, and their memory
> Shall as a pattern or a measure live,
> By which his Grace must mete the lives of other,
> Turning past evils to advantages.

(IV, iv, 73–78)

In other words, Hal lives among these lower elements only to learn. We greet this estimation with mixed feelings for we know how much Hal will relinquish when he does cast off the world of Falstaff and the tavern.

We also note something else. Henry as yet does not express worry for Hal, as a father might for a son. Henry's concerns are strictly public concerns, and we recognize that the political figure in Henry has supplanted the private man. He even expresses doubts about Warwick's reassurance:

> 'Tis seldom when the bee doth leave her comb
> In the dead carrion.

(IV, iv, 79–80)

So little does Henry know Hal that he doubts the Prince's capacity to abandon harmful influences.

Westmerland enters to report that Mowbray and Archbishop Scroop have been subdued, but before the King can take any pleasure, he learns that Northumberland and Bardolph still maintain their martial stance (IV, iv, 97–101). Historically Henry survived for years after this rebellion ended, but Shakespeare here encapsulates victory and death in one tableau, in which Henry gradually withers under the pressure of inexorable assault:

> And wherefore should these good news make me sick?
> Will Fortune never come with both hands full,
> But [write] her fair words still in foulest terms?

(IV, iv, 102–104)

He is paying the full penalty for his ambition as well as for the responsibilities of kingship he has assumed. Henry's looking to Fortune for salvation suggests he knows that forces greater than himself, perhaps divine retribution, now wreak havoc on him.

In Act IV, scene v, the dying King is placed in bed, where he rests until Hal makes his way in. For the third time in the play the anguish of the King is placed in the context of sleep, this time by Hal:

> O polish'd perturbation! golden care!
> That keep'st the ports of slumber open wide

To many a watchful night, sleep with it now!

> (IV, v, 23–25)

When he sees a feather lying motionless on the pillow, Hal assumes his father has died:

> My gracious lord! My father!
> This sleep is sound indeed, this is a sleep
> That from this golden rigol hath divorc'd
> So many English kings.

> (IV, v, 34–37)

For the first time he speaks gently of Henry as his father. Since these lines are spoken in private, we should assume his despondency is real. Then, in a gesture without historical substantiation, Hal places the crown on his head and leaves:

> Lo where it sits,
> Which God shall guard; and put the world's whole strength
> Into one giant arm, it shall not force
> This lineal honor from me.

> (IV, v, 43–46)

He accepts the throne not with greedy eagerness but with a sense of historical inevitability and responsibility.

When Henry awakens to discover the missing crown, he is furious, and when told that Hal visited the room, shouts an accusation:

> See, sons, what things you are!
> How quickly nature falls into revolt
> When gold becomes her object!

> (IV, v, 64–66)

But a change in attitude is about to occur.

When Hal enters, he utters a line whose meaning is ambiguous: "I never thought to hear you speak again" (IV, v, 91). A neutral listener could not be certain whether Hal says these words with joy or disappointment. But we who saw his earlier sorrow recognize that he is happy to see his father alive. Henry, though, chooses to believe the opposite and accuses Hal of robbing him of the crown and wishing the King dead (IV, v, 92–96).

Suddenly his voice softens, and his anger turns to regret and sympathy:

> O foolish youth,
> Thou seek'st the greatness that will overwhelm thee,
> Stay but a little, for my cloud of dignity
> Is held from falling with so weak a wind
> That it will quickly drop; my day is dim.

> (IV, v, 96–100)

For the first time we see the King speaking with fatherly concern. Quickly, however, he reverts to anger, and his strongest objections are against his son's apparent ruthlessness (IV, v, 109–112) an odd accusation from a man who risked everything and now endures such tribulation:

> Give that which gave thee life unto the worms,
> Pluck down my officers, break my decrees,
> For now a time is come to mock at form.
> Harry the Fift is crown'd! Up, vanity!
> Down, royal state! All you sage counsellors, hence!
>
> (IV, v, 116–120)

He fears the nation will degenerate into chaos, and in his warnings he sounds like Richard II:

> O my poor kingdom, sick with civil blows!
> When that my care could not withhold thy riots,
> What wilt thou do when riot is thy care?
>
> (IV, v, 133–135)

All sorts of emotions swirl around this final address: anger at his son, sympathy for his son's plight, jealousy over the power he himself has usurped, concern for the kingdom he has nurtured. The enormous stress Henry has contained under the discipline of a public persona he now releases. Hal allows him to exorcise his torments, then answers with his most emotional words of the play:

> O, pardon me, my liege! but for my tears,
> The moist impediments unto my speech,
> I had forestall'd this dear and deep rebuke
> Ere you with grief had spoke and I had heard
> The course of it so far. There is your crown;
> And He that wears the crown immortally
> Long guard it yours!
>
> (IV, v, 138–144)

He even anticipates the King's possible objection to these words:

> If I do feign,
> O, let me in my present wildness die,
> And never live to show th' incredulous world
> The noble change that I have purposed!
>
> (IV, v, 151–154)

He goes on about how in hesitating to put the crown on his head he reflected upon the paradoxical images of gold. We know he never expressed such reservations out loud. Thus we could look upon Hal's entire apology, including the reminder of his reformation, as the work of the consummate politician, soothing his dying King. Still, Hal has never been such a hypocrite. He has kept his emotions tightly reined, but he has never lied to that extent. Were John the speaker here, we might be justifiably dubious. But this confession, coming right after the King's, is believable.

Certainly Henry believes it, and at last the two are reconciled not only as

King and Prince, but as father and son. Historically their rivalry went on for years, and in 1410–11 Hal virtually controlled the nation's Parliament and worked against his father. But Shakespeare dispenses with that episode. Here the King accepts Hal's reformation, then offers fatherly and political advice. The first step is confession:

> God knows, my son,
> By what by-paths and indirect crook'd ways
> I met this crown, and I myself know well
> How troublesome it sate upon my head.
>
> (IV, v, 183–186)

"I met this crown" suggests that Henry ended up King by accident. We know that he took the crown directly from Richard, that nothing about the taking was fortuitous. Still, the second part of the line is accurate. Perhaps the King is seeking absolution, recognizing that in committing an act against God he has brought punishment on himself. Yet Henry also knows that through his struggle he has legitimized the reign of his son:

> And now my death
> Changes the mood, for what in me was purchas'd
> Falls upon thee in a more fairer sort . . .
>
> (IV, v, 198–200)

His sacrifice of his own life thus has meaning. Henry is also conscious of the perpetual threat of rebellion against his son, and cautions Hal about strategy:

> Therefore, my Harry,
> Be it thy course to busy giddy minds
> With foreign quarrels, that action, hence borne out,
> May waste the memory of the former days.
>
> (IV, v, 212–215)

This advice has guided the rulers of countless countries before and since. Until the moment of his death Henry IV remains the pragmatist. As he is carried off, regretful that his journey to the Holy Land will remain unfulfilled, he has come to grips with his own life. Whether we see him as an illegal usurper or a bold challenger of the political structure, he has suffered profoundly for the direction of his life.

We move to Justice Shallow's house, where the dialogue reverts to the prose of the lower classes. Falstaff insists he must be allowed to leave, and Shallow is just as insistent that the knight must remain. The Justice is preoccupied, however, with his servant Davy, who is equally busy with his own tasks, and the similarity in attitude between master and servant is humorous counterpoint. When Davy inquires ironically whether "the man of war stay all night . . . " (V, i, 29), Shallow indicates that Falstaff's stay has some purpose:

> Yes, Davy, I will use him well. A friend i'
> th' court is better than a penny in purse.
>
> (V, i, 30–31)

He still believes the Prince's once intimate friend has influence. Sadly, Falstaff also trusts that the Prince will have nothing better to do than listen to Falstaff's witticisms:

> I will devise matter enough out of this Shallow to keep
> Prince Harry in continual laughter the wearing out of
> six fashions, which is four terms, or two actions,
> and 'a shall laugh without intervallums.
>
> (V, i, 78–81)

Given Hal's last scene, these plans seem silly. They are also set off by Davy, who, for all his roguishness, has a fundamental sense of justice and order:

> I have serv'd your worship truly, sir, this eight
> years; and I cannot once or twice in a quarter bear out
> a knave against an honest man, I have little credit with
> your worship. The knave is mine honest friend, sir,
> therefore I beseech you let him be countenanc'd.
>
> (V, i, 47–51)

This theme of equity becomes far more important in the next scene, when the Chief Justice returns to settle his score with Hal, soon to be Henry V. The episode is fictitious but important. The Justice is nervous about dealing with the young monarch (V, ii, 10–13) and even Warwick, who earlier spoke so optimistically about Hal, is uneasy. Hal remains a cipher to them, and they wonder whether he will bring them down to the level of his lowlife cronies. Speaking of Hal's three brothers, Warwick comments:

> O that the living Harry had the temper
> Of he, the worst of these three gentlemen!
>
> (V, ii, 15–16)

But when Hal enters, he establishes at once that different rules will apply in court than flourished at the tavern:

> This is the English, not the Turkish court,
> Not Amurath an Amurath succeeds,
> But Harry Harry. Yet be sad, good brothers,
> For by my faith it very well becomes you.
>
> (V, ii, 47–50)

His listeners, nevertheless, are apprehensive, especially when Hal turns to the Justice and recalls the " . . . great indignities you laid upon me" (V, ii, 69). The Chief Justice summons his courage and warns the man soon to be King that the earlier chastisement was intended only to hold up the sovereign law of obedience to the King (V, ii, 73–80). And the Justice bids Hal imagine he were ruler under such circumstances:

> Hear your own dignity so much profan'd,
> See your most dreadful laws so loosely slighted,
> Behold yourself so by a son disdained;
> And then imagine me taking your part,
> And in your power soft silencing your son.
>
> (V, ii, 93–97)

The proposal is a challenge. Will Hal as King hold the law above all? He has been anticipating this question:

> You did commit me;
> For which I do commit into your hand
> Th' unstained sword that you have us'd to bear,
> With this remembrance, that you use the same
> With the like bold, just, and impartial spirit
> As you have done 'gainst me. There is my hand.
> You shall be as a father to my youth.
>
> (V, ii, 112–118)

The paternal image rounds out his development in the two plays:

> The tide of blood in me
> Hath proudly flow'd in vanity till now;
> Now doth it turn and ebb back to the sea,
> Where it shall mingle with the state of floods,
> And flow henceforth in formal majesty.
>
> (V, ii, 129–133)

Here are the words his listeners have been waiting to hear. And the audience is just as moved. Hal's reformation is complete, and we have no doubt of his priorities. We also see his words as a tribute to the sense of order and lawfulness England seeks.

One character, however, has not learned this truth, and the moment he does is one of the most despairing in all of Shakespeare's plays. First, however, the action moves back to Shallow's house, specifically the orchard, where Falstaff and his companions indulge in drinking and singing. Falstaff, ever calculating, works to flatter Shallow and Davy (V, iii, 10–11), hoping to ingratiate himself with them. His mood brightens even more when he learns from Pistol that Henry IV is as dead "as nail in door" (V, iii, 121), and Falstaff leaps to the same conclusion that the Chief Justice did:

> I know the young King is sick for me. Let us
> take any man's horses, the laws of England are at
> my commandement. Blessed are they that have been

my friends, and woe to my Lord Chief Justice!

(V, iii, 134–137)

But the arrests of Hostess Quickly and Doll Tearsheet in scene iv are the first indication that Falstaff is mistaken, and that the law is beginning to tighten. The arresting Beadle is thin, like Shallow, perhaps emphasizing that such leanness will be associated with order, while gross figures like Falstaff represent an anti-order to be tamed.

At the coronation scene, Falstaff still does not know what lies ahead and boasts of his relationship with the new King. When Henry V enters, Falstaff calls out: "God save thy Grace, King Hal! my royal Hal!" (V, v, 41). And once more: "My King, my Jove! I speak to thee, my heart!" (V, v, 46). Such antics are woefully misplaced. Nonetheless, the royal answer chills both Falstaff and us:

> I know thee not, old man, fall to thy prayers.
> How ill white hair becomes a fool and jester.
> I have long dreamt of such a kind of man,
> So surfeit-swell'd, so old, and so profane;
> But being awak'd, I do despise my dream.

(V, v, 47–51)

Then Hal coldly justifies the rejection:

> Reply not to me with a fool-born jest,
> Presume not that I am the thing I was,
> For God doth know, so shall the world perceive,
> That I have turn'd away my former self;
> So will I those that kept me company.

(V, v, 55–59)

His tone is absolute. The King does grant Falstaff a pension (V, v, 69–70), but the bequest does not reduce the impact of his pronouncement. Even as Falstaff tries to bluff his way through his embarrassment (V, v, 76–80), we understand what has occurred. And that John approves it is not cheering:

> I like this fair proceeding of the King's.
> He hath intent his wonted followers
> Shall all be very well provided for,
> But all are banish'd till their conversations
> Appear more wise and modest to the world.

(V, vi, 96–101)

Lumping Falstaff with all the rest is a misjustice, and Falstaff can never change enough that he will accommodate himself to the world at large. Thus this banishment is permanent. But one lesson of this play, indeed, of all the history plays, is that those who would achieve political success must make personal sacrifices. The loss of Falstaff's company is one of Hal's. We hope that he does not lose Falstaff's spiritual influence, but we note that the final words of the play belong to John, who eagerly anticipates war with France. For the new King, holding on to any of joyous youth will be difficult.

The two parts of *Henry IV* dramatize Shakespeare's vision of the nature of political life. Henry IV does make remarkable achievements: he takes a kingship shaken by usurpation, consolidates it, and passes it on intact to his son, who stands prepared to carry the crown to ever more impressive victories. Yet these glories do not eclipse the personal toll exacted on Henry IV and the country he serves. This balance of glory and loss, set against the social panorama of England and accompanied by the wise, sometimes ribald, sometimes wistful, laughter of Falstaff, gives these plays a unique place in Shakespeare's canon.

SUGGESTIONS FOR FURTHER READING

Blanpied, John W. " 'Unfathered heirs and loathly birds of nature': Bringing History to Crisis in *2 Henry IV*." *English Literary Renaissance* 5 (1975): 212–231.

Carrington, Norman Thomas. *Shakespeare:* King Henry IV, Part 2. London: Brodie, 1955.

Jorgensen, Paul A. "The 'Dastardly Treachery' of Prince John of Lancaster." *PMLA* 76 (1961): 488–492.

Leech, Clifford. "The Unity of *2 Henry IV*." *Shakespeare Survey* 6 (1953): 16–24.

Palmer, D. J. "Casting Off the Old Man: History and St. Paul in *Henry IV*." *Critical Quarterly* 12 (1970): 267–283.

Spencer, Benjamin T. "*2 Henry IV* and the Theme of Time." *University of Toronto Quarterly* 13 (1944): 394–399.

Young, David, ed. *Twentieth Century Interpretations of* Henry IV, Part Two. Englewood Cliffs, N.J.: Prentice-Hall, 1968.

HENRY V

This play poses difficult challenges of interpretation. It depicts the military successes of a man who, despite his death at age thirty-four, after less than ten years on the throne, stands as perhaps England's most revered king. It has the massive scope of an ancient epic and contains some of the most rousing, if jingoistic, poetry Shakespeare ever composed. Is the play, then, one of glorification? If so, just what or whom is glorified? The title character is a bold commander who leads his charges with audacity and inspiration. Yet he is a consummate politician, in important ways unchanged from the often unemotional, astute Prince of *Henry IV*. The plot also encompasses some of the most renowned battlefield triumphs the English nation has known. Yet the events themselves are dramatized with little glamor, and at times the work focuses on the ugliest aspects of war. Can these apparently contradictory qualities be synthesized into a unified vision?

In the Prologue, a curious device, Shakespeare seems to protest that the stage is of too small a scope to handle the drama:

> Can this cockpit hold
> The vasty fields of France? Or may we cram
> Within this wooden O the very casques
> That did affright the air at Agincourt?
>
> (Prologue, 11–14)

The playwright also begs indulgence for the jumps from scene to scene and country to country. Why does he make such excuses?

The answer emerges from the nature of the drama Shakespeare offers. Henry V, the man, is a titanic hero, beyond criticism. The act of warfare, however, is never portrayed by Shakespeare as heroic, but invariably as brutal and dehumanizing. Thus this play has a split vision. The king and his victories are exalted, but the battles themselves are not. In addition, the political strategies of the King are beneficial to England, but they are the tactics of a man who must carry out his duties while taking into account his own past, his country's history, and the values of the world in which he finds himself. Furthermore, he must yield to the demands of his own complicated personality. Thus the great shifts of action and emotion for which the Prologue offers apology.

That this play, for all its military talk, is grounded in the world of politics is clear from the opening action. The Archbishop of Canterbury and his colleague plot to gain funds for themselves, but they are frustrated by a bill intended to cut off church possessions (II, i, 1–5). During the reign of Henry IV, the bill was pushed aside because of internal squabbling that beset the kingdom. Now, with the new King in place, the Church is vulnerable once more, and the two clerics go into considerable detail about how many funds and resources they might lose (I, i, 11–19). These clerics are not the first we have seen who give their time to worldly concerns.

Next they move to a discussion of politics, and this centers on Henry V. Both men are relieved that he has proven such a beneficent figure, loyal to the church, and they go on to describe the transformation dramatized in the two parts of *Henry IV*:

> The breath no sooner left his father's body,
> But that his wildness, mortified in him,
> Seemd'd to die too . . .
>
> (I, i, 25–27)

Shakespeare uplifts his hero, who after the reign of his father took important steps to bind the nation's wounds. He assumed office in 1413, and by the spring of 1414, the start of this play, had already ordered the remains of Richard II moved to Westminster and made peace with the Earl of March, Richard's descendant. Most important, he had restored the land of the Percy family to the sons of the late Hotspur.

But the discussion here involves more immediate political crises. In an attempt to take the King's attention away from the Church bill, the Archbishop has challenged him:

> For I have made an offer to his Majesty,
> Upon our spiritual convocation
> And in regard of causes now in hand,
> Which I have open'd to his Grace at large,
> As touching France, to give a greater sum
> Than ever at one time the clergy yet
> Did to his predecessors part withal.
>
> (I, i, 75–82)

In other words, the church intends to bribe the king and support a war with France. We remember the words of Henry IV to his son, that he should busy local minds with foreign wars to avoid civil disorder (*Henry IV, Part 2*, IV, v, 213–216). Here those tactics are used by those who are supposed to be far more involved in the spiritual world. The demands of politics invade all levels of life.

In the next scene the persuasion begins. But how necessary is it? Shakespeare cannot show Henry V being manipulated by clerics, no matter how noble the cause. Instead he shows that Henry is already inclined to fight but seeks justification from the Archbishop of Canterbury:

> My learned lord, we pray you to proceed,
> And justly and religiously unfold
> Why the law Salique, that they have in France,
> Or should, or should not, bar us in our claim . . .
>
>   (I, ii, 9–12)

The point is subtle but essential. Henry V is depicted as a man who fights only for legitimate causes, for he understands the suffering war brings:

> For God doth know how many now in health
> Shall drop their blood in approbation
> Of what your reverence shall incite us to.
> Therefore take heed how you impawn our person,
> How you awake our sleeping sword of war—
> We charge you, in the name of God, take heed . . .
>
>   (I, ii, 18–23)

Henry wants war against France so as to regain territory won by Edward III, but he wants someone else to "incite us." He also believes in the order of law. Thus he seeks religious approval and warns the cleric to be sure that the sanction is clear. Shakespeare, in other words, makes Henry V politically, morally, and humanly aware: an ideal king.

In response to this order, which is historically unsubstantiated, the Archbishop embarks on a convoluted explanation of the Salique Law, which barred succession to the throne through a female line. This ruling had a logical basis. If a woman of the ruling French family married into another country, as was often the case, her loyalties might be divided. The Salique Law also prevented the French throne from passing to a foreign heir. In the play, the French deny the legality of Henry's claim since it is based on inheritance through a woman, Isabella of France, wife of Edward II, but the Archbishop establishes that the Salique land is in fact part of Germany and not subject to such a decree (I, ii, 50–55). He goes on to cite numerous precedents whereby the French have defied their own ruling. Thus Henry does have the legal basis on which to fight.

After this lengthy and at times baffling explanation, the King restates the question: "May I with right and conscience make this claim?" (I, ii, 96). The effect is comic, but nonetheless we feel that Henry is making every attempt to be a humane monarch. In answering, the Archbishop invokes the Bible and the conquests of Henry's great-uncle, Edward the Black Prince (I, ii, 101–114). Then the Bishop of Ely reaches the desired conclusion:

> Awake remembrance of these valiant dead,
> And with your puissant arm renew their feats.
> You are their heir, you sit upon their throne;
> The blood and courage that renowned them

Runs in your veins; and my thrice-puissant liege
Is in the very May-morn of his youth,
Ripe for exploits and mighty enterprises.

(I, ii, 115–121)

Exeter and Westmerland add to the urging, but Henry remains cautious, warning
about the traditional dangers posed by the Scots (I, ii, 136–139). Again, Shakespeare portrays Henry as wary and protective of his people. His comment also
invites reassurance, first from Canterbury, then from Ely:

But there's an old saying very old and true,
"If that you will France win,
Then with Scotland first begin."

(I, ii, 166–168)

Exeter, too, agrees that the battle can be won on two fronts. Here again Henry
appears not as a militaristic, battle-hungry warrior, but as a responsible leader
willing to listen to well-meaning counselors. Finally, we note that no one raises
even a hint about the King's being the son of a usurper. Everyone speaks of
him as a completely legitimate ruler, the unchallenged inheritor of royalty.

The crux of the argument in favor of war is offered by the Archbishop, who
invokes the image of honey bees working under the guidance of a ruler (I, ii,
187–189). His emphasis is on order and obedience (I, ii, 204–213). To this
picture Henry responds:

Now are we well resolv'd, and by God's help
And yours, the noble sinews of our power,
France being ours, we'll bend it to our awe,
Or break it all to pieces . . .
Either our history shall with full mouth
Speak freely of our acts, or else our grave,
Like Turkish mute, shall have a tongueless mouth,
Not worshipp'd with a waxen epitaph.

(I, ii, 221–233)

The speech is emotional, but politically sophisticated as well. Henry pays tribute
to God, acknowledging his own responsibility to divine sustenance. He also
acknowledges a debt to his nobles; thus he appears proud, yet humble. This
combination allows Henry to pursue his own political ends without antagonizing
anyone, and simultaneously to maintain his own idealized place. In sum, Henry
proves himself at every step a politician supreme, but one whose strategies are
devoted towards proper ends.

The Ambassadors from France then enter, answering contentions Henry has
made about certain dukedoms. The rejection is framed with insinuations about
Henry's revelrous youth (I, ii, 250–257), and the insult is compounded with a
gift of tennis balls, equipment used in a sport then thought to be a frivolity in
which English youth indulged excessively. Historically this incident never oc-

curred, but Shakespeare uses it to great effect. Henry's response is cool, and even utilizes puns about the game:

> We will in France, by God's grace, play a set
> Shall strike his father's crown into the hazard.
> Tell him he hath made a match with such a wrangler
> That all the courts of France will be disturb'd
> With chaces.
>
> (I, ii, 262–266)

("Hazard" refers to the walls of a real tennis court, as well as a state of danger. "Chaces" refers to missed returns and pursuits.) Henry also pretends that this moment of impudence is justification for combat:

> But I will rise there with so full a glory
> That I will dazzle all the eyes of France,
> Yea, strike the Dolphin blind to look on us.
> And tell the pleasant prince this mock of his
> Hath turned his balls to gun-stones, and his soul
> Shall stand sore charged for the wasteful vengeance
> That shall fly with them . . .
>
> (I, ii, 278–285)

The images sound straight from the young Hal, the sun rising to dazzle all around him (*Henry IV, Part 1*, I, ii, 196–217). But Henry is not finished:

> And some are yet ungotten and unborn
> That shall have cause to curse the Dolphin's scorn.
> But this lies all within the will of God,
> To whom I do appeal, and in whose name
> Tell you the Dolphin I am coming on
> To venge me as I may, and to put forth
> My rightful hand in a well-hallow'd cause.
>
> (I, ii, 287–293)

The King is politically adept. First he personalizes the war, giving the English a specific object of hate: the insulting Dolphin. Then he again makes this challenge seem spontaneous, as if he had not considered the option before, when we know he had. Finally he again sanctifies his attack under God's name. Without doubt Henry is heroic; yet his heroism is gauged. He does not charge recklessly into war but makes sure that his campaign is justified according to every standard. The war against France will inspire the King's countrymen with patriotic fervor, but we see political craft underneath.

Act II begins with another Prologue, this more blatantly patriotic than the first:

> Now all the youth of England are on fire,
> And silken dalliance in the wardrobe lies;
> Now thrive the armorers, and honor's thought

Reigns solely in the breast of every man.

(II, prologue, 1–4)

We have seen no evidence that anyone outside Henry and a few advisors are
fired with zeal. Nevertheless, the speaker claims that the entire nation is taken
with a desire for war. At the same time the presence of ''honor'' alerts us to
the possibility of irony. Characters throughout these plays have so misused the
word that we cannot take it seriously. Thus here again Shakespeare seems to be
arousing nationalism; yet the cause is undercut. Even the rest of the Chorus's
words, so passionate, seem overstated.

The grandeur of military action is further mocked in scene one, with Nym,
Bardolph, and later Pistol. Here is the seamier side of war, and we are spared
little of it. The boisterous comic spirit of the lower classes has disappeared, and
instead we hear speculation on mortality (II, i, 5–10) and a fatalism about war:

Men may sleep, and they may have their throats about
them at that time . . .

(II, i, 20–21)

Resignation turns to anger when Pistol and Nym draw their swords, and the
quarrel has such little substance that we cannot help thinking of the previous
scene and Henry's rationalizing a war with France over causes that are of greater
scope but equally the product of ego. This dramatic structure occurs frequently
through the play. One episode in which royal plotting turns into patriotic ardor
is followed by another in which behavior from the lower class satirizes such
pretension.

Also mocking the procedure of warfare is the presence of Pistol, whose extravagant language and gestures reduce virtually any military action to a charade:

I [thee defy] again.
O hound of Crete, think'st thou my spouse to get?
No, to the spittle go,
And from the powd'ring-tub of infamy
Fetch forth the lazar kite of Cressid's kind,
Doll Tearsheet she by name, and her espouse.

(II, i, 72–77)

The classical images, interspliced with the boisterous tone, are ludicrous, and
the implication that all fighting is equally pointless remains.

The moment is tempered by the news from the Boy that Falstaff is critically
ill (II, i, 81–85) and the two antagonists put down their arms and agree to share
Pistol's profits in the army (II, i, 107–115). Again, the nobility of military
conflict is diminished by the attitude of these participants, for whom warfare is
only a means of lining their own pockets.

The situation turns serious in the next scene, as Henry brings forth the conspirators mentioned earlier by the Chorus (II, Prologue, 21–30). He knows about
the collusion, but he approaches the three obliquely, inquiring about the devotion

of his troops in general (II, i, 20–24). The trio assures him that everyone is loyal to the throne. Then Henry shifts tactics, bringing up the case of a man who, while drunk, spoke out against the King. When Henry proposes pardon, Scroop challenges him:

> That's mercy, but too much security.
> Let him be punish'd, sovereign, lest example
> Breed, by his sufferance, more of such a kind.

(II, ii, 44–46)

Henry poses again the possibility of mercy, but the others are insistent. Then Henry asks once more:

> If little faults, proceeding on distemper,
> Shall not be wink'd at, how shall we stretch our eye
> When capital crimes, chew'd, shallow'd, and digested,
> Appear before us?

(II, ii, 54–57)

The King appears willing to err on the side of generosity as he frees the accused man, but suddenly he calls on Cambridge, Scroop, and Grey, and thrusts before them incriminating letters. For a moment they are silent, while Henry taunts them:

> What see you in those papers that you lose
> So much complexion?

(II, ii, 72–73)

Within seconds all three confess, allowing Henry to release his full anger.

Why has he followed such a method? Why not simply bring forth the accusations right away? Again Henry plays politics. He permits the three to put self-condemning words in their own mouths. When their treason is thereafter uncovered, Henry himself seems not harsh, but just, according to the precedent the three themselves have established.

Next Henry goes off on a tirade, linking treachery and murder (II, ii, 102–110) and expressing shock at the disloyalty the conspirators have demonstrated (II, ii, 126–140). The climactic lines have a peculiar echo:

> I will weep for thee;
> For this revolt of thine, methinks, is like
> Another fall of man.

(II, ii, 140–142)

Here Henry V sounds like Richard II, placing the kingship in its divine perspective. He also seems to be harking back to Richard's removal from office at the hand of Henry's father. The outrage may be genuine, but we set it in the context of earlier plays and recognize that the King is here victim of the kind of opposition that enabled his father to gain the throne. Henry, of course, does not point to any parallels. The implication, however, is that once a man has

become King, certain values and attitudes take over. He is taken with his own
need for security, and in a sense he isolates himself from everyone. From this
point on Henry becomes more and more the figure of the King, and the emotional
detachment that was part of Hal prevails.

After Exeter proclaims the formal charges, all three conspirators claim loyalty,
but whether they are sincerely repentant is not clear. As Cambridge says:

> For me, the gold of France did not seduce,
> Although I did admit it as a motive
> The sooner to effect what I intended.
> But God be thanked for prevention,
> Which [I] in sufferance heartily will rejoice,
> Beseeching God, and you, to pardon me.
>
> (II, ii, 155–160)

What is pushed aside is that Cambridge's claim to the throne, although through
the female line, is based on his marriage to Anne Mortimer, a descendant of
Edward III's third son, Lionel; according to the rules of succession, Cambridge
should have priority over Henry V, a grandson of Edward III's fourth son, John
of Gaunt. Earlier Henry was declared entitled to fight for a claim based on
succession through a female line, but no one bothers to point out this contradiction.

In any case, Henry is not interested in excuses from the conspirators and
condemns them to death:

> Get you therefore hence,
> Poor miserable wretches, to your death;
> The taste whereof God of his mercy give
> You patience to endure, and true repentance
> Of all your dear offenses!
>
> (II, ii, 177–181)

He leavens the moment by inciting the troops to war in God's name (II, ii, 182–
190). Henry has certainly taken his father's advice about busying his subjects
"With foreign quarrels" (*Henry IV, Part 2*, IV, v, 213–214).

The next episode is set up beautifully. We leave Henry V, the politician
supreme, and immediately learn of the death of Falstaff, a death that parallels
to an extent the disappearance of the more fun-loving "Hal" part of Henry. The
description of Falstaff's expiration is also intriguing, for he seems to have
repented to a degree on his deathbed (II, iii, 18–20). Perhaps we are meant to
see Henry's single-minded intensity reflected in Falstaff's change in his final
moments.

Also interesting here is Pistol's invocation to his cohorts as they head off to
war. Henry roused the troops by appealing to God, the kingship, and a spirit of
national glory. Pistol's approach is different:

> Yoke-fellows in arms,
> Let us to France, like horse-leeches, my boys,

To suck, to suck, the very blood to suck!

(II, iii, 54–56)

Here is war for the great mass of soldiers: an enterprise without dignity, without honor, just profit. And no matter how it is dressed up in pageantry and rhetoric, that truth pervades.

Scene iv is an introduction to the French court, which is depicted with all the derision we might expect. The first quality we note is their misreading of the English king. They still think of Henry as "a vain, giddy, shallow, humorous youth" (II, iv, 28). We also note that the French king is wiser than his son, the Dolphin, for the King remembers the military skill of Edward, the Black Prince, Henry's ancestor (II, iv, 50–62). What neither man recognizes is Henry's political shrewdness, which is apparent with the entrance of Exeter, Henry's representative, who enters bearing a powerful message. In the name of his King, Exeter essentially claims France for England, "By the law of nature and of nations" (II, iv, 80). The message also asks the King of France to spare his country the violence that will ensue:

Therefore in fierce tempest is he coming,
In thunder and in earthquake, like a Jove,
That if requiring fail he will compel;
And bids you, in the bowels of the Lord,
Deliver up the crown, and to take mercy
On the poor souls for whom this hungry war
Opens his vasty jaws; and on your head
Turning the widows' tears, the orphans' cries,
The dead men's blood, the privy maidens' groans,
For husbands, fathers, and betrothed lovers,
That shall be swallowed in this controversy.

(II, iv, 99–109)

Here again is the political Henry. Earlier he legitimized his military aggression with legal and divine approval. Now he turns responsibility for his action to the French if they refuse to capitulate. He dramatizes his duty as a mandate to fulfill his mission as King, but makes the French guilty of aggression if they choose to defend themselves.

Then Henry, through Exeter, adds one more touch: a personal insult to the hot-headed Dolphin, to "sweeten the bitter mock you sent his Majesty . . ." (II, iv, 122). The challenge naturally infuriates the Dolphin, who shouts in return: " . . . I desire/Nothing but odds with England" (II, iv, 129). Henry has thus shifted his stance so that France now seems the aggressor.

Act III begins with one of the great calls to glory in English literature. First the Chorus romanticizes the military entourage, adding that England itself is to be left guarded by only "grandsires, babies, and old women . . ." (III, i, 20). Historically this plan was not the case, but Shakespeare's liberties are understandable. Then Henry himself takes stage:

> Once more unto the breach, dear friends, once more;
> Or close the wall up with our English dead.
> In peace there's nothing so becomes a man
> As modest stillness and humility;

>   (III, i, 1–4)

He lists in detail the physical transformation that should overtake his troops. In fact, Henry deliberately urges his men to turn into beasts:

> But when the blast of war blows in our ears,
> Then imitate the action of the tiger;
> Stiffen the sinews, [conjure] up the blood,
> Disguise fair nature with hard-favor'd rage . . .

>   (III, i, 5–9)

Once again we are reminded of the reality of war in contrast to its image.
    How seriously is this call to be taken? Consider the first line of the next scene:

> On, on, on, on, on! To the breach, to the
> breach!

>   (III, ii, 1–2)

So shouts Bardolph as he rouses his two comrades, Nym and Pistol. What is our reaction now to Henry's own cheering? The irony becomes sharper when the Boy relates the adventures of the three reprobates, all of whom he describes as thieves and swindlers (III, ii, 28–53). That the Boy resists joining them does not minimize their destructiveness.

    If these three represent one dark side of war, the next who enter reflect a more patriotic version. MacMorris, Jamy, Gower, and the long-winded Fluellen are not nobles, and they do squabble amidst themselves. Yet in spite of their comically disparate dialects, they also work in concert in support of Henry, and thus we may assume that since these representatives from traditionally rival countries join together, the King's call to action has touched the spirits of all the kingdom.

    The next scene returns us to the reality of combat. Henry stands before the gates of Harfleur, waiting for the French to surrender. At this moment he is hardly the magnanimous ruler, for he threatens the city with destruction:

> The gates of mercy shall be all shut up,
> And the flesh'd soldier, rough and hard of heart,
> In liberty of bloody hand, shall range
> With conscience wide as hell, mowing like grass
> Your fresh fair virgins and your flowr'ing infants . . .
>   Therefore, you men of Harflew
> Take pity of your town and of your people,
> Whiles yet my soldiers are in my command,
> Whiles yet the cool and temperate winds of grace
> O'erblows the filthy and contagious clouds

Of headly murther, spoil, and villainy.

(III, iii, 10–32)

On the one hand, Henry warns the town of the disaster that awaits them. On the other hand, he frames his warning as if he does not wish any of this savagery to occur. Again he manages to remove himself from the center of action. His only purpose seems to be to prevent bloodshed, but he also seeks to avoid fighting for another reason. If his troops do embark on a rampage, Henry will not be able to control them. Thus his generosity towards Harfleur is actually an attempt to maintain command over his own soldiers. We should not be surprised, therefore, that the Governor of Harfleur surrenders (III, iii, 47–50), and that Henry is doubly pleased to be merciful.

After a brief introduction to the charm and innocence of Katherine, the future wife of Henry V, we move again to the French court, once more set up to contrast with the English. The King, the Dolphin, and Constable are derisive towards their enemies, but their hatred seems more like pettiness:

> O, for honor of our land,
> Let us not hang like roping icicles
> Upon our houses' thatch, whiles a more frosty people
> Sweat drops of gallant youth in our rich fields!

(III, v, 22–25)

We should also keep in mind that the Elizabethan audience knew the outcome of the battles about to take place. Thus when the French boast of taking Henry prisoner (III, vi, 53–55), and crow about the illness besetting the English troops (III, vi, 57), the audience of Shakespeare's time must have reacted with knowing smiles.

But Shakespeare does not leave his audience smug. From the French side he moves back to the baser aspect of the English, where Pistol reveals that Bardolph has stolen sacraments from a church and been condemned to death by Exeter (III, vi, 39–45). This crime is more vicious than the pranks or bribes we earlier associated with this crew, and Fluellen, wordy as always but determined to maintain military order, urges punishment to Henry (III, vi, 99–106). We know that Henry has long been a consort of Bardolph at the tavern, but here he brooks no breaches of discipline and does not attempt to pardon Bardolph. Indeed, he ignores his erstwhile companion and establishes a precedent: "We would have all such offenders so cut off" (III, vi, 107–108). Morally and politically he emerges triumphant again, as he diverts every incident to his own advantage.

In addition, this moment reminds us of one of Falstaff's lines from early in *Henry IV, Part 1*: "Do not when thou art king, hang a thief" (I, ii, 62). At that juncture Falstaff was being semi-comic, petitioning a still casual Hal not to forget his best friend. At the same time, Falstaff was asking for royal protection. Here Henry V demonstrates that Falstaff's fears have come to pass, for under the burden of kingship, the one-time "wag" must act responsibly.

He also contrasts himself with the French in two other ways. Speaking to

Montjoy, a herald from France who warns of retribution for any military action, Henry decries bravado:

> Yet forgive me, God,
> That I do brag thus! This your air of France
> Hath blown that vice in me.
>
> (III, vi, 150–152)

He also takes to heart the suffering his army would endure:

> We would not seek a battle as we are,
> Nor, as we are, we say we will not shun it.
>
> (III, vi, 164–165)

Never does Henry allow himself to be seen as ruthless. Instead he always works to appear as the reluctant upholder of a noble cause with potentially tragic consequences.

Scene vii builds up to the climactic battle by taking us to the French side. The most important point of contrast remains that between Henry and the Dolphin. The latter is once again portrayed as a braggart, essentially shallow, as his poetic devotion to his horse suggests (III, iii, 11–18, 20–25). Moreover, his troops are aware of his inadequacy, as the Constable comments about the Dolphin's reputed valor: " . . . never anybody saw it but his lackey" (III, vii, 110–112). This reservation, however, is contrasted by the French anticipation of the morning's battle:

> What a wretched and peevish fellow is this
> King of England, to mope with his fat-brain'd follow-
> ers so far out of his knowledge!
>
> (III, vii, 132–134)

For the Elizabethan audience the irony of such short-sighted remarks must have been exhilarating and contributive to the loyalty that surrounds Henry. Again, such fervor may be transferred to the war itself, but the essence of the play is the accomplishment of Henry, not the glory of war.

Act IV dramatizes the famous battle at Agincourt, which took place in October 1415. Before the first scene, the Chorus emphasizes themes already familiar: the overconfidence of the French, the struggles of the English, and the inspirational leadership of Henry. The Chorus also apologizes for what will prove an inadequate representation of battle. Why is such an apology necessary? Because the war hardly appears onstage, and the battles are depicted in the barest outlines. Far more important to the playwright are the consequences of war and the character of the participants.

One scene that brings these elements to the fore is the first of Act IV. Henry offers support to his troops by ruminating on the nearby French army:

> Besides, they are our outward consciences
> And preachers to us all, admonishing

That we should dress up fairly for our end.

(IV, i, 8–10)

He optimistically takes the proximity of the enemy as beneficial, for they inspire his own forces to remain alert. He then borrows the cloak of Thomas Erpingham, and wanders through his camp. Perhaps we should take this gesture as indication that the King has not entirely lost the common touch that originally made him so winsome a public figure.

His affection for the lower classes is apparent right away in his treatment of Pistol, who, unaware of the stranger's identity, describes Henry in a bluff, familiar tone:

> The King's a bawcock, and a heart of gold,
> A lad of life, an imp of fame,
> Of parents good, of fist most valient.

(IV, i, 44–46)

Pistol, though, has his own preoccupation, for he inquires whether this stranger knows Fluellen, and promises to knock Fluellen's "leek about his pate" (IV, i, 56). (The leek, an onion-like herb, is a symbol of the Welsh, and was commonly worn on the soldiers' hats). Apparently Pistol has not forgotten Fluellen's attitude toward the captured Bardolph, and means to take revenge.

Just as Pistol departs, Fluellen enters with Gower, and the Welshman's bombastic tones ring out:

> If you would take the pains but
> to examine the wars of Pompey the Great, you shall
> find, I warrant you, that there is no tiddle taddle
> nor pibble pabble in Pompey's camp.

(IV, i, 68–71)

In his own well-meaning, pretentious way, Fluellen, too, is trying to maintain English spirits.

Henry gains a more accurate measure of morale when he continues anonymously on his path. When he encounters Bates, Court, and Williams, the King, speaking as just another soldier, tries to justify the conflict:

> Methinks I could not die any
> where so contented as in the King's company, his cause
> being just and his quarrel honorable.

(IV, i, 126–128)

Michael Williams, however, is not impressed:

> I am afeard there are few die
> well that die in a battle; for how can they charitably
> dispose of any thing, when blood is their argument?
> Now, if these men do not die well, it will be a black
> matter for the King that led them to it; who to disobey

were against all proportion of subjection.

(IV, i, 141–146)

This argument touches the king closely. Throughout this play he has positioned himself so that he appears to be responding to antagonistic forces rather than arousing them. He has arranged matters so that he is obeying legal and religious law as well as answering French insult. Here Williams does not permit the King such a pose, but insists that he is in the end responsible for his actions. Henry is not eager to bear this burden.

Thus he turns on Williams with a vengeance. Still in disguise, he compares the King to a father whose son turns scoundrel:

> The King is not bound to answer the
> particular endings of his soldiers, the father of his
> son, nor the master of his servant; for they purpose not
> their death when they purpose their services.

(IV, i, 155–158)

But this argument is not convincing. Again Henry is trying to deny responsibility for the predicament of others, and the longer he speaks, the more we feel the emptiness of his arguments. Of course a master is responsible for his servant, just as a father is responsible for his son. Henry does not stop here, though:

> Every subject's
> duty is the King's, but every subject's soul is his own.
> Therefore should every soldier in the wars do as every
> sick man in his bed, wash every mote out of his con-
> science; and dying so, death is to him advantage . . .

(IV, i, 176–180)

This argument, too, is unimpressive. Henry wants authority, but he resists the responsibility that comes with authority. Williams, however, accepts this prem-ise, perhaps overcome by the length and passion of the interloper's argument. Henry is still not satisfied. He claims that the King has said he would not be ransomed (IV, i, 191) (so as to survive while his troops are killed), but Williams doubts this claim, too. Henry reasserts himself, but Williams remains unmoved: "You pay him then" (IV, i, 197). Henry is sufficiently outraged that he chal-lenges Williams to a duel, an action that makes the King look foolish. The two swap gloves, agree to wear the other's apparel as a sign, and resolve to fight when they next meet (IV, i, 211–220). What stays with us is the King's insecurity. He seems desperate to be freed of the weight of kingship, and his subsequent soliloquy explains why:

> What infinite heart's ease
> Must kings neglect, that private men enjoy!
> And what have kings, that privates have not too,

Save ceremony, save general ceremony?

(IV, i, 236–239)

As his father spoke in *Henry IV, Part 2* about the obligations of the crown, so
Henry V here is oppressed by those duties. At line 265 he invokes, as his father
did years before, the image of sleeplessness. The cumulative effect of this speech
is the question of the price of greatness, a familiar issue from the history plays.
We remember Henry VI musing over the tranquility of the shepherd's life. We remember Richard II disposing happily of the cares of office. We remember Henry IV
collapsing under the pressures of his position. Now even Henry V, young, energetic,
supported by his people, and free from civil unrest, seems overcome by them:

> No, not all these, thrice-gorgeous ceremony,
> Not all these, laid in bed majestical,
> Can sleep so soundly as the wretched slave . . .

(IV, i, 266–268)

Yet he manages to carry off his tasks with stunning effectiveness. Throughout
this play he has manipulated political situations with aplomb, harnessing the will
of a nation. But at what cost? Henry tells us in a speech that may be regarded
as revealing the center of his character:

> O God of battles, steel my soldiers' hearts,
> Possess them not with fear! Take from them now
> The sense of reck'ning, [if] th' opposed numbers
> Pluck their hearts from them. Not to-day, O Lord,
> O, not to-day, think not upon the fault
> My father made in compassing the crown!
> I Richard's body have interred new,
> And on it have bestowed more contrite tears,
> Than from it issued forced drops of blood.
> Five hundred poor I have in yearly pay,
> Who twice a day their wither'd hands hold up
> Toward heaven, to pardon blood; and I have built
> Two chauntries, where the sad and solemn priests
> Sing still for Richard's soul. More will I do;
> Though all that I can do is nothing worth,
> Since that my penitence comes after all,
> Imploring pardon.

(IV, i, 289–305)

For all his political sophistication, for all his military boldness, for all his ability
to inspire his countrymen, Henry V knows he remains trapped by the crimes of
his father. He has tried to redress some wrongs by giving Richard II proper
burial, and he has tried to escape the legacy of murder and blood that his father
wrought. But in this scene he is helpless, and we feel a man battling against
forces of history and divine retribution. He is nonetheless striving to keep his
nation whole and to fulfill what he believes is its destiny. At the same time we

are aware of his innate political disposition. All these elements are intertwined with the always brutal nature of war and the remarkable triumphs Henry leads. Thus the complexity of Shakespeare's portrait of this King.

After a tableau of the French forces, who still mock the English (IV, ii, 24–29), the portrait of Henry becomes even more complicated when we hear his brilliant call to the troops in scene iii. So much of the speech is focused on honor, a word we have come to mistrust (IV, iii, 22, 28, 31). He is conscious, too, of the odds his army faces, but he is not deterred:

> We would not die in that man's company
> That fears his fellowship to die with us.
>
> (IV, iii, 38–39)

Finally he makes his greatest appeal to national unity:

> We few, we happy few, we band of brothers;
> For he to-day that sheds his blood with me
> Shall be my brother; be he ne'er so vile,
> This day shall gentle his condition . . .
>
> (IV, iii, 60–63)

All the principles of Henry V are in this speech. His call for honor is a way of justifying national pride and legalizing the war against the French. The attempt to claim the free will of all the participants (IV, iii, 34–39) is a way to escape the ultimate responsibility for this battle. And the call for national solidarity is the charismatic Hal at his best.

When the next challenge comes from the French through Montjoy (IV, iii, 80–87), Henry reacts, as we might expect, with shock and sadness (IV, iii, 91–97). But even in his anger his quandary is revealed. Speaking of his troops he warns the French:

> And those that leave their valiant bones in France,
> Dying like men, though buried in your dunghills,
> They shall be fam'd; for there the sun shall greet them,
> And draw their honors reeking up to heaven,
> Leaving their earthly parts to choke your clime,
> The smell whereof shall breed a plague in France.
>
> (IV, iii, 98–103)

The word "sun" reminds us of the dominant image associated with Henry V ever since his first appearance in the tavern. Here he retreats back to his old persona to frighten the enemy and rouse himself. He also invokes the help of God (IV, iii, 120), in a modest appositive intended to remind all on both sides that the English are divinely inspired. How successful is he? One measure of Henry V's efficacy is the momentary appearance of York, who volunteers to lead the charge (IV, iii, 130–131). What makes this offer remarkable is that York is none other than Aumerle, who has not taken the stage since the last act of *Richard II*. This gesture may be taken as reflective of the King's capacity to unite the nation, for Aumerle was once violently opposed to Henry IV. Now he is willing to die in the name of Henry IV's son.

But the import of battle is derided in scene iv, as Pistol and a French soldier go at one another. When they depart, the Boy places the encounter in perspective:

> I did never know so full a voice
> issue from so empty a heart; but the saying is true,
> "The empty vessel makes the greatest sound."
> Bardolph and Nym had ten times more valor than
> this roaring devil i' th' old play, that every one may
> pare his nails with a wooden dagger, and they are both
> hang'd, and so would this be, if he durst steal any thing
> adventurously.
>
> (IV, iv, 68–74)

The false bravery of Pistol survives, while the daring, if immoral, boldness of Nym and Bardolph ends on the gallows. Such is the way of the world in which Henry struggles to maintain honor.

Part of Shakespeare's strategy in this play is that we see only fragments of the war itself. In scene v we view the frustrations of the French in defeat as they berate themselves and the English:

> O perdurable shame! let's stab ourselves.
> Be these the wretches that we play'd at dice for?
>
> (IV, v, 7–8)

Then we move in scene vi to a report of the battlefield glory of York, who turns into a model of chivalry. (In fact, York, who was excessively fat, died after he fell off his horse.) But the concept of "honor" sounds hollow when Henry learns that the French have regathered their troops: "Then every soldier kill his prisoners" (IV, vi, 37). Historically the sequence of events was different, for Henry ordered prisoners and noncombatants killed before the French reorganized. Yet if Shakespeare chooses to ignore that reality, he undercuts this brutality in a more subtle way, when Fluellen asks one question: "What call you the town's name where Alexander the Pig was born?" (IV, vi, 12–13). Gower corrects the misnomer, but if Fluellen remembers one of the world's foremost soldiers with such a sobriquet, what does that say about war in general? In fact, Fluellen can remember hardly anything accurate about Alexander, a devastating comment upon the transiency of military glory. When Fluellen adds that Alexander killed his own best friend, Clytus, (IV, vii, 45–50), we think immediately of Falstaff. Gower denies that Henry ever committed so cruel an act, but Fluellen remembers the fat knight, and also approves of Henry's rejection of him (IV, vii, 46–48). Consider, then, the next gesture by Henry, following right upon the memory of Falstaff:

> Besides, we'll cut the throats of those we have,
> And not a man of them that we shall take

> Shall taste our mercy.
>
>   (IV, vi, 63–65)

The ruthlessness that has manifested itself in Henry's political dealings shows up in his military triumph. Yet in warfare, as in politics, the only barometer is victory. And Henry is victorious.

At the peak of Henry's triumph, the French ambassador, Montjoy, enters to ask permission to bury his dead:

> For many of our princes (woe the while!)
> Lie drown'd and soak'd in mercenary blood;
> So do our vulgar drench their peasant limbs
> In blood of princes, and [their] wounded steeds
> Fret fetlock deep in gore, and with wild rage
> Yerk out their armed heels at their dead masters,
> Killing them twice.
>
>   (IV, vii, 75–81)

For all of Henry's renown, suffering like this is an inevitable result of combat. Henry, however, always the pragmatist, replies that he still sees Frenchmen galloping "o'er the field" (IV, vii, 86). Then Montjoy officially surrenders: "The day is yours" (IV, vii, 86). And suddenly Henry's attitude turns from aggressor to humble victor: "Praised be God and not our strength, for it!" (IV, vii, 87). When he defeated Hotspur at Shrewsbury, his win was a personal one. Here all England shares the triumph. The King's modesty is shown in an even warmer light by the brief encounter with Fluellen, whose bluntness is an effective counterpoint to the grandeur of other speeches:

> I need not to be ashamed of your Majesty,
> praised be God, so long as your Majesty is an honest
> man.
>
>   (IV, vii, 113–115)

Such comparatively rough treatment gives Henry an endearing humanity, as if a hint of Hal remains within him. He even retains some of the tavern-like feel for deception and prank. He meets Williams, and demands why the soldier is wearing in his hat the glove the King gave him in the earlier scene (IV, vii, 120–121). After Williams explains the circumstances, then leaves, Henry orders Fluellen to wear Williams' glove under the excuse that it belongs to a French soldier, Alanson (IV, vii, 157). To Warwick and Gloucester, Henry attempts to justify his behavior:

> If that the soldier strike him, as I judge
> By his blunt bearing he will keep his word,
> Some sudden mischief may arise of it;
> For I do know Fluellen valiant
> And touch'd with choler, hot as gunpowder,

And quickly will return an injury.

(IV, vii, 176–181)

This entire charade seems roundabout, but in scene viii Fluellen and Williams do meet and immediately begin to fight. Williams is taken as a traitor to Henry, who then reveals himself:

'Twas indeed thou promisedst to strike,
And thou hast given me most bitter terms.

(IV, viii, 41–42)

Williams apologizes profusely, insisting he spoke only honestly (IV, viii, 50–56), and the King quickly forgives him, even offering money. Williams, always proud and upright, declines the offer: ''I will none of your money'' (IV, viii, 67), but Fluellen is insistent.

Why is the King so desperate to assert himself over Williams, and why does Henry take so circuitous a course? Perhaps because Williams tapped something deep with Henry, and this scene is an attempt at exoneration, aimed at both revealing Henry's generosity and asserting his authority as King.

That business completed, Henry returns to the primary action of the play: the story of the triumph over France. Historically the battle at Agincourt was miraculous. Only 400 English died, while 10,000 French soldiers were killed, primarily because the English had lighter and more mobile armaments. But Shakespeare makes the victory even more stunning, with only twenty-five English announced as dead. Then in three consecutive speeches Henry announces that the victory belongs to God (IV, viii, 111–112, 115–116, 120). He thereby insinuates that this battle, and by implication all of Henry V's reign, was divinely ordained. The overthrow of Richard II by Henry IV was an act against God, and the reign of Henry VI will be punishment for the act. Yet the conquests by Henry V were possible only because of Richard's downfall. Thus that event was tragic, but it permitted one of the great moments in English history. This pattern underlies this tetralogy.

Act V is an anticlimax, given how much of this play and the three preceding are devoted to the spectacle of military battle and the more subtle battles of politics. The Chorus's opening address implies that the battle at Agincourt essentially ended the war with France. But historically the fighting carried on for five more years until the Treaty of Noyes in 1420. The splendor of victory is diminished, however, by a scene containing the less reputable elements of war, as Fluellen, in retaliation for earlier humiliation, forces Pistol to eat leek. Pistol has no chance to retaliate, yet his reactions after Fluellen leaves are telling, especially in the context of the play as a whole:

News have I that my Doll is dead i' th' spittle
Of a malady of France,
And there my rendezvous is quite cut off.
Old I do wax, and from my weary limbs
Honor is cudgell'd. Well, bawd I'll turn.

And something lean to cutpurse of quick hand.
To England will I steal, and there I'll steal;
And patches will I get unto these cudgell'd scars,
And [swear] I got them in the Gallia wars.

(V, i, 81–89)

Lest we imagine that Henry's triumph has changed the nature of humanity or English society, Pistol reverts to type. His willingness to live by stealing, his unchanging immorality, and his general disrepute emphasize the anti-romantic side of this play. For all his triumphs, Henry V is but one man, and his influence, though that of a king, is finite.

The play can hardly end on such a gloomy note, and thus in the final scene we are taken to the court of France, where all pomp and ceremony are carried out. The general sense of triumph is darkened, though, by Burgundy, who relates the tragic condition of his country after the war. His use of natural imagery is particularly moving:

Her vine, the merry cheerer of the heart,
Unpruned dies; her hedges even-pleach'd,
Like prisoners wildly overgrown with hair,
Put forth disorder'd twigs . . .
And all our vineyards, fallows, meads, and hedges,
Defective in their natures, grow to wildness.
Even so our houses, and ourselves, and children,
Have lost, or do not learn for want of time,
The sciences that should become our country,
But grow like savages—as soldiers will
That nothing do but meditate on blood—
To swearing and stern looks, defus'd attire,
And every thing that seems unnatural.

(V, ii, 41–62)

Throughout the history plays, the health of a nation and its throne have been concretized in imagery of nature. Here Burgundy gives the other side of that picture: the agony of a country's hardships. He also clarifies the inhumanity of war, and the image of Pistol charging off to England, still fresh in our minds, emphasizes that such "unnaturalness" is not limited to the losing side. Henry is strict in his settlement, allowing the French to agree to terms established by the English. He also adds one more stipulation, asking for Katherine, to whom he refers pecularily as "our capital demand" (V, ii, 96).

This request sets up a strange wooing scene, for Henry has a minimum of grace in these matters, and even speaks prose. The actual betrothal, by the way, took place in May 1420, five years after Agincourt. Making the situation even more humorous is that Katherine speaks little English, and thus Henry's awkward protestations go right by her. Nonetheless, the King is an unpretentious and honest suitor, squarely facing his soldierly strengths and deficiencies:

If thou would have such a one, take me! and take
me, take a soldier; take a soldier, take a king.

                                        (V, ii, 165–166)

Even at such a moment Henry plays politics. His strongest selling point is his
own stature, and he uses it for all it is worth.

He also exhibits some of the boyish charm we associate with the younger Hal.
When he asks Kate "Canst thou love me?" (V, ii, 194), she innocently replies,
"I cannot tell" (V, ii, 195), inspiring the comically exasperated "Can any of
your neighbors tell, Kate?" (IV, i, 196).

But national ramifications are never far from view. Earlier Katherine asks "Is
it possible dat I should love de ennemie of France?" (V, ii, 169–170). Henry
assures her that he is now a friend of France, and many of his subsequent remarks
imply the unity not only of two people, but also of two countries:

                        Put off your
maiden blushes, avouch the thoughts of your heart
with the looks of an empress, take me by the hand, and
say, "Harry of England, I am thine"; which word
thou shalt no sooner bless mine ear withal, but I will
tell thee aloud, "England is thine, Ireland is thine,
France is thine, and Henry Plantagenet is thine" . . .

                                        (V, ii, 234–240)

Such comments lead to the speech of reconciliation by the French king (V, ii,
348–355). Before that, however, Henry plays politician once more, demanding
that he be named inheritor of France. He also orders that the guarantee be made
in Latin as well as French, for the former was the more formal language of
Europe (V, ii, 336–342). His last words remind the Lord of Burgundy that all
the French lords shall swear to the appointed terms on the day of the wedding.
Thus this closing scene presents Henry as the awkward, sincere lover, who even
in the throes of what passes for his passion maintains political acuity.

Shakespeare could have ended the play on such a triumphant note. Yet the
Chorus's final words are unhappy ones. The address includes praise of Henry:

Small time; but in that small most greatly lived
This star of England. Fortune made his sword;
By which the world's best garden he achieved,
And of it left his son imperial lord.

                                        (V, Epilogue, 5–9)

The mention of the "garden" recalls that dominant image from *Richard II*. Then
the speech takes a downward turn, as the Chorus outlines events to come: The
loss of territories and the suffering of England.

Therefore the play ends on the same note that has resounded throughout this
tetralogy. Certain individuals have been celebrated, notably Henry V. But what
we have felt all along is the inevitable destruction caused by the overthrow of

Richard II. No matter how egregious Richard's sins or how blatant his incompetence, no matter how sharp Henry IV's political acumen, no matter how startling the transformation of Henry V, and no matter how inspiring his conquests, the overthrow of Richard brought civil disorder down on England. And such disorder, dramatized with less subtlety in the first tetralogy, is what Shakespeare's audience feared. Thus in this play as in all the history plays, there is victory, there is loss, there is warning, and, above all, there is understanding of the nature of political reality and the forces that would take control of those who participate in the struggle for power.

SUGGESTIONS FOR FURTHER READING

Berman, Ronald. *Twentieth Century Interpretations of* Henry V. Englewood Cliffs, N.J.: Prentice-Hall, 1967.

Hobday, C. H. "Imagery and Irony in *Henry V*." *Shakespeare Survey* 21 (1968): 107–114.

Jorgensen, Paul A. "The Courtship Scene in *Henry V*." *Modern Language Quarterly* 11 (1950): 180–188.

———. "Accidental Judgments, Casual Slaughters, and Purposes Mistook: Critical Reactions to Shakespeare's *Henry the Fifth*." *Shakespeare Association Bulletin* 22, no. 2 (1947): 51–61.

Milward, Peter. "The Function of the Chorus in *Henry V*." *Shakespeare Studies* 22 (1983–84): 1–9.

O'Brien, M. A. *A Critical Commentary on Shakespeare's* Henry V. New York: Macmillan, 1967.

Newman, Franklin B. "The Rejection of Falstaff and the Rigorous Charity of the King." *Shakespeare Studies* 2 (1966): 153–161.

Richmond, Hugh. *Shakespeare's Political Plays*. New York: Random House, 1967.

Wentersdorf, Karl P. "The Conspiracy of Silence in *Henry V*." *Shakespeare Quarterly* 27 (1976): 264–287.

HENRY VIII

The final history play of Shakespeare is likely the last work to which he was a contributor. Its authorship remains a subject of dispute, the specific question being whether John Fletcher had a significant hand in its composition. Fletcher, who lived from 1579–1625, collaborated with several playwrights, most notably Francis Beaumont, and their output includes *Philaster* (c.1610) and *The Maid's Tragedy* (c.1611). Our chief concern will be how *Henry VIII* reflects and diverges from themes and techniques that have recurred throughout Shakespeare's other history plays.

One major variation is that this play contains great spectacle, and therefore many critics assume it was written for a special ceremony. In addition, the characters are largely one-dimensional, and we feel little of the intricate or contradictory inner passions that distinguished leading figures from earlier plays. Furthermore, the action is limited to the world of the court, and thus we have no sense of how events on stage influence the populace at large.

The play covers a period of thirteen years: from the meeting with France at the Field of the Cloth of Gold in Flanders in June 1520 (an extravagant celebration that marked a period of relative calm between the two nations) to the christening of the King's daughter Elizabeth in 1533. This time frame is not, however, strictly observed, for the play also dramatizes the death of Katherine, Henry's first wife, who died in 1536, as well as the conspiracy in 1544 against Cranmer, the Archbishop of Canterbury. In addition, other events are presented out of sequence. For instance, Henry's infatuation with Anne Bullen (the last name is usually spelled "Boleyn") actually preceded by a couple of years the arrival of Cardinal Campeius to adjudicate the matter of divorce from Katherine. Finally, the King himself is presented with extraordinary generosity. True, Henry was the first English ruler in more than 100 years to succeed to the throne with an undisputed title. But we do not see or hear that he ravaged the English monasteries, that he married six wives and executed two of them, or that he turned himself from a handsome young sportsman into a grotesquely bloated victim of his own hedonism. Such omissions are understandable, for Henry VIII lived too close to Shakespeare's own age for the playwright to dramatize him without regard for political ramifications.

Instead the play depicts Henry's gradual mastery of the political realities of his court. He is portrayed as fundamentally benign, with the best interests of his country at heart, but through most of the play he is naive and unaware. The thrust of the action thus emerges from the more energetic Cardinal Wolsey, Henry's chief advisor and the court power broker, who wreaks havoc with the lives of rivals. Yet for all his ability to dominate royal politics, Wolsey is a comparatively straightforward figure, driven toward authority and uncomplicated by moral scruples. Not until his very end does he reveal a more subtle dimension. These deficiencies in character development add to the play's diffuseness.

Another unusual but more positive aspect of the play is the role of Katherine. Unlike other women in the history plays, who are either power-mad or helpless, Katherine is intelligent, incisive, and sympathetic to the needs of the people and her husband. She, too, is a victim of Wolsey's machinations, but her suffering is more affecting than that of anyone else.

The Prologue sets the tone for the play, as Shakespeare establishes one motif:

> Such noble scenes as draw the eye to flow,
> We now present.
>
> (Prologue, 4–5)

The play's emphasis is thus on pageant and the nobility of the characters. Another essential point is made:

> Think ye see
> The very persons of our noble story
> As they were living. Think you see them great,
> And follow'd with the general throng and sweat
> Of thousand friends; then, in a moment, see
> How soon this mightiness meets misery . . .
>
> (Prologue, 25–27)

The play is intended to be a realistic portrait of royal life. The Prologue suggests that the nobility themselves are not to blame for their misfortunes, but that these result from the inevitable burdens of royal life, brought on by other forces. Chief among those forces is Wolsey, who, we are regularly reminded, is the son of a butcher, a commoner risen to power.

The conflict between royal pageantry and the ruthless ambition of Wolsey is apparent in the opening scene. To Buckingham, Norfolk praises the spectacular celebration with Henry and the King of France at the Field of the Cloth of Gold (I, i, 14–37, 39–45), but their joy is undercut by knowledge that the occasion was arranged by Wolsey, whom they loathe:

> The devil speed him! no man's pie is freed
> From his ambitious finger. What had he
> To do in these fierce vanities? I wonder

That such a keech can with his very bulk
Take up the rays o' th' beneficial sun,
And keep it from the earth.

(I, i, 51–57)

As the pair exchange venemous comments about the Cardinal's manipulations, Wolsey appears briefly in a very effective moment. He speaks only a few lines (I, i, 114–119), but his entrance silences the others and communicates with great efficacy the nature of political influence. That influence is stressed when Norfolk warns Buckingham against opposing Wolsey:

Be advis'd:
Heat not a furnace for your foe so hot
That it do singe yourself.

(I, i, 139–141)

Political reality has not changed from the first of these plays. Norfolk knows that those who risk confrontation also risk retribution. We think back to the world of Richard III and remember Stanley, who remained seemingly neutral while his son gathered forces in opposition to the King. We also remember Buckingham, the father of the present character, and the advisor who overplayed his hand with Richard. Both father and son misjudge their respective political environments, and both pay the ultimate price.

Punishment follows swiftly, as Buckingham is arrested within moments. The officer claims that the command comes from the King, but Buckingham knows the truth:

My surveyor is false; the o'er-great Cardinal
Hath show'd him gold; my life is spann'd already.
I am the shadow of poor Buckingham,
Whose figure even this instant cloud puts on
By dark'ning my clear sun.

(I, i, 222–226)

The word "sun" retains implications of royalty, and here, as in the other histories, when characters refer to the sun, we see parallels to the king and the kingship. Yet this scene is not as effective as it could be, for we do not know Buckingham well enough to feel his suffering, nor do we know Wolsey well enough to be involved in his treachery.

In scene ii Henry takes the stage "leaning on the Cardinal's shoulder," but he does not fit the compelling image history has created. As the issue of taxation is raised and his wife speaks in opposition (I, ii, 18–29), Henry seems strangely detached: "Taxation? Wherein? and what taxation?" (I, i, 37–38). He turns to Wolsey for advice, and the Cardinal shifts responsibility elsewhere:

I have no further gone in this than by
A single voice, and that not pass'd me but

By learned approbation of the judges.

(I, ii, 69–71)

When Henry pardons those unfairly punished for protesting the tax (I, ii, 98–102) Wolsey orders his confederate to make the King's decree seem to spring from Wolsey's intervention (I, ii, 103–107).

The Cardinal is thus a master manipulator. Clearly he is the villain of the piece, although he is just as clearly no monster like Richard III. He simply fights by every means possible for political dominance. Although he is absorbing, he is also frustrating, for we have little insight into what makes him so relentless. Thus we are kept at a distance, and the play as a whole suffers.

Of Katherine, however, we understand more. She is a voice of conscience, as in this scene, when Henry confesses his affection for Buckingham:

> The gentleman is learn'd, and a most rare speaker,
> To nature none more bound; his training such
> That he may furnish and instruct great teachers
> And never seek for aid out of himself.

(I, ii, 111–114)

At Wolsey's urging a surveyor then reports that Buckingham had expressed an eagerness to be King, as well as a desire to be revenged against Wolsey (I, ii, 132–138). Katherine points out that the informer was once fired by Buckingham (I, ii, 171–176), but Henry is not willing to listen to her. She is thus turned into a noble, if ineffective, figure, a woman of morality forced to compete in the cutthroat world of court politics. She is also set against Wolsey, with Henry VIII in the middle, the object of their competition.

Although he is here passive, Henry is always presented as independent. He may be deceived by Wolsey, but he is not under his advisor's thumb. This distinction is important, for when the truth about Wolsey becomes known, the King takes appropriate action. Furthermore, throughout the play, as when Henry changes the tax policy in this scene, his fundamental sense of justice is evident.

Scene iii is a respite from the political machinations, as three lords of the court discuss various trends and fashions of the French court. The discussion contributes to the general atmosphere of spectacle, and ends with mention of a party to be given by Wolsey. The event is dramatized in scene iv, but from its start the tone is one of forced levity. As Guilford says, speaking for the Cardinal:

> He would have all as merry
> As, first, good company, good wine, good welcome,
> Can make good people.

(I, iv, 5–7)

And when Wolsey enters, he maintains that tense spirit:

> Y' are welcome, my fair guests. That noble lady
> Or gentleman that is not freely merry

Is not my friend.

(I, iv, 35–37)

The celebration is joined by a group of maskers, including the King, all disguised
as shepherds. When the King chooses to dance with Anne Bullen, Wolsey
shrewdly identifies him, and the King is impressed:

You hold a fair assembly; you do well lord,
You are a churchman, or I'll tell you, Cardinal,
I should judge now unhappily.

(I, iv, 87–89)

The remark indicates that the King respects Wolsey, but also recognizes Wolsey's
ambition and cunning.

Another way favorable light is cast on the King is through Buckingham, who
in the first scene of Act II is condemned to death. He accepts this verdict with
equanimity:

The law I bear no malice for my death;
'T has done, upon the premises, but justice;
But those that sought it I could wish more Christians.
Be what they will, I heartily forgive 'em . . .

My vows and prayers
Yet are the King's; and, till my soul forsake,
Shall cry for blessings on him. May he live
Longer than I have time to tell his years;
Ever belov'd and loving may his rule be;
And when old Time shall lead him to his end,
Goodness and he fill up one monument!

(II, i, 62–64, 88–94)

He conveys two crucial ideas. One is faith in the law. He is, he says, the victim
of a single miscarriage of justice, not an evil system. The second is loyalty to
the King. Buckingham thus emphasizes that his adversity is not the result of a
misdirected court or a misguided monarch, but a certain corrupting force, i.e.,
Wolsey. Once that force is removed, Buckingham believes, the country will
right itself.

Buckingham also adds one important piece of political advice:

Where you are liberal of your loves and counsels,
Be sure you be not loose; for those you make friends
And give your hearts to, when they once perceive
The least rub in your fortunes, fall away
Like water from ye, never found again
But where they mean to sink ye.

(II, i, 126–131)

The same lesson his father learned at the hands of Richard III Buckingham now
teaches others. Indeed, this lesson applies to all the history plays. One of the

verities of politics, Buckingham suggests, is that people who are not friends are enemies. And once our friends can no longer rely on us, we are their enemy.

In opposition to such ruthlessness is Katherine, who in the eyes of others stands as a nonpareil. As Norfolk says, speaking of Wolsey's influence:

> And out of all these to restore the King,
> He counsels a divorce, a loss of her
> That, like a jewel, has hung twenty years
> About his neck, yet never lost her lustre;
> Of her that loves him with that excellence
> That angels love good men with; even of her
> That when the greatest stroke of fortune falls
> Will bless the King.
>
> (II, ii, 29–36)

A painful theme of the play is that such virtue is helpless against the unscrupulousness of one like Wolsey, especially when the King himself is ingenuous. What makes Katherine's situation more touching is that Henry does attempt to be decent.

But at present he is still blind to Wolsey's policies, and other nobles are frustrated. In Act II, scene ii the Lord Chamberlain, Norfolk, and Suffolk review their complaints, which are encapsulated in Norfolk's calling Wolsey the "king-cardinal" (II, ii, 19). The three attempt to talk with the King, but he is preoccupied with the matter of his divorce from Katherine. The problem is that divorce is against the precepts of the Catholic Church, to which England is bound. Historically this divorce led to the break between England and Rome, and the subsequent development of the Church of England. Here, however, we concentrate on the political and emotional ramifications of events leading to the divorce. Wolsey brings with him Cardinal Campeius, a representative of the Pope, who intends to help with "the impartial judging of this business" (II, ii, 106). Wolsey assures Henry that "scholars" have been selected to argue for Katherine, and the King gladly accepts this report that she is being treated justly (II, ii, 112–113). Yet Wolsey's tactics are never far from sight. He calls in Gardiner, the King's new secretary, to explain Gardiner's priorities: "You are the King's now" (II, ii, 118). But Gardiner understands where power is currently to be found:

> But to be commanded
> For ever by your Grace, whose hand has rais'd me.
>
> (II, ii, 118–119)

For the moment Wolsey looks invulnerable, even as the King takes Gardiner aside and whispers to him. Then Campeius warns Wolsey of jealousy surrounding him. Wolsey, however, remains truculent: "We live not to be grip'd by meaner persons" (II, ii, 135). He is unwilling to see any threats. The King, meanwhile, struggles to do right:

> O my lord,
> Would it not grieve an able man to leave
> So sweet a bedfellow? But conscience, conscience!
> O, 'tis a tender place, and I must leave her.
>
> (II, ii, 140–143)

These words are not those of an unfeeling man. Rather they are the words of an unimaginative man, whose greatest deficiency is shortsightedness. But in the world of politics, as Shakespeare depicts it, that particular weakness may have devastating consequences. In this play the victim is Katherine.

Also interesting in Shakespeare's portrait of this era is that Katherine's rival, Anne Bullen, is not a villain, either. She is an unaffected girl, who in Act II, scene iii is taken aback by all the attention thrust on her:

> I do not know
> What kind of my obedience I should tender.
> More than my all is nothing: nor my prayers
> Are not words duly hallowed, nor my wishes
> More worth than empty vanities; yet prayers and wishes
> Are all I can return.
>
> (II, iii, 65–70)

But if Anne is harmless, she scarcely approaches the dignity of Katherine, who in Act II, scene iv offers a stirring defense of herself and her life:

> I have been to you a true and humble wife,
> At all times to your will conformable;
> Ever in fear to kindle your dislike,
> Yea, subject to your countenance—glad, or sorry,
> As I saw inclin'd.
>
> (II, iv, 23–27)

She has a sense of history that Henry lacks, as she refers back to his father, Henry VII, and her own father, Ferdinand of Spain, and the international dimensions of their marriage. But in the face of Wolsey, who has chosen her defense lawyers, Katherine is impotent, as she admits to the Cardinal:

> Y' are meek and humble-mouth'd,
> You sign your place and calling, in full seeming,
> With meekness and humility; but your heart
> Is cramm'd with arrogancy, spleen, and pride.
> You have, by fortune and his Highness' favors,
> Gone slightly o'er low steps and now are mounted
> Where pow'rs are your retainers, and your words
> (Domestics to you) serve your will as't please
> Yourself pronounce their office. I must tell you,
> You tender more your person's honor than

Your high profession spiritual . . .

(II, iv, 107–117)

This speech not only reflects the heart of this play but also recalls moments from
the other histories when characters remonstrate against those who abuse power.
However, those outraged speakers are almost always themselves frustrated in
their desire for authority. We think of Constance in *King John*, or Margaret in
any part of *Henry VI*, or Worcester or Northumberland from *Henry IV*. All these
characters protest vociferously against political opponents, but the sentiments
mask jealousy and ambition. Katherine, however, is motivated only by a willingness to serve her King. Furthermore, her insights into Wolsey could be applied
not only to him but to many others in these works for whom power is an end
in itself. Perhaps as much as any other figure in the history plays, Katherine is
a voice of decency and political perception.

   Henry, sadly, is blind to her wisdom, and his reaction is also typical of the
political world:

Go thy ways, Kate.
That man i' th' world who shall report he has
A better wife, let him in nought be trusted
For speaking false in that.

(II, iv, 134–137)

He appreciates her values. Yet, he also attempts to justify his request for divorce
in a lengthy explanation (II, iv, 156–209) that has two main points: one, that
because Katherine is the widow of Henry's brother, her marriage to Henry has
always been illegal; second, that their failure to have a male child is evidence
of divine intervention. Thus he claims he seeks the divorce for the good of his
kingdom:

Then follows, that
I weigh'd the danger which my realms stood in
By this my issue's fail, and that gave to me
Many a groaning throe.

(II, iv, 197–200)

Here is another example of a man whose political life supersedes his personal
life. The dramatic problem in this play, however, is that Henry VIII is not as
energetic a figure as Henry IV or V, or even Richard II.

   Here the Bishop of Lincoln approves of Henry's petition, as does Canterbury.
Henry puts up a final front to the pair:

Prove but our marriage lawful, by my life
And kingly dignity, we are contented
To wear our mortal state to come with her,
Katherine our queen, before the primest creature

That's paragon'd o' th' world.

(II, iv, 227–231)

We know that Henry retains feelings for Katherine, but these lines are hypo-critical, for we know equally well that he wants the divorce. And that he resents having to pretend is clear from his last aside:

> I may perceive
> These Cardinals trifle with me; I abhor
> This dilatory sloth and tricks of Rome.
> My learn'd and well-beloved servant, Cranmer,
> Prithee return; with thy approach, I know,
> My comfort comes along.

(II, iv, 236–241)

The antagonism to Rome establishes Henry's independence of spirit, and places him in better favor historically for the Elizabethan audience. But his inability to act at this point means that we do not feel his anguish as we feel that of other rulers in the history plays. Instead we feel the anguish of Katherine.

Even at this nadir of her life, she never loses her stature:

> There's nothing I have done yet, o' my conscience,
> Deserves a corner. Would all other women
> Could speak this with as free a soul as I do!

(III, i, 30–32)

Nor does she allow herself to maintain illusions about her enemies, Wolsey and Campeius, who have come ostensibly to give solace:

> The more shame for ye! Holy men I thought ye,
> Upon my soul, two reverend cardinal virtues;
> But cardinal sins and hollow hearts I fear ye.

(III, i, 102–104)

As the two continue their outpouring of false sympathy, she resists any plans they might conceive: "Nothing but death/ Shall e'er divorce my dignities" (III, i, 141–142). Yet, like Buckingham, Katherine does not lose faith in Henry:

> Pray do my service to his Majesty;
> He has my heart yet and shall have my prayers
> While I shall have my life.

(III, i, 179–181)

Again, we think back to the other history plays. The Queen does not call for chaos or destruction, as does York in *Henry VI, Part 2* (III, i), and Northum-berland in *Henry IV, Part 2* (I, i). She believes in the ultimate authority of the king and his place on the throne.

From here the play shifts to what ought to be the climactic scene: the downfall of Wolsey. Yet the moment is unsatisfying. First we learn that Wolsey's deceit has been discovered:

> The King hath found
> Matter against him that for ever mars
> The honey of his language.

> (III, ii, 20–22)

That we are simply told this vital information is weak. The scene is strengthened, however, as details are revealed, and suspense builds. Suffolk adds that Wolsey attempted to communicate privately with the Pope to prevent the marriage of Henry and Anne (III, ii, 30–36), but that the King has already married her. Moreover, Campieus has returned to Rome, leaving the entire situation unsettled (III, ii, 56–58). Perhaps most important, Cranmer and all the King's other religious advisors support Henry's decision (III, ii, 63–66). Hence Wolsey is utterly isolated, although he is unaware of his predicament.

Therefore the moment is ripe with dramatic irony when the Cardinal enters with Norfolk. In asides, Wolsey schemes to have Henry marry a Frenchwoman, the Duchess of Alanson (III, ii, 85), and to eliminate Cranmer, whom he describes as "An heretic, an arch-one . . . " (III, ii, 102). The intensity increases when the King enters, shocked over the profits he at last realizes Wolsey has accumulated (III, ii, 107–110). And he confirms Suffolk's earlier news about the newly discovered packet of papers.

Irony builds more as the King flatters Wolsey, who unknowingly continues to feign devotion:

> My sovereign, I confess your royal graces
> Show'r'd on me daily have been more than could
> My studied purposes requite, which went
> Beyond all man's endeavors.

> (III, ii, 166–169)

With new-found acuity, the King invites Wolsey to condemn himself, challenging the Cardinal's loyalty:

> I presume
> That, as my hand has open'd bounty to you,
> My heart dropp'd love, my pow'r rain'd honor, more
> On you than any, so your hand and heart,
> Your brain, and every function of your power,
> Should, notwithstanding that your bond of duty,
> As 'twere in love's particular, be more
> To me, your friend, than any.

> (III, ii, 183–189)

We feel his barely disguised rage. And Wolsey's sanctimonious reply increases the tension until Henry tosses him the packet of telltale papers. Wolsey then realizes the truth, and that he is undone.

Historically this incident seems to have been based on the fall of a bishop of Durham, who was ruined by Wolsey on evidence of a similarly misplaced missive. Wolsey himself was eventually accused by Henry on the basis of charges relating to Papal interference in English affairs.

In the play Wolsey's downfall does not stir us for it comes not from weakness of his own nor even from a conspiracy of his enemies, but rather from circumstances. The problem is compounded when Wolsey begins to reveal himself:

> I have touch'd the highest point of all my greatness,
> And, from that full meridian of my glory,
> I haste now to my setting. I shall fall
> Like a bright exhalation in the evening,
> And no man see me more.
>
> (III, ii, 223–227)

Wolsey's ego is suddenly in full view, as his imagery suggests the path of the sun, a symbol more often associated with the King. But Wolsey has virtually usurped Henry's power, so perhaps the image does fit. Still, this moment is the first where we feel the Cardinal's inner self, which rages on as he assaults his former subordinates for their jealousy:

> How eagerly ye follow my disgraces
> As if it fed ye, and how sleek and wanton
> Ye appear in every thing may bring my ruin!
> Follow your envious courses, men of malice!
>
> (III, ii, 240–243)

Here is manifestation of a misanthropy that partially explains his all-encompassing ambition. But it has come too late to make him more engrossing.

Wolsey's denials receive extensive rebuffing. Surrey recounts several whom the Cardinal has betrayed, including Buckingham, Surrey's father-in-law (III, ii, 254–264). Wolsey denies all these accusations. But Surrey is indefatigable, and with aid from Norfolk embarks on a recital of Wolsey's illegalities and selfish acts against the Crown. So harsh is Surrey's attack that the Lord Chamberlain cries out:

> Press not a falling man too far! 'tis virtue.
> His faults lie open to the laws, let them,
> Not you, correct him. My heart weeps to see him
> So little of his great self.
>
> (III, ii, 333–336)

Whether this outcry is intended by the playwright to give Wolsey a measure of tragic stature is unclear, as is the question of whether Wolsey is as beaten down as the Lord Chamberlain implies. At any rate, Surrey relents, and all that remains is for Suffolk to pronounce the sentence that Wolsey must surrender all his lands and possessions, as well as the protection of the King. All four nobles then leave, with Norfolk tossing the final note of humiliation: "So fare you well, my little good Lord Cardinal" (III, ii, 349).

When Wolsey is left alone, his personality shifts again, and he is more self-aware and vulnerable:

> My high-blown pride
> At length broke under me, and now has left me,
> Weary and old with service, to the mercy
> Of a rude stream that must for ever hide me.
> Vain pomp and glory of this world, I hate ye!
>
> (III, ii, 361–365)

This epiphany leads immediately to yet another new emotion:

> I feel my heart new open'd. O how wretched
> Is that poor man that hangs on princes' favors!
>
> (III, ii, 366–367)

The theme is not uninteresting, but the transition from conspirator to confessor is too quick to be persuasive. Were some of these doubts apparent earlier, were we able to see Wolsey as anything but an indefatigable plotter, this outburst would be more cogent.

It leads to a more public statement, as Wolsey claims a new inner peace:

> Never so truly happy, my good Cromwell;
> I know myself now, and I feel within me
> A peace above all earthly dignities,
> A still and quiet conscience.
>
> (III, ii, 377–380)

Had we earlier inkling of inner conflict, this revelation would carry greater weight. So would his final proclamation:

> Cromwell, I charge thee, fling away ambition!
> By that sin fell the angels; how can man then
> (The image of his Maker) hope to win by it? . . .
> Had I but serv'd my God with half the zeal
> I serv'd my king, He would not in mine age
> Have left me naked to mine enemies.
>
> (II, ii, 440–457)

Here theme overtakes character. These values are ones the play seems intended to communicate, and Wolsey is the proper vehicle to expound them. But even though we have now had time to feel Wolsey's transformation, the scene is not completely successful.

In Act IV, scene i we see that public affection for Katherine is transferred to Anne, as the pageantry so much a part of this play takes center stage. Even amidst this celebration, however, dissension arises, as the second Gentleman indicates:

> He of Winchester
> Is held no great good lover of the Archbishop's,

The virtuous Cranmer.

(IV, i, 103–105)

Such factionalism seems to be an inevitability in court life, and by implication all of political life. We have seen that for decades the legitimacy of the occupant of the English throne was in question, and that the fight for power centered on who would be king. Now, for the first time in over a century, the place of the king is unquestioned. But power is still to be had. Thus the battle shifts to who will be closest to the king, who is to be his chief advisor. For a time Wolsey had that position, and all were opposed to him. Now Cranmer takes over, and everyone turns on him. The conflict is unabated.

In Act IV, scene ii we hear of the death of Wolsey, who repented on his deathbed (IV, ii, 27–30). Katherine is curiously sympathetic to the man who brought her to ruin: "So may he rest, his faults lie gently on him" (IV, ii, 31). Griffith adds a reflection of his own:

> Men's evil manners live in brass, their virtues
> We write in water.

(IV, ii, 45–46)

His words are reminiscent of Antony's oration over the body of Julius Caesar:

> The evil that men do lives after them,
> The good is oft interred with their bones.

(*Julius Caesar*, III, ii, 75–76)

Griffith also offers a different perspective on the young Wolsey:

> From his cradle
> He was a scholar, and a ripe and good one;
> Exceeding wise, fair-spoken, and persuading;
> Lofty and sour to them that lov'd him not,
> But to those men that sought him, sweet as summer.

(IV, ii, 50–54)

If this evaluation is to be believed, Wolsey is another one of Shakespeare's figures whose better qualities are destroyed in the irresistible struggle for power.

Katherine's vision and her directions for her funeral contribute to her stature. She may be seen as like Juliet, who also dies nobly and poetically. Yet, again like Juliet, Katherine never reaches tragic stature because of her essential passivity.

We also should note the organization of the scene. Wolsey and Katherine die together, not geographically, but at the same time within the structure of the play. One is the perpetrator, one the victim. They are the two major influences on Henry VIII, and in a sense the rest of the play is evidence of their contributions to his life.

At the beginning of Act V we learn that the new queen, Anne, is in labor, and that her own life is at risk (V, i, 18–20). Yet this vital matter is put aside, as political squabbling comes to the fore in Gardiner's fulminations against Cranmer:

> Sir (I may tell it you), I think I have
> Incens'd the lords o' th' Council that he is
> (For so I know he is, they know he is)
> A most arch-heretic, a pestilence
> That does infect the land . . .
>
> (V, i, 42–46)

The qualifying parentheses that dominate Gardiner's dialogue suggest duplicity. But when the King enters, his new manner reveals that no matter how Gardiner and the others conspire the King will control them. At this moment he stands with his ally, unswayed by specious arguments as he was with Wolsey. Instead he draws the battle lines for Cranmer:

> Know you not
> How your state stands i' th' world, with the whole world?
> Your enemies are many, and not small . . . At what ease
> Might corrupt minds procure knaves as corrupt
> To swear against you? Such things have been done.
>
> (V, i, 126–133)

The King has come a long way from the man who in Act I could not grasp problems about taxation. We also note that he gives his ring to Cranmer (V, i, 150–151). Thus the King is both suspicious of those who plot against him and loyal to those who support him. Such conduct suggests that the lives of Wolsey and Katherine have not been in vain, that Henry is now prepared to lead the country.

The scene concludes with word from an Old Lady that Anne has given birth to a girl, and that this birth "Promises boys hereafter" (V, i, 166). The logic is peculiar, but the political ramifications clear. This girl is to become the future Queen Elizabeth, and in no way can her birth be denigrated.

The King's awareness is further manifested in Act V, scene ii, as Cranmer is accused, and Henry stands listening above, unseen. Gardiner is again the most vicious attacker, and, like Wolsey before him, claims the King's authority for his actions:

> 'Tis his Highness' pleasure
> And our consent, for better trial of you,
> From hence you be committed to the Tower,
> Where being but a private man again,
> You shall know many dare accuse you boldly,
> More than (I fear) you are provided for.
>
> (V, ii, 87–92)

As always, Gardiner's appositives cast doubt on his veracity. The case suddenly weakens, however, when Cranmer indicates the ring Henry gave him. Suffolk sees the truth at once:

'Tis the right ring, by heavn'n! I told ye all,
When we first put this dangerous tone a-rolling,
'Twould fall upon ourselves.

                                                    (V, ii, 138–140)

Once again a plotter is tripped up. Now the King has heard enough and steps
in grandly to announce his verdict:

You were ever good at sudden commendations,
Bishop of Winchester. But know I come not
To hear such flattery now, and in my presence
They are too thin and base to hide offenses.
To me you cannot reach you play the spaniel,
And think with wagging of your tongue to win me;
But whatso'er thou tak'st me for, I'm sure
Thou hast a nature cruel and a bloody.

                                                    (V, ii, 157–164)

Rather than invoke punishment, though, Henry seeks alliances between the
opponents: "Be friends, for shame, my lords!" (V, ii, 194). Even Gardiner is
softened: "With a true heart/ and brother-love I do it." (V, ii, 205–206). An
aura of forgiveness and unity hangs over the moment, thanks to the King's
wisdom and compassion.

The last part of Act V is essentially a celebration. From the porters in scene
iii to Cranmer is scene iv, all offer tribute to the baby, Elizabeth:

She shall be lov'd and fear'd: her own shall bless her;
Her foes shake like a field of beaten corn,
And hang their heads with sorrow.

                                                    (V, iv, 30–32)

The play thereby ends on an uplifting note.

That historically the King was infuriated to learn he had fathered a daughter
is ignored. So, as indicated before, are most of the Henry's long list of flaws.
But in evaluating the King's character we must keep in mind that the playwright
was dealing with extraordinarily sensitive material, and could not afford to say
anything truly unattractive about the father of the recent Queen. Nonetheless,
its deficiencies aside, the play stands as tribute to two people: Henry, portrayed
as everything a King should eventually become, and Elizabeth, who will carry
on the tradition of royal excellence.

Even though it was written nearly a decade after the rest of the history plays,
Henry VIII nonetheless reminds us of issues that have dominated this series of
works. We have seen the responsibilities of a monarch, how these weigh heavily
on all who sit on the throne, and how they break certain individuals. We have
seen how the nature of power attracts, alters, and destroys those who compete
for it. And we have seen how that struggle destroys innocent victims as well.

What may touch us most deeply, however, is the timelessness of these conflicts. Specific issues, such as primogeniture and succession, are long gone.

Nevertheless, the political struggles and their consequences, the triumphs and defeats of individuals, parties, and nations, are endemic to the human predicament, and nowhere is this aspect of our existence dramatized more tellingly than in the history plays of Shakespeare.

SUGGESTIONS FOR FURTHER READING

Berman, Ronald, "*King Henry the Eighth*: History and Romance." *English Studies* 48 (1967): 112–121.

Berry, Edward I. "*Henry VIII* and the Dynamics of Spectacle." *Shakespeare Studies* 12 (1979).

Bliss, Lee. "The Wheel of Fortune and the Maiden Phoenix of Shakespeare's *King Henry the Eighth*." *ELH* 42 (1975): 1–25.

Clark, Cumberland. *A Study of Shakespeare's* Henry VIII. New York: Golden Vista Press, 1931.

Knight, G. Wilson. "Henry VIII and the Poetry of Conversion." *The Crown of Life: Essays in Interpretation of Shakespeare's Final Plays*. London: Methuen, 1948.

Mincoff, Marco. "*Henry VIII* and Fletcher." *Shakespeare Quarterly* 12 (1961): 230–260.

Waage, Frederick O., Jr. "*Henry VIII* and the Crisis of the English History Play." *Shakespeare Quarterly* 24 (1972): 459–462.

THE COMEDIES

Shakespeare's comedies dramatize a remarkable variety of moods and characters. The tones range from the farcical to the gentle to the satirical, and the casts encompass royals, buffoons, and legions in between. Furthermore, all the plays have multiple plot lines in which events at one stratum of society reflect events at another. The works also have one unifying theme: love in all its myriad facets. In every play we watch men and women struggle with their own drives and emotions: sometimes trying to resist, sometimes trying to gain control, sometimes trying to understand. We see love in its purest, most spiritual form. And we hear about love in its lustiest, most physical aspects. Virtually all the plays conclude with marriages that not only maintain the social and political order, but that also exalt human passion.

The comedies are usually classified in three groups. The "early" plays, including the first five discussed here, are those in which Shakespeare is often judged to be exploring technique and character. These works are laden with elements of farce, i.e., humor based primarily on physical action and intricacies of plot. Some of the characters are subtle emotionally and intellectually, but by and large the depictions lack sophistication.

In the next five plays, the "mature" comedies, the characters are more complicated. Their attitudes, actions, and values are less obvious and the ramifications more profound. In addition, these plays are set against a social system that often invades the story, and the efforts of the characters to achieve happiness are often hindered by environmental conditions. Thus these works have greater intensity, and at times we feel a satiric attitude on the part of the playwright.

The final three comedies are the "problem" plays, written later in Shakespeare's career, and sometimes referred to as the "dark comedies" or "tragicomedies." They are classified together not by what they have in common but by the fact that each one differs in its own way from the other twelve comedies. These three plays are at moments funny, but their essential crises are grim, and the laughter is often cut off by painful turns of plot. The satire is powerful, and the targets are individual characters as well as societies at large. Two of these plays have endings that are in accord with conventional comic structure. Yet the vision of human nature that emerges from all three works is fundamentally gloomy.

The focus of the following essays is on the characters and how their individual psychological unity is manifested in language and behavior. Two themes dominate. One, the women in these plays are at the center of the action. Given the social constrictions of Shakespeare's age, a young woman at that time had to make her chief concerns romance and marriage. Therefore we should not be surprised that the female characters here are portrayed as having an understanding and maturity about matters of love that far exceed those of their male counterparts. Moreover, the men in the comedies are generally callous or unthinking, and leave these intelligent, loving women frustrated at the lack of appreciation. Indeed, so admirable are many of the women that few seem to end up with men of comparable worth.

One other motif dominates the discussions that follow, and it demands a brief preliminary analysis. In all successful comedy, characters regard themselves seriously. Whether we are observing a dramatic or real-life dilemma, a good portion of our laughter comes from individuals battling to maintain dignity amid circumstances that conspire to steal that dignity. What distinguishes specific comedies is the perspective from which these endeavors are presented.

For instance, in works of pure farce, such as plays of Plautus or films of the Marx Brothers, the audience is never allowed to take the characters' pain seriously. Whether the suffering is physical or emotional, we keep our distance. We do not wonder about characters' hopes and dreams, nor do we ponder motivation. In fact, if a work that begins as farce suddenly shifts tone and demands that we offer compassion, we usually feel instead betrayal on the part of the dramatist. The rules of the game have been altered, and we are uncomfortable.

In higher comedy, however, laughter is accompanied by sensibility. No matter how foolish the characters appear or how misguided their behavior, their situations have potentially grave overtones. We often realize that were the playwright so inclined, the crisis could just as easily be resolved unhappily. The protagonist may be opposed by other characters, the society outside, forces of nature, or the protagonist's own personality, but whatever the stakes, the predicament touches us, and we care how it is decided. Such caring is endemic to Shakespeare's comedies. Even in his earliest works, we sense beneath the laughter a sympathy for human aspiration and emotion. This balance between comic perspective and tragic awareness is the cornerstone of Shakespearean comedy.

SUGGESTIONS FOR FURTHER READING

Barber, C. L. *Shakespeare's Festive Comedy*. Princeton: Princeton University Press, 1959.

Berry, Ralph. *Shakespeare's Comedies*. Princeton: Princeton University Press, 1972.

Bradbrook, M. C. *The Growth and Structure of Elizabethan Comedy*. London: Chatto & Windus, 1961.

Brown, John Russell. *Shakespeare and His Comedies*. London: Methuen, 1957.

Charlton, H. B. *Shakespearean Comedy*. New York: Macmillan, 1938.

Evans, Bertrand. *Shakespeare's Comedies*. Oxford: Clarendon Press, 1960.

Frye, Northrop. *The Myth of Deliverance: Reflections on Shakespeare's Problem Comedies*. Toronto: University of Toronto Press, 1983.

Knight, G. Wilson. *The Sovereign Flower*. London: Methuen, 1958.

Lerner, Laurence, ed. *Shakespeare's Comedies: An Anthology of Modern Criticism*. Harmondsworth, England: Penguin Books, 1967.

Muir, Kenneth, ed. *Shakespeare: The Comedies*. Englewood Cliffs, N.J.: Prentice-Hall, 1965.

———. *Shakespeare's Comic Sequence*. Liverpool: Liverpool University Press, 1979.

Newman, Karen. *Shakespeare's Rhetoric of Comic Character*. New York and London: Methuen, 1985.

Palmer, David John, ed. *Shakespeare's Later Comedies: An Anthology of Modern Criticism*. Harmondsworth, England: Penguin Books, 1971.

Parrott, Thomas Marc. *Shakespearean Comedy*. New York: Oxford University Press, 1949.

Phialas, Peter G. *Shakespeare's Romantic Comedies: The Development of Their Form and Meaning*. Chapel Hill: University of North Carolina Press, 1966.

Salingar, Leo. *Shakespeare and the Traditions of Comedy*. London: Cambridge University Press, 1974.

Swinden, Patrick. *An Introduction to Shakespeare's Comedies*. London: Methuen, 1957.

Tillyard, E.M.W. *Shakespeare's Problem Plays*. Toronto: University of Toronto Press, 1950.

Traversi, Derek. *Shakespeare: The Early Comedies*. London: Longmans, Green, 1960.

Wilson, J. Dover. *Shakespeare's Happy Comedies*. London: Faber, 1962.

THE COMEDY OF ERRORS

So dexterously manipulated is the plot of what is likely Shakespeare's first comedy and so brisk its pace that we are liable to dismiss the work as frivolous and unfeeling. Such an attitude is unfair. *The Comedy of Errors* is an ingratiating play, hardly flawless, but one that reveals a budding genius exploring themes and developing techniques that emerge triumphantly in later masterpieces.

The basic story comes from *The Menaechmi* of the Roman playwright Plautus, whose creative life extended from roughly 205 to 184 B.C. Shakespeare's play involves Plautus's twin masters, who undergo confusions compounded by the presence of identical twin servants, a twist taken from another of Plautus's works, *Amphitryon*. *The Comedy of Errors* stays loyal to its classical antecedent by maintaining unities of time and place, but in more important ways moves beyond the sheer farce that marks Roman comedy.

First, the added characters of Egeon, Luciana, and the Abbess contribute to a tension created by the mixture of both comic and dramatic episodes. In addition, the play has moments of intense romanticism as well as suspense that verges on the melodramatic. And the ending is a catharsis of sorts, wherein all conflicts resolve amidst universal joy.

Several other elements here return in subsequent comedies of Shakespeare. The mainspring of the plot is a shipwreck, after which a family is broken apart, then reunited. The language is suffused with references to dreaming and sorcery. The surrounding community is preoccupied with money, a devotion that invades private lives. Several characters suffer dilemmas in which they are left stranded, uncertain of their identity. Other characters undergo a metamorphosis, as the trials they endure lead to permanent changes of personality and values.

One distinction that separates this play from others to follow is that no single character schemes to set off the plot, and consequently no character can explain everything we see. All participants are confused. Thus we do not find ourselves rooting for a hero and against a villain. In fact, the play has no truly dark figure, and therefore risks keeping us detached observers: amused, but not emotionally committed to the outcome. However, the passion of several characters as well as the labyrinth of perplexities ensures that we remain anxious about the resolution.

The opening two lines by Egeon are melancholy for a comedy:

> Proceed, Solinus, to procure my fall,
> And by the doom of death end woes and all.
>
> (I, i, 1–2)

Egeon remains gloomy throughout, and his presence undercuts the rollicking proceedings. The Duke's response is equally serious, recalling the enmity between the two cities, Syracuse and the present setting, Ephesus. Such discord anticipates the ensuing disorder. We note also the gravity of the Duke's pronouncement, which ends with threat of death against Egeon for illegally visiting Ephesus without a thousand marks ransom (I, i, 21–25). In his reply Egeon is characteristically somber:

> Yet this my comfort, when your words are done,
> My woes end likewise with the evening sun.
>
> (I, i, 26–27)

He seems almost suicidal.

Egeon's narrative is lengthy and dramatically awkward, and Shakespeare even interrupts it (I, i, 96–97, 121–123) to keep us alert. But it has serious implications. Long ago Egeon's wife in Syracuse gave birth to twins, as did one of Egeon's serving women. On a voyage to Epidamium, a storm left the family alone on the ship, which itself split apart. This "unjust divorce" (I, i, 104) left Egeon with one son and servant, and his wife with the other two boys. When Egeon's surviving son turned eighteen, he set out in search of his brother, while Egeon assumed his own quest for his missing son.

All this information unfolds slowly, but given the conventions of the comic genre, we soon anticipate a family reunion. On the other hand, the details are muted by the general tone of melancholy, as when Egeon again expresses his willingness to accept death (I, i, 69). His most important motif is the loss of love (I, i, 131), a theme that recurs regularly in the play. The result of this solemn exposition is that whatever humorous muddles unfold before us, we remain conscious of Egeon's sorrow and how his need for love is paralleled by that same void in others.

Although the Duke is moved by Egeon's story (I, i, 142–145), the decree for punishment stays in effect:

> Beg thou, or borrow, to make up the sum,
> And live: if no, then thou art doom'd to die.
>
> (I, i, 153–154)

In this environment feelings are less important than finances, a condition that pervades the world of Shakespeare's comedies.

Antipholus of Syracuse enters in scene ii, and instructs his servant, Dromio, to take the money given by the merchant and return it to the Centaur, the inn

where they are lodging. When Antipholus is left alone, his comments clarify
that the strain of sadness has passed from father to son:

> A trusty villain, sir, that very oft,
> When I am dull with care and melancholy,
> Lightens my humor with his merry jests.

(I, ii, 19–21)

Antipholus also reveals that he will wander the city: "I will go lose myself..."
(I, ii, 30). And when left alone, he reasserts his isolation:

> I to the world am like a drop of water,
> That in the ocean seeks another drop,
> Who, falling there to find his fellow forth
> (Unseen, inquisitive), confounds himself.
> So I, to find a mother and a brother,
> In quest of them (unhappy), ah, lose myself.

(I, ii, 35–40)

He believes that he is to find himself only through love, and at this moment
assumes its source to be a member of his family. Later he "discovers" himself
through romantic love, a manner of self-fulfillment experienced by many characters in comedies to follow. Indeed, one of the pervasive themes of these plays
is that an individual can be complete only when willing to give of him or herself
to another.

 With the entrance of Dromio of Ephesus, plot confusions begin to flow, for
this Dromio assumes he is talking to his own master, whose wife awaits him
for dinner. Meanwhile Antipholus is appropriately bewildered by the strange
turns of conversation with a man he takes to be his servant (I, i, 68–70, 77–
81). After driving away Dromio with blows, Antipholus expresses telling concerns:

> Upon my life, by some device or other
> The villain is o'erraught of all my money.
> They say this town is full of cozenage:
> As nimble jugglers that deceive the eye,
> Dark-working sorcerers that change the mind,
> Soul-killing witches that deform the body,
> Disguised cheaters, prating mountebanks,
> And many such-like liberties of sin:
> If it prove so, I will be gone the sooner.
> I'll to the Centaur to go seek this slave;
> I greatly fear my money is not safe.

(I, ii, 95–105)

He is preoccupied with money, an appropriate reaction in the world of this play.
He also speculates on the presence of supernatural beings that may be infiltrating
the society. Such imagery develops atmosphere, but here does little more, for

no outside agents influence the plot. In later comedies, magical elements are built into the text and therefore contribute more significantly.

Furthermore, the confusions that dominate this work are arbitrary. They do arise not out of personality or quirks of behavior, but from outlandish coincidence. Thus we do not feel a link between character and destiny. Such artificiality could diminish audience involvement, but because characters are developed sufficiently, we empathize with those caught in this maze of uncertainty.

In Act II, scene i, we meet the two principal women who are drawn more subtly than their male counterparts. Adriana, wife of Antipholus of Ephesus, whom we have yet to meet, is nervous about her missing husband, but her sister, Luciana, dismisses this worry:

> Good sister, let us dine, and never fret;
> A man is master of his liberty:
> Time is their master, and when they see time,
> They'll go or come; if so, be patient, sister.
>
> (II, i, 6–9)

An unmarried woman, Luciana has no emotional stake in male behavior. Adriana, however, retorts that such weakness is the very reason Luciana has been unable to find a husband (II, i, 26). Men, Adriana implies, seek a partner of substance, not submission. Perhaps the speech is an attempt by Adriana to reassure herself of her own attractiveness. At the same time, she is tormented by the powerlessness of a married woman's position (II, ii, 34–41). Such humorless griping in combination with her harping on her own desperation communicates why Antipholus would want to stay away as long as possible.

Still, her character is not one-dimensional. After Dromio enters to complain about the incomprehensible beating by his master, Adriana confesses her plight:

> His company must do his minions grace,
> Whilst I at home starve for a merry look:
> Hath homely age th' alluring beauty took
> From my poor cheek? Then he hath wasted it.
> Are my discourses dull? Barren my wit?
> If voluble and sharp discourse be marr'd,
> Unkindness blunts it more than marble hard.
>
> (II, i, 88–93)

She communicates with a variety of emotions. She is possessive, but also wants to be loved. She is afraid that her husband is losing interest in her, but also knows that she has much to offer. She does not seek to rule Antipholus, but needs to be loved by him. She is bitter at his ill treatment but eager for his pleasure with her to be revived.

Adriana is the first of many women in Shakespeare's comedies who feel such anguish in love. And Adriana's drastic solution to her dilemma is echoed in plays to follow:

> Since that my beauty cannot please his eye,
> I'll weep what's left away, and weeping die.

> (II, i, 114–115)

Luciana's closing line, "How many fond fools serve mad jealousy" (II, i, 116), partially satirizes Adriana's outcry. Yet her desperation is moving, and eventually we sympathize with her as we do with no other character in the play.

In Act II, scene ii, Antipholus meets his own Dromio and, thinking him the rude servant of the previous scene, beats him. Antipholus also emphasizes propriety: " . . . learn to jest in good time . . . " (II, ii, 64). Often in Shakespeare's plays the concept of time stands for order, and here the warning about an inappropriate occasion reminds us of the chaos slowly spreading. It extends further with the entrance of the searching Adriana, who comes across her husband's twin and speaks to him with an anger tempered by love. That she is attempting to win back the wrong man keeps the scene light, but her depth of feeling is apparent:

> How comes it now, my husband, O, how comes it,
> That thou art then estranged from thyself?
> Thyself I call it, being strange to me,
> That, undividable incorporate,
> Am better than thy dear self's better part.

> (II, ii, 119–123)

She has unintentionally hit upon a part of Antipholus that he earlier noted about himself: his longing for identity and love. Two lines later she uses the image of the drop of water that Antipholus invoked (I, ii, 36). The irony of her addressing the wrong man, yet pinpointing his vulnerabilities, gives her address a measure of pathos.

Emotions become more intense as she pleads with Antipholus not to break away from her:

> My blood is mingled with the crime of lust:
> For if we two be one, and thou play false,
> I do digest the poison of thy flesh,
> Being strumpeted by thy contagion.

> (II, ii, 141–144)

Marriage is the foundation of her life, and betrayal by her husband will cause her great pain. Few males in any play of Shakespeare's speak so ardently about fidelity.

At this moment, though, Adriana's fervor is mocked and the comic mood sustained by Antipholus's innocent response: "Plead you to me, fair dame?" (II, ii, 147). And after she claims that she sent Dromio (her servant) to fetch him, Antipholus wonders just whom he can trust (II, ii, 163–164). But when she continues her assault, Antipholus, who in fact seeks the affection she offers, complies with her request to come home with her:

> To me she speaks, she moves me for her theme;
> What, was I married to her in my dream?
> Or sleep I now and think I hear all this?
>
> (II, ii, 181–183)

A few lines later, Dromio remarks, "This is the fairy land" (II, ii, 189), then adds "I am transformed" (II, ii, 195). The references to dreams, fairies, and transformation anticipate *A Midsummer Night's Dream*, another comedy about confused lovers. In *The Comedy of Errors*, however, such images are mentioned only in passing, while in the later play Shakespeare creates, through language, action, and character, an entire world of dreams. Here the town of Ephesus, despite the occasional allusion, remains realistic and colorless, and the lovers, despite occasional bursts of poetry, rarely exceed the prosaic.

Nevertheless, Antipholus' comment as he leaves with Adriana is thematically important:

> Am I in earth, in heaven, or in hell?
> Sleeping or waking, mad or well-advis'd?
>
> (II, ii, 212–213)

His delight in his befuddlement and his willingness to surrender to this predicament he knows to be absurd suggest the power of infatuation. We also note that Adriana orders Dromio to refuse anyone entrance to the house (II, ii, 209–211), a command that leads to the confusion of the next scene.

In Act III we at last meet Antipholus of Ephesus, a man more self-possessed than his twin, and a jauntier, less thoughtful, one as well. He is mildly concerned that when he is late his wife will become "shrewish" (III, i, 2), but his feelings extend no further. Thus when he and his Dromio are refused admittance to Antipholus's own house, his first reaction is immature: to break down the door (III, i, 59). In response Bathazar pays tribute to Adriana:

> Once this—your long experience of [her] wisdom,
> Her sober virtue, years, and modesty,
> Plead on [her] part some cause to you unknown;
> And doubt not, sir, but she will well excuse
> Why at this time the doors are made against you.
>
> (III, i, 89–93)

This warning reveals another side of Adriana's character. She may be, as her husband suggests, "shrewish," but she is also virtuous and trustworthy. This consideration calms Antipholus, but he nonetheless retreats to a female companion, "a wench of excellent discourse . . ." (III, i, 109), about whom his wife is already suspicious (III, i, 111–114). He appears to be acting out of vengeance, and if earlier we regarded Adriana as excessively jealous, we now understand that her husband's insensitivity contributes to her suspicion and tenaciousness as well as her hatred of infidelity.

Such balance between the silliness of the situation and our sympathy for some of the characters continues in Act III, scene ii, as Luciana tries to persuade the wrong Antipholus to treat Adriana more kindly:

> Alas, poor women, make us [but] believe
> (Being compact of credit) that you love us;
> Though others have the arm, show us the sleeve:
> We in your motion turn, and you may move us.

> (III, ii, 21–24)

She claims that even a hypocritical love is better than none at all. Whether Luciana means these sentiments to reflect the feelings of all women, those of her sister, or those of herself is not clear. In any case, her ability to utter such powerful sentiments shows her own need and capacity for love. But the result of her petition is a surprise, as Antipholus disclaims all affection for Adriana, and instead offers himself to Luciana:

> Are you a god? Would you create me new?
> Transform me then, and to your pow'r I'll yield.

> (III, ii, 39–40)

Gradually he grows more lyrical, in lines that are among the most stirring of the play:

> O, train me not, sweet mermaid, with thy note,
> To drown me in thy [sister's] flood of tears.
> Sing, siren, for thyself, and I will dote;
> Spread o'er the silver waves thy golden hairs,
> And as a [bed] I'll take [them], and there lie,
> And in that glorious supposition think
> He gains by death that hath such means to die:
> Let love, being light, be drowned if she sink!

> (III, ii, 45–52)

That Luciana's name means "light" adds to the wit of the moment, as do the sexual overtones of "lie" and "die." But we also realize that Antipholus is smitten, and that he sees in Luciana, who has exposed her own vulnerability, the identity he has sought:

> It is thyself, mine own self's better part:
> Mine eye's clear eye, my dear heart's dearer heart,
> My food, my fortune, and my sweet hope's aim,
> My sole earth's heaven, and my heaven's claim.

> (III, ii, 61–64)

The extravagance of his language is amusing, but his idealized passion is legitimate.

The entrance of Dromio changes the tone, as the servant describes in bawdy terms the body of the aggressive Luce. Such lustiness is endemic to Shakespeare's comic sense and part of all his comedies. Within this scene, however, are also further references to witches and magic (III, ii, 140 ff.), and so unnerved are the two men that they resolve to leave this strange community. Their confusion is exacerbated by Angelo's delivery of the gold chain, meant for the other Antipholus as a present to his wife (III, ii, 172–175). The inability of this Antipholus and his Dromio to comprehend the behavior of those around them suggests a theme prevalent in many comedies of Shakespeare: the conflict between appearance and reality. Here this motif is barely suggested, but in subsequent works it is crucial.

In Act IV matters become scrambled almost beyond explanation. Angelo creates a greater sense of urgency with his promise that he will repay his merchant friend when Angelo receives his own money for the chain (IV, i, 10–13). Meanwhile Antipholus of Epheseus orders his servant to buy a rope to punish Adriana for locking him out, but the threat seems idle (IV, i, 15–20). Whatever his less attractive aspects, Antipholus never becomes genuinely villainous. Yet we do enjoy the comic reversal when Angelo asks Antipholus to pay for the gold chain that we saw delivered to his twin (IV, i, 62–66), and when Antipholus is subsequently taken off to jail. The bully in the first part of the scene now needs his wife's aid, and commands the wrong Dromio to bring the bail money from Adriana (IV, i, 102–107). These plot twists are ingenious and amusing, especially when Dromio of Syracuse enters to mistake this Antipholus for his master and announces that he has purchased not a rope, but tickets for passage. Yet because the convolutions do not further expose character, the scene has a manufactured quality. At this point we are eager for the inevitable resolution, since we have learned all we shall about the principals.

In the next scene Luciana complains to her sister about the changeable affections of the Antipholus both women assume to be Adriana's husband (IV, ii, 7–28), but even this exchange does little more than propel the plot forward. The most significant words are uttered by Dromio of Syracuse, who has returned home seeking bail money, and his reflections on time and the brevity of human life echo through Shakespeare's plays:

> Time is a very bankrout and owes more than he's worth to season.
> Nay, he's a thief too: have you not heard men say,
> That Time comes stealing on by night and day?
> If ['a] be in debt and theft, and a sergeant in the way,
> Hath he not reason to turn back an hour in a day?
>
> (IV, ii, 58–62)

Such a sense of life's transience haunts a spectrum of characters ranging from Jaques in *As You Like It* to Falstaff in *Henry IV* to Macbeth. Dromio's words change Adriana's attitude, and she gives him the money at once. Again we feel her desire to love and to be loved.

In scene iii Antipholus of Syracuse has another bewildering conversation with his Dromio, who seems to find the puzzlement more amusing than perturbing. Here the subject is the bail money that Dromio is delivering to the wrong

Antipholus. As his master asks short, pointed questions, Dromio responds with a circumlocution that leaves Antipholus eager to escape:

> The fellow is distract, and so am I,
> And here we wander in illusions:
> Some blessed power deliver us from hence.

(IV, iii, 42–44)

Were some divine being actually responsible for the predicament, the comment would be amusing. That the entire confusion could be resolved with one simple bit of information makes the story less exotic, and thus the dream imagery seems imposed rather than intrinsic.

The Courtesan then conveniently enters to mistake this Antipholus for her own. She demands a gold chain for a ring she claims to have given Antipholus (IV, iii, 68–70), but he assumes that she is a witch and rushes off in self-preservation. She, in turn, decides he is mad, and resolves to tell Adriana of her husband's cruelty (IV, iii, 92–95). First, however, in scene iv the imprisoned Antipholus is furious with his Dromio, who has bought a rope, as originally ordered, but not the bail money, as ordered later. This use of props to confuse matters is most effective.

In this scene the suspicions of insanity lead to the confrontation with the fraudulent Dr. Pinch. Antipholus is still beating Dromio, but at the Doctor's first attempts at examination, Antipholus switches and attacks him. Pinch immediately assumes Antipholus to be mad, and after evidence from the women, as well as corroboration from a flustered Dromio, decrees that this Antipholus is to be "bound and laid in some dark room" (IV, iv, 93). Such a plot turn is developed more fully in *Twelfth Night*, when Malvolio is imprisoned at length, and suffers great torments. Here the possibility of humiliation is not so moving, for this Antipholus is too self-possessed to suffer severe stress. However, his invulnerability keeps the play's jaunty tone, while his harshness towards his wife guarantees that we feel little for him. As he says to her:

> Dissembling harlot, thou art false in all,
> And art confederate with a damned pack
> To make a loathsome abject scorn of me;
> But with these nails I'll pluck out these false eyes
> That would behold in me this shameful sport.

(IV, iv, 101–105)

Even after he utters these vicious lines, Adriana pays his debt to Angelo rather than see her husband imprisoned, for she has compassion for what she perceives as his insanity (IV, iv, 119–123). Thus her shrewishness gradually fades, although whether Antipholus deserves such kindness is another matter.

At the end of the scene, Shakespeare demonstrates his skill at audience manipulation, for just as the plot is about to reach a climax, Antipholus of Syracuse and his Dromio enter. They are taken by the others for the men just left in prison, and the imbroglio leaves everyone in panic. Antipholus decides that proceedings have become too bizarre, and that he and his servant should return home at once (IV, iv, 149–150). We, however, are desperate for them to remain and help solve the discord we have endured, and thus even the possibility that they will leave increases our apprehension. Such strategy has been used in countless plays and films, when by postponing events of resolution or by threatening to bypass them altogether, dramatists and directors make the audience more nervous about the outcome. In his first play Shakespeare shows mastery of the technique.

That long-awaited resolution occurs in Act V. First Antipholus of Syracuse, still wearing the chain, is assaulted by Angelo and the merchant, and in desperation the perplexed man and his Dromio seek sanctuary in the priory. When Adriana enters to retrieve her husband, the Abbess suddenly appears to lecture her sternly, blaming Adriana for her husband's supposed lunacy. Adriana defends herself, and we understand that fault lies on both sides, but the Abbess lays responsibility for the success of a marriage squarely on the woman:

> The venom clamors of a jealous woman
> Poisons more deadly than a mad dog's tooth.
>
> (V, i, 69–70)

Later the Abbess adds:

> The consequence is then, thy jealous fits
> Hath scar'd thy husband from the use of wits.
>
> (V, i, 85–86)

Luciana tries to support her sister:

> She never reprehended him but mildly,
> When he demean'd himself rough, rude, and wildly.
>
> (V, i, 87–88)

But Adriana soon capitulates:

> I will attend my husband, be his nurse,
> Diet his sickness, for it is my office,
> And will have no attorney but myself,
> And therefore let me have him home with me.
>
> (V, i, 98–101)

The Abbess reaffirms what was accepted doctrine in Shakespeare's time, that a wife should be subordinate to her husband, and therefore Adriana's transformation is thematically vital. Such character development also helps lift the play out of the realm of farce and suggests the more profound relationships between men and women that Shakespeare offers in later works.

Never, though, does the playwright resolve marriage crises with the simplistic solution that a husband should always rule his wife. Rather Shakespeare dramatizes that true love often inspires feelings of possession from both partners, and

this mutual respect within certain socially defined perameters is the foundation
of a happy union. Here such balance is implied but not articulated.

Curiously, the Abbess is not ready to release Antipholus:

> Be patient, for I will not let him stir
> Till I have us'd the approved means I have,
> With wholesome syrups, drugs, and holy prayers,
> To make of him a formal man again:
> It is a branch and parcel of mine oath,
> A charitable duty of my order,
> Therefore depart, and leave him here with me.
>
>   (V, i, 102–108)

We wonder why she is delaying, but in retrospect, the Abbess's decision to
prepare Antipholus for his entrance is understandable.

When the Duke enters, he sadly intends to carry out Egeon's execution. But
Adriana interrupts with her convoluted version of events that have transpired.
The Duke intends to impose a verdict, but this decision, too, is cut short when
a messenger reports that Antipholus and Dromio have escaped from jail. When
Antipholus's shout is heard offstage, Adriana approaches hysteria:

> Ay me, it is my husband! Witness you,
> That he is borne about invisible . . .
>
>   (V, i, 186–187)

Antipholus soon bursts in, inspiring recognition from Egeon, who tempers even
a moment of joy with a characteristically gloomy expression:

> Unless the fear of death doth make my dote,
> I see my son Antipholus and Dromio.
>
>   (V, i, 195–196)

Antipholus is thereafter permitted to tell his own story, which is even longer
and more manic than his wife's. In a sense the two tales both satisfy and frustrate
us, for while they bring out some truths, they leave room for mutual accusations
to fly back and forth. These grow increasingly energetic and exhausting, so that
we enjoy the spectacle but are grateful when the Duke sends for the Abbess: "I
think you are all mated, or stark mad" (V, i, 282). ("Mated" here means
"confounded.") The line reaffirms a familiar theme.

Egeon takes us one step closer to resolution. He at last approaches his son
Antipholus, but when the citizen of Ephesus does not recognize his father,
Egeon's pain is touching:

> Not know my voice! O time's extremity,
> Hast thou so crack'd and splitted my poor tongue
> In seven short years, that here my only son

Knows not my feeble key of untun'd cares?

(V, i, 308–311)

He reminds us that underneath the comic turmoil lie loneliness and loss, and for a few moments our laughter stops.

At last the Abbess brings out the other Antipholus and Dromio, and explanations follow quickly. After so long a delay, we, too, find the discovery as exhilarating as do the characters. The Abbess also surprises Egeon and perhaps the audience by disclosing that she is his wife, Amelia (V, i, 345–346). In only one other play, *The Winter's Tale*, does Shakespeare withhold information this way. The revelation is moving, but we also realize that the Abbess's lecture to Adriana on wifely submission was not merely from one woman to another, but from mother-in-law to daughter-in-law, and we therefore may regard it more quizzically.

After all details are clarified, the couples pair off in a spirit of mutual forgiveness and celebration, but Shakespeare leaves one very minor confusion, as the two Dromios remain onstage to dicker over seniority. However, they, too, reconcile, and the play ends in harmony. Given the antagonism between the cities of Ephesus and Syracuse that was announced in the opening scene, we might expect a political treaty to accompany the reuniting of the family but no such agreement is discussed.

What *A Comedy of Errors* lacks most is the sophistication of character and language that distinguishes the best of Shakespeare's comedies. But much here can be appreciated. The ingenious plot resolves into a series of satisfying relationships that lead to marriage. The laughter does not obscure potentially serious ramifications, particularly about the complicated relations between men and women and the myriad aspects of love. Finally, the play dramatizes women with great sympathy, and in subsequent comedies their role in the social organism proves rich material.

SUGGESTIONS FOR FURTHER READING

Brooks, Charles. "Shakespeare's Romantic Shrews." *Shakespeare Quarterly* 11 (1960): 351–356.

Elliott, G. R. "Weirdness in *The Comedy of Errors*." *University of Toronto Quarterly* 9 (1939): 95–106.

Grivelet, Michael. "Shakespeare, Moliere, and the Comedy of Ambiguity." *Shakespeare Survey* 22 (1969): 15–26.

Hamilton, A. C. *The Early Shakespeare*. San Marino, Calif.: The Huntington Library, 1967.

Petronella, V. T. "Structure and Theme Through Separation and Union in *The Comedy of Errors*." *Modern Language Review* 49 (July, 1979): 481–488.

Salgado, R.G.N. "Time's Deformed Hand: Sequence, Consequence, and Inconsequence in *The Comedy of Errors*." *Shakespeare Survey* 25 (1973): 81–91.

THE TAMING OF THE SHREW

No plot line is as pleasing to audiences as that of a woman and man beginning their relationship in enmity and resolving it in love. So irresistible is the situation that even mediocre renditions can have considerable charm. The paradigm of the scenario is *The Taming of the Shrew*, which Shakespeare may have adapted from an earlier play called *The Taming of a Shrew*. The subplot, concerning Bianca and her suitors, was apparently adapted from a work by George Gascoigne, *The Supposes* (1566), a translation of Ariosto's *I Suppositi* (1509).

Many productions of *The Taming of the Shrew* emphasize its farcical qualities, for here is opportunity for endless horseplay: hitting, slapping, shoving, tickling, kicking, and shouting. But to focus narrowly on such slapstick is to miss elements of great warmth and to do a disservice to the playwright's vision. The two protagonists achieve a relationship both subtle and complicated, and one easily misunderstood.

The play begins with an Induction often omitted from performances, for it is long and roundabout. But thematically it anticipates the heart of *The Taming of the Shrew*. Christopher Sly falls asleep drunk, and the patrons of the alehouse amuse themselves by making him believe he is a lord. As one hunter claims, "He is no less than what we say he is" (Induction, i, 71). The crowd thereafter treats Sly as if he were of royalty, and before long he is convinced that he is a nobleman who has been asleep for fifteen years. The climax of the charade is Sly's astonishment at the news that a lady of stature, actually a disguised page, is in love with him:

> Am I a lord, and have I such a lady?
> Or do I dream? Or have I dream'd till now?
> I do not sleep: I see, I hear, I speak;
> I smell sweet savors, and I feel soft things.

> (Induction, ii, 68–71)

The crude Sly has been altered into a man of delicacy, and his change suggests that our character is determined as much by how people treat us as by what we intrinsically are. That theme is the core of the play to follow, which ostensibly unfolds before Sly himself. However, after one more brief appearance, he disappears, leaving us with the memory of his transformation.

With the beginning of the play proper, we are in Padua, and meet Lucentio and his servant Tranio. Lucentio has come to the town's famous university, and plans to devote himself to work:

> And therefore, Tranio, for the time I study,
> Virtue and that part of philosophy
> Will I apply that treats of happiness
> By virtue specially to be achiev'd.
>
> (I, i, 17–20)

But Tranio warns his master of the dangers of exclusive devotion to matters of intellect:

> Let's be no Stoics nor no stocks, I pray,
> Or so devote to Aristotle's checks
> As Ovid be an outcast quite abjur'd.
>
> (I, i, 31–33)

As if to confirm this advice not to forswear love, Baptista and his daughters, Bianca and Katherine, take the stage. They are surrounded by a company of Bianca's suitors, none of whom is dramatically compelling. Their vacuousness to a degree weakens the play, but also sets off Petruchio and Katherine, who loom powerfully over the other characters.

Baptista has decreed that Bianca will not marry until Katherine has a husband, and this vow is the springboard for the action. But more important are the personalities of the principals. Our initial impression of Baptista is that he cares for both his daughters, but soon we grasp that Bianca is by far his favorite (I, i, 74–77). He relishes her apparent appreciation of talented men (I, i, 92–100), and therefore seeks tutors to keep her company. Meanwhile he has no hesitation in ordering Katherine inside while he continues "to commune with Bianca" (I, i, 101). Before long, Baptista's mercenary attitude is evident, and we understand that he regards both his daughters less as people and more as commodities. Bianca herself remains demurely quiet, but with her first lines we sense a hypocrite beneath:

> Sister, content you in my discontent.
> Sir, to your pleasure humbly I subscribe:
> My books and instruments shall be my company,
> On them to look and practice by myself.
>
> (I, i, 80–83)

Her modesty is too good to be legitimate, and one subplot of this play is the revelation of Bianca's true nature.

And what of Katherine? Her initial words to her father tell a great deal:

he upon finding a rich wife that we suspect he has more substance than he allows us to view. Presently such a surmise proves correct.

Hortensio has a convenient solution:

> I can, Petruchio, help thee to a wife
> With wealth enough, and young and beauteous,
> Brought up as best becomes a gentlewoman.
> Her only fault, and that is faults enough,
> Is that she is intolerable curst
> And shrowd and froward, so beyond all measure,
> That were my state far worser than it is,
> I would not wed her for a mine of gold.
>
>   (I, ii, 85–92)

Far from being discouraged, Petruchio is intrigued:

> For I will board her, though she chide as loud
> As thunder when the clouds in autumn crack.
>
>   (I, ii, 95–96)

He also knows of Katherine's family, so Petruchio is eager to meet her. Grumio, in fact, thinks his master clearly up to the occasion:

> I'll tell you what,
> sir, and she stand him but a little, he will throw a
> figure in her face, and so disfigure her with it, that
> she shall have no more eyes to see withal than a cat.
> You know him not, sir.
>
>   (I, ii, 112–116)

At this prediction we anticipate more eagerly than ever the meeting of these two energetic figures.

In return for the information about Katherine, Hortensio asks that Petruchio introduce him to Baptista as a teacher of music (I, ii, 132–137). But before Petruchio can answer, he and Hortensio are joined by Gremio and Lucentio, now calling himself Cambio, a tutor of literature who claims he will plead for Gremio to Bianca (I, ii, 154–158). Gremio assumes that his introduction of "Cambio" to Baptista will help Gremio himself win Bianca (I, ii, 176), while we enjoy that the tutor he presents is actually a romantic rival. All these plotters flutter about in astonishment when they learn that Petruchio will actually woo Katherine, and his self-assurance is ever more impressive:

> Have I not in a pitched battle heard
> Loud 'larums, neighing steeds, and trumpets' clang?
> And do you tell me of a woman's tongue,
> That gives not half so great a blow to hear
> As will a chestnut in a farmer's fire?

Tush, tush, fear boys with bugs.

(I, i, 205–210)

He has all the signs of a man who is bored and who seeks a fresh spark. But he does not imagine one to be available, and thus his claims about marrying merely for money reflect his suspicion that he will not come upon any other reason to do so. He also has little patience with these trivial men around him, and perhaps their awe of Katherine suggests to Petruchio that she may in fact be the vibrant soul he seeks.

During the last part of the scene the suitors of Bianca all declare their intentions, but Tranio realizes that they must temporarily put aside their own ambitions to work in support of Petruchio:

And if you break the ice, and do this [feat],
Achieve the elder, set the younger free
For our access—whose hap shall be to have her
Will not so graceless be to be ingrate.

(I, ii, 265–268)

No doubt "the ice" refers to Katherine. Petruchio does not answer, but surely he suspects he needs little help from any of these weaker souls.

The squabble between Katherine and Bianca that opens Act II recalls the argument between Luciana and Adriana in their initial appearance in *A Comedy of Errors*. Bianca is normally more at ease with herself, while Katherine, furious at life in general, takes out her resentment on her sibling and anyone else available. These two sisters are also drawn more vividly than the ones from the earlier play. Katherine, in particular, is less passive and more dynamic, especially at this moment, when she has bound Bianca's hands behind her. Katherine's anger with her sister reflects her own despondency:

Of all thy suitors here I charge [thee] tell
Whom thou lov'st best; see thou dissemble not.

(II, i, 8–9)

She is enraged by Bianca's capacity for deceit. Bianca's response indicates her own temperament:

Believe me, sister, of all the men alive,
I never yet beheld that special face
Which I could fancy more than any other.

(II, i, 10–12)

The lines could mean that Bianca has yet to fall in love. The more likely implication is that she has never found one man whose attentions could supplant those of many men at once.

After Baptista permits Bianca to escape, Katherine cries to her father about the depths of her unhappiness:

> What, will you not suffer me? Nay, now I see
> She is your treasure, she must have a husband;
> I must dance barefoot on her wedding-day,
> And for your love to her lead apes in hell.

> (II, i, 31–34)

She feels bored, frustrated, and loveless. In fact, she has the same needs as Petruchio, though each reacts to desperation differently. Petruchio expresses his unhappiness through cynicism, Katherine through rage.

After Katherine's convenient exit, Petruchio enters the house, and his unvarnished approach contrasts sharply with the machinations of the other suitors. Gremio even warns him: "You are too blunt, go to it orderly" (II, i, 45). In other words, lie. But Petruchio maintains his attitude, speaking of Katherine in the most flattering terms (II, i, 47–53). The great irony is that these extravagant praises eventually prove true.

Baptista is momentarily distracted by the supposed tutors for Bianca, as Hortensio, Lucentio (as Cambio), and Tranio (as Lucentio) present themselves and are led off to meet with Bianca. Petruchio then puts the important matter squarely before Baptista:

> Then tell me, if I get your daughter's love,
> What dowry shall I have with her to wife?

> (II, i, 119–120)

Baptista promises half his lands and 20,000 crowns, and Petruchio insists that proper documents be drawn. This bargaining over a potential wife may seem distasteful, but it was standard Elizabethan form. Nonetheless, we sense that Baptista truly regards Katherine as mere property, bribing Petruchio with promise of a dowry and an inheritance, then pretending to avoid that implication;

> Ay, when the special thing is well obtain'd,
> That is, her love; for that is all in all.

> (II, i, 128–129)

Baptista sees no further value to his daughter. But Petruchio does, especially when Hortensio reveals that Katherine has smashed his head with a lute (II, i, 148–150). Petruchio is now genuinely taken:

> Now by the world, it is a lusty wench!
> I love her ten times more than e'er I did
> O, how I long to have some chat with her!

> (II, i, 160–162)

Her actions tell him that she is by far the most energetic person Petruchio has met in a long time. And he announces his strategy in dealing with a woman of such spirit:

> Say that she rail, why then I'll tell her plain
> She sings as sweetly as a nightingale;

Say that she frown, I'll say she looks as clear
As morning roses newly wash'd with dew;
Say she be mute, and will not speak a word,
Then I'll commend her volubility . . .

						(II, i, 170–175)

How does he know this tactic will work? Because even without meeting Katherine, he understands her plight.

Their initial encounter is a brilliant scene. From the outset we feel that these two characters are a match, but that before the relationship can be fulfilled, certain ground rules must be established. For instance, Petruchio establishes his approach at once:

Take this of me, Kate of my consolation—
Hearing thy mildness prais'd in every town,
Thy virtues spoke of, and thy beauty sounded,
Yet not so deeply as to thee belongs,
Myself am mov'd to woo thee for my wife.

						(II, i, 190–194)

Katherine responds by defining herself in terms of angry wit: "I knew you at the first/ You were a moveable" (II, i, 196–197). And the badinage flies fast, each speaker playing according to the personality established at the outset. Gradually, however, the tone of the encounter shifts. Petruchio discovers his delight with Katherine, as she becomes worth "taming" not only for the money, but also for the wit and spirit that lies underneath the shrewish surface. For her part Katherine finds pleasure with this man who shows himself her equal in intellect and energy, but she confirms as well that her temperament is still out of control, and that she is hardly reconciled to submitting to any man.

A moment where these feelings are apparent occurs after Katherine strikes Petruchio. For roughly thirty-five lines the pair have bantered bawdily in a parody of romantic convention, and they have proven themselves equal. Now Katherine challenges him further. Her slap is meant for insult more than injury, and thus for Petruchio to strike back would be against the unstated rules. Thus Petruchio responds: "I swear I'll cuff you, if you strike again" (II, i, 220), and Katherine challenges him back: "So may you lose your arms" (II, i, 221). Both understand that he could hurt her, but both also know that to be fair he must subdue her by less painful means.

Their mutual affection slowly blossoms. After further salacious verbal dueling, Petruchio rhapsodizes about Kate's charms:

No, not a whit, I find you passing gentle:
'Twas told me you were rough and coy and sullen,
And now I find report a very liar;
For thou art pleasant, gamesome, passing courteous,
But slow in speech, yet sweet as spring-time flowers.
Thou canst not frown, thou canst not look askance,

Nor bite the lip, as angry wenches will,
Nor hast thou pleasure to be cross in talk;
But thou with mildness entertain'st thy wooers,
With gentle conference, soft, and affable.

(II, i, 242–251)

He is speaking ironically. Yet he is also speaking a version of the truth. Underneath, she is all that he says she is, and to an extent both realize that he is accurate. Thus when a few lines later Katherine asks, "Where did you study all this goodly speech?" (II, i, 262), she seems to reveal reluctantly her admiration of his style.

Petruchio continues his tributes, and, when the other men return, announces that he will have Katherine for his wife (II, i, 280). Here she reverts to her former manner, for the decision is too abrupt, and she has not been consulted. Furthermore, she will not drop her long-standing personality without a struggle. But her protests seem to subside momentarily when Petruchio says, "If she and I be pleas'd, what's that to you?" (II, i, 303). Surely no man has ever spoken of her as his ally, and Katherine is probably secretly gratified. She may be taken as well with Petruchio's imaginary narrative about how she kissed him passionately (II, i, 307–313), for deep down she wishes that such events actually occurred. Thus her silence as Petruchio carries her out expresses a combination of consternation and curiosity.

The eventual bond between Petruchio and Katherine is set off by the rest of the scene, when Baptista essentially offers Bianca to the highest bidder:

'Tis deeds must win the prize, and he of both
That can assure my daughter greatest dower
Shall have my Bianca's love.

(II, i, 342–344)

He means that the winner will have Bianca in marriage, but we suspect that the richest will also be the one she prefers. Gremio and Tranio, still pretending to be Lucentio, boast of their wealth, but the atmosphere of mistrust is thick, especially when Baptista accepts the bid by Tranio (II, i, 386–389). Baptista insists, however, that the man he takes as Lucentio provide his father's assurance about the money to be given to Baptista. And Baptista's willingness to change his mind if the money is not forthcoming adds to the nastiness. Such trickery continues in Act III, scene i, when Lucentio and Hortensio, both disguised as tutors, try to appeal to Bianca during their lessons. She, in turn, plays one off against the other, and we realize that in her own way Bianca is the true shrew. Furthermore, whatever suitor wins her, she and he will deserve each other.

The wedding scene changes the mood of the play, as Petruchio alters his tactics. No matter how attracted to him Katherine may be after what passes for their scene of courtship, her personality is too firmly ingrained to change overnight, and thus Petruchio still has lessons for her to learn. When he does not appear on time for the wedding, she is naturally upset, for she wants a legitimate ceremony:

> Now must the world point at poor Katherine,
> And say, "Lo, there is mad Petruchio's wife,
> If it would please him come and marry her!"
>
> (III, ii, 18–20)

She is tormented most by the thought of public humiliation. What Petruchio attempts to teach her during the rest of the play is that what should matter most is not her public image but her private reality.

His first lesson is arriving late and dressed outlandishly for the ceremony. After Petruchio innocently inquires as to his bride's location, then strides off to marry her, Tranio senses the truth: "He hath some meaning in his mad attire" (III, ii, 124). That meaning is to judge not by appearance, but by substance, a truth reinforced when the situation turns momentarily to Bianca, and her fraudulent suitors resume plotting to win her.

After the bizarre marriage, the details of which we learn through Gremio's report, Petruchio is ready to depart. But Katherine refuses, insisting that her own priorities take precedence:

> Do what thou canst, I will not go to-day,
> No, nor to-morrow—not till I please myself.
>
> (III, ii, 208–209)

> I will be angry, what hast thou to do?
> Father, be quiet, he shall stay my leisure.
>
> (III, ii, 216–217)

> Gentlemen, forward to the bridal dinner.
> I see a woman may be made a fool,
> If she had not a spirit to resist.
>
> (III, ii, 219–221)

In response to these assertions of her own will and her emphasis on "I," Petruchio goes to the other extreme, proclaiming that as his wife she is his possession, devoid of personal identity:

> She is my goods, my chattels, she is my house,
> My household stuff, my field, my barn,
> My horse, my ox, my ass, my any thing:
> And here she stands, touch her whoever dare,
> I'll bring mine action on the proudest he
> That stops my way in Padua.
>
> (III, ii, 230–235)

By reducing her to the level of an object, without privilege, without dignity, without rights of any kind, Petruchio hopes that Kate will in essence start over, rediscovering who she is. The mockery of the onlookers (III, ii, 240–253), themselves both empty-headed and confident, confirms our faith that Petruchio and Katherine are soon to find happiness together.

The instruction continues in Act IV at Petruchio's home. Before the couple enters, Grumio recounts to Curtis some of the treatment Petruchio has inflicted and the personal humiliation Katherine is enduring (IV, i, 72–84). Curtis grasps the import: "By this reck'ning he is more shrew than she" (IV, i, 85–86). Such will be the underlying theme of the scenes to follow. When Petruchio arrives he brutally orders and abuses his servants, to such an extent that Katherine herself begs him to relent (IV, i, 168–169). But he is absolutely gentle with his wife. Peter understands one point of Petruchio's behavior: "He kills her in her own humor" (IV, i, 180). Petruchio is also holding a mirror up to Katherine's face, showing her the preposterousness of her own behavior. In addition, by subsequently denying her food and sleep, he makes her susceptible to change.

These scenes of what amounts to behavior modification continue for quite a while, and they are excessive. Nevertheless, Petruchio's motives are benign:

> Thus have I politicly begun my reign,
> And 'tis my hope to end successfully.
> My falcon now is sharp and passing empty,
> And till she stoop, she must not be full-gorg'd,
> For then she never looks upon her lure . . .
> Ay, and amid this hurly I intend
> That all is done in reverend care of her,
> And in conclusion, she shall watch all night,
> And if she chance to nod I'll rail and brawl,
> And with the clamor keep her still awake.
> This is a way to kill a wife with kindness,
> And thus I'll curb her mad and headstrong humor.
> He that knows better how to tame a shrew,
> Now let him speak; 'tis charity to shew.
>
> (IV, i, 188–211)

These tactics should not be understood as fulfilling sadistic pleasure, for Petruchio does not enjoy seeing Katherine suffer. Rather he is doing what he believes he has to do, not so much changing her as allowing her real personality to emerge. The product of his efforts is not a conditioned Katherine, but a true Katherine, who reflects the soul that has lain dormant inside her, thwarted by her father and his world.

In Act IV, scene ii, such development is again contrasted with Bianca and her suitors. Hortensio has agreed to marry a wealthy widow (IV, ii, 36–43), and we realize that although earlier Petruchio claimed to seek marriage only for money, Hortensio is actually following that precept. We also see Tranio indulge in yet another lie, persuading a traveling pedant to pose as Vicentio, Lucentio's father (IV, ii, 103–112). The deceptions in Padua grow more elaborate, while Katherine and Petruchio gradually break down their own.

In Act IV, scene iii Katherine still cannot understand her husband's attitude

(IV, iii, 2–14), but Petruchio's "taming" continues through the scene. When Gremio torments her by hesitating with his offer of beef and mustard, Katherine resorts to violence, and Petruchio kindly, but gently, seems to accede to her wishes by taking the food away (IV, iii, 38–44). He then treats the haberdasher rudely, finding fault with every one of his offerings, but when Petruchio has Hortensio reimburse the tailor (IV, iii, 164–165), we realize the entire episode was staged. Petruchio is determined to teach Katherine not only the importance of amenities that preserve the social order, but also the value of judging by quality and not appearance:

> Our purses shall be proud, our garments poor,
> For 'tis the mind that makes the body rich;
> And as the sun breaks through the darkest clouds,
> So honor peereth in the meanest habit.

(IV, iii, 171–174)

The man who utters these lines is a fellow of substance, and the woman who listens and follows the advice recognizes him as such.

Before we see their relationship blossom, though, we once more are taken back to Padua, where Baptista, taken in by the false Vicentio, gives his daughter Bianca to Tranio, thinking him Lucentio. As Baptista consents to the marriage, he ironically judges himself clever:

> Right true it is, your son Lucentio here
> Doth love my daughter, and she loveth him,
> Or both dissemble deeply their affections . . .

(IV, iv, 40–42)

In fact, they are dissembling, and so busy is Baptista ensuring his financial future that he sends the real Lucentio, still disguised as Cambio, to deliver the marriage plans to Bianca (IV, iv, 62–66). Lucentio, of course, has his own ideas, and schemes with his other servant, Biondello, to take bride and contract, and carry out a secret marriage.

The contrast between such goings-on and the relationship Katherine and Petruchio share is winning. Their bond reaches fruition in Act IV, scene v, when during their journey to Padua Petruchio vacillates about whether the sun or moon shines down warmly. In a quiet climax to so noisy a play, Katherine joins in the game, and as she says the following lines, her pleasure glows:

> Then God be blest, it [is] the blessed sun,
> But sun it is not, when you say it is not;
> And the moon changes even as your mind.
> What you will have it nam'd, even that it is,
> And so it shall be so for Katherine.

(IV, v, 18–22)

Whereas only a short time before Petruchio was playing a parody of the role Katherine used to play, now she acts a parody of the role he has set out for her.

And she takes the game one step further when she greets the aged Vincentio, Lucentio's father:

> Young budding virgin, fair, and fresh, and sweet,
> Whither away, or [where] is thy abode?
> Happy the parents of so fair a child!
> Happier the man whom favorable stars
> Allots thee for his lovely bedfellow.

(IV, v, 37–41)

Petruchio protests that he hopes she has not gone mad, although he surely knows that her comments are part of the sport he started. Katherine graciously restates her judgment, which she claims was hampered by the "sun" (IV, v, 46), a witty reference to Petruchio's own game of moments earlier. She and Petruchio never precisely clarify their relationship in words, but their mutual affection is evident here and after. This meeting with the real Vincentio, by the way, reunites the two stories, and allows us to look forward to further mix-ups when all reach Padua.

In Act V the subplots reach their climax, as those in disguise encounter the people they are pretending to be. As if to reflect their emotional and intellectual separation from such deception, Petruchio and Katherine gracefully stand aside (V, i, 61–62). The mass confusion is embodied in one stage direction: "*Exeunt Biondello, Tranio, and Pedant as fast as may be* (V, i, 111)." After Lucentio's explanation (V, i, 124–130), all antagonisms are eventually reconciled, although both Baptista and Vincentio feel slighted that the marriage between Lucentio and Bianca has taken place without the permission of the fathers (V, i, 133–136). Such disorder is again set in contrast with the relationship of Katherine and Petruchio, as when they are alone he asks for a kiss. She is embarrassed to embrace in the middle of the street, but when he threatens to turn back home, she relents: "Nay, I will give thee a kiss, now pray thee, love, stay" (V, i, 148). His response is equally warm:

> Is not this well? Come, my sweet Kate:
> Better once than never, for never too late.

(V, i, 149–150)

At such a moment we think back to the initial meeting of this pair (II, i), when Petruchio lavished praise on Katherine. At the time we thought his words sarcastic. Now he has been proven right, for Katherine has been transformed into all that Petruchio described. His love, singular though its manner, created hers.

In the final scene Petruchio sits with Katherine at the banquet, while Lucentio joins with Bianca, and Hortensio with his rich widow. When the widow makes a disparaging remark about Petruchio's being saddled with a shrew (V, ii, 28), Katherine retorts sharply. She has not lost any of her spunk, and Petruchio's cheering her on (V, ii, 33, 35) indicates he enjoys it. He has not crushed her vitality. He has instead brought out her softer side, previously suppressed by a society unable to appreciate her.

For contemporary audiences the summoning of the three wives and Katherine's obedience in appearing so quickly may seem demeaning, while her lengthy tribute to her status as wife resounds uncomfortably. But to understand her address as an expression of complete surrender is to misinterpret. Certainly Shakespeare, as typical of his age, believed a woman's place subordinate to her husband's. But Katherine's tone and words, stated to a quietly rapt assemblage, communicate not servitude, but sharing:

> Thy husband is thy lord, thy life, thy keeper,
> Thy head, thy sovereign, one that cares for thee,
> And for thy maintenance; commits his body
> To painful labor, both by sea and land;
> To watch the night in storms, the day in cold,
> Whilst thou li'st warm at home, secure and safe;
> And craves no other tribute at thy hands
> But love, fair looks, and true obedience—
> Too little payment for so great a debt.

(V, ii, 146–154)

She advocates what for the time would be an equilibrium between husband and wife. When she goes on to compare marriage to the political relationship between prince and subject (V, ii, 155), she clarifies that just as a society's health is based on a proper hierarchical structure, so the happiness of a marriage is inextricably tied to order. To have all in balance and proportion: that was an ideal of Shakespeare's age, and that is the ideal Katherine advocates. In our time the social mores are far different from those of the Renaissance, and our perceptions of propriety have changed. But for his era, Shakespeare, in this play and many others, shows deep respect for the contribution of women to the moral and emotional health of the society.

The raucous physicality in a production of *The Taming of the Shrew* may prove so dominant that it diverts an audience from the thematic import. Furthermore, the extended scenes of Katherine's abuse are antithetical to the ethos of our time. But for its day, and beyond, the play offers a winning theatrical spectacle, as well as two characters whose vibrancy makes them among Shakespeare's most successful creations. We may not approve completely of the relationship they establish, but we cannot doubt that on their own terms they have achieved a love that surpasses any in their world.

SUGGESTIONS FOR FURTHER READING

Bradbrook, M. C. "Dramatic Role as Social Image: A Study of *The Taming of the Shrew*." *Shakespeare Jarbuch* 94 (1958): 132–150.

Dusinberre, Juliet. *Shakespeare and the Nature of Women*. New York: Barnes and Noble, 1975.

Greenfield, Thelma N. "The Transformation of Christopher Sly." *Philological Quarterly* 33 (1954): 34–43.

Heilman, Robert B. "The Taming Untamed, or, The Return of the Shrew." *Modern Language Quarterly* 27 (1966): 147–161.

Hense, Richard. "Role Playing in *The Taming of the Shrew*." *Southern Humanities Review* 4 (1969): 231–240.

Seronsy, C. C. "*Supposes* as the Unifying Theme in *The Shrew*." *Shakespeare Quarterly* 14 (1963): 15–30.

THE TWO GENTLEMEN OF VERONA

For many audiences this play is one of the least satisfying in the Shakespearean canon. The key problem is character development, for neither hero is especially attractive, and one, Proteus, conducts a series of machinations that completely antagonize us. Even more problematical, his instantaneous apology at the end and Valentine's equally quick acceptance of that turnabout are, to many, dramatically unconvincing. The major question in analyzing this work is whether these difficulties are intrinsic to a unified vision on the playwright's part. The primary source of the play is the episode of Felix and Felismena in the pastoral romance *Diana Enamorada* (1542) by the Portuguese author Montemayor.

The opening scene presents two conventional Renaissance youths about to go separate ways. Valentine is preparing to depart from his home city, hoping to learn more of life: "To see the wonders of the world abroad . . . " (I, i, 6). He has tried to persuade his friend Proteus to join this excursion, but the latter is in love and unwilling to leave. Proteus adds that he will be with Valentine in spirit: "thy beadsman" (I, ii, 18). Valentine gently mocks Proteus's stereotypical infatuation:

> To be in love—where scorn is bought with groans;
> Coy looks with heart-sore sighs; one fading moment's mirth
> With twenty watchful, weary, tedious nights:
> If happ'ly won, perhaps a hapless gain;
> If lost, why then a grievous labor won;
> However—but a folly bought with wit,
> Or else a wit by folly vanquished.
>
> (I, i, 29–35)

A moment later he adds:

> But wherefore waste I time to counsel thee
> That art a votary to fond desire?
>
> (I, i, 51–52)

Proteus has his own interpretation of their respective attitudes. Of Valentine he comments:

> Yet writers say: as in the sweetest bud
> The eating canker dwells, so eating love
> Inhabits in the finest wits of all.

                                                            (I, i, 42–44)

Proteus doubts Valentine's invulnerability to romance. And when Valentine departs, Proteus evaluates their priorities:

> He after honor hunts, I after love:
> He leaves his friends, to dignify them more;
> I [leave] myself, my friends, and all, for love.

                                                            (I, i, 63–65)

In this brief scene we discover the core of these two men. Valentine is a stock figure from Renaissance literature, the scorner of romance soon to fall madly in love. His conventional desire to travel masks superficiality. Proteus's equally conventional claims about love disguise his lack of substance:

> Thou, Julia, thou hast metamorphis'd me,
> Made me neglect my studies, lose my time,
> War with good counsel, set the world at nought;
> Made wit with musing weak, heart sick with thought.

                                                            (I, i, 66–69)

He seems to be pining over his love, but he does not specify what is wonderful about her. Rather he uses his preoccupation with her to excuse his own weaknesses and stupidities. Proteus should therefore be understood as a man taken with his own obsession, and nothing about that state is romantic.

Both these young men are, in their own way, foolish, and both are objects of satire. The play is thus a mockery of their pretension, and the unlikely turns of events that follow are equally mocking.

The problem theatrically is that the audience is forced to accompany these two fellows, neither of whom is attractive. Even if we appreciate the implications of their behavior, we do not necessarily enjoy their company.

Proteus's unpleasant manner is emphasized in his exchange with Valentine's servant, Speed, who returns after having given Proteus's missives to Julia. The servant is long-winded in his explanation of Julia's lack of interest, but Proteus has no patience with puns and other wordplay, and Speed leaves in a snit: " . . . henceforth carry your letters yourself . . . " (I, i, 145–146). Proteus places blame for the failure on Speed:

> I must go send some better messenger:
> I fear my Julia would not deign my lines,
> Receiving them from such a worthless post.

                                                            (I, i, 151–153)

But Speed is a sophisticated young servant. Unlike either one of the Dromios (*The Comedy of Errors*) he is clever in his use of language, and his series of puns on "shepherd" and "mutton" (I, i, 75–100) sparkles in a work too often darkened by the protagonists. Proteus, however, is an egotist, and cannot imagine that either he or his letter is the problem.

In scene ii we encounter Julia, with her woman in waiting, Lucetta. Julia has a range of suitors, two of whom, Sir Eglamour and Mercatio, Lucetta dismisses lightly, much as Portia mocks her lovers in *The Merchant of Venice*. At the mention of Proteus, though, Lucetta's tone changes:

> Pardon, dear madam, 'tis a passing shame
> That I (unworthy body as I am)
> Should censure thus on lovely gentlemen.
>
> (I, ii, 16–18)

When Julia asks the reason for Lucetta's affection, the reply is telling:

> I have no other reason but a woman's reason:
> I think him so, because I think him so.
>
> (I, ii, 22–23)

Such instinctive reaction turns out to be far stronger than the supposedly reasoned love of the male characters. Julia is nonetheless suspicious of Proteus, who seems unresponsive: "They do not love that do not show their love" (I, ii, 30). But when she hears that Proteus's letter has been accepted, she rebukes Lucetta:

> Dare you presume to harbor wanton lines?
> To whisper and conspire against my youth?
>
> (I, ii, 42–43)

She is also insulted that it has been delivered by a servant rather than by Proteus himself, as propriety would demand. Earlier Speed claimed to have brought the letter to Julia personally, but this contradiction is never explained.

More important, after tossing the letter aside, Julia immediately regrets rejecting it (I, ii, 50). She is caught between conflicting emotions:

> How angerly I taught my brow to frown,
> When inward joy enforc'd my heart to smile.
>
> (I, ii, 62–63)

She is conscious of the role she plays, that of the virtuous young lady awaiting her lover's attention, but the passivity of her part frustrates her, and for the moment she dispenses with it by recalling Lucetta. Even then Julia cannot confess her eagerness to read Proteus's words, and the two exchange byplay built on the metaphor of music, which disguises the vigor of Julia's feeling. She ineffectively feigns indifference by tearing the letter, but as soon as Lucetta departs, Julia scrambles about the floor, picking up the pieces and seizing upon choice phrases.

Like Proteus, Julia indulges in the game of love, and in a sense she watches herself playing, but because she, as a woman in these times, must be the reactive agent, we feel more deeply for her:

> Lo, here in one line is his name twice writ,
> "Poor forlorn Proteus, passionate Proteus:
> To the sweet Julia"—that I'll tear away—
> And yet will I not, sith so prettily
> He couples it to his complaining names.
> Thus will I fold them one upon another;
> Now, kiss, embrace, contend, do what you will.
>
> (I, ii, 120–126)

The complexity of her emotions is winning, for although she enjoys games with her suitor, her affection for him outweighs any cruelty she might impose. Her ambivalence makes her a good match for Proteus, while her fundamental kindness elevates her above him.

In scene iii we are offered a glimpse of why Proteus is a maladjusted young man. Panthino asks Antonio, Proteus's father, why his son has been allowed to remain home all these years while other young men his age have traveled or served in the army, and thereby matured. The implication is that Proteus, sheltered for so long, has been stifled:

> I have consider'd well his loss of time,
> And how he cannot be a perfect man,
> Not being tried and tutor'd in the world:
> Experience is by industry achiev'd,
> And perfected by the swift course of time.
>
> (I, iii, 19–23)

Antonio's evaluation may explain Proteus's subsequent behavior. An overly protected youth, he releases his frustrations in ruthless deception.

Proteus enters with a letter ostensibly from Valentine. And Antonio orders Proteus to leave for Milan at once, the son's protests notwithstanding (I, iii, 66–71). Left alone, Proteus tells us the letter was actually from Julia, and that he was afraid to show it to his father, who objects to Proteus's affections for her. Again the play obliquely implies that the father is ultimately responsible for his son's antisocial actions. As further emphasis, Proteus's last lines suggest a poetic soul lurking underneath:

> O, how this spring of love resembleth
> The uncertain glory of an April day,
> Which now shows all the beauty of the sun,
> And by and by a cloud takes all away.
>
> (I, iii, 84–87)

These words anticipate some of the eloquent lyrics Proteus offers later. Whatever he does later, we know that a measure of decency lies within him, and we remember that he is a victim of his father's treatment.

When we next meet Valentine, the erstwhile scorner of love has fallen completely for Silvia, daughter of the Duke of Milan, and is now mocked by Speed,

> . . . first, you
> have larn'd, like Sir Proteus, to wreathe your arms,
> like a malecontent, to relish a love-song, like a
> robin-redbreast, to walk alone, like one that had the
> pestilence, like a schoolboy that had lost his
> ABC . . . and now you are metamorphis'd
> with a mistress, that when I look on you, I can hardly
> think you my master.

(II, i, 18–32)

Later, Speed again compares Valentine's new attitude to that of Proteus earlier:

> O that you had
> mine eyes, or your own eyes had the lights they were
> wont to have when you chid at Sir Proteus for
> going ungarter'd!

(II, i, 70–73)

Speed's accuracy is made clear when Valentine gives Silvia a love letter he has written at her behest to an imaginary third-party (II, i, 104–105). Speeds grasps that "she woos you by a figure" (II, i, 148), another reference to music and the metaphor of the dance of courtship, but Valentine, new to the world of love, does not grasp that he is that unnamed party (II, i, 152–153). We laugh at Valentine, the object of Silvia's mockery, but we also realize that love is dramatized here as a demanding competition, in which boldness and wit are necessary for survival. That Proteus must operate in such an environment does not excuse his subsequent actions, but it does explain further why they are so extreme.

Thus the shift to the farewell scene between Proteus and Julia has other overtones. We see no evidence that Proteus is being deceptive when he promises fidelity and accepts Julia's ring, but he soon changes his allegiance. The reason is unclear, and we must assume his own nature is at fault, but previous scenes reveal other factors that may influence him. Julia's last line has important overtones: "For truth hath better deeds than words to grace it" (II, ii, 17). Her trust in Proteus's actions rather than his statements proves ironically accurate.

In the next scene, Proteus's attitude and behavior are contrasted with that of Launce, whose loyalty to his dog proves greater than Proteus's loyalty to Julia. The servant's narrative about leaving his mother also mocks Proteus's tearful departure. Launce is the first of several buffoons who populate the world of Shakespeare's comedies, and in his unaffected manner and corruption of language he resembles Bottom (*A Midsummer Night's Dream*), Dogberry (*Much Ado About Nothing*), and others. Launce is entertaining, and his values do offset those of the protagonists, but he seems an amendment to the primary plot, not an integral part of it. In later plays Shakespeare uses the clowns more effectively, but few have more charm than Launce.

In the first part of Act II, scene iv, Silvia arranges matters so that Valentine and the older suitor Thurio exchange uninspired insults in their quest for her hand. The potential physical confrontation stops with the entrance of the Duke, who asks Valentine about Proteus. Valentine pays a stirring tribute, ending with:

> He is complete in feature and in mind
> With all good grace to grace a gentleman.
>
> (II, iv, 73–74)

When the Duke announces that Proteus is about to arrive, Valentine adds that his longtime friend would have come originally, but that ''his mistress/ Did hold his eyes lock'd in her crystal looks'' (II, iv, 88–89). When Proteus enters moments later, however, he proves this judgment wrong, for almost immediately he follows the meaning of his name, and changes his affections to Silvia. He brushes aside questions about Julia (II, iv, 126–127), cuts off Valentine's extended confession of infatuation (II, iv, 142), refers to Silvia as ''an earthly paragon'' (II, iv, 146), and orders Valentine, who proclaims that Silvia is ''alone'' (II, iv, 167), ''Then let her alone'' (II, iv, 167). The obvious threat to his happiness flies by Valentine, but the tension inherent in that retort does not escape us.

Valentine reveals his plot to elope with his beloved (II, iv, 179–183), but upon his exit Proteus speaks openly of his newly discovered infatuation:

> Even as one heat another heat expels,
> Or as one nail by strength drives out another,
> So the remembrance of my former love
> Is by a newer object quite forgotten.
>
> (II, iv, 191–195)

This shift in emotion takes place rapidly. Yet it is understandable and even forgiveable, given Proteus's earlier statements of ardor for romance. More difficult to accept is the calculation that follows:

> Methinks my zeal to Valentine is cold,
> And that I love him not as I wont;
> O, but I love his lady too too much,
> And that's the reason I love him so little.
>
> (II, iv, 203–206)

He rationalizes acts of treachery:

> If I can check my erring love, I will;
> If not, to compass her I'll use my skill.
>
> (II, iv, 213–214)

And after an interlude where Launce and Speed weigh whether Proteus and Julia are yet married according to custom, Proteus returns to delineate his plan more specifically. With virtually every line he annoys us more.

He initially places blame for his tactics elsewhere:

> Love bade me swear, and Love bids me forswear.
> O sweet-suggesting Love, if thou hast sinn'd,

Teach me, thy tempted subject, to excuse it!

(II, vi, 6–8)

As if he knows that his plans are unethical, he envisions himself as the prisoner of forces beyond his control. He is also becoming completely egocentric:

I to myself am dearer than a friend,
For love is still most precious in itself . . .

(II, vi, 23–24)

Such self-love is directly opposed to the traditional values of friendship, and presently turns into a hatred of others:

I will forget that Julia is alive,
Rememb'ring that my love to her is dead.

(II, vi, 27–28)

By denying all previous emotions, he denies his humanity. All that remains for him is to announce that any deceptions he takes hereafter are justified:

Love, lend me wings to make my purpose swift,
As thou hast lent me wit to plot this drift.

(II, vi, 42–43)

He claims that Love has inspired him to act. Therefore the power of Love vindicates the damage he will wreak.

Does Proteus deserve sympathy? Or is he but a suddenly vicious young man, whose actions repulse us?

Certainly his love at first sight is comprehensible. But other forces are shaping him. In the first scene he was an object of mockery, a young man whose infatuation drove him to extreme behavior. Next he was depicted as the sheltered son of a difficult father. In sum, then, we should see Proteus as a naive yet headstrong young man who falls in love and loses all sense of responsibility to his best friend and to the woman he has left behind. His actions are those of an intense, pressured boy, whose perspective becomes painfully narrowed. In this light all that he does from this point on becomes understandable if still dislikable.

Scene vii offers an effective contrast to the treachery of Proteus, as Julia asks of Lucetta:

. . . tell me some good mean
How with my honor I may undertake
A journey to my loving Proteus.

(II, vii, 5–7)

Lucetta warns about the difficulties, but Julia is determined, and decides to disguise herself as a man and go to Milan (II, vii, 40–43). Her fortitude is undercut, however, by her concern about Proteus's nature:

His words are bonds, his oaths are oracles,
His love sincere, his thoughts immaculate,

> His tears pure messengers sent from his heart,
> His heart as far from fraud as heaven from earth.
>
> (III, vii, 75–78)

The unintentional irony of her trust is painful.

In Act III Silvia's father takes the stage, and his manner and scheming reflect the society in which such plotting as Proteus has exhibited is necessary. First the Duke dismisses his own man Thurio, who is soon to be shown as fatuous. Then Proteus takes over, claiming that because of friendship he speaks reluctantly, but that Valentine intends to run away with Silvia (III, i, 11–12) in spite of the Duke's plans to have his daughter marry Thurio. After the Duke broods over his blindness, Proteus compounds the treachery by supplying the details of Valentine's plan (III, i, 38–43).

When Valentine innocently enters, the Duke embarks on his own scheme. First he derogates his daughter (III, i, 68–71), supposedly justifying his eagerness to marry another woman to whom he will leave his fortune (III, i, 76–79). When the Duke then pretends to solicit advice for this imaginary courtship, Valentine eagerly boasts of his skill, and the deceptions he advocates ironically confirm Proteus's earlier estimation (II, vii, 93–95). When the Duke accidentally uncovers the rope Valentine will use to elope with Silvia plus the love letter written to her (III, i, 137–138), Valentine is expelled.

The impact of this scene is darkly comic. We sense a moral miasma here, a cold-blooded approach to romance that makes all these men dislikable. Even Valentine, essentially good-hearted, makes the stereotypical Renaissance courting of a woman a nasty business:

> Flatter and praise, commend, extol their graces;
> Though ne'er so black, say they have angels' faces.
> That man that hath a tongue, I say is no man,
> If with his tongue he cannot win a woman.
>
> (III, i, 102–105)

Moments later, after the Duke's order of banishment (III, i, 161–169), Valentine confesses his pain at losing Silvia. Yet the emotions seem excessive for one who was so taken with his own chicanery:

> Unless I look on Silvia in the day,
> There is no day for me to look upon.
> She is my essence, and I leave to be,
> If I be not by her fair influence
> Foster'd, illumin'd, cherish'd, kept alive.
>
> (III, i, 180–184)

In light of his previous attitude, such overflow may inspire moderate compassion from us, although when Proteus enters, our feelings may shift further to Valentine, who naively believes Proteus's description of Silvia's pain (III, i, 224–228). Valentine even accepts Proteus's promise to deliver letters to Silvia (III, i, 250–252). But if we feel pity for Valentine, our distaste for the entire proceedings is stronger than our affection for any character. Thus the parodying lines of Launce (III, i, 262–280) are some comfort, for as he weighs the reasons for his love, his practicality is more dignified than all the affected verses and sentimentality of the more traditional lovers.

Our displeasure is exacerbated in the next scene, after Thurio confesses his inability to win Silvia. When the Duke requests advice, Proteus suggests that Valentine be slandered (III, ii, 31–32); Proteus himself is initially reluctant to do so:

> 'Tis an ill office for a gentleman,
> Especially against his very friend.
>
> (III, ii, 40–41)

But such scruples do not impress the Duke:

> Where your good word cannot advantage him,
> Your slander never can endamage him;
> Therefore the office is indifferent
> Being entreated to it by your friend.
>
> (III, i, 42–45)

With every sentence the Duke proves himself more slippery. This last comment is also foolish, and thus we are torn between conflicting emotions. We are glad to see the Duke outwitted, as he embraces Proteus as "Love's firm votary" (III, ii, 58), an ironic echo of Valentine's earlier remark (I, i, 51–52). But that Proteus is the successful plotter takes away our pleasure. At this point we want all confusions resolved and all characters punished.

The male characters, that is. Our antipathy grows during Act IV, scene i, in which Valentine is accosted in the forest by thieves, but then embraced after claiming to have killed a man, and to be living regretfully for the act. The entire situation seems forced, a gimmick to keep Valentine occupied away from the court. Meanwhile, outside the Duke's palace, Julia, as Sebastian, joins Proteus. The gambit of a woman dressing in men's clothes is used often in the comedies, for the obvious reason that all women's roles were played by boys. But thematically the maneuver gives Shakespeare opportunity for creating scenes of great pathos. Often the disguised women find themselves privy to conversations they are not meant to hear, and their being trapped in their role prevents them from reacting honestly. Thus they must repress feeling, and our sympathy for their plight increases.

Such is the case here. Before Julia enters, Proteus has what may be a pang of conscience:

> Already have I been false to Valentine,
> And now I must be as unjust to Thurio:
> Under the color of commending him,

I have access my own love to prefer—
But Silvia is too fair, too true, too holy,
To be corrupted with my worthless gifts.

                                                        (IV, ii, 1–6)

Whether he is stricken by guilt or his own inability is uncertain. Nonetheless, when Julia enters, she overhears Proteus's eloquent song, and her gloom is apparent to the Host (IV, i, 54–56). The subsequent encounter between Proteus and Silvia, overheard by the disguised Julia, is painful for her and us.

At first Silvia completely dismisses Proteus's affections:

I am so far from granting thy request,
That I despise thee for thy wrongful suit,
And by and by intend to chide myself
Even for this time I spend talking to thee.

                                                        (IV, ii, 101–104)

Desperate, Proteus lies seemingly without conscience:

I grant, sweet love, that I did love a lady;
But she is dead.

                                                        (IV, ii, 105–106)

As Proteus continues his claims of love, Silvia begins to capitulate, almost against her will consenting to Proteus's request for a picture of her:

I am very loath to be your idol, sir;
But since your falsehood shall become you well
To worship shadows and adore false shapes.
Send to me in the morning, and I'll send it;
And so, good rest.

                                                        (IV, ii, 128–132)

Perhaps we should understand the beauty of his earlier song and this triumph as evidence of some decency within him. Julia's closing remark reveals her helplessness:

Not so; but it hath been the longest night
That e'er I watch'd, and the most heaviest.

                                                        (IV, ii, 139–140)

Her speech reflects part of the problem with this play. The mixed-up lovers are fundamentally comic, but the fineness of the women set off against the foolishness of the men lends a melancholy to the proceedings. Such unhappiness underlies much of Shakespearean comedy, but in other plays it is leavened by the likability of the men. Here that attribute is lacking, and thus the comedy is blunted.

In scene iii Sir Eglamour (not the unseen suitor of Act I, scene ii) agrees to help Silvia escape from Milan to live with Valentine. His courtly ways are an effective counterpoint to the unattractive scheming of the other men in the play. So is Launce's tale of his loyalty to his dog in scene iv. But the second part of this scene, wherein Proteus and Julia (still as Sebastian) speak, is a high point of the play.

Julia tries to bring Proteus to his senses. He appears to have a momentary pang of guilt when he says of Julia "I think she lives" (IV, iv, 75), and this admission emboldens Julia, who tries to guide him from his current love and back to her:

> Because methinks that she lov'd you as well
> As do you love your lady Silvia:
> She dreams on him that has forgot her love;
> You dote on her that cares not for your love.
> 'Tis pity love should be so contrary;
> And thinking on it makes me cry "alas!"
>
> (IV, iv, 79–84)

The moment anticipates the best of Shakespeare's comedies. Julia cannot reveal her identity, she cannot become angry with Proteus, and she cannot say much of what she feels. Instead, in the comic predicament of disguise, she must offer touching, if indirect, remarks that still fail to move Proteus as much as she and the audience would wish.

But Proteus remains obsessed, and gives her the ring and message for Silvia. Then he departs to leave Julia to her own unhappiness:

> Alas, poor fool, why do I pity him
> That with his very heart despiseth me?
> Because he loves her, he despiseth me;
> Because I love him, I must pity him.
>
> (IV, iv, 93–96)

The complexity of her feelings reflects the dilemma of many of Shakespeare's women. They love for reasons they often do not understand, and such love often goes for a long time unrequited. Even when the men finally respond, the women may still be discontent. But they must carry on. Their capacity for affection is almost beyond fulfillment, and often their partners for life can satisfy only a small portion of their needs.

When Silvia and Julia (as Sebastian) finally meet, they transcend Julia's disguise to form a bond. Silvia is shocked at Proteus's gift of the ring (IV, iv, 133–137), for she knows it was given to him by Julia. Then Silvia inquires about Julia herself, and "Sebastian" replies subtly:

> She hath been fairer, madam, than she is:
> When she did think my master lov'd her well,
> She, in my judgment, was as fair as you . . .
>
> (IV, iv, 149–151)

We smile at Julia's combination of cattiness and wistfulness. She is not angry at Silvia, but something within Julia drives her to establish her own worth, and she does so at length (IV, iv, 158–173). Julia's words move Silvia as well:

> Here, youth, there is my purse; I give thee this
> For they sweet mistress' sake, because thou lov'st her.
>
> (IV, iv, 176–177)

Julia's decency and lovingness shine through her deception so that even Silvia is taken with her. This motif pervades Shakespearean comedy: an individual's nature cannot be truly hidden, no matter what the outward appearance.

When Julia is left alone to ponder Silvia's picture, her brave front fades:

> O thou senseless form,
> Thou shalt be worshipp'd, kiss'd, lov'd, and ador'd;
> And were there sense in his idolatry,
> My substance should be statue in thy stead.
>
> (IV, iv, 198–201)

Her sadness is one more element that darkens this play.

Act V offers a problematic resolution. In scene i Sir Eglamour helps Silvia escape, and in scene ii the Duke, Proteus, Thurio, and Julia follow into the forest. The departure for the chase allows Thurio to reveal his true nature:

> Why, this it is to be a peevish girl,
> That flies her fortune when it follows her.
> I'll after, more to be reveng'd on Eglamour
> Than for the love of reckless Silvia.
>
> (V, ii, 49–52)

He cannot believe that she is not as impressed by his money as he is. Suspense builds, though, as Proteus and Julia hurry right behind, each desperate to locate Silvia. She, meanwhile, is taken prisoner by the outlaws, while Eglamour apparently scampers for his own safety. His courtly manners do not cover his cowardice.

In scene iv Valentine enters, mourning his lost love, but when he hears a hubbub coming towards him, he takes strategic cover. Proteus still cannot see the error of his ways, and continues to solicit Silvia's love:

> Unhappy were you madam, ere I came;
> But by my coming I have made you happy.
>
> (V, iv, 29–30)

Silvia continues to insist on her love for Valentine, and we feel Proteus growing more manic:

> O, 'tis the curse in love, and still approv'd,
> When women cannot love where they're belov'd.
>
> (V, iv, 43–44)

At this point he scorns the entire tradition of courtly love. As a last resort Silvia claims that Proteus is betraying Valentine, his "true friend" (V, iv, 53), but now Proteus rejects even that revered bond: "In love/ Who respects friend?" (V, iv, 53–54). Finally, consumed with lust or ardor, Proteus threatens rape:

"I'll force thee yield to my desire" (V, iv, 59). He has reached a point of madness. Here Valentine steps forward to accuse his friend of treachery:

> Proteus,
> I am sorry I must never trust thee more,
> But count the world a stranger for thy sake.
> The private wound is deepest: O time most accurst!
> 'Mongst all foes that a friend should be the worst!
>
> (V, iv, 68–72)

Now follow two twists that leave often audiences dissatisfied. First, Proteus has a sudden change of heart:

> My shame and guilt confounds me.
> Forgive me, Valentine; if hearty sorrow
> Be a sufficient ransom for offense,
> I render't here: I do as truly suffer
> As e'er I did commit.
>
> (V, iv, 73–77)

Is such a shift of personality credible? It is if we see Proteus's earlier changes as equally sudden. His story is that of a young man who becomes possessed by desire and thereby loses all reason, including his bond to his best friend. He cheats, lies, and bullies, and in his passion almost rapes Silvia. Then, in one flash of reality, he sees the damage he has done to himself and others, and relents. Repentance comes over him as abruptly as did infatuation.

The second awkward moment is Valentine's immediate acceptance of this apology and his subsequent peculiar gift: "All that was mine in Silvia I give thee" (V, iv, 83). Valentine's gesture may be taken as manifestation of the Renaissance ideal of supreme male friendship, but even so, his surrender of Silvia appears unreasonable. Yet we should remember that Valentine, a former skeptic about love and shaken by his experience during this course of events, knows the romantically impetuous nature of his friend. Therefore Valentine's willingness to step aside is consistent with his character from the start.

Julia's fainting at Valentine's offer inspires the revelation of identity, and the last 100 lines of the play are marked by forgiveness and reconciliation. After Julia removes her disguise, Proteus comes to his senses and realizes that she is actually the woman with whom he belongs:

> What is in Silvia's face, but I may spy
> More fresh in Julia's with a constant eye?
>
> (V, iv, 114–115)

He means to compliment Julia, but the back-handed slap at Silvia partially undoes Proteus's claim of devotion by implying that it is based partly on his pleasure in rejecting Silvia. Thurio then steps forward to claim Silvia (V, iv, 125), but under Valentine's threats withdraws his demand, with the pathetic excuse that since she no longer cares for him, he no longer has interest in her (V, iv, 132–

135). The feebleness of Thurio's affections may cast a kinder light on the intense if ill-directed passions of Proteus and Valentine.

One odd component of the scene is that Silvia says nothing during the exchanges of affection. Perhaps Proteus's threatened assault has left her beyond words. In any case, even the Duke forgives Valentine, and also pardons the band of thieves in the forest. Such generosity springing forth so fast seems artificial, but the theme of forgiveness as the ultimate gesture of humanity returns again and again in Shakespeare's comedies. Also notable are Valentine's last lines:

> Come Proteus, 'tis your penance but to hear
> The story of your loves discovered;
> That done, our day of marriage shall be yours,
> One feast, one house, one mutual happiness.

(V, iv, 170–173)

Such unity of emotion emerges at the end of almost every comedy.

The Two Gentlemen of Verona presents problems of characterization, but these diminish if the play is regarded as a work about obsession. According to that perspective, the characters' sharp turns of thought and emotion become dramatically coherent, as does the generally gloomy tone. The sophistication with which the women, especially Julia, are drawn suggests Shakespeare's mature comedies. Most important, the play has few elements of farce. Instead, the turmoil endured by the central figures grows out of both circumstance and personality, and that strategy is the mark of a master dramatist.

SUGGESTIONS FOR FURTHER READING

Danby, John. "Shakespeare Criticism and *Two Gentlemen of Verona.*" *Critical Quarterly* 2 (1960): 309–321.

Lindenbaum, Peter. "Education in *The Two Gentlemen of Verona.*" *Studies in English Literature* 15 (1974): 229–244.

Perry, Thomas. "Proteus, Wry-Transformed Traveller." *Shakespeare Quarterly* 5 (1954): 33–40.

Thompson, Karl F. "Shakespeare's Romantic Comedies." *PMLA* 67 (1952): 1079–1093.

Velie, Alan R. *Shakespeare's Repentance Plays: The Search for an Adequate Form.* Rutherford, N.J.: Fairleigh Dickinson University Press, 1972.

Weimann, R. "Laughing With the Audience: *The Two Gentlemen of Verona and the Popular Tradition of Comedy.*" *Shakespeare Survey* 22 (1970): 35–42.

LOVE'S LABOR'S LOST

Of all Shakespeare's plays, this one is in some ways the most remote. No specific literary source has been found. Instead several characters are likely modeled after contemporary celebrities, and a substantial portion of the dialogue is satire of literary and poetic fashions of the playwright's day. Parody of topicalities, however, rarely lasts beyond the immediate time. Still, for our purpose, the examination of character, the play offers rewards, for the figures at the center of the comedy reflect several of Shakespeare's major themes.

The opening lines set the tone. They clarify that the King's goal is to make himself and his colleagues "heirs of all eternity" (I, i, 7), and such vanity makes us regard the rest of his speech none too seriously. The King then decrees that his court will become a sanctuary for his three colleagues:

> Your oaths are pass'd, and now subscribe your names,
> That his own hand may strike his honor down
> That violates the smallest branch herein.
> If you are arm'd to do, as sworn to do,
> Subscribe to your deep oaths, and keep it too.
>
> (I, i, 19–23)

The convoluted, pompous language clarifies the personality of the King and also suggests that his scheme of remaining in isolation for three years is ill-conceived. To deny all company is to force unnaturalness on oneself, and we suspect that the foolishness of the King's directive is soon to become apparent.

Berowne realizes this truth immediately and protests that they will be denying themselves the company of women (I, i, 47–48), but he is willing to play along:

> . . . all delights are vain, but that most vain
> Which, with pain purchas'd, doth inherit pain:
> As, painfully to pore upon a book
> To see the light of truth, while truth the while
> Doth falsely blind the eyesight of his look.
>
> (I, i, 72–76)

He resounds with the key theme of this play: the egoism of the major characters, especially the men. They are completely absorbed by their own values. Berowne recognizes the pretension, but he himself is subject to such affectation, as his language reflects and his behavior reveals. For the moment, though, he is a voice of moderation in a chorus of extremes.

The oaths the four men swear reach a climax with their plans to deny themselves all contact with women (I, i, 129–132). Berowne again points out the absurdity, noting first that the King himself is soon to meet with the daughter of the French King. That aspect of the decree is therefore abandoned. However, before the other rules are enforced, Berowne inquires: "But is there no quick recreation granted?" (I, i, 161). Perhaps he hopes for a final fling. The King answers that one potential source of entertainment, Don Armado of Spain, is nearby:

> One who the music of his own vain tongue
> Doth ravish like enchanting harmony;
> A man of complements, whom right and wrong
> Have chose as umpeer of their mutiny.

(I, i, 166–169)

The King points out Armado's pretensions, but as often in Shakespeare, a speaker who condemns another fails to recognize the same weaknesses in himself.

With the entrance of Dull and Costard, the tone temporarily changes. Dull's first lines indicate that he is prone to the corruptions of language that characterize Bottom (*A Midsummer Night's Dream*) and Dogberry (*Much Ado About Nothing*):

> I myself reprehend his own person, for I am
> his Grace's farborough; but I would see his own
> person in flesh and blood.

(I, i, 183–185)

Such gaucherie also sets off the linguistic bombast to follow. The pedants and other purveyors of nonsense may be more sophisticated than Dull, but all are objects of Shakespeare's ridicule. In fact, the aristocrats may be more so, for they ought to be cognizant of their foolishness. Dull can know no better.

His task at the moment is bringing in Costard, who has been accused of dallying with a maid named Jaquenetta, a crime delineated in overblown prose in a letter from the very same Armado:

> "So it is, besieged with sablecolored
> melancholy, I did commend the black oppressing
> humor to the most wholesome physic of
> thy health-giving air; and as a gentleman, betook
> myself to walk . . . "

(I, i, 231–235)

Costard has an excuse: " . . . it is the manner of a man to speak to a woman . . . " (I, i, 209–210), but the King remains unimpressed by what the audience knows to be truth. Costard's punishment is to serve Armado (I, i, 304–305), who in scene ii is revealed to be unbearably pompous, a version of the braggart soldier from Roman comedy yet humorously vulnerable to his servant's jibes. For instance, when Armado explains "I have promised to study three years with the Duke" (I, ii, 35–36), Moth replies, "You may do it in an hour, sir" (I, ii, 37). Armado also reveals that he is in love with the maid Jaquenetta:

> Boy, I do love that country girl that I took
> in the park with the rational hind Costard. She
> deserves well.
>
> (I, ii, 117–119)

But when she enters, Jaquenetta treats him with the same disrespect as does his servant. "I will tell thee wonders" (I, ii, 139), he boasts. "With that face?" (I, ii, 140), she answers. But Armado is blind to her distaste. Like the other characters, he is too preoccupied with his own concerns to grasp the feelings of others.

Yet the audience enjoys his foppery for several reasons. One, we delight in seeing a man of his social and literary pretension in love with a woman who belittles him:

> I will hereupon confess I am in love; and
> as it is base for a soldier to love, so I am in love with
> a base wench.
>
> (I, ii, 57–59)

Two, we recognize the hypocrisy of someone who is subject to the same passions he decries in others:

> Love is a familiar; Love is a devil; there
> is no evil angel but Love.
>
> (I, ii, 172–173)

And three, we know that we shall continue to be amused by his avalanche of words, which occasionally include something memorable:

> Cupid's
> butt-shaft is too hard for Hercules' club, and therefore
> too much odds for a Spaniard's rapier. The first
> and second cause will not serve my turn; the passado
> he respects not; the duello he regards not: his dis-
> grace is to be called boy, but his glory is to sub-
> due men.
>
> (I, ii, 175–181)

Armado is also one example of the topicality in this play. He has been suggested to be a parody of Sir Walter Raleigh, an enemy of Spain who married the commoner Elizabeth Throckmorton, or to be a portrait of Antonio Perez, the former secretary of Philip II of Spain. Perez, who lived in England for more than two years, was a homosexual and notorious snob, and thus Armado's affair with the maid may be considered an inside joke. Even Armado's name, which sounds like "Armada," has satiric overtones that would have pleased a sophisticated Elizabethan audience.

The play is filled with such references, and how precisely Shakespeare meant them to reflect actual people is uncertain. Armado has also been suggested to be a satiric portrait of playwright John Lyly. Holofernes is probably a version of either the scholar John Florio or Shakespeare's own schoolmaster Thomas Jenkins. Boyet may be a parody of George Chapman, poet, playwright and translator of *The Iliad*. Other possible models for characters include Thomas Nashe and Robert Greene. The names of Berowne and his two colleagues, Dumaine and Longaville, belong to actual Frenchmen. Intriguing though these speculations may be, more important are the universal targets of Shakespeare's satire: pomposity and hypocrisy. They are timeless.

In Act II we meet the women of the play, and they are well matched with the men, although, as usual in Shakespeare's comedies, more sensitive and perceptive than their male counterparts. For instance, the Princess, who knows of the King's vow against the presence of women, immediately shows herself worldly about human nature and love:

> Beauty is bought by judgment of the eye,
> Not utt'red by base sale of chapmen's tongues.
> I am less proud to hear you tell my worth
> Than you much willing to be counted wise
> In spending your wit in the praise of mine.

(II, i, 15–19)

Her practical voice is welcome contrast to the fraudulent and high-flown romanticism of the men.

The women are also conscious of the personalities of the men, and each woman recites the surface attractions of the one she has selected. In the midst of such idolatry, the Princess maintains her detachment:

> God bless my ladies! are they all in love,
> That every one her own hath garnished
> With such bedecking ornaments of praise?

(II, i, 77–79)

In her tone is the resilience and tough-mindedness that characterizes the most striking of Shakespeare's women, such as Rosalind (*As You Like It*), Viola (*Twelfth Night*), and Beatrice (*Much Ado About Nothing*). All are independent spirits, confident and vigorous in speech and action.

Such energy is apparent when the King greets her: "Fair Princess, welcome to the court of Navarre" (II, i, 90). She has already been informed by Boyet that because of the King's vow, she and her ladies will have to lodge "in the field" (II, i, 85), and she is unwilling to tolerate this order passively:

"Fair" I give you back again, and "welcome"
I have not yet. The roof of this court is too high to
be yours, and welcome to the wide fields too base to
be mine.

(II, i, 91–94)

The attraction of this response is evident by how quickly the King is won over.
The problem of the 100,000 crowns owed by the Princess's father, or rather the
absence of proof that the loan has been repaid (II, i, 157–159), demands that
certain proprieties be observed, but the King of Navarre nonetheless seems
smitten:

You may not come, fair Princess, within my gates,
But here without you shall be so receiv'd
As you shall deem yourself lodg'd in my heart,
Though so denied fair harbor in my house.

(II, i, 171–174)

The firm celibate of Act I is wavering, as Boyet notes later:

Why, all his behaviors did make their retire
To the court of his eye, peeping thorough desire:
His heart like an agot with your print impressed,
Proud with his form, in his eye pride expressed;
His tongue, all impatient to speak and not see,
Did stumble with haste in his eyesight to be;
All senses to that sense did make their repair,
To feel only looking on fairest of fair . . .

(II, i, 234–241)

Equally taken are his colleagues, each of whom returns to inquire of Boyet
about one of the ladies. We soon realize that all the men and women are infatuated, but their love is expressed solely through wit and verbal play, through
clever rhyme and imagery. Their passion, therefore, lacks substance. The characters have charm, and we enjoy seeing them squirm under their own desires,
but these figures are vacuous. This exposition builds to the turnabout in Act V,
when such shallowness strikes the women hard.

From mild affectation the play moves to the absurd pretensions of Don Armado, who in Act III, scene i, accepts advice from Moth on matters of the heart.
The pervasive imagery of music and dance is reflective of the world of this play,
in which courtship is a stylized, insubstantial ritual, and we visualize Moth
putting both himself and Armado through a series of physical contortions to
communicate proper techniques. Yet Armado's own ludicrous sentiments remain
the comic highlight:

A most acute juvenal, volable and free of grace!
By thy favor, sweet welkin, I must sigh in thy face:

Most rude melancholy, valor gives thee place.

(III, i, 66–68)

Through such feigned emotion Armado turns himself into a parody of Renaissance style. Costard is brought into the proceedings, assigned by Armado to
deliver a love letter to Jaquenetta, but when Berowne gives Costard a different
letter to take to Rosaline, the mix-up is ensured. Such inevitability takes away
from the plot of the play, which concentrates more on style than story. The work
should therefore be regarded as a portrait of the quality of a certain level of life,
and therefore the intricacies of circumstances are comparatively unimportant.
What matters is how characters conduct themselves: how they act and speak,
how they weigh value and morality, and how they function in the artificial
environment they have established.

An example is Berowne's soliloquy at the end of Act III:

O, and I, forsooth, in love! I, that have been love's whip,
A very beadle to a humorous sigh,
A critic, nay, a night-watch constable,
A domineering pedant o'er the boy,
Than whom no mortal so magnificent!

(III, i, 174–178)

He is both tormented and enthralled by his passion, embarrassed that after so
many years of scorning love he is now subject to its irresistible attraction. Then
his mockery of other lovers turns into self-mockery. He knows that he will be
ridiculous, but he accepts his foolishness. Even more telling, Berowne has no
idea why he loves this woman:

What! I love, I sue, I seek a wife—
A woman, that is like a German [clock],
Still a-repairing, ever out of frame,
And never going aright, being a watch,
But being watch'd that it may still go right!

(III, i, 189–193)

The mystery of his affections amuses and annoys him. Yet he manages to
reconcile himself:

And I to sigh for her, to watch for her,
To pray for her, go to! It is a plague
That Cupid will impose for my neglect
Of his almighty dreadful little might.
Well, I will love, write, sigh, pray, sue, groan:
Some men must love my lady, and some Joan.

(III, i, 200–205)

Berowne's bemused but healthy perspective is a great relief after the posturings
of Armado.

In Act IV the Princess further reveals her intellect and wit by bantering at the expense of the Forester. Within her remarks, however, lie truths about attempts to achieve eminence:

> Glory grows guilty of detested crimes,
> When for fame's sake, for praise, an outward part,
> We bend to that the working of the heart;
> As I for praise alone now seek to spill
> The poor deer's blood, that my heart means no ill.
>
> (IV, i, 31–35)

She communicates a sad cognizance of the transience of things, especially in light of the Princess's holding a bow that suggests Cupid's weapon. Thus the hunt for "deer" is paralleled with the hunt for human love. Such sentiments set up the ending of the play, when reality supersedes the games.

Then Costard delivers the first of his misplaced missives, and Boyet reads Armado's letter aloud. The prose is grotesquely convoluted and earns appropriate scorn from the Princess:

> What plume of feathers is he that indited this letter?
> What vane? What weathercock? Did you ever hear better?
>
> (IV, i, 94–95)

Nonetheless, the letter inspires from the listeners an extended byplay, in which the imagery of shooting and targets is blended with sexual implications. The episode emphasizes the wit of the participants as well as their superficiality.

In scene ii the distortion of language is carried to new heights by Holofernes the pedant:

> The preyful Princess pierc'd and prick'd a pretty pleasing pricket;
> Some say a sore, but not a sore, till now made sore with shooting.
>
> (IV, ii, 56–57)

Such bizarre alliteration is entertaining, and to overestimate its gravity would be wrong, but we also realize the emptiness of the speaker, along with that of his colleague, Nathaniel. Their style is contrasted by that of the letter from Berowne, whose simple dignity reveals far greater depths of feeling:

> If knowledge be the mark, to know thee shall suffice;
> Well learned is that tongue that well can thee commend,
> All ignorant that soul that sees thee without wonder;
> Which is to me some praise that I thy parts admire.
>
> (IV, ii, 111–114)

He takes the images of knowledge and targets and turns them into poetry. Such is the difference between legitimate feeling and pedantic affectation.

Act IV, scene iii is a scene of great charm as well as one where character and theme join. Berowne enters to bemoan his fate: "I will not love; if I do, hang me; i' faith, I will not." He is aware of the duality of his love as well as his foolishness and vulnerability. Yet he is helpless to resolve the dilemma. His only solace would be if his three companions were similarly possessed: "I would not care a pin, if the other three were in" (IV, iii, 18). His wishes are soon fulfilled.

First the King enters, reading a poem intended for the Princess:

> Do but behold the tears that swell in me,
> And they thy glory through my grief will show.
> But do not love thyself, then thou [wilt] keep
> My tears for glasses, and still make me weep.

(IV, iii, 35–38)

He, too, wallows in the melancholy of the love-sick suitor. Longaville then enters, and the King, like Berowne, takes his own place of hiding, while Longaville reads a sonnet that justifies his love:

> Vows for thee broke deserve not punishment.
> A woman I forswore, but I will prove,
> Thou being a goddess, I forswore not thee.

(IV, iii, 61–62)

His approach is more intellectual, closer to the tradition of the metaphysical poets, as he plays with contradiction to explain his love. Finally Dumaine enters to muse over his poem, another expression of love and suffering, although the least mature effort in this episode.

What adds to the comedy of the scene are the ironic comments of the listeners, each of whom imagines himself hidden from the others. Eventually all are revealed, but Berowne is the one who most strongly mocks the others:

> O, what a scene of fool'ry have I seen,
> Of signs, of groans, of sorrow, and of teen.

(IV, iii, 161–162)

The inevitable then occurs, as Berowne's own letter to Rosaline is exposed by Costard and Jaquenetta, and the author is forced to confess and seek pardon from the others:

> We cannot cross the cause why we were born;
> Therefore of all hands must we be forsworn.

(IV, iii, 214–215)

For the next several lines he defends his actions and affections.

Part of the joy of this scene is its harmlessness. We never feel malevolence on anyone's part. Instead we feel a sense of camaraderie, a jollity from four men who have discovered that their own weaknesses are shared by friends. As the King says: "But what of this, are we not all in love?" (IV, iii, 278). The lightheartedness also sets up the final scene, when events force the participants to weigh the substance of their lives.

The climax here is a lengthy address by Berowne, who puts in perspective the follies the men have imposed on themselves:

From women's eyes this doctrine I derive:
They are the ground, the books, the academes,
From whence doth spring the true Promethean fire.

> (IV, iii, 298–300)

Then he repeats the thought fifty lines later (IV, iii, 347–351). So much for the King's ambition to achieve a purely scholarly environment. Berowne also emphasizes the naturalness of relations between men and women:

Then when ourselves we see in ladies eyes,
Within ourselves,
Do we not likewise see our learning there?

> (IV, iii, 312–314)

[Let] us once lose our oaths to find ourselves,
Or else we lose ourselves to keep our oaths.

> (IV, iii, 358–359)

His theme is one familiar from other comedies of Shakespeare: self-discovery through love.

This scene of revelation and the unmasking of hypocrisy is followed by one in which hypocrisy is maintained, as Holofernes, Nathaniel, and Dull, soon to be joined by Armado, plan a presentation for the court. Their self-importance is ridiculous, and none more so than Armado's:

By the world, I
recount no fable: some certain special honors it pleaseth
his greatness to impart to Armado, a soldier, a man of
travel, that hath seen the world; but let that pass.

> (V, i, 105–108)

This gathering sets up the final play-within-a-play, which is mercilessly mocked. Here we realize that it deserves no better treatment.

The final scene of the play is long, yet clear in theme and structure. It is a proper climax to a play built upon the superficialities of its characters. At the beginning the Princess and her friends muse on tokens offered by their suitors, but gloom quickly intrudes when the memory of Katherine's sister is raised:

He made her melancholy, sad, and heavy,
And so she died.

> (V, ii, 14–15)

They resolve to remain "light" (V, ii, 15) so as to avoid the potential pain of a disappointing love. Yet by thus far keeping their love on such a level, the women find themselves frustrated by the foolish gifts and excessive poetry of the men. Rosaline speaks for all when she wishes she could make Berowne suffer for the games he plays:

How I would make him fawn, and beg, and seek,
And wait the season, and observe the times,

> And spend his prodigal wits in bootless rhymes,
> And shape his service wholly to my device,
> And make him proud to make me proud that jests!
>
> (V, ii, 62–66)

We sense her fury at a woman's socially determined role in the courtship ritual. We also sense her impatience at the lack of depth in the relationships the women and men have maintained, for she seeks genuine affection. All these sentiments prepare us for the final twist of the plot.

When Boyet discloses the disguises their suitors will wear (V, ii, 94–118), the women resolve to torment the men by masking themselves. The Princess explains the reasoning behind the scheme:

> The effect of my intent is to cross theirs:
> They do it but in mockery merriment,
> And mock for mock is only my intent.
>
> (V, ii, 138–140)

That she bothers to explain herself suggests that her scheme has a crueler purpose. And in light of the comments above, that purpose is to express anger.

The men enter disguised as Muscovites, a costume typical of court masquerades, and the women enjoy themselves by flirting, then denying the suitors' advances. Boyet in particular relishes the spectacle:

> The tongues of mocking wenches are as keen
> As the razor's edge invisible,
> Cutting a smaller hair than may be seen;
> Above the sense of sense, so sensible
> Seemeth their conference, their conceits have wings
> Fleeter than arrows, bullets, wind, thought, swifter things.
>
> (V, ii, 256–261)

In his own way he embodies the spirit of this play. He is an ironic chorus, mocking everyone's aspirations and values. Yet he gives no evidence of being anything but a commentator, capable only of belittling others. Though this role is entertaining to himself and to us, we recognize his insubstantiality.

His pose eventually arouses anger from the men. But before they return in normal dress, Rosaline suggests the women keep up their attitude:

> Let us complain to them what fools were here,
> Disguis'd like Muscovites, in shapeless gear . . .
>
> (V, ii, 302–303)

Then Boyet acts as go-between for the men, announcing them to the women offstage. Berowne has no stomach for this privilege:

> This fellow pecks up wit as pigeons pease,
> And utters it again when God doth please.
> . . . The ladies call him sweet;

The stairs as he treads on them kiss his feet.

(V, ii, 315–316, 329–330)

Although the suitors must endure the taunts and jibes of the women, the couples will eventually unite, while Boyet will be left alone. His detachment spares him a certain unhappiness, but his failure to risk pain means that he will never know the joy the couples share.

The women return to resume their game, and they play it for all they can, mocking male pretensions, until Berowne surrenders:

O, never will I trust to speeches penn'd.
Nor to the motion of a schoolboy's tongue,
Nor never come in vizard to my friend.
Nor woo in rhyme, like a blind harper's song!
Taffeta phrases, silken terms precise,
Three-pil'd hyperboles, spruce affection,
Figures pedantical—these summer flies
Have blown me full of maggot ostentation . . .
Henceforth my wooing mind shall be express'd
In russet yeas and honest kersey noes.

(V, ii, 402–413)

His rejection of poetic pretension serves almost as a moral for the play. Before long the men realize that they have been victims of a prank (V, ii, 459–462), and all is forgiven.

The Pageant of the Nine Worthies follows, and it anticipates the more amusing play inside *A Midsummer Night's Dream*. We notice here how eagerly the men in the audience heckle the performers. The women are more tolerant, but the men seem to derive some perverse satisfaction by transferring their degradation onto someone else. The two sharpest wits, Boyet and Berowne, even turn from antagonists into allies, as the latter says in response to one remark: "Well said, old mocker. I must needs be friends with thee" (V, ii, 549). The implication is that the men, ever shallow, find a bond only by attacking others. The women, on the other hand, are moved by the efforts of the players, or perhaps by the grandeur of the characters. One remark of the Princess is characteristic: "Speak, brave Hector, we are much delighted" (V, ii, 665).

Even as we laugh at the pretenses of the actors, we are reminded of the foolishness of the suitors and the roles they played to win the women of their choice. Similarly, we think of the women and the games they played to humiliate the men. Affectation takes place offstage and on, vanity and ego rule in both arenas, and the performances are merely different versions of the same plot.

The merriment is interrupted by a rare tragic moment in Shakespearean comedy: the announcement of the death of the Princess's father. As the characters begin to reflect on the situation, we grasp the uselessness of so much of what has occurred. Berowne put matters in perspective:

> For your fair sakes have we neglected time,
> Play'd foul play with our oaths. Your beauty, ladies,
> Hath much deformed us, fashioning our humors
> Even to the opposed end of our intents . . .
>
> (V, ii, 755–758)

He even points out the fundamental deception they have played not only on the ladies but on themselves as well:

> We to ourselves prove false,
> By being once false for ever to be true
> To those that make us both—fair ladies, you;
> And even that falsehood, in itself a sin,
> Thus purifies itself and turns to grace.
>
> (V, ii, 772–776)

He tries to excuse his shallowness. But the Princess and the other ladies will have no apologies. The men are assigned to complete various trials for a year, after which time the women will consider capitulating. Berowne is asked to endure the greatest suffering:

> You shall this twelvemonth term from day to day
> Visit the speechless sick, and still converse
> With groaning wretches; and your task shall be,
> With all the fierce endeavour of your wit,
> To enforce the pained impotent to smile.
>
> (V, ii, 850–854)

Rosaline reasons that Berowne has been the most scornful of love and emotion (V, ii, 841–846); therefore he should have to face reality most severely. She wonders whether the sick will respond to his humor:

> But if they will not, throw away that spirit,
> And I shall find you empty of that fault,
> Right joyful of your reformation.
>
> (V, ii, 867–869)

She will be grateful to find a man who does not need to hide behind jests. Even Armado is changed, for he promises to farm for three years to win Jaquenetta (V, ii, 883–884). The purpose of all these trials is to force the participants to think beyond the immediate physical pleasures of their relationships and to seek more purified and spiritual qualities.

The play ends with a melancholy song about the passing of the seasons. It emphasizes the ephemerality of human aspiration, placing the pain of human existence as part of a grander continuum of birth, life, and death. Our sense is that overlooking all the pageant of life is the spectre of mortality.

Such a conclusion may seem out of place in a comedy devoted almost completely to parody and nonsense. But the ending is curiously appropriate. For almost an entire play we have enjoyed the triviality of a life lived within the narrow bounds of aristocratic and aesthetic egoism. How better to understand the inconsequence of that existence then to see it set against the inevitable pain of reality.

SUGGESTIONS FOR FURTHER READING

Anderson, J. J. "The Morality of *Love's Labour's Lost*." *Shakespeare Survey* 24 (1974): 55–62.

Carroll, William C. *The Great Feast of Language in* Love's Labour's Lost. Princeton: Princeton University Press, 1976.

Draper, John W. "Tempo in *Love's Labour's Lost*." *English Studies* 29 (1948): 129–137.

Goldstein, N. L. "*Love's Labour's Lost* and the Renaissance Vision of Love." *Shakespeare Quarterly* 25 (1974): 935–950.

Greene, Thomas M. "*Love's Labour's Lost*: The Grace of Society." *Shakespeare Quarterly* 22 (1971): 315–328.

McLay, Catherine. "The Dialogues of Spring and Winter: A Key to *Love's Labour's Lost*." *Shakespeare Quarterly* 18 (1967): 119–127.

Yates, Frances A. *A Study of* Love's Labour's Lost. Cambridge: Cambridge University Press, 1936.

A Midsummer Night's Dream

Here is the first comedy of Shakespeare in which the playwright is in absolute control. The plot, which is Shakespeare's invention, brings together four stories, each of which skillfully intertwines with and reflects the others. The characters, who come from all levels of life, are sharply drawn: laughable, but sympathetic. The language is vivid, and through his poetry the playwright creates a world in which magic and marriage harmonize eloquently.

All these elements combine to dramatize several themes that pervade the comedies. We see the power of imagination in romance as well as parody of romantic convention. We see the pain suffered by women to whom men are foolish, insensitive, and even brutal. We see the self-deception to which people in love are vulnerable. We see the potential tragedy underlying comic complications about love. And we see the glory of marriage as a celebration of the cycle of fertility and affirmation of life.

Theseus and Hippolyta, characters taken from Chaucer's "The Knight's Tale," bring out several of these themes in their opening tableau. They are the embodiment of an elegant couple in love; yet beneath their formal exchange lurks a tension in their relationship. From the start Theseus is impatient:

> Now, fair Hippolyta, our nuptial hour
> Draws on apace. Four happy days bring in
> Another moon; but, O, methinks, how slow
> This old moon [wanes]! She lingers my desires,
> Like to a step-dame, or a dowager,
> Long withering out a young man's revenue.

(I, i, 1–6)

His emphasis on the moon, with its traditional connotations of "lunacy," suggests the disorder to follow as well as the potential madness that in this play characterizes love itself. In addition, the image of the changing phases of the moon intimates the changeableness of the lovers. Finally, the restlessness of his lines reflects his own frustrated energy.

Hippolyta's response invokes the same image, but in a different spirit:

> Four days will quickly steep themselves in night;
> Four nights will quickly dream away the time;
> And then the moon, like to a silver bow
> [New] bent in heaven, shall behold the night
> Of our solemnities.

(I, i, 7–11)

The evenness of her lines, her palliative tone, and the words "dream," "time," "silver," and "heaven" all reflect the controlled romanticism typical of Shakespeare's women.

The plot complications begin with the narrative of Egeus, a father figure who gains no sympathy from us. First he orders Demetrius, Egeus's own choice for his daughter Hermia's husband, to "stand forth" (I, i, 24), and from that point on Egeus tries to manipulate everyone. His description of Lysander's crimes is particularly unconvincing:

> Thou, thou, Lysander, thou hast given her rhymes,
> And interchang'd love-tokens with my child;
> Thou hast by moonlight at her window sung
> With faining voice verses of faining love,
> And stol'n the impression of her fantasy
> With bracelets of thy hair, rings, gawds, conceits,
> Knacks, trifles, nosegays, sweetmeats—messengers
> Of strong prevailment in unhardened youth.

(I, i, 28–35)

Lysander's tactics sound like nothing more than the stereotypical gestures of a young man in the throes of romance, and therefore what may bother Egeus is that such techniques should be successful. However, he mentions Lysander's "faining love," and in the context of what follows that line has intriguing overtones.

In response to Theseus's query and tribute to Demetrius (I, i, 46–52), Hermia proves her mettle with a brief but effective answer: "So is Lysander" (I, i, 53). Then she adds: "I would my father look'd but with my eyes" (I, i, 56). Her energy is clear, and Lysander's standing by dumbly says little for him. True, questions are not coming his way, but his torpidity does not suggest great passion. More important, Hermia's mention of "eyes" and Theseus's echo of the image (I, i, 56–57) establish that the concept of "seeing" will loom important. Characters here are constantly deceived by what they think they view, and they constantly lack "insight," or understanding of what they see. Therefore self-deception is commonplace.

Theseus threatens Hermia with the full power of the law, and his threat temporarily darkens the mood:

> You can endure the livery of a nun,
> For aye to be in shady cloister mew'd,

To live a barren sister all your life,
Chaunting faint hymns to the cold fruitless moon.

(I, i, 70–73)

At this moment his sympathies are uncertain. In any case, Hermia's vigorous rejoinder (I, i, 79–82) indicates that she will not accept her fate meekly, and, as is typical in Shakespeare's comedies, we empathize with the woman, the victim of society's rules that have been determined by males.

Lysander and Demetrius at last contribute to the discussion, but from the start they seem petty. We resent Demetrius for obvious reasons: he pursues a woman who doesn't want him, he interferes with her genuine affection for another man, and he has the support of a father of whom we disapprove. His two lines here are also not encouraging:

Relent, sweet Hermia, and, Lysander, yield,
Thy crazed title to my certain right.

(I, i, 91–92)

He whines, and his putting the issue of love in the context of a "certain" right does not speak well of his romantic inclinations. Lysander's response (I, i, 93–94) shows his capacity for biting wit, but when he has opportunity to express more fully his values, the emphasis is less on his love for Hermia and more on his own stature:

I am, my lord, as well deriv'd as he,
As well possess'd; my love is more than his:
My fortunes every way as fairly rank'd
(If not with vantage) as Demetrius' . . .

(I, i, 99–103)

A few lines later he speaks of his "right" to her. Again, the light of romance is dim. Then he accuses Demetrius of inconstancy for having wooed Helena. The indictment proves powerfully ironic.

Theseus's perspective on the crisis remains unclear, but he does pull Demetrius and Egeus away, claiming that he needs to discuss business with them. Thus Lysander and Hermia are left to formulate their plans and to reveal themselves further to us. From the start of this encounter, Hermia's spirit is ever more apparent, and Lysander seems the respondent rather than the instigator. After she states her anger (I, i, 130–131) he muses on their predicament: "The course of true love never did run smooth . . . " (I, i, 134). Then they indulge in alternating lines. Each one of hers is full of fury, while his are only attempts to soothe (I, i, 136–140). Even his extended response (I, i, 141–149) communicates helplessness rather than dynamism.

Hermia then puts their dilemma in proper context:

If then true lovers have been ever cross'd,
It stands as an edict in destiny.

(I, i, 150–151)

Her words sound like the opening lines of the Chorus in *Romeo and Juliet*, about "star-cross'd lovers" (Prologue, 6). Hermia makes us aware that this story could have serious consequences, and her order to "teach our trial patience" (I, i, 152) suggests her desire to proceed cautiously and avoid fatal errors.

Lysander, though, is more immature, and schemes how they might run away to the woods, where, he discloses, he once met with Helena (I, i, 166). Earlier he chided Demetrius for straying from Hermia. Now Lysander blindly confesses the same crime. Hermia does not appear to notice this slip, but when she swears to meet him and communicates her devotion "By all the vows that ever men have broke . . . " (I, i, 175), we are aware that she knows the character of the man with whom she is dealing. And we share her mistrust.

At this moment Helena conveniently enters, in anguish over her frustrated love for Demetrius. For some reason Lysander reveals his and Hermia's plans to run away:

To-morrow night, when Phoebe doth behold
Her silver visage in the wat'ry glass,
Decking with liquid pearl the bladed grass
(A time that lovers' flights doth still conceal),
Through Athens gates have we devis'd to steal.

(I, i, 209–213)

Perhaps Lysander, who here speaks more alluringly than we have heard before, is trying to torment Helena with news of his elopement. Or perhaps he is trying to entice her to follow and intercept. Surely he makes their escape sound attractive. Hermia adds her own confirmation of the story, then departs, leaving Lysander to offer Helena one more word of encouragement to Helena: "As you dote on him, Demetrius dote on you!" (I, i, 225). Whether this expression is out of sympathy for Helena or a desire to ensure that Demetrius leaves Hermia alone is open to question.

Helena, stranded, pours out her heart for Demetrius, but also focuses on key themes of this play:

Things base and vile, holding no quantity,
Love can transpose to form and dignity.
Love looks not with the eyes but with the mind;
And therefore is wing'd Cupid painted blind.
Nor hath Love's mind of any judgment taste;
Wings, and no eyes, figure unheedy haste;
And therefore is Love said to be a child,

Because in choice he is so oft beguil'd.

(I, i, 232–239)

In the first line, she recalls a theme familiar from other plays: the power of love to transform the human personality. Her next line recalls a comment of Berowne from *Love's Labor's Lost*:

> From women's eyes this doctrine I derive:
> They are the ground, the books, the academes,
> From whence doth spring the true Promethean fire.

(IV, iii, 298–300)

Helena has less faith in appearance. She recognizes that eyes and faces may deceive, and subsequent events confirm her impression. Lastly, she resolves to tell Demetrius of "Hermia's flight" (I, i, 246). Apparently Helena assumes her loyalty will inspire Demetrius's love, but the complications go in another direction. The conflict between the two women also reveals their individual personalities. Hermia, short and dark, is feistier, more of a battler. Helena, tall and fair, is reflective, mournful over past events.

Scene ii introduces us to the "mechanicals," a group of simple laborers, and in particular Nick Bottom, the weaver. They are planning a performance of *The most lamentable comedy and most cruel death of Pyramus and Thisbe*, a story from Ovid that reflects the main action of this play. Most of these men are timid souls, but Bottom has enough intrepidity for all, as he volunteers to play every part in the script. At this moment he is outside the primary plot, but we look forward to seeing him involved. Quince foresees such involvement when he urges his comrades to gather outside town "by moonlight" (I, ii, 102), where no doubt they, too, will be subject to the lunacy that affects others.

The final social stratum appears in the first scene of Act II. Puck, like the rest of the fairies a figure from English folklore, opens the proceedings by inquiring of a fairy where she has traveled: "How now, spirit, whither wander you?" (II, i, 1). And the fairy's answer helps break the earthbound dimensions that have characterized the action thus far:

> Over hill, over dale,
> Thorough bush, thorough brier,
> Over park, over pale,
> Thorough flood, thorough fire,
> I do wander every where,
> Swifter than the moon's sphere . . .

(II, i, 2–7)

From here on, time and place no longer restrict the action of the play. This speech, in combination with many to follow, establishes an atmosphere of magic and wonder that brings the "Dream" of the title to life. Puck further develops this aura when he identifies himself for the fairy:

> I am that merry wanderer of the night.
> I jest to Oberon and make him smile
> When I a fat and bean-fed horse beguile,
> Neighing in likeness of a filly foal . . .

(II, i, 43–46)

He is a practiced confuser of lovers of all types. And the rest of this speech intimates that he unleashes his trickery with manic delight.

When Oberon and Titania enter, their bickering reveals how the jealousies that afflict human men and women flourish in the fairy world as well. Both King and Queen are possessive of the other, and their marital discord has taken the form of natural disorder, as Titania explains:

> But with thy brawls thou hast disturb'd our sport.
> Therefore the winds, piping to us in vain,
> As in revenge, have suck'd up from the sea
> Contagious fogs; which, falling in the land,
> Hath every pelting river made so proud
> That they have overborne their continents.

(II, i, 87–92)

She goes on to describe a series of phenomena that have interfered with "mortal" comfort.

On one hand, Titania's description and imagery communicate the hidden role of the fairies in this play and make us believe in a stage world in which anything is possible. More important, it dramatizes that love, whether among human beings or fairies, is in fact part of the natural cycle; that the celebration of the marriage rite is at heart glorification of the human role in the chain of being.

Titania's jealousy over her adopted changeling boy perturbs Oberon (II, i, 119–121), who wants him for his own attendant, and Oberon decides to take action against her. He orders Puck to retrieve the juice of a magic flower:

> The juice of it on sleeping eyelids laid
> Will make or man or woman madly dote
> Upon the next live creature that it sees.

(II, i, 170–172)

This form of retribution reaffirms the theme of sight, for when Titania awakens she will fall in love with the next creature she "looks upon" (II, i, 179).

The mood of mischief is shattered when Demetrius enters, Helena on his trail. His first line breaks the tone: "I love thee not; therefore pursue me not" (II, i, 188). He is annoyed that someone for whom he has no affection refuses to give up. Oddly, Demetrius never connects that same sentiment to his own relationship with Hermia, whom he pursues and who had told him to leave her alone. Furthermore, in this scene and throughout the play, the denials of love by Demetrius and later by Lysander are always more convincing than the claims of affection. Both articulate their hate more forcefully than they do other emotions, as Demetrius demonstrates here:

Tempt not too much the hatred of my spirit,
For I am sick when I do look on thee.

(II, i, 211–212)

His protestations, however, only further arouse Helena's passion, which has implications beyond this play:

Your wrongs do set a scandal on my sex.
We cannot fight for love, as men may do.
We should be woo'd, and were not made to woo.

(II, i, 240–242)

Her helplessness reminds us of the frustrations of women from other comedies of Shakespeare. Societal rules prevent them from acting according to their wishes, and they are compelled to remain passive in romance. Here, as elsewhere, we feel the torment women undergo, for in these plays their lives are bound up in love. Yet according to the conventions of Shakespeare's day, women are unable to give full rein to their desires.

Helena, incidentally, repeats one of the central linguistic themes of the play when she makes a pun on "woo'd" and "woo." The words should be seen in the context of "wood," for all three sound like "wode," meaning "mad," a quality that may be applied to individuals here as well as to the overall proceedings and the love these characters undergo.

Helena's plea moves Oberon, and he resolves to aid her. But his instructions to Puck to anoint the eyes of "a disdainful youth" (II, i, 261) invite confusion. In fact, both Lysander and Demetrius are disdainful, and thus Puck's error is not only understandable but thematically appropriate.

We should also note Oberon's language at the beginning of this speech. Throughout the play a variety of speakers create scenes through words alone, but none is more beautiful than Oberon's here:

I know a bank where the wild thyme blows,
Where oxlips and the nodding violet grows,
Quite over-canopied with luscious woodbine,
With sweet musk-roses and with eglantine . . .

(II, i, 249–252)

The stages of Shakespeare's era were almost bare of scenery. Thus through language alone does Shakespeare create the magical environment of this play.

In the next scene Titania enters with her fairy contingent, and when she lies down to rest, Oberon squeezes the flower on her eyelids. This magical moment is contrasted by the prosaic entrance of Lysander with Hermia, and his first comment lowers him deeper in our estimation:

> Fair love, you faint with wand'ring in the wood;
> And to speak troth I have forgot our way.
>
> (II, ii, 35–36)

He has managed to lose direction, hardly a sign of acuity. He then suggests they lie down together, but Hermia demurs, adding "Thy love ne'er alter till thy sweet life end" (II, ii, 61). Again she implies doubts about his faithfulness.

Puck then mistakenly puts the magic potion on the sleeping Lysander, who awakens to find Helena, abandoned by Demetrius. Lysander's sudden claims of love are thematically telling:

> Who will not change a raven for a dove?
> The will of man is by his reason sway'd;
> And reason says you are the worthier maid.
> Things growing are not ripe until their season,
> So I, being young, till now ripe not to reason;
> And touching now the point of human skill,
> Reason becomes the marshall to my will,
> And leads me to your eyes, where I o'erlook
> Love's stories written in love's richest book.
>
> (II, ii, 114–122)

His claims are undercut by his actions, for in fact his reason is powerless to determine his will. In addition, he mentions Helena's eyes, reminding us of the fallibility of human vision. He also brings out the natural imagery of the play, the cycles of the seasons and the concept of "ripeness." Finally, we hear in his voice the preoccupation with self, the egoism that dominates both male human lovers. What concerns Lysander here are not Helena's qualities but his own desires to fall in love.

Only when he speaks of his hate for Hermia do his emotions seem legitimate:

> For as a surfeit of the sweetest things
> The deepest loathing to the stomach brings,
> Or as the heresies that men do leave
> Are hated most of those they did deceive,
> So thou, my surfeit and my heresy,
> Of all be hated, but the most of me!
>
> (II, ii, 137–142)

The brutality of his words apparently awakens Hermia, terrified by a dream:

> Lysander, look how I do quake with fear.
> Methought a serpent eat my heart away,
> And you sate smiling at his cruel prey.
>
> (II, ii, 148–150)

She intuits the meanness within Lysander's spirit. Throughout this play several characters, even those under the influence of magic, nonetheless reveal truths of their world. Shakespeare's unspoken implication is that an individual's personality, no matter what the forces that toy with it, inevitably exposes itself. No magic or potion can change a person's fundamental character. Hermia's last line as she races off touches us: "Either death, or you, I'll find immediately" (II, ii, 156). We are not worried that she will die, for we recognize that the fairies hold sway over all, but Hermia's anguish hints at the potential tragedy underneath the story. All resolves happily, but were circumstances slightly different, like those in which Romeo and Juliet find themselves, the unraveling of such a mix-up could be sad indeed.

The action pauses when the mechanicals take the stage to resume rehearsing. Their antics do resound thematically, for they are concerned particularly with making their production as realistic as possible. They even go so far as to decide that one of their players must play the part of "Wall." For them, reality and illusion are separate entities. These men do not grasp how the world of dreams and imagination can have any relation to reality. If a literal wall is not present, then the audience will be unable to imagine one. One theme of Shakespeare's play is the power of imagination to assert itself on reality. Human beings, especially those in love, often choose to accept what they want to see, what they dream they see, far more readily than they accept literal truth.

Bottom temporarily departs the stage, and when he returns under Puck's spell, he wears an ass's head and is, in Quince's word, "translated" (III, i, 119). In his own way Quince hits a central motif of the play: the mutability of human emotion. When Titania awakens, her infatuation both mirrors and mocks the alternating affections of the Athenian men, for she is taken in the same way as they: "So is mine eye enthralled to thy shape . . . " (III, i, 139). Bottom, still a buffoon, responds with a sentiment appropriate to the play:

> Methinks, mistress, you should have little
> reason for that. And yet, to say the truth, reason
> and love keep little company together now-a-days.

> > (III, i, 142–144)

No doubt Bottom is less sophisticated than the Athenian men. Yet in his own way he understands more of life than they do. The men and women in love imagine that they are rational and in control of their will and senses. Bottom understands that human beings have no such mastery, and thus he is at ease with the suggestion that a being such as Titania could fall in love with him. Such an infatuation makes no sense, but then Bottom never expects that it should. Thus as the two exchange puns on "wood" (madness), Bottom comprehends completely. He has the capacity to yield to wonder, and he comfortably adapts when Titania's fairy servants come to wait on him.

In the next scene Puck tells Oberon of Titania's predicament: "My mistress with a monster is in love" (III, ii, 6). And the fairy King delights in her foolishness. But when a bickering Hermia and Demetrius enter, Puck and Oberon realize that Puck has anointed the eyes of the wrong mortal (III, ii, 41–42), and they listen as Hermia spouts vituperative accusations. As is usual in this play, expressions of dislike are more concrete and vivid than those of affection. For instance, Hermia brands Demetrius a liar:

> And has thou kill'd him sleeping? O brave touch!
> Could not a worm, an adder, do so much?
> An adder did it! for with doubler tongue
> Than thine, thou serpent, never adder stung.
>
> (III, ii, 70–73)

After Hermia flees and Demetrius demonstrates his vigor by going to sleep, Puck applies the drops to his eyes. Then Lysander and Helena enter, he violently claiming his love, and she just as violently resisting. His expressions, however, are so extravagant as to be laughable:

> Why should you think that I should woo in scorn?
> Scorn and derision never come in tears.
> Look when I vow, I weep; and vows so born,
> In their nativity all truth appears.
> How can these things in me seem scorn to you,
> Bearing the badge of faith to prove them true?
>
> (III, ii, 122–127)

Even under the influence of the potion, his personality emerges. He cannot speak directly. Instead, his words are smooth but his thoughts fraudulent. The poetry is graceful but deceptive, adjectives that apply equally to Lysander himself. We also enjoy the irony underlying such comments as his claim that ''I had no judgment when to her I swore'' (III, ii, 133). Lysander blindly insists upon his own capacity for rationality.

When Demetrius awakens, his protestations are even more bizarre:

> O Helen, goddess, nymph, perfect, divine!
> To what, my love, shall I compare thine eyne?
> Crystal is muddy. O, how ripe in show
> Thy lips, those kissing cherries, tempting grow!
>
> (III, ii, 137–140)

He is under a spell, but the gross images are still his. In a curious way, both men, under the influence of the potion, reveal their shallowness. That they talk as they do normally, rather than with genuine claims of affection for Helena, brings out their vacuity. This emptiness takes different forms: insidious wordplay from Lysander, overblown imagery from Demetrius.

Helena logically assumes the two are conspiring to humiliate her (III, ii, 145–146), and attacks their fundamental character:

> If you were men, as men you are in show,
> You would not use a gentle lady so;
> To vow, and swear, and superpraise my parts,

When I am sure you hate me with your hearts.

(III, ii, 151–154)

Both men are under spells, but we recognize that even in their natural state the two would deserve Helena's chastisement.

When Hermia joins the trio, the two women are led by circumstance to accuse each other of treachery. Helena articulates their predicament:

Is all the counsel that we two have shar'd,
The sisters' vows, the hours that we have spent,
When we have chid the hasty-footed time
For parting us—O, is all forgot?
All school-days friendship, childhood innocence?

(III, ii, 198–202)

The intrusion of the two men in their lives has shattered their long-standing bond.

All four personalities grow more vivid in their antipathy. Lysander and Demetrius argue like little boys over the depth of their affections. First Lysander claims to Helena ''I say I love thee more than he can do'' (III, ii, 254). Then Demetrius, ever pompous, challenges back: ''If thou say so, withdraw, and prove it too'' (III, ii, 255). When Hermia finds herself the target of both men's hate, her pugnaciousness emerges against Helena:

O me, you juggler, you canker-blossom,
You thief of love! What, have you come by night
And stol'n my love's heart from him?

(III, ii, 282–284)

Helena's response reflects her more reflective nature:

Have you no modesty, no maiden shame,
No touch of bashfulness? What, will you tear
Impatient answers from my gentle tongue?
Fie, fie, you counterfeit, you puppet, you!

(III, ii, 285–288)

The accusations in the last line are directed to Hermia, but they should be turned against the two men, the actual counterfeits and puppets of this play.

The argument grows in intensity as Hermia's anger against Helena rises, especially when anyone uses a word that has connotations of height (III, ii, 297–298, 305, 326–328). Helena, however, is more melancholy than angry:

I evermore did love you, Hermia,
Did ever keep your counsels, never wrong'd you;
Save that, in love unto Demetrius,
I told him of your stealth unto this wood.

(III, ii, 307–310)

Hermia remains insulted, but never do her gibes measure up in cruelty to the men's. For instance, Lysander says to Hermia:

Get you gone, you dwarf; You minimus, of hind'ring knot-grass made;
You bead, you acorn.

(III, ii, 328–330)

Such attacks are more memorable than any claims of love.

Soon the four angry lovers depart, Lysander and Demetrius threatening each
other with physical harm. The confusion is overheard by Oberon and Puck, who
resolve to unravel it. As Oberon says:

When they next wake, all this derision
Shall seem a dream and fruitless vision.

(III, ii, 370–371)

But all will not be so forgettable as he insinuates, even after Puck anoints the
eyes of the sleeping Lysander.

During the rest of this scene Puck assumes various voices to lead all four
lovers racing around the woods. Each man starts in violent pursuit of a voice
he assumes to be that of his rival, but both eventually tire, and their willingness
to sleep rather than maintain the chase is one more undercutting of their claims
of passion.

Act IV returns us to the relationship between Titania and Bottom, who still
wears his ass's head, and who is still comfortable amidst the fairies. What is
surprising is that Oberon is now moved by his wife's predicament:

Her dotage now I do begin to pity.
For meeting her of late behind the wood,
Seeking sweet favors for this hateful fool,
I did upbraid her, and fall out with her.

(IV, i, 47–50)

He seems almost jealous of her infatuation. After all, Titania is not suffering.
Thus Oberon removes the spell, and her attitude towards Bottom immediately
changes: "O, how mine eyes do loathe his visage now" (IV, i, 79). Somehow
the enchanted Titania was able to see through the "visage" to appreciate the
inner qualities of Bottom.

The stage is next taken by the royal couple, whose words summarize the
events that we have seen. Speaking of his hounds, Theseus comments on "the
musical confusion" (IV, i, 110) of their voices. Then Hippolyta recalls a hunt
from her own memory:

I never heard
So musical a discord, such sweet thunder.

(IV, i, 117–118)

Such has been the pattern of this play. Voices have intermingled, and confusion
has been rampant. Yet never have we feared the consequences, and thus the
clash of harmonies was never painfully dissonant.

The lovers are awakened, the males in particular blind to what has transpired.

Egeus is still eager to have Hermia marry Demetrius, but the former suitor is now smitten with Helena. Even at this moment, though, Demetrius manages to make his uglier side vivid:

> To her, my lord,
> Was I betrothed ere I [saw] Hermia,
> But like a sickness did I loathe this food;
> But, as in health, come to my natural taste,
> Now I do wish it, love it, long for it,
> And will for evermore be true to it.
>
> (IV, i, 171–176)

As the four lovers head off, Hermia comments on the uncertainties of sight (IV, i, 189–190), but Demetrius, as yet under the spell of Puck's magic flower, utters the key sentiment:

> Are you sure
> That we are awake? It seems to me
> That yet we sleep, we dream. Do not you think
> The Duke was here, and bid us follow him?
>
> (IV, i, 192–195)

Amidst the words of reconciliation, the lovers conveniently forget Demetrius's loathing of Hermia.

Another reaction to the awakening from a dream is that of Bottom: "I have had a most rare vision" (IV, i, 204–205). Here again Bottom is content with what he has experienced, and he characterizes it with typical charm:

> It shall be call'd "Bottom's
> Dream," because it hath no bottom, and I will
> sing it in the latter end of a play, before the Duke.
>
> (IV, i, 215–217)

He has no hesitation in accepting what he cannot understand, and his happiness with his lot gives him a stature unique in this play. And when he rejoins his companions, their free and open delight is a welcome contrast to the lovers' affectations.

With the plot resolved, Act V is, in a sense, an epilogue, but it is nonetheless important. First Theseus offers reflections on love, and his words may be said to summarize some of the themes of the play:

> The lunatic, the lover, and the poet
> Are of imagination all compact.
> One sees more devils than vast hell can hold;
> That is the madman. The lover, all as frantic,
> Sees Helen's beauty in a brow of Egypt.
> The poet's eye, in a fine frenzy rolling,
> Doth glance from heaven to earth, from earth to heaven;
> And as imagination bodies forth

> The forms of things unknown, the poet's pen
> Turns them to shapes, and gives to aery nothing
> A local habitation and a name.
>
> (V, i, 7–17)

We have seen examples of all three types. But what gives this speech a special irony is that at times all three have appeared in the same bodies, notably those of Lysander and Demetrius, who under Puck's spell have experienced a wide range of emotions. Theseus's comments, both comic and melancholy, thus reflect the laughable but moving story of the play.

One more spectacle serves as commentary on that story: the performance of *Pyramus and Thisbe* by Bottom and his cohorts. Following an announcement by Philostrate, Theseus urges his companions to be sympathetic to the efforts forthcoming:

> Our sport shall be to take what they mistake:
> And what poor duty cannot do, noble respect
> Takes in might, not merit.
>
> (V, i, 90–92)

His advice, though, is not taken seriously by the audience, in particular Demetrius. As the play unfolds, with blunders galore, we are conscious that the tragic story of Pyramus and Thisbe, a tale of frustrated lovers who die because of their love, is uncomfortably close to the story in the previous four acts. Demetrius, however, is as callous about this narrative as he was during earlier events. For instance, when Theseus comments about whether the lion will speak, Demetrius retorts, "No wonder, my lord; one lion may, when many asses do" (V, i, 153–154). This speaker, however, is still hypnotized, and thus his nasty gibes reflect him far more than he knows.

The play is staged with hilarious incompetence. For instance, when Quince reads the Prologue, he confuses his punctuation, so that lines run together and subvert his meaning:

> Our true intent is. All for your delight
> We are not here.
>
> (V, i, 114–115)

Second, the language becomes a parody of bad drama, with particular delight in excessive alliteration:

> Whereat, with blade, with bloody, blameful, blade,
> He bravely broach'd his boiling, bloody, breast . . .
>
> (V, i, 146–147)

And a most intriguing blunder is made by Bottom as Pyramus, who while acting overhears a comment by Theseus, and breaks character to explain the situation:

> No, in truth sir, he should not. "Deceiving
> me" is Thisbe's cue. She is to enter now, and

I am to spy her through the wall. You shall see it
will fall pat as I told you. Yonder she comes.

(V, i, 184–187)

As always, he moves innocently between the world of art, or imagination, and
the world of reality.

Despite all the missteps, the tragic potential of the story is evident, as Pyramus's grief, even in so burlesque a version, moves the spectators. Theseus
comments:

This passion, and the death of a dear friend,
would go near to make a man look sad.

(V, i, 288–289)

And Hippolyta adds, "Beshrew my heart, but I pity the man" (V, i, 290). And
when "Thisbe" recites her death speech of Pyramus's body (V, i, 324–347),
the elegy goes uninterrupted. Regardless of the awkward poetry we can imagine
both actor and audience onstage suddenly infused with the sadness of the moment.
The two quiet lines that follow, offered by the chief scoffers, Theseus and
Demetrius, perhaps reflect their involvement in the passion before them. But
then the mood is shattered by Bottom's awakening, an ironic encore of his earlier
emergence from enchantment in Act IV, scene i.

All the acting in this burlesque, as indicated by the language, must be ex-
travagantly overdone. But then the emotions of the lovers earlier in the main
action were equally overdone. What emerges from both stories is Shakespeare's
combination of sympathy and mockery for those caught in the joy as well as the
potential anguish of love.

The play ends with two statements, one by Oberon, the last by Puck. Oberon
emphasizes the theme of nature that has pervaded this work:

So shall all the couples three
Ever true in loving be;
And the blot of Nature's hand
Shall not in their issue stand . . .

(V, i, 407–410)

Puck's final words, asking forgiveness for any offenses the play might have
caused, emphasize the movement from chaos to order that both the play and the
institution of marriage bring.

What might impress us most about *A Midsummer Night's Dream* is the playwright's superb balancing of several stories. Like the voices of a fugue, they
weave in and out, one shaping another, a third influencing the second. All,
however, revolve around the multitudinous aspects of love and the complexity
of human emotion. Yet despite the sadness and frustration that loom dangerously
close, we are charmed and amused by the predicament of men and women whose
minds and emotions leave them bewildered and beguiled.

SUGGESTIONS FOR FURTHER READING

Dent, R. W. "Imagination in *A Midsummer Night's Dream*." *Shakespeare Quarterly* 15 (1964): 115–129.

Dillingham, William B. "Bottom: The Third Ingredient." *Emory University Quarterly* 12 (1956): 230–237.

Fender, Stephen. *Shakespeare:* A Midsummer Night's Dream. London: Edward Arnold, 1968.

Garber, Majorie. *Dream in Shakespeare*. New Haven: Yale University Press, 1974.

Hemingway, Samuel B. "The Relation of *A Midsummer Night's Dream* to *Romeo and Juliet*." *Modern Language Notes* 24 (1911): 78–80.

Miller, R. E. "*Midsummer Night's Dream*: The Fairies, Bottom and the Mystery of Things." *Shakespeare Quarterly* 26 (1975): 254–268.

Olson, Paul A. "*A Midsummer Night's Dream* and the Meaning of Court Marriage." *Journal of English Literary History* 24 (1957): 95–119.

Schanzer, E. "The Moon and the Fairies in *A Midsummer Night's Dream*." *University of Toronto Quarterly* 24 (1955): 234–246.

Young, David P. *Something of Great Constancy: The Art of* A Midsummer Night's Dream. New Haven: Yale University Press, 1966.

THE MERCHANT OF VENICE

The title character of this work is not the figure of greatest interest. Indeed, during most productions, Antonio fades from audience concern, and Shylock dominates the action the way he has dominated centuries of criticism. No character of Shakespeare's has aroused more passionate debate, to such an extent that *The Merchant of Venice* has been attacked, censored, and even banned across our country and the world on the grounds that it is anti-Semitic. We shall consider this issue presently.

The primary source of the play is the story of Gianetto, found in a medieval Italian anthology called *Il Pecorone* (*The Simpleton*) by Ser Giovanni Florentino. This tale contains the crucial element of the pound of flesh as well as the woman disguised as a lawyer appearing in the courtroom to ensure that not a single drop of blood is shed. The casket story may have come from another medieval collection, the *Gesta Romanorum*, first translated from Latin about 1524.

Shylock does not take the stage for some time. Instead, Antonio opens the play by establishing a tone that pervades the story:

> In sooth, I know not why I am so sad;
> It wearies me, you say it wearies you;
> But how I caught it, found it, or came by it,
> What stuff 'tis made of, whereof it is born,
> I am to learn;
> And such a want-wit sadness makes of me,
> That I have much ado to know myself.

(I, i, 1–7)

Antonio communicates his unhappiness as well as his inability to fathom that condition. Life itself, or at least life as he knows it, enervates him spiritually, and at this moment we wonder why he should be so unhappy. So do his friends, Salerio and Solanio, who try to assure him that his ships and financial affairs are secure. As will prove typical of almost everyone in Venice, they assume that a person's emotional state is directly related to that person's financial state. But Antonio denies any connection (I, i, 45). Solanio next assumes that Antonio is in the throes of love (I, i, 46), but Antonio dismisses that prospect, too. Soon, however, the matter of his affections surfaces again.

With the entrance of Bassanio, Lorenzo, and Gratiano, a new energy takes over. Gratiano notices that Antonio is depressed, and Antonio acknowledges this mood:

> I hold the world but as the world, Gratiano,
> A stage, where every man must play a part,
> And mine a sad one.
>
> (I, i, 77–79)

He invites commiseration, but no one cares to probe further. Indeed, Gratiano takes this last line as a cue for his own recitation: "Let me play the fool" (I, i, 79). And he makes fun of Antonio's predicament, while embarking on an extended monologue that implies the emptiness of all around him. Gratiano proves himself light-hearted, but also shallow and callous, as Bassanio indicates when Lorenzo and Gratiano depart:

> Gratiano speaks an infinite deal of nothing,
> more than any man in all Venice.
>
> (I, i, 114–115)

Yet Bassanio, ostensibly Antonio's best friend, is himself too self-absorbed to inquire the reason for Antonio's unhappiness, and instead discloses his own troubles:

> To you, Antonio,
> I owe the most in money and in love,
> And from your love I have a warranty
> To unburthen all my plots and purposes
> How to get clear of all the debts I owe.
>
> (I, i, 130–134)

Once again money and happiness are linked. Antonio's reply suggests another attitude:

> I pray you, good Bassanio, let me know it,
> And if it stand, as you yourself still do,
> Within the eye of honor, be assur'd
> My purse, my person, my extremest means,
> Lie all unlock'd to your occasions.
>
> (I, i, 135–139)

He is willing to give financial help, but his offer also goes much deeper. He is making an emotional overture to Bassanio, and reaffirms so in his next speech:

> Then do but say to me what I should do
> That in your knowledge may by me be done,

And I am prest unto it; therefore speak.

(I, i, 158–160)

Bassanio, however, has other concerns, as he extols the virtues of his new love, Portia. His first line reveals that she is "richly left" (I, i, 161), and he soon raves that she is, like "a golden fleece" (I, i, 170), the object of many suitors. Bassanio's request is that Antonio lend him enough money so that Bassanio might compete for her. For a third time money and emotional contentment are intertwined.

Antonio's reply to Bassanio's plea is far less energetic than his earlier statements of allegiance:

> Thou know'st that all my fortunes are at sea,
> Neither have I money nor commodity
> To raise a present sum; therefore go forth,
> Try what my credit can in Venice do.
> That shall be rack'd, even to the uttermost,
> To furnish thee to Belmont, to fair Portia.
> Go presently inquire, and so will I,
> Where money is, and I no question make
> To have it of my trust, or for my sake.

(I, i, 177–185)

The melancholy strain returns. Antonio is not eager to talk about money, and the placement of the words "to fair Portia" suggests little enthusiasm. In fact, the entire speech is devoid of passion, as the two part company. Antonio has tried to open his heart to Bassanio, but the latter has not responded and has instead shown himself absorbed with someone else.

Thus this opening scene establishes several points. Antonio is unhappy with existence itself. The initial presentation of Venice's population suggests that they are inordinately preoccupied with money and their own pleasure. And Antonio's devotion to Bassanio, who is occupied with wealth, is appreciated, but returned only mildly. In sum, the world of this play is not attractive, and Antonio's sadness seems to emerge directly from his place in this rollicking society.

He is not the only character who feels alienation, as the first lines of the next scene indicate:

> By my troth, Nerissa, my little body is
> a-weary of this great world.

(I, ii, 1–2)

The speaker is Portia, a woman with money, stature, and, as we soon learn, a supply of suitors. In other words, she has what the Venetians we have met would consider an ideal life. But Portia lives in Belmont, and here she is frustrated. The primary cause of her unhappiness is her late father's decree that her future husband will be the man who wins a "lott'ry" (I, ii, 29), and Portia's impotence annoys her no end, so much so that she resents virtually all the men who come after her. Her dismissal of each shows her intelligence but also her capacity for cruel wit. The only one who intrigues her is Bassanio (I, ii, 120–121).

Portia's plight is far removed from Antonio's, but they have two qualities in common: each is unhappy, and each looks to Bassanio for relief from that unhappiness.

Scene iii, which takes us back to Venice, introduces us to one more figure detached from his society: Shylock. Questions immediately leap to the fore. Is the portrait of Shylock evidence that Shakespeare was anti-Semitic? The play is a comedy, but does Shylock belong to the world of tragedy? How did Shakespeare's age regard him? And how are we to do so?

First we should note that Shakespeare probably never met any Jews, for they were expelled from England in 1290 during the reign of Edward I. A small Jewish enclave survived by living in accordance with the religious law of the land, although privately some held their own services. The only Jew of prominence in England during this era was Dr. Roderigo Lopez, a Portuguese physician to Queen Elizabeth. Brutally executed in 1594 on a dubious charge of treason, he might have inspired Shakespeare to center a play on a Jewish character. The other famous Jewish figure of the time was fictional: Barrabas, the vengeful protagonist of Marlowe's *The Jew of Malta*. His bloody treachery was in accordance with the then common image of Jews, and we may assume that the Elizabethan audience regarded Shylock with equal distaste.

Yet that Shakespeare had no dealings with Jews suggests that what makes Shylock a villain is not only his Jewishness but also his place as an alien in a Christian society. Just as Othello suffers not specifically because of his black skin but because he is alone in this same cosmopolitan yet insulated Venice, so Shylock is apart: a man whose values, traditions, and beliefs isolate him. Malvolio in *Twelfth Night* suffers from a similar predicament, for the source of his villainy, too, is that he is different. The stereotypical Jewish characteristics that Shakespeare ascribes to Shylock turn him into a grotesque, an easy target for the laughter of the Elizabethan audience, which thrived on harsh racial and ethnic humor that recurs throughout Shakespeare's plays and other Renaissance drama.

But the portrait of Shylock is not this simple. Whatever Shakespeare's intention might have been, Shylock has some of the dignity and pride that Othello exudes, and this balance makes Shylock difficult to grasp. He is greedy, puritanical, and vengeful. He is also proud, honest, and acutely sensitive to religious bigotry. He is also a bigot himself. What becomes apparent through the play is that his hatred for Venice and Venice's hatred for him feed off one another.

This condition is clear in scene iii of Act I, when Bassanio and Antonio confront Shylock with the request for a loan of 3,000 ducats. Shylock's opening lines, all ironic repetitions, reveal his exaggerated circumspection, as well as his luxuriating in the possibility of earning money. So does his description of Antonio as a ''good'' man because of his available funds (I, iii, 12, 15–17). The opening glimpse of Shylock, then, is the caricature of the Jewish moneylender. We should note, however, that in Shakespeare's England usurers were not Jews, but Puritans. Thus Shakespeare is portraying a foreign stereotype, not a familiar figure.

The first religious antagonism also comes from Shylock as he turns down Bassanio's invitation to dinner:

> Yes, to smell pork, to eat of the habitation
> which your prophet the Nazarite conjur'd the devil
> into. I will buy with you, sell with you, talk
> with you, walk with you, and so following; but I
> will not eat with you, drink with you, nor pray with
> you. What news on the Rialto? Who is he comes
> here?
>
> (I, iii, 33–38)

With Antonio's entrance, Shylock grows angrier:

> How like a fawning publican he looks!
> I hate him for he is a Christian;
> But more, for that in low simplicity
> He lends out money gratis, and brings down
> The rate of usance here with us in Venice.
>
> (I, iii, 41–45)

Shylock's hatred initially seems to be sheer prejudice. Next it emerges from economic competition. Then a new element is added:

> He hates our sacred nation, and he rails
> Even there where merchants most do congregate
> On me, my bargains, and my well-won thrift,
> Which he calls interest. Cursed be my tribe
> If I forgive him!
>
> (I, iii, 48–52)

Shylock feels that he is only responding to the enmity Antonio has towards him. Here is part of the tension of Shylock's character. Is his hatred for Christians the reason Christians hate him? Or does he personally inspire resentment? Were he not Jewish but otherwise the same man, would he be so despised? Does he react to an enmity directed at all Jews? Or is he reacting to the treatment accorded him alone? These questions are never fully resolved.

The issue grows more complicated when the deal is debated. Shylock's roundabout story of Jacob and Laban from the Old Testament (I, iii, 71–90) reflects two qualities that annoy his listeners: his dwelling on his religious heritage, and his sententiousness. Antonio is not even impressed with the use of Biblical authority: "The devil can cite scripture for his purpose" (I, iii, 98). Insulted once more, Shylock moves directly to business, and defends his policies:

> You call me misbeliever, cut-throat dog,
> And spet upon my Jewish gaberdine . . .
> You, that did void your rheum upon my beard,

> And foot me as you spurn a stranger cur
> Over your threshold; moneys is your suit.
>
> (I, iii, 111–119)

But Antonio has similar bitterness inside him:

> I am as like to call thee so again,
> To spet on thee again, to spurn thee too.
> If thou wilt lend this money, lend it not
> As to thy friends, for when did friendship take
> A breed for barren metal of his friend?
> But lend it rather to thine enemy,
> Who if he break, thou mayst with better face
> Exact the penalty.
>
> (I, iii, 130–137)

Earlier Antonio revealed his estrangement from the community of Venice. Here Antonio's anger with his own life finds an outlet in an attack on Shylock, another alienated man, whom Antonio invites to make the rate of interest on the loan as strict as possible.

We might expect Shylock to impose an inordinate penalty for interest, but we would also expect that penalty to be money. Instead we hear something shocking:

> . . . let the forfeit
> Be nominated for an equal pound
> Of your fair flesh, to be cut off and taken
> In what part of your body pleaseth me.
>
> (I, iii, 148–151)

What can be Shylock's motivation? The Elizabethan audience would likely have taken this stipulation as a sign of Shylock's depravity. But we may see it as more subtle. Shylock's hatred for Antonio is palpable, and Antonio has here brought that hatred to the surface. Thus Shylock is so angered that he gives vent to some latent violence within him. He cannot strike back at Antonio physically. But the thought of violating him with a knife provides vicarious pleasure. Shylock makes his demand not with the hope of fulfilling it but with the unconscious desire to communicate his distaste and to make Antonio squirm.

Over Bassanio's objection, Antonio agrees to the bond, confident his ships will return on time. We suspect, however, as the first scene hinted, that the ships might not return on schedule.

So uncomfortable is this last episode that we could lose sense of the romantic and comic elements of the play. They return in the opening scenes of Act II, in Belmont, where the Prince of Morocco enters as Portia's first suitor. He is a quiet, noble man, apologetic about the darkness of his skin, and as Portia ushers him in for his chance to choose the casket in which her picture may be found, she is forced to withhold her frustration. We note, however, that Morocco is another alien, and he does not receive a warm greeting:

> You must take your chance,
> And either not attempt to choose at all,
> Or swear before you choose, if you choose wrong
> Never to speak to lady afterward
> In way of marriage; therefore be advis'd.
>
>   (II, i, 38–42)

Portia seems to pronounce this penalty with glee.

Grosser comic elements appear in scene ii with the appearance of Launcelot Gobbo, Shylock's servant. Gobbo is not especially witty, and his banter with his blind father is more cruel than amusing. Yet one of Launcelot's lines is memorable: " . . . it is a wise father that knows his own child" (II, ii, 76). We think of Portia's father, condemning his daughter to passive frustration as she must wait for a man to win her. Soon Shylock is in conflict with his daughter, failing to appreciate her desires.

The scene ends with a brief interlude by Gratiano and Bassanio, who urges his friend to be more serious:

>   Pray thee take pain
> To allay with some cold drops of modesty
> Thy skipping spirit, lest through thy wild behavior
> I be misconst'red in the place I go to,
> 'And lose my hopes.
>
>   (II, ii, 185–189)

Gratiano's reply might stand for the spirit of Venice, at least as Shakespeare dramatizes it, for while Gratiano indicates that he will put on a sober expression, he clarifies that it is entirely a mask (II, ii, 189–197). Such is the personality of Venice itself: seemingly decent and reverent, but ugly underneath.

Scene iii introduces us to Shylock's daughter, Jessica, and this brief episode suggests her unhappiness. As she says after Launcelot leaves:

> Alack, what heinous sin is it in me
> To be ashamed to be my father's child!
> But though I am a daughter to his blood,
> I am not to his manners. O Lorenzo,
> If thou keep promise, I shall end this strife,
> Become a Christian and thy loving wife.
>
>   (II, iii, 16–21)

The interlude emphasizes first the parallel between Jessica and Portia, two women held prisoner by their fathers' values. The speech also brings out the romantic side of what is, after all, a comedy. Here Jessica offers sentiments familiar from other comedies, as she proclaims her desire to break away from her father and go with the man she loves. Here, though, the stereotypical situation is complicated by the religious separation Jessica also seeks.

This intricacy builds in the next scene, as Lorenzo plots to steal Jessica away:

> She hath directed
> How I shall take her from her father's house,
> What gold and jewels she is furnish'd with,
> What page's suit she hath in readiness.
>
> (II, iv, 29–32)

He seems the familiar romantic hero, preparing to elope with his love and leave her frustrated father behind. And although like almost everyone else in this city he focuses on money, ordinarily we would root for him, as we do for almost all young couples. But Lorenzo's next lines add extra bitterness to the secrecy:

> If e'er the Jew her father come to heaven,
> It will be for his gentle daughter's sake,
> And never dare misfortune cross her foot,
> Unless she do it under this excuse,
> That she is issue to a faithless Jew.
>
> (II, iv, 33–37)

That Jessica is herself Jewish does not bother Lorenzo at all. Thus the cause of Shylock's alienation may not be his religion, but other aspects of his personality.

These surface in the next scene, when he rails to Jessica against the masques scheduled for the evening:

> Lock up my doors, and when you hear the drum
> And the vile squealing of the wry-neck'd fife,
> Clamber not you up to the casements then,
> Nor thrust your head into the public street
> To gaze on Christian fools with varnish'd faces;
> But stop my house's ears, I mean my casements;
> Let not the sound of shallow fopp'ry enter
> My sober house.
>
> (II, v, 29–36)

He despises the hedonistic life of Venice, but his antagonism raises additional questions. Does Shylock dislike these parties because they are as decadent as he says, or does he dislike them because he does not feel welcome in the revelry? Again, which comes first? His detachment from Venice, or Venice's resentment of him? Then again, is Venice as debauched as Shylock indicates? Gratiano's personality and the comments of other characters have suggested that the city is devoted to pleasure, but is that impression fair? And if it is accurate, does Shakespeare disapprove of such behavior? In some comedies, such as *Measure for Measure*, Shakespeare mocks the hypocrisy behind a seemingly strait-laced figure like Angelo. In *Twelfth Night* Malvolio is ridiculed, but the revelers who hate him are also dislikable. The issue is not easily resolved.

In any case, the relationship between Shylock and Venice is complex. That both sides seem unattractive suggests that Shakespeare here dramatizes a pervasive hypocrisy and corruption. Such an atmosphere becomes more blatant in subsequent comedies.

In scene vi, a scene that could be part of any romantic comedy of the era, Jessica makes her escape with Lorenzo. She disguises herself as a boy, a familiar convention. But the added sting of the scene is that Jessica is not only leaving her father but robbing him, and therefore she lacks the pristine charm of other heroines:

> I will make fast the doors, and gild myself
> With some moe ducats, and be with you straight.
>
> (II, vi, 49–50)

As always in this society, love and money are intertwined.

Scene vii takes us back to Belmont, where the Prince of Morocco attempts to choose the correct casket. As he reads the inscriptions on each (II, vii, 5–10), the words always return to the theme of appearance versus reality, a motif that resounds through the comedies. The inscriptions are ambiguous, and each suitor may interpret them differently. Morocco's debate with himself over which casket to choose is particularly long and may increase tension. Finally he chooses the gold, thinking he will win "what many men desire" (II, vii, 37). When he finds he has selected incorrectly, we are not surprised, for given the traditions of the comedy form, we are confident that Portia will be won by Bassanio. Still, Morocco is a decent man, and Portia's sneering dismissal reflects a hardened personality: "Let all of his complexion choose me so" (II, vii, 79).

The entrance of Salerio and Solanio to relate Shylock's reaction to his daughter's elopement is a skillful move by Shakespeare, as Shylock's fury is communicated and simultaneously derided:

> I never heard a passion so confus'd,
> So strange, outrageous, and so variable
> As the dog Jew did utter in the streets.
> "My daughter! O my ducats! O my daughter!
> Fled with Christian! O my Christian ducats!
>
> (II, viii, 12–16)

The exaggerated narrative ensures that we shall not have excessive sympathy for Shylock. At the same time we know that the loathing Shylock has for Antonio and Venice now has been concretized, so that when we next see him, his fury is likely to be more concentrated. In addition, the phrase "dog Jew" suggests the antagonism the Venetians bear against Shylock, and our view of him remains complex.

The Prince of Aragon is the next of Portia's suitors to try his luck at finding the right casket. When he notes the inscription on the silver box, " 'Who chooseth me shall get as much as he deserves' " (II, ix, 36), his ego leads him in this direction, and he, too, is proven wrong. Both Morocco and Aragon are too literal in their love. Bassanio, who at the end of the scene makes his way to Portia's room, proves to be the poet and the fitting lover.

In Act III, scene i, Salerio and Solanio enter with news that Antonio's ships may have been lost. Shylock then reappears, with all the bitterness we expect, eager to carry out the bond with Antonio:

> To bait fish withal—if it will feed nothing
> else, it will feed my revenge.
>
> (III, i, 53–54)

He continues with a plea that has come to stand as the paradigm of all statements against racial intolerance:

> Hath not a Jew eyes? Hath not a Jew hands, organs,
> dimensions, senses, affections, passions; fed with
> the same food, hurt with the same weapons, subject
> to the same diseases, heal'd by the same means,
> warm'd and cool'd by the same winter and summer,
> as a Christian is?
>
> (III, i, 59–64)

Such words suggests that Shakespeare was acutely sensitive to the injustice of bigotry. But that conclusion should be tempered, for the tone of the speech changes towards the end, and the seemingly humanistic spirit turns venomous:

> And if you wrong us, shall
> we not revenge? If we are like you in the rest, we
> will resemble you in that. If a Jew wrong a Christian,
> what is his humility? Revenge. If a Christian wrong
> a Jew, what should his sufferance be by Chris-
> tian example? Why, revenge. The villainy you teach
> me, I will execute, and it shall go hard but I will
> better the instruction.
>
> (III, i, 66–73)

Shylock now sounds more vicious than anyone in the play. A spirit of vengeance has infected him, but we cannot be certain whether he is innately so motivated or responding to Venice and its ill treatment of him.

When Tubal enters, Shylock storms against his daughter and her actions, and so furious is he that he wishes his daughter dead: "Would she were hears'd at my foot, and the ducats in her coffin!" (III, i, 89–90). Shylock seems unable to distinguish between his daughter and his money, and we feel him losing all human feeling. Then Tubal offers the news that Antonio's ships have indeed been lost, and Shylock is delighted: "I thank God, I thank God. Is it true, is it true?" (III, i, 101–102). But his joy is cut off when he learns that his daughter has been throwing away his money, and in addition has sold a precious family ring for a monkey. Such news drives Shylock further towards irrationality and madness:

> Out upon her! Thou torturest me, Tubal.
> It was my turkis, I had it of Leah when I was a
> bachelor. I would not have given it for a wilder-

ness of monkeys.

(III, i, 120–123)

As he gradually veers out of control, his insistence on the literal carrying out of the bond becomes more comprehensible.

Such violent intention is contrasted by the resolution of the casket story, as Bassanio comes to make his choice. Portia's helplessness is ingratiating, for her position does not permit her to express her love for Bassanio, and after a rambling address she is reduced to confessing:

> I speak too long, but 'tis to peize the time,
> To eche it, and to draw it out in length,
> To stay you from election.

(III, ii, 22–24)

To see such a self-possessed woman tongue-tied is enjoyable and also communicates the extent of her love for Bassanio. Then Bassanio reveals his own anguish (III, ii, 24–25), and Portia seems to relax and revert to her customary wordplay. Again Shakespeare extends the scene to create further suspense, but Bassanio eventually picks the right casket. His reasoning is significant:

> There is no [vice] so simple but assumes
> Some mark of virtue on his outward parts.

(III, ii, 81–82)

> Thus ornament is but the guiled shore
> To a most dangerous sea; the beauteous scarf
> Veiling an Indian beauty; in a word
> The seeming truth which cunning times put on
> To entrap the wisest. Therefore then, thou gaudy gold,
> Hard food for Midas, I will none of thee;
> Nor none of thee, thou pale and common drudge
> 'Tween man and man; but thou, thou meagre lead,
> Which rather threaten'st than dost promise aught,
> Thy paleness moves me more than eloquence,
> And here choose I.

(III, ii, 97–107)

Bassanio has the capacity to distinguish between reality and appearance. What specific qualities he has that enable him to make such a distinction are not apparent, but perhaps we are meant to assume that he is simply in love, and therefore empowered to see certain aspects of life more clearly. His behavior also contrasts with that of Shylock, who in previous scenes has been unable to distinguish between the value of human beings and that of money.

Portia and Bassanio rejoice with rapturous language although even at this moment financial terminology invades Portia's language:

> To wish myself much better, yet for you,
> I would be trebled twenty times myself,

> A thousand times more fair, ten thousand times more rich,
> That only to stand high in your account,
> I might in virtues, beauties, livings, friends,
> Exceed account. But the full sum of me
> Is sum of something . . .

(III, ii, 153–158)

Portia also reaffirms what seems to be the eternal doubt of Shakespeare's women characters by giving Bassanio a ring:

> This house, these servants, and this same myself
> Are yours—my lord's!—I give them with this ring,
> Which when you part from, lose, or give away,
> Let it presage the ruin of your love,
> And be my vantage to exclaim on you.

(III, ii, 170–174)

The pair are then joined by Gratiano and Nerissa, also in love, and their relationship adds a ribald tone to the hitherto poetic proceedings, as Gratiano says: "We'll play with them the first boy for a thousand ducats" (III, ii, 213–214). The romance brightens further when Lorenzo and Jessica enter, thereby uniting the worlds of Belmont and Venice.

However, reality and money intrude when Salerio brings a letter from Antonio reporting losses that leave Bassanio stunned (III, ii, 266–271). And Jessica casts further gloom by emphasizing that her father has indicated he will seek the literal bond rather than even twenty times the money involved (III, ii, 284–290). Bassanio wavers, caught between helping Antonio and staying with Portia. But her energy and determination take over as she orders immediate action:

> First go with me to church and call me wife,
> And then away to Venice to your friend;
> For never shall you lie by Portia's side
> With an unquiet soul. You shall have gold
> To pay the petty debt twenty times over.

(III, ii, 303–307)

Such vitality is in sharp contrast to Antonio's attitude in jail. For in the next scene, as Shylock turns down all requests for mercy, repeating the word "bond" with infuriating determination, Antonio seems strangely fatalistic:

> Let him alone,
> I'll follow him no more with bootless prayers.
> He seeks my life; his reason well I know:
> I oft deliver'd from his forfeitures
> Many that have at times made moan to me;
> Therefore he hates me.

(III, iii, 19–24)

A bit later he adds:

Pray God Bassanio come
To see me pay his debt, and then I care not!

(III, iii, 35–36)

Antonio sounds as if he will receive perverse satisfaction in making sure Bassanio knows the sacrifice that he, Antonio, has made. Indeed, Antonio seems eager to die and to let Bassanio carry that burden through life. Perhaps Antonio feels that Bassanio's affection for Portia has tainted the friendship the two men share. Perhaps Antonio is a frustrated homosexual whose unhappiness throughout the play is a reaction to the lack of reciprocal affection from Bassanio. Perhaps Antonio is tormented by an inability to express these desires, or perhaps he is baffled by certain longings within himself that he cannot fathom. Whatever the reason, Antonio's melancholy is parallel to Shylock's intention to revenge. Both characters are outcasts.

Such detachment is set off by the next two brief scenes. First Portia reaffirms to Jessica and Lorenzo the ideal of friendship (III, iv, 11–18). And she determines with Nerissa to proceed disguised to Venice to take further action (III, iv, 60–62). But throughout the delineation of her plan her tone is hardly noble, especially at its culmination:

I have within my mind
A thousand raw tricks of these bragging Jacks,
Which I will practice.

(III, v, 76–78)

Portia seems less interested in rescuing her husband's friend than in asserting her own wit. We sense a woman who finally has the opportunity to break out of the passive role her father forced on her, and who is eager to pay back all the men whose advances she has been forced to accept. At the trial Portia will play her role to the hilt, fairly lusting over the misery she causes. Perhaps her grandiose performance is the consequence of pent-up frustration.

In scene v, Jessica banters with Launcelot, to whom she remarks:

I shall be sav'd by my husband, he hath
made me a Christian!

(III, v, 19–20)

In light of Shylock's fate, that line has serious ramifications that are clear later. Now Lorenzo enters, and Jessica continues her bright conversation. The impact of the scene is that she has escaped her father's oppressive household and thereafter blossomed into a more self-possessed, secure young woman. Such is the power of love, even in the dark world of this work.

The lengthy trial is the climax of the play, both theatrically and thematically. From the Duke's early lines to Antonio, the situation is clear:

I am sorry for thee. Thou art come to answer
A stony adversary, an inhuman wretch,
Uncapable of pity, void and empty

From any dram of mercy.

(IV, i, 3–6)

The sympathy of all characters onstage, and certainly all those in the Elizabethan audience, is with Antonio. Shylock stands alone, a Jew in a Christian society. But Antonio's response shows his own singular position:

> I do oppose
> My patience to his fury, and am arm'd
> To suffer, with a quietness of spirit,
> The very tyranny and rage of his.

(IV, i, 10–13)

Such resignation sets him apart from every other character.

The Duke offers Shylock a chance to retract his claim: "... thy strange apparent cruelty" (IV, i, 21). But the Duke completes his request with "We all expect a gentle answer, Jew" (IV, i, 34). The phrasing invites hostility from Shylock, who responds in kind:

> So can I give no reason, nor I will not
> More than a lodg'd hate, and a certain loathing
> I bear Antonio, that I follow thus
> A losing suit against him.

(IV, i, 59–62)

Shylock essentially confesses that he himself does not understand his reason, but that he is motivated by so strong a detestation that he is beyond rationality. We may speculate that on a deeper level Shylock is answering the cruel spirit of Venice with a greater cruelty of his own, as if determined to outdo the Christian world at its own game. He may even be judged to feel that his actions are justified because the society around him has treated him as an unfeeling monster. They have treated him as though he acts this way, he implies. Now he will do so.

After Antonio restates his curious acceptance of sentence (IV, i, 80–83), Shylock retorts bitterly upon how the Venetians themselves deal in human beings as barter:

> You have among you many a purchas'd slave,
> Which like your asses, and your dogs and mules,
> You use in abject and in slavish parts,
> Because you bought them . . .
> The pound of flesh which I demand of him
> Is dearly bought as mine, and I will have it.

(IV, i, 90–100)

He is only giving back what they deserve, he says.

Antonio once more reaffirms his surrender:

> I am a tainted wether of the flock,
> Meetest for death; the weakest kind of fruit
> Drops earliest to the ground, and so let me.

You cannot better be employ'd, Bassanio,
Than to live still and write mine epitaph.

(IV, i, 114–118)

With the word "wether," which means a castrated ram, Antonio insinuates his asexuality, his estrangement from that dimension of human emotion. His affection for Bassanio, we can thus conclude, is a profound friendship, and when Bassanio compromises that devotion by sharing his life with Portia, Antonio abandons all loyalty. Here, too, his last lines suggest a desire that Bassanio live with the memories of Antonio's death, forever haunted by what Antonio considers a betrayal.

After Nerissa enters dressed as a lawyer, Gratiano drops his pose as a charming "fool" and releases his personal loathing for Shylock:

Thy currish spirit
Govern'd a wolf, who hang'd for human slaughter,
Even from the gallows did his fell soul fleet,
And whilst thou layest in thy unhallowed dam,
Infus'd itself in thee; for thy desires
Are wolvish, bloody, starv'd, and ravenous.

(IV, i, 133–138)

Such vituperation reflects the genuine spirit of Gratiano as well as Venice and although Gratiano means to humiliate Shylock and thereby sway him from his intention, his words only harden Shylock, as if they are confirmation of what he has always believed about Venice:

Repair thy wit, good youth, or it will fall
To cureless ruin. I stand here for law.

(IV, i, 141–142)

He relishes the assault. So possessed is Shylock by hatred that the more the onlookers hurl abuse, the more he enjoys it.

Portia soon enters, dressed as Balthazar, the lawyer, and in the tradition of comedy inveigles herself into handling Antonio's case. Her first question is crucial: "Which is the merchant here? and which the Jew?" (IV, i, 174). She cannot distinguish them. Whether either wants to believe so, both are possessed by animosity, both base their lives on monetary reward, and both are outcasts in their hedonistic society.

Portia soon offers a moving plea to Shylock, a speech that has survived as an eloquent plea for justice and compassion:

The quality of mercy is not strain'd,
It droppeth as the gentle rain from heaven
Upon the place beneath.

(IV, i, 184–186)

She continues reverently until the last few lines:

> I have spoken thus much
> To mitigate the justice of thy plea,
> Which if thou follow, this strict court of Venice
> Must needs give sentence 'gainst the merchant there.
>
> (IV, i, 202–205)

Suddenly she switches her tone and challenges Shylock to press for punishment. Her previous call for mercy, then, was hypocritical. She does not want to see the suit dropped. She knows the trick she has waiting, and she wants to see Shylock suffer. Indeed, she soon ignores the very call for mercy she has advocated so movingly.

Whether Shylock is touched by her earlier words is unclear, but after this last invitation he restates his determination to see the bond fulfilled, and enthusiastically lauds Portia:

> A Daniel come to judgment! yea, a Daniel!
> O wise young judge, how I do honor thee!
>
> (IV, i, 223–224)

His glee makes his attitude all the more repulsive. But in response to her further comments, Shylock has a curious line:

> An oath, an oath, I have an oath in heaven!
> Shall I lay perjury upon my soul?
> [No], not for Venice.
>
> (IV, i, 228–230)

The last words have two possible meanings. Does Shylock mean he would not abandon his oath for all the wealth of Venice? Or does he mean that he will not relent so as to do a kindness for Venice? The second meaning is more consistent with his values and behavior, which now borders on the demonic, especially when he brings forth the scales to weigh Antonio's flesh (IV, i, 255).

Antonio then offers his farewell, and it communicates the fatalism he manifested earlier:

> Repent but you that you shall lose your friend,
> And he repents not that he pays your debt.
>
> (IV, i, 278–279)

Bassanio responds with equal fervor:

> Antonio, I am married to a wife
> Which is as dear to me as life itself,
> But life itself, my wife, and all the world,
> Are not with me esteem'd above thy life.
> I would lose all, ay, sacrifice them all
> Here to this devil, to deliver you.
>
> (IV, i, 282–287)

During these two speeches Portia stands by quietly, and we wonder why she allows these men to suffer so. She even jokes to Bassanio:

Your wife would give you little thanks for that
If she were by to hear you make the offer.

(IV, i, 288–289)

Such banter maintains the comic mood but also reflects a nasty streak in Portia. Not only is she about to allow Shylock to entrap himself, but she lets her husband and his best friend agonize over the latter's impending death. Again, we wonder about Portia's attitude toward "the quality of mercy."

With her line "Tarry a little, there is something else" (IV, i, 305), Portia reverses herself on Shylock and craftily points out that he must take the flesh without shedding a drop of blood. Shylock realizes his predicament and hurriedly offers to take money instead, but Portia is relentless. Interestingly, Bassanio is not nearly as hard, and is prepared to give Shylock the money: "I have it ready for thee, here it is" (IV, i, 337). But Portia is as unwavering as Shylock was, and eagerly dispenses the strict punishment:

If it be proved against an alien,
That by direct or indirect attempts
He seek the life of any citizen,
The party 'gainst which he doth contrive
Shall seize one half his good; the other half
Comes to the privy coffer of the state,
And the offender's life lies in the mercy
Of the Duke only, 'gainst all other voice . . .

(IV, i, 349–356)

She then orders Shylock to beg for mercy.

No clear indication is provided as to whether Shylock kneels, but Shakespeare does make Shylock a somewhat pitiable victim by including Gratiano's taunt:

Thou hast not left the value of a cord;
Therefore thou must be hang'd at the state's charge.

(IV, i, 366–367)

The judge, however, spares Shylock's life "before thou ask it" (IV, i, 369), and rules that half of Shylock's money will go to the state, and the other half to Antonio. After Shylock numbly agrees, and apparently is willing to die (IV, i, 374–377), Antonio surprisingly takes mercy on him. First Antonio asks for only half of what Shylock has been ordered to pay him if Shylock will carry out two other stipulations. One, upon his death those funds must go to Lorenzo and Jessica. Two, Shylock must become a Christian.

To audiences of our day, both commands seem unusually cruel. Yet to Shakespeare's audience they must have appeared beneficent. After all, Lorenzo and Jessica are the most romantic characters in the play, and their reward is thereby deserved. In addition, becoming a Christian would be, according to the Elizabethans, Shylock's only opportunity to achieve salvation. Jessica felt the same way earlier (III, v, 19–20).

Shylock's compliance with such strictures may be played in a variety of ways.

For instance, his line "I am content" may be whispered with helpless acceptance or muttered with barely restrained resentment. His last lines, too, are open to interpretation:

> I pray you give me leave to go from hence,
> I am not well. Send the deed after me,
> And I will sign it.
>
> (IV, i, 395–397)

Should these words be spoken with resignation or with tightly controlled fury? To emphasize the helplessness of Shylock would bring out those elements of his character that approach tragic loneliness. To emphasize the resentment and frustration would emphasize his villainy and tilt the play more toward the comic.

Once Shylock leaves, we might expect Portia to reveal herself to Bassanio. Yet she maintains her disguise and goes so far as to force Bassanio to surrender the ring he swore he would keep forever. Only Antonio seems untroubled by the sacrifice:

> My Lord Bassanio, let him have the ring.
> Let his deservings and my love withal
> Be valued 'gainst your wive's commandment.
>
> (IV, i, 449–451)

Perhaps he is eager to have Portia angry with Bassanio, and for Bassanio in turn to give his devotion back to Antonio. In any case, Portia's request is further evidence that she delights in tormenting the man she loves. In the next scene she whispers an aside to Nerissa:

> We shall have old swearing
> That they did give the rings away to men;
> But we'll outface them, and outswear them too.
>
> (IV, ii, 15–17)

Why is this trickery necessary? The only apparent reason is Portia's pleasure in toying with her husband. True, such games are typical of romantic comedy, but after Portia's treatment of Shylock in court, this mischief confirms her malicious wit.

The final scene of the play brings out its romance. Lorenzo and Jessica begin with an elegant recitation of stories of illicit lovers. More moving, however, are Lorenzo's lines about their own world:

> How sweet the moonlight sleeps upon this bank!
> Here will we sit, and let the sounds of music
> Creep in our ears. Soft stillness and the night
> Become the touches of sweet harmony.
>
> (V, i, 54–57)

The scene as a whole intimates that once the figure of Shylock has been purged, once the figure of hate has been banished, love can flourish.

But the resolution is not so simple. First Portia and Nerissa enter, and Portia's opening line reflects the appearance of purity she tries to present:

> How far that little candle throws his beams!
> So shines a good deed in a naughty world.
>
> (V, i, 90–91)

She contradicts this sentiment, however, when she and Nerissa taunt Gratiano and Bassanio about surrendering their rings. The two men are reduced to begging for forgiveness, and although their desperation is comic, we wonder what Portia and Nerissa hope to gain from this humiliation. Portia even offers herself to the mysterious "doctor" to whom Bassanio gave his ring:

> I'll not deny him any thing I have,
> No, not my body nor my husband's bed.
>
> (V, i, 227–228)

The sharp-tongued woman who in Act I, scene ii mocked all her suitors is still here.

Her irony is undercut by the intrusion of Antonio: "I am th' unhappy subject of these quarrels" (V, i, 238). Possibly the lonely Antonio is bothered to see a loving couple arguing—he recognizes that they have something precious, and he does not want them to waste it. More likely he is wallowing in his misery, for a few lines later he again suggests himself as ransom for Bassanio's bond:

> I dare be bound again,
> My soul upon the forfeit, that your lord
> Will never more break faith advisedly.
>
> (V, i, 251–253)

Antonio still appears eager to lose his life in devotion to Bassanio. Thus even in this comically romantic situation, Antonio's desperate affection for Bassanio casts a pall. We recognize that as the other three couples pair up and head off for a happy life, he is left as unhappy as when the play began.

Even when Antonio learns from Portia that three of his ships have miraculously "come to harbor" (V, i, 277), all he can say is "I am dumb" (V, i, 279). Without a reason to drown in dejection, he has nothing to say, except a few lines later when he thanks Portia for restoring his money and giving him "life and living" (V, i, 286). Here for the last time is a similarity between Antonio and Shylock, two men reduced to existing for money. The other three couples are then happily married.

What ties together all the strands of *The Merchant of Venice* is the egoism of virtually the entire cast. Shylock is obsessed with his money, his only daughter, and his hatred for Christian Venice. Antonio is preoccupied with his loneliness and his finances as well as with his frustrated desire for Bassanio's complete devotion. Portia is dedicated to her own satisfaction, which includes having the man she wants, but also with exercising her wit and power at the expense of others, even those for whom she cares. Lorenzo and Jessica are attracted to one

The Comedies

another, but he is absorbed with her money, and she uses him as a passport to her freedom. The other citizens of Venice are busy with their own pleasures. In sum, self-absorption clouds the romantic tone of the play.

So do the characters of Shylock and Antonio. The former is, for the sake of comedy, a partial caricature, but Shakespeare invests him with sufficient dignity that we feel the anguish of an outsider forced to deal with a society that rejects him. Antonio's unhappiness, too, permeates the play, and even the romantic finale is suffused with his melancholy. The spirit of these two characters suggests a darker vision that dominates Shakespeare's later comic works.

SUGGESTIONS FOR FURTHER READING

Andrews, Mark Edwin. *Law versus Equity in* The Merchant of Venice. Boulder: Colorado University Press, 1965.

Barnet, Sylvan, ed. *Twentieth Century Interpretations of* The Merchant of Venice. Englewood Cliffs, N.J.: Prentice-Hall, 1970.

Burckhardt, Sigurd. "*The Merchant of Venice*: The Gentle Bond." *ELH* 29 (1962): 239–262.

Carrington, Norman. *Shakespeare:* The Merchant of Venice. London: Brodil, 1958.

Coolidge, J. S. "Law and Love in *The Merchant of Venice*." *Shakespeare Quarterly* 27 (1976): 243–263.

Grebanier, Bernard. *The Truth About Shylock*. New York: Random House, 1962.

Henye, R. "Which is the Merchant Here? And Which the Jew?" *Criticism* 16 (1974): 287–300.

Landa, M. J. *The Shylock Myth*. London: Allen, 1942.

Lewalski, Barbara K. "Biblical Allusion and Allegory in *The Merchant of Venice*." *Shakespeare Quarterly* 13 (1962): 327–343.

Moody, Anthony David. *Shakespeare:* The Merchant of Venice. London: Edward Arnold, 1964.

Sinsheimer, Herman. *Shylock, The History of a Character*. New York: B. Blom, 1968.

THE MERRY WIVES OF WINDSOR

Tradition has it that this work was composed in two weeks after a request from Queen Elizabeth, who wished to see a play about Falstaff in love. It is the only comedy of Shakespeare set in an English setting, here Windsor, and it is his only portrait of contemporary, middle-class English life. More important, it is his only pure farce and consequently has less character development than any of his other plays. Yet even as farce the play poses problems. Its charm comes from its generally sunny tone. But for many audiences, that lightness, in combination with the two-dimensional characters, robs the play of interest. Still, the story, which has no known literary source, is sufficiently involving and attractive that it has been adapted successfully into opera, notably by Verdi as *Falstaff* and by Vaughan Williams as *Sir John in Love*.

The key element of the play, and for some the key difficulty, is the character of Falstaff. He is a far cry from the great knight of *Henry IV*. That figure is a brilliant wit, a worthy companion to a future king, and, above all, a man of dignity. His intellect is sharper than any other on stage, and when characters laugh at him, Falstaff is always aware of the joke and able to take it steps further. In sum, whatever his points of vulnerability, such as his girth, capacity for drink, cowardice, and general lecherousness, and Falstaff of the history plays is a man of substance, greater than his world.

In *The Merry Wives of Windsor* that Falstaff is no longer present. His weight remains enormous and he does enjoy a good jest, but his stature has faded. In addition, many of Falstaff's companions from the history plays, including Bardolph, Pistol, and Nym, appear here as fun-loving but essentially harmless rogues. And their sanitation, as it were, takes away part of the threat in this play. Even in farce, no matter how light, someone must pose a danger to someone else. The audience needs to feel substantial pressure or conflict. In this play that threat is so mild that we are kept at a distance, watching rather than worrying.

For instance, at the start we learn that Justice Shallow, another figure from the history plays, has a grievance against Falstaff and wants him punished (I, i, 1–4). This claim brings to mind the fat knight's adventures in *Henry IV*, but the accusation here is lost when Sir Hugh Evans distracts Shallow with the suggestion that Shallow might find profit were his cousin Slender to marry Mistress Anne Page (I, i, 42–46). Here is the first of several instances in which marriage and money are intertwined. Slender, as his name suggests, is later described by Mistress Quickly as follows:

> . . . he hath but a little [whey]-face,
> with a little yellow beard, a Cain-color'd beard.

(I, iv, 22–23)

The image of his courting anyone evokes laughter. But in scene i Slender is immediately intrigued, for he knows of the young woman's inherited wealth (I, i, 47–65). Evans, too, is the object of mockery, for with his Welsh dialect he creates memorably awful phrases: "It were a goot motion if we leave our pribbles and prabbles . . ." (I, i, 54). Thus here we have amusing characters and silly situations, but no more. We have little about which to worry or think.

When Falstaff enters, he is accompanied by familiar associates: Nym, Bardolph, and Pistol. Shallow immediately states his charge (I, i, 111–112), and Falstaff admits guilt, but advises against Shallow's pressing the case: "You'll be laughed at" (I, i, 119). In light of what happens to Falstaff himself, that warning is ironic. Pistol then is accused of having picked Shallow's pocket, but with Falstaff's support that crime is denied. Again, the fat knight is momentarily in command, but he will not remain so for long.

After Mistress Page, her daughter Anne, and Mistress Ford appear, Page invites all for dinner. Slender, however, resists, and angles to remain with Anne. Shallow and Evans try to offer counsel, but Slender wants only to be alone (I, i, 270–272). When he does make his attempts to woo Anne, however, he blunders. He feigns an absence of hunger, as if in the throes of romantic passion (I, i, 279–280), then boasts at having been wounded dueling for "stewed prunes" (I, i, 285), food common to brothels and therefore slang for prostitutes. Yet despite these weak efforts, Slender does have support, for in scene ii Evans sends Slender's servant, Simple, to Mistress Quickly so as to solicit her aid in Slender's cause (I, ii, 9–11).

The courtship by Slender is soon to be complicated by other figures who seek Anne Page's hand, while that overall story is paralleled by Falstaff's own efforts in romance. In scene iii he tells Pistol:

> Briefly—I do mean to
> make love to Ford's wife. I spy entertainment in
> her. She discourses, she carves, she gives the leer
> of invitation. I can construe the action of her fa-
> miliar style, and the hardest voice of her behavior
> (to be English'd rightly) is, "I am Sir John Falstaff's."

(I, iii, 43–48)

He is also attracted to Mistress Ford's closest friend, Mistress Page, and has written amorous letters to both of them:

                                        I will
be cheaters to them both, and they shall be
exchequers to me. They will be my East and West
Indies, and I will trade to them both.

                                                (I, iii, 69–72)

The plan has such an obvious weakness that any tension is broken. Falstaff will
attempt to woo separately two women almost certain to share their correspondence and thus almost certain to realize his deception. As if this realization were
not enough to undermine our expectations that Falstaff has any chance of success,
Nym and Pistol, both of whom are rejected by Falstaff in this scene, resolve to
have revenge on him by revealing his schemes to the women involved (I, iii,
90–104).

     That Falstaff as cheater will be the victim of his own plottings has the potential
for dramatic irony, and that theme may be considered vital overall. It is developed
further in the next scene, when Mistress Quickly is recruited privately to help
each of the suitors of Anne Page. First Quickly assures Simple: "Tell Master
Parson Evans I will do what I can for your master" (I, iv, 33). Dr. Caius then
enters, pretentiously spouting a combination of English and French. He, too,
seeks to marry Anne, and the aspirations of the two suitors, each with his own
bizarre version of English, contrast throughout the play. Quickly assures Caius
that she will further his plan (I, iv, 120–121), but also reveals that his attempts
will be fruitless:

     You shall have Anne—fool's-head of your
     own. No, I know Anne's mind for that.

                                                (I, iv, 126–127)

Finally she agrees to aid young Fenton, but her private words about him are
hardly encouraging:

     Truly, an honest gentleman; but Anne loves him
     not; for I know Anne's mind as well as another does.

                                                (I, iv, 163–165)

We suspect, however, that Anne will eventually end up with Fenton. One reason
is that Mistress Quickly describes him as "honest," and that quality is rare in
this play. A second is that Mistress Quickly herself appreciates him, and we
have no reason to doubt her opinion, for she is the only character aware of all
the conflicting ambitions, and as such becomes a voice of authority and reason.
Finally, the other two suitors are entirely unacceptable.

     In Act II, scene i, mistresses Ford and Page discover that they are both objects
of Falstaff's attention (II, i, 70–71), and they resolve to punish the knight for
his effrontery. Equally intriguing as this plot line, however, are the reactions of
the husbands, who have learned from Pistol and Nym of Falstaff's aim. Page
remains confident of his wife's loyalty (II, i, 181–184), but Ford is suspicious:

> I do not misdoubt my wife; but I would be
> loath to turn them together. A man may be too
> confident. I would have nothing lie on my head.
> I cannot be thus satisfied.
>
> (II, i, 185–188)

He resolves to test his wife by disguising himself and visiting Falstaff (II, i, 233–240).

We also learn of events in the parallel story, for Shallow announces that Evans and Dr. Caius are to fight a duel, but Shallow confides to the page and us that the Host has sabotaged the contest by sending the combatants to different locations (II, i, 200–210).

In scene ii Falstaff again demonstrates his self-assurance by turning down Pistol's request for a loan, simultaneously reproving his friend over his general impropriety (II, ii, 15–29). With every word Falstaff seems to set himself as a target. Mistress Quickly then enters with messages, first one from Mistress Ford that Ford will be away between ten and eleven, then one from Mistress Page that Falstaff should send his own page to her. As Falstaff grandly pays for this information, he settles back smugly:

> Say's thou so, old Jack? go thy ways.
> I'll make more of thy old body than I have done.
>
> (II, ii, 138–139)

He is asking for a fall.

Ford's scheme leads to a winning scene between Falstaff and Ford, masquerading as "Brook," and supposedly seeking his own fling with Mistress Ford. "Brook" admits to Falstaff his hope to "lay open mine own imperfection" (II, ii, 184–185), but one irony of the scene is that while Ford fools Falstaff, he himself undergoes considerable anguish. Ultimately Ford becomes aware of his own brand of folly, but until then he appears slightly mad. For instance, he claims to be infatuated with Mistress Ford but has thus far been rejected by her (II, ii, 194–208). He even professes to Falstaff:

> Some say that, though she appear
> honest to me, yet in other places she enlargeth her
> mirth so far that there is shrewd construction made
> of her.
>
> (II, ii, 221–224)

Therefore, Ford claims, he seeks Falstaff's aid in wooing her (II, ii, 235–237). Afterwards "Brook" will take action:

> Now, could I come to
> her with any detection in my hand, my desires
> had instance and argument to commend themselves.
> I could drive her then from the ward of her purity,
> her reputation, her marriage vow, and a thousand

other her defenses, which now are too too strongly
embettled against me.

(II, ii, 245–251)

Falstaff, flattered at his reputation, boasts that by coincidence he will be with
Mistress Ford "between ten and eleven..." (II, ii, 265). And we anticipate
his entrapment. But Falstaff is not the only victim here.

Ford's doubts about his wife are played for comic effect, especially when
Falstaff, unaware of the identity of his visitor, comments on Ford's reputation:

> Hang him, poor cuckoldly knave, I know
> him not. Yet I wrong him to call him poor. They
> say the jealous wittolly knave hath masses of money,
> for the which his wife seems to me well-favor'd. I will
> use her as the key of the cuckoldly rogue's coffer,
> and there's my harvest-home.

(II, ii, 270–275)

Ford is forced to listen while Falstaff derides him. But the derision has thematic
import. Here again love and money are brought together, and Ford is as guilty
as any in his sense of possession, both of his money and his wife.

When Ford is left alone onstage, he blusters furiously:

> See the hell of
> having a false woman! My bed shall be abus'd, my
> coffers ransack'd, my reputation gnawn at, and
> I shall not only receive this villainous wrong, but
> stand under the adoption of abominable terms, and
> by him that does me this wrong.

(II, ii, 291–296)

In the context of this dramatic situation, these lines strike us as those of a buffoon.
But were the same words placed in another context, they could reflect a mind
preoccupied with infidelity and loss of money. In subsequent plays, such as
Othello and *The Winter's Tale*, Shakespeare brings out the darkest side of jealousy
through characters so fixated that they go virtually mad. The actor playing Ford
may hint at such obsession, but the text steers clear of any truly grim possibilities.
We are never encouraged to take his ravings seriously, although they sometimes
are extreme.

Before these are revealed, however, scene ii dramatizes Dr. Caius's pre-duel
moments. He boasts and threatens but we know nothing will happen, and Caius
too seems relieved when the contest is postponed (II, iii, 90–93). Act III, scene
i is a parallel scene, in which Evans awaits his rival. When all the principals
arrive, the Host admits his deception (III, i, 107–108), and all adjourn for dinner,
although Caius and Evans mumble discontentedly. The petty suitors are not so
easily assuaged.

In Act III, scene ii Ford returns to the action, as he anticipates catching his
wife and Falstaff together:

> Good plots,
> they are laid and our revolted wives share damnation
> together. Well, I will take him, then torture
> my wife, pluck the borrow'd veil of modesty from
> the so-seeming Mistress Page, divulge Page himself
> for a secure and willful Actaeon; and to these violent
> proceedings all my neighbors shall cry aim.
>
> (III, ii, 38–44)

At such a moment Ford sounds like an avenging spirit, determined to wipe from his world all hypocrisy and sexual license. In addition, the lines could be enacted with lasciviousness so that the character could be depicted as finding such thoughts in themselves arousing. From such a perspective Ford anticipates Angelo from *Measure for Measure*, who hides his unattractive desires for pleasure under an even more unattractive veneer of purity. But the comparison should not be overemphasized. Angelo is a perpetually solemn character in a story with many unpleasant overtones. Here Ford rails in the midst of a society populated by characters we know to be harmless. Thus his protests and schemes seem out of place. We never doubt that all complications will resolve happily, and we always accept Ford as a foolish, deluded husband, not an unbalanced, dangerous one.

The physicality of the comedy is developed further in the next scene. Falstaff is attempting his courtship of Mistress Ford, when Mistress Page rushes in shouting that Ford himself is coming (III, ii, 106–110). Falstaff is forced to hide in a laundry basket, and the servants, at Mistress Page's order, unknowingly remove him for a dunking in the Thames. Ford is naturally frustrated in his search, and Mistress Ford seizes the pith of the moment:

> I know not which pleases me better,
> that my husband is deceiv'd, or Sir John.
>
> (III, iii, 178–179)

The sight of the fat knight scrambling is funny, but to enjoy it we have to dismiss all thoughts of the Falstaff from *Henry IV*, for to imagine that character so humiliated is sad. This Falstaff, however, is far less dignified, and thus to see him shoved about is laughable. So is Ford's frustration at not finding Falstaff, especially amid Mistress Ford's seemingly innocent expression "buck-washing" (III, iii, 155–156), a reference to cuckolding.

Scene iv continues the more traditional romantic story line, as Fenton and Anne Page exchange conventional expressions of affection. Fenton's key lines reflect one of the main themes of the play:

> Albeit I will confess thy father's wealth
> Was the first motive that I woo'd thee, Anne;
> Yet wooing thee, I found thee of more value
> Than stamps in gold, or sums in sealed bag;
> And 'tis the very riches of thyself

That now I aim at.

(III, iv, 13–18)

He is one of the few figures who realize the relative values of money and human character, and his admission is one of the rare statements of true affection in the play. We would not want to overemphasize the seriousness of the work, but surely the desire for money as a substitute for love dominates the action, as it does in so many of Shakespeare's comedies. Page, an essentially decent man, nonetheless dismisses Fenton for lack of funds (IV, iii, 68–70), as does Mistress Page, although she does so with a gentle word for the poor fellow (IV, iii, 88–93). At the end of this scene, Mistress Quickly, still acting as marriage broker for all three suitors, emphasizes Fenton's quality:

> A kind heart he hath. A woman
> would run through fire and water for such a kind
> heart.

(III, iv, 102–104)

After such praise, we assume more than ever that Fenton will marry Anne.

In scene v Falstaff again encounters Ford disguised as Brook, and the knight relates the story of his imprisonment in the laundry basket. The narrative is filled with the grandiose imagery and vocabulary we associate with Falstaff:

> I suffer'd
> the pangs of three several deaths: first, an intolerable
> fright, to be detected with a jealous rotten
> bell-wether; next, to be compass'd like a good
> bilbo in the circumference of a peck, hilt to point,
> heel to head; and then to be stopp'd in like a strong
> distillation with stinking clothes that fretted
> in their own grease.

(III, v, 107–114)

The impact of the speech, though, is blunted by the nature of the speaker. His skill with language is undeniable, but if he is so witty, how he can so easily be fooled? Throughout this play Falstaff is trivialized, and even so grand a passage cannot turn him into the formidable figure of *Henry IV*.

The other interesting element of the scene is the dilemma of Ford. On the one hand, he is pleased to learn that Falstaff's lusting has been thwarted. On the other hand, Ford is frustrated that he himself was played for a dupe by his wife. The character does not have many lines until Falstaff leaves, and thus the actor must communicate the contradictory emotions through tone and gesture.

Act IV, scene i is a respite from the main action, as Evans, William, and Mistress Quickly engage in reflections on learning. Quickly has little patience for book knowledge (IV, i, 65–68), and her worldliness, in contrast with Evans's dim pomposity, suggests the impracticality of classroom education. In Act IV, scene ii Falstaff resumes his wooing of Mistress Ford, but when word once more comes of Ford's imminent arrival, the fat knight refuses to retreat to the basket, and instead is forced to disguise himself as the Witch of Brainford. This time his punishment is more severe, as Ford is allowed to discover the intruder, and, unaware that he is attacking Falstaff in disguise, swats the figure about the room. Such physical comedy can be entertaining, but again, we may find ourselves squirming to see an old man battered. Whatever his stature in this play, Falstaff is an enjoyable character, and to see him undergo such pain leaves us uneasy, especially when the attacker is the dislikeable Ford. The cruelty of the moment no doubt appealed to the Elizabethans, who derived considerable pleasure from seeing figures on stage in physical torment.

In Act IV, scene iv, Ford has been made aware of his own victimization, and he begs forgiveness of his wife:

> I rather will suspect the sun with [cold]
> Than thee with wantoness.

$$(IV, iv, 7–8)$$

But his gentle spirit quickly disappears, as the women and men conspire to create one more punishment for Falstaff. Evans seeks to impose severe suffering:

> Methinks there should be terrors in him that he should
> not come; methinks his flesh is punish'd, he shall have
> no desires.

$$(IV, iv, 21–23)$$

Mistress Page takes up this cue, imagining an entire pageant of torture for Falstaff:

> Then let them all encircle him about,
> And fairy-like to pinch the unclean knight . . .

$$(IV, i, 57–58)$$

Mistress Ford adds:

>   And till he tell the truth,
> Let the supposed fairies pinch him sound,
> And burn him with their tapers.

$$(IV, iv, 61–63)$$

Their sadistic glee is entertaining. Meanwhile the plotters themselves are being deceived, as Page, in an aside, schemes to have his daughter elope with Slender (IV, iv, 74), while Mistress Page intends her daughter to run off with Dr. Caius (IV, iv, 84–85). That virtually everyone in the play is the object of deception makes the work consistent, for we therefore have no heroes, just victims.

The next set of short scenes builds to the great final spectacle. Falstaff is told that Mistress Ford has been beaten by her husband (IV, v, 111–113), and Quickly convinces Falstaff that other revelations will require action. In Act IV, scene vi, the Host accepts 100 pounds to help Fenton marry Anne, and the Host seems to find particular pleasure in deceiving both sets of parents (IV, vi, 46). In Act V, scene i, Mistress Quickly sets up Falstaff for his third try at seduction, while the knight still smarts over the beating from Ford and swears revenge (V, i, 26–

29). In scene ii, the other major plot line continues, as Slender learns the password by which he will recognize Anne, who will be in white. Meanwhile in scene iii, Caius is told that Anne will be in green, and in scene iv Evans gathers the would-be fairies.

In scene v Falstaff finally appears as directed, trying to give himself dignity by recalling various disguises the god Jupiter wore during his seductions (V, i, 3–11). When Mistress Ford calls for her "deer" (V, i, 16), Falstaff does not realize that he is about to be hunted, and before long his final humiliation is underway. The disguised fairies sing and dance their way around the horned victim, then put candles to his fingers, as Mistress Quickly taunts him unmercifully:

> Corrupt, corrupt, and tainted in desire!
> About him, fairies, sing a scornful rhyme,
> And as you trip, still pinch him to your time.
>
> (V, v, 90–92)

This scene appears like an exorcism of sorts, as the evil in Falstaff is purged in this parody of a ritual. But the physical suffering is ultimately less hurtful to the knight than the humiliation he must bear when he realizes that he has been the butt of a series of pranks: "I do begin to perceive that I am made an ass" (V, v, 119). Moments later, after Evans mocks him, Falstaff adds:

> Have I liv'd to stand
> at the taunt of one that makes fritters of English?
> This is enough to be the decay of lust and late-walking
> through the realm.
>
> (V, v, 142–145)

Were anyone but Falstaff uttering these lines, we would find them satisfying. To hear this once titanic personality reveal such denseness, however, is depressing.

The final twists of the plot include the deceptions on Slender and Dr. Caius, both of whom discover they have run away not with Anne Page, but with disguised boys (V, v, 184, 206). Yet little bitterness or anger surfaces, especially when Fenton enters with the truth:

> You would have married her most shamefully,
> Where there was no proportion held in love.
> The truth is, she and I (long since contracted)
> Are now so sure that nothing can dissolve us.
>
> (V, v, 221–225)

Immediately the couple is forgiven, even by Page, and the play ends amid expressions of love and reconciliation. Ford has the last line, reminding all of the confusion that has taken place:

> Sir John.
> To Master [Brook] you yet shall hold your word,

> For he to-night shall lie with Mistress Ford.
>
> (V, v, 245–246)

He emphasizes that of all the victims of the play, none has been so foolish as Falstaff, but also that general affection and forgiveness triumph.

The pleasure of *The Merry Wives of Windsor* is its genial spirit, involved plot, and physical humor. For some audiences, however, such qualities are insufficient, because the simplistic characters, in particular Falstaff, make the play inconsequential. From Shakespeare we expect comedy that makes us think and feel as well as laugh, and in this play those attributes are muted.

SUGGESTIONS FOR FURTHER READING

Battenhouse, Roy. "Falstaff as Parodist and Perhaps Holy Fool." *PMLA* 90 (1974): 32–52.

Bryant, J. A. "Falstaff and the Renewal of *Windsor*." *PMLA* 89 (1973): 296–301.

Goldshalk, William L. "An Apology for *The Merry Wives of Windsor*." *Renaissance Papers* (1973): 97–108.

Green, William. *Shakespeare's* Merry Wives of Windsor. Princeton: Princeton University Press, 1962.

Roberts, J. A. "Falstaff in Windsor Forest: Villain or Victim?" *Shakespeare Quarterly* 26 (1975): 8–15.

Steadman, John M. "Falstaff as Actaeon: A Dramatic Emblem." *Shakespeare Quarterly* 14 (1963): 231–244.

MUCH ADO ABOUT NOTHING

One theme that appears throughout the early comedies of Shakespeare is the self-love of characters preoccupied with their own needs and desires and oblivious to the needs and desires of others. Male characters, in particular, are subject to such egoism. We think of Proteus in *Two Gentlemen of Verona*, any of the men in *Love's Labor's Lost*, and Demetrius and Lysander in *A Midsummer Night's Dream*. Bianca in *The Taming of the Shrew* is an example of a female character devoted to her own pleasures. In Shakespeare's later comedies this theme comes to the fore, as many characters must escape self-absorption before they can find happiness in the love of others.

In *Much Ado About Nothing*, such vanity is complicated by a spirit of deception, for almost all characters involve themselves in plots in which they attempt to carry out one trick but end up victims of another. The title word ''Nothing'' may be taken as a pun on ''noting,'' or overhearing, and much of the action involves eavesdropping and the partial discernment of truth. One overall motif, therefore, is that of characters too preoccupied with themselves to appreciate what happens around them.

The sources for the play's two main plot lines are unclear. Shakespeare may have come across the Claudio-Hero story in the tale of Ginevora and Ariodante, which was dramatized by Ariosto in his epic *Orlando Furioso* (1516), as well as in Matteo Bandello's tale of Sir Timbreo and Fenicia in a collection titled *Novelliere* (1554). The Beatrice-Benedick plot seems to have been Shakespeare's own, inspired by passages in Baldassar Castiglione's *Il Libro del Cortegiano* (*The Courtier*), which was translated in English in 1561.

The play begins with the news that Don Pedro and Claudio, fresh from triumph in war, are headed to Messina (I, i, 12–17). The first comment that strikes us is Beatrice's question about whether Benedick, too, is returning. When she learns that he is, she rushes to mock his manhood:

> In our last
> conflict four of his five wits went halting off, and
> now is the whole man govern'd with one; so that

if he have wit enough to keep himself warm, let
him bear it for a difference between himself and
his horse . . .

(I, i, 65–70)

She also asks:

Who is his
companion now? he hath every month a new sworn
brother.

(I, i, 71–73)

That Beatrice brings up Benedick's name suggests her interest in him. That she
rails against him without provocation suggests her attraction to him. And that
she worries about his companion and his popularity among colleagues suggests
she is jealous of any attention he gives to someone other than her. Beatrice may
try to seem antagonistic to Benedick, but her opening sallies confirm her fascination with him.

When Benedick enters a few lines later, he refers to Beatrice as "Lady Disdain" (I, i, 118), and his responses to her insults clarify his regard for her:

But it is
certain I am lov'd of all ladies, only you excepted;
and I would I could find in my heart that I had not a
hard heart, for truly I love none.

(I, i, 124–127)

To this last line he might add "except myself." The speech anticipates a great
deal of the action to come, for any man who proudly relates his independence
from emotion is virtually begging to yield to someone. And Benedick's singling
out Beatrice for rejection also has the effect of announcing how intrigued he is
with her. Both characters, in fact, remind us that the opposite of love is not hate
but indifference. The more they gibe at one another, the more we realize that
each hopes the other will break down the linguistic barriers between them and
allow their latent affection to bloom.

Their relationship recalls that between Katherine and Petruchio in *The Taming
of the Shrew*. One major difference between the two situations is that Beatrice
(whose name means "blesser") and Benedick (meaning "the blessed one") are
social equals. In addition, both maintain the pose of hostility towards the other.
In the earlier play, Petruchio is always open with his affection, and the difference
between his station and Katherine's enables him to employ a variety of physical
punishments and deprivations to make Katherine yield to him. Here such physical
tactics are forbidden, and the characters must meet strictly on emotional and
intellectual grounds.

These two characters are the most interesting in the play. However, the inevitable resolution of the tension between them means that they cannot be the
prime focus of the action. Some other story must take center stage, and that is
the relationship between Hero and Claudio.

When Claudio and Benedick are left alone, Benedick claims hardly to have noticed Hero Leonato's daughter, but Claudio expresses his interest in curious terms: "Can the world buy such a jewel?" (I, i, 181). Does he mean that he seeks to possess her, as he does wealth? He adds: "In mine eye, she is the sweetest lady that ever I look'd on" (I, i, 187–188). Imagery of sight recurs throughout the play, as characters frequently judge by appearance and are unable to distinguish truth from fraudulence. We also note that to this point in the play Hero has said not a word. Thus Claudio's affections seem based on surface values: her money and her appearance. Later, at the marriage altar, we remember these weak statements of affection. Throughout the rest of this scene, as Don Pedro and Claudio together mock Benedick's devotion to bachelorhood and his future victimization as a cuckold, Claudio never becomes any more profound in his estimation of Hero. Indeed, he even asks Don Pedro: "Hath Leonato any son, my lord?" (I, i, 293). The implication is whether Hero will have to share her fortune with any siblings. Again, the genuineness of Claudio's affection is open to question.

Moments later Don Pedro further lowers the audience's opinion of Claudio. First he criticizes Claudio's courting technique:

> Thou wilt be like a lover presently,
> And tire the hearer with a book of words.

> (I, i, 306–307)

Then Don Pedro compounds the insult:

> I know we shall have revelling to-night;
> I will assume thy part in some disguise,
> And tell fair Hero I am Claudio
> And in her bosom I'll unclasp my heart . . .

> (I, i, 320–323)

Claudio's silently accepting this offer for someone else to court for him intimates he is hardly bold. Indeed, he is an unlikely romantic hero, and that he proves disappointing is not surprising.

Scene ii places the information communicated at the end of the last scene in a different context, as Antonio tells his brother Leonato that Don Pedro has confessed love for Hero, and intends to court her at the dance (I, ii, 11–13). The confusion of detail reflects a world in which overhearing and spying lead to misunderstanding.

Scene iii of Act I introduces the villain of the play, Don John, Don Pedro's bastard brother. John is a curious instrument of darkness, for his self-awareness leaves him detached from his own emotions. To Conrade's queries about this melancholy, Don John comments:

> I cannot hide what I am: I must be sad when I
> have cause, and smile at no man's jests; eat

when I have stomach, and wait for no man's leisure . . .

(I, iii, 13–15)

Moments later he adds:

I had rather be a canker in a hedge
than a rose in his grace, and it better fits my blood
to be disdain'd of all than to fashion a carriage to
rob love from any . . . In the mean time let me be that I
am, and seek not to alter me.

(I, iii, 27–37)

Like Iago in *Othello*, Don John has no explanation for his behavior. In that respect he is another example of what Coleridge called "motiveless malignity." Yet Don John is different from Iago in that the latter tries to devise reasons for his hatred and thereby pervert himself into a perpetual rage. And in those ravings Iago reveals the depth of his sexual wounds and frustrations. The second quote above, however, shows that Don John does not seek explanation for his attitude. He accepts his estrangement and satisfies his needs with unpleasant intrusions into the happiness of others. He probes no further.

Thus when he learns of Claudio's affection for Hero and of Don Pedro's plan to court for Claudio (I, iii, 60–64), he resolves to sabotage the courtship: "That young start-up hath all the glory of my overthrow" (I, iii, 65–66). Whether Claudio did steal Don John's glory is beside the point. For Don John the opportunity to cause mischief is enough reason to do so.

In Act II Beatrice's first comment confirms her intelligence as she evaluates Don John correctly: "How tartly that gentlemen looks" (II, i, 3). But her own problems distract her, and she feels compelled to bring Benedick into the discussion (II, i, 8–17). The more she protests, both at him and at the institution of marriage, the more convinced we are that because they share parallel attitudes and manners, Beatrice and Benedick are bound to end up together.

Her speeches are thematically powerful. After she disparages marriage (II, i, 27–29), she uses the phrase "lead his apes into hell" (II, i, 41), the proverbial punishment for old maids, as opportunity to comment on the nature of men and on her unwillingness to subordinate herself to any:

Would it not grieve a woman
to be overmaster'd with a piece of valiant dust? to
make an account of her life to a clod of wayward
marl?

(II, i, 60–63)

Her independent spirit emphasizes her worth. Yet her speech in lines 69–80 contains several references to dancing, including "measure." Such imagery reflects the pattern of social convention to which the characters respond as well as the reluctance of Beatrice and Benedick to "dance" by those rules until the very end, when they, too, surrender to the conventional sense of order.

At this point the celebrants don masks, an appropriate action for the world of this play. Hero dances with Don Pedro, who pretends to be Claudio, and Beatrice eventually dances with Benedick. The last pair has an effective bit of irony, for Benedick recognizes Beatrice, and thus talks about himself in the hope of hearing flattering remarks in return. Instead Beatrice insults him:

> Why, he is the Prince's jester, a very dull
> fool; only his gift is in devising impossible slanders.

> (II, i, 137–138)

We cannot be certain whether Beatrice recognizes Benedick, or whether she is speaking unaware, but the scene is effective either way. Soon Beatrice decides they must dance and "follow the leaders" (II, i, 151), and Benedick responds in rhythm: "In every good thing" (II, i, 152). By the end of the play they are such conformists.

The plot darkens for the first time when Borachio recognizes Claudio (II, i, 159–160), and Don John beings to work his plan. He easily dupes Claudio into believing that Don Pedro woos Hero only for himself (II, i, 163–164), and Claudio's reaction sets up the remaining tension of the play:

> 'Tis certain so, the Prince woos for himself.
> Friendship is constant in all other things
> Save in the office and affairs of love;
> Therefore all hearts in love use their own tongues.
> Let every eye negotiate for itself,
> And trust no agent . . .

> (II, i, 174–178)

The first key element here is Claudio's receptivity. He never questions Don John's accusations. Second, he is willing to generalize on the basis of this one incident, so that suddenly no one is to be trusted. Finally, the one person who will in fact be unfaithful is Claudio himself. Thus here he ironically condemns himself. Moments later Benedick wanders over to assure Claudio that "the Prince hath got your Hero" (II, i, 191–192). The phrasing confirms Claudio's suspicions and he grumbles in return: "I wish him joy of her" (II, i, 193). Soon Claudio departs, as Benedick's own situation takes over. Yet Claudio's anger remains in our minds.

Benedick's perpetual assault on the character of Beatrice continues (II, i, 202–210), and more than ever we are assured that such a confounded man must end up married. Benedick then reports that Claudio is "melancholy" (II, i, 214), and explains obtusely that Claudio feels he has been the victim of treachery:

> The flat transgression of a schoolboy,
> who being overjoy'd with finding a bird's nest,
> shows it his companion, and he steals it.

> (II, i, 222–224)

Don Pedro does not take this mood seriously, then switches the topic back to Beatrice, thereby leaving Benedick blustering in an extended harangue on Beatrice's manner: "She speaks poniards, and every word stabs" (II, i, 247–248). Yet the more he protests, the more we feel his captivation. When Don Pedro announces that Beatrice is approaching, Benedick satirizes courtly behavior, as he volunteers to do a series of extraordinary feats not to win his lady's hand, but to escape her presence:

> I will go on the slightest arrand
> now to the Antipodes that you can devise to send
> me on; I will fetch you a toothpicker now from
> the furthest inch of Asia, bring you the length of
> Prester John's foot . . .
>
>   (II, i, 264–268)

Such outlandish deeds were the tasks lovers traditionally fulfilled to win their ladies. Here Benedick uses them as a means of escape. That he indulges in such a literary game at the time of his supposed panic affirms yet again that he is taken with Beatrice and hardly horrified by her presence. And when he runs away seconds later, he is escaping not her, but feelings inside him that he is afraid to reveal.

Next follows a curious moment. When Beatrice enters, she is accompanied by Claudio, Leonato, and Hero, who stands silently. After Don Pedro gently reproves Beatrice for her attitude towards Benedick, the conversation turns to Claudio, and Don Pedro tries to brighten the young man's mood:

> Here, Claudio, I have woo'd in thy name,
> and fair Hero is won.
>
>   (II, i, 297–298)

And Leonato confirms his own pleasure at this news (II, i, 302–304). After the interlude with Don John moments before, we expect Claudio to speak out. Instead, he stands passively until Beatrice urges him to speak (II, i, 305). Finally he does:

> Silence is the perfectest herald of joy; I were
> but little happy, if I could say how much!
> Lady, as you are mine, I am yours. I give away
> myself for you, and dote upon the exchange.
>
>   (II, i, 306–309)

Apparently he has forgotten his recent antagonism. For some audiences this shift in mood is a misstep by Shakespeare, for Don John's first attempt at sabotage goes nowhere. However, Claudio's early willingness to believe the worst sets up his gullibility, and his reversion to trusting Hero and Don Pedro does not disguise his vapidness. We shall not be surprised when he succumbs to another plot.

During this scene Hero remains silent while Beatrice seemingly cannot keep her mouth closed. Her volubility is caused by more than wit, for as her friend Hero is happily betrothed, Beatrice must feel frustration. Thus her excuse, "I was born to speak all mirth and no matter'' (II, i, 330) manifests her need to let a wall of words hide her emptiness. Don Pedro is sophisticated enough to recognize the latent affection in her: ''She were an excellent wife for Benedick'' (II, i, 351–352), and Leonato, too, is taken with the prospect:

> O Lord, my lord, if they were but a week
> married, they would talk themselves mad.
>
> (II, i, 352–353)

The two and Claudio then resolve to make Beatrice and Benedick fall in love. What the plotters do not realize, though, or at least what they never say, is that the two victims instinctively love one another already. All they require are circumstances in which they are allowed to tell each other.

In Act II, scene ii, Don John attempts a more complicated trick to destroy the love between Hero and Claudio. First he mentions the word ''sick'' (II, ii, 5). Gradually the motif of illness dominates the play's language and expresses the state of those in love, as here it reflects the mood of one in anguish over lack of love. In addition, Don John seems yet to have no serious reason for his treachery: ''Only to despite them, I will endeavor any thing'' (II, ii, 31–32). He does not want Hero for himself, and he seems to have lost sight of his jealousy of Claudio. He seeks only some peculiar pleasure at disrupting their happiness. As Borachio explains: ''The poison of that lies in you to temper'' (II, ii, 21). The image of poison again reminds us of Iago. Borachio then outlines a scheme wherein Don Pedro and Claudio will be led to see Margaret pretending to be Hero at her window. The plan emphasizes the theme of deceptive appearance, especially as Borachio speaks of ''seeming truth'' (II, ii, 48).

In Act II, scene iii, Benedick takes up his struggle with himself. He dwells first on Claudio's infatuation, invoking familiar images of music and dance. Then he turns to self-examination:

> May I be so coverted and see with these eyes?
> I cannot tell; I think not. I will not be sworn but
> love may transform me to an oyster, but I'll take
> my oath on it, till he have made [an] oyster of
> me, he shall never make me such a fool.
>
> (II, iii, 22–26)

Even as he denies his capacity to be so taken with a woman, he enumerates the qualities he seeks:

> Rich she shall be, that's certain;
> wise, or I'll none; virtuous, or I'll never cheapen
> her; fair, or I'll never look on her . . .
>
> (II, iii, 30–32)

As much as he tries, Benedick cannot fight his own instincts. Here he claims to demand perfection in a woman. In fact, he is waiting to fall in love; he simply needs the push to confess that need.

The final urging comes as his male colleagues gather nearby to carry out a charade about Beatrice's supposed longing for Benedick. Don Pedro begins the performance (II, iii, 90–91), and before long Benedick is utterly convinced, as Claudio indicates: "He hath ta'en th' infection" (II, iii, 121). With Leonato's help he goes on to describe Beatrice in the pangs of frustrated love:

> Then down upon her knees she falls,
> weeps, sobs, beats her heart, tears her hair, prays,
> curses: "O sweet Benedick! God give me pa-
> tience!"

(II, iii, 146–149)

Don Pedro then turns the conversation to Benedick himself, remarking on his "contemptible spirit" (II, iii, 180–181), but the other men switch to flattery, while Don Pedro modifies each of their claims. The deception works wonderfully, as Benedick, heretofore a man who uses words skillfully as weapons and a shield, believes their criticism and turns to self-analysis:

> I may chance
> have some odd quirks and remnants of wit broken
> on me, because I have rail'd so against marriage . . .

(II, iii, 235–237)

Then he seizes the new information and resolves to do what we have long felt he has always wanted to do: pursue Beatrice. He convinces himself, however, with a different perspective:

> When
> I said I would die a bachelor, I did not think
> I should live till I were married. Here comes Beatrice.
> By this day, she's a fair lady. I do spy some marks of
> love in her.

(II, iii, 242–246)

The last line is especially revealing. Now that he believes Beatrice is infatuated with him, Benedick sees in her the affections he desires. Again, as in many comedies of Shakespeare, love is what characters want to see, not what is necessarily there. Even after Beatrice announces that she is merely calling him to dinner, Benedick manages in his own mind to twist her words so that they mean what he wants to hear (II, iii, 257–262).

In Act III, scene i, the women conduct the same kind of treatment to entrap Beatrice, and she, too, falls for the performance. Ursula and Hero try a different approach, however, as they criticize Beatrice sharply:

> But nature never fram'd a woman's heart
> Of prouder stuff than that of Beatrice.

Disdain and scorn ride sparkling in her eyes . . .

(III, i, 49–51)

But who dare tell her so? If I should speak,
She would mock me into air . . .

(III, i, 74–75)

The men flattered Benedick into acting. The women instead try to humiliate
Beatrice into behaving. Hero also feigns warning Benedick against Beatrice's
sharp tongue:

No, rather I will go to Benedick,
And counsel him to fight against his passion,
And truly I'll devise some honest slanders
To stain my cousin with. One doth not know
How much an ill word may empoison liking.

(III, i, 82–86)

What Hero and Ursula do not know is that they are soon to be the victims of
such venom. Beatrice, in the meantime, is struck by their words, both the tributes
to Benedick and the criticism of her:

Stand I condemn'd for pride and scorn so much?
Contempt, farewell, and maiden pride, adieu!
No glory lives behind the back of such.
And, Benedick, love on, I will requite thee,
Taming my wild heart to thy loving hand.
If thou dost love, my kindness shall incite thee
To bind our loves up in a holy band;
For others say thou dost deserve, and I
Believe it better than reportingly.

(III, i, 108–116)

The women Beatrice overheard were acting, yet they were not acting. Their
evaluations of Beatrice's wit was done for their own amusement, yet it was
honest. Underneath the joke lies truth. And the women, perhaps unaware, told
Beatrice what they really felt about her.

Her own reaction tells us that Beatrice understands this truth. And her willingness to go after Benedick reminds us that beneath the veneer of the cynic
lies the incurable romantic. Her invocation to have her heart "tamed" suggests
that despite her protestations, she is, deep down, a woman who wants to abide
by certain conventions of her time. She has no intention of giving in completely,
but her words indicate that partial surrender is desirable.

In the next scene we return to the more melodramatic story, as Claudio,
oblivious to his new marital responsibilities, offers to accompany Don Pedro
back to Arragon (III, ii, 3–4). Both men laugh at Benedick, who claims to have
a toothache (III, ii, 21), another image in which pain suggests emotional disorder,
here love. Claudio reasserts that Benedick is in love (III, ii, 30), and after Don
Pedro mockingly asks for traditional signs of a smitten man's moods, Claudio

and he eagerly debate Benedick's behavior and appearance (III, ii, 31–62). But the tone of the play turns gloomy once more when Don John enters with what he claims is serious news. As he describes Hero's supposed disloyalty (III, ii, 104–110), Claudio believes the worst:

> If I see any thing to-night why I should
> not marry her, to-morrow in the congregation,
> where I should wed, there will I shame her.

(III, ii, 123–125)

The precise nature of Claudio's personality is not easy to ascertain. He is not stupid, but he is remarkably naive, once more accepting the obviously untrustworthy Don John on nothing more than rumor. But Claudio also seems eager to punish Hero, and thus within him is a touch of cruelty. He is a passionate young man: quick to fall in love and quick to fall out again. Never is he likeable. He is not evil, but he is petty. Hero herself is a quiet woman, and she does not prove herself especially winning. Yet in this play as in other comedies, when the relationship is resolved we feel a superior woman settling for an inferior man.

In Act III, scene iii, the tone of the play changes once more, as Dogberry and his cohorts take the stage. Dogberry is noteworthy for his constant misuse of language, as he earnestly but thickly tries to establish his legal authority. For instance, he compliments his Watch:

> You are thought here to be the most
> senseless and fit man for the constable of the watch . . .

(III, iii, 22–23)

Thematically his awkward distortion of English reflects the use of language throughout this play, as many characters who imagine that they are speaking intelligently and understanding others are actually deceived. But Dogberry has a more important function: his very presence onstage creates an aura of innocence. No matter what the threat Don John poses and no matter how ugly Claudio and Leonato turn, Dogberry's existence removes malice.

Borachio and Conrade enter in rowdy fashion, and as two of Dogberry's cohorts overhear, Borachio proudly, and perhaps drunkenly, relates how he carried out the plot he laid out for Don John (III, iii, 144–163). His immediate arrest reassures us that all will resolve happily.

Scene iv dramatizes Hero's preparations for the wedding. She is naively enthusiastic about the beauty of her gown: "God give me joy to wear it, for my heart is exceeding heavy" (III, iv, 24–25). And her idealism is countered by Margaret's bawdy realism: " 'Twill be heavier soon by the weight of a man" (III, iv, 26–27). When Beatrice joins them, she complains of her own sickness (III, iv, 72), and we recognize how the same disease that infected Benedick (III, ii) now possesses her.

In scene v the purely comic takes over again, as Dogberry desperately tries to communicate to Leonato the earlier arrest. So entranced is Dogberry within his own position, though, and so eager is he to make himself sound important that the information drags, and Leonato finally orders that Dogberry himself carry out the questioning (III, v, 49–50). The earnest officer accepts his responsibility with singular dignity: "It shall be suffigance" (III, v, 52).

The episode at the window, when a disguised Borachio speaks to Margaret, also in disguise, is never dramatized. Instead the climactic scene of the play is the wedding, which swiftly turns from joyous anticipation to harsh disappointment when Claudio interrupts his vows:

> There, Leonato, take her back again.
> Give not this rotten orange to your friend,
> She's but the sign and semblance of her honor . . .
> All you that see her, that she were a maid,
> By these exterior shows? But she is none:
> She knows the heat of a luxurious bed;
> Her blush is guiltiness, not modesty.
>
> (IV, i, 31–42)

Margaret is not here to explain that she was the one at her window and that Borachio was the man who called to her. More important, Claudio thinks he is seeing the truth beneath the surface, but he has been deceived by the image given to him by Don John. Yet other, more painful, questions about his character arise. Why does he choose to make his revelation public? Why does he humiliate not only Hero but also her father and everyone else in the assemblage? Perhaps something in Claudio's ego demands that he be the center of attention, that he make decisions and take decisive action.

He is not the only egoistic character onstage. Don Pedro responds the crisis with similar self-regard:

> I stand dishonor'd, that have gone about
> To link my dear friend to a common stale.
>
> (IV, i, 64–65)

He accepts Claudio's claim without question. Benedick, too, reacts with his customary wit: "This looks not like a nuptial" (IV, i, 68). The line is amusing but also reflects Benedick's fear of emotion and his hiding behind words rather than meeting life head-on. Hero, who has always been passive and reactive, is here again helpless:

> O God defend me, how am I beset!
> What kind of catechizing call you this?
>
> (IV, i, 77–78)

Don Pedro then follows with what he believes to be corroborative evidence (IV, i, 87–94), an unsympathetic rendering that adds to the overall ugliness of the scene. Don John then adds his malevolent wit, manipulating others with a fraudulent morality: "Thus, pretty lady, I am sorry for thy much misgovernment"

(IV, i, 98–99). Claudio follows with melodramatics (IV, i, 100–108), and seconds later Hero characteristically swoons. After Claudio callously leaves with Don Pedro and Don John, Leonato speaks and embodies all the self-centeredness of this society:

> Why ever wast thou lovely in my eyes?
> Why had I not with charitable hand
> Took up a beggar's issue at my gates
> Who smirched thus and mir'd with infamy,
> I might have said, "No part of it is mine;
> This shame derives itself from unknown loins"?
>
> (IV, i, 133–135)

In a speech of roughly twenty lines he uses the first person more than twenty times. He never feels sympathy for his daughter nor mourns her mortification. Instead, he dwells solely on his pain and embarrassment, as he berates "her foul tainted flesh" (IV, i, 143).

Beatrice defends Hero, and then the Friar objects to Leonato's attitude, claiming belief in Hero's purity (IV, i, 164–170), while Hero herself declares her innocence. When Benedick suggests that Don John is responsible for the slander (IV, i, 188–189), Leonato comes to his senses and swears revenge on those who wronged his daughter (IV, i, 190–200). What makes the scene dramatically awkward is that the comments in support of Hero come too late, and we wonder why those who believe in her did not speak earlier. Perhaps Benedick's reticence can be explained by the fact that he does not think of Don John until later. Nonetheless, that such an attack on Hero goes unanswered does not seem believable, but calculated by the playwright to set up the Friar's scheme and the final twists of the plot.

The Friar suggests that word of Hero's death should be spread (IV, i, 203–208), so Claudio will assume that his accusation has killed her. The scheme is somewhat like the plot line of *Romeo and Juliet*, although here the comic side is never lost as Leonato bursts out in confusion, "What shall become of this? what will this do?" (IV, i, 209). The Friar anticipates Claudio's reaction:

> When he shall hear she died upon his words,
> Th' idea of her life shall sweetly creep
> Into his study of imagination,
> And every lovely organ of her life
> Shall come apparell'd in more precious habit,
> More moving, delicate, and full of life,
> Into the eye and prospect of his soul,
> Than when she liv'd indeed.
>
> (IV, i, 223–230)

This thought is peculiar, for heretofore Claudio has demonstrated neither sensitivity nor intelligence, and we wonder whether anything will change him.

Perhaps the victimization of Hero should therefore be judged as a necessary suffering for the redemption of Claudio.

When Beatrice and Benedick are left alone, they commiserate, and Benedick is astonished to see tears from Beatrice. In response he tentatively confesses his affections:

> I do love nothing in the world so well as
> you—is not that strange?

(IV, i, 267–268)

He even boasts of his willingness to fulfill any demand she makes, but she shocks him with one brutal order: "Kill Claudio" (IV, i, 289). We wonder if she is serious. After all, Hero is still alive and the Friar has predicted that Claudio will eventually reform. More likely Beatrice is still angry with Claudio, and in her rage irrationally commands his death. She may also be testing Benedick. Where are his loyalties: with her or with his friend? Benedick's answer comically deflates the tension: "Ha, not for the wide world" (IV, i, 290). Nonetheless, Beatrice remains angry, frustrated that as a woman she cannot take proper revenge on Claudio (IV, i, 317–324). But Benedick's steadfastness ensures that this relationship will thrive as soon as the one between Hero and Claudio is restored.

In the next scene Dogberry's plodding if awkward inquisition of Borachio and Conrade brings that revelation one step closer. While we enjoy the emergence of the truth, we take even greater pleasure in Dogberry's corruption of language, as when he condemns Borachio's plot:

> O villain! thou wilt be condemn'd into ever-
> lasting redemption for this.

(IV, ii, 56–57)

Again, we relax. We especially delight in his reaction to Conrade's assault on his high office (IV, ii, 73):

> But, masters, remember that
> I am an ass; though it be not written down, yet forget
> not that I am ass.

(IV, ii, 76–78)

The opening scene of Act V moves slowly, for we know resolution is imminent. Instead we watch characters suffer, in particular Leonato, still brooding over his own predicament (V, i, 5–20). He bears punishment for his mistrust of his daughter, and thus in one sense his pain is justified. But because he knows she is alive, his performance is overdone, as when he criticizes Antonio for trying to provide comfort:

> No, no, 'tis all men's office to speak patience
> To those that wring under the load of sorrow,
> But no man's virtue nor sufficiency
> To be so moral when he shall endure
> The like himself. Therefore give me no counsel,

My griefs cry louder than advertisement.

(V, i, 27–32)

His concern remains primarily with himself. When Claudio and Don Pedro enter, Leonato castigates them, in particular Claudio:

> I say thou hast belied mine innocent child!
> Thy slander hath gone through and through her heart,
> And she lies buried with her ancestors . . .

(V, i, 67–69)

But Claudio refuses to relent, and even Antonio finds such stubbornness intolerable:

> Scambling, outfacing, fashion-monging boys,
> That lie and cog and flout, deprave and slander,
> Go anticly, and show outward hideousness . . .

(V, i, 94–96)

These accusations make Claudio's sudden redemption in the final scene less believable. Don Pedro, too, comes off badly here, as his earlier worldliness here turns into a kind of smug moralizing:

> My heart is sorry for your daughter's death;
> But on my honor she was charg'd with nothing
> But what was true, and very full of proof.

(V, i, 103–105)

When Benedick enters, Claudio and Don Pedro tastelessly banter with him, as if immune to all the feelings around them. They mock Benedick, but he remains genuinely angry at Hero's mistreatment. He even whispers an aside to Claudio:

> You have kill'd a sweet lady,
> and her death shall fall heavy on you.

(V, i, 148–149)

Claudio's nonchalance through this scene is unsettling. He should be wounded by his loss, or he should at least pretend to be hurt. Yet he is casual, and his capacity to laugh about love borders on the callous. The Friar's prediction that Claudio would suffer great emotional distress is proven false, and more and more he seems unworthy of Hero. Indeed, Benedick finally cannot tolerate the joking. He reports that Don John has left Messina, and repeats that Claudio has killed "a sweet and innocent lady" (V, i, 190–191).

Dogberry now enters, prepared to condemn Borachio and Conrade, and infused with his mission:

> Marry, sir, they have committed false report,
> moreover they have spoken untruths; secondarily,
> they are slanders; sixt and lastly, they
> have belied a lady, thirdly, they have verified unjust

things; and to conclude, they are lying knaves.

(V, i, 215–219)

Despite this convoluted list of charges, Borachio confesses the entire plot (V, i, 230–243). Claudio's shift in mood is so quick that again we wonder about the substance of his character:

Sweet Hero, now thy image doth appear
In the rare semblance that I lov'd it first.

(V, i, 251–252)

He still speaks in terms of sight and surface appreciation:

Choose your revenge yourself,
Impose me to what penance your invention
Can lay upon my sin, yet sinn'd I not,
But in mistaking.

(V, i, 272–273)

He admits only a mistake, not a tragic mistrust of one he claimed to love. Even as he offers to repent, he makes excuses that blunt his emotion.

In response, Leonato offers a peculiar alternative:

My brother hath a daughter,
Almost the copy of my child that's dead,
And she alone is heir to both of us.
Give her the right you should have giv'n her cousin,
And so dies my revenge.

(V, i, 288–292)

This gambit is awkward for at least two reasons. One, are we persuaded that Claudio would believe this offer? Previously Leonato excoriated Claudio. Would Leonato now have Claudio marry Antonio's daughter? What about the daughter's feelings? Would Antonio and Leonato be so insensitive as to give her away so high-handedly and without asking her permission? Whether the turn of plot is believable, it is necessary for Shakespeare's final scene. The episode ends on one more comic upturn, as Dogberry takes his leave:

I humbly give you leave to depart, and if a merry
meeting may be wish'd, God prohibit it!

(V, i, 324–325)

Of all Shakespeare's clowns, none is more loveable than this good-willed minion of the law.

In Act V, scene ii, Beatrice and Benedick, fighting themselves, draw closer together. As Benedick explains:

Suffer love! a good epithet! I do suffer
love indeed, for I love thee against my will.

(V, ii, 66–67)

But he is not completely willing to play the conventional romantic hero. After Ursula enters to reveal that Hero has been proven innocent and Don John guilty

(V, i, 95–99), Beatrice asks Benedick to accompany her. His acceptance is framed in terms that suggest that their relationship will always be marked by wit:

> I will live in thy heart, die in thy lap, and
> be buried in thy eyes; and moreover I will go with
> thee to thy uncle's.

(V, ii, 102–104)

Beatrice offers no reply, but the two depart together, and we imagine that they are permanently bound.

After a brief scene in a churchyard, where a repentant Don Pedro and Claudio mourn Hero, the play concludes in Leonato's home. He instructs the women to enter the wedding scene masked, although before they do Benedick asks the Friar to perform the marriage to Beatrice later on (V, iv, 29–31). Claudio and Don Pedro then enter, and both still joke their way through the preliminaries. Claudio, in particular, tosses ribald images to Benedick (V, iii, 43–44) whose response to Claudio is acidulous:

> Bull Jove, sir, had an amiable low,
> And some such strange bull leapt your father's cow,
> And got a calf in that same noble feat
> Much like to you, for you have just his bleat.

(V, iv, 48–51)

Now seriously committed to a woman, Benedick has little tolerance for so shallow a man as Claudio. When the masked Hero appears with the other women, Claudio remains graceless: "Which is the lady I must seize upon?" (V, iv, 53). At the moment of revelation, Hero removes her mask, and Claudio has only a brief remark: "Another Hero!" (V, iv, 62). Perhaps we are to take him as one stunned into joyful silence, but he offers no apology or expression of faith confirming the lack of substance he has shown throughout the play.

The more passionate expressions are offered by Beatrice and Benedick. When he asks for her, Beatrice responds with surprising gentleness: "I answer to that name. What is your will?" (V, iv, 72). Her tone may seem to be a compromise of her independence, but that returns as the two immediately banter about the misadventures they have undergone. Yet their manner has changed, for they speak not with enmity, but with mutual embracing, until Benedick brings the byplay to a sudden end: "Peace, I will stop thy mouth" (V, iv, 97). He kisses her, and thereafter Beatrice says not another word. Like Katherine in *The Taming of the Shrew*, she seems to be submitting to the will of a man. And this acquiescence may bother modern audiences. Still, in Shakespeare's time such an attitude on the part of a woman was the sign of a healthy state of a marriage.

Almost as an afterthought a messenger mentions at the very end that Don John has been captured and will be returned for punishment. Benedick concludes the play with a call to dance, his joyous capitulation to conformity and marriage and his affirmation of the social rituals he has so long derided.

During *Much Ado About Nothing* we see several different unmaskings. The one by Beatrice and Benedick is the most complicated, as they unmask not only each other's public faces but also their own private personalities. Theirs is the true marriage of this play: one of the mind and heart. We do not have much faith that Claudio and Hero will remain happy, for even by the end they offer hardly any signs of maturity or understanding. We are confident, though, that Beatrice and Benedick will continue to find one another a constant source of amusement.

The relationship between Beatrice and Benedick also reflects the conceit and self-deception that dominates almost all the characters. During much of the action the two indulge in civilized triviality, fussing over minor affronts and retreating behind stylized wit. They disguise and deceive to hide from both one another and themselves. The breakdown of such masking, the emergence of honest thought and emotion, results in their happiness and fulfillment. That theme is hardly unfamiliar to audiences of Shakespeare's comedies.

SUGGESTIONS FOR FURTHER READING

Allen, John A. "Dogberry." *Shakespeare Quarterly* 24 (1973): 35–53.

Davis, Walter, ed. *Twentieth Century Interpretations of* Much Ado About Nothing. Englewood Cliffs, N.J.: Prentice-Hall, 1969.

Jorgensen, Paul A. "*Much Ado About Nothing*." *Shakespeare Quarterly* 5 (1954): 287–295.

Lewalski, Barbara K. "Love, Appearance, and Reality: Much Ado About Something." *Studies in English Literature, 1500–1900* 8 (1968): 235–251.

McCollom, William G. "The Role of Wit in *Much Ado About Nothing*." *Shakespeare Quarterly* 19 (1968): 165–174.

Mulryne, J. R. *Shakespeare:* Much Ado About Nothing. London: Edward Arnold, 1965.

Ormerod, D. "Faith and Fashion in *Much Ado About Nothing*." *Shakespeare Survey* 25 (1973): 93–105.

As You Like It

As its title suggests, *As You Like It* dramatizes characters who offer a variety of perspectives and attitudes. Almost all these figures are subject to satire, but of a very mild sort, and thus this play may be the most affectionate and forgiving of Shakespeare's first ten comedies. Its villains are primarily a necessity of plot and soon drift to the periphery of the story. All the other characters are essentially likeable, and our pleasure is watching them deal with one another's quirks and egos.

The wide range of characters also offers a series of oppositions of both ideas and values. Most important is the contrast of life in court to that in the country. We are also conscious of the differences in spirit between age and youth, between genuine love and love that gratifies one's own pride or lust, and between honest emotion and emotion feigned for effect. Yet however certain characters are criticized or mocked, the tone of the play is gentle, and we never feel that anyone is seriously threatened. Instead we find ourselves amused and enlightened by a panorama of social interminglings that shows Shakespeare at his warmest. The primary source of the play is Thomas Lodge's pastoral romance *Rosalynde: Euphes' Golden Legacie* (1590), which was derived from *The Tale of Gamelyn*, a fourteenth-century poem of uncertain authorship.

The opening scenes create the crucial tension of the play. To his servant Adam, Orlando explains that his older brother, Oliver, has cheated Orlando out of his fortune.

> He lets me feed with his hinds, bars me at the
> place of a brother, and as much as in him lies,
> mines my gentility with my education.

(I, i, 19–21)

This information is delivered in one continuous speech of prose, and we feel Shakespeare moving through preliminaries of the story to reach the main action as quickly as possible. Oliver's entrance gives Orlando a chance to personalize the accusation:

> The courtesy of nations allows you my better, in
> that you are the first born, but the same tradition
> takes not away my blood, were there twenty brothers
> betwixt us.

(I, i, 46–49)

Orlando takes a stand for the traditional rule of primogeniture, and Oliver's response, to strike his brother, establishes him as an enemy of the social order. Again Orlando tries to assert his rights:

> My father charg'd you in his will to give me good
> education. You have train'd me like a peasant,
> obscuring and hiding from me all gentleman-like
> qualities.

(I, i, 67–70)

But Oliver remains unfeeling, and no more so than in his cruel dismissal of Adam: "Get you with him, you old dog" (I, i, 81). Despite Oliver's malevolence, he is without guile or sophistication and therefore more of a prop than a well-developed character.

This impression is reinforced when Oliver confers with the wrestler Charles, who informs Oliver first that "the old Duke is banish'd by his younger brother the new Duke" (I, ii, 99–100). Here is another pair of brothers in conflict, and again the issue is primogeniture. In this case, however, the younger has cheated the older. Oliver, somewhat mechanically for the sake of plot, also inquires about Rosalind (I, i, 105–106) and about the Old Duke himself, who, we learn, is living among voluntary exiles in the forest of Arden: There they "fleet the time carelessly, as they did in the golden world" (I, i, 118–119).

Charles then announces that Orlando intends to wrestle him tomorrow. Charles, who does not wish to hurt Orlando (I, i, 127–129), seeks advice from Oliver, who instead urges Charles to do all the damage he can. Indeed, Oliver speaks at length about Orlando's gross defects (I, i, 141–157). Why is he so antagonistic? Oliver himself cannot say, as he reveals when Charles departs:

>   I hope I shall see an end
> of him; for my soul (yet I know not why) hates
> nothing more than he. Yet he's gentle, never school'd
> and yet learn'd, full of noble device, of all sorts
> enchantingly belov'd, and indeed so much in the
> heart of the world, and especially of my own
> people who best know him, that I am altogether mispris'd.

(I, i, 164–171)

In his blind hatred and resentment of goodness, Oliver reminds us of Don John in *Much Ado About Nothing*, but Oliver never acquires further depth, and his villainy stays on the surface. Still, his violation of family loyalty is a serious offense.

In scene ii another pair, this one female, takes the stage. Rosalind, the older and more mature, mourns her banished father, the older Duke (I, ii, 5–7). Celia, daughter of the younger Duke, Frederick, tries to cheer her friend, reminding her that whatever Celia will inherit will be Rosalind's as well (I, ii, 19–21). At this news Rosalind brightens, and we note the first hint of a major theme of the play: the restorative powers of love. Rosalind, too, senses it, and wonders out loud whether she should try to fall in love herself. Celia partially agrees:

> But love no man in good earnest, nor no further
> in sport neither, than with safety of a pure blush
> thou mayest in honor come off again.

> (I, ii, 27–29)

Their intent to restrain their passions is foolish, for once infatuated, both girls find themselves at the mercy of their emotions. Furthermore, their desire to mock the fortunes of others suggests that these two are ripe for a lesson about the power of love.

The byplay is interrupted by Touchstone, who summons Celia to her father. Touchstone is a peculiar figure, for unlike earlier clownish figures, like Launce and Gobbo, he is more of a wit. In other words, a courtly clown. And his name, taken from the stone used to test the purity of gold and silver, suggests he will be a standard by which other characters are measured. But Touchstone's presence is ironic for two reasons. One, he is not nearly as funny as he thinks. For example, here he comments: ''The more pity that fools may not speak wisely what wise men do foolishly'' (I, ii, 86–87). The sentiment is familiar and heavy-handed. Second, the measure of other characters turns out not to be what Touchstone thinks of them, but what they think of him. The ones who find him puzzling or disturbing turn out to be the smartest; the ones who approve of him turn out to be the more foolish.

Le Beau then enters to invite Rosalind and Celia to the wrestling match. He is a pretentious fellow, but seems to have respect and affection for the two women:

> I will tell you the beginning; and if it
> please your ladyships, you may see then end, for
> the best is yet to do, and here where you are, they
> are coming to perform it.

> (I, ii, 113–116)

In addition, Le Beau demonstrates a clear lack of interest in Touchstone's remarks, another sign of wisdom.

Before the match, Orlando resists the attempt by Rosalind and Celia to subvert the contest, as he modestly explains that no one will suffer for his pains but himself (I, ii, 189–193). Rosalind's next line indicates she is sympathetic to such an unpretentious speaker, but before they can proceed further Orlando is called to the match.

To everyone's surprise he is victorious, but when Orlando reveals that he is the son of Rowland de Boys, a colleague of the banished Duke, the new Duke

Frederick withdraws his praise and stalks away. Rosalind, however, is smitten with Orlando, and offers him a chain from around her neck. The gesture reveals her spirit. Rather than conform to the values of the courtly love tradition by which the man is responsible for making overtures, Rosalind takes the first step herself, and such assertiveness marks her behavior throughout the play. Orlando himself is so taken that he is unable to offer a formal reply:

> My better parts
> Are all thrown down, and that which here stands up
> Is but a quintain, a mere liveless block.
>
> (I, ii, 249–251)

Rosalind pretends that Orlando has called after them, then acknowledges a bond with him by picking up the key image:

> Sir, you have wrastled well, and overthrown
> More than your enemies.
>
> (I, ii, 254–255)

After Rosalind and Celia exit, Le Beau returns to urge Orlando to leave and thereby escape Frederick's wrath (I, ii, 261–267). Le Beau also clarifies that the Duke is angered with Rosalind because she is popular with the people at large (I, ii, 277–281). We remember Oliver's rage with Orlando, which is similarly unreasonable. Both men will eventually be cured. Before Orlando departs he learns that Rosalind is the daughter of the banished Duke and Celia the daughter of Frederick. Armed with this knowledge, Orlando scurries away:

> Hereafter, in a better world than this,
> I shall desire more love and knowledge of you.
>
> (I, ii, 284–285)

His implication, that somewhere else happiness may be found, underlies the succeeding action in the Forest of Arden.

By scene iii Rosalind has resumed her melancholy state. "O how full of briers is this working-day world!" (I, ii, 11–12). And Celia grasps the cause only gradually:

>   Is
> it possible, on such a sudden, you should fall into so
> strong a liking with old Sir Rowland's youngest son?
>
> (I, iii, 26–28)

The banter the two shared in scene i about maintaining detachment where love is concerned now looms ironically. But before the pair can explore the emotion, the Duke enters to expel Rosalind from the court (I, iii, 41–42). He is unwilling to give a specific reason. "Let it suffice thee that I trust thee not" (I, iii, 55). Then he adds one more telling accusation: "Thou art thy father's daughter, there's enough" (I, iii, 58). Even in the world of comedy a usurper like the Duke may well be insecure enough to want the daughter of the legitimate ruler

as far away as possible. Celia demonstrates her own love by standing by her
friend: "If she be traitor,/ Why, so am I" (I, iii, 72–73). Frederick's reply,
"You are a fool" (I, iii, 87), emphasizes his shallowness.

After Celia suggests escaping to the Forest of Arden, the two women resolve
to disguise themselves as men, a familiar gambit in the plays of Shakespeare.
But in this play the masking has more profound implications, as Rosalind indicates:

> A gallant curtle-axe upon my thigh,
> A boar-spear in my hand, and—in my heart
> Lie there what hidden woman's fear there will—
> We'll have a swashing and a martial outside,
> As many other mannish cowards have
> That do outface it with their semblances.
>
>   (I, iii, 117–122)

She unintentionally hits upon her most intriguing quality: the combination of
masculine boldness and feminine sensitivity that makes her so alluring to Orlando. Then she and Celia depart, soon to be joined by Touchstone (I, iii, 130–
131).

The scene then switches to the Forest of Arden, where the exiled Duke is
gathered with a few supporters. In his opening words the Duke extols the virtues
of his exile: "Are not these woods/ More free from peril than the envious court?"
(II, i, 3–4). But his sentiments seemed forced:

> Sweet are the uses of adversity,
> Which like the toad, ugly and venomous,
> Wears yet a precious jewel in his head;
> And this our life, exempt from public haunt,
> Finds tongues in trees, books in the running brooks,
> Sermons in stones, and good in everything.
>
>   (II, i, 12–17)

His devotion to the pastoral mirrors a preoccupation of Shakespeare's day.
Here the Duke appears to be making the best of an awkward situation. That
he finds "good in every thing" suggests he is trying hard to remain blind to
all else, and thus at this moment he is an engaging, yet somewhat impractical, figure.

In this scene we also hear for the first time about "The melancholy Jaques"
(II, i, 26), a self-appointed mocker of the pastoral life, as the first Lord explains
in a lengthy narrative about Jaques' objecting to the hunting of a deer (II, i, 45–
63). The report dramatizes Jaques as wailing uncontrollably:

> Thus most invectively he pierceth through
> The body of [the] country, city, court,
> Yea, and of this our life, swearing that we

Are mere usurpers, tyrants . . .

(II, i, 58–61)

When Jaques does appear, he provides balance for the Duke's enthusiasm, but as this initial description suggests, Jaques himself turns into an object of ridicule.

Scene ii is essentially exposition, in which Frederick learns that Celia and Rosalind have run away. When he hears that they were seen in Orlando's company, Frederick demands that Orlando or Oliver be brought to him. Thus we anticipate Oliver's following the two women into Arden.

In scene iii we see another form of affection, this between master and servant. Adam's devotion is absolute, and here he counsels Orlando to escape for the wrestling triumph has become public news, and in revenge Oliver intends to burn Orlando's house. Adam adds, however, that if the scheme should fail, "He will have other means to cut you off . . . " (II, iii, 25). Were the threat of burning real, its likely failure would not be mentioned so quickly. In any case, Orlando is uncertain where to go or what to do, but he and Adam hurry off to parts unknown. Adam also offers his life savings to Orlando, who praises the "constant service of the antique world . . . " (I, iii, 57). Such kinship reaffirms the essential goodness that permeates this play. Orlando goes on to ruminate sadly on a selfish world: "Where none will sweat but for promotion . . . " (II, iii, 60). The implication is that Orlando seeks a pure devotion that we expect he will find with Rosalind.

In scene iv she enters in disguise as Ganymed, along with Celia, dressed as Aliena, and Touchstone. All are exhausted, and Touchstone tries to be witty about their predicament:

Ay, now am I in Arden, the more fool I.
When I was at home, I was in a better place, but
travellers must be content.

(II, iv, 16–18)

This remark, like his others in the early part of the scene, earns no more than mere acknowledgment from either woman. He simply is not worth more. All three then overhear Corin and Silvius, as the latter pines for his disdainful lover, Phebe (II, iv, 33–43). Rosalind sympathizes with the frustrated love: "I have by hard adventure found mine own" (II, iv, 45). Touchstone, though, mocks the shepherd, then recalls a gift of two peapods to Jane Smile, an ironic reference to Rosalind's present to Orlando. She, in turn, acknowledges his recognition of human folly in love (II, iv, 57), but this temporary approval of Touchstone's insight fades, for during the play his perspective never matures. His view of love remains cynical and selfish, while Rosalind's feelings for Orlando bloom gloriously.

Indeed, Rosalind's impatience with Touchstone is clear only a few lines later, when he greets the shepherd Corin with "Holla! you clown!" (II, iv, 66). Rosalind rebukes him at once: "Peace, fool, he's not thy kinsman" (II, iv, 67). But Touchstone is insensitive to mockery, for to Corin he identifies himself and the women as "Your betters, sir" (II, iv, 68). On the other side, Corin's modest reply, "Else are they very wretched" (II, iv, 68), suggests a becoming modesty Touchstone lacks. When Corin reveals that his master plans to sell all possessions to Silvius, who is otherwise preoccupied, Rosalind quickly works to make the purchase herself (II, iv, 91–93). Here is one more way she acts like a man, as she deals decisively with financial matters.

In scene v, Amiens' song is a conventional pastoral ditty, but Jaques, in his initial appearance, insists on mocking it, brooding theatrically: "I can suck melancholy out of a song, as a weasel sucks eggs" (II, v, 12–13). At first he seems to provide realistic commentary on the praise for country life others have offered, but eventually we realize that Jaques devotes himself to contrariness, in finding pleasure when others are unhappy, and in pretending unhappiness when others find joy:

> I'll go sleep, if I can; if I cannot, I'll rail
> against all the first-born of Egypt.

(II, v, 60–61)

He virtually admits that his complaining is artificial, a way to compensate for inner weakness.

An image of human relationships opposite to that offered by Jaques occurs immediately, when Orlando and Adam enter. The old servant is out of energy, but Orlando cheers him along:

> For my sake be comfortable, hold
> death a while at the arm's end. I will here be with
> thee presently, and if I bring thee not something to
> eat, I will give thee leave to die; but if thou diest
> before I come, thou art a mocker of my labor.

(II, vi, 9–13)

His gentle banter, strategically placed between two scenes where Jaques expounds, is a reminder of order and affection, a stark contrast to the cynic's egoism.

That attitude is dramatized full force in the next scene, when Jaques bursts in with news: "A fool, a fool! I met a fool i' th' forest . . ." (II, vii, 12). We learn eventually that this figure is none other than Touchstone, but from the arrogance and paucity of wit that Jaques quotes we might guess as much right now. For instance, Jaques is taken with his fool's philosophy:

> 'Tis but an hour ago since it was nine,
> And after one hour more 'twill be eleven,
> And so from hour to hour, we ripe and ripe,
> And then from hour to hour, we rot and rot;
> And thereby hangs a tale.

(II, vii, 24–28)

Why these lines are inspiring is unclear, although they do parallel some of Jaques' pessimistic reflections. We do recognize that what pleases Jaques most about his discovery is that Jaques himself has found him. He enjoys the philosophy, but takes greater pleasure in his own singular appreciation of this hitherto unknown wit.

The Duke senses this egoism, and reprimands Jaques for criticizing crimes of which Jaques, too, has been guilty:

> Most mischievous foul sin, in chiding sin:
> For thou thyself has been a libertine,
> As sensual as the brutish sting itself . . .

(II, vii, 64–66)

Jaques defends his satire, pointing out at length the pride and hypocrisy of the world (II, vii, 70–83). Yet something in his tone is hysterical, and we sense a man desperate to arouse an audience, and through his act to maintain contact with society.

He is interrupted by Orlando, who yells out in hunger. The Duke questions whether Orlando is rude because of circumstance or nature (II, vii, 91–93), and the intruder's reply reaffirms a key theme of the play: "I thought that all things had been savage here . . . " (II, vii, 107). He is not certain whether so-called "civilized" behavior is to be found in city or country, and by the end of the play the controversy is not resolved. Instead we are expected to judge each person on individual merits.

Orlando is grateful for the kindness of the reception, then asks to be allowed to find Adam:

> There is an old poor man,
> Who after me hath many a weary step
> Limp'd in pure love . . .

(II, vii, 129–131)

Such empathy underlies whatever cynicism Jaques and Touchstone propagate. The Duke commiserates with Orlando's plight, then reminds Jaques that "Thou seest we are not all alone unhappy . . . " (II, vii, 136). This line inspires one of the most famous passages in all of Shakespeare's plays:

> All the world's a stage,
> And all the men and women merely players;
> They have their exits and their entrances,
> And one man in his time plays many parts,
> His acts being seven ages.

(II, vii, 139–143)

Jaques continues to delineate those seven stages, each, according to him, a time of misery. The entire speech has a set quality, as if Jaques has been waiting for the proper moment to unleash his well-rehearsed misanthropy. Furthermore, whatever its rhetorical attraction, the sentiments are unattractive, and emphasize not Jaques' wit, as he imagines, but his vacuity, his inability or unwillingness to see anything substantial in human life. Indeed, his negativism is contradicted again by Orlando, who enters carrying Adam, thus reaffirming their friendship. And when during Amiens' song Orlando reveals his parentage to the Duke, the latter's warmth shows the power of friendship to be even stronger.

At the beginning of Act III, back at court, Frederick orders Oliver to capture Orlando or else suffer banishment (III, i, 6–8). The command ensures that Oliver ends up in Arden, where we next see Orlando carving verses on trees. On the one hand, his actions are those of a laughably lovesick young man. On the other hand, such passion contrasts Oliver and Frederick's coldness as well as the unpleasant wit of Touchstone, who is about to take the stage.

He and Corin resume debate about the merits of country and city life. Corin does not understand most of Touchstone's puns and other wordplay, but nonetheless Corin's unaffected manner reduces Touchstone to humorless curses:

> Truly, thou art damn'd, like an ill-roasted
> egg, all on one side.
>
> (III, ii, 37–38)

Touchstone continues his attack, and although he puts on a genial front, his insults sting:

> Why, if thou never wast at court, thou
> never saw'st good manners; if thou never saw'st
> good manners, then thy manners must be wicked,
> and wickedness is sin, and sin is damnation.
>
> (III, ii, 40–43)

Later Touchstone will show the ill manners he claims Corin demonstrates. Corin, however, remains unbowed, and even manages to match his antagonist line for line:

> You told me you salute
> not at the court, but you kiss your hands; that
> courtesy would be uncleanly if courtiers were shepherds.
>
> (III, ii, 48–50)

However, as most characters in this play eventually tire of Touchstone or Jaques, so does Corin: "You have too courtly a wit for me, I'll rest" (III, ii, 70). Then he adds:

> Sir, I am a true laborer: I earn that I eat,
> get that I wear, owe no man hate, envy no man's
> happiness, glad of other men's good, content with my
> harm, and the greatest of my pride is to see my ewes
> graze and my lambs suck.
>
> (III, ii, 73–77)

In his own way, Corin understands the dignity of the individual, and his perspective buttresses the spirit of the play.

Touchstone's inadequacies are emphasized further when Rosalind appears, reading aloud one of Orlando's extravagant poems. Touchstone spoofs this effort with a poem of his own but Rosalind has no patience with his criticism (III, ii, 117–120). He is unable to appreciate the sentiment behind the poetry, while Rosalind, although aware that the verses are maudlin, retains her capacity for romance. She discerns the love behind the language. From this point Touchstone remains quiet until he departs with Corin, someone he can dazzle. In the face of genuine sentiment, Touchstone has nothing to offer.

When Celia enters, she is reading yet another poem she has found, and she and Rosalind ridicule this one as well. Yet Rosalind is eager to know the author, and when Celia reveals that he is Orlando (III, ii, 216), Rosalind is immediately overcome:

> What did he when thou saw'st him?
> What said he? How look'd he? Wherein went he?
> What makes he here? Did he ask for me? Where
> remains he? How parted he with thee? And when
> shalt thou see him again? Answer me in one word.
>
> (III, ii, 220–224)

For all her self-possession and wit, Rosalind is vulnerable to her passions. As she explains:

> Do you not know I am a woman? when
> I think, I must speak. Sweet, say on.
>
> (III, ii, 249–250)

Her mind and her heart are in battle against each other. She is in command of everyone but herself.

At this moment Orlando enters with Jaques. The two are at odds, exchanging insults, particularly because Jaques claims to have no tolerance for Orlando's infatuation. As Jaques drones on, we realize that for all his claims to preferring his own company (III, ii, 253–254), he needs the presence of others precisely to tell them that he prefers his own company. He needs an audience to derogate; when he is alone, he is without the behavior of others to serve as the object of mockery (III, ii, 277–279). Thus his unfortunate predicament, in which he revels.

When Orlando continues to get the best of him, Jaques departs, and Rosalind, still dressed as a man, emerges from her hiding place to speak to Orlando. According to the comedy conventions of the Elizabethan stage, he fails to recognize her, even when she talks about the poems to Rosalind she has found on the trees (III, ii, 358–366). Orlando confesses that he is the mystery poet, but Rosalind claims he cannot be that man for he lacks all the traditional symptoms of the infatuated lover (III, ii, 373–384). Dual levels of meaning dominate, as Rosalind insists that Orlando prove his love:

> Me believe it? You may as soon make her
> that you love believe it, which I warrant she is

apter to do than confess she does.

(III, ii, 387–389)

She describes her own situation exactly: she is unable to confess her infatuation. As a further test, Rosalind offers to cure Orlando of his "madness" (III, ii, 400), and in that cause volunteers to serve as his lady:

> I would cure you, if you would but call me
> Rosalind, and come every day to my cote and woo me.

(III, ii, 426–427)

Here, too, Rosalind must control her passion, for she seeks the very wooing Orlando will reluctantly present. Thus the war within Rosalind still rages. She cannot reveal her affection, but she manages to arrange a situation in which she can express her feelings ostensibly in the guise of another, but in fact for herself. The combination of frustration and joy makes her predicament theatrically winning.

Before their relationship develops, we witness a less admirable one, this between Touchstone and Audrey. He has managed to find the least sophisticated woman available, and easily dazzles her with his attempts at wit.

> . . . for the truest poetry is the most
> feigning, and lovers' are given to poetry;
> and what they swear in poetry may be said as lovers
> they do feign.

(III, iii, 19–22)

Even here he insists on mocking human feeling. He also has little interest in her as a woman:

> Well, prais'd be the gods for thy foulness!
> sluttishness may come hereafter.

(III, iii, 40–41)

And after she agrees to marry him, Touchstone arranges to have a ceremony performed by one Sir Oliver Martext, a local vicar of dubious standing. Touchstone, however, is not bothered by the shady circumstances:

> I am not in the mind but I were
> better to be married of him than of another, for
> he is not like to marry me well; and not being well
> married, it will be a good excuse for me hereafter
> to leave my wife.

(III, iii, 89–94)

Touchstone has no sense of morality, and that Jaques overhears and approves this scheme further diminishes its value (III, iii, 83–89). Indeed, Jaques and the simpleminded Audrey are the only characters in the play who have any use for Touchstone. They are also the only characters in the play who have so little to recommend them.

At the beginning of scene iv Rosalind is almost in tears, as she desperately awaits the arrival of Orlando:

> But why did he swear he would come this
> morning, and comes not?

(III, iv, 18–19)

When Celia suggests that Orlando may be helping out Rosalind's father, she is distracted, but only for a moment:

> But what talk we of fathers, when
> there is such a man as Orlando?

(III, iv, 38–39)

The disparity between Rosalind's normal assurance and her anxiety to see again the man she loves is comic and touching. The tension of their waiting is interrupted by Corin, who invites them to watch yet another pair of lovers who serve as additional counterpoint to Rosalind and Orlando.

Silvius's opening poem in scene v is a stereotypical expression of courtly love, hopelessly passionate. And Phebe plays her part of the disdainful object of that love, although her denial is extremely harsh:

> Now I do frown on thee with all my heart,
> And if my eyes can wound, not let them kill thee.

(III, v, 15–16)

Nonetheless, Silvius relentlessly plays his role, and pines after the woman who scorns him. Rosalind, however, becomes so upset that she cannot help bursting out:

> Who might be your mother,
> That you insult, exult, and all at once,
> over the wretched?

(III, v, 35–37)

Herself deeply in love, Rosalind sympathizes with a man as smitten as Silvius. She also makes clear that Silvius is considerably more handsome than Phebe is pretty:

> But, mistress, know yourself, down on your knees,
> And thank heaven, fasting, for a good man's love. . . .

(III, v, 57–58)

Here is Rosalind the woman, dressed as a man, lecturing another woman on the preciousness of love. We sense that Rosalind is speaking her own ardor, and that she feels that though the conventions of love may appear ridiculous, the sentiments themselves are not. As always, she responds to life with a combination of intellect and passion. And so moving is Rosalind's statement that Phebe falls in love with her, for she is still dressed as Ganymed (III, v, 81–82). The moment suggests, first, that women talk of love on a plane far apart from that of men;

second, that only women understand what women feel; and, third, that women seek in love what only women can provide.

Silvius, however, is still lost in his own romantic aura, and fails to notice Phebe's new focus. Therefore when Rosalind leaves with Celia and Corin and Phebe suddenly finds Silvius more useful, he blindly maintains devotion. Phebe, however, is beset by more complicated emotions about the bold Ganymed:

> 'Tis but a peevish boy—yet he talks well—
> But what care I for words? Yet words do well
> When he that speaks them pleases those that hear.
>
> (III, v, 110–112)

Moments ago Phebe was disdainful of Silvius and his poetry. Now she finds herself attracted to someone else's language. In her inconsistency and selfishness, Phebe is a parody of the woman of Petrarchan romance. And she eagerly recites all the features that make Ganymed so attractive (III, iv, 113–131). The description is an intriguing combination of traditionally masculine and feminine characteristics, and in her contemplation Phebe appears to lose awareness of all around her. When she regains her senses, though (III, v, 134), she reasserts her manipulative skills, and convinces Silvius to deliver a letter to Ganymed.

In Act IV Rosalind and Celia await Orlando, but in the meantime they are hounded by Jaques, as usual trying pompously to justify his own gloomy wit (IV, i, 10–20). And, as usual, he loses. Rosalind has no patience for him (IV, i, 21–25), and when Orlando enters, he dismisses Jaques contemptuously, so that "Monsieur Traveller" (IV, i, 33) must depart without a word.

What follows is the most endearing scene of the play, as Rosalind invites Orlando to act out his affections. He is a few minutes late, however, so first Rosalind scolds him, ostensibly as part of her role, but clearly as an expression of her own anguish (IV, i, 44–49). Then she invites his courtship:

> Come, woo me, woo me; for now I am in a
> holiday humor, and like enough to consent. What
> would you say to me now, and I were your very very
> Rosalind?
>
> (IV, i, 68–71)

Rosalind receives partial satisfaction from this wooing, for she hears Orlando say the right words to her. Yet because he is not aware to whom he speaks, she remains frustrated. Thus she emerges from what was then women's conventional role and orders Orlando: "Then you must say, 'I take thee, Rosalind, for wife' " (IV, i, 135–136). And he obeys those instructions. Yet we must imagine that even as she is thrilled to hear the offer, she aches at withholding her true joy. Indeed, so profound is her feeling that at moments Rosalind almost breaks character. For instance, after Orlando states he will be away for two hours, Rosalind almost pulls him back physically: "Alas, dear love, I cannot lack thee two hours!" (IV, i, 178). Here she orders him away, accusing him of deception, but just as quickly welcomes him back (IV, i, 182–186). Her passion overflows, ever in conflict with the intellectual male she portrays, as she tells Celia moments later:

> O coz, coz, coz, my pretty little coz, that
> thou didst know how many fathom deep I am
> in love!
>
> (IV, i, 205–207)

The intense romanticism is leavened in the brief scene ii, as Jaques jokes about a deer's horns, the traditional symbol of cuckoldry. But quickly complications are augmented when Silvius arrives in scene iii, bearing Phebe's letter, which he has not read (IV, i, 21–22). At first Rosalind tries to convince him that the letter berates Ganymed. But when she reads passages out loud, Silvius recognizes the letter as a plea for love (IV, iii, 50–63). Rosalind has no choice but to admit that truth, but although she has little sympathy for Silvius's passivity (IV, i, 66–70), she conceives a plan to restore Silvius to Phebe's affections:

> . . . say this to her:
> that if she love me, I charge her to love thee; if she
> will not, I will never have her unless thou entreat for
> her. If you be a true lover, hence, and not a word;
> for here comes more company.
>
> (IV, iii, 71–74)

In other words, if Phebe is to remain loyal to Ganymed, she must love Silvius. The absurdity of these instructions is further satire of traditional pastoral romance.

Oliver's entrance is unexpected, but no more so than the revelation of his swift repentance. Oliver relates how he was sleeping in the forest when a snake worked itself around his neck. But at Orlando's entrance "it unlink'd itself" (IV, iii, 111). Nearby, however, a lionness was waiting for Oliver to awaken:

> . . . for 'tis
> The royal disposition of that beast
> To prey on nothing that doth seem as dead.
>
> (IV, iii, 116–118)

To save his brother, Orlando killed the lionness, at which point Oliver woke up:

> I do not shame
> To tell you what I was; since my conversion
> So sweetly tastes; being the thing I am.
>
> (IV, iii, 135–137)

Thus reconciled, the brothers retreated to the Duke's camp, where Orlando revealed a wound caused by the lionness, and Oliver now presents a bloody handkerchief as proof of Orlando's battle:

As You Like It   661

> . . . unto the shepherd youth
> That he in sport doth call his Rosalind.

(IV, iii, 155–156)

Immediately, however, Rosalind faints. Oliver sympathizes: "Many will swoon when they do look on blood" (IV, iii, 158), while Celia struggles to maintain the Ganymed illusion: "There is more in it" (IV, iii, 159). When Rosalind recovers, Oliver offers unintentionally ironic comfort: "You lack a man's heart" (IV, iii, 164). We recognize that throughout the play Rosalind has never lacked a man's courage, but it has always been tempered by a woman's affections. A few lines later Oliver tells Rosalind to "counterfeit to be a man" (IV, iii, 173–174). She agrees, adding, "I should have been a woman by right" (IV, iii, 175–176). Her comment seems recognition that her womanly nature will always permeate her actions. We, however, have seen her exude both traditionally masculine and feminine values and actions. Thus as much as any character in any play of Shakespeare, Rosalind embodies the best of both genders.

In Act V we detour from the main romantic story to return to Touchstone and his relationship with Audrey, who still tries to bring him to the altar. When William enters to claim, very mildly, Audrey for himself, Touchstone subdues the simple fellow with a barrage of words (V, i, 46–57). Gradually Touchstone has turned from an innocuous wit into something of a bully.

The main plot resumes with Oliver's confession that he has fallen in love with Aliena, the disguised Celia (V, ii, 8–12). The suddenness of this attraction, which is mutual, is accepted by both Rosalind and Orlando, and thus we believe it (V, ii, 31–43). But in its own way, the infatuation is as much a parody of romantic love as the Silvius-Phebe relationship. When the marriage of Oliver and Celia is set for the next day, Orlando confesses that "I can live no longer by thinking" (V, ii, 50). He himself is prepared to yield to feeling and marry. Rosalind promises that because of certain magical powers, she can arrange Orlando's marriage (V, ii, 58–64). He is hardly surprised, nor should we be. The forest of Arden is not quite the haven of the supernatural as is the forest in *A Midsummer Night's Dream*. Nevertheless, in this play, all sorts of creatures, including lions, snakes, and sheep, have flourished together. In addition, we have seen one major character transformation, and another, that of Frederick, is forthcoming. In addition, we should remember that belief in all sorts of magical powers prevailed during Shakespeare's day.

But before Rosalind departs, Silvius and Phebe enter, and the four lovers offer a poetic counterpoint to reflect their frustrated love (V, ii, 85–108). The lines are almost operatic; the balance between character, plot, and verse are beautifully structured. And Rosalind's whirling farewell to each member of the group is both ingenius and amusing.

Scene iii allows us one more glimpse of Touchstone, who may be changed by his adventures. He still insults the simple pages (V, iii, 34–36), but his affection for Audrey could be genuine, as he leads her off to marriage.

In the final scene of the play, all plot complications are untangled, but what makes this resolution unusual for a play of the Elizabethan era is that it follows directly from Rosalind, a woman. She commands this situation, as she indicates in the opening lines, giving orders to the Duke, Orlando, Phebe, and finally Silvius:

> Keep you your word, O Duke, to give your daughter;
> You, yours, Orlando, to receive his daughter;
> Keep you your word, Phebe, that you'll marry me,
> Or else, refusing me, to wed this shepherd;
> Keep your word, Silvius, that you'll marry her
> If she refuse me, and from hence I go
> To make these doubts all even.
>
> (V, iv, 19–25)

She then departs to remove her disguise. Meanwhile the Duke and Orlando comment on "Ganymed's" resemblance to Rosalind.

While we await her return, Jaques and Touchstone engage in elaborate banter. Touchstone clarifies his completely unromantic and unemotional attitude toward Audrey:

> A poor virgin, sir, an
> ill-favor'd thing, sir, but mine own; a poor humor of
> mine, sir, to take that that no man else will.
>
> (V, iv, 57–59)

His coldness confirms one of the play's themes. We have heard a great deal of romantic verse that has been mocked as pretentious or foolish. Yet beneath that poetry is genuine love and commitment. Shakespeare seems to suggest that romantic conventions themselves deserve some mockery but also that they play a vital role in human relations, and thus these rituals need not be abandoned. Touchstone offers no grand verse and no courting, but then he offers no substantial feeling, either. His debate with Jaques about the "Lie Circumstantial" and the "Lie Direct" is further evidence of the emptiness of both men, as the Duke says of Touchstone:

> He uses his folly like a stalking-horse,
> and under the presentation of that he shoots his wit.
>
> (V, iv, 106–107)

The tone of the play changes slightly in the last few moments as the god Hymen enters with Rosalind and Celia. Amidst dance and song a series of unmaskings and embraces takes place, including Phebe's sudden desire for Silvius (V, iv, 149–150). Whether or not this change is believable, it is necessary for the unified structure of the conclusion.

The final revelation, also unexpected, concerns Duke Frederick. Jaques de Boys enters to report that Frederick was planning to kill his brother, but in the forest encountered "an old religious man" (V, iv, 160) who miraculously was able to convert Frederick. The changed Duke has subsequently relinquished his claims and become a hermit, and all lands and rights have thus been restored to the Duke senior. Perhaps more than any twist in the plot, this one strains credulity, but we are supposed to trust in the regenerative powers of the forest. Furthermore, the restoration of the proper son to the throne is the final step in the establishment of the old order.

After all the marriages, one character remains unattached: Jaques. Fittingly, he does not choose to join the Duke back at the court. Instead he sends everyone off and resolves to join Frederick as a hermit:

> Out of these convertites
> There is much matter to be heard and learn'd.
>
> (V, iv, 184–185)

He yet insists that he alone knows the path to truth and wisdom. We recognize that he has no place in court nor in any establishment, for he finds his identity not in himself but in being different from everyone else.

Rosalind ends the play, one more twist on male-female roles, for traditionally a male character spoke the epilogue to the audience. But in this work she is the dominant character. Like the other figures in love, she is the object of gentle laughter on the playwright's part, as she finds herself unable to express feelings as freely as she would like. But she never falters. She is steadfast in her devotion. And her combination of wit and sentiment, of daring and sensitivity, makes her perhaps the most alluring of Shakespeare's heroines.

SUGGESTIONS FOR FURTHER READING

Cole, Howard C. "The Moral Vision of *As You Like It.*" *College Literature* 3 (1976): 17–32.

Halio, Jay L., ed. *Twentieth Century Interpretations of* As You Like It. Englewood Cliffs, N.J.: Prentice-Hall, 1968.

Hotson, Leslie. *Shakespeare's Motley.* 1952. Reprint. New York: Haskell House, 1971.

Jamieson, Michael. *Shakespeare*: As You Like It. London: Edward Arnold, 1965.

Jenkins, Harold. "*As You Like It.*" *Shakespeare Survey* 8 (1955): 40–51.

Leggatt, Alexander. *Shakespeare's Comedy of Love.* London: Methuen, 1974.

Shaw, John. "Fortune and Nature in *As You Like It.*" *Shakespeare Quarterly* 6 (1955): 45–50.

Wilcox, John. "Putting Jaques into *As You Like It.*" *Modern Language Review* 36 (1941): 388–394.

Twelfth Night, or What You Will

The title *Twelfth Night* suggests the final day of the Christmas season, a traditional time of feasting and revelry. Accordingly, the play has certain entertaining elements that we might see as typical of Shakespearean comedy: self-involved lovers, mistaken identity, a large measure of boisterous humor, and a comic villain who is appropriately punished. But the alternative title, *What You Will*, the only such subtitle Shakespeare provided, suggests a more subtle vision. Indeed, this play is about excess, the abuse of "will," and despite the surface good humor, something ugly permeates the characters and their world. Although the plot complications and situations offer a great deal of laughter, this work may be seen as the transition between Shakespeare's lighter, more traditional comedies and the three "problem" comedies to follow. The primary source of the main plot is the story of Apolonius and Silla, in *Farewell to Militaire Profession* (1581) by Barnabe Riche.

We sense this darker quality from Duke Orsino's opening lines:

> If music be the food of love, play on,
> Give me excess of it; that surfeiting,
> The appetite may sicken, and so die.
> That strain again, it had a dying fall;
> O, it came o'er my ear like the sweet sound
> That breathes upon a bank of violets,
> Stealing and giving odor. Enough, no more,
> 'Tis not so sweet now as it was before.
>
> (I, i, 1–8)

Initially he seems the conventional lovestruck young romantic, like Orlando in *As You Like It* or Bassanio in *The Merchant of Venice*. But the words "excess," "surfeiting," "sicken," "die," and "dying" betoken passion that borders on decadence. Orsino seems not simply to seek pleasure but to wallow in it. When the music temporarily loses its charm, he angrily grows bored and cuts off the sound. He requires constant stimulation, and when that stimulation is not fulfilling, he grows impatient.

His self-absorption is paralleled by that of Olivia, the object of Orsino's passion:

> O, when mine eyes did see Olivia first,
> Methought she purg'd the air of pestilence!
> That instant was I turn'd into a hart,
> And my desires, like fell and cruel hounds,
> E'er since pursue me.
>
> (I, i, 18–22)

After hearing Orsino's first speeches, we wonder whether this infatuation is genuine or whether the Duke is seizing Olivia as a momentary target for love. Our suspicions are aroused further when the report comes from Valentine about Olivia's behavior:

> The element itself, till seven years' heat,
> Shall not behold her face at ample view;
> But like a cloistress she will veiled walk,
> And water once a day her chamber round
> With eye-offending brine, all this to season
> A brother's dead love, which she would keep fresh
> And lasting in her sad remembrance.
>
> (I, i, 25–31)

Like Orsino, Olivia drowns in exaggerated feeling, carrying the mourning for her brother to bizarre extremes. Yet Orsino finds this extravagant emotion attractive:

> How will she love when the rich golden shaft
> Hath kill'd the flock of all affections else
> That live in her . . .
>
> (I, i, 34–36)

Both characters yield entirely to their "wills," their capacities for self-indulgence.

The opposite to such behavior is dramatized in the next scene, with the appearance of Viola. From her opening question (I, ii, 1), she reveals her realistic attitude toward the world. She has been shipwrecked and must find her way alone in an unfamiliar country. She has heard of Orsino, though. Furthermore, she herself is mourning her own brother, so far unnamed, who is supposed to have drowned. But when Viola hears of Olivia and her cause for sorrow (I, ii, 36–38), Viola resolves to serve her. Toward that end Viola plans to disguise herself as a man and work at Orsino's court, where she will win him over with "many sorts of music" (I, ii, 58), a phrase that recalls Orsino's own imagery. In her attitude and actions we see Viola's intuitive understanding of people. She trusts the Captain, and he proves reliable. She will also intuit the best qualities of Orsino and Olivia. In sum, Viola's strength provides ballast to the weaknesses of the other characters.

In scene iii the play turns from romance to lower comedy. Sir Toby Belch, Olivia's uncle, announces that "I am sure care's an enemy to life" (I, iii, 2–3), and when Maria accuses him of extravagant revelry and warns him to obey rules of order, he accepts no criticism:

> Confine? I'll confine myself no finer than
> I am. These clothes are good enough to drink in, and
> so be these boots too; and they be not, let them hang
> themselves in their own straps.

(I, iii, 10–13)

His tone and excessive girth remind us of Falstaff, but Sir Toby is different. Falstaff's lustiness and capacity for food and drink is modulated by two qualities: a supreme wit and a good will. True, Falstaff is a corrupt army officer, and at times that corruption is intolerable. But at the core of Falstaff is a geniality and affection for others. Sir Toby is never so warm. For instance, in lines 18–41 in this scene he speaks of his companion Sir Andrew Aguecheek, whose qualities he extols, but the affection for Sir Andrew is based on the latter's income (I, iii, 22). Furthermore, Sir Toby lives at Olivia's house only because he requires her money. He has no affection for her, either, as he will reveal. Therefore he would not mind seeing Andrew married to Olivia so that Sir Toby himself could benefit from the additional money. Throughout the play his wit tends to be less humorous than cruel, more vulgar than sharp. He embodies not the joyous revelry of Falstaff, but a gross debauchery. He is the dark side of pleasure, much as Orsino and Olivia are the dark side of romantic obsession.

When Sir Andrew Aguecheek enters, he is a ridiculous figure, hardly the romantic to win Olivia's hand. He is shriveled in both body and personality, and Maria's jests about his being "dry," with the implied meaning of "impotent," ensure that we always regard him as a joke. He takes himself seriously, but his blindness suggests foolish self-delusion:

> I am a fellow o'
> th' strangest mind i' th' world; I delight in masques and
> revel sometimes altogether.

(I, iii, 112–114)

His is the type of vanity that is vulnerable to deft manipulation, such as carried out by Sir Toby, who here convinces Sir Andrew to remain at Olivia's house to maintain his courtship (I, iii, 109–111). And Sir Andrew's enjoyment of pleasure is in the form of a decadence that underlies this play.

Scene iv takes us back to Orsino's court, where Viola, disguised as Cesario, has within three days won the affection of Orsino. But to Valentine Viola asks the key question about Orsino: "Is he inconstant, sir, in his favors?" (I, iv, 7). She has already fallen in love with the Duke. Yet Viola is also aware of Orsino's desire for Olivia. Thus Viola wants the answer to be both negative and positive: negative because she wants the man she loves to be unswerving in his affections, positive because she wants him to transfer those affections to her. Valentine answers that Orsino is constant, but after Orsino's performance in scene i, we are not convinced that his affections are steady.

The situation is further complicated when Orsino asks "Cesario" to woo Olivia in the Duke's name. Orsino's reasoning is telling, as he praises Cesario's features:

> Diana's lip
> Is not more smooth and rubious, thy small pipe
> Is as the maiden's organ, shrill and sound,
> And all is semblative a woman's part.

(I, iv, 31–34)

Whether he is aware or not, Orsino is falling in love with the young man in front of him. His words communicate that he senses Viola's womanliness, but at the moment he does not know her identity. Viola herself will soon be in the bizarre position of wooing another woman in the name of the man she loves. Thus her psychology grows more complex as her emotions become tangled.

The final scene of Act I introduces the play's remaining major characters. Feste appears first, bantering with Maria. He is called a "clown" by Shakespeare, but the term is deceiving, for he is not a buffoon in the tradition of Dogberry in *Much Ado About Nothing* or Launce in *The Two Gentlemen of Verona*, but a "wit" somewhat like Touchstone in *As You Like It*. Yet Feste's humor is by and large cleverer than Touchstone's and often tinged with melancholy. Although he participates in the action of the play and even dominates the cruelest comic scene, we feel his disengagement. His first line captures this emotion:

> Let her hang me! He that is well hang'd in
> this world needs to fear no colors.

(I, v, 5–6)

He puns gracefully, the word "colors" being part of a proverbial phrase as well as a reference to the noose of a hangman. The line also communicates a measure of resignation, of Feste's belief in the brevity and ultimate unimportance of things. Throughout the play, in both song and dialogue, he makes this attitude apparent.

Olivia then enters, accompanied by Malvolio, her steward. At Feste's opening jests she appears intolerant: "Take the fool away" (I, v, 38). But her reasons for keeping him about soon are obvious, for she enjoys his playfulness and even tolerates his speculations on her dead brother: "I think his soul is in hell, madonna" (I, v, 68). To which Olivia firmly answers, "I know his soul is in heaven, fool" (I, v, 69). That Olivia can accept such light-hearted comments suggests her good nature, also that her exaggerated grief is a pose to garner attention.

Contrary to Olivia's enjoyment of Feste is Malvolio's haughtiness. The steward refers to Feste as a "barren rascal" (I, v, 84), and confesses himself amazed that Olivia can endure such an annoyance. Olivia dismisses Malvolio's complaints with one of the central lines of the play:

> O, you are sick of self-love, Malvolio, and
> taste with a distemper'd appetite.
>
> (I, v, 90–91)

The accusation is not only correct toward Malvolio, but may also be applied to many other characters, including Orsino, Sir Toby, Sir Andrew, and Olivia herself. All are preoccupied with their own feelings and desires. Malvolio is perhaps the guiltiest of all, and thus he is the appropriate victim for a plot based on his vanity. Still, the environment in which he must function is run by Sir Toby, who here appears half-drunk. Feste enjoys some humor at the knight's expense (I, v, 131–133), but the interruption is unattractive.

On the other hand, Malvolio's snobbishness toward anyone he judges beneath his station is apparent when he describes the visiting Cesario:

> Not yet old enough for a man, nor young
> enough for a boy; as a squash is before 'tis a peascod,
> or a codling when 'tis almost an apple. 'Tis with
> him in standing water, between boy and man. He
> is very well-favor'd, and he speaks very shrewishly.
> One would think his mother's milk were scarce out
> of him.
>
> (I, v, 156–162)

Malvolio dismisses any man who is remotely attractive and who might be a rival for Olivia's hand. His attitude is supercilious, his language arrogant. Yet Malvolio is more complicated than his first impression suggests. And his relationship with the other members of Olivia's household also becomes complex.

Before that situation evolves, however, Olivia encounters Viola, and from their opening lines Shakespeare exploits Viola's disguise masterfully. In *As You Like It*, Rosalind's impersonation of Ganymed was touching in just a couple of scenes, most of all during Orlando's mock courtship. In *Twelfth Night*, though, the confusion of identity is developed as richly as possible. Here Viola speaks for Orsino, proclaiming love for Olivia:

> My lord and master loves you. O, such love
> Could be but recompens'd, though you were crown'd
> The nonpareil of beauty.
>
> (I, v, 252–254)

Viola even captures the extravagant tone of Orsino's passion:

> With adorations, fertile tears,
> With groans that thunder love, with sighs of fire.
>
> (I, v, 255–256)

But when Olivia invites Cesario to offer "his" version of courtship, Viola responds with lines that reflect her own temperament:

> Make me a willow cabin at your gate,
> And call upon my soul within the house;

Write loyal cantons of contemned love,
And sing them loud even in the dead of night . . .

(I, v, 268–271)

Viola wants to address such sentiments to Orsino, but Olivia takes them as a
manifestation of Cesario's capacity for affection, and she falls for "him," although at this point she controls herself: "You might do much" (I, v, 276).
And she invites not Orsino but Cesario to return (I, v, 280–281). Viola hurries
away, but Olivia sends Malvolio after her with a fabrication about a ring left
behind (I, v, 301–305), while to herself she wonders how the matter will proceed:

I do I know not what, and fear to find
Mine eye too great a flatterer for my mind.
Fate, show thy force: ourselves we do not owe;
What is decreed must be; and be this so.

(I, v, 308–311)

The Viola-Olivia relationship has no future, but just as we acknowledge that
fact, Shakespeare brings in the last major character, Sebastian, who appears in
Act II, scene i. Although he believes his twin sister Viola dead, just as she
believes him drowned, he remains loyal to her (II, i, 25–31). And when he
announces his intention to go to Orsino's court, we recognize that confusion is
soon bound to take hold of everyone. This scene also brings in Antonio, whose
devotion to Sebastian, especially as articulated in Act II, scene i, lines 44–48,
contrasts with the self-love that motivates other characters.

Act II, scene ii, returns us to Viola's predicament and reveals the intricate
emotions she bears. First Malvolio, reluctantly following Olivia's orders, rudely
invites Cesario to return with the ring Olivia gave him (II, ii, 13–16). After he
stalks off, Viola is left to ponder her dilemma:

She loves me sure, the cunning of her passion
Invites me in this churlish messenger

(II, ii, 22–23)

Viola is bothered that her deception may cause another woman pain, for Viola
is aware of how acute a woman's feelings may be:

How easy it is for the proper-false
In women's waxen hearts to set their forms!
Alas, [our] frailty is the cause, not we,
For such as we are made [of,] such we be.

(II, ii, 29–32)

We know that Viola's sympathies are not only for Olivia but for herself as well:

As I am man,
My state is desperate for my master's love;
As I am woman (now alas the day!),
What thriftless sighs shall poor Olivia breathe!
O time, thou must untangle this, not I,

It is too hard a knot for me t' untie.

(II, ii, 36–41)

She is both puzzled and intrigued by the confusion of which she is a part. Her reflections show the mixture of feminine and masculine instincts within her as well as Shakespeare's perspective on the differences in attitude between men and women in love.

In scene iii we discover more about Malvolio. First, however, we are prepared for his entrance by the raucous celebration of Sir Toby and Sir Andrew. They are joined by Feste, who characteristically offers two verses that conflict with the general attitude of merriment. The first dramatizes lost love (II, iii, 39–44), the second the transience of all human emotion (II, iii, 47–52). Both themes continue to preoccupy him. When Maria enters, the noise reaches its apex, at which point Malvolio enters to subdue the revelry.

> My masters, are you mad? or what are you?
> Have you not wit, manners, or honesty, but to gabble
> like tinkers at this time of night?

(II, iii, 86–88)

Sir Toby's first response is a sneer at Malvolio's status: "Art any more than a steward?" (II, iii, 114). Sir Toby, after all, is a knight, and Malvolio's social superior. Then Sir Toby dismisses all complaints eloquently:

> Dost
> thou think because thou art virtuous there shall be no
> more cakes and ale?

(II, iii, 114–116)

Moments later, after a furious Malvolio departs following a series of insults from Sir Toby, Maria adds:

> The dev'l a puritan that he is, or any thing
> constantly but a time-pleaser, an affection'd ass, that
> cons state without book, and utters it by great
> swarths; the best persuaded of himself, so cramm'd
> (as he thinks) with excellencies, that it is his grounds
> of faith that all that look on him love him; and on that
> vice in him will my revenge find notable cause to work.

(II, iii, 147–153)

Their hatred for him has two causes: his disapproval of their hedonistic life and his high estimation of himself.

Puritanical figures appear elsewhere in Shakespeare, and they are always disparaged. Shylock in *The Merchant of Venice* is an outsider not only because of his religion but because of his humorless demeanor. Octavius in *Antony and Cleopatra* and Prince John in *Henry IV, Part 2* are both cold politicians with little emotion or affection and little capacity for joy. All are presented as unpleasant and even untrustworthy because of their reluctance to participate in parties and celebrations. Malvolio follows in that tradition. Yet the celebrations surrounding him are at least as unpleasant as he is. We remember Sir Toby's earlier line "Lechery! I defy lechery" (I, v, 125), his insults and crude laughter. Who, then, is more taken with himself than Sir Toby? Who is more affected and deceiving? Certainly Malvolio has his eye on Olivia, but who else considers himself attractive to her? Sir Andrew, for one. Furthermore, Malvolio does seem to care sincerely for Olivia, and that cannot be said of either Sir Toby or Sir Andrew, who care for no one. Even as this scene ends, Sir Toby urges Andrew to send for more money (II, iii, 186), the only reason Sir Toby cares to associate with him. Finally, what exactly has Malvolio done but demand, albeit condescendingly, for the tone of his household to be more sober? In doing so he is only carrying out Olivia's orders. Thus our assessment of him is mixed. His snootiness requires comeuppance, but this group is too unpleasant to deserve the right to punish anybody.

Scene iv returns us to the other main story, when we meet Orsino, whose preoccupations remain the same. In his first line he demands music (II, iv, 1), and he yet enjoys suffering his own anguished love. As he says to Viola, still disguised as Cesario:

> Come hither, boy. If ever thou shalt love,
> In the sweet pangs of it remember me;
> For such as I am, all true lovers are,
> Unstaid and skittish in all motions else,
> Save in the constant image of the creature
> That is belov'd.

(II, iv, 15–20)

A double irony is at work here. One, Orsino soon proves just as "skittish" as he describes others. Two, the person to whom he speaks, Viola, is more devoted to him than Orsino at this moment recognizes. Viola, of course, is helpless to express her affection, as she is throughout this scene, while Orsino reflects upon the emphemerality and quality of love. Meanwhile Feste sings "Come away, come away, death . . . '' (II, iv, 51), and his lyrics affirm the dark tone underlying the comic confusion.

The most powerful irony occurs when Orsino ruminates upon the comparative weakness of woman's love:

> Alas, their love may be call'd appetite,
> No motion of the liver, but the palate,
> That suffer surfeit, cloyment, and revolt,
> But mine is all as hungry as the sea,
> And can digest as much. Make no compare
> Between that love a woman can bear me
> And that I owe Olivia.

(II, iv, 97–103)

At this Viola cannot resist responding:

My father had a daughter lov'd a man
As it might be perhaps, were I a woman,
I should your lordship.

(II, iv, 107–109)

We men may say more, swear more, but indeed
Our shows are more than will; for still we prove
Much in our vows, but little in our love.

(II, iv, 116–118)

At this moment her pain overflows. Here is one way in which Viola differs from Rosalind, who never truly suffers because of her deception, for she never sees Orlando dedicate himself to another woman. But Viola must stand by helplessly as the man she loves gives of himself elsewhere. Thus Viola's deception has both comic and serious repercussions.

The next scene reverts to the other plot, the gulling of Malvolio. He is strolling through the garden, luxuriating in what he imagines is his place in Olivia's affections (II, v, 23–28). Sir Toby and Sir Andrew eavesdrop, as Malvolio fantasizes about disciplining them for their drinking, and gaining authority over them. Even at this moment, though, Malvolio is not evil or malevolent. He is instead an officious spoilsport, but that crime is enough to arouse the hatred of the likes of Sir Toby who grumbles threateningly: "Shall this fellow live?" (II, v, 62). When Malvolio discovers Maria's letter, ostensibly from Olivia, his imagination runs amuck, and he deludes himself into assuming that the Countess is in love with him:

Some are [born] great, some [achieve] greatness, and
some have greatness thrust upon 'em.

(II, v, 145–146)

His attempts to dignify his romantic aspirations are ridiculous, but they complement the other misplaced loves in the play. The key directions in the letter are for Malvolio to wear yellow stockings in a cross-gartered fashion, so that they pass bizarrely both above and below the knee (II, v, 153–154). Maria maliciously explains how Olivia will respond:

He will come
to her in yellow stockings, and 'tis a color she abhors,
and cross-garter'd, a fashion she detests; and he will
smile upon her, which will now be so unsuitable
to her disposition, being addicted to a melancholy as
she is, that it cannot but turn him into a notable contempt.

(II, v, 197–204)

We anticipate the moment almost as much as Maria does.

With Malvolio fooled, the other story returns, as Viola prepares to continue pleading to Olivia in Orsino's name. At the start of Act III, scene i, she chats with Feste, and these two keen minds get along contentedly. Eventually Viola acknowledges his superiority in the verbal fencing:

> Nay, and thou pass upon me, I'll no more
> with thee.
>
> (III, i, 42–43)

And in tribute to his skill she gives him some money. Feste, though, offers one more sally, this one emphasizing Viola's youthful appearance:

> Now, Jove, in his next commodity of hair,
> send thee a beard!
>
> (III, i, 44–45)

Viola agrees, offering as well a reflection meant for us alone:

> By my troth, I'll tell thee, I am almost sick
> for one—(*aside*) though I would not have it grow
> on my chin.
>
> (III, i, 46–48)

She is nervous that her pose may be discovered, but also comfortable enough in Feste's presence to joke to herself.

When Feste leaves, Sir Andrew and Sir Toby enter, and exchange formal greetings with Viola, who stands her ground confidently. Upon Olivia's appearance, though, Viola speaks more generously:

> Most excellent accomplish'd lady, the heavens rain
> odors on you.
>
> (III, i, 84–85)

Even Sir Andrew is impressed by the young "man's" style:

> That youth's a rare courtier—"rain
> odors," well.
>
> (III, i, 86–87)

Viola and Olivia are soon left alone, and the courtship resumes, although it is hopelessly complicated by Olivia's desire not for Orsino, but for Viola:

> I bade you never speak again of him;
> But would you undertake another suit,
> I had rather hear you to solicit that
> Than music from the spheres.
>
> (III, i, 107–110)

The intricacies build to four alternating lines (III, i, 139–142) that express Olivia's hopes and Viola's recognition of reality. They also communicate the pathos of unfulfilled desire. At last Olivia can no longer restrain herself:

> I love thee so, that maugre all thy pride,
> Nor wit nor reason can my passion hide.

Do not extort thy reasons from this clause,
For that I woo, thou therefore hast no cause;
But rather reason thus with reason fetter;
Love sought is good, but given unsought is better.

(III, i, 151–156)

She reminds us of a theme familiar from other comedies, such as *Two Gentlemen of Verona* and *A Midsummer Night's Dream*: the conflict between reason and emotion in matters of love. Viola has no choice but to refuse Olivia's affections, but her anguish is clear:

I have one heart, one bosom, and one truth,
And that no woman has, nor never none
Shall mistress be of it, save I alone.

(III, i, 158–160)

A further irony is that as Olivia has long dismissed Orsino's suit, now she shares his plight, pining for a love who rejects her. The situation is comic, and we are confident it will resolve happily. Nonetheless, the emotions of both characters in this episode are powerful.

The next two scenes propel the plot quickly. First Sir Andrew reveals how he is frustrated that his courtship for Olivia goes nowhere. Therefore, under prodding from Sir Toby, Sir Andrew resolves to take action against his supposed rival, Cesario (III, ii, 42–50). Sir Toby looks forward to the challenge:

For Andrew, if he
were open'd and you find so much blood in his liver as
will clog the foot of a flea, I'll eat the rest of th'
anatomy.

(III, ii, 61–64)

Clearly Sir Toby cares little for the welfare of his comrade. Meanwhile Maria's description of Malvolio's new affectation leaves us awaiting his next entrance.

Scene iii brings in another element of this superbly balanced story, as Antonio's devotion to Sebastian is further dramatized. Even at risk to his own safety Antonio is willing to stay with Sebastian, who is somewhat bemused by this attention:

I can no other answer make but thanks,
And thanks; and ever oft good turns
Are shuffled off with such uncurrent pay;
But were my worth as is my conscience firm,
You should find better dealing.

(III, iii, 14–18)

The passionate nature of Antonio's affection for the younger man is never explored fully, but we should accept it not as homosexual love, but as the epitome of male friendship. That the mix-up of the two twins is imminent becomes clear when Sebastian gives Antonio the purse and they agree to meet in an hour (III, iii, 38–48).

All these plot lines meld ingeniously in Act III, scene iv, as Olivia calls for
Malvolio, whom she describes as "sad and civil" (III, iv, 5). Evidently she
prefers him as he has always been. When she sees him now, however, dressed
according to the description in Maria's letter, her first reaction is revealing:

> I am as mad as he,
> If sad and merry madness equal be.
> How now, Malvolio?

(III, iv, 14–16)

Olivia seems to acknowledge that extremes of passion, whether from self-love
or devotion to another, are all varieties of madness. We think back to the alternative title, *What You Will*. But when Malvolio begins to spew sentiments
from the letter written by Maria, Olivia is unable to grasp what he says, and
thus to her he seems out of touch with reality. The comedy is rich but under-
lined by a measure of sadness, for Malvolio does seek her affection and believes he is following her wishes. Even as he raves, she remains solicitous:

> Let some of my people have a special care of him. I
> would not have him miscarry for the half of my dowry.

(III, iv, 62–63)

Olivia is a decent, caring person, and her affection for Malvolio remains unflagging. Thus the ill treatment he is about to receive seems even more unjustified.
First Sir Toby refers to him as "an enemy to mankind" (III, iv, 98), a harsh
overstatement. Then Malvolio himself hits at another version of the truth:

> You are idle shallow
> things, I am not of your element.

(III, iv, 123–124)

No evidence in the play suggests that Malvolio is evaluating Sir Toby, Maria,
or Fabian incorrectly. Yet his manner infuriates them, and after he leaves they
clarify their intention to have him imprisoned.

The comparative legitimacy of Malvolio's affections is then parodied unconsciously by the ridiculous Sir Andrew, whose challenge to Cesario is read aloud
by Sir Toby. The prose is stilted and pretentious, and therefore appropriate to
Sir Andrew:

> "Wonder not, nor admire not in
> thy mind, why I do call thee so, for I will show thee no
> reason for't."

(III, iv, 150–152)

But rather than deliver the letter itself to Viola, Toby schemes with Fabian and
Maria to make the challenge personally. After all, Cesario will obviously recognize that the prose comes from "a clodpole" (III, iv, 190). Thus when Viola
enters, still fending off Olivia's affections (III, iv, 201–205), she is assaulted
by Sir Toby, who is eager to see a fight:

              . . . therefore on, or
strip you sword stark naked; for meddle you must,
that's certain, or forswear to wear iron about you.

                                        (III, iv, 250–252)

While Viola quivers in terror, Sir Toby brings on Sir Andrew, all the while praising Cesario's skills (III, iv, 273–279). At this news Sir Andrew's bravado fades: "Pox on't, I'll not meddle with him" (III, iv, 280). And Viola, too, is genuinely frightened:

                    A little thing
would make me tell them how much I lack of a man.

                                        (III, iv, 302–303)

We know that Viola's fears are misdirected, for her opponent is incapable of harming anyone. But the confrontation soon occurs in a scene that may be played to great comic effect, as two incompetent and terrified combatants delicately wield their weapons. They are interrupted with several moments of energy, first by Antonio defending Cesario (whom he mistakes for Sebastian), then by the entrance of the police arresting Antonio. At the appearance of the law, Sir Toby scurries away: "I'll be with you anon" (III, iv, 320). Here is one more bit of evidence that Malvolio's estimate of his character is correct, for why should Toby be frightened of the police unless he has something to hide?

The romantic and comic elements of the play unite in Antonio's mistaking Viola for Sebastian (III, iv, 332–338). She, of course, knows nothing of him (III, iv, 352–357), and Antonio's loyalty is tested severely:

But O, how vild an idol proves this god!
Thou hast, Sebastian, done good feature shame.

                                        (III, iv, 365–366)

As he is taken away, however, Viola senses the cause of the confusion:

Prove true, imagination, O, prove true,
That I, dear brother, be now ta'en for you!

                                        (III, iv, 375–376)

In this play we have observed all sorts of dreams and madnesses. Now Viola hopes that one will prove legitimate.

Act III, scene iii is remarkable for the range of emotions Shakespeare dramatizes. We see the comic delusions of Malvolio, the petty bitterness of the plot against him, the passion of Olivia, the farce of the swordfight, the loyalty of Antonio, and the desperate hope of Viola.

In Act IV Sebastian finds himself the object of confusion. First Feste takes him for Cesario, then Sir Andrew, Sir Toby, and Fabian do the same. When

Olivia enters to see the fighting, she reacts as we have been anticipating. First she dismisses Sir Toby and his cohorts:

> Ungracious wretch,
> Fit for the mountains and the barbarous caves,
> Where manners ne'er were preach'd! Out of my sight!
>
> (IV, i, 47–49)

Olivia may be unaware of the circumstances, but Sir Toby deserves the admonishment. She then turns to Sebastian and attempts to comfort what she assumes are the same delicate sensibilities she found in Cesario (IV, i, 52–59). Sebastian is puzzled but pleased, and he expresses his delight in familiar terms:

> What relish is in this? How runs the stream?
> Or I am mad, or else this is a dream.
>
> (IV, i, 60–61)

Her invitation is strong: "Would thou'dst be rul'd by me!" (IV, i, 64). And he answers with a reminder of the title of the play: "I will" (IV, i, 65). Sebastian senses that his spirit is best exercised not in the unbridled exercise of his own prerogative, but in submission to affection and love. The lesser characters in the play never achieve that realization.

The action shifts to the plight of Malvolio, now imprisoned and forced to appeal to Feste, who enters in the disguise of Sir Topas the Curate:

> Good, Sir Topas, do not think I am mad; they have laid
> me here in hideous darkness.
>
> (IV, ii, 29–30)

No doubt his cries for help would have amused the Elizabethans, who enjoyed making sport of the insane. But if the actor playing Malvolio injects any pathos into his words, the scene can be moving. If Malvolio remains outraged rather than hurt, we can laugh. But if his cries are of genuine suffering, the injustice of his treatment pierces through, as in this line:

> Fool, there was never man so notoriously
> abus'd; I am as well in my wits, fool, as thou art.
>
> (IV, ii, 87–88)

Here the chief agent of Malvolio's misery is Feste, who torments Malvolio, first in front of Sir Toby and Maria, then alone, switching from voice to voice. But Feste's attitude during this scene is less anger at Malvolio and more delight in the opportunity to perform. As Maria says:

> Thou mightst have done this without thy
> beard and gown, he sees thee not.
>
> (IV, ii, 64–65)

Indeed, once Sir Toby and Maria depart Feste has only himself to please and ends his extravaganza with another melancholy song, as if this episode were not enough to cure his constant sadness.

Sebastian's soliloquy takes up that theme of madness:

This is the air, that is the glorious sun,
This pearl she gave me, I do feel't and see't,
And though 'tis wonder that enwraps me thus,
Yet 'tis not madness.

(IV, iii, 1–4)

At this juncture the relationship between falling madly in love and being genuinely mad is before us, and perhaps we think back to Theseus's line in *A
Midsummer Night's Dream*:

Lovers and madmen have such seething brains,
Such shaping fantasies, that apprehend
More than cool reason ever comprehends.

(V, i, 4–6)

Sebastian feels himself under such an influence, and he happily accepts the
condition:

For though my soul disputes well with my sense,
That this may be some error, but no madness . . .

(IV, iii, 9–10)

He has fallen in love quickly, perhaps unrealistically, and when Olivia enters
we believe in her willingness to marry Sebastian. But then such acceptance on
our part, like our willingness to believe that male and female twins could be
confused, is endemic to comic convention. Furthermore, if we accept such
passion as a kind of benign madness (and that supposition is the spirit of this
play), then their mutual infatuation is well within the bounds of theatrical reality.

The single scene of Act V resolves all plot lines, and in doing so allows the
main figures to react characteristically to the crisis. Feste brings Malvolio's letter
to Olivia, although he indulges himself with Fabian by refusing to allow him to
see the letter (V, i, 5). Feste's amusement is interrupted by the entrance of Viola
and Orsino, who seek Olivia. Even at this tense moment, Feste's wit proves so
charming that Orsino twice gives him gold, with the promise of more (V, i, 27–
28, 35). But before Feste can retrieve his lady, the police bring in Antonio,
whom Orsino remembers as an enemy but nonetheless valiant (V, i, 52–59). In
his own defense Antonio, always noble and upright, insists on his honesty. He
then relates his own story, in the meantime mistaking Viola for Sebastian (V,
i, 82–92). And while that confusion remains, Olivia enters and the Duke immediately becomes distracted.

This meeting is the first of two that bring the play to a resolution, for Olivia
and Orsino have never appeared onstage together. She behaves in typically grand
style, dismissing Orsino's desires:

If it be aught to the old tune, my lord,
It is as fat and fulsome to mine ear

As howling after music.

(V, i, 108–110)

She takes Orsino's own metaphor of music and love and turns it back to him. Orsino then reacts with his customary excess by threatening to kill Cesario, whom he takes for a traitor:

I'll sacrifice the lamb that I do love,
To spite a raven's heart within a dove.

(V, i, 130–131)

Viola then proclaims loyalty to Orsino (V, i, 134–138), leaving Olivia shocked: "Whither, my lord? Cesario, husband, stay" (V, i, 143).

With the entrance of the priest who married Olivia to Sebastian, the tension is compounded skillfully, as all onstage are hopelessly bewildered, while the audience is desperate to unravel their confusion. We also recognize that the plight that currently besets Malvolio has spread. All the characters are confused, victims of false accusations, and all are reduced to shouting and threatening to no useful end. The tension brings out some of Orsino's uglier aspects, as he berates Viola for the traitorous act of marrying Olivia:

O thou dissembling cub! what wilt thou be
When time hath sow'd a grizzle on thy case?

(V, i, 164–165)

We are pained at this unjust accusation, but we are gratified to see Sir Andrew blaming Sir Toby for one portion of the trouble (V, i, 193–194), and that Sir Toby is finally forced to confess his true feelings for his supposed friend:

Will you help!—an ass-head and a coxcomb
and a knave, a thin-fac'd knave, a gull!

(V, i, 206–207)

At this point Sebastian enters, and complications at last are unraveled: In Olivia's words: "Most wonderful" (V, i, 225). The reunion between Sebastian and Viola is genuinely moving, as is the change that overcomes Orsino:

Boy, that hast said to me a thousand times
Thou never shouldst love woman like to me.

(V, i, 267–268)

He finally understands the extent of his folly.

The lovers now pair off, although we are not completely satisfied at the result. Somehow the noble and loving Viola deserves better than Orsino (V, i, 272–273). Still, one character in love is left loose: Malvolio. His letter to Olivia is brought by Feste, then read aloud, and Malvolio himself enters to demand apology. Again, this scene can be played for pathos, as the steward states his case:

Why have you suffer'd me to be imprison'd,
Kept in a dark house, visited by the priest,

And made the most notorious geck and gull
That e'er invention play'd on? Tell me why!

(V, i, 341–344)

Were the plot of this play less rollicking and the ending less joyful, Malvolio's final question might be unsettling. Why should he have suffered simply for obeying Olivia's orders and seeking to devote himself to her? The question has implications for Shakespeare's tragic plays, which grapple more directly with the mystery of human evil and unhappiness. Here the query is never answered. Instead Fabian reports that Toby has rewarded Maria for writing the letter by marrying her (V, i, 362–364), an appropriate union, for in their capacity for cruel humor these two will punish each other sufficiently. Feste then recalls some of the highlights of the deception (V, i, 370–376), as if the gulling were an endearing spectacle: "And thus the whirligig of time brings in his revenges" (V, i, 376–377). Malvolio's exit line is also intriguing: "I'll be revenged on the whole pack of you" (V, i, 378). The words may be delivered with genuine malice or as an expression of temporary insult. If the latter tone is used, we laugh, comfortable the mood will pass. If the former tone is adopted, Olivia and Orsino's genial order to soothe his hurt feelings may seem insufficient and even callous.

The final song of the play is a fitting ending from Feste. He, too, remains unattached, and his song might be seen as his version of Jaques' "seven ages of man" speech from *As You Like It*. Feste's emphasis, however, is not on the misery of human existence but on its brevity, and his refrain, "For the rain it raineth every day" (V, i, 392), is an antidote to the vanity and egoism that has dominated the previous action. "A great while ago the world began" (V, i, 405), and it will continue irrespective of what we do. Feste sees our lives as short and therefore laughable, for to him nothing we do really matters. At the same time because nothing we do really matters, he sees our lives as short and therefore sad.

This split attitude towards human existence underlies *Twelfth Night*. That it ends with affirmations of love is comforting. Nonetheless, until those final moments the unpleasantness of several characters dominates the action and the bright humor of the earlier comedies is faded. Succeeding works in this genre are dominated by strains of gloom and stinging satire that reflect Shakespeare's darkening vision of human nature and existence.

SUGGESTIONS FOR FURTHER READING

Crane, Milton. "*Twelfth Night* and Shakespearean Comedy." *Shakespeare Quarterly* 6 (1955): 1–8.

Draper, John. *The Twelfth Night of Shakespeare's Audience*. Stanford: Stanford University Press, 1950.

Goldsmith, Robert H. *Wise Fools in Shakespeare*. East Lansing: Michigan State University Press, 1955.

Hardy, Barbara Gladys. *Twelfth Night*. Oxford: Basil Blackwell, 1962.

King, Walter, ed. *Twentieth Century Interpretations of* Twelfth Night. Englewood Cliffs, N.J.: Prentice-Hall, 1968.

Leech, Clifford. Twelfth Night *and Shakespearean Comedy*. Toronto: University of Toronto Press, 1965.

Lyons, Charles R. *Shakespeare and the Ambiguity of Love's Triumph*. The Hague: Mouton, 1977.

Salingar, Leo G. "The Design of *Twelfth Night*." *Shakespeare Quarterly* 9 (1958): 117–139.

Summers, Joseph. "The Masks of *Twelfth Night*." *University of Kansas Review* 22 (1955): 25–32.

Yearling, Elizabeth M. "Language, Theme, and Character in *Twelfth Night*." *Shakespeare Survey* 35 (1982): 79–86.

TROILUS AND CRESSIDA

The tone of this play is established in the Prologue:

> Sixty and nine, that wore
> Their crownets regal, from th' Athenian bay
> Put forth toward Phrygia, and their vow is made
> To ransack Troy, within whose strong immures
> The ravish'd Helen, Menelaus' queen,
> With wanton Paris sleeps—and that's the quarrel.

(Prologue, 5–10)

The flippancy of those last four words suggests the folly of the enterprise to unfold before us. Shakespeare takes the most famous military adventure in history, the siege of Troy, and turns it upside down. Here are no extraordinary heroes fighting boldly in a struggle complicated by the actions of the gods. Here instead are petty and vicious plotters caught up in an endless war that never made much sense, and now, after seven years of slaughter, makes even less. That *Troilus and Cressida* apparently was not performed before 1898, yet has been staged regularly since, is appropriate. For this play, perhaps more than any of Shakespeare's, speaks especially to our century, when so many works of art have dramatized the madness of war.

The story of Troilus and Cressida was a popular medieval tale, and Shakespeare was probably acquainted with Chaucer's romantic retelling, *Troilus and Criseyde*. But medieval writers also exalted courtly love and scorned what they judged to be the crude customs and mores of the Greeks. Cressida herself is mocked in several medieval works, and Shakespeare probably knew one of the most famous, Robert Henryson's *Testament of Cressid*, composed in the latter part of the fifteenth century.

Many of the events of this play are taken from the *Iliad* of Homer, and Shakespeare was likely influenced by Chapman's translation. Dominating the *Iliad*, however, is a sense of tragedy, as human beings of stature, always conscious of their mortality, battle fiercely in a drive for national and personal glory.

By the medieval era, however, when the concept of chivalry had taken hold, Greek and Trojan warriors, with the exception of Hector, were regarded as barbarians and cowards. Shakespeare's key influences for this perspective were William Caxton's *Recuyell of the Historyes of Troy* (1475) and John Lydgate's *The Troy Book* (c. 1412–1420). Both volumes, as well as Chaucer's poem, drew heavily from the medieval tales of Troy gathered by Guido delle Colonne in *Historia Troiana* (1287).

In Shakespeare's play, the cause of the war, the kidnapping of Helen, Menelaus's wife, by Paris, is the same as in Homer's epic, and the characters' insistence on personal pride remains. But, as in so many works of Shakespeare, that pride is not a legitimate reason for action but a feeble excuse. The word ''honor'' is invoked dozens of times, and never can we take it seriously. For some audiences the plight of Hector makes the play tragic, but he is the only figure worthy of any respect, and, he, too, is subject to the play's pervasive irony. Even at solemn moments, rhetorical excess and emotional bombast makes the characters' values and aspirations ridiculous, and the gap between their words and their actions makes virtually all comic.

Finally, this play has about it a sense of detachment. With the possible exceptions of Hector and Andromache, we do not become emotionally committed to the characters. Instead we observe them manipulating one another, and they do so with little feeling or conscience. The egoism apparent in many of the comedies is here thrust full force before us. But the plot, instead of an intimate story of love and romance, is part of a titanic struggle in which tens of thousands perish while a few struggle to salvage wounded self-respect.

Act I, scene i establishes the spirit of the play. We meet none of the important leaders or fighters. Instead we see the lovesick Troilus with Pandarus, uncle of Cressida, the woman Troilus idealizes, and the daughter of Calchas, a Trojan priest who has deserted to the Greeks. The infatuated young man has little concern with military business:

> Call here my varlet, I'll unarm again.
> Why should I war without the walls of Troy,
> That find such cruel battle here within?

> (I, i, 1–3)

He ignores all civic and family loyalty. His language, too, suggests his shallowness:

> I tell thee I am mad
> In Cressid's love; thou answer'st she is fair,
> Pourest in the open ulcer of my heart
> Her eyes, her hair, her cheek, her gait, her voice . . .

> (I, i, 51–54)

Throughout the play, imagery of the body suggests the lack of intellect and nobility that marks the roster of figures. This imagery is often complemented by imagery of food, which reflects the appetite for all sorts of pleasure, especially sexual, that dominates the characters. Furthermore, Troilus's weakness is clarified by his asking Pandarus to set up a meeting with Cressida. Troilus does not have the courage to pursue her himself. Pandarus, meanwhile, with no more sense of duty, is not offended by Troilus's preoccupation, but departs without agreeing to serve as go-between. Troilus's subsequent soliloquy emphasizes that his desires are no worse than those that gave rise to this war:

> Fools on both sides, Helen must needs be fair,
> When with your blood you daily paint her thus.
>
> (I, i, 90–91)

He reminds us that this massive conflict has been fought for a woman, and his implication is that the woman hardly merits such attention.

Aeneas then enters to bring Troilus to battle. Aeneas also reports that Paris has been wounded by Menelaus, but this news brings only more contempt from Troilus:

> Let Paris bleed, 'tis but a scar to scorn;
> Paris is gor'd with Menelaus' horn.
>
> (I, i, 111–112)

Even Paris's own brother has little respect for him, and the reference to Menelaus and "horns" emphasizes that this entire conflict is being waged because one husband was cuckolded by a faithless wife.

When we meet Cressida, the object of Troilus's idolatry, she is clearly more sophisticated than he. For instance, after her servant Alexander comments about Ajax, "They say he is a very man *per se* and stands alone" (I, ii, 16), Cressida responds, "So do all men, unless th' are drunk, sick, or have no legs" (I, ii, 17). Her words suggest she has known quite a few men, and remains unimpressed by most. Her worldiness is even more apparent when Pandarus enters to promote his client, Troilus. Each line that Pandarus offers in praise Cressida subtly deflects, demonstrating that she knows Pandarus's purpose and will not play his victim. For instance, Pandarus attempts to prove Troilus's appeal: "I swear to you, I think Helen loves him better than Paris" (I, ii, 107–108). But Cressida is not fooled: "Then she's a merry Greek indeed" (I, ii, 109). "Merry" and other words that suggest loose morals are often applied to the Greeks by the Trojans, who view the invaders as brutal primitives.

Cressida remains aloof even during the parade of retreating Trojan heroes. As each man passes, Pandarus extols the wonders of Troilus, who enters last, in Cressida's words, a "sneaking fellow" (I, ii, 226). The effect is twofold. One, Pandarus's constant praise of Troilus undermines the nobility of the other soldiers. Two, Troilus's anticlimactic entrance mocks not only himself, but Pandarus, the other fighters, and the war. No matter what happens from this point on, Troilus's skulking about and Pandarus's shameless promotion diminish the dignity of everyone and everything.

That Cressida is aware of matters is clear from her last line to Pandarus (I,
ii, 281) and her soliloquy at the end of the scene:

> Women are angels, wooing:
> Things won are done, joy's soul lies in the doing.
> That she belov'd knows nought that knows not this:
> Men prize the thing ungain'd more than it is.
> That she was never yet that ever knew
> Love got so sweet as when desire did sue.
> Therefore this maxim out of love I teach:
> Achievement is command; ungain'd, beseech;
> Then though my heart's content firm love doth bear,
> Nothing of that shall from mine eyes appear.
>
> (I, ii, 286–295)

The sexual connotations of the word "doing" reaffirm Cressida's view of men
as fundamentally animalistic. Furthermore, she concludes, once a man has won
her, she must be subservient to him. Until a man has won her, however, she
remains in command of herself, him, and their relationship. From this point on,
as she deals with Troilus and other men, we keep in mind Cressida's worldliness.

Scene iii introduces the Greek side of the war, and these men are a curious
lot. The first to speak is Agamemnon, who attempts to inspire his disheartened
troops:

> Why then, you princes,
> Do you with cheeks abash'd behold our works,
> And call them shames which are indeed nought else
> But the protractive trials of great Jove
> To find persistive constancy in men?
>
> (I, iii, 17–21)

These lines are but a few from a long address, and the convoluted passage
suggests that, as is often the case in Shakespeare, the voluble speaker is talking
primarily to overwhelm his listeners with words. Furthermore, the thrust of his
urging is that suffering is worthwhile, and here his logic is faulty. Were the
Greeks winning, Agamemnon would take their victories as a positive sign. He
also takes their losing as benign, a test of the gods. In other words, whatever
happens, the war must go on.

Nestor, even more long-winded, echoes Agamemnon's thoughts:

> Even so
> Doth valor's show and valor's worth divide
> In storms of fortune . . .
>
> (I, iii, 45–47)

The circumlocution, in support of a horrific war, belittles both the conflict and
the participants.

The primary orator is Ulysses, who shrewdly acknowledges the worth of the
two previous speakers, then offers an extended address that extols order:

The heavens themselves, the planets, and this centre
Observe degree, priority, and place,
Insisture, course, proportion, season, form,
Office, and custom, in all line of order . . .

(I, iii, 85–88)

Then he describes what happens when that order is broken:

Then every thing include itself in power,
Power into will, will into appetite,
And appetite, an universal wolf
(So doubly seconded with will and power),
Must make perforce an universal prey,
And last eat up himself.

(I, iii, 119–124)

According to Ulysses, the only way to avoid anarchy is absolute obedience. His speech is impressive, but never does Ulysses justify his cause. He never explains why the war is legitimate. Instead, Ulysses is on the side of authority, and his central point is that authority must be obeyed just because it is authority. In light of the chaos that soon takes hold of this play, Ulysses' paean to order and control is superbly ironic. His attitude has motivated many a totalitarian government throughout history, but there no one objects.

Instead Agamemnon asks for a solution to the ennui that besets the army. He points to Achilles as the chief cause, for the Greeks' greatest warrior is mocking his leaders by dallying in his tent with Patroclus (I, iii, 146–151). In the *Iliad*, the cause of Achilles' anger is Agamemnon's taking of Briseis, Achilles' female captive. In the play, the cause of Achilles' resentment of both Agamemnon and the war is not clarified at this point. Ulysses goes on to argue that Achilles' frivolity has spread disorder throughout the army, infecting, as Nestor notes, Ajax, "grown self-will'd" (I, iii, 188), and Thersites, "A slave whose gall coins slanders like a mint . . . " (I, iii, 193). In other words, the chaos Ulysses described earlier in a more philosophical vein has come to pass. Here is another belittling of the war and its leaders. We have not yet met Thersites, but that one man's snickering, in combination with Achilles' indolence, can demoralize the Greek forces suggests poor motivation. One more bit of burlesque is provided by the silent presence of Menelaus, the cuckolded husband of Helen. Here he stands dumbly while colleagues debate the merits of a war fought for the sake of his manhood. He speaks only two words, indicating the entrance of Aeneas: "From Troy" (I, iii, 214).

In a scene not found in the *Iliad*, Aeneas brings a challenge from the greatest of the Trojan fighters, Hector, to meet any Greek soldier. The grandness of this boast, presented in the style of medieval chivalry, is undercut by the frequent use of the word "honor" to describe Hector, and Aeneas's almost boyish insults about Greek women (I, iii, 282–283). Agamemnon accepts the challenge, but Nestor deflates the acceptance by seconding it (I, iii, 291–301). He unintentionally belittles once again, when Ulysses claims that the challenge is obviously aimed at arousing Achilles (I, iii, 321–323). Nestor responds with an intricate and wordy reply (I, iii, 333–356) that misses Ulysses' point completely. The latter plans to spur Achilles' pride by selecting "blockish Ajax" (I, iii, 374) to challenge Hector. Ulysses is obviously the wiliest of the Greeks, but he is just as obviously a ruthless man who has no hesitancy in using anyone else to further his own goal: the continuation of this war. Any time he speaks, despite the ostensible reason of the moment, that motivation underlies every word.

In Act II, scene i, Thersites takes the stage and immediately insults everyone he meets or mentions. His language is filled with physical imagery, his implication that as individual bodies are diseased and scarred, so the body politic is corrupted. He is a satiric version of the Greek chorus, and although we may be tempted to hear Shakespeare's voice in Thersites' condemnation of everyone, the universal detestation is itself egocentric and undignified. Rather we should think of Thersites as one honest if crude voice that mocks the war and its participants.

The scene begins with Ajax and Thersites' tearing into one another verbally. The blundering Ajax resents Thersites' cynicism, but can offer only threats and simple insults, while Thersites' venom is memorable:

> I wouldst thou didst itch from head to foot;
> and I had the scratching of thee; I would make thee the
> loathsomest scab in Greece.
>
> (II, i, 27–29)

Thersites is also perceptive, as he correctly points out Ajax's jealousy of Achilles (II, i, 32–35). In response Ajax resorts to violence. When Achilles steps in, the conflict does not end, as Thersites sneers that Hector would defeat both Achilles and Ajax in competition. Yet Achilles, who is also disdainful of his fellow Greeks, finds Thersites amusing, even though the satirist attacks Achilles himself:

> I will see you hang'd like clatpoles ere I
> come any more to your tents. I will keep where there
> is wit stirring, and leave the faction of fools.
>
> (II, i, 117–119)

Achilles enjoys the sarcasm, but he is conscious of his stature, as he speaks of Hector's challenge: "He knew his man" (II, i, 129). Achilles recognizes that he is the best on the Greek side and therefore Hector's unspoken target. We recognize that Ulysses' estimate of Achilles' ego is accurate.

Scene ii is one of the most intriguing in the play. Priam announces that the Greeks have made a proposal: if the Trojans will free Helen, the war will end (II, ii, 2–6). In response to Priam's question, Hector, leader of the Trojans, urges that Helen be released:

> What merit's in that reason which denies
> The yielding of her up?
>
> (II, ii, 24–25)

Troilus, however, is outraged, and part of his response reveals his shallowness:

> Nay, if we talk of reason,
> [Let's] shut our gates and sleep. Manhood and honor
> Should have hare hearts, would they but fat their thoughts
> With this cramm'd reason; reason and respect
> Make livers pale and lustihood deject.
>
> (II, ii, 46–50)

For someone who has remained outside the fighting, he is remarkably enthusiastic. Furthermore, no one opposes his rejection of reason in the name of "manhood and honor," hardly justification for the wholesale slaughter the city currently endures. Hector offers a cautionary perspective: "Brother, she is not worth what she doth cost/ The Keeping" (II, ii, 51–52). But Troilus is insistent: "What's aught but as 'tis valued?" (II, ii, 52). In other words, if the Trojans want to believe that the stakes are high enough, then the fighting is justified. Troilus then offers a lengthy harangue, urging that the Trojans maintain the war for Helen. He mentions his own plan to marry, and from this point on we realize that he is in the throes of romantic ador. When he mentions "honor" once more (II, ii, 68), his words carry less authority. Finally he reminds his listeners that they encouraged Paris to steal Helen (II, ii, 85), and he concludes as follows:

> O theft most base,
> That we have stol'n what we do fear to keep!
> But thieves unworthy of a thing so stol'n,
> That in their country did them that disgrace
> We fear to warrant in our native place!
>
> (II, ii, 92–97)

The repetition of "stol'n" and "thief" suggests the error of taking Helen initially, but Troilus insists that to return her would be to acknowledge that the action was wrong. Therefore the only proper course is to pretend that the crime was legitimate. Were the rationale not so destructive, it would be laughable.

Cassandra interrupts, predicting disaster: "Troy burns, or else let Helen go" (II, ii, 112). Yet as in Homer, her curse is to know the future but to be ignored. Troilus and Paris continue to argue on the basis of passion, both invoking "honor" to a ridiculous extent. Priam correctly interprets that Paris's motive is simply his lust for Helen:

> Paris, you speak
> Like one besotted on your sweet delights.
>
> (Ii, ii, 142–143)

But the old man's evaluation is disregarded.

Hector then offers a remarkable address, for first he provides incontrovertible argument in support of returning Helen and ending the war:

> Nature craves
> All dues be rend'red to their owners: now,
> What nearer debt in all humanity

Than wife is to the husband?
                                    . . . Thus to persist
In doing wrong extenuates not wrong,
But makes it much more heavy.

                                    (II, ii, 173–176, 186–188)

Then, having marshalled all the evidence, Hector suddenly makes an astonishing
reversal:

                                    . . . yet ne'er the less,
My spritely brethren, I propend to you
In resolution to keep Helen still,
For 'tis a cause that hath no mean dependance
Upon our joint and several dignities.

                                    (II, ii, 189–193)

He has capitulated to the attractions of military renown. Even though he knows
the cause to be ignoble, Hector cannot resist the impulse to seek honor. If the
play has a tragic element, it may be found in this decision. Yet so bizarre and
misguided is Hector's concession that its implications are grotesque rather than
tragic. And that Troilus approves is not encouraging:

She is a theme of honor and renown,
A spur to valiant and magnanimous deeds . . .

                                    (II, ii, 199–200)

The next scene returns us to the Greeks, and Thersites' impudence. In front
of Achilles and Patroclus, he derogates universally:

Agamemnon is a fool, Achilles is a fool,
Thersites is a fool, and, as aforesaid, Patroclus is a fool.

                                    (II, iii, 58–60)

The inclusion of himself in the tirade, as well as the modifying ''as aforesaid,''
reveals Thersites conscious of the role he plays, and aware of the extremity of
his attitude.

But before he departs, and as the Greek leaders enter, Thersites provides one
of the key lines of the play:

                All the argument is a whore and a
cuckold, a good quarrel to draw emulous factions and
bleed to death upon. [Now the dry suppeago on the
subject, and war and lechery confound all!]

                                    (II, iii, 72–75)

He will repeat this sentiment, which pierces to the heart of the drama. We might
think of other plays of Shakespeare and moments when battle is reduced to a
meaningless charade: for instance, Falstaff's musing on honor at the end of
Henry IV, Part 1. The grossness of Thersites' exaggerations and denunciations
makes identification with the playwright impossible; nonetheless, Thersites has

captured the essence of this struggle with a clear-sightedness that escapes all the other characters on stage.

At the sight of the Greek hierarchy Achilles retreats to his tent. To these visitors Patroclus claims that Achilles is sick, but Ulysses denies the assertion (II, iii, 85). While Patroclus confers with Achilles, the others are left onstage childishly dickering, until Patroclus returns with yet another refusal from Achilles (II, iii, 107–112). At this effrontery Agamemnon accuses Achilles of excessive pride (II, iii, 123); an accurate evaluation, but an ironic one, given the egos of all these men, especially Ajax, who announces again how he hates arrogance (II, iii, 158–159). Even Nestor realizes the fatuousness of this remark, but the others are uncertain how to proceed, until Ulysses, ever the plotter, schemes to rouse Achilles from his torpor by elevating Ajax:

> We'll consecrate the steps that Ajax makes
> When they go to Achilles.
>
> (II, iii, 183–184)

This praise of Ajax swells his ego to even greater dimensions:

> If I go to him, with my armed fist
> I'll [pash] him o'er the face.
>
> (II, iii, 202–203)

Gradually Ajax is sucked in, as the others flatter him, then in asides mock his stupidity. Eventually Ajax's ego is so bloated that he is willing to fight Achilles (II, iii, 233–234). Ulysses, however, continues to offer preposterous adulation of a figure at whom all the Greeks sneer, but the upshot is the Ajax is ostensibly chosen to fight Hector (II, iii, 264). The real plan, however, is that after this one-on-one combat is arranged, Achilles' pride will spur him back to action.

Despite its success, the manipulation is so obvious and the asides by the others so disparaging, that all appear like malicious schoolboys rather than expert tacticians.

From the attempted seduction of Achilles and the successful seduction of Ajax, the play moves to a seduction already fulfilled: that of Helen by Paris. This appearance is Helen's only one, and she is as unimpressive as the rest of the characters. When she enters, Pandarus works to appeal to her and Paris:

> Fair be to you, my lord, and to all this fair
> company! fair desires, in all fair measure, fairly guide
> them! Especially to you, fair queen, fair thoughts be
> your fair pillow!
>
> (III, i, 43–46)

He is desperate to ingratiate himself, but Helen keeps him at a distance: ''Dear lord, you are full of fair words'' (III, i, 47). Pandarus wants Paris to accompany him for a private talk with Paris, but Helen playfully interrupts, and her tone is appropriately lusty and in the spirit of this work (III, i, 68–69). Finally Pandarus is forced to articulate Troilus's request:

> And, my lord, he desires you, that if the King
> call for him at supper, you will make his excuse.
>
> (III, i, 76–77)

Paris accurately guesses that the cause is Cressida, a claim Pandarus denies, to
comic effect (III, i, 88–89). Meanwhile Paris and Helen banter as Paris sings,
maintaining the general spirit of lechery. But the comedy takes an ironic turn
when Paris invites Helen to greet the warriors returning from battle:

> You shall do more
> Than all the island kings—disarm great Hector.
>
> (III, i, 153–154)

Ultimately Helen is the agent that destroys Hector, for were she not the traitorous
woman she is, the entire war would not have taken place. The impact of this
brief scene is to emphasize the link between war and lust that metaphorically
unites the play.

In scene ii Troilus prepares to greet Cressida, and his idealized desire remains
unabated:

> I am giddy; expectation whirls me round;
> Th'imaginary relish is so sweet
> That it enchants my sense; what will it be,
> When that wat'ry palates taste indeed
> Love's thrice-repured nectar?
>
> (III, ii, 18–22)

But these words, like so many in the play, are underscored by irony, for we
remember the worldly Cressida of Act I, scene ii. When she enters here, she
proves her earlier predictions accurate, for she feigns shyness and innocence.
Pandarus lasciviously sets the tone: "So, so, rub on and kiss the mistress" (III,
ii, 49–50). Then Troilus attempts to arouse her passions:

> This [is] the monstruosity in love, lady, that
> the will is infinite and the execution confin'd, that the
> desire is boundless and the act a slave to limit.
>
> (III, ii, 81–83)

Her response reveals her sophistication:

> They say all lovers swear more performance
> than they are able, and yet reserve an ability that
> they never perform . . .
>
> (III, ii, 84–86)

She pretends that she has only heard rumors. We suspect her comments are
based on more personal experience.

After Pandarus interrupts, frustrated that the two are still only talking, Cressida
continues to play her role. First she confesses that she has always loved Troilus
(III, ii, 114–115), then takes back her claim, as if in torment at her own boldness

and desire: "Sweet, bid me hold my tongue . . . " (III, ii, 129). When he does kiss her, she withdraws in mock embarrassment (III, ii, 136–139), manipulating him unerringly. She even admits her skill, but her clever phrasing veils the thought:

> Perchance, my lord, I show more craft than love,
> And fell so roundly to a large confession,
> To angle for your thoughts, but you are wise,
> Or else you love not . . .
>
> (III, ii, 153–156)

Troilus remains impassioned (III, ii, 168–170), and the two express mutual fidelity, as Cressida in particular states her devotion with fervor (III, ii, 184–196). But the emotions of this scene mocked by the irony of Cressida's performance, are obliterated by Pandarus's final claim:

> If ever you prove false to one another . . .
>   Let all constant men be
> Troiluses, all false women Cressids, and all brokers-
> between Pandars!
>
> (III, ii, 199–204)

That warning becomes actuality.

The general atmosphere of mistrust continues in the next scene as Calchas confesses his treason from Troy (III, iii, 5–10), and asks the Greeks a favor: if they will return the prisoner Antenor, he will give them his daughter Cressida. This gesture fuses for the first time the two primary stories, one of war, the other of lust, and reaffirms Thersites' general accusation about the relationship of the two. But even as this arrangement is accepted, and Diomedes is sent to retrieve Cressida, the Greek leaders are further mocked for they are still attempting to involve Achilles in the war. At Agamemnon's urging they ignore him, hoping disdain will arouse his concern (III, iii, 50–54). Thus we see the ludicrous spectacle of eminent Greek soldiers, like spoiled children, walking by Achilles' tent but barely acknowledging his greetings. What is even more foolish is that Achilles is taken in and seeks an explanation for his apparently lost "honor" (III, iii, 81) from the most deceptive of the Greeks, Ulysses.

In characteristically lengthy and intricate speeches, Ulysses plays on all Achilles' points of vulnerability. After emphasizing that virtue must be reaffirmed (III, iii, 100–102) and that Ajax has done precisely that (III, iii, 123–141), Ulysses returns once more to the theme of lost honor:

> Perseverance, dear my lord,
> Keeps honor bright; to have done is to hang
> Quite out of fashion, like a rusty nail
> In monumental mock'ry.
>
> (III, iii, 150–153)

Skillfully he makes a transition to the specific issue: Achilles' retreat inside his tent (III, iii, 184–190). In response to Achilles' protestations, Ulysses suggests that Achilles' affection for Polyxena, Hector's sister, may be blunting responsibility (III, iii, 205–208). This relationship has basis in legend, but is not part of the *Iliad*. With insidious skill Ulysses climaxes by speaking of Achilles' son:

> But it must grieve young Pyrrhus now at home,
> When fame shall in our islands sound her trump,
> And all the Greekish girls shall tripping sing,
> "Great Hector's sister did Achilles win,
> But our great Ajax bravely beat down him."
>
> (III, iii, 209–213)

All of Ulysses' not-so-subtle hints refer to images of manhood, a dominant theme here. After all, the Trojan War started because of Menelaus's being cuckolded by Paris, and the subsequent carnage may be seen as an attempt to salvage Greek masculine pride. Troilus has been fulfilling his own lust as Paris has satisfied his. Now Ulysses personalizes the matter for Achilles, and it is more acutely articulated by Patroclus. In the *Iliad*, Achilles and Patroclus share a noble friendship. In this play, Patroclus is regarded as Achilles' male lover, as Patroclus himself admits:

> A woman impudent and mannish grown
> Is not more loath'd than an effeminate man
> In time of action. I stand condemn'd for this;
> They think my little stomach to the war,
> And your great love to me, restrains you thus.
>
> (III, iii, 217–221)

At this confession Achilles finally responds:

> I see my reputation is at stake,
> My fame is shrowdly gor'd.
>
> (III, iii, 227–228).

He has Thersites brought in and seeks to meet with both Ajax and Hector. Even this decision, though, is mocked by Thersites:

> Would the fountain of your mind were clear
> again, that I might water an ass at it! I had rather be a
> tick in a sheep than such a valiant ignorance.
>
> (III, iii, 310–312)

Those last two words apply to many characters across the play.

The general spirit of lechery flourishes again in Act IV, scene i, when Aeneas expresses surprise that Paris is on the street, away from Helen:

> . . . nothing but heavenly business
> Should rob my bed-mate of my company.
>
> (IV, i, 5–6)

Diomedes, the Greek representative, agrees. Yet that both men offer such suggestive remarks does not seem to bother Paris at all. Then the discussion turns to

procedures for moving Cressida to the Greeks (IV, i, 38–39). Paris and Aeneas
both note how upset Troilus will be, but no one mentions the fundamental irony
of the scene: that the Trojans are willing to surrender Cressida to help end the war,
but they have been and still are unwilling to give up Helen, who is worth no more.
In fact, the issue is approached with unintentional irony by Paris, who asks
Diomedes who better deserves Helen, Paris himself or Menelaus. The answer is
hardly diplomatic. Diomedes refers to Menelaus as "a puling cuckold" (IV, i,
62), Paris as a "lecher" (IV, i, 64), and Helen as "a whore" (IV, i, 67).
Diomedes also adds bitter comments on the battles fought over this lust (IV, i,
69–75). This speech as much as any encapsulates the overall action of the play.

The corruption of such love is further emphasized in scene ii, when Troilus
and Cressida are in bed. He is still attempting to turn their affair into an idealized
romance by winning her with passionate lyrics and images, but Cressida's worldliness shines through, as she jests with him and the intruding Pandarus. She asks
Troilus, "Are you a-weary of me?" (IV, ii, 7), then comments "You men will
never tarry" (IV, ii, 16). When Pandarus enters to ascertain what is happening,
she has a gibe for him:

> Go hang yourself, you naughty mocking uncle!
> You bring me to do—and then you flout me too.
>
> (IV, ii, 25–26)

Never do we forget that Cressida is conscious of her role.

Her will, however, is tested when Aeneas brings word that Cressida is to leave
and go over to the Greek side. Troilus is, not surprisingly, frustrated: "How
my achievements mock me!" (IV, ii, 69). But he is not so overcome with love
that he forgets his reputation:

> . . . and, my Lord Aeneas,
> We met by chance, you did not find me here.
>
> (IV, ii, 70–71)

Pandarus, too, is frustrated (IV, ii, 74–77), but the real anguish emerges from
Cressida, who bursts out with protest:

> O you gods divine,
> Make Cressida's name the very crown of falsehood,
> If ever she leave Troilus! Time, force, and death,
> Do to this body what extremes you can;
> But the strong base and building of my love
> Is as the very centre of the earth
> Drawing all things to it.
>
> (IV, ii, 99–105)

The words seem powerful. Yet within two scenes they prove fraudulent.

Even before that reversal, though, scene ii mocks almost any sensibility, as
Paris instructs Troilus about Cressida's surrender (IV, iii, 1–5). Troilus characterizes himself as a priest about to make a sacrifice, and Paris responds sym-

pathetically: "I know what 'tis to love . . . " (IV, iii, 10). The sight of one illicit lover comforting another prohibits us from taking almost any of this seriously.

We have an inkling of the inevitable turnabout between Cressida and Troilus in scene iv, as each offers parting expressions of faithfulness. Troilus seems to overdo his role (IV, ii, 33–48), and so emphasizes that he wants Cressida to be true (IV, iv, 67) that she is struck by the repetition: "O heavens, 'be true' again?" (IV, ii, 74). They exchange love tokens (IV, ii, 70–71), but Troilus nonetheless is preoccupied with Cressida's vulnerability to temptation: "The Grecian youths are full of quality . . . " (IV, ii, 76). And during the rest of their tearful parting, the two insist on their loyalty so fervently that we know it cannot survive. The scene ends with yet another ironic comment, as Paris blames Troilus for the delay in reaching Hector. For Paris, the instigator of the entire war, to blame Troilus for excessive passion in ludicrous.

The burlesque of war and its participants continues in scene v, as the Greek leaders gather in preparation for Ajax's fight with Hector. Ajax calls for a trumpet, which sounds (IV, v, 11), but no response is forthcoming, and the anticlimax deflates whatever battle is to take place. The fighting is temporarily suspended with the entrance of Cressida, escorted by Diomedes. The "merry" Greeks live up to their reputation, as several, including Agamemnon, kiss her in greeting. Even Menelaus participates, although as usual he endures a snide comment about his being cuckolded:

> No, Paris is not, for you know 'tis true
> That you are odd, and he is even with you.
>
> (IV, v, 43–44)

What makes this remark particularly annoying for Menelaus is that it comes from Cressida, who is surprisingly content amidst the affection of her enemies. Once more we are reminded of her experience with men and her pleasure at manipulating them. Even Nestor seems entranced: "A woman of quick sense" (IV, v, 54), but only Ulysses evaluates her accurately:

> There's language in her eye, her cheek, her lip,   ·
> Nay, her foot speaks; her wanton spirits look out
> At every joint and motive of her body.
>
> (IV, v, 55–57)

The scene is interrupted by the entrance of the Trojan leaders. An exchange of insults follows, each side accusing the other of, ironically, pride. Ulysses' tribute to Troilus (IV, v, 96–112) seems laughably inaccurate, but in light of Troilus's later success in battle, Ulysses, crafty as always, senses the danger Troilus poses.

The battle between Hector and Ajax begins, but is quickly stopped by Diomedes, who announces that Hector must agree to end this particular fight. Hector concurs, clarifying that he and Ajax are cousins (IV, v, 120). Thus the conflict is suspended. The result for the audience is once again a profound irony.

Soldiers on both sides maintain rituals and politeness, the veneer of civilization. Even Ajax is willing to lay down arms, although he still seeks glory (IV, v, 138–141). The scene then turns into a temporary truce, as enemies of long standing express respect for one another. Yet they will soon insist on resuming a bloody and pointless war. Over and over that theme is played out. So is the underlying reason for that war, as lust finally infects Hector, the noblest soldier on either side. When he meets Menelaus, Hector, too, turns the encounter into a dirty joke:

> Mock not [that I] affect the untraded [oath],
> Your quondam wife swears still by Venus' glove.
> She's well, but bade me not commend her to you
>
> (IV, v, 178–180)

He apologizes at once, but the point is made.

Achilles and Hector do meet fact to face, and the challenge is established. Throughout the scene, though, Achilles' ego is on full display:

> Tell me, you heavens, in which part of his body
> Shall I destroy him—whether there or there, or there?—
> That I may give the local wound a name,
> And make distinct the very breach whereout
> Hector's great spirit flew.
>
> (IV, v, 242–246)

Such confidence arouses the usually proper Hector: "I'll kill thee every where, yea, o'er and o'er" (IV, v, 256). Yet even this threat is undercut as Ulysses ends the scene by escorting Troilus to Menelaus's tent, where Cressida is kept. Ulysses asks innocently about Cressida's past in Troy: "Had she no lover there/ That wails her absence?" (IV, v 289–290). Troilus's response is characteristic:

> O, sir, to such as boasting show their scars
> A mock is due. Will you walk on, my lord?
> She was belov'd, [she lov'd]; she is, and doth:
> But still sweet love is food for fortune's tooth.
>
> (IV, v, 290–293)

He virtually admits that he is that lover left behind. And his reference to food suggests again that his preoccupation is not so much love as appetite, the hunger that dominates the play.

In the first scene of Act V, Achilles is preparing for his showdown with Hector when Thersites enters. He and Achilles indulge in mutual insult, particularly about Patroclus, who, Thersites insists, is said to be Achilles' "masculine whore" (V, i, 17), but then Achilles reads a letter from Hecuba, Hector's mother. The message reminds Achilles of a promise made to Hecuba and Polyxena, and implores him not to fight Hector (V, i, 40–42). Moved, Achilles instead orders Patroclus to prepare a banquet in Hector's honor. But this moment of quiet, like so many others, is shattered, first by Thersites' soliloquy insulting all the Greeks, then by the Greek and Trojan leaders entering but befuddled about the proper direction (V, i, 67–69). Even their comparatively dignified partings are mocked by Diomedes, who explains that he has "important business" (V, i, 83). Ulysses knows this "business" to be Cressida, and urges Troilus to follow while the others depart, leaving Thersites alone to mock everyone once more, ending with "nothing but lechery" (V, i, 97). Shakespeare is relentless in his diminution of these figures and in his insistence on the relationship between sex and war.

That relationship is clarified once more in the next scene, as Diomedes continues his pursuit of Cressida. Again Ulysses offers his estimation of her worth: "She will sing any man at first sight" (V, ii, 9). and we are not surprised that the eavesdropping Thersites agrees:

> And any man may sing her, if he can take
> her cliff; she's noted.
>
> (V, ii, 10–11)

The comedy of the moment is irresistible, as these two and Troilus overhear Cressida's flirting with Diomedes: "Sweet honey Greek, tempt me no more to folly" (V, ii, 18). We are never clear exactly how she feels about Troilus, whether her affection for him is entirely pretense or whether she simply enjoys the company of all men. In any case, Troilus, listening with Ulysses, is infuriated (V, ii, 29, 51, 65), especially when Cressida surrenders the love token Troilus had bestowed to symbolize their mutual trust: "O beauty, where is thy faith?" (V, ii, 67). The treachery is also noted by Thersites, for whom the episode is confirmation of his entire view of life:

> How the devil Luxury, with his fat rump
> and potato finger, tickles [these] together! Fry,
> lechery, fry!
>
> (V, ii, 55–57)

But Diomedes proves to be less malleable than Cressida expects, for he asks the origin of that token. She continues to dangle it before him:

> Well, well, 'tis done, 'tis past. And yet it is not;
> I will not keep my word.
>
> (V, ii, 97–98)

In a curious way she is honest, for she does confess her duplicity. But he does not tolerate such behavior: "Thou never shalt mock Diomed again" (V, ii, 99). Even after this rejection, or perhaps because of it, Cressida's affections have changed:

> Troilus, farewell! one eye yet looks on thee,
> But with my heart the other eye doth see.
> Ah, poor our sex! this fault in us I find;
> The error of our eye directs our mind.
>
> (V, ii, 107–109)

Once again, Thersites summarizes most effectively:

A proof of strength she could not publish more,
Unless she said, "My mind is now turn'd whore."

(V, ii, 113–114)

On any occasion in which Thersites participates, all emotions, even those of the wounded Troilus, are laughable.

The extent of Troilus's anguish is apparent in a lengthy triade against Cressida, but the speech is marked by outlandish contradiction, climaxing with "This is, and is not, Cressid" (V, ii, 146). He wants to believe in her loyalty; yet what he observes leaves him helpless to trust her. Ulysses slyly eggs Troilus on (V, ii, 161–162), to which Troilus responds with wild overstatement of his devotion:

O Cressid! O false Cressid! false, false, false!
Let all untruths stand by thy stained name,
And they'll seem glorious.

(V, ii, 178–180)

Ulysses' warning (V, ii, 180–181) is one more comic deflation, but the result of his anger is that Troilus is now ready to go to war, specifically against Diomedes. The reason is clarified by Thersites:

Lechery, lechery, still
wars and lechery, nothing else holds fashion.

(V, ii, 194–195)

Act V, scene iii may be compared to Book Six of the *Iliad*, in which Andromache urges her husband Hector not to fight Achilles:

. . . for I have dreamt
of bloody turbulence, and this whole night
Hath nothing been but shapes and forms of slaughter.

(V, iii, 10–12)

Despite her pleas, Hector resolves to go to battle even though he is aware that he is fated to die. He is devoted to his city and its cause, and thus his acceptance of inevitable defeat has a tragic dignity. Here, however, his goal seems far less glorious:

Mine honor keeps the weather of my fate.
Life every man holds dear, but the dear man
Holds honor far more precious-dear than life.

(V, ii, 26–28)

Throughout this play the word "honor" has been abused. We recognize that Hector is fighting for hollow values, and thus his passion is not tragic but misguided.

Yet he appears noble in comparison to Troilus, who enters full of energy for battle. First he mocks Hector's unwillingness to allow defeated enemies to live (V, iii, 40–42). Then he explains his own motivations to fight:

And when we have our armors buckled on,
The venom'd vengeance ride upon our swords,
Spur them to ruthful work, rein them from 'ruth.

(V, iii, 46–48)

He fights in a spirit of revenge, but we also sense that he is recklessly eager to assert his masculinity, to prove with his sword the quality of the man Cressida deserted. Hector is offended by such crudity, for throughout the play he has acted as though battle were a noble adventure. Again, given what we have seen of the brutality of war in this play and how Shakespeare has dramatized its savagery throughout his works, Hector is deluded.

Virtually every notable on the Trojan side warns Hector of impending disaster. In Priam's words:

Thy wife hath dreamt, thy mother hath had visions,
Cassandra doth foresee, and I myself
Am like a prophet suddenly enrapt
To tell thee that this day is ominous:
Therefore come back.

(V, iii, 63–67).

But Hector is unwilling to listen. Yet even at this moving moment, too, the drama is mocked as Pandarus enters, coughing and carrying a letter from Cressida. Troilus tears the letter to pieces, but its intrusion diminishes the moment.

The final scenes of the play are short, and the action moves quickly, reflecting the chaos of war. Before the fighting is underway, Thersites offers one more tirade, this one mocking virtually every participant in the play (V, iv, 1–17). He insults them as politicians, soldiers, and individuals, and his malice is so overwhelming that by the time Troilus and Diomedes take the stage, they are ridiculous. The satire continues when Hector enters, challenging Thersites, who announces himself "a rascal, a scurvy railing knave, a very filthy rogue" (V, iv, 28–29). At this evaluation Hector seeks other foes, leaving Thersites one more opportunity to lash out at both sides (V, iv, 31–35). His mutterings remain ironic commentary on the furor around him.

In scene v the battle rages and bodies drop. Word that Patroclus has been killed brings Achilles roaring against Hector, whom he derides as a "boy-queller" (V, v, 45). We also learn that Troilus has acquitted himself effectively (V, v, 37–38), thereby arousing the wrath of Ajax, who rumbles across the stage calling for Troilus. In scene vi Ajax vies with Diomedes for the right to fight Troilus, then ends the squabble by taking on both of them (V, vi, 9–11). This action, though, is subordinate to the meeting between Hector and Achilles. But just when we think they are about to embark on the long-awaited battle, Hector asks for respite, and Achilles agrees that he, too, needs rest.

This civility disappears, when in scene vii Achilles gathers his comrades, the Myrmidons:

And when I have the bloody Hector found
Empale him with your weapons round about,
In fellest manner execute your arms.

(V, vii, 4–6)

After all the preliminary talk and for all his pride and bluster, Achilles does not have the courage to meet Hector one-on-one.

Even now Thersites intrudes comically, as Menelaus and Paris go after each other: ''The cuckold and the cuckold-maker are at it'' (V, vii, 9). When Thersites himself is challenged, he turns away the opponent with a praise to bastards that mocks the entire situation:

Take heed, the quarrel's most ominous
to us. If the son of a whore fight for a whore, he
tempts judgment.

(V, vii, 20–22)

This evaluation leads to the final brawl between Achilles and Hector, but the meeting is hardly the grand struggle we have been anticipating. Instead, the Myrmidons strike Hector from behind, and Achilles stands proudly over the body, ordering his supporters to spread the report: '' 'Achilles hath the mighty Hector slain!' '' (V, vii, 14). The most exalted of the Greek warriors has turned into a treacherous thug. His next order is even more disgraceful:

Come tie his body to my horse's tail,
Along the field I will the Troyan trail.

(V, viii, 21–22)

Here is no glorious triumph but the humiliation of a worthy foe, whose manner of death reflects the degeneracy of his world.

In scene ix the news of Hector's death spreads, and in scene x Troilus resolves to revenge his brother's murder by killing Achilles. In his tribute to Hector (V, x, 31), he seems more resolved, and thus one aspect of the play is Troilus's maturation. But his spirit is sparked only by revenge, as it was earlier by revenge against Diomedes, and Troilus's energy then came only after the faithless Cressida failed to live up to Troilus's foolish idealization. As usual, passion is shrunk by irony.

The final words of the play belong appropriately to Pandarus, whose presence onstage, which parallels his appearance in the first scene of Act I, reaffirms the themes of war and lechery. True, Troilus does dismiss Pandarus, but the old man has the last words, in which he speaks to his fellow ''good traders in the flesh'' (V, x, 46). The implication of his peroration is that his trade is society's chief mode of barter. But the world refuses to acknowledge such a reality (V, x, 38–39). Pandarus concludes the play by bequeathing his ''diseases'' (V, x, 56), an apt word to end a work preoccupied with corruption of so many varieties.

Goethe wrote that *Troilus and Cressida* is the product of Shakespeare's mind "unfettered." Surely the play has the feel of anger nearly out of control. It has scarcely any likeable characters, and even Hector, the most dignified, looks foolish on several occasions. The pageant of the Trojan War is reduced to a barbaric farce, motivated by pride and lust, and in no other work is Shakespeare's profoundly antiwar spirit so evident. Here is corrosive comedy in the tradition of Juvenal and Swift. Yet underlying the anger is a profound sadness for the human folly that sanctions such behavior under the guise of civilization.

SUGGESTIONS FOR FURTHER READING

Bowden, William R. "The Human Shakespeare and *Troilus and Cressida*." *Shakespeare Quarterly* 8, (1957): 167–177.

Campbell, Oscar J. *Comical Satyre and Shakespeare's* Troilus and Cressida. San Marino, Calif.: The Huntington Library, 1938.

Elton, W. R. "Shakespeare's Ulysses and the Problem of Value." *Shakespeare Studies* 2 (1966): 95–111.

Farnham, Willard. "Troilus in Shapes of Infinite Desire." *Shakespeare Quarterly* 15 (1964): 257–264.

Foakes, R. A. "*Troilus and Cressida* Reconsidered." *University of Toronto Quarterly* 32 (1962–1963): 142–154.

Kaula, David. "Will and Reason in *Troilus and Cressida*." *Shakespeare Quarterly* 12 (1961): 271–283.

Oates, J. C. "The Ambiguity of *Troilus and Cressida*." *Shakespeare Quarterly* 17 (1966): 142–150.

Presson, Robert K. *Shakespeare's* Troilus and Cressida *and the Legends of Troy*. Madison: University of Wisconsin Press, 1953.

Tillyard, E. M. W. *Shakespeare's Problem Plays*. London: Chatto & Windus, 1950.

Ure, Peter. *Shakespeare: The Problems Plays*. London: Longmans, Green, 1961.

ALL'S WELL THAT ENDS WELL

Conflict between generations is a theme prevalent in many of Shakespeare's tragedies, histories, and comedies. Romeo and Juliet struggle against their parents' feud and values. Hamlet battles within himself to deal with the ethics of his father's order for revenge. Hal and his biological father, Henry IV, work out an uneasy coexistence, while the Prince simultaneously resolves his relationship with his spiritual father, Falstaff. In *A Midsummer Night's Dream*, the mainspring of the plot is the willingness of Lysander and Hermia to go against the wishes of Egeus. In such works audience sympathy is usually with the younger generation, which often embodies a tolerance and understanding unrestricted by narrow beliefs and codes of behavior.

In *All's Well That Ends Well*, however, wisdom lies with the older characters, who frequently harken back to past years as a better, happier time. The younger figures, in particular Bertram, are not especially likeable or sympathetic. Indeed, one reason this play is difficult to interpret is Bertram himself, doubtless Shakespeare's least amiable hero. That the story ends with a marriage suggests the play is a comedy, but the road to this moment of contentment is so rocky and the antagonisms between characters so harsh that we enjoy little laughter, and the disentangling of the plot is far from joyous. Thus whether all "ends well" is problematic. The source of the story is "Giletta of Narbona," the ninth novella of the third day in Boccaccio's *Decameron* (1353), a collection of 100 fables and folk tales ostensibly told by ten people who have taken refuge from the plague in France. Shakespeare probably read these stories in William Painter's *Palace of Pleasure* (1567).

The play's opening scene communicates the gloomy tone that dominates the work. In the first line the Countess mourns that the imminent departure of her son will be like the loss of a second husband. That son, Bertram, mourns his dead father, while the King he is soon to attend is himself mortally ill (I, i, 11–16). Furthermore, the one physician who might have cured the King, Helena's father, is also deceased. Helena, who has been raised by the Countess, reveals that she, too, is possessed by sadness (I, i, 54), but she does not publicly specify its source. Thus a sense of mortality and human futility in the face of that mortality loom heavily.

The plot moves underway with the Countess's advice to Bertram, who is to leave for the court in Paris:

> Thy blood and virtue
> Contend for empire in thee, and thy goodness
> Share with thy birthright! Love all, trust a few,
> Do wrong to none. Be able for thine enemy
> Rather in power than use, and keep thy friend
> Under thy own life's key. Be check'd for silence,
> But never tax'd for speech.

(I, i, 62–68)

Her tone is like that of Polonius in *Hamlet*, but her counsel is wiser, and observations more perceptive. To Lafew she adds:

> Farewell, my lord,
> 'Tis an unseason'd courtier, good my lord,
> Advise him.

(I, i, 70–72)

The Countess has little faith in either Bertram's judgment or his nature. He is not only inexperienced, but inclined to follow the advice and actions of less sterling characters.

In contrast to these reservations is the attitude of Helena. Left alone, she reveals that she is weeping not for her long-gone father, but over her unrequited love for Bertram:

> 'Twere all one
> That I should love a bright particular star
> And think to wed it, he is so above me.
> In his bright radiance and collateral light
> Must I be comforted, not in his sphere.

(I, i, 85–89)

She is tormented by the difference in their classes. We, however, consider the object of her fascination. Thus far Bertram has given no evidence of being worthy of idolatry. We ponder, therefore, whether Helena intuits something deep within him or if she will in some way work to redeem him.

Our impression of Bertram is reinforced with the entrance of Parolles, a braggart soldier whom Helena describes:

> One that goes with him. I love him for his sake,
> And yet I know him a notorious liar,
> Think him a great way fool, soly a coward . . .

(I, i, 99–101)

Bertram's choice of companions is dubious, as his mother suggested. Parolles' vulgarity is obvious at once, when he begins a comic discourse with Helena concerning her virginity. He emphasizes the unnaturalness of her state (I, i, 126–127), but far from being perturbed at his gibes (I, i, 133–134), she remains unruffled. She is not uncomfortable discussing the physical aspects of a relationship although she is upset by the temptations Bertram will encounter in France (I, i, 166–178). Yet she is also occupied with more spiritual matters, as she indicates when Parolles leaves to join Bertram:

> Our remedies oft in ourselves do lie,
> Which we ascribe to heaven. The fated sky
> Gives us free scope, only doth backward pull
> Our slow designs when we ourselves are dull.
> What power is it which mounts my love so high,
> That makes me see, and cannot feed mine eye?
> The mightiest space in fortune nature brings
> To join like likes, and kiss like native things.
>
> (I, i, 216–223)

Throughout the play, heavenly or divine influences are often mentioned in conjunction with Helena. These references, in combination with her own awareness of the physical nature of things, make her a combination of the spiritual and the earthly. In that light, some of her seemingly contradictory or puzzling actions are better understood.

In scene ii Bertram's inadequacy is reinforced, as we meet the ill King of France who is urging his soldiers to prepare for war (I, ii, 13–15). Even in his sickly state the King muses on the fine qualities of Bertram's father (I, ii, 24–47), and Bertram's response (I, ii, 48–51), though formally correct, adds little to his image. The King also dwells on the inadequacies of the current generation, quoting Bertram's father:

> "Let me not live," quoth he,
> "After my flame lacks oil, to be the snuff
> Of younger spirits, whose apprehensive senses
> All but new things disdain; whose judgments are
> Mere fathers of their garments; whose constancies
> Expire before their fashions."
>
> (I, ii, 58–63)

Whether these judgments were based on his father's knowledge of Bertram is not certain, but the possibility exists, and subsequent events reveal that the young man is as shallow and as taken with appearance as his father claimed the new generation is. The King also asks about Helena's father, the eminent physician (I, ii, 70). Given the King's earlier reflections on the generations, we wonder whether Helena has acquired her father's skills.

In scene iii the Countess and the Steward attempt to discuss Helena, but they are interrupted by their Clown, who insists upon his own interests in marriage. Although his intrusions are not particularly witty, they do have thematic relevance. First he comments: " . . . and indeed I do marry that I may repent" (I, iii, 36–37). After commenting crudely on the physical pleasures of marriage and his cynical belief that his wife will be unfaithful (I, iii, 42–55), the clown is asked by the Countess whether he shall always be "a foul-mouth'd and calumnious knave" (I, iii, 56–57). The question remains unanswered, but the clown's interlude raises the issue of whether character can be changed. Is repentance possible? The question will eventually be applied to Bertram.

After the Steward tells the Countess that the cause of Helena's sadness is a desperate love for Bertram (I, iii, 107–116), the Countess orders him to "keep it to yourself" (I, i, 121–122), then ruminates on her own past romances:

> Even so it was with me when I was young.
> If ever we are nature's, these are ours. This thorn
> Doth to our rose of youth rightly belong,
> Our blood to us, this to our blood is born.
>
> (I, iii, 128–131)

Like the King in the previous scene, the Countess remembers her own youth, and her memories leave her fundamentally generous.

Helena enters, and the Countess gently comforts her (I, iii, 170–179), drawing out Helena's love for Bertram:

> I know I love in vain, strive against hope;
> Yet in this captious and intenible sieve
> I still pour in the waters of my love
> And lack not to lose still.
>
> (I, iii, 201–204)

She is determined to make herself worthy. What surprises Helena is that the Countess is not put off by the disparity between Bertram's class and Helena's. Thus when Helena offers her plan to go to Paris and use her father's remedies to cure the King, the Countess is sympathetic:

> Why, Helen, thou shalt have my leave and love,
> Means and attendants, and my loving greetings
> To those of mine in court.
>
> (I, iii, 251–253)

Unlike her son, whose bigotry is soon revealed, the Countess is free from prejudices based on class and heritage.

In Act II, scene i, the King urges his young lords off to war, warning them about the dangers of Italian women (II, i, 19–22). Meanwhile, Bertram, left behind, grumbles about his predicament (II, i, 27–28), but reveals his immaturity by following Parolles' brazen suggestion to "steal away bravely" (II, i, 29). Parolles then clarifies his priorities:

> Use a more spacious ceremony to the noble
> lords: you have restrain'd yourself within the list of
> too cold an adieu. Be more expressive to them, for
> they wear themselves in the cap of time, there do

muster true gait; eat, speak, and move under the
influence of the most receiv'd star, and though the
devil lead the measure, such are to be follow'd.

(II, i, 50–56)

Parolles is preoccupied with fashion, with the style of the moment, with appearance rather than substance. His influence on Bertram will become apparent in Bertram's own reliance on such values.

At this point Lafew enters, first to try to cheer the King out of despair (II, i, 72–78), then to report the presence of a woman doctor of amazing skills (II, i, 79–87). Helena appears, explains that her father was Gerard de Narbon, and pleads to be allowed to try to cure the King. Her faith in herself is almost mystical:

He that of greatest works is finisher
Oft does them by the weakest minister:
So holy writ in babes hath judgment shown,
When judges have been babes; great floods have flown
From simple sources; and great seas have dried
When miracles have by the great'st been denied.

(II, i, 136–141)

Her insistence is so powerful that the King is moved to believe in her:

Methinks in thee some blessed spirit doth speak
His powerful sound within an organ weak . . .
Sweet practicer, thy physic I will try,
That ministers thine own death if I die.

(II, i, 175–186)

The threat of punishment is daunting, but Helena's self-assurance reminds us of Joan of Pucelle's almost supernatural strength of will in *Henry VI, Part 1*. If we see Helena this way, the play may be regarded as a dramatization of the redemption of Bertram, a prodigal wastrel, by Helena, an angel or other divine being. To be sure, Helena's earthier side means that such a perspective only partially explains the overall structure, but the notion of Helena as a redeemer is doubtless present.

Helena is allowed to choose a potential reward should she cure the King:

Then shalt thou give me with thy kingly hand
What husband in thy power I will command.

(II, i, 193–194)

She is careful to modify her request:

Exempted be from me the arrogance
To choose from forth the royal blood of France,
My low and humble name to propagate

> With any branch or image of thy state . . .
>
> (II, i, 195–198)

She is perpetually conscious of class distinction, but she is also a driven woman, and her desires are the energy that propels the play. Here the King agrees to her proposal (II, i, 209–210).

Scene ii is a brief parody of court life, as the Clown demonstrates how one response, "O Lord, sir," can answer virtually all questions. Such repartee may be satire of the affected environment to which Bertram aspires. Its superficiality is contrasted with Lafew's address beginning scene iii in which he comments to Parolles on the astonishing recovery of the King:

> They say miracles are past, and we have our
> philosophical persons, to make modern and familiar,
> things supernatural and causeless. Hence is it that we
> make trifles of terrors, ensconcing ourselves into seem-
> ing knowledge, when we should submit ourselves to an
> unknown fear.
>
> (II, iii, 1–6)

A bit later he reads from a report: "A showing of heavenly effect in an earthly actor" (II, iii, 23–24). Both lines suggest the presence of divine providence, a willingness to believe in some agent beyond human knowledge and skill. Helena is that agent, a contrast to the worldly concerns of Bertram and others.

Now Helena and the King enter, and she reasserts this theme: "Heaven hath through me restor'd the King to health" (II, iii, 64). The King then stands by his word, and allows her to choose her husband:

> Make choice and see,
> Who shuns thy love shuns all his love in me.
>
> (II, iii, 72–73)

The King anticipates that her choice will reject her. After moments of suspense, during which Helena stands before four others, she moves to Bertram:

> I dare not say I take you, but I give
> Me and my service, ever whilst I live,
> Into your guiding power.
>
> (II, iii, 102–104)

Her humility in "giving" herself rather than "taking" Bertram is consistent with her expressions of faith.

Bertram, however, is outraged, and despite the King's protest (II, iii, 108–109) reveals the nasty side of his personality:

> She had her breeding at my father's charge—
> A poor physician's daughter my wife! Disdain
> Rather corrupt me ever!
>
> (II, iii, 114–116)

The rebuff frustrates the King:

> Good alone
> Is good, without a name; vileness is so:
> The property by what [it] is should go,
> Not by the title . . .
> Virtue and she
> Is her own dower; Honor and wealth from me.

(II, iii, 128–130, 143–144)

The King is aware that Bertram's anger is not without justification. After all, by forcing Bertram to marry beneath his rank and to a woman who provides no dowry, the King has disregarded the law. But the King is subtly reassuring Bertram that by marrying Helena he will be supported. In short, the King is putting his own ''honor'' (II, iii, 149) on the line. Thus when Bertram announces, ''I cannot love her, nor will strive to do't'' (II, iii, 145), he is insulting the King.

The King therefore invokes his authority:

> Check thy contempt;
> Obey our will, which travails in thy good;
> Believe not thy disdain, but presently
> Do thine own fortunes that obedient right
> Which both thy duty owes and our power claims . . .

(II, iii, 157–161)

At this command Bertram has no choice but to acquiesce:

> When I consider
> What great creation and what dole of honor
> Flies where you bid it, I find that she, which late
> Was in my nobler thoughts most base, is now
> The praised of the King, who so ennobled,
> Is as 'twere born so.

(II, iii, 167–173)

Bertram's apology hints at mockery of the King's earlier claims. But as unpleasant as Bertram has been, his resentment is not unreasonable, for the King is using him to fulfill a debt that is not Bertram's. Still, so rude is Bertram that our sympathy goes to Helena, who must endure his insults.

When the party leaves for the wedding, Lafew and Parolles remain. Lafew is convinced that Bertram has acted properly (II, ii, 186), but Parolles disagrees, inviting accusation by Lafew about Parolles' own deceptions and conceits (II, iii, 201–208). Lafew departs momentarily with the warning that eventually Parolles will be unmasked (II, iii, 224–229), and that threat leaves us looking forward to a plot against Bertram's ally. That anticipation is whetted when Lafew returns, as if unable to resist attacking Parolles further:

> Methink'st thou art a general offense, and every
> man should beat thee. I think thou wast created for

men to breathe themselves upon thee.

(II, iii, 254–256)

Soon Bertram returns, married and furious:

> O my Parolles, they have married me!
> I'll to the Tuscan wars, and never bed her.

(II, iii, 272–273)

And Parolles agrees (II, iii, 278), for he himself is eager to escape Lafew. More important, Bertram here becomes downright vicious when he prepares to send Helena to his mother with a letter revealing his hatred (II, iii, 286–289). At this point his actions appear inexcusable. He also fails to recognize the fineness of his mother, who, he assumes, shares his intolerance.

In scene iv Helena and the clown are speaking of the Countess, and he comments on the Countess's health, saying that she is well except for two things:

> One, that she's not in heaven, whither God
> send her quickly! the other that she's in earth, from
> whence God send her quickly.

(II, iv, 11–13)

The lines seem to mock Helena's dual perspective, for she alternates between acting as a divine agent infused with religious fervor, and as a poor woman aggressively scheming to marry a man who is her social superior. Such a dichotomy raises the issue of whether we should regard Helena as a miraculous being who brings redemption, or as a fortune-hunter determined to raise herself socially. The question remains open when Parolles enters, bringing a message from Bertram that he is leaving at once, and that therefore Helena's "great prerogative and rite of love" (II, iv, 41) must be put off. Helena remains undaunted: "In every thing I wait upon his will" (II, iv, 54). Should we regard her patience as saint-like, or as evidence of ruthless persistence?

The second major plot line, the gulling of Parolles, begins in scene v, when Lafew and Bertram talk about him. Bertram insists upon the quality of his associate:

> I do assure you, my lord, he is very great in
> knowledge, and accordingly valiant.

(II, v, 8–9)

Parolles' name means "words" in French, and language is part of the key to his character, for he hides his corruption behind bombastic speech. His relationship to Bertram may be compared to that of Falstaff to young Henry IV. Yet although both soldiers come from the tradition of the braggart from Roman comedy, Parolles' intolerance of Helena is but one example of his reinforcing Bertram's own bigotries rather than humanizing his young charge, as Falstaff does. Indeed, Lafew sneers of Parolles that "the soul of this man is his clothes" (II, v, 43–44), and that image of dressing characterizes the fraudulent figure

Parolles presents to the world. We recall earlier mention of that theme in the King's quotation from Helena's father (I, ii, 61–62). Therefore in his insistence on Parolles' worth, Bertram proves himself not only blind to human nature but also proud and even foolish for ignoring the wisdom of Lafew, a more experienced man. Indeed, subsequently everyone who meets Parolles disparages him. Furthermore, with almost every scene, Bertram becomes more dislikable, and we wonder why Helena is so taken with him. Her devotion becomes less comprehensible at the end of this scene when Bertram refers to her as "my clog" (II, v, 53), then coldly dismisses her with a letter for the Countess.

Act III, scene i recalls a motif familiar from other comedies: the futility of war. The Duke of Florence has attempted to justify the fighting (III, i, 1–4), the reasons for which go unspoken. Yet the Duke is also disturbed that the King of France has remained neutral (III, i, 7–9). The Duke takes comfort, however, in that certain younger Frenchmen will be eager to participate (III, i, 17–19). Here is one more instance in the play where the younger generation, and by implication Bertram, embodies destructive values.

In scene ii, the Countess returns, having received from the clown the letter from Bertram disavowing affection for Helena. The Countess is pained by her son's impolitic callousness:

> This is not well, rash and unbridled boy,
> To fly the favors of so good a king,
> To pluck his indignation on thy head
> By the misprising of a maid too virtuous
> For the contempt of empires.
>
> (II, ii, 28–32)

Helena soon enters and gloomily reads aloud Bertram's letter, which stipulates what she must accomplish to win him as her husband:

> "When thou canst get the ring upon my
> finger, which never shall come off, and show me a child
> begotten of thy body that I am father to, then call
> me husband . . . "
>
> (III, ii, 57–60)

The Countess is profoundly disappointed in her son:

> He was my son,
> But I do wash his name out of my blood,
> And thou art all my child.
>
> (III, ii, 66–68)

Yet she finds an explanation that partially redeems him. Speaking of Parolles, the Countess comments:

A very tainted fellow, and full of wickedness.
My son corrupts a well-derived nature
With his inducement.

(III, iii, 87–89)

By blaming another agent for Bertram's transgressions, the Countess keeps alive
the hope of his rehabilitation. She also reminds the second Lord to tell her son
that "his sword can never win the honor that he loses" (III, ii, 93–94). She
recognizes the feebleness of military glory in contrast to the reward of personal
integrity. So does Helena, who at the end of this scene resolves to leave France
so that Bertram can come home:

No, come thou home, Rossillion,
Whence honor but of danger wins a scar,
As oft it loses all.

(III, ii, 120–122)

With this sentiment, Helena herself recalls Falstaff's "catechism" at the end of
Henry IV, Part I. Her reflection undercuts the news in scene ii that Bertram's
efforts in warfare have been notable. He enjoys fighting (III, iii, 8–11), but his
pleasure in destruction confirms his vacuity.

Helena's nature is developed further in scene iv, in her plan to disguise herself
as a pilgrim, further indication of possible divine influence.

"I am Saint Jaques' pilgrim, thither gone.
Ambitious love hath so in me offended
That barefoot plod I the cold ground upon
With sainted vow my faults to have amended"

(III, iv, 4–7)

The Countess also suggests Helena's restorative powers:

What angel shall
Bless this unworthy husband? He cannot thrive,
Unless her prayers, whom heaven delights to hear,
And loves to grant, reprieve him from the wrath
of greatest justice.

(III, iv, 25–29)

No matter how far Bertram falls, redemption remains possible.

In Act III, scene v, Bertram's military achievements are repeated by the Widow
of Florence as well as by her daughters. Oddly enough, however, the greater
his triumphs in battle, the lower he falls morally. He is still associated with
Parolles, whom Mariana dismisses as a "filthy officer" (III, v, 17), and she
warns her sister about both officers:

Beware of them, Diana, their promises, enticements,
oaths, tokens, and all these engines of lust,

are not the things they go under.

$$(III, v, 18-20)$$

When Helena enters in disguise, Diana clarifies that she has taken the advice to
heart, for she recounts Bertram's past, including the existence of his wife, while
Helena dismisses the wife's name as unimportant (III, v, 60–61). When Helena
confirms for herself that Diana is aware of Bertram's dishonesty (III, v, 78),
Helena arranges with the Widow to dine with Diana that night (III, v, 93–96).
The plot against Bertram is thus begun, but the nature of Helena's disguise
ensures that it looks less like revenge and more like the salvation of a wayward
soul.

Such is not the case with the plot against Parolles, which gets underway in
scene vi. Before he enters, the two lords scheme to reveal his deceit (III, vi,
24–33), and with Bertram's permission send him on a fraudulent mission to
retrieve a drum (III, vi, 34–35). As Parolles dashes off with enthusiasm, his
final words are ironic: "I love not many words" (III, vi, 84). The second Lord
views the matter differently:

> Nor more than a fish loves water. Is not
> this a strange fellow, my lord, that so confidently
> seems to undertake this business, which he knows is
> not to be done, damns himself to do, and dares better
> to be damn'd than to do't?

$$(III, vi, 85-89)$$

He pierces right to the heart of Parolles' combination of verbosity and deceit.
What is surprising is how easily Bertram consents to have his supposed friend
made the dupe. His lack of compassion continues to diminish his stature, as
does his detachment in his comments about Diana at the end of the scene (III,
vi, 112–117). He treats her as just another conquest, with no regard for her
personally.

In scene vii Helena reveals that Bertram is her husband, then asks for the
Widow's help in exposing him (III, vii, 8–12). Bertram is to be allowed to
continue to court Diana, who will demand Bertram's ring in exchange for sleeping
with him. But Helena adds that she herself will appear "to fill the time" (III,
vii, 33), and will in addition give Diana 3,000 crowns. The deception is unattractive and clashes with Helena's almost religious nature. Yet the plan does fall
into the acceptable realm of behavior in a comedy and emphasizes that Helena
is not simply a divine symbol but also a human being. She is determined to win
Bertram back, and in her mind the ends justify the means:

> Let us assay our plot, which if it speed,
> Is wicked meaning in a lawful deed,
> And lawful meaning in a lawful act,

> Where both not sin, and yet a sinful act.
>
> (III, vii, 44–48)

In other words, Bertram will assume he is committing a sin, when in fact he will be with his own wife. Accordingly, Helena remains within her own moral precepts.

In Act IV, scene i, Parolles tries to talk himself out of carrying out his assignment:

> What the devil should move me to undertake
> the recovery of this drum, being not ignorant of the
> impossibility, and knowing I had no such purpose.
>
> (IV, i, 34–36)

But just as he is about to salvage any drum available, the French soldiers capture him, and from then on make him believe he is in the hands of the enemy. The particular fun is that the abuser of words is himself fooled by a fake language his captors create. We also enjoy seeing his cowardice exposed:

> O, let me live,
> And all the secrets of our camp I'll show,
> Their force, their purposes; nay, I'll speak that
> Which you will wonder at.
>
> (IV, i, 83–86)

Such emptiness of character is paralleled in the next scene by Bertram's behavior with Diana. She reminds him of his responsibility to his wife (IV, ii, 12–13), but he claims that the relationship was forced upon him and that now he cares only for Diana (IV, ii, 15–17). He follows by spewing empty romantic cliches, playing the conventional spurned lover:

> Be not so holy-cruel. Love is holy,
> And my integrity ne'er knew the crafts
> That you do change men with. Stand no more off,
> But give thyself unto my sick desires,
> Who then recovers.
>
> (IV, ii, 32–36)

Diana then demands the ring, and he protests that it was "Bequeathed down from many ancestors" (IV, ii, 43), but under her mocking repetition (IV, ii, 47) he releases it. We know that she is satirizing the falsity of his vows. Perhaps he takes her humor as a challenge to his manhood, an insinuation that he is afraid to release the ring. She then promises him another (IV, ii, 61), an artificial point of plot, for the exchange is not well motivated. But when Bertram leaves, agreeing to meet her later that night, Diana derides his personality and method of courtship:

> My mother told me just how he would woo,
> As if she sate in 's heart. She says all men

Have the like oaths.

(IV, ii, 69–71)

Her bitterness adds to the general discomfort of both this scene and this aspect of the plot. Although Bertram believes his wife dead, he will soon go to bed with her, and she will give him that second ring from the King.

Scene iii dramatizes at length the trick played on Parolles, but before that takes place, the two lords review the extent of Bertram's perfidy:

> He has much worthy blame laid upon
> him for shaking off so good a wife and so sweet a lady.

(IV, iii, 6–7)

> He hath perverted a young gentlewoman
> here in Florence, of a most chaste renown,
> and this night he fleshes his will in the spoil of her
> honor. He hath given her his monumental ring, and
> thinks himself made in the unchaste composition.

(IV, iii, 14–18)

Both men also assume Helena to be dead (IV, iii, 47–53), and remind us of the punishment Bertram is to face:

> The great dignity that his
> valor hath here acquir'd for him shall at home be
> encount'red with a shame as ample.

(IV, iii, 68–70)

The second lord is confident that the proper order of things will be restored. Bertram then enters, blithely unaware of their judgment of him, and boasts of the deceptions he has carried off:

> I have congied with the Duke, done my adieu with his
> nearest; buried a wife, mourn'd for her, writ to my
> lady mother I am returning, entertain'd my con-
> voy, and between these main parcels of dispatch
> [effected] many nicer needs.

(IV, iii, 87–91)

This moment may be his lowest, as he is virtually asking to be exposed.

First, though, we see Parolles brought before him, and Bertram is eager to see his erstwhile friend humiliated:

> Come, bring forth
> this counterfeit module, h'as deceiv'd me like a
> double-meaning prophesier.

(IV, iii, 98–100)

As yet without proof, Bertram is willing to believe the worst. His loyalty does not extend far.

The rest of the scene is Parolles' confession of the lies to which he has been a part. He reveals various troop strengths (IV, iii, 160–169), thus demonstrating his treachery (although we doubt his accuracy). He slanders Captain Dumaine (IV, iii, 185–188), then is shown to have written a letter to Diana in which he insults Bertram:

> . . . for I knew the young Count
> to be a dangerous and lascivious boy, who is a whale to
> virginity, and devours up all the fry it finds.
>
> (IV, iii, 219–221)

The report shocks Bertram: "He shall be whipt through the army with this rhyme in 's forehead" (IV, iii, 233–234), but this surprise is just the first comeuppance Bertram will receive. Parolles' confession shows his life to be such a parade of fraud that one of the lords is almost won over: "I begin to love him for this" (IV, iii, 262). But when all have been unmasked, Parolles still is unrepentant: "Simply the thing I am/Shall make me live" (IV, iii, 333–334). In his self-awareness and steadfastness to his own character, Parolles emerges with a minor dignity, a strength that escapes Bertram.

The next two scenes serve primarily to advance plot, but several lines have repercussions. For instance, Helena comforts the Widow and Diana:

> Doubt not but heaven
> Hath brought me up to be your daughter's dower,
> As it hath fated her to be my motive
> And helper to a husband.
>
> (IV, iv, 18–21)

She also adds a conclusion that hints at how all this pain must be endured for a greater cause:

> You, Diana,
> Under my poor instructions yet must suffer
> Something in my behalf.
>
> (IV, iv, 26–28)

The play is grounded in reality. Yet Helena's numerous references to herself as a divine agency make us question whether she believes herself in some way a holy force, or, indeed, if we should take her as such, whether she believes so or not. Her final two lines here also imply a greater purpose is at work:

> All's well that ends well! still the fine's the crown;
> What e'er the course, the end is the renown.
>
> (IV, iv, 35–36)

She intimates that she has all matters under control, that the resolution is almost ordained. Such confidence again hints at supernatural powers.

In scene v the Countess and Lafew lament what they believe to be Helena's death (IV, v, 4–15). Perhaps the clown's humor is intended to keep the scene light, but the wit seems forced, and Lafew finally ends it (VI, v, 56–59). Then he raises the possibility of a marriage between his daughter and Bertram (IV, v, 71–75), a gesture that implies that Lafew sees in Bertram growth and maturity. Nonetheless, that proposal is darkened by the wit of the clown, who speaks of a "patch of velvet" (IV, v, 95) on the approaching Bertram's face. Lafew suggests that the bandage covers an honorable wound sustained in war, but the clown hints that the bandage might cover a syphilitic sore. The joke is out of place in this mournful atmosphere, but reflects the awkward mixture of tension and laughter in much of this play, specifically the last act.

Its first two scenes give the characters opportunity to work their way to the Count's palace in Rossillion. In scene i Helena gives the gentleman a message for the King (V, i, 30–35), and we assume it contains information that will lead to the resolution of all these complications. The most intriguing exchange is between Lafew and Parolles, as the latter begs forgiveness: "My lord, I am a man whom Fortune hath cruelly scratch'd" (V, ii, 26–27). After Parolles begs further, Lafew relents:

> I had
> talk of you last night; though you are a fool and a
> knave, you shall eat.
>
> (V, ii, 53–54)

This generosity establishes the tone of forgiveness of the final scene.

At its start the Countess begs the King to forgive Bertram (V, iii, 4–8), and the King concedes that he has done so (V, iii, 9–11). When Bertram arrives, he, too, is remorseful (V, iii, 44–55), and agrees to marry Lafew's daughter (V, ii, 44–46). But such apology and reconciliation cover only Bertram's public errors. His private sins, his boasting and cheating, have yet to be disclosed, and that process begins when as an expression of loyalty Bertram surrenders the ring given him by Diana but given to her by Helena (V, iii, 76). The King recognizes the jewel as the one he gave Helena (V, iii, 83–86), and under the pressure of severe questioning, Bertram reverts to lying:

> In Florence was it from a casement thrown me,
> Wrapp'd in a paper, which contain'd the name
> of her that threw it.
>
> (V, iii, 93–95)

The King insists that he himself gave Helena the ring (V, iii, 104–112), and Bertram is thereafter accused of murdering his wife. He furiously denies that crime:

> If you shall prove
> This ring was ever hers, you shall as easy
> Prove that I husbanded her bed in Florence,

Where yet she never was.

(V, iii, 124–127)

The statement is ironic, for Bertram is unaware of the truth of his protestation.

After Bertram is removed, his case grows shakier when the letter arrives from Diana:

>   " . . . Now is the Count Rossillion
> a widower, his vows are forfeited to me, and my
> honor's paid to him. He stole from Florence, taking
> no leave, and I follow him to his country for justice.
> Grant it me, O King, in you it best lies; otherwise a
> seducer flourishes, and a poor maid is undone . . . "

(V, iii, 141–146)

Even after Bertram returns, and Diana appears and announces herself to be his wife (V, iii, 170–175), Bertram remains contemptuous:

> My lord, this is a fond and desp'rate creature,
> When sometime I have laugh'd with. Let your Highness
> Lay a more noble thought upon mine honor
> Than for to think that I would sink it here.

(V, iii, 178–181)

He reiterates the snobbishness he demonstrated in Act II, scene iii, when he originally disdained Helena. He then sneers at Diana as "a common gamester to the camp" (V, iii, 188), and soon implies that she seduced him (V, iii, 210–219), but in her defense she points to the ancestral ring he gave her, then calls Parolles as a witness. Bertram understandably belittles his former aide as "a most perfidious slave" (V, iii, 205), but Parolles' testimony is no help anyway, as he seems incapable of uttering a clear truth. Thus the King is forced to turn back to Diana, and to demand of her how she came to possess the ring. She, however, plays out the confusion as long as possible:

> Because he's guilty, and he is not guilty.
> He knows I am no maid, and he'll swear to't;
> I'll swear I am a maid, and he knows not.
> Great King, I am no strumpet, by my life;
> I am either maid, or else this old man's wife.

(V, iii, 289–293)

At last Helena enters, and the King is appropriately amazed:

>   Is there no exorcist
> Beguiles the truer office of mine eyes?
> Is't real that I see?

(V, iii, 304–306)

With unstoppable determination Helena marches to Bertram, presents his original letter and reviews its orders, then claims Bertram for her own: "Will you be mine now you are doubly won?'' (V, iii, 314). Any saintly overtones have vanished from her manner. Indeed, these words could be said with an icy control, or perhaps with intense passion, for they reduce Bertram to two lines of helpless resignation:

> If she, my liege, can make me know this clearly,
> I'll love her dearly, ever, ever dearly.

> (V, iii, 315–316)

Perhaps we are meant to believe that the appearance of Helena, her virtual rebirth, causes Bertram's transformation. The moment is strained, however, for Bertram has been too long dislikeable for us to believe him capable of an instantaneous change. Nevertheless, such reversal of character under similar circumstances is invoked by Shakespeare in subsequent plays, where the technique is more effective. The King, with promise of a dowry, unites Bertram and Helena in marriage but ends the action with a peculiar couplet:

> All yet seems well, and if it end so meet,
> The bitter past, more welcome is the sweet.

> (V, iii, 333–334)

The word "seems" implies that all is not happy.

This ambiguity is a fitting conclusion to a play filled with contradictions. The structure, with a hero and heroine who undergo trials, then are united in marriage, is that of traditional comedy. But the mood of the work, in combination with the sour personality of the leading male figure, robs the play of much of its joy. Helena's triumph at the end, with her conversion of Bertram, may be taken as symbolic of the regenerative power of youth. Yet that conclusion is not exultant. It is tempered by the play's conflicting elements of comedy and drama, a tension that may reflect a playwright whose appetite for pure comedy was diminishing and whose need for a different form of dramatic expression would lead to the creation of such a genre in the final portion of his career.

SUGGESTIONS FOR FURTHER READING

Carter, Albert H. "In Defense of Bertram." *Shakespeare Quarterly* 7 (1956): 21–31.

Leech, Clifford. "The Theme of Ambition in *All's Well That Ends Well*." *ELH* 21 (1954): 17–29.

Pearce, Frances M. "In Quest of Unity: A Study of Failure and Redemption in *All's Well That Ends Well*." *Shakespeare Quarterly* 25 (1975): 71–89.

Price, Joseph G. *The Unfortunate Comedy: A Study of* All's Well That Ends Well. Toronto: University of Toronto Press, 1968.

Rothman, Jules. "A Vindication of Parolles." *Shakespeare Quarterly* 23 (1972): 183–196.

Tuner, Robert Y. "Dramatic Convention in *All's Well That Ends Well*." *PMLA* 85 (1960): 497–502.

Wilson, Harold S. "Dramatic Emphasis in *All's Well That Ends Well*." *Huntington Library Quarterly* 13 (1949–50): 217–240.

MEASURE FOR MEASURE

As its title suggests, this play is about judgment, retribution, and mercy. It is also about the balance between freedom and restraint and between legitimate exercise of power and abuse of that power. The dramatic matrix Shakespeare creates is fundamentally serious. Yet he brings in comic elements, and the resolution of the story is carried out in the tradition of comedy. Thus the "problem" of this play: the mood constantly shifts, as do our perspectives. Throughout the work we tend to sympathize with certain characters and remain antagonistic to others. Yet the lines of demarcation blur. Even at the end, no absolute clarification is achieved, for we still find ourselves weighing the merits of opposing forces and evaluating the significance of what we have experienced.

The primary source of the work, which is set in sixteenth-century Vienna, is George Whetstone's play *Promos and Cassandra* (1578), which itself was derived from Giraldi Cinthio's collection of tales known as *Hecatommithi* (1565). This book is the one from which Shakespeare took the story that became *Othello*.

The opening scene establishes the curious atmosphere. The Duke begins by praising the wisdom and skill of his advisor Escalus (I, i, 3–13). Thus we are surprised when the Duke orders the presence of Angelo:

> What figure of us think you he will bear?
> For you must know, we have with special soul
> Elected him our absence to supply,
> Lent him our terror, dress'd him with our love,
> And given his deputation all the organs
> Of our own pow'r. What think you of it?

(I, i, 16–21)

Escalus's answer is neutral (I, i, 22–24), but questions remain: first, why is the Duke bestowing authority on someone else, and second, why does he choose a seemingly unknown quantity like Angelo instead of a reliable counselor like Escalus?

The second problem is answered partially when Angelo enters and the Duke
utters a quiet warning: "Look where he comes" (I, i, 24). He compliments
Angelo's reputation for strict morality, then offers a lengthy address on the
nature of goodness:

> . . . for if our virtues
> Did not go forth of us, 'twere all alike
> As if we had them not.
>
> (I, i, 33–35)

In other words, good intentions are not enough. Good actions are the test of a
human being. Thus the Duke implies that this experience in office is an examination of Angelo's character: under the responsibilities and privileges of power
will he maintain his standards of morality?

Angelo modestly denies his worth (I, i, 47–50), but the Duke insists, adding
that he will write to Angelo to learn how matters proceed. Subtly the Duke
clarifies that he will be too far away to interfere, and he further reminds Angelo
of the absolute nature of the jurisdiction he is to assume:

> Your scope is as mine own,
> So to enforce or qualify the laws
> As to your soul seems good.
>
> (I, i, 64–66)

Finally he invites Angelo to exert command without fear of reprisal. All these
warnings hint that the Duke suspects how Angelo will conduct himself. Therefore
this tenure is less of a test and more of an opportunity for confirmation.

But why is the Duke carrying out this elaborate scheme? The answer is never
certain, but one way to look at this plan, and, indeed, the entire play, is as a
chance for the Duke to teach Angelo and all who will be involved with him the
strength of mercy. The Elizabethan audience would have understood the Duke
as ruler of both the secular and the religious life of Vienna. Hence the Duke's
scheme may be seen as an attempt to teach to the population of the city Christian
humility and forgiveness.

But this explanation is only partially satisfactory, for as scene ii reveals,
Vienna, under the Duke's leadership, is hardly a virtuous place. Instead, it is
rife with corruption and a variety of illegal activities. The conversation between
Lucio and the two gentlemen skirts casually about matters of grace (I, ii, 24–
26) and hints at a scorn for religious values. But with the appearance of the
bawd Mistress Overdone, the discussion turns decidedly obscene, filled with the
puns based on sexual innuendo. She also brings news of Claudio's impending
execution because of Juliet's pregnancy (I, ii, 72–73), and such information
reaffirms that vice is widespread. Pompey, a pimp, then enters, and crudely
repeats the news about Claudio, which for some reason Mistress Overdone does
not seem to remember. Pompey adds that all the houses of prostitution have
been ordered shut, but he comforts the distressed Mistress Overdone:

Come; fear not you; good counsellors lack no
clients. Though you change your place, you need not
change your trade; I'll be your tapster still.

(I, ii, 106–108)

No matter what the laws, business will flourish. Apparently beneath the veneer
of civilization, Vienna suffers rampant immorality.

Into this atmosphere comes Claudio, on his way to jail. Although he is the
romantic hero, in this environment his behavior is already tainted, especially
when he describes his crime:

From too much liberty, my Lucio, liberty:
As surfeit is the father of much fast,
So every scope by the immoderate use
Turns to restraint. Our natures do pursue,
Like rats that ravin down their proper bane,
A thirsty evil, and when we drink we die.

(I, ii, 125–130)

Such language, describing a lack of sexual restraint, does not befit a hero. Nor
does Claudio's more detailed description. He claims that he and Juliet are married
in all but name:

This we came not to,
Only for propogation of a dow'r
Remaining in the coffer of her friends,
From whom we thought it meet to hide our love
Till time had made them for us.

(I, ii, 149–153)

In the age of this play, public declaration of intent to marry created a valid
marriage, but confirmation by church ceremony was necessary for the union to
be religiously sanctioned. Nonetheless, Claudio's explanation sounds suspi-
ciously like that of a man seeking more money before he commits himself. And
after he explains that the new governor, whom we know to be Angelo, has
invoked an ancient law and ruled Claudio guilty (I, ii, 165–171), Claudio urges
Lucio to find Isabella, Claudio's sister:

This day my sister should the cloister enter,
And there receive her approbation.
Acquaint her with the danger of my state;
Implore her, in my voice, that she make friends
To the strict deputy; bid herself assay him.

(I, ii, 177–181)

Here, too, Claudio sounds unheroic. He knows that his sister is entering a holy
order. Yet his urging suggests that she can use her charm to entrance the governor.
Throughout Claudio's explanation, Juliet, obviously pregnant, stands right by
him. Yet never does he acknowledge her, and never does he express sympathy

for her plight. Therefore throughout this scene Claudio is in the midst of a crisis for which we feel sympathy; yet because of his language and actions that sympathy is modified, and the tone of the play overall is ambiguous.

Such uncertainty continues in scene iii, when the Duke explains his strategy to Friar Thomas. The Duke denies seeking to carry on a secret love affair (I, iii, 1–3), but the denial suggests that he has previously conducted other illicit activities, a peculiar confession to a friar. He then explains why he has placed Angelo in charge:

> We have strict statutes and most biting laws
> (The needful bits and curbs to headstrong weeds),
> Which for this fourteen years we have let slip,
> Even like an o'ergrown lion in a cave,
> That goes not out to prey.
>
> (I, iii, 19–23)

The implication is that the Duke has been neglectful of his responsibilities, and that the current unhealthy state of the city is a result of his failure. He continues with the other half of his plan:

> Therefore indeed, my father,
> I have on Angelo impos'd the office,
> Who may, in th' ambush of my name, strike home,
> And yet my nature never in the fight
> To do in slander . . . Lord Angelo is precise;
> Stands at a guard with envy, scarce confesses
> That his blood flows; or that his appetite
> Is more to bread than stone: hence shall we see
> If power change purpose: what our seemers be.
>
> (I, iii, 39–54)

The first section intimates that the Duke is using Angelo as a hatchet man. Knowing Angelo's tendencies, the Duke has put him in charge, hoping that Angelo will impose harsh measures and thereby put the city in order without the Duke's being blamed. The last lines suggest that the Duke is conducting an experiment, examining the effects of unlimited power on a man who claims to live by a strict personal code. In sum, his purpose is confusing as is his morality. On a realistic level the Duke is using another man to undo the Duke's errors. On a symbolic level he is studying aspects of human nature.

Scene iv takes place at the nunnery, where Isabella seeks entrance and petitions Francisca with a curious request:

> I speak not as desiring more,
> But rather wishing a more strict restraint
> Upon the sisterhood, the votarists of Saint Clare.
>
> (I, iv, 3–5)

She may be seeking escape from reality. Whatever her motivation, this request for an additionally ascetic existence hints at neurotic tendencies in Isabella, who represents one more extreme. The city itself revels in sexual license, Angelo embodies puritanical strictness, and Isabella is an example of unwavering religious devotion. The clash of these forces, all in their own way unyielding, is the crux of the drama.

Lucio enters to explain Claudio's predicament, and Isabella surmises correctly that the woman involved is Juliet (I, iv, 45), but her attitude towards her brother's actions goes unspoken. The contrast between Lucio's playful banter and Isabella's earnestness is striking, but eventually Lucio clarifies that because of Angelo, "a man whose blood/ Is very snow-broth" (I, iv, 57–58), Claudio faces death:

> All hope is gone,
> Unless you have the grace by your fair prayer
> To soften Angelo.
>
> (I, iv, 68–70)

The irony of the words "grace" and "prayers" are soon apparent, for Angelo will be moved by Isabella's devotion, but not in the direction she or Lucio anticipates.

In Act II, scene i, Angelo's character is further revealed. Escalus seeks mercy for Claudio, wondering whether Angelo, too, might have been guilty of some undiscovered sexual sin (II, i, 8–16). But Angelo is unswerving:

> 'Tis one thing to be tempted, Escalus,
> Another thing to fall . . . What's open made to justice,
> That justice seizes.
>
> (II, i, 17–22)

Angelo virtually sets himself up as a target, and from this point on we await the moment when he will be unable to resist temptation. In his cold-blooded approach to matters of law, Angelo reminds us of Shylock from *The Merchant of Venice*. Although both are legally correct, both lack compassion and are emotionally repellent. The crucial difference between them is that we understand to a much greater degree the social circumstances that have made Shylock, a Jew in a Christian society, what he is. Of Angelo we have no such knowledge, and thus his intolerance seems arbitrary and Angelo himself more villainous.

A long comic interlude follows, in which Froth is brought in by Elbow and Pompey before Angelo for judgment. The crime in question is the supposed rape of Mistress Elbow, but Elbow's numerous verbal blunderings ensure that we do take little of the session seriously. For instance, he refers to a woman "cardinally given" (II, i, 80) instead of "carnally." And he transposes phrases:

> Prove it before these varlets here, thou
> honorable man, prove it.
>
> (II, i, 86–87)

But one of his misusages is telling. He refers to "precise villains" (II, i, 54), and the word "precise" recalls the Duke's description of Angelo (I, iii, 50).

The subtle implication is that Angelo has more in common with these lecherous characters than appearances would suggest, an impression that turns out to be accurate.

Pompey offers a convoluted explanation about a pregnant Mistress Elbow entering a brothel (II, i, 88–94, 96–104), but the story leaves Escalus at a loss:

> Come, you are a tedious fool. To the pur-
> pose: what was done to Elbow's wife, that he hath
> cause to complain of? Come me to what was done to her.
>
> (II, i, 115–118)

Eventually the charge is dismissed, but the intrusion of all three characters and their bawdy dialogue reinforces the general foulness that infects Vienna. They are also a subtle echo of the crime committed by Claudio, an implication particularly clear at II, i, 97–104. Indeed, when Escalus notes that Pompey's trade (pimping) is outlawed in Vienna, the accused asks innocently: "Does your worship mean to geld and splay all the youth of the city?" (II, i, 230–231). Finally, the scene reveals further the personalities of Angelo and Escalus. The Deputy never laughs, and eventually stalks out with the suggestion that all should be whipped (II, i, 135–137). Escalus, however, finds the trio entertaining and even humorous. Right before they appear, he comments:

> Some rise by sin; and some by virtue fall;
> Some run from brakes of ice and answer none,
> And some condemned for a fault alone.
>
> (II, i, 38–40)

Such a charitable attitude underlies the spirit of the play.

Scene ii is the first of the encounters between Angelo and Isabella, two high points of the play. Before Isabella enters, Angelo hints that not only is he a strict observer of legal procedure, but also he is possessed by a heartlessness he has so far kept submerged. For instance, when the Provost asks about Juliet, soon to give birth, Angelo's response is curt:

> Dispose of her
> To some more fitter place, and that with speed.
>
> (II,ii, 16-17)

At this moment a servant announces that Claudio's sister wishes to see Angelo. Immediately he is intrigued: "Hath he a sister?" (II, ii, 19), and in retrospect we shall wonder if the notion of sexual blackmail occurs to Angelo at the very moment he learns of Isabella's existence. She then enters, with Lucio in support. At first her pleas are surprisingly restrained:

> I have a brother is condemn'd to die;
> I do beseech you let it be his fault,

And not my brother.

> (II, ii, 34–36)

Perhaps, as was hinted earlier, she is repulsed by his crime and unable to plead for him. But Lucio urges her to proceed with more feeling:

> Give't not o'er so. To him again, entreat him,
> Kneel down before him, hang upon his gown;
> You are too cold.

> (II, ii, 43–45)

Meanwhile Angelo, speaking brusquely, dismisses her petition: "He's sentenc'd; 'tis too late" (II, ii, 55). Gradually Isabella grows more impassioned, and her thoughts have more powerful implications:

> How would you be
> If He, which is the top of judgment, should
> But judge you as you are? O, think on that,
> And mercy then will breathe within your lips,
> Like man new made.

> (II, ii, 75–79)

Her address emphasizes the religious necessity of mercy, that Angelo's denial is anti-Christian. But Angelo remains rigorously secular: "It is the law, not I, condemn your brother" (II, ii, 80). Such a claim has long been the retreat of those who impose relentless, if legal, punishment. Angelo's insistence on the strict imposition of the law thus reflects his lack of feeling.

Isabella's passion approaches its apex:

> O, it is excellent
> To have a giant's strength; but it is tyrannous
> To use it like a giant.

> (II, ii, 107–109)

This condemnation of the abuse of power is followed by an overwhelming tribute to the fact that God shows mercy, but that man does not (II, ii, 110–123). She also insists on the universality of human sin:

> Go to your bosom,
> Knock there, and ask your heart what it doth know
> That's like my brother's fault. If it confess
> A natural guiltiness such as is his,
> Let it not sound a thought upon your tongue
> Against my brother's life.

> (II, ii, 136–138)

This challenge obviously strikes Angelo hard, for he begins to waver:

> She speaks, and 'tis˙
> Such sense that my sense breeds with it.
>
> (II, ii, 142–143)

His self-control falters, and, against his will, he finds himself drawn to her.
When Isabella uses the word "bribe" (II, ii, 144), meaning she will approach
him with a prayer, Angelo seizes the other connotation of the word (II, ii, 146).
And when left alone, he regards his own feelings with a combination of fascination and revulsion:

> What's this? what's this? Is this her fault, or mine?
> The tempter, or the tempted, who sins most, ha? . . .
> What dost thou? or what art thou, Angelo?
> Dost thou desire her foully for those things
> That make her good? . . .
> O cunning enemy, that to catch a saint,
> With saints dost bait thy hook! Most dangerous
> Is that temptation that doth goad us on
> To sin in loving virtue.
>
> (II, ii, 162–182)

Here is the first moment where Angelo earns sympathy. His feelings are immoral,
but that he is helpless to stifle them means that he is not a one-dimensional prude
but a man tormented by his own drives. Thus our feelings toward him, even as
he grows more ruthless, remain complex.

Scene iii, a transition between the Isabella-Angelo encounters, also serves two
other purposes. It dramatizes the character of Juliet, who is visited by the Duke,
and whose courage in the face of Claudio's death and the birth of her own
illegitimate child is stirring. She repents her "sin," as the Duke calls it, but
without regret:

> I do repent me as it is an evil,
> And take the shame with joy.
>
> (II, iii, 35–36)

The scene also shows us the Duke understanding Juliet's character, thereby
setting up subsequent twists of plot.

Scene iv begins with Angelo's still brooding over what he sees as his inexplicable attraction to Isabella:

> O place, O form,
> How often dost thou with thy case, thy habit,
> Wrench awe from fools, and tie the wiser souls
> To thy false seeming! Blood, thou art blood.
> Let's write "good angel" on the devil's horn,
> 'Tis not the devil's crest.
>
> (II, iv, 12–17)

He is infuriated by his own vulnerability to passions he has long derided. And
after a servant announces Isabella's proximity, Angelo again feels uncontrollable
urges:

What does my blood thus muster to my heart,
Making both it unable for itself,
And dispossessing all my other parts
Of necessary fitness?

(II, iv, 20–23)

Isabella's first line reflects her naivete: "I am come to know your pleasure" (II, iv, 31). Innocent of the sexual implications, she remains unaware of Angelo's feelings for several moments. For instance, Angelo poses an alternative to her:

Which had you rather, that the most just law
Now took your brother's life, [or], to redeem him,
Give up your body to such sweet uncleanness
As she that he hath stain'd?

(II, iv, 52–55)

We feel Angelo's self-consciousness, as he phrases the question in delicate religious terms. He is unable to restrain his desires for Isabella; yet he is unwilling to confess them openly:

Might there not be a charity in sin
To save this brother's life?

(II, iv, 63–64)

He gradually makes his proposal more blatant (II, iv, 96–97), but still Isabella resists:

Better it were a brother died at once,
Than that a sister, by redeeming him,
Should die for ever.

(II, iv, 106–108)

She clarifies what becomes her central conflict: the temporal life of her brother versus her own eternal life. And for Isabella the issue is beyond discussion. She will not sacrifice her soul (II, iv, 112–113).

Isabella admits that out of love she has overlooked her brother's crime:

I something do excuse the thing I hate,
For his advantage that I dearly love.

(II, iv, 119–120)

Angelo, however, slyly tries to persuade her by dwelling on pervasive moral vulnerability: "Nay, women are frail too" (II, iv, 124). He insinuates that she has the capacity to be corrupted, and this implication is a manifestation of his desire to soil her purity. Her virtue is what attracts him.

At last Angelo can no longer control himself: "Plainly conceive, I love you" (II, iv, 141). And he clarifies his demand (II, iv, 144). She resorts to the worldly threat of exposure (II, iv, 153–154), but at the warning he dispenses with all civility:

> I have begun
> And now I give my sensual race the rein.
> Fit thy consent to my sharp appetite,
> Lay by all nicety and prolixious blushes
> That banish what they sue for. Redeem thy brother
> By yielding up thy body to my will . . .
>
> (II, iv, 159–164)

With this acknowledgement of his own lust, he leaves Isabella alone. She, in turn, vows to go to her brother, who, she is confident, will prefer to die rather than see her surrender herself (II, iv, 177–183). The conflict between the temporal and the eternal remains foremost in her mind.

Tension subsides only slightly in the next scene, when the Duke, disguised as a friar, comes to the prison. He attempts to comfort Claudio with a sermon on the solace offered by heaven:

> What's yet in this
> That bears the name of life? Yet in this life
> Lie hid moe thousand deaths; yet death we fear
> That makes these odds all even.
>
> (III, i, 38–41)

And Claudio seems to accept this vision (III, i, 41–43). We wonder, however, why the Duke carries on this masquerade. He has the power to save Claudio at any time. Why, then, does the Duke allow Claudio, and soon Isabella, to suffer so? Perhaps, as we suggested earlier, the Duke seeks to teach mercy and justice to the citizens of his city. But although at this moment he speaks as a figure of divine compassion, he gradually becomes more manipulative, and looms less holy and ethical.

Isabella enters to confront Claudio with the alternative offered by Angelo:

> Lord Angelo, having affairs to heaven,
> Intends you for his swift ambassador . . .
>
> (III, i, 56–57)

The humor is dark, but Isabella is confident that Claudio will accept death rather than her dishonor. Thereafter she proceeds slowly, delaying revelation of Angelo's offer by dwelling on its horrible consequences. Perhaps, then, she is not as confident about her brother as she earlier claimed, and is building up his dread. At last she states the details:

> Dost thou think, Claudio,
> If I would yield him my virginity,
> Thou mightst be freed!
>
> (III, i, 96–98)

Claudio is shocked, but his dismay is undercut in the next few lines, as Isabella states her unwillingness to surrender:

O, were it but my life,
I'd throw it down for your deliverance
As frankly as a pin.

(III, i, 103–105)

With grim humor Claudio mutters: "Thanks, dear Isabel" (III, i, 105), as if to imply, what good would that do? She seeks an answer from him, and he weighs the issue carefully, at last offering a terrifying vision of hell (III, i, 117–127). Clearly the Duke's earlier portrait of heaven was unconvincing to Claudio, at least now that he has a chance to escape, and Claudio's own images are far more stark and passionate. Thus he asks Isabella to make the awful sacrifice:

Sweet sister, let me live.
What sin you do to save a brother's life,
Nature dispenses with the deed so far,
That it becomes a virtue.

(III, i, 132–135)

Now Isabella is horrified:

O you beast!
O faithless coward! O dishonest wretch!
Wilt thou be made a man out of my vice?
Is't not a kind of incest, to take life
From thine own sister's shame?

(III, i, 135–139)

To audiences in our day, her outrage may be unacceptable. Surely her brother's life is worth any price. Yet we must judge her reaction in light of the values that dominated Shakespeare's time, which held that the eternal fate of a soul is of greater consequence than the mere earthly life of the body. Thus Isabella sees Claudio as willing to damn her eternally for a few years of existence. And she dismisses his cause:

Mercy to thee would prove itself a bawd,
'Tis best that thou diest quickly.

(III, i, 149–150)

However, so callous is this last line that Isabella herself, even granting her religious passion, seems extreme. From her first appearance her devotion has been inordinate; now, as her brother faces death, that zeal robs her of sympathy. We understand Claudio's desperation in asking his sister to make such a sacrifice, though by doing so he diminishes his own stature severely. But even if we grasp her reasons for refusing, we do not appreciate her intolerance for him.

At this moment the play has reached an impasse, for the dilemma appears insoluble by the characters themselves. Claudio and Isabella are locked into irreconcilable positions. What occurs, therefore, is a complete change in tone and dramatic strategy. The Duke, still disguised as a friar, emerges from the shadows, and tells Claudio that Angelo never intended to pardon him (III, i,

164–167). At this news Claudio, rather unheroically, begs to be allowed to apologize to his sister and accept his death gracefully. And Isabella stands by her earlier resolve (III, i, 189–191). The Duke then offers an elaborate plan to fool Angelo, including bringing back Mariana, to whom Angelo was once to be married, but whom he deserted for lack of a dowry (III, i, 207–223). At this point we recall that Claudio did not marry Juliet over a similar lack of money. Isabella is outraged: "What corruption in this life, that it will let this man live?" (III, i, 232–233). The line must hit the Duke hard, for he is responsible not only for life in the city, but for elevating Angelo to his present authority. Thus the Duke may feel a special urgency, and explains at length that he has a scheme for undoing Angelo. The key point is the switching of Mariana for Isabella in bed, a tactic similar to the plot carried out in *All's Well That Ends Well*. Here it is equally distasteful, but Isabella agrees, a surprising concession from a woman of such absolute morality.

From here on the play turns from a study of character into a heavily plotted piece, as the other characters become objects for the Duke's manipulation. Why does he not end the tension by simply pardoning Claudio and removing Angelo from office? If we do regard the Duke as a savior, then all these machinations, no matter how outlandish, may be interpreted as part of a divine plan. But if we regard him as a realistic figure, then he appears overly deceptive and to no particular end.

Scene ii is a continuation, as Pompey appears as a manifestation of the low life of Vienna. He has been arrested again for pimping, and the disguised Duke has little tolerance for the crime:

> Canst thou believe thy living is a life,
> So stinkingly depending?
>
> (III, ii, 26–27)

And he orders Pompey imprisoned. The swiftness of this intended punishment suggests that the Duke has forgotten he is in disguise, for Elbow reminds him and us that Pompey must be taken before Angelo for judgement (III, ii, 34–36).

We also see the darker side of Lucio, who enters to find Pompey in custody and begins to mock his comrade (III, ii, 43–52). The Duke listens to this cruel if witty banter, and begins an extended discussion with Lucio, who reveals that he estimates the Duke to be a far less rigorous judge than Angelo (III, ii, 94–95), especially about matters having to do with sex:

> He had some feeling of the sport; he knew
> the service, and that instructed him to mercy.
>
> (III, ii, 119–120)

The Duke struggles to defend his own reputation, but only invites more offensive remarks from Lucio, who describes the Duke as a "very superficial, ignorant, unweighing fellow" (III, ii, 139–140), then continues his slander with a mixture of bawdiness and elegance:

The Duke (I say to thee again) would eat mutton on
Fridays. He's now past it, yet (and I say to thee) he
would mouth with a beggar, though she smelt brown
bread and garlic. Say that I said so. Farewell.

(III, ii, 181–184)

Lucio accentuates his insults by claiming not to care whether they are reported
to the Duke. Such effrontery in tandem with his general lewdness lessens Lucio's
standing. Yet the Duke's allowing Lucio to condemn himself and the Duke's
subsequent revenge is also unseemly, especially for a man of such rank.

Escalus then enters with the Provost and Mistress Overdone, who is under
arrest for being a "bawd of eleven years' continuance" (III, ii, 196). Because
Lucio is the one who turned her in, Mistress Overdone reveals that Lucio is the
father of a child by one Kate Keepdown, whom he deserted after promising to
marry her. Knowing the Duke's antagonism for Lucio, we expect this information
to return.

In introducing himself to Escalus, the disguised Duke tells a minor lie about
his origins. He carries on the falsehood, however, by going on about the general
decay of the world (III, ii, 229). Perhaps the Duke is here subconsciously
excusing his own failures. In this scene he has been confronted with heavy
evidence of the corruption of the city for which he was responsible. The diatribe
about immorality running rampant may be an attempt to excuse his own failure
(III, ii, 222–231). He also listens to Escalus praise him (III, ii, 235–241), and
that tribute both counteracts Lucio's disparagement and confirms the Duke's
eminence. Without that stature, his plotting would be less acceptable in the
audience's eyes. The Duke also hears word about Angelo's strictness, and promises justice of another sort:

If his own life answer the straitness of his
proceeding, it shall become him well; wherein if he
chance to fail, he hath sentenc'd himself.

(III, ii, 255–257)

As the Friar, the Duke seems to be implying heavenly punishment. But when
left alone he changes his tone:

Twice treble shame on Angelo,
To weed my vice, and let his grow!
O, what may man within him hide,
Though angel on the outward side!

(III, ii, 269–272)

The rest of the play is devoted to the revelation of Angelo's inner demon.

Act IV is a series of shorter scenes in which the Duke keeps his plot moving.
First he visits Mariana, still in mourning and listening to a song of lost love
(IV, i, 1–6). Isabella enters to tell the Duke that Angelo has agreed to meet her
(IV, i, 32–35), then leaves with Mariana to explain the details of the plan.

Apparently Isabella has already acceded to Angelo's proposal, a scene we are spared. When Mariana and Isabella return and announce that Mariana has agreed to participate (IV, i, 65–66), the Duke notes again that Mariana and Angelo were once engaged (IV, i, 71). Thus this "bed-switch" has a certain moral basis.

Scene ii returns to the life of the prison, where the peculiar morality of this society surfaces again. Pompey is offered a reduced sentence if he is willing to serve as the executioner's assistant (IV, ii, 8–11). However, the head executioner, named Abhorson, reacts with comic distaste: "A bawd, sir? fie upon him, he will discredit our mystery" (IV, ii, 28–29). Abhorson's absurd pride is an ironic counterpoint to Angelo's stiffnecked insistence on fidelity to the law. Nonetheless, Pompey's banter wins approval, and he takes to his new job with enthusiasm and another round of bawdy jokes:

> I do desire to learn, sir; and I hope, if you
> have occasion to use me for your own turn, you shall
> find me yare; for truly, sir, for your kindness, I owe
> you a good turn.

> (IV, ii, 56–59)

The word "turn" has connotations of both sex and hanging.

Claudio is reminded of his execution scheduled for the next morning (IV, ii, 63–64), but his muted reaction is less than intrepid. The Duke then enters, to hear what he imagines will be a pardon from Angelo. In response to the Provost's denunciation of the Deputy, therefore, the Duke offers an explanation of Angelo's strictness:

> He doth with holy abstinence subdue
> That in himself which he spurs on his pow'r
> To qualify in others. Were he meal'd with that
> Which he corrects, then were he tyrannous.

> (IV, ii, 81–82)

Instead, the message retains the order for Claudio to be put to death by four o'clock (IV, ii, 120–121).

What follows is dramatically weak, for the Duke expresses no shock at Angelo's betrayal even though the Duke knows that by this time Angelo has already been to bed with a woman he assumes to have been Isabella. Thus he has not only destroyed her purity (or thinks he has), but has gone back on his word and maintained the order for Claudio's death. Whatever feeling we might have had for him vanishes almost entirely. Yet that all this action takes place offstage ensures that we are emotionally removed.

The Duke now switches tactics and inquires about a prisoner named Barnardine, earlier mentioned as due for execution. He is described by the Provost:

> A man that apprehends death no more
> dreadfully but as a drunken sleep, careless, reakless,

and fearless of what's past, present, or to come;
insensible of morality, and desperately mortal.

(IV, ii, 142–145)

Such audacity is rare in the world of this play. Nonetheless, Barnardine seems doomed, for the Duke suggests that after the execution, Barnardine's head should be disfigured and taken to Angelo in place of Claudio's head (IV, ii, 170–171, 175–176). The Provost fears the consequences: "Pardon me, good father, it is against my oath" (IV, ii, 181). But the Duke subtly exerts authority: "Were you sworn to the Duke, or to the Deputy?" (IV, iii, 181). The incongruity of a friar's resorting to political manipulation places the Duke's entire role in an uncertain light. When he brings forth the letter from the Duke himself (IV, ii, 192), the willingness of the Provost to accept this evidence is another awkward plot manipulation. Furthermore, the Duke tells the Provost that Angelo has already received "letters of strange tenor" (IV, ii, 200), telling of the Duke's death or entrance to a monastery. Such compilation of detail in seemingly arbitrary fashion further strains credibility.

Scene iii continues in the prison, which has become the dominant setting, adding to the gloomy atmosphere. But Pompey's zest in reviewing the roster of his former clients, also frequenters of Mistress Overdone's house, restores some of the comic flavor. We finally meet Barnardine, who lives up to his reputation for gruffness by ignoring the call for execution (IV, iii, 28–29, 43–44). His strongest gesture is to refuse absolution offered by the Duke:

Friar, not I; I have been drinking hard all
night, and I will have more time to prepare me, or
they shall beat out my brains with billets. I will not
consent to die this day, that's certain.

(IV, iii, 53–56)

So outlandish is Barnardine's attitude that the Provost offers to substitute instead the head of another prisoner, already dead, the pirate Rogozine (IV, iii, 71–76). To keep anyone from revealing his plan, the Duke orders that both Barnardine and Claudio be kept "in secret holds" (IV, ii, 87). This command is followed by the entrance of Isabella, who expects to learn her brother has been pardoned. When she hears the Duke's report, her tone changes: "O I will to him, and pluck out his eyes!" (IV, iii, 119), a line that sounds inappropriate from the novice nun of early in the play. So does her next line:

Unhappy Claudio! Wretched Isabel!
Injurious world! Most damned Angelo!

(IV, iii, 121–122)

Her participation in the secular world has certainly changed her language and attitude. But we wonder why the Duke puts Isabella through such an ordeal. One possible answer is that this strategy will build our anticipation for the final revelation. But the torment is painful, although it may be important for Isabella to undergo this trial if she is to learn the lesson that the final scene teaches her.

The last part of this episode is Lucio's once more telling tales about the Duke. Lucio even admits to having fathered a child (IV, iii, 169–174), a story that confirms Mistress Overdone's claim about Kate Keepdown (III, ii, 198–201). But the boasting to the friar is another example of Lucio's foolishness, for why should he confide in a man who has already promised to report him to the Duke (III, ii, 161–162)?

In scene iv Angelo takes the stage briefly. He is concerned about conflicting letters coming from the Duke (IV, iv, 1) but, more important, privately confesses guilt over what he thinks was his behavior with Isabella:

> A deflow'red maid!
> And by an eminent body that enforc'd
> The law against it!
>
> (IV, iv, 21–23)

What continues to make him deserving of some sympathy, despite his ruthlessness, is this shock at his own deception. He knows that she could publicly humiliate him (IV, iv, 23–25) but also that his own reputation will protect him. At the same time, Angelo regrets that Claudio had to be killed, for otherwise he "Might in the times to come have ta'en revenge . . ." (IV, iv, 30). Such a confession hardly absolves Angelo, but it does remind us that he suffers inner turmoil. Furthermore, such psychological contortion in the midst of an unwieldy plot mechanism gives the play a depth that has vanished during the last several scenes. Thus Angelo is the villain of the play, but he is also its richest character.

In scene v the Duke continues to engineer his plan for revelation, establishing that the Provost is aware of the plot, then sending Peter to set up a processional greeting. In scene vi Isabella and Mariana review their roles in the plan. Isabella is uncomfortable making her accusations against Angelo public, but the Duke has assured her that the tactic is "a physic/ That's bitter to sweet end" (IV, vi, 7–8). Perhaps in retrospect we should understand that the Duke's scheme is not only to ensure that Angelo receive his comeuppance, but also to break down the ruthless piety Isabella has built around herself. Thus his not revealing Claudio's survival is part of that overall strategy.

We now move into the single scene of Act V, wherein the Duke maneuvers all the characters into disclosure. This scene is the only one that takes place before the populace, and thus we feel the goal of teaching and edification the Duke seeks. He makes his public return with great enthusiasm, embracing in particular Angelo:

> Give [me] your hand,
> And let the subject see, to make them know
> That outward courtesies would fain proclaim
> Favors that keep within.
>
> (V, i, 13–16)

The Duke's emphasis on secret feeling and false appearance resounds ironically.

Isabella then rushes before him to plead the cause of her brother's life. She simultaneously accuses Angelo, but the Duke seems to dismiss her (V, i, 47–48). He knows the truth, but clearly he is waiting for the proper moment and for Angelo to condemn himself. Isabella's determination recalls her earlier passion:

> O Prince, I conjure thee, as thou believ'st
> There is another comfort than this world,
> That thou neglect me not, with that opinion
> That I am touch'd with madness.
>
> (V, i, 48–51)

Once again she hints at the religious elements of the Duke's role. But she also demonstrates more earthly qualities, as she categorizes the Deputy who has victimized her:

> Even so may Angelo
> In all his dressings, caracts, titles, forms,
> Be an arch-villain. Believe it, royal Prince,
> If he be less, he's nothing, but he's more,
> Had I more name for badness.
>
> (V, i, 55–59)

As she presents her evidence, Lucio interrupts twice to support her claims, but each time the Duke autocratically cuts him off, maintaining the balance of comedy and drama. Isabella then accuses Angelo with a specific charge:

> He would not, but by gift of my chaste body
> To his concupiscible intemperate lust,
> Release my brother . . .
>
> (V, i, 97–99)

This time the Duke is even more insistent in his anger against Isabella and his defense of Angelo (V, i, 105–114). Apparently he wants all information brought out before he reveals the truth. But despite our pleasure in anticipation, we feel Shakespeare's extending the scene, albeit skillfully, for drama's sake.

Isabella needs Friar Lodowick, the Duke's alter ego, to substantiate her story (V, i, 125), and Lucio confirms their meeting. Why Lucio, ostensibly on her side, should confirm that Isabella was consorting with the mysterious friar is unclear, but after Friar Peter's accusations (V, i, 139–142) Isabella is taken away under guard. The moment gives the Duke another occasion to offer support of Angelo (V, i, 163–167), thus making the ultimate unmasking that much more powerful.

The situation is complicated by the entrance of the veiled Mariana. After a lewd suggestion by Lucio (V, i, 179–180), who is again silenced by the Duke,

Mariana denies Isabella's charge against Angelo, claiming that she was the woman he "knew" (V, i, 203). She then reveals her identity (V, i, 207–213), forcing Angelo to admit part of the truth (V, i, 216–224). But he smugly maintains he has not seen her for five years. Mariana, however, insists:

> Noble Prince
> As there comes light from heaven, and words from breath,
> As there is sense in truth, and truth in virtue,
> I am affianc'd this man's wife as strongly
> As words could make up vows; and, my good lord,
> But Tuesday night last gone, in 's garden-house,
> He knew me as a wife.
>
>   (V, i, 223–230)

This confession brings out of Angelo an ugly self-confidence:

> I do perceive
> These poor informal women are no more
> But instruments of some more mightier member
> That sets them on.
>
>   (V, i, 235–238)

Once more he speaks the truth, although he is ironically unaware of the identity of the "mightier member," and the Duke seems to go along with Angelo's claim. The Duke then follows the Provost, ostensibly to search for Friar Lodowick. With each step the Duke allows Angelo to further incriminate himself.

After Lucio mocks the absent Friar and offers some suggestive remarks about Isabella, the Duke returns, dressed in his friar's cloak, and all point to him as the instigator. The audience, meanwhile, enjoys the dramatic irony of characters, especially Lucio (V, i, 283, 304) speaking while ignorant of the deception played upon them. After enduring taunts from all, even Escalus (V, i, 305–313), who defends Angelo, the Duke, still as the Friar, speaks out:

> My business in this state
> Made me a looker-on here in Vienna,
> Where I have seen corruption boil and bubble,
> Till it o'errun the stew; laws for all faults,
> But faults so countenanc'd, that the strong statutes
> Stand like the forfeits in a barber shop,
> As much in mock as mark.
>
>   (V, i, 316–322)

Such accusation arouses anger across the stage. But the Duke's tirade is in part self-accusatory, for as he explained in Act I, scene iii, he left the city in a condition where law could be so abused and people exploited. The Duke's attacks against himself also give Lucio one last opportunity to fall into a trap, as he further blunders by claiming the Friar and not Lucio himself slandered the Duke (V, i, 331, 333–335, 339–340). How fitting, then, that Lucio should become so taken with his part that he pulls off the friar's hood and reveals Duke Vicentio.

The thrill of the moment is mocked by Lucio's guilty retreat: "This may prove worse than hanging" (V, i, 360). But then the serious consequences unfold. The first person to confess is, surprisingly, Angelo:

> O my dread lord,
> I should be guiltier than my guiltiness,
> To think I can be undiscernible,
> When I perceive your Grace, like pow'r divine,
> Hath look'd upon my passes. Then, good Prince,
> No longer session hold upon my shame,
> But let my trial be mine own confession.
> Immediate sentence then, and sequent death,
> Is all the grace I beg.
>
> (V, i, 366–374)

The immediacy of this admission is dramatically problematic. Yet throughout the play Angelo has been at war with himself, and can be understood as one who has come to hate instincts he cannot master. Thus to him this disclosure of his hypocrisy and immorality may be a relief. Yet now that he has been exposed, he can no longer live in such humiliation, and therefore seeks death. The Duke, however, orders him to marry Mariana, who is silently led away with Angelo. Neither comments, another peculiar moment.

The Duke is not yet finished, for he maintains one more fiction: that Claudio has been executed. The Duke claims to Isabella that he arrived too late to reveal himself and save her brother (V, i, 387–396). Then he comforts her in terms she has invoked constantly:

> That life is better life, past fearing death,
> Than that which lives to fear. Make it your comfort,
> So happy is your brother.
>
> (V, i, 396–399)

Perhaps this prayer-like solace is one more attempt by the Duke to shake Isabella from her state of religious fervor, and to turn her attention to this life. Given his final plans for her, that strategy is understandable. When Angelo and Mariana return, now married, the Duke insists that Angelo be punished for Claudio's death:

> The very mercy of the law cries out
> Most audible, even from his proper tongue,
> "An Angelo for Claudio, death for death!"
> Haste still pays haste, and leisure answers leisure;
> Like doth quit like, and *Measure* still *for Measure*.
>
> (V, i, 407–411)

Mariana is horrified by this decree, even when the Duke promises her a dowry and the opportunity to find a better husband (V, i, 422–425). Like Helena in *All's Well That Ends Well*, Mariana is devoted to one man, whatever his earlier slander and his flaws. Mariana then turns to Isabella to beg for Angelo's life (V, i, 430–432), and Isabella, too, joins her plea:

> I partly think
> A due sincerity governed his deeds,
> Till he did look on me. Since it is so,
> Let him not die. My brother had but justice,
> In that he did the thing for which he died;
> For Angelo,
> His act did not o'ertake his bad intent,
> And must be buried but as an intent
> That perish'd by the way.
>
> (V, i, 445–453)

"Till he did look on me" suggests that Isabella realizes and even takes some pride in her appeal to Angelo. She also demonstrates the capacity for forgiveness that has been one point of the Duke's performance from the start. Even now, though, his mission is not complete. He berates the Provost for beheading Claudio at the wrong time (V, i, 455–458) then demands Barnardine be brought before him. This respite allows Escalus to express sorrow for Angelo's transgressions, and Angelo himself to apologize again:

> I am sorry that such sorrow I procure,
> And so deep sticks it in my penitent heart
> That I crave death more willingly than mercy:
> 'Tis my deserving, and I do entreat it.
>
> (V, i, 474–477)

Once more Angelo says that he would prefer to die rather than live with the memory of his sins. By now we recognize that no matter how instantaneous his transformation may appear, he, too, has learned the strength of mercy. Thus the two extremes, Isabella and Angelo, have both softened.

After Barnardine is brought in and pardoned by the Duke (V, i, 482–485), Claudio is at last uncovered. No one but the Duke reacts orally, and his comments must capture the responses of others. In a gesture for which we have virtually no preparation, the Duke proposes to Isabella, whose silence must be accepted as assent. Now, however, we understand the Duke's treatment of Isabella, for he expects her to renounce the vows she was about to take when she appeared for the first time in Act I. Perhaps her adversity has been a curative of sorts, and we should see her as emotionally and spiritually healthy as she enters into marriage with the Duke.

Oddly, Juliet never returns to join Claudio, and thus that relationship does not resolve happily before us. But Angelo is sent off with Mariana, and we hear no objection, so we must assume that both participants are satisfied.

At this point the only character whose fate remains undecided is Lucio. In response to the Duke's threat, he begs to be let off with only a whipping, but the Duke orders him whipped, then hanged. Yet we know the play could not end with such a likeable rogue suffering execution, so we are not surprised when the Duke recalls the woman by whom Lucio fathered a child:

> Upon mine honor, thou shalt marry her.
> Thy slanders I forgive, and therewithal
> Remit thy other forfeits.
>
> (V, i, 518–520)

We remember Mistress Overdone's comment in Act III, scene ii about Lucio's promising to marry Kate Keepdown, who bore his children. And Lucio himself confessed to the Friar (IV, iv, 172–174). Thus the punishment, despite Lucio's protests (V, i, 514–517), seems fitting. Like Claudio and Angelo, Lucio has made a commitment, and he must fulfill the responsibility. The Duke then ends the play by emphasizing the theme of forgiveness, with gratitude to all.

That no one else offers any concluding sentiment emphasizes the Duke's superior status, his semi-divine role. Yet that reticence also reflects some of the difficulties this work poses. The Duke seeks to teach to both individuals and his society a lesson about justice, but even at the end we are not clear just why the Duke placed Angelo in charge, and why he allowed Angelo to abuse his power so extensively. Isabella is admirable in her courage yet so single-minded in her religious devotion that she is willing to sacrifice her brother's life. Claudio is caught in the throes of romantic passion, but has refrained from sanctioned marriage and is willing to have his sister forfeit her salvation for his life. Angelo is a merciless hypocrite but unable to control himself despite awareness of his offenses. Lucio, Elbow, and the other lower-class citizens of Vienna are good humored, but their amiability does not disguise the essential corruption of their existence.

All these contradictory elements make *Measure for Measure* difficult to grasp. The path to the happy ending is dark, and the universal manipulation by the Duke leads to a conclusion that emerges not as a natural outgrowth of the dilemma Shakespeare created but as a forced resolution imposed by him. Thus here, as at the end of *All's Well That Ends Well*, we sense a playwright stretching comedy to its limits, as if the rules of the form do not permit what he wishes to express. In his next work in the comic/romantic vein, he goes beyond those boundaries.

SUGGESTIONS FOR FURTHER READING

Battenhouse, Roy. "*Measure for Measure* and Christian Doctrine of Atonement." *PMLA* 61 (1946): 1029–1059.

Bennett, Josephine Waters. Measure for Measure *as Royal Entertainment*. New York: Columbia University Press, 1966.

Geckle, George L., ed. *Twentieth Century Interpretations of* Measure for Measure. Englewood Cliffs, N.J.: Prentice-Hall, 1970.

Hyman, L. W. "Unity in *Measure for Measure*." *Modern Language Quarterly* 36 (1975): 3–20.

Knights, L. C. "The Ambiguity of *Measure for Measure.*" *Scrutiny* 10 (1941–42): 222–233.

Lascelles, Mary. *Shakespeare's* Measure for Measure. London: University of London, The Athlone Press, 1953.

Leavis, F. R. "The Greatness of *Measure for Measure.*" *Scrutiny* 10 (1941–42): 234–247.

Miles, Rosalind. *The Problem of* Measure for Measure. New York: Barnes & Noble, 1976.

Stevenson, David Lloyd. *The Achievement of Shakespeare's* Measure for Measure. Ithaca, N.Y.: Cornell University Press, 1966.

Price, Jonathan R. "*Measure for Measure* and the Critics: Towards a New Approach." *Shakespeare Quarterly* 20 (1969): 179–204.

THE ROMANCES

In the last of his tragedies, *Timon of Athens,* Shakespeare abandoned what for him had become traditional character development and instead created a work more allegorical in nature. That tendency may be observed more fully in his final four plays, known often as "the romances," in which the playwright seems to be striving for a new dramatic form, one that incorporates elements of tragedy, comedy, and history, as well as music and dance and even fairy tales. In addition, the works have a didactic quality, as if the playwright intended to teach the audience about the meaning of life and the beliefs human beings ought to hold. Some critics have speculated that this experimental genre with its elaborate spectacle was created for the more affluent and sophisticated audience at Black-friars, a private theater.

The romances have several plot characteristics in common, many familiar from folklore. All the stories concern conflict between generations, royal families divided and children lost over extended periods of time, and the reconciliation of these families. Such accords become manifestations not only of love, but also of political and social stability. All the works involve substantial journeys, many across expanses of water, and one prevalent image is that of water as both the embodiment of chaos and the sustainer of life. In all the plays, major characters undergo great suffering, and several approach death. Yet the endings are happy, achieved with the help of magic or the influence of the supernatural. Furthermore, the good characters are almost always rewarded and the wicked punished. Thus the plays have tragic potential, but their fairy-tale-like qualities ensure that the resolutions are joyous.

Thematically the romances have several points in common. In Shakespeare's more traditional tragedies, comedies, and histories, trials endured by the characters are usually the product of the interplay between character and circumstance. Figures find themselves in situations where their own personalities and values lead to conflict. In the romances, on the other hand, a chain of causality is not always present, and characters may be victimized through no fault of their own. This arbitrariness leads them to question the purpose of existence, and a sense of mystery exists in these plays as it does in the tragedies. Yet here those characters who maintain faith and fortitude in the face of adversity are rewarded by the alleviation of their suffering.

One more element should be noted. The most important familial relationship in these plays is that between father and daughter. In each of the four romances the father suffers profoundly, and in each his daughter represents hope, the spirit of regeneration. All these daughters marry. Yet the love they have for their husband seems to reflect a love for their father. This motif is familiar from other plays of Shakespeare, most notably the greatest of his tragedies, *King Lear,* in which the title character and his daughter Cordelia, after agonizing separation, are rejoined and survive briefly together in scenes of unsurpassed beauty.

We can only speculate on why this particular relationship should be at the heart of so many of Shakespeare's plays. To be sure, it was a dominant theme of Renaissance literature and thought. But critics have also speculated that the writing of the romances coincided with the marriage of Shakespeare's daughter Susannah and the birth of his granddaughter, Elizabeth. Whatever the reason, the bond between father and daughter seems to have been profoundly meaningful to Shakespeare, embodying what these plays dramatize: joy and sadness, the transience of life, and the endurance of love.

SUGGESTIONS FOR FURTHER READING

Adams, Robert M. *Shakespeare: The Four Romances.* New York: W. W. Norton, 1989.

Felperin, Howard. *Shakespearean Romance.* Princeton: Princeton University Press, 1972.

Foakes, R. A. *Shakespeare: The Dark Comedies to the Last Plays.* Charlottesville: University Press of Virginia, 1971.

Frye, Northrop. *A Natural Perspective: The Development of Shakespearean Comedy and Romance.* New York: Columbia University Press, 1965.

Hartwig, Joan. *Shakespeare's Tragicomic Vision.* Baton Rouge: Louisiana State University Press, 1972.

Kermode, Frank. *Shakespeare: The Final Plays.* London: Longmans, 1963.

Knight, G. Wilson: *The Crown of Life.* London: Oxford University Press, 1947.

Leech, Clifford. "The Structure of the Last Plays." *Shakespeare Survey* 11 (1958): 19–30.

Marsh, D. R. C. *The Recurring Miracle: A Study of Cymbeline and the Last Plays.* Lincoln: University of Nebraska Press, 1962.

Peterson, Douglas L. *Time, Tide, and Tempest: A Study of Shakespeare's Romances.* San Marino: The Huntington Library, 1973.

Pettet, E. C. *Shakespeare and the Romance Tradition.* London: Staples, 1949.

Smith, Hallet. *Shakespeare's Romances: A Study of Some Ways of the Imagination.* San Marino: The Huntington Library, 1972.

Tillyard, E. M. W. *Shakespeare's Last Plays.* London: Chatto & Windus, 1968.

Traversi, Derek. *Shakespeare: The Last Phase.* London: Hollis & Carter, 1954.

PERICLES

Of the thirty-seven plays traditionally included in the Shakespearean canon, *Pericles* was the only one not in the First Folio, which appeared in 1623. The play's authorship remains uncertain, but the consensus of scholars is that Shakespeare may have had a hand in the first two acts, and that the last three are likely his alone. The original source of the story is the Latin tale "Appolonius of Tyre," as adapted by John Gower in *Confessio Amantis* (1385–1393). The changing of the protagonist's name was perhaps made to accommodate the lines of iambic pentameter.

Even though the opening acts may be largely the work of another writer, their structure is important. The presence of the narrator Gower lends a sense of artificiality, so that we do not react as if the story were entirely realistic. In his opening address Gower provides background about the incestuous relationship between King Antiochus and his daughter (I, 25–28), then sets the plot moving by detailing the challenge the King has established: the man who solves a particular riddle will win the daughter's hand, while anyone who attempts a solution and fails will be executed (I, 37–38).

Several aspects of the initial scene are awkward. The Princess is unnamed and speaks only a few lines, so we must accept that she is worth the risk Pericles takes by falling in love with her (I, i, 12–24). Antiochus then praises his daughter's beauty (I, ii, 27–33) and clarifies the strictness of the penalty for suitors who fail:

> Here they stand martyrs, slain in Cupid's wars;
> And with dead cheeks advise thee to desist
> For going on death's net, whom none resist.

(I, i, 38–40)

But Pericles graciously accepts the challenge (I, i, 41–55). We also note that the Princess herself hopes Pericles will win her (I, i, 59–60), and thus we accept his attractiveness, despite the lack of additional evidence.

The answer to the riddle, which is not at all complicated, is "incest," and we wonder why the King would risk discovery of such a dark secret. Furthermore, Pericles is horrified by his realization, and reveals his dismay to the Princess:

> Fair glass of light, I lov'd you, and could still,
> Were not this glorious casket stor'd with ill.
> But I must tell you, now my thoughts revolt,
> For he's no man on whom perfections wait
> That, knowing sin, within, will touch the gate.

(I, i, 76–80)

When Pericles guesses the solution, he is aware that the truth may be dangerous, as he hints to Antiochus:

> Great King,
> Few love to hear the sins they love to act;
> 'Twould braid yourself too near for me to tell it.

(I, i, 91–93)

The King, recognizing that Pericles may expose him, allows him forty days to reveal the answer. Pericles, meanwhile, knows that his life is in danger:

> One sin, I know, another doth provoke:
> Murther's as near to lust as flame to smoke;
> Poison and treason are the hands of sin,
> Ay, and the targets to put off the shame;
> Then lest my life be cropp'd to keep you clear,
> By flight I'll shun the danger which I fear.

(I, i, 137–142)

After Pericles leaves, the King orders Thaliard to kill Pericles immediately (I, i, 155–156), but the visitor has already escaped back to Tyre. Antiochus then commands Thaliard to follow Pericles and kill him, and Thaliard, invoking a charming anachronism, swears that if he can place Pericles "within my pistol's length" (I, i, 166), the murder will be carried out.

This opening scene introduces the theme of the father-daughter relationship. It also introduces the air of unreality characteristic of Shakespearean romance, as the plot proceeds independent of the individuals involved. Indeed, characters are given little opportunity for reflection or revelation of their qualities. Even Pericles remains a cipher. We have no reason to assume that he is in any way malicious, and certainly his horror at the behavior of Antiochus suggests strong morality, but otherwise we know little about him. We do not sense any conflict or struggle within him; instead he is a reactive agent. Yet we must identify with him since he is the focus of the story.

Back in Tyre, Pericles is fearful that Antiochus will ravage the city (I, ii, 16–33), and in reviewing his adventure with Hericanus, worries that Antiochus will "fill this land with arms,/ And make pretense of wrong that I have done him . . ." (I, ii, 90–91). Hericanus, with a fidelity that recalls that of Kent in *King*

Lear, suggests that both for Pericles' safety and the good of Tyre the Prince should "go travel for a while" (I, ii, 106), and Pericles agrees. Thus when Thaliard arrives, he overhears that Pericles is no longer there (I, iii, 10–13). Thaliard is grateful he need not commit murder, then departs the play. Here is another example of loose construction, for several characters in this play appear on stage briefly, contribute to the narrative, then disappear.

Scene iv introduces Cleon and Dionyza, King and Queen of Tharsus. Their city is suffering terrible famine, and Pericles' ships are, by coincidence, well stored with food. How or why we do not know. The King expresses gratitude for Pericles' aid (I, iv, 101–104), but in light of the treachery to come, that promise is ironic, the first of several ironies in the play. Yet these are ironies of circumstance, not character: thus they emphasize the arbitrary nature of existence and humanity's need to accept that arbitrariness.

For instance, at the very beginning of Act II, before scene i, Gower tells us, and the incident is acted in mime, of a message from Helicanus about Thaliard (II, 23–24), and Pericles' subsequent departure from Tharsus, when he is caught in a terrible storm at sea:

> All perishen of man, of pelf,
> Ne aught escapend but himself;
> Till Fortune, tir'd with doing bad,
> Threw him ashore, to give him glad.
>
> (II, 35–39)

Fortune buffets men about the world. And when Pericles reaches land, he resigns himself to being a victim of such force:

> Yet cease your ire, you angry stars of heaven!
> Wind, rain, and thunder, remember earthly man
> Is but a substance that must yield to you;
> And I (as fits my nature) do obey you.
>
> (II, i, 1–4)

This passage recalls King Lear's bold call to the universe, when he finds himself left at the mercy of a raging storm (III, ii, 1–9). Lear, however, challenges the heavens, daring them to do their worst. Part of the grandeur of *King Lear* and the other tragedies is humanity's struggle against the unfathomable universe. The dominant spirit of the other romances, on the other hand, is a fortitude that enables one to endure great suffering and eventually overcome it.

Pericles is rescued by three fishermen, to whom he describes himself:

> A man whom both the waters and the wind,
> In that vast tennis-court, hath made the ball
> For them to play upon, entreats you pity him.
> He asks of you that never us'd to beg.
>
> (II, i, 59–62)

Here again is the theme of man's helplessness in the face of forces greater than himself. The sea storms that literally toss Pericles and other characters about are

a symbol of those powers. At the same time the sea also protects certain characters, and thus it has qualities of a benign deity as well.

From the genial trio Pericles learns that a tournament is to be held and that
the victor will win the daughter of the king, "good Simonides" (II, i, 100).
Pericles is eager to enter but lacks armor. One of the fishermen, however,
suddenly discovers in his net weaponry that turns out to be armor left to Pericles
by his dead father. Such coincidence goes beyond credibility and suggests the
divine intervention essential to the romances. At their core is a faith in the
fundamental rightness of the world, a belief that good ultimately triumphs no
matter what the trials that must be endured. In Pericles' words:

> Thanks, Fortune, yet that after all [thy] crosses,
> Thou givest me somewhat to repair myself . . .
>
> (II, i, 121–122)

In his shabby, rusted armor, Pericles joins the parade of knights marching
before the King and his daughter, Thaisa. Their thoughtful relationship, as
dramatized initially (II, ii, 8–15), is a strong contrast to that between Antiochus
and his daughter. After five knights pass by grandly, Pericles appears, and other
lords are suspicious of him (II, ii, 48–55), but the King is intrigued:

> Opinion's but a fool, that makes us scan
> The outward habit by the inward man.
>
> (II, ii, 56–57)

He confirms a theme familiar from many of Shakespeare's works: the substance
of a person is not to be found in clothing or manner but in actions and values.

Pericles, not surprisingly, triumphs in the contest, and in scene iii Thaisa finds
herself infatuated with him: "To me he seems like diamond to glass" (II, iii,
36). Simonides, too, is impressed, and urges his daughter to approach Pericles
and learn more of him (II, ii, 64–65, 73–74). Pericles introduces himself as "a
gentleman of Tyre" (II, iii, 81), but omits his royal heritage. The King therefore
continues to assume that Pericles is merely another knight, as Simonides alleged
earlier (II, iii, 33–35), one more moment that reminds us of the theme of reality
versus appearance.

While Pericles celebrates with Simonides and Thaisa, back in Tyre comes
news that Antiochus and his daughter have been killed by lightning. Helicanus
sees the significance of this phenomenon:

> And yet but justice; for though
> This king were great, his greatness was no guard
> To bar heaven's shaft, but sin had his reward.
>
> (II, iv, 13–15)

He, too, believes in the fundamental justice of the world. With the threat of
Antiochus gone, other lords, suspecting that Pericles is dead (II, ii, 27–33),
come before Helicanus to proclaim him their sovereign. But he demurs, asking
for one year to find Pericles. The moment is strange, for we cannot be certain

what this character is thinking. Helicanus is loyal to his absent ally, but expresses no more subtle feelings about government or friendship.

Scene v returns us to Pentapolis, where Thaisa has resolved, for reasons that her father does not specify, not to marry for a year. She has, however, written to him that she intends to marry Pericles, and the presence of the other knights suggests that her oath may be a trick to discourage other suitors. The King recognizes the strength of Thaisa's will (II, v, 19), and he also approves of Pericles (II, v, 21). Nonetheless, a peculiar scene follows, when Pericles enters and Simonides shows him Thaisa's letter. Pericles thinks that he is being trapped by another father and therefore denies any passion for Thaisa (II, v, 42–48). At this rejection Simonides accuses him of bewitching Thaisa, a charge Pericles repudiates vehemently. Simonides' asides assure us that he is not serious in his denunciations, but we wonder why he puts on the charade, even after Thaisa enters. Perhaps Simonides is conducting a test of Pericles' courage or determination. In any case, until Simonides playfully forces the two to marry (II, v, 81–88), the joke is cruel although its resolution happy.

Act III opens with a speech by Gower, which is accompanied by another dumb show. We learn that Pericles and Thaisa have been married, that they are expecting a child (III, 9–11), and that Pericles has been informed of the nobles' intention to place the crown of Tyre on Helicanus. These events are told, not dramatized, as if in themselves they are of no import. What matters, instead, is the overall story and the general lesson it teaches.

In Act III, scene i, where, critical opinion suggests, Shakespeare took over the play, the tone changes;

> The god of this great vast, rebuke these surges,
> Which wash both heaven and hell; and thou that hast
> Upon the winds command, bind them in brass,
> Having call'd them from the deep! O, still
> Thy deaf'ning, dreadful thunders, gently quench
> Thy nimble, sulphurous flashes!
>
> (II, i, 1–6)

The language is more concentrated, the imagery sharper and more vivid than earlier in the play. As the storm rages over Pericles, who is on deck, Lychorida, Thaisa's nurse, tells Pericles that his wife has died giving birth. Pericles' response reflects a philosophical depth the work has not attained until now:

> O you gods!
> Why do you make us love your goodly gifts
> And snatch them straight away?
>
> (III, i, 22–24)

He begins to question the meaning of events. Like the heroes of the tragedies, Pericles searches for a pattern to existence. Yet unlike those figures, Pericles suffers solely from what happens *to* him, not because *of* him.

His shock at the death of his wife is compounded by a demand from the sailors on ship, who claim that the storm will not end until Thaisa's body is tossed overboard (III, i, 47–49). Pericles agonizes, then consents and decides to sail for Tharsus, where he hopes to leave his child, too weak to survive the sea journey, in the care of Cleon (III, i, 77–80). Pericles' instructions to Lychorida include putting his jewels in the casket with Thaisa (III, i, 65), and the word "jewels" recurs through the rest of the story. It reflects the theme of appearance and reality, for what turns out to be precious to Pericles is not stones and money but the love of family he will be so long denied.

In scene ii, back in Ephesus, Thaisa's body is recovered and brought to Lord Cerimon, whose philosophy embodies one aspect of the play:

> I hold it ever
> Virtue and cunning were endowments greater
> Than nobleness and riches. Careless heirs
> May the latter two darken and expend;
> But immortality attends the former,
> Making a man a god.
>
> (III, ii, 26–31)

His emphasis on the timelessness of human values as superior to possessions is a theme that pervades the romances. Cerimon finds within the coffin a letter from Pericles explaining that Thaisa is a queen and deserving of royal burial. Cerimon, however, is a physician of remarkable powers, and brings Thaisa back to life:

> She is alive, behold
> Her eyelids, cases to those heavenly jewels
> Which Pericles hath lost, begin to part
> Their fringes of bright gold.
>
> (III, ii, 97–100)

This intrusion of magic is an additional quality of the romances, in which natural law is suspended. We sense a playwright who wishes no longer to be confined by reality, but to dramatize beneficence and kindness rewarded, no matter how improbable the plot mechanism.

In scene iii Pericles reaches Tharsus where he tells his sad story to Cleon and Dionyza:

> We cannot but obey
> The powers above us. Could I rage and roar
> As doth the sea she lies in, yet the end
> Must be as 'tis.
>
> (III, ii, 9–12)

Here once more is resignation to the heavens. Pericles then leaves his child, named Marina (after "the sea"), and vows never to cut his hair until she is married (III, iii, 27–30). In light of subsequent events, the oath provides a way for Pericles' inner turmoil to be manifested in his appearance. This scene is followed by the brief appearance of Thaisa, who does not remember her child and expects never to see her husband again. She chooses, therefore, to devote herself to the goddess Diana. Like Pericles, Thaisa endures a time of penance or private suffering until a reunion occurs.

Act IV, which takes place years later, begins the second half of the play. Gower tells us that Marina is now grown, and we learn that for an unspecified reason Pericles has never returned to Tharsus to acknowledge her. She has been raised by Cleon and Dionyza, along with their own daughter, Philoten. But the latter has become jealous of Marina, as has Dionyza, who, as the act begins, plots Marina's death (IV, 35–40). Here again character development is weak, as all this information is told and not dramatized. Thematically, the device of the wicked stepmother further emphasizes the fairy-tale quality of the play.

Dionzya orders her servant Leonine to murder Marina (IV, i, 1–8), although he has reservations: "I will do't, but yet she is a goodly creature" (IV, i, 9). Marina then enters, mourning the death of her mother years ago in the storm. Dionyza offers a few encouraging words of love (IV, i, 31–41), then leaves Marina with Leonine, who listens to her reminiscences, then suddenly exclaims: "Come say your prayers" (IV, i, 65). Marina is shocked, for she recognizes she is about to be murdered:

> Why would she have me kill'd now?
> As I can remember, by my troth,
> I never did her hurt in all my life.
> I never spake bad word, nor did ill turn
> To any living creature.

(IV, i, 72–76)

Marina's question reflects the nature of the world of the romances. She sees no reason Dionyza would want to kill her, and neither do we. In this dramatic universe certain events take place independent of human action. Yet the world itself is not aimless and purposeless, for the evil are punished and the good do survive happily. Thus human beings are responsible for their behavior and ultimately treated as they deserve; still, the workings of providence remain inscrutable.

Leonine is moved by Marina's plea, but he cannot go against orders. Before he can act, though, pirates appear to kidnap her, and Leonine assumes that they will do his job for him (IV, i, 98–99). Instead of harming Marina, however, they take her to Mytilene, where she is sold to a brothel. The playwright's arbitrariness is never so strong as in this scene, in which the intrusion of the pirates is outlandish. But it does allow Marina to escape Tharsus and encounter a new society, where her character resonates in the most realistic portion of the work.

The brothel humor of Act IV, scene ii reminds us of similar scenes from other plays, among them *Measure for Measure*. Pander and Boult complain about the quality of women they can afford (IV, ii, 10–12), and the earthiness of their

conversation clashes with the dreamlike quality of the other action. When Boult
brings Marina to the brothel, he seeks reassurance from the pirates that she is a
virgin (IV, ii, 40–41), then assures the Bawd of the new girl's qualities:

> She has a good face, speaks well, and has
> excellent good clothes; there's no farther necessity of
> qualities can make her be refus'd.
>
> (IV, ii, 47–49)

That Marina is a virgin ordinarily would mean that she is a valuable commodity,
and thus the Bawd attempts to cheer her: '' . . . you shall live in pleasure'' (IV,
ii, 76).

But Marina's self-righteousness is dramatically intriguing, as she has no understanding of what is happening around her. Nevertheless, she sticks firmly to
her morals (IV, ii, 85). The Bawd, however, does not grasp such a perspective.
After Boult returns from advertising Marina, and reports that she is attracting
clients, the Bawd offers Marina advice on how to play the part of virgin:

> Mark me: you
> must seem to do that fearfully which you commit
> willingly, despise profit where you have most gain.
> To weep that you live as ye do makes pity in your
> lovers; seldom but that pity begets you a good opinion,
> and that opinion a mere profit.
>
> (IV, ii, 116–121)

The Bawd intends for Marina to follow such pretense. The irony is that Marina
intends to be unswerving in her purity:

> If fires be hot, knives sharp, or waters deep,
> Untied I still my virgin knot will keep.
> Diana aid my purpose!
>
> (IV, ii, 146–148)

To which the Bawd can only reply: ''What have we to do with Diana?'' (IV,
ii, 149). The contrast between the naive stubbornness of Marina and the good-
natured, if immoral, practicality of the trio provides the play's sharpest comedy.

Scene iii returns us to Tharsus, where Cleon blames his wife for what they
believe is Marina's murder by pirates (IV, iii, 2–3). But Dionzya remains un-
remorseful:

> She died at night; I'll say so. Who can cross it?
> Unless you play the [pious] innocent,
> And for an honest attribute cry out,
> ''She died by foul play.''
>
> (IV, iii, 16–19)

And she berates Cleon for cowardice (IV, iii, 23–25). They end the scene with
mutual accusations (IV, iii, 46–51), and their evil begins to turn on itself. Hence
this encounter, too, hints at affirmation of the essential justice of the world.

The next episode is pure narration by Gower, buttressed by a dumb show. Pericles at long last returns to Tharsus, learns what Cleon and Dionzya believe is the fate of his daughter, and carries out his earlier promise by swearing to withdraw from the world (IV, iv, 27–30). The scene is moving and pathetic, as the good Pericles is once again seemingly the victim of implacable fate.

The solemnity of this spectacle is balanced by the comedy of the next two scenes. Marina's influence is spreading, as the two gentlemen explain in scene v (IV, v, 6–9), and as the Bawd states with fury in scene vi:

> Fie, fie upon her, she's able to freeze the god
> Priapus, and undo a whole generation.
>
> (IV, vi, 3–4)

Despite her reluctance, Marina is the choice of a visiting dignitary, the governor Lysimachus, who, in the spirit of this play, is taken with her on sight: "Faith, she would serve after a long voyage at sea" (IV, ii, 44–45). The Bawd's warning to Marina is unintentionally ironic:

> First, I would have you
> note, this is an honorable man.
>
> (IV, vi, 49–50)

The discrepancy between the earnest admonition and the immoral profession escapes the Bawd, but we enjoy it. Lysimachus attempts to charm Marina, but she refuses to accept that she belongs in this house and profession, and her straightforward replies leave him bewildered (IV, vi, 85–91). She eventually explains that she has been made a prisoner, and Lysimachus is sufficiently moved that he gives her money and departs:

> Fare thee well, thou art a piece of virtue, and
> I doubt not but thy training hath been noble.
>
> (IV, vi, 111–112)

This persuasion enrages the keepers, and Boult in particular speaks with comic vexation. First he complains that Marina has " . . . spoken holy words to the Lord Lysimachus" (IV, ii, 133), then adds that she "makes our profession as it were to stink afore the face of the gods" (IV, ii, 135–136). The Bawd has a solution, and orders Boult to rape her and thereby break down Marina's resistance to subsequent clients:

> Boult, take her away, use her at thy pleasure
> Crack the glass of her virginity, and make the rest
> malleable.
>
> (IV, vi, 141–143)

But Marina's powers are such that she is able to resist this threat as well. First she appeals to Boult's self-worth:

> Neither of these are so bad as thou art,
> Since they do better thee in their command.

> Thou hold'st a place for which the paindest fiend
> Of hell would not in reputation change.

(IV, vi, 161–164)

He helplessly asks how else he should survive, and Marina promises to give him skills:

> Here, here's gold for thee.
> If that thy master would gain by me,
> Proclaim that I can sing, weave, sew, and dance,
> With other virtues, which I'll keep from boast,
> And will undertake all these to teach.

(IV, vi, 181–185)

So strong is Marina's faith that he agrees with her. Without force, without legal compulsion, her instinctive good surpasses evil. Such are the miracles that occur in the world of the Shakespearean romance.

At the beginning of Act V Gower reports that Marina has escaped the brothel, and now works in comparative happiness. Pericles, meanwhile, has once more been driven ashore by a storm, and arrives at Mytilene. Lysimachus, still governor, boards the ship and is told by Helicanus of Pericles' state:

> A man who for this three months hath not spoken
> To any one, nor taken sustenance
> But to prorogue his grief.

(V, i, 24–26)

Lysimachus, however, whose own perspective on life has been changed by Marina, believes she might do the same for Pericles:

> She questionless with her sweet harmony,
> And other chosen attractions, would allure
> And make a batt'ry through his [deafen'd] parts . . .

(V, i, 45–47)

Marina is soon brought before Pericles in a moment that recalls the reunion between King Lear and his daughter Cordelia. Marina speaks first, about her own troubled past (V, i, 84–94), but in an aside is touched by something else she cannot articulate:

> I will desist,
> But there is something glows upon my cheek,
> And whispers in mine ear, "Go not till he speak."

(V, i, 94–96)

Upon hearing her voice and words, Pericles has a similar intuition:

> Pray you turn your eyes upon me.
> You're like something that—What country [woman]?

Here of these [shores]?

(V, i, 101–103)

Her tone and manner remind Pericles of his wife (V, i, 106–113), and he even uses the word "jewel-like" (V, i, 110). The imminent reunion is stirring, but what also touches us is that both father and daughter instinctively sense their bond.

Pericles continues delicately to ask questions, and as Marina reveals details of her past, including the fate of her mother (V, i, 157–160), the moment of discovery grows inevitably closer. The suspense is extended to excruciating lengths, as Marina reveals her name, her royal birth (V, i, 147–149), the tragic circumstances of her birth aboard the ship (V, i, 155–156), and her father's identity (V, i, 178–179). At last Pericles bursts out with joy:

> O, come hither,
> Thou that beget'st him that did thee beget;
> Thou that wast born at sea, buried at Tharsus,
> And found at sea again!

(V, i, 194–197)

After Marina offers confirmation of her identity by revealing that her mother's name was Thaisa, the divine presence that looms over this play appears once more. First Pericles hears music that escapes everyone else (V, i, 223–226). It causes him to fall asleep, and in his dream Diana appears, telling him to go to the temple at Ephesus where he will learn the fate of his wife. Before he can hurry off, however, Lysimachus quickly proposes marriage to Marina, and Pericles consents (V, ii, 260–263). This circumstance is approved by Gower in his narrative that provides a transition to scene ii (V, ii, 9–16).

At the temple Pericles announces why he has come (V, iii, 1–13) and Thaisa, overhearing his voice, faints. In a moment of restoration that encapsulates the entire play, Thaisa regains consciousness, and mother, father, and daughter are at last reunited. Pericles tells Thaisa of the forthcoming marriage (V, iii, 70–72), and thus all the good people in the play are rewarded. Gower, in his final speech, emphasizes that the evil characters have been punished, for Antiochus and his daughter are dead, and Cleon and Dionyza have also been killed:

> The gods for murder seemed so content
> To punish, although not done, but meant.

(V, iii, 99–100)

Divine justice holds sway.

Whatever Shakespeare's precise contribution, *Pericles* remains a difficult play to evaluate. Its plot is chaotic and its language is of inconsistent quality. It may be regarded as an experiment, as the playwright grasps at a new dramatic form. The plot spans not just days or years, but generations. Royalty is lost, then rediscovered, as are family bonds. Theme, not character, dominates this work. The most important motifs are reconciliation, acceptance of adversity, and the healing powers of time and patience. Like Job, Pericles endures great and inexplicable pain, but is eventually honored for his faith.

Perhaps writing such a piece fulfilled a need in Shakespeare himself. No longer does he work within the bounds of reality or even of theatrical probability. Instead, he deals in fantasy, in which the playwright can ensure that the ending is fair and just. Such is not always the way of the world, as Shakespeare's plays have dramatized. But then the romances are not the way of the world. They are, rather, the way of Shakespeare's faith and imagination.

SUGGESTIONS FOR FURTHER READING

Arthos, John. "*Pericles, Prince of Tyre*: A Study in the Dramatic Use of Romantic Narrative." *Shakespeare Quarterly* 4 (1953): 257–270.

Brockbank, J. P. "*Pericles* and the Dream of Immortality." *Shakespeare Survey* 24 (1971): 105–116.

Cutts, John O. "*Pericles*' Downright Violence." *Shakespeare Studies* 4 (1968): 275–293.

Muir, Kenneth. "The Problem of *Pericles*." *English Studies* 30 (1948): 65–83.

Taylor, Gary. "The Transmission of *Pericles*." *Papers of the Bibliographical Society of America* 80 (1986): 193–217.

Thomas, Sidney. "The Problem of *Pericles*." *Shakespeare Quarterly* 34 (1983): 448–450.

CYMBELINE

Of all Shakespeare's plays, this one has perhaps the most intricate plot. It balances three separate stories, all intertwined and eventually resolved together. It combines qualities of tragedy, comedy, history, and pastoral with episodes of fantasy and other incidents that defy probability. Yet we never feel the playwright out of control. The dramatic technique is that of a virtuoso, and the unity of work is never in doubt.

Holinshed's *Chronicles* was probably Shakespeare's source for the background material on Cymbeline, who supposedly became King in 33 B.C., when Britain was occupied by the Romans. The playwright may also have used Geoffrey of Monmouth's *History of the Kings of Britain*. The wager story was most likely adapted from the ninth novel of the second day of Boccaccio's *Decameron*. And the third plot line, that of Belarius and his sons, was probably taken from an anonymous romantic play called *The Rare Triumphs of Love and Fortune*, first presented in 1582 and printed in 1589.

Certain elements of characterization and plot here are similar to those of other romances. Characters are separated, then reunited after extended journeys and suffering. Few of the characters are developed thoroughly, and several are little more than stereotypes. The good survive happily, and the evil are punished, so that a certain purification takes place. Nonetheless, the sequences of events implies a mystery to the workings of the world, if ultimately its beneficence.

Complications begin in the opening scene, as one gentleman outlines the situation for another and for us. The time period is that of *King Lear,* and in this play as well a father misjudges the quality of his children. Imogen, daughter of King Cymbeline by a former wife, has disobeyed her father by marrying his foster-son Posthumus rather than her stepbrother, Cloten:

> She's wedded,
> Her husband banish'd, she imprison'd: all
> Is outward sorrow, though I think the King
> Be touch'd at very heart.

(I, i, 7–10)

The last few words let us know that like Lear, this King should be understood not as villainous but as misguided. We learn further that Posthumus was the son of Sicinius Leonatus, a noble soldier who served Cymbeline well. Posthumus was orphaned soon after birth, and brought up by Cymbeline as his own. The young man has come to be regarded with respect:

> . . . most prais'd, most lov'd,
> A sample to the youngest, to th' more mature
> A glass that feated them, and to the graver
> A child that guided dotards.

(I, i, 47–50)

In fact, Imogen's choice of him confirms the worthiness of both:

> To his mistress
> (For whom he now is banish'd), her own price
> Proclaims how she esteem'd him; and his virtue
> By her election may be truly read,
> What kind of man he is.

(I, i, 50–54)

The imagery of price and value permeates the play, as does the image of jewelry in *Pericles*. Here, too, the language reflects characters' understanding the value of others and a capacity to judge by more than appearance. The second gentleman finishes his background narrative by telling of Cymbeline's other two sons by his first wife. Twenty years ago they were lost, and their fate remains unknown. Even at this early mention we anticipate the reuniting of Imogen and her brothers.

The Queen, Imogen's stepmother, enters to assuage her daughter and Posthumus:

> No, be assur'd you shall not find me, daughter,
> After the slander of most stepmothers
> Evil-ey'd unto you.

(I, i, 70–72)

The denial of the stereotype proves ironic, however, a first instance in this play of appearance being inaccurate. Not to Imogen, however, who already sees through the Queen (I, i, 84–85). Left alone, Imogen and Posthumus exchange tokens: he accepts a ring that was her mother's, she takes a bracelet. The tenderness of the emotion is undercut by the entrance of Cymbeline: "Thou basest thing, avoid hence, from my sight!" (I, i, 125). The imagery of sight recalls the anger of King Lear, who banished Cordelia and Kent in a similar tirade (I, i, 157). Like Lear, Cymbeline mistrusts his loyal children and blindly punishes them. But unlike Lear, Cymbeline is ultimately saved. Such are the conventions of romance.

Imogen and Cymbeline argue about the comparative worth of the two men involved, Cloten and Posthumus, and what impresses us most is Imogen's cour-

age. Like Cordelia, she is unafraid to speak what she knows is the truth, and
she is equally willing to express her anger:

> Would I were
> A neat-herd's daughter, and my Leonatus
> Our neighbor shepherd's son!

(I, i, 148–150)

These lines prove ironic, for Imogen's brothers are discovered in a similar
condition.

We have yet to meet the Queen's son, heretofore unnamed, but called Cloten.
Now the servant Pisanio enters to report that the prince has just been fighting
with Posthumus, who apparently did not take Cloten at all seriously (I, i, 162–
163). In the next scene we learn why, for Cloten, whose name hints at "clod"
and "clotpole," is a braggart, a parody of a young English courtier. Even his
two colleagues mutter asides about his inadequacies. He is so outlandishly arrogant that he is never a threat, and thus his outrage is comic rather than dangerous: "And that she should love this fellow, and refuse me!" (I, ii, 26).

This comedy is contrasted by the next scene, in which Pisanio tells Imogen
of Posthumus's departure. She is both comforted and pained by every detail (I,
iii, 8–14), but the quality that stands out is her loyalty, as articulated in one
speech expressing regret that she never had time to offer one parting kiss (I, iii,
25–37). This devotion becomes the strongest emotion in the play. Whatever
travails she experiences, Imogen's passion for Posthumus remains the dramatic
fulcrum.

In discussion of the comedies, we noted that women are often in love with
men undeserving of that affection. Such proves the case here, when Posthumus
is in Rome. In scene iv he participates in a debate with Jachimo, an Italian, as
well as with a Frenchman, a Dutchman, and a Spaniard. Before Posthumus
enters, the others discuss his life and banishment, but when he joins the group,
the conversation turns to the fidelity of women. Jachimo doubts that any woman
is faithful (I, iv, 63), but Posthumus affirms his trust in Imogen (I, iv, 64).
Jachimo remains skeptical:

> With five times so much conversation, I
> should get ground of your fair mistress; make her go
> back, even to the yielding, had I admittance, and
> opportunity to friend.

(I, iv, 103–106)

He is confident of his skill at winning any woman (I, iv, 110–113), and Posthumus's insistence on Imogen's devotion leads Jachimo to make a formal wager:

> I will lay you ten [thousand] ducats to your
> ring, that, commend me to the court where your lady is,
> with no more advantage than the opportunity of a
> second conference, and I will bring from thence that

honor of hers which you imagine so reserv'd.

(I, iv, 127–131)

Jachimo may be interpreted as the Italian equivalent of Cloten: an immoral young courtier, with what in Shakespeare's time was considered a characteristic Italian capacity for plotting. Yet his outright effrontery suggests he is not a pure villain but something of a scoundrel. His bet is reprehensible; yet his belief in his own attractiveness is bold. In fact, from our perspective the unseemly participant in the wager is Posthumus, who is willing to put his love to such a test. He becomes even more unattractive when he imposes a stipulation:

> . . . if you
> make your voyage upon her and give me directly to
> understand you have prevail'd, I am no further your
> enemy; she is not worth our debate. If she remain
> unseduc'd, you not making it appear otherwise, for
> your ill opinion and th' assault you have made to her
> chastity, you shall answer me with your sword.

(I, iv, 157–163)

We understand Posthumus's perspective: if Imogen does give in, she has no honor, and therefore is not worth a fight. Only if she refuses Jachimo is she the woman Posthumus believes her to be. But that he acknowledges the possibility of her capitulation suggests his faith is not as strong as he claims. And that he would put his wife through such a trial is more distressing.

Scene v, back in Britain, reveals the true nature of the Queen, who has commanded her doctor, Cornelius, to provide a poison that causes a slow, lingering death (I, v, 8–10). The depth of her malice is apparent when she pretends to have a plan to experiment with the poison on animals (I, v, 18–21). Cornelius realizes her depravity, and substitutes a poison that only feigns death:

> She is fool'd
> With a most false effect; and I the truer,
> So to be false with her.

(I, v, 42–44)

The theme of appearance versus reality recurs again. The Queen promises Pisanio a reward if he can make Imogen love Cloten, then drops what she imagines is poison and allows Pisanio to pick it up. Claiming that the box contains powerful medicine "which hath the King/ Five times redeem'd from death" (I, v, 62–63), she gives it to Pisanio, insisting it reflects future reward. But when Pisanio leaves, she refers to him as "A sly and constant knave" (I, v, 75), and indicates she hopes he will swallow the "poison" and leave Imogen friendless (I, v, 79–80). When Pisanio returns with her ladies, however, he clarifies the strength of his devotion to Posthumus:

> But when to my good lord I prove untrue,
> I'll choke myself. There's all I'll do for you.
>
> (I, v, 86–87)

His fidelity to Posthumus, like Imogen's, proves stronger than Posthumus's own character.

Scene vi is one of the most intriguing in the play. First Imogen, isolated, bemoans her fate:

> A father cruel, and a step-dame false,
> A foolish suitor to a wedded lady
> That hath her husband banish'd.
>
> (I, vi, 1–3)

She also mourns her two lost brothers, then reflects unknowingly on what will prove to be their quality of spirit:

> Blessed be those,
> How mean so'er, that have their honest wills,
> Which seasons comfort.
>
> (I, vi, 7–9)

A walking contradiction to such sentiments enters in the person of Jachimo, who has come to carry out the seduction of Imogen. He is taken immediately with her beauty:

> All of her that is out of door most rich!
> If she be furnish'd with a mind so rare,
> She is alone th' Arabian bird, and I
> Have lost the wager.
>
> (I, vi, 15–18)

Throughout the rest of the scene he is caught between two emotions: his attempt to win his wager and his infatuation with Imogen. In his plotting, Jachimo may be compared to Iago in *Othello,* who also manipulates the mind and emotions of others. But whereas Iago's attitude toward sexuality and emotion is perverse, as he clarifies in his soliloquies, Jachimo is comparatively healthy. He is lustful and unscrupulous, but he is also sufficiently sensitive that he is vulnerable to Imogen's allure.

His initial strategy is to hint that Posthumus has already broken his bond with Imogen. While she ruminates on Posthumus's letter, Jachimo pretends to talk to himself, but allows his sentiments to be overheard:

> What, are men mad? Hath nature given them eyes
> To see this vaulted arch and the rich crop
> Of sea and land, which can distinguish 'twixt
> The fiery orbs above, and the twinn'd stones
> Upon the number'd beach, and can we not
> Partition make with spectacles so precious

'Twixt fair and foul?

(I, vi, 32–38)

In his pretense, Jachimo reveals a poet within him, another distinction between
him and Iago, who has no such emotion. Here Jachimo seems more like Richard
III, who plays the role of wounded lover to entrap Lady Anne.

Imogen is intrigued by Jachimo's brooding, and she probes until he confesses
with seeming reluctance about Posthumus's self-indulgence: "He is called/ The
Britain reveller" (I, vi, 60–61). Jachimo claims to pity Imogen, then hints that
she ought to take action of her own:

> That others do
> (I was about to say) enjoy your—But
> It is an office of the gods to venge it,
> Not mine to speak on't.

(I, vi, 90–93)

Imogen notes that "both you spur and stop" (I, vi, 99), but she fails to see any
calculation behind his hesitancy. Jachimo continues to speak romantically:

> Had I this cheek
> To bathe my lips upon; this hand, whose touch
> (Whose every touch) would force the feeler's soul
> To th' oath of loyalty; this object, which
> Takes prisoner the wild motion of mine eye,
> Firing it only here . . .

(I, vi, 99–104)

He is simulating attraction to her, but that he can speak with such passion suggests
that he is not altogether without feeling. He does, however, keep up the charade,
and finally pretends to be unable to restrain himself:

> Be reveng'd
> Or she that bore you was no queen, and you
> Recoil from your great stock.

(I, vi, 126–128)

Imogen, however, is horrified by this suggestion, and even more so when Jachimo
volunteers to aid her: "I dedicate myself to your sweet pleasure . . ." (I, vi,
136). But Imogen dismisses him:

> If thou wert honorable,
> Thou wouldst have told this tale for virtue, not
> For such an end thou seek'st—as base as strange.

(I, vi, 142–144)

At this condemnation, Jachimo has no recourse but to pretend that he was only
testing her (I, vi, 162–168), and Imogen believes him. Immediately Jachimo
switches to his alternate plan. He asks Imogen to store a large box of treasures,
and she offers to place it in her bedroom. So convincing is his performance that

Imogen regrets that he must depart Britain so soon (I, vi, 204). He also entreats her to write a letter to Posthumus, a missive Jachimo will use to his own advantage. At this point Jachimo acts without any moral restraint. In subsequent scenes he becomes more complicated.

Act II returns Cloten to the stage, and his reflections on gambling losses reaffirm his shallowness and pomposity (II, i, 1–5). Even his associates scorn him:

> That such a crafty devil as is his mother
> Should yield the world this ass! a woman that
> Bears all down with her brain, and this her son
> Cannot take two from twenty, for his heart,
> And leave eighteen.
>
> (II, i, 52–56)

Such a speech distinguishes Cloten from Jachimo, two proud young courtiers. Moreover, so often is the word "Italian" brandished about during the play, as in this scene (II, i, 37, 48), that a contrast is established between the proud but indolent and even stupid English youth, and the proud but manipulative Italian. That contrast has intriguing ramifications when set against the political crisis to be dramatized presently.

A version of the social disorder is delineated by the second Lord at the end of his speech:

> Alas, poor Princess,
> Thou divine Imogen, what thou endur'st,
> Betwixt a father by thy step-dame govern'd,
> A mother hourly coining plots, a wooer
> More hateful than the foul expulsion is
> Of thy dear husband, than that horrid act
> Of the divorce he'ld make. The heavens hold firm
> The walls of thy dear honor; keep unshak'd
> That temple, thy fair mind, that thou mayst stand
> T' enjoy thy banish'd lord and this great land.
>
> (II, i, 56–65)

The parallel between Imogen and England is clear. As the country is beset by unnaturalness (a queen ruling her husband), so Imogen is under attack by forces seeking to separate her from her husband. The restoration of order in the kingdom, the dominant theme of Shakespeare's history plays, is here compared with the restoration of order in Imogen's own life.

Scene ii takes place in Imogen's room, where she is sleeping. To our mild surprise, Jachimo emerges from the large box that, as promised, has been placed there, and such an action, treacherous though it is, nonetheless comes from the tradition of farce, and prevents us from regarding Jachimo with complete detestation. So does his commentary as he circles the room, seeking evidence to prove that he has actually been with Imogen:

How bravely though becom'st thy bed! fresh lily,
And whiter than the sheets! That I might touch!
But kiss, one kiss! Rubies unparagon'd,
How dearly they do't!

(II, ii, 15–18)

Such language reveals that he is not simply trying to win a bet, but that he indeed desires her. Within Jachimo is frustrated love, and as he slinks about the room and peruses her body, the combination of pleasure and anguish grows:

Swift, swift, you dragons of the night, that dawning
May bare the raven's eye! I lodge in fear;
Though this a heavenly angel, hell is here.

(II, ii, 48–50)

After removing the bracelet and observing the mole on Imogen's breast (II, ii, 37–38), Jachimo crawls back into the trunk. If Imogen may be said to represent the nation of Britain, then Jachimo is a symbolic invader.

He is contrasted by Cloten, the representation of forces within the country that seek to destroy Imogen. In scene iii he admits he wants her only for her money (II, iii, 8–9), then attempts to woo her with music. But his lyrics are mocked by his own ugly sexual innuendo, as when he speaks of the song as if it could "penetrate" (II, iii, 27). Although Imogen ignores him, his mother encourages him to continue courtly rituals (II, iii, 44–53), so Cloten offers one of his own: bribing one of Imogen's ladies. Such tactics reflect his belief in the power of money: "What/ Can it not do, and undo?" (II, iii, 72–73). The implication is that Imogen is no more than a prostitute to be bought.

After the lady's refusal to cooperate, Imogen at last dismisses Cloten's claims of love:

... and learn now, for all,
That I, which know my heart, do here pronounce
By th' very truth of it, I care not for you ...

(II, iii, 106–108)

Cloten retorts with accusations, claiming that Imogen goes against her father, and that the marriage with "that base wretch" (II, iii, 113) Posthumus is illegal because he is not of royal birth. Imogen finally convinces Cloten of her detestation for him:

His mean'st garment
That ever hath but clipt his body, is dearer
In my respect than all the hairs above thee,
Were they all made such men.

(II, iii, 133–135)

The insult is daunting, and Cloten is so astonished by it that he cannot help repeating the phrase "his meanest garment" four times. His dazed response lends a comic touch, despite his threat of revenge (II, iii, 155), which recalls

Malvolio's closing line in *Twelfth Night*. Meanwhile Imogen notices her bracelet is missing, and asks Pisanio to order a search for it.

The action moves to Rome, where Jachimo is to confront Posthumus with verification of the conquest of Imogen. Before that demonstration, however, Posthumus and Philario consider the quarrel between Rome and Britain as to whether Cymbeline will pay tribute to the Emperor. Posthumus fears the situation could cause war:

> Our countrymen
> Are men more order'd than when Julius Caesar
> Smil'd at their lack of skill, but found their courage
> Worthy his frowning at.
>
> (II, iv, 20–23)

He is confident that his nation's army is strong. But he himself is vulnerable to another sort of attack from Rome, this in the form of Jachimo, who now enters. In a tale that he draws out in painful detail, he claims to have won Imogen's "honor" (II, iv, 53). He provides particulars of the room (II, iv, 66–75, 80–85, 87–91), then offers the bracelet. He never states absolutely that he slept with Imogen, but merely hints, and the result is similar to Iago's seduction of Othello. The victim denies what he fears, but eventually succumbs to apparently overwhelming evidence. In torment Posthumus denounces women universally:

> Let there be no honor
> Where there is beauty; truth, where semblance; love,
> Where there's another man. The vows of women
> Of no more bondage be to where they are made
> Than they are to their virtues, which is nothing. ·
> O, above measure false.
>
> (II, iv, 108–113)

His fury recalls the diatribes of Hamlet and Othello. After letting Posthumus wallow further in misery, Jachimo provides the final proof:

> If you seek
> For further satisfying, under her breast
> (Worthy her pressing) lies a mole, right proud
> Of that most delicate lodging.
>
> (II, iv, 133–136)

At this detail Posthumus begins to rage:

> If you will swear you have not done't, you lie,
> And I will kill thee if thou dost deny
> Thou'st made me cuckold.
>
> (II, iv, 144–146)

Jachimo's reply to this tirade, "I'll deny nothing" (II, iv, 146) reminds us further of Iago, whose brief responses throughout Act III, scene iii of *Othello* also let the victim destroy himself.

Left alone, Posthumus storms against all women in a lengthy soliloquy that climaxes in frenzied hatred (II, v, 19–35). We understand that Imogen has done nothing to deserve such hatred. Rather, the fault lies with Posthumus, who allowed himself to be deceived and who proved that his faith in Imogen was not nearly as strong as he had claimed. Irony resounds through his speech:

> O vengeance, vengeance!
> Me of my lawful pleasure she restrain'd,
> And pray'd me oft forbearance . . .
>
> (II, v, 8–10)

Earlier Jachimo urged Imogen take action against Posthumus, but she resisted. Now Posthumus seeks his own retribution (II, v, 32–35). We should also recognize this scene as the conquering of an Englishman by an Italian invader.

The other political struggle returns in Act III, scene i, in which Cloten has his few moments of stature. Lucius, the Roman general, is in Britain to demand tribute, but Cloten dismisses the order crudely:

> Britain's a world
> By itself, and we will nothing pay
> For wearing our own noses.
>
> (III, i, 12–14)

The Queen and eventually Cymbeline add more graceful refusals, insisting on their country's independence from Rome (III, i, 22–24, 48–61), but the impact is the same. As Lucius says:

> Receive it from me then: war and confusion
> In Caesar's name pronounce I 'gainst thee . . .
>
> (III, i, 65–66)

Cymbeline nonetheless maintains a civilized manner, and the ambassador is treated with dignity. The allegorical implication seems to be the importance of a united Britain against Rome. This image is in contrast to the family split over the marriage of Imogen and the treachery and conflict that have resulted.

In scene ii Pisanio receives a letter from Posthumus that slanders Imogen and threatens her death. The servant has no idea why Posthumus should be so enraged, and gives Imogen only the first part of the letter, which explains that Posthumus is now in Wales. Imogen's passion at this information overflows, and her faithfulness emphasizes the foolish delusions of Posthumus:

> Then, true Pisanio,
> Who long'st like me to see thy lord; who long'st
> (O let me bate!)—but not like me—yet long'st,
> But in a fainter kind—o, not like me,
> For mine's beyond beyond—say, and speak thick
> (Love's counsellor should fill the bores of hearing,
> To th' smothering of the sense), how far it is

To this same blessed Milford.

(III, ii, 52–59)

So deep are her feelings that she can barely articulate them. And over Pisanio's objections she insists on going to Milford.

When the scene switches to Wales, a new theme is introduced: the pastoral. Belarius lives with his sons in tranquility, and he extols the glories of their existence (III, iii, 1–9). Yet their restlessness reflects their true parentage of which they remain unaware. Guiderius clarifies their anxiety:

> Happ'ly this life is best,
> If quiet life be best; sweeter to you
> That have a sharper known; well corresponding
> With your stiff age; but unto us it is
> A cell of ignorance, travelling a-bed,
> A prison, or a debtor that not dares
> To stride a limit.

(III, iii, 29–35)

Belarius defends his life, dramatizing the fearful corruption by society (III, iii, 45–55), and relating the story of the false accusations of treachery that caused him to be banished from his friend Cymbeline's court (III, iii, 66–73). But when left alone he reflects sadly that he stole Cymbeline's sons. He recognizes that their royal breeding is taking hold of them, as when he relates stories from his past and they become determined to live such adventures themselves. Their clothing and mean existence cannot disguise their royal nature, and in this respect they are another variation on the theme of appearance versus reality. The two boys may also be regarded as counterparts of Cloten: English nobility uncorrupted by the ways of the court. Belarius's theft also disrupted the royal family, as Cymbeline destroyed Belarius's (III, iii, 99–103). Thus we anticipate that the reunification of that family will be accompanied by the resolution of the political controversy against Rome and the restoration of the marriage between Imogen and Posthumus.

When Pisanio and Imogen enter in scene iv, he has yet to show her the other portion of Posthumus's letter. She insists he do so (III, iv, 11–18), and the contents horrify her:

> Jachimo,
> Thou didst accuse him of incontinency;
> Thou then look'dst like a villain; now methinks
> Thy favor's good enough . . .
> Men's vows are women's traitors. All good seeming,
> By thy revolt, O husband, shall be thought
> Put on for villainy; not born where't grows,

>But worn a bait for ladies.

(III, iv, 46–57)

She blames men for the anguish women undergo. Throughout Shakespeare's comedies and romances we have seen considerable evidence in support of that belief.

Imogen then orders Pisanio to kill her (III, iv, 66–73). She would commit the act herself, but even in her fury she is, like Hamlet (I, ii, 131–132), conscious of moral law:

>Against self-slaughter
>There is a prohibition so divine
>That cravens my weak hand.

(III, iv, 76–78)

Pisanio, however, has an alternative plan. He will communicate to Posthumus that Imogen has been killed (news that should convince the Queen that her order has been obeyed), and send along a piece of bloodied clothing as proof (III, iv, 124–127). For her own survival, Imogen, who refuses to go back to court to deal with Cloten, will disguise herself as a man (III, iv, 154–155) and enter the service of Lucius, who has just come to Milford-Haven and will soon head to Rome. Such a strategy will keep her near Posthumus so that she can discover the cause of his anger. Pisanio also warns her to appear aggressive and masculine so that her masquerade will not be discovered (III, iv, 155–165). Finally, before they part, he gives her the doctor's potion, which he imagines is medicine but which is actually sleeping potion. All these strategies are appropriate to a play in which a key theme is how human nature inevitably emerges through disguise and deception.

Back at the court of Britain, Cymbeline continues his argument with Lucius over the matter of tribute to Rome. Though civility is maintained, no agreement is reached, and with the threat of war ever greater, Cymbeline agrees to have Lucius escorted to Milford-Haven. Even at this moment, Cloten remains his rude self, disdaining Lucius's hand (III, v, 12–14).

Cymbeline then turns to the matter of Imogen, whom he has not seen about the court (III, v, 29–32). The Queen fabricates an excuse:

>Since the exile of Posthumus, most retir'd
>Hath her life been, the cure wherof, my lord,
>'Tis time must do.

(III, v, 36–38)

But when a servant reports that Imogen is not to be found in her room, the Queen eagerly assumes that Imogen has run away to be with Posthumus, as she indicates to Pisanio, whom she believes loyal to her:

>Gone she is
>To death or to dishonor, and my end
>Can make good use of either. She being down,

I have the placing of the British crown.

(III, v, 62–65)

Left alone, Cloten articulates his own feelings:

> I love and hate her; for she's fair and royal,
> And that she hath all courtly parts more exquisite
> Than lady, ladies, woman, from every one
> The best she hath, and she, of all compounded,
> Outsells them all. I love her therefore, but
> Disdaining me and throwing favors on
> The low Posthumous slanders so her judgment
> That what's else rare is chok'd; and in that point
> I will conclude to hate her, nay indeed,
> To be reveng'd upon her.

(III, v, 70–79)

He has affection for her not as a person but as a commodity, as his use of the word "sells" indicates. Furthermore, her rejection of him leads to a rationalized hatred, and that, in combination with his cold passion, leaves Cloten totally unsympathetic.

After bullying Pisanio and reading the letter that reveals Posthumus's location, Cloten concocts a scheme consistent with his values. He asks Pisanio, who is pretending cooperation, for some of Posthumus's clothing; then, still replaying Imogen's remark about the "mean'st garment" (II, iii, 133–135), Cloten reveals his ulterior motive:

> With that suit upon my back will
> I ravish her; first kill him, and in her eyes . . .

(III, v, 137–138)

Pisanio brings the raiment, and Cloten, thinking he has an ally, heads off, but the servant remains loyal to Imogen and Posthumus:

> Thou bid'st me to my loss; for true to thee
> Were to prove false, which I will never be
> To him that is most true.

(III, v, 157–159)

Back in the forest, Imogen wearily wanders alone in disguise. In her loneliness she ponders the quality of citizens less fortunate than she:

> Will poor folks lie,
> That have afflictions on them, knowing 'tis
> A punishment or trial?

(III, vi, 9–11)

Like Lear stranded on the heath, she reflects how the lives of those she has never known reflect her own existence. Soon she is discovered by Belarius and his sons, and Belarius's reaction upon seeing her suggests that he intuits Imogen's nature immediately:

By Jupiter, an angel! or if not
An earthly paragon! Behold divineness
No elder than a boy!

(III, vi, 42–44)

Imogen is initially frightened by the three men, and in desperation offers them money for their food, but they refuse it. In Arviragus's words:

All gold and silver rather turn to dirt,
As 'tis no better reckon'd, but of those
Who worship dirty gods.

(III, vi, 53–55)

At this moment we think back to Cloten and Jachimo, two young men with a different perspective on wealth. Imogen refers to herself as Fidele, and a bond quickly develops between the two boys and Imogen (III, vi, 68–74). Though the disguise works, Imogen's true nature emerges, as does the instinctive affinity of royal brothers and sister.

After a brief scene between Roman senators and tribunes, which keeps before us the threat of war, Cloten enters, dressed in Posthumus's clothes: "How fit his garments serve me!" (IV, i, 2–3). He is still taken with appearance, not substance, still unable to grasp the difference between the inner and external man. He is also confident that although his "rough usage" of Imogen may anger Cymbeline, the Queen will be able to smooth matters (IV, i, 20–22). The irony here is that he will soon have to accept responsibility for his own actions.

Scene ii brings back Belarius, his sons, and Imogen, and the latter demurs from hunting because of illness. Guiderius offers to stay with "Fidele," but Imogen, whose indisposition is doubtless based on her pining for Posthumus, insists she is strong enough to remain alone (IV, ii, 9–16). The devotion of his two sons to this stranger moves Belarius:

O noble strain!
O worthiness of nature! breed of greatness!
Cowards father cowards and base things sire base:
Nature hath meal and bran, contempt and grace.

(IV, ii, 24–27)

Their nobility also impresses Imogen:

These are kind creatures. Gods, what lies I have heard!
Our courtiers say all's savage but at court.
Experience, O, thou disprov'st report!

(IV, ii, 32–34)

Both speakers, from their own perspective, emphasize the theme that true nobility may emerge in any environment. Imogen then downs what she has been told is medicine but which we know to be sleeping potion.

As the boys pay tribute to Imogen's mixture of qualities (IV, ii, 52–58), Cloten enters and is recognized by Belarius, who is afraid of being discovered and scampers away with Arviragus. Cloten attempts to establish his social status with insults (IV, ii, 72, 74–75) and his familiar values: "Know'st me not by my clothes?" (IV, ii, 81). He continues to boast and insults Guiderius, who remains unimpressed, even after Cloten identifies himself as "son to th' Queen" (IV, ii, 93). Soon they begin to duel, carrying their battle offstage. The effect is as much comic as dramatic, for Cloten is consistently belittled by Guiderius's retorts: "At fools I laugh, not fear them" (IV, ii, 96).

Belarius and Arviragus return, and Guiderius soon follows, carrying Cloten's severed head:

> This Cloten was a fool, an empty purse,
> There was no money in't.
>
> (IV, ii, 113–114)

The effect is tragicomic. To be sure, a man is dead, but that man is the irredeemable Cloten, and his slaying is characterized by the imagery of money on which he so long relied. Fearing discovery, the brothers remove the headless corpse. Belarius, meanwhile, takes pride in his sons:

> O thou goddess,
> Thou divine Nature, thou thyself thou blazon'st
> In these two princely boys! . . . 'Tis wonder
> That an invisible instinct should frame them to
> Royalty unlearn'd, honor untaught,
> Civility not seen from other, valor
> That wildly grows in them but yields a crop
> As if it had been sow'd.
>
> (IV, ii, 169–181)

He reaffirms once more the view that essential goodness emerges in any setting, and that the world itself, under the guiding hand of Nature, is fundamentally beneficent.

Back at the cave, Belarius and Guiderius hear music that they have not experienced, Guiderius notes fearfully, since the death of his mother. Under this supernatural intrusion Arviragus enters carrying the sleeping Imogen, whom they assume to be dead. Their mourning is conducted in language filled with imagery of nature. Arviragus speaks of Fidele: "The bird is dead/ That we have made so much on" (IV, ii, 197–198). And Guiderius adds: "O, sweetest, fairest lily!" (IV, ii, 201). In the rest of this episode, the mourning is conducted in language appropriate to the body of a woman, reflective of the instinctive love the brothers feel for Imogen.

Belarius still worries about the fate of Cloten (IV, ii, 243–251), and goes to retrieve the corpse. After a moving song by the brothers, he returns with Cloten's headless body, which he lays beside Imogen, intending to bury both later. This gesture leads to one of the most curious scenes in all of Shakespeare's plays, when Imogen awakens beside the corpse. At first she cannot believe her predicament: "I hope I dream" (IV, ii, 297). But gradually she recognizes the clothing of Posthumus and imagines she recognizes the rest of the body:

> I know the shape of 's leg; this is his hand,
> His foot Mercurial, his Martial thigh,
> The brawns of Hercules; but his Jovial face . . .
>
> (IV, ii, 309–311)

The recital is partially comic, especially when Imogen asks: "O Posthumus, alas,/ Where is thy head?" (IV, ii, 320–321). But it turns more serious when she conjectures that Pisanio and Cloten have conspired to murder Posthumus, and faints over the body. We think of the symbolic qualities of the scene, for the presence of Cloten's body in Posthumus's clothing, and Imogen's confusing the two men, suggests some likeness between them. Perhaps in Posthumus's current state of anger against Imogen and in his acceptance of her faithlessness, he has acquired some of Cloten's worst characteristics. Ultimately, however, Posthumus has opportunity to redeem himself, a chance Cloten is forever denied.

Imogen is discovered by Lucius and his Roman troops, including some led by Jachimo (IV, ii, 340). A soothsayer envisioned one of Jove's eagles, a symbol of Rome, as flying toward Wales and fading into the sun, and here he interprets that sign as an omen of victory (IV, ii, 352). Under questioning, Imogen, still disguised as a man, claims that the body next to her is that of her master, one Richard du Champ, and in an aside she pardons her own lie (IV, ii, 377–379). She then volunteers to serve Lucius (IV, ii, 393–394), as Pisanio originally planned, and all prepare to bury Cloten.

Back in court, disorder reigns as the fracture of the royal family grows worse. The Queen is growing ill over the absence of her son (IV, iii, 2–3), and Cymbeline wonders about the location of Imogen. Even under threat of torture (IV, iii, 11–12) Pisanio cannot help, for he truly does not know where she is. This confusion is set against the ever-approaching war (IV, iii, 23–26), and once more the connection between political and familial turmoil arises. Furthermore, Pisanio still awaits news from Posthumus over the supposed death of Imogen (IV, iii, 35–41).

In scene iv fear of war spreads into the countryside, as Belarius and his sons realize that fighting surrounds them. As Guiderius states:

> Nay, what hope
> Have we in hiding us? This way, the Romans
> Must or for Britains slay us or receive us
> For barbarous and unnatural revolts
> During their use, and slay us after.
>
> (IV, iv, 3–7)

Because of Cloten's death, Belarius hesitates to side with the Britains (IV, iv, 8–14), but both his sons are eager to fight, as their noble instincts ascend once more. Taken with their courage, Belarius joins them:

Have with you, boys!
If in your country wars you chance to die,
That is my bed too, lads, and there I'll lie.

(IV, v, 50–52)

Act V returns Posthumus to the story, as he enters alone, carrying the bloodied cloth sent by Pisanio. Posthumus blames the servant for following instructions all too well (V, i, 5–9). But Posthumus is also beginning to forgive Imogen, whatever sins she might have committed:

Gods, if you
Should have ta'en vengeance on my faults, I never
Had liv'd to put on this; so had you saved
The noble Imogen to repent, and strook
Me, wretch, more worth your venegance.

(V, i, 7–11)

And he takes off his "Italian" garments, one way of returning to his original values.

Such pangs of conscience have also struck Jachimo, as is revealed in the next scene:

The heaviness and guilt within my bosom
Takes off my manhood. I have belied a lady,
The Princess of this country . . .

(V, ii, 1–3)

Such a transformation may seem improbable, but we remember that even as he carried out his plot against Imogen, Jachimo was fighting his affection for her. Thus his repentance is not totally unexpected.

The battle then rages full force. Cymbeline is captured but quickly rescued by, of all people, Belarius and his two sons, with the help of Posthumus. This episode is retold in scene iii, by a nameless lord and Posthumus, who comments on the bravery of Belarius and the two boys in holding a wave of Romans in a narrow passage. Posthumus never mentions his own contribution, but when left alone, confesses that he sought death in battle (V, iii, 68–70). Though still a Britain, he is dressed as a Roman, and at this point almost suicidal. We may interpret his willingness to die as recognition of the error in his judgment of Imogen. He cannot know the complete story of her victimization, but he senses that truth and is haunted by it. He is then taken prisoner by Britains, who fail to recognize him as one of those who helped rescue Cymbeline.

As he lies imprisoned, Posthumus's repentance grows fuller:

My conscience, thou art fetter'd
More than my shanks and wrists. You good gods, give me
The penitent instrument to pick that bolt,

Then free for ever! Is't enough I am sorry?

                                                         (V, iv, 8–11)

Once more he offers his own life in place of Imogen's:

> For Imogen's dear life take mine, and though
> 'Tis not so dear, yet 'tis a life; you coined it.

                                                         (V, iv, 22–23)

He then falls into a sleep, during which the ghosts of his family speak of him
in rhymed verse. Sicilius, his father, lauds Posthumus's character:

> Great nature, like his ancestry,
> Moulded the stuff so fair,
> That he deserv'd the praise o' th' world,
> As great Sicilius' heir.

                                                         (V, iv, 48–51)

His mother pities the loss of his marriage (V, iv, 58–62), and his father then
blames Jachimo (V, iv, 58–68). Finally, his brothers pay tribute to his bravery
in fighting for Britain.

   This Christian spirit of forgiveness in the light of repentance is answered by
Jupiter, who descends in thunder and lightning:

> Be content,
> Your low-laid son our godhead will uplift.
> His comforts thrive, his trials well are spent.
> Our Jovial star reign'd at his birth, and in
> Our temple was he married. Rise, and fade.
> He shall be lord of Lady Imogen,
> And happier much by his affliction made.

                                                         (V, iv, 102–108)

The scene is full of contradictory religious imagery, the mythological all-pow-
erful Jupiter speaking in terms of redemption through suffering. Thematically,
however, the moment embodies the spirit of the romances. Posthumus has suffered, and will suffer more. But a benign Providence shapes the world, and
Posthumus's endurance and fortitude eventually bring him divine reward.

   Posthumus awakens to find beside him a book with a message inside:

> "When as a lion's whelp shall, to himself
> unknown, without seeking find, and be embrac'd by a
> piece of tender air; and when from a stately cedar
> shall be lopp'd branches, which, being dead many
> years, shall after revive, be jointed to the old stock, and
> freshly grow; then shall Posthumus end his miseries,
> Britain be fortunate and flourish in peace and plenty."

                                                         (V, iv, 138–144)

At the moment Posthumus understands none of this, so when his jailers come
to retrieve him, he is prepared to die: "Overroasted rather; ready long ago" (V,

iv, 152). At such a moment Shakespeare injects a touch of comedy, for the jailer demonstrates a mordant wit that recalls that of the gravedigger in *Hamlet*. The jailer even counsels Posthumus that death holds certain advantages:

> But the
> comfort is, you shall be call'd to no more payments,
> fear no more tavern-bills, which are often the sadness
> of parting, as the procuring of mirth.

> (V, iv, 157–160)

Both the jailer and the messenger who arrives moments later have sympathy for Posthumus, despite the fact they they think he is Roman. The interlude lightens the play before the final scene and the numerous revelations to come.

In Cymbeline's tent the King still searches for the young man who helped rescue him (V, v, 2–7). In the meantime Cymbeline knights the other two heroes, Guiderius and Arviragus, still unaware that they are his sons (V, v, 20–22). This ironic step is the first in restoring order to the King's family and the country itself.

Cornelius then announces the death of the Queen, who in the moments before her death managed to make a confession. She admitted that she never loved Cymbeline, but used him only to gain power, and that she also hated Imogen (V, v, 43–47), whom the Queen believed was killed with poison. Cymbeline's reaction is thematically crucial:

> It had been vicious
> To have mistrusted her; yet, O my daughter,
> That it was folly in me, thou mayst say,
> And prove it in thy feeling. Heaven mend all!

> (V, v, 65–68)

Like Lear, Cymbeline is staggered at the recognition of his blindness about his daughter, and like other figures at the center of the romances, he places his trust in Providence to right all.

When Lucius is brought in as prisoner, he asks that Fidele, his page, who harmed no one, be spared (V, iv, 83–92). Cymbeline, observing what he assumes is a young man, senses something familiar about the boy, and not only agrees to spare him, but to grant "him" a favor. While Cymbeline and Imogen confer, the stage is abuzz with asides, as Belarius, Guiderius, and Arviragus are amazed that Fidele still lives, while Pisanio notes the same about his mistress. The playwright's balancing of all these stories and characters is most adroit.

At last Imogen comes forward to ask one question of Jachimo, who had been brought in with Lucius:

> My boon is, that this gentlemen may render
> Of whom he had this ring.

> (V, v, 135–136)

The question astonishes Posthumus, who still has no idea that Fidele and Imogen are one and the same. What is particularly intriguing, though, is Jachimo's eagerness to relate all the villainy he has done (V, iv, 141–146), and the emotional toll his confession takes:

> That paragon, thy daughter,
> For whom my heart drops blood, and my false spirits
> Quail to remember—Give me leave, I faint.
>
> (V, v, 147–149)

His lengthy recital includes substantial tribute to Posthumus:

> (. . . He was too good to be
> Where ill men were, and was the best of all
> Amongst the rar'st of good ones) . . .
>
> (V, v, 158–160)

> This Posthumus,
> Most like noble lord in love and one
> That had a royal lover . . .
>
> (V, v, 170–172)

> He, true knight,
> No lesser of her honor confident
> Than I did truly find her . . .
>
> (V, v, 186–188)

Jachimo conveniently ignores all the sordid aspects of the bet and Posthumus's attitude that we observed in Act I, scene iv. The long speeches, which are interrupted comically by an impatient Cymbeline, also include a humorous note, when Jachimo reflects on his days visiting Cymbeline's court before he attempted to win the wager:

> Being thus quench'd
> Of hope, not longing, mine Italian brain
> Gan in your duller Britain operate
> Most vildly . . .
>
> (V, v, 195–198)

The contrast between the two cultures is emphasized repeatedly.

At Jachimo's revelations, Posthumus charges in fury, angry more with his own blindness and stupidity than with Jachimo:

> I am Posthumus,
> That kill'd thy daughter—villain-like, I lie—
> That caus'd a lesser villain than myself,
> A sacrilegious thief, to do't.
>
> (V, v, 217–220)

At his agonizing cry for Imogen she rushes forward, but Posthumus is still unaware of her disguise and strikes her, causing Pisanio to hurry to her aid. Her identity is then revealed, but she is still angry at Pisanio for giving her what she imagines was poison (V, iv, 236–237). Cornelius, conveniently, is present to explain that particular confusion (V, iv, 240–258), and Imogen and Pisanio are reconciled. Most important, Imogen kneels before Cymbeline to ask his blessing, and father and daughter are at last together.

After Cymbeline reveals the Queen's death, his only remaining question concerns the fate of Cloten, and Pisanio is forced to confess that he directed Cloten to Milford-Haven (V, v, 278–285). Guiderius supplies the rest of the information:

> The wrongs he did me
> Were nothing prince-like; for he did provoke me
> With language that would make me spurn the sea
> If it could so roar to me. I cut off 's head,
> And am right glad he is not standing here
> To tell this tale of mine.

(V, v, 292–297)

At this report Cymbeline reluctantly orders Guiderius condemned for killing Cloten (V, v, 299). But now, at long last, Belarius is forced to reveal himself (V, v, 332–352) and the kidnapping years before of Cymbeline's sons. Belarius imparts this information to the wonderment of all, especially Cymbeline:

> O, what, am I
> A mother to the birth of three? Ne'er mother
> Rejoic'd deliverance more. Blest pray you be,
> That after this strange starting from your orbs,
> You may reign in them now! O Imogen,
> Thou has lost by this a kingdom.

(V, v, 368–373)

He characteristically refers to the political implications of this discovery, for the reuniting of the royal family is also the re-establishment of the ruling dynasty. Imogen, with the warmth and love she has demonstrated throughout the play, sees the bringing together of family and kingdom from a different perspective: "I have got two worlds by't" (V, v, 374). Indeed, so pervasive is the atmosphere of absolution that even Jachimo is influenced. He offers the ring and bracelet to Posthumus and begs forgiveness, and Posthumus pardons him (V, v, 412–420).

All that remains is for the soothsayer to explain the message from Jupiter. Leonatus, Posthumus's father, was the lion, and Posthumus the whelp embraced by Imogen, the "piece of tender air" (V, v, 446). Cymbeline is the stately cedar, Guiderius and Arviragus the branches. The political implications take hold when Cymbeline agrees to pay tribute to Caesar, and the two empires of Britain and Rome are united. Such an alliance should not be viewed as the conquering of Britain by Rome, for in the play Britain triumphs militarily. Instead, the combination of the two countries, before Christianity, and centuries before the split between Rome and the Church of England, should be understood as the foundation for an English culture that endured through Shakespeare's day. Thus the two nations become one, as does the family, and Cymbeline ends the play with the appropriate tribute:

> Laud we the gods,
> And let our crooked smokes climb to their nostrils
> From our blest altars.

(V, v, 476–478)

The final thought is an expression of faith in the benign universe.

The dazzling plot is a most impressive aspect of *Cymbeline*. But its most stirring figure is Imogen, who embodies the best of Shakespeare's heroines. Like Desdemona in *Othello,* she is accused unjustly by an irrationally jealous husband in whom she never loses faith. Like Rosalind in *As You Like It,* she bravely retreats to the forest where she carries on successfully in the disguise of men's clothes. Like Cordelia in *King Lear,* she forgives her father and is ultimately reunited with him.

Yet the conjunctive character is Cymbeline. He has comparatively little stage time, but in him are integrated the two major lines of the story: the schisms in political and family order. His words, actions, and values separate the family, and his learning and growth bring the family and nation together. Most important, in his development from a despot blind to reality to a noble king redeemed by love and forgiveness is the spirit of Shakespearean romance.

SUGGESTIONS FOR FURTHER READINGS

Brockbank, J. P. "History and Histrionics in *Cymbeline." Shakespeare Survey* 11 (1958): 42–49.

Carrington, Norman. *Cymbeline.* London: Brodie, 1954.

Kirsch, Arthur C. "*Cymbeline* and Coterie Dramaturgy." *ELH* 34 (1967): 285–306.

Ribner, Irving. "Shakespeare and Legendary History: *Lear* and *Cymbeline." Shakespeare Quarterly* 7 (1956): 47–52.

Siemon, James E. "The Significance of *Cymbeline." Shakespeare Survey* 10 (1976): 41–49.

Taylor, Michael. "The Pastoral Reckoning in *Cymbeline." Shakespeare Survey* 36 (1983): 97–106.

Thorne, William B. "*Cymbeline*: 'Lopp'd Branches' and the Concept of Regeneration." *Shakespeare Quarterly* 20 (1969): 143–159.

THE WINTER'S TALE

The themes of reconciliation and forgiveness integral to Shakespearean romance are nowhere more movingly dramatized than in *The Winter's Tale,* a work that shows the playwright gaining control as he works in this yet experimental form. The story, adapted from the novel *Pandasto* (1588) by Robert Greene, is carefully structured in two parts, and, like *Cymbeline,* incorporates elements of tragedy, history, comedy, and pastoral. Here, too, we feel an allegorical tone, although it is balanced by realistic emotions and desires.

The work begins with a scene of exposition, as Camillo and Archidamus provide the background on Leontes, King of Sicilia, and his friend from boyhood, Polixenes, King of Bohemia. After Archidamus comments on the insufficiency of Bohemian hospitality, and hints at competition between the countries, Camillo dramatizes in detail the friendship of the two rulers (I, i, 21–32), and this bond appears so extraordinary that it invites challenge. The two speakers also dwell briefly on the winsomeness of Mamillius, Leontes's son:

> They that went on
> crutches ere he was born desire yet their life to see
> him a man.

(I, i, 39–41)

Mamillius is thus presented as the embodiment of the future: the spirit of life manifested in youth. In light of subsequent events, such faith in this particular young person proves ironic.

Scene ii introduces the main characters, and minor tension between them arises at once. Polixenes announces that he has been away from his homeland for nine months and is now prepared to return home (I, ii, 1–9). Leontes, somewhat perfunctorily, requests that his friend stay, and as Polixenes refuses elegantly, Leontes insists, although with curt sentences (I, ii, 9–10, 15–16, 17, 18–19). Thus the anxiety is exacerbated. Leontes then asks Hermione to make the request, and she complies, although not without a gibe at Leontes: "You, sir,/ Charge him too coldly" (I, ii, 29–30). She then attempts her persuasion playfully, first hinting that Polixenes wishes to see his son (I, i, 34), then joking that she will keep Polixenes prisoner (I, i, 52). All this badinage seems genial, but a hint of sexual innuendo lies beneath.

That insinuation begins to surface when Hermione asks the two men about their youth. Polixenes responds that both were innocent then (I, ii, 67–74), but Hermione does not accept this answer: "By this we gather/ You have tripp'd since" (I, ii, 75–76). She anticipates hearing their sins. Polixenes then speaks of both his wife and Hermione as "temptations" (I, ii, 77), and Hermione picks up his cue:

> Yet go on,
> Th' offenses we have made you do we'll answer,
> If you first sinn'd with us, and that with us
> You did continue fault, and that you slipp'd not
> With any but with us.
>
> (I, ii, 82–86)

After such suggestive remarks, which imply that women have led men down a path of evil, Leontes returns from another conversation to ask if Polixenes will be staying. "He'll stay, my lord" (I, ii, 87) is Hermione's confident answer, but Leontes is disturbed: "At my request he would not" (I, ii, 87). Hermione turns to flirt with Leontes, recalling their courtship, all the while keeping an eye on Polixenes:

> Why, lo you now! I have spoke to th' purpose twice:
> The one for ever earn'd a royal husband;
> Th' other for some while a friend.
>
> (I, ii, 106–108)

At this moment the atmosphere, sexually charged since the reference to nine months in the opening line of the scene, invades Leontes' personality. He mutters an aside:

> Too hot, too hot!
> To mingle friendship far is mingling bloods.
>
> (I, ii, 108–109)

And he seethes over the frivolous comments and gestures his wife and best friend have exchanged. Angrier still, he calls over his son: "Art thou my boy?" (I, i, 120). Then he looks back to Hermione and Polixenes: "Still virginalling/ Upon his palm?" (I, ii, 125–126). Once more he asks Mamillius a question: "Art thou my calf?" (I, ii, 127).

The impact here is peculiar. Leontes has no specific evidence on which to base his suspicion, but the emotion nonetheless consumes him. Yet Shakespeare has provided just enough detail so that the overwhelming jealousy is understandable. Leontes is no Othello, who is gradually twisted by Iago into a state of irrational rage. Instead Leontes is possessed by a madness from within himself, spurred on by circumstantial evidence.

Indeed, so wound up is Leontes that his lines become contorted almost beyond comprehension:

> Affection! thy intention stabs the centre.
> Thou dost make possible things not so held,
> Communicat'st with dreams (how can this be?)
> With what's unreal thou co-active art,
> And fellow'st nothing. Then 'tis very credent
> Thou mayst co-join with something, and thou dost
> (And that beyond commission), and I find it
> (And that to the infection of my brains
> And hard'ning of my brows).
>
> (I, ii, 138–146)

The thought here seems to be that what Leontes views before him has the capacity to destroy his rationality, but the speech is very confusing, so much so that we identify with Polixenes as he asks: "What means Sicilia?" (I, ii, 147). At last Hermione, who has been blissfully casual throughout the scene, notices that Leontes is perturbed:

> You look
> As if you held a brow of much distraction.
> Are you mov'd, my lord?
>
> (I, ii, 148–150)

Leontes does not answer directly, but rambles about his past, then asks Polixenes his feelings about Mamillius. The response is affectionate, as we might expect (I, ii, 165–171), but we sense that for Leontes it is further proof of Polixenes' adultery with Hermione, who tells Leontes that she and Polixenes are headed to the "garden" (I, ii, 178), a word with connotations of Eden and corrupted innocence.

Although Leontes does not articulate such ideas, he is horrified by the signals of intimacy between his wife and best friend. Left alone, he withdraws into himself, like Posthumus in *Cymbeline,* universalizing his dilemma into a general condemnation of female infidelity:

> Nay, there's comfort in't,
> Whiles other men have gates, and those gates open'd,
> As mine, against their will. Should all despair
> That have revolted wives, the tenth of mankind
> Would hang themselves.
>
> (I, ii, 196–200)

Even Mamillius's statement, "I am like you [they] say" (I, ii, 207), cannot soothe Leontes. He calls over Camillo and begins a roundabout sequence of questions and ironic commentary, revealing his own warped state.

But the trusted servant has no idea what Leontes is suggesting. Thus he responds innocently when Leontes asks why Polixenes is staying:

To satisfy your Highness and the entreaties
Of our most gracious mistress.

(I, ii, 232–233)

Leontes, however, seizes the word "satisfy" and its sexual implications as further proof of Hermione's infidelity and accuses Camillo himself of treachery (I, ii, 235–241).

The dramatization of Leontes' madness feeding on itself is gripping. He pays no attention to Camillo, who calmly defends himself against Leontes' charges of negligence, foolishness, and cowardice (I, ii, 249–267). Instead Leontes relentlessly articulates his accusations in long, windy sentences that betoken a man out of control:

If thou wilt confess,
Or else be impudently negative,
To have eyes nor ears nor thought, then say
My wife's a [hobby]-horse, deserves a name
As rank as any flax-wench that puts to
Before her troth-plight: say't and justify't.

(I, ii, 273–278)

When Camillo continues to support Hermione, Leontes rants tellingly:

Is whispering nothing?
Is leaning cheek to cheek? is meeting noses?
Kissing with inside lip? stopping the career
Of laughter with a sigh (a note fallible
Of breaking honesty)? horsing foot on foot?
Skulking in corners? wishing clocks more swift?
Hours, minutes? noon, midnight? and all eyes
Blind with the pin and web but theirs, theirs only,
That would unseen be wicked? Is this nothing?
Why then the world and all that's in't is nothing,
The covering sky is nothing, Bohemia nothing,
My wife is nothing, nor nothing have these nothings,
If this be nothing.

(I, ii, 284–296)

In the first part of this speech Leontes is plainly fabricating evidence. Something in his makeup causes him to see every action in the worst light, and possibly to imagine others. How much detail we can believe is uncertain, as is the matter of whether this behavior is the result of frustrated sexual desire on Leontes' part or some other psychological imbalance. We do know that Leontes is driving himself toward madness. In the second part of the speech, his emphasis on "nothing" recalls King Lear, who dwells on that same word. Here Leontes is ironically accurate, for his fanaticism will in fact leave him with "nothing," and all his world will soon be as meaningless as he intimates it has become.

A few lines later Leontes invokes one of the central images of the play:

> Were my wive's liver
> Infected as her life, she would not live
> The running of one glass.
>
> (I, ii, 304–306)

Camillo picks up that image of disease: "Who does infect her?" (I, ii, 306). Leontes blames Polixenes; and Camillo, who speaks with the courage of Kent from *King Lear,* professes astonishment (I, ii, 321–324). But Leontes refuses to listen and orders Camillo to poison Polixenes (I, ii, 316–318, 347–349). Left alone after Leontes storms off, Camillo realizes he is torn between obedience to his lord and to his own conscience, and resolves to leave Sicilia (I, ii, 351–363).

At this moment Polixenes enters, and comments on Leontes' altered manner (I, ii, 368–375). Camillo broaches the subject gently, reaffirming the central motif of this opening act:

> There is a sickness
> Which puts some of us in distemper, but
> I cannot name the disease, and it is caught
> Of you that yet are well.
>
> (I, ii, 384–387)

At first Polixenes is baffled: "A sickness caught of me, and yet I well?" (I, ii, 398). But Camillo reluctantly clarifies Leontes' order: "I am appointed him to murther you" (I, ii, 412). When he realizes his predicament, Polixenes echoes the same theme:

> O then, my best blood turn
> To an infected jelly, and my name
> Be yok'd with his that did betray the Best!
>
> (I, ii, 417–419)

The last reference is to Jesus, and is one of several that suggest to some commentators that the play is in part a Christian allegory about transgression and forgiveness. Camillo then offers his services to Polixenes (I, ii, 437–441), who articulates the danger of a great man's anger (I, ii, 451–457). Thus the two have no choice but to escape.

Act II, scene i offers a brief respite from Leontes' fury, as Mamillius charmingly jokes with his mother's ladies. His mocking of women's faces (II, i, 12) may be an ironic echo of Leontes' accusations. This appearance is Mamillius's last, and his manner confirms for us the familial joy Leontes is about to shatter. Mamillius also echoes the play's title when he offers to tell a story: "A sad tale's best for winter" (II, i, 25). Perhaps this line is a suggestion that the entire play may be regarded as a fairy tale.

But the momentary happiness disappears with the entrance of Leontes. When he learns that Polixenes and Camillo have left by ship, he shouts that his suspicions were justified:

> There may be in the cup
> A spider steep'd, and one may drink; depart,
> And yet partake no venom (for his knowledge
> Is not infected), but if one present
> Th' abhorr'd ingredient to his eye, make known
> How he hath drunk, he cracks his gorge, his sides,
> With violent hefts. I have drunk, and seen the spider.

(II, i, 39–45)

In this bizarre image we sense madness, a man fixated on proving his misconceptions to be reality. Now he turns to Mamillius and Hermione:

> Bear the boy hence, he shall not come about her.
> Away with him! and let her sport herself
> With that she's big with, for 'tis Polixenes
> Has made thee swell thus.

(II, i, 59–62)

His attack grows increasingly vulgar:

> Praise her but for this her without-door form,
> (Which on my faith deserves high speech) and straight
> The shrug, the hum or ha (these petty brands
> That calumny doth use—O, I am out—
> That mercy does, for calumny will sear
> Virtue itself) . . .

(II, i, 69–74)

> . . . that she's
> A bed-swerver, even as bad as those
> That vulgars give bold'st titles; ay, and privy
> To this their late escape.

(II, i, 93–95)

The contorted, irregular rhythms of his verse reflect the twisted paths of his mind. In *Othello,* the language of the title character changes under Iago's influence. Here Leontes does all the damage to himself. Yet Hermione maintains her dignity:

> Should a villain say so,
> The most replenish'd villain in the world,
> He were as much more villain: you, my lord,
> Do but mistake.

(II, i, 78–81)

Even after Leontes orders her to prison, she tries to excuse him:

> There's some ill planet reigns;
> I must be patient, till the heavens look

With an aspect more favorable.

(II, i, 105–107)

The responsibility, though, rests with Leontes. Moments later, with her husband still fuming, Hermione departs with her ladies-in-waiting.

At her exit, Leontes is beseiged by protests, notably from Antigonus, who swears by his own children that Hermione must be true (II, i, 143–150). But Leontes is maddeningly confident of his own judgment: "We need no more of your advice" (II, i, 168). And in his irrationality he continues to take all events, such as the flight of Camillo and Polixenes (II, i, 174–179), as evidence. Yet he makes one peculiar order:

> ... I have dispatch'd in post
> To sacred Delphos, to Apollo's temple,
> Cleomines and Dion, whom you know
> Of stuff'd sufficiency. Now, from the oracle
> They will bring all, whose spiritual counsel had,
> Shall stop or spur me.

(II, i, 182–187)

He claims his reason for this errand is to "Give rest to th' minds of others ... " (II, i, 191). But his doing so is not consistent with his mental state, for he seems so far gone that he would not care what anyone else thinks. Nonetheless, the possibility of the revelation builds audience anticipation that the truth will come out and that Leontes will be brought to his senses.

Before that news arrives, however, the action moves to prison, where Hermione has just given birth to a little girl. Paulina, Antigonus's wife and Hermione's confidante, asks to see the Queen, but when denied permission (II, ii, 7–8), manages to speak to Emilia, one of the ladies in attendance. Learning that the baby is a girl, Paulina hopes the infant will change Leontes' perspective:

> We do not know
> How he may soften at the sight o' th' child:
> The silence often of pure innocence
> Persuades when speaking fails.

(II, ii, 37–40)

Eventually this child does change Leontes. But that time is far off, and presently Paulina's hope is thwarted. One measure of her character, though, is indicated when a prison guard challenges her right to take the child out (II, ii, 54–56). Paulina's reply leaves no doubt as to her inner strength:

> This child was prisoner to the womb, and is
> By law and process of great Nature thence
> Freed and enfranchis'd, not a party to
> The anger of the King, nor guilty of

(If any be) the trespass of the Queen.

(II, ii, 57–61)

Faced with such intrepidity, the guard lets her pass.

In scene iii Leontes has not changed his attitude. Like Macbeth, he suffers from lack of sleep (II, iii, 1), and he continues to talk himself into a state of anger (II, iii, 3–6). A servant brings the news that Mamillius is ill, but Leontes has an explanation:

> To see his nobleness,
> Conceiving the dishonor of his mother!

(II, iii, 12–13)

We suspect another reason. The boy may well suffer because he sees the mother he loves injured and humiliated. But so absorbed is Leontes in his own antagonism that he is incapable of judging rationally, as he indicates by assuming that Camillo and Polixenes are somewhere mocking him (II, iii, 23–24).

When Paulina works her way past Antigonus to see Leontes, the King mocks her husband: "What? canst not rule her?" (II, iii, 46). He is bolstering his own ego by sneering at other married men. Leontes orders her away, but Paulina stands her ground: "Let him that makes but trifles of his eyes/ First hand me" (II, iii, 63–64). In many external ways, including age and occupation, Paulina reminds us of semi-comic figures like the Nurse in *Romeo and Juliet*. But throughout her scenes she displays courage that gives the play an underlying sense of hope. At this point she brings the infant to Leontes, but the King's reaction is not what she expected. To Antigonus he exclaims:

> Give her the bastard,
> Thou dotard, thou art woman-tir'd; unroosted
> By thy Dame Partlet here. Take up the bastard,
> Take't up, I say; give't to thy crone.

(II, iii, 74–77)

When Paulina fights back, claiming the child is his, Leontes' vituperation grows more extreme:

> This brat is none of mine,
> It is the issue of Polixenes.
> Hence with it, and together with the dam
> Commit them to the fire!

(II, iii, 93–96)

The reference to Hermione with the animalistic term "dam" and the order to burn mother and child are so extreme that Leontes is virtually beyond sympathy. The fury of the moment is temporarily undercut, however, when Antigonus, ordered to hang Paulina, comments:

> Hang all the husbands
> That cannot do that feat, you'll leave yourself

Hardly one subject.

(II, iii, 110–112)

But the comic desperation does not change Leontes' mood. Nor does it alter the horror of this episode. The only redeeming words are spoken by Paulina, who reacts to Leontes' brutality with resoluteness:

> I'll not call you tyrant;
> But this most cruel usage of your queen
> (Not able to produce more accusation
> Than your own weak-hing'd fancy) something savors
> Of tyranny, and will ignoble make you,
> Yes, scandalous to the world.

(II, iii, 116–121)

Despite her efforts, Paulina is expelled from the room, although she leaves the child behind, perhaps in the hope that it may soften Leontes. He again orders it burnt (II, iii, 140–141), but under pleas from Antigonus and other lords relents (II, iii, 157–158). He does, however, demand a terrible act of retribution from Antigonus:

> We enjoin thee,
> As thou art liegeman to us, that thou carry
> This female bastard hence, and that thou bear it
> To some remote and desert place quite out
> Of our dominions, and that there thou leave it
> (Without more mercy) to its own protection,
> And favor of the climate.

(II, iii, 173–179)

Such stranding of a child recalls many stories from mythology, the most famous being that of Oedipus. The order is meant to be a sentence of death, but given the conventions of the genre, we expect to see this child again. Antigonus departs with resignation, a tone in vital contrast to his wife's defiance:

> Come on, poor babe.
> Some powerful spirit instruct the kites and ravens
> To be thy nurses!

(II, iii, 185–187)

The scene closes with the news that messengers from the oracle have returned, and Leontes eagerly anticipates the condemnation of "Our most disloyal lady . . ." (II, iii, 203), although he ends by pretending he seeks "A just and open trial" (II, iii, 205).

Act III, scene i allows us another moment's respite from the tension of the main story, as Cleomines claims that he, like all others but Leontes, believes in Hermione's innocence:

> These proclamations,
> So forcing faults upon Hermione,

I little like.

(III, i, 15–17)

In addition, Dion's awestruck words emphasize the authority of the oracle's decree:

> When the oracle
> (Thus by Apollo's great divine seal'd up)
> Shall the contents discover, something rare
> Even then will rush to knowledge.

(III, i, 18–21)

After these remarks, opposition to the divine words will be understood as blasphemous.

In scene ii, Leontes announces that he intends the trial to be fair (III, ii, 1–8), but we suspect the outcome is ordained. The charges are read, and they also include one beyond adultery:

> . . . and conspiring with
> Camillo to take away the life of our sovereign lord the
> King, thy royal husband . . .

(III, ii, 15–17)

This accusation has not been made before, but given the extent of Leontes' fury and his separation from reality, we should not be surprised at his extending the accusations as far as possible.

Hermione conducts herself with her accustomed dignity and articulates her faith with assurity:

> But thus, if pow'rs divine
> Behold our human actions (as they do),
> I doubt not then but innocence shall make
> False accusation blush, and tyranny
> Tremble at patience.

(III, ii, 28–32)

She does not avoid the concept of tyranny, as Paulina did (II, iii, 116). And her composed answers to Leontes' charges suggest her innocence:

> For Polixenes
> (With whom I am accus'd), I do confess
> I lov'd him as in honor he required . . .
> Now for conspiracy,
> I know not how it tastes, though it be dish'd
> For me to try how. All I know of it
> Is that Camillo was an honest man . . .

(III, ii, 61–74)

Leontes, though, pays no attention, and attacks her once more: "Your actions are my dreams" (III, ii, 82). He virtually acknowledges that he is the victim of his own delusions:

You had a bastard by Polixenes,
And I but dream'd it.

(III, ii, 83–84)

Then he demonstrates that his trial is in fact a sham when he admits that he has
already punished the newly born child:

... for as
Thy brat hath been cast out, like to itself,
No father owning it (which is indeed
More criminal in thee than it), so thou
Shalt feel our justice; in whose easiest passage
Look for no less than death.

(III, ii, 86–91)

As his anger grows more intense, Hermione becomes more sedate, even resigned.
She confesses that life holds nothing for her:

The crown and comfort of my life, your favor,
I do give lost, for I do feel it gone,
But know not how it went. My second joy
And first-fruits of my body, from his presence
I am barr'd, like one infectious. My third comfort
(Starr'd most unluckily) is from my breast
(The innocent milk in it most innocent mouth)
Hal'd out to murther ...

(III, ii, 94–102)

The repetition of the word "infectious" suggests that a disease has taken over
the court, and we accept that illness to be Leontes' madness. When Cleomines
and Dion enter with the judgment of the oracle, events follow swiftly. First the
order is read:

"Hermione is chaste, Polixenes
blameless, Camillo a true subject, Leontes a jealous
tyrant, his innocent babe truly begotten, and the King
shall live without an heir, if that which is lost be not
found."

(III, ii, 132–136)

The brevity of this speech, with one statement of fact succeeding another, increases the dramatic potency. So do the quick rejoinders in support, but they
are negated by Leontes' stunning rejection:

There is no truth at all i' th' oracle.
The sessions shall proceed; this is more falsehood.

(III, ii, 140–141)

No one has time to respond to this outrageous breach of order. Instead a servant
rushes in to reveal the death of Mamillius. Hermione faints, and Paulina im-

mediately claims that her mistress is dying. Leontes denies that charge, but clearly takes the death of Mamillius as punishment for his own transgression:

> I have too much believ'd mine own suspicion.
> Beseech you tenderly apply to her
> Some remedies for life.

(III, ii, 151–153)

And after Hermione is carried out, Leontes offers a universal apology (III, ii, 155–172).

The suddenness of this reversal is in keeping with the tone of the play. Leontes' original fixation upon his wife's treachery came upon him almost instantaneously. Thus the relinquishing of his fury should follow with equal speed. Furthermore, this play is not about the psychological development of jealousy. It is about the consequences of that jealousy and the time for repentance. The first half of the story has therefore almost ended.

It does not conclude until Paulina lashes out against Leontes, restating all his crimes (III, ii, 175–198). She waits until the end of her indictment to announce the most tragic news: the death of Hermione. Leontes has no immediate reply, and Paulina assumes he is beyond redemption:

> Do not repent these things, for they are heavier
> Than all thy woes can stir; therefore betake thee
> To nothing but despair.

(III, ii, 208–210)

Leontes, though, has changed, as he reveals when he does not dispute her charge:

> Thou canst not speak too much, I have deserv'd
> All tongues to talk their bitt'rest.

(III, ii, 215–216)

Such a response takes Paulina aback, and she apologizes for her denunciation (III, ii, 218–225). Her words indicate further that she does in fact see potential for repentance. She also swears that no longer will she speak of the Queen or of Leontes' children (III, ii, 229–231). For his part, Leontes promises to visit daily the chapel where his wife and child will be buried (III, ii, 236–240). Thus his spiritual renewal begins.

Scene iii concludes the first half of the play, as Antigonus, according to Leontes' orders, prepares to leave the infant in the wilds. The mariner offers a word of caution that seems irrelevant, but which proves ironic:

> Besides, this place is famous for the creatures
> Of prey that keep upon't.

(III, iii, 10–13)

The line will refer not only to animals, but also to a comic human equivalent.

Unaware of events at court, Antigonus is haunted by the image of Hermione that appeared to him in a dream, for she promised that by committing this act he would never see again his own wife, Paulina (III, iii, 27–36). As a storm approaches, he lays down the child, named Perdita according to the vision's command. Antigonus is sad that the infant will die because of the sins of the mother (III, iii, 50), but surprisingly he is the one who perishes, as a notorious stage direction indicates at line 58: "*Exit pursued by a bear.*" This death may seem unjustified, for we recognize that Antigonus is a decent man. Yet he has followed what he knows to be an immoral command from Leontes, and therefore unlike those who have risked their lives to act according to conscience, including Camillo and Paulina, Antigonus is forced to surrender his life.

The child is discovered by a shepherd, who complains of the indolence of the youth of his day (III, iii, 59–64). His is a light-hearted version of the conflict between age and youth that dominates the latter part of the play. The shepherd is joined by a clown who has seen the wounded Antigonus. Both take pity on the helpless infant, and the shepherd clarifies the primary theme of the rest of the play:

> Now bless thyself: thou met'st with
> things dying, I with things new-born.

> (III, iii, 113–114)

A few lines later the clown brings in another key thought:

> You're a [made] old man; if the sins of your
> youth are forgiven you, you're well to live.

> (III, iii, 120–121)

Thus the crucial motifs of the second half: rebirth and repentance.

Act IV, scene i is a transition, in which "Time," as speaker, dominates. Its strength is its capacity for healing and reconciliation (IV, i, 9–15), and those two words reflect the final two acts of the play. The passage of time is also the subject of scene ii, as Camillo muses on his fifteen years away from the court of Sicilia (IV, ii, 4–9). Now Leontes has sent for him, and Camillo is eager to return. Polixenes, kind though he means to be, asks Camillo to stay (IV, ii, 11–20), and, before Camillo has a chance to reply, inquires about Polixenes' son, Florizel, who has been missing for several days. In fact, Polixenes is being deceptive: he knows the boy has been with the daughter of a shepherd. Camillo is familiar with this shepherd, and Polixenes resolves that the two of them should disguise themselves and investigate. This scene, too, is primarily one of exposition, but also introduces the theme of young love, a principal subject of the last two acts.

In scene iii the tone of the play changes entirely as we move near the Shepherd's cottage, and Autolycus takes the stage. The lyrics of his opening song are a combination of the bawdy and the pastoral:

> The lark, that tirra-lyra chants,
>   With heigh, [with heigh,] the thrush and the jay!
> Are summer songs for me and my aunts,

While we lie tumbling in the hay.

                                                              (IV, iii, 8–12)

That "aunts" is a euphemism for "whores" takes away from some of the pastoral innocence of the ditty. Autolycus was once in the employ of Florizel, but now is out of service, and living a vaguely criminal life:

> With die
> and drab I purchas'd this caparison, and my revenue
> is the silly cheat. Gallows and knock are too powerful
> on the highway. Beating and hanging are terrors to
> me. For the life to come, I sleep out the thought of it.

                                                              (IV, iii, 26–30)

231In the tranquil world of the country, Autolycus is the closest to an evil presence. But as opposed to the malice that emerged from Leontes, Autolycus is more of a scamp, taking advantage of human folly. Indeed, he is soon to be a help to the more heroic characters, so that despite his shady antics he never poses a danger.

He provides an example of his skills with his dexterous manipulation of the Clown, who enters carrying a lengthy grocery list (IV, iii, 37–49). While Autolycus feigns having been robbed, he picks the pocket of the Clown who stops to help him. To the Clown's solicitous question, "What manner of fellow was he that robb'd you?" (IV, iii, 85–86), Autolycus tells his own story, or at least a version of it, then calls the imaginary thief Autolycus. Yet whatever his morality, Autolycus is a likeable rogue, and presents a humorous counterpoint to the serious events around him. Furthermore, his capacity for fantasy provides another comic contrast, this with Leontes' obsessions and delusions.

The lengthy scene iv brings in Florizel and Perdita, preparing to attend a sheep-shearing. In their love and simplicity they embody all the promise of youth, untainted by worldly experience. Perdita speaks of herself as unworthy of Florizel's high station (IV, iv, 7–10), but he has partially removed the barriers between them by changing into humble country attire. Both characters are devoid of pride, and their humility as well as their contentment in one another's company stands in sharp contrast to the more formal society elsewhere in the play.

Perdita worries about Polixenes, how he will regard her dressed as a princess while his son is dressed so meanly (IV, iv, 18–24), but Florizel comforts her:

> Or I'll be thine, my fair,
> Or not my father's; for I cannot be
> Mine own, nor any thing to any, if
> I be not thine. To this I am most constant,
> Though destiny say no.

                                                              (IV, iv, 42–46)

His devotion is impressive, but we are conscious of the underlying irony. Perdita is a princess, but that truth will not become public for some time.

The conflict between age and youth takes over in the next portion of the scene, as the Shepherd, accompanied by Camillo and Polixenes in disguise, as well as Mopsa, Dorcas, and servants, enters to criticize Perdita for neglecting her duties. He harkens back to his wife, who, he claims, did her job more efficiently (IV, iv, 55–62). Perdita modestly accepts his judgment and greets the newcomers with flowers:

> Reverend sirs,
> For you there's rosemary and rue; these keep
> Seeming and savor all the winter long.
>
> (IV, iv, 73–75)

The flowers she chooses, which Polixenes approves because they are appropriate to his age, invites a discussion on the quality of flowers from nature versus those created by artificial cross-breeding. This subject, a particularized version of a long-standing Renaissance debate on the value of the "natural" versus the "artificial," brings out Perdita's personality. She, the child of nature, argues for the purity of nature's flowers (IV, iv, 87–88) while Polixenes suggests that the influence of man can improve nature's art:

> This is an art
> Which does mend Nature—change it rather; but
> The art itself is Nature.
>
> (IV, iv, 95–97)

Later we recall this judgment.

Perdita distributes flowers to the rest of the men, finally turning to Florizel, who is still in disguise and calling himself Doricles. Her gift to him invokes a series of images of fertility and growth (IV, iv, 112–129), so that Perdita becomes almost a force of nature: sexual, passionate, yet pure. Florizel responds with similar intensity:

> When you do dance, I wish you
> A wave o' th' sea, that you might ever do
> Nothing but that; move still, still so,
> And own no other function. Each your doing
> (So singular in each particular)
> Crowns what you are doing in the present deeds,
> That all your acts are queens.
>
> (IV, iv, 140–146)

The irony of the last line escapes Florizel, but his tribute to her is nevertheless moving. Even Polixenes is struck:

> This is the prettiest low-born lass that ever
> Ran on the green-sord. Nothing she does, or seems,
> But smacks of something greater than herself,

Too noble for this place.

(IV, iv, 156–159)

This theme is familiar from other comedies and romances. Whatever the outward demeanor of the individual, true nobility shines through.

The idealized vision of the pastoral is interrupted by the announcement that a peddler is soon to appear, and after some discussion about what wares he is selling, Autolycus enters. His presence is the cue for a good deal of humor, as the Clown confesses that because he is love with Mopsa, he will have to buy something. The revelry continues for some time amidst song and dance, and the bawdy exchanges between the rustics (IV, iv, 242–248, 262–265) set off the poetic strains between Perdita and Florizel.

Eventually Polixenes declares to Camillo: "'Tis time to part them . . . " (IV, iv, 344). And he mocks Florizel for not buying his love any presents from the peddler (IV, iv, 347–356). Florizel replies that Perdita has no interest in such trinkets, and before long he is preparing to marry her in a non-religious ceremony that will nonetheless be legal and binding (IV, iv, 386–389). Faced with this prospect, Polixenes suggests that Florizel's father should be advised, but the young man, still failing to see through Polixenes' disguise, refuses (IV, iv, 411–413).

At this obstinacy Polixenes tears off his mask and explodes in a rage that recalls Leontes' fury:

> For thee, fond boy,
> If I may ever know thou dost but sigh
> That thou no more shalt this knack (as never
> I mean thou shalt), we'll bar thee from succession,
> Not hold thee of our blood, no, not our kin,
> Farre than Deucalion off.

(IV, iv, 426–431)

Only moments before Polixenes advocated marrying "A gentler scion to the wildest stock . . . " (IV, iv, 93). Now he disinherits his son, then threatens Perdita:

> I will devise a death as cruel for thee
> As thou art tender to't.

(IV, iv, 440–441)

With this warning he departs. Once again irrational anger possesses a ruler.

The shepherd also becomes outraged, blaming first Florizel, then Perdita his daughter (IV, iv, 452–462), but both young people retain their dignity and determination. Camillo is, as he was in Act I, a conciliatory voice, but Florizel remains resolved.

> It cannot fail, but by
> The violation of my faith, and then
> Let nature crush the sides o' th' earth together,

And mar the seeds within! Lift up thy looks.
From my succession wipe me, father, I
Am heir to my affection.

(IV, iv, 476–481)

He will not desert Perdita, and the images of fertility emphasize the natural energy of his passion.

Now the plot moves quickly. Florizel continues that he will not surrender Perdita "for Bohemia" (IV, iv, 488), and that Perdita and he will escape by sea (IV, iv, 498–502). Camillo modifies this strategy by suggesting that the two head for Sicilia:

> Methinks I see
> Leontes opening his free arms, and weeping,
> His welcomes forth; asks thee there, son, forgiveness,
> As 'twere i' th' father's person; kisses the hands
> Of your fresh princess . . .

(IV, iv, 547–551)

Camillo hopes that the invitation he received earlier from Leontes will carry over for the others. He explains how Florizel will gain entrance to the court:

> Sir,
> The manner of your bearing twards him, with
> What you (as from your father) shall deliver,
> Things known betwixt us three, I'll write you down,
> The which shall point you forth at every sitting
> What you just say . . .

(IV, iv, 557–562)

Florizel agrees to the plan, but points out that he is not dressed royally (IV, iv, 588). At this moment Autolycus returns, recounting all the swindles he has conducted. After Camillo offers sufficient money (IV, iv, 637), Autolycus and Florizel exchange clothes, and the two lovers and Camillo leave. Camillo is uncertain how he will explain the circumstances to Polixenes, but hopes the confusion will lead him back to Sicilia (IV, iv, 662–667). Autolycus, meanwhile, feels he has triumphed once more (IV, iv, 670–682), and resolves to pass himself off as a courtier. When the Clown and the Shepherd enter, promising to deliver to the King news of the lovers' escape (IV, iv, 693–702), Autolycus takes on a royal manner: "Though I am not naturally honest, I am so sometimes by chance" (IV, iv, 712–713). Thus he removes his disguise, bullies the two into revealing their intentions, and terrifies them with horrors that await them once the King hears their report about Perdita (IV, iv, 768–770). Autolycus promises to escort the men for a fee (IV, iv, 794–799). And when they have followed his direction, he ruminates on how Fortune will not allow him to be honest (IV, iv, 831–832). His reflections are a comic version of the role of fate in human life.

This last episode complicates the portrait of rural life in this play. The rustics are by and large decent, but they are also naive, and their pastoral existence, although tranquil, is far from ideal when they can be gulled by such as Autolycus. As is usual in those of Shakespeare's plays in which the controversy of country life versus city life is presented, no verdict is offered, and the quality of the existence finally depends on the individuals involved.

Act V returns us to Sicilia, where a resigned Leontes has mourned all these years. As Cleomines indicates:

> At the last
> Do as the heavens have done, forget your evil,
> With them, forgive yourself.
>
> (V, i, 4–6)

But Leontes is still haunted by the memory of Hermione, and Paulina, too, does not let him forget her:

> If, one by one, you wedded all the world,
> Or, from the all that are, took something good
> To make a perfect woman, she you kill'd
> Would be unparallel'd.
>
> (V, i, 13–16)

Dion delicately reminds Paulina that if she disapproves of a new wife and child for the King, she denies his responsibility to the country:

> You pity not the state, nor the remembrance
> Of his most sovereign name; consider little
> What dangers, by his Highness' fail of issue,
> May drop upon his kingdom, and devour
> Certain lookers-on.
>
> (V, i, 24–29)

Paulina responds by recalling certain prophetic words:

> Is't not the tenor of his oracle,
> That King Leontes shall not have an heir
> Till his lost child be found?
>
> (V, i, 38–40)

This issue relates directly to the health of the kingdom, for in the eyes of Shakespeare's audience the absence of a suitable heir could mean that the power of the kingship, divinely ordained, would be diluted, and disorder would spread. Paulina also manages to force Leontes to agree to her dictum about any future marriage partner:

> She shall not be so young
> As was your former, but she shall be such
> As (walk'd your first queen's ghost) it should take joy

To see her in your arms.

(V, i, 78–81)

Such badgering by Paulina may seem unrealistic. How would a king tolerate it? But we must imagine that this episode is a concentrated version of events that have occurred slowly over the course of sixteen years. Besides, the play itself is not entirely realistic. Thus the emphasis on Leontes' submission and repentance supersedes the credibility.

A servant enters to announce the arrival of Florizel and a young princess:

Ay; the most peerless piece of earth, I think,
That e'er the sun shone bright on.

(V, i, 94–95)

After the servant extols Perdita's beauty, claiming that women as well as men will love her (V, i, 110–112), Paulina reminds Leontes of the fate of his own sons:

Had our prince,
Jewel of children, seen this hour, he had pair'd
Well with this lord; there was not full a month
Between their births.

(V, i, 115–118)

Leontes is struck by this sentiment, as well as by the appearance of both young people. First Florizel:

Were I but twenty-one,
Your father's image is so hit in you
(His very air) that I should call you brother,
As I did him . . .

(V, i, 126–129)

Then Perdita:

And your fair princess—goddess! O! alas,
I lost a couple, that twixt heaven and earth
Might thus have stood, begetting wonder, as
You, gracious couple, do . . .

(V, i, 131–134)

He also expresses deep remorse for ever doubting Polixenes' friendship (V, i, 148–151). Leontes then greets the young couple in appropriate terms: "Welcome hither,/ As is the spring to th' earth" (V, i, 151–152). Even to him they are a symbol of renewal, of a rebirth of life. In addition, their presence inspires Leontes to dwell again on his own lost children:

What might I have been,
Might I a son and daughter now have look'd on,

Such goodly things as you?

                                                        (V, i, 176–178)

At the news of Polixenes' arrival (V, i, 181–185), Leontes is overjoyed, but Florizel assumes that he has been betrayed by Camillo (V, i, 193–195). Florizel explains the predicament he and Perdita share, and Leontes is sympathetic but firm:

                                I am sorry,
          Most sorry, you have broken from his liking,
          Where you were tied in duty; and as sorry
          Your choice is not so rich in worth as beauty,
          That you might well enjoy her.

                                                        (V, i, 211–215)

Florizel, however, is adamant in his love for Perdita, and asks Leontes to intervene with Polixenes, who will surely listen (V, i, 218–222). Leontes' response does not surprise us:

          Would he do so, I'ld beg your precious mistress,
          Which he counts but a trifle.

                                                        (V, i, 223–224)

Unbeknownst to himself, he sees in Perdita the image of Hermione. Paulina warns immediately that Perdita is much too young for Leontes to consider marrying her, then reminds him that the girl is the image of his dead wife. But Leontes' response reveals his sudden awareness of the situation: "I thought of her,/ Even in these looks I made" (V, i, 227–228). And he volunteers to speak to Polixenes.

Scene ii is a curious episode, for it is all narrative about events that take place offstage. Though the conversation of three gentlemen we learn with Autolycus of the moment of recognition, when Leontes realized that Perdita is his daughter. The celebratory occasion was marred only by Leontes' mourning for Hermione: "O, thy mother, thy mother!" (V, ii, 51–52). We hear again of the fate of Antigonus (V, ii, 63–66), then of the "noble combat that 'twixt joy and sorrow was fought in Paulina!" (V, ii, 73–74). We know that sight of Perdita in combination with the news of her husband's death is a shock. But we are soon to learn that she has one more revelation that she must struggle to withhold. Finally we hear that Perdita was told of her mother's statue, and will go see it (V, ii, 94–103). Apparently Paulina has, for some unknown reason, visited that location every day. Such detail almost challenges us to suspend our insistence on reality. The telling is not nearly as effective as the showing might be, but then a greater surprise awaits in the final scene, and that one might be diminished were it part of a sequence, rather than unto itself.

Before that climactic unveiling, however, members of the lower class make one final appearance. Autolycus regrets that his fraudulent nature prevented him from revealing the truth to Leontes and thereby gaining the reward (V, ii, 113–

123). Now he must deal with "those I have done good to against my will" (V, ii, 124). At this moment the Clown enters, dressed in royal robes, for in the joy of the occasion the two kings have elevated him socially (V, ii, 139–145). Autolycus tries to ingratiate himself with the newly raised pair (V, ii, 149–151), and while the Shepherd remains humble (V, ii, 152–153), the Clown's bombastic confidence suggests that he has already been corrupted by his rank (V, ii, 162–168). But we do feel that Autolycus has been at least partially reformed.

The final scene takes place appropriately before the public, for the actions of the royal family have universal ramifications. Leontes is eager to see the statue (V, iii, 9–10), but Paulina delays long enough to warn him how realistic it is:

> But here it is; prepare
> To see the life as lively mock'd as ever
> Still sleep mock'd death.
>
> (V, iii, 18–20)

Leontes' astonishment at the statue is comically undercut:

> But yet, Paulina
> Hermione was not so much wrinkled, nothing
> So aged as this seems.
>
> (V, iii, 27–29)

But thereafter Leontes and Perdita are both moved profoundly. Meanwhile Paulina struggles to prevent anyone from touching the statue, or even drawing too close:

> O, patience!
> The statue is but newly fix'd; the color's
> Not dry.
>
> (V, iii, 46–48)

> No longer shall you gaze on't, lest your fancy
> May think anon it moves.
>
> (V, iii, 60–61)

Leontes imagines the statue is alive (V, iii, 65–66), then bids Paulina let him continue to suffer the mixture of torment at Hermione's loss and of delight at seeing her recreated with such astonishing fidelity:

> For this affliction has a taste as sweet
> As any cordial comfort.
>
> (V, iii, 76–77)

And again he imagines the statue moves. Once more reality and illusion intertwine.

Paulina draws the moment out, claiming she has the magical ability to bring the statue to life, but adds this stipulation: "It is requir'd/ You do awake your faith" (V, iii, 94–95). At Leontes' affirmation, she orders music, then announces "'Tis time" (V, iii, 99). Her words remind us of a theme throughout the romances: the healing powers of time. She then commands the statue come to life: " . . . for from him/ Dear life redeems you" (V, iii, 102–103). Except for a revelation by the Abbess in *A Comedy of Errors,* this moment is unique in Shakespeare, as information has been withheld from us. We especially remember Paulina's insistence on Hermione's death in Act III.

As much as any moment in Shakespeare's plays, this resurrection is supremely theatrical. On the page it cannot make nearly as profound an impression, especially because several lines comment on action that readers must imagine (V, iii, 111–120). Furthermore, when Hermione speaks, we have not heard her voice for so long, and it ought to seem from another world:

> You gods, look down
> And from your sacred vials pour your graces
> Upon my daughter's head!
>
> (V, iii, 121–123)

Finally, the notion that Hermione has been hidden nearby for sixteen years may seem unbelievable. So, too, may be the sudden marriage of Paulina, widowed for sixteen years, to Camillo. But such practicality is irrelevant to the allegorical nature of the moment. Hermione's return, the reunion with Perdita, the marriage of the young couple, and the marriage of the older: all are essential to a story that dramatizes sin, repentence, and redemption.

The play ends with the restoration of family unity as well as harmony within the nation and between nations. Only one character is missing: Mamillius, whose death will forever be the price Leontes paid for his tragic misjudgment. Nevertheless, the play is an optimistic work. It affirms the power of friendship and of faith in humanity. Perhaps most of all, it dramatizes life reborn through youth and love renewed through forgiveness.

SUGGESTIONS FOR FURTHER READING

Bethell, S. L. The Winter's Tale: *A Study.* New York: Staples, 1947.

Bonjour, Adrien. "The Final Scene of *The Winter's Tale.*" *English Studies* 33 (1952): 193–208.

Cox, Lee Sheridan. "The Role of Autolycus in *The Winter's Tale.*" *Studies in English Literature, 1500–1900* 9 (1969): 283–301.

Fox, G. P. *The Winter's Tale.* Oxford, Basil Blackwell, 1967.

Hoeniger, F. David. "The Meaning of the *Winter's Tale.*" *University of Toronto Quarterly* 20 (1950–51): 11–26.

Muir, Kenneth, ed. *Shakespeare*: The Winter's Tale. *A Casebook.* London: Macmillan, 1968.

Pyle, Fitzroy. The Winter's Tale: *A Commentary on the Structure.* New York: Barnes & Noble, 1969.

Siegel, Paul N. "Leontes, a Jealous Tyrant." *Review of English Studies.* New Series I (1950): 302–307.

Taylor, Michael. "Shakespeare's *The Winter's Tale*: Speaking in the Freedom of Knowledge." *The Critical Quarterly* 14 (1972): 49–56.

Triemens, Roger J. "The Inception of Leontes' Jealousy in *The Winter's Tale*." *Shakespeare Quarterly* 4 (1953): 321–326.

THE TEMPEST

This play is traditionally regarded as the final one of which Shakespeare is the sole author. No direct source has been found. Its plot, set in the fifteenth century, is simple, especially compared to the overwhelming intricacies of the other romances, but the story suggests so many allegorical levels that it has inspired a great variety of interpretations. We shall focus on three perspectives: the political, the artistic, and the familial.

The Tempest is one of only two of Shakespeare's plays (*The Comedy of Errors* is the other) that largely obeys the classical unities of time, place, and action. More important, events are tightly controlled, for early on we recognize that Prospero is in command of everything that happens. No matter what alliances and conspiracies form, no matter what personal struggles characters undergo, all will resolve happily because Prospero can determine the course of action. Thus the play has little conflict and less suspense. The questions that occupy us concern the significance of what unfolds.

The story begins on a ship amidst a terrifying storm. In this moment of crisis the personalities of several principal characters are revealed. The Boatswain, for instance, has little regard for the royal standing of his superiors:

> Use your authority. If you cannot,
> give thanks you have liv'd so long, and make
> yourself ready in your cabin for the mischance of
> the hour, if it so hap.
>
> (I, i, 23–26)

He dismisses useless or ill-used authority. Later the issue of power properly wielded becomes crucial. The Boatswain's bluster is overheard by Gonzalo, whose response reveals his nature:

> I have great comfort from this fellow. Methinks
> he hath no drowning mark upon him, his complexion
> is perfect gallows . . . If he be not born to
> be hang'd, our case is miserable.
>
> (I, i, 28–33)

Such good-humored faith marks Gonzalo throughout the play.

The darker characters are also clarified. Antonio, the usurping Duke who is soon to begin another conspiracy on the island, slanders the hard-working sailor:

> We are merely cheated of our lives by drunkards.
> This wide-chopp'd rascal—would thou mightst lie drowning
> The washing of ten tides!
>
> (I, i, 56–58)

He has no respect for jurisdiction or work. Sebastian, his cohort, is equally intolerant (I, i, 40–41), and follows Antonio's lead in attitude and action both on the boat and later on the island.

The tempest itself becomes reflective of several issues. As we soon learn, it is the product of Prospero's art, and thus a manifestation of his anger. It also reflects the political disorder in Milan and the conflict between that city and Naples. Lastly it reflects the fragmented royal families.

Scene ii provides the background information to these conflicts. Miranda's trusting nature emerges in her pleas to her father that he calm the storm:

> Had I been any god of power, I would
> Have sunk the sea within the earth or ere
> It should the good ship so have swallow'd, and
> The fraughting souls within her.
>
> (I, ii, 10–13)

Prospero reassures her, then offers a lengthy narrative about their own history. Theatrically this exposition is awkward and is interrupted several times when Prospero demands not only his daughter's attention but ours as well.

He begins his tale with what seems a threat: "What seest thou else/ In the dark backward and abysm of time?" (I, ii, 49–50). He appears to be ready to teach her about the painful aspects of life from which she has heretofore been spared. He establishes his own place as Duke of Milan, then continues with details of how his brother Antonio usurped power through political appointments and subterfuge:

> Being once perfected how to grant suits,
> How to deny them, who t' advance, and who
> To trash for overtopping, new created
> The creatures that were mine, I say, or chang'd 'em,
> Or else new form'd 'em; having both the key
> Of officer and office, set all hearts i' th' state
> To what tune pleas'd his ear, that now he was
> The ivy which had hid my princely trunk,
> And suck'd my verdure out on't.
>
> (I, ii, 79–87)

The crucial element of his story is that Prospero was expelled from his lawful office by Antonio. However, Prospero himself was not entirely blameless:

I, thus neglecting wordly ends, all dedicated
To closeness and the bettering of my mind
With that which, but by being so retir'd,
O'er-prized all popular rate, in my false brother
Awak'd an evil nature . . .

(I, ii, 89–93)

Prospero failed as leader of his people, a position ordained by God. Thus his exile and subsequent retaking of authority is the fulfillment of his responsibility to his city, not just a personal vendetta, although his long-lasting bitterness is evident. Still, whatever his shortcomings, Prospero was a popular and learned ruler, and his place is on the throne.

Antonio was joined in conspiracy against Prospero by Alonso, the King of Naples: "... an enemy/ To me inveterate" (I, ii, 121–122). Antonio, knowing he had Alonso's support, allowed an invading army into Milan, and they carried off Prospero and Miranda. At this moment she wonders why they were not killed at once. Prospero's answer reveals both his sense of self-worth and the value of his character:

Dear, they durst not,
So dear the love my people bore me; nor set
A mark so bloody on the business; but
With colors fairer painted their foul ends.

(I, ii, 140–143)

Instead the pair were set adrift at sea (I, ii, 149–151), but ended up on the island, as Prospero explains, "By divine Providence" (I, ii, 159). This intervention took the form of Gonzalo, originally charged with the task of setting them adrift. Instead he provided necessities as well as books (I, ii, 161–168).

Now, on this day, Providence has interfered again:

By accident most strange, bountiful Fortune
(Now my dear lady) hath mine enemies
Brought to this shore; and by my prescience
I find my zenith doth depend upon
A most auspicious star, whose influence
If now I court not, but omit, my fortunes
Will ever after droop.

(I, ii, 178–184)

Here is a motif familiar from other romances. The universe is ultimately benign, but man is responsible for his own fate. Providence has been kind to Prospero and Miranda on two occasions. Nonetheless, Prospero's charge is to take advantage of this opportunity and to fulfill his duties appropriately.

After putting Miranda to sleep, Prospero calls the spirit, Ariel, who dramatizes the storm (I, ii, 195–206), then reports that all have been taken safely from the ship, including Ferdinand, Alonso's son. (I, ii, 221–224). The other vessels of the fleet have been sent onward (I, ii, 230–235). Pleased at Prospero's approval,

Ariel recalls promises of liberty, but Prospero reminds him of the privileges
Ariel enjoys:

> Thou dost; and think'st it much to tread the ooze
> Of the salt deep,
> To run upon the sharp wind of the north,
> To do me business in the veins o' th' earth
> When it is bak'd with frost.
>
> (I, ii, 252–256)

Ariel, too, has responsibilities, and Prospero expects his rule to be followed.
Ariel has the capacity to move through the traditional elements of the world:
Prospero notes water, air, and earth. And we have already observed Ariel as
fire, in scene i. Yet Ariel also has human qualities, which becomes apparent in
his emotional responses to Ferdinand and others. This combination of magical
and realistic qualities makes Ariel something other than a literal character, who
should be taken metaphorically, perhaps as a symbol of imagination or fantasy
or some spiritual aspect of humanity.

Despite his affection for Ariel, Prospero is still stern when the spirit claims
to have forgotten his unhappy past:

> Thou liest, malignant thing! Hast thou forgot
> The foul witch Sycorax, who with age and envy
> Was grown into a hoop? Hast thou forget her?
>
> (I, ii, 257–259)

And Prospero details with vengeful pride how he rescued Ariel from Sycorax's
control (I, ii, 270–282). Throughout the play Prospero seems to be compensating
for the negligence of his earlier career by carrying out his current duties with
absolute authority. Here he orders Ariel's actions, but also promises to maintain
their bond by freeing Ariel in two days (I, ii, 297–298).

Whatever Ariel's specific nature, he is contrasted by the earthly Caliban,
Sycorax's son, who frightens the awakened Miranda. Caliban, whose name is
a near anagram of "cannibal," also suggests a variety of allegorical interpretations. His first words reveal the brutality that is part of his nature:

> As wicked dew as e'er my mother brush'd
> With raven's feather from unwholesome fen
> Drop on you both! A south-west blow on ye,
> And blister you all o'er!
>
> (I, ii, 321–324)

Yet he also has a capacity for love, as he recalls Prospero's initial affection
towards him:

> When thou cam'st first,
> Thou strok'st me and made much of me, wouldst give me
> Water with berries in't, and teach me how
> To name the bigger light, and how the less,

That burn by day and night; and then I lov'd thee
And show'd thee all the qualities o' th' isle . . .

(I, ii, 332–337)

Caliban may be regarded as savage man, instinctive and untutored. One of the central debates of Shakespeare's day concerned man's nature: is it essentially good, or must good be inculcated by civilization? The portrait of Caliban does not solve the issue, for he has several opposing aspects: he is at various moments vicious, pathetic, vengeful, and naive. He occasionally offers the charm of innocence, and an animalistic affection. But without the guiding hand of society he reverts to savagery, as Prospero indicates:

I have us'd thee
(Filth as thou art) with human care, and lodg'd thee
In mine own cell, till thou didst seek to violate
The honor of my child.

(I, ii, 345–348)

Miranda insists that she, too, tried to help Caliban:

I pitied thee,
Took pains to make thee speak, taught thee each hour
One thing or other.

(I, ii, 353–355)

Yet such society has its price, as Caliban himself says: "The red-plague rid you/ For learning me your language" (I, ii, 363–65). Civilization has also given him the ability to exercise his baser instincts.

The opposition between Ariel and Caliban is but one in the play. We should also consider the contrast between the magic of Prospero and that of the unseen Sycorax. Shakespeare's audience believed in two kinds of magic: black magic, which came from the devil and which in this context was practiced by Sycorax, and white magic, the variety practiced by Prospero, and which denotes a mastery of the elements. The latter is fundamentally beneficient and acquired through study. Thus for Shakespeare's audience, Prospero's skills and actions reveal his intellect and his proper place on the throne of Milan.

The final character to be introduced in this scene is Ferdinand, who enters listening to Ariel's singing. Ferdinand is sensitive to the power of that voice:

Sitting on a bank,
Weeping again the King my father's wrack,
This music crept by me upon the waters,
Allaying both their fury and my passion
With its sweet air . . .

(I, ii, 390–394)

One of the lyrics, however, hints a key theme:

Nothing of him that doth fade,
But doth suffer a sea-change

> Into something rich and strange.
>
> (I, ii, 400–402)

The "him" is Alonso, Ferdinand's father. But the process of change might refer to any of several characters who during the course of the play undergo a crisis, then emerge altered spiritually and emotionally.

When Ferdinand and Miranda meet, they are immediately smitten with one another. Miranda's first words reflect both her innocence and her capacity for love:

> What, is't a spirit?
> Lord, how it looks about! Believe me, sir.
> It carries a brave form. But 'tis a spirit.
>
> (I, ii, 410–412)

Prospero seems pleased: "It goes on, I see . . . " (I, ii, 420). But he is not willing to make matter easy for the young couple. He challenges Ferdinand's claims about his background so that even Miranda is pained: "Pity move my father/ To be inclin'd my way!" (I, ii, 447–448). And such passion inspires Ferdinand further:

> O, if a virgin,
> And your affection not gone forth, I'll make you
> The Queen of Naples.
>
> (I, ii, 448–450)

In his insistence on Miranda's purity, Ferdinand mirrors Prospero, who still chooses to make their courtship a trial:

> They are both in either's powers; but this swift business
> I must uneasy make, lest too light winning
> Make the prize light.
>
> (I, ii, 451–453)

Ferdinand, too, must grow before he and Miranda may be joined. Therefore Prospero accuses him of being a spy (I, ii, 454–457), but Miranda protests: "There's nothing ill can dwell in such a temple" (I, ii, 458). When her objections grow strenuous, Prospero asserts his order: "My foot my tutor?" (I, ii, 470). Quashing his daughter's rebellious streak, he re-establishes the hierarchical authority at the core of Shakespeare's political world, as dramatized in all the history plays. Despite Prospero's derogation (I, ii, 480–482), Miranda continues to express her devotion to Ferdinand, whose feelings are at this moment tangled:

> My spirits, as in a dream, are all bound up.
> My father's loss, the weakness which I feel,
> The wrack of all my friends, nor this man's threats
> To whom I am subdu'd, are but light to me,
> Might I but through my prison once a day

Behold this maid.

(I, ii, 487–492)

The image of a dream reminds us of other similarly entranced young heroes from Shakespeare's comedies, including Antipholus from *The Comedy of Errors* (II, ii, 181–182, 212–213) and Sebastian from *Twelfth Night* (IV, i, 61–63). Here Ferdinand is comforted by Miranda (I, ii, 497–498), and thus willingly follows Prospero's directive.

Act II, scene i brings to us the other stranded royals. Gonzalo is characteristically optimistic, looking on the best side of the survival (II, i, 1–9). Alonso, however, is too saddened by what he believes is the loss of his son to take any comfort. Sebastian and, in particular, Antonio, grouse obnoxiously, and in lines 10–68 mock the more cheerful words of Gonzalo and Adrian with cynical retorts. For instance, Gonzalo reflects contentedly: "Here is every thing advantageous to life" (II, i, 50). To which Antonio replies "True, save means to live" (II, i, 51) and Sebastian, ever the follower, adds, "Of that there's none, or little" (II, i, 52).

The maliciousness grows more serious, however, with the reflections on the marriage of Alonso's daughter, Claribel, to the King of Tunis. Alonso muses that this journey has caused him to suffer a double loss: his daughter by marriage and his son by drowning on the return trip. Even Francisco's report that Ferdinand might have survived (II, i, 116–123) does not move the King, perhaps because he feels guilt over his aiding Antonio's usurpation of the throne from Prospero. This regret is clarified later.

At present, however, Sebastian does not spare blaming Alonso for their predicament, for everyone opposed the recent marriage (II, i, 129–136). But we must keep Sebastian's comments in perspective, for he is Alonso's brother, and thus a rival for the throne of Naples. Indeed, as Antonio took Milan from Prospero, so Sebastian, with Antonio's help, will try to undo Alonso. Gonzalo, ever loyal, attempts to defend Alonso (II, i, 137–140). Then, in a reflective speech that emerges somewhat arbitrarily, Gonzalo reflects on his ideal political state:

I' th' commonwealth I would, by contraries,
Execute all things; for no kind of traffic
Would I admit; no name of magistrate;
Letters should not be known; riches, poverty,
And use of service, none; contract, succession,
Bourn, bound of land, tithe, vineyard, none . . .

(II, i, 148–153)

This vision of what Gonzalo calls "the golden age" (II, i, 169) is undercut, though, by Sebastian and Antonio. The former asks mockingly "No marrying 'mong his subjects?" (II, i, 166), and the latter responds, "None, man, all idle— whores and knaves" (II, i, 167). Gonzalo's utopian vision is based on a faith in man's natural goodness, but the presence of Antonio and Sebastian as well as that of Caliban suggests that such idealism is unrealistic. Antonio and Sebastian represent a corruption acquired in civilization, Caliban such instincts in nature. As long as these forces are present in the world, Gonzalo's vision must remain unfulfilled.

Ariel, unseen, plays music that puts to sleep all except Antonio and Sebastian. Antonio takes this opportunity to work on Sebastian's ambition:

> My strong imagination sees a crown
> Dropping upon thy head.
>
> (II, i, 207–208)

Sebastian is comically slow to pick up the implications of Antonio's words:

> Thou dost snore distinctly,
> There's meaning in thy snores.
>
> (II, i, 217–218)

But Antonio points out that Ferdinand is gone (II, i, 235–238) and thus the nearest successor to the throne of Naples is Claribel, now in Tunis (II, i, 246–248). Then Antonio points to Alonso:

> O that you bore
> The mind that I do! what a sleep were this
> For your advancement! Do you understand me?
>
> (II, i, 266–268)

Sebastian, however, is reluctant, and recalls Antonio's own action against Prospero (II, i, 270–271). Then Sebastian asks the crucial question: "But, for your conscience?" (II, i, 275). Antonio brushes the query aside: "Ay, sir; where lies that?" (II, i, 276). And in a lengthy diatribe he shows himself beyond the realm of moral or ethical restraint (I, i, 276–290). Here he aligns himself with such characters as Iago in *Othello,* Edmund in *King Lear,* Richard III, and Don John in *Much Ado About Nothing.* He thinks only of himself, and his will is paramount over all other instincts. What is strange about Antonio is that he plans his murder on an island from which they have no hope of rescue. Such considerations make Antonio seem even more cold-blooded, for the murder of Alonso is without immediate purpose. It emerges strictly from Antonio's own desires, and thus stands as one more piece of evidence counteracting Gonzalo's vision of an ideal society.

The two conspirators draw their swords, Antonio assigned to kill Alonso and Sebastian to slay Gonzalo. But as if in a moment of weakness, Sebastian draws Antonio aside, just as Ariel enters. He sings in Gonzalo's ear, and he and Alonso soon awaken to see Sebastian and Antonio with swords poised.

Ariel then awakens the others, forcing Antonio and Sebastian to concoct a lie about hearing wild beasts; then the party heads off to search for Ferdinand. But the image of Antonio and Sebastian as animals themselves remains with us, especially when Gonzalo says of Ferdinand: "Heavens keep him from these beasts!" (II, i, 324).

In scene ii a comic version of this conspiracy surfaces. First Caliban enters, cursing Prospero. His poetry is cruel but graphic (II, i, 1–14). We recognize his spirit of vengeance, but he is only brute force, unaided by the more dangerous weapon, intellect. Then Trinculo the jester arrives, drunk, and Caliban, thinking him another of Prospero's spirits, hides. Trinculo discovers the odd creature, which he imagines displaying for profit in England (II, ii, 27–31). Then he hides with it to escape an approaching storm.

Finally Stephano the butler staggers on, and he, too, has been drinking. After some investigation of this "monster," he discovers Trinculo, and the two slowly come to the recognition that both are alive (II, ii, 99–114). Caliban is terrified of them, but also awestruck, especially at Stephano: "Hast thou not dropp'd from heaven?" (II, ii, 137). Caliban is eager to worship them, and in his trust he becomes a perverse version of Miranda, who fell in love on sight of Ferdinand. Caliban is pathetic in his own way: "I'll kiss thy foot. I'll swear myself thy subject" (II, ii, 152). He is also eager to serve:

> I'll show thee the best springs; I'll pluck thee berries;
> I'll fish for thee, and get thee wood enough.
>
> (II, ii, 160–161)

He seeks to exchange one master, Prospero, for another, Stephano, who is soon intoxicated not just with drink but with ambition (II, ii, 173–177). A conspiracy is thus formed against Prospero, a burlesque of the one in the previous scene. Stephano is here the instigator, as Antonio is in the other plot, and Trinculo is, like Sebastian, the follower. Furthermore, Caliban's wild song about freedom (II, ii, 180–187) is a parody of Gonzalo's vision of the golden age.

In Act III, scene i, Ferdinand carries out his assigned tasks, but the pain is partially alleviated by the thought of Miranda:

> The mistress which I serve quickens what's dead,
> And makes my labors pleasures.
>
> (III, i, 6–7)

In this respect he is the archetypal courtly hero of Renaissance literature, striving nobly to win the hand of his beloved. Miranda enters, so smitten that she volunteers to help (III, i, 23–25). Prospero is touched by her infatuation: "Poor worm, thou art infected!" (III, i, 31). Yet he remains reluctant to let her share any passion beyond love of daughter for father. Perhaps he regards her love for Ferdinand, ideal though it may be, as a kind of corruption that must accompany her immersion into human society. Therefore his struggle to ensure that Miranda and Ferdinand remain pure until marriage may be judged both as Prospero's way of shielding his daughter from evil, and as another way of exercising the authority he disregarded years before in Milan.

Ferdinand, too, is in love. He admits he has met many women:

> . . . and many a time
> Th' harmony of their tongues hath into bondage

> Brought my too diligent ear . . .
>   But you, O you,
> So perfect and so peerless, are created
> Of every creature's best!

(II, ii, 40–48)

Ferdinand as well relishes Miranda's purity, and views her as a force of nature, immune from the taints of civilization that make other women less pleasurable.
   What stands out most in the scene is Miranda's innocence:

>   I do not know
> One of my sex; no woman's face remember,
> Save, from my glass, mine own; nor have I seen
> More that I may call men than you, good friend,
> And my dear father.

(III, i, 48–52)

The word "friend" seems out of place in a romantic context. And yet Miranda's use of it is appropriate, for she and Ferdinand are friends before they fall in love. Ferdinand himself maintains some poetic conventions expected from the traditional romantic hero:

>   Here my soul speak:
> The very instant that I saw you, did
> My heart fly to your service, there resides,
> To make me slave to it, and for your sake
> Am I this patient log-man.

(III, i, 63–67)

But he is disarmed by Miranda'a unaffected simplicity: "Do you love me?" (III, i, 67). And they pledge themselves to each other. Even Prospero is moved:

>   Fair encounter
> Of two most rare affections! Heavens rain grace
> On that which breeds between 'em!

(III, i, 74–76)

Yet before he can truly rejoice in their union, he has other work to perform (III, i, 92–96).
   The action returns to the comic conspiracy, where Stephano is even more drunk on power (III, ii, 15–16). Trinculo, himself still stumbling, remains something of a commentator, sneering at both Stephano and Caliban (III, ii, 19–20). Caliban, seeking to establish a legitimate ruling structure to replace Prospero's, is offended by Trinculo's rudeness, and begs Stephano to take action: "Bite him to death, I prithee" (III, ii, 34). And eventually Stephano does take action and pummel the jester (III, ii, 76). Meanwhile, in between intrusive comments of "Thou liest" by the invisible Ariel, Caliban articulates his desire for revenge against Prospero:

I say by sorcery he got this isle;
From me he got it. If thy greatness will
Revenge it on him—for I know thou dar'st,
But this thing dare not—

(III, ii, 52–55)

This speech reflects the multiple aspects of Caliban's character. His hatred for Prospero reflects the depravity that seems endemic to him, while his trust in Stephano reveals his helplessness and gullibility. These aspects are revealed in other speeches. First Caliban delineates his scheme for conquering Prospero:

Why, as I told thee, 'tis a custom with him
I' th' afternoon to sleep. There thou mayst brain him,
Having first seiz'd his books; or with a log
Batter his skull, or paunch him with a stake,
Or cut his wezand with thy knife.

(III, ii, 87–91)

Here degeneracy dominates Caliban. Yet the creature is not stupid:

                    Remember
First to possess his books; for without them
He's but a sot, as I am; nor hath not
One spirit to command; they all do hate him
As rootedly as I.

(III, ii, 91–95)

Moreover, he recognizes that Prospero's point of vulnerability is Miranda, and that information inspires Stephano:

Monster, I will kill this man. His daughter
and I will be king and queen—'save our Graces! And
Trinculo and thyself shall be viceroys.

(III, ii, 106–108)

Once the three are united, Stephano apologizes for attacking Trinculo (III, ii, 111), and begins to sing. When Ariel, still invisible, accompanies the ditty, the other two are frightened, and Caliban comforts them with poetry of unexpected beauty:

Be not afeard, the isle is full of noises,
Sounds, and sweet airs, that give delight and hurt not.
Sometimes a thousand twangling instruments
Will hum about mine ears; and sometimes voices,
That if I then had wak'd after long sleep,
Will make me sleep again, and then in dreaming,
The clouds methought would open, and show riches
Ready to drop upon me, that when I wak'd

I cried to dream again.

(III, ii, 135–143)

Such eloquence lifts Caliban far above the two drunken men beside him. Thus he is a puzzling combination: cruel, yet sensitive; naive, yet conniving. Perhaps Caliban is, as has been suggested by a variety of commentators, Shakespeare's version of primitive man, untutored in the ways of civilization, but with potential for both evil and good.

The more serious conspiracy resurfaces in scene iii. Gonzalo and Alonso are hungry and exhausted from their trek about the island, and Alonso is further enervated by the thought that his son is dead (III, iii, 6–10). Meanwhile Antonio and Sebastian maintain their plot against Alonso. Suddenly all are confounded by the appearance of spirits providing a banquet for their sustenance. Gonzalo, as befits his character, offers thanks to the people of the island and praises their generosity (III, iii, 29–34), but just as the group is ready to satisfy their hunger, the food disappears amidst thunder and lightning, revealing Ariel, "like a harpy," and he accuses them of crimes against Prospero:

> You are three men of sin, whom Destiny,
> That hath to instrument this lower world
> And what is in't, the never-surfeited sea
> Hath caus'd to belch up you . . .

(III, iii, 53–56)

Ariel omits that a crucial aspect of such "Destiny" is the power of Prospero.

Ariel then specifies that "I have made you mad" (III, iii, 58), and such psychological torment is distinguished from the comical physical punishment to be borne by Stephano and Trinculo. Next Ariel clarifies the crimes committed by Sebastian, Antonio, and Alonso:

> But remember
> (For that's my business to you) that you three
> From Milan did supplant good Prospero,
> Expos'd unto the sea (which hath requit it)
> Him, and his innocent child; for which foul deed
> The pow'rs, delaying (not forgetting), have
> Incens'd the seas and shores—yea, all the creatures,
> Against your peace.

(III, iii, 68–75)

Ariel also clarifies that the death of Alonso's son is direct punishment for his participation (III, iii, 75–76). Lastly, Ariel condemns the other two to "Ling'ring perdition" (III, iii, 77), a purgation of their sins, then leaves in a blaze of thunder. Prospero approves the performance: "They now are in my pow'r . . ." (III, iii, 90). Indeed, Alonso's conscience is so wounded that he rushes out:

> Therefore my son i' th' ooze is bedded; and
> I'll seek him deeper than e'er plummet sounded,

And with him there lie mudded.

> (III, iii, 100–102)

He intimates he will commit suicide. Antonio and Sebastian, however, as yet unrepentant, keep their swords high (III, iii, 102–103). But Gonzalo understands what is happening:

> All three of them are desperate: their great guilt
> (Like poison given to work a great time after)
> Now gins to bite the spirits.

> (III, iii, 104–106)

Although he knows of their guilt, he nonetheless orders Adrian and Francisco to follow them. Gonzalo has thus forgiven the conspirators their transgressions, and such generosity resounds through the last two acts.

In Act IV, scene i, Prospero ends Ferdinand's time of penance:

> All thy vexations
> Were but my trials of thy love, and thou
> Hast strangely stood the test.

> (IV, i, 5–7)

"Strangely" here means "well." But before the marriage Prospero has a serious stipulation:

> But
> If thou dost break her virgin-knot before
> All sanctimonious ceremonies may
> With full and holy rite be minist'red,
> No sweet aspersion shall the heavens let fall
> To make this contract grow . . .

> (IV, i, 14–19)

Prospero insists that these young people maintain the highest ethical standards. In no way does he want them to yield to animal passions, perhaps as others on the island would be tempted to do. Not surprisingly, Ferdinand consents:

> As I hope
> For quiet days, fair issue, and long life,
> With such love as 'tis now, the murkiest den,
> The most opportune place, the strong'st suggestion,
> Our worser genius can, shall never melt
> Mine honor into lust, to take away
> The edge of that day's celebration,
> When I shall think or Phoebus' steeds are founder'd
> Or Night kept chained below.

> (IV, i, 23–31)

Ferdinand shares Prospero's desire for a chaste wife and therefore a pure marriage.

Prospero then calls Ariel to bring together the "rabble" (IV, i, 37) to perform for the young couple, and Ariel summons spirits resembling various goddesses from mythology: Iris, goddess of the rainbow and Juno's messenger; Ceres, goddess of agriculture; and Juno herself, queen of the gods. Joined by images of harvesters, they perform a ritual masque that ensures that the union of Ferdinand and Miranda is fertile and otherwise blessed by nature. At Ceres' request, though, Venus and Cupid are excluded from the ceremony (IV, i, 87–91), and with them is absent the element of romantic love, or, in Iris' words, "some wanton charm" (IV, i, 95). Such an omission is consistent with Prospero's intentions.

In the midst of the dance Prospero recalls the conspiracy of Stephano, Trinculo, and Caliban, and stops the celebration to attend to it. He dismisses the performers, and as partial explanation for his fit of temper offers one of the most celebrated speeches in all of Shakespeare's plays:

> Our revels now are ended. These our actors
> (As I foretold you) were all spirits, and
> Are melted into air, into thin air,
> And like the baseless fabric of this vision,
> The cloud-capp'd tow'rs, the gorgeous palaces,
> The solemn temples, the great globe itself,
> Yea, all which it inherit, shall dissolve,
> And like this insubstantial pageant faded
> Leave not a rack behind. We are such stuff
> As dreams are made on; and our little life
> Is rounded with a sleep.

> > (IV, i, 148–157)

Elsewhere Shakespeare has compared human existence to the world of the stage. Macbeth speaks of life as " . . . a poor player,/ That struts and frets his hour upon the stage" (*Macbeth*, V, v, 24–25), and Jaques proclaims that "All the world's a stage" (*As You Like It*, II, vii, 139). The description here may be the most poignant, for it dwells on the transience not only of the individual human life but of all human achievement. The declamation seems apart from the action of the play, although its presence is meant to contribute to the tone of forgiveness. After all, the reference to "the great globe," the name of Shakespeare's theater, indicates that even art itself ultimately fades. If life is so transitory, we must be compassionate towards human weakness.

Prospero's attention turns back to Caliban and his cohorts. Ariel has tormented them all over the island, finally leaving them dunked:

> I' th' filthy-mantled pool beyond your cell,
> There dancing up to th' chins, that the foul lake
> O'erstunk their feet.

> > (IV, i, 181–184)

Prospero is still angry at Caliban:

And as with age his body uglier grows,
So his mind cankers.

                                            (IV, i, 191–192)

He reminds us of a Renaissance theme that pervades the Shakespearean canon:
how the state of a human spirit is reflected in the individual's body. The three
enter "all wet," but Stephano and Trinculo are bothered most by the squandering
of their wine (IV, i, 208):

There is not only disgrace and dishonor in that,
monster, but an infinite loss.

                                            (IV, i, 209–210)

Their mourning over "honor" is parody of figures from many plays who dwell
on such a loss. Caliban urges the pair to be more circumspect, but they are
entranced by the royal clothing they find, and begin to change, leaving Caliban
frustrated:

We shall lose our time,
And all be turn'd to barnacles, or to apes
With foreheads villainous low.

                                            (IV, i, 247–249)

Suddenly a group of spirits sets upon them, and the three are routed to suffer
further physical pain, while to Ariel Prospero muses that his work is almost
completed:

At this hour
Lies at my mercy all mine enemies.
Shortly shall all my labors end, and thou
Shalt have the air at freedom. For a little
Follow, and do me service.

                                            (IV, i, 262–266)

At the start of Act V, Prospero reaffirms that he has reached the apex of his
plan (V, i, 1–2), and Ariel reports back that his victims are now imprisoned:

Your charm so strongly works 'em
That if you now beheld them, your affections
Would become tender.

                                            (V, i, 17–19)

In one of the most touching moments of the play, Prospero asks whether Ariel's
emotions have been reached: "Dost thou think so, spirit?" (V, i, 19). And Ariel
replies: "Mine would, sir, were I human" (V, 1, 20). This line brings out the
complicated nature of Ariel: part human, part supernatural. And the human side
moves Prospero:

And mine shall.
Hast thou, which art but air, a touch, a feeling
Of their afflictions, and shall not myself,

> One of their kind, that relish all as sharply
> Passion as they, be kindlier mov'd than thou art?
> Though with their high wrongs I am strook to th' quick,
> Yet, with my nobler reason, 'gainst my fury
> Do I take part. The rarer action is
> In virtue than in vengeance.

                                                        (V, i, 20–27)

This speech, and in particular the last sentence, resounds with implications that pervade Shakespeare's plays. We think of Romeo, pursuing revenge after Mercutio slays Tybalt. We think of Hamlet, trapped by a revenge ethic perpetuated by his society. We remember Macbeth, ordering the death of Macduff's wife and children, so possessed by a longing for power that he imagines them a threat to his throne. We think of the long sequence of history plays, in which ambition, revenge, and intrafamily conflict run rampant through England for nearly a century. *The Tempest* has all these forces of potential destruction, but they are contained by Prospero.

Left alone, Prospero summons all his powers (V, i, 33–50), then prepares to turn them aside:

> But this rough magic
> I here abjure; and when I have requir'd
> Some heavenly music (which even now I do)
> To work mine end upon their senses that
> This airy charm is for, I'll break my staff,
> Bury it certain fadoms in the earth,
> And deeper than did ever plummet sound
> I'll drown my book.

                                                        (V, i, 50–57)

Numerous critics have suggested that this soliloquy is Shakespeare's farewell to his own magic, that of artistic creation. We cannot be sure, but the words, especially in conjunction with the speech in Act IV that "Our revels now are ended" (IV, i, 147–158), and the Epilogue to follow seem to imply that the playwright was conscious that the end of his career was imminent.

Ariel returns, bringing with him the company of enchanted prisoners. Prospero praises Gonzalo (V, i, 62–70), then accuses Alonso, Sebastian, and Antonio. But Prospero concludes as he promised: "I do forgive thee,/ Unnatural though thou art." (V, i, 78–79). This forgiveness unites all the disparate elements of the play. Prospero pardons the political and familial transgressions of his enemies, and further forgiveness follows.

After Prospero dresses himself in the robes of the Duke of Milan, he orders Ariel to retrieve the rest of the boat's crew (V, i, 96–101). In the meantime Prospero appears for the first time before the royal members. At this astonishing vision, Alonso immediately confesses:

Thy dukedom I resign, and do entreat
Thou pardon me my wrongs.

(V, i, 118–119)

Prospero then clarifies the treacherous behavior of Sebastian and Antonio (V, i, 126–129). In response Antonio says nothing, but Sebastian mutters aside: "The devil speaks in him" (V, i, 129). Prospero denies the accusation, then once more indicts Antonio (V, i, 130–131), the one who conceived the plan of regicide, and still the most hardened villain of the play. Yet Prospero forgives even him, and simultaneously reclaims the Dukedom (V, i, 132–134). Whether Antonio's silence is genuine acceptance or temporary restraint is not clear. In any case, the return of Prospero to power is part of the restoration of political order.

Some small tension remains, though, and Prospero extends it by speaking of Ferdinand and Miranda as though they are lost. Alonso seems truly repentant:

O heavens, that they were living both in Naples,
The King and Queen there! That they were, I wish
Myself were mudded in that oozy bed
Where my son lies.

(V, i, 149–152)

At this confession, Prospero reunites the family by revealing Ferdinand and Miranda playing chess.

Even Sebastian is struck by this sight: "A most high miracle!" (V, i, 177). The image of the game suggests the end of the ancient rivalry between the two cities, Milan and Naples. And the marriage between the two may be seen as uniting of two warring families.

Miranda is overcome at the men before her:

O wonder!
How many goodly creatures are there here!
How beauteous mankind is! O brave new world
That has such people in't!

(V, i, 181–184)

Prospero tempers her optimism: "'Tis new to thee" (V, i, 184). He implies that for all the miracles he has wrought on the island, he cannot change human nature. Thus Miranda has much to learn.

After Ferdinand's expression of love for Miranda, Alonso demonstrates that some of Prospero's magic has worked:

I am hers.
But O, how oddly will it sound that I
Must ask my child forgiveness.

(V, i, 196–198)

Here is another speech that reverberates with implications from numerous other plays of Shakespeare. So many of these works dramatize the conflict between generations, the clash of old values and new. And how often the parents cause destruction for their children. We recall Romeo and Juliet, Hamlet, Othello and Desdemona, and Coriolanus, as well as Shylock, Leonatus, Cymbeline, and other figures from the comedies and romances. Perhaps most of all we remember King Lear, who expels his daughter Cordelia, then after unbearable suffering begs forgiveness of her.

Ariel returns with the rest of the crew, including the steadfast Boatswain, who describes the magical experience he has undergone (V, i, 230–240). Finally Caliban, Stephano, and Trinculo are brought in, with the two aspiring rulers still drunk and Stephano still lost in his own grandeur:

> Every man shift for all the rest, and let no man
> take care for himself; for all is but fortune. *Coraggio,*
> bully-monster, *corragio!*

(V, i, 256–258)

But Prospero chastises them, and his tone keeps us aware of the parallel between this harmless trio and the other, more sinister, conspiracy (V, i, 267–276). As the butler and the jester squirm in discomfort, Prospero sneers at Stephano's aspirations: "You'ld be king o' the isle, sirrah?" (V, i, 288). And Caliban at last sees the foolishness of his dream:

> . . . I'll be wise hereafter,
> And seek for grace. What a thrice-double ass
> Was I to take this drunkard for a god,
> And worship this dull fool!

(V, i, 295–298)

But we still see no sign that his nature has changed completely, and thus he remains outside the bounds of civilization. Here is one more element beyond Prospero's magic. But the calming of the tempest, promised by Prospero (V, i, 314–317), and the freeing of Ariel (V, i, 317–319) represent the re-establishment of order and the ultimate expression of forgiveness.

The Epilogue, delivered by Prospero, sounds like one more speech directly from Shakespeare to his audience:

> Now my charms are all o'erthrown,
> And what strength I have's mine own,
> Which is most faint . . .
> As you from crimes would pardon'd be,
> Let your indulgence set me free.

(Epilogue, 1–20)

At the conclusion of a play that has been dominated by the motif of forgiveness, Prospero, the shaper of this drama, asks exoneration for any anger he may have incurred. The thought that this voice is Shakespeare's offering his own farewell is impossible to resist.

In some respects *The Tempest* is a play about wish-fulfillment. Many of the

conflicts that have recurred throughout the plays of Shakespeare and which have
wreaked havoc are here whisked away literally by magic. Thus the play seems
a fantasy. Still, the story has so many angles, some realistic, that to limit it to
a single interpretation is unfair. But one meaning certainly is communicated
here: faith in the goodness of humanity. Throughout the plays of Shakespeare
we see that evil cannot be eradicated from our existence. Nonetheless, throughout
those same plays humanity is ultimately redeemable, and therefore our struggles,
whether political, social, emotional, or, as in the case of Shakespeare, artistic,
help make that existence meaningful.

SUGGESTIONS FOR FURTHER READING

Brown, John Russell. *Shakespeare:* The Tempest. London: Edward Arnold, 1969.

Gesner, Carol. "*The Tempest* as Pastoral Romance." *Shakespeare Quarterly* 5 (1959):
531–539.

Hunt, John Dixon. *A Critical Commentary on Shakespeare's* The Tempest. London:
Macmillan, 1968.

James, David G. *The Dream of Prospero*. Oxford: Clarendon Press, 1967.

Knox, Bernard. "*The Tempest* and the Ancient Comic Tradition." *Virginia Quarterly
Review* 31 (1954): 73–89.

Nuttall, A. D. *Two Concepts of Allegory: A Study of Shakespeare's* The Tempest *and
the Logic of Allegorical Expression*. London: Routledge and Kegan Paul, 1967.

Palmer, D. J., ed. *Shakespeare:* The Tempest: *A Casebook*. London: Macmillan, 1968.

Sisson, C. J. "The Magic of Prospero." *Shakespeare Survey* 11 (1958): 70–77.

Smith, Hallet, ed. *Twentieth Century Interpretations of* The Tempest. Englewood Cliffs,
N.J.: Prentice-Hall, 1969.

Wilson, John Dover. *The Meaning of* The Tempest. Newcastle-upon-Tyne: Literary and
Philosophical Society, 1936.

APPENDIX 1: THE TWO NOBLE KINSMEN

Current critical judgment attributes most of this work to John Fletcher, with Shakespeare contributing individual scenes, including parts of Acts I and III, and the bulk of Act V. As such, the play is worth considering briefly for elements that reflect themes and images found in Shakespeare's own works.

The plot of *The Two Noble Kinsmen* is taken from "The Knight's Tale" in *The Canterbury Tales,* and includes Theseus and Hippolyta, two characters featured in *A Midsummer Night's Dream.* The primary tension is between Palamon and Arcite, nephews of Creon, king of Thebes. They are best friends; in Arcite's words, "dearer in love than blood . . . " (I, ii, 1). And throughout the play they are much alike in action and attitude. The two loathe their uncle, whom we never see, but who is described unsympathetically in Act I. His refusal to surrender to three queens the bodies of their husbands killed in war starts a conflict between Thebes and Theseus's city, Athens. And under that pressure Arcite and Palamon are moved by patriotism to fight for their city. Thus a primary issue of the play is a conflict between priorities: antagonism to Creon and his ethical posture versus loyalty to Thebes.

In the war the two fight nobly, but they are captured and put in prison, where they again affirm their mutual devotion:

> Let's think this prison holy sanctuary
> To keep us from corruption of worse men.
> We are young and yet desire the ways of honor,
> That liberty and common conversation,
> The poison of pure spirits, might, like women,
> Woo us to wander from.
>
> (II, ii, 71–76)

Arcite's earnestness invites a third party to cause a fissure between the two friends.

That intruder turns out to be Emilia, the sister of Hippolyta, the bride of Theseus. Earlier Emilia had forsworn men, praising instead the loyalty of women

(I, iii, 78–82). When the two boys see her from jail, both are smitten, and within moments have turned into enemies. Thus they manifest a motif common to Renaissance literature: the importance of male friendship set against love for a woman. Before either of the two can take action against the other, Arcite is freed and expelled from the kingdom while Palamon is left in jail.

Palamon is rescued, however, by the jailer's daughter, a curious figure. She finds herself in love with Palamon, and despite her recognition of the difference in their social stations, she allows her affection to reach the level of obsession (II, iv, 1–33), and frees him. He escapes to the forest where he meets Arcite, who in disguise has won a position as servant to Emilia. The shackled Palamon accuses Arcite of treachery, and they resume their rivalry (III, i). During this scene, and even more so during Act III, scene iii, Palamon's passion remains unabated, while Arcite urges his friend to remain calm. Perhaps such differences in attitude are meant to indicate that Palamon deserves to win Emilia. Meanwhile, the jailer's daughter, frustrated that Palamon has deserted her, goes mad with desire (III, ii).

Her intense feeling is contrasted with Emilia's lack of passion. When Palamon and Arcite are discovered in the woods fighting, both declare before Theseus their love for his sister-in-law. Yet she remains unable to choose between them, and the irony of the situation is that the comparatively cold Emilia is pursued by two men, while the jailer's daughter, overflowing with devotion, is stranded in the country.

Theseus rules that Arcite and Palamon should fight for Emilia, with the loser to be executed. Even with this brutal alternative, however, Emilia cannot choose, as she expounds in a long soliloquy (IV, ii, 1–54). Her inaction leads to what may be regarded as the climax of the play: the prayers to the gods in Act V, scene i. Arcite pleads with Mars for strength during combat:

> . . . me thy pupil,
> Youngest follower of thy drum, instruct this day
> With military skill, that to thy laud
> I may advance my streamer, and by thee
> Be styl'd the lord o' th' day.
>
> (V, i, 56–60)

Palamon, on the other hand, implores Venus:

> O then, most soft sweet goddess,
> Give me the victory of this question, which
> Is true love's merit, and bless me with a sign
> Of thy great pleasure.
>
> (V, i, 126–129)

Palamon's prayer is more an expression of love than Arcite's call for triumph in battle, and should probably be understood as further evidence that Palamon belongs with Emilia. She herself prays to Diana:

> O mistress,
> Thou here dischargest me. I shall be gather'd,

I think so, but I know not thine own will:
Unclasp thy mystery.

(V, i, 169–172)

She remains passive, hoping a divinity will choose the man most in love with her. At the opening of Act V, scene iii, however, she seems to admit a subtle preference for Palamon:

But Palamon's sadness is a kind of mirth,
So mingled as if mirth did make him sad,
And sadness merry; those darker humors that
Stick misbecomingly on others, on [him]
Live in fair dwelling.

(V, iii, 51–55)

Unfortunately such distinctions of character are not apparent throughout the play.

The jailer's daughter, in the meantime, is courted by a longtime suitor disguised as Palamon. Eventually the suitor brings her out of her madness, but the resolution of that plot is partially unsatisfactory, for the daughter, so full of yearning, ends up with a man who loves her, but whom she has previously discarded.

The main story resolves in more interesting fashion. The duel between the two suitors takes place offstage, and we only hear reports of the action. Eventually Arcite is returned in triumph, but Emilia now realizes that she prefers Palamon and prays to the gods for rescue (V, iii, 138–144). The measure of Palamon's affection is clear from his words as he hears that Emilia is to be married, and as his own head is placed upon the block:

By my short life,
I am most glad on't. 'Tis the latest thing
I shall be glad of, prithee tell her so.

(V, iv, 28–30)

Soon the gods do intervene, as Arcite is thrown from his horse and brought in dying. He confesses that he was deceitful, gives Emilia to Palamon, then expires.

Palamon acknowledges the hollowness of his victory:

O, cousin,
That we should things desire which do cost us
The loss of our desire! that nought could buy
Dear love but loss of dear love!

(V, iv, 109–112)

This sentiment, intimating a fundamental irony at the core of human existence, is developed by Theseus:

O you heavenly charmers,
What things you make of us! For what we lack
We laugh, for what we have are sorry, still
Are children in some kind. Let us be thankful
For that which is, and with you leave disputes

> That are above our question. Let's go off,
> And bear us like the time.
>
> (V, iv, 131–137)

He concludes this play with the reiteration of a theme familiar from Shakespeare's romances: the mystery of the universe and man's inability to comprehend the workings of Providence. These words, among the last Shakespeare wrote, affirm that at least part of his vision of our lives remained consistent through the final portion of his career.

SUGGESTIONS FOR FURTHER READING

Bertram, Paul. *Shakespeare and* The Two Noble Kinsmen. New Brunswick, N.J.: Rutgers University Press, 1965.

Edwards, Philip. "On the Design of *The Two Noble Kinsmen.*" *Review of English Literature* 5, no. 4 (October, 1964): 89–105.

Muir, Kenneth. *Shakespeare as Collaborator*. London: Methuen, 1960.

APPENDIX 2: THE ROYAL FIGURES FROM THE HISTORY TETRALOGIES— WHO THEY ARE AND WHERE THEY APPEAR

The following is a genealogy of royal figures from Shakespeare's two tetralogies based on events in English history from 1399 to 1485. At left are the sons of Edward III (1312–1377). Below are the descendants of each man, aligned according to generation; the plays in which they appear are indicated by bold letters.

Edward the Black Prince

    Richard II **a**

William of Hatfield

Lionel, Duke of Clarence

    Phillipa

  m Edmund Mortimer, 3d Earl of March

      Elizabeth Mortimer **bc**

     m Hotspur, Sir Henry Percy **ab**

      Roger Mortimer, 4th Earl of March

        Edmund Mortimer, 5th Earl of March* **e**

       m Anne Stafford (see House of Gloucester)

        Anne Mortimer

       m Richard, Earl of Cambridge **d** (see House of York)

      Sir Edmund Mortimer***b**

     m Daughter of Owen Glendower **b**

HOUSE OF LANCASTER (Red Rose)

John of Gaunt, Duke of Lancaster **a**

m 1. Blanche of Lancaster

  Henry Bullingbrook, Duke of Herford, Henry IV **abc**

    Prince Hal, Henry V **bcd**

   m Katharine of France **d**

      Henry VI **efg**

     m Margaret of Anjou **efgh**

        Edward, Prince of Wales **g**

       m Anne Neville (Daughter of Richard Neville, Earl of Warwick; later wife of Richard III) **h**

    Thomas, Duke of Clarence **bc**

    Prince John of Lancaster, Duke of Bedford **bcde**

    Humphrey, Duke of Gloucester **bcde**

m 3. Katherine Swynford

  Thomas Beaufort, Duke of Exeter **deg**

  Henry Beaufort, Bishop of Winchester, Cardinal **ef**

  John Beaufort, Earl of Somerset

    John Beaufort, Duke of Somerset **e**

      Margaret Beaufort

     m Edmund Tudor, Earl of Richmond

        Henry Tudor, Earl of Richmond, Henry VII **gh**

       m Elizabeth Plantagenet (Daughter of Edward IV)

        Henry VIII

    Edmund Beaufort, 2d Duke of Somerset **f**

     Henry Beaufort, 3d Duke of Somerset **g**

HOUSE OF YORK (White Rose)

Edmund of Langley, Duke of York

    Edward (Aumerle), Earl of Rutland, 2d Duke of York **ad**

    Richard, Earl of Cambridge **d**
  m Anne Mortimer (see House of Clarence)

        Richard Plantagenet, 3d Duke of York **efg**
      m Cicely Neville, Duchess of York **h**

           Edward, Earl of March, Edward IV **fgh**
          m Elizabeth Woodville, Lady Grey **gh**

               Edward, Prince of Wales, Edward V **h**

               Richard, Duke of York **h**

               Elizabeth Plantagenet
              m Henry, Earl of Richmond, Henry VII (see House of Lancaster) **gh**

           Edmund, Earl of Rutland **g**

           George, Duke of Clarence **fgh**
          m Isabel Neville (Daughter of Richard Neville)

               Edward Plantagenet, Earl of Warwick, **h**
               Margaret Plantagenet, Countess of Salisbury **h**

           Richard, Duke of Gloucester, Richard III **fgh**
          m Lady Anne, Anne Neville (Widow of Edward, Prince of Wales) **h**

  Thomas of Woodstock, Earl of Buckingham, Duke of Gloucester

    Anne
  m Edmund, Lord Stafford **bc**

        Humphrey, Earl of Stafford, 1st Duke of Buckingham **f**

        Humphrey, Earl of Stafford **fg**

        Henry Stafford, 2d Duke of Buckingham **h**

  William of Windsor

*Shakespeare combined Sir Edmund Mortimer and his nephew Edmund Mortimer, Earl of March (named by Richard II as heir to the throne) in *Richard II*.

SELECT BIBLIOGRAPHY

Bentley, Gerald Eades. *Shakespeare: A Biographical Handbook*. New Haven: Yale University Press, 1961.

Calderwood, James L., and Harold E. Toliver, eds. *Essays in Shakespearean Criticism*. Englewood Cliffs, N.J.: Prentice-Hall, 1970.

Chute, Marchette. *Shakespeare of London*. New York: E. P. Dutton: 1949.

Clemen, Wolfgang H. *The Development of Shakespeare's Imagery*. Cambridge: Harvard University Press, 1951.

Dean, Leonard, ed. *Shakespeare: Modern Essays in Criticism*. Revised edition. New York: Oxford University Press, 1967.

Frye, Northrop. *Northrop Frye on Shakespeare*. New Haven and London: Yale University Press, 1986.

Goddard, Harold C. *The Meaning of Shakespeare*. Chicago: University of Chicago Press, 1951.

Granville-Barker, Harley. *Prefaces to Shakespeare*. Princeton: Princeton University Press, 1946–47.

Harbage, Alfred. *William Shakespeare: A Reader's Guide*. New York: Noonday Press, 1963.

———. *Shakespeare and the Rival Traditions*. New York: Macmillan, 1952.

———. *Shakespeare's Audience*. New York: Columbia University Press, 1941.

Kott, Jan. *Shakespeare Our Contemporary*. Garden City, N.Y.: Doubleday, 1966.

Righter, Anne. *Shakespeare and the Idea of a Play*. London: Chatto & Windus, 1962.

Schoenbaum, Samuel. *William Shakespeare: A Documentary Life*. Oxford: Clarendon Press, 1975.

Spurgeon, Caroline F. E. *Shakespeare's Imagery and What It Tells Us*. New York: Macmillan, 1935.

Tillyard, E. M. W. *The Elizabethan World Picture*. New York: Macmillan, 1943. Reprint. New York: Random House, 1961.

Traversi, Derek. *An Approach to Shakespeare*. New York: Doubleday, 1956.

Van Doren, Mark. *Shakespeare*. New York: Holt, 1939. Reprint. New York: Anchor Books, 1953.

Wells, Stanley, ed. *The Cambridge Companion to Shakespeare Studies*. Cambridge: Cambridge University Press, 1986.

Character Index

INDEX